American
Theatre Companies,
1749–1887

American Theatre Companies, 1749–1887

EDITED BY

WELDON B. DURHAM

GREENWOOD PRESS
NEW YORK • WESTPORT, CONNECTICUT • LONDON

Library of Congress Cataloging-in-Publication Data

Main entry title:

American theatre companies, 1749–1887.

Includes bibliographies and indexes.
1. Theater—United States—History—18th century.
2. Theater—United States—History—19th century.
I. Durham, Weldon B.
PN2237.A43   1986   792′.0973   84–27947
ISBN 0–313–20886–7 (lib. bdg.)

Library of Congress Catalog Card Number: 84–27947
ISBN: 0–313–20886–7

First published in 1986

Greenwood Press, Inc.
88 Post Road West, Westport, Connecticut 06881

Printed in the United States of America

The paper used in this book complies with the
Permanent Paper Standard issued by the National
Information Standards Organization (Z39.48–1984).

10 9 8 7 6 5 4 3 2 1

Contents

Preface

A commonplace of theatrical wisdom has been that theatre is a communal art, an experience arising out of the coordinated efforts of the members of a group. Withal, theatre historians have conventionally organized their field of study into biographical studies of performers, playwrights, and other artists, or they have studied the structure of playhouses and the organization of theatrical business ventures. Histories of theatre buildings and of the theatre communities large and small, as well as the history of the crafts of acting and directing, have been common topics. In our century, a great deal of scholarship has been accomplished that both tangentially and directly acknowledges and explores the communal aspects of the making of theatre. The theatrical company, especially the resident company, has become a topic of interest and investigation. Concern for the relationship between American theatre and American society, as well as for the sociology of theatre, has focused attention on the theatrical company as a phenomenon worthy of close study.

American Theatre Companies, 1749–1887, is the first of a series of three books providing salient facts about resident acting companies in the American colonies and the United States. This book covers the period from 1749, the date of the organization of the first significant English-speaking company in the American colonies, to 1887, the date of the formation of the last company organized and operated in the mode imported to the colonies from England in the eighteenth century. The second book will treat organizations formed in the United States from 1888 to 1930, a period in which the stock-company mode of organization was revived and modified to achieve great currency. A third work will treat groups formed from 1931 to 1986, including especially the histories of nonprofit resident performing groups, other groups devoted to experimentation and political action, and professional art theatres and repertory companies.

This book contains eighty-one group biographies arranged alphabetically. In addition to the general subject index, entries with cross-references provide access to entries on companies known by alternate names. An asterisk following the mention of a company in a narrative indicates that the book includes an entry on the company named. Authors of the entries have distilled vital information from published and unpublished sources relating to the dates, places, personnel, policies, and repertories of the most durable organizations assembled to produce more than one non-musical play while residing for at least twenty consecutive weeks in a single location. Each entry includes dates and locations of the company's operations, the manager's name(s), and an analysis of the group's artistic and business practices. An assessment of the company's commerical and artistic significance adds a critical dimension to each item. Each entry also includes a list of names, when known, of performers, designers, technicians, and other support and managerial personnel. Dates of the association of key persons (names in italics) are included in parentheses following the person's names. The narrative portion of each entry contains an analysis and an assessment of the group's repertory. A variety of techniques has been used to cope with the great volume of play titles properly associated with the most durable repertory companies of the eighteenth and nineteenth centuries. When a company's efforts have been calendared in already available research, individual contributors have been asked to make an expert judgment about how much, if any, of the calendar should be reproduced in *American Theatre Companies*. Some entries include a representative sample of the titles of plays produced by the group. Usually, a sample season's bill is listed in the order the pieces were presented. Some entries include no lists of plays, because the repertory of the group has not been or cannot be researched. A few entries include an exhaustive listing of all plays known to have been produced by the group. No one universally meaningful format for reporting the results of research into the repertory of all these companies was found to be appropriate. Spelling of play titles has been standardized according to Allardyce Nicoll, *A History of English Drama, 1600–1900*, vol. 6: *A Short-Title Alphabetical Catalogue of Plays Produced or Printed in England from 1660 to 1900* (Cambridge: Cambridge University Press, 1969). Each entry concludes with a bibliography of published sources used in compiling the entry and a guide to archival resources for further study, when such primary material is known to exist.

American Theatre Companies encapsulates information from many sources, some rare and hard to find; arranges it for easy access; and presents it succinctly. Users will find it an indispensable guide to an aspect of American theatre covered by no other reference work.

Weldon B. Durham

American
Theatre Companies,
1749–1887

A

ACADEMY OF MUSIC COMPANY. The Academy of Music, originally known as The Cleveland Theatre, was constructed in the winter of 1852 by Charles Foster of Pittsburgh. Foster unceremoniously opened the theatre on April 16, 1853, with a production of *The School for Scandal* enacted by a small stock company headed by Ben Maginley. Located on the top floor of a three-story brick building on the east side of Bank Street between Superior and St. Clair streets (1371 West Sixth Street), Cleveland, Ohio, this new playhouse staked its claim as Cleveland's premier "temple of the Thespian Art" when John A. Ellsler leased it from Foster in the spring of 1855.

For thirty-five years (since the *Cleveland Herald* advertised the first theatrical performance for the city on May 23, 1820), Cleveland had yielded to circuses, traveling theatrical companies with one-night stands, and occasional special exhibits. John Ellsler terminated that trend when he opened his first Academy of Music season on April 3, 1855, with James Sheridan Knowles' five-act drama *The Wife; or, A Tale of Mantua*, followed by the comic afterpiece *Sweethearts and Wives*. The history of nineteenth-century Cleveland theatre is largely the history of Ellsler's activities from 1855 to 1878.

"Uncle John," as he was to be affectionately called by the people of Cleveland, developed a resident stock company that eventually bore the reputation of being one of the most complete in the West, organized one of the first dramatic schools in the nation, and provided Clevelanders a never-ending array of distinguished guest artists. Ellsler was one of the few managers who successfully bridged the gap between resident companies and visiting guest stars.

Ellsler's success with his inaugural season (April 3 to August 20, 1855), gave impetus to enterprising competitors. The Cleveland Theatre (eventually named Academy of Music by Ellsler) reopened for the fall/winter season on September 22, 1855, and was forced to share the spotlight with the Athenaeum Theatre and Melodeon Hall. The former, built on Superior Street opposite Bank by the great showman P. T. Barnum, employed E. L. Tilton as manager and boasted a stock company fresh from New York. In addition to providing the acting company, which gave Cleveland its first showing of John Baldwin Buckstone's *Leap Year; or, The Ladies' Privilege,* the Athenaeum offered the French Ballet Troupe and the Grand National Dancers. Melodeon Hall, originally Brainard's Music Hall, specialized in novelty acts and variety pieces, such as the Original Christy's Minstrels. Ellsler's company prevailed, however, with consistent reviews from the *Cleveland Leader* touting "the excellent abilities of the various members of his corps," and by December 3, 1855, Tilton was replaced by E.T. Nichols, who was forced to manage the Athenaeum as a vaudeville house. The novelties of the Melodeon were countered with the Academy's star parade from 1855 to 1858: Fanny Davenport, Charles W. Couldock, James E. Murdoch, Matilda Heron, Charlotte Cushman, and Edwin Forrest.

John A. Ellsler (1822–1903), the actor-manager of the Academy, was a native Philadelphian, but his managerial activity began in Georgia and South Carolina, when he formed a partnership with Joseph Jefferson III in the early 1850s. Ellsler, often credited with teaching Jefferson the Dutch dialect for his famous role of Rip Van Winkle, tired of this strenuous traveling partnership and decided to settle down as a resident actor-manager. Cleveland, an already established agricultural center of the Midwest and a thriving seaport town with a steadily increasing population, provided Ellsler a culturally untapped locale.

For three years (1855–58) Ellsler; his wife, Effie, and his ever-changing but solid stock companies labored with scarcely a break between the spring/ summer and fall/winter seasons. Although Ellsler was regarded as a fine artistic manager and versatile actor, he was not a good financier. This economic instability is evidenced by the number of hands attempting to juggle bank accounts. Charles S. Reese, the first to be billed as treasurer and coproprietor, gave way to Felix A. Vincent in 1856. T. L. Wilcox followed in 1857. Meanwhile, the positions of acting manager, stage manager, and prompter fluctuated between Ellsler, W. H. Maddock, G. H. Gilbert, and Fred W. Hildreth. From 1855 to 1858 gallery seats remained at twenty-five cents, but prices for the orchestra, dress circle, and private boxes escalated from fifty cents to $1 and from $1 to $5 or $10, respectively. Additionally, national economics were strained before the Civil War, and Ellsler was forced to close the theatre for several months in 1856 due to a prohibitive license tax. Ellsler finally made frequent tours to Columbus, Toledo, Cincinnati, and Pittsburgh in search of larger audiences. He left Cleveland in June 1858 to return for only two brief engagements in the next four years.

Remarkably, Ellsler's tenacity prevailed, and he returned to Cleveland with a newly formed dramatic corps in April 1862. The *Cleveland Leader* (April 23, 1862) stated: "the excellent performance gave proof that the company is a very superior one . . . in short, Cleveland has not been so favored with so pleasing and satisfactory a company for a long time." For the next sixteen years (1862–78) Ellsler and his Academy of Music gave Cleveland a notable variety of plays, from Shakespeare to popular melodrama, music spectacles, and opera, and complemented his fine stock companies with a host of guest stars, including Frank Mayo, James H. Hackett, E. A. Sothern, Charles Kean, John McCullough, Lawrence Barrett, Joseph Jefferson, Frank S. Chanfrau, Lotta Crabtree, Joseph Proctor, Edwin Booth, and Booth's infamous brother John Wilkes. The Academy of Music relinquished its position as Cleveland's theatrical entertainment mecca for three years (1875–79), when Ellsler helped construct, organize, and manage the Euclid Avenue Opera House.

In addition to maintaining his acting company (which ranged from fifteen to twenty members at a time), Ellsler employed a treasurer, prompter, stage manager, acting manager, music director, scenic artist, costumer, property maker, and machinist. Although Ellsler brought in guest artists, his organization featured a strong, versatile ensemble with the ability to sing, act, dance, and perform a large repertory of old and new plays with or without a visiting star. His dramatic school was formed to serve the apprentices in his company as well as to provide experimental opportunities for the established performers. Ellsler not only brought stars to Cleveland, but he also developed some of his own. Graduating from the Academy's boards as either apprentices or full company members were Mrs. G. H. Gilbert (1856–58) and James Lewis (1862–65), both of whom became bright stars with Augustin Daly's Fifth Avenue Theatre; John McCullough (1850s), the heir apparent to Edwin Forrest's muscle roles; Lawrence Barrett (early 1870s), a struggling young genius when taken in by Ellsler; James O'Neill (1870), who later gained fame as Edmond Dantes in *The Count of Monte Cristo*; James Whiting (1874–75), eventually known as "Jim the Penman"; the Ellslers' own daughter, little Effie E. Ellsler (1862–78), who rose to stardom with Steele MacKaye's Madison Avenue Theatre; and Clara Morris (1862–68), destined to become one of America's leading actresses in the nineteenth century. Morris, whose real name was Clara Morrison, debuted as a star-struck thirteen year old in a rival company (The Theatre Comique) headed by I. H. Carter. She quickly joined Ellsler's newly re-opened Academy in 1862.

The Academy of Music passed through three periods under Ellsler: the premiere seasons from 1855 to 1858; the sparkling and golden era from 1862 to 1875; and the declining era from 1878 to 1885. The latter period followed Ellsler's artistically successful, but financially disastrous, three-year management of the newly constructed Euclid Avenue Opera House.

Ellsler went bankrupt, and the Opera House was auctioned in a sheriff's sale. Ellsler attempted a third stay at the Academy in 1878. Again, due to financial difficulties, he surrendered the managerial reins of the Academy in 1885. The theatre served mostly as a cheap variety house for the next four years. In 1889 the playhouse was partially destroyed by fire and then was reconstructed as a Quaker church. It suffered a second fire in 1892 and survived its last years as a dance hall, labor meeting room, and factory.

Following a brief two-year engagement as actor-manager for the Park Theatre (1886–88), Ellsler finally retired from theatre management. In the 1890s, both the Park Theatre (renamed The Lyceum) and Ellsler's Euclid Avenue Opera House became properties of the powerful New York syndicate headed by Charles Frohman, Marc Klaw, and Abraham Erlanger. Ironically, Erlanger began his career as a Cleveland schoolboy selling peanuts and candy in the gallery of that same Euclid Avenue Opera House.

PERSONNEL

Management: John A. Ellsler (1855–58, 1862–75, 1879–85); W. H. Maddock (1856–57); Felix Vincent (1857–58); James Dickinson (1863); Effie Ellsler (1873–75).

Treasurers: Charles S. Reese (1855–57); T. L. Wilcox (1857–58); C. Busch (1863); Richard Geary (1864–68).

Prompters: Fred W. Hildreth (1855–57); G. H. Gilbert (1857–58); W. H. Young (1860s).

Scenic Technicians: Professor Andrieu, artist (1855–56); Charles O'Hart, artist (1856–58); L. Cowdry, machinist (1856–58); Christopher Scheein, costumer (1856–58); Seth Simmons, property maker (1856–58); Samuel Culbert, artist (1862–65); Simon Maesto, artist (1865–75); James Flemming, gas man (1865–75).

Musical Directors: Mr. Loland (1855–58); Mr. Noverre (1855–58); Sandy Jamison (1866–75).

Actors and Actresses: Rebecca Adams (1864–65), Annie Allen (1855), *G. J. Arnold* (1855–56), Miss Barrett (1856–57), *Lawrence Barrett* (1870–73), *Mark Bates* (1866–67), *Mrs. Mark Bates* (1866–67), Miss Bennett (1856–57), G. C. Boniface (1855–56), Lida Bonque (1862), Mrs. Bradshaw (1862–65), *Blanch Bradshaw* (1862–65), W. H. Briggs (1862), A. R. Brooks (1873–75), Mrs. Cappell (1855), *Cordelia Cappell* (1855), T. Chandler (1855), J. M. Charles (1862), Florence Chase (1873–75), Ed Clifford (1866–72), Fannie Clifford (1857–58), Mills Colcraft (1856–57), John J. Collins (1873–75), *J. B. Curran* (1872–76), W. C. Davenport (1872–73), H. H. Davis (1862), *E. Murray Day* (1866–75), C. P. DeGroot (1862), Susan Denin (1855), Mr. Dickson (1856–57), *James W. Dickson* (1862–64), Mrs. J. W. Dickson (1862–64), Mrs. Douglas (1857–58), T. B. Douglas (1857–58), Miss M. Dunn (1856–57), Miss Eleanor (1856–57), Henry A. Ellen (1867–72), *Mrs. Effie Ellsler* (1855–85), *Miss Effie E. Ellsler* (1862–78), *John A. Ellsler* (1855–85), *Mr. Evelyn Evans* (1864–65), N. Fay (1857–58), A. W. Fenno (1857–58), *A. Fitzgerald* (1855), *Harold Forsberg* (1872–75), Mr. Fyffe (1856–57), Mrs. G. H. Gilbert (1856–58), G. W. Gile (1856–57), W. R. Goodall (1855–58), B. R. Graham (1873–75), *Charles Graham* (1858), Miss Granger (1862–64), Mrs. Gregory (1857–58), E. T. Gregory

(1857–58), Walter Hannon (1864–65), Aggie Hardy (1862), Alice Hastings (1873–75), J. Hegberne (1864–67), Lizzie Herbert (1867–72), *J. Wesley Hill* (1867–70), Miss Horn (1856–57), *Isabella Howitt* (1864–66), George Hudson (1864–67), Matilda Hughes (1862–64), *Edwin Irving* (1865–72), Miss Irving (1856–57), Miss J. E. Irving (1865–72), W. M. Jamison (1856–57), Clark Jeffrey (1862–64), Mr. Johnson (1865–67), Ada Jones (1865–73), L. B. Kellogg (1862–64), Jenny Kendall (1855), Lizzie Kendall (1855), Emma Keough (1856–57), Annie Keyser (1862–67), W. King (1857–58), Fanny La Forrest (1864–65), Minnie Lannier (1864–65), Simcoe Lee (1864–67), D. W. Leeson (1856–57), Mrs. Lennex (1857–58), *James Lewis* (1862–65), R. A. Locke (1864–65), Louisa Lyle (1872–73), Lizzie Madden (1857–58), Mary Madden (1857–58), W. H. Maddocks (1856–57), Eliza Mann (1856–57), J. Marble (1865–67), C. B. Martin (1864–65), *J. C. McCullom* (1862–64, 1866–67, 1870), Hattie McKee (1867–70), Miss Melville (1862), Marion Moore (1862–64), *Clara (Morrison) Morris* (1862–68), T. Morrow (1857–58), E. Mortimer (1857–58), F. T. Murdock (1865–66), James Murray (1873–76), Joseph Nagle (1865–66), Rachael Noah (1862), J. F. Noyes (1862), John Ogden (1867–73), *James O'Neill* (1870–72), T. E. Owens (1855), J. B. Pardon (1856–57), Hattie Parker (1855), Jane Parker (1865–67), Mr. Phillips (1865–67), Estelle Potter (1872–76), A. Purcell (1862–64), G. Robinson (1867–70), J. B. Robinson (1862–64), Josie Robinson (1873–75), C. Stuart Rogers (1873–75), Miss Rosalie (1856–57), E. Rossiter (1857–58), Harry Rowe (1867–72), D. A. Ryan (1856–57), Mr. Schenck (1856–57), Sidney S. Smith (1867–72), C. A. Stedman (1873–74), E. Stephens (1865–72), *Collin Stewart* (1862–64), Miss Townsend (1856–57), *Felix A. Vincent* (1856–58), T. Vinton (1857–58), Ed Voltz (1865–67), Mrs. Walcot (1870–72), Mary Wall (1867–71), C. F. Walters (1856–57), *James Whiting* (1874–76), Mr. Wilder (1869–70), H. Wright (1864–65), Eliza Young (1867–71, Nellie Young (1867–71), W. H. Young (1866–72).

REPERTORY

1855–56: *The Wife; or A Tale of Mantua; Sweethearts and Wives; Hamlet; Good for Nothing; Thérèse, The Orphan of Geneva; The Married Rake; Young America; Damon and Pythias; The Rough Diamond; Faint Heart ne'er Won Fair Lady; The Serious Family; Comedy Triumphant; London Assurance; The Stranger; Eustache Baudin; The Eton Boy; Duel in the Dark; Two Buzzards; Richelieu; or, The Conspiracy; King Lear; Louis XI; Othello; Betrothal; Ingomar; The Mountain Sylph; Time Altered; Italian Wife; The Wandering Boys of Switzerland; Raffalle; The Reprobate; Town and Country; Another Glass; Carpenter of Rouen; Love in a Mist; Romeo and Juliet; Camille; The Actress of Padua; The Banker's Wife; The London Merchant; The Lady of Lyons; Money; Wine Works Wonders; or, The Inconstant; Macbeth; The Robbers; DeSoto: The Hero of the Mississippi; The School for Scandal; Richard III; The Fugitive Slave; or, The Convict's Niece; The Poor Gentleman* (opened the fall/winter season of 1855–56); *My Precious Betsey; The Loan of a Lover; Love; or, The Countess and the Serf*; the following afterpieces: *The Alpine Maid, Love under a Cleveland Lamppost, Poor Pillicoddy, Flying Colors in Crossing the Frontier, Phenomenon in a Smock Frock, Bamboozling Is a Wife for a Half Hour*, and *Women's Rights Convention; or, Cleveland in 1956* (a special fantasy especially for Mrs. Effie Ellsler); *The Road of Life; The Daughter of the Stars;*

Green Bushes; or, 100 Years Ago; Don Caesar de Bazan; Much Ado about Nothing; Hunchback; The Wonder, A Woman Keeps a Secret; As You Like It; A Glance at New York; Courier of Lyons; Rip Van Winkle; Jack Cade; or, The Kentish Rebellion; Aladdin (first big long run—twenty-five nights); *A New Way to Pay Old Debts; The Drunkard; Fashion; Cherry and Fair Star.*

1856–57: *The Rent Day; Ingomar; Herne the Hunter; Rookwood; or, Bonnie Black Bess* (equestrian dramas with the horse "Will Watch"); *Rookwood; or, Dick Turbin's Ride and the Forty Thieves; Love in Humble Life; Rob Roy McGregor; Irish Assurance; Working the Oracle; Paddy Miles; The Seven Ages of Woman; Satan in Paris; The Clown Prince; The Rights and Wrongs of Women; Pizarro; or, The Death of Rolla; Nick of the Woods; Wallace: Hero of Scotland; William Tell; The Green Mountain Boy; Yankee Land; The Yankee Duelist; A Wife for a Day; The Corsican Brothers* (assorted specialty acts).

1857–58: *Paul Jones* (nautical drama*); Othello; The Barber of Seville; The Beggar's Opera; Pocahontas; The French Spy; Shocking Events; Love in Livery; The Maid of Munster; A Day after the Wedding; The School for Scandal; Macbeth; Guy Mannering* (Charlotte Cushman as Meg Merrilies); *Virginius; Richelieu; Metamora; The Gladiator; Jack Cade; Damon and Pythias* (the preceding six plays starred Edwin Forrest); *Thérèse, the Orphan of Geneva; Giralda; Romeo and Juliet* (with Charlotte Cushman playing Romeo to Mrs. Effie Ellsler's Juliet); *Aladdin; London Assurance; Camille; Sketches in India; Swiss Swain; Limerick Boy.*

1862–63: *Mysterious Stranger; or, The Satan in Paris; Peggy Green; The French Spy; or, The Fall of Algiers; Hypochondriac; Green Bushes; or, 100 Years Ago; My Young Wife and My Old Umbrella; The Marble Heart; or, The Sculptor's Dream; The Fairy of Home; The White Terror; The Hidden Hand; The Siege of Lucknow; The Soldier's Daughter;* the following three plays starring F. S. Chanfrau: *The Mysteries and Miseries of New York, The Octoroon,* and *A Glance at New York; Richard III; Hamlet; The Stranger; Black Eyed Susan; or, All in the Downs; Jack Cade; The Advocate; Richelieu; The Chimney Corner; The Corsican Brothers; Uncle Tom's Cabin* (first Cleveland showing with debut of little Effie E. Ellsler as "Little Eva"); *Still Waters Run Deep; The Serious Family; The Sea of Ice; The Seven Sisters; The Poor Gentleman; She Stoops to Conquer* (opened the fall/winter season of 1862–63); *The Loan of a Lover; Honey Moon; or, How to Rule a Wife; Ingomar; Margot; The Poultry Dealer; The Swiss Cottage; The Spectre Gambler; or, The Greek Slave; The Lady of Lyons; The Sea of Ice; The French Spy; The Young Actress; Yankee Land; Fashion; The Daughter of the Regiment; Claude Bonheur; The Guide of the Alps; Ambition; Belphegor, the Mountebank; Three Hundred and Fifty Nights; Jessie Brown; or, The Siege of Lucknow; The Gypsy Girl; The Faery of Home; A Trip to Richmond; The Young Rebel; The Husband's Revenge; The Serious Family;* all of the following afterpieces spotlighting the company's new stock comedian Jimmie Lewis: *The College Boy, A Ghost in Spite of Himself, The Corporal's Wedding, Mr. and Mrs. Peter White, The Lord and Cobbler, An Object of Interest, The Factory Girl; or, All That Glitters Is Not Gold;* and the seasonal ending costume-equestrian spectacle *Bluebeard; or, Woman's Curiosity.*

1863–64: *Henry IV* and *The Merry Wives of Windsor* (both starring James H. Hackett as Falstaff); *The Woman in White; Our American Cousin; Wizard Skiff; or, The Ship on Fire; Dot, Dot, Dot; The Lady of Lyons; Richard III; Othello; The Marble Heart; A Conjugal Lesson; Cricket; The Dead Heart and the Heretic;*

The Belle of the Season; East Lynne; Aurora Floyd; Lady Edith; or, The Earl's Daughter (Matilda Heron's own manuscript copy used); *The Ticket-of-Leave Man.*

1864–65: Still Waters Run Deep; Two Buzzards; Hamlet; A Life's Revenge; The Ticket-of-Leave Man; Bibio; Aladdin (another long run); *Macbeth; The People's Lawyer; Ten Nights in a Bar-Room* (little Effie Ellsler as Mary Morgan and specialty guest George "Yankee" Locke as Sample Switchel); *Henry VIII; Hamlet; The Merchant of Venice.*

1865–66 (Mostly old repertory with the following new plays added): *Rosedale; or, The Rifle Ball; The Red League; Louis XI; Ireland as It Was; The Good-for-Nothing; The Female Detective; Fanchon, The Cricket* (with Lotta Crabtree); *My Poll and My Partner Joe; Dunderketty's Pic-nic! Bull in a China Shop; Sam.*

1866–75 (The following new pieces added to previous repertory): *The Ice Witch; The Naiad Queen; or, The Water Sprites of the Rhine; Little Strawberry Girl; Our Country Cousin* (with "giant" actor Colonel Goshen who was eight feet tall and weighed 575 pounds); *The Black Crook; Luna; or, The Little Boy Who Cried for the Moon; Leah the Forsaken; Amrie's New Year; Checkmate; Davy Crockett* (with Frank Mayo in title role); *Eileen Oge; or, Dark Is the Horn Before Dawn.*

BIBLIOGRAPHY

Published Sources: *Cleveland Herald* (1820–53); *Cleveland Leader* (1855–85); William Ganson Rose, *Cleveland: The Making of a City* (World Publishing Co., 1950); Samuel P. Orth, *A History of Cleveland, Ohio* (S. J. Clarke Publishing Co., 1910); James H. Kennedy, *A History of the City of Cleveland* (The Imperial Press, 1896).

Archival Sources: Western Reserve Historical Society Museum in Cleveland has an incomplete collection of memorabilia of which the following items are most noteworthy: The Leo and Maurice Weidenthal Collection of photographs of stock and guest stars with the Academy, artifacts and documents from old trunks owned by Effie E. Ellsler (Mrs. Frank Weston), and a copy of "Stage Memories of John A. Ellsler" (Historical Society's manuscript, no. 3025, edited by Effie Ellsler Weston).

Charles Schultz

ADELPHI THEATRE COMPANY. Chartered in 1849 by an act of the Tennessee legislature, the Adelphi Theatre Company proposed to erect a handsome building in Nashville, therein to produce legitimate drama of an elevated sort.

The Adelphi Theatre, on Cherry Street (now Fourth Avenue) near Cedar, opened July 1, 1850, under the management of John Greene. Although the company consisted largely of local, untried talent, it fared well with daily changes of bill that included a drama, farce, and program of songs. Greene's first company continued through December 15, 1851, during which time the stock produced the standard repertory of the period with visiting stars such as Julia Dean, Eliza Logan (later Mrs. George Wood), Charlotte Cushman, Mr. and Mrs. G. C. Howard, Richard Graham, and J. B. Roberts.

After a four-month hiatus, Greene brought forth a new company of experienced actors, supplemented by a scenic artist and an orchestra. The group opened with Knowles' *Love Chase* and the farce *Nipped in the Bud* but turned to extravaganzas a month later after appearances by stars J. B. Roberts and Conrad Clarke. *Cherry and Fair Star* ran six nights; *Forty Thieves* followed later in the month. Greene's management ended when the theatre closed June 9, 1852.

A short season under new management commenced January 22, 1853, and lasted until February 16. In September 1853 the managers introduced a new and very poor stock company. Another much superior company headed by G. K. Dickenson, with E. L. Tilton and Joe Cowell, followed in 1854. Eliza Logan, George Jameson, and Annette Ince appeared in starring engagements. The visit of noted tragedian James E. Murdoch was the highlight of the 1855–56 season.

Joel Davis assumed control of the theatre in 1856, renaming it the Nashville Theatre. Although the company's effort in the first season was reasonably pleasing, the organization suffered through a period of stinging criticism and declining patronage after the opening of the 1857–58 season. Davis closed the theatre and disbanded the company on November 14, 1857.

PERSONNEL

Managers: John Greene, Joel Davis.
Actors and Actresses: Only names of visiting stars have been documented.

REPERTORY

1850–51 (Partial list): *Lucrezia Borgia; Evadne; or, The Statue; Romeo and Juliet; Macbeth; Fazio; or, The Italian Wife; The Merchant of Venice; Gabrielle; or, The Wager; The Lady of Lyons; Trevanion; or, The False Position; The Barricade Room; Rip Van Winkle; The People's Lawyer; The Forest Rose.*

1851–52 (Partial list): *The Lady of Lyons; London Assurance; Sir Giles Overreach; Hamlet; Romeo and Juliet; The Duke's Wages* (closing December 18, 1851). Opening April 1852: *The Love Chase; Nipped in the Bud; Romeo and Juliet; Hamlet; Richard III; Othello; Julius Caesar; Werner; Cherry and Fair Star; The Forty Thieves.*

1852–53: No record in sources.

1853–54 (Partial list): *Honey Moon; The Hunchback; Mohammed, the Arabian Prophet.*

1854–55 (Partial list): *Adrienne, the Actress; The Old Plantation; or, The Real Uncle Tom.*

1855–56 (Partial list): *Hamlet; Adrienne, the Actress; Mona Lisa; or, da Vinci's Masterpiece; The Hunchback.*

1857–58: No record in sources.

BIBLIOGRAPHY

Published Sources: Francis G. Davenport, *Cultural Life in Nashville on the Eve of the Civil War* (Chapel Hill: University of North Carolina Press, 1941); *Nashville Daily Gazette* (title varies) (1849–60); *Republican Banner and Nashville Whig* (1849–

60); *Nashville Union and American* (1856–57); *Nashville Daily News* (1857–59); *Nashville Patriot* (1856–60).

Weldon B. Durham

AFRICAN THEATRE. The first black repertory company in the United States opened in September 1821 in New York City in rooms near a garden called the African Grove. Conceived in an effort to provide acting opportunities for black performers and entertainment for black audiences, the small, all-male group first attempted Shakespeare's *Richard III*. The group expanded in October 1821, and another production of *Richard III* was mounted in a conventional theatre with pit, box, and gallery at the corner of Mercer and Bleecker streets. This evening's bill included the ballet *Asawa* and a concert of songs, for which customers paid a top price of seventy-five cents. By January 1822 the troupe had moved to a hotel next door to the Park Theatre, where they met stiff resistance from elements of the white population. Police closed the theatre and detained the performers. The group returned to the Mercer Street Theatre for the remainder of the 1822–23 season but disbanded about July 1, 1823.

The group's leading actor was James Hewlett, whom Charles Mathews satirized in an "At Home" called "A Trip to America." Hewlett performed in the United States until at least 1831 and visited Great Britain in an effort to confront Mathews. Ira Aldridge also appeared with the group.

PERSONNEL

Manager: Mr. Brown.
Actors and Actresses: Ira Aldridge, James Hewlett, Miss Welsh.

REPERTORY

1821–23: *Richard III*; the ballet *Asawa*; the ballet *Balilion*; *Othello*; the pantomime *Obi; or, Three-Fingered Jack;* an afterpiece, *The Poor Soldier*; an original play, *King Shotaway; Tom and Jerry*.

BIBLIOGRAPHY

Published Source: Yvonne Shafer, "Black Actors in the Nineteenth Century American Theatre," *CLA Journal* 20 (March 1977): 387–400.

Weldon B. Durham

AIKIN'S MUSEUM STOCK COMPANY. See WOOD'S MUSEUM STOCK COMPANY.

ALCAZAR THEATRE STOCK COMPANY. (SAN FRANCISCO, CALIFORNIA, 1886–1930) See AMERICAN THEATRE COMPANIES, 1888–1930.

AMERICAN COMPANY. (1752–92) This company was also known as the Company of Comedians from England, the London Company of Comedians, Company of Comedians from London, the American Company of Comedians, and the [Old] American Company*. The organization performed throughout the American colonies, 1752–55; in Jamaica, 1755–58; again in the American colonies, 1758–74; in Jamaica, 1775–85; and in the new American republic, 1785–92. The reorganized group established nearly permanent residence in New York City in 1792 and became the Park Theatre Company (1806)*.

Encouraged by the news of the success of John Moody's troupe in Jamaica, 1745–49, William Hallam, a bankrupt London theatre manager, assembled a small group; put his brother Lewis (1714–56) in charge; equipped them with costumes, scenery, decorations, and drama scripts salvaged from Hallam's failed theatre in Goodman's Fields; and sent them to the American colonies. Ten performers and a vocalist were hired for the tour. William Rigby and Mrs. Lewis Hallam were assigned to play leads, Patrick Malone was the heavy, John Singleton was the light comedian, and Lewis Hallam was the manager and low comedian. Mrs. Rigby, Mr. and Mrs. Thomas Clarkson, Mr. Herbert, Mr. Wynell, and Mrs. William Adcock rounded out the adult acting corps. William Adcock was the group's vocalist, and the Hallam children—Lewis, Jr. (c.1740–1808), Adam, and Helen—played small roles. Miss Palmer apparently joined the company in England, but any appearance with it in the colonies has left no trace. Members of the group shared profits split into eighteen parts. Each adult performer received one share, Lewis Hallam received one more as company manager, and one was reserved for the Hallam children. Four shares were split between Lewis and William Hallam as proprietors of the company. Company members were also allowed occasional benefit performances at which the company shares went to the beneficiary.

A usual evening's fare was a full-length play and a farce, comic opera, pantomime, or burlesque performed as an afterpiece, as well as two or three recitations, playlets, or other entertainments, with songs and dances before the curtain and at intermissions. In longer stands, the group performed Monday, Wednesday, and Friday nights, charging a substantial five shillings per admission. They operated no box office. Patrons purchased tickets at taverns, inns, and coffeehouses. The Hallam company was conventionally organized for the period, and they played a conventional repertory in a conventional manner. Their corporate acting style was probably declamatory and broad. The mere availability—rather than the high artistry of the ensemble—was featured in their advertising. Leading players were assigned the most significant roles, but they were not stars. The scenery William Hallam furnished was a collection of wings, drops, shutters, and borders that could be rolled up for easy hauling. The settings made from these pieces were generalized interiors and exteriors. The costumes came from the performers' personal wardrobes, with some special pieces supplied by the company.

The actors rehearsed their repertory of twenty plays in passage to America on the *Charming Sally*. They disembarked at Williamsburg, Virginia, and on September 15, 1752, "New Style" performed Shakespeare's *Merchant of Venice* with either Garrick's *Lethe* or Edward Ravenscroft's *Anatomist* as the afterpiece. Their sojourn at the Play House on the east side of Eastern (now Waller) Street, just behind the capitol, lasted eleven months. Few records of it remain.

In June 1753 they embarked by coastal packet for New York, arriving about July 2. They immediately set up in the Play House used by the Murray and Kean Company* in 1750, on the east side of Nassau Street between John Street and Maiden Lane. They struggled for a month to get permission to perform from a wary city government. They opened their first stand in New York on September 17, featuring Richard Steele's impeccably moral *Conscious Lovers*. They continued to perform regularly until March 18, 1754, when they closed to depart for Philadelphia.

Patrick Malone, Hallam's advance agent, had been in the Quaker city since early February. His efforts to remove legal bars to theatrical performances in the city met intense resistance. Appeals to the governor of the colony of Pennsylvania finally availed, however, and the troupe was licensed to present a season of twenty-four plays and afterpieces in the New Theatre in Water Street. William Plumstead's warehouse, for that's what it was, had been altered to accommodate the Murray and Kean Company and stood ready in the suitably remote precinct of Southwark. The Hallam troupe opened April 15 in Nicholas Rowe's *Fair Penitent* and continued through June 27. In the interim, William Hallam visited them and sold his company shares to Lewis, who became sole proprietor.

In Charleston, South Carolina, they performed in a theatre built to serve their needs from October 7, 1754, to about January 27, 1755. After Charleston the troupe temporarily disbanded, and the Hallam family retired to Kingston, Jamaica, where they joined forces with David Douglass (? – 1789) and Mr. and Mrs. Owen Morris, former members of the Moody troupe. The Hallams achieved much in thirty months in the colonies. They refurbished three theatres and built a fourth, they allayed some of the Puritan disdain for theatre and for actors by taking themselves seriously and maintaining a high standard of decorum, and they presented, in addition to their original repertory, fourteen full-length plays and several afterpieces.

In 1756 Lewis Hallam died, leaving the company to his wife. Shortly thereafter, Mrs. Hallam married David Douglass, who became the new company manager. The reorganized troupe returned to the American colonies in the fall of 1758 for what was to be a sixteen-year residency. During the American Company's second period, which ended at Charleston on May 19, 1774, Douglass, Mrs. Hallam Douglass, and their partners and employees built four permanent theatres, introduced to American audiences the first native-written, professionally produced American play, and, by stubbornly refusing to yield to oppression, strengthened and expanded the position of theatre in the culture of colonial America. In addition, they added to their repertory thirty-five full-length plays and more short pieces, many seen in the colonies only a year or two after the London premiere.

The Hallam-Douglass Company of Comedians from London built their first new theatre in New York City on Cruger's Wharf in the East River. They were at first denied permission to perform plays, so they established the Histrionic Academy as an outlet for their talents. On December 28, 1757, after gaining permission, they opened the new theatre with a production of Nicholas Rowe's "she-tragedy" *Jane Shore*. They closed February 7, 1759, and may have spent part of the ensuing spring performing in Perth Amboy, New Jersey. On June 25 the troupe began a six month's residency in Philadelphia. Despite much opposition from religious quarters, Douglass built a new theatre in Southwark and had it equipped with a new set of scenery painted by William Williams. From Philadelphia, the group moved to Annapolis where yet a third new theatre was built for an initial five-week residency. From Annapolis, Douglass led his company to Upper Marlborough (May 22, 1760 to July 1, 1760) and then to Williamsburg (c. October 2, 1760 to May 1761), with brief forays into Norfolk, Suffolk, and Petersburg, Virginia, and Fredericksburg, Maryland.

Late in the spring of 1761, armed with a good conduct certificate from Governor Dinwiddie of Virginia, Douglass ventured north to the less hospitable Newport, Rhode Island. Despite public objection, he built a temporary theatre on Eastern Point and presented his company in "moral dialogues," a euphemism for standard dramas in the repertory, from June to October 31, 1761. In November he moved back to New York City, where a third new theatre was being readied for his use. This building, ninety feet by forty feet and seating about 325 people, was situated on Beekman Street (then Chapel), below Nassau Street. The group wintered in New York, leaving there in early May 1762 for brief visits to Newport and Providence, where they again encountered public opposition. Forced out of a performance space in the new "school house" in Meeting Street, east of Benefit Street in Providence in August 1762, the group journeyed south. They spent one year in Williamsburg and Petersburg and almost three years in Charleston and Barbados, where they were welcomed in November 1763 as "The American Company of Comedians." Douglass built a new theatre in Queen Street, Charleston, for a residency beginning December 14, 1763. The theatre was dark most of 1765 while the group was in Barbados, but Charlestonians enjoyed a four-month season in early 1766.

In the summer of 1766, Douglass took his company north to Philadelphia; equipped it with new players, new scenery, and new plays; and set it up in a new theatre in the city's northeast district of Southwark. The building on Cedar, or South, Street, between Fourth and Fifth streets, was the first permanent theatre in America. In the American Company was the first native American to become a professional actor, Samuel Greville, and one of the group's first tasks was the production of Thomas Godfrey's *Prince of Parthia*, a new play by an American author. The Philadelphia season of 1766–67 (to July 6), in addition to claiming so many firsts, may have been the most accomplished of the Douglass era.

The American Company played a supplemental season in Philadelphia from October 9 to November 25, 1767, while a new theatre was being built on John Street, New York City. The company's inaugural performance in the second permanent theatre in America was on December 7, 1767. They did not draw well in the John Street Theatre that first season, so they returned to Philadelphia in July, where they again experienced heavy financial losses in a season of six month's duration. On January 9, 1769, they returned to the John Street Theatre, New York City, playing there to modest receipts until July, when they ventured up the Hudson to Albany for a month of performances in the city hospital. In September 1769 they traveled to Philadelphia, where they stayed until June 1, 1770, producing many new plays in an effort to attract patrons and weather this period of severe financial distress.

In mid-1770 they went to Williamsburg for a summer. The next year found the troupe in Annapolis, Williamsburg, and other Virginia and Maryland cities. The company slowly recovered its economic health, and Douglass was able to open a permanent theatre in Williamsburg, his third in the colonies, on September 9, 1771, and to purchase new scenery, painted in London. In October 1772 the restored American company, again near the peak of its power, returned to Philadelphia's Southwark Theatre for a successful season, highlighted by the most spectacular production in the twenty-one-year history of the company, a rendition of George Cockling's *Conquest of Canada; or, The Siege of Quebec,* presented February 17, 1773. Some performances in Philadelphia were disrupted by jeering patriots in the gallery, men who condemned the probably apolitical players as Loyalists. Similar incidents checked the otherwise smooth surface of the group's New York visit, April 14 to August 5, 1773. From New York Douglass sailed to Charleston to secure the theatre, leaving the company under the management of the temperamental and possessive leading man John Henry (1738–94). Henry led his charges to Annapolis for the racing season, ending in mid-October, and then withdrew them to Philadelphia to await ocean transportation to Charleston. Meanwhile, Douglass was supervising the construction of a new theatre on Church Street in Charleston, which the American Company opened December 22, 1773. The Charleston season, which closed May 19, 1774, was to be the group's last in the colonies until 1785. The company temporarily disbanded in Charleston, and before they could reassemble in Philadelphia, the Continental Congress forbade public amusements as a mobilization measure.

Mrs. Hallam Douglass passed away in Philadelphia in the autumn of 1774. The American Company's third period ended as the group reassembled in Jamaica, where they occupied a theatre in Kingston, on the Parade, near the barracks in Victoria Park. Still later, they built a new home in Spanish Town, on Montego Bay. David Douglass headed the company until 1779, when he abandoned his career in theatre to become the king's printer in Jamaica, a post he held until his death in 1789.

Lewis Hallam, Jr., assumed proprietorship and management of the company in 1779 and steered it through a period of financial hardship in 1780. When John Henry rejoined the group in 1781, he assumed copartnership with young Hallam. As the colonial Revolution ended in 1781, Hallam and Henry planned a return to America. Henry left for the new nation in January 1782 to secure property rights and titles to company theatres in Annapolis, Philadelphia, and New York. Hallam embarked on a talent search in London theatres. Thomas Godwin managed the group until Henry returned in January 1784. Meanwhile, Lewis Hallam returned to Philadelphia in January 1784 and joined with Mr. Allen to manage a small troupe until his associates could leave Jamaica. The Hallam-Allen company played in Philadelphia from December 1784 to July 29, 1785, and then moved to New York, in the throes of postwar turmoil, for a brief season of "lectures" (subterfuge for "plays") at the John Street Theatre, beginning about August 11, 1785, and ending in November. Hallam then rejoined John Henry and the Old American Company for a season at the John Street Theatre beginning November 21, 1785. Allen went to Albany to build and manage the first theatre in that city.

The Old American Company dominated theatre in New York until 1792. Opposition to the theatre persisted, but Hallam and Henry steered a carefully nationalistic and prudential course. The old regulars (Lewis Hallam, Jr., John Henry, Stephen Woolls, and Owen Morris) were aging. The second Mrs. Morris (formerly Elizabeth Walker), Fanny Storer, and Maria Storer Henry played female leads, and Thomas Wignell aspired to the best roles for men. In this first season in the new nation, the company produced its first hit: Richard Brinsley Sheridan's *The School for Scandal*, which ran first seven and then eighteen nights in succession.

In 1786 the troupe opened a new theatre in Baltimore, on Philpot's Hill, near Pratt and Albermarle streets, and remained there a month. They visited Richmond in October and November, again inaugurating a new theatre built by Alexander Quesnoy. A fortnight in Philadelphia started the new year of 1787, followed by four months at the John Street Theatre in New York City. During this stand they produced Royall Tyler's *The Contrast*, the first American comedy to be performed by professional actors. They also experienced an episode of internal strife that seriously undermined the integrity of the organization. Thomas Wignell and Mrs. Kenna wanted roles assigned to Lewis Hallam, John Henry, and Elizabeth Morris. The oldsters refused to yield. Mrs. Kenna was forced out of the company, and Wignell's disenchantment smouldered. The Old American Company in this period had a virtual monopoly on theatre in the new nation, and Hallam and Henry were indisposed to allow younger performers into the management fold or to help other groups get started.

Tours in 1787 took the group to Philadelphia, Annapolis, Baltimore, and, probably, to Richmond. The winter season in New York (December 21, 1787, to May 31, 1788) was very modestly profitable. There followed a tour to Philadelphia, Baltimore, and back to Philadelphia, the last season in the Quaker City in which it was necessary to resort to the subterfuge of calling plays "lectures" and "dialogs" to evade the letter of the law. Two notable events occurred in the New York season of April 14 to December 15, 1789. In September, the Old American Company produced its first piece by William Dunlap (1766–1839), *The Father; or, American Shandyism.* Dunlap was the first American to attempt to make a profession of playwriting. *The Father* was his second play. The Old American Company produced two more of his comedies, two tragedies, and an opera in the next few years. Dunlap bought into the company in 1796 and became its sole proprietor and manager in 1798. Internal strife grew as Maria Storer Henry's incontinent use of alcohol created embarrassment behind the scenes and on stage.

By 1790 the company was regularly at the John Street Theatre for six months, spending the rest of the year in Philadelphia, Baltimore, and Annapolis. In 1791 Wignell and Mr. and Mrs. Owen Morris left the company over Henry's refusal to allow Wignell greater managerial and artistic power and responsibility. At the same time, artistic pressure mounted as newspaper commentators assailed the management for its failure to strengthen the company with new talent from England. The effects of monopoly were pervasive. The Old American Company left Philadelphia in July 1791 and took up nearly permanent residence in New York. They played their last season in Philadelphia's Southwark Theatre from May 28 to July 2, 1792. By this time the company was in shambles. Wignell and the Morrises were gone. Mrs. Joseph Harper died in October 1791, and her husband was on the verge of retirement. Lewis Hallam, nearing the end of his career, was about to marry Miss Tuke and was avidly promoting her career. John Henry was loath to bring in an actress to compete with Mrs. Henry, and the proprietors wanted to protect their lines of acting business, so the organization languished. At the conclusion of the Philadelphia run, the group disbanded, and the company was dissolved. Meanwhile, John Henry yielded to his business sense and went to England to recruit new players. When he returned in the summer of 1792, he and Hallam formed a new organization under the old name, and he hired many of the old performers, persons who had been company shareholders. When the Old American Company reappeared at the Southwark Theatre, Philadelphia, on September 26, 1792, it was a salaried company under the partnership management of John Henry and Lewis Hallam, Jr., and it featured a group of strong, new performers from England, led by John Hodgkinson.

PERSONNEL

Managers: William Hallam, Lewis Hallam (1752–54); Lewis Hallam (1754–c.56); Mrs. Lewis Hallam (1756–c.57); David Douglass (c.1757–79); Lewis Hallam, Jr. (1779–85); Lewis Hallam, Jr., John Henry (1785–92).

Other: Mr. Broadbelt, business manager (c.1767); Jacob Snyder, scenic artist (1762– ?).

Actors, Actresses, Dancers, Pantomimists and Instrumentalists: George Abbington, dancer (1759– ?); William Adcock, violinist (1752–55); Mrs. William Adcock (1752–55); *Adam Allyn* (1759–68); Mr. Ashton (c.1791–92); Mr. Barry (1763– ?); Mrs. Becceley (1753–55); Charles Bell (1753–55); Mr. Biddle (1784–89); Mr. Bisset (c.1791–94), Mr. Bylerly (c.1773); *Margaret Cheer*, later Mrs. Long (1764– ?, 1773–74, 1781–94); Thomas Clarkson (1752–55); Mrs. Thomas Clarkson (1752–55); Mr. Dermot (1773– ?); *David Douglass* (1756–79); *Mr. Douthwaitt* (1760–61, 1763–68); *Mrs. Douthwaitt* (1760–61, 1763–68); Mr. Emmett (1763–c.66); Mr. Furell (1763– ?); Mr. Gay (1790); Mrs. Gifford (c.1787); *James Verling Godwin* (1767–c.75), Richard Goodman (1771– ?, 1779–c.81); Mrs. Gray (c.1791–92); *Samuel Greville* (1767–c.73); *Adam Hallam* (1752–c.64); *Helen Hallam* (1752–c.55); *Lewis Hallam* (1752–c.56); *Mrs. Lewis Hallam*, later *Mrs. David Douglass* (1752–c.74); *Lewis Hallam*, Jr. (1752–1806); Mrs. Lewis Hallam, Jr. (1761); *Nancy Hallam* (c.1755–60, 1766–c.84); Mrs. Hamilton (1779– ?, 1788– ?); Mr. Hammond (1791–94); Mr. Harman (1755–c.59); *Catherine Maria Harman* (1755–c.73); *Mr. Joseph Harper* (c.1784–92); *Mrs. Joseph Harper* (c.1784–c.91); Mr. Heard (1786–c.93); *Ann Storer Henry* (1767– ?, 1774– ?); as *Mrs. Hogg* (1798–1817); *John Henry* (1767–74, 1781–94); *Maria Storer Henry* (1768–94); Mr. Herbert (1752–53); Mr. Horne (c.1755–c.59); *George Hughes* (1773–81); William Hulett, dancer, singer (1753–55); *Joseph Jefferson* (1791–1803); I. or J. Kenna (1786); Miss Kenna (1786); Mr. Kenna (1786); Mrs. Kenna (1786–87); Mr. Lake (1785–89); Charles Love, harpsichordist, and Mrs. Charles Love, singer (1753–c.59); *Patrick Malone* (1752–55, 1767–69); *John Martin* (1790–c.1807); Mr. Mathews, dancer (1766–67); Mr. McPherson (1786); Francis Mentges (? –c.1774); Mr. Miller (1753–55); Isaac Morales (1779–c.84); *Elizabeth Walker Morris* (1771–90); *Owen Morris* (1755–90); *Mrs. Owen Morris* (1755–d.67); Walter Murray (1760); Henrietta Osborne (1766); Miss Palmer (1752); John Palmer (1759–60); Mr. Platt (1767– ?); Mr. Quelch (1761– ?); Mrs. Rankin (1791–93); Mrs. Raymond (c.1779); Mr. Reed (c.1755–c.62); Mary Richardson (? –c.1774); William Rigby (1752–c.55); Mr. Roberts (c.1779–c.84); Mr. Robinson (1791); Mr. Ryan, prompter (1785–c.95); Mr. Sale (c.1779); Mr. Scott (1759); Mrs. Sewall (c.1788); John Singleton (1752–c.58); *Fanny Storer* (1768–69, c.1785– ?); Mr. Sturt (1760–62); *Mr. Tomlinson* (c.1755–c.64); *Mrs. Tomlinson* (c.1755–c.64); John Tremain (1761); *Miss Tuke*, later *Mrs. Lewis Hallam, Jr.* (1785–1806); Mr. Vaughn (1791–92); William Verling (1766); *Miss Wainright*, later *Mrs.*

Miranda, and *Mrs. Isaac Morales* (c.1766–84); *Thomas Wall* (1766–c.74); *Mrs. Thomas Wall* (1767–c.74); *Thomas Wignell* (1774–90); William Wignell (c.1774–?); *Stephen Woolls* (1766–99); Mr. Wynell (1752–53).

REPERTORY

Dates in parentheses indicate the first performance by the company.

1752–54: *The Merchant of Venice, Lethe,* and/or *The Anatomist* (9/15/52); *Othello* (11/9/52); *Damon and Phillada* (9/15/53); *The Conscious Lovers* (9/17/53); *Tunbridge Walks* (9/24/53); *The Constant Couple* (10/1/53); *Virgin Unmasked* (10/8/53); *Love for Love* (10/22/53); *Tom Thumb* (10/22/53); *George Barnwell* (10/29/53); *Lying Valet* (10/29/53); *The Distrest Mother* (11/5/53); *Hob in the Well* (11/5/53); *Richard III* (11/12/53); *The Devil to Pay* (11/12/53); *The Beggar's Opera* (11/19/53); *The Committee* (11/26/53); *The Spanish Fryar* (11/30/53); *The Careless Husband* (12/3/53); *Beaux Stratagem* (12/10/53); *Harlequin Collector* (12/10/53); *Miss in Her Teens* (12/17/53); *The Fair Penitent* (12/17/53); *The Twin Rivals* (12/26/53); *The Drummer* (1/7/54); *King Lear* (1/14/54); *Woman Is a Riddle* (1/21/54); *Romeo and Juliet* (1/28/54); *The Gamester* (2/4/54); *The Earl of Essex* (2/11/54); *The Miller of Mansfield* (2/11/54); *The Suspicious Husband* (2/18/54); *Harlequin Skeleton* (2/15/54); *The Albion Queens* (2/25/54); *The Virgin Unmasked* (2/25/54); *The Tragedy of Jane Shore* (3/4/54); *The Stagecoach* (3/11/54); *Tamerlane* (6/12/54); *A Wife Well Managed* (6/12/54); *The Provok'd Husband* (6/24/54); *The Orphan* (?/54); *A Bold Stroke for a Wife* (?/54); *Cato* (11/6/54); *The Recruiting Officer* (11/13/54).

1759–60: *The Inconstant* (1/1/59); *The Mock Doctor* (1/1/60); *Lovers' Quarrels* (1/8/60); *Venice Preserved* (1/15/60); *Douglas* (1/24/60); *Honest Yorkshireman* (7/6/60); *Adventures of Half an Hour* (7/20/60); *Hamlet* (7/27/60); *Theodosius* (8/10/60); *The School Boy* (8/31/60); *The Toy Shop* (10/5/60); *Macbeth* (10/26/60); *The Busybody* (3/24/60); *The Revenge* (3/27/60).

1761–66: *Henry IV, Part 1* (12/18/61); *The Mourning Bride* (12/22/63); *The Jealous Wife* (3/17/64); *The Orphan of China* (3/26/64); *A Wonder, A Woman Keeps a Secret* (4/25); *Love in a Village* (2/10/66); *The Way to Keep Him* (3/20/66); *The School for Lovers* (4/3/66); *Catherine and Petruchio* (11/21/66); *The Old Maid* (11/28/66); *The Oracle* (12/5/66).

1767: *The Upholsterer* (1/23); *High Life below Stairs* (1/26); *The Citizen* (1/30); *The Reprisal* (2/2); *The Miser* (2/9); *Thomas and Sally* (2/20); *The Mayor of Garratt* (2/23); *All for Love* (3/9); *Love Makes a Man* (3/14); *The Deuce in Him* (3/14); *The Brave Irishman* (3/17); *The Witches: A Pantomime* (4/2); *The Contrivances* (4/20); *The Prince of Parthia* (4/24); *The Apprentice* (5/4); *A Picture of a Playhouse* (5/11); *The Spirit of Contradiction* (5/11); *Don Quixote in England* (5/21); *Cymbeline* (5/25); *The Country Lasses* (6/4); *The Chaplet* (6/4); *Coriolanus* (6/8); *Neck or Nothing* (6/12); *Double Disappointment* (6/15); *The Roman Father* (6/18); *Harlequin Restored* (10/9); *The Clandestine Marriage* (11/19).

1768: *All in the Wrong* (4/6); *Polly Honeycomb* (4/21); *Taste, an interlude* (5/2); *Love à la Mode* (5/13); *Cock-Lane Ghost* (6/2); *King John* (12/12); *False Delicacy* (12/16); *Zara* (12/26); *Alexander the Great* (12/30); "Dissertation upon Noses" (12/30).

1769: *The Guardian* (2/2); *The English Merchant* (2/6); *Every Man in His Humour*

(2/20); *The Tender Husband* (3/25); *The Musical Lady* (4/3); *The Maid of the Milk* (5/4); *Padlock* (5/29); *Midas* (11/24); *The Siege of Damascus* (12/19).

1770: *The Tempest* (1/19); *Neptune and Amphitrite* (1/19); *Edward: The Black Prince* (2/6); *The Funeral* (2/9); *The Merry Wives of Windsor* (3/2); *Comus* (3/9); *The Good-Natured Man* (5/3); *Wits Last Stake* (5/10); *Julius Caesar* (6/1).

1771: *The Brothers* (3/?); *A School for Libertines; or, A Word to the Wise* (3/26); *The West Indian* (10/23).

1772: *The Fashionable Lover* (11/30); *Lionel and Clarissa* (12/14).

1773: *Englishman in Paris* (1/20); *Edgar and Emmaline* (2/15); *The Conquest of Canada* (2/17); *Cymon* (3/3); *The Register Office* (3/29); *Cross Purposes* (5/28); *The Irish Widow* (6/28); *She Stoops to Conquer* (8/2).

1774: *School for Fathers* (3/4); *Young America in London* (4/22).

1777 At Montego Bay: *The Gamester* (4/19).

1779 At Kingston: *Percy* (5/15); *Choleric Man* (6/1); *Devil upon Two Sticks* (10/30); *Duenna* (11/27).

1780 At Kingston: *Lyar* (2/16); *Theatrical Candidate* (2/16); *Countess of Salisbury* (3/18); *The Genii* (4/1); *The Rivals* (6/3); *The Ghost* (6/28); *Law of Lombardy* (7/1); *The Duke and No Duke* (10/21); *Rule a Wife and Have a Wife* (12/9).

1781 At Kingston: *The Vintner Tricked* (2/6); *Virginia* (6/12); *Tony Lumpkin in Town* (4/28); *She Wou'd and She Wou'd Not* (5/12); *The Triumph of Genius*, pantomime (5/12); *The School for Scandal* and *Shadows of Shakespeare* (6/12); *Chapter of Accidents* (6/30); *Measure for Measure* (7/18); *Linco's Travels* (7/18); *Daphne and Amintor* (7/18); *Maid of the Oaks* (8/4); *Author* (8/18); *School for Soldiers* (8/25); *The Quakers* (8/25); *Lilliputian Camp* (9/1); *West Indian Lady's Arrival in London* (9/1); *The Belle's Stratagem* (12/8); *Kingston Privateer* (12/8).

1782 At Kingston: *The Grecian Daughter* (1/19); *Scandal Club* (2/7); *Edward and Eleanora* (7/3).

1783 At Montego Bay: *Cleone* (9/3); *Isabella* (10/11).

1784 At Montego Bay: *The Chances* (4/15).

1785 At New York's John Street Theatre: *Touchstone; or Harlequin Traveler* (9/1); *Flitch of Bacon* (9/27); *Elopement*, pantomime (9/30); *The Poor Soldier* (12/2); *Sir Thomas Overbury* (12/26).

1786: *The Benevolent Merchant* (1/6); *Robinson Crusoe* (1/11); *More Ways Than One* (3/6); *Rosina* (4/19); *Harlequin's Invasion* and *As You Like It* (7/14).

1787: *Agreeable Surprise* (1/27); *Harlequin's Frolic* (1/31); *Much Ado about Nothing* (3/19); *The Widow's Vow* (3/23); *Love in a Camp* (4/13); *The Contrast* (4/16); *The Deaf Lover* (5/7); *The School for Wives* (5/8); *May Day* (5/19); *All in the Wrong* (5/23); *Selima and Azor* (6/1); *The Deserter* (6/8); *The Mysterious Husband* (12/21).

1788: *The First Floor* (2/6); *The Madcap* (2/11); *The Heiress* (2/25); *Convention; or, Columbian Father* (4/7); *The Castle of Andalusia* (4/21); *True Blue* (4/24).

1789: *Who's the Dupe?* (6/12); *He Would Be a Soldier* (6/22); *Inkle and Yarico* (7/1); *The Father* (7/7); *Like Master, Like Man* (9/9); *Dead Alive* (9/24); *All's Well That Ends Well* (10/1); *Duplicity* (10/9); *The Critic* (10/12); *Cheats of Scapin* (10/19); *Gustavus Vasa* (10/22); *The Fair American* (11/9); *Invasion* (11/13); *Wapping Landlady* (11/16); *The Toy* (11/24); *Darby's Return* (11/24); *Prisoner at Large* (11/28).

1790: *The Wrangling Lovers* (2/26); *The Widow of Malabar* (5/7); *Half an Hour after Supper* (5/17); *All the World's a Stage* (5/17); *Shakespeare Jubilee* (6/3); *Harlequin Cook* (6/10); *Patie and Roger* (7/1).

1791: *Seeing's Believing* (3/11); *The Recess* (4/27); *The Dramatist* (5/2); *Death of Harlequin* (5/19); *As It Should Be* (5/19); *Little Hunchback* (5/27); *Harlequin Shipwrecked* (6/13); *The Rival Candidates* (6/13); *Constitutional Follies* (6/30); *Birth of Harlequin* (7/7); *Divorce* (11/28).

1792: *King of the Genii* (1/2); *The Bird Catcher*, ballet (1/25); *Two Philosophers*, ballet (2/3); *Return of the Laborers*, ballet, and *Harlequin Wood Cutter*, ballet (2/10); *The Restoration of Harlequin* (2/13); *La Belle Dorothee*, ballet (2/17); *Columbine Invisible*, ballet (2/24); *Silver Rock* (3/26); *Yorker's Stratagem* (4/24); *Harlequin Balloonist*, ballet (5/3); *The New Peerage* (5/8); *Enchanted Nosegay*, ballet (6/5); *Merry Girl* (6/7); *Harlequin Tobacconist*, ballet (6/20).

BIBLIOGRAPHY

McCosker, Susan, "The American Company, 1752–1791, Founders of the American Theatre." M.A. thesis, Catholic University of America, 1968.

Odell, George C.D. *Annals of the New York Stage*. Vol. 1. New York: Columbia University Press, 1927.

Rankin, Hugh F. *The Theatre in Colonial America*. Chapel Hill: University of North Carolina Press, 1965.

Seilhamer, George O. *History of the American Theatre*. Vols 1–2. Philadelphia: Globe Printing House, 1889.

Weldon B. Durham

[OLD] AMERICAN COMPANY. (Reorganized: 1792–1806). The salaried company under the dual proprietorship and management of Lewis Hallam, Jr. (1740–1808), and John Henry (1738–94) appeared first at Philadelphia's Southwark Theatre on September 26, 1792, in *Wonder*, by Susannah Centlivre, and in *Padlock*, by Isaac Bickerstaffe. John Hodgkinson (1766–1805), age twenty-six, in the eleventh year of a long career in theatre, debuted as second leading man (comedy) with Hallam and Henry's forces. Mrs. Hodgkinson, flaxen haired and blue eyed, assumed roles in the soubrette line of business and contributed dances and songs in the *entr'acte*. Other performers recruited in England and debuting at this time were William King, W. H. Prigmore, and James West. Later, Hallam and Henry hired Mrs. James Wrighten (later Mrs. Pownall) to play female leads, and they employed Miss Brett (later Mrs. King), Mrs. Hodgkinson's younger sister, in a utility line. Several members of the old sharing company were hired, including Mr. Ryan (box keeper and utility actor), John Durang (dancer), Miss Tuke (soon to be Mrs. Lewis Hallam, Jr.), Mrs. Henry, and Stephen Woolls (with the company since 1766).

Although blame is difficult to assign, the new organization was beset by internal strife, apparently originating in the belligerent efforts of John Hodgkinson to promote his own career and that of his wife, her sister, and her mother. Hodgkinson also favored the use of English recruits in lines of business and roles formerly in the possession of the longtime shareholders. Turmoil in the company ultimately created a rift between Hallam and Henry, and the unity of the group was further undermined. Hodgkinson's maneuvers particularly affected Mr. and Mrs. John Henry. Hodgkinson, a very popular actor and singer, had ordered the repertory to make light use of Mr. and Mrs. Henry, but he had also subordinated a splendid leading actress, Mrs. Pownall, to Mrs. Hodgkinson. In 1794 Mr. and Mrs. Henry left the company. Henry sold his partnership to Lewis Hallam, Jr., who resold some or all of Henry's share to John Hodgkinson.

The Hallam-Henry Company played a season in Philadelphia that ended January 12, 1793, after which they moved to New York's John Street Theatre for a spring and summer season ending July 14, 1793. The new pieces entering the group's repertory in this first year were primarily farces such as the long-popular *No Song, No Supper* of Prince Hoare, introduced December 10, 1792, in Philadelphia, and Charles Dibdin's *Waterman*, first played by the group in New York on May 20, 1793. The opportunities in Philadelphia were rapidly decreasing in the face of stiff competition from Thomas Wignell's powerful company at the New Theatre in Chestnut Street. A brief season at the Southwark, Philadelphia, scheduled while the Wignell troupe was in Baltimore, ended abruptly in August 1793, as a yellow-fever epidemic seized the Quaker City. The reorganized Old American Company, streamlined by the addition of Mrs. Melmoth in tragic leads, was idle until November 11, 1793, when they returned to the John Street Theatre in New York for a long season ending June 28, 1794. Most of the new works in the repertory were farces and comediettas, such as those from the pen of John O'Keeffe *(Farmer, Wild Oats, Highland Reel, The World in a Village, The Young Quaker)* and Mrs. Inchbald *(Child of Nature, Such Things Are, Animal Magnetism, I'll Tell You What, Every One Has His Fault, Midnight Hour)*. In New York the company met a heavy demand for nationalistic plays on the theme of liberty, a demand they seldom satisfied. But the public also wanted comedy and spectacle, which the reorganized Old American Company ably provided. The old tragedies, the staple of the company before the Revolution, were seldom performed. William Dunlap (1766–1839) contributed regularly to the repertory in the years before he stepped into the management of the group. His *Wedding* appeared on May 20, 1793. Eleven months later the group presented his tragedy *The Fatal Deception* and the interlude *Shelty's Travels*. Dunlap's *Fontainville Abbey*, a gothic thriller adapted from a popular novel, premiered February 16, 1795. None of them was remarkably successful.

After Hodgkinson became Lewis Hallam's partner, the company played only one season in Philadelphia (September 22 to December 4, 1794), again while the Chestnut Street Theatre Company* was in Baltimore. Thomas Morton's *Children in the Wood* was the hit of the season, although a spectacular production of *Macbeth* with special scenery by the Old

American Company's scenic artist Charles Ciceri was exceptional in its departure from stock production heretofore given the old tragedies. While the Philadelphia link was weakening, a New England connection was being forged. John Martin led a contingent of Old American Company performers to Hartford in 1794, and Hodgkinson led another splinter group into Hartford for a season beginning August 3, 1795. At the same time, elements of the company played a season in Providence, Rhode Island. The two joined and, with members of the Boston ["Federal Street"] Theatre Company*, played a brief but brilliant season at Boston's Federal Street Theatre from November 2, 1795, to January 13, 1796. The combined Boston company was one of the most talented assemblages yet seen on the American stage, including Mr. and Mrs. Snelling Powell of the Boston Theatre, the Hodgkinsons, the Joseph Tylers, John and Elizabeth Johnson, the Joseph Harpers, and young Joseph Jefferson of the New York troupe. The combined company began the new year with a production of Charles Dibdin's musical burletta *Poor Vulcan,* an early example of an entertainment form that captured and held the hearts of American audiences during the next half-century. Summer trips to New England cities continued for several years after the Old American Company settled somewhat permanently into a residency at the John Street Theatre in New York on February 10, 1796.

At John Hodgkinson's request, William Dunlap became associate manager of the Old American Company for the winter/spring season at the John Street Theatre. Dunlap hoped to have more of his own works produced, a hope temporarily dashed by Hallam's refusal to sign contracts for Dunlap's plays. Nevertheless, Dunlap's *The Archers,* an opera with music by Benjamin Carr, was the first of twenty-two new works presented in this season. George Odell assessed the season as one of the most brilliant in the history of the John Street Theatre, a history rapidly coming to an end. The season in Hartford (July 17 to September 13, 1796) was the first under joint management of Dunlap, Hallam, and Hodgkinson, and it ended with Lewis Hallam's retirement from management. When he sold his share of the property to Dunlap and Hodgkinson, Lewis Hallam, Jr., ended forty-five years of Hallam family interest in the Old American Company. He and Mrs. Hallam stayed on as hirelings until 1806. The end of the season of 1796–97 also was the beginning of the end for the John Street Theatre. Plans were underway for the construction of a new theatre on Park Row, near Ann Street, as Hodgkinson left for Hartford and Boston. The Boston season netted poor financial returns, but Hodgkinson held on while awaiting the completion of the New Theatre, as it was then called. The company returned to the John Street Theatre for a brief interim December 11, 1797, to January 13, 1798. The interlude is memorable for the first appearance, on January 5, 1798, with the Old American Company of Thomas Abthorpe Cooper, later owner, manager, and leading light of the company and for nearly thirty years a regular visiting star (his last starring engagement was in June 1830).

On January 29, 1798, the Old American Company opened the New Theatre on Park Row with Shakespeare's *As You Like It,* followed by J. C. Cross' farce afterpiece *The Purse.* The New Theatre and its successor on the same site was the company's home for the next fifty years and New York's premier theatre for most of that time. The first Park Theatre seated 2,000 in box, pit, and gallery. A month later, to bolster declining box-office receipts, T. A. Cooper joined the company for an extended starring engagement. The first Park Theatre season also marked the advent of several new romantic dramas. Morton's *Zorinski* and Dunlap's *Major André* were among the first of a string of "dramas dealing with tyrants, wronged misanthropes, impregnable castles, and persecuted maidens, in Poland or Russia, or other semi-barbarous lands" (Odell, 2:17). The tide of romance peaked in the season of 1798–99, when, under William Dunlap's management, the company produced a spate of gothic dramas, among them several Dunlap adaptations of the plays of August Kotzebue (1761–1819): *The Stranger, The Natural Son, Count Benyowski, The Italian Father,* and *Indians in England.* Friedrich von Schiller's *Don Carlos* and *Love and Intrigue* also appeared, as did Dunlap's own *Sterne's Maria* and *The Natural Daughter.* The Kotzebue craze continued in 1799–1800, when Dunlap's adaptation of *Pizarro in Peru; or, the Death of Rolla* played an unprecedented six-night run beginning March 26, 1800, after Kotzebue's *Virgin of the Sun* had thrilled Park Theatre audiences for five consecutive nights beginning March 12. Fourteen new Kotzebue dramas were performed for Park Theatre audiences in this long season.

The energy and industry of the organization is clear from the variety and novelty of each season. The 1798 New York season of seventy-six performances was made up of fifty-five main plays (mostly comedies) and fifty-three afterpieces. In 1798–99 a season of eighty-eight performances was made up of forty-eight main plays and forty-seven afterpieces.

At the end of the Old American Company's first Park Theatre season, John Hodgkinson left to assume the management of Boston's Federal Street Theatre Company. Dunlap became sole manager and proprietor and brought in Mrs. Oldmixon (? –1835) (formerly Miss George, the singing star of London's Haymarket Theatre in the 1780s) from Wignell's Chestnut Street Theatre Company in Philadelphia. The company, despite the leadership of Thomas Abthorpe Cooper and Mrs. Oldmixon and the support of Joseph Jefferson (1774–1832) and John Hogg (1770–1813), was not strong. However, Dunlap's introduction of new romantic drama carried the group through the seasons of 1798–99 and 1799–80. Despite receiving the group's highest salary, Mrs. Oldmixon stayed only one year, and on March 10, 1800, Cooper withdrew, apparently unhappy with the company's commitment to romance, a mode to which his crisp, classical sensibility was hardly adaptable.

John Hodgkinson returned to the Old American Company with his retinue (Mrs. Hodgkinson, Miss Brett, Mrs. Brett, Miss Harding, and Mrs. King) for the 1799–1800 season; James Fennell (1766–1816) appeared with the group in 1800–1801, as did Mr. and Mrs. Snelling Powell, stars of the Boston stage. Mrs. Joseph Jefferson (*nee* Fortune) appeared in December 1800 and stayed with the company until she and her husband left in 1803. Additionally, Hopkins Robinson (d.1819), later Robertson, an employee in the Park Theatre costume department, began to play small roles but rapidly advanced to greater responsibility, thereby launching a twenty-year career in which he played a prominent role in the life of the company. J.H.D. Zschokke's *Abaellino; or, The Great Bandit* was the hit of the season, playing eight consecutive performances in February 1801.

The following season, carried on day to day by the Hodgkinsons in popular farces as afterpieces, was remarkable for its most successful production, that of *Bluebeard* by George Colman, the younger, seen first on March 8, 1802, and the two-week engagement in April of Mrs. Merry. *Bluebeard* was the Old American Company's most successful production in Dunlap's years in management, being presented twelve times in this season, six in succession. Mrs. Merry's appearance marked, according to Odell, the pinnacle of excellence in acting for Dunlap's management. Despite these surges of success, the company was slowly slipping into bankruptcy, a condition that ended Dunlap's management in 1805.

T. A. Cooper returned to the Old American Company in 1801 to play leading men, resigning in January 1803 to go to London to replace Kemble at Drury Lane, and returning only in starring attractions until he became theatre lessee and manager of the company in 1806. Dunlap's group incandesced briefly in 1802–3 and then rapidly declined. Mrs. Hodgkinson died in September 1803, and John Hodgkinson began looking for other employment (he later joined Alexander Placide's company in the 1803–4 season in Charleston, South Carolina). This was also the last season with the Old American Company for Joseph Jefferson. The theatre was in bad repair, and the plays Dunlap selected were not attracting adequate patronage to keep the group solvent. Moreover, this year marked the beginning of a long tradition of fine descriptive and critical writing in New York's *Morning Chronicle* and *Evening Post* newspapers. The criticism of William Coleman and of "Jonathan Oldstyle" (Washington Irving) in the *Post* and the *Chronicle*, respectively, was especially troublesome for the Old American Company. Coleman leveled a broadside of complaints against Dunlap's management, against Hodgkinson (for his obstinacy as a company member and for his increasing corpulency), and against the "buckram crew," the company's supernumeraries, who were condemned for their inattentive behavior and for their poor and dirty costumes. The company and its manager, repertory, stars, and home were commonly the butt of critical and humorous jibes. Leading ladies Mrs. Whitlock and Mrs. Johnson failed to please, and with Cooper's departure, the company was without an attractive leading man. After a flurry of interest in Morton's *Voice of Nature* in February, the profitability of the season dropped sharply in the spring.

A yellow-fever plague forced the late opening of the Park in mid-November 1803. Dunlap was seeking concessions from his stockholders and trying to hold the company together. John E. Harwood (1771–1809), a fine comic actor, was recruited from Philadelphia and scored well in the first new play of the season, *John Bull; or, An Englishman's Fireside*, seen November 21 and repeated often throughout the season. Declining attendance and competition from a company at the Grove Theatre in Bedlow Street forced a temporary closing in mid-March.

The truncated season of 1804–5 was Dunlap's last in management. A weak company headed by John Darley and Ellen Westray Darley needed a twelve-night starring engagement from T. A. Cooper to stay in business in the fall. Again, competition from the Grove Theatre Company was telling, but they, too, failed to overcome the poverty and freezing cold that stilled the city's life in this bitter winter. The Park closed briefly in January but revived in February to present Dunlap's *Nina*, and then closed permanently February 22, 1805.

Dunlap's regime brought to New York many successes of the London stage and, in adaptations, many from his own pen, the best of contemporary French and German drama. Dunlap's repertoire featured modern plays. The stock tragedies were performed when Cooper was in residency, but Dunlap focused attention on new plays, especially his own. The Old American Company produced six of Dunlap's plays before he became a manager, thirty-eight in the nine years of his management. Fifteen were from his own pen, eight adapted from French, and seventeen from German sources. Eight other pieces have been attributed to him by subsequent scholarship. The great successes of the Dunlap era were Dunlap's own adaptations of the plays of the German August Kotzebue. Although Dunlap was a great importer of plays, he had little to do with the importation of players, one of the very successful revitalizing devices of his predecessors and successors.

The unemployed actors met in late February to form a cooperative under the comanagement of John Johnson (1759–1819) and Joseph Tyler (1751–1823); the so-called Theatrical Commonwealth reopened the Park Theatre on March 5, 1805. The most notable addition to the company was the comic actor William Twaits (1781–1814), brought to New York from Birmingham, England, via Philadelphia. A season of comedy ensued featuring a company strong in such material on the female side. The Commonwealth (Johnson and Tyler managing) resumed business on November 18, 1805. The company had no strong leading man who could play tragic roles and no adequate male juvenile. Starring attractions by Mrs. Jones, later a popular comic actress with the Park Theatre Company; T. A. Cooper; Joseph Jefferson; John E. Harwood; and William Twaits attracted patrons in modest but profitable numbers. The company introduced few new pieces, ten in the three-month season in 1805 and ten in the six-and-one-half-month season of 1805–6.

In 1806 the shareholders of the Park Theatre sold out to John K. Beekman and John Jacob Astor, who leased the property to Thomas A. Cooper. Meanwhile, on June 2, 1806, Lewis Hallam, Jr., retired from the New York stage, no longer a popular actor. His son Mirvan (1771–1811) carried on the family tradition in New York and in theatres in the South, when the new manager, Cooper, refused to hire the old actor-manager or his wife for the Park Theatre Company season of 1806–7.

PERSONNEL

Actors and Actresses: Andrew Jackson Allen (1805–8); Mr. Ashton (1792–95); Master George Barrett (1798); Giles L. Barrett (1798–99, 1805–6); Mrs. Giles L. Barrett (1798–99, 1805–6); Miss Bates (1798–99); Mr. Bates (1798–99); Mr. Bergman (1793); Mr. Berwick (1794–95); Mr. Bisset (1791–94); *Miss Brett*, later Mrs. William King (1792–96, 1799–1802); *Mrs. Brett* (1795–98, 1799–1803); *Arabella Brett* (1795–1803); Miss Broadhurst (1795–98); Mr. Burd (1803–6); Benjamin Carr, singer and composer (1794–95); Mr. Chalmers (1798); Mr. Charnock (1805–6); Miss Chaucer (1794–95); Mr. Claude (1803–4); *Mrs. Claude*, formerly Miss Hogg (1798–1803); Mr. Cleveland (1796); Mrs. Cleveland (1796); Mr. Collins (1796–97); Mrs. Collins (1797); *Thomas A. Cooper* (1798–1800, 1802–3); *Richard Crosby* (1793–97, 1799–1802); Mrs. Darby, formerly Miss Melbourne (1803–4); *John Darley* (1804–5); Miss Dellinger (1804–21); John Durang, dancer (1791–92, 1796–97); Mrs. John Durang (1794–97); John Fawcett (1795–98); *James Fennell* (1799–1804); *Gilbert Fox* (1799–1802); Mme. Gardie, dancer (1794–96); Miss Graham (1805–6); *Lewis Hallam, Jr.* (1792–1806); *Mrs. Lewis Hallam, Jr.*, formerly Miss Tuke (1792–1806); *Mirvan Hallam* (1792–93, 1794–1812); Mrs. Hamilton (1792–95); Mr. Hammond (1792–94); *Miss Harding*, later Mrs. Clark, later Mrs. G. Marshall (1794–98, 1799–1802, 1805–6); *Joseph Harper* (1800–1805); Mrs. Joseph Harper (1800–1801); *John E. Harwood* (1803–09); Mr. Heard (1792–94); *John Henry* (1792–94); *Mrs. John Henry* (1792–94); *John Hodgkinson* (1792–98, 1799–1803); *Mrs. John Hodgkinson* (1792–98, 1799–1803); *Ann Storer Henry Hogg* (1798–1805); *John Hogg* (1796–1807); *Joseph Jefferson* (1795–1803); *Mrs. Joseph Jefferson*, formerly Miss Fortune (1800–1803); *Elizabeth Johnson* (1795–1806); *John Johnson* (1795–1806); Mrs. Jones (1805–6); Mr. Kenna (1792–94); Mrs. Kenna (1792–94); *William King* (1792–96); *Mr. Lee*, actor and property master (1794–1802); *Mr. Leonard* (1794–1801); Mrs. Long, formerly Miss Cheer (1793–94); Mr. Macdonald (1799–1804); Mr. Marriott (1794–95); Mrs. Marriott (1794–95); *John Martin*, actor, stage manager, and property master (1794–95, 1796–1807); Mr. McKnight (1796–97); *Charlotte Melmoth* (1793–1802, 1804–5); *Mrs. Merry* (1801–2); John D. Miller (1793–95, 1796–99); Mrs. Miller, formerly Mrs. Rankin(?)(1793–95); Mr. Minton (1794–97); Mrs. Minton (1796–97); Mr. Nelson (1794–95); *Mrs. Oldmixon* (1798–

99); Miss Patton (1803–4); Mr. Perkins (1798–1800); Mrs. Perkins (1798–1800); Alexander Placide (1801); Mrs. Alexander Placide (1801); C. S. Powell (1797); Mrs. C. S. Powell (1797); Snelling Powell (1800–1801); Mrs. Snelling Powell (1800–1801); *Mrs. Pownall*, formerly Mrs. Wrighten (1792–95); William H. Prigmore (1792–96, 1797–98, 1802–3); Mrs. Rankin (1791–93); Mr. Richards (1793–95); Mr. Ringwood (1805–6); *Hopkins Robinson*, later Robertson (1800–1819); Miss Ross, later Mrs. F. Wheatley (1805–7); Mr. Ryan, boxkeeper, prompter, and actor (1792–95); Mr. Saubere, dancer (1804–7); Mr. Saunderson (1803–4); Mr. Serson (1803–4); *Mr. Seymour* (1796–99, 1803–4); Mrs. Seymour (1796–1800, 1803–4); Mr. Shapter (1798–1809); J. Simpson (1797–98, 1800–1802); *Mrs. J. Simpson* (1797–98, 1800–1802, 1805–8); Miss Solomons (1794); Mrs. Solomons (1794); Mrs. Spencer (1795); *Master Stockwell* (1795–1806); Mr. Tompkins (1795–97); Mr. Turnbull (1802–3); *William Twaits* (1805); *Joseph Tyler* (1795–1806); *Mrs. Joseph Tyler* (1795–98); Mr. Utt (1805–6); James West (1792–93); James West, Jr. (1792–93); *Elizabeth Westray*, later *Mrs. Villiers*, later *Mrs. William Twaits* (1801–2, 1805–7); *Ellen Westray*, later *Mrs. John Darley* (1797–1800, 1804–5); Juliana Westray (1797–99); Miss White (1798, 1803); Mr. Whitlock (1802–3); Mr. Williamson, singer (1797); Mr. Wilse (1802–3); Mrs. Wilson (1794–95); Bland Wilson (1801–3); *Stephen Woolls* (1796–99); Charles Young (1805–6); Mrs. Charles Young (1805–6).

Other: Mr. Audin, scenic artist and machinist (1798– ?); Charles Ciceri, scenic artist (1794–98, 1798– ?); Mr. Faulkner, also Joseph Falconer (?), treasurer (c.1794– ?); James Hewitt, orchestra leader (c.1794– ?); Mr. Hughes, prompter (1798– ?); Mr. Morris, scenic artist (1798); M. Pellissier, composer (1798– ?).

REPERTORY

Dates in parenthesis indicated the first performance by the company.

1792: *The Romp* (10/22); *The Farmer* (11/16); *No Song, No Supper* (12/10).

1793: *The Child of Nature* (1/7); *Ways and Means* (1/9); *The Dramatist* (1/28); *The Road to Ruin* (2/28); *Don Juan; or, The Libertine Destroyed* (3/13); *Wild Oats* (3/18); *St. Patrick's Day* (4/15); *Notoriety* (4/22); *Such Things Are* (5/13); *Look before You Leap* (5/17); *The Wedding* (5/20); *The Chapter of Accidents* (5/22); *The Waterman* (5/23); *Animal Magnetism* (5/31); *Hunt the Slipper* (5/31); *The Death of Captain Cook* (5/31); *The Irishman in London* (6/5); *Percy* (12/13); *I'll Tell You What* (12/18); *Needs Must; or, The Ballad Singers* (12/26).

1794: *The Highland Reel* (1/20); *The Carmelite* (2/1); *Tammany; or, The Indian Chief* (3/3); *The Battle of Hexham* (3/20); *The World in a Village* (4/9); *The Surrender of Calais* (4/21); *The Fatal Deception; or, The Progress of Guilt* (4/24); *Every One Has His Fault* (4/26); *Liberty Restored* (4/28); *The Wedding Ring* (4/28); *Robin Hood; or, Love in Sherwood Forest* (4/30); *How to Grow Rich* (5/5); *The Sultan* (5/5); *The Guardian Outwitted*, an adaptation of *A Bold Stroke for a Husband* (5/19); *The Midnight Hour* (5/23); *The Patriot; or, Liberty Asserted* (6/4); *Nootka Sound* (6/5); *The Huntress; or, Tammany's Frolics* (6/11); *Spoil'd Child* (6/23); *The Danaides; or, Vice Punished* (10/13); *Sophia of Brabant; or, The False Friend* (11/1); *Intrigues of a Morning* (11/3); *Chimera; or, Effusions of Fancy* (11/17); *Love's Frailties* (11/21); *The Country Girl* (11/19); *The Children in the Wood* (11/24); *The Haunted Tower* (12/2); *The Quaker* (12/23).

1795: *Mahomet* (1/21); *The Prize* (2/11); *Fontainville Abbey* (2/16); *The Purse*

(2/23); *The Jew; or, The Benevolent Hebrew* (2/25); *The Deaf Lover* (3/9); *Heigho for a Husband* (3/16); *La Forêt Noire* (3/20); *The Village Lawyer* (3/25); *The School for Greybeards; or, The Mourning Bride* (4/20); *Know Your Own Mind* (4/24); *The Natural Son* (4/27); *The Double Disguise* (4/29); *Zenobia* (5/2); *Which Is the Man?* (5/7); *The Farm House* (5/9); *The Robbers* (5/?); *The Rage* (5/25); *Modern Antiques* (5/29); *Florizel and Perdita*, revision of *The Winter's Tale* (6/1); *The Gentle Shepherd* (6/5); *Seduction; or, The Libertine Exposed* (6/20); *Try Again!* (6/23); *Tyranny Suppressed* (6/23); *The Triumph of Mirth* (8/3). (For repertory of the Old American Company joined with the Federal Street Theatre Company, Boston, see Boston ["Federal Street"] Theatre Company.).

1796: *The Deserted Daughter* (2/24); *The Wheel of Fortune* (3/4); *Poor Vulcan* (3/16); *The Whims of Galatea* (3/26); *The Mountaineers* (3/30); *Bon Ton; or, High Life above Stairs* (4/8); *The Archers; or, The Mountaineers of Switzerland* (4/18). (Benefits begin and last for two months.) *The Enraged Musicians* (4/21); *The Sicilian Romance* (4/27); *The American Heroine* (5/3); *The Prisoner* (5/4); *Speculation* (5/6); *Charlotte and Werther* (5/9); *Crotchet Lodge* (5/11); *The Masked Apparition* (5/13); *Tancred and Sigismunda* (5/18); *Old Men Grown Young* (5/18); *First Love* (5/20); *Auld Robin Gray* (5/20); *The Adopted Child* (5/23); *The Earl of Warwick* (5/25); *My Grandmother* (5/30); *The Son-in-Law* (6/3); *The Independence of America* (6/8); *Better Late Than Never* (6/13). The Old American Company was in residence in Hartford, Connecticut, from July 17 through September 13 and returned to New York's John Street Theatre on September 26, 1796. *The Mysterious Monk* (10/31); *Edwin and Angelina; or, The Bandit* (12/19); *Two Strings to Your Bow* (12/21); *The Siege of Belgrade* (12/30).

1797: *The Man of Ten Thousand* (1/6); *Tell Truth and Shame the Devil* (1/9); *Bourville Castle* (1/16); *The Comet* (2/1); *The School for Arrogance* (2/20); *Lock and Key* (3/8); *The New York Balloon* (3/13); *The Way to Get Married* (4/7); *Next Door Neighbours* (4/17); *Alonzo and Imogene* (4/21); *Ariadne Abandoned by Theseus* (4/26); *Life's Vagaries* (4/28); *The Midnight Wanderers* (5/3); *Quality Binding* (5/5); *Fortune's Fool* (5/10); *Fontainebleau* (5/15); *The Doldrum; or, 1797 and 1804* (5/17); *No One's Enemy but His Own* (5/19); *Old Thomas Day* (5/24); *The First Floor* (5/29); *The Panel* (5/31); *Mogul Tale* (6/5); *The Man of Fortitude* (6/7); *Cure for the Heart-Ache* (12/29).

1798: *Penruddock* (1/6); *Wives as They Were and Maids as They Are* (1/12); *All in a Bustle; or, The New House (2/2); King John (3/2); The Doctor and the Apothecary* (3/4); *Zorinski* (3/23); *Major André* (c.3/29); *The Will* (4/11); *Female Patriotism; or, The Death of Joan d'Arc* (4/13); *Flash in the Pan* (4/20); *The Lad of Spirit; or, Fool of Fashion* (4/27); *The London Hermit* (4/30); *The Wandering Jew; or, Love's Masquerade* (5/2); *The Mysteries of the Castle* (5/12); *The Count of Narbonne* (5/14); *Wives Pleased and Maids Happy* (5/16); *Cheap Living* (5/21); *The Castle Spectre* (6/1); *The Touchstone of Truth* (6/1); *The Italian Monk* (6/5); *Knave or Not* (6/8); *The Wedding Day* (6/13); *Preparation for a Cruise; or, The American Tars*, revision of *The Positive Man* (12/5); *The Stranger* (12/10); *Secrets Worth Knowing* (12/19); *The Telegraph* (12/24); *Rule a Wife and Have a Wife* (12/31).

1799: *He's Much to Blame* (1/9); *Sterne's Maria* (1/14); *The Natural Daughter; or, Old Sins with New Faces* (2/8); *The Shipwreck* (2/18); *The Temple of American Independence* (2/21); *Every Man in His Humour* (2/27); *Lovers' Vows* (3/11); *Count Benyowski* (4/1); *The Italian Father* (4/15); *The Heir-at-Law* (4/24); *Don Carlos* (5/

6); *False and True; or, The Warrior Triumphant* (5/8); *A Pick Nick* (5/8); *Both-eration* (5/8); *The Minister; or, Cabal and Love* (5/10); *Henry VIII* (5/13); *The Mouth of the Nile* (5/13); *The Follies of a Day* (5/20); *The Prodigal* (5/24); *The Constellation; or, American Triumph* (5/24); *The Town before You* (5/30); *Indians in England* (6/14); *The School for Soldiers* (7/14); *Self-Immolation; or, The Sacrifice of Love* (11/29); *False Shame; or, The American Orphan in Germany* (12/11); *The Smugglers; or, The Generous Tar* (12/13); *The Robbery* (12/30).

1800: *The Wild Goose Chase* (1/24); *The Force of Calumny* (2/5); *Laugh When You Can* (2/12); *The Count of Burgandy* (3/3); *The Virgin of the Sun* (3/12); *Pizarro in Peru; or, The Death of Rolla* (3/26); *Sighs; or, The Daughter* (4/16); *The Corsicans; or, The Dawnings of Love* (4/21); *The Stranger's Birthday* (4/23); *King Arthur* (4/25); *The Castle of Almunecar* (4/28); *Cyrus; or, The Follies of Superstition* (5/5); *The Horse and the Widow* (5/5); *King Henry II; or, The Death of Fair Rosamond* (5/7); *The Recruiting Sargeant* (5/12); *The Sailor's Triumph* (5/12); *Duplicity* (5/14); *Peru Revenged; or, The Death of Pizarro* (5/19); *Richard Coeur de Lion* (5/21); *Washington* (5/26); *Joanna of Montfaucon* (5/28); *Wise Man of the East* (5/30); *The Happy Family* (6/2); *Medea and Jason* (6/6); *Fraternal Discord* (10/24); *Speed the Plough* (11/5); *The East Indian* (11/17); *Bunker Hill* (11/25); *The Spanish Castle* (12/5); *The Country Heiress; or, The Man of Quality* (12/8); *Braganza; or, The Revolution in Portugal* (12/17).

1801: *Management* (1/12); *Abaellino; or, The Great Bandit* (2/11); *The Soldier of '76; or, The Birthday of Washington* (2/23); *Abbé de l'Epée; or, The Dumb Made Eloquent* (3/19); *The Captive of Spilburg* (3/25); *De Montfort* (4/13); *Life* (4/24); *The Cottagers* (5/6); *A New Way to Pay Old Debts* (5/15); *The Balse of Diamonds; or, What Is She?* (5/18); *Little Hunch-Back; or, A Frolic in Baghdad* (5/20); *Five Thousand a Year* (5/25); *The Lie of a Day* (5/25); *Obi; or, Three-Fingered Jack* (5/21); *The Turnpike Gate* (6/8); *Where Is He?* (12/2).

1802: *The Poor Gentleman* (1/8); *Modern Magic; or, The Writing Desk* (1/25); *The Merry Gardener; or, Night of Adventures* (2/3); *Folly as It Flies* (2/10); *Adelmorn, the Outlaw* (2/25); *Bluebeard* (3/8); *The Ladies' Frolic; or, The Farm House* (3/17); *Fresco* (3/27); *Paul and Virginia* (5/7); *The Manager in Distress* (5/10); *The Positive Man* (5/10); *The Irish Mimic; or, Blunder upon Blunder* (5/19); *Follies of Fashion* (5/24); *Il Bondocani* (6/7); *The Votary of Wealth; or, Modern Friendship* (6/14); *Peter the Great* (11/15); *Gil Blas* (12/10).

1803: *The Wheel of Truth* (1/12); *First Love; or, The French Emigrant* (1/17); *Liberal Opinions* (1/21); *The Voice of Nature* (2/4); *The Good Neighbor* (2/25); *Alfonso: King of Castile* (3/2); *Retaliation* (3/4); *A Tale of Mystery* (3/16); *A Blind Boy* (3/25); *The Tournament* (4/20); *Hear Both Sides* (5/4); *Delays and Blunders* (5/11); *The Review; or, The Wags of Windsor, The Man of the World* (5/20); *Charlotte Corder* [sic] (5/23); *A House to Be Sold* (5/25); *The Fair Fugitive* (5/27); *The Glory of Columbia: Her Yeomenry* (7/4); *John Bull; or, An Englishman's Fireside* (11/21); *The Sixty-third Letter* (11/30); *The First Floor* (12/7); *The Maid of Bristol* (12/9); *Mrs. Wiggins* (12/14); *Bonaparte in England* (12/19).

1804: *The Marriage Promise* (1/11); *Raymond and Agnes* (1/16); *A Tale of Terror* (1/23); *Chains of the Heart* (2/1); *Conceit Can Cure, Conceit Can Kill* (2/20); *Lewis of Monte Blanco* (3/12); *Raising the Wind* (3/14); *Wife of Two Husbands* (4/4); *The Soldier's Daughter* (4/18); *The Hero of the North* (5/7); *Liberty in Louisiana* (5/12); *Hearts of Oak* (5/14); *Love Laughs at Locksmiths* (5/23); *The Comedy of*

Errors (5/25); *Twelfth Night* (6/11); *The History and Exploits of the Renowned Don Quixote* (6/11); *Black Beard* (7/4); *Guilty or Not Guilty* (11/16).

1805: *Nina* (2/4); *The Sailor's Daughter* (3/15); *Sprigs of Laurel* (3/22); *Valentine and Orson* (4/15); *The Generous Farmers* (5/6); *The Blind Bargain* (5/13); *Crochet Lodge* (5/20); *Harlequin's Invasion* (5/22); *The Hunter of the Alps* (5/22); *Honey Moon* (5/29); *Oberon; or, The Siege of Mexico* (6/5); *Too Many Cooks* (12/13).

1806: *Who Wants a Guinea?* (c.1/25); *The Farm House* (2/5); *Julia; or, The Wanderer* (2/7); *Tars from Tripoli; or, A Tribute of Respect to the Mediterranean Heroes* (2/24); *The Will for the Deed* (3/26); *The Manhattan Stage; or, Cupid in His Vagaries* (4/11); *The School for Reform* (4/16); *The Delinquent; or, Seeing Company* (4/28); *The School for Friends* (5/14).

BIBLIOGRAPHY

Published Sources: Joseph N. Ireland, *Records of the New York Stage from 1750 to 1860*, 2 vols. (New York: T. H. Morrell, 1866–67); George C. D. Odell, *Annals of the New York Stage*, vols. 2–3 (New York: Columbia University Press, 1929, 1930); George O. Seilhamer, *A History of the American Theatre*, 3 vols. (Philadelphia: Globe Printing House, 1888–91).

Weldon B. Durham

[CALDWELL'S] AMERICAN COMPANY. (1819–43) Caldwell's American Company was organized in the fall of 1819 in New Orleans, Louisiana, by actor-manager James H. Caldwell (1793–1863). He acquired a lease on an eighteenth-century-style playhouse, the St. Philip Street Theatre (built in 1808 on St. Philip Street, between Royal and Bourbon streets), and opened it on January 7, 1820, with John Tobin's comedy *The Honey Moon* and Prince Hoare's farce *The Three and the Deuce*.

New Orleans was ripe for a high-quality, English-language theatre company in 1820. The French populace had attended French-language performances for some three decades before Caldwell's arrival, and several traveling English-language companies had played limited seasons in the preceding decade. Between 1815 and 1820 the Faubourg Ste. Marie (St. Mary Suburb), the "American Quarter" above Canal Street, had begun to develop as more and more Americans arrived in New Orleans. As the English-speaking population grew, the need for familiar entertainment became significant. James Caldwell, an entrepreneur of the first order, grasped this opportunity to organize the first high-quality resident stock company, featuring star attractions, in the commercial center of the South. For more than two decades he maintained a near monopoly on theatre in New Orleans. The only companies competing with Caldwell's company between 1820 and 1843 were those managed by Aaron Phillips (1820), Richard Russell and James S. Rowe (1833–38), and Noah Ludlow and Sol Smith (1840–43). Caldwell absorbed Phillips' company intact into his American Company during the 1820 season. During Caldwell's years of temporary retirement from theatre management (1833–35), Russell and

Rowe (who had been stage manager and treasurer for the American Company during the previous decade) successfully managed the Camp Street Theatre, using many actors formerly employed by Caldwell and maintaining the visiting-star system established by Caldwell in 1821 but widening their theatrical fare to include circuses, magicians, acrobats, menageries, and other such showpieces.

When Caldwell came out of retirement in 1835 as manager of the St. Charles Theatre, determined to offer nothing but the purest of legitimate drama, he found formidable opponents in the popular entertainments of Russell and Rowe. Despite the death of James Rowe in 1835, Richard Russell continued to compete with Caldwell with great success until Russell died in 1838. Caldwell then regained the lease on the Camp Street Theatre and organized a second company there, under the management of George Barrett, who relied on standard plays performed by excellent stock actors and visiting stars rather than on novelties. The theatre flourished for two seasons before the building was converted to the Camp Street Exchange in 1840. During his last three seasons as manager of the St. Charles and New American Theatres, Caldwell battled Ludlow and Smith for theatrical supremacy in New Orleans. This was not merely a local three-year feud; it was a struggle for supremacy in the Mississippi Valley. Since the mid-1820s Caldwell had competed with the same duo in his efforts to establish a theatre circuit connecting Cincinnati, St. Louis, Nashville, Huntsville, Mobile, Natchez, and New Orleans.

James H. Caldwell was an English actor who began his managerial career in Washington, D.C., in 1817 and developed a theatrical circuit in Virginia between 1817 and 1820. Aware of the inherent limitations of theatre business on the Eastern Seaboard, caused by strong competition among several companies for use of a few small theatres, Caldwell shifted his center of operations to the Mississippi Valley and chose New Orleans as the hub of his new circuit. Although financial success and theatrical monopoly were high on Caldwell's list of priorities, he was also determined to offer New Orleans the finest in legitimate English-language drama performed by proven professionals and the finest English and American stars.

Within a few weeks of his opening at the St. Philip Street Theatre, Caldwell occupied a second theatre, the Orleans. He shared each theatre with French companies and managed to play four or five nights each week at a top ticket price of $1.00. The 1820 season lasted twelve weeks. Although reports differ regarding the net income of the season, Caldwell accumulated a substantial profit (between $1,740.00 and $6,540.00), an amount sufficient to encourage him to continue his New Orleans effort. He took a three-year lease on the Orleans Theatre (at $10,000.00 a year) and left with his company for a summer campaign in Virginia. Caldwell discontinued the summer seasons in Virginia after 1825 and devoted his summers to developing the Mississippi Valley circuit until his retirement from management in 1843. During his second season at the Orleans, Caldwell introduced the "star system" in New Orleans, presenting Thomas A. Cooper in repertory. Admission to the boxes and parquet was raised from $1.00 to $1.50, an increase resulting from the manager's increased expenses (Cooper received $3,333.33 for sixteen nights, and the engagement was extended to twenty-four nights). From Cooper's appearance, according to Caldwell, the high level of the drama in the manager's New Orleans ventures was established, and he continued to present British and American stars for the next two decades.

Between 1821 and 1833 Caldwell maintained a monopoly on the New Orleans theatre, and his business boomed. Indeed, during that period he constructed the New American Theatre on Camp Street (at a cost of $70,000) and on several occasions altered its interior to improve its looks and increase its seating capacity. When the 1,000–seat theatre opened in 1824, prices ranged from twenty-five cents for seats apportioned to the "colored population" to $1 for boxes and parquet. Whenever stars visited, those prices increased.

Caldwell's business activities were not limited to theatre. He had an exclusive city franchise for the manufacture and sale of illuminating gas, and his was the first theatre in the South to introduce gas lighting. To finance his gas operation he formed the New Orleans Gas Light and Banking Company in 1833 and, realizing that this was a full-time job, temporarily abandoned his theatrical career.

Two years later, when he returned to theatrical management at the St. Charles, Caldwell faced keen competition from Russell and Rowe at the Camp Street. His first season (1835–36) was a disappointment: increased prices and public apathy toward legitimate drama resulted in poor patronage. Thereafter Caldwell attempted to diversify his program: he offered opera, melodrama, ballet, and spectacles to attract the common citizens, while he continued to present visiting stars in legitimate dramas. With such variety (and with the demise of Russell's company in 1838), Caldwell recaptured the public's favor. With the appearance of the Ludlow and Smith Company* in 1840, however, Caldwell once again lost his monopoly. With their fine company of actors and their popular productions of horse opera and lighter drama, Ludlow and Smith outdrew Caldwell and caused his final three seasons in New Orleans to be financial disasters.

Caldwell selected a quality repertory, maintained an excellent stock company, and engaged the most popular American and British stars and performers throughout his career as a manager in New Orleans; accordingly, discerning reviewers consistently noted the high level of dramatic presentation at Caldwell's theatres. During the seasons at the Camp Street, reviewers were occasionally disappointed by the singing voices of some of the stock performers and by the weakness of the small orchestra. When opera stars Mr. and Mrs. Pearman appeared in 1831, they supplemented the orchestra with their own musicians, and the Louisiana *Courier* reviewer expressed overwhelming approval. Caldwell was an excellent light comedian but a less impressive tragedian, and several reviewers despaired when he chose to act in tragedy. But Caldwell was aware of his limitations and often allowed visiting stars or other company members to replace him in the larger tragic roles. Reviewers always praised Caldwell's decisions to produce native playwrights (often they were New Orleans citizens) and to celebrate important holidays and celebrity visits with special productions. Scenery in Caldwell's theatres was consistently praised by reviewers, particularly that in musical and melodramatic spectacles. Caldwell's attempts to enforce a decorus attitude among his patrons by policing the audience also drew the critics' appreciation.

Caldwell sought to emphasize legitimate drama, but in his repertory he included light comedy, serious and comic opera, farce, melodrama, spectacle, plays commemorating holidays and honoring celebrity visitors, ballet, dioramas, circus acts, acrobats, equestrian plays, and canine shows. Major roles in legitimate dramas were most often performed by visiting stars or stars who had been engaged as company members. In an attempt to provide a diversified program of entertainment, he instigated, during his first year in New Orleans, a seasonal organization that remained fairly consistent throughout his tenure. He opened with a popular favorite, usually a comedy, to spur the public's excitement over the new season. He then introduced his new company members (another audience enticement) in several productions of varying kinds of plays. He next presented the visiting stars in repertory but alternated the stars' performances with lighter fare— spectacles, musicals, and opera. Finally, he renewed the public's interest by offering benefit performances for the principal company members, the visiting stars, the scene designers, the stage manager, and sometimes the playwrights.

The Honey Moon and *The Three and the Deuce*, a comedy and farce with which Caldwell initiated his New Orleans venture in 1820, were perennial favorites in New Orleans. Indeed, comedy was most popular at Caldwell's theatres. T. H. Bayly's *Perfection*, Bulwer-Lytton's *Lady of Lyons*, Richard Sheridan's *School for Scandal*, and Oliver Goldsmith's *She Stoops to Conquer* had numerous productions. Of the musicals that abounded, M. R. Lacy's *Cinderella* was the most popular, followed by Isaac Pocock's musical version of *Rob Roy*. Melodramas, such as M. G. Lewis' *Timour, the Tartar*, were second only to comedies in popularity; English translations of European works (for example, Sheridan's adaptation of August Kotzebue's *Pizarro*) were also popular. The most popular of the legitimate dramatists was William Shakespeare, whose plays comprised a large portion of the repertories of visiting stars. J. B. Booth, Thomas Cooper, Charlotte Cushman, Edwin Forrest, James Hackett, James Murdoch, and Ellen Tree, among other stars, presented plays such as

Richard III, Hamlet, Macbeth, and *Othello.* Certain of Shakespeare's comedies, such as *The Taming of the Shrew*, provided vehicles as well. Another popular dramatist was John Baldwin Buckstone, whose most produced plays were the farces *Dead Shot, A Husband at Sight,* and *Mischief Making.* Buckstone's spectacle *The Ice Witch* was also popular.

The intense rivalry that existed between American and French citizens in New Orleans may have been partly responsible for the enthusiastic reception Caldwell received when he produced native authors. John Howard Payne's *Thérèse* was often produced, as were William Dunlap's *Stranger,* Payne and Washington Irving's *Charles II*, and Mordecai Noah's *She Would Be a Soldier.* New Orleans' interest in native writers stimulated Caldwell to produce local playwrights such as James Rees, whose *Lafitte: The Pirate of the Gulf* was popular. Visiting stars often played their most famous pieces. Edwin Forrest presented *Damon and Pythias, Virginius,* and *The Gladiator* and low comedian Dan Marble performed in Yankee plays. Other popular performers presented their specialties: the famous Ravel family performed acrobatics and presented pantomimes; Celeste and Madame Le Compte danced ballets; Joe Blackburn, the famous clown, performed comic pieces; Herr Cline, a seasonal favorite, performed on the "elastic cord"; and Fanny Elssler, the celebrated danseuse, appeared in ballets.

Caldwell employed a secretary-treasurer, a musical director, a small orchestra, several scenic technicians, a property master, a stage manager, and a company of actors usually numbering between twenty and thirty. Supernumeraries were engaged irregularly, and visiting stars were engaged every season beginning in 1821. Most members of the acting company did not remain with Caldwell for extended periods, although some actors were steadfast and continued with the manager for a decade or more. In many cases, players from former seasons returned and became stock members again; in other instances, players left to achieve stardom in New York and returned as visiting stars. The list of visiting celebrities engaged by Caldwell is striking. Thomas Cooper was the first in 1821, and Cooper returned to New Orleans for eight additional engagements between 1822 and 1836. Cooper, J. B. Booth, Edwin Forrest, Jane Placide, George Sloman, Mr. and Mrs. Sol Smith, and Mrs. Alexander Drake all appeared during the 1829 season, when Caldwell's company was among the strongest in the English-speaking theatre. Other major stars who appeared were Charlotte Cushman, Mrs. Mary Duff, Clara Fisher, William C. Forbes, James H. Hackett, Charles Kean, Dan Marble, James E. Murdoch, William Pelby, Tyrone Power, Ellen Tree, and James W. Wallack. Caldwell engaged a number of excellent opera companies during his management: Signor Brichta's Italian Opera starring Madame Brichta, Signor Montresor's Company, and a company starring Madame Feron. Vocalist John Sinclair was among the many singing stars engaged by Caldwell.

In organizing his company each season, Caldwell had to consider the variety of his repertory. During his first season, for example, he employed Jackson Gray and Joseph Hutton for second leads in tragedy. Mrs. Jackson Gray, Irish tenor Arthur Keene, and Mr. and Mrs. Richard Russell were leads in opera and musical farce, and Mr. Goll directed ballets and entertained between plays with his comic dances. Jackson Gray remained with Caldwell's company until 1833, as did stage manager Richard Russell, who, with James Rowe, subsequently leased the Camp Street Theatre and organized a company during Caldwell's temporary retirement. Two of Caldwell's company, Jane Placide and Edwin Forrest, served their apprenticeships under Caldwell before attaining star status in New York. Noah Ludlow, Sol Smith, and Alexander Drake all played leads for Caldwell before becoming theatre managers on the American frontier. Other notable company members were Mrs. Alexander Drake, undisputed leading lady of the Western theatre; celebrated vocalist Mrs. Edward Knight; Covent Garden tragedienne Mrs. George Sloman; low comedian George Holland; and Ben DeBar, later manager of the new St. Charles Theatre.

Caldwell's final three seasons at the St. Charles and New American theatres were financial disasters. In 1840 Ludlow and Smith organized a company at the American Theatre on Poydras Street, where they relied on equestrian shows to win the New Orleans audience. Their success brought an end to Caldwell's "Temple of the Drama" in 1842. The St. Charles Theatre burned to the ground at the end of that season, and Caldwell's last gasp—the construction of the New American Theatre in 1842—resulted in even harsher financial woes and his retirement from management in 1843.

PERSONNEL

Management: James Henry Caldwell, lessee and manager, St. Philip Street Theatre (1820) and Orleans Theatre (1820–23); proprietor and manager, Camp Street Theatre (1823–33) and St. Charles Theatre (1835–42); and lessee and manager, American Theatre (1842–43); James Rowe, treasurer (1823–33); George Holland, secretary-treasurer (1835–41).

Scenic Technicians: Antonio Mondelli (1824–32, 1835–38); Hugh Reinagle (1832–33); S. M. Lee (1838–39); John Varden, principal machinist (1824–30).

Musical Directors: Noke (1823–28); P. Lewis (1829–30); J. G. Maeder, H. Willis (1835–36); Fallon (1836–37); H. W. Jonas (1838–39).

Stage Managers: Richard Russell (1823–32); J. W. Forbes (1835–36); W. H. Lathan (1836–37); Henry Pearson (1838–39); George Barrett (1840–42); John Barton (1838–42).

Actors and Actresses: A. A. Adams (1837); *William Anderson* (1820, 1827–31, 1841–42); *Mrs. William Anderson* (1820, 1822); *Mr. Archer* (1837–42); Mrs. W. H. Bailey (1838); Mrs. Baker (1823–24); *James Balls* (1836–37, 1839–40); *N. H. Bannister* (1835–37); *Mrs. N. H. Bannister (Miss Legg)* (1821, 1835–37); Mr. and Mrs. Barker (1837); *Charlotte Barnes* (1837–40); *Mr. and Mrs. John Barnes* (1837–

40); *George H. Barrett* (1837–42); *Mrs. George Barrett* (1838–39); H. N. Barry; John H. Barton (1832–33, 1835–42); Mrs. Battersby (1825); W. H. Benton; Thomas Bishop (1836–38); Mr. and Mrs. Bloxton; W. F. Brough (1840); John Mills Brown; Mrs. Frederick Browne; James S. Browne (1838–39, 1842); Mr. and Mrs. Brunton (1841–42); John Baldwin Buckstone (1841); Mr. and Mrs. Burke; Master Joseph Burke (1832, 1837–39); Thomas Burke (1821), Mrs. Thomas (Cornelia) Burke (1821); Samuel Butler; Edward Caldwell; *James H. Caldwell* (1820–33, 1837–39, 1841); Thomas Caldwell; H. N. Cambridge (1828); *Mr. Carr* (1827–33, 1837–39); *Mrs. Carr* (1828–33, 1837–39); Mr. and Mrs. Carter; William Chapman; Mr. Charnock (1831–33); Mr. and Mrs. Chipps; George Clarke; Miss Josephine Clifton (1838–39); T. S. Cline (1841); *Mrs. Conduit*, later *Mrs. Ben DeBar* (1837–41); William Conway (1825); Miss Copeland (1835–36); *Mr. and Mrs. Joseph Cowell* (1830–32, 1835–36, 1838–39, 1841–42); *Sam Cowell* (1830–32, 1838–40); Miss Sidney Cowell, later Mrs. Bateman (1838); Mrs. H. Cramer (1837–38); Miss Charlotte Crampton; H. Crampton (1827–29); Mrs. H. Crampton; Robert Crooke (1828–29); *Mrs. Robert Crooke, formerly Mrs. Entwhistle* (1820–21, 1828–31); Charlotte Cushman (1835–36); John Dalton (1823–24); Mr. and Mrs. Davenport; Miss Jean Davenport (1839); *Miss DeBar* (1835–38); *Mr. and Mrs. Ben DeBar* (1835–41); Vincent DeCamp (1835–36); Alexander Drake (1823); *Mrs. Alexander Drake* (1823, 1828–29); *William C. Drummond* (1820, 1826); William Duffy; John Dwyer (1823); Samuel Emberton; Mr. and Mrs. George P. Farren (Miss Mary Ann Russell) (1838–39); A. W. Fenno; *Joseph M. Field* (1832–33, 1836, 1838–41); *Mrs. Joseph M. Field (Eliza Riddle)* (1839–41); Thomas Fielding; Henry J. Finn (1832, 1835–39); *Miss Clara Fisher*, later *Mrs. James Maeder* (1829–36); J. W. Forbes (1835–36); Edwin Forrest (1824–25); *William Forrest* (1823–26); George Frethy; Mrs. Gibbs (1835–36, 1838); John Gilbert (1829–33); Mrs. Gray (1829–33); *Jackson Gray* (1820–33); *Mrs. Jackson Gray* (1820); *John Greene* (1825, 1841–42); *Mrs. John Greene* (1825, 1838–39, 1841–42); Thomas S. Hamblin (1829–30); Mr. and Mrs. Harrison (1838–39); John Herbert (1831); *George Hernizen* (1828–33); Mr. and Mrs. William Hield (1837–38); *John Higgins* (1820–33); *Mrs. John Higgins* (1823–33); Mr. and Mrs. Hill; George H. Hill (1836); Thomas Hilson (1821, 1832–33); Mrs. Thomas Hilson (1832–33); *George Holland* (1829–33, 1835–42); *Mr. Houpt* (1831–33); James Howard (1829–30); Mrs. Hughes (1821–23); C. W. Hunt; Henry Hunt (1836–37); *Mrs. Henry Hunt (Miss Louisa Lane)* (1829, 1835–37); Mr. and Mrs. Joseph Hutton (1820–21); Mr. and Mrs. Jackson; Thomas Jefferson; W. F. Johnson; John Jones (1840); *Samuel P. Jones* (1824–29); Mr. and Mrs. Robert Keeley (1837); *Arthur Keene* (1820–23); *Lydia Kelly* (1827, 1830); Miss Blanche Kemble (1841–42); Mr. and Mrs. Kenny; William H. Keppell (1832, 1836–37, 1839–40); Mrs. William H. Keppell; Mrs. Edward Knight (1829, 1832–33); *W. H. Latham* (1835–37); Mr. Lear (1827–29); Mr. and Mrs. G. Lewellen; Mr. and Mrs. Henry Lewis; *Noah Ludlow* (1821–24, 1830–33); *Mrs. Noah Ludlow* (1823–24, 1831–33); Mr. and Mrs. Madden, A. J. Marks; Charles Mason (1836, 1840); *William McCafferty* (1820–28); *Mr. and Mrs. McClure* (1829–31); Miss Meadows (1838); *Miss Melton* (1836–37, 1839–40); Mrs. Minnich (1836); Miss Mongin; Mrs. Mongin (1824); John Moore; Miss Morgan (1840–41); *Mr. Morton* (1828–33, 1841); Miss Mowbray (1840–41); Mr. and Mrs. Charles E. Muzzy; Mrs. Noke (1823–24); Mme. Otto (1840); *Mr. Page* (1837–39); *Joseph Page* (1824–25, 1831–33); Mr. and Mrs. Parker; Mr. and Mrs. Pearman (1831); *Henry G. Pearson* (1828–31, 1835–42); Mrs. Pemberton, Mr. and Mrs.

Petrie; Miss Eliza Petrie (1831–32); Miss Lydia Phillips (1836); Moses S. Phillips (1840); Thomas Phillips (1823); *Alexander L. Pickering* (1837–38, 1840–42); Miss Eliza Placide; Miss Jane Placide (1823–27, 1829–33); Thomas Placide; *Mr. and Mrs. Charles Plumer* (1838–39);Mr. and Mrs. Cramer Plumer (1831); *Mr. and Mrs. Price; Thomas Radcliffe* (1836–37, 1839–41); *Mrs. Thomas Radcliffe; William Ranger* (1841); *Edward Raymond; Mr. and Mrs. Reeder; T. D. Rice* (1842); *Eugene Robertson; Miss Rock* (1842); Mrs. Rowe (1824); Mrs. George Rowe (1841–41); James Rowe; Miss Mary Ann Russell; Mr. and Mrs. Richard Russell (1820–32); Master Richard Russell, Jr.; J. Sandford; Mr. and Mrs. Saunders; James Scholes; James M. Scott (1822, 1830–33); *Moses Scott* (1823–27); *Mr. and Mrs. Seguin* (1842); Miss and Master Sergeant; Mrs. G. W. Sergeant (1841–42); *Miss Rosina Seymour (Mrs. James Rowe)* (1823–33); Mrs. Sharpe (1837); Mrs. Shaw (1836–37); *Mr. and Mrs. George Sloman* (1829, 1840–42); Master C. F. Smith (1823); Lemuel Smith; *Mr. and Mrs. Sol Smith* (1827–31); *Joseph Still* (1826–28); *Mrs. Stuart,* formerly *Mrs. Vos* (1831, 1839–40, 1842); *Mrs. Tatnall,* later *Mrs. Pritchard and Mrs. Hartwig* (1827–28, 1837, 1841); Mr. and Mrs. Ternan (1835–36); James Thorne (1832–33); Henry Vaughan; Mrs. Watson (1838); Mr. and Mrs. Williams (Miss Verity); Mr. and Mrs. H. A. Williams (1820–22, 1828–32); T. Williamson; Alexander Wilson (1824–26).

REPERTORY

During his twenty-two seasons in New Orleans, Caldwell premiered several thousand plays and revived a large percentage of them from season to season. Accordingly, a complete list of his repertory is prohibitive. Moreover, Caldwell adjusted his repertoire to accommodate changes in the city's theatrical climate and to fight competition from other companies. Accordingly, the repertory of selected seasons that follows reflects some of those necessary adjustments and serves as a representative list of plays produced by the manager.

1828–29 (Significant starring performances indicated in parentheses): *Soldier's Daughter; Of Age Tomorrow; Honey Moon; No Song, No Supper; Much Ado about Nothing; Poor Soldier; Douglas; Spoil'd Child; Town and Country; All on the Wing; Pizarro; Family Jars; Guy Mannering; Rendezvous; George Barnwell; Paul Pry; Lovers' Vows; Fortune's Frolic; Rob Roy; 'Twas I; School for Scandal; Adelgitha; Hunter of the Alps; Lafayette; Hundred-Pound Note; Hamlet; Gambler's Fate; Lyar; Richard III; Lock and Key; Glory of Columbia: Her Yeomanry; Young Widow; New Way to Pay Old Debts; Three Deep; The Merchant of Venice; Poachers; West Indian; Macbeth; Tom Thumb; Children in the Wood; Stranger; All the World's a Stage; King Lear; Othello; Sprigs of Laurel; Town and Country; Sweethearts and Wives; Day after the Fair; Mountaineers; Raising the Wind; The Secret; Turnpike Gate; Whims of a Comedian; Haunted Tower; Deaf as a Post; Love in a Village; Katherine and Petruchio; The Secret; She Stoops to Conquer; Dramatist; Whims of a Comedian; Guy Mannering; Turn Out; The Will; Somnambulist; The Romp; Brother and Sister; Secret; Gretna Green; Love and Reason; Fontainebleau; Tom and Jerry; Frederick the Great; Laugh When You Can; Invincibles; The Hypocrite; The Prize; Paul and Virginia; Lord of the Manor; Iron Chest; Brutus; Wool Gathering; Bertram; Fortune's Frolic; Agreeable Surprise; Virginius; Distrest Mother; Mayor of Garratt; Damon and Pythias; Isabella; Fish Out of Water; Venice Preserved*

(Cooper, E. Booth, Mrs. Sloman); *Foundling of the Forest; The Wonder; Animal Magnetism; Pizarro; Haunted Inn; The Critic; Othello* (Booth, Cooper, Caldwell, Mrs. Sloman, Jane Placide); *Jane Shore; Macbeth; Rendezvous; Lottery Ticket; Jealous Wife; Wives as They Were; Modern Antiques; Provok'd Husband; Old and Young; Intrigue; Gamester; Romeo and Juliet; Actress of All Work; Julius Caesar; Twelve Precisely; Heir-at-Law; The Rivals; Sergeant's Wife; Paris and London; Thérèse; Village Lawyer; Virginius* (Forrest); *Blue Devils; William Tell; Touch and Take; King Lear* (Forrest, Booth, Caldwell, J. Placide); *Highland Reel; High Life below Stairs; Magpie and the Maid; Dumb Girl of Genoa; Half an Hour's Courtship; Venice Preserved; The Purse; Rienzi; Wandering Boys; Raising the Wind; Bertram; Valentine and Orson; School of Reform; Lovers' Quarrels; Wheel of Fortune; Winning a Husband; Monsieur Tonson; Is It a Lie?; Belle's Stratagem; Falls of Clyde.*

1841–42: In response to the lack of patronage the previous season, and to compete with Ludlow and Smith's popular entertainments, Caldwell erected an equestrian arena on stage for the 1841–42 season, and he diversified his program. The list below characterizes his season, listing major attractions and several representative works from each engagement. October 25 to November 6 (Equestrian shows and pantomimes): *Jeremiah Blackstitch; Harlequin Frolics.* November 7 to December 5 (Minor stars, comedies, comic ballets and pantomimes, nautical dramas, melodramas, animal acts, spectacles): *Wandering Minstrel; The Murdered Boatman and His Dog; Timour, the Tartar; Turnpike Gate; The Stranger; Forty Thieves.* December 6 to December 13 (James Hackett engagement): *King Henry IV, Part 1; Rip Van Winkle; Merry Wives of Windsor.* December 14 to December 19 (Levi North—"greatest equestrian rider in the world"—engagement): *The Pride of the Navy; Middy Ashore; Poor Soldier; Handsome Husband.* December 20: *London Assurance* engagement begins (eighteen performances in two and one-half months). December 27–December 31: James Hackett return engagement. January 5 (Opera season begins with Mr. and Mrs. Sequin's engagement): *Norma; The Mummy; Wild Boy of Bohemia; La sonnambula.* January 9 to January 21 (Dan Marble's Yankee plays alternate with opera): *American Farmer; Yankee in Time; Luke, the Labourer.* February 11 (Miss Rock—comedienne—engagement begins): *Belle's Stratagem; Fish Out of Water; New Orleans Assurance.* February 16 to February 21 (T. D. Rice—impersonator—engagement): *Jumbo Jim; Jim Crow in London; Peacock and Crow; Robert Macaire.* February 22 (Italian Opera Company—Havana—engagement begins): *Lucia di Lammermoor; Naiad Queen; Beatrice di Tenda; Sleep Walker.* March 13, 1842: Theatre destroyed by fire.

BIBLIOGRAPHY

Dorman, James. *The Theatre in the Ante-bellum South, 1815–1861.* Chapel Hill: University of North Carolina Press, 1967.

Gafford, Lucile. *A History of the St. Charles Theatre in New Orleans, 1835–43.* Chicago: University of Chicago Press, 1932.

Smither, Nelle Kroger. "A History of the English Theatre in New Orleans, 1806–1842," *Louisiana Historical Quarterly* 28 (January–April 1945): 85–276, 361–572.

C. Alex Pinkston, Jr.

AMERICAN COMPANY OF COMEDIANS. See AMERICAN COMPANY (1752–92).

AMERICAN MUSEUM STOCK COMPANY. The American Museum, on the southeast corner of Broadway and Ann Street, New York City, opened in 1841 under the management of Phineas Taylor Barnum (1810–91). A genius of promotion and press-agentry, Barnum capitalized on native American curiosity and Protestant antipathy toward conventional theatre in creating an institution that combined an exhibit of some 600,000 curios with uplifting and instructive entertainment to which a refined Christian mother could take her children, presented in a "Moral Lecture Hall." Barnum admired, copied, and improved upon the formula developed by his close Bostonian friend, Moses E. Kimball, founder of the Boston Museum (1841) and the fabled Boston Museum Company* (1843). Occasional dramatic performances were given at the American Museum as early as 1844, but the promise of a regular stock company was not redeemed until 1849, when Barnum placed Francis Courtney Weymss (1797–1859), longtime manager of Philadelphia's Chestnut Street Theatre Company*, at the head of a small troupe regularly reinforced by lesser well-known or fading stars, such as the Martinetti Family, with Louis Ellsler, or the aging blackfaced farceur T. D. Rice. In April and May 1850, Barnum enlarged (to 3,000 seats) and redecorated the lecture room, opening it June 17, 1850, with a larger company. The opening production was a revival of William H. Smith's temperance drama *The Drunkard* (1844). Barnum's excellent company, managed by Wemyss and featuring first William R. Goodall and then Corson W. Clarke (1814–67), Thomas Hadaway (1801–92), and Alexina Fisher, played *The Drunkard* throughout the summer and into October, in the longest New York run up to that time. Clarke and Hadaway became regulars with the company for the next fifteen years. Dramatic bills at the American Museum thereafter changed each week, but Barnum would let a hit run until its appeal was exhausted. The American Museum Stock Company was the first in American theatre to rely on long-running plays.

Theatre in New York was at a low ebb in the late 1840s. The venerable Park Theatre was in its rat-infested last days, its place in the first rank taken by the Broadway Theatre Stock Company*, where stars of every magnitude held forth. Mitchell's Olympic Theatre* and Burton's Stock Company* attracted a clientele drawn to comedy and burlesque; Hamblin's Bowery Theatre Company* and [Purdy's] National Theatre Stock Company* featured robust and spectacular melodrama. Wherever one went, the gallery, or third tier, was a haven for prostitutes and an arena of assignation for sporting bloods and their "dates." Drunkenness and profanity undermined the respectability of most theatres, and a woman without an escort was unable to attend even in a box or orchestra seat. Barnum raised the price of admission to the third tier, policed the area to keep out prostitutes, banned the sale of liquor on the premises, and barred free reentry to those leaving his theatre for drinks between the acts. He made the theatre available and attractive to women and children, with morning, afternoon, and evening performances.

In 1885 Barnum sold the collection to his assistant, John Greenleaf, Jr. Greenleaf and his partner, Henry D. Butler, also rented the theatre and took over management of the American Museum Stock Company. They tampered little with the Barnum formula of curiosities and moralism during the next five years. On March 31, 1860, Barnum returned to management and proprietorship, recalling Clarke and Emily Mestayer (1814–82), favorites who had been lured, meanwhile, to other theatres. Barnum still headed the organization when the American Museum burned July 13, 1865, with the loss of almost all the menagerie and the entire collection of curios. He moved the company to a concert hall known as the Chinese Rooms at 539–541 Broadway. In August the building was taken down and the new Museum and Lecture Hall was ready for business on September 6, 1865. The popularity of a circus Barnum engaged was such that he cut a ring in the Lecture Hall stage, covering it with boards during the play so that the circus could share the bill with the play, as it did most of the season of 1865–66 and 1866–67. In 1866 Van Amburgh's Museum and Menagerie was added to the attraction, and the name of the institution changed to Barnum and Van Amburgh's Museum and Menagerie. A revival of *Uncle Tom's Cabin* (H. J. Conway's version with a happy ending) was the attraction onstage when the second museum burned March 3, 1868, with a total loss of exhibits, animals, and theatre equipment. Barnum assisted George Wood briefly in the general management of Wood's museum, but he never again assembled a dramatic company.

The repertory of the American Museum Stock Company featured melodrama because of its spectacular excitement and because of its portrayal of virtue triumphant: Andrew Cherry's *Soldier's Daughter* (1804), Bulwer-Lytton's *Lady of Lyons* (1838), an adaptation of Susannah Rowson's sentimental novel (1791) *Charlotte Temple*, and G. A. à Beckett's *Don Caesar de Bazan* (1844). Farces and pantomimes lightened the bill. A prize drama by Louisa Reeder, *Mary Morton; or, The Shirt Sewers*, brought out on October 11, 1855, was a typical Museum play. It appealed to the Museum's working-class audience with a vigorous affirmation of that sentimental faith in the dignity of honest labor. J. B. Buckstone's *Victorine: The Orphan of Paris* (1831) was offered at the Museum as *The Seamstress of Paris*. One could also see *Katy, the Hot Corn Girl; or, Life Scenes in New York* and *Gotham; or, Daylight and Gaslight*, as well as Buckstone's *Luke, the Labourer* (1826) and C. A. Logan's *Vermont Wool Dealer* (1845). George Lillo's *London Merchant; or, The History of George Barnwell* (1731) continued to alert apprentices to the dangers of being suborned to fraud and murder by an alluring female.

The long-running and often-revived plays most closely associated with Barnum's American Museum were *The Drunkard* and *Hop o' My Thumb*, a piece devised by Englishman Albert Smith to show off Barnum's prize dwarf, Tom Thumb (Charles Stratton). Tom Taylor's *Vicar of Wakefield*, an adaptation of Oliver Goldsmith's novel, had a long run in 1851, as did *Rosina Meadows: The Village Maid* (1843), by C. H. Saunders. Tom Taylor's temperance play *The Bottle* (1847) became a part of the Museum repertoire with a long run in 1852. Other hits the same year were two plays by anonymous authors, *Orphan's Dream* and *Old Folks at Home*, in which Emily Mestayer sang the popular title song. H. J. Conway's *Uncle Tom's Cabin* was the event of the autumn season. Conway (1800–1860), the house dramatist, churned out an adaptation of Harriet Beecher Stowe's novel to meet the competition posed by the National Theatre production of George L. Aiken's dramatization of the same story. Conway's *Tom* ran for two months, followed shortly by a popular production of *The Old Brewery*, another Conway adaptation from the novel form. *Mary Morton* was the hit of the 1855–1856 season, a season in which Conway wrote and Barnum produced yet another popular play of the American Revolution, *New York Patriots; or, The Battle of Saratoga*. It ran from June 2 to July 5, 1856. Conway's next effort was an adaptation of another Stowe novel, *Dred: A Tale of the Great Dismal Swamp*. The play was not so good as John Brougham's adaptation for the Bowery, September 29, 1856, but Conway provided the company with a vehicle that held up from October 16 to November 22, 1856. J. T. Trowbridge's *Neighbor Jackwood*, dealing with a white runaway slave, had a long run in May 1857. Sentiment surrounding the slavery issue was a deep well into which Barnum dipped frequently. In 1857 Harry Watkins (1825–94), an actor-playwright in the company, succeeded Corson W. Clarke as Barnum's director of amusements. Watkins, a prolific, if pedestrian, author, larded the season with plays of his own hand: *A Mother's Prayer; or, The Rose of Penrith; Our Country's Sinews* (about the Mexican War); and a dramatization of Sylvanus Cobb's novel *The Pioneer Patriot; or, The Maid of the Warpath*. Watkin's dramatization of Mrs. Emma Southworth's story *The Bride of the Evening* ran a month, its closing followed immediately by Watkins' *Heart of the World*, a moral drama on the evils of ingratitude, the benefits of self-reliance, and the inspiring influence of a true woman. Barnum put Watkins in charge of the company, because business was falling off, and Watkins promised to write plays that would draw out the public, despite the financial depression crippling commerce. Watkins did as he promised, but Barnum would pay him no more for the plays than he was contracted to earn as an actor: $40 a week. Watkins quit his job as director of amusements at the end of the 1857–58 season, and the next season at the Museum did not start until February 28, 1859. This brief outing was highlighted by the March 28 production of Conway's *Our Irish Cousin* (capitalizing on the phenomenal success of Tom Taylor's *Our American Cousin*). Conway continued writing plays for the Museum company in 1859–1860, but none was as successful as his *Uncle Tom's Cabin*. Dion Boucicault's *Octoroon* (1859) had a profitable run of nearly seven weeks, a run that marked the end of the Blackwood management of the American Museum Company. A revival of Royall Tyler's moral and religious spectacle *Joseph and His Brethren* began the season of 1860–61 and was its strongest attraction. In 1863–64 a mania for ghost plays swept the city, and Barnum capitalized on the trend with a series of pieces that included the anonymous *Mariette; or, The Warning of Death*. The season's grand spectacle, replete with ghost effects, was *Aphrosa; or, The Spirit of Beauty*. It ran six weeks.

Barnum's formula of action and sentiment blended in a play with a simple Protestant moral continued to attract patrons in large numbers. Laura Keene's *Workmen of New York; or, The Curse of Intemperance*, which featured the interior of an iron foundry with the machinery in full operation, ran a month in February and March 1865. In 1866 George L. Aiken's *Moses; or, Israel in Egypt* ran eight weeks, and *Pale Janet*, a new drama by American Museum Company stalwart Milnes Levick (1825–97), ran six weeks in 1867. Levick had first appeared as George Harris in *Uncle Tom's Cabin* in 1853. He was the stage manager (director) of the company in its last season and the author of its last hit.

The personnel of the company changed only slightly each year. This home of moral drama attracted a loyal public: although the theatre's prestige was slight, the pay was sure. Corson W. Clarke, Thomas Hadaway, and Emily Mestayer, along with Sylvester Bleecker, Milnes Levick, and Harry Watkins, performed year-in and year-out for Barnum and managed to acquire a notable reputation, sometimes for writing plays as well as for acting. But others among Barnum's hardy performers labored long but left little or no trace on the history of the profession: Mrs. R. G. France, who worked regularly from 1855 to 1868; John Bridgman, seen in dozens of Museum plays from 1855 to 1866; and Mrs. J. J. Prior (Louisa Young) (1830–83), a company regular for ten years, 1858 to 1868. They contributed much to the success of the American Museum Company, a minor but vital and innovative organization assembled and directed by America's master showman, Phineas T. Barnum.

PERSONNEL

Management: Phineas T. Barnum (1849–55, 1860–68); John Greenleaf, Jr., and Henry D. Butler (1855–60).

Musical Director: F.W. Peterschen (c.1863).

Orchestra Leader: Mr. Lerch (1857– ?).

Scenic Artists: *George Hielge* (1861–67), M. de la Mans (1857– ?).

Property Masters: Mr. Kiernan (1857–58), Robert Cutler (1863–67).

Carpenter-Machinists: Charles Burns (1857–64), W. Demelt (c.1866).

Actors and Actresses: Irene Acton (1859–60); Ellen Adair (1852–53); Kate Adair (1852–53); Miss B. Albertine (1850–51); Miss M. Albertine (1850–51); Miss S.

Albertine (1850–51); Miss Alderman (1852–53, 1856–57); *Carrie Alford,* later *Mrs. W.L. Jamieson* (1859–65); Miss H. Alford (1860–61); *Mr. R. Anderson* (1860–68); Mr. A. Andrews (1850–54); Hattie Arnold (1859–60); Miss Atkins (1866–68); T. S. Atkins (1865–68); Miss M. Augustin (1852–53); Miss Barton (1849); Ellen Bateman (1849); Kate Bateman (1849); Mr. Beane (1860–61); Sallie Bishop (1853–54); *Sylvester Bleecker* (1850–57, 1865–66); *John Bridgman* (1855–66); Miss Britman (1855–56); Mr. Brogan (1862–63); George Brooks (1860–62, 1866–67); Mrs. George Brooks (1866–67); Miss Brown (1853–54); Mr. Brown (1860–61); Mrs. Bruce (1855–56); Mr. Brude (1852–53); Mrs. Burroughs (1852–58); Charles Carroll (1857–58); Mr. Cavanaugh (1856–57); Caroline Chapman (1850–51); E. Chapman (1867–68); *H.E. Chapman* (1860–64); George C. Charles (1852–54); Mary Ann Charles (1853–54); Miss Chiarini (1853–54); Agnes Clare (1860–61); Adele Clark (1866–67); *Corson W. Clarke* (1850–58, 1860–61, 1865–68); *George H. Clarke* (1849–57, 1860–67); Harry G. Clarke (1866–67); Josephine Clarke (1859–60); Jennie Cleaver (1846–66); Miss Coburn (1859–60); Miss Colevolini (1852–53); J. J. Collins (1865–66); J. Colson (1866–67); *James Conner* (1852– 59); Kate Conner (1857–58); Miss Connolly (1867–68); Mr. Cooke (1860–61); J. M. Craig (1859); *Harry Cunningham* (1853–57, 1860–65); W. Cunningham (1853–54, 1859–61); Henry F. Daly (1853–54, 1855–56); W. H. Daly (1863–64, 1866–67); Miss Dayton (1859); Mrs. Deering (1850–51); Miss F. Deering (1850–51); Miss Rebeckah Deering (1850–51); J. C. DeForrest (1859–61); Tony Denier (1864–65); Kate Denin (1850–51, 1858–59); Susan Denin (1850–51, 1858–59); Miss Dennis (1860–61); Mrs. Dickson (1856–57); Anna E. Dillingham (1859); Miss Dodge (1852–53); Miss Douglas (1862–63); Mrs. Frank Drew (1856–57); Mr. Dubois (1861–64); Mr. Duncalf (1856–57); Mrs. J. Dunn (1860–61); Mr. Eden (1863–64); Mary Eilert (1859–60); *Louisa Mortimer Eldredge* (1852–61); Mr. Ellis (1860–61); R. H. Ellsworth (1867–68); Louis Elssler (1849); Miss Everitt (1855–56); L. H. Everitt (1859); Miss Fenton (1865–68); J. B. Ferdon (1860–61); Frank S. Finn (1863–64); Alexina Fisher (1850–51); Mrs. Fitzgerald (1857–58); Lizzie Fleming (1863–64); Miss Flood (1863–64); John Flood (1863–64); Miss Flynn (1853–54); J. Folwell (1866–67); Mr. Forbes (1856–57); Mr. Foster (1857–60); Miss F. France (1860–61); R. G. France (1864–65); *Mrs. R. G. France* (1855–68); *Rosa France* (1861–68); *Shirley Henry France* (1855–60); Banks Garrett (1859–60); Miss Garthwaite or Goldthwaite (1852–53); Mr. Gates (1855–56); Irene Gay (1867–68); Mr. George (1853–57); Letitia George (1859–60); Sarah Germaine (1863–64); Miss Gladstone (1852–53); Mr. Gladstone (1855–56); William R. Goodall (1850); Mr. Gowen (1856–57); J. Delmon Grace (1859–61, 1864–65); J. D. Grace (1864–65); Rowena Granice (1852–54); Mr. Grosvenor (1850); H. P. Grattan (1857–58); Mrs. H. P. Grattan (1857–58); H. D. Guion (1866–67); *Thomas Hadaway* (1850–57, 1860–65); Charles Hale (1858–60); Miss Hall (1853–54); Agnes Hampton (1859–60); T. Hampton (1859–60); Frank Hardenberg (1857–58); Mr. Harris (1855–56); Mr. J. Harrison (1860–61); W. B. Harrison, singer (1850–51, 1865–66); Mr. Havelock (1856–57); *Mr. E. Haviland,* sometimes *Hayland* (1860–66); W. Henderson (1867–68); H. Henkins (1850–53); Miss Henry (1865–66); Mr. Henry (1853–54); W. J. Herbert (1856–57); H. Higbie (1865–66); Mr. Higgins (1849); Miss Hill (1865–66); W. M. Holland (1862–64); Mrs. Charles Howard (1857–59); *Cordelia Howard* (1855–59); *George C. Howard* (1853–59); Mrs.

H. Howard (1859–61); Mr. Hughes (1860–63); Miss Jackson (1852–56); Mr. Jackson (1859–60); T. E. Jackson (1867–68); Mr. James (1860–61); William L. Jamieson (1859–66); Mr. Jardine (1860–61); Miss Johnson (1865–66); R. J. Johnson (1865–66); Miss Keogh (1850–51); Lydia Knight (1859–60); Mr. Knowlton (1852–56); Mrs. Kook (1864–65); Charlotte Lacy (1851–52); Miss Laing (1863–64); Miss La Porte (1860–61); Mr. Laws (1863–64); *Miss Le Brun* (1860–64); *Mrs. Le Brun* (1861–64); *Mr. Addie Le Brun* (1861–66); Miss Le Moyne (1865–66); Emma Leslie (1849–51); *Milnes Levick* (1853–58, 1864–68); Mrs. Milnes Levick (1856–57); Mr. Livingston (1852–53); Miss Livingston (1866–67); *George Lingard* (1855–57); *James W. Lingard* (1855–57); *Mrs. J. W. Lingard* (1855–57); George F. MacDonald (1859–60); G. W. Malmberg (1867–68); Miss Marks (1866–67); William Marsden (1852–53); Miss Marshall (1851–53); Mr. Martin (1852–53); Mrs. Martin (1855–56); Martinetti Family (1849); Mrs. Massen (1866–68); L. F. Massen (1867–68); Mrs. Mawe (1856–57); J. J. McClosky (1855–56); Miss McCormack (1860–62); R. S. Meldrum (1859–60); Miss Melissa (1857–58); Emilie Melville (1865–66); Jerry Merrifield (1849); *Emily Mestayer* (1851–60); Louis J. Mestayer (1863–64); George Mitchell (1866–68); *Carrie Monell* (1863–66); Pat Morris (1849); Miss Mortimer (1852–53); Miss Morton (1852–53); F. A. Munroe (1853–54); J. L. Munroe (1853–54); Mrs. J. L. Munroe (1853–54); *Joseph E. Nagle* (1860–64); Mrs. C. Newman (1866–67); J. W. Norris (1866–67); D. Oakley (1857–58); William O'Neill (1859–60); Mrs. Orient (1855–56); Miss Josephine Orton (1856–57); Robert Otis (1855–56); Miss Palmer (1855–57); Sefton Parry (1852–53); *Mrs. Sefton Parry* (1852–56); *Sallie Partington* (1857–60, 1865–66); Miss Pelham (1856–57); Mrs. Penson (1851–52); Mr. Pierrepont (1852–53); B. C. Porter (1864–65); Olive Priestly (1863–64); *Mrs. James J. Prior (Louisa Young)* (1858–68); Miss Radford (1865–66); Mr. Radinski (1855–57); Mrs. Radinski (1855–56); Miss Randolph (1850–51); T. G. Roberts (1867–68); Miss E. Robinson (1857–58); Mrs. Rogers (1850–51, 1857–58); Mr. Rose (1849); Mr. Ryley (1861–62); Harry Ryner (1857–58); Mrs. Harry Ryner (1857–60); Milly Sackett (1857–58); Agnes St. Clair (1860–62); Mrs. St. John (1855–56); Miss Salmon (1856–57); Kate Saxon (1856–57); Emma Schell, danseuse (1865–66); Miss Sherman (1867–68); Mr. Simpson, later Dan Setchell (1852–53); Percy Skerrett (1859–60); Master Smith (1853–54); Mr. Smith (1850–51); T. Soutain (1865–66); J. R. Spackman (1857–58); Mr. Stafford (1850–51); Miss Stanhope (1849–51); Henry Stapleton (1859–60); Mr. Sternes (1855–56); Ernest Stevens (1865–66); L. Stevens (1858–60); Mrs. L. Stevens (1859–60); *Charles Stratton*, "Tom Thumb" (1850–65); Miss Taglioni (1852–53); *Edward Fenton Taylor* (1855–65); Stage Manager (1860–65); Mr. Thomason, or Thompson (1852–53); J. S. Thompson (1857–64); Miss M. Thompson (1863–66); Cassie Troy (1867–68); M. Vigotty (1865–66); *Harriet Walby* (1859–65); Julia Walby (1858–60); H. H. Wall (1860–61); Miss Walker (1865–67); J. L. Wallis (1859–60); John C. Walsh (1867–68); *Jenny Walters* (1860–68); Miss Ward (1863–64); Mr. Warner (1855–56); Charles Warwick (1849, 1852–53); *Harry Watkins* (1857– ?); Miss Watson (1855–56); J. Weaver (1850–51); *Sarah Weinlich* (1859); *F.C. Wemyss* (1849–50); Mr. Wentworth (1853–54); C. Wesley (1866–67); Josephine West (1849–51); Mr. Whitman (1852–53); Mr. Whitmore (1852–53, 1855–56); Mr. Wilson (1850–51); Miss Winter (1855–56); F. Wood (1863–64); S. Wright (1867–68); Charles Van Kleeck (1851–53); Mrs. Yeomans (1850–51).

REPERTORY

The performance history of the American Museum Stock Company has not been calendared. T. Allston Brown's *History of the New York Stage* registers the highlights of several of the seasons; George Odell's *Annals of the New York Stage* is more thorough, although by no means exhaustive.

BIBLIOGRAPHY

Brown, T. Allston. *A History of the New York Stage*. Vols. 1–2. New York: Dodd, Mead and Company, 1903.
Harris, Neil. *Humbug: The Art of P.T. Barnum*. Boston: Little, Brown and Company, 1973. Neatly places Barnum's many show-business achievements in the context of cultural history.
Odell, George C. D. *Annals of the New York Stage*. Vols. 5–8. New York: Columbia University Press, 1931–36.
Wallace, Irving. *The Fabulous Showman*. New York: Alfred A. Knopf, 1959.

Weldon B. Durham

AMERICAN OPERA HOUSE COMPANY. After the failure of Noah M. Ludlow as manager of the Chatham Garden Theatre Company * in Chatham Street (New York City), the house fell into desuetude, being used primarily as a rental hall for masquerade balls. Early in 1829 the nomadic actor James Henry Hackett announced his intention of opening Barrière's old theatre as the American Opera House, Chatham Street. The premiere performance (May 20, 1829) of the new enterprise featured Richard Sheridan's *Rivals* and John O'Keeffe's *The Agreeable Surprise*, a comic opera.

Hackett's venture was another attempt to unseat the Park Theatre as the major metropolitan playhouse, but in this he proved unsuccessful, partly because 1829 was what George Odell (3:420) called "one of the worst of theatrical years," but largely because he presented little of extraordinary interest. The fate of the American Opera House might have been different had the manager remained in residence and dominated the repertory with his own popular characterizations, but Hackett devoted much of his time to other interests. His soon-to-be-legendary Falstaff was not seen in Chatham Street, nor were any of his Yankee impersonations except those of *Jonathan in England* and its literary source *Paul Pry*. In addition to appearing in these presentations, Hackett was seen by Chathamites only in *Pizarro, The Road to Ruin*, and *Monsieur Tonson*. After a fairly disastrous summer in which Hackett promised novelties that never materialized, he booked a magician into the theatre. In October he announced his decision to convert the theatre into a saloon and ballroom. By December 31, 1829, the American Opera House was a thing of the past, and Hackett was involved in the management of the Bowery Theatre Company*.

Critical reaction to this short-lived company was not particularly supportive; there was, in fact, more response to Hackett's renovation of the theatre than to the performances of his company. The usual run of Gaelic plays (*The Irish Tutor*), Scottish dramas (*Guy Mannering, Rob Roy, The Lady of the Lake*), and an occasional Shakespearean piece (*Richard III, The Comedy of Errors, The Merchant of Venice*) provided contrast to the predictable repertory of musicals, farces, and melodramas. The principal novelty was a production of *John Overry; or, The Miser of Southwark Ferry*. Forty-eight plays were presented during the summer and fewer than a dozen in the autumn. Henry Wallack supervised the productions.

The principal guest artists—J. J. Adams, George Washington Dixon, Thomas Kilner, George Holland, and occasionally Hackett himself—were supported by a fairly mediocre company, details of which are sparse because newspaper references were infrequent. Mrs. Stickney, once a leading woman, was now reduced to assuming old women's parts. The remainder of the troupe mostly was composed of holdovers from the Chatham Garden Company of recent years.

Presumably there was little to mourn when Hackett relinquished the building and released his company to find situations elsewhere. So disappeared the American Opera House Company.

PERSONNEL

Management: James H. Hackett.

Stage Director: W. H. (Henry) Wallack.

Actors and Actresses: Mlle. Adolph, James Anderson, Mr. Archer, George Barrett, Mrs. W. R. Blake, William Rufus Blake, Mrs. Frederick Brown, W. B. Chapman, William Chapman, Sr., Mr. Clarke, Thomas Comer, Sam Cowell, Mrs. Sam Cowell, Miss Emery, Amelia Fisher, Clara Fisher, Mr. Foot, W. Forrest, Ann Marie French, W. F. Gates, Mrs. Golden, Mr. Grierson, Mrs. J. H. Hackett, Mr. Horton, Mrs. Hughes, H. B. Hunt, Mr. Kelsey, Miss Kent, Mr. Laidley, Mr. McGuire, D. D. McKinney, J. Mercer, Master Charles Mestayer, Emily Mestayer, James Myers, Miss Phillips, Moses S. Phillips, Thomas H. Quin, James Roberts, Mrs. James Roberts, James M. Scott, John Sefton, Alexander Simpson, Mrs. G. G. Stevenson, George G. Stevenson, Mr. Stickney, Mrs. Stickney, J. A. Stone, Mr. Tuthill, Mrs. Walstein, Mr. Wells, A. W. Wright, Charles Young.

REPERTORY

1829: *The Rivals; The Agreeable Surprise; Of Age Tomorrow; Thérèse; 'Twas I; The Poor Gentleman; Tekeli; Turn Out; My Grandmother; The Blind Boy; The Mountaineers; Ways and Means; Jonathan in England; Pizarro; The Road to Ruin; The Romp; Monsieur Tonson; The Devil's Bridge; No Song, No Supper; Simpson and Company; Actress of All Work; The Wandering Boys; Brother and Sister; Rosina; Guy Mannering; Rob Roy; The Barber of Seville; The Death Fetch; The Irish Tutor; Paul Pry; Richard III; The Turnpike Gate; The Forger; Cure for the Heart-Ache; The Lady of the Lake; The Comedy of Errors; The Hundred-Pound Note; The Anaconda; Honey Moon; Alexander the Great; Paul Jones; Sweethearts and Wives; The Lottery Ticket; Othello; The Hypocrite; Rienzi; John Overry; Ambrose Gwinnett; The Merchant of Venice; The Young Widow; The Jealous Wife; Lovers' Quarrels; A Day after the Fair; Nature and Philosophy.*

BIBLIOGRAPHY

Published Sources: Joseph N. Ireland, *Records of the New York Stage from 1750 to 1860*, 2 vols. (New York: T. H. Morrell, 1866–67); George C. D.Odell, *Annals of the New York Stage*, vol. 3 (New York: Columbia University Press, 1928).

George B. Bryan

AMERICAN THEATRE COMPANY. Philadelphia's Walnut Street Theatre, opened in 1820, had endured a steady turnover of managers and a turbulent metamorphosis from circus amphitheatre to legitimate dramatic facility, when actor-manager Francis Courtney Wemyss secured the theatre's lease in the fall of 1834. Wemyss (1797–1859), born and trained in England, made his American debut in Philadelphia in 1822 with the Chestnut Street Theatre Company*. He played with that company sporadically during the next decade, primarily in serious roles. Wemyss had also managed theatres in Baltimore and Pittsburgh when he took up the management of the Walnut Street Theatre. Keenly sensitive to popular sentiments of nationalism and nativism that permeated American consciousness in the 1830s and 1840s, Wemyss' first undertaking was to Americanize the decor of his theatre. American history from the Declaration of Independence to the Battle of New Orleans was the decorative theme, and patriotism was its tone. Scenes of American battles adorned the boxes, medallions of the heads of presidents decorated the dress circle, and portraits of generals and naval heroes embellished the second and third tiers, respectively. Gold stars against a pink background completed the design by casting a soft, romantic aura over the images of American military might. A drop curtain by artist Harry Williams copied Trumbull's famous painting of "The Battle of Bunker Hill." The most enduring new symbol was a huge American eagle with widespread wings at the center of the proscenium arch. It remained the theatre's emblem until the 1920s. Appropriately, the theatre's name was changed to the "American Theatre."

Wemyss planned to cultivate a lower- and middle-class audience for his American Theatre by responding to the popular interest in native entertainment. The Chestnut (also spelled "Chesnut") Street Theatre had long been Philadelphia's only permanent legitimate theatre. Nicknamed "Old Drury," it was the embodiment of aristocratic, British theatrical traditions; it appealed primarily to the upper and middle classes with its British and continental opera and theatre personalities. To create a new theatrical audience that would support a second permanent resident company, Wemyss initially charged low admission prices of twenty-five to fifty cents and later halved those prices. (The top price at the Chestnut was seventy-five cents.) Wemyss especially endeared his theatre to lower-class Philadelphians by producing an unprecedented number of benefits for the local volunteer fire companies, which were comprised predominantly of working-class young men.

Wemyss assembled a resident company of twenty-two male and female performers. Many were well known to Philadelphia audiences, having appeared previously with the Chestnut Street Theatre Company; they included Mrs. Mary Ann Duff, Thomas Hadaway, Mr. and Mrs. Kent, and Charles S. Porter. The company opened during the Christmas week of 1834 and was well received by local critics, although its lavish scenery and detailed production methods were even more highly touted. Commented Philadelphia actor-manager William Burke Wood, "Dramas of show and spectacle . . . and every variety of pageantry . . . were produced in a truly magnificent style . . . with little regard to expense" (Wood, 401). Initially, Miss Mary Duff, daughter of the noted tragedienne Mrs. Mary Ann Duff, drew strong local support and aided in the company's mounting popularity. The troupe remained fairly stable, typically replacing five to ten performers each year. Several of the company's young performers went on to outstanding theatrical careers. A teenaged Mrs. Hunt, who appeared in 1839 and 1840, later became the famous actress-manager Mrs. John Drew, known especially in Philadelphia for her long tenure as manager of the Arch Street Theatre Company*. Fifteen-year-old Barney Williams also performed with the troupe in 1839 and 1840, gaining experience at the beginning of a forty-year career as America's most-loved Irish comedian. Popular comedian William E. Burton, later to become a noted manager of Philadelphia's National Theatre Company (1840–42)*, [Burton's] Arch Street Theatre Company*, Philadelphia, and Burton's Stock Company*, New York, transferred from the Chestnut to the American during Wemyss' management. One of the American Theatre Company's most versatile and seasoned members, Charles Durang—an actor, stage manager, and playwright particularly known for his specialty dance "Rickett's Hornpipe" and for his whimsical portrayals in pantomimes and children's pieces—later became a major historian of the Philadelphia stage. Older Philadelphia favorites, such as genteel comedian William Burke Wood, also appeared.

The American Theatre Company operated primarily as a resident stock troupe in which each actor specialized in a stock role. Visiting stars and their vehicles often were chosen to complement the company's overall purpose and to appeal to local needs. Delineators of the Yankee and other American characters abounded, including Joseph Jefferson, George H. Hill, Dan Marble, Sol Smith, James H. Hackett, and Henry J. Finn. Thomas D. Rice performed with the company on a regular basis from 1835 until 1838, making his burnt-cork Negro and other American characters—Jim Crow, Gumbo Chaff, Sambo, Ginger Blue, and Sylvester Daggerwood—highly popular. Occasional performers, who appeared by engagement rather than by season, supplemented the company, as was the standard practice of the day.

Bills of the American Theatre Company followed the traditional combination of main piece, usually a full-length drama or comedy, and a shorter afterpiece, usually a comedy, farce, or musical burletta. Stock company actors headlined the afterpiece almost without exception. Since traveling stars were given the most complex and challenging tragic, especially Shakespearean, roles, it is not surprising that many stock actors concentrated their talents in comedy. Voguish operettas and operas were also produced, although the regular company boasted only four vocalists. Wemyss planned to minimize musicals, which he viewed as basically foreign products. Their continued popularity, however, forced him to retreat somewhat from this stand, although the American Theatre never challenged the Chestnut as the city's opera emporium. Wemyss did enhance the evening's dramatic fare with both musical and nonmusical specialty acts, for which he often hired additional variety performers, such as Cony and his dogs; Master Blanchard the ape-boy; Signor Sciarra, the Ninth Wonder of the World; Hervio Nano, the man-fly; and Monsieur Bihin, the Belgian giant. Barkham Cony, known as the "dog star," and his famous trained canines, Hector and Bruin, regularly appeared with the American Theatre Company in the seasons of 1835–37. During this period the company produced several plays featuring the animals, including *Love Me, Love My Dog; Planter and His Dog*; and *Cherokee Chief*.

An abundance of both serious and comic plays treating American themes in a patriotic fashion distinguished the company's repertory. A long list of Yankee plays included *Jonathan Doubikins, The Yankee Valet, Lion of the East, Seth Slope, The Yankee Pedlar, Yankee Bill Sticker*, and *Jonathan in England*. Wemyss attempted to produce as many as possible of the newer American plays, making a special point to offer such fare on national memorial days. They included works such as J. S. Jones' *Liberty Tree; or, The Boston Boys of '76*; and Samuel Woodworth's *Forest Rose; or, American Farmers* and *The Spirit of '76; or, Washington*. Local, topical plays occasionally were offered, such as T. D. Rice's farce *Discoveries in the Moon; or, Herschel Out-Herscheled*, which reacted to articles by astronomer Sir John Herschel, who then resided in Philadelphia and wrote for the local press. Wemyss encouraged new playwrights continually, producing pieces by his stage managers, prompters, and actors; he also produced his own plays, such as *The Jewess*. Other plays presented came from the standard London stage repertory and from adapted German and French works. British theatrical traditions, which Wemyss' company openly embraced, were the offering of Christmas pantomimes and occasional processionals. Ironically, one of the American Theatre Company's most acclaimed productions was its spectacle-procession *The Coronation of Queen Victoria* in August 1838.

Seasons at the American Theatre varied considerably in length. The 1834–35 winter season ran from Christmas week until April, and a shorter summer season followed from May until July. In 1835–36 the company operated during the full theatrical year, from late August 1835 until early July 1836, and then recessed for the summer. Wemyss operated in the traditional mode from August until April during the 1836–37 season and then shocked local critics by implementing a summer season to run from June through September, Philadelphia's hottest and most humid months. The latter season's success prompted Wemyss to operate year-round for the next two years, until a dispute with the theater's stockholders halted the company's operation in late January 1840. In September 1839 the theatre's board compelled Wemyss to raise his admission prices by fifty percent in the pit. Purportedly, Wemyss lost $6,000 in the months following and simply refused to continue production until he regained control of ticket prices. When the stockholders succumbed, the company resumed, running from February until late July 1840.

However, a long and bitter series of disputes between Wemyss and the theatre's stockholders, headed by president G. H. Freeman, threatened the company's existence. First, Wemyss and stockholders disagreed about liquor sales in the theatre's lobby: when the law that prohibited liquor in theatres was rescinded, Wemyss, virulently against the effects of drink, lobbied to keep his theatre dry. The stockholders resisted his appeals, insisting that liquor sales raised their annual profits by $3,000. In 1837 Wemyss and the stockholders clashed on the installation of gaslights, which Wemyss deemed essential to compete effectively with the Chestnut Street Theatre. (This theatre had recently modernized the primitive gas lighting system it had installed in 1816.) Wemyss prevailed but was forced to pay $1,000 in advance on the theatre's annual rent of $4,150. Another battle occurred in 1837 regarding Wemyss' right to sublease the theatre. George A. Cooke, an impresario of the Baltimore theatre and a financial backer of Wemyss, wanted to bring his circus to Philadelphia for an engagement at the American Theatre when his own Baltimore amphitheatre burned down. The stockholders refused, angering both Wemyss and Cooke, and Cooke retaliated by erecting the Chestnut Street Circus at Ninth and Chestnut streets, just one block north of the American. An agreement eventually was negotiated whereby Cooke brought a traveling company of actors to the American Theatre for the period April 2 to May 5, 1838. This troupe presented the equestrian drama *Mazeppa* while the regular resident company remained inactive. The stockholders continually protested Wemyss' aggressive investment practices, especially his expenditures for theatre renovations, scenery, and regular operations, which they alleged exceeded his receipts, despite good attendance and his company's overall popularity. A rift with the stockholders over the theatre's redecoration followed the disagreement over ticket prices. Their differences finally proved irreconcilable, and in the late spring of 1840, Wemyss secured the lease of the newest and most modern of the main Philadelphia playhouses, the Arch Street Theatre, thereby ending his association with the American Theatre. The last performance of the American Theatre Company took place on July 25, 1840. The theatre then remained dark until its new manager, Ethelbert A. Marshall, assumed control in October, renaming the theatre and its company, for the third time, the Walnut Street Theatre Stock Company (1840–79)*.

PERSONNEL

Management: Francis Courtney Wemyss, proprietor and manager; P. Warren, treasurer.

Scenic Artists: Mr. Landers, Russell Smith.

Musical Director: J. G. Clemens.

Directors: W. Barrymore, Mr. Ward, and Charles Durang, stage managers; C. Porter, acting manager.

Actors and Actresses: J. P. Adams; Miss Anderson; Miss Angelica; *Mr. and Mrs. N. H. Bannister* (1837–39); Mr. and Mrs. Bennie; T. Bishops; Yankee Bowman; J. M. Brown; Mr. Burgess; *William E. Burton* (1839–40); Miss Charnock; Miss Chester; Mr. Chippendale; *N. B. Clarke* (1835–37); Mr. Clemens; S. Collingbourne; J. H. Collins; Mr. Conner; *E. S. Conner* (1834–39); *Mrs. F. B. Conway* (1835–36); Barkham Cony (and his dogs Hector and Bruin); Mr. Cunningham; G. K. Dickenson; *Mary Duff* (1834–36); Mrs. Mary Ann Duff; Mr. and Mrs. Charles Durang; C. H. Eaton; Mr. Edwards; Mr. Ferrers; J. M. Field; H. J. Finn; Mr. Frimbley; T. E. Garson; M. and Mme. Gouffe; Mr. Grierson; Polly Hadaway; *Thomas Hadaway* (1834–40); J. R. Hall; Miss Hamblin; Mr. Harrison; Mr. and Mrs. John Herbert; Miss Hichie; *Mr. and Mrs. George Hield* (1838–39); *Mrs. Hunt*, later known as Mrs. John Drew (1839–40); Mr. Ingersoll; Mr. Jackson; N. Johnston; Mr. Joseph; Mr. and Mrs. Kemble; Mr. and Mrs. W. Kent; *Mr. and Mrs. J. P. Knight* (1834–36); *Mr. and Mrs. LaForest* (1838–40); Mme. LaTrust; Mr. Lennox; Mrs. Maeder, formerly Clara Fisher; Miss H. Matthews; T. Matthews; Mr. McConachy; Mr. McCormick; Mr. McCutchen; Miss Meadows; J. Mestayer; Mr. Morley; Mr. Morton; Mr. Mossop; Miss Murray; *Mr. and Mrs. William Muzzy* (1834–36); F. S. Myers; Mr. Neafie; John H. Oxley; Miss A. Packard; Miss E. Packard; Miss S. Packard; Miss Parker; Mr. Percival; Mr. Pickering; Miss A. Porter; *Mr. Powell* (1839–40); Mr. and Mrs. Preston; Mrs. Pritchard; Mr. and Mrs. J. Proctor; *D. Reed* (1834–39); Miss Reynolds; Mr. and Mrs. J. B. Rice; T. D. Rice; Eliza Riddle; T. B. Russell; Miss Ruth; Miss Scott; Joseph O. Sefton (1834–35); *W. Sefton* (1834–35); *Mrs. W. Sefton* (1839–40); Joseph Smith; Mr. and Mrs. W. H. Smith; Mrs. Thorne; W. A. Vache; Mr. Walstein; Mr. Walters; Mr. Ward; *Ann D. Waring* (1835–36); Mary Ann Warren; William Warren; Mr. and Mrs. C. Watson; *Francis Courtney Wemyss* (1834–46); Miss White; Mrs. G.B.S. Wilks; Barney Williams; Mrs. Willis; Mr. Wills; John Winnan; William B. Wood; Mr. Woodhull.

Guest Artists: Augustus A. Addams; Mme. Augusta; Miss Barnes; Mr. and Mrs. John Barnes; Mrs. W. Barrymore; Miss E. Booth; Junius Brutus Booth; William E. Burton; D. L. Carpenter; Mlle. Celeste; Mrs. Samuel Chapman; T. S. Cline;

Mr. Cooper; Miss Priscilla Cooper; Joe Cowell; Mrs. E. L. Davenport; Miss Jean Margaret Davenport; Mr. DeLarue; Mr. Denvil; H. J. Finn; Mme. Fitzwilliams; Mr. Forbes; Miss Gannon; Mr. and Mrs. John Greene; J. Hackett; Mr. Hall (Zip Coon); Mme. Hazard; George H. Hill; Mr. Horncastle; Emma Ince; Mr. and Mrs. Joseph Jefferson; Miss Kerr; Mr. Klishing; Mrs. A. Knight, formerly Miss Povey; Mrs. Edward Knight; James Sheridan Knowles; Miss Lee; Dan Marble; Mrs. Meer; Masters R. and J. Meer; Virginia Monier; Mr. Morley; J. E. Murdoch; T. C. Parsloe; Mrs. Parsons; Mrs. J. B. Phillips; Mr. Porter (the Kentucky Giant); John Sefton; Mrs. Sequin; Sol Smith; Mlle. Stephan; Mrs. Thayer; W. Wood.

SAMPLE REPERTORY

1835–36: *Richard III; My Neighbor's Wife; A New Way to Pay Old Debts; Maid and Magpie; Hamlet; Affair of Honor; Brutus; Siamese Twins; Virginius; Congress Hall; Othello; King Lear; Julius Caesar; Mayor of Garratt; William Tell; In the Wrong Box; Damon and Pythias; Virginia Mummy; Macbeth; Oh, Hush!; A Woman's Life; Pizarro; Discoveries in the Moon; The Stranger; Romeo and Juliet; Fazio; Skeleton Witness; Alexander the Great; Dead Shot; Hypocrite; Pitcairn's Island; Biena; Dumb Savoyard and His Monkey; Illustrious Stranger; The Secret; Jocko; Wild Woman of Our Village; Lying Valet; 102!; Three and Deuce; Spirit of '76; Lo Zingaro; The Young Widow; Secret Service; The Merchant of Venice; Cherokee Chief; Sylvester Daggerwood; Seven Clerks; Four Sisters; Love Me, Love My Dog; Perfection; Ourang Outang; The Exile; Forest of Bondy; Gretna Green; Hyder Ali; Wild Boy; Aladdin; Englishmen in India; Loan of a Lover; Murder of the Blind Boy; Zenocles and the Greek Chief; Mountain Devil; Jack Robinson and His Monkey; Knight of the Golden Fleece; Green Mountain Boy; Jonathan in England; Lion of the East; Jonathan Doubikins; Infidel; Note Forger; Isabella; The Gamester; Jane Shore; Botheration; Arab Chief; Adelgitha; Robber's Wife; Young Reefer; The Gipsy of Ashburnham Dell; The Brigand; The French Washerwoman; Spoil'd Child; Tower de Nesle; I'll Be Your Second; Miser's Miseries; Fieschi; Wreckers; The Review; Cherry Bounce; Miller and His Men; Turnpike Gate; Spanish Pirates; Victoire; Spirit Bride; The Kentuckian; Monsieur Tonson; Catching an Heiress; Black Angus of the Evil Eye; The Golden Farmer; Thérèse; Bone Squash Diavolo; Fatal Prophecies; Is He Jealous?; Ambrose Gwinnett; Jack Cade; Luke, the Labourer; Nature and Philosophy; Raising the Wind; Weathercock; Venice Preserved; Agreeable Surprise; Two Gregories; Kaspar Hauser; Crowded Houses; Adventure; The Forest Rose; Yankee Pedlar; Gray Man of Tottenham; Love Laughs at Locksmiths; O-I-E-O-E; George Barnwell; Idiot Witness; The Poor Soldier; Lodoiska; Uda and Magnus; Harlequin Hurry Scurry; Ida Stephanoff; Black Eyed Susan; Douglas; The Purse; Tom Thumb, the Great; The Maid of New Orleans; A Fish Out of Water; Passion and Repentance; Diamond Arrow; Hunting a Turtle; The Iron Chest; No!; The Apostate; The Mountaineer; Harlequin Tom: The Piper's Son; The Children of Chittigong; Yellow Kids; Henriette the Forsaken; My Poll and My Partner Joe; Three Hunchbacks; Who Owns the Hand?; The Ladies' Man; Rienzi; The Rent Day; The Wonder; My Aunt; Hazard of the Die; The Wolf and the Lamb; Spring and Autumn; The Adopted Child; The Jewess; Dumb Belle; Wild Oats; The Broken Heart; Norman Leslie; Cure for the Heart-Ache; Laugh When You Can; Barbarossa; Henry IV; Tom and Jerry; The Spirit of the Black Mantle; Comfortable Service;*

Carnival Scene; The Busybody; Job Fox; The Yankee Valet; Fortune's Frolic; Rip Van Winkle; Monsieur Mallet; Caswallon; Sledge Driver; The Widow's Victim; The Youthful Queen; Alberti Contradine; 23 John Street; Disowned; The French Tutor; Military Execution; The Heart of Midlothian; Tekeli; Heir-at-Law; The Mummy; Council of the Inquisition; Popping the Question; The Old Gentleman; Dream at Sea; The Somnambulist; Circumstantial Evidence; Paul Ulric; Wenlock of Wenlock; The May Queen; The Lady and the Devil; Honest Thieves; Town and Country; The Married Rake; The Lottery Ticket; The Daughter; Caradora; Brian Boroihme; Forty and Fifty; The Actress of Padua; Point of Honour; Frank Fox Phipps; The Last Nail; Lucille; Pocahontas; The Wood Demon; Dick, the Apprentice; A Husband at Sight; Judgement of Solomon; Liberty Tree.

1839–40: Virginius; Nipped in the Bud; The Gladiator; Ask No Questions; Damon and Pythias; The Padlock; Metamora; The Conquering Game; Rum Old Commodore; Othello; Thérèse; Richelieu; Love Laughs at Locksmiths; William Tell; Mazeppa; The Romp; Blanche of Navarre; Freemason; Paul Pry; Sweethearts and Wives; His First Champagne; Peter the Great; Mayor of Garratt; Plots; State Secrets; The Mummy; Whigs and Democrats; Peeping Tom of Coventry; The Emigrant; Robinson Crusoe; The Wandering Minstrel; Murder at the Inn; John Jones; The Irish Tutor; But, However!; Der Wachter; Love, Law, and Physic; Knight of the Golden Fleece; New Notions; Jonathan in England; Forest Rose; Loan of a Lover; A Wife for a Day; The Yankee Pedlar; Seth Slope; Man and Wife; Cramond Brig; Kaspar Hauser; The Tourists; Lady of Munster; Der Freischutz; Clari; The Will; The Warlock of the Glen; The Secret; Marriage of Figaro; Cinderella; No Song, No Supper; Fra Diavolo; Swiss Cottage; Charles XII; The Battle of Austerlitz; The Innkeeper's Daughter; Is He Jealous?; The Idiot Witness; Jacques Strop; Doctor Dilworth; The Dead Shot; Macbeth; Hunting a Turtle; Hamlet; My Neighbor's Wife; The Robber's Wife; King Lear; Gretna Green; The Lady of Lyons; Sea Captain; Bachelor's Buttons; Forty Thieves; Love; Marmion; The Daring Man; The Secret Mine; Black Eyed Susan; Mother Shipton; Two Drovers; Siege of Tripoli; Kenilworth; Billy Button; Rob Roy; Is the Philadelphian Dead?; Woman's Wit; Pizarro; The Adopted Child; George Barnwell; Jane Shore; The Hunchback; Amateurs and Actors; Perfection; Rory O'More; Hofer; Tekeli; Luke, the Labourer; Bluebeard; Don Juan; Jack Sheppard; Yankee Bill Sticker; La Bayadère; Wallace; The Golden Farmer; Sadak and Kalasrade; Dew Drop; The Happy Man; The White Eagle; The Negro Doorkeeper; Alice Gray; Paddy Murphy's Weather Almanac; The Review; The Lear of Private Life; Who's the Murderer?; The Death Token; The Rivals; The Siamese Twins; The Chain of Guilt; Lafitte; School of Reform; Hunters of the Pyrenees; Henri Quatre; The Philadelphia Fireman; Six Degrees of Crime; Brother and Sister; The Handsome Husband; Richard III; The Cradle of Liberty; Cherry and Fair Star; A Quiet Day; Ambrose Gwinett; Joan of Arc; Romanzo; The Old Oak Chest; Paul Jones; Brutus; Snakes in the Grass; The Irish Lion; Point of Honour; The Exile; Monsieur Jacques; The Light Ship; Humbug; Emigration; Begone Dull Care; A Good Night's Rest; The Dark Lady; Stag Hall; Little Sins and Pretty Sinners; Paul: The Patriot; The Manic Lover; Napoleon Bonaparte's Invasion of Russia; What Have I Done?; Bold Dragoons; The Little Back Parlor; Ugolino; Children in the Wood; Caswallon; Faint Heart ne'er Won Fair Lady; If the Cap Fits You, Wear It; His Last Legs; Love's Frailties; The Fortunate Couple; Robert Macaire; Edgar the Idiot; My Young Wife and My Old Umbrella; Victoire; Frightened *to Death; Turning the Tables; Winning a Husband; The Man in the Iron Mask; Corsair's Revenge; Disguise; The Miller's Maid; The Country Girl; Nicholas Nickleby; The Iron Chest; The Sentinel; The Giant of Palestine; The Sorcerer; Marco Bombo; The Truth; Gig Gig; Henriette; The Vampire; Omnibus; The Devil's Daughters; The Falls of Clyde; Hamlet Travestie; The Bleeding Nun of Lindenberg; A New Way to Pay Old Debts; Pleasant Neighbors; The Stranger; The Apostate; Lovers' Quarrels; The Distrest Mother; Oroonoko; Two Greens; Douglas; The Merchant of Venice; The Mountaineers; The Ladder of Love; Comfortable Service; Valentine and Orson; Conquest of Taranto; The Purse; Adelgitha; Wreck Ashore; The Dying Gift; Patriotism; The White Farm; Affair of Honor; The Miller and His Men; Oh, Hush!; The Innkeeper of Abbeville; The Evil Eye; Tom and Jerry; Dumb Girl of Genoa; Bombastes Furioso; Matheo Falcone; The Little Tiger; Bee Hive; Wild Oats; Two Brothers; Alpine Hunters; The Pet of the Admiral; The Floating Beacon; Turnpike Gate.*

BIBLIOGRAPHY

Published Sources: Reese D. James, *Old Drury of Philadelphia* (Philadelphia: University of Pennsylvania Press, 1932); Francis Courtney Wemyss, *Twenty-Six Years in the Life of an Actor and Manager* (New York: Burgess, Stringer, and Company, 1847); Arthur Herman Wilson, *A History of the Philadelphia Theatre, 1835–1855* (Philadelphia: University of Pennsylvania Press, 1935); William Burke Wood, *Personal Recollections of the Stage* (Philadelphia: Henry Carey Baird, 1855).

Unpublished Source: Mary Helps, "The Walnut Street Theatre" (Paper presented as partial fulfillment of the M.L.S. degree, Drexel University, Philadelphia, 1966).

Archival Sources: Walnut Street Theatre File, Philadelphia Theatre Collection, Free Library of Philadelphia (Logan Square). The Philadelphia Theatre Collection also has files on many of the managers and performers connected with the Walnut Street Theatre.

Mari Kathleen Fielder

[BURTON'S] ARCH STREET THEATRE COMPANY. (1844–50) William E. Burton (1804–60) returned to the field of theatre management on June 1, 1844, at Philadelphia's 2,000-seat Arch Street Theatre. His first management ventures at Philadelphia's [New] National Theatre Company (1840–42)* and at New York's National Theatre (1841) had ended disastrously. Misfortune and mismanagement riddled Burton's earlier enterprises, so his selection of the dusty, deplorably located Arch Street Theatre for his new undertaking augered simply more failure. A succession of managers, beginning with William Burke Wood (1779–1861), who had successfully managed the rival Chestnut Street Theatre Company* for decades, had failed to establish a regular clientele for the Arch Street Theatre, built in 1828. Charles Durang, a knowledgeable analyst of events in Philadelphia's theatre history, thought Burton's effort was absurd.

Burton aimed once more to profit from light, varied, and attractive entertainment offered by a small, hardworking corps of stock performers.

Moreover, he dedicated himself to cleaning up the infamous third tier, the gallery to which was drawn a disorderly, crude, drunk, and womanizing element. He closed the saloon at that level, at some sacrifice to profit, refused admission to those who looked like troublemakers, and ejected those who got in and became rowdy. He aimed to make the Arch Street a profitable family theatre.

The company opened June 1, 1844, with an all-farce bill consisting of Sophia Lee's *Chapter of Accidents* (1780), based loosely on Denis Diderot's *Le pere de famille* (1761); R. B. Peake's *One Hundred-Pound Note* (1827); J. T. Haines' *White Squall* (1839); and J. B. Buckstone's *Kiss in the Dark* (1840). Prices at the opening were but fifty cents for box seats and twenty-five cents elsewhere, which was considerably below the prevailing scale.

Burton's group played at the Arch Street Theatre from June 1, 1844, to January 4, 1845. Burton sent a contingent of players to Baltimore for a three-month season at the Front Street Theatre beginning December 23, 1844, and he took a small group to Washington, D.C., for a three-month season beginning January 13, 1845. Brief seasons in Baltimore by Burton's satellite groups were common until July 1848. All of Burton's employees reassembled at the Arch Street Theatre to begin another short season in Philadelphia on March 22, 1845. After a brief recess, Burton's forces began anew on July 14, holding forth until January 24, 1846, before recessing for one week. Meantime, Burton had opened Philadelphia's Chestnut Street Theatre on August 3, 1845, forming a company around a nucleus of players from the Arch Street Theatre. The first Chestnut Street Theatre season ran until December 8, 1845; the second from December 19, 1845, to January 20, 1846; the third, and final, from April 27, 1846, to June 1, 1846. So, for periods in 1845–46, Burton was managing three theatres and stocking two of them with performers assigned from the Arch Street Theatre Company. Burton's third Arch Street season began January 30, 1846, and ended June 9. A short summer season followed, and then the group launched a long fall and winter season on August 26, 1846. They recessed February 17, 1847, and then regrouped on April 25 for an unbroken engagement of two years and two months, ending June 20, 1849. During this period the Arch Street Theatre was the premier entertainment outlet in Philadelphia. Burton used the profits from his Philadelphia business to establish Burton's Stock Company* in the nation's theatre center, New York City, at the Chambers Street Theatre. The last Burton season at the Arch, then operating without Burton's personal supervision, lasted from August 15, 1849, to January 2, 1850.

His small company featured several performers who had worked in the New National Theatre Company: George Graham, an excellent comedian, had failed Burton as a young star, but he had served well as a company member in 1841–42; Thomas à Beckett, a versatile actor, accomplished singer, and instrumentalist; tragedian John R. Scott; and, briefly, the rapidly rising Charlotte Cushman. William Jones and Edmund S. Conner, journeyman performers formerly with Burton at the New National, signed on with the new company at the Arch Street Theatre. They were joined by Mrs. Junius B. Booth, Jr., the former Clementine DeBar, a good dramatic actress and an excellent singing burletta comedienne; George H. Barrett, one of the best light comedians in the country; and Nick Johnson, a competent utility actor and an accomplished equestrian. Burton's mainstays were Charles Burke (1822–54) and Esther Hughes. Burke, a half-brother to Joseph Jefferson III and, like his relative, a famous interpreter of Rip Van Winkle, was an excellent foil to Burton. Burke's comic style was subtle and refined; Burton's, broad and expansive. Burke was lithe and graceful; Burton, strong, portly, even ungainly. Mrs. Hughes became the feminine half of one of the most famous comic couples in U.S. theatrical history, Mr. and Mrs. Toodles, in *The Toodles* (1849), Burton's hilarious adaptation of D. W. Jerrold's sentimental play *The Broken Heart; or, The Farmer's Daughter* (1832). Joseph Jefferson III was a company regular in May and June 1845 and appeared occasionally in nonstarring roles in 1846. Caroline Chapman (sister of William Chapman, the originator of the American showboat), one of the most vivacious soubrettes on the American stage, joined the company for the 1846–47 season. John Brougham appeared intermittently with the company beginning in 1845, thus marking the beginning of a long and brilliant professional relationship with Burton. Brougham was the consummate stage Irishman but was effective also as Dazzle in Dion Boucicault's *London Assurance*.

Burton hired stars for short engagements, but from first to last, he depended most heavily for his success on a strong, diversely talented company in a varied bill of plays. The first summer he used no stars and appeared himself each night in up to three roles. In 1844 he engaged the English tragedian William Charles Macready (1793–1873). Macready's repertory both tested and complemented the strength of Burton's company. James Robert Anderson, another English tragedian, followed Macready, but Anderson's engagement was unsuccessful. A production of George Heilge's *Putnam* drew well, as did two fairy extravaganzas, J. R. Planché's *Beauty and the Beast* (1841) and Gilbert A. à Beckett's *Yellow Dwarf* (1842). Joshua Silsbee and James H. Hackett, stars who specialized in popular Yankee characters, played brief engagements in 1844. Mr. and Mrs. George Skerrett appeared a week the following season, and Anderson returned briefly. In the fall of 1845, Burton engaged the team of William Crisp (c.1820–74) and Anna Cora Mowatt (1819–70), authoress of the new American comedy-satire *Fashion*. T. D. "Jim Crow" Rice, blackface comedian Silsbee, and W. F. Wood, the pantomime star, followed. Tragedians John R. Scott, Charles Thorne, Augustus A. Addams, and W. S. Conner starred briefly in the next four years, as did comedians John Brougham, Benjamin DeBar (both of whom became company regulars), and James W. Wallack, Jr. Female stars included Julia Dean and Catherine Weymss. Generally, though, the resident company bore the burden of making the venture a success, which they did, at a time when such a practice was dangerously old fashioned.

The repertory of Burton's Arch Street Theatre Company was extensive, including 690 plays produced between June 1, 1844, and January 2, 1850. In 1847–48, a season in which Burton's company dominated the theatre scene in Philadelphia, the group produced more than 220 pieces in about 300 nights of operation between July 5, 1847, and June 30, 1848. Other seasons were similarly varied, Burton's company bringing out, on the average, two pieces every three days. In the same period, Burton had a virtual monopoly on new visiting players for long and short engagements, and he brought twice as many new plays to the Philadelphia stage as did all other Quaker City theatres combined. Long runs were unusual. Only twenty-nine plays were produced twelve times or more. The diversity of the most popular plays indicates the diversity of Burton's repertoire. The most popular piece in the group's history was *A Glance at Philadelphia*, Burton's adaptation of Benjamin A. Baker's *Glance at New York*, the great success of Mitchell's Olympic Theatre Company in 1848, and one of the greatest successes of the New York stage. *A Glance at Philadelphia*, like its prototype, featured Mose, a volunteer fireman who befriends and protects a country friend who is beset by every type of sharper known to the city's slums. Mose beats every trickster at his game, all the while courting a charming shop girl. Baker's one-act play, technically a burletta, or farce, with interpolated songs and dances, and its sequels from Baker's own pen, *New York as It Is, Three Years After*, and *Mose in China*, spawned countless imitations from other hands, Burton's Philadelphia version being one of the most successful. *A Glance at Philadelphia*, featuring scenes of city locales painted by George Heilge, premiered April 25, 1848, and ran eighteen nights in succession and fifty-four nights in all.

The next most popular piece in Burton's repertoire was a "crook" melodrama adapted by J. B. Buckstone from William Harrison Ainsworth's popular novel *Jack Sheppard, the Housebreaker*. The play about the life and death by hanging of a famous English robber and prison breaker of the 1720s opened at the Arch Street Theatre on September 24, 1845, and was revived forty-one times in the next four years. Traditionally, the hero's was a "breeches" role, played by the company's tragedienne. *The Lady of Lyons* (1838), by Edward Bulwer, Lord Lytton, one of the era's most popular romantic dramas, was brought out thirty-six times. Other often-performed plays, in the order of their popularity, were J. R. Planché's extravaganza *Beauty and the Beast* (1841), seen twenty-eight times; Shakespeare's *Richard III*, the most-often-produced play in Philadelphia in the period 1835 to 1855, seen twenty-seven times; and the anonymously authored drama *Margaret Catchpole: The Female Horsethief* (1845), seen twenty-six times. George Heilge's scenic spectacle *Putnam; or, The Eagle Eye and Hand of Steel*, based on N. H. Bannister's very successful dramatization of the exploits of Putnam, a hero of the American Revolution, *Putnam: The Iron Son of '76* (1844), was featured twenty-five times. Of the twenty-nine most popular pieces Burton presented, twelve were light entertainments such as farces, burlesques, burlettas, and extravaganzas; one was a comedy, H. J. Conway's *Charles O'Malley; or, The Irish Dragoon*; and four were tragedies of Shakespeare: *Richard III, Hamlet, Macbeth*, and *Romeo and Juliet*. Burton's reputation, as well as that of his company, has been based on excellence in production of lighter, shorter forms, especially farce, but an analysis of the most-often-revived scripts reveals that dramas, melodramas, and tragedies were more popular.

Credit for the success of the Arch Street Theatre Company goes largely to the men and women of the ensemble, to Burton's acting manager J. M. Scott (not the tragedian), and to his stage managers H. E. Stevens, Wyzeman Marshall, and Edmund S. Conner. However, Burton contributed much hard work, by which he set the tone for the company's professional behavior. Burton was intelligent, articulate, experienced, and well trained as a performer and manager. He was also crusty, imperious, penurious, meddlesome, and combative. A portion of the credit for the success of the company is attributable to his dogged committment to an idea of a stock company virtually without stars, an idea out of currency for at least twenty years. Burton's efforts to resuscitate the old style of theatre management, while initially unrewarding at the New National Theatre, 1840–42, finally made him, according to Arthur H. Wilson, "the figure that stands at the keystone of the Philadelphia theatre through the fifth decade of the Nineteenth Century" (Wilson, 35).

PERSONNEL

Proprietor: William E. Burton.
Acting Manager: J. M. Scott.
Scenic Artists: George Heilge, Thomas Glessing.
Stage Managers: H. E. Stevens, Wyzeman Marshall, E. S. Conner.
Orchestra Leader: Sandy Jamison.
Treasurer: Mr. Edmonds.
Actors and Actresses: Thomas à Beckett; John B. Addis; Mrs. J. K. Altemus; G. J. Arnold; John Lewis Baker; *George A. Barrett* (1844–46); Mrs. Bell; Mr. Blankman; *Mrs. J. B. Booth, Jr.*(1844–45); *David P. Bowers* (1844–45, 1848–49); Mr. Bradford; John J. Bradshaw; Mr. Brazier; Mr. Brierson; *John Brougham* (1845–46); *Charles Burke* (1844– ?); *Mrs. Charles Burke* (1844– ?); *William E. Burton* (1844–48); Mr. Cadell; Mr. Calladine; Mrs. Capell, or Cappell; *Caroline Chapman* (1846–47); Harry Chapman; Mr. and Mrs. N. B. Clarke; Miss Coad; Edmund S. Conner; Mrs. H. Cramer; Mrs. Davis; Benjamin DeBar; Thomas Duff; *James Dunn* (1844–46); David Eberle; John Ellsler; Mr. and Mrs. Thomas Faulkner; Alexina Fisher, later Mrs. Baker; W. S. Fredericks; George Graham; *Anne*

N. Greene (1844–46); R. Hamilton; Mr. Hawks; W. Harrison; Mr. Henkins; Mr. Hickman; Miss J. Hill; Mrs. Hilson; *Mr. and Mrs. Charles Howard* (1844–45); *Esther Hughes* (1844– ?); Mr. Jackson; Mrs. Jamar; Mr. James; Joseph Jefferson III; Mr. Jervis; Nick Johnson; Robert Johnson; *T. B. Johnston* (1844– ?); William G. Jones; Mr. Keyser; Miss Kirby; Mrs. A. Knight; Mary Ann Lee, dancer; Mr. and Mrs. Henry Lewis; Mr. Marsh; Wyzeman Marshall; James Martin; Mrs. Mason; Mrs. McClure; Mrs. McLean; Mr. and Mrs. Charles Mestayer; Eliza Moore; Miss Moran; Miss Morgan; Mr. Mortimer; Mrs. Mossop, formerly Mrs. H. Knight; Mr. Mulholland; Frederick S. Myers; Miss Nelson; Mr. Neville; Mrs. H. Nicholls; *John E. Owens* (1846– ?); Eliza Place Petrie; Mr. Philips; George James Rea; Mrs. Ribas; James Hale Robinson; Margaret Rogers; Miss Rogers; Henry Russell; Mrs. T. B. Russell; Mr. G.V.M. Ryder; Sallie St. Clair; J. R. Scott; E. J. Shaw; Rosina Shaw; Anna Sinclair; Mr. C. Smith; George Smith; *Mrs. William H. Smith* (1844– 46, 1848–50); *Edward N. Thayer* (1845–46, 1848–49); Fanny Wallack; Mr. and Mrs. James Wallack, Sr.; Mr. Walters; Mrs. Harry Watkins; George Weston; Mrs. Wilkerson; Miss Wilson; Mrs. Winstanley; Mrs. Wood; Miss E. Wood; Thomas J. Worrell; Mr. Wright.

REPERTORY

The Arch Street Theatre Company's repertory is calendared in Arthur H. Wilson, *A History of the Philadelphia Theatre, 1835 to 1855* (Philadelphia: University of Pennsylvania Press, 1935), and Rue C. Johnson, "The Theatrical Career of William E. Burton" (Ph.D. diss., Indiana University, 1967). Typical Burton repertories are appended to the entries [Burton's New] National Theatre Company* and Burton's Stock Company*.

BIBLIOGRAPHY

Johnson, Rue C. "The Theatrical Career of William E. Burton." Ph.D. diss., Indiana University, 1967.
Wilson, Arthur H. *A History of Philadelphia Theatre, 1835 to 1855*. Philadelphia: University of Pennsylvania Press, 1935.

Weldon B. Durham

ARCH STREET THEATRE COMPANY. (1861–76) Louisa Lane Drew (1820–97) assumed the management of the Arch Street Theatre in Philadelphia in June 1861 at the request of its stockholders. Designed by William Strickland and built in 1828, the Arch Street Theatre had housed various companies, and its early managers included William B. Wood, W. E. Burton, William Forrest, Francis Wemyss, William Wheatley, J. S. Clarke, and John Drew. Following a summer of renovations to the building, Mrs. Drew's company began its premiere season on August 31, 1861, with a gala production of *The School for Scandal*, the type of play with which the Arch Street Theatre Company thereafter usually began its season and to which it turned when stars were delayed.

Louisa Lane Drew was a widely known and respected actress who had both starred and served as a leading stock player for most of the major theatre managers in the East, performing with the distinguished actors of the day. To these obvious advantages to a novice manager she could add a long and favorable reputation in Philadelphia and a lifetime of experience with management, from her step-father's, when she was a child star, to her husband's successful management of the Arch Street (with William Wheatley, 1853–55) and his disastrous experience with Philadelphia's National Theatre (from May to August 1857). Managing, like acting, was a family business then and Mrs. Drew's company from time to time involved her husband, John Drew, her brother-in-law Frank Drew and his wife, her half-sister Georgina Kinlock Stephens, her niece Adine Stephens, and her children Georgiana Drew (Barrymore) and John Drew, Jr.

Louisa Lane Drew maintained a resident stock company at the Arch Street from the fall of 1861 through the spring of 1876, although from the 1872–73 season the company served mainly as support for touring combinations or played afterpieces. For these fifteen seasons, acting by the resident company was augmented with stars, as few as possible so as to enlarge house profits, yet steadily increasing over time. Stars included F. S. Chanfrau, Lester Wallack, E. L. Davenport, Lotta Crabtree, Lawrence Barrett, James E. Murdoch, Julia Dean, Edwin Adams, Charles Fox, Lydia Thompson, Charles Mathews, Charles Fechter, Frank Mayo, Oliver Doud Byron, and Buffalo Bill.

While typical in many respects, the Arch Street Theatre Company under Louisa Lane Drew is notable because she taught acting. Mrs. Drew had a good eye for and was regularly robbed of promising novices—Ada Rehan, Fanny Davenport, Clara Fisher Maeder, John Drew, Jr., and Clara Morris became the stars of the next generation—but all members of her company were subject to the same discipline. Regular rehearsals were held at 10 A.M., including Sundays. Afternoons were to be given over to study, with performances at 8 P.M.; hence there were no matinees at the Arch Street until competition forced them in 1874–75, and then they were added only on Saturdays. All who recalled her teaching during this period and after considered it unique in its thoroughness and rigor. Although training no doubt centered upon performing as well as possible a large and scenically complex repertory, Mrs. Drew's view of acting was sophisticated and strikingly modern: "Acting is a matter of feeling and experience. One must be in reality the character personated; self-consciousness must not appear; one's identity must be lost in that of the part assumed" (New Orleans *Daily Picayune*, March 27, 1894).

The common conception—even John Drew, Jr., repeated it in his autobiography—is that the Arch Street Company specialized in comic classics (Oliver Goldsmith, Richard Sheridan, George Colman, the younger, and David Garrick, William Shakespeare). In fact, the repertory consisted primarily of recent and new melodramas, comedies, and novelties. Following a trend in her own career away from tragedy, Mrs. Drew gradually culled as much of it out of the Arch Street repertory as she could. By providing mixed fare, the Arch Street sought to serve both a popular and a fashionable audience, a combination rare in New York at the time. The critical response to this policy was primarily favorable until 1872, when a number of stock regulars left, and the company's well-remembered although few performances of comic classics were no longer praised.

The mixed repertory also reflected the Arch Street's competition in Philadelphia, beginning with the fall of 1863 when Edwin Booth and J. S. Clarke took over the Walnut Street Theatre and began to feature stars like Forrest, John Brougham, and Joseph Jefferson. New plays provided a way successfully to stand off the Walnut's name stars in the classics. When E. L. Davenport took over the Chestnut Street Theatre Company*, however, he altered its policy from long-running sensational melodrama to more varied stock fare. By 1871 this company and local variety houses were having an impact upon the Arch's receipts. Davenport gave up the Chestnut about 1873, and stock gradually disappeared there and at the Walnut after 1876. The Arch's company succumbed with them in this decade to the pressures of the touring combination. (Mrs. Drew apparently hung on to a stock company past 1872 in order to launch her children's careers in the theatre. When John went to work for Augustin Daly in New York in 1875— Daly had managed Davenport's Chestnut Street Theatre, 1872–73—and Georgie in April of 1876, a resident stock company at the Arch was abandoned.)

What Louisa Lane Drew did that her contemporaries like Wallack in New York, with whose company hers favorably compared, did not do was encourage native plays, plays untried in Philadelphia and sometimes U.S. or world premieres. She had a knack for picking plays that went over well and for giving them good technical presentation in terms of spectacle, scenery, and rehearsal. Unafraid of the untried (in plays or actors), Mrs. Drew did not depend solely upon it. She had an arrangement with Lester Wallack to option the plays he did in New York that she considered suitable for the Arch Street Company and Philadelphia; thus she acquired *Ours, Rosedale, The Veteran*, and many others. Neither the tried nor the new parts of her repertory are still performed, but Mrs. Drew's support of the native product deserves to be noted.

A season at the Arch began approximately the first Saturday in September and initially extended to the fourth of July. During the summer months bell ringers, minstrels, protean actors, and the like would perform at the Arch, and Mrs. Drew would make up a company and tour, a practice that began, in 1875, to extend into the regular year because of combinations. Indeed, from 1876 to 1879 Mrs. Drew assembled nonresident companies during the regular season to support herself at the Arch or on tour or to support the few visiting stars at the Arch who still toured without support.

The lease to the Arch Street Theatre was managed by the Board of Agents for the stockholders. It was never even advertised as available after it was given to Mrs. Drew in 1861, despite the fact that her first season was a financial failure and she had to borrow money for salaries. Her rent is not known, but several times she asked to have it reduced. In the best years of her resident stock company, a lead was paid $50 a week, a utility player $12, and a star reputedly between $300 and $500. With house prices in the 1860s at fifty cents for the dress circle and parquet, $1 for the orchestra, seventy-five cents for single box seats (boxes $6 to $8), twenty-five cents for the family circle, and fifteen cents for the amphitheatre, salary expenses alone were considerable. Wartime inflation and postwar depression exerted their own pressures upon repertory companies. Mrs. Drew, a widow since 1862 with six dependants, survived by augmenting her income from management with an income from acting, the attraction to management for many during the period.

What makes Louisa Lane Drew's management of the Arch Street Theatre notable is the evidence it provides of what we now call directing. Accounts indicate that Mrs. Drew was skilled at picturization and movement. She supervised three alterations of the theatre—renovations of the auditorium in 1861, of the rear of the house and the facade in 1863, and of the auditorium and the stage (during which a shutter system was apparently removed) in 1871. Mrs. Drew attended to all aspects of production from cleanliness backstage to play selection and interpretation. Frank Stull, once a member of her company, said of her management, "She [did] it better than any man in the country" (*Lippincott's Monthly*, March 1905, p. 377), but the most telling evaluation was recorded by T. Allston Brown, when he said, "She produced a reform in the manner of placing pieces on the stage. A great many old actors have told me that she is the best stage director ever seen" (Brown, 133).

In 1879 Louisa Lane Drew succumbed to booking only combinations. She kept the Arch Street lease until her retirement from management in 1892. To augment her income, she undertook a series of tours, including her celebrated engagements with Joseph Jefferson in *The Rivals* beginning in 1880. By that time, the stock theatre in which an eight-week starring engagement was a long run, making John Drew's never equaled Arch Street record of 101 nights (1861–62) seem miraculous, had essentially disappeared. To the stock company tradition she knew and valued, Louisa Lane Drew contributed her art as an actress, her experience to other actors, her encouragement to unknown native playwrights, and her skill at the artistic management of the stage.

PERSONNEL

Management: Louisa Lane Drew (Mrs. John Drew), lessee and manager (1861–92); Joseph D. Murphy, treasurer (1861– ?).

Scenery and Costumes: S. E. Hayes, C. Hawthorne, C. Long, George Harris, Frank S. Johnson, Mrs. Griffiths.

Musical Director: C. R. Dodsworth (1861– ?).

Stage Managers: William S. Frederick (1861–65); W. A. Moore (1865–67), E. F. Taylor (1867–68), Barton Hill (1868–73), Charles H. Morton (1873–76).

Actors and Actresses: There were too many stock company members during the fifteen years to list all. Here are listings for the Arch Company at intervals.

1861–62: Alexina Fisher Baker, Frank Drew, Mrs. John Drew, John Gilbert, Charles Henri, Mrs. Charles Henri, S. D. Johnson, Frank Lawler, W. H. Leak, J. K. Mortimer, Eliza Price, B. T. and/or F. R. Ringold, William Scallan, L. R. Shewell, Clara Stoneall, Emma Taylor, Charlotte Thompson, William Wallis, and Mary Wells.

1865–66: Lizzie Creese, T. A. Creese, Mr. Everham, P. Fitzgerald, Mr. Gale, Mr. Goldson, Ms. Griffiths, Ms. Harris, Mr. S. Hemple, Charles Henri, Mrs. Charles Henri, Mr. Holt, Ms. Howard, Lewis L. James, Ms. Jones, Ms. Levi, F. F. Mackay, Owen Marlowe, Mr. Nagle, Ms. C. Price, McKee Rankin, Clara Reed, Fanny Reeves, Mrs. W. H. Reeves, Stuart Robson, Charles Rogers, Ms. Styles, Ms. Summerfield, Mrs. Thayer, E. L. Tilton, William Wallis, Rosa Wood, and Mrs. Worrell.

1870–71: Jennie Arnot, Louise Arnott, Harry Beckett, W. B. Cahill, Mary Claire, R. Craig, Willie Edwards, Mr. Fetters, C. Hawthorne, Samuel Hemple, Nellie Henderson, Barton Hill, Lewis L. James, Alfred Kelleher, Emily Kiehl, F. F. Mackay, Clara Fisher Maeder, Mrs. E. W. Maeder, Mr. McManus, Alice Placide, Lizzie Price, D. Ralton, Mrs. Thayer, William Wallis, Jennie Wheatleigh, and Eliza Wethersby.

1875–76: (the "Star Dramatic Company"): Alexina Fisher Baker, Josephine Baker, Georgie Drew, Gertie Granville, Samuel Hemple, George Howard, Alfred Hudson, Milnes Levick, Frank Lord, Fred Maeder, Florence Noble, Edwin Price, and Madrigal Royce.

REPERTORY

There were too many plays presented during the fifteen years to list all here; thus samples of that repertory at intervals are provided. The first season is omitted owing to John Drew's untypically long star engagement in Irish roles. Note throughout the list the preponderance of popular fare and comic classics.

1862–63: *Money; Fanchon, the Cricket; Margot: The Poultry Dealer; The Wife's Secret; Fazio; or, The Italian Wife; Love's Sacrifice; The World of Fashion; The Lady of Lyons; Ada: Princess of Lombardy; The Hunchback; Romeo and Juliet; London Assurance; Honey Moon; Geraldine; or, Love's Victory; Macbeth; The School for Scandal; Rosa Gregorio; The Madonna of Art; The Rivals; She Stoops to Conquer; Speed the Plough; The Poor Gentleman; The School of Reform; Babes in the Wood; Leap Year; or, The Ladies Privilege; Paul Pry; Giralda; or, The Invisible Husband; Peter Waxem; The Eton Boy; Turning the Tables; Everybody's Friend; All That Glitters Is Not Gold; Sweethearts and Wives; Our American Cousin;*

The Octoroon; Sudden Thoughts; The Naiad Queen; The Daughter of the Regiment; Fashion; Extremes; Court Cards; The Enchantress; Satanella; or, The Power of Love; Love's Sacrifice; The Wife; or, A Tale of Mantua; The Stranger; Love; or, The Countess and the Serf; Evadne; Ingomar, the Barbarian; The Marble Heart; Wild Oats; Dreams of Delusion; Richard III; The Apostate; The Merchant of Venice; The Robbers; Hamlet; Money; Macbeth; Aurora Floyd; The Cricket on the Hearth; Nell Gwynne; The Countess and the Grisette; Lucie D'Arville; Rip Van Winkle; Camille; The Female Gambler; Masks and Faces; Lucrezia Borgia; The Duelist; The Heretic; The Dead Heart; Women; or, Love Against the World; Up at the Hills; George Barnwell; Grist to the Mill.

1865–66: *The School for Scandal; Old Heads and Young Hearts; The Rivals; Wives as They Were and Maids as They Are; The Jealous Wife; Know Your Own Mind; How She Loves Him; Rosedale; The Serf; or, Love Levels All; The Dead Heart; Adrienne Lecouvreur; Charlotte Corday; Masks and Faces; Joan of Arc; The Stranger; The Fairy Circle; Ireland as It Was; Born to Good Luck; Rory O'More; Shandy Maguire; The Irish Post; All Hallow's Eve; or, Snap-Apple Night; Yankee Courtship; Willie O'Reilly; Connie Soogah; Green Bushes; St. Mary's Eve; Robert Emmet; The Fenian of '98; The Woman in Red; The House on the Bridge of Notre Dame; Honey Moon; The Lady of Lyons; Macbeth; Lost in London; The Needful; Fortunio; Follies of a Night; Camille, Fazio; Lucrezia Borgia; Evadne; Love; or, The Countess and the Serf; Ingomar, the Barbarian; Ion; Duchess of Malfi; Guy Mannering; Othello; Naomi, the Deserted; Hamlet; Sam; Streets of New York; Belphegor, the Montebank; Virginius; A New Way to Pay Old Debts; King Lear; Waiting for the Verdict; Wild Oats; Wine Works Wonders; Money; The Dramatist; The Duke's Motto; The Robbers; The Marble Heart; Richard III; The Flying Dutchman; Fanchon; Who Killed Cock Robin?; The Gunmaker of Moscow; Silver Lining; Waiting for the Verdict; A Sheep in Wolf's Clothing; Old Phil's Birthday; The Mischievous Boy; Nick of the Woods; The Irish Immigrant; As You Like It; Pauline; The Black Domino; London Assurance; Nine Points of the Law; Agnes de Vere; The Dead Shot; Victorine; The Sea Flower; Giralda; Youthful Days of Richelieu; Satan in Paris; Kathleen Mavourneen; The Hidden Hand; Child of the Regiment; Ticket-of-Leave Man's Wife; Arrah-na-Pogue.*

1870–71: *She Stoops to Conquer; Swiss Swains; Fernande; Camille; Central Park; The House with Two Doors; A Victim of Circumstances; Sixteen String Jack; Rann the Reiver; Man and Wife; London Assurance; The Man and the Tiger; The School for Scandal; A Thumping Legacy; The Love Chase; The Toodles; The Floating Beacon; The Norwegian Wreckers; Down by the Gate; The Two Roses; The Marble Heart; The Swiss Cottage; A Morning Call; The Pilot; Leap Year; Rosedale; As You Like It; Faint Heart ne'er Won Fair Lady; Honey Moon; How to Rule a Wife; Edwin Drood; The Good-for-Nothing; The Widow's Victim; The Jealous Wife; Love's Sacrifice; The Rival Merchants; The Miller and His Men; The Lady of Lyons; The Victim of Circumstances; The Merchant of Venice; Faust and Marguerite; Across the Continent; Ours; Secret Love; Coquettes; or, The Two Joneses; Lost at Sea; Much Ado about Nothing; The Wonder; The Willow Copse; Paris; or, The Apple of Discord; The Brigands; Lurline; Sinbad; The Stump Speech; The Idiot Witness; A Talk of Blood; Black Eyed Susan; Captain Coriolanus Crabtree; Hamlet; The Hypocrite; The Cracked Heart; John Wopps; The Wandering Minstrel; The Spitfire; The Drunkard; Henry IV; The Irish Lion; East Lynne; Mag's Diversion; Satan in*

*Paris; A Kiss in the Dark; Much Ado about a Merchant of Venice; The Happiest
Day of My Life; Playing with Fire; The Golden Farmer; Red Light; Nobody's
Daughter; The Serpent on the Hearth; The Comedy of Errors; The Serious Family;
Dick Turpin; Borrowing a Husband; The Bonnie Fish Wife; Our American Cousin.*

1875–76: *A New Way to Pay Old Debts; Hamlet; Othello; Richelieu; Macbeth;
The Stranger; Queen Mary; Girofle-Girofla; Divorce; Oliver Twist; Frou-Frou;
Across the Continent; The Spy of the Neutral Ground; Little Emily; The Good for
Nothing; The Two Orphans; Wild Oats; The Dead Heart; The Marble Heart; The
School for Scandal; Madame Angot's Child; The Princess of Trebizonde; La Jolie
Parfumuese; Trial by Jury; The Belles of the Kitchen; Fun in a Fog; The Wrong
Man in the Right Place; Nan; Armed; The Captive Prince; The Deadly Challenge;
East Lynne; Romeo and Juliet; The Family Circle; Customs of the Country; Ireland
as It Was; The Latest from New York; All Hallow's Eve; The Connecticut Court;
Running a Corner; The Spitfire; The Golden Farmer; Love in '76; Law in New
York; Richelieu; Othello; King Lear; Virginius; Harvey Birch; The Centennial; The
Rose of Tyrol; The Gladiator; Richard III; The Lady of Lyons; Metamora; Uncle
Tom's Cabin; The Idiot Witness; Rip Van Winkle; Nick; Sentenced to Death; She
Stoops to Conquer; Pygmalion and Galatea; Grist to the Mill; Rose Michel; Ferreol;
Little Nell and the Marchioness; Little Barefoot; Fanchon; A Bunch of Blueberries.*

BIBLIOGRAPHY

    The Arch Street Theatre under Mrs. Drew advertised regularly in the Philadel-
phia *Public Ledger* and the *Philadelphia Inquirer*. Extensive collections of playbills
and like materials may be found in the Furness Collection of the University of
Pennsylvania Library and the theatre collection of the Free Library of Philadelphia.
The most complete history is Dorothy E. Stolp, "Mrs. John Drew, American
Actress-Manager, 1820–1897" (Ph.D. diss., Louisiana State University, 1953). Particularly germane published sources include: Louisa Lane Drew, *Autobiographical
Sketch of Mrs. John Drew* (New York: Scribner's Sons, 1899); Lionel Barrymore,
as told to Cameron Shipps, *We Barrymores* (New York: Appleton-Century-Crofts,
1951); Ethel Barrymore, *Memories, An Autobiography* (New York: Harper and
Brothers, 1955); Otis Skinner, *Footlights and Spotlights* (Indianapolis: Bobbs-Mer-
rill Co., 1924); John Drew, *My Years on the Stage* (New York: Dutton, 1922). T.
Allston Brown's study of Mrs. Drew in F. E. McKay and C.E.L. Wingate, eds.,
Famous American Actors of Today (New York: Crowell, 1896), pp. 127-34; Clara
Morris' "The Dressing Room Reception Where I First Met Ellen Terry and Mrs.
John Drew," *McClure's Magazine* (December, 1903); and Frank Stull's "Where
Famous Actors Learned Their Art," *Lippincott's Monthly* (March 1905).

Rosemarie K. Bank

B

BARNUM'S THEATRE COMPANY. See AMERICAN MUSEUM STOCK COMPANY.

BLANCHARD'S AMPHITHEATRE STOCK COMPANY. Extensive remodeling of the Chatham Garden Theatre (New York City) enabled equestrian G. Blanchard to venture into theatrical management on January 18, 1830. His performing horses and equestrian company held the stage and arena for nearly three weeks; then on February 5 his dramatic company under the direction of James Roberts presented *The Mine of Blood* with appropriate variety acts and an afterpiece.

In fairness to Blanchard it must be said that he rivaled the Park Theatre for a brief time, but his major accomplishment was his ability to remain in business during eight months of troublous theatrical times. His tenure at the old Chatham Garden Theatre marks the penultimate degradation of Barrière's achievement.

G. Blanchard and his family of horsemen provided the principal equestrian entertainment at the Amphitheatre during the winter months, and on Mondays, Wednesdays, and Fridays in the sweltering summer they performed in Vauxhall Gardens, leaving the actors to manage as well as they could in Chatham Street. Even in the Amphitheatre, though, drama capitulated to variety acts. By the middle of August, Blanchard and company had exhausted their resources and their energy, and the old theatre passed into other hands.

Blanchard's repertory was in no way remarkable except as it tended toward extravaganzas such as *The Forty Thieves, Bluebeard,* and *The Fairy of the North Star*. No equestrian theatre, moreover, could resist a production of *Mazeppa*, but Adah Isaacs Menken's celebrated performance of the title role lay a generation in the future. Only thirty-four dramas were presented, and the sole visiting stars of note were George Washington Dixon, Henry J. Finn, and Danforth Marble.

PERSONNEL

Management: G. Blanchard.

Stage Director: James Roberts.

Actors and Actresses: Mr. Archer, James Anderson, Mr. Bacon, Mr. Beckwell, William Rufus Blake, Cecilia Blanchard, Elizabeth Blanchard, George Blanchard, Master William Blanchard, Mrs. Frederick Brown, Thomas Burke, D. Callahan, Mr. Clarke, Mr. De Angelis, Mr. Downie, Mr. Eagleston, Mr. Eberle, Calvin Edson, Mr. Farren, Alexina Fisher, Thomas Flynn, Mrs. French, Mr. Gallott, Mrs. Charles Gilfert, Mrs. Golden, Mr. Grierson, Mr. Horton, Mrs. Hughes, George F. Hyatt, Mr. Jervis, Emanuel Judah, G. Keane, D. D. McKinney, Mrs. Nelson, William Pelby, Moses S. Phillips, Edward Raymond, Mrs. Richer, James Roberts, Mrs. James Roberts, Mr. Rockwell, Mr. Rose, Master Spencer, Mrs. G. G. Stevenson, George G. Stevenson, Mr. Stickney, Mrs. Stickney, Mrs. E. N. Thayer, Edward N. Thayer, Mrs. Walstein, Ann Duff Waring, Mr. Weir, A. W. Wright.

REPERTORY

1830: *The Mine of Blood; The Forty Thieves; False and True; Timour, the Tartar; The Tiger Horde; Bluebeard; The Independents of Bohemia; The Death of Captain Cook; Manfredi; The Chieftains of Ireland; Rob Roy; The Battle of Bothwell Brig; X.Y.Z.; The Hundred-Pound Note; The Falls of Clyde; The Mountaineers; Tekeli; Black Eyed Susan; My Master's Rival; Metamora; The Sisters; The Happiest Day of My Life; The Irish Tutor; Animal Magnetism; Lovers' Quarrels; The Rendezvous; Cerenza; The Turnpike Gate; The Fairy of the North Star; Teddy, the Tiler; The Solitary of the Heath; Thérèse; The Wandering Boys.*

BIBLIOGRAPHY

Published Sources: Joseph N. Ireland, *Records of the New York Stage from 1750 to 1860*, 2 vols. (New York, 1866–67); George C. D. Odell, *Annals of the New York Stage*, vol. 3 (New York: Columbia University Press, 1928).

George B. Bryan

BOARD ALLEY THEATRE COMPANY. Boston's New Exhibition Room, popularly known as the Board Alley Theatre, and its company under the management of Joseph Harper, Jr. (1759-1811), and Alexander Placide (d. 1812) became a test of the laws prohibiting theatrical performances in Massachusetts. In the summer of 1792, the hope that the antitheatre law would be repealed, if the public could be aroused against it, led five of Boston's leading citizens to build a public theatre on what is now Devonshire Street. The group, which included John Russell, newspaper owner and Boston town treasurer, 1790-95, built a 500-seat facility on land owned by wealthy tradesman Joseph Barrell.

The manager of the new theatre was Joseph Harper, Jr., late of the

[Old] American Company* in New York City. Harper brought from New York Mr. and Mrs. Alexander Placide and Stephen Woolls, who, with the acrobat Martine, formed the nucleus of the Board Alley Theatre Company. The New Exhibition Room, as the theatre was advertised, opened August 16, 1792, to admissions of 6 shillings, 4 shillings, 6 pence, and 3 shillings. Performances were on Monday, Wednesday, and Friday, with curtain times varying from 6:00 to 7:30 P.M. The early bills were made up of recitations, pantomimic ballets by Mr. and Mrs. Placide, songs, and acrobatic feats. The company was enlarged on August 28, when sixteen new players joined. A repertory season began September 26, 1792, with a production of John Home's *Douglas*, followed by John O'Keeffe's farce *Poor Soldier*. The season ended abruptly on December 5, when a sheriff served Joseph Harper with a warrant for his arrest for violating laws against theatrical entertainments. The warrant was issued upon application by the attorney-general, under orders from Massachusetts Governor John Hancock. Harper was tried the next day and acquitted on a legal technicality. Friends urged Placide and Harper to leave Boston, which they did, Harper taking parts of the company to Providence, Placide leading another contingent to Salem. In January 1793 they returned to Boston and announced that they would open the Board Alley Theatre. A mob, which threatened to destroy the theatre, was stopped only by a justice of the peace.

Shortly after Harper's arrest, a citizen's committee, which included patriots John Q. Adams and Paul Revere, set to the task of gaining the repeal of the antitheatre law of 1750. A repeal bill was issued, although Governor Hancock refused to sign it. However, he vowed on March 28 to make no further efforts to impede theatrical performances in Massachusetts. The law was not formally repealed until 1806. Meanwhile, Harper and Placide produced plays occasionally at the Board Alley Theatre until its doors closed permanently on June 10, 1793.

During the repertory season, the Board Alley Theatre Company presented twenty-five tragedies and comedies, most by William Shakespeare, Richard Sheridan, George Lillo, and Thomas Otway. Thirty-five afterpieces, four full-length French operas, and a full-length comic opera were also seen. The repertory and the company were clearly English; only one American play—Royall Tyler's *Contrast* (a piece deeply indebted to Sheridan's *School for Scandal*)—was produced.

PERSONNEL

Mr. Adams, Miss Chapman, Mr. and Mrs. Joseph Harper, Jr., Mr. Kenna, Mr. Kenny, Martine, Mr. and Mrs. Morris, Mr. Murray, Mr. and Mrs. Alexander Placide, Charles Stuart Powell, Mr. Redfield, Mr. Robinson, Miss Smith, Mr. and Mrs. Solomon, Mr. Tucker, Mr. Watts, and Stephen Woolls.

REPERTORY

Numbers in parentheses indicate the number of times the play was performed this season, if more than once.

Placide's pantomimes commencing August 16: *The Bird Catcher; The Old Soldier; Harlequin Doctor* (2); *Harlequin Supposed Gentleman; Harlequin Skeleton; Two Philosophers; Grand Italian Shades; Two Woodcutters; Birth of Harlequin; Robinson Crusoe.*

The repertory plays: *Douglas* (2); *Poor Soldier* (2); *Beaux Stratagem; Miss in Her Teens* (2); *The London Merchant* (2); *Madcap; Poor Soldier* (concert); *Jane Shore* (2); *Thomas and Sally; Venice Preserved; The Duenna; She Stoops to Conquer* (2); *Rosina* (2); *The Mock Doctor; The Contrast* (2); *The Lying Valet* (2); *The Busybody; The Register Office; The Suspicious Husband* (2); *Polly Honeycomb; The True-born Irishman* (2); *The Gamester; The West Indian; The Bird Catcher; The Ghost; Katherine and Petruchio* (2); *The Miller of Mansfield; Harlequin Balloonist; The School for Scandal* (2); *The Padlock* (2); *The Rivals* (2); *Love à la Mode* (2); *Old Schoolmaster Grown Young; High Life below Stairs; Inkle and Yarico; Love in a Village; Two Woodcutters; The Citizen; The Bear Hunters; Clandestine Marriage; The Devil to Pay; Hamlet; Richard III; The Romp.*

BIBLIOGRAPHY

Ruff, Loren K. "Joseph Harper and Boston's Board Alley Theatre, 1792–1793."
     Educational Theatre Journal 26 (March 1974): 45–52.
Seilhamer, George O. *History of American Theatre*. Vol. 3. *New Foundations.
     1888–91*. Reprint. New York: B. Blom, 1968.

Weldon B. Durham

BOSTON MUSEUM COMPANY. Moses Kimball opened an exhibit of curiosities on Bromfield Street in Boston June 14, 1841. The admission price included a concert, recitation, panorama, or, beginning February 6, 1843, a dramatic presentation. Plays continued to be performed at this location until 1846, when the collection (eventually to include paintings, engravings, statuary, Chinese curios, stuffed birds and mammals, mechanical models and dioramas, live reptiles and animals, "freaks," and wax statuary) was moved to a new building erected for it, located on Tremont Street between Court and School streets and designed by H. and J. E. Billings. The auditorium seating capacity in this facility is given in the *Boston Transcript*, June 14, 1841, as 1,500, but recent estimates suggest 600 (Golden, 95), with a proscenium opening of thirty feet, gas lighting, and a stage fifty feet deep by ninety feet wide equipped with iron grooves and a windlass to shift scenery (the box set was introduced in 1862). At the time of the first performance there on November 2, 1846, the stage and auditorium were on the second story, while support spaces took a small part of the museum's grand gallery on the first floor and an exhibition hall occupied the third floor. The auditorium was renovated in 1868, 1872, and 1876, and in 1880 a new entrance was cut at the north side of the building, the stage and auditorium were lowered one story, and a second gallery was added to the house, raising its capacity to an estimated 900 seats (various museum collections were also removed at this time). The Museum actress Catherine Reignolds reported that before this renovation the backstage area had only a three-foot passageway between the grooves and the scenery stacked against the walls and that the green room and dressing rooms were similarly cramped. The Museum's scenery remained extensive, including by 1886 eighteen room sets with center doors and thirteen complete sets of furniture. The last performance in the Boston Museum was by a touring combination on June 1, 1903, after which the theatre was demolished.

A repertory company was part of the Boston Museum for fifty years, beginning September 4, 1843, at the Bromfield Street building and ending with the theatrical season in 1893 at the facility on Tremont Street. Its longevity is due primarily to the proprietorship of dry goods merchant, publisher, and entrepreneur Moses Kimball. When he began to withdraw from active managerial duties in the 1860s to concentrate upon politics, and when his overworked producer-actor-stage manager E. F. Keach died in harness, Kimball introduced the then-unprecedented position of managing producer, ably filled by Richard Montgomery Field from 1864 to 1893. Before his election to the legislature, however, Kimball had proved that he understood the theatrical preferences of Bostonians and the practical needs of the theatre. He managed to get the Boston Museum associated with morality by controlling the plays as to subject matter and swearing (*The Drunkard* premiered there February 25, 1844, and many abolition and Yankee plays were performed), by not playing on Sabbath eves until 1871 (Wednesday and Saturday matinees were offered as compensation), by preserving etiquette backstage, by acquiescing to Bostonian objections to visiting stars as steady Museum policy, and the like. Because of its museum character, some early patrons may actually have been unaware that they were attending a theatre, and the Museum remained the favorite of conservative Bostonians throughout its life. It was also cheap to patronize, the twenty-five-cent 1843 admission price having risen only a dime by 1883.

The quality of the company Kimball and Field assembled for fifty years is what gave the Boston Museum a national reputation for good repertory acting. Salaries were reliably paid but were less than those at theatres of equal rank, and even the six to eight stars who visited each season were paid a flat fee rather than the usual percentage of receipts. Records reveal that Museum leads made $30 to $50 and other players $2 to $20 a week in the 1850s, while Wallack's in New York paid $35 to $80 to leads and $6 to $30 for others. An 1863–64 salary list shows established players at $20 to $30, an amount equivalent to the weekly pay of the Museum's ballet master, conductor, and scenic artist. By the 1880s, beginners were paid $3 to $6, utility players $7 to $15, walking ladies and gentlemen $20 to $35, and leads $70 to $80 (Mammen, 51; Ryan, 245–47).

To compensate for lower salaries, contract performers and some house personnel could count upon benefits. William Warren recorded that his benefits were worth $1,000 at the Museum in 1864, when his weekly salary as a stock lead was $60 (Ball, 60). The number of benefits was stipulated in contracts and declined steadily over the years. Utility players had neither contracts nor benefits as a rule, only a verbal agreement cancelable at a week's notice. Catherine Reignolds recorded that solely on a salary of $4 a week, a utility player in the early 1860s kept herself and two children (Winslow, 158). There was a Museum fund for sick actors and destitute dependents and fines for infractions of a long list of rules. Actors could depend upon a full season, initially as long as eleven months—variety shows filled in the off-month—although the length of a season declined in later years.

Stability marked not only the management of the Boston Museum but also its players. Of nearly 600 stock actors from 1843 to 1893, 25 percent could be classified as permanent, some staying a decade, some a quarter-century (William Warren, Mrs. Vincent, James Nolan, and Annie Clarke, among others). These actors had loyal followers in Boston, particularly the Museum's most famous actor (1847 to 1883), comedian William Warren. Of the remaining 75 percent, 57 percent were transient and left after a year or two, and the rest remained three to five years. Thus in an average season, the Museum Company would be about half new and half old, roughly the same ratio as at the better companies in other cities (Mammen, 16; McConnell, 68).

The Boston Museum Repertory Company averaged eighteen men and about twelve women members in the traditional lines of acting, plus extras and dancers as needed. The number of parts each actor performed in a season varied considerably. For example, in the 1850–51 season when 126 plays were done, one actor had 103 roles, while 11 members played more than 70 roles, 8 played 50 to 70 parts, 5 had 25 to 40 roles, and 5 had fewer than 20 parts. In the 1843–60 period, male utility players performed every night and averaged 100 roles for the season. By 1875 they were down to 30 to 40 roles, with women utilities about equal to them, and by 1890 all utility players were down to 5 to 10 roles a season, augmented with public "rehearsals" of the lead parts they understudied (Mammen, 102–7).

To handle the volume of roles, actors rehearsed from 10 A.M. until 1 or 2 P.M., with the rest of the afternoon and after-performance hours given over to studying lines and to costume preparation (even lower-rank actors supplied their own costumes, although the theatre had a stock of special garments). From 1848 to 1875 the Museum allowed one to three rehearsals for a revival, a week for a new play (lines were to be perfect by the third rehearsal), and three to five sessions for an afterpiece. An actor might see a new script a week before rehearsals or be told on Friday what the next week's bill would be, but usually the actual rehearsal period was all the time an actor had for study. Beginning in the late 1870s, rehearsals lengthened to as much as two weeks for a new play, but even then, as Museum actress Kate Ryan reported, some actors still found repertory work onerous.

Although essentially a school of experience, the Boston Museum and other companies offered classes until the 1870s in fencing, dancing, walking, and grace, to which some actors added private lessons in elocution and singing. No acting was taught at the Museum except, during rehearsal, for a specific role. As in other fields in the nineteenth century, theatre provided an apprenticeship whereby in four years one moved from super or utility to responsible utility, to walking lady or gentleman, to juveniles or seconds in the various lines. This was followed by a journeyman period of two years to achieve roles of any size in the line chosen. Kate Ryan reported that she got her first Museum contract after a six-year trial period of this sort (Ryan, 247). Actors learned from masters such as William Warren, said to have played 577 parts in his career, and by observing the stars who visited the Museum. They included E. L. Davenport; Junius Brutus, John Wilkes, and Edwin Booth; George Vandenhoff; Charlotte Cushman; James W. Wallack; C. Dibdin Pitt; Matilda Heron; Kate Bateman; E. A. Sothern; Blanche Ring; Dion Boucicault; Mrs. John Drew; Richard Mansfield; Fanny Janauschek; Helena Modjeska; Lester Wallack; Clara Morris; Tommaso Salvini; Sol Smith Russell; Edward Harrigan; James A. Herne; and Lawrence Barrett. Museum actors were also kept occupied and were trained by spring tours of New England and Canada, beginning in 1877, which were scheduled whenever combinations played the home theatre or long runs released enough members for touring.

If Kimball and Field succeeded because they provided Boston with good acting companies for fifty years, one must also credit their choice of plays. In addition to a well-publicized high moral tone, the Boston Museum offered $100 prizes for moral dramas adapted to the needs of the Museum Company. Plays by local writers Joseph Stevens Jones, S. S. Steele, and Charles H. Saunders were presented along with Oliver Goldsmith, Richard Sheridan, William Shakespeare, and a plethora of English and American comedies and melodramas. In its first year (1843–44), two or three short plays separated by interludes made up the Museum's bill, lasting as long as five hours, but they quickly gave way to longer plays, an afterpiece, and a shorter program, usually changed daily, a Museum policy into the 1870s. Farce, pantomime, extravaganza, and burlesque augmented the regular fare; the Museum was still presenting five farces in one night, a house specialty, as late as 1880. In short, Museum patrons were offered large, varied, and frequently changing selections of plays throughout most of the Museum stock company's history.

Because of its longevity and the continuity and preservation of its records, the Boston Museum provides a nearly perfect example of the policies that led to the dissolution of even the most successful repertory companies in the late nineteenth century. From 1843 to 1863 the Museum presented an average of 130 pieces each season, half new and the remainder revivals of seventeenth-, eighteenth-, and earlier nineteenth-century plays. By comparison, theatres in New York with a larger population from which to draw presented fewer pieces; for example, Wallack's did about 60 in the 1855–56 season. During its first two decades, successful new plays would run seven to twenty consecutive performances at the Museum and then be revived for, say, fourteen scattered performances, although *Uncle Tom's Cabin* lasted eighty-six in the 1852–53 season. From 1863 to 1883 the Museum averaged only 40 to 70 pieces each season, divided between repertory blocks of the old comedies (Shakespeare, Goldsmith, and Sheridan) and blocks of performances of new plays and recent successes. The number of farces was much reduced. A successful play would now run twice as long as in the earlier period, 14 to 40 consecutive performances, compared with a New York company's repertory of only 15 to 30 plays a season, the most successful of which would run even longer. From 1883 to the dissolution of the company in 1893, the average number of plays dropped from 40 to 15, almost all of them new or recent successes. In the 1887–88 season, the Museum offered only three plays from August to March (Mammen, 9–12). As was the case throughout its history, during this decade the Museum offered much the same sort of fare—preponderantly comedy and melodrama—that was popular throughout the United States.

The Boston Museum preserved a repertory company by limiting stars and combinations and by holding its actors with regular playing and tours. The company's zenith is said to have occurred between 1873 and 1883 when companies of similar quality in other cities were collapsing. With the retirement of Warren and other longtime company members came a decrease in performances of old comedies and standard pieces and the presentation of ever fewer plays for ever longer runs. Whether it was Kimball's age— he died at eighty-six in 1895, although he appears to have owned the Museum to the end of its stock company's existence in 1893—the passing of the older actors and the conditions that trained them, a change in public taste away from the old plays and the same old players, or some combination of these or other factors that caused the demise of this company has not been precisely determined. What is certain is that the Boston Museum Company was the premier repertory company of Boston, equal for most of its history to the best groups of other cities, such as Wallack's in New York and the Arch Street in Philadelphia, and perhaps the longest-lived professional repertory company in the nation's history.

PERSONNEL

Management: Moses Kimball, manager (1841–64) and owner (1841–93) of the Boston Museum; Richard Montgomery Field, managing producer (1864–93).
Scenery and Costumes: Mr. Glessing, G. Heister, T. Joyce, Susan Mason.

Musical Directors: Tom Comer (1843–54), J. Eichberg, George Purdy.

Ballet Mistress or Master: L. Szollosy, Ann Jeanette Kerr.

Stage Managers: William Sedley-Smith (1843–60), E. F. Keach (1860–64), James R. Pitman, Fred Williams, Theodore Grahame, H. F. Daly, William Seymour, A. Robertson, H. M. Pitt, and E. E. Rose.

Prompters: J. W. Thoman, J. P. Price, J. H. Ring (1843–59), J. Crouta, R. M. Eberle, Fred Williams (1860–69), James R. Pitman (1869–93).

Actors and Actresses: There were too many stock-company members during the fifty years to list all. Here is a partial listing of the Boston Museum Company as provided in various histories.

1843–63: Elizabeth Anderson, Jane Anderson, Tom Comer, George H. Finn, Caroline Fox, Greenbury C. Germon, George C. Howard, C. W. Hunt, W. F. Johnson, Mrs. Emanuel Judah, Ann Jeanette Kerr, Louis Mestayer, Adelaide Phillips, Kate Reignolds, Charles H. Saunders, J. A. Smith, William Sedley-Smith, Jacob W. Thoman, Mrs. J. R. Vincent, William Warren, Frank Whitman.

1873–83: Amy Ames, Charles Barron, Ms. Bowne, James Burrows, E. N. Catlin, Annie Clarke, May Davenport, Nellie Downing, Frank Carlos Griffiths, Frank Hardenberg, Joseph Haworth, R. H. Lucas, Ms. Marden, Fanny Marsh, Sadie Martinot, W. S. Mason, R. F. McClannin, James Nolan, Margaret Parker, Laura Phillips, J. R. Pitman, J. H. Ring, Kate Ryan, Nate Salsbury, Fanny Skerritt, J. A. Smith, Georgia Tyler, Mrs. J. R. Vincent, William Warren, Ms. Watkins, Fred Williams, Mrs. Fred Williams, George W. Wilson, H. N. Wilson, Josie Wright.

1883–93: Fanny Addison, Viola Allen, Charles Barron, Marie Burress, Evelyn Campbell, Annie Clarke, E. L. Davenport, May Davenport, Erroll Dunbar, Robert Edeson, Isabel Eveson, Arthur Falkland, Mary Hampton, Joseph Haworth, Sadie Martinot, John Mason, Barney Nolan, H. M. Pitt, Eben Plympton, Kate Ryan, William Seymour, Emma Sheridan, Helen Standish, Mrs. J. R. Vincent, George W. Wilson.

REPERTORY

There were too many plays presented during the fifty years to list all here; thus samples of the repertory as provided in various histories are given. Note the predominance of melodramas, "Warren comedies," regional subjects, and a sizeable although decreasing number of extravaganzas and short farces.

1843–53: *As You Like It; Romeo and Juliet; Richard III; Hamlet; The Merchant of Venice; Othello; King Lear; Macbeth; Much Ado about Nothing; Katherine and Petruchio; The School for Scandal; The Rivals; She Stoops to Conquer; Lady of Lyons; Money; Richelieu; The Hunchback; The Love Chase; London Assurance; Love's Sacrifice; The Wife's Secret; The Apostate; Evadne; Wives as They Were and Maids as They Are; The Belle's Stratagem; The Jealous Wife; The Stranger; Wild Oats; The Rent Day; A New Way to Pay Old Debts; The King and the Commons; Guy Mannering; Rob Roy; Oliver Twist; Nicholas Nickleby; One Hour; Moll Pitcher; The Gambler; The Drunkard; The Dream; The Carpenter of Rouen; Old Job and Jacob Gray; The Last of the Kings; A Tale of Boston; The Last Dollar; Luke, the Labourer; The Christmas Gift; or, The Golden Axe; The Busy Bee; Bluebeard; Forty Thieves; The Enchanted Horse; The Enchanted Beauty; Riquet with the Tuft; Fortunio; Cinderella; The Children of Cyprus; The Paint King; The Review; Grist to the Mill; Loan of a Lover; Paul Pry; A Roland for an Oliver; Black Eyed Susan; Perfection; Naval Engagements; Poor Pillicoddy; Box and Cox; Friend Waggles;*

Slasher and Crasher; Lend Me Five Shillings; Pet of the Petticoats; Speed the Plough;
musical versions of works by Dickens and Scott.

1853–63: *The Ladies' Battle; Number One 'Round the Corner; Family Jars; Hot
Corn; Andy Blake; The Maid with the Milking Pail; To Parents and Guardians; A
Pretty Piece of Business; The Bottle Imp; Two Buzzards; The Talisman; The Road
to Ruin; Extremes; The Willow Copse; Hard Times; Peter Wilkins; The Stranger;
Swiss Swains; Black Eyed Susan; The Magic Mirror; Tit for Tat; A Dead Shot;
Breach of Promise; First Night; Peg Woffington; Aladdin; Our Wife; St. Mary's
Eve; Neighbor Jackwood; Dred; The Sea of Ice; The Liberty Tree; The Naiad Queen;
The Flying Dutchman; The Rich and Poor of Boston; A Quiet Family; Gold; The
Winter's Tale; Sinbad the Sailor; Our American Cousin; Retained for the Defense;
Nine Points of the Law; A Husband to Order; Bluebeard; The Hidden Hand; The
Serious Family; Babes in the Wood; The Colleen Bawn; Jeanie Deans; Belphegor,
the Mountebank; Fashion; Uncle Robert; Fanchon; Angel of Midnight; Pauvrette;
The Octoroon; The Home Guard; Great Expectations; The Rivals; She Stoops to
Conquer; Union Boys of '62; A Conjugal Lesson; Jeannette; Doing for the Best;
Magnolia; Crossing the Quicksands; Nell Gwynne; Aurora Floyd; Port Royal; Mrs.
Winthrop's Boarders; The Spectre Bridegroom; The School for Scandal*; plays by
Shakespeare.

1863–73: *Turn Him Out; Camilla's Husband; Leap Year; Rosedale; The Merry
Widow; Town and Country; The Steeple Chase; On the Sly; Sons of the Cape; The
Outcast; Lost in London; The Frozen Deep; My Turn Next; Rochambole; Hilda;
Caste; A Dangerous Game; Nobody's Daughter; The Long Strike; Foul Play; Surf;
Blow for Blow; Cyril's Success; A Victim of Circumstances; A Cup of Tea; Arrah-
na-Pogue; Uncle Dick's Darling; Frou-Frou; Fernande; Central Park; The Two
Roses; Man and Wife; Elfie; The Streets of New York; The Veteran; Divorce; Rachel
the Reaper; The Overland Route; The Christmas Supper; The Rivals; The School
for Scandal; She Stoops to Conquer*; plays by Shakespeare.

1873–83: *The Geneva Cross; Little Emily; Led Astray; Heart's Delight; Mimi;
Daddy O'Dowd; The Lancashire Lass; The Big Bonanza; Rose Michael; Our Friends;
Paul Revere and the Sons of Liberty; The Minute Man; Ferreol; Vendôme; Poor
Jo; Our Boarding House; Cricket on the Hearth; A Celebrated Case; Olivia; My
Son; A Fool and His Money; Dr. Clyde; The Shaugraun; Our Girls; The Guv'nor;
Jeannie Deans; The Colonel; The False Friend; The Parvenue; The Romany Rye;
The Banker's Daughter; A Quiet Family; East Lynne; Macbeth; King Lear; She
Stoops to Conquer; Heir-at-Law; The School for Scandal; Pinafore; Patience; Ruy
Blas; The Iron Chest; Midsummer Madness.*

1883–93: *The Marble Heart; Macbeth; Katherine and Petruchio; Shore Acres;
Harbor Lights; Hands across the Sea; Held by the Enemy; Dr. Jekyll and Mr. Hyde;
Little Lord Fauntleroy; Shenandoah; Sweet Lavender; All the Comforts of Home;
Prince Pro Tem; A Parisian Romance; The Belles of Haslemere; The English Rose;
Ye Airlie Trouble; The Jilt.*

BIBLIOGRAPHY

The Boston Museum advertised and/or was reviewed in the Boston *Transcript,
Herald, Commercial Bulletin, Gazette, Advertiser,* and *Courier.* Extensive collections of playbills and like materials can be found in the Channing Pollock Theatre

Collection of Howard University, Washington, D.C.; the Harvard Theatre Collection, Cambridge, Massachussetts; and the Princeton Library, Princeton, New Jersey. The most complete histories of the Boston Museum are Edward Mammen's "The Old Stock Company: The Boston Museum and Other 19th Century Theatres," *More Books*, 19 (January 1944): 3–18; (February 1944): 49–63; (March 1944): 100–107; Kate Ryan's *Old Boston Museum Days* (Boston: Little, 1915); and Claire McGlinchee's *First Decade of the Boston Museum* (Boston: B. Humphries, 1940). Other germane sources include Margaret E. McConnell's "William Warren II: The Boston Comedian" (Ph.D. diss., Indiana University, 1963); Edwin J. Golden's "Funny Man in the Snake Shop: The Art of William Warren, Jr." (Ph.D. diss., Tufts University, 1973); Frederic E. McKay's and C.E.L. Wingate's *Famous Actors of Today*, Vol. 1 (New York: Crowell, 1896); and Henry Austin Clapp's *Reminiscences of a Dramatic Critic* (Boston: Houghton Mifflin Co., 1902); Catherine Reignolds-Winslow's *Yesterdays with Actors* (Boston: Cupples and Hurd, 1887, reprint, 1972); William W. Clapp, Jr., *A Record of the Boston Stage* (Boston: James Munroe and Company, 1853); idem, "The Drama in Boston," in *The Memorial History of Boston, Including Suffolk County, Mass., 1630–1880*, vol. 4, edited by Justin Winsor (Boston: James R. Osgood and Company, 1881), pp. 357–382; Henry C. Barnabee's *My Wanderings* (Boston: Chapple Publishing Co., 1913); and Charles A. Grandgent's "The Stage in Boston in the Last Fifty Years," *A Memorial Volume Issued in Commemoration of the Tercentenary Committee, 1930* (Boston: Sub-Committee on Memorial History of the Boston Tercentenary Committee, 1932). The museum is also mentioned in the memoirs of the articles about numerous actors who worked there. The names of many of these persons and works can be found in the bibliographies of the histories named above.

Rosemarie K. Bank

BOSTON ["FEDERAL STREET"] THEATRE COMPANY. The Boston Theatre, the first in America to be professionally designed by a native architect, was built in 1793 at the corner of Federal and Franklin streets, Boston, Massachusetts, by a joint stock association composed of wealthy Bostonians. Since the theatre was underwritten by some of Boston's most respectable citizens, its erection marked the beginning of an era in Boston heretofore beset by bigotry and prejudice against the stage, its players, and its patrons. Designed by Charles Bulfinch, one of the stockholders, the lofty and spacious edifice of brick and stone offered an aproned proscenium stage before two tiers of boxes, a pit and a gallery, the whole seating 1,105. Its capacity was later reduced to 1,050 to make patrons more comfortable. The trustees engaged Charles Stuart Powell (d.1811) to manage the theatre. Powell, a minor London actor with few qualifications for management, had arrived in Boston with a small group of actors in mid-1792. Powell and his friends joined a short-lived company managed by Joseph Harper (1759–1811) and Alexander Placide (d.1812) in Boston's New Exhibition Room, also called the Board Alley Theatre*.

In June 1793 Powell visited England and secured a new company of players, none of whom was an acknowledged artist. The managers (Powell was assisted by Thomas Baker, also an actor in the company) and the trustees, the better to appease critics, maintained a high degree of formality and decorum in the theatre. They appointed Colonel John Steel Tyler (brother of early American comic dramatist Royall Tyler) as master of ceremonies and charged him to preserve order both within and about the theatre. Any theatrical employee risked instant dismissal for any social impropriety.

Although the theatre was well attended three evenings each week the first season, which began February 3, 1794, with a production of the impeccably moral and intensely patriotic *Gustavus Vasa*, the company was a commercial and artistic failure. Powell ended the season July 4, 1794, with a debt of almost $8,000.

The theatre was dark from July 5 to December 15, 1794, during which time Powell again voyaged to England to recruit players. The new group was little more capable than the first. Powell's fiscal management, his failure to recruit an attractive company, his ongoing battle with his comanager Thomas Baker, and perpetual discord in the company provoked the trustees and led them to ask for his resignation at the end of the second season, June 19, 1795. Powell was bankrupt. A contingent of players departed immediately for Charleston to join John Sollee's City Theatre Company*.

The trustees asked Colonel Tyler to manage the theatre, and with motives of personal profit paramount, he took the job. He quickly engaged members of the [Old] American Company* of New York, who had been performing in Providence and Hartford. The groups complemented each other artistically, and the combination was a critical and popular success after its opening November 2, 1795. The enlarged and improved band proved to be not only attractive to patrons but also expensive for the trustees, who raised prices to reflect prevailing rates at the nation's principal theatres: boxes, $1; pit, seventy-five cents; gallery, fifty cents. Bostonians hoped the Yankee-born Tyler would develop American playwriting and acting talent and reduce dependence on foreign artists. He could not do so. The marriage of the two companies was not always amiable, but Tyler quelled trouble before it became serious. The New York detachment returned to its home, the John Street Theatre, on January 20, 1796. The Boston company continued with *Othello* on January 25, to fair business. John Brown Williamson (d.1802) appeared in the title role, and his wife, formerly Miss Fontenelle, a popular soubrette, pleased audience and critics alike. Williamson succeeded Tyler in management in April and headed the company through the season's close on May 16, when most members traveled to Providence for a summer season.

In 1796–97 the Boston Theatre Company was beset by competition as The Haymarket Theatre Company* opened December 26 under the management of Charles Stuart Powell and with the Boston Theatre Company's leading performers, Mr. and Mrs. Snelling Powell, on the payroll.

Boston, population less than 20,000, could hardly support one theatre; two were sure to compete to the ruin of both. The business competition was fierce, the situation made more tense by professional jealousy and political enmity (the Haymarket catered to "the Jacobin spirit in the lower ranks," while the Boston Theatre depended on Federalist, upper-class Anglophiles). The season was a financial disaster for the Boston Theatre Company, which lost nearly $17,000. Williamson retired from management at season's end, June 17, 1797, the entire corporation in virtual collapse.

John Sollee managed the company for a belated season beginning December 6, 1797. He was succeeded on January 22, 1798, by Giles Leonard Barrett and Joseph Harper. On February 2 a fire gutted the building, forcing the temporary dissolution of the acting company.

The second "Federal Street" Theatre, designed, like the first, by Charles Bulfinch, opened October 29, 1798, under the management of John Hodgkinson (1767–1805), formerly a leading actor and comanager of the Old American Company, New York. To match the large capacity of the Haymarket, Bulfinch added a third tier of boxes so that the new theatre could seat 1,819, nearly double its former capacity. However, neither Hodgkinson nor Giles Leonard Barrett, who managed in the season of 1799–1800, was able to turn a profit. Similarly, the 1800–1801 season under Charles E. Whitlock's management was a financial failure.

For the 1801–1802 season, the trustees hired Snelling Powell (1758–1821) to manage the company. Snelling, brother to Charles Stuart Powell, was the company's most popular actor in its first few seasons. His marriage, in 1794, to Elizabeth Harrison (1774–1843), the group's most popular actress, did much to endear the company to Boston, for these local favorites were models of social correctness. Powell was ably assisted by Joseph Harper. The season was not profitable, but the managers paid their bills, a breakthrough for the now eight-year-old organization. The next season, 1802–1803, was the first successful season in the history of the company. The Haymarket Theatre failed and was demolished in June 1803, an event that marked the beginning of twenty-four years of competition-free business for the Boston Theatre Company.

Powell continued in sole management until 1806, when he was joined by actors John Bernard (1756–1828) and James H. Dickson (1774–1853), Powell's brother-in-law. Bernard, who joined the company in 1803, comanaged the group, with Dickson and Powell, from 1806 to 1811. The duo of Powell and Dickson comanaged until 1817. The summer of 1811 marked the beginning of regular summer engagements in Providence, Rhode Island. John Duff (1787–1831), an actor with the company from 1810 to 1812, joined the management team in 1817 after a residency in Philadelphia and Baltimore.

In 1821 the Boston Theatre was incorporated, and the joint stock venture that built the theatre sold out. At the beginning of its declining years,

Elizabeth Harrison Powell leased the theatre from the corporation and engaged Thomas Kilner (1777–1862) and John Clarke (1788–1838) as acting managers. Clarke retired from management in 1826, succeeded by the very popular actor Henry James Finn (1787–1840), with the company since 1822. Finn, Mrs. Snelling Powell's son-in-law, apparently was a more vital leader than his comanager Kilner.

Of the company regulars, Elizabeth Harrison Powell, an actress of large range and great force, was surely the best among the women. The dignity and reserve of both her acting and her conduct in private life set the prevailing tone for the company and exemplified the quality of the group's relations with its host community. Except for a brief stint with the Haymarket Theatre Company in 1796 and a season on tour in 1800–1801, she was a mainstay of the Boston Theatre Company from 1794 to 1828. Likewise, Snelling Powell, although noted for his versatility as an actor and for his acumen as a manager, was as much remembered after his death in 1821 as a gentleman of "undoubted probity" and as a respected citizen. The London-born Dickson's reputation for being charitable and responsible (he closed the theatre on public and church holidays) further enhanced the respectability of the company, as did his more than forty sojourns to England in search of theatrical talent. The actor-managers John Bernard, regarded by his biographer as "the most finished comedian this country had yet seen," and John Duff, a distinguished actor of genteel Irish characters, were as good as could be found in the ranks of resident companies in the young United States. Thomas Kilner was an excellent actor in old men's parts, and Henry James Finn was widely admired for the eccentric comedy of his "Yankee" characters. Mrs. Mary Ann Dyke Duff (1794–1857) had her American debut with the Boston Theatre Company in 1819 and appeared regularly with the group for the next nineteen years. Tall, dark, and graceful, she was acclaimed one of the greatest tragic actresses of her time, a reputation based on her appeal to audiences in Boston and Philadelphia.

In its earliest period, from its opening in 1793 to 1807, the end of Snelling Powell's solo management, the most popular playwrights in the company's broad repertory were William Shakespeare and Richard Sheridan. William Dunlap was the most often produced American playwright. His melodrama *Abaellino: The Great Bandit*, produced fourteen times in the season 1802–3, was one of the group's early successes.

The August von Kotzebue craze struck Boston in 1799, when Sheridan's translation of the German's *Pizarro* (1799) was seen eight times. Kotzebue's *Happy Family* (1799) and his *Point of Honour* (1800), in a translation by Charles Kemble, were also popular in 1802–3. In the following year, Kotzebue's popularity began to wane. In 1803–4 James Broaden's *Voice of Nature* (1802) and Charles Coleman, the younger's *John Bull* (1803) were popular, although the appetite for gothic melodrama remained strong for several seasons as shown by the frequency of performances of Monk

Lewis' *Castle Spectre* (1797), *Adelmorn, the Outlaw* (1801), and *Alfonso: King of Castile* (1801), as well as regular revivals of Thomas Holcroft's *Tale of Mystery* (1802). An average of about seventy pieces were brought out each of the first thirteen seasons, but only about 10 percent were new to the company's repertory each year.

In the group's middle period, the public taste for spectacle grew, and the Boston Theatre Company responded, first in 1807 with *Cinderella* (anonymous, 1804), featuring scenes and machines purchased in London by John Bernard. In 1809 they offered a spectacular production of T. E. Hook's *Tekeli* (1806), which was seen ten times during this season and seven the next. On March 12, 1810, came the younger Coleman's *Forty Thieves* (1806), presented six times before season's close and fifteen times in 1810–11. For years to come, a scenic spectacle emerged each spring to recall audiences from their winter's hibernation. On February 28, 1812, a new version of *Cinderella*, with new scenery by John Worrall, launched the spring season. Worrall's scenery was a key ingredient in the annual success of the Boston Theatre Company until his retirement in 1822.

By 1812, as the United States slipped into a disastrous war with England, the Boston Theatre Company catered to the less literate with novelties and spectacles and to pugnacious nationalists with the anonymous *Constitution and the Guerriere*, a "patriotic effusion" first seen October 2, 1812, and with *American Tars: or, Huzza for the Navy; Huzza for the Constitution; The Constitution and Java*, and *American Commerce and Freedom* in April just after the annual spectacle, Monk Lewis' *Timour, the Tartar* (1811). The vital English roots of the company were temporarily protected by a heavy mulch of American patriotism.

More discriminating patrons began to return to the theatre after the war. William Clapp averred that by 1815 "the Boston Theatre held undisputed reign" with a company reknowned for the tastefulness of its programs and for the high moral calibre of its personnel (Clapp, 145). William Dimond's ghostly *Aethiop* (1812), first produced March 27, 1815, after a two-week recess to prepare the scenes and machines, was one of the great successes of the group's middle period, which ended with the demise of the founding association of stockholders.

Until 1827 a season was organized much the same each year: an attractive resident company of about thirty actors and actresses supported a regular succession of stars in brief engagements of two to three weeks; between star engagements, the company drew well with artful reproductions of stock favorites; and the whole was anchored around a popular spring extravaganza. Seasons from 1800 to 1819 lasted about 110 nights, during each of which the group produced about sixty main plays and as many afterpieces. Seasons in the eighteen twenties ran nearly 150 nights, after the company began opening five nights each week in 1819.

The stars appearing with the Boston Theatre Company were the brightest of the day: Thomas Abthorpe Cooper (annually from 1804); James Finnell from the Philadelphia theatre; William Twaits, an extremely popular low comedian; the youthful John Howard Payne; George Frederick Cooke; Elizabeth Kemble Whitlock; Joseph G. Holman and his daughter Miss Agnes Holman (later Mrs. Charles Gilbert); the singer Mr. Incledon; James W. Wallack; and in 1821, Edmund Kean. Kean was engaged for nine nights to begin February 12; the star drew well and extended the visit for six more nights. He reappeared in May, against manager Dickson's advice, and drew poorly. Kean played two nights but refused to appear the third, although a good house assembled. Bostonians were annoyed by his rebuff, so much so that they held a grudge for four years. When Kean reappeared on December 21, 1825, he was greeted by a riot of protest, which forced the closure of the theatre for four days.

Charles Mathews starred in 1822, playing seventeen nights. Edwin Forrest and Charles Macready starred in 1826.

A strong Tremont Theatre Company* opened September 24, 1827, at a new theatre in a better location. Clapp believed the Kean riot was the beginning of the end for the Boston Theatre Company. Thereafter the theatre drew poorly, appealing mainly to an older clientele, the longtime patrons of the establishment. Although it was widely asserted that the Boston Theatre Company failed to cater to public taste, the Kean appearances and the resultant disturbances reestablished the image of the Boston Theatre Company as a pocket of Loyalist sentiment. Under the pressure of public disapproval, the morale of the group disintegrated, and the new managers, Finn and Kilner, were unable to reverse the tide. The season of 1828–29, the last for the Boston Theatre Company, began September 22. Finn reduced prices shortly after opening and engaged a rapid succession of stars, including Clara Fisher, Thomas A. Cooper, and James Caldwell, of the New Orleans theatre, all clearly established "native" performers. The Boston Theatre, as it had been called since 1805, was almost deserted, while the new Tremont Theatre Company thrived. The Boston Theatre closed in June 1829, and the company disbanded. Finn and a few other members were absorbed into the rival company.

The Boston Theatre was used as a lecture room until 1846, when Oliver C. Wyman leased it, restored the interior, and installed a stock company to support Mr. and Mrs. John Gilbert. The group performed from August 2 until March 15, 1847, when it disbanded. Charles R. Thorne, noted tragedian, headed a stock company at the Boston Theatre in 1847–48. The following seasons, the theatre was leased to equestrian groups, pantomime companies, and dramatic stars. It was razed in 1852 after Boston's National Theatre Stock Company* (1836–39) used it for a brief season.

PERSONNEL

Managers: Charles Stuart Powell, 1793–95; Colonel John A. Tyler, 1795–96; John Brown Williamson, 1796–97; John Sollee, 1797–98; Giles L. Barrett, Joseph Harper, 1798; John Hodgkinson, 1798–99; Giles Barrett, 1799–1800; Charles E. Whitlock, 1800–1801; Snelling Powell, 1801–6; Snelling Powell, John Bernard, John Dickson, 1806–11; Snelling Powell, John Dickson, 1811–17; Snelling Powell, John Dickson, John Duff, 1817–21; Thomas Kilner, John Clarke, 1821–26; Thomas Kilner, Henry James Finn, 1826–29.

Scenic Artists: Christian Gallagher, 1793–97; Emmanuel Jones, 1793–94; Anthony Audin, the younger, 1798–99; Mr. Melbourmle, 1805–6; John Worrall, 1806–22; assisted by J. R. Penneman from 1813.

Orchestra Leaders: Johann Gottlieb Graupner, c.1795–c.1803, occasional actor, Mr. Hewett, c.1810– ?

Ballet Masters: Signior Cipriani, 1806– ?; E. H. Conway, 1824– ?

Actors and Actresses: Miss Abbott, 1794; Mr. Adamson, low comedian, 1817– ?; Mr. Allen, c.1809–11, 1813– ?; George Andrews, low comedian, 1827–28; Mrs. Arnold, 1796; Mr. and Mrs. Ashton, c.1796–97; Eliza Baker, 1794; Thomas Baker, 1794, 1797– ?; Mrs. Thomas Baker, 1794, 1796– ?; *John Barnes*, regular, 1800–1810, and star, 1827; *Mrs. John Barnes*, 1821–29; George Barrett, child, 1799, adult, 1822–25, and star, 1825–26; *Mrs. Giles Barrett*, 1797–98, later *Mrs. Drummond*, 1816–c.22; *Mr. Giles Seward Barrett*, 1797–98, 1799–1800, 1802– ?; Mr. Bartlett, 1794–96; Miss Bates, 1804– ?; *William Bates*, 1796–97, 1799–1800, 1801–4, 1809– ?; Mrs. William Bates, 1797–98, 1802– ?; Mr. Bernard, 1821–22, 1824–29; Mrs. Bernard, formerly Miss Tilden, 1827–28; *John Bernard*, 1803–11, 1815–29; *Mr. Bignall*, 1801–5; *Mrs. Bignall*, 1803–5; Mr. Blanchard, 1816– ?; Mr. Bray, 1814–16; Mrs. Bray, 1814–16; Miss Amelia Brett, 1796– ?; Frederick Brown, 1816– ?; Mrs. Frederick Brown, ? –1818; *J. Mills Brown*, 1821–27; Mr. Caulfield, 1806–c.10; Mr. and Mrs. Chambers, 1796; *James Chalmers*, 1796–c.1805; *Mr. Charnock* 1822–28; Miss Clarke, 1827– ?; Mr. Clarke, 1796– ?; *John Clarke*, 1811–16, 1822–28; W. Clarke, 1815–16, 1823–24; Mrs. W. Clarke, 1815–16; Mr. Claude, 1809– ?; Mrs. Claude, formerly Miss Hogg, 1809– ?; Mr. and Mrs. Thomas Cleveland, 1796–97; Mr. Cole, 1813–15; Mr. Coles, 1796– ?, 1800– ?; Mrs. Collins, 1793–94; Mr. and Mrs. Collins, 1794–95, 1796–97; Miss Cramer, 1829; Miss Cunningham, 1808–9; *Eleanora Westray Darley*, 1799–1800, 1802–3, 1805–6, 1809–11; *John Darley*, 1802–3, 1805–6, 1809–11; Miss Deblin, dancer, 1824– ?; Miss Dellinger, c.1811–12; *Mrs. James Dickens*, formerly Miss Harrison, 1794–1816; *James H. Dickens*, 1801–17, continued in management; Mrs. Doige, 1810–12; Mr. Downie, 1796–1803, 1805– ?; Mrs. Downs, 1806– ?; Julia Drake, 1810–12; Samuel Drake, 1810–12; Mrs. Samuel Drake, 1810–12; Mr. Drummond, 1816–17; *John Duff*, 1810–12, 1817–23, 1828–29; *Mary Ann Duff*, 1810–12, 1817–23, star, 1827; Mr. Durang, dancer (?), 1795– ?; Mr. Dwyer, star, 1809–13, company regular, 1815– ?; Mrs. Dykes, 1806–7, 1815–16; Mr. Edgar, 1825– ?; Mr. Entwistle, 1810–14; Mr. Faulkner, 1828–29; Mr. Fawcett, 1796–97; James Fennell, Jr., 1814–c.17; Miss Field, 1800– ?; Mr. Fielding, 1823– ?; *Elizabeth Powell Finn*, 1822–29; *Henry James Finn*, 1822–29; Thomas Flynn, 1828–29; Mr. Fox, 1804–c.6; Mme. Gardie, 1796– ?; Mr. Gardner, singer, 1813– ?; Miss Graham, 1803– ?; Miss Green, 1796– ?; Mr. and Mrs. Green, c.1815–c.20; *Mrs. Johann Graupner*, formerly Mrs. Hillyer, 1793–94, 1796–1803, 1807–c.16; Mr. Hamilton, 1795–97; *Joseph Harper*, 1795–1800, 1801–3; *Mrs. Joseph Harper*, 1795–96, 1799–1803; Mr. Hayman, 1803– ?; Mr. Heeley, 1795–96; Mr. Henry, c.1809–16; Mrs. Henry, 1823–24; Mr. Hepworth, 1794–95; Mr. and Mrs. John Hodgkinson, 1798; Ann Storer Hogg, 1796–97; John Hogg, 1796–97; Mr. Homwe, 1798–99; Mr. Hughes, 1794–96, 1813–17; Mrs. Hughes, 1794–96; Mr. Hunt, 1798–99, 1803– ?; Joseph Jefferson, 1795–96; Miss Johnson, later Mrs. Thomas Hilson, 1816– ?; Mr. Johnson, 1824–25; Mr. and Mrs. John Johnson, 1795–96; Mr. Johnston, c.1810–c.13; *Mr. Jones*, 1794–96, 1800–c.1805; *Mrs. Jones*, 1794–96, 1798–99, 1800–c.1806; Mr. W. Jones, dancer, 1813–15; Mr. Kedey, 1798– ?; Mr. Keene, vocalist, 1818–23; *Jonathan (?) Kenny*, 1794–1806; *Thomas Kilner*, 1821– 28; *Mrs. Thomas Kilner*, 1821–28; Mr. King, 1827–29; Miss Labotture, 1809– ?; Mr. Lathy, 1798– ?; Mr. Lege, 1796– ?; Mr. Legg, 1814–16; Mr. Leonard, 1795– ?; Mr. Lindsley, ? –1812; Mr. Maginnis, 1796– ?; Mr. and Mrs. James Marshall, 1796–97; Mr. Martin, 1795– ?; Miss C. McBride, 1825–28; Mr. McFarland, 1813– 15; D. McKenzie, 1796–97, 1814–15; Mr. McMurtrie, 1816– ?; *Mrs. Mills*, 1809– 16; Mr. Moore, 1800–1803; Mr. Moreland, 1821– ?; Mr. Morgan, 1805– ?; Mr. Morse, 1810– ?; Mr. Mortimer, 1816– ?; Mr. and Mrs. Munto, 1797–98; Mr. Nelson, 1793– ?; Mr. and Mrs. Papanti, 1826–28; Mrs. Parker, 1821– ?; Mr. Parsons, c.1809– 15; Mr. Pearson, 1814– ?; Miss Pelby, 1820– ?; William Pelby, 1815– ?, 1825–26 and starring engagements, 1823–24 and 1826–27; Mrs. William Pelby, 1820– ?, 1825–26; Mr. Perkins, 1821– ?; *Mr. Persons*, 1803–11; Mr. Phillips, singer, 1818– ?; Mrs. Pick, 1796; Miss Placide, 1824– ?; David Poe, Jr., 1806–8; Elizabeth Arnold Poe, 1806–8; Miss Poole, 1810– ?; Miss Powell, 1797–98; Mrs. C. S. Powell, 1797– 98; *Charles Stewart Powell*, 1793–95, 1797–98, 1806–7, 1808–9; *Elizabeth Harrison Powell*, 1794–96, 1800, 1801–28; *Snelling Powell*, 1794–96, 1797–1821; Mrs. Pown-all, 1794; Mr. Price, 1798– ?; Mr. Prigmore, 1803– ?; Mr. Ratcliff, c.1794–c.96; Mr. Reed, 1825– ?; Miss Rivers, 1827–29; Mr. Roberts, 1810–13; *Mr. and Mrs. Robertson*, or *Robinson*, 1808–13; Charlotte Rowson, 1796–97; Susannah Haswell Rowson, 1796–97; William Rowson, 1796–97; Mr. Rutley, 1800–1802; Mr. Saubere, 1804– ?; Mr. Savage, 1814–15; Mrs. Savage, formerly Miss White, 1813–15; Mr. Shaw, 1807–8; Mrs. Shaw, 1805–8; Mr. Simpson, 1798–1801; Mrs. Simpson, 1798– 1801, 1809–10; Mr. Solomon, 1796– ?; Mrs. Solomon, 1796– ?; Miss C. Solomon, 1797–98; Mr. Spear, 1821–25; Mrs. Spencer, 1796– ?; Mr. Spiller, 1812–14; Mr. Spooner, 1824–?; Mr. Stamp, c.1815; Mr. Stanley, 1826– ?; Miss Stockwell, later Mrs. George H. Barrett, 1813–15; *Mr. Stockwell*, c.1809–12, 1813–16; Mr. Story, 1800– ?; Mr. Stowell, c.1809– ?; Miss Sully, 1796; *Mr. Sumes*, c.1809–16; Mr. Taylor, 1794–96, 1802–3; Mr. Thayer, 1820–22; Mr. Turnbull, 1806– ?; Mrs. Turner, 1809– ?; Mr. Twaits, 1807– ?; Mr. and Mrs. Joseph Tyler, 1795–96, 1813–14 (?); Mr. Tyron, 1824– ?; Mr. Usher, 1805–8; Mrs. Usher, 1807–8; Mr. H. Vaughn, 1810–12; *Mr. Villiers*, 1794–99; Mrs. Villiers, 1807– ?; Mr. Vining, singer, 1806– ?, 1810– ?; Tom Walton, 1827– ?; Mr. Waring, 1812– ?; Anne Brunton Warren, 1806– ?; Mr. Warren, 1805– ?; Mrs. Warren, 1823– ?; William Warren, child debut, 1822; Mr. Webster, singer, 1807– ?; *Mr. and Mrs. Wheatley*, 1812–18; William Charles White, 1796–97; *Charles E. Whitlock*, 1798–c.1801; *Elizabeth Kemble Whitlock*, 1796–c.1802; Henry Whitlock, 1803; Mr. Williamson, 1825–26; John Williamson, 1796–97, 1798–?; Mrs. John Williamson, 1796–97; J. Willis, c.1815; Mr. Wilmot, 1802–4; Mr. Wilson, 1803–5; Mrs. Woodham, later Mrs. Moore, 1809–

?, 1815–17; Mr. Wooley, 1811–12; Miss Worrall, c.1809– ?; *Mr. Young*, 1824–29; Mrs. Young, debut as Miss Blandford, 1819; Mr. and Mrs. Charles Young, 1805–6, 1812–15.

REPERTORY

Plays are listed by season in order of first production, indicating in parentheses the number of times the play was produced that season, if more than once.

1794: *Gustavus Vasa* (2); *Modern Antiques* (2); *The Belle's Stratagem* (3); *The Farmer* (3); *The Busybody; The Midnight Hour* (2); *A Natural Son* (3); *The Quaker* (4); *Barbarossa; The Provok'd Husband* (2); *The Child of Nature* (3); *An Agreeable Surprise* (4); *The Foundling* (2); *Bon Ton* (3); *Which Is the Man?* (2); *The Old Maid* (3); *Wonder* (2); *Rosina* (3); *George Barnwell* (2); *She Stoops to Conquer; Jane Shore; Douglas; Who's the Dupe?* (2); *The School for Scandal* (2); *The Revenge; The West Indian* (2); *The Citizen* (2); *A Bold Stroke for a Wife* (2); *The Miller of Mansfield; Ways and Means* (2); *A Chapter of Accidents* (4); *Midas* (5); *Love in a Village; Miss in Her Teens; Hamlet* (2); *Barnaby Brittle* (2); *Padlock* (2); *Romeo and Juliet* (2); *All in Good Humor; Richard III; Twelfth Night; Inkle and Yarico* (4); *The Mourning Bride; The Lying Valet; The Drummer; The Virgin Unmasked; A Poor Soldier* (3); *No Song, No Supper; The Waterman* (2); *The Merchant of Venice; The Son-in-Law* (2); *A Clandestine Marriage; Animal Magnetism; The Rivals; A Grecian Daughter; Hunt the Slipper; The Examination of Dr. Last; The Road to Ruin; An Irish Tailor; Three Weeks after Marriage; All the World's a Stage; Lyar.*

1794–95: *As You Like It* (2); *Rosina* (3); *Manager in Distress; Romp* (2); *Jew* (7); *Who's the Dupe?; Bon Ton; Dramatist* (4); *Modern Antiques; Farmer* (4); *Poor Soldier* (2); *Such Things Are* (2); *Wrangling Lovers* (2); *George Barnwell; Lying Valet* (2); *Every One Has His Fault* (5); *Barnaby Brittle; Deaf Lover; Ways and Means* (3); *Inkle and Yarico* (4); *Midnight Hour* (3); *Henry IV; West Indian; Miller of Mansfield* (2); *Wild Oats* (4); *Waterman; Mock Doctor; All in a Good Humour; Child of Nature; Village Lawyer* (3); *Rivals; Irishman in London* (2); *Padlock* (2); *Young Quaker* (2); *Road to Ruin* (2); *Romeo and Juliet* (3); *Seeing Is Believing; The School for Scandal; Medium; All the World's a Stage; Beaux Stratagem; How to Grow Rich* (3); *She Stoops to Conquer; Busybody; Deuce Is in Him* (4); *Three Weeks after Marriage; Old Maid; Natural Son; Cato* (2); *Miss in Her Teens; Prize* (4); *Virgin Unmasked; Mountaineers* (7); *As It Should Be; Dramatist; Midas* (2); *Belle's Stratagem; Lyar; Robinson Crusoe* (3); *Quaker; Contrast; Agreeable Surprise; High Life below Stairs* (2); *Notoriety* (2); *Catherine and Petruchio* (2); *Venice Preserved; Orphan; Mayor of Garratt; Richard III; Suspicious Husband; No Song, No Supper; Hamlet; Prisoner at Large; Percy; Bold Stroke for a Wife; Neck or Nothing; Gamester; Wedding Day; Wonder; The Merchant of Venice.*

1795–96 (Combined Boston Theatre Company and Old American Company): *Know Your Own Mind; Caledonia; Frolic; Purse* (2); *Provok'd Husband; Rosina; The School for Scandal; Children in the Wood* (4); *Jane Shore; Highland Reel* (2); *Dramatist; Harlequin Restored; Midnight Hour; Two Philosophers; or, The Merry Girl; The Rivals; The Sultan* (2); *The Clandestine Marriage; The Bird Catcher* (2); *Spoil'd Child* (2); *I'll Tell You What; Poor Jack* (2); *The Rage; Padlock; The Haunted Tower* (2); *Love à la Mode; Bon Ton; The Battle of Hexham; Romp; The*

Deserted Daughter (2); *Don Juan* (2); *A School for Soldiers; or, The Deserters* (3); *Country Girl; Harlequin Gardener; Robin Hood; Bold Stroke for a Wife; Macbeth; Tempest; Le Forêt Noire; Richard III* (2); *Which Is the Man?; Irish Widow; He Would Be a Soldier; Poor Vulcan; Wheel of Fortune; Tammany; Alexander the Great; Beggar's Opera; Inkle and Yarico; Harlequin Shipwrecked; The Slaves Released from Algiers; The School for Wives; Othello; Man and Wife; or, The Shakespeare Jubilee; The Inconstant; Les Deux Chasseurs; The West Indian; Harlequin Skeleton; No Song, No Supper; Florizel and Perdita; Flitch of Bacon; The Critic.*

1796: *Othello; Spoil'd Child* (5); *Every One Has His Fault* (3); *The Romp* (3); *The Mountaineers* (5); *The Old Maid* (2); *She Stoops to Conquer; The Mock Doctor; The Gamester; The Foundling; The Virgin Unmasked; Love in a Village* (2); *The Deuce Is in Him; The Jew* (3); *Crotchet Lodge* (2); *George Barnwell; The Lying Valet* (2); *The True-born Irishman* (2); *The Wrangling Lovers; Monody to the Chiefs; High Life below Stairs; Brothers; Shipwreck* (2); *The Prize* (2); *The Devil to Pay* (2); *The Child of Nature* (2); *Wild Oats; All the World's a Stage; The Miller of Mansfield; The Traveller Returned* (3); *The Prize* (2); *Oscar and Malvina* (7); *First Love* (2); *The Bank Note* (2); *The Quaker; Romeo and Juliet; Midas; The Recess; A Peep behind the Curtain; Orpheus; The Seduction; The Prisoner at Large; Cymon and Sylvia; The Conscious Lovers; The Farmer; A Bold Stroke for a Husband* (2); *Love in a Camp; Hob in the Well; The Witches; The Mysteries of the Castle; Rosina; Better Late Than Never; Sicilian Romance* (2); *Half an Hour after Supper; The Village Lawyer; The Fashionable Lover; No Song, No Supper; King Lear; The Mogul Tale; The World in a Village; The Old Soldier; The Love of Fame; The Farm House; The Jealous Wife; An Agreeable Surprise; The Children in the Wood; Who's the Dupe?; The Highland Reel; The Maid of the Oaks.*

1796–97 (September 19 to June 22): *The Dramatist* (3); *The Farmer* (2); *The School for Scandal; Lyar* (2); *The West Indian; Spoil'd Child* (5); *Much Ado about Nothing; Modern Antiques; Romeo and Juliet* (3); *The Apprentice; Know Your Own Mind; Rosina* (4); *Isabella* (2); *The Provok'd Husband; The Maid of the Oaks; Percy; The Purse* (4); *Oscar and Malvina* (4); *Venice Preserved; The Way to Keep Him* (2); *Cymbeline; The Romp* (2); *The Jealous Wife* (2); *The Fontainville Forest; The Irishman in London; Love à la Mode; The Fair Penitent; The Virgin Unmasked* (3); *The Roman Father; The Highland Reel* (3); *The Mountaineers* (5); *Inkle and Yarico* (2); *The First Floor; Love in a Village; The Lying Valet; As You Like It* (3); *My Grandmother* (5); *The Suspicious Husband* (2); *Tom Thumb, the Great* (3); *Lionel and Clarissa* (2); *The Sultan* (2); *The Miser; Catherine and Petruchio; Hamlet* (3); *George Barnwell; Peeping Tom of Coventry* (2); *Speculation; The Virgin Unmasked; The Poor Soldier* (4); *The Belle's Stratagem; Harlequin's Invasion* (4); *The Patriot; Harlequin Skeleton; The Beggar on Horseback; The Chances; The Busybody; An Agreeable Surprise* (5); *Henry IV; The Death of Captain Cook* (3); *Douglas* (2); *Oroonoko; Richard III; The Way to get Married* (4); *Three Weeks after Marriage* (2); *Critic* (4); *Tancred and Sigismunda* (2); *Next Door Neighbours* (2); *Children in the Wood* (4); *Rivals* (2); *Castle of Andalusia* (2); *Wedding Day* (4); *She Wou'd and She Wou'd Not; All the World's a Stage; Richard Coeur de Lion* (4); *Count of Narbonne; The Merchant of Venice* (2); *Two Hunters and the Milkmaid* (3); *Spanish Barber* (4); *Merry Wives of Windsor* (2); *American Heroine* (3); *The Jew; Man of Ten Thousand; Birthday* (2); *Young Quaker; Preservation* (3); *Two Philosophers; Maid of the Mill* (2); *Cripples; Orlando* (2); *La Boiteuse*

(2); *Midnight Hour* (3); *St. Patrick's Day; Le Forêt Noire; The Prisoner* (4); *Day in Turkey; Miraculous Mill* (3); *The Old Maid; Lethe; The Country Girl; The Bird Catcher; Midas; Lock and Key* (3); *Life's Vagaries; Devil upon Two Sticks; Selima and Azor; Follies of a Day* (2); *The Iron Mask; Deserted Daughter; The Triumph of Washington* (2); *Island of Calypso; Little Yankee Sailor; Americans in England* (5); *Shipwrecked Mariners Preserved* (3); *Heigho for a Husband* (2); *La petite espiegle; Day in Boston; Mahomet; Cure for the Heart-Ache; No Song, No Supper* (2); *Slaves in Algiers; The Mock Doctor; Pygmalion; Paul and Virginia; Wonder; Jane Shore; Wild Oats; Town before You; Taste of the Times* (3); *Such Things Are; Ways and Oddities; Melocosmiotis; The Son-in-Law; All in a Good Humour; Wheel of Fortune; Ghost.*

1797–98: *Wonder; Two Philosophers; Adopted Child* (2); *Hamlet; Old Maid; Jew; Rosina; Richard III; Valiant Soldier; Jane Shore; Oscar and Malvina; Roman Father; Bon Ton; Recruiting Officer; No Song, No Supper; Alexander the Great; True-born Irishman; Provok'd Husband; Power of Magic* (harlequinade). The Federal Street Theatre burned February 2, 1798. Some players rented Dearborn's Exhibition Room and continued with *Purse, Child of Nature, Amanthis, Wrangling Lovers.*

1798–99: *Wives as They Were; Purse; Cure for the Heart-Ache* (2); *Adopted Child; Shipwreck; Honest Thieves; New Way to Win Hearts* (2); *Double Disguise; The Grecian Daughter; Lyar; Duenna; Three Weeks after Marriage; All in the Wrong; Highland Reel* (2); *Cheap Living* (3); *Widow's Vow; Lock and Key; Castle Spectre* (9); *Launch* (2); *Quaker; Robbers; Secrets Worth Knowing; Agreeable Surprise; Jealous Wife; Two Strings to Your Bow; All the World's a Stage; The Will; Farmer; Animal Magnetism; Ghost; Isabella* (2); *Village Lawyer* (4); *Who's the Dupe?; The School for Scandal; School for Wives; Irishman in London* (2); *Jane Shore; The Deuce Is in Him; Mountaineers; The Merchant of Venice; Midnight Hour* (2); *The Way to Get Married; Tamerlane; Critic; Lovers' Vows* (3); *Author; Mourning Bride; Sicilian Romance; Macbeth; Bonaparte in Egypt; The Follies of a Day; All's Well That Ends Well* (John Philip Kemble alteration); *No Song, No Supper; Wives Pleased and Maids Happy; Prize; Siege of Belgrade; Child of Nature; False Impressions; Oscar and Malvina; Stranger* (3); *Group of Lovers; Inkle and Yarico; Son-in-Law; Heir-at-Law; Cymon and Sylvia* (2); *Haunted Castle; Man and Wife* (The Shakespeare Jubilee); *Americans in England; Haunted Tower; Major André; Tempest* (Dryden's alteration); *Children of the Wood; Plymouth Rock.*

1799–1800: *Laugh When You Can, Be Happy When You May; Preparations for a Cruise* (3); *Belle's Stratagem; The Jew and the Doctor* (4); *He's Much to Blame; Castle Spectre; Old Maid* (2); *Count Benyowski* (3); *Indians in England* (2); *Catherine and Petruchio* (2); *The Horse and the Widow* (3); *Poor Soldier; Stranger* (2); *Animal Magnetism; Roman Father* (2); *High Life below Stairs* (2); *Italian Father* (2); *Deuce Is in Him; Ghost* (2); *Siege of Quebec; Henry IV; Pizarro* (8); *Harlequin's Frolic; Purse; Oroonoko; Gil Blas* (2); *Spanish Fair* (2); *Merchant of Venice; Witches; or, Harlequin Salamander* (2); *Wild Oats; Douglas; The Prodigal* (2); *Bluebeard* (2); *Harlequin's Wishing Cap* (2); *Bon Ton; Five Thousand a Year; Daranzel* (2); *Mountaineers* (2); *Constellation* (2); *True-born Irishman; Battle of Bunker Hill* (2); *Spoil'd Child; Secret; Waterman* (2); *False Shame; Lovers' Vows; Village Lawyer; American Volunteers* (2); *Henry VIII; Deserter of Naples; Reparations* (2); *Thomas and Sally; Alexander the Great; or, The Rival Queens; Oscar and Malvina; Rivals;*

Inkle and Yarico; New England Captive; Tournament (2); *Highland Reel; Widow of Malabar; Maid of the Oaks; Harlequin Pantomime; Next Door Neighbours* (2); *Agreeable Surprise; Robinson Crusoe; Citizen; Such Things Are; Harlequin Medley; Henry II; Miller of Mansfield; Life and Death of Harlequin; Self-Immolation; The Times; West Point Preserved; Mother Pitcher; Spanish Barber; Rosina; Garden of Love; Mayor of Garratt; Modern Antiques; Bold Stroke for a Husband; Botheration.*

1800–1801: *Speed the Plough* (2); *Rosina; The School for Scandal; Adopted Child; Sighs* (4); *Agreeable Surprise; The Jew and the Doctor; Mock Doctor; Stranger* (3); *Ghost; Castle Spectre* (2); *Lying Valet; Birthday; Preparations for a Cruise; Waterman* (2); *Purse* (4); *Aurelio and Miranda; The Deuce Is in Him; Mountaineers* (2); *Fortune's Frolic* (4); *Romeo and Juliet; Spoil'd Child* (3); *Votary of Wealth; Padlock; Grecian Daughter; Turnpike Gate* (2); *George Barnwell; Indiscretion* (2); *Julia* (3); *Inkle and Yarico; Management (3); Comus* (2); *Regent; Carmelite; Blue Devils; Maid of the Oaks; Zorinski; All the World's a Stage; Lock and Key* (4); *Law of Lombardy* (2); *Every One Has His Fault; Harlequin's Frolic; Retaliation* (4); *Jealous Wife* (2); *Pizarro* (5); *Clandestine Marriage; Prize; As It Should Be* (2); *West Indian; Tournament; Son-in-Law; Country Girl; Highland Reel; Paul and Virginia* (4); *Tell the Truth and Shame the Devil; Provok'd Husband; The Way to Keep Him; Percy; Obi* (4); *Next Door Neighbours* (2); *Richard III; Venice Preserved; He Would Be a Soldier; Castle of Sorento; The Will; My Grandmother; Abbe de l'Epee; Bluebeard; Harlequin's Invasion of the Realms of Shakespeare; Robinson Crusoe; Honest Thieves; The Way to Get Married; Macbeth; Spirit of Contradiction; Alexander the Great; Oscar and Malvina.*

1801–2: *The School for Scandal* (2); *No Song, No Supper* (3); *Lovers' Vows* (2); *Catherine and Petruchio; Wise Man of the East; Inkle and Yarico* (2); *Speed the Plough; Sultan; False Shame; Bluebeard* (2); *Romeo and Juliet; Romp; Life* (2); *Turnpike Gate* (2); *East Indian* (3); *Purse; Child of Nature; Hunt the Slipper* (4); *Mountaineers; Oscar and Malvina; Harlequin's Invasion of the Realms of Shakespeare; Richard III; Castle Spectre* (3); *Village Lawyer* (2); *Poor Gentleman* (6); *Lying Valet* (2); *Spoil'd Child; Wheel of Fortune; Agreeable Surprise; Mock Doctor; The Dumb Made Eloquent* (2); *Fortune's Frolic* (4); *Highland Reel; St. Patrick's Day* (2); *Every One Has His Fault; Prize* (2); *Columbus* (3); *All the World's a Stage; Children in the Wood* (2); *Sighs; Poor Soldier; Major André; Jew; The Sailor's Festival; What Is She?* (2); *Folly as It Flies* (2); *The Benevolent Quaker; My Grandmother; Zorinski; Henry IV* (3); *Hob in the Well; The Will; Peep behind the Curtain; Soldier's Festival* (3); *Way to Get Married; Harlequin's Frolics; London Hermit; Padlock; Obi; Deserted Daughter* (2); *Farmer* (2); *Wives as They Were; La Forêt Noire; Chapter of Accidents; Harlequin Free-Mason* (3); *Heir-at-Law; Heigho for a Husband; Irishman in London; Pizarro* (2); *Midnight Hour; Wild Oats; Island of Barataria; Young Quaker; Prisoner* (2); *The Dash of the Day; Spanish Barber; Lock and Key; Liberal Opinions* (2); *Landing of Our Forefathers; Jane Shore; Rosina; Cure for the Heart-Ache; Merry Wives of Windsor* (2); *Robinson Crusoe; George Barnwell; Adelmorn* (3); *Retaliation; Female Duelist; He Would Be a Soldier.*

1802–3: *The Poor Gentleman; Purse; False Shame; Padlock; Sighs; Prize; Romeo and Juliet; Inkle and Yarico* (2); *Columbus* (2); *Village Lawyer; Dramatist; Adopted Child* (2); *Macbeth; Hunt the Slipper; The School for Scandal; Rosina* (2); *Abaellino, the Great Bandit (14); Fortune's Frolic; Lock and Key; No Song, No Supper; Children in the Wood; Happy Family* (2); *Highland Reel* (2); *Obi* (3); *Zorinski;*

Richard III; Who's the Dupe? (2); *West Indian; Land of the Potatoe; Death of Captain Cook* (3); *Castle Spectre* (2); *Douglas; Rivals; Battle of Bunker Hill; Blunders at Brighton* (2); *Such Things Are; Turnpike Gate; Heir-at-Law; Mogul Tale; Count Benyowski; Catherine and Petruchio* (2); *The Deuce Is in Him; Oscar and Malvina; Management* (2); *Spoil'd Child; Hamlet; Double Disguise; Point of Honour* (7); *Shipwreck* (2); *Alexander the Great; Lying Valet; Paul and Virginia* (2); *Clandestine Marriage; Harlequin Ranger* (2); *Adelmorn; Romp; Pizarro; Retaliation; Speed the Plough; English Merchant; Harlequin Free-Mason* (3); *Julius Caesar; Siege of Quebec; Fair Penitent; The Three and the Deuce; Belle's Stratagem; Robinson Crusoe; Suspicious Husband; Ramon and Agnes; Tempest; Much Ado about Nothing; Shakespearean Jubilee; Secrets Worth Knowing; Farmer; Busybody; Son-in-Law; Spanish Barber; Mountaineers; Wild Oats.*

1803–4: *Cure for the Heart-Ache; Turnpike Gate; Will; Rosina* (2); *Douglas; Padlock; Country Girl; Farmer; Jane Shore; Tripolitan Prize; or, American Tars Triumphant* (3); *The Voice of Nature* (8); *Shipwreck; Battle of Hexham* (2); *The Jew and the Doctor* (2); *He Would Be a Soldier; George Barnwell; Highland Reel* (2); *Point of Honour; Two Strings to Your Bow* (2); *John Bull* (8); *Wrangling Lovers; Purse* (2); *My Grandmother* (2); *Poor Gentleman; King Lear; Wonder* (2); *Romp* (2); *Speed the Plough; Adopted Child; Abaellino* (2); *Bon Ton* (2); *Agreeable Surprise* (2); *Rival Soldiers* (2); *Alfonso; King of Castile* (5); *Deaf Lover; Harlequin's Invasion; All in a Good Humour; Delays and Blunders* (2); *Inkle and Yarico; Columbus; Castle Spectre; Buonaparte in England; Three Weeks after Marriage; The Horse and the Widow; A Tale of Mystery* (4); *Old Maid* (2); *Miss in Her Teens; Wags of Windsor* (2); *Pizarro; Marriage Promise* (2); *Catherine and Petruchio; Paul and Virginia* (3); *Alexander the Great; Mrs. Wiggins; Stranger* (2); *Maid of Briton; Review; Cheap Living; Bluebeard* (3); *Duplicity; Don Juan* (2); *Hear Both Sides; Secret; Richard III; Rule a Wife and Have a Wife; Maid of the Oaks; Young Quaker; Asylum* (2); *Follies of a Day; She Wou'd and She Wou'd Not; Prize; How to Grow Rich* (2); *Poor Soldier; Leap Year; Every One Has His Fault; Shipwrecked Mariners Preserved; Double Disguise; Midnight Hour; Soldier's Daughter; Midas; Dramatist; Shipwreck; Wives as They Were; American Heroism; Sailor's Frolic.*

1804–5: *Speed the Plough; Quaker; Castle Spectre* (2); *Rival Soldiers; Jew* (2); *Double Disguise* (2); *Miss in Her Teens; Tale of Mystery* (2); *Lyar* (2); *Notoriety; Three Savoyards; The Jew and the Doctor; The School for Scandal; Fortune's Frolic; Macbeth; Purse; Clandestine Marriage* (2); *Millers; Romeo and Juliet* (2); *Raising the Wind* (3); *Beaux Stratagem; Next Door Neighbours; Offering to Love; Mirza and Lindor; Provok'd Husband; Belle's Stratagem; Ghost; John Bull* (3); *My Grandmother; Guilty or Not Guilty* (2); *Country Girl; The Sixty-third Letter* (4); *Every One Has His Fault; As You Like It* (2); *Hunt the Slipper; Hearts of Oak* (5); *Paul and Virginia* (2); *Padlock; Obi; Deaf Lovers; Bluebeard* (2); *La Forêt Noire; Inkle and Yarico; Wife of Two Husbands* (5); *Who's the Dupe?; Old Maid; Lovers' Vows; Battle of Hexham; Don Juan* (2); *Like Master Like Man; Wags of Windsor; Maid of the Oaks; Miser; Witches; or, Harlequin Salamander* (2); *Votary of Wealth; Midas; Wild Oats; Abaellino; Robinson Crusoe; Wheel of Fortune; Douglas; Jack in Distress; Highland Reel; Richard III; Robin Hood; Venice Preserved; Agreeable Surprise; Osmond; Othello; Romp.*

1805–6: *Speed the Plough; Wags of Windsor* (2); *Douglas; Turnpike Gate* (2); *John Bull; Hamlet* (2); *Lovers' Vows; Farmer; Othello* (3); *Romp; Every One Has*

His Fault; Fortune's Frolic; Who's the Dupe?; Heir-at-Law; Inkle and Yarico; Macbeth (2); *Too Many Crooks* (3); *Richard III; Honey Moon* (8); *My Grandmother; Don Juan* (2); *Bluebeard; Revenge; Miser; Paul and Virginia* (2); *Jane Shore; Witches; or, Harlequin Salamander* (2); *To Marry or Not to Marry* (4); *No Song, No Supper; 'Tis All a Farce; West Indian; Children in the Wood* (2); *Alexander the Great* (3); *Sixty-third Letter; Wheel of Fortune; Love Laughs at Locksmiths* (5); *Castle Spectre; Mountaineers; Coriolanus* (2); *Poor Soldier* (2); *The School for Scandal; Who Wants a Guinea?; Padlock; Macbeth; Lying Valet; Gamester* (3); *Oscar and Malvina* (2); *Romeo and Juliet; Of Age Tomorrow* (3); *Abaellino; Rule a Wife and Have a Wife; Irishman in London; Revenge; Venice Preserved; Richard III; Birthday; Lodoiska* (4); *Hearts of Oak; Voice of Nature; The Will for the Deed; Bold Stroke for a Husband; Fire King; The Rage; Four Seasons; or, Harlequin in Boston; King Lear; Sylvester Daggerwood; Adelmorn.*

1806–7: *Speed the Plough; Rosina; Cure for the Heart-Ache; La Forêt Noire; Richard III* (2); *Poor Soldier; Secrets Worth Knowing; Don Juan; Jane Shore; Harlequin Frolics; Rival Soldiers; Wife of Two Husbands; Bluebeard* (2); *Iron Chest* (2); *Lying Valet; Village Lawyer; School of Reform* (5); *Romp; The Jew and the Doctor* (2); *Provok'd Husband; Quaker; Dr. Last's Examination before the College of Physicians; Dermot and Kathlane* (2); *Every One Has His Fault; Sultan; Five Miles Off* (2); *Lodoiska* (2); *Fair Penitent; Purse; Secret; Robin Hood; Hamlet; Gamester; Macbeth* (2); *Othello* (2); *Coriolanus; Venice Preserved* (2); *Rule a Wife and Have a Wife; Romeo and Juliet; Ghost; Rivals; Four Seasons; Alexander the Great; La Perouse* (3); *The School for Scandal; Double Valet; High Life below Stairs* (2); *Earl of Essex; Paul and Virginia; Sixty-third Letter* (2); *King John; Highland Reel; King Lear; Stranger; Honey Moon; Wheel of Fortune; Douglas; Agreeable Surprise; Tempest; Ramahdroog; Much Ado about Nothing; Oscar and Malvina; Algerine Pirate; Harlequin in the Moon; The Glory of Columbia; Her Yeomanry; Love Laughs at Locksmiths.*

1807–8: *Love in a Village; The Jew and the Doctor; Rivals; Paul and Virginia* (2); *Rosina; Belville; Robin Hood; Village Lawyer; Duenna; Irishman in London; Othello* (3); *Romp; King Lear* (3); *Rival Soldiers* (2); *Town and Country; Sultan and Seraglio* (2); *Belvidera; Grecian Daughter; Highland Reel; School for Scandal; A Turkish pas trios; Tom Thumb; Pizarro* (3); *Weathercock* (4); *Romeo and Juliet; Cinderella* (6); *Miss in Her Teens; Maid of the Oaks; Raising the Wind* (2); *Sultan; Every One Has His Fault; Wags of Windsor* (2); *She Stoops to Conquer; Of Age Tomorrow; Cure for the Heart-Ache; 'Tis All a Farce; Mumps; Animal Magnetism; My Grandmother; Road to Ruin; Agreeable Surprise; Adrian and Orrila* (3); *La Perouse; Richard III; Prize; Venice Preserved; Purse; Macbeth; Wives as They Were* (3); *Barbarossa; The Will; Julius Caesar; Douglas; Chinese in Boston; More Ways Than One; Bluebeard; Adelmorn; Adopted Child; Belle's Stratagem; Virgin of the Sun; Tale of Mystery* (2); *Such Things Are; Female Prisoner; Harlequin's Choice; Time's a Tell-Tale* (2); *Wood Daemon* (2); *Robbers; A New Way to Pay a Reckoning* (2); *Ella Rosenberg; Manager in Distress; Next Door Neighbours; Embargo; Harlequin in the Moon; Charlotte and Werther; Life.*

1808–9: *Soldier's Daughter; Spoil'd Child* (2); *Belle's Stratagem; Rosina* (2); *West Indian; Poor Soldier; Poor Gentleman; Cinderella* (2); *She Stoops to Conquer; Blind Girl* (3); *Agreeable Surprise; Harlequin Medley; Weathercock* (2); *Begone Dull Care; Miss in Her Teens; Wood Daemon* (5); *Man of the World* (2); *Two*

Strings to Your Bow; Curfew (2); *Adrian and Orrila; Three Savoyards; Matrimony* (3); *More Ways Than One; Honey Moon; Woodcutters; Tom Thumb; School of Reform; Tale of Mystery; Heir-at-Law; Sixty-third Letter; Henry V; The Genius of Columbia; Jew; La Perouse* (2); *The World* (4); *Quaker's Wedding; The Pilgrim* (2); *Battle of Hexham; The School for Scandal; Romp; Quaker; Brazen Mask* (3); *Every One Has His Fault; False Alarms; Catherine and Petruchio; Town and Country* (2); *Midas* (3); *Henry IV; Pizarro* (2); *Oscar and Malvina; Folly as It Flies; Cheap Living; Wife of Two Husbands; Rival Soldiers; Deserved Daughter; Paul and Virginia; Gustavus Vasa; Raising the Embargo; Wives as They Were; La Forêt Noire; Laugh When You Can; Feudal Times; John Bull; Rival Sisters; We Fly by Night; Douglas; Lovers' Vows; Revenge.*

1809–10: *Man and Wife; Wood Daemon* (2); *George Barnwell* (2); *Brazen Mask* (3); *Lovers' Quarrels; The Jew and the Doctor* (2); *King Lear* (3); *Deaf Lover* (2); *Deuce Is in Him* (3); *Tekeli (10); Raising the Wind; Grieving's a Folly; La Perouse; Animal Magnetism* (3); *Werter; Dramatist; Julius Caesar; Virginius; Mountaineers; Two Misers* (3); *She Stoops to Conquer; The Foundling of the Forest* (3); *We Fly by Night; Hamlet; Spoil'd Child; Rule a Wife and Have a Wife; Highland Reel; Macbeth; My Grandmother; Othello* (2); *High Life below Stairs* (2); *Adelgitha* (4); *A Flitch of Bacon; Sixty-third Letter* (2); *Hunt the Slipper; Clergyman's Daughter* (5); *Purse; Sultan; Honey Moon; Pilgrims; Poor Soldier* (2); *Venice Preserved; Robin Hood* (2); *School of Reform; No Song, No Supper* (2); *Heir-at-Law; Lyar; Valentine and Orson* (4); *Tancred and Sigismunda; Adopted Child; Romeo and Juliet; Barbarossa; Mahomet; Register Office* (2); *Forty Thieves* (6); *Fortune's Frolic; Catherine and Petruchio; Ghost; Quality Binding; Rival Soldiers; Stranger; All the World's a Stage; Busybody; Little Bob and Little Ben; A Picnic; Manager in Distress; Blind Boy* (2); *Mayor of Garratt; Wild Oats; Sicilian Romance; Wives as They Were; Wedding Day; Battle of Hexham; Scotch Ghost; Robinson Crusoe; West Indian; Hunt the Slipper.*

1810–11, Opened October 8, 1810: *Speed the Plough; Love Laughs at Locksmiths* (3); *The Soldier's Daughter; Padlock; The School of Reform* (2); *Honey Moon* (2); *Paul and Virginia* (3); *John Bull; Of Age Tomorrow* (3); *Man and Wife* (2); *Tekeli* (7); *She Stoops to Conquer; American Generosity; or, Moorish Ingratitude* (4); *Town and Country* (2); *The Wanderer* (2); *Fortune's Frolic* (3); *Forty Thieves (15); The Mountaineers* (2); *Laugh When You Can* (2); *Raising the Wind* (2); *Douglas* (2); *The West Indian; The Farmer; Jane Shore* (2); *The Point of Honour* (2); *George Barnwell* (2); *Pizarro; The Way to Get Married; Tom Thumb; Werter; Valentine and Orson* (3); *The Midnight Hour* (2); *Hamlet; No Song, No Supper* (2); *Hearts of Oak* (3); *Blind Boy* (4); *Weathercock* (3); *Barbarossa; The Foundling of the Forest* (2); *The Paragraph; Hunter of the Alps; The Poor Lodger* (5); *The Jew and the Doctor* (2); *Rosina; Romeo and Juliet; Turnpike Gate (2);* George F. Cooke's repertory from January 3 to January 23, 1811: *Richard III* (3); *The Man of the World* (2); *My Grandmother* (2); *The Merchant of Venice* (3); *Love à la Mode; Sixty-third Letter; Othello* (2); *Macbeth; Rival Soldiers* and *Henry IV, Part I* (2); *Lying Valet; Quaker; Busybody; Oscar and Malvina* (2); *The Castle Spectre; Four Seasons; Tamerlane; Country Girl* (2); *Abaellino* (3); *Black Beard* (6); *Dramatist; Jew; The Belle's Stratagem* (2); *Cure for the Heart-Ache; Mazeppa* (4); *Don Juan; Oroonoko; Such Things Are; Village Lawyer; Death of Captain Cook; Children of the World; The Fortress* (4); *The School for Scandal; Bluebeard* (3); *The Clandestine*

Marriage; Hunt the Slipper; More Ways Than One; The Voice of Nature; Columbus; Tale of Mystery; Every One Has His Fault; The Budget of Blunders; The Three and the Deuce (2); *A Bold Stroke for a Husband; Lodoiska* (2); *The Poor Gentleman; The Drummer; Alexander the Great* (2).

1811–12: *Laugh When You Can; The Midnight Hour* (3); *The Castle Spectre; No Song, No Supper* (2); *The School of Reform* (2); *The Brazen Mask; Pizarro* (4); *Fortune's Frolics* (2); *The Way to Get Married* (4); *My Grandmother* (2); *Tekeli* (3); *Adrian and Orrila; Animal Magnetism; Of Age Tomorrow* (3); *The Curfew* (2); *Hamlet* (2); *Isabella; The Sultan* (2); *Jane Shore; The Blind Boy* (2); *The Belle's Stratagem; Raising the Wind* (2); *Romeo and Juliet; The Grecian Daughter; The Three and the Deuce* (3); *Alexander the Great* (2); *The Wood Daemon* (2); *Honey Moon; Shipwreck* (2); *Speed the Plough; The Exile* (7); *Plot and Counterplot* (6); *George Barnwell* (2); *Forty Thieves* (3); *Such Things Are; The Voice of Nature; The Stranger; The American Captive; or, The Siege of Tripoli* (4); *The Quaker* (2); *Abaellino* (2); *Yes or No?* (2); *The Battle of Bunker Hill* (2); *Tamerlane; High Life below Stairs; Music Mad* (3); *Adelmorn* (2); *Hurry Scurry; Richard III* (2); *The Merchant of Venice* (3); *The Man of the World; Henry IV, Part I; The Weathercock* (2); *Othello* (2); *The Wheel of Fortune; Venice Preserved; Love à la Mode* (2); *A Tale of Mystery* (2); *The Turnpike Gate* (2); *A New Way to Pay Old Debts* (2); *The Fortress; The Revenge* (2); *Purse* (2); *Macbeth* (2); *King Lear* (2); *The Jew and the Doctor; The Ghost* (2); *The Mountaineers; Douglas* (2); *Inkle and Yarico; The Paragraph* (2); *Lovers' Vows* (2); *The Highland Reel; Modern Antiques* (3); *Oroonoko; The Hunter of the Alps; Adelgitha; Tom Thumb* (2); *Cinderella* (9); *Barbarossa; Tancred and Sigismunda; Like Master, Like Man; Is He a Prince?* (2); *The Busybody; Folly as It Flies; The Critic; The Knights of Snowdown* (4); *Two Strings to Your Bow; The Foundling of the Forest; The Lying Valet; The School for Scandal; The Rival Soldiers; The Battle of Hexham; Rule a Wife and Have a Wife; The Wags of Windsor; Sylvester Daggerwood; Oscar and Malvina; Wives as They Were; The Duel; Love Laughs at Locksmiths; Harlequin Salamander* (2); *Secrets Worth Knowing; The Maid of the Oaks; Caravan; or, The Driver and His Dog* (4); *The Point of Honour; He Would Be a Sailor; The Glory of Columbia.*

1812–13: *The Exile* (2); *Catherine and Petruchio* (2); *Honey Moon* (3); *The Three and the Deuce; The Foundling of the Forest* (2); *The Constitution and the Guerriere* (3); *Romeo and Juliet; The Knights of Snowdown; Bluebeard* (2); *The Dramatist* (2); *The American Camp; The Wags of Windsor; The Castle Spectre; The Kiss* (5); *The Fortress; Cinderella* (2); *Jane Shore; Lodoiska; The Critic; The Shipwreck* (3); *The Doubtful Son* (4); *Plot and Counterplot* (2); *The Maid of the Oaks; Tom Thumb* (2); *The Sons of Erin* (4); *Spoil'd Child* (3); *Yes or No?* (2); *La Perouse* (6); *The Iron Chest* (2); *Is He a Prince?; George Barnwell; Darkness Visible* (4); *Lost and Found* (3); *Tekeli* (2); *Folly as It Flies; Rich and Poor* (4); *A Tale of Mystery; Forty Thieves* (4); *Paul and Virginia; The Gazette Extraordinary* (3); *Valentine and Orson* (4); *Isabella* (2); *The Jealous Wife; The Grecian Daughter; American Tars; or, Huzza for the Navy* (7); *Music Mad; The Gamester* (2); *The Mourning Bride; Inkle and Yarico; The Farm House; The Blue Devils* (2); *Percy; How to Die for Love* (4); *The Roman Father; Hamlet* (2); *The Turnpike Gate; The Provok'd Husband* (3); *Venice Preserved; No Song, No Supper* (2); *The Fair Penitent; The Midnight Hour* (2); *The Wonder* (2); *Modern Antiques; Fortune's Frolics* (2); *Othello* (2); *The Earl of Essex; Much Ado about Nothing* (2); *Of Age Tomorrow; Honey Moon*

(2); *The Sultan; Alexander the Great; The Votary of Wealth; The Wedding Day; As You Like It* (2); *The School for Scandal; The Weathercock; Macbeth; Purse* (2); *Rule a Wife and Have a Wife; Like Master, Like Man; Coriolanus; Love Laughs at Locksmiths; Abaellino; The Hunter of the Alps; Richard III; My Grandmother; The Merchant of Venice; The Constitution and Java* (2); *Timour, the Tartar (10); Ways and Means; All the World's a Stage; The Jew and the Doctor; Prisoner at Large* (2); *Laugh When You Can; The West Indian* (2); *The Budget of Blunders; Lyar; The Suspicious Husband; Every One Has His Fault; American Commerce and Freedom* (3); *He Would Be a Soldier; Hamlet Travestie* (3); *The Road to Ruin; The Adopted Child; The Stranger; The Romp; Speed the Plough; The Curfew; Eight to One* (3); *The Soldier's Daughter; The Sailor's Daughter; The Caravan; She Stoops to Conquer.*

1813–14: *Man and Wife* (2); *The Wags of Windsor* (3); *The Heir-at-Law; Rosina; The Exile* (2); *No Song, No Supper* (2); *Speed the Plough; Lodoiska; The Road to Ruin* (2); *The Poor Soldier; The School of Reform; She Stoops to Conquer; The Heroes of the Lake; or, The Glorious 10th of September* (4); *Rich and Poor* (3); *The Foundling of the Forest; The Sixty-third Letter; Timour, the Tartar* (6); *Inkle and Yarico; Ourselves* (3); *Valentine and Orson* (4); *Bluebeard* (4); *The Gazette Extraordinary; Love Laughs at Locksmiths; The Sleepwalker* (5); *The Sons of Erin* (2); *John Bull; George Barnwell; Tekeli* (3); *The School for Friends* (3); *Mr. H; The Soldier's Daughter; The Sailor's Daughter* (2); *The Romp* (3); *The Poor Gentleman* (3); *An Irishman in London* (2); *La Perouse* (2); *Who Wants a Guinea?* (4); *The Grecian Daughter; Time's a Tell-Tale* (2); *The Purse; American Commerce and Freedom; Forty Thieves (12); Jane Shore* (2); *Abaellino* (2); *The American Captive; Botheration; Love in a Village; Plot and Counterplot* (3); *The Peasant Boy* (4); *How to Die for Love; The Africans* (3); *Hamlet; Othello; The Mountaineers; Catherine and Petruchio; The Shipwreck; Macbeth; Spoil'd Child* (2); *Rule a Wife and Have a Wife; The Quaker; Richard III; The Turnpike Gate; Honey Moon; My Grandmother; The Merchant of Venice; Coriolanus; Provok'd Husband* (2); *Much Ado about Nothing; As You Like It; Hamlet Travestie; Alexander the Great; The School for Scandal; The Wonder* (2); *The Castle Spectre; Cymbeline* (2); *Paul and Virginia; Wives as They Were* (2); *Alexis* (2); *The Sultan; Padlock; The Battle of York; or, The Death of General Pike* (4); *Anything New; Life; Town and Country* (2); *The Faithful Wife; Folly as It Flies; Laugh When You Can; Return of the Constitution; Ella Rosenberg* (2); *The Will* (2); *The Rivals; The Hero of the North* (2); *Wife of Two Husbands; The Hunter of the Alps.*

1814–15: *The Soldier's Daughter* (2); *The Honest Thieves* (4); *The Castle Spectre; The Wags of Windsor* (2); *Speed the Plough* (2); *An Irishman in London* (3); *Venice Preserved; The Boarding House* (6); *Man and Wife* (2); *The Toothache* (3); *The Genius of America; Adelgitha* (2); *The Battle of York; He Would Be a Soldier; Valentine and Orson* (2); *Tekeli* (3); *Point of Honour* (2); *Wife of Two Husbands* (2); *Abaellino* (3); *The Sleepwalker* (2); *The Glory of Columbia; George Barnwell; The Witches' Cave* (3); *The Romp* (2); *La Perouse* (2); *Bunker Hill* (2); *Like Master, Like Man* (3); *The Turnpike Gate* (2); *The Foundling of the Forest* (2); *Lodoiska; The Poor Gentleman* (3); *John Bull* (2); *Love à la Mode* (2); *The Kiss; Alexander the Great; Forty Thieves* (4); *The Doubtful Son; Adelmorn; The Hero of the North* (2); *The Highland Reel; The Voice of Nature; Lafitte and the Pirates of Barataria; The Midnight Hour* (3); *Fortune's Frolic* (2); *Pizarro* (2); *The Revenge; The Mer-*

chant of Venice; The Stranger; Animal Magnetism; Romeo and Juliet; My Grand-
mother (2); How to Die for Love (3); Richard III; Anything New?; The Adopted
Child; The Miller and His Men (8); Town and Country (3); Spoil'd Child; The
School for Scandal; As You Like It; The Provok'd Husband; Darkness Visible (2);
Wives as They Were; Education (3); Henry VIII (2); Peace (4); The Wonder; Much
Ado about Nothing; The Sultan; The Peasant Boy (3); The Prisoner-at-Large; The
Will (2); The Exile; Timour, the Tartar; Who Wants a Guinea?; The Aethiop (12);
A Quarter of an Hour before Dinner (2); 'Tis All a Farce (2); Botheration; All the
World's a Stage; Hamlet Travestie; Paul and Virginia (2); Marmion (2); Little Red
Riding Hood; The Genii (3); The World as It Goes; Such Things Are; The Wood
Daemon (2); The Man of the World; Rich and Poor; The Rivals; The Magic Rock;
The Purse; A Sailor's Return; The Rival Lasses; The Sons of Erin.

1815–16: The Dramatist (2); The Children in the Wood (4); Little Red Riding
Hood (2); The Weathercock (2); The Birthday (3); Education; My Grandmother
(2); Every One Has His Fault (2); The Sleepwalker (2); The Foundling of the Forest
(2); Honest Thieves (4); The Miller and His Men (4); The Boarding House (4);
Speed the Plough (2); The Prize (4); Laugh When You Can (2); No Song, No
Supper; The West Indian (3); Raising the Wind (2); The Belle's Stratagem (3); The
Heir-at-Law; The Wood Daemon (2); The Aethiop (3); Lyar (3); Richard III; The
Merchant of Venice (2); The Man of the World (2); Tom Thumb (3); Love à la
Mode; The Adopted Child; The Poor Gentleman; Paul and Virginia (2); George
Barnwell (2); He Would Be a Soldier; The Critic (3); An Irishman in London; John
Bull; First Impressions (2); The Death of Captain Cook (3); Hamlet; The Wags of
Windsor (3); Alexander the Great; Honey Moon; Agreeable Surprise (3); Othello;
The Curfew; Henry IV, Part I (2); Fortune's Frolic; Rule a Wife and Have a Wife;
Macbeth; The Turnpike Gate; The Mountaineers (3); Timour, the Tartar; The Witches'
Cave; The Gamester; Catherine and Petruchio; Illusion (3); How to Die for Love
(2); The Rival Soldiers; Tekeli (3); Wild Oats; The Soldier's Daughter (2); Spoil'd
Child (3); Much Ado about Nothing; Past Ten O'Clock (2); The School for Scandal
(2); The Country Girl (2); The Romp (4); The Sultan; Of Age Tomorrow (2); Man
and Wife; The Will; Wonder; Turn Out!; The Way to Get Married (2); The Magpie
or the Maid? (14); Douglas; Love Laughs at Locksmiths (2); Wives as They Were;
Love, Law, and Physic; 'Tis All a Farce (2); Plot and Counterplot (2); Cure for
the Heart-Ache; All the World's a Stage; The Deserted Daughter; The Highland Reel
(2); As You Like It; Three Weeks after Marriage (2); Zembuca (11); The Hunter
of the Alps; Two Strings to Your Bow; Matrimony (2); The Wedding Day (2); La
Perouse; Cheap Living; Bluebeard (2); Like Master, Like Man (2); Slaves of Algiers
(2); Adrian and Orrila; Oscar and Malvina (2); Adelmorn; Inkle and Yarico; Zorinski; Pizarro; A Tale of Mystery; Harlequin Shipwrecked; Bold Stroke for a
Husband (2); Music Mad; King Lear; The Purse; The School of Reform; The
Woodman's Hut (4); The Point of Honour; Harlequin Conjurer. The repertory of
Boston Theatre Company has not been calendared after 1816. Clapp names a few
plays each season to 1829.

BIBLIOGRAPHY

Alden, J. "A Season in Federal Street: J. B. Williamson and the Boston Theatre,
    1796–1797." Proceedings, American Antiquarian Society 65 (1955): 12–74.
Ball, William T. W. "The Old Federal Street Theatre." Bostonian Society Publi-
    cations 8 (1911): 41–92.

Bonowitz, Dorothy M. "The History of the Boston Stage from the Beginning to 1810." Ph.D. diss., Pennsylvania State University, 1936.

Clapp, William W., Jr. "The Drama in Boston." In *The Memorial History of Boston, 1630–1880*. Vol. 4. Edited by Justin Winsor. Boston: James R. Osgood and Company, 1881, pp. 357–382.

————. *A Record of the Boston Stage*. Boston: James Monroe and Company, 1853.

Coad, Oral Sumner. "Henry James Finn". In *Dictionary of American Biography*. Vol. 6. New York: Charles Scribner's Sons, 1943.

Edgett, Edwin Francis. "Snelling Powell." In *Dictionary of American Biography*. Vol. 15. New York: Charles Scribner's Sons, 1943.

Michael, Mary Ruth. "A History of the Professional Theatre in Boston from the Beginning to 1815." Ph.D. diss., Radcliffe College, 1941.

Seilhamer, George O. *History of the American Theatre*. Vol. 3. New York, 1891.

Shaver, Muriel. "Mary Ann Dyke Duff." In *Dictionary of American Biography*. Vol. 5. New York, Charles Scribner's Sons, 1943.

Stoddard, Richard F. "The Architecture and Technology of Boston Theatres, 1794–1854." DFA diss., Yale University, 1971.

Toscan, Richard E. "The Organization and Operation of the Federal Street Theatre from 1793 to 1806." Ph.D. diss., University of Illinois at Urbana-Champaign, 1970.

Weldon B. Durham

BOSTON THEATRE STOCK COMPANY.   In *A Record of the Boston Stage* (1853), William W. Clapp, Jr., quoted from a letter written to him by Thomas Barry, an actor-manager of considerable repute in New York and Boston: "You will have, sooner or later, a first-class theatre in Boston, and if properly built and properly conducted, it will prove a boon to the public and a fortune to the manager" (p. 479). The facility to which Barry referred was very shortly to be built at the corner of Washington and Mason streets. Just a few weeks after the destruction by fire of the Old Boston Theatre in Federal Street (1852), a group of Boston citizens formed a theatre corporation. The group selected the site and sold subscriptions that financed construction. The theatre they built opened its door to the public on September 11, 1854, and it stood in regular use until 1926. Until 1885 it housed a company of actors, the Boston Theatre Stock Company. Along with the Boston Museum Company*, which ended its fifty-year career in 1893, and the companies of Lester Wallack, A.M. Palmer, Augustin Daly, and Daniel and Charles Frohman, which lasted another decade, the Boston Theatre Stock Company was among the most durable stock companies of the late nineteenth century.

The Boston Theatre of 1854 seated 3,140 in an orchestra, two balconies, and a gallery before a proscenium stage with a commodious apron (removed in 1888). Four private boxes were included for purely decorative effect at the ends of the apron. The auditorium was nearly circular, slightly raked, and about ninety feet in diameter at its widest. Public spaces were generous.

A free-standing spiral staircase, nine feet wide, carried patrons from the Washington Street lobby to the gallery. A ladies room off the first-floor lobby, a smoking room off the second-floor (first balcony) lobby, with a family circle in the second balcony, were richly paneled, draped, and lighted to show off the massive but elegant balustrades and archways. A paneled clock, unique in the United States, filled the space directly above the proscenium. The stage opening was forty-eight feet wide and forty-one feet high. A cellar beneath the stage plunged to a depth of thirty feet to admit sinking flats and wings. The circularity and size of the auditorium and negligible seating for aristocrats were emblems of the purpose of the theatre: to provide quality entertainment for Boston's burgeoning middle class and liberal profits for the theatre's managers.

The Boston Theatre opened under the management of Thomas Barry on September 11, 1854. The company produced Richard Sheridan's *Rivals* and J. R. Planché's musical farce *Loan of a Lover*, certainly a most conventional stock-company bill. The company, numbering forty-three, with an equal number employed behind the scenes and in the house, was led by James Bennett and his daughter Julia Bennett Barrow. Mr. and Mrs. John Gilbert and Mr. and Mrs. John Wood played second leads and characters, respectively. The theatre operated Monday through Friday, with curtain at 7:30 P.M. Matinees on Monday, Tuesday, Thursday, and Friday commenced October 7. Not until 1859 did the theatre open on Wednesday afternoon or Saturday night.

The stock performed without addition until October 9 (*Merchant of Venice, A New Way to Pay Old Debts*, and *Virginius* stand out in a typical stock repertory). The company's first visiting star was Julia Dean, who played four weeks in standard fare such as *The Lady of Lyons, The Stranger, The Gamester*, and *Romeo and Juliet*. Edwin Forrest's three-week stand followed; it included *Richelieu, A New Way to Pay Old Debts, Virginius* (again!), and *Jack Cade*.

On November 27 Louisa Fanny Pyne's English Opera Company appeared, the regular company assisting with small roles and playing a farce each evening. The stock held forth for two weeks and then supported E. L. Davenport for a fortnight. Italian Opera followed, the stock filling all matinees and each Tuesday and Thursday evening bill. James H. Hackett appeared intermittently with the stock during the visit of the Italians. On February 12 a Boston Theatre Company tradition, the spring extravaganza, opened a five-week run. Julia Dean returned for two weeks and then the stock performed a travesty of the opera *Norma*. English Opera reappeared, as did Italian opera, with the stock filling in between the opera stands. The ravel family, a troupe of pantomimists performed the stock in farces, until July 4, the traditional season's close, when the Ravels played to $189. The largest receipts for a single night, $4,225 came on Monday, January 22, when the Italian Opera presented *Norma*.

In summary, the stock company was featured for eighteen of the first season's thirty weeks. It supported stars for another eleven weeks and filled in around visiting opera companies for the remainder of the time. The repertory was conventional but reasonably sophisticated. One new play was introduced. Julia Dean starred in *The Priestess*, a five-act tragedy by an anonymous author, from March 19 to 23, on April 5 and 6, and again in mid-May, during a stock stand.

Under Thomas Barry's management the company flourished for three seasons. The Barry formula called for eighteen to twenty weeks of unembellished work by the stock company, including a spring spectacular (which, like Christmas at the gift shop, was supposed to provide the company's major surge of profits), four or five star visits (each with some nationalistic or ethnic flavor), Italian or English opera, and pantomimes and burlesques, with the company in farces. In the 1855–56 season, Edwin Booth, at age twenty-three, made the first of his many regular starring engagements at the Boston Theatre. The group's profitability was undermined by the financial panic of 1857, when Barry had to cut prices in half to attract enough patrons to keep the doors open. In 1858 the old corporation failed, but a new one was formed, the formal transfer of property taking place on October 9, 1858. Barry continued to manage for the new proprietors, although the company of 1858–59 retained only a few of the regulars who had been with the organization for four years. Mr. and Mrs. E. L. Davenport took leading roles in a company that numbered thirty-four. The pattern of the season was slightly changed. From September 13 to June 11, 1859, the theatre operated thirty-five weeks; the stock company stood alone for fifteen weeks, assisted stars for eleven weeks, and filled in around Italian opera the remaining nine weeks. The theatre auditorium was floored over and the building used for balls for six weeks after Barry's lease expired in February. During this period the company prepared its spring extravaganza *Faust and Marguerita*.

The proprietors of the Boston Theatre engaged no regular company for the next four seasons. In June 1863 Wyzeman Marshall formed a company and secured a lease. Under the Marshall management the company supported a steady succession of stars: James H. Hackett, Mr. and Mrs. W. J. Florence, Charlotte Cushman and Joseph Proctor, Isabella Cubas, Daniel Bandmann, and others, with occasional breaks for opera.

In 1864 the theatre was purchased by Benjamin W. Thayer and Orlando Tompkins, who held the property during all of its remaining years as a home to a resident company of performers. Henry Jarrett was the resident manager for two seasons, 1864–66. In 1866 Edwin Booth and John S. Clarke, Booth's brother-in-law, leased the theatre for one year and installed Junius B. Booth, Jr., as resident manager. The youngest Booth took up the lease and continued in management from 1867 to 1873. The Booth regime ended when Thayer and Tompkins emerged from behind the cover of a lease agreement to assume openly the ownership and management of the theatre and the company. Lemington R. Shewall directed the company for five years, to 1878, and Eugene Tompkins took over for the last seven years of the acting company's residency, to 1885. Tompkins claimed that the theatre experienced not even one unprofitable season after 1864, although in some seasons the margin of gain was slight.

Although the theatre and the company remained a financially sound venture, the makeup and function of the resident company altered slowly in these twenty-one years. The processes of change are apparent in several components of the company's life. The company managers engaged leading men and women of lesser reknown in the company's later years. In 1864–65 E. L. Davenport and J. W. Wallack shared the roles assigned to leading men in the Boston Theatre Company; Rose Eytinge took the female leads. The next two years the company was led by Frank Mayo. Charles R. Thorne, Jr., led the group in two seasons, but when he defected to the company's arch rival, the Selwyn Company, in 1869, he was replaced by Frank Roche. Roche was a competent performer, but he did not have the glamour that Thorne brought to the company. Later leading men were little more than good stock leads; none had significant star experience: Neil Warner (1870–71), Louis Aldrich (1871–72), H. S. Murdoch (1872–74), Alexander Fitzgerald (1874–75), L. R. Shewall (1875–76), C. Leslie Allen (1876–78), Louis James (1878–79), Thomas W. Keene (1879–80). Mark Price (1880–81), and William Redmund (1881–85). In the choice of leading women the managers opted even more obviously for stability rather than luminescence. Rose Eytinge played the leads opposite Davenport and Wallack in 1864–65, but the next year a longtime company toiler, Rachel Noah, stepped up from second leads. She was succeeded by Agnes Perry, who shortly married J. B. Booth, Jr., and remained, playing leads for seven years, from 1866–73. From 1881 to 1891 Mrs. Booth was the leading lady of Palmer's Madison Square Theatre Stock Company* in New York City. Mrs. Thomas Barry (formerly Clara Biddles, an ingenue with the Boston Theatre Company from 1854 to 1856) returned to the company in 1873 and played leads until 1880, when she sat out one year in favor of Margaret Linner. Mrs. Barry returned in 1881 and led the company on the distaff side for four more years. Mrs. Barry was a fixture of theatre in Boston, having played leads at a rival theatre, Selwyn's, later the Globe Theatre, from 1867 to 1873.

The changing function of the resident company can also be seen in the way the managers employed its stock of performers. The Boston Theatre season averaged forty weeks during the twenty-one years from 1864 to 1885. In the first Thompkins-Thayer season, the stock supported visiting stars thirteen weeks, stood alone for fifteen weeks, supplemented visiting opera companies for seven weeks, and stood aside entirely for five weeks, as the William Warren Comedy Company held the stage. The total displacement of the Boston Theatre Company by a visiting company was an anomaly in the period, but the curiosity became more common as the years passed. In 1865–66 the company supported stars for twenty weeks, supplemented opera and pantomime companies for five weeks, and stood alone for fifteen weeks. The solo stands were twelve weeks long in 1866–67 and sixteen weeks in 1867-68 but only four weeks in 1868–69 and six and one-half weeks in 1869–70.

During the early 1870s this formula prevailed: three-fifths of the season the company supported visiting stars in one-, two-, or three-week stands; one-fifth of the season the company supplemented opera and pantomime companies (by filling in as dancers and chorus singers and by performing matinees and some evenings while the visiting troupe rested), and one-fifth of the season the company itself was the featured bill. Furthermore, after 1868 the company ceased offering a repertory of old plays, unless a star visited, and spent most of its solo time each season in a run of a month or more of the season's spectacular. For instance, in 1870–71 the company ran *The Twelve Temptations* for four of the six weeks it appeared solus; in 1871–72 it ran the *The Black Crook* for five of its seven independent weeks. However, in 1876–77 the company supported stars for thirty-eight of its forty weeks, including a three-week run of the annual spectacular, when F. C. Bangs was imported to star in *Sardanapoulas*.

According to Eugene Tompkins, a turning point in the history of the Boston Theatre Company was reached on December 12, 1877. Tompkins had acquired exclusive rights to an American production of an adaptation of Victorien Sardou's *Exiles*. Tompkins and Noble Hill (who had purchased a share of the organization after Benjamin Thayer died in December 1875) spared no expense in this year's spectacular. It ran for ten weeks, during which time the managers began to believe they had a new kind of property to sell—a property that could compete with the productions mounted in New York City for extensive and profitable tours of the major cities of the United States. The company continued in residence until May 6, when Tompkins and Hill tested their belief in the regional appeal of the company with a six-week tour, while visiting companies occupied the Boston Theatre.

The following season, the stock company opened with *The Two Mothers*, which ran three weeks. Five weeks later the company assayed *Cosette*, an adaptation of *Les Miserables*, which ran five weeks but stirred up no great enthusiasm. A revival of *The Exiles* followed and held up for four weeks. The stock continued with another week of *The Two Mothers* and a week of *Uncle Tom's Cabin*. Still later in the spring, the stock produced another Sardou piece, this one written especially for the Boston Theatre Company and entitled *André Fortier: The Hero of the Calaveras*. It failed to spark the interest the Boston public had shown in *The Exiles*. By April the stock company had been featured in eighteen of the theatre's thirty-two weeks of operation. Clearly, Tompkins and Hill were trying to capitalize on the success of *The Exiles* by increasing the use in Boston of the company that had produced it. Somehow, the strategy failed. Eugene Tompkins reported that this season was the least profitable in recent memory—the organization was losing money. In April the managers mounted a production of *H.M.S. Pinafore*, using only a few of the stock, the main body of which was sent to Portland, Maine, for a brief residency. *Pinafore* was the season's only profitable venture. It ran for seven weeks and allowed the managers to balance their books. Moreover, the Boston Theatre Company drew well in Portland.

The effect of the experience of the seasons 1877–78 and 1878–79 was obvious in the life of the Boston Theatre Company. In 1879–80 the stock company stood one week on its own, it supported stars for eleven weeks, and for thirty-one weeks it toured the northeastern United States, performing its most profitable material: *The Exiles; Two Mothers; André Fortier; Boulogne*, the farce with which the Boston Theatre Company opened the 1879–80 season; and *Drink*, a modestly successful temperance drama that played for four weeks at the Boston Theatre. Visiting companies filled the theatre's time while the Boston Theatre Company was on tour. In 1880–81 the company was on tour twenty-four of the forty-one weeks of the theatre season. In 1881–82 a full-time touring company was engaged, while the parent group stayed in Boston, during which time the resident company turned out two eleven-week runs of spectacular and melodramatic material. In 1882–83 the resident company spent twenty-four weeks in Boston, fifteen of which were concentrated in two long-run hits. In 1883–84 the Boston Theatre Company produced its greatest hit, the spectacular drama *Jalma*, written especially for the company by Charles Gayler. The production, which featured "The March of the Silver Army," a parade of 100 armor-clad girls down a giant jeweled staircase into a glittering palace hall, played to very large receipts for twelve weeks and then toured to Philadelphia, Baltimore, Chicago, and elsewhere for twelve weeks. In 1884–85 the last season in which a resident company was engaged, the company played in Boston fourteen weeks, two in support of F. S. Chanfrau in *Kit: The Arkansas Traveller* (the last of the thirteen years in which Mose appeared at the Boston Theatre), and twelve in the musical comedy *Zanita*, by Eugene Tompkins and Dexter Smith. It spent twenty-two weeks on tour.

The stock company Thomas Barry established in 1854 and directed for five years performed on the repertory plan. The company assembled barely a week before its opening; yet they led off with a four-week stand of sixteen plays and afterpieces. The stars who followed changed the bill about three times a week, with the company offering afterpieces at an even greater rate of change. Moreover, foreign-language opera played a large part in the theatre's life, as did ethnic and national stars. In the last five years of its life, the Boston Theatre Company was predominantly a touring organization producing a single play or a few pieces, usually more or less originated by the group. Its home stands were concentrated not in a repertory of familiar plays and not in the support of stars but in the run of a single new play. Until about 1890, five years after its detachment from its home, the Boston Theatre Company existed only as a touring group. The precise date it permanently disbanded is unclear.

PERSONNEL, 1854–59

Lessee and Manager: Thomas Barry (1854–59).

Assistant Managers: J. B. Wright (1855–58), J. P. Price (1858–59).

Musical Director: Thomas Comer (1854–59).

Orchestra Leader: H. W. Durlang (1854–59).

Scenic Artists: C. Lehr (1854–55), Mr. Hayes (1855–59), John H. Selwyn (1855–59).

Machinist: Jacob T. Johnson (1854–59).

Property Maker: J. Jeffries (1854–59).

Costumer: A. Howell (1854–59).

Treasurers: F. Fleming (1854–56), William Ellison (1856–59).

Actors and Actresses: Mrs. Abbott (1857–58); Edwin Adams (1858–59); Mrs. Edwin Adams (1858–59); J. Adams (1858–59); George H. Andrews (1857–58); Miss Barrett (1854–55); Miss E. Barrett (1854–55); *Julia Bennett Barrow* (1854–57); *Thomas Barry* (1854–59); Charles Bass (1858–59); Mr. Belton (1855–57); Mrs. Belton (1855–57); *James Bennett* (1854–57); Mr. Biddles (1854–55); Mrs. Biddles (1854–55); *Adelaide Biddles* (1854–57); *Clara Biddles*; later *Mrs. Thomas Barry* (1854–59); Miss Burbank (1858–59); Mrs. Burroughs (1858–59); Miss Christy (1855–56); *Thomas Comer* (1854–59); *Joe Cowell* (1854–58); Charlotte Crampton (1858–59); Mr. Cunningham (1858–59); E. Curran (1854–55); W. H. Curtis (1857–59); H. F. Daly (1854–57); *E. L. Davenport* (1858–59); Mrs. E. L. Davenport (1858–59); Lizzie Weston Davenport (1857–58); *N. T. Davenport* (1854–59); William Davidge (1857–58); Mr. Davis (1858–59); Mr. Daymond (1855–59); Mr. Dayton (1855–57); Mary Devlin (1858–59); Mrs. Dixon (1854–57); *W. A. Donaldson* (1854–58); Lizzie Emmons (1857–59); Mr. Finn (1857–59); Mrs. Fiske (1854–55); *Moses Fiske* (1854–57); Miss Florence (1857–58); Mr. Forrester (1854–57); Mrs. France (1858–59); Fanny France (1858–59); Mr. French (1854–55); *John Gilbert* (1854–58); Mrs. John Gilbert (1854–58); Mr. Gouldson (1854–57); Mr. Harcourt (1854–55); Miss Harris (1854–55); Miss Hayward (1858–59); Miss Heaney (1858–59); *George Holland* (1858–59); Mr. Holmes (1854–58); F. J. Horton (1858–59); *J. B. Howe* (1854–58); Miss Howell (1855–57); Mr. Howell (1854–55); Miss Irving (1854–55); G. Johnson (1854–58); G. W. Johnson (1854–57); *S. D. Johnson* (1854–58); Mrs. T. Johnson (1857–58); Mrs. Hudson Kirby (1855–58); Miss Kuhn (1858–59); Mr. Lingham (1858–59); Mr. Lyster (1854–55); Josephine Manners (1857–58); Mrs. Marshall (1857–59); Miss Marshall (1857–59); T. E. Morris (1854–57); Miss Munroe (1857–58); Josephine Orton (1858–59); Mr. Pauncefort (1854–55); Charles Pope (1857–58); Mr. Price (1855–58); Mr. Reed (1858–59); Miss Robinson (1854–57); Miss Rose (1855–59); *John H. Selwyn* (1854–59); Dan Setchell (1858–59); Mrs. W. H. Smith (1854–57); Mr. Stephens (1858–59); *J. H. Stoddart* (1855–57); *Emma*

Taylor (1854–57); *George Vandenhoff* (1857–58); Mr. Verney (1857–58); Ida Vernon (1857–58); Miss Walters (1854–57); *John Woods* (1854–57); *Mrs. John Woods* (1854–57).

PERSONNEL, 1863–85

Proprietors: Wyzeman Marshall (1863–64), Benjamin W. Thayer (1864–75), Orlando Tompkins (1864–85), Noble H. Hill (1876–85).

Lessees: Edwin Booth, John S. Clarke (1866–73).

Acting Managers: Wyzeman Marshall (1863–64), Henry C. Jarrett (1864–66), Junius B. Booth, Jr. (1866–73), Lemington R. Shewall (1873–78), Eugene Thompkins (1878–85).

Stage Managers (Stage Directors): J. G. Hanley (1863–64), Junius B. Booth, Jr. (1866–73), Napier Lothian, Jr. (1870–85), Lemington R. Shewall (1873–78).

Treasurers: John M. Ward (1863–85), Quincy Kilby (1881–83).

Orchestra Leaders: F. Suck (1863–65), Charles Koppitz (1865–67), Napier Lothian (1867–85).

Scenic Artists: Charles Witham (1863– ?), George Heister (1866–71), George Tirrell (1871–73), Charles S. Getz (1873–c.80), John Sommer (1873–c.80), J. S. Getz (1880– ?), Richard Gannon (1880– ?).

Costumers: Charlotte Gilbert (1871– ?), Miss A. Endress (1877–85).

Machinists: Henry Rough (1865–66), W. P. Prescott (1866–85).

Property Master: J. B. Sullivan (1867–85).

Gas Engineer: George Wilkerson (1871– ?).

Traveling Company Managers: Fred Stinson (1881–82), Frank Carlos Griffith (1882–83).

Actors and Actresses: *Louis Aldrich* (1865–66, 1867–68, 1870–71); Laura Alexander (1870–71); *C. Leslie Allen* (1869–81); *Mrs. C. Leslie Allen* (1870–86); D. R. Allen (1867–68); E. H. Allen (1881–82); Miss Amelia (1863–64); Lizzie Anderson (1882–83); R. A. Anderson (1875–76); J. Armstrong (1879–80); R. Arnott (1866–67), a/k/a Russell Clarke (1865–66), a/k/a J. D. Russell (1870–72); E. Y. Backus (1878–85); F. C. Baker (1863–64); Alice Banicoat (1878–79); O. H. Barr (1875–77); E. Barry (1863–64); *Mrs. Thomas Barry* (1873–80, 1881–84); Maurice Barrymore (1881–82); H. L. Bascombe (1865–67); E. W. Beattie (1863–64); Clara Bell (1878–79); J. Biddles (1863–64); Mrs. J. Biddles (1863–64); T. Bingham (1866–67); Charlotte Blair, later Lottie Blair Parker (1878–79); Gertie Blanchard (1879–80); Harry Bloodgood, minstrel (1876–77); George Boles (1874–77); George C. Boniface, Jr. (1876–77); J. Bowan (1875–76); May Bowers (1878–79); J. B. Bradford (1872–73); Annie L. Brown (1864–65); E. P. Brown (1883–85); J. H. Browne (1865–66); *Mrs. J. H. Browne* (1865–68); *E. J. Buckley* (1876–80); Frank Burbeck (1881–82, 1884–85); W. F. Burroughs (1866–68); Carrie Burton (1884–85); E. Burton (1863–64); Miss A. Byron (1867–68); Lillian Calef (1883–84); Victoria Cameron (1881–82); Mary Carr (1866–67); Miss Carter (1871–72); T. Chandler (1863–64); Mrs. F. S. Chanfrau (1863–64); Emma Chase (1881–82); *H. E. Chase* (1877–85); Vilella Chase (1878–79); A. Z. Chipman (1878–80); George Clair (1864–65); George H. Clarke (1864–65); Stuart Clarke (1870–71, 1882–83); Florence Clifford (1876–77); Susie Cluer (1866–68); W. H. Collings (1865–66, 1869–70); Harvey Collins (1873–74); J. H. Connor (1871–72); *Frazer Coulter* (1881–85); Anna Cowell (1863–64); *H. A. Cripps* (1874–77, 1879–80); C. H. Currier (1883–84); W.

H. Curtis (1863–64); Mrs. E. L. Davenport (1865–66); Fanny Davenport (1865–66); N. T. Davenport (1863–64); Mrs. N. T. Davenport (1863–64); *H. Rees Davies* (1874–78); C. M. Davis (1863–64); May Davis (1871–72); W.E. Davis (1881–84); J.W. Dawson (1863–64); Elma Delano (1884–85); Adelaide Detchon (1879–81); Julia Dillon (1872–75); R. J. Dillon (1872–75); *Nellie Downing* (1874–78); Belle Dudley (1870–71); Fanny Dudley (1878–80); E. A. Eberle (1882–83); Mrs. E. A. Eberle (1882–83); *Harry Edwards* (1878–81); Mary Edwards (1876–77); T. N. Edwards (1878–79); Walter Edwards (1882–83); Miss Ellwood (1863–64); Lizzie Emmons (1857–58); John P. Endres, Jr. (1881–83); Rose Eytinge (1864–65); *W. R. Falls* (1879–84); Raymond Finley (1881–84); May Fiske (1872–75); *Alexander Fitzgerald* (1874–75); Mrs. Alexander Fitzgerald (1874–75); F. H. Fitzpatrick (1873–74, 1881–82); Clara B. Flagg (1879–80); S. Flood (1867–68); Miss Florence (1857–58, 1863–64); *Marion Follett* (1873–78); S. H. Forsberg (1865–68); Horace Frail (1865–66, 1869–70); Rosa France (1881–84); *Shirley France* (1864–65, 1868–72); C. H. Frye (1865–66); J. W. Gardiner (1873–74); Julia Gaylord (1867–68); May Germon (1884–85); H. T. Gibson (1878–79); *John D. Gilbert* (1884–85); *Doris Goldthwaite* (1869–72); William Gomersol (1865–66); Mrs. William Gomersol (1865–66); Howard Gould (1881–83); Blanche Gray (1863–64); George H. Griffiths (1881–82); J. F. Hagan (1870–71); *J. W. Hague* (1871–74, 1878–80); Miss E. Hall (1863–64); Josie Hall (1884–85); Fred P. Ham (1884–85); W. H. Hamblin (1863–64); Frank Hardenberg (1866–67); Miss Harding (1865–66); Anita Harris (1884–85); Hamilton Harris (1883–84); Frank S. Hartshorn (1880–81); *Blanche Hayden* (1873–78); J. A. Hendrie (1883–84); *Marie Henley* (1874–78); Sadie Henley (1877–78); Miss Hoffman (1873–74); E. B. Holmes (1872–75); Frank Holland (1865–66); T. C. Howard (1865–66, 1870–71); J. H. Howland (1877–78); R. C. Hudson (1883–84); W. Hudson (1863–64); *Lizzie Hunt* (1874–78); *T. M. Hunter* (1873–78); *Mrs. T. M. Hunter* (1874–78, 1882–83); John E. Ince (1881–82); Will S. Ingersoll (1883–85); *Louis James* (1878–79); Miss E. Johnson (1863–64); Carrie Jones (1873–74); N. D. Jones (1869–70); M. J. Jordan (1880–81); Gus Kammerlee (1884–85); George Karnes (1864–65); J. P. Keefe (1868–69); Thomas W. Keene (1879–80); Miss Kendrick (1863–64);*Charles Kent* (1881–84; J. F. Kenway (1870–71); Jennie Kimball (1865–66); *Edith Kingdon* (1881–84); Frank Lamb (1883–84); Harry Lampee (1872–73); *Margaret Lanner* (1880–81); Phineas Leach (1882–85); Miss Lees (1863–64); Helen Leigh (1881–82); Walter Leman (1866–68); *Ambrose Leonard* (1868–72); E. M. Leslie (1866–67); Mrs. E. M. Leslie (1866–68); J. F. L'Estrange (1871–72); Gustavus Levick (1874–78); Horace Lewis (1878–79); James Lewis (1868–69); J. W. Lonergan (1882–83); Eliza Long (1869–70); *Napier Lothian, Jr.* (1874–78); Charles Maddern (1873–74); Clara Fisher Maeder (1881–82); *D. S. Maguinnis* (1867–85); Miss Malvina (1863–64); Mrs. Marshall (1864–67); Ella Mayer (1882–83, 1884–85); *Frank Mayo* (1865–67); L. M. McCormack (1881–82); James McCoy (1863–64); Thomas H. McGrath (1882–83, 1884–85); Kate Meek (1881–82); Eleanor Merron (1882–83); Edwin Millikin (1882–83); Joseph Mitchell (1875–77); Ada Monk (1864–65); Minnie Monk (1864–65); Lizzie A. Moore (1879–80); Miss Morgan (1873–74); Sadie Morris (1879–80); Louisa Morse (1867–68, 1871–72); Arthur Moulton (1880–82); Louise Muldener (1882–83); *H. S. Murdock* (1869–71, 1872–74); May Newman (1883–84); *Rachel Noah* (1864–68, 1870–72); Frank M. Norcross (1883–84); W. H. Norton (1871–78); Miss Oakley (1871–72); Harriet Orton (1864–65); *George R. Parks* (1877–82); Charles T. Parslow (1865–66); W. A. Paul (1882–

83); Louise Paullin (1884–85); Henry Peakes (1865–66); James Peakes (1865–66); *Mrs. M. A. Pennoyer* (1879–81, 1884–85); *Agnes Perry*, later *Mrs. Junius Brutus Booth, Jr.* (1866–67, 1868–69, 1870–74); Henry Pierson (1877–78); *Mrs. Charles Poole* (1870–78); W. H. Pope (1871–72); *Carrie Prescott* (1873–78; T. Preston (1863–64); *Mark Price* (1876–82); Annie Proctor (1881–82); *Olivia Rand* (1873–78); William Raynor (1873–74); Alvin Read (1863–64); *M. D. Rebus* (1875–78); Lizzie Rechelle (1879–80); *William Redmund* (1881–84); Georgie Reignolds (1870–71); J. P. Reynolds (1865–67); Walter Reynolds (1883–84); Harry Richmond (1873–74); Mrs. Robinson (1866–67); M. Robinson (1875–77); Frank Roche (1869–70); Benjamin G. Rogers (1864–65); Mrs. Howard Rogers (1865–66); C. Rolfe (1877–78); F. Rooney, later Frank Roberts (1869–72); Frank Oakes Rose (1882–83); Master Tommy Russell (1882–83); Ruby St. Clair (1876–77); W. St. Maur (1867–68); J. L. Sandford (1863–64); F. O. Savage (1863–64); J. R. William Scanlan (1863–66); J. R. Scott (1865–68); Rufus Scott (1873–75); G. A. Selwyn (1874–75); Blanch Sherwood (1884–85); Romie Sherwood (1884–85); Lemington R. Shewall (1875–78); Otis Skinner (1880–81); *Emma Smiley* (1871–78, 1879–80); *Iola Smiley* (1873–78); C. Somerville (1863–64); William H. Spencer (1879–80); *S. E. Springer* (1874–84); H. Stanford (1865–66); C. A. Stedman (1872–73); May Stembler (1884–85); Hattie Stevens (1873–74); J. O. Stevens (1873–74); Mrs. E. F. Stewart (1866–67); L. R. Stockwell (1869–72); Mrs. Stonewall (1863–64); Anna Warren Storey (1878–79); D. J. Sullivan (1882–85); J. J. Sullivan (1871–72); Miss Swindlehorst (1863–64); Miss Sylvester (1863–64); Mrs. Sylvester (1863–64); E. D. Tannehill (1881–82); *J. W. Taylor* (1863–72, 1874–85); J. W. Thomas (1867–68); Ida F. Thoreau (1878–79); *Charles R. Thorne, Jr.* (1866–69); Grace Thorne (1882–85); Helen Tracy (1868–69); H. H. Train (1876–77); Mary Tucker (1880–81); Zoe Tuttle (1880–81); *Marie Uart* (1870–74); Viola Vance (1872–73); Charles H. Vandenhoff (1881–82); Alice Veazie (1884–85); J. J. Wallace (1865–66); *J. W. Wallack* (1864–65); F. W. Wallis (1876–77); *Neil Warner* (1870–71); H. A. Weaver (1872–73); Mrs. H. A. Weaver (1872–73); Charlene Weidman (1880–81); Norma Wells (1884–85); W. H. Whalley (1863–64); J. P. Weid (1874–75); *Eugene Wiley*, later *Eugene Wiley Presprey* (1876–80); J. S. Williams (1882–84); C. H. Wilson (1864–65); *George W. Wilson* (1871–75, 1876–77); *Miss Georgie Wilson* (1874–77); H. N. Wilson (1882–83); Kate Wilson (1883–84); R. G. Wilson (1882–83); Annie Winslow (1866–67, 1876–77); F. Woodhull (1866–67); Master Harry Woodruff (1880–81); D. B. Wylie (1865–66); *Emma Wyman* (1877–80).

REPERTORY

1854–55, September 11: *The Rivals; Loan of a Lover; The Wonder; Mr. and Mrs. Peter White; The Love Chase; The Merchant of Venice; The Swiss Cottage; John Bull; A New Way to Pay Old Debts; The Poor Gentleman; The Wandering Minstrel; Virginius; The Two Gregories; A Kiss in the Dark; Man and Wife.* In support of Julia Dean: *The Hunchback; The Lady of Lyons; The Wife; The Love Chase; Lot; The Stranger; Evadne; Honey Moon; The Gamester; Romeo and Juliet; Ingomar; The Follies of a Night* (four weeks). November 6: in support of Edwin Forrest in *Richelieu; Damon and Pythias; A New Way to Pay Old Debts; Virginius; King Lear; Othello; The Gladiator; Metamora; Jack Cade; Hamlet* (three weeks). November 27: The Boston Theatre Company regulars played small roles in support of the Louisa Pyne English Opera Company for three weeks; they also played a farce each evening. December 18: *The Merry Wives of Windsor; Hamlet; The School for Scandal; Money; The Merchant of Venice; Richard III* (two weeks). January 1, 1855, in support of E. L. Davenport: *Hamlet; Othello: St. Marc; The Stranger: Richard III; Brutus; Black Eyed Susan; The Wife; The Morning Call* (two weeks). January 15: The Boston Theatre Company supported Madame Grisi and Signor Mario in Italian opera on Monday, Wednesday, and Friday; on Tuesday and Thursday the stock performed alone, until January 30, and then in support of James H. Hackett in *Henry IV, Part 1; Merry Wives of Windsor; The Kentuckians;* and *Monsieur Mallet* (four weeks). February 12: *The Invisible Prince; or, the Island of Tranquil Delights* (five weeks). March 19: in support of Julia Dean: *The Wife, The Lady of Lyons, The Priestess,* which new, anonymous tragedy played until March 23 and then on April 2, 5, and 6. Miss Dean's farewell benefit was *The Jealous Wife* and *Honey Moon* on April 9. April 11–13: "The *Norma* Travesties" played. April 16: The Pyne English Opera Company (three weeks). May 7, stock: *Rule a Wife and Have a Wife; The Bridal; The Jealous Wife; The Priestess; Henry IV, Part 1; The Invisible Prince; King John; As You Like It; Twelfth Night; Wild Oats; The King and the Mimic* (two weeks). May 21: Italian opera (three weeks), the regular stock filling off nights (Tuesday and Thursday). June 5: Niblo's celebrated Ravel Troupe of pantomimists played until July 4, the season's traditional closing date.

1855–56, September 10: *Much Ado about Nothing; The Stranger; Wild Oats; The Poor Gentleman; The Hunchback; Paul Pry; The School for Scandal; Cure for the Heart-Ache; Twelfth Night; Wives as They Were and Maids as They Are* (two weeks). September 24, in support of Mr. and Mrs. George Vandenhoff: *Hamlet; Money; Town and Country; The School for Scandal; The Lady of Lyons* (one week). October 1, in support of Mr. and Mrs. Barney Williams: *The Custom of the Country; Born to Good Luck; Barney, the Baron; The Irish Tiger; Ireland as It Is; Our Gal; Patience and Perseverence; Irish Assurance and Yankee Modesty; The Happy Man; Ireland and America; Law for Ladies; Teddy, the Tiler; The Fairy Circle; The Irish Ambassador; In and Out of Place; The Irish Tutor; Shandy Maguire; O'Flanagan and the Fairies; The Limerick Boy; Yankee Courting; The Modern Mephistopheles; Brian O'Linn; The Bashful Man; The Irish Thrush and the Swedish Nightingale* (three weeks). October 22: the stock was unemployed in the two-week engagement of Rachel and Company, except on October 31, when Rachel was ill, it presented *Wives as They Were and Maids as They Are.* November 5: in support of Edwin Forrest (four weeks). December 2: in support of Adelaide Phillips: *The Devil's Bridge, The Duenna, The Cabinet* (one week). December 10: Various comedies, including, on December 24, *The Tempest,* which ran for two weeks. January 27, 1856: Italian opera (four weeks), Boston Theatre Company on Monday, Wednesday, and Friday, in support of Joseph Proctor. February 25: in support of Wyzeman Marshall: *Zafari; Hamlet; Pizarro; Julius Caesar; Macbeth* (one week). March 10, in support of Julia Bennett Barrow: *Olympia,* a new play anonymously authored for Mrs. Barrow (two weeks). March 24: *The Wife* (one week). March 31: *It Is Ill Playing with Edged Tools,* by an anonymous gentleman (two weeks). April 14: *A Midsummer Night's Dream* (seven weeks). June 4: The Vestvali Italian Opera Troupe (two weeks).

1856–57, September 3: *A Midsummer Night's Dream; The Tempest; Old Heads and Young Hearts; Much Ado about Nothing; Retributions* (an American premiere); *The Marble Heart* (Boston premiere) (four weeks). October 6: in support of Fanny

Davenport: *Love; The Maid of Mariendorpt; Lady of Lyons; Hunchback; Adrienne, the Actress; Camille; Mona Lisa* (two weeks). October 20: Italian opera (three weeks). November 10: in support of Edwin Forrest (five weeks), during which appeared *William Tell* (a Boston premiere). December 15: Boston premiere of *Self* and *My Wife's Mirror* (one week). December 22: the Ravels in pantomimes and ballets; Boston Theatre Company in farces each night (six weeks). February 2, 1857: Brough's burlesque *The Corsair* (two weeks). February 13–14: the burlesque *Hiawatha; or, Ardent Spirits and Laughing Waters*. February 16: a week of benefits. February 23: in support of Mrs. McMahon: *The Hunchback; The School for Scandal; Romeo and Juliet; Fazio; Lady of Lyons* (one week). March 2: week of benefits. March 9: in support of Agnes Robertson and Dion Boucicault in *Life of an Actress; The Phantom; Young Actress; Bob Nettles; Andy Blake; Bluebell; Pauline; The Little Treasure; The Chameleon; Used Up* (three weeks). March 30–31: in support of Ruth Oakley. April 1: German opera (one week). April 6: in support of George Vandenhoff in *Henry V, Hamlet, Macbeth* (one week). April 20: in support of Edwin Booth: *A New Way to Pay Old Debts; Richelieu; Richard III; The Apostate; Bertram; Little Toddlekins; Hamlet; King Lear; Brutus; The Iron Chest; Katherine and Petruchio* (two weeks). May 4, in support of Matilda Heron: *Camille* (one week). May 11: in support of Miss Heron in *Medea, Camille, Fazio* (one week). May 18: in support of Avonia Jones: *Ingomar, the Barbarian; The Lady of Lyons; Romeo and Juliet; The School for Scandal; Armond* (one week). May 25: A week of benefits. June 1: *London Assurance* (one week).

1857–58, September 7: *Evadne; The Poor Gentleman; Romeo and Juliet; The Victims; Masks and Faces;* farces (one week). September 14: in support of Edwin Booth (two weeks); October 5: in support of Charles Mathews: *Patter vs. Clatter; Domestic Economy; Married for Money; A Game of Speculations; Cool as a Cucumber; Used Up; Little Toddlekins; The Busybody; A Curious Case; Trying It On; Bachelor of Arts; The Practical Man; The Captain of the Watch; London Assurance* (three weeks). October 26: the company in comedies and farces (two weeks). November 9: the Ronzani Ballet Troupe (four weeks). December 7, in support of Mr. and Mrs. Charles R. Thorne: *Don Caesar de Bazan; Rob Roy; Ernest Maltravers; The Stranger; Alexander the Great; Uncle Tom's Cabin* (two weeks). December 21: in support of Mrs. Anna Senter: *A Snake in the Grass, Satan in Paris* (one week). December 28, stock: *The Scarlet Letter, The Money Panic of '57* (one week). January 4, 1858: in support of Matilda Heron: *The Maid's Tragedy; Camille; Medea; Phaedra; Fazio; Vice and Virtue; Masks and Faces; Leonore* (two weeks). January 18: the Ravels in pantomime and ballet; the regular company in farces (nine weeks). March 22 (for one night): *A Hard Struggle, Gwynneth Vaughn* (benefit for Mrs. Hudson Kirby). March 23: in support of Edwin Booth: (two weeks). Arpil 6: in support of Agnes Robertson: *Jessie Brown; or, The Siege of Lucknow; Andy Blake; Bluebells; The Young Actress; Bob Nettles* (three weeks). April 26: in support of E. L. Davenport and Joseph Proctor in *Julius Caesar; Damon and Pythias; Othello; Richard III; Macbeth; St. Marc; Jibbenainosay* (two weeks).

1858–59, September 13: stock in standard plays, including *Othello* (one week). September 20: in support of Julia Dean Hayne: *The Duke's Wage* and other plays (two weeks). October 5: Strakosch's Italian Opera Company (two weeks). October 11: in support of William E. Burton: *Dombey and Son; A Serious Family; Wanted: 1,000 Spirited Young Milliners; The Breach of Promise; The Toodles; Blue Devils;*

The Dutch Governor; The Mummy; David Copperfield; Twelfth Night; John Jones (two weeks). October 25: in support of Edwin Booth: (three weeks). November 15: stock (one week). November 22: in support of J. H. Hackett: *Rip Van Winkle; Henry IV, Part 1; Merry Wives of Windsor; A Yankee in England; The Man of the World; A Kentuckian's Trip to New York in 1815*. December 8: Italian opera (four weeks). December 24: the Boston Theatre Company offered its first Saturday night performance. January 6, 1859: *The Corsican* (two weeks). January 17: *The Cataract of the Ganges* (six weeks). February 26: Barry's lease terminated, and the theatre closed for six weeks. April 5: the spring spectacular *Faust and Marguerite* (four weeks); May 2: in support of William E. Burton: (one and one-half weeks); Italian opera closed the season with a five-week stand ending June 11. The stock company offered benefits on the opera's off-nights.

No regular dramatic company was engaged for the next four seasons.

1863–64, August 24: in support of James H. Hackett: *Henry IV; The Merry Wives of Windsor; Rip Van Winkle; Monsieur Mallet* (one week). August 31: in support of Mr. and Mrs. W. J. Florence: *The Death Fetch* and other plays (four weeks). September 26: in support of Charlotte Cushman and Joseph Proctor: *Macbeth*. September 28: in support of Isabella Cubas and W. H. Edgar: *The French Spy; Narramatta; The Wizard Stiff; The Flying Dutchman* (four weeks). October 24: in support of Daniel E. Bandmann, one night only: *The Merchant of Venice*. October 28: in support of Edwin Booth (five weeks). November 30: in support of Maggie Mitchell: *Fanchon; Margot; Little Barefoot; The Pearl of Savoy; Petite Marie; Katty O'Sheil* (five weeks). January 4, 1864: Italian opera (four weeks). February 1: in support of Edwin Forrest and Daniel Bandmann: (six weeks). March 14: Italian opera (two weeks). March 28: in support of Vestvali: *Gamea; or, The Jewish Mother; The Duke's Motto; Lucrezia Borgia*; (three weeks). April 18: in support of Marie Zoe, the Cuban Sylph: *The French Spy, The Wizard Skiff, Esmeralda*; (two weeks). May 2: German opera (two weeks). May 16: Maggie Mitchell (four weeks). Season ended on June 10.

1864–65, August 29: in support of E. L. Davenport and J. W. Wallack: *The Lady of the Lake; Hamlet; The Iron Mask; Macbeth; Amisis; or the Last of the Pharoahs; Richard III; Still Waters Run Deep; The Forty Thieves; The King of the Commons; Oliver Twist; St. Marc; Black Eyed Susan; Honey Moon* (six weeks). October 10: German opera (four weeks). November 7: the company moved to the Melodeon Theatre next door for two and one-half weeks. November 24: in support of Mrs. D. P. Bowers: her repertory, including *East Lynne* and *The Jewess of Madrid* (three weeks). December 12: The William Warren Comedy Company displaced the Boston Theatre Company for three weeks. January 2, 1865: Boston Theatre Company supplemented Italian opera (four and one-half weeks). February 1: *Enoch Arden* (one week). February 8: *The Naiad Queen* (five weeks). March 13: in support of Laura Keene: *The Workmen of Boston* and *Our American Cousin* (two weeks). March 29: in support of Edwin Booth, but his engagement was halted and the theatre darkened for five nights in response to the assassination of President Lincoln. April 20: in support of Mr. and Mrs. Barney Williams: Irish and Yankee plays (two and one-half weeks). May 8: Mrs. D. P. Bowers (three weeks). May 31: William Warren Comedy Company (two weeks). June 12: benefits continuing until season's end on June 21, 1865.

1865–66, August 28: *The Streets of New York* (four weeks). September 25: in support of Charles Kean and Ellen Tree: *Henry VIII; The Jealous Wife; Macbeth; Louis XI; The Merchant of Venice; King Lear; Hamlet.* October 9: in support of Maggie Mitchell (four weeks). November 7: *Arrah-na-Pogue* (four weeks). December 4: *The Ice Witch* (five weeks). January 8, 1866: in support of Frank Dwight Denny: *Hamlet, Romeo and Juliet, Richard III* (one week). January 15: Italian opera (two weeks). February 5: in support of Caroline Richings, with Peter Richings: *The Enchantress.* February 12: the Ravels in pantomime and ballet (three weeks). March 7: in support of Kate Bateman: *Leah the Forsaken; Romeo and Juliet; Lady of Lyons; Fazio.* April 2: in support of Charles Kean and Ellen Tree (one week). April 16: the stock in *The Streets of New York* (two weeks). April 23: in support of John E. Owen in Yankee plays, such as *Solon Shingle* and *The Happiest Day of My Life* (nine days). May 14: in support of Maggie Mitchell (three weeks). June 11: in support of Lucille Western: *East Lynne; The Stranger; Macbeth; Jane Shore; Oliver Twist.* June 29: the season of forty weeks closed.

1866–67, from August 20, stock: *Money; The Loan of a Lover; Ingomar; The Romance of a Poor Young Man; Jack Cade; The Marble Heart; St. Tropaz; Faint Heart ne'er Won Fair Lady; A Life's Revenge; Nan: The Good-for-Nothing; The Dead Heart; Trying It On.* September 3: in support of Edwin Booth: *Othello; Hamlet* (which ran three weeks); *Romeo and Juliet; Merchant of Venice; Richard III; Brutus, or, The Folly of Tarquin; Don Caesar de Bazan; The Fool's Revenge; Ruy Blas; Katherine and Petruchio; The Stranger* (six weeks). October 14: in support of John S. Clarke, Booth's brother-in-law: *Everybody's Friend; Toodles; Babes in the Wood; Nicholas Nickleby* (two weeks). October 29: Adelaide Ristori's Italian Opera Company featured, the stock in *Ticket-of-Leave Man* or *The Octoroon* on Wednesday and Saturday. November 12: Italian opera continued without Ristori (two weeks). November 26: in support of John Brougham: *The Captain; or, The Watch; His Last Legs; Playing with Fire; David Copperfield;* a burlesque of *Columbus; Dombey and Son; A Bull in a China Shop; The Irish Lion; The Irish Immigrant* (four weeks). December 24: in support of J. B. Roberts: *Faust and Marguerite; The Iron Chest; The Corsican Brothers; Richard III* (two weeks). January 7: in support of Lawrence Barrett: *Rosedale, Hamlet, The Lady of Lyons* (two weeks). January 21: Italian opera (two weeks). February 4: in support of Mrs. D. P. Bowers (two weeks). February 18: stock: *The Streets of New York; Ours; The Colleen Bawn; Brian Boroihme; The Idiot Witness; The Three Guardsmen; The Veteran; Waiting for the Verdict* (seven weeks). March 8: Italian opera (one week). March 15: in support of Edwin Booth (six weeks). April 26: stock: *The Naiad Queen* (three weeks). The season of forty-two weeks ended May 14.

1867–68, September 2, in support of Edmund Falconer and Kate Reignolds: *Innisfallen; or, The Man in the Pit* (two weeks). September 16: in support of Jean Davenport Lavender and James H. Taylor: *Elizabeth, Mary Stuart,* with *Fanchon, the Cricket* on Saturday nights (two weeks). September 30: in support of Mr. and Mrs. W. J. Florence: *Caste; Handy Andy; The Yankee Housekeeper; The Young Actress; The Irish Lion; Thrice Married; Return of the Volunteers; Shandy Maguire; Kathleen Mavourneen; Born to Good Luck; Mischievous Annie; Ireland as It Was; Lord Flanigan; The Irish Immigrant; A Lesson for Husbands* (four weeks). October 28: in support of the Hanlons, a vaudeville company (two weeks). November 11: in support of Italian opera (three weeks), one with Adelaide Ristori. December 2: in support of English opera company (four weeks). December 30: stock: *La*

Grand Duchesse (three weeks). January 20, 1868: in support of Robert Johnson and Nellie Garmon: *The Heart of a Great City* (one week). January 27: stock: *The Streets of New York* (two weeks). February 10: *The White Fawn,* (eleven weeks). April 28: benefits for the regular company (two weeks). May 12: in support of Adelaide Ristori (one week). May 19: in support of New Orleans French Opera Company (three weeks). The thirty-nine week season concluded June 6.

1868–69, August 27: stock: *A Flash of Lightning* (one week). September 3: stock: *Foul Play* (two weeks). September 14: in support of Lotta Crabtree: *Little Nell; The Pet of the Petticoats; Family Jars; Firefly* (three weeks). October 4: in support of Edwin Booth (four weeks). November 1: stock: *After Dark* (two weeks). November 15: stock: *The Lancashire Lass* (one week). November 22: in support of Mrs. Landers, with James H. Taylor and George Becks: *Elizabeth; Marie Antoinette; Mary Stuart; Macbeth* (two weeks). December 7: in support of Edwin Forrest in his last Boston engagement (three weeks). December 28: in support of James H. Hackett: *Merry Wives of Windsor; Rip Van Winkle; Monsieur Mallet; His Last Legs* (one week). January 5, 1869: in support of Italian opera (four weeks). February 2: in support of Kate Reignolds: *Peg Woffington; The Shadow of the Crime; Two Can Play at that Game; Richelieu at Sixteen,* with Elise Holt, and her own company of six in burlesques (one week). February 9: in support of the French Opera Bouffe Company of James Fisk, Jr.: *Barbe Bene, La Perichole* (three weeks). March 2: in support of English opera (two weeks). March 16: in support of Lizzie Inez St. John: in *Leah the Forsaken;* Lotta Crabtree: *Little Nell and the Marchioness; Firefly; Uncle Tom's Cabin; The Female Detective; An Object of Interest;* Mrs. D. B. Bowers; with J. C. McCollum: *Lady Audley's Secret; East Lynne; Snare; or, What Money Can't Do; Romeo and Juliet; Love's Masquerade; Lucrezia Borgia; The King's Rival; Leah the Forsaken;* Joseph Jefferson: *Rip Van Winkle* (twelve weeks).

1869–70, August 16: stock: *The Seven Dwarfs,* with the R. W. Butler Company and the Morlacchi Ballet Troupe (five weeks). September 13: in support of Mr. and Mrs. Barney Williams, Irish comedians (four weeks). October 20: stock: *Formosa* (ten days). October 31: in support of George L. Fox: *Hickory Dickory Dock* (one week). November 7: in support of Edwin Booth (ten performances). November 15: in support of Maggie Mitchell: *The Pearl of Savoy; Little Barefoot; Lorle; Margot; Katty O'Sheil; Fanchon;* on Saturday nights the stock presented *Moll Pitcher,* with Mrs. H. P. Grattan, as well as *The Octoroon* and *The Long Strike,* and on November 20, *Richard III* with Edwin Booth, a benefit for J. B. Booth, Jr. (four weeks). December 13: in support of Mrs. Scott-Siddons: *As You Like It; Honey Moon; King René's Daughter; Twelfth Night; Masks and Faces* (one week). December 20: in support of Lucille Western and James A. Herne: *East Lynne; The Child Stealer; Green Bushes; Oliver Twist,* with McKee Rankin (three weeks). January 10, 1870: Parepa Rose Grand English Opera Company (two weeks). February 1: in support of Mrs. Emma Waller: *Guy Mannering* (one week). February 7: in support of Frank S. Chanfrau: *Sam; Joe; Kit: The Arkansas Traveller* (two weeks). February 21: in support of Charles Fechter and Carlotta Leclercq: *Hamlet; Ruy Blas; The Lady of Lyons; Jessie Brown; The Long Strike.* February 22: stock in a matinee performance of *Uncle Tom's Cabin.* March 7: in support of Lester Wallack: *The Captain of the Watch; Woodcock's Little Game; Ours; Home; Ernestine; A Regular Fix* (one week). March 14: in support of Italian opera (three weeks). April 4: in support of Charles Fechter and Carlotta Leclercq: *The Duke's Motto; The Lady of Lyons: Hamlet; Ruy Blas; Don Caesar de Bazan* (three weeks). April 25: in support of Joseph Jefferson in *Rip Van Winkle* with Charles Fechter featured in occasional matinees (three weeks). May 9: in support of Lotta Crabtree: *Firefly; The Little Detective; Heartsease* (three weeks). May 30: in support of Catherine Reignolds and Neil Warner: *Armadale; Camille; Ingomar; Kathleen Mavourneen; The Angel of Midnight* (three weeks).

1870–71, September 12: in support of Lydia Thompson Troupe in burlesques (three weeks). October 2: in support of Mr. and Mrs. Barney Williams in their repertory of Irish comedies, *The Connie Soogah* added (three weeks). October 12: in support of Lotta Crabtree: *Little Nell; The Ticket-of-Leave Man; The Little Detective; Heartsease; Captain Charlotte; Andy Blake* (three weeks). November 14: in support of Mrs. D. P. Bowers: *Man and Wife; Lady Audley's Secret; Honey Moon; The Rose of Mayence; East Lynne* (two weeks). November 28: in support of Stuart Robson: *Barnaby Rudge*, with Mary Stuart (one week); then *Billiards; Everybody's Friend; Toodles; Paul Pry; The Spitfire; Gole Breezely; Robert Macaire; Camille; or, The Cracked Heart* (one week). December 12: in support of Hess's English Opera (two weeks). December 26: in support of Walter Montgomery (three weeks): *Antony and Cleopatra* (one week); then *King John; Louis XI; Othello; Hamlet; Macbeth; The Merchant of Venice; The Stranger; Honey Moon; Romeo and Juliet; Richard III; Not a Bad Judge; The Iron Chest* (two weeks). January 16, 1871: in support of German Opera (two and one-half weeks). February 1: in support of Neil Warner and Stuart Robson: *Rob Roy; Crummond Brig; The Lady of Lyons: The Long Strike; Richard III; Handy Andy; Paddy Mile's Boy* (four days). February 6: the season's spectacular, *The Twelve Temptations*, with Nully Pieris (six weeks). March 20: in support of Charles Fechter and Carlotta Leclercq: *The Lady of Lyons; Ruy Blas; Don Caesar de Bazan; No Thoroughfare; Hamlet* (three weeks). April 16: the company moved to Continental Theatre, Boston, one week, while the Boston Theatre presented a fair. April 24: in support of William Creswick, James Bennett, Walter Montgomery, and Charles Kemble Mason: *Othello; Julius Caesar; Romeo and Juliet; Macbeth* (one week). May 1: in support of Joseph Jefferson in *Rip Van Winkle* (three weeks). May 22: in support of French opera (two weeks). June 5: in support of Johnny Thompson in the "protean drama" *On Hand* (two weeks).

1871–72, August 1: Season began with a series of eccentric dramas: Gwaine Buckley in protean role in *On the Track* (two weeks); Joseph Proctor in *Nick of the Woods, Ambition, O'Neill* (one week); Little Nell, later Helene Dauvray, in *Katy-Did* (one week); D. L. Morris, German dialect comic, in *Dollars* (one week); and Joseph Murphy in protean role in *Help* (one week). September 11: in support of Effie Germon, Charles Wheatleigh, and Charles Fisher, from Wallach's Theatre Company: *Elfie: the Maid of Cherry Tree Inn* (two weeks). September 25: in support of Lydia Thompson Troupe (two weeks). October 9: in support of Italian opera (two weeks). October 23: in support of Edwin Booth (three weeks). November 13: in support of Lotta Crabtree (two weeks). November 27: stock: *The French Spy*, with Mlle. Morlacchi and the Mazilton Family of Grotesque Dancers (two weeks). December 11: stock: with Mlle. Morlacchi and the Mazilton Family of Grotesque Dancers and in *The Wizard Skiff, O'Flanagan and the Fairies* (one week). December 18: in support of E. A. Sothern, Amy Roselle, and Charles Wheatleigh:

Our American Cousin (three weeks). January 8, 1872: in support of English opera (three weeks). January 29: in support of Frank Mayo and Charles T. Parsloe: *The Streets of New York* (three weeks). February 19: in support of Italian opera (three weeks). March 4: stock: *The Black Crook* (five weeks). April 8: in support of Oliver Doud Byron: *Across the Continent* (two weeks). April 22: in support of Mrs. John Wood and the St. James Theatre Company of London in farces and burlesques (one week). April 29: in support of Maggie Mitchell: *Fanchon, Jane Eyre, The Pearl of Savoy* (two weeks). May 13: in support of Joseph Jefferson III in *Rip Van Winkle* (three weeks). June 3: Some members of the stock company supported the Vokes Family in a six-week summer engagement.

1872–73, August 19: in support of Lisa Weber burlesque troupe (two weeks). September 2: in support of Joseph Proctor: *The Red Pocketbook, Nick of the Woods,* and other plays (two weeks). September 23: in support of F. S. Chanfrau in the first of thirteen regular autumn visits in *Kit: The Arkansas Traveller* (three weeks). October 14: in support of Lester Wallack, with Effie Gannon: *Rosedale, Ours, John Garth* (three weeks). November 14: in support of Charlotte Cushman: *Macbeth; Guy Mannering; Henry VIII; Simpson and Company* (three weeks). November 25: stock: *The Cataract of the Ganges,* with *Mazeppa* added the final weeks (five weeks). December 30: stock: *The Streets of New York* (one week). January 7, 1873: in support of Italian opera (three weeks). January 27: in support of Oliver Doud Byron: *Across the Continent, Nick of the Woods* added February 1 (one week). February 3: in support of Adelaide Neilson (her Boston debut), with Joseph Wheelock and H. S. Murdock: *Romeo and Juliet, As You Like It* (two weeks). February 17: in support of Charles R. Thorne, Jr.: *The Three Guardsmen; Amos Clarke; The Octoroon; Foul Play* (two weeks). March 2: in support of William F. "Buffalo Bill" Cody, Texas Jack (J. B. Omohundro), Ned Buntline (E.Z.C. Judson), and Mlle. Morlacchi's grotesque dancers in *The Scouts of the Plains* (one week). March 10: in support of Maggie Mitchell: *Jane Eyre; Fanchon; The Pearl of Savoy; Little Barefoot* (three weeks). March 31: in support of Edwin Adams: *Enoch Arden; The Marble Heart; Wild Oats; Black Eyed Susan; The Drunkard* (two weeks). April 14: in support of Mrs. F. S. Chanfrau: stock: *Two Wives, Christie Johnstone, Dora* (two weeks). April 28: stock: *Under the Gaslight,* with the Carroll Family of Dancers (one week). May 5: stock: *Jack Harkaway* (one week). May 12: in support of Mr. and Mrs. J. W. Albaugh in *Poverty Flat,* with benefits interspersed (one week). May 19: in support of the Vokes Family: *The Belles of the Kitchen, Fun in a Fog, The Wrong Man in the Right Place* (five weeks). June 23: a visiting combination company displaces the stock for two weeks. June 30: stock in benefit performance of *A Quiet Family.* July 5: regular season ends, but a few of the stock stay on for two weeks to light business.

1873–74, September 1: stock in *Polaris; or, The Northern Lights* (two weeks). September 15: in support of F. S. Chanfrau in *Kit: The Arkansas Traveller* (three weeks). October 6: in support of Edwin Booth (three weeks). October 27: in support of Italian opera (two weeks). November 10: in support of Mr. and Mrs. W. J. Florence: *Inshavogue; The Yankee Housekeeper; The Ticket-of-Leave Man; The Irish Lion; Thrice Married; Return of the Volunteers; Eileen Oge; Thrice Married* (two weeks). November 24: in support of Tommaso Salvini and Italian company (one week). December 1: in support of Charles Fechter: *Hamlet; Don Caesar de Bazan; Ruy Blas; The Lady of Lyons* (one week). December 8: in support of

Charlotte Cushman: *Guy Mannering, Henry VIII* (one week, her last in Boston). December 15: stock: *The Naiad Queen*, with the Kirafly Family, specialities, caricaturists, trapeze artists, a boy's choir, and a child violinist (five weeks). January 19, 1874: in support of Frank Mayo in *Davy Crockett* (two weeks). February 3: in support of Italian opera (two weeks). February 16: in support of E. A. Sothern in *Our American Cousin* (one week) and *Brother Sam; Lord Dundreary Married and Settled; David Garrick; A Regular Fix;* with Lytton Sothern, Vining Bowers, and Minnie Walton (one week). March 9: in support of Kellogg English Opera (two weeks). March 23: in support of Maggie Mitchell: *Jane Eyre; The Pearl of Savoy; Fanchon; Little Barefoot* (three weeks). April 13: in support of Marie Aimée and the French Opera Company (one week). April 20: in support of Carlotta Leclercq: *The New Magdalen; Fate; or, Women's Trials;* and *East Lynne* (two weeks). May 4: in support of Tommaso Salvini, split week with Carlotta Leclerq (one week). May 13: in support of H. S. Murdock in *The Lottery of Life* (four days). May 18: stock in benefits (one week). May 25: in suport of Lawrence Barrett: *Richelieu, Hamlet, Julius Caesar* (one week). June 1: in support of Alice (Mrs. James A.) Oates and her Comic Opera Company (two weeks). June 15: in support of Buffalo Bill, Texas Jack, and Mlle. Moracchi in *The Scouts of the Plains* [one week). June 22: in support of Schumann's Transatlantic Novelty Company (vaudeville) (three weeks). July 20: closed one week. July 27: in support of Josh Hart's Theatre Comique Company (five weeks). August 22: Closed.

1874–75, August 24: in support of Frank Mayo in *Davy Crockett, Streets of New York* (three weeks). September 14: in support of F. S. Chanfrau in *Kit: The Arkansas Traveller* (three weeks). October 5: in suport of Carlotta Leclerq: *The New Magdalen, East Lynne* (one week). October 12: stock in *Belle Lamar* (three weeks). November 2: in support of Mr. and Mrs. Barney Williams: *The Connie Soogah, The Fairy Circle* (two weeks). November 16: in support of Carlotta Leclercq: *The New Magdalen; Masks and Faces; East Lynne; The Hunchback*. November 23: stock in *Lost at Sea* (one week). November 30: in support of Annie Oates' Comic Opera Company (two weeks). December 14: stock in spectacle *Azael, the Prodigal* (two weeks). December 28: in support of Lotta Crabtree: *Zip, Musette* (three weeks). January 18, 1875: in support of Maggie Mitchell: *Fanchon; The Pearl of Savoy; Lorle; Little Barefoot* (three weeks). January 23: benefit performance of *Under the Gaslight*, with Ray Trafford played by Maurice Barrymore, his first appearance in the United States. February 8: in support of Lester Wallack in *Rosedale, Ours* (two weeks). February 22: in support of Mr. and Mrs. W. J. Florence: *The Colleen Bawn, The Yankee Housekeeper* (one week). March 1: in support of Lawrence Barrett: *Richelieu; Hamlet; The Merchant of Venice; The Lady of Lyons; Julius Caesar; The Man o' Arlie* (two weeks). March 15: in support of Edwin Booth (three weeks). April 5: in support of Maurice Barrymore and Dion Boucicault in *The Shaughraun* (four weeks). May 3: in support of Joseph Jefferson III in *Rip Van Winkle* (two weeks). May 17: in support of Frank Mayo in *Davy Crockett, The Streets of New York* (two weeks). June 1: stock company benefits (one week). June 7: minstrels (one week). June 14: *La Bayadère*, with dancers from the Boston Theatre Company (three weeks). July 5: minstrels (two weeks).

1875–76, August 2: in support of Katie Putnam: *The Old Curiosity Shop; The Child of the Regiment; The Little Rebel; Blade O' Grass; The Little Detective* (two weeks). August 16: minstrels (one week). August 23: closed (one week). August

30: in support of Frank S. Chanfrau in *Kit: The Arkansas Traveller* (three weeks). September 20: in support of Lotta Crabtree: *Zip; Little Nell; Musette* (three weeks). October 9: in support of Barry Sullivan: *Richelieu; Richard III; Hamlet; The Lady of Lyons; The Gamester; Macbeth; The Stranger* (two weeks). October 23: in support of English opera (two weeks). November 8: in support of Geroge Belmore in *The Flying Scud* (one week). November 15: in support of George Fawcett Rowe in *Little Emily* (one week). November 22: in support of George Rignold in *Henry V* (three weeks). December 12: in support of Joseph F. Wheelock and Kate Claxton in *The Two Orphans* (eleven weeks). January 31, 1876: in support of John Mc-Cullough: *The Gladiator* (company produces *The Cricket on the Hearth* and *Sarah's Young Man*, when star is ill); *Virginius; Richelieu; Jack Cade; Othello; The Lady of Lyons; Richard III; Metamora* (two weeks). February 14: in support of E. A. Sothern: *Our American Cousin; David Garrick; Lord Dundreary Married and Settled* (two weeks). February 28: in support of Italian Opera (two weeks). March 13: in support of Joseph Proctor: *The Colleen Bawn, Richard III* in German, and *Nick of the Woods* (one week). March 20: in support of Opera (two weeks). April 3: in support of Mr. and Mrs. G. C. Howard and George Kunkel in *Uncle Tom's Cabin* (one week). April 10: in support of E. L. Davenport, Lawrence Barrett, Frank C. Bangs, and Milnes Levick in *Julius Caesar* (one week). April 17: in support of Mr. and Mrs. W. J. Florence in *The Mighty Dollar* (two weeks). May 1: in support of Italian opera (one week). May 8: in support of Mrs. D. P. Bowers and J. C. McCullom: *Elizabeth; Mary Stuart; Lady Audley's Secret; The Hunchback* (two weeks). May 22: two weeks, unknown. June 5: in support of the Vokes Family: *The Belles of the Kitchen; A Bunch of Berries; Fun in a Fog; Nan: The Good-for-Nothing;* and *The Wrong Man in the Right Place* (two weeks). June 19: in support of French opera (one week).

1876–77, August 28: in support of Frank Mayo in *The Streets of New York* (one week). September 4: in support of F. S. Chanfrau in *Kit: The Arkansas Traveller* (two weeks). September 18: in support of Kate Claxton and Marie Wilkins in *The Two Orphans* (two weeks). October 1: in support of Dion Boucicault in *The Shaughraun* (four weeks). October 30: in support of Madame Janauschek: *Bleak House, Macbeth, Mary Stuart* (two weeks). November 13: in support of John T. Raymond in *Colonel Sellers* (one week). November 20: in support of Kate Claxton in *Conscience* (one week), *The Two Orphans* (one week). December 4: in support of Louise Pomeroy in *Romeo and Juliet; As You Like It; The Lady of Lyons; Macbeth,* and the stock in *The Chimney Corner* Saturday evening. December 11: in support of F. C. Bangs in *Sardanapalus* (three weeks). January 1, 1877: in support of Mrs. Lander and Theodore Hamilton in *The Scarlet Letter* (three weeks). January 22: in support of Joseph Murphy in *Kerry Gow* (two weeks). February 15: in support of John E. Owen: *The Victim; Self; The Happiest Day of My Life; Solon Shingle* (two weeks). February 19: in support of Maggie Mitchell: *Mignon; Jane Eyre; The Pearl of Savoy; Little Barefoot* (three weeks). March 12: in support of Charles Fechter: *Monte Cristo, Hamlet, Ruy Blas, Don Caesar de Bazan* (two weeks). March 26: in support of opera, one week, except March 31, George Riddle in *The Romance of a Poor Young Man.* April 2: in support of Madame Janauschek: *Medea; Bleak House; Deborah; Mary Stuart; Macbeth; Brunhilde* (two weeks). April 16: in support of opera (one week). April 23: in support of Charles Fechter with Lizzie Price: *The Corsican Brothers; Hamlet; The Lady of Lyons* (two weeks). May 7: in support of Clara Morris: *Camille, Miss Multon* (two weeks). May 21: Union Square Theatre Stock Company in *The Danicheffs* (two weeks). June 4: in support of opera (two weeks). June 10: benefits (one week).

1877–78, September 17: in support of F. S. Chanfrau in *Kit: The Arkansas Traveller* (two weeks). October 1: in support of Lydia Thompson and Co. (two weeks). October 15: in support of Mary Anderson: *Evadne; Guy Mannering; Ion; Romeo and Juliet; Ingomar, the Barbarian* (one week). October 22: in support of opera, interspersed with E. A. Sothern and Company in benefit and *The Danites*, with McKee Rankin, Kittie Blanchard, and Louis Aldrich (two weeks). November 5: in support of Maggie Mitchell: *Mignon; Fanchon; The Pearl of Savoy* (two weeks). November 19: in support of John T. Raymond in *Colonel Sellers* (two weeks). November 26: in support of Gertrude Kellogg in *The Two Orphans* (two weeks). December 10: in support of Louis James and Marie Wainwright in *The Exiles* (ten weeks). February 11, 1878: in support of John C. McCullough: *Coriolanus* (two weeks) and *Richard III; Virginius; Othello; King Lear; The Gladiators; Jack Cade* (one week). March 4: in support of Edwin Booth with Joseph Wheelock and J. Clinton Hall (three weeks). March 21: in support of McKee Rankin and Kittie Blanchard, Louis Aldrich, and Charles T. Parsloe in *The Danites* (two weeks). April 4: in support of opera (two weeks). April 22: in support of Joseph Jefferson III in *Rip Van Winkle* (two weeks). May 6: in support of J. C. Williamson, Maggie Moore and members of Palmer's Company: *Struck Oil, The Chinese Question* (one week). May 13: in support of Colville Folly Company (five weeks). June 17: closed. After May 6: stock on tour.

1878–79, August 26: stock in *The Two Mothers* (three weeks). September 16: in support of F. S. Chanfrau in *Kit: The Arkansas Traveller* (two weeks). September 30: in support of Mary Anderson: *The Hunchback; Romeo and Juliet; Macbeth; Ingomar, the Barbarian* (two weeks). October 14: stock in *Cosette [Les Miserables]* (five weeks). November 18: stock in *The Exiles* (four weeks). December 16: stock in *The Two Mothers* (one week). December 23: stock in *Uncle Tom's Cabin* (one week). December 30: in support of Italian Opera (two weeks). January 13, 1879: in support of John C. McCullough: *Pizarro; Brutus; Virginius; Richard III; Henry VIII; Julius Caesar; Macbeth; Othello; Jack Cade* (three weeks). February 3: in support of Italian Opera (two weeks). February 17: in support of Dion Boucicault in *The Shaughraun* (two weeks). March 4: in support of John Brougham in *Arrah-na-Pogue* (one week). March 11: stock in *André Fortier: The Hero of the Calaveras* (four weeks). April 7: in support of Genevieve Ward: *Jane Shore; Henry VIII; The Merchant of Venice; Macbeth* (one week). April 14: *H.M.S. Pinafore*, with only a few of the stock in the cast, the regular company being on tour to Portland, Maine, in *The Merchant of Venice; Katherine and Petruchio; The Hunchback; Cosette* (seven weeks). June 2: in support of *Fatinitza*, with *Pinafore* Company plus Adelaide Phillips, W. H. Fessenden, Alice Carle, Rachel Noah, George Parks, and John Craven (two weeks). June 16: minstrels (one week).

1879–80, September 1: in support of Dickie Lingard and W. H. Lytell in *Boulogne* (two weeks). September 15: in support of F. S. Chanfrau in *Kit: The Arkansas Traveller* (two weeks). September 29: Boston Theatre Company on tour in *Boulogne* (eight weeks). November 24: in support of L. R. Shewall, Florence Chase, and Ada Gilman in *Drink* (four weeks). December 22: stock: *Dot; Katherine and Petruchio; Richard III* (one week). December 29: Boston Theatre Company on tour in *The Voyagers of the Southern Seas* (eight weeks). February 23, 1880: Boston

Theatre Company on tour (six weeks). April 5: in support of John A. Stevens in *The Unknown* (one week). April 12: in support of Joseph Jefferson III and Henrietta Vaders in *Rip Van Winkle* (two weeks). April 26: Boston Theatre Company on tour (four weeks). May 15: in support of Thomas W. Keene and Mary Anderson in *Love* (one week). May 24: Boston Theatre Company on tour in New England (five weeks).

1880–81, August 23: James A. Herne, Frank E. Aiken, W. H. Compton, and Genevieve Rogers in *Hearts of Oak* (three weeks). September 13: F. S. Chanfrau in *Kit: The Arkansas Traveller* (two weeks). September 27: Boston Theatre Company in rehearsal or on tour (four weeks). October 26: in support of Frank Lawlor and an imported ballet in *The Voyagers of the Southern Seas* (ten weeks). December 27: Boston Theatre Company on tour (thirteen weeks). March 28: in support of Sarah Bernhardt (one week). April 4: in support of Frank Mayo in *The Streets of New York* (one week). April 11: Boston Theatre Company on tour (eight weeks).

1881–82, September 5: in support of F. S. Chanfrau in *Kit: The Arkansas Traveller* (two weeks). September 19: in support of Annie Pixley in *M'liss* (two weeks). October 5: stock in *Michael Strogoff* (eleven weeks). December 26: Boston Theatre Company on tour (twelve weeks). March 21, 1892: stock in *The World* (eleven weeks).

1882–83, August 14: stock in *A Free Pardon* (three weeks). September 4: in support of F. S. Chanfrau in *Kit: The Arkansas Traveller* (two weeks). September 19: stock in *Youth* (ten weeks). November 27: stock in *The White Slave* (four weeks). December 25: stock in *The World* (three weeks). January 15, 1883: Boston Theatre Company on tour (nine weeks). March 20: stock in *Fifty Thousand Pounds: A Story of Pluck* (five weeks). April 23: stock in *Love and Money* (two weeks). May 7: Boston Theatre Company on tour (four weeks).

1883–84, September 3: in support of F. S. Chanfrau in *Kit: The Arkansas Traveller* (two weeks). September 19: Stock in *Jalma* (twelve weeks). December 10: Boston Theatre Company on tour (eight weeks). February 4, 1884: in support of Margaret Mather, Alexander Salvini, and Milnes Levick: *Romeo and Juliet; Leah the Forsaken; As You Like It; The Lady of Lyons; The Hunchback* (three weeks). February 25: Boston Theatre Company in rehearsal or on tour (three weeks). March 17: stock in *The Silver King* (six weeks). April 28: in support of Frank Mayo in *The Streets of New York* (one week). May 5: stock in *Jalma* (three weeks).

1884–85, September 1: in support of F. S. Chanfrau in *Kit: The Arkansas Traveller* (two weeks). September 16: stock in *Zanita* (twelve weeks). December 8: Boston Theatre Company on tour (six weeks). January 19, 1885: stock in *The Shadows of a Great City* (one week). January 26: Boston Theatre Company on tour (sixteen weeks).

BIBLIOGRAPHY

Published Sources: Eugene Tompkins, *The History of the Boston Theatre* (Boston and New York: Houghton Mifflin Company, 1908); *Boston Evening Transcript*, September 9, 1854, p. 1; John Perry, "The Boston Theatre," *Players* 43 (August–September 1968): 184–87.

Weldon B. Durham

BOWERY SLAUGHTERHOUSE. See BOWERY THEATRE COMPANY.

BOWERY THEATRE COMPANY. The Bowery Theatre was built in 1826 by the New York Association—comprised of Henry Astor, Rodman Bowne, George W. Brown, Samuel Gouverneur, Daniel P. Ingraham, Matthew Reed, Thomas S. Smith, and Prosper M. Wetmore—and remained controlled by these men until 1836. The land upon which the theatre was built, just south of Canal Street, fronting on Bowery and back to Elizabeth Street, originally held an abattoir and stockyards, a likely source for the pun associating blood and thunder melodrama with the theatre under the sobriquet "the Bowery Slaughterhouse."

In its first decade, the Bowery was managed by Charles Antonio Gilfert (1784–1829) and then by Thomas Sowerby Hamblin (1800–1853). The theatre that opened October 23, 1826, seated 3,000 and had a stage almost seventy-five feet wide, with most of the basement leased for refreshments during performances. This theatre burned May 26, 1828, part of a conflagration that raged through the neighborhood. The second Bowery, opened on August 20, 1828, was said to have the largest stage in the United States at that time (eighty-four feet deep, with at least five grooves, and seventy-five feet wide, with wings that could be moved eight feet to widen the proscenium even further). The boxes were arranged in a horseshoe, flattened at the center. The theatre was lit throughout, as its predecessor had been, by gas. A print of the exterior of the 1828 Bowery Theatre, which burned September 22, 1836, can be found in the Harvard Theatre Collection and in George Odell's *Annals of the New York Stage* (3:414). The interior is described in the August 23, 1828, *Mirror*.

Gilfert managed the Bowery until May 2, 1829, when, since he was several months in arrears on his rent, the owners seized the theatre's scenery, wardrobe, and other property but allowed him to reopen June 4. The lease passed in July to James H. Hackett at a rent of $7,000 a year. Gilfert died July 30, at the age of 42. Under his management, the Bowery repertoire consisted of established English comedies (36 percent of performances, according to Theodore Shank), melodramas (26 percent), and tragedies (23 percent), rarely played two nights consecutively. Gilfert established an exchange of plays and stars with F. C. Wemyss of the (Second) Walnut Street Theatre Company* in Philadelphia, and his lucrative renting out of Edwin Forrest made Gilfert solvent, if temporarily, within his first year's operation. Other stars included Gilfert's wife, Miss Holman (Gilfert himself was a businessman, not an actor); Thomas Hamblin; T. A. Cooper; J. B. Booth; William A. Conway; Mrs. Edward Knight; Mary Ann Rock; and Mr. and Mrs. John Sloman. In addition to having the legitimate repertoire, Gilfert rented horses for equestrian melodramas, produced opera and ballet, and presented spectacular melodramas, beginning in 1827 and 1828, that ran twenty-four (William Dunlap's *Flying Dutchman*) and twenty-eight times (*Peter Wilkins; or, The Flying Indians*) before the seasons ended. According to Joe Cowell, Gilfert hired a man to arrange playbills and ads and to write letters to or articles for newspapers praising the theatre; indeed, Odell said Gilfert introduced press agentry in the United States. Since the Bowery at this time ran six nights a week for a season of ten months, longer than everywhere else, publicity kept the public abreast of the continuously changing bills. For their efforts with a repertoire embracing scores of plays a season, company actors were paid $10–$40 a week and subject to a list of forty-one regulations, still in effect years after Gilfert's death.

Hackett's purpose in assuming the Bowery lease was to restrict legitimate drama to the Park. The Bowery was open only twenty-six nights from September 1, 1829, to August 2, 1830, with nondramatic entertainment, at the end of which period the lease was awarded to Thomas Hamblin. Hamblin continued Gilfert's practice of exchanging plays and stars with F. C. Wemyss and of publicizing the theatre, identifying it from 1831 as the American Theatre, Bowery. His efforts on behalf of the "the nursery of native talent" and against the Park's foreign stars and plays did much to advance American acting and drama (house playwrights during this period included Louisa Medina, Charles W. Taylor, and James B. Phillips) and won Hamblin a loyal Bowery audience. His patrons were scorned by the bon ton as plebian in taste and manners, an association that continued in some critical quarters long after the Park burned in 1848 and Andy Jackson had died.

The decade of the thirties was Hamblin's most successful, artistically and financially. He started the practice of long continuous runs of a week's to a month's duration (unprecedented in his predecessors or competitors) for successful spectacular melodramas, including, between 1830 and 1836, *Miantonimah; or, The Wept of Wish-Ton-Wish; The Elephant of Siam and the Fire Fiend* (with real elephant); *The Water Witch; Cagliostro; or, The Mysterious Confederates; The Ice Witch; or, The Frozen Hand; The French Spy; The Tower of Nesle; The Warden of Galway; Mazeppa; Jonathan Bradford; or, The Murder at the Road-Side Inn; Wacousta; or, The Curse; The Maid of the Mist; or, Anne of Geierstein; The Six Degrees of Crime; The Demon Duke; or, The Cloisters of St. Rosalie; Tom Cringle's Log; The Last Days of Pompeii; Norman Leslie; The Jewess; Rienzi;* and *Santa Ana; or, The Liberation of Texas*. Many of these plays—melodramas constituted 84 percent of Bowery performances by 1836, according to Shank—became and remained house favorites and successful vehicles for visiting stars such as Madame Celeste and Edwin Forrest. When company plays did not succeed, stars appeared in the standard repertoire of classics and popular pieces familiar to students of the careers of T. A. Cooper, J. B. Booth, James Hackett, Madame Feron, T. D. Rice, Dan Marble, and Charlotte Cushman. Although new plays contributed greatly to Hamblin's success over the Park, he was from time to time obliged to resort to horse or dog dramas, elephants, slack-wire performers, or other novelties, a practice that increased (as did the use of stars) in the 1840s, much to the detriment of the Bowery and Hamblin's reputations.

In May of 1834 Hamblin bought six shares of New York Association stock from William B. Astor—a total of sixty had been issued—for $3,900, the manager's first installment toward buying the theatre. In October 1835 Hamblin bought forty shares for $26,000 and was thus the major owner of the building and its contents when the Bowery was destroyed by fire a second time in September 1836. T. Allston Brown put Hamblin's losses at $30,000 for the building and $70,000 in scenery, music, props, and wardrobe. Undaunted, Hamblin bought the remaining fourteen shares, and the New York Association was dissolved (Astor retained a mortgage on the property for $50,000, as surviving records reveal). Hamblin liquidated his debts and for the next three years functioned primarily as a touring star and advisor to W. E. Dinneford and Thomas Flynn, who rented the site.

Dinneford put together a stock company and raised a third Bowery Theatre, which opened January 2, 1837. His acting company came largely from the Franklin, which Dinneford also managed, and the *Knickerbocker* called his theatre the largest in the city and unsurpassed in scenery, machinery, and decoration. Dinneford continued the Bowery's tradition of long-running, spectacular melodrama with *Hernani* and a full equestrian *Mazeppa*. He revived the house successes and featured favorite Bowery stars but could not meet his debts. As a result, the Bowery opened August 14, 1837, "under the supervision of [Dinneford's] assignees for the benefit of the creditors," although he continued to manage it until January of 1838 (Odell, 4:230). At that point, Flynn assumed the management, continuing a rapid change of plays and players in house pieces until February 18, 1838, when the theatre again burned to the ground.

The fourth Bowery Theatre did not open until the following year. Hamblin was producing at Wallack's National in March of 1838 and was thereafter embroiled throughout much of the year in personal and professional scandals of the sort that delighted his enemies. On May 6, 1839, Hamblin was once again in charge of the Bowery, where he was essentially to remain until his death. The new theatre had a splendid edifice by Calvin Pollard of fluted columns and friezes, with the interior of the house divided into four tiers containing twelve private boxes and a gallery, the tiers capable of seating 3,000. It was fifty-two feet from the boxes to the stage, and the 800-seat pit was thirty-nine feet wide. The stage of this Bowery was eighty-five feet deep and seventy-one feet wide, with a thirty-two-foot proscenium opening that could be extended. The interior decorations included murals of the Muses, the arms of the states, and portraits of American heroes and statesmen, with medallion portraits of Washington and Franklin above the proscenium flanking a Phoenix rising from the flames (*Ladies Companion*, May 1839). The building was home to the Bowery Company until this theatre also burned April 25, 1845.

Theatrical conditions in New York had altered considerably during the three years Hamblin was away from active management. There were many more theatres to appeal to his audience, and the National was well on its way to becoming the premier house for the legitimate drama, replacing the Park and dwarfing Hamblin's attempts at the classical repertory. The years from 1839 to 1845 saw an increase in the blood and thunder melodramas—an equestrian *Rookwood; or, Dick Turpin, the Highwayman; The Lion King* (with a real lion); a spectacular *Giafar al Barmeki; or, The Fire Worshippers; The Surgeon of Paris; The Carpenter of Rouen; Putnam; or, The Iron Son of '76; The Mysteries of Paris; The Butchers of Ghent*— and an endless repetition of the successes of the early 1830s. All attempts to produce lavishly new Bowery melodramas (house playwrights included J. S. Jones and C. H. Saunders) seemed doomed to failure, although Hamblin continued his long-run policy when he could. While Forrest, Celeste, Marble, Rice, Joseph Proctor, Booth, Mrs. Shaw, and other favored stars continued to appear, so did giants and dwarfs, animal imitators, circus, aqua dramas, boxing matches, and variety stars. Hamblin employed his company actors on short contracts with a resulting lack of continuity throughout a season and from season to season.

Hamblin's new Bowery Theatre—the fifth—opened August 4, 1845, some three months after its predecessor was destroyed by fire. This theatre, which sat 4,000 when built and had a stage 126 feet deep, "with corresponding width," was still standing in 1929, when it was taken for a final time by fire. The building proved sturdier than Hamblin, who, until his death January 8, 1853, suffered a variety of ills both physical and financial. The Bowery continued to offer operas, ballets, and house melodramas, including equestrian and canine versions, and to introduce topical spectacles such as *Hoboken, Lola Montez in Bavaria*, and *The Siege of Monterey*, but successes equal to those in the second Bowery eluded Hamblin. From 1845 to 1848 A. W. Jackson managed the theatre, and his account books (Harvard Theatre Collection) indicate large outlays for replacement of costumes, dry goods, and properties, with salaries not as high as those paid by the Park in 1799 (Odell 5:192) and amounting to $762.82 a week. Jackson gave $104,432.50 and $94,543.22 as the receipts for a season of some 192 plays and farces, with $741.87 earned on a season's best night.

Hamblin appeared rarely in the bills from 1845 to 1853. During the 1847–48 season, he bought out Edmund Simpson's interest in the Park, renovated that house, and ran a dual company, with himself in Shakespearean and other classic roles. The Park theatre burned December 16, 1848, and Hamblin thereafter restricted his Bowery playing to benefits and infrequent star engagements with his wife (Mrs. Shaw), making one of a trio of Macbeth's with Forrest and William Charles Macready during the 1849 engagements that resulted in the Astor Place Riot. The season of 1849–50 saw a strong Bowery company, including J. W. Wallack and his wife, Lester Wallack, and John Gilbert, few stars, and a return to long-running spectacular melodramas, for example, *Mose and Jack, The Three Guardsmen, The Four Musketeers,* and other costume pieces. The respite was short, however, and star tours or the company in a continuously changing sequence of old house favorites once again typified the Bowery bill in the early 1850s, with occasional successes, such as *The Corsican Brothers,* and popular company leads in Edward Eddy and Matilda Heron to hearken back to earlier days. Although Hamblin's will left his family well provided for, Brown asserted that Bowery earnings from 1849 to 1852 often showed expenses in excess of receipts.

From 1853 until 1867 the Bowery remained the property of Hamblin's heirs and was run for them by a variety of managers, most notable of whom was George L. Fox. Stars appearing included F. S. Chanfrau, Fanny Herring, Proctor, Adah Isaacs Menken, Mr. and Mrs. Davenport, Mrs. Farren, William Wheatley, and Helen and Lucille Western. The company continued to appear in the Bowery standards, augmented with productions new to the house, such as *Uncle Tom's Cabin; Katy, the Hot Corn Girl; Seven Temptations; or, Virtue and Vice Contrasted; The Enchanted Temple; or, The Spectre of the Nile; The Invasion of Britain; or, The Sea King's Vow; Pirates of the Mississippi; Life in New York; Tippoo Saib; or, The Storming of Seringapatum;* and plays by the house dramatist, for example, John F. Pool, author of *War Eagle* and *Hubert, the Foundling.* John Brougham's company (1856–57) and George Wood's company (1860) were of exceptional merit, but neither thrived at the Bowery, which soon reverted to the circus, Saturday matinees, and house favorites. Beginning in 1859, George L. Fox and James Lingard (who managed the Bowery, 1858–59) opened the New Bowery Theatre between Canal and Hester streets with many Bowery company members. They prospered until 1861, when Fox broke with his partner and resumed the lease of the original theatre (the New Bowery burned in 1866 and was never rebuilt as a theatre).

Hamblin's Bowery was badly run down in the three years between Fox's going and returning by circus and by a military occupation during which much of the theatre's property was stolen or destroyed. Fox renovated it completely and opened with a company of Boweryites, a series of spectacles, and his popular pantomimes. A night's bill at this time still ran to three and four pieces, although Wallack Theatre Company* and Laura Keene's Theater* did only a main bill. In the tradition of energetic Bowery managers (Eddy played 203 nights the year he managed), Fox appeared 150 times in farces, comedies, pantomimes, and extravaganzas; stars were seldom or never employed during the season. The successes of the 1830s and the 1840s—*The Last Days of Pompeii, The Wept of Wish-Ton-Wish, The Carpenter of Rouen,* and so on—continued to reappear throughout Fox's management, a policy continued when W. B. Freligh replaced Fox in May 1867. In the summer of that year, the Bowery was offered at auction to satisfy a mortgage and settle the claims of Hamblin's heirs. According to Brown (1:142), the building and it contents sold for $100,700.

Freligh managed the Bowery for its new owners until 1875. His policy was to play the company in house pieces, augmented by clog dancing, performing dogs, acrobats, and other variety acts, with the introduction of some new sensation dramas, but stars were soon very much in evidence. Despite remodeling and increased prices, the Bowery had sunk to the status of a minor theatre by decade's end, ninth in yearly gross ($107,263) among the seventeen theatres in a *Times* survey. Edward Eddy, Matilda Heron, Kate Fisher, the Ravels, the Blanchards and their dogs, and other Bowery favorites continued star visits, and faithful fans could still witness in 1875 the melodramatic successes of the 1830s and the comedies of Fox's day.

From 1875 to 1879 the Bowery entered a second period of impermanence, similar to that following Hamblin's death. The fare remained as usual, with some newer entertainments, appearances by Ada Rehan and Oliver Doud Byron (1875–76), star combos (beginning 1876–77), Buffalo Bill (in a piece with Hamblin's daughter Constance, 1877), and others. Double and triple bills were offered in which star combos would be preceeded or followed by company pieces or variety acts. In September 1879 the building became the Thalia Theatre, home to plays and operettas in German, thus concluding fifty-three years as the Bowery. Yet the theatre continued to make history, for it was here that the Meininger Company played on November 17, 1891, and here that the Thalia Theatre Company* presented Gerhardt Hauptmann's *vor Sonnenaufgang* (January 6, 1892). In August 1893 the Thalia became a Yiddish theatre, which it remained for many years, eventually succumbing to fire in 1929.

PERSONNEL

Gilfert's Management, 1826–29: George H. Barrett and Charles Young, stage managers; William Taylor, orchestra leader; Henry Liebenau, Mr. Boudet, and Mr. Ferri, scene painters.

Acting Company: George H. Barrett, comic lead; Edwin Forrest, romantic lead; Thomas Faulkner, old man; George Hyatt, James Roberts, John Augustus Stone, comedians; John Duff, heavy man; J. Barry, Mr. Beckwell, John Bernard, Charles Durang, Mr. Essender, Mr. Hamilton, Edward Lamb, Mr. Laws, Cornelius A. Logan, Mr. Read, Mr. C. Scott, Charles Young, walking gents and utility; Mrs. John Duff, lead; Mrs. George Barrett, lighter leads; Agnes Holman Gilfert, romantic leads; Mrs. H. A. Williams, comedienne; Mrs. Brazier, Mrs. Hughes, Mrs. Roberts, Mrs. Young, walking ladies and utility. Also playing part of the year: Thomas Archer, William Chapman, Thomas Comer, Vincent DeCamp, Jane and John Fisher, Amelia George, Mrs. Gill, George Holland, George Vernon, Henry Wallack, Alexander Wilson.

Hamblin's Management, 1830–53: William R. Blake, George Farren, Thomas Flynn, A. W. Jackson, stage managers; St. Luke, Woolf, orchestra leaders; Peter Grain, George Heister, Mr. Lehr, Henry Liebenau, Duke White, scene painters;

John Anderson, R. Williams, prompters; Mr. Burton, Thomas Danes, machinists; Nehemiah Lewis, R. Williams, property maker; George G. Stevenson, I. P. Waldron, H. E. Willard, treasurers; Mr. Deverna, carpenter; Mrs. Downie, wardrobe mistress.

Acting Company, 1830–36: Augustus Addams, James Anderson, Mr. and Mrs. George Barrett, Eliza Bell, Master Blanchard, Josephine Clifton, E. S. Conner, Barkham Cony, Ferdinand Durang, George P. Farren, Mrs. Farren, Alexina Fisher, Mrs. and Mrs. Flynn, Mr. and Mrs. George Gale, William F. Gates, G. C. Germon, Thomas Hadaway, Elizabeth Blanchard Hamblin, Mr. and Mrs. Augustus Herbert, George Holland, David Ingersoll, Louisa Johnson, George Jones, Sophia Judah, Thomas Kilner, Mrs. Kinlock, Louisa Lane, Mr. and Mrs. Charles McClure, D. D. McKinney, Mrs. William Pelby, Mr. and Mrs. Charles Percival, Alexander Pickering, John R. Scott, William Sefton, Frank Sowerby, Mr. and Mrs. George Stevenson, Mr. and Mrs. J. A. Stone, Charles R. Thorne, Henry Tuthill, Naomi Vincent, Henry Wallack, Ann Waring, William Wheatley, John Woodhull, Mrs. Wray.

1845–52: James Anderson, E. and M. Barber, E. and M. Bell, Mrs. Broadley, George Brookes, C. W. Clarke, E. L. Davenport, Edward Eddy, Miss Flynn, Mr. Gouldson, Thomas Hadaway, Harry Henkens (or Henkins), Mrs. Henry, Mrs. Thomas Hilson, Mrs. Isherwood, Mr. Johnson, Miss Johnson, Mrs. Jones, Mr. Lewis, Mrs. Madison, Mr. McKeon, Mr. Milner, Mrs. Phillips, Miss Plumer, Mr. Rose, Mrs. Sargeant, J. R. Scott, Mrs. Stickney, Mr. Sutherland, Mrs. Sutherland, W. Taylor, William A. Vache, Mr. and Mrs. Yeomans.

Varied Managements, 1853–67: Lessees, F. C. Wemyss (1853–?), John Brougham (1856–57), T. S. Murphy (1857), Edward Eddy (1857–58), George L. Fox and James W. Lingard (1858–59), J. H. Allen and G. C. Boniface (1859–60), Robert Johnson and W. E. Briggs (1860), George Wood (1860), Mr. Spaulding and Mr. Rogers (1860–61), George L. Fox (1861–67); stage managers, Robert Johnston (for Murphy), James Anderson ("stage director" for Eddy), E. L. Tilton (for circus operators Spaulding and Rogers), G. C. Howard (acting manager for Fox); treasurer, W. Tryon (Fox); scenery, J. P. Smith; machinist, W. Crane; properties, N. Walder; costumes, L. Phillips; prompter, W. Crane; music, A. Tyre.

W. B. Freligh's Management, 1867–75.

Varied Managements, 1875–79: Lessees, W. A. Robbins (1875–76); W. B. Freligh (?) (1876–77); L. H. Everitt, business manager (1877–78); "Ferdinand Hofele was still in charge" (Odell, 10:606) (1878–79).

REPERTORY

Incompletely sketched in George C. D. Odell, *Annals of the New York Stage*, vols. 3–5, and in T. Allston Brown, *A History of the New York Stage*, 1:100–172.

BIBLIOGRAPHY

Primary sources concerning the Bowery are housed primarily in the Harvard Theatre Collection, Cambridge, Massachusetts, including playbills, promptbooks, 1831 lease, receipt book for 1845–47, prints of T. D. "Jumping Jim Crow" Rice (November 26, 1832) and of the 1828 theatre, Hamblin's 1836 license to operate, letters to and from Hamblin, his will (1836), and the New York Association Transfer

Book, 1826–36. The Folger Library, Washington, D.C., has the Bowery receipt books for 1829–38, and Bowery related materials are held by the New York Public Library Theatre Collection.

Major secondary sources about the Bowery are T. Allston Brown, *A History of the New York Stage*, 3 vols. (New York: Dodd, 1903); Joseph Ireland, *Records of the New York Stage from 1750 to 1860,* 2 vols. (New York: T. H. Morrow, 1866–67); George C. D Odell, *Annals of the New York Stage*, vols. 3–5 (New York: Columbia University Press, 1928–31); and Theodore J. Shank, "The Bowery Theatre, 1826–1836" (Ph.D. diss., Stanford University, 1956). The theatre's major house playwright during these early years is dealt with in Rosemarie K. Bank, "Theatre and Narrative Fiction in the Work of the Nineteenth- Century American Playwright Louisa Medina,"*Theatre History Studies* 3 (1983: 55–68). The Bowery is the subject of numerous features and reviews in the *New York Mirror,* the *Ladies Companion, The Spirit of the Times,* and other periodicals cited in the sources named above. Autobiographies and biographies mentioning the theatre or its managers in one capacity or another include Joseph Cowell, *Thirty Years Passed among the Players in England and America* (New York: Harper, 1844); Lester Wallack, *Memories of Fifty Years* (New York: Charles Scribner's, Sons, 1889); F. C. Wemyss, *Twenty-Six Years in the Life of an Actor and Manager,* 2 vols. (New York : Burgess, Stringer and Co., 1847); and Laurence Senelick, "George L. Fox and Bowery Pantomine," in *American Popular Entertainment,* ed. M. Matlaw (Westport, Conn.: Greenwood Press, 1979), pp. 97-110.

Rosemarie K. Bank

BROADWAY THEATRE STOCK COMPANY. Erected by the famous New York theatre builder John Trimble, the Broadway Theatre (New York) stood on Broadway between Pearl and Anthony streets. It was commissioned by Alvah Mann, a circus promoter, and opened September 27, 1847, with *School for Scandal* and *Used Up.*

E. A. Marshall of the Walnut Street Theatre in Philadelphia joined Mann in the venture in 1848, but the partnership was dissolved in October of that year, leaving Marshall in full control. The original intention had been to present a resident company without stars, but the scheme was abandoned when the Park Theatre burned. Marshall decided to capture this audience, and thereafter he was committed to a star policy. The theatre became known as the house of stars, although it had initial competition in this from the Astor Place Opera House. Burton's Chamber Street Theatre, Broughman's Lyceum, and later Wallack Theatre Company and Laura Keene's Theatre were formidable rivals.

The ravages of the then thirty-year-old star system were nowhere more evident than at the Broadway. During this period, any actor who had appeared on the London stage might take license to star in America, and Marshall was the most gullible (or unscrupulous) of managers in this regard. Some of his attractions were genuine, even great: Edwin Forrest, Charlotte Cushman, James H. Hackett, Charles Mathews, the younger, Mr. and Mrs. Barney Williams, and Josh Silsbee. Far more frequently, however, the principal attractions proved to be overpublicized individuals with little talent and even less real claim to the star appellation.

The general format was to to present the star in his or her individual repertory for one to three weeks, with a resident company of actors in support. The quality of this company varied considerably from season to season, but many of the best actors on the American stage in later years appeared or debuted here: Mr. and Mrs. G. H. Barrett, Lester Wallack, Charles Burke, W. B. Chapman, George Vandenhoff, William Rufus Blake, John Dyott, George Jordan, Mme. Ponisi, Mrs. George Vernon, John Dean, Fanny Morant, and Jean M. Davenport.

The fortunes of the Broadway were typical of the period. The feast of a truly stellar attraction could be blotted out by the famine of several weeks of mediocre or even disastrous business. The ticket price scale was $1 for the parquet and dress (there was no pit), fifty cents for the upper boxes and family circle, and twenty five cents for the galleries.

Critical opinion varied depending on the individual attactions; Forrest and Cushman, for instance, never failed to draw ecstatic reviews (even in their monotonous repertories). The resident company, occasionally appearing without a headliner in old comedies and stock pieces, met with almost unswervingly denigratory reception.

In ten seasons, Marshall presented the full spectrum of dramatic fare. Notable productions included *The Count of Monte Cristo, The Enchantress, Faustus, The Vision of The Sun, Ingomar, The Cataract of the Ganges, A Midsummer Night's Dream, The Sea of Ice,* and *Herne the Hunter.* All of these plays were examples of the spectacular, where the sumptuousness of scenery and costumes often swept dramatic considerations aside. Old English comedies rarely succeeded. The afterpiece was obligatory and generally so successful in drawing audiences that it hardly mattered what was played before it. Every season was liberally spiced with opera, ballet, juvenile troupes, elephant acts, and the circus, and these events were life saving to the theatre after weeks of presenting stars who could not shine and would not draw business.

The Broadway regularly employed a stage manager, prompter, large scenic department, and full orchestra with leader. The size of the resident company usually remained at an average of twenty-five performers, plus supernumeraries.

Unable to withstand the financial panic of 1857, Marshall left after the closing of the season, May 1, 1858. The disjointed organization, run now by Edward Eddy, managed to limp into the 1858–59 season. The theatre was demolished in 1859.

PERSONNEL

Management: Alvah Mann (1847–48), E. A. Marshall (1848–58).
Scenic Technicians: J. R. Smith, George Heister.
Musical Director: J. St. Luke.

Stage Managers: George H. Barrett (1847–53); Thomas Barry, W. R. Blake (1853–57).

Actors and Actresses: Mrs. G. Abbott, Laura Addison, *James R. Anderson* (1848–52), G. H. Andrews, Mr. Aymar, *Mr. G. H. Barrett* (1847–53), Kate and Ellen Bateman, L. Bernard, *William Rufus Blake* (1853–57), Dion Boucicault, John Broughman, James S. Browne, McKean Buchanan, Mrs. Buckland, Mrs. G. Chapman, Mme. Celeste, Frederick Chippendale, Rosaline Cline, John Collins, Mr. and Mrs. F. B. Conway, Jane Coombs, *Joe Cowell* (1853–56), William F. Cutter, A. H. Davenport, William P. Davidge, J. M. Dawson, *John Dean* (1852–54), Mrs. Dooley, John Dyott, Marcus Elmore, Teressa Esmonde, S. Eytinge, B. Fairclough, Henry Farren, A. W. Fenno, Alexina Fisler, Charles Fisler, Emma Fitzpatrick, W. M. Fleming, W. J. Florence, Mrs. J. C. Frost, *Adelaide Gougenheim* (1850–53), Josephine Gougenheim, Julia Gould, Joseph Grosvenor, Emma Hall, Barton Hill, Kate Horn, H. Howard, L. Howard, James Hudson, Mrs. W. Isherwood, Mrs. A. Knight, Annie Lamdale, Mrs. George Loder, Harry Lorraine, Harry Lyme, G. F. Marchant, Lola Montez, Anna Cara Mowatt, Mrs. Joseph E. Nagle, Julia Oatley, *Henry Placide*, Thomas Placide, Charles Pope, Adelaide Price (1856–57), Emeline Raymond, Eveline Reed, W. H. Reeves, W. H. Reynolds, Mr. and Mrs. Peter Riching, B. T. Ringgold, *Agnes Robertson* (1853), J. R. Scott, Mrs. Sergeaub, Mrs. John Setton, E. Shaw, *Rose Telbin* (1847–50), General Tom Thumb, Mr. Vache, George Vandenhoff, Gustavus Vaughn, Mrs. George Vernon, Fanny Wallack, Henry Wallack, *Mr. and Mrs. W. J. Wallack* (1848–52), Wilmarth Waller, Mrs. Winstanley, J. B. Wright.

REPERTORY

1847–48: *The School for Scandal; Used Up; Love's Sacrifice; Ladies Beware; The Lady of Lyons; The Captain of the Watch; The Hunchback; The Rivals; The Jacobite; Beatrice and Benedict; What Do They Take Me For?; The Prisoner of War; Temper; Faint Heart ne'er Won Fair Lady; Lyar; A Trip to Kissinger; The Flowers of the Forest; Hamlet;* (first star production); *Romeo; The Stranger; Ernestine; Wild Oats; Young America; The Emigrant's Dream; Macarthy Mare; Speed the Plough; The Poor Gentleman; John Bull; Macbeth; Othello; The Merchant of Venice; Werner; The Rent Day; The Bridal; Box and Cox; Key of the Commons; Monsieur Jacques; The Love Chase; Lucrezia Borgia; The Ransom; Old Heads and Young Hearts; The Last Man; London Assurance; The Trumpeter's Daughter; The Elder Brother; Glencoe; The Advocate; Romance and Reality; Metamora Burlesque; The Irish Ambassador; Teddy, the Tiler; The Wrong Passenger; The Angel in the Attic; My Companion in Arms; The Patrician's Daughter; Town and Country; The Hunter of the Alps; The Gamester; Lyar; Fashion; A Model of a Wife; Virginia; She Would Be a Soldier; Robert Macaire; The Follies of a Night; Napoleon's Old Guard.*

1848–49: *The Captain of the Watch; Richelieu; Spartacus; Jack Cade; Metamora; Key Hour; The Broker of Bogota; The Eton Boy; Is He Jealous?; Kissing Goes by Favor; The Irish Ambassador; Born to Good Luck; The Irish Post; The Irish Attorney; The Happy Man; The Nervous Man; King O'Neil; Rory O'More; His Last Legs; The Bird Dragoons; The Loan of a Lover; Our Mary Anne; The Poor Gentleman; Charles II; Born to Good Luck; The Arcade; Richard III; Savile of Haysted; Poor Pillicoddy; The Mountaineer; The Dramatist; The Nervous Man;*

The Honest Thieves; The Chronicles of Hop o' My Thumb; or The Seven League Boots; Bombastes Furioso; The Married Rake; Every One Has His Fault; The Count of Monte Cristo (long run)*; Founded on Facts; Kate Woodhull; The Midnight Watch; The West End; The Enchantress; Falstaff; The Man of the World; Cockneys in California; The Kentuckian; Rip Van Winkle; The Merry Wives of Windsor; Monsieur Mallet; The Yankee in England; Your Life's in Danger; Which Is the King?; Who Speaks First; Love's Sacrifice; Skeleton in India; The Witch of Windermere.*

1849–50: *A Kiss in the Dark; The Knight of Arva; The Irish Secretary; Henry VIII; As You Like It; Taken in and Done For; Spoil'd Child; The Swiss Cottage; The Four Mowbrays; My Aunt; Walter Raymond; or, The Lovers of Accomac; The Spirit of Gold; The Jealous Wife; Laugh When You Can; The Serious Family; Wild Oats; Extremes; Irish Honor; Remorse; The Venetian; The Barrack Room; The Belle's Stratagem; Poor Cousin Walter; The Spirit of Gold; Friend Waggler.*

1850–51: *A Thumping Legacy; The Crown Prince; Shocking Events; The Irish Fortune Hunter; Venice Preserved; The Inconstant; Petticoat Government; Honey Moon; The Daughters of the Stars; 102; or, The Veteran and His Progeny; Dave on Both Sides; A Village Tale; Single Life; An Alarming Sacrifice; Platonic Attachments; The Betrothal; My Friend in the Straps; The Loan of a Lover; The Fair One with the Golden Locks; Faustus* (long run)*; The Husband of My Heart; Betsy Baker; The Old Love and the New; Sent to the Tower; The Day after the Wedding; The Housekeeper; Belphegor; All that Glitters Is Not Gold; Who's Your Friend?; The Vision of the Sun; Cure for the Heart-Ache; I'll Be Your Second; The Teacher Taught; That Odious Captain Cutter; A Morning Call; The Day of Reckoning; Retired from Business; Azael, the Prodigal.*

1851–52: *Catarina; The Wonder; Delicate Crowd; Honesty, the Best Policy; The Village Doctor; The Double-Bedded Room; My Young Wife and My Old Umbrella; The Bengal Tiger; Left in a Cab; The Queen's Secret; The Flowers of the Forest; Taming a Tartar; The Wept of Wish-Ton-Wish; Marie Ducange; The Cabin Boy; Ingomar; The Modern Masaniello; The Alderman's Gown; The Two Bonnycastles; Paul Clifford; The Guardian Angel; The Truth; or, A Glass too Much; A Lady and a Gentleman in a Peculiarly Perplexing Predicament; Simpson and Co.; The Banker's Wife; The Poor Relation; The Rifle Brigade; Victorine; The Valet de Sham; La Manola; The Lottery Ticket; Born to Good Luck; Time Out of Place; The Limerick Boy; This the Custom of the Country; Shandy Maguire; The Omnibus; The Irish Liar; Ireland and America; Barney O'Toole.*

1852–53: *The Good-for-Nothing; The Swiss Cottage; The Old School and the New; The Dumb Belle; Ireland as It Is; Our Gal; Brian O'Lynn; The Duke's Wager; The Woman I Adore; Married and Settled; Her Royal Highness; The Poor Dependent; Box and Cox; Married and Settled; The Peri; The Postillion of Longjumeau; Anne Blatte; Rob Roy.*

1853–54: *The Forest Rose; Yankee Land; The Wool Dealer; The Green Mountain Boy; The Yankee in France; Fazio; The Camp at Catham; Evadne; The Belle of Faubourg; The Goat; Law for Ladies; Civilization; A Morning Call; The Maid of Mariendorpf; Adrienne, the Actress; The Cataract of the Ganges; The Two Buzzards; Domestic Economy; The Hope of the Family; A Midsummer Night's Dream; Leonardi Guzman; The Fatal Mask; The Irish Thrush; Irish Assurance and Yankee Modesty; The Bashful Irishman; To Oblige Benson; Crossing the Atlantic.*

1854–55: *A Lover by Proxy; Wildrake; Ganem; or, The Slave of Love; Black*

Eyed Susan; A Desperate Game; A Hopeless Passion; The Invisible Prince; The Young Actress; The Fairy Star; Used Up; To Parents and Guardians; A Blighted Being; Sophia's Supper; Bona Fide Travellers; Charity's Love; Love and Loyalty; A Game of Romps.

1855–56: *Francesca da Rimini; The Maid with the Milking Pail; The Bankrupt; King Charming; Don't Judge by Appearances; Catching a Mermaid; The Sea of Ice; Twenty Minutes on a Tiger; The Iron Mask; Windsor Castle; Herne the Hunter; Mazeppa; That Blessed Baby; Uncle Pat's Cabin; The Widow Bedott Papers; Darby O'Donnell.*

1856–57: *Nature and Philosophy; The New Footman; The Usurper of Siam; The Last Days of Pompeii; De Soto; The Son of the Night.*

1857–58: *Married for Money; Patter vs. Clatter; The Maid of Croissey; A Game of Speculation; Cool as a Cucumber; A Curious Case; That Aggravating Sam; Mesmerism; The Busy Body; Not a Bad Judge; The Practical Man; A Conjugal Lesson; The Duchess of Malfi; Philip of France and Marie de Meranie.*

BIBLIOGRAPHY

Published Sources: Seasonal accounts appear in T. Allston Brown's *A History of the New York Stage*, 3 vols. (New York: Dodd, 1903); Joseph Ireland's *Records of the New York Stage from 1750 to 1860*, 2 vols. (New York: T. H. Morell, 1866–67); and George C. D. Odell's *Annals of the New York Stage*, vols. 5–7 (New York: Columbia University Press, 1931). A personal account of the 1850–55 seasons is found in William P. Davidge's *Footlight Flashes* (New York: American News Co., 1866).

Archival Sources: New York Public Library and Harvard Theatre Collection, Cambridge, Massachusetts, have some playbills as well as scrapbooks of the individual stars who appeared at the Broadway.

James Burge

BROOKLYN THEATRE COMPANY. (1871–75) After a successful seven years at Brooklyn's Park Theatre, Mr. and Mrs. Frederick B. Conway decided they needed a larger house for their work. Since Brooklyn lacked adequate playhouses, they arranged for a new one to be built at the southwest corner of Johnson and Washington streets, where St. John's Episcopal Church had stood since 1826. Their elaborate new playhouse, the 1,500-seat Brooklyn Theatre, opened on October 2, 1871, with Edward Bulwer-Lytton's *Money*.

Forty-six actors belonged to the initial stock company. Mr. and Mrs. Conway were the leading players, although illness prevented each from appearing as often as formerly. They charged $10.00 for private boxes holding six persons, $1.50 for reserved orchestra seats, $1.00 for the dress circle (fifty cents extra for reserved), seventy-five cents for the parquet, and fifty cents for the family circle.

For four years the Conways struggled to keep their theatre open. Times were bad economically; one reason cited by the press was the damage recently done to money markets by the great Chicago fire. Mrs. Conway performed most of the managerial duties at the new theatre, as before. She offered the better class of standard contemporary plays and revivals. On one occasion during her first season she achieved great success with Augustin Daly's *Divorce*, then being played at Daly's own theatre in New York. Daly permitted Mrs. Conway's company to do it simultaneously, and the press found the local version not far behind that of the better-known Manhattan company. A four-week run helped Mrs. Conway sustain her troupe's livelihood.

Mrs. Conway presented the stock company as the main attraction in a variety of offerings ranging from standard legitimate plays to more modern society dramas and comedies. A few stars, including Edwin Booth, John Brougham, and Charles Mathews, played with the company in 1871–72. Even fewer came the next year. The stars failed to boost business, but a letter to the local press expressed public disappointment at the nonstar policy. By 1872–73 Mr. Conway's health was too poor for him to act, and a stock player, Frank Roche, took over all leading roles Conway would have played. Mrs. Conway, contending with the theatre's problems, an ailing husband, and her failing health, greatly decreased her own stage activities as well.

The company's leading players were retained each season, but most of the lesser actors were replaced. An occasional star was booked when appropriate, but one such player, the German tragedienne Fanny Janauschek, cancelled an engagement at the Brooklyn in 1874, precipitating a violent public quarrel with the normally reticent Mrs. Conway. In a rare interview she expressed her dissatisfaction with all stars. She preferred the unity the stock company brought to a play and thought the presence of an outsider disruptive to artistic harmony. Nevertheless, a new business manager, John P. Smith, hired in 1874, seems to have convinced her that stars would boost attendance. A large number of well-known players soon were acting on the Brooklyn's stage. The press lauded the move, but the public continued to stay away. One element that appears to have hurt Mrs. Conway was her nepotistic policy of starring her young daughter Lillian in major roles. The fledgling actress had just debuted in November 1873.

Frederick B. Conway, popular for his jovial and flamboyant character, died on September 8, 1874. He had been a strong force in the making of theatre in Brooklyn, and his death was mourned by all local theatregoers.

Business manager Smith's star policy continued in force in 1874–75; finally, the policy began to pay off. The appearance of famous players in familiar plays and recent New York successes drew sizable crowds and profits rapidly accumulated. It was too late for Sarah Conway, however; on April 28, 1875, eight months after her husband died, she too passed away. When she died, the play on stage at the theatre was Hart Jackson's adaptation of Adolphe P. D'Ennery's *Two Orphans*, the same piece that was being played there on December 5, 1876, the night the theatre burned down. Minnie, the elder daughter of the Conways, took over the management after her mother's death. She was soon in financial difficulty because her mother had failed to pay the theatre's rent after January 1, 1875. The landlords were willing to forgive the debt of $9,000 if she agreed to give up the lease, but Minnie resisted until legal pressure forced her to concede. With the demise of the Conway management, the Brooklyn *Eagle* noted that the couple had been guilty of "treating the theatre as a tribute" to their own presence and that they had overexposed themselves to the point of becoming boring.

A new management, that of Sheridan Shook and Arnold Palmer, took control of the theatre in August 1875.

PERSONNEL

Management: Mrs. Frederick B. (Sarah) Conway.
Business Manager: John P. Smith.
Musical Director: F. Peterschen.
Actors and Actresses: Maria Atkins, O. H. Barr, S. Branscombe, Kate Brevoort, Mrs. Brutone, Ione Burke, Ella Burns, Sallie Campbell, B. Carter, G. C. Charles, F. Chippendale, *Frederick B. Conway,* Minnie Conway, *Sarah Conway*, Sophie Crosbie, Mary Dallas, W. Dallas, Arthur Davis, Frank Edwards, Maud Ernest, Julie Evans, H. Eytinge, Mrs. Farren, May Fiske, Martha Grey, J. Hetherington, J. Hoskins, Emma Howson, George C. Jordan, Gertrude Kellogg, M. A. Kennedy, Edward Lamb, Mrs. W. H. Leighton. Jane Lennox, Walter Lennox, Anna Lewis, T. Lipscomb, L. Loveday, Mr. Mackay, S. Marshall, Adelaide Merry, S. Moreley, Andrew Queen, Augusta Raymond, Fanny Reeves, Frank Roche, Mark Russel, Ida Saunders, Ida Savory, G. C. Spear, Emma Stanley, Neil Warner, Georgie Watson, R. White, A. S. Wright, P. Wright.

REPERTORY

Not available.

BIBLIOGRAPHY

Unpublished Source: Samuel L. Leiter, "The Legitimate Theatre in Brooklyn, 1861–1898," 2 vols. (Ph.D. diss., New York University, 1968).

Samuel L. Leiter

BROOKLYN THEATRE COMPANY. (1875–76) After the deaths of Mr. and Mrs. Conway, and the subsequent managerial failure of their daughter, the Brooklyn Theatre was leased to Lester Wallack and Theodore N. Moss, but the lease soon changed hands, and the important team of Sheridan Shook and Arnold M. Palmer took control. This pair was to run its famed Union Square Theatre in New York in conjunction with the new enterprise. The facilities of the Manhattan house, including its actors, could thus be at their disposal for use in Brooklyn.

Shook and Palmer planned to alternate stock and star engagements with single-play attractions at the Brooklyn. Some weeks would be devoted solely to the stock company, with or without a star in the lead, and other weeks would see an entire combination booked, with all or most of the roles filled by actors hired especially for that production alone. The first stock presentation on October 4 featured Agnes Ethel, a famous actress who had retired in 1873. She acted in Augustin Daly's adaptation of *Frou-Frou*, a work that had been a great success for her under Daly's management.

Shook and Palmer's 1875–76 season was the most brilliant ever seen at the theatre. The alternating star and stock system was followed, and the stars who appeared included Kate Claxton, John Gilbert, J. J. Montague, Steele MacKaye, E. A. Sothern, and Lester Wallack. Young Maud Harrison, later an important actress, debuted October 18, 1875, in *The Flying Scud*.

The standard legitimate fare of the day occupied the Brooklyn's boards, augmented by a great number of recent New York successes. *The Flying Scud, Around the World in Eighty Days, Ferreol, Colonel Sellers, False Shame, Queen and Woman, Rose Michel, The Two Orphans*, and George Rignold's production of *Henry V* were among them. The control of a New York theatre allowed Shook and Palmer to give Brooklyn current hits while they were still popular across the river. Brooklyn had never seen such lavish productions. The *Eagle* of October 10, 1876, reported that Shook and Palmer had "produced more new plays, better plays, acted by better artists and supported by better scenery than Brooklyn playgoers ever saw before in any of their theatres."

Alternating stars and stock continued in the fall of 1876. On December 4 *The Two Orphans* opened (it had closed a previous run on the same date a year earlier) with Kate Claxton in the starring role. The next night the theatre burned down with a great loss of life in what was then America's most tragic theatre fire. Several hundred people died, including two actors, Claude Burroughs and H. S. Murdoch. A new Brooklyn Theatre went up on the site in 1879 but was used solely by combination companies.

PERSONNEL

Management: Sheridan Shook and Arnold M. Palmer.

Actors and Actresses: Blanche Brey, Claude Burroughs, Mrs. Farren, Kate Giraud, Dora Goldthwaite, Annie Gordon, Maud Harrison, Edward Lamb, H. S. Murdoch, Eben Plympton, Augusta Raymond, F. Robson, Katherine Rogers, Louise Sylvester, Hattie Thorpe, Ida Vernon.

REPERTORY

Not available.

BIBLIOGRAPHY

Unpublished Source: Samuel L. Leiter, "The Legitimate Theatre in Brooklyn, 1861–1898," 2 vols. (Ph.D. diss., New York University, 1968).

Samuel L. Leiter

BROUGHAM'S LYCEUM THEATRE STOCK COMPANY. Brougham's Lyceum Theatre Company (New York City) was formed by comedian John Brougham (1810–80) shortly before the Lyceum's belated opening December 23, 1850. His tenure there was brief. The Lyceum, newly erected on the west side of Broadway, next door to the southwest corner of Broome Street, was designed and built by theatre architect J. M. Trimble. This house reputedly held between 1,800 and 2,000 persons. The inaugural bill was Brougham's "occasional rigmarole," *Brougham and Co.*, which introduced "the entire company" (or nearly so); followed by a musical intermezzo and a dance; succeeded in turn by the farce *Deeds of Dreadful Note [Crimson Crimes]* and the comedy *The Light Guard; or, Women's Rights.* Opening-night admission prices were fifty cents for dress circle and parquet, twenty-five cents for family circle, $1 for an orchestra stall, and $5 for a private box.

By clinging to Olympic manager William Mitchell's durable but then outmoded formula of three or four light farces, comedies, burlettas, and/ or operettas each night, Brougham lagged behind his more flexible former partner, William E. Burton (1804–60), at the Chambers Street Theatre. His initial company included "an array of female talent and beauty that should have brought profit and fame to any management" (Hutton, 58): Mary Taylor, Mrs. Vernon (Jane Fisher), Mrs. Blake (Caroline Placide), Kate Horn, and later Julia Gould. Besides offering Brougham, its male comic ranks were fortified by tyro W. J. Florence (late of Niblo's) and Burton protégé John E. Owens (New York debut). Yet the Lyceum "had no leading man of metropolitan calibre, whereas Burton had...Lester [Wallack] and George Jordan....Brougham's game was a losing one, almost from the start" (Odell, 6:52).

Even Brougham's timely adaptation of *David Copperfield* failed to draw, and a rival dramatization of Dickens' novel almost nightly thrived at Burton's. Intermittent hits scored by two of Brougham's topical novelties, *A Row at the Lyceum* and *What Shall We Do for Something New?* were vitiated by the actor-manager's alternately old-fashioned and experimental bills and bookings, perhaps too by a plethora of benefit nights during the second season. The harried actor-manager's concurrent, ill-starred editorship of the comic journal *The Lantern* doubtless also undermined his conduct of affairs at the Lyceum. Laurence Hutton, a partisan chronicler, was wont to blame the "unsympathetic and *porco-cephalic* public" for Brougham's declining fortunes; but Burton, catering to these same audiences with a different budget of plays and players, managed to sustain nightly profits. With evident success, the Lyceum comedy troupe expanded its histronic range into tragic and classic pieces, in the fall of 1851, supporting star-actress Charlotte Cushman; and their box-office receipts peaked, early in 1852, with the stage debut in English comedies of Catherine Sinclair Forrest (the recently divorced wife of American tragedian Edwin Forrest). But Brougham's house then abruptly closed its doors on March 17, 1852 (St. Patrick's Day), and the staff and acting company dispersed.

After a brief apprenticeship at London's Tottenham Street Theatre, Dublin-born Brougham had acted comic parts for more than a decade at the Olympic and Covent Garden, under Madame Vestris' inspired aegis. He had ventured into management at the English Opera House [Lyceum] in the summer of 1840, coauthored *London Assurance* with Dion Boucicault in 1841, and made his American debut October 4, 1842, at the Park Theatre, New York. After a season in major eastern U.S. cities, he embarked on a one-year starring western tour. He was comedian, stage manager, and house playwright in Philadelphia for a season, and he comanaged the Adelphi Theatre, in Boston, for two years. Brougham was resident playwright and star-actor at Burton's Chambers Street Theatre during 1848–50, and he briefly comanaged Niblo's Garden, New York, in 1850. In late 1850 he undertook direction of the Lyceum.

He would later manage the Bowery Theatre, in 1856–57, but he spent the Civil War years in England. He made two highly profitable starring tours of America in 1865–68 and, in a disastrous partnership with financier Jim Fisk, briefly conducted Brougham's Theatre, New York, in early 1869. During the early and mid–1870s he was a featured member alternately of Lester Wallack's and Augustin Daly's companies.

The gifted, genial Brougham was a prodigious fabricator of scripts for the stages of London, New York, New Orleans, Boston, Philadelphia, and other cities. He supplied vehicles for numerous touring stars (Burton, Cushman, Wallack, Florence, Charles Fechter, Lotta Crabtree, Barney Williams, John Drew) and provided plays of many kinds for the leading New York managers (Burton, the Wallacks, Daly, A. M. Palmer)—more than 160 pieces in all. He was undoubtedly the most effective American dramatic satirist of his own or any time. Brougham was handsome, stylishly dressed, and a versatile, popular comic actor. Esteemed over a long career for his portrayals of Irish gentlemen, he persistently failed in repeated attempts at independent theatrical management.

The Lyceum's inaugural bill gave way within a fortnight to *The Serious Family* and *My Friend in the Straps*. *A Kiss in the Dark*, *The Rough Diamond*, and Brougham's *Esmeralda and Her Gifted Goat* successively entered the bills through the year's end, and *David Copperfield* (emphasizing the novel's eccentric and comic figures) was introduced early in January 1851 for a three-week run. In short, hurried succession, *Jenny Lind*, *The Wild Indian*,

The King's Gardener, The Happiest Day in My Life, Where There's a Will There's a Way, Paul Pry, Serve Him Right, Sent to the Tower, Betsy Baker, and Auber's opera *The Ambassadress* crowded the Lyceum stage into early February. Constant changes in the bills and a heavy reliance on recent English scripts marked the company's repertory throughout the first season. Reviewers were friendly enough. When Brougham's new "Cosmopolitan Wonder," *The World's Fair; or, London in 1851*, emerged on February 10, the *Herald* claimed (February 13, 1851) there was "not a subject of interest passing at the time which is not wittily commented on." But *The World's Fair* soon vanished from the boards—as, in turn, did the actor-manager-playwright's satirical *Ye Deville and Dr. Faustus, The Spirit of the Air, The Bloomers*, and even *A Row at the Lyceum*. (No other authors' comedies except one—*The Fortunes of War*—were premiered on this stage.) The fast rising Owens departed the company after a farewell benefit in February. Florence, also destined for wider fame, did not renew his contract, nor did any of the troupe's original leading women renew theirs. In June George Jordan and Tom Johnston (both late of Burton's), William Chippendale, and Julia Bennett (briefly, from the Broadway) demonstrably bolstered the Lyceum's ranks, which also included stage manager Harry Lynne, Stephen Leach, David Palmer, H. B. Phillips, Mr. Bristol, Annette Brougham, Mrs. Loder, and dancers Louise Ducy-Barre and G. W. Smith. Their first season closed on July 7.

Emulating Burton's recent innovation, Brougham opened the 1851–52 Lyceum season with a bill of but two pieces, *What Shall We Do for Something New?* (Bellini's *La sonnambula* in modern dress) and *Romance and Reality*. The company now comprised the Broughams, Lynne, Leach, Palmer, Phillips, Bristol, and Mrs. Loder, all of the original ranks; late arrivals Gould, Chippendale, Jordan, and Johnston; and newcomers George and Emma Skerrett and Clara Fisher Maeder. At first sustaining only light comic roles (in a half-dozen English pieces and three more Brougham scripts), these players gamely joined Cushman in tragedy, melodrama, and Shakespearean comedy, after which Cushman shared their enlarging comic repertoire. Brougham booked the Roussets (dancers) and western tragedian J.A.J. Neafie into the Lyceum during October and November. His resilient troupe again supported Cushman in Shakespearean repertory (for example, the star in the title part of *Hamlet*) and English comedies. The theatre was visited by a French company, playing in French, in mid-January 1852 (a hiatus for the Lyceum troupe), and at length the house descended to notoriety on February 2 with Mrs. Forrest's advent as Lady Teazle in *The School for Scandal*, supported by her acting coach, English tragedian George Vandenhoft. The divorcée-debutante's five-week engagement comprised the Lyceum's last noteworthy event—"the only great and positive success"— during Brougham's brief managerial term. It was also the last.

After a disastrous season, Brougham had to surrender the Lyceum to his friend Major Rodgers. Rodgers promptly entered negotiations with actor-manager James W. Wallack, who in September 1852 would launch a long and distinguished era of management at this theatre, with Brougham as a company regular.

During Brougham's regime, the Lyceum regularly employed a stage manager, musical director, treasurer, chorus master, ballet master, two scenic artists, a costumer, a machinist, a small orchestra, and a large company of comedy specialists (about ten men and a half-dozen women), each seasoned in a specific line of business. All of the plays performed, chiefly British, were royalty-free (since still unprotected by copyright). Brougham's own productions—farces, comedies, burlettas, melodramas, adaptations— may have specially attracted because of their novelty and/or topicality. The Lyceum's normally frequent changes of bill reflect a collision of heavy overhead and light houses, and except for his last-ditch, bar-sinister triumph with Mrs. Forrest, Brougham's occasional booking of visiting stars and outside troupes probably did little to improve his house's faltering finances.

Clara Fisher Maeder, long absent, was an admired but fading star, whereas Mrs. Blake, Mrs. Vernon, Kate Horn, and Mary Taylor all had gained celebrity on other stages. Julia Gould, from England, made her American debut at Brougham's Lyceum and played there two seasons, and dancer Malvina Pray found a fleeting showcase for her budding talents in *What Shall We Do for Something New?* Advancing George Jordan was already esteemed one of the city's handsomest young leading men when he joined Brougham, and W. J. Florence, hitherto a utility player, advanced along his way to stardom in *A Row at the Lyceum.* Low comedian John E. Owens also attracted favorable notice during his short tenure, as Sleek in *The Serious Family* and Uriah Heep in *David Copperfield.* Yet none of these young artists was at the Lyceum long enough to have developed there the sort of polish Brougham had gained while with Lucy Eliza Vestris, her talented husband Charles Mathews, and playwright-designer J. R. Planché.

PERSONNEL

Management: John Brougham, lessee and proprietor; John Buckland, treasurer.

Mise en scène: Charles Thorne and Mr. Roberts, scene-painters; W. DeMilt, machinist; G. Taylor, costumer.

Music: George Loder, musical director; Fred Lyster, chorus master.

Stage Direction: Harry Lynne, stage manager; G. W. Smith, ballet master; Henry B. Phillips, prompter.

Actors and Actresses: Julia Bennett, Caroline Placide Blake, Mr. Bristol, Annette Nelson Brougham, John Brougham, William Chippendale, Louise Ducy-Barre, W. J. Florence, Julia Gould, Kate Horn, Thomas B. Johnston, George Jordan, Stephen Leach, Mrs. George Loder, Harry Lynne, Clara Fisher Maeder, John E. Owens, David Palmer, Henry B. Phillips, Malvina Pray, Emma Skerrett, George Skerrett, G. W. Smith, Mary Taylor, Jane Fisher Vernon.

REPERTORY

1850–51: *Brougham and Co.; Deeds of Dreadful Note [Crimson Crimes]; The Light Guard; or, Women's Rights; The Serious Family; My Friend in the Straps; A Kiss in the Dark; Esmeralda and Her Gifted Goat; The Rough Diamond; David Copperfield; Jenny Lind; The Wild Indian; The King's Gardener; The Happiest Day of My Life; Where There's a Will There's a Way; Paul Pry; Serve Him Right; Sent to the Tower; Betsy Baker; The Ambassadress* (opera); *The World's Fair; or, London in 1851; A Curious Case; The Old Love and the New; Allow Me to Apologize; The Fast Man; Ye Deville and Dr. Faustus; A Lesson for Lovers; Love in a Maze; The Spirit of the Air; or, The Enchanted Isle; The Teacher Taught; That Odious Captain Cutter; A Row at the Lyceum; or, Green Room Secrets; The Child of the Regiment; The Devil in Paris; London Assurance; The Fortunes of War* (Lester Wallack's first produced play); *La Fille du Danube* (ballet); *Don Giovanni in London; The Invincibles; The National Guard; The Home Book of Beauty* (benefit performances); *Naval Engagements; Dombey and Son; The School for Scandal; Grist to the Mill; The Loan of a Lover; The Ransom; The Ladies' Battle; The Lady of Lyons; Queen of the Frogs; The Bloomers; or, Pets in Pants* (benefit performances).

1851–52: *What Shall We Do for Something New?; Romance and Reality; The Ladies' Battle; The Fire Eater; The School for Tigers; Alcestis; The Yacht Race; The Card Case; Wanted: A Wizard [The Rival Magicians]; See Saw; or, Paddy's Sliding Scale; David Copperfield; The Stranger [Menschenhass und Rue]; The Actress of Padua [Angelo]; Guy Mannering; As You Like It; London Assurance; The School for Scandal; The Lady of Lyons; A Lesson of the Heart* (farces October 13 et seq.); *Mohammed; King Richard III; Kossuth's Kum; The Money Market; or, Romance of Wall Street [Mercadet]; Hamlet; King Henry IV, Part 1; The Merchant of Venice; She Stoops to Conquer;* (light comedies and farces); *A Christmas Carol; A Row at the Lyceum;* (French plays performed by visiting troupe); *Love's Sacrifice; Much Ado about Nothing; The Patrician's Daughter.*

BIBLIOGRAPHY

Published Sources: Frank G. Bangs, "Recollections of Players: V. [John Brougham]," *New York Dramatic Mirror*, March 19, 1898; George Clement Boase, "John Brougham," *Dictionary of National Biography* (New York: Oxford University Press, 1938), 2:1366–67; John Brougham, *Life, Stories, and Poems*, ed. William Winter (Boston: James R. Osgood and Company, 1881), reprints several previously published biographical sources, Brougham's diary, and so on; "John Brougham," *Appleton's Cyclopedia of American Biography* (New York: Appleton and Company, 1887), 1:391–93; Walter Prichard Eaton, "John Brougham," *Dictionary of American Biography* (New York: Charles Scribner's Sons, 1929), 3:95–96; Laurence Hutton, "John Brougham," in *Plays and Players* (New York: Hurd and Houghton, 1875), pp. 49–89; "John Brougham," *New York Clipper*, February 19, 1910; *New York Herald*, 1850–52; *New York Times*, 1851–52; George C. D. Odell, *Annals of the New York Stage*, vol. 6 (New York: Columbia University Press, 1931); Pat M. Ryan, Jr., "John Brougham: The Gentle Satirist—A Critique, with a Handlist and Census," *Bulletin of the New York Public Library* 63 (December 1959): 619–40; William Winter, "John Brougham," in Winter's *Shadows of the Stage*, 2nd ser. (New York: Macmillan, 1893), pp. 95–112.

Unpublished Source: David S. Hawes, "John Brougham as American Playwright and Man of the Theatre" (Ph.D. diss., Stanford University, 1953).

Archival Sources: Playbills, scrapbooks, and clippings at Harvard Theatre Collection, Cambridge, Massachusetts, and Library for the Performing Arts, Lincoln Center, New York.

Pat M. Ryan

BURTON'S STOCK COMPANY. Burton's Stock Company's (New York City) premiere performance was on July 10, 1848, in a proscenium-equipped theatre at 39 and 41 Chambers Street. Opened under the management of actor-manager William E. Burton (1804–60), the troupe's initial offering included *Maidens Beware, Raising the Wind*, and *The Irish Dragoon*. Burton purchased the 800-seat theatre (formerly Palmo's Opera House) for $15,000. Upon completing a new proscenium, adding private boxes and new chandeliers, and having the theatre seats stuffed and lobbies carpeted, he rechristened it Burton's Chambers Street Theatre (known also as Burton's Theatre).

Offering a varied bill of full-length plays, burlesques, farces, and vaudeville entertainment, modeled partially on the successful style of William Mitchell's Olympic Theatre, and with a top admission price of only fifty cents, Burton's Theatre did not immediately generate the enthusiasm of the New York theatregoers. Burton, a former manager of theatres in Baltimore, Philadelphia, and Washington, D.C., had decided to form a company to perform without the use of stars. Since visiting stars were the staple attractions of profitable theatres of the time, associates of the novelty-seeking Burton predicted an early failure. With the tumultuous reception (in early August 1848) of John Brougham's adaptation of Charles Dickens' *Dombey and Son*, however, Burton's new formula gained the support and popularity that earned his theatre the position of "the most popular playhouse in New York" (Odell, 6:127).

The achievements of the theatre on Chambers Street were due largely to the exhaustive energy of its key figure. Outside as well as inside the theatre, Burton was a man of broad interests and versatile talent. From being an accomplished author and public speaker to winning prizes for his flowers in horticultural shows to cofounding and presiding over the American Shakespeare Club, Burton's list of accomplishments was one to envy. His passion, however, was for the theatre, and there he achieved his greatest successes. Not only did Burton attempt to manage more than one theatre at a time (he took on the failed Olympic Theatre for a short time in 1852), but he also directed rehearsals, wrote plays and adapted other works, and was known throughout the country as a proficient comedian. Trained in the comic style of London's John Liston (1776–1846), Burton gained recognition for his skill in delighting patrons to such an extent that "the very sound of his voice off-stage could send an audience into an uproar"

(Wilson, *Three Hundred Years of American Drama and Theatre*, 163). Burton's style was enhanced by his stocky build, his flexible voice, and his broad, genial face that allowed for a full range of expression. His success as an actor derived from his ability to intensify any characterization or emotion through the use of his physical self and facial and vocal expressiveness. His style was broad but not limited. Burton created hundreds of characters throughout his lifetime, from William Shakespeare's to Richard Sheridan's to Charles Dickens', each with an adeptness that became synonymous with Burton's name. Although he ventured into more serious roles occasionally, comedy was Burton's forte and what he was most famous for. Laurence Hutton, in agreement with many others, called Burton "the greatest comedian of our day" (Hutton, 240).

John Brougham (1810–80), who later established his Lyceum Theatre as a rival of Burton's, proved to be a pillar of strength in the early years at the Chambers Street Theatre. As an actor, stage manager, and playwright of the company, he assisted in making Burton's a prominent place. In his adaptations and burlesques of popular material, Burton found many successes that would last as long as the company itself.

The Chambers Street Theatre's regular offerings were varied but featured mainly modern, broad comedy, for which the troupe became renowned. Adaptations of Charles Dickens' novels as well as plays by William Shakespeare, Dion Boucicault, and Richard Brinsley Sheridan were frequently performed. Apart from the triumphant productions of Brougham's adaptation of *Dombey and Son*, Morris Barnett's *Serious Family*, and Burton's *Toodles*, the ensemble's ensuing successes included a vast array of old comedy (for example, Sheridan's *School for Scandal* and Oliver Goldsmith's *She Stoops to Conquer*) revivals, the likes of which had not been seen in New York for quite a while. Several Shakespearean productions mounted in the historically accurate style of Charles Kean added to Burton's growing list of novelties. These types of innovations "set [Burton's] enterprise in considerably higher artistic acclaim" (Odell, 6:17) than the company's original offerings did.

Critically, popularly, and financially, "everything seemed to succeed in those day's at Burton's" (Odell, 6:20). *Dombey and Son* had captured the attention of audiences and reviewers alike, and because of equally successful productions between 1848 and 1856, Burton's Theatre became the most respected company in America. In the early years critics particularly admired individual performances. The Toots of Oliver B. Raymond, Susan Nipper of Caroline Chapman, and Captain Cuttle of Burton were lauded in *Dombey and Son*, as was T. B. Johnston's Uriah Heep in *David Copperfield*. Two other productions, *The Toodles* and *The Serious Family* (which, before the era of the long run even began, played 123 performances in its first season alone), gained further accolades for Burton in the characters of Timothy Toodles and Aminadab Sleek, respectively. These personal accomplishments together with innovations such as the old comedy revivals and the Shakespearean productions produced for Burton's Chambers Street Theatre Company a reputation for artistic worth.

Burton's domination of the New York theatrical scene went unchallenged until the opening of James W. Wallack's Lyceum Theatre. Not only did Wallack employ some of Burton's top performers, but he also scored an equal (and eventually greater) success following the style of Burton's organization. Wallack's Lyceum provided the first able competition to the Chambers Street Theatre. The company continued to thrive, though, until Laura Keene established her own troupe in New York. This, in addition to the threat of Wallack's new theatre and Burton's futile attempts to find a permanent leading lady, led Burton to the decision to relocate his company nearer to his competitors, in anticipation of increasing his edge. (The Chambers Street Theatre was located so far downtown that when Ferdinand Palmo opened his opera house there in 1844, he included this convenience for patrons: "Arrangements have been made by the management with the Rail Road Company, for the accommodation of ladies and gentlemen living uptown, so that a large car . . . will start after the Theatre closes. . . . The car will run from the corner of Chambers and Centre Streets as far as 42nd Street" [Ireland, 2:424]). In the early summer of 1856, Burton displaced Laura Keene by purchasing the Metropolitan Theatre on the west side of Broadway opposite Bond Street. On September 6 the troupe gave a fitting farewell to the Chambers Street Theatre by performing *The Toodles* and *The Serious Family*. It signaled the end of Burton's company's popularity and domination, for Burton's New Theatre, one of the largest in the country, was too big to achieve the intimacy that was possible in the little theatre on Chambers Street. After correcting the faulty construction, removing the boxes in the second tier, reconstructing the proscenium, and redecorating, Burton opened his New Theatre on September 8, 1856, with productions of *The Rivals* and *The Loan of a Lover*. In the beginning (at Chambers Street) Burton had brought in guests (for example, W. Chippendale, Frank S. Chanfrau, and Charles Burke) primarily on a one- or two-night basis. In return, members of Burton's company often appeared in other theatres. Failing to create excitement about his New Theatre, Burton came to depend upon stars to insure financial success. Even failing stars J. B. Roberts, James Rogers, Ana Maria Quinn, and James E. Murdoch appeared in a desperate attempt to restore Burton's quickly fading eminence. Burton's dependence on stars, however, fell short of saving the company, and in October 1858 Burton, after opening his eleventh season with alternate nights devoted entirely to opera, closed his theatre's doors permanently.

The personnel in Burton's employment included a treasurer, a stage manager, a musical director, a ballet master, and various scenic artists, machinists, and costumers. Specialty performers were a staple of the early entertainment, and occasionally a featured guest made an appearance at the Chambers Street Theatre: Mrs. Mary Amelia Warner of Sadlers Wells; Morris Barnett, author of *The Serious Family*; Dr. Northall, adapter of *David Copperfield*; and George H. Barrett. In Burton's New Theatre the visiting stars included Edwin Booth (who made his New York debut at Burton's), Charlotte Cushman, Mr. and Mrs. E. L. Davenport, Charles Mathews, James H. Hackett, the W. J. Florences, and Julia Bennett Barrow. Called by Thomas Allston Brown "a perfection of ensemble which have never been surpassed in this country" (Brown, 1:358), Burton's regular company boasted over the years of the talents of Henry Placide, Lester Wallack, Charles Fisher, George Holland, William Rufus Blake, and Lawrence Barrett. In addition to these noted actors, many other performers deserve to be ranked high in the history of Burton's: Oliver B. Raymond, T. B. Johnston, Caroline Chapman, Mrs. Esther Hughes, Charles Walcot, Agnes Robertson, Dion Boucicault, Lizzie Weston, Lysander Thompson, Maggie Mitchell, and Humphrey Bland. These regulars and many more like them formed the core of the acting troupe, the source of the triumphant popularity achieved by Burton's.

Despite the faded success of his New Theatre, due largely to the expense of competing with his rivals, Burton established a norm for theatrical excellence with his Chambers Street Theatre. Memorable for demonstrating that success did not require stars, Burton provided a constant source of entertainment, achievement, and originality, which was hailed as "the beginning of modern times in [New York City]'s theatres" (Odell, 5:430).

PERSONNEL

Management: William E. Burton, proprietor and manager (1848–58); J. C. Barnet, treasurer (1848–58).

Stage Managers: John Brougham (1848–49), John Sefton (1852), John Moore (1853–58).

Acting Manager: Henry C. Jarrett (1857).

Musical Directors: George Loder (1848), J. Cooke (1852–54).

Ballet Master: Monsieur Frederic (1848–58).

Scenic Artist: Mr. Heigle (1848–54).

Machinists: Mr. DeMilt (1848), William Foudray (1853).

Costumer: Mr. Keyser (1853).

Actors and Actresses: *Charles F. Addams* (1849), *Mary Agnes* (1855), Miss Alderman, Mr. Alleyn, James K. Anderson, Mr. Anderton, *A. Andrews* (1849, 1854), *George H. Andrews* (1853), Mr. Baccianti, Master Baker, *Alexina Fisher Baker* (1854), J. Lewis Baker, John L. Baker, Miss Barber, Miss E. Barber, Mrs. Barker, *Joseph L. Barrett* (1857), *Lawrence P. Barrett* (1856–57), G. Barton, Maria Barton, *Charles Bass* (1848–49), Miss Bell, Mr. Belton, *Mrs. Bernard* (1852), L. C. Bishop, Caroline Blake, *William Rufus Blake* (1850–51), *Humphrey Bland* (1850–52, 1856–57), *George C. Boniface* (1857), *Dion Boucicault* (1855, 1856), *Brookhouse Bowler* (1858), Mr. Bradley, *Mrs. J. P. Brelsford* (1855), *W. H. Briggs* (1857–

58), Miss Brooks, *Annette Brougham* (1848–49), *John Brougham* (1848–49, 1856–57), Miss Brown, Fanny Brown, James Brown, Mrs. Helen Mathews Brunton, *Mrs. Kate Horn Buckland* (1852–53), W. Burke, Mr. Burnett, *William E. Burton* (1848–58), James Canoll, Mrs. Carpenter, *Caroline Chapman* (1848–49, 1851), W. B. Chapman, Thomas Christian, *Constantia Clarke* (1849–50), *Corson W. Clarke* (1848–49), *Ada Clifton* (1857), Miss Cohen, Miss E. Cohen, Miss L. Cohen, *John Collins* (1858), Miss Connor, Miss Cooke, Mrs. J. Cooke, *Jane Coombs* (1856), C. W. Couldock (1849), Miss Crawford, *W. H. Crisp* (1848), Julia Daly, *A. H. Davenport* (1856), Miss Day, Miss Deering, Mr. Denham, Mary Ann Denham, *Susan Denin* (1857), Mr. De Silveria, Miss Devere, T. B. DeWalden, Sir William Don, Clarisse Doria, Mrs. Dowling, Miss Dummie, Mrs. J. C. Dunn, James C. Dunn, *John Dunn* (1848, 1851), *Rosalie Durand* (1855), *John Dyott* (1848, 1851–52), Miss Everett, Mr. Everett, Mr. Eytinge, Boothroyd Fairclough, Miss Farresa, Miss C. Fielding, Miss S. Fielding, Mr. Fish, Mrs. Fish, Miss Fisher, *Charles Fisher* (1852–54, 1856–57), Georgette Fisher, Mr. Fisk, Mrs. Fisk, Mr. Fitzgerald, Mr. Fletcher, Miss Florence, Monsieur Frederic, *Mary Gannon* (1857), Mr. Gardiner, Mr. Gaspard, Miss Gimber, Mr. Gledhill, *Lionel Goldschmid* (1855), Mr. Gourlay, Mrs. Gourlay, Jenny Gourlay, J. Delmon Grace, John Greene, Joseph Grosvenor, *Thomas Hadaway* (1849), Mrs. Hale, Miss Hall, *Harry Hall* (1854), Mr. Hamilton, Mr. Harcourt, Mr. Hayes, Mr. Heath, John Milton Hengler, Master Henry, Mr. Henry, Mrs. Henry, *Caroline Hiffert* (1848–49), Mrs. C. Barton Hill, *Jane Hill* (Mrs. Burton) (1848–53), *Thomas J. Hind* (1849), H. Holbrand, *George Holman* (1849–57), *Mrs. George Holman* (1849–57), *George Holland* (1848, 1854), *Clarence Holt* (1857), *Mrs. Clarence Holt* (1857), *Lotty Hough* (1853–54), Charles Howard, *Mrs. Charles Howard* (1855–56), D. Howard, H. Howard, Louisa Howard, Miss Howe, *Mrs. Esther Hughes* (1848–58), Mr. Hurley, Mr. Hutchinson, Mr. Jack, Mrs. Jansen, Mr. Jeffries, Miss Johnson, Sam Johnston, *T. B. Johnston* (1848–51, 1852–54), *George Jordan* (1848–50, 1853–56), H. C. Jordan, Mr. Kain, Mlle. Katrina, Walter Keeble, Mr. Kemp, Miss Keys, M. Keyser, Master Kinchin, *Mrs. Hudson Kirby* (1857), Master Kneass, *Mrs. A. Knight* (1848), Nellie Knowles, Mr. Lawson, Mr. Layskin, Stephen Leach, Annie Lee, J. S. Lee, *M. W. Leffingwell* (1855), Miss Leoline, Kate Leslie, Mr. Levere, Mrs. George Loder, Cornelius Logan, Harry Lorraine, Henry Lynne, *Fred Lyster* (1855), *Harry B. MacCarthy* (1854), *Marian MacCarthy* (1854), G. F. Marchant (1854–55), Louisa Marshall, *Polly Marshall* (1856–57), Wyzeman Marshall, Miss Mason, *Lizzie Weston Davenport Mathews* (1850–52, 1856–57), Mr. Mattison, Miss Maxwell, Miss McCormick, Mr. McFarland, Mr. McRea, *J. H. McVicker* (1855), Mr. Mears, F. Meyer, Miss Julia Miles, Miss Miller, Miss Mitchell, *Maggie Mitchell* (1850, 1857), *Charlotte Mitchell* (1853, 1855), *John Moore* (1853–58), Master Alfred Moore, Charles Moorhouse, Miss Morgan, Miss Mortimer, John K. Mortimer, A. Morton, Charlotte Nikinson, John Nikinson, Miss Norton, *William H. Norton* (1852–53), Wayne Olwin, Josephine Orton, H. O. Pardley, *Amelia Parker* (1855–58), *Charles T. Parsloe, Jr.* (1851–53), *Charles T. Parsloe, Sr.* (1848–55), Mr. Paul, *Julia Pelby* (1853), Kate Pennoyer, *Harry A. Perry* (1855), Eliza Petrie, H. B. Phillips, *Henry Placide* (1849, 1851–52), *Thomas Placide* (1856), Mr. Potts, Ada Stetson Plunkett (1856), Mr. Radcliff, Mrs. Radcliff, Mrs. Rainford, *Milton Rainford* (1855–56), Master Ralph, Master Raphael, Emiline Raymond, *Oliver B. Raymond* (1848–49), Mrs. Rea, Frank Rea, *Kate Reignolds* (1855), *W. H. Reynolds* (1855), Miss Richardson, Miss Robertson, *Agnes Robertson* (1853, 1855, 1856), Miss Robinson, Miss Rose, Henry Russell, *Mrs. Josephine Russell* (1848–50), Redmond Ryan, *Kate Saxon* (1854), *Dan E. Setchell* (1855–57), Mrs. Seymour, James Seymour, Mary Shaw, Paul Shirley, Miss Sinclair, Mr. Sinclair, George Skerrett, *Mrs. George Skerrett* (1850, 1852), *Mrs. John Sloan* (1849), Miss Smith, Mr. Smith, *C. J. Smith* (1857), *Mark Smith* (1856–58), Mrs. Mark Smith, *Mrs. W. H. Smith* (1856–57), *Sallie St. Clair* (1857), Miss Stella, *Sara Stevens* (1856), *J. H. Stoddart* (1854), Miss Talbot, Miss Taylor, Emma Taylor, *Mary Taylor* (1848, 1851), Miss Terry, *E. N. Thayer* (1848), *Lysander S. Thompson* (1852), Mrs. Charles R. Thorne, *Emily Thorne* (1855), Mr. Tree, Mr. Trevor, Edwin Varrey, Mr. Vernon, Mrs. Vernon, Herr Von Jansen, *Fanny Wallack* (1848, 1851), *J. W. Wallack, Jr.* (1852, 1856), Mrs. J. W. Wallack, Jr., *John Johnstone (Lester) Wallack* (1850–51), Miss Walters, Annie Walters, Miss Walton, Mr. Warden, Mr. Warren, Harry Watkins, Mr. Wenslee, Miss White, Miss Williams, Miss Wilson, Mr. Wilson, *Mrs. Winstanley* (1849), William A. Wood, W. Wright.

REPERTORY

1848–49: *Maidens Beware; Raising the Wind; The Irish Dragoon; The Weathercock; The Miller's Maid; Irish Help; Paul Pry; That Rascal Jack; Cure for the Heart-Ache; John Bull; Mr. and Mrs. Peter White; The Omnibus; Sweethearts and Wives; Dombey and Son; The Angel in the Attic; Lucy Did Sham Amour; The Tipperary Legacy; or, A Voice from Old Ireland; Valentine and Orson; The Old Guard; The Revolt of the Sextons; or, The Undertaker's Dream; Old Honesty; Valet de Sham; The Invisible Prince; The Capture of Captain Cuttle and Barnaby's Wedding; Poor Pillicoddy; Comus; Seeing the Elephant; Monsieur Jacques; The Dancing Barber; The Woman Hater; The Toodles; Mr. Lobjoit and His Papa; New York in Slices; The Dead Shot; Living Pictures; Don Keyser de Bassoon; The Poor Gentleman; Anything for a Change; Breach of Promise; The Winterbottoms; A Counterfeit Presentment; The Mummy; An Irish Engagement; Pas de fascination; Metamora; Musical Arrivals; Thomas and Jeremiah in America; The Printer's Apprentice; The Tragedy Queen; Where's Barnum? The California Gold Mines; The Midnight Watch; Slasher and Crasher; The Haunted Man and the Ghost's Bargain; The Enchanted Isle; A Day Well Spent; Luke, the Labourer; Jeremiah Clip; Vanity Fair; Monto Cristy; Fistimania; or, The Man Who Saw the Fight; The King of the Peacocks; The Fast Man; Your Life's in Danger; Punch in New York; A Wife for a Day; Napolean's Old Guard; The Nervous Man; St. Patrick's Eve; Beauty and the Beast; Who Speaks First?; Macbeth Travestie; The Hemlock Draught; Forty Winks; or, Blunders in a Bedroom; Socialism; or, Modern Philosophy Put in Practice; Perfection; The Illustrious Stranger; Pickels; or, Ye Broken Hearted Brigand; Romance and Reality; Herr Nanny; His First Peccadillo; The Wager; The Adopted Child; The Review; The Wigwam; The Pet of the Petticoats; The Eton Boy; Chloroform; The Siamese Twins; The Heir-at-Law; Begone Dull Care; The Cabinet Question; London Assurance; The Dumb Belle; Turning the Tables; The Hundred-Pound Note; The Confidence Man; Don Giovanni; The Haunted House; Day after the Fair; Taken in and Done For; John Dobbs; Kinge Richarde Ye Thirde; The Merchant of Venice; Horn's Last; Keeping the Line; The Rivals; Romeo and Juliet; Buy It, Dear; Jenny Lind; Married Life; A Most Unwarrantable Intrusion; The Unfinished Gentleman; The Widow's Victim; Money; The Abduction of Rea.*

1849–50: *Faint Heart ne'er Won Fair Lady; The Sphinx; Turning the Tables; The Toodles; Paul Pry; Temptation; or, The Price of Happiness; Cousin Cherry; The Marriage of Figaro; 'Tis Only My Aunt; A Mother's Bequest; Dombey and Son; Lola Montez; How to Pay Your Washerwoman; Mr. and Mrs. Peter White; Somebody Else; Young America; Spring Gardens; Love Laughs at Locksmiths; Kingcraft in 1852; A Day after the Fair; The Demon Jester; or, The Dutchman's Dream; Burton's New York Directory; or, The Cockney in America; A Peep from a Parlour Window; Breach of Promise; The Platform; All Guilty; Hearts Are Trumps; The Old Dutch Governor; Peggy Green; Love in a Village; Who Do They Take Me For?; The Jersey Monopoly; Romance and Reality; Ask No Questions; A Bird of Passage; Mammon and Gammon; Mrs. Bonbury's Spoons; The Queen's Husband; The Serious Family; Methinks I See My Father; The Laughing Hyena; Santa Claus: A Christmas Dream; The Haunted Man; A Lady in a Fix; The Poor Gentleman; The Heir-at-Law; My Wife's Second Floor; Wild Ducks; Leap Year; Forty Winks; Poor Pillicoddy; The Old English Gentleman; An Alarming Sacrifice; King René's Daughter; A Scene in the Life of an Unprotected Female; Domestic Economy; Wreck Ashore; My Precious Betsey; The Vicar of Wakefield; The Merry Family; or, Sleek in New York; The Rent Day; Mysterious Knockings; The Catspaw; The Three Cuckoos; Speed the Plough; The Rivals; London Assurance; Charles XII; X.Y.Z.; Upside Down; Friend Waggles; The Merry Wives of Windsor; Honey Moon.*

1850–51: *The Rough Diamond; Second Thoughts; The Serious Family; The Toodles; Breach of Promise; Poor Pillicoddy; My Precious Betsey; The Laughing Hyena; Forty Winks; Crimson Crimes; Love under a Lamp Post; Consuelo, la Cantatrice; The School for Scandal; The Poor Gentleman; The Heir-at-Law; London Assurance; The Rivals; Old Heads and Young Hearts; Wild Oats; Speed the Plough; She Stoops to Conquer; Secrets Worth Knowing; Man and Wife; She's Come; Jenny's Come!; Bachelor's Torments; The Bold Dragoons; Four Sisters; Without Incumbrances; Ernestine; Dombey and Son; Henry V; Giralda; Used Up; Education; The Young Quaker; My Friend's in the Straps; The Road to Ruin; Married an Actress; The Deserted; David Copperfield; The Pickwick Club; Leap Year; Woman's Life; Sent to the Tower; My Heart's Idol; Lucy Did Sham Amour; The Hypocrite; Betsy Baker; She Wou'd and She Wou'd Not; The World's Fair; or, London in 1851; The Old Love and the New; A Short Reign and a Merry One; Love in a Maze; The School for Tigers; A Morning Call; The School of Reform; Mimi; Valet de Sham; Cure for the Heart-Ache; The Soldier's Daughter; The Old English Gentleman.*

1851–52: *Married Life; That Rascal Jack; Alcestis; The Original Strong-minded Woman; Grimshaw, Bagshaw, and Bradshaw; Sweethearts and Wives; Charles II; Perfection; The Rough Diamond; Not so Bad as We Seem; Midas; The Last Man; The Winter's Tale; Macbeth; The School for Scandal; Nature's Nobleman; I Have Eaten My Friend; The New Park; The Son and Stranger; Mad Dogs; A New Peculiarity; As You Like It; Old Heads and Young Hearts; Paul Pry; She Stoops to Conquer; London Assurance; The Road to Ruin; Who Wants a Guinea?; The School of Reform; Dombey and Son; The Serious Family; The Toodles; A Hopeless Passion; Wig Wag; The First Night; Clari; Every One Has His Fault; Speed the Plough; The Ladies' Man; or, Love and Pastry; Weak Points; Caught in His Own Trap; The Smuggler's Son and the Exciseman's Daughter; The Pickwick Club; Oliver Twist; The Highway Robbery; The West End; Cinderella; The Old Commodore; Wild Oats; The Mummy; The Belle's Stratagem; The Poor Gentleman; The Way to Get*

Married; The Critic; Rather Excited; or, an Organic Affection; The J.J.'s; Twelfth Night; The Maid of the Mountains; The Connubial Bliss Association; Our Clerks; Who Stole the Pocketbook?; Delicate Ground; The Happiest Day of My Life; The Child of the Regiment; The Fire Eater; The School for Tigers; David Copperfield; The Good for Nothing; John Bull; Bamboozling; Mind Your Own Business; Paris and London; Young America.

1852–53: *The Gardener's Wife; The Eton Boy; The Toodles; David Copperfield; The School for Reform; The Good for Nothing; The Heir-at-Law; The Two Queens; Dombey and Son; The Miller's Maid; The Wreck Ashore; Love's Frailties; A Novel Expedient; Cure for the Heart-Ache; Fortune's Frolic; The Rivals; Robert Macaire; Sink or Swim; The Poor Gentleman; The School for Scandal; Grandfather White-head; Begone Dull Care; Old York and New York; The Serious Family; One Thou-sand Milliners Wanted for the Gold Diggin's of California; City Politics; The Woman I Adore; Patrician and Parvenu; Victorine; The Work of an Artist; Paris and Lon-don; New Year's Day in New England; Laugh and Grow Fat; A New Way to Pay Old Debts; Nicholas Nickleby; Money; The Lady of Lyons; St. Cupid; A Phenom-enon; Twelfth Night; The Smiths; The Merry Wives of Windsor; William and Susan; Civilization; A Bold Stroke for a Husband; She Wou'd and She Wou'd Not; The Custom of the Country; The Irish Lion; The Haunted Chamber; Uncle Pat's Cabin; John Bull.*

1853–54: *A Capital Match; A Duel in the Dark; The Secret; Rappings and Table Movings; Luke, the Labourer; A Day after the Fair; X.Y.Z.; Lend Me Five Shillings; One Thousand Milliners Wanted for the Gold Diggin's of California; Turn Out; The Lawyers; She Stoops to Conquer; The Heir-at-Law; Grist to the Mill; The Serious Family; Delicate Ground; The Poor Gentleman; A.S.S.; Love in a Maze; The Mysterious Lady; Trying It On; David Copperfield; Dombey and Son; Every Man in His Humour; Perfection; My Uncle's Card; Paul Pry; Twelfth Night; Paris and London; The Young Actress; To Parents and Guardians; Shylock; or, The Merchant of Venice Preserved; The Lawyers; The Toodles; Antony and Cleopatra; The Fox Hunt; My Guardian Angel; Christmas Eve in Connecticut; The Comedy of Errors; The Maid with the Milking Pail; Black and White; Masks and Faces; Advertising for a Wife; A Pretty Piece of Business; Married by Force; How to Make a Home Happy; Our Best Society; A Midsummer Night's Dream; Rather Excited; The Lancers; William Tell; Robert Macaire; The Beaux Stratagem; The Automaton Man; The Tempest; The Tempest in a Teapot; Charles XII; Married, Unmarried; Away with Melancholy; Asmodeus; Wild Oats; Honey Moon.*

1854–55: *The Serious Family; The Toodles; The Little Devil's Share; Poor Pil-licoddy; The Rivals; Away with Melancholy; A Midsummer Night's Dream; Heads or Tails; As Like as Two Peas; The Filibuster; Sunshine through the Clouds; Now-adays; The Moustache Mania; Dombey and Son; To Parents and Guardians; Family Jars; Ben Bolt; The Tempest; Patrick: The Poor Sailor; The Heart of Gold; The Good-for-Nothing; The Upper Ten and the Lower Twenty; A Tale of a Tub; A Blighted Being; Living too Fast; or, A Twelve Month Honeymoon; Apollo in New York; Monsieur Jacques; A Nice Young Man; Sophia's Supper; Pride Shall Have a Fall; Circe and Her Magic Cup; Old Adam; The Balance of Comfort; Our Set; or, The Vacant Consulship; Woman's Life in Three Eras: The Girl, the Wife, and the Mother; Fashion; The Player's Plot; or, The Manager and the Minister; As You Like It; Where Shall I Dine?; The Spectre Bridegroom; The Black Swan; Aggravating*

Sam; Trying It On; The Steward; or, The Deserted Daughter; The Invincibles; John
Bull; The Miller's Maid; Legerdemain; or, The Conjuror and His Wife; The Soldier's
Daughter; Janet Pride; David Copperfield; The Siamese Twins; The Youthful Days
of Louis XIV, or, The Secret Agent; Take That Girl Away!; The Thimblerig; Out
for a Holiday; The Ladies' Battle; The Post of Honour; A Day after the Fair; That
Rascal Jack.

1855–56: Breach of Promise; A Kiss in the Dark; Deaf as a Post; Paul Pry; The
Wandering Minstrel; Asmodeus; A New Way to Pay Old Debts; Mr. Burton's
Adventures in Russia; Still Waters Run Deep; The Clockmaker's Hat; An Anony-
mous Correspondent; The Sentinel; Love and Reason; The Daughter of the Regi-
ment; John of Paris; The Toodles; The Serious Family; The Picnic, or, The Water
Party; The Man of Many Friends; Dombey and Son; Lend Me Five Shillings; David
Copperfield; Doleful Life and Dismal Death of a Pair of True Lovers; The Little
Treasure; False Pretenses; or, Both Sides of Good Society; Hamlet; An Impudent
Puppy; or, The man Who Followed the Ladies; Only a Penny; The Dutch Governor;
A Trip to Niagara; New Year's Eve; Burton's New York Directory; Heads or Tails;
The Barber's Tale; Twenty Minutes with a Tiger; Sweethearts and Wives; The Upper
Ten and the Lower Twenty; Laugh When You Can; Young Rapid; The Lady of
Lyons; Sam Patch in France; The Gamecock of the Wilderness; Take That Girl
Away!; The Winter's Tale; Grist to the Mill; Urgent Private Affairs; Jenny Lind;
The Belle's Stratagem; Fortunio; A Cosy Couple; That Blessed Baby; Helping Hands;
Taking the Chances; or, Our Cousin from the Country; Young Tarnation; Ganem;
Queen of Spades; or, The Gambler's Fate; A Scene from the Life of an Unprotected
Female; 'Tis Ill Playing with Edged Tools; One Thousand Milliners Wanted for the
Gold Diggin's of California; The Swiss Cottage; The Evil Genius; A Prince for an
Hour; The Unfinished Gentleman; Catching an Heiress; Monsieur Tonson; Andy
Blake; The Young Actress; Used Up; The Chameleon; Cool as a Cucumber; Maid
with the Milking Pail; Violet; or, The Life of an Actress; A Dose of Champagne;
The Follies of a Night.

1856–57: The Serious Family; The Toodles; The Rivals; The Loan of a Lover;
Honey Moon; Charity's Love; Faint Heart ne'er Won Fair Lady; Catching a Gov-
ernor; An Object of Interest; The Witch Wife; The Poor Scholar; Twice Killed; The
Queen's Husband; The Wreckers, or, A Dream at Sea; Hamlet; Wild Oats; The
School for Scandal; Self; Who Did You Vote For?; Presented at Court; or, The City
Heiress; Genevieve; or, The Reign of Terror; To Parents and Guardians; The Life
of an Actress; Blue Belle; Victor and Hortense; The Young Actress; The Phantom;
Rights and Wrongs of Women; The Slave Actress; Dombey and Son; The Jealous
Wife; The Wonder; Twelfth Night; The Bottle Imp; Fascination; The Invisible Prince;
Our Wife; Perfection; She Wou'd and She Wou'd Not; Much Ado about Nothing;
Vice and Virtue; or, Woman's Heart; Olympia; As You Like It; Trying It On; John
Bull; Duality; The Nervous Man; The Siamese Twins; The Comedy of Errors;
Retribution; The Four Phantoms, or, The Legend of St. Mark; A New Camille;
Time Tries All; Wat Tyler; A Peep from a Parlour Window; Wall Street; The Rules
of the House; or, The Revolt of the Borders of a Bleecker Street Boarding House;
The Winter's Tale; The Crown Diamonds; The Bohemian Girl; The Daughter of
the Regiment; Maritana; La sonnambula; Fra Diavolo; Midas; Hearts Are Trumps;
Our Best Society; Richard III; Richelieu; A New Way to Pay Old Debts; The
Merchant of Venice; King Lear; Romeo and Juliet; The Lady of Lyons; Othello;

The Iron Chest; The Taming of the Shrew; The Wife; The Stranger; The Apostate; Little Toddlekins; Julius Caesar; The Coroner's Inquisition; The Stage Struck Tailor; Married Life.

Summer 1857: *The Irish Emigrant; A Lesson for Husbands; The Yankee House-keeper; Sunshine through the Clouds; Trying It On; The Irish Lion; Twice Married; Mischievous Annie; Ireland as It Is; The Young Actress; The Limerick Boy; The Naiad Queen; The French Spy; Katty O'Sheil; The Toodles; The Serious Family; The Printer's Apprentice; Naramattah; Antony and Cleopatra; The Pet of the Petticoats; The Little Treasure; The Four Sisters; Satan in Paris; The Maid with the Milking Pail; Turning the Tables; Duality; Lucrezia Borgia; Giulietta e Romeo; Ernani.*

1857–58: *A New Way to Pay Old Debts; Julius Caesar; Richelieu; The Apostate; The Iron Chest; The Taming of the Shrew; Richard III; The Irish Broom-maker; The Inconstant; Hamlet; The Stranger; The Dramatist; A Fearful Murder Downtown; Money; Wild Oats; The Robbers; Honey Moon; The School for Scandal; Much Ado about Nothing; Fazio; Romeo and Juliet; As You Like It; Guy Mannering; The Actress of Padua; Was I to Blame?; Macbeth; Janet Pride; London Assurance; Simpson and Co.; Henry VIII; A Lesson of the Heart; My Overcoat; My Son Diana; The Actress of All Work; The Little Treasure; Little Pickle; Arthur; Paris and London; A Day in New York; Vanity Fair; Burton Worried by Brougham; You're Sure to Be Shot; Hamlet Travestie; Angels and Lucifers; An Appeal to the Public; Cure for the Heart-Ache; The Dowager; You're Another; An Eligible Investment; The Critic; A Nice Firm; The Great Gun Trick; Crinoline; He Would Be an Actor; Columbus el Filibustero; The Comical Countess; A Bachelor's Wife; Twelfth Night; A Day of Reckoning; Cool as a Cucumber; Old Heads and Young Hearts; The Merry Wives of Windsor; Pocahontas; The Serious Family; The Toodles; David Copperfield; Nicholas Nickleby; Romance and Reality; The Review; The Head of a Pin; The Road to Ruin; The Comedy of Errors; The Savage and the Maiden; The Metropolitan Policeman; A Struggle for Gold; The Coup d'Etat; The Mormons; or, Life in Salt Lake City; Sarah's Young Man; Damon and Calanthe; The Hard Struggle; Dombey and Son; A Great Tragic Revival; Life Among the Players in England and America; The Musard Ball; or, Love at the Academy; This House to Be Sold; My Friend's in the Straps; The Man without a Head; Love and Murder; Nothing to Nurse; The Obstinate Family; Henry VI; The Kentuckian; Monsieur Mallet.*

Summer 1858: *L'Elisir d'amour; Il Barbiere di Siviglia; Linda di Chamounix; The Handsome Husband; The Eton Boy; Before Breakfast; Belphegor, the Mountebank; or, Woman's Constancy; Love's Sacrifice; The Lady of Lyons; Black Eyed Susan; Ambition; or, The Throne, the Tomb, and the Scaffold.*

1858: *The Irish Ambassador; How to Pay the Rent; The Soldier of Fortune; The Nervous Man; The Wrong Passenger; Fortune Hunters; The Happy Man; King O'Neil; The Irish Genius; Lucrezia Borgia; Rory O'More; La Figlia del Reggimento; A New Way to Pay Old Debts; Richard III; La Traviata; King Lear; Il Trovatore; Richelieu; Othello; Venice Preserved; The Troubadour; The Bohemian Girl.*

BIBLIOGRAPHY

Published sources: T. Allston Brown, *A History of the New York Stage from the First Performance in 1732 to 1901*, 3 vols. (New York: Dodd, 1903); Walter Prichard Eaton, "William Evans Burton," *Dictionary of American Biography*, ed. Allen

Johnson (New York: Charles Scribner's Sons, 1943), 3:346–47; Phyllis Hartnoll, ed., *The Oxford Companion to the Theatre*, 2nd ed. (London: Oxford University Press, 1957); Laurence Hutton, *Plays and Players* (New York, 1875); Joseph N. Ireland, *Records of the New York Stage: 1750 to 1860*, 2 vols. (New York: T. H. Morrell, 1866–67); William L. Keese, *William E. Burton: A Sketch of His Career Other Than That of Actor, with Glimpses of His Home Life and Extracts from His Theatrical Journal* (New York, 1891); George C. D. Odell, *Annals of the New York Stage*, 15 vols. (New York: Columbia University Press, 1929–50); Garff B. Wilson, *A History of American Acting* (Bloomington: Indiana University Press, 1966); idem, *Three Hundred Years of American Drama and Theatre: From 'Ye Bear and Ye Cubb' to 'Hair'* (New York: Prentice-Hall, 1973).

Daniel A. Kelin II

C

CALIFORNIA THEATRE STOCK COMPANY. The theatre life of San Francisco was enriched in 1869 with the erection of the California Theatre on the north side of Bush Street, between Kearney and Dupont (now Grant) streets. William C. Ralston, head of the powerful Bank of California, envisioned a San Francisco with wealth, vitality, and culture to rival any city of the world. The establishment of a superb new "temple of the Muses" was a necessary step to that end. Nearly a dozen theatres had been built in San Francisco since the first professionals performed in English in the gold-rush year of 1849. The Metropolitan, San Francisco's first brick theatre, was opened in 1853 and hosted various stock companies for more than twenty years. However, no resident stock company remained intact longer than a year until the California Theatre Stock Company was assembled in 1869, an event that marked the beginning of a brilliant theatrical era in San Francisco.

To manage his new theatre, Ralston engaged two successful actors, John McCullough (1832–85) and Lawrence Barrett (1838–91). John McCullough came to San Francisco in May 1866 at the age of thirty-four in the company of the great tragedian Edwin Forrest. Nearing the end of his career, Forrest passed his mantle to McCullough, an unpublicized actor, with the advice that he stay in San Francisco. Thomas Maguire, San Francisco's leading theatrical promoter, engaged McCullough as leading man in his stock company at Maguire's Opera House. Young Shakespearean star Lawrence Barrett arrived in San Francisco in 1868 and starred at Maguire's in tandem with McCullough. Barrett, tall, classically featured, with deep-set eyes, was a scrupulous and competent man of the theatre. McCullough was a big man whose forceful, easygoing personality appealed to his coworkers. Beside sharing duties as managers, both men also appeared periodically as stars at the head of the California Theatre Stock Company.

The California Theatre's dignified facade of tall, windowed arches supported by Corinthian columns was unusual for San Francisco, where theatres generally looked like store buildings. The California breathed elegance and comfort, from the twin gas lamps flanking the stone step placed for theatre patrons alighting from carriages to the luxurious, commodious reclining seats in the parquet and dress circles. Seating capacity was 1,478, but this could be increased by extra seats and standing room to 2,150. The proscenium arch was large by the standards of the day, forty-five feet wide and forty feet high. A spacious stage almost eighty feet square featured seven pairs of grooves for laterally moving scenery and a rigging floor fifty feet above the stage for flying scenery. Noiseless rollers made scene shifting quick and easy. An understage chamber, the full size of the stage and fifteen feet deep, contained the latest stage machinery. The theatre was lighted by gas, illumination throughout and onstage controlled by an elaborate system of valves in the backstage wings. The builders announced that except for the gas fittings, carpets, and a few decorations, all materials were of California growth or manufacture. To improve the acoustics, an entirely new wood ceiling was constructed in the late summer of 1872. At the same time, drafts were eliminated by walling up many of the doors to the dress circle and by installing a ventilating system. Finally, seating capacity was increased by 300 seats.

The opening of the California Theatre in 1869 under the management of McCullough and Barrett brought the quality of San Francisco theatre to a new high. Given a free hand in assembling a stock company, McCullough and Barrett hired the best local talent, thereby depleting the local companies. In addition, eight actors were imported from first-rate eastern theatres.

Most of the local actors were from Maguire's Opera House, where, with shrewdness and good judgment, Tom Maguire had formed a strong company. Heading the list of local players was Annette Ince. The first leading lady of the California Theatre Stock Company was a member of a theatrical family, her father having managed the Baltimore Museum. Ince had performed in San Francisco since 1857 and was near the end of her career in 1869. After the first year of operation, she appeared only on rare occasions. Emelie Melville, an attractive actress-singer who had debuted in San Francisco in 1868, was engaged as the leading soubrette. Mrs. C. R. Saunders and Mrs. Judah filled the crucial roles of old women. Both ladies were popular favorites in San Francisco and remained so throughout the decade of the seventies. Harry Edwards, a man of varied theatrical experience, but most recently manager of San Francisco's Metropolitan Theatre, was hired to play leading-man roles. John Wilson, formerly manager of the Lyceum Theatre, San Francisco, contracted to play "heavy-man" parts. Other locals included Willie Edouin, Mr. and Mrs. Frederick Franks, Mr. and Mrs. E. J. Buckley, and Stephen W. Leach.

On January 8, 1869, a steamer brought eight additional company members from the East. Loraine Rogers came out to be business manager. W. H. Sedley-Smith undertook the dual responsibility of stage director and first old man. Sedley-Smith (more commonly known as W. H. Smith in the East) had enjoyed a long and successful career in the theatres of Boston. He was an instant favorite in San Francisco and remained popular until his death in January 1872. John T. Raymond, low comedian, came from the Theatre Comique in New York, after having toured London and Paris with the American star E. A. Sothern. Raymond was one of America's best in his line of business, and in 1873 he left California to become a touring star. Other less important newcomers included brothers William and Claude Burroughs and E. B. Holmes, most recently seen at New York's Niblo's Gardens Theatre. E. S. Marble, son of Dan Marble, the famous character actor, joined the company as second low comedian. Marie Gordon, wife of John Raymond, was engaged as light comedienne, and Fanny Marsh of Boston was placed in the juvenile-lady line. Unlike any other stock company in the city, the group at the California Theatre proved to be an institution in itself, flourishing for eight years with only small changes.

The first season at the California ran for eighteen months. Performances were given Monday through Saturday evenings, with Saturday matinees. Ticket prices were similar to those at Maguire's Opera House and at the Metropolitan. Opera and dress boxes sold at $10.00 and $12.00 a performance, depending on the location of the box. Seats in the Orchestra stalls and in the Dress Circle were reserved for $1.50. Prices in the balconies varied from twenty-five cents to seventy-five cents. Scalping tickets for the better seats was common.

The company was introduced to an expectant public on January 18, 1869, in a production of Edward Bulwer, Lord Lytton's comedy *Money* (1848). John McCullough and Marie Gordon took the leading roles. Amelia Neville, a San Francisco socialite, attended the opening and recorded her memory of the occasion:

The city's wealth, beauty, and fashion were all there, the ladies in light silks with fluttering fans and their hair done in the new mode with long "follow-me-lad" curls over one shoulder—an audience of "carriage folk." Those who did not own clarence or barouche commandeered public hacks for the evening, and they rolled up Bush Street from Kearney, the horses' hoofs clattering on cobble-stones. The lobby with its mirrors fairly glittered with elated people assembling, long silk skirts sweeping the tessellated marble floor; and the elegant Barrett, in full evening regalia, stood smiling like a host welcoming his guests. (Neville, 212)

As many as 2,479 spectators jammed every inch of space, including the aisles, alcoves, and lobbies. Barrett recited a dedicatory address in verse written by Bret Harte, who also was present. Between Acts I and II, a much-heralded new act curtain, the achievement of marine artist Gideon J. Denny, was revealed. Significantly, Denny used a local setting and filled it with the symbols of trade that represented the lifeblood of the city. J. S. Knowles' popular drama *The Hunchback* (1832), E. Falconer's old-fashioned comedy *Extremes* (1858), and G. W. Lovell's tragedy *Love's Sacrifice* (1829, 1842) were vehicles to demonstrate the versatility of the company and its leading performers. Each evening's program consisted of a full-length play and a short, farcical afterpiece. Programs changed nightly throughout the first three weeks, and the press began to notice the strain on the company. Audiences crowded every performance, despite heavy rainfall and foul weather. Barrett did not make his debut until February 1869, when he appeared in Charles Selby's romantic drama *The Marble Heart* (1854). In March 1869 the company presented a two-week season of Shakespeare. *Hamlet*, the opener, used every male member of the company. Critical notes ranged from good to excellent, but evidence of inadequate preparation again appeared, the result of too few rehearsals. Barrett did not fare well with the critics, but McCullough was praised as Othello and Macbeth, roles well suited to his talents.

Prominent stars John E. Owens, Charlotte Thompson, and John Brougham appeared at the California during the spring and summer of 1869. Company members temporarily displaced by stars would make a tour of smaller towns in the California interior, where they played the larger parts ordinarily reserved for the leads and stars, thereby improving their range. Barrett and McCullough used these trips to try out new plays and parts before presenting them in the city. On January 3, 1870, almost one year after its opening, the theatre counted its 300th performance. With total receipts of $278,000, the company averaged more than $900 nightly. On January 18, 1870, an anniversary performance of *Money* was given, for which occasion the interior of the theatre was newly decorated and the front was illuminated. In the spring of 1870 business conditions in general were not very good, for the opening of the transcontinental railroad had not brought the expected wave of prosperity. Other managers of legitimate theatres lowered the standard of their repertoire to include spectacle and burlesque, but McCullough and Barrett resisted, capitulating only with a production of the pantomime *Cherry and Fair Star* and with the month-long engagement of Lydia Thompson and her company of "British Blondes," who had thrilled America with delightful theatrical parodies to which had been added the element of feminine allure. Fortunately, business conditions improved, and the managers were able to return to a policy of legitimate drama. Barrett terminated his association with the company in the summer of 1870 to pursue his acting career in New York.

When the California Theatre Stock Company opened its second regular season August 29, 1870, competition from other theatres had almost ceased. Both the Metropolitan and the Alhambra were closed, and a troupe of

Japanese gymnasts performed at Maguire's Opera House. The California was the only legitimate theatre operating.

For the next six years McCullough guided the activities of the California Theatre Stock Company through a period in which it dominated the theatrical scene in San Francisco. McCullough occasionally played starring engagements in the East, but he maintained a uniformly good stock company, many of whom eventually found stardom. By skillfully negotiating rights to produce recent hits and by maintaining an excellent technical staff, McCullough assured the regular availability of excellent fare. Stars were a regular feature of the California Theatre. The three-week visit of Jean Davenport (Mrs. J. W. Lander, 1829–1903) beginning May 8, 1871, was the company's most successful starring engagement up to that time. Mrs. Davenport Lander was the company's leading lady in the season beginning July 31, 1871. The years 1873–74 saw the greatest array of talent ever to reach the West Coast. E. A. Sothern (1826–81), then at the height of his fame as Lord Dundreary in Tom Taylor's *Our American Cousin* (1858), played the first of three engagements at the California Theatre (he appeared again in 1877 and in 1880). Frank Mayo brought to the California Theatre his version of Davy Crockett, the rugged frontiersman with the arm of iron and the heart of gold, four times in six years, to become one of the most popular stars to appear with the company. McCullough also engaged the international luminary Adelaide Neilson (1846–80), then on the first of her two extremely successful tours of the states. McCullough himself, having achieved stardom, played a lucrative four-week engagement in his own theatre. Barton Hill was acting manager while McCullough pursued his acting career during the prosperous years of 1874 and the first half of 1875.

In early April 1872 the group presented its most successful production, W. S. Gilbert's *Palace of Truth* (1870), featuring scenery by William T. Porter. The piece ran until May 4, an exceptional term for this company given to rapid change of bill to attract an audience. Porter's scenery was commonly an ingredient in the group's most successful pieces. His work was first mentioned in September 1869 in a revival of Dion Boucicault's *Streets of New York* (1857), which closed with a final tableau of a burning building with a real engine, hose, and firemen. The presentation of John Brougham's *Duke's Motto* (1853), the great success of the spring of 1870, combined acting, ballet, and gymnastic feats with magnificent scenery and costumes. Porter was at his best in preparing landscapes with distant views in deep perspective. His representation of the Gypsy Dell in Brougham's extravaganza was noted for its "massive grandeur." The reporter for the *Bulletin* noted on March 22, 1870, that "when the curtain rolled up on this scene, a storm of applause swept through the house and continued for several minutes." Much of the success of the 1871 production of Fred Lyster's *Ready! or, California in 1871* rested on local allusions and on

Porter's scenic views of sights such as Seal Rock and the Farallones with clippers and steamships entering the Golden Gate. The company basked in the warmth of public praise from 1873 to 1876, and the whole operation seemed to be financially solvent. A business recession in 1876, close on the heels of the death of the group's principal benefactor, William C. Ralston, spelled the eventual end of this great company.

On August 26, 1875, the Bank of California closed its doors, and San Francisco experienced a severe financial panic, which set off a prolonged depression lasting to the end of the decade. McCullough attempted to salvage the fortunes of the company in 1876 by engaging Edwin Booth, America's foremost tragedian, for a triumphal return to the San Francisco stage, where he had debuted as a boy in his father's company in 1849. Barton Hill went to Chicago to escort Booth and his family to San Francisco in a special railway car. McCullough remained in the city to supervise arrangements for Booth's appearance. He installed large windows in the wall between the dress circle and the lobby to increase standing room, and he organized an auction of choice seats. An enthusiastic public paid enormous premiums for tickets and filled the theatre every night. He procured additional scenery and costumes and strengthened an already strong company by engaging Kate Denin to support Booth. Luring Booth to the West Coast was the high point of McCullough's career as a theatrical manager. Booth's starring engagement temporarily halted the decline of the company, as did the American debut of the great Polish actress Mme. Helena Modjeska in 1877. Nevertheless, the 1876–77 season was the poorest in the group's history.

In 1877 McCullough added to his duties the management of Baldwin's Theatre in San Francisco. With a confidence that amounted to foolhardiness in these depressed times, McCullough set about engaging an entirely new dramatic company from the East. Baldwin refurbished the theatre, and McCullough ordered new scenery. Despite these promising arrangements, business lagged. In only two and a half months of managing two theatres, McCullough lost a reported $28,000.

Having learned a bitter lesson, McCullough ended all of his managerial ventures. He sold a half interest in the California Theatre to his acting manager, Barton Hill, recovering in the sale the amount he had recently lost in managing the Baldwin. His Hamlet on August 27, 1877, was the last role he played in San Francisco. Eight months later he sold the remaining half interest to George Barton and Frank Lawlor and withdrew entirely from the San Francisco theatre scene. A report in the San Francisco *Chronicle* of June 30, 1878, revealed some of the sad financial details of the operation of the California Theatre. McCullough had put up $12,000 at the beginning of the McCullough-Barrett lease in 1869. Barrett's contribution was not revealed, but the *Chronicle* reported that Barrett sold out for $5,000 a year later. McCullough had to borrow heavily from banker

William C. Ralston, owing him, at Ralston's death in 1875, about $75,000. Booth's engagement in 1876 permitted the liquidation of a $20,000 debt to the Bank of California, but the cost of subsequent stars such as Frank Mayo and E. A. Sothern exceeded income. On June 30, 1878, the California Theatre Stock Company was $55,000 in debt. Sources do not reveal fully and precisely the financial history of the company, but it seems throughout its life to have been an occasionally glittering artistic success but a consistent financial failure.

Neither of the new managers, Barton or Lawlor, had sufficient experience to make the California Theatre either a financial or an artistic success. The fortunes of the theatre declined sadly in 1878. Players drifted away and were not replaced. Touring productions gradually replaced the stock organization. Reorganization was attempted in the late spring of 1878 and again in August 1878, but the new companies were short lived. The California Theatre was closed the summer of 1879 for repairs. It reopened August 25 for two months, then closed a month, opened again November 20, and remained in business to the end of the year. In 1880 the theatre was open less than half of the time and employed, for the most part, performers jobbed in to support stars when touring companies were not available. Successive managements of Charles E. Locke and the team of Thomas Maguire and A. W. Field relied ever more heavily on traveling productions. By the end of 1881, the stock company mode of organization had been totally abandoned.

PERSONNEL

Lessees and Managers: Lawrence Barrett, John McCullough (1869–70); John McCullough (1870–77); John McCullough, Barton Hill (1877–78); Barton Hill, George Barton, Frank Lawlor (1878–81); Charles E. Locke (1881); Tom Maguire, A. W. Field (1881).

Acting Manager: Barton Hill (1873–77).

Stage Managers: W. H. Sedley-Smith (1869–72), Robert Eberle (1877– ?).

Business Managers: Loraine Rogers (1869–70), Frank B. Cilley (1870– ?).

Scenic Artists: John Wilkins, Herr Habbe, William T. Porter (1869–77).

Machinist: John Torrance.

Costumer: J. H. Paulin.

Orchestra Leader: Charles Schultz (1869– ?).

Actors and Actresses: Sarah Alexander, Harry Atkinson, *William Barry* (1873–74), *Mr. and Mrs. E. J. Buckley* (1869– ?), J. B. Burnett, Clyde Burroughs, W. F. Burroughs, W. Caldwell, James Carden, Eleanor Carey, *George D. Chaplin* (1872–73), Belle Chapman, J. Chapman, G. Cleaves, Nellie Cummings, *Jean Davenport* (1872–73), Rellie Deaves, *Nelson Decker* (1874–77), Willie Edouin, *Harry Edwards* (1869–78), *Sophie Edwin* (c.1870–76), Mr. and Mrs. Frederick Franks, *Marie Gordon* (1869–71), *Annie Graham* (1872–73), *Alice Harrison* (c.1876–78), Charles Henry, E. B. Holmes, *May Howard* (1870–72), *Annette Ince* (1869–70), L. Johnson, *Mrs. Judah* (1869–78), *Thomas W. Keane* (1874–78), H. King, *Stephen W. Leach* (1869–

78), *Carlotta Leclercq* (1873–74), Jennie Lee, *Walter Leman* (1870–78), Kate Lynch, E. S. Marble, Fanny March, *Owen Marlow* (1870–73), *Emelie Melville* (1869–70), *W. A. Mestayer* (1872–78), Miss Mitchell, *Maggie Moore* (1872–74), *Bella Pateman* (1874–75), *Robert Pateman* (1874–75), Eban Plympton, *John T. Raymond* (1869–71), Betty Rigl, Emily Rigl, *Mrs. C. R. Saunders* (1869–81), *William R. Sedley-Smith* (1869–70), J. A. Smith, *Charlotte Thompson* (1873), Helen Tracy, J. Walters, *Minnie Walton* (1870, 1871–73), *J. C. Williamson* (1871–74), Mrs. Wilson, John Wilson, Ellie Wilton (1875–78).

REPERTORY

No calendar of the California Theatre for the period 1869–81 has come to light. The *Annals of the San Francisco Stage* sketches an outline of the offerings of the California Theatre Stock Company.

BIBLIOGRAPHY

Federal Theatre Project, San Francisco. *Annals of the San Francisco Stage*. Vol. 1, 1850–80. Edited by L. M. Foster. Vol. 2, 1880–1924. Edited by C. E. Marshall. San Francisco: Federal Theatre Project, 1937.
Gagey, Edmund M. *The San Francisco Stage*. New York: Columbia University Press, 1950.
Krumm, Walter C. "The San Francisco Stage, 1869–79." Ph.D. diss., Stanford University, 1961.
McElhaney, John Scott. "The Professional Theatre in San Francisco, 1880–1889." Ph.D. diss., Stanford University, 1972.
Neville, Amelia (Ransome). *The Fantastic City*. New York: Houghton Mifflin Co., 1932.

Weldon B. Durham

CHAMBERS STREET THEATRE COMPANY. (1848–56) See BURTON'S STOCK COMPANY.

CHARLESTON COMPANY OF COMEDIANS. (1792–96) See [THOMAS WADE] WEST COMPANY.

CHARLESTON COMPANY OF COMEDIANS. (1815–24) The Charleston Company of Comedians, Charleston, South Carolina, was organized by Joseph G. Holman (1764–1817) in October 1815, when he reopened the "Old" Charleston Theatre after the end of the War of 1812.

After Alexander Placide's death in the summer of 1812, his widow, Charlotte Wrighten Placide, continued with Placide's Company* at the Charleston theatre until January 1813, but the war and declining attendance forced her to close the theatre. It remained closed until eight months after the Peace of Ghent was declared in February 1815, when Joseph G. Holman reopened it. Holman continued as manager until a dispute with his leading man, James Caldwell, convinced him to cede his management to his son-in-law Charles Gilfert.

Joseph Holman debuted at Covent Garden in 1784, coming to America in 1812 to perform with the Park Theatre Company (1806–26)* in New York under Stephen Price and Thomas A. Cooper. After an engagement in Boston with his daughter Agnes (who married Gilfert in 1815), he went to Charleston to open the theatre for the 1815–16 season. Charles Gilfert (1787–1829), an orchestra leader, immigrated to Charleston from his native Germany as a young man and quickly became a leader of the music community there, for he was a composer and music critic as well as a conductor. He and his wife, Agnes, participated in Charleston theatre from 1815 to 1825. He extended his theatrical interests to Savannah, Richmond, and other southern cities, furthering theatre in the South. After leaving the southern circuit, he met with ill fortune and died a pauper.

After the opening of the theatre October 25, 1815, Holman played six nights a week to large audiences eager to celebrate the end of the war. Holman's two seasons with the Charleston Theatre were profitable financially, but his career with the company ended with a contractual dispute with Caldwell in 1817. On March 8, 1817, Holman dismissed Caldwell without warning or public explanation. The argument was carried to the public when personal letters between the adversaries were printed in the city newspaper. It eventually went to the Court of Common Pleas, which granted Caldwell a final benefit performance but upheld Holman's right to discharge his recalcitrant player. Facing an irate town deprived of a favorite actor, Holman ceded his management to Charles Gilfert and left Charleston shortly after. The Panic of 1819 and the resultant nationwide depression deprived the theatre of financial support, and the slow business convinced Gilfert to take his troupe to Savannah twice during the 1818–19 season, once in November and again in February. By May 1819, unable to make expenses in Charleston, he spent a long winter season in Savannah from November 1821 to February 1822. There was no Charleston season in 1822–23, for the Gilfert company remained in Savannah. They returned for a short season from May 22 to June 1821. By 1824, with an upswing in the economy, there was a revival of interest in the theatre, but Gilfert's refusal to compromise the quality of his performances resulted in financial losses until he resigned his management in 1825.

The first postwar Charleston season opened with *The Road to Ruin* on October 25, 1815. The theatre drew packed houses eager to enjoy themselves. The repertory included most of the standard fare for the day, including harlequinades, contemporary melodramas, classics (including Shakespeare's major plays), and pieces by local authors (usually performed in hopes of boosting attendance). These pieces included *Alberti* by Isaac Harby, a local journalist; *The Sea Serpent* by William Crafts, a Charleston lawyer; and *Fauntleroy* by J. A. Strong, a stock player. On February 18, 1818, the company presented the first American performance of Edwin C. Holland's *Corsair*, with special music by Charles Gilfert. On March 12,

1824, Vincent DeCamp, Henry Wallack, and Mrs. Amelia Gilfert joined forces for a presentation of *Henry IV*. Later that same year, on April 12, the Charleston audience was treated to the first American performance of James W. Simmon's *Master of Ravenwood*.

The stock company under both Holman and Gilfert was usually headed by a strong leading man, such as Thomas Hilson or James Henry Caldwell, liberally supplemented by visiting stars. Agnes Gilfert played the female leads; she continued with the stock company for eight years and then returned as a visiting star after her husband left for Albany. In 1816 Thomas A. Cooper returned for his fifth starring engagement, opening in *Hamlet*. He appeared for a total of four engagements during the Holman-Gilfert management. Holman brought James Caldwell from London for his first American appearance, also bringing with him at that time Miss Lattimer, a singer and dancer, who later became Holman's wife.

After a final profitless season, 1824–25, Gilfert left for Albany, hoping for better opportunities. After his resignation, there was a steady decline in Charleston theatre and a long string of unsuccessful managers.

PERSONNEL

Management: Joseph G. Holman, manager (1815–17); Charles Gilfert, manager (1817–25); Charles Young, acting manager (1817–19); Thomas Hilson, acting manager (1819–22); F. Brown, acting manager (1822–25).

Box keeper: Edward Young (1817–20).

Treasurer: Mr. Miller (1823–24).

Scenists: J. West (1815–20), Mr. Spanoletti (1817–20), Mr. Grain (1821–24), C. Bernard (1824–25), Mr. Sera (1824–25).

Orchestra Leaders: Charles Gilfert (1815–25), R. R. Bishop (1821–22), J. Eckhardt Nicola (1823–24).

Ballet Masters: T. Williams (1822–23), Mr. Trebuchet (1823–24).

Actors and Actresses: Mr. Adamson, Mr. Allen, Mr. Andes, Mr. Andrews, Mr. and Mrs. G. H. Barrett, Mrs. G. L. Barrett, Mr. Barry, Mr. C. Bernard, *J. B. Booth* (1821–22, 1825), Mr. Brazier, Mr. Brennen, Mr. Brooks, Mr. J. Brosa, Mr. and Mrs. F. Browns, James H. Caldwell, Master Carey, Mr. Carpenter, Mr. and Mrs. Clarke, Miss C. Clarke, Master E. Clarke, Mrs. J. Claude, *Mr. Cleary* (1819), *William A. Conway* (1824–25), Mr. J. Cooke, *Thomas A. Cooper* (1816, 1818–20), Mr. Cregier, Mr. Cross, Mr. Dalton, *Vincent DeCamp* (1823–24), Mrs. De Sylvia, Mr. and Mrs. W.C. Drummond, Mr. F. Durang, *John H. Dwyer* (1818), Mr. Dyball, Mr. Dykes, Mr. and Mrs. T. Faulkner, Mr. J. Fennell, Jr., Mr. H. J. Finn, Master Foucard, Mr. Fuller, Mrs. Fulmer, *Agnes Holman Gilfert* (1817–23), Mrs. Gray, Mr. Green, Miss Haines, Mr. Hanna, Mr. and Mrs. Harper, Mr. Hatton, Mr. and Mrs. Hayes, Mr. Hedderley, Mr. Higgins, Mr. Thomas Hilson, Mr. Holloway, Mrs. J. G. Holman, Mr. Holmes, Mr. Hopkins, Mr. and Mrs. Horton, Mr. J. Howard, Mr. and Mrs. Hughes, Mr. Humber, Mr. Hume, Mr. Hunter, Mr. G. Hyatt, *Benjamin Charles Incledon* (1818), Mr. A. Keene, Mr. Kenyon, Mr. Lamb, Miss Lattimer, Master C. Lege, Mr. Legg, Miss Lettine, Miss Lewin, Mr. Lindsley, Mr. Lowry, Mr. C. Lyons, Mr. Major, Mr. H. Marks, Mr. Marshall, Mr. Mason,

Mr. Mayberry, Mr. Meholla, Mr. H. Moreland, Miss Morre, Mr. Mude, Mr. W. Nichols, Mr. Page, Mr. Palmer, *William Pelby* (1824), Mr. Pemberton, *Aaron Phillips* (1816, 1818, 1819), Elizabeth Placide, Henry Placide, Mr. J. Pritchard, Mr. Quin, Mrs. Reeves, Mr. Ringwood, Mr. Rivers, Mr. W. Robertson, Mr. Robinson, Miss Russell, Mr. Saunders, Mr. Schinotti, Mr. Seward, Mr. Singleton, Miss Smith, Mrs. Smith, Mr. Somerville, Mr. and Mrs. Spiller, Mr. Steele, Mr. Stevenson, Mr. Stewart, Mrs. J. A. Stone, Mr. Taylor, Mr. and Mrs. Thomas, Miss Tilden, Mr. Trevor, Mr. Tyke, Mr. J. Tyler, Mrs. Utt, *Henry Wallack* (1820, 1824), Mrs. Leigh Waring, Mr. Warrell, Mrs. James West, Mr. and Mrs. Frederick Wheatley, Mrs. S. Wheatley, Master William Wheatley, *Mr. Williams* (1818), Mrs. E. Young.

REPERTORY

1815–16: *The Road to Ruin; 'Tis All a Farce; Sleep Walker; The Merchant of Venice; The Agreeable Surprise; She Stoops to Conquer; The Miller and His Men; George Barnwell; Sons of Erin; Venice Preserved; The Fair Penitent; The School for Scandal; Much Ado about Nothing; The Highland Reel; Jane Shore; Macbeth; Votary of Wealth; Alexander the Great; The Devil to Pay; The Maid and the Magpie; The Prize; Ten Thousand Pounds; Richard III; Spoil'd Child; Othello; Coriolanus; Catherine and Petruchio; The Cooper; Pizarro; Romeo and Juliet; Douglas; Point of Honour; The Bridal Ring; The Child of Nature; Ella Rosenberg.*

1816–17: *The Will; The Review; The West Indian; The Farmer's Wife; Cymbeline; Fortune's Frolic; The Prisoner at Large; Foundling of the Forest; The Jew and the Doctor; The Forest of Bondy; Bombastes Furioso; Wives as They Were and Maids as They Are; Aethiop; No Song, No Supper; Bertram; Lyar; Matrimony; The Glory of Columbia; Henry VIII; John of Paris; Sylvester Daggerwood; Tekeli; King Lear; Harlequin Skeleton; Pas de Deux; The Death of Captain Cook; The Haunted Tower; For Freedom! Ho!*

1817–18: *Speed the Plough; The Way to Get Married; Of Age Tomorrow; John Bull; The Battle of New Orleans; The Merchant of Venice; The Sprigs of Laurel; As You Like It; The Apostate; Henry IV; The Belle's Stratagem; Punch's Festival; Much Ado about Nothing; Corsair; The Innkeeper's Daughter; Wild Oats; Richard III; Accusation; Brother and Sister; Honey Moon; The Romp; Rule a Wife and Have a Wife; The Wheel of Fortune; The Quaker; The Waterman; Love in a Village; The Village Lawyer; Julius Caesar; The Wandering Minstrel; The Tempest; Out of Place; Married Yesterday; Mayor of Garratt; Two Strings to Your Bow; Siege of Belgrade; Honest Thieves; Battle of Hexham; Surrender of Calais; Animal Magnetism; Timour, the Tartar; L'Ambique Comique.*

1818–19: *Falls of Clyde; Devil's Bridge; Maid of the Mill; The Cabinet; Fontainbleu Races; Love Laughs at Locksmiths; My Grandmother; Forty Thieves; Laugh When You Can; The Green Man; Cure for the Heart-Ache; Cinderella; The Sleeping Draught; Robbers; Tale of Mystery; The Iron Chest; Alberti; Rob Roy MacGregor; Castle Spectre; The Sea Serpent.*

1819–20: *Brutus; She Would Be a Soldier; Shelty's Frolic; Blue Devils; Personation; Wanted: A Wife; High Life below Stairs; The Jew of Lubeck; Flora's Birthday; Bluebeard; Evadne; The Wonder; Votary of Wealth; Forest of Bondy; The Broken Sword; The Hunter of the Alps; Barber of Seville; The Midnight Hour; Ways and*

Means; Lodoiska; La Perouse; Origin of Harlequin; The Provok'd Husband; Revenge; Lady of the Lake; Actress of All Work; Dermot and Kathleen; The Steward.

1820–21: *Guy Mannering; Henry Quatre; Don Giovanni; The Suspicious Husband; Marmion; The Young Quaker; The Vampire; The Country Girl; Three Weeks after Marriage; Virginius; Secrets Worth Knowing; Exile; Budget of Blunders; The Promissory Note; The Apprentice; Mountaineers; King Lear; The Woodman's Hut; The Heart of Midlothian; Who Wants a Guinea?; Battle of Bunker Hill; The Warlock of the Glen.*

1821–22: *The Heir-at-Law; Lovers' Quarrels; Damon and Pythias; Roland for an Oliver; Thérèse; Wallace; Nature and Philosophy; The Poor Soldier; Too Late for Dinner; A New Way to Pay Old Debts; Town and Country; The Distrest Mother; Irishman in London; The Lady and the Devil; Harlequin Woodcutter; The Spectre Bridegroom; The Virgin of the Sun; Fraternal Discord; The Merry Wives of Windsor; Riches; Is He Jealous?; Hamlet Travestie; How to Grow Rich; Know Your Own Mind; Wandering Boys.*

1822–23 (May–July): *Monsieur Tonson; Don and Patty; King John; John Buzzby; Rochester; Adrian and Orrila; Gilderoy; Manager in Distress; The Festival of the Fourth of July.*

1823–24: *Raising the Wind; Isabella; Two Pages of Frederick the Great; Spy; Fazio; Clari; The Duel; Tom Thumb, the Great; Washington; Wine Does Wonders; Love among the Roses; Forest of Rosenwald; Ladies at Home; The Way to Get Married; Tom and Jerry; Family Jars; Rendezvous; The Adopted Child; Deaf as a Post; Greece and Liberty; Zembuca; Lady of the Lake; Master of Ravenswood; Youthful Days of Mr. Hyatt; Shakespeare's Jubilee; The Boarding House; Gile Tout Soul.*

1824–25: *The Dramatist; Rule a Wife and Have a Wife; The Stranger; Simpson and Co.; The Gamester; Married and Single; The Day after the Wedding; Lafayette; Aladdin; The Vampire; The Bride of Abydos; The Steward; Alasco; Smiles and Tears; Caius Gracchus; Fauntleroy; Eight to One; Restoration; Trick upon Trick.*

BIBLIOGRAPHY

James H. Dormon, Jr. *Theatre in the Ante-bellum South: 1815–1861.* Chapel Hill: University of North Carolina Press, 1967.

W. Stanley Hoole. *The Ante-Bellum Charleston Theatre.* Tuscaloosa: University of Alabama, 1946.

Nan Louise Stephenson. "The Charleston Theatre Management of Joseph George Holman, 1815 to 1817." B.S. thesis, Louisiana State University, 1976.

Jerri Cummins Crawford

[THE "NEW"] CHARLESTON THEATRE COMPANY. The "New" Charleston Theatre Company, Charleston, South Carolina, was organized by William C. Forbes after he extended his Georgian circuit to include Charleston in 1842.

The "New" Charleston Theatre, Meeting Street, was built by a group of local businessmen and opened under the management of William Abbott, December 15, 1827. W. H. Lathan assumed the management in 1841 after

Abbott's resignation. In 1842 Charles Gilfert added the theatre to his southeastern circuit.

Forbes' first Charleston appearance was at the Queen Street Theatre in 1835. He went on to play at the Park Theatre, New York, and Philadelphia's Walnut Street Theatre, where he married the actress Fannie Marie Gee. He opened theatres in Savannah and Augusta in 1837, extending this circuit to Charleston in December 1842.

Forbes boasted packed houses and profitable limited engagements for his stars until his resignation in 1847. This first season was interrupted by a fire in April 1838, which destroyed a large part of the city (excluding the theatre). Forbes gave a benefit in Savannah for the Charleston fire sufferers in May 1838. He continued with annual seasons from mid-November to April or May to coincide with the winter social season.

During the bleak years of Charleston theatre from 1825 to 1861, Forbes' astute management provided the city with brilliant, if short, seasons. During his first season, he engaged ten internationally known artists in five months. He continued with this formula, offering variety, a large number of celebrities, a capable orchestra, and an excellent stock company throughout his management.

Forbes opened his management of the New Charleston Theatre with a performance of *Honey Moon* prefaced by a poetical address written by a local citizen and delivered by the manager's wife. In keeping with local tastes, he opened April 1843 for a brief season of opera and engaged the Seguin Opera Company in 1844 for their fourth annual visit to the city. Also in 1844 the Robinson Equestrians presented *Mazeppa* and *Timour, the Tartar* with live horses. If his standards of production were slightly lowered for this second season, he certainly knew how to keep his audiences happy.

Forbes engaged many fine performers during his management, notably William Charles Macready, who performed *Macbeth, Richelieu*, and *Othello*. Another favorite with Charleston audiences was Anna Cora Mowatt, author of *Fashion* and an accomplished actress, who appeared in 1844.

No financial accounting indicates a reason for Forbe's withdrawal from Charleston. He may have been prophetic, for the next five years saw five different managers unsuccessfully try to attract an audience to the theatre. The Civil War finally destroyed any semblance of legitimate theatre as the city turned its full attention to survival. On December 11, 1861, the New Charleston Theatre, as well as one-third of the city, was destroyed by a fire (not related to the war).

PERSONNEL

Management: W. C. Forbes, manager (1842–47); H. J. Conway, acting manager (1844–45); J. B. Fuller, acting manager (1846–47).

Treasurer: Mr. Dennison (1846–47).

Scenists: H. Isherwood (1842–43), Mr. Milner (1843–44), J. C. Lamb (1844–47).

Orchestra Leaders: Mr. Tscheruer (1842–43), Mr. Rink (1842–44), F. C. Cook (1845–46), A. Gambati (1846–47).

Machinists: Mr. Galbrath (1844–45); Mr. Valentine (1844–45).

Actors and Actresses: A. J. Allen, Mrs. D. C. Anderson, *James R. Anderson* (1847), E. W. Anderton, G. J. Arnold, Mrs. G. Barrett, W. H. Bellamy, Mr. and Mrs. Bennie, Mr. Berger, Mrs. O. Berger, *J. B. Booth* (1844), *Mrs. J. Brougham* (1844), Mr. and Mrs. J. Byrne, Miss Celeste, Miss Charles, Mr. and Mrs. J. S. Charles, Mrs. W. Chippendale, Mrs. Clairville, *Josephine Clifton* (1845), *Herr Andre Cline* (1845), *John Collins* (1846–47), *Edward L. Davenport* (1846), Mrs. Dearing, T. B. de Walden, Mrs. Duvenelle, Mrs. Eastcoat, *Clara Ellis* (1846), Mr. and Mrs. W. Ellis, *Louis and Gustave Ellsler* (1844, 1845), W. M. Fleming, Mrs. W. C. Forbes, *Edwin Forrest* (1844, 1847), Mrs. Frary, J. B. Fuller, Miss M. Gannon, Mr. Gowan, Miss Grove, J. H. Hall, *James Hackett* (1843), Mrs. Hardwick, W. Hardy, G. H. Hill, Miss Homer, Mrs. Hughes, C. Hunt, Miss E. Ince, Mrs. H. Isherwood, Mrs. James, T. B. Johnston, W. G. Jones, Mr. and Mrs. Kemble, Mr. Larkins, Miss M. A. Lee, *William Charles Macready* (1844), *Dan Marble* (1847), Mrs. C. Matthewes, Miss H. Matthewes, T. Matthewes, Mrs. M. Maywood, R. C. Maywood, T. McCutcheon, Mr. M'Cluskey, Miss M'Duall, Mrs. McGowan, W. H. Meekes, Mr. Milot, W. Mitchell, *Anna Cora Mowatt* (1844), Mr. Muillar, Mr. Nagel, J. Oxley, Mons. Paul (1843), H. Pearson, Miss Phillips, Mr. and Mrs. H. B. Phillips, *Henry Placide* (1844, 1847), J. Proctor, T. Radcliffe, Mr. Raphael, W. Ryder, J. R. Scott, *J. S. Silsbee* (1844, 1845), *John Sloman* (1843, 1847), G. H. Smith, Mr. Sullivan, *James W. Wallack, Sr.* (1844, 1846), T. Ward, *Falvy Williams* (1844), Mrs. Wray.

REPERTORY

1842–43: *The Lady of Lyons; State Secrets; Bertram; Hamlet; Kinsmen; Maid of Croissey; Conscripts; Dream of Fate; Nick of the Woods; Carpenter of Rouen; Pleasant Neighbors; Lottery Ticket; Our Mary Anne; Mons. Paul; Spectre Bridegroom; Henry IV; Prince and the Peasant; Virginius; La Bayadère; Charles II; Hylas and Hebe; London Assurance; Macbeth; Actress of All Work; Don Juan; Sergeant's Wife; Last Days of Pompey; Barrack Room; De Montalt; Rendezvous; Blue Devils; What Will the World Say?; Quiet Day; Day after the Wedding; Joan of Arc; Man with the Carpet Bag; Wreck Ashore; Lucky Stars; Faustus; Wives as They Were and Maids as They Are; Tom and Jerry; Naval Engagements; The School for Scandal; Richard III; Animal Magnetism; Rent Day; Exile; Siege of Charleston; My Uncle Foozle; Boots at the Swan; Othello; La sonnambula; Barber of Seville; Raising the Wind; Fra Diavolo; Massaniello; Postillion of Longjumeau; Marriage of Figaro; Olympic Revels; Gazza ladra; Mutiny at the Nore; Der Freischutz; Rob Roy MacGregor; Two Greens; Dead Shot; Jane Shore; Tekeli; Macbeth; Brutus; The Merchant of Venice; Valet de Sham; Wonder; Thérèse.*

1843–44: *The Belle's Stratagem; Waterman; She Stoops to Conquer; Nature and Philosophy; Sweethearts and Wives; Simpson and Co.; La Bayadère; Merchant and His Clerks; La sylphide; His Last Legs; Three Weeks after Marriage; Alma Mater; Dumb Girl of Genoa; Double Bedded Room; La Polacco; William Tell; Wife for a Day; Knight of the Golden Fleece; Cut and Come Again; Hunting a Turtle; Green*

Mountain Boy; Star Spangled Banner; Forest Rose; Macbeth; Virginius; Richard III; Othello; Richelieu; Love's Sacrifice; Henry IV; Rip Van Winkle; Merry Wives of Windsor; Man of the World; Monsieur Mallet; Militia Training; Jonathan in England; Kentuckian; Monsieur Tonson; Richard III; Alma Mater; Cherry and Fair Star; Two Friends; My Wife's Second Floor; Werner; Love Chase; Centogenarian; Youthful Queen; Grandfather Whitehead; Hunchback; Rivals; Married Rake; Metamora; New Way to Pay Old Debts; Iron Chest; Apostate; King Lear; Mayor of Garratt; Rent Day; Children in the Wood; My Aunt; Town and Country; Much Ado about Nothing; Wild Oats; Brigand; Katherine and Petruchio; Agnes de Vere; Charles XII; Graveyard Murder; Mazeppa; Spanish Exile; Yankee Land; Wool Pedlar; Boston Tea Party; Bumps.

1844–45: *Love's Sacrifice; Roland for an Oliver; Crusaders; King's Gardener; Hercules of Brittany; Valentine and Orson; Chapter of Accidents; Sam Slick; Vermont Wool Dealer; Red Wood; New Footman; Rights of Women; Turning the Tables; Millionaire; Maiden's Vow; Perfection; Bride of Lammermoor; My Wife's Come; Tam O'Shanter; Poor Gentleman; Is He Jealous?; Speed the Plough; Uncle Sam; John Bull; Bombastes Furioso; Uncle John; Paul Pry; Anatomist; Forty Thieves; Bertram; Riches; Amateurs and Actors; Fraternal Discord; Fortunio; Yemassee; Follies of a Night; College Boy; Putnam; Post of Honor; Asmodeus; Mysteries of Paris; Stranger; Bohemian Girl; Young Widow; Ballet de Sham; Cinderella; Patrician's Daughter; Tower of London; Married Bachelor; Norman Leslie; William Tell; Columbus; Timour, the Tartar; Virginny Mummy; Black Eyed Susan; Ben, the Boatswain; Tom Cringle; Rival Pages; Happiest Day of My Life; Golden Farmer; Lady and the Devil.*

1845–46: *Money; Young America; Evadne; Wife; Loan of a Lover; Fazio; Old Heads and Young Hearts; Wrecker's Daughter; Love Chase; Two Queens; Time Works Wonders; Sam Patch in France; Backwoodsman; Hue and Cry; All the World's a Stage; People's Lawyer; Peaceful Pelton; Larboard Finn; Honey Moon; Used Up; Romeo and Juliet; Bride of Lammermoor; Faint Heart ne'ver Won Fair Lady; Fashion; Robert Macaire; Jane Shore; Weathercock; Don Caesar de Bazan; Venice Preserved; Uncle John; West End; La cracovienne; King and I; Point of Honour; Buy It, Dear, 'Tis Made of Cashmere; Momentous Question; Man and Wife; Review; Spy; Farmer's Story; Maidens Beware; 'Twas I; As You Like It; Gamester; Ion; Twelfth Night; Somebody Else; Corporal's Wedding; Cricket on the Hearth.*

1846–47: *Iron Chest; Giselle; Lend Me Five Shillings; La fleur de champ; Turned Head; Wept of Wish-Ton-Wish; Clari; Soldier's Daughter; Done Brown; Make Your Wills; Money; Evadne; Mary Stuart, Queen of Scotland; Illustrious Stranger; King of the Commoners; Love, Law, and Physic; My Aunt; Rent Day; Swiss Swains; Ernestine; Love's Sacrifice; Love; Trumpeter's Daughter; Did You Ever Send Your Wife to Mount Pleasant?; Irish Ambassador; Teddy, the Tiler; Born to Good Luck; How to Pay the Rent; Nervous Man and the Man of Nerve; Irish Attorney; Soldier of Fortune; Irish Post; Pleasant Neighbors; Happy Man; You Can't Marry Your Grandmother; Wizard of the Wave; Wandering Minstrel; Family Jars; Imagination; Fish Out of Water; Patriot's Wife; My Master's Rival; Deaf as a Post; King of Clubs; Palo Alto; Napoleon's Old Guard; Prophecy; Robbers; Elder Brother; Damon and Pythias; Wolf and Lamb; Spectre Bridegroom; Gladiator; Dumb Belle; Skeleton Hand; Bob Short; Uncle Foozle's Wedding Day; Hue and Cry; Married Rake; Family Ties; Fortune's Frolic; Norma; Don Pasquale; Brewer of Preston.*

BIBLIOGRAPHY

James H. Dormon, Jr. *Theatre in the Ante-bellum South: 1815–1861.* Chapel Hill: University of North Carolina Press, 1967.
W. Stanley Hoole. *The Ante-Bellum Charleston Theatre.* Tuscaloosa: University of Alabama, 1946.

Jerri Cummins Crawford

CHATHAM GARDEN THEATRE COMPANY. The Chatham Garden Theatre, New York City, opened on March 17, 1824, under the management of Hippolite ("Henry") B. Barrière. His successful productions in a tent in Chatham Garden in 1822 and 1823 so angered Stephen Price, the doughty manager of the Park Theatre, that he invoked an antiquated fire statute to eliminate Barrière's competition. Barrière, consequently, dismantled his Pavilion Theatre and erected the Chatham Garden Theatre, a brick-and-mortar testament to his business acumen. The new proscenium theatre in Chatham Street, which accommodated 1,300 patrons in two circles of boxes and a pit, featured a stage thirty-two feet wide by twenty-nine feet, nine inches, high by about forty feet deep. The company performing there, according to George Odell, provided "the most important opposition the Park had ever encountered" (3:160).

Barrière's initial offering of *The Soldier's Daughter* and *Raising the Wind* signaled the end of the Park Theatre's sole domination of the theatrical scene in New York. Like Price, Barrière assembled a first-rate stock company to support a respectable procession of visiting stars. The former ice cream merchant was also hospitable to new dramatists as he sought to break the hegemony of the Park. The first season was celebrated indeed but gave way to a somewhat less distinguished second year, notable primarily for the addition of thirty feet of stage depth and the installation of gas lighting throughout the theatre, the earliest so-equipped American house. Barrière's death on February 21, 1826, ushered in a succession of managers and companies, each somewhat drearier than the last. As Odell said, "The theatre never again raised its head very proudly above the waters; it passed from one manager to another, and sank lower and lower in the estimation of the fashionable and the fastidious" (3:286).

H. B. Barrière first came to notice as a purveyor of summer entertainments and confections, excelling both as a man of business and as an entrepreneur. He was a gifted judge of and caterer to the public appetite. At his theatre, boxes were rented for fifty cents and the pit for twenty-five cents. An evening's diversion usually included two full-length plays and an afterpiece, with dancing and variety stunts as *entr'actes*.

In 1827 Thomas Megary, the new manager, refurbished the theatre, raising the height of the proscenium, providing backs and cushions for the seats, and adding a "Shakespeare," a twenty-five-cent gallery. Boxes were still available for fifty cents, but the pit cost thirty-seven and a half cents.

The new accommodations, though, did not insure the financial success of the Chatham Garden. There was ever the competition of the Park, and in 1826 the Bowery Theatre opened its doors. The three theatres, then, drew crowds in proportion to the eminence of their visiting stars and the novelty of their offerings. New York, in fact, was not large enough to support three theatres presenting virtually identical programs. When the Bowery burned in May 1828, the Park Theatre reasserted its preeminence, and the Chatham Garden Theatre Company descended to further transmogrifications under the guises of the American Opera House Company*, Blanchard's Amphitheatre Stock Company*, and the Chatham Theatre Company*. In 1832 the theatre was converted into a Presbyterian chapel and used for performances by the Sacred Music Society.

Under Barrière's direction, the Chatham Garden competed successfully with the Park and later with the Bowery. Since at that time stars were conspicuously peripatetic, it is difficult to judge one of the three theatres as superior to the others, especially since their repertories were much the same. The *New York Mirror* of June 5 and 12, 1824, catalogued the company's merits, concluding that it was a very good assemblage of talent. Frequent shifts of management, however, caused a fluctuation of the company's worth. Under R. C. Maywood and Thomas Kilner, the personnel of the Chatham Garden was notable, but no subsequent manager recaptured the excellence of Barrière's troupe. The *Mirror* of September 27, 1826, denominated the Park the lower house, the Chatham the middle house, and the Bowery (now rebuilt) the upper house.

Each manager from Barrière to Maywood and Kilner constructed a season's offerings of standard dramas of all forms, largely dependent on the repertories of visiting stars and "novelties"—new plays or old plays in new guises. When Junius Brutus Booth appeared at the Chatham (1826–28), for example, Shakespearean tragedy and Georgian melodrama dominated the bills. In the absence of stars, farces (for example, James Kenney's *Raising the Wind*), musicals (for example, W. T. Moncrieff's *Tom and Jerry*), and melodramas (for example, George Colman, the younger's *Iron Chest*) usually exhibited the troupe to best advantage. Chatham novelties included John Augustus Stone's *Restoration; or, The Diamond Cross*; Micah Hawkins' *The Sawmill; or, A Yankee Trick*; Samuel Woodworth's *Forest Rose*; and *Old Hickory; or, A Day in New Orleans* "by two gentlemen of this city." Barrière presented "an astonishingly large and varied repertory of all types" (Odell, 3:160), his first season including more than 120 plays and the second almost 100.

Barrière and his successors apparently adjusted the company roster to the demands of each season. In addition to choosing a stage manager from the ranks of the acting company, the managers hired costumers, scenic artists, and machinists. No mention is made of a treasurer, but such an officer doubtless was required. The original acting troupe included fourteen men and nine women, each of whom specialized in a line of business. When required, supernumeraries were hired, as occasionally were specialty performers. Visiting stars, however, added distinction to the company, which over the years supported Junius Brutus Booth, Henry J. Finn, Francis C. Wemyss, Mr. and Mrs. John Barnes, Thomas Barry, Mr. and Mrs. T. S. Hamblin, Edward N. Thayer, and the exceptionally gifted Mary Ann Duff.

The permanent company (under Barrière's management) included Henry Wallack, an English actor whose presence uplifted the stage of America; he was the Chatham's leading man. The principal comedian was George H. Barrett, called by Francis Wemyss "one of the best Genteel Comedians ever attached to the American Stage" (Wemyss, 25). Thomas Kilner, respected as actor and manager, excelled in old men's roles, and Alexander Simpson, the first of the Yankee impersonators, also played comic parts. The leading actress was Mrs. Entwhistle, sometimes called the greatest actress of her time in America. The eccentric Andrew Jackson Allen, Edwin Forrest's "Dummy" Allen, acted in the company and served as costumer. The composition of the acting corps at the Chatham was so fluid that any further attempt to describe the main performers would be futile.

The Chatham Garden Theatre, then, is memorable both for competing seriously with the Park and Bowery Theatres and for providing an additional metropolitan outlet for the talents of established and burgeoning performers. That it started with great promise and ended desultorily is more attributable to the financial exigencies of the period than culpable failure on the parts of its inhabitants.

PERSONNEL

Management: Hippolite B. Barrière, proprietor and manager (May 1824–February 1826); Henry Wallack, manager (March 1826–May 1827); Thomas Megary, manager (June 1827–February 1828); Thomas Flynn, manager (May–March 1828); R. C. Maywood and Thomas Kilner, managers (June–August 1828); Thomas A. Cooper, manager (September 1828); Noah M. Ludlow, manager (September–October 1828).

Stage Directors: Thomas Kilner (1824–26), Watkins Burroughs (1825), Junius Brutus Booth (1826), R. C. Maywood (1827–28).

Scenic Artists: Hugh Reinagle, Mr. Coyle, P. Grain, F. Grain, P. Grain, Jr.

Costumer: Andrew Jackson Allen (1824).

Actors and Actresses: *John J. Adams* (1826, 1828), Mrs. A. J. Allen, *Andrew Jackson Allen* (1824), *James Anderson* (1824–26), George H. Andrews, Thomas Archer, *Mrs. G. Barrett* (1827), *George Barrett* (1824, 1827), Charles Bernard, *Mrs. W. R. Blake* (1824, 1828), *William Rufus Blake* (1824–28), Mr. Blakeley, Mrs. F. Brown, Frederick Brown, *John Mills Brown* (1827–28), *Thomas Burke* (1824), *Mrs. Thomas Burke* (1824–25), Caroline Chapman, W. B. Chapman, William Chapman, Sr., Miss P. M. Clark, Isaac S. Clason, Mr. Collingbourne, Mr. Collins, Thomas Comer, *E. H. Conway* (1825), W. A. Conway, *Thomas A. Cooper* (1828), *Joseph Cowell* (1828), *Sam Cowell* (1828), *Mrs. Sam Cowell* (1828), Mrs.

Crooke, Mr. Darke, Ellen W. Darley, Mr. Denman, Mrs. Dennis, Mrs. W. Dinneford, *William Dinneford* (1825), *George Washington Dixon* (1828), Mrs. A. Drake, *Alexander Drake* (1824, 1828), William Duffy, Mrs. C. Durang, *Charles Durang* (1824–27), Richard F. Durang, John H. Dwyer, Charles Eberle, Elizabeth Eberle, Mr. Edgar, Mr. Edwards, Miss Emery, *Mrs. Entwhistle* (1824–27), Mr. Essender, Mr. Field, Mr. Fielding, Alexina Fisher, *Amelia Fisher* (1827–28), John Fisher, Oceana Fisher, Palmer Fisher, *Thomas Flynn* (1827–28), Mrs. Thomas Flynn, Mr. Foot, Mrs. Forbes, W. S. Forrest, Mr. Garner, W. F. Gates, *Agnes Holman, later Mrs. Charles Gilfert* (1827), Mr. Gray, Mrs. Green, Mrs. Hartwig, *Ann Jane Henry* (1824), John Herbert, Mr. Higgs, Mrs. Mary Hill, *Thomas Hilson* (1827), Mrs. Thomas Hilson, *George Holland* (1827), Mr. Howard, Mr. Hughes, Mrs. Hughes, Henry B. Hunt, William Isherwood, Mrs. Joseph Jefferson, *Joseph Jefferson II* (1824), George F. Jervis, Mrs. Jones, John Jones, Arthur Keene, Mr. Kelsey, Mr. Kenny, *Thomas Kilner* (1824–25, 1827–28), *Mrs. Eliza Kinlock* (1827), Mrs. LaCombe, Mr. Lindsley, *Noah M. Ludlow* (1828), *R. C. Maywood* (1825–28), Mrs. C. F. McClure, Charles F. McClure, Mr. Miller, George H. Moreland, Mr. Morrison, Miss Oliff, Mrs. Papanti, Mr. Parker, *Charles B. Parsons* (1828), William Pelby, Mr. Pemberton, Mr. Petrie, Miss Phillips, Aaron J. Phillips, *Moses S. Phillips* (1826–27), Jane Placide, *Thomas Placide* (1825–27), Thomas H. Quin, Mr. Richards, Miss Riddle, *James Roberts* (1824–28), W. Robertson, Mary Ann Russell, Mr. Sarzedas, *James M. Scott* (1825–28), John Sefton, *Alexander Simpson* (1824–28), Mr. Somerville, Mr. Spiller, Mrs. G. G. Stevenson, George G. Stevenson, *Mrs. Stickney* (1828), John A. Still, Mrs. J. A. Stone, John A. Stone, Charles W. Taylor, Mr. Thompson, Miss Tilden, Mr. Turnbull, Miss C. Turnbull, Miss E. Turnbull, Misses Turner, Mrs. Turner, Mr. Tuthill, Mr. Twibill, George Vernon, Jane Vernon, Mrs. H. Wallack, *Henry Wallack* (1824–28), Mr. Walstein, Mrs. Walstein, W. J. Walton, Ann Duff Waring, Mrs. Caroline Waring, Charles Webb, *F. C. Wemyss* (1824), H. A. Williams, Mrs. H. A. Williams, Mr. Williamson, Alexander Wilson, John Woodhull, Mr. Wray, Charles Young.

REPERTORY

1824–25: *The Soldier's Daughter; Raising the Wind; The Belle's Stratagem; The Day after the Wedding; Wives as They Were and Maids as They Are; Turn Out; The Rivals; Three Weeks after Marriage; Cure for the Heart-Ache; The Irishman in London; Honey Moon; No Song, No Supper; Of Age Tomorrow; Matrimony; Town and Country; Love among the Roses; High Life below Stairs; The Mountaineers; The Wonder; The Critic; The Poor Gentleman; Rosina; The Review; The Heir-at-Law; The Stranger; Love Laughs at Locksmiths; Adelgitha; The Foundling of the Forest; Guy Mannering; Spoil'd Child; Jane Shore; The Merchant of Venice; The Way to Get Married; Othello; The Steward; The Purse; The Iron Chest; Damon and Pythias; The Apostate; Virginius; Three and the Deuce; The Point of Honour; Agreeable Surprise; Abaellino; Sylvester Daggerwood; The Weathercock; Every One Has His Fault; A Roland for an Oliver; John Bull; My Grandmother; The Prize; She Stoops to Conquer; Who's the Dupe?; Rob Roy; St. Patrick's Day; All the World's a Stage; The Brothers; Lovers' Quarrels; Hamlet; Twelfth Night; Richard III; Tom and Jerry; Modern Antiques; Venice Preserved; Adrian and Orrila; Man and Wife; The West Indian; The Hunter of the Alps; The Road to Ruin; The Young*

Widow; Paul and Virginia; Thérèse; The Dramatist; The Devil's Bridge; The Busy Body; The Slave; The Lady and the Devil; Is He Jealous?; Wild Oats; Fire and Water; The Wedding Day; Too Late for Dinner; Smiles and Tears; Romeo and Juliet; Pizarro; The Gamester; Macbeth; Speed the Plough; The Broken Sword; The Will; The Sawmill; A Race for a Wife; Woman's Will a Riddle; The Innkeeper of Abbeville; False and True; Cherry Bounce; Fazio; Kenilworth; The Countess of Leicester; The Turnpike Gate; Melmoth; Old Hickory; Manoeuvring; Caius Gracchus; The Bridal Ring; Marmion; The Fatal Curiosity; The Children in the Wood; The Maid and the Magpie; The Inconstant; Myrtil and Myrtilla; Sweethearts and Wives; The Midnight Hour; Tom Thumb; The Young Hussar; Alexander the Great; The Ruffian Boy; The Reprobate; The Protean Bandit; The Forty Thieves; Lafayette; The Rendezvous.

1825–26: *Honey Moon; Red Riding Hood; Fortune's Frolic; Sweethearts and Wives; Tribulation; The Poor Gentleman; Brother and Sister; Guy Mannering; Charles II; Simpson and Co.; The Heir-at-Law; Paul and Virginia; Rob Roy; Pizarro; Jane Shore; The Forty Thieves; The Mountaineers; The Soldier's Daughter; Tom and Jerry; The Lady of the Lake; Love in a Village; The Forest Rose; The Merchant of Venice; The Falls of Clyde; Town and Country; The Wandering Boys; Adrian and Orrila; Too Late for Dinner; Virginius; The Iron Chest; The Stranger; Othello; The Slave; Thérèse; The Spoil'd Child; Smiles and Tears; The Jew; The Man of the World; King Lear; The Grand Canal; Richard III; Washington; The Busy Body; The Castle Spectre; The Two Pages; The Miller and His Men; The School of Reform; Speed the Plough; The Sultan; George Barnwell; Mr. H.; The Foundling of the Forest; The Romp; Rosina; A Day at Elizabethtown; The Aethiop; The Heart of Midlothian; Buskin at Home; The Rochester of France; The Fortunes of Nigel; Damon and Pythias; Sons of Erin; The Wicklow Goldmines; The Gentle Shepherd; Coriolanus; The Road to Ruin; A Tale of Mystery; Charlotte Temple; Sylvester Daggerwood; The Poor Soldier; Much Ado about Nothing; The Castle of Andalusia; Robinson Crusoe; The Weathercock; Love and Gout; Family Jars; Three Singles and the Deuce; Don Giovanni; The Apostate; The Spy; Love à la Mode; The Gamester; Venice Preserved; Romeo and Juliet; Brier Cliff; Crazy Bet; Macbeth; Julius Caesar; Lyar; Roberts at Home; The School for Scandal; The Mogul Tale; Douglas; Love, Law, and Physic; The Turnpike Gate.*

1826–27: *Speed the Plough; Three and the Deuce; Rob Roy; The Wonder; The Heir-at-Law; Guy Mannering; Ella Rosenberg; Richard III; Hamlet; The Iron Chest; Othello; Brutus; Brother and Sister; The Mountaineers; Town and Country; Virginius; A New Way to Pay Old Debts; The Mayor of Garratt; The Lady of the Lake; Pizarro; Damon and Pythias; Macbeth; William Tell; Michel et Christine; Julius Caesar; The Falls of Clyde; Brier Cliff; Smiles and Tears; Wallace; Douglas; The Road to Ruin; The School for Scandal; The West Indian; Lyar; Laugh When You Can; Deaf and Dumb; King Lear; The Aethiop; George Barnwell; Botheration; Sylla; Brian Boroihme; The London Hermit; Adelgitha; My Uncle Commodore; Marmion; Old Bachelors; Paul Jones; The Battle of Bothwell Brig; The North Pole; The Bride of Lammermoor; Valdemar; Feudal Times; The Stranger; The Maid and the Magpie; Romeo and Juliet; Is He Jealous?; The Children in the Wood; Catherine and Petruchio; The Grecian Daughter; Love in a Village; The Forty Thieves; Lovers' Quarrels; The Busy Body; The Merchant of Venice; The Merry Wives of Windsor;*

Venice Preserved; Honey Moon; The Wandering Boys; Clari; Alonzo, the Brave; The Fair Imogene; The Slave; Wild Oats; The Dramatist; The Snow Storm.

1827–28: *The Man of the World; Family Jars; Paul Pry; The Poor Gentleman; Rob Roy; Tom and Jerry; The Prize; The Castle Spectre; The Warlock of the Glen; The Spy; The Day after the Fair; Pizarro; The Apostate; High Life below Stairs; The Robbers; The Snow Storm; The Soldier's Daughter; Cramond Brig; Douglas; Alonzo, the Brave; The Fair Imogene; The Mountaineers; The Riever's Ransom; Gilderoy; Turn Out; The Poor Soldier; The Battle of New Orleans; The Heir-at-Law; The Wood Demon; Raising the Wind; Mary Stuart; Bears not Beasts; Macbeth; Julius Caesar; The Hundred-Pound Note; Othello; Wild Oats; The Merchant of Venice; The Review; A Bold Stroke for a Husband; Three Weeks after Marriage; Jane Shore; The Revenge; Don Giovanni; Cure for the Heart-Ache; Too Late for Dinner; The Turnpike Gate; The West Indian; Romeo and Juliet; The Weathercock; The Children in the Wood; Laugh When You Can; The Way to Get Married; The Hero of the North; The Ruined Chateau; The Falls of Clyde; She Would Be a Soldier; Fazio; Don Juan; Robinson Crusoe; Venice Preserved; Bellamira; Crazy Jane; Virginius; Evadne; Honey Moon; The Lady of the Lake; Thérèse; The Reapers; The Murderer; The Rivals; Of Age Tomorrow; The School for Scandal; Luke, the Labourer; The Stranger; Agreeable Surprise; Is He Jealous?; Rosina; The Foundling of the Forest; The Slave; Adrian and Orrila; The Comedy of Errors; Brother and Sister; Adelgitha; Sweethearts and Wives; The Citizen; Isabella; The Prodigal Son; Charlotte Temple; Phoebe; King John; Roses and Thorns; Monster and Magician; Paul Jones; A Tale of Mystery.*

1828–29: *Honey Moon; The Poor Soldier; Othello; Spoil'd Child; Love and Sausages; The Irish Tutor; Rosina; The Review; Rule a Wife and Have a Wife; Virginius; Guy Mannering; The Prize; Damon and Pythias; The Lady and the Devil; The Wheel of Fortune; Catherine and Petruchio; The Pilot; Valentine and Orson; The Child of Nature; Alonzo, the Brave; William Tell; The Apostate; Three Singles and the Deuce; Mr. H.; Jane Shore; The Two Galley Slaves; Wild Oats.*

BIBLIOGRAPHY

Published Sources: Joseph N. Ireland, *Records of the New York Stage from 1750 to 1860*, 2 vols. (New York, 1866–67); George C. D. Odell, *Annals of the New York Stage*, vol. 3 (New York: Columbia University Press, 1930); Francis C. Wemyss, *Chronology of the American Stage from 1752–1852* (New York, 1852). An engraving of the interior of the theatre appears in William C. Young, *Famous American Playhouses, 1716–1899*. Vol. 1 of *Documents of American Theater History* (Chicago: American Library Association, 1973), p. 72.

George B. Bryan

CHATHAM THEATRE COMPANY. After Blanchard's Ampitheatre closed in the summer of 1830, the building once known as the Chatham Garden Theatre (New York City) passed from the public's notice until Moses S. Phillips reopened it as the Chatham Theatre. John Banim's tragedy of *Damon and Pythias*, brought out at the theatre's inauguration on March 11, 1831, presaged the ensuing tone of the managements that strove to make a success of the theatre.

Phillips might have had a sentimental attachment to the Chatham, for he had spent the previous four years as a member of the various stock companies that had inhabited the house; perhaps the opportunity to be master in one's own theatre was irresistible to him. If so, his dream became a nightmare. Seventeen-year-old Charles R. Thorne entered the management with Phillips on April 5, but the new talent was unable to subvene financial disaster. The *New York Mirror* of June 25, 1831, observed that the Chatham "closed with the suddenness of an apoplectic fit." The theatre was unoccupied until October, when Thomas S. Hamblin mounted a brief season of opera and drama, but his venture also failed. In 1832, consequently, the Sacred Music Society started to perform in the old theatre, which had by then been converted into a Presbyterian chapel.

Augustus A. Addams, J. J. Adams, Henry J. Finn, George Washington Dixon, and George H. ("Yankee") Hill were the most distinguished guest performers at the Chatham, and they were supported by a troupe headed by Charles R. Thorne as leading man. The *Mirror* of June 25, 1831, noted, "There were several actors of merit at this establishment, whose merits were almost neutralized by want of support." Might this refer to someone like Danforth Marble, who paid Phillips and Thorne $20 to be allowed to perform?

The repertory, containing the new play *Tom Bowline*, was predictable and included only one notable production, that of John Howard Payne's *Oswali of Athens*, which was seen on June 13. Increasingly, variety acts took precedence over plays, the last indignity being the appearance of the Royal Elephant. Hamblin's autumnal season was devoted largely to the musical productions of the French Opera Company, which was followed by a round of variety acts under the direction of Villalave. After Thomas Hilson's brief, unsuccessful tenure in early 1832, the Chatham Theatre ceased to exist.

PERSONNEL

Management: Moses S. Phillips, March–June 1831; Charles R. Thorne, April–June 1831; Thomas S. Hamblin, October 1831; Mr. Villalave, November–December 1831; Thomas Hilson, January 1832.

Stage Director: W. R. Blake, May 1831.

Prompter: Mr. Nelson.

Actors and Actresses: Mr. Archer, Mr. Beckwell, W. R. Blake, E. Blanchard, Mr. Clarke, Mr. Farren, Thomas Flynn, Mr. Foot, Mrs. French, Mr. Gallott, Mrs. Gilfert, Mr. and Mrs. John Greene, Mr. Hazard, Mr. and Mrs. Hilson, Mrs. Hughes, Mr. Hyatt, Mr. Jervis, Emanuel Judah, D. D. McKinney, Emily Mestayer, Mr. and Mrs. Nelson, William Pelby, Aaron J. Phillips, Mrs. Richer, Mr. Rose, Mrs. G. G. Stevenson, E. N. Thayer, Mr. and Mrs. C. R. Thorne, Mrs. Walstein, Ann Duff Waring.

REPERTORY

1831–32: *Damon and Pythias; Thérèse; A Race for a Dinner; Raising the Wind; Gretna Green; The Phantom Bride; Richard III; The Arrest of Daniel O'Connell; Laugh When You Can; Will Watch: The Bold Smuggler; The Forest of Bondy; Fortune's Frolic; The Revenge; Honey Moon; High Life below Stairs; Brutus; Hamlet; Paul Pry; His Master's Rival; 102!; The Hypocrite; The Poor Gentleman; The Hundred-Pound Note; The Merchant of Venice; The Two Thompsons; A Year in an Hour; The School for Scandal; The Prize; Sweethearts and Wives; The Happiest Day of My Life; Married and Single; Alexander the Great; A Tale of the Sea; Rule a Wife and Have a Wife; The Castle Spectre; Pizarro; Spoil'd Child; Tom Bowline; Oswali of Athens; Fra Diavolo; Vatel; The Barber of Seville; La Marraine; The Marriage of Figaro; La muette de Portici; Le Jésuite; L'Ambassadeur; La clochette; La héritière; La pie voleuse; Le menteur véridique; The School for Scandal; Nature and Philosophy; Black Eyed Susan; She Would Be a Soldier.*

BIBLIOGRAPHY

Published Sources: Joseph N. Ireland, *Records of the New York Stage from 1750 to 1860*, 2 vols. (New York, 1866–67); George C. D. Odell, *Annals of the New York Stage*, vol. 3 (New York: Columbia University Press, 1930).

George B. Bryan

[NEW] CHATHAM THEATRE STOCK COMPANY. The New Chatham Theatre, New York City, between James and Roosevelt streets on Chatham Street, was a phoenix risen from its own ashes, for Thomas Flynn and Henry E. Willard's theatre was erected according to Samuel Purdy's designs on the charred ground where its predecessor had stood. The new structure accommodated 2,200 patrons in three tiers of boxes, a pit, and a gallery. When the house opened on September 11, 1839, with J. R. Scott in the tired *New Way to Pay Old Debts* and John Barnes in *Family Jars*, playgoers surely felt the pangs of ennui. George Odell lamented "the utter sameness of offerings at all the houses, one and several" (4:375).

Incapable of providing the sort of leadership necessary to make the Chatham a worthy competitor of the Park, Bowery, and Olympic theatres, Flynn and Willard "drifted aimlessly because [their] seas were not charted" (Odell, 4:378). By January 1840 Willard withdrew from the management, and Charles R. Thorne attempted to work in tandem with Flynn, but the latter was so inept that Thorne emerged as sole manager in March. Unlike Flynn, Thorne had a policy: to stress the lighter sorts of entertainment to which his company was particularly suited. Under Thorne's direction, the Chatham showed some profit but was no real threat to Mitchell's Olympic and produced little that deserves remembrance. He was able, though, to keep the theatre operative during nearly two and a half years with negligible hiatuses, perhaps the longest extended run to that time in the metropolis.

Charles Robert Thorne (1814–93) made his debut as an actor in 1829 and soon made a name for himself in "a lower range of parts. As manager, he . . . had, at various times, control of several minor theatres in the city, in some of which he catered most successfully for that kind of dramatic appetite which is best pleased with coarse, high-seasoned fare": Thus Joseph Ireland (1:599) disposed of C. R. Thorne.

When Thorne relinquished control of the Chatham, A. W. Jackson and Willard assumed responsibility and mounted a summer season starting on July 20, 1843. The house thereafter passed to William S. Deverna, whose managerial career commenced on September 4, 1843; he later took Benedict DeBar as a partner, an arrangement that lasted a mere eighteen months. Finally, in July 1847 Deverna resigned, and the Chatham passed into the hands of J. Fletcher, who held on for only six months. The theatre then entered a new phase of its existence under Frank S. Chanfrau, who renamed it Chanfrau's National Theatre.

The greatest boon to Flynn and Willard's management was not of their own doing; it was the burning of Wallack's National Theatre and dissolution of his company, which freed some good actors and diminished competition among the minor theatres. The Chatham's first-tier boxes sold for fifty cents; twenty-five cents bought admission to the second and third tiers, and the gallery went for twelve and a half cents. When Edwin Forrest was lured to the Chatham Theatre, Thorne raised his prices to seventy-five, fifty, and twenty-five cents and restored the lower rates when Forrest departed. In 1842 the range of ticket prices had sunk to thirty-seven and one-half, eighteen and three-quarters, and ten cents. A further reduction brought twenty-five-cent, twelve-and-a-half-cent, and six-and-a-quarter cent tickets. Prices were temporarily raised to a fifty-cent top for the engagement of Mr. and Mrs. John Brougham and then lowered to twenty-five cents. When DeBar joined the management in 1845, ticket prices were raised, but necessity restored them to a twenty-five-cent ceiling. This fluctuation of admission fees speaks eloquently of the financial position of the organization.

The New Chatham was definitely viewed by the newspaper as a minor theatre. Notices of its offerings were abbreviated, and comments on its productions were sketchy indeed. Journalists notwithstanding, audiences could be lured in great numbers to the Chatham, especially when the stars were attractive or the repertory inviting.

Thorne deluged his patrons with a dizzying round of shows, more notable for their number than for their quality. In 1840–41 Chathamites saw 187 plays; in 1841–42, 167; in 1842–43, 276. One supposes that the prompter worked hard for his salary as he tried to keep the dialogue from faltering. Occasionally, Thorne gauged the public's taste and staged a lucrative production. *Night and Morning*, adapted from Edward Bulwer-Lytton's work, ran for an entire week, and *Undine; or, The Spirit of Water* proved to be so popular tht 2,500 people were said to have been turned away. Thorne pirated *The Surgeon of Paris* and mounted it two days before its opening at the Bowery. He even turned to opera as a means of capturing audiences: *The Escape* drew fairly well. He also booked the Virginia Minstrels and started a tradition of minstrelsy at the Chatham. Eventually, though, the pursuit of novelty became too much even for Thorne, so he surrendered his managerial responsibilities.

Under the aegis of William Deverna, the Chatham housed a circus for two months in 1844. When he later produced *The Monks of Monk Hall*, a lurid play that had been banned in Philadelphia, the lusty Chathamites were greatly attracted by a scene laid in a brothel. The repertory was appreciably elevated when Mrs. George Jones appeared in *Margaret Catchpole, The Female Horse Thief*, which had a long and profitable run. The management excelled in extravaganzas, two of which accounted for the greatest successes of 1845–46. *The Enchantress*, an equestrian drama, was played for two successive weeks before becoming an afterpiece, and *The Seven Escapes of Adelaide of Dresden* dominated the bills from August to October.

Deverna again rented his theatre to a circus late in 1846, a few months before the season's most notable production, H. B Mattison's *Witch; or, A Legend of the Catskill*, which lasted for two weeks. Under J. Fletcher's banner, the repertory proved even more vapid than under Deverna. The only thing of note was the two-week run of *The Lonely Man of the Ocean*. A final observation about the Chatham's repertory should be made: none of its managers scrupled against presenting old plays under new names, nor did any of them resist the temptation to plagiarize dramas slated for production in other theatres.

To delineate the companies employed at the Chatham during this period is rendered difficult by frequent shifts of loyalty on the part of the actors; the managers, too, ever in pursuit of novelty, drastically altered the composition of the troupe. Flynn and Willard's principal actors were John Barnes, comedian, and Mrs. Flynn and Mrs. Bannister, leading women. Leading roles were shared by a number of males. J. S. Browne was also prominent, and in the second season, J. Hudson Kirby, who specialized in roaring melodramas, was the leading man. E. S. Conner led the company in 1843–44, with light leading roles assigned to Miss Reynolds, heavy parts to Mrs. McClure. During the last season the principals were Anna Cruise and A. W. Fenno. Although the calibre of the company was not stable, there was an almost clocklike predictability to the visits of the stars.

The three mainstays of the Chatham were Junius Brutus Booth, T. D. Rice, and George H. Hill—an eminent tragedian, the creator of Jim Crow, and the embodiment of the stage Yankee. Each of these actors performed at the Chatham nearly every season and sometimes more than once. Edwin Forrest and John Brougham acted there with less frequency but with no less success. Other favorites were Dan Marble, Joshua Silsbee, George Vandenhoff, W. E. Burton, and Frank S. Chanfrau. Additional stars of merit appeared numerous times: J. R. Scott, W. R. Blake, H. J. Finn, J. W. Wallack, W. Wood, John Sefton, Mrs. George Jones, Josephine Clifton, and Charles H. Eaton, to name but a few. One believes that the Chatham by their talents was elevated, only to be plunged beneath waves of mediocrity in their absence.

PERSONNEL

Management: Thomas Flynn, Henry E. Willard (September 1839–January 1840); Thomas Flynn, Charles R. Thorne (January–March 1840); C. R. Thorne (March 1840–July 1843); A. W. Jackson, H. E. Willard (July–August 1843); William S. Deverna (September 1843–July 1847); Benedict DeBar (April 1845–October 1846); J. Fletcher (July 1847–February 1828).

Stage Directors: James Anderson, J. M. Scott, Henry E. Stevens, Charles Freer, Benedict DeBar.

Prompter: J. Crouta.

Scenic Artists: Marmaduke White, P. Grain, Mr. Hielge.

Machinists: Mr. McMillan, Mr. Torrence.

Properties Master: Mr. Stevens.

Costumer: Mme. de Grouche.

Orchestra: Mr. St. Luke.

Treasurer: P. C. Palmer.

Police: J. L. Smith.

Actors and Actresses: James Anderson, Mr. Anderton, N. H. Bannister, *Mrs. N. H. Bannister*, Mr. Barber, Mr. Barnard, *John Barnes* (1839, 1843), Mr. Barton, Mr. Bedford, Miss Beerman, Mr. Bellamy, Mr. Blaike, Mrs. Blake, Mr. Blakeley, Mr. Bland, Mrs. Bland, Mr. Bloomer, J. B. Booth, Jr., T. G. Booth, Mr. Boswell, Mr. Brandon, J. Mills Brown, Miss Bruce, Mr. Brunton, Mrs. Brunton, Mlle. Celeste, Mr. Canito, Mr. Carter, J. S. Charles, Mr. Chesbrough, Miss Clarendon, Mr. Clark, Master Clemence, Miss Clemence, Miss Clements, T. S. Cline, Mrs. Coad, Miss Cohen, Master Coleman, Mr. Collins, *E. S. Conner* (1844), Mr. Conover, Miss Crauford, J. Crouta, *Anna Cruise* (1845), Mr. Davenport, *Benedict DeBar* (1845–46), Mr. Dent, Miss De Zosier, Master Diamond, William Dinneford, Mr. Donaldson, Mrs. Du Bois, Mary Duff, John Dunn, Mr. Durivage, H. Eberle, Mr. Edwards, Mr. Edwin, Rosalie Edwin, Henry Eytinge, A. W. Fenno, Mr. Field, Miss Flynn, *Mrs. Thomas Flynn* (1839, 1844), W. C. Forbes, Mr. Forrester, Mr. Franklin, Charles Freer, Mary Ann Gannon, Mrs. Gibbs, Mr. Gibson, Mr. Goodenow, Mr. Goodwin, George Graham, H. P. Grattan, J. Greene, Mrs. J. Greene, Mr. Gregg, Mrs. Griffith, Miss Gullen, Miss Gwineanoh, J. H. Hall, Mr. Hamilton, Mr. Harrison, Mrs. Harrison, Mrs. Hautonville, Miss Heber, J. Herbert, Mrs. J. Herbert, Mrs. Herring, Miss S. Hildreth, Mr. Hield, Mrs. Hield, Miss Hilson, Miss Homer, Mr. Hope, Henry Horncastle, Mrs. W. Hoskins, C. W. Hunt, Mrs. H. Hunt, George Jamieson, Mr. Jessaline, Mr. Johnson, Miss Johnston, J. Jones, W. G. Jones, Mrs. W. G. Jones, Mrs. Judah, *J. Hudson Kirby* (1841), Miss S. Kirby, Mrs. La Forest, Mr. Lambert, Mr. Langrishe, Mr. Lawrence, Mrs. Le Comte, Mary Ann Lee, Miss Le Mure, Mr. Lennox, Mr. Lewellen, Bertha Lewis, H. Lewis, Mrs. H. Lewis, Mr. Madison, Mrs. Madison, Mrs. Marsden, *Wyzeman Marshall* (1842, 1845), C. K. Mason, Mr. Matthews, *Mrs. McClure* (1844), T.

McCutcheon, Mr. McDougal, Mr. McKeon, Charles Mestayer, *Emily Mestayer* (1840–41), H. Mestayer, L. Mestayer, Mr. Miller, Miss Montgomery, F. S. Morris, George Mossop, Mrs. George Mossop, Mr. Myers, Hervio Nano, Mr. Nelson, Mrs. Nelson, Mrs. Horace F. Nichols, Mr. Ollier, Mr. Oxley, Mr. Parker, Miss Partington, R. W. Pelham, Miss Penson, Mrs. Penson, Harry A. Perry, Adelaide Phillips, Matilda Phillips, Mr. Porter, Mr. Pray, Mrs. Preston, Joseph Proctor, Mrs. Joseph Proctor, A. H. Purdy, Mr. Rae, Miss E. Randolph, Jean Ravel, Victor Ravel, Mr. Resor, Mrs. Rivers, Mr. Russell, Mr. Salisbury, Mr. Sanford, Mrs. W. Sefton, Miss Sharpe, Mr. Sinclair, John Sloman, Mrs. John Sloman, *C. J. Smith* (1841), John Smith, W. H. Smith, Mr. Sprague, George Stanley, Henry E. Stevens, Paul Taglioni, L. F. Tasistro, E. N. Thayer, Mr. Thompson, *C. R. Thorne* (1840–43), Mrs. C. R. Thorne, Mr. Tuthill, Miss Vallée, Mr. Vanstavoren, Dr. Valentine, Charles Walcot, Mr. Walkins, Fanny Wallack, Julia Wallack, Miss Walters, Mr. Walton, Mrs. Ward, Mr. Watts, Mr. Wells, Harriet Wells, A. L. West, Mrs. Western, Mr. Wharam, Miss Wheeler, Cool White, Mr. Whitlock, Mr. Wilkinson, Amelia Williams, P. F. Williams, Alexander Wilson, John Winans, Mr. Winchell, Master Wood, Emily Wood, Guelph Wood, Charles Wyndham, Miss Yates.

REPERTORY

1839–40: *A New Way to Pay Old Debts; Family Jars; The Comedy of Errors; The Iron Chest; Richard III; Virginius; The Youthful Brigand; Spoil'd Child; Douglas; Seven's the Main; The Hunchback; The Swiss Cottage; George Barnwell; Exchange No Robbery; Twelve Precisely; The Destruction of Jerusalem; Old and Young; A Day in New York; Monongahela; The Merchant of Venice; Sprigs of Laurel; The Rivals; Scene in a Madhouse; The Poachers; Othello; Damon and Pythias; Faith and Falsehood; Catherine and Petruchio; Crockett in Texas; Ugolino; The Conscript; The Irish Lion; England's Iron Days; Town and Country; Ion; Raising the Wind; Paul Pry; Sweethearts and Wives; Monsieur Jacques; Kate Kearney; The Hypocrite; 102; The Hundred-Pound Note; The Heir-at-Law; Tom and Jerry; Pizarro; The Maid of Croissey; Robert Macaire; Victorine; A Nabob for an Hour; An Irishman's Home; Bombastes Furioso; Charles XII; Brian Boroihme; The Happy Man; The Unfinished Gentleman; The Old English Gentleman; The King's Gardener; Rob Roy; Too Late for Dinner; Billy Snivel; Frightened to Death; My Young Wife and My Old Umbrella; The Wandering Minstrel; The Poor Idiot; Harlequin Margery Daw; Ancient Statues; The Ogre of Brackenburg; The Way to Get Married; The Wife; The Wolf and the Lamb; The Brigand; The Rent Day; The Adopted Child; The Mountaineers; Honey Moon; Obi; The Review; The Old Block; Three Chips; Tom Cringle's Log; The False Friend; Robert Emmet; Giovanni in London; His First Champagne; Christophe: King of Hayti; The Maine Question; The Battle of Sedgemoor; Romeo and Juliet Travestie; Alice Gray; The Yellow Kids; The Critic; Brutus; Black Eyed Susan; The Forest of Bondy; Paul Jones; The Emerald Isle; The Grenadier; Infidelity; The Children in the Wood; The Last Pardon; Avarice; Kairrissah; Alive and Merry; Oh! Pshaw!; The First Night; The Knight of the Golden Fleece; The Yankee Pedlar; The Green Mountain Boy; Seth Slope; The Forest Rose; The Yankee in England; New Notions; Kaspar Hauser; The Tourists; A Wife for a Day; Old Manhattan; The Golden Farmer; The Mayor of Garratt; The Apostate; Amateurs and Actors; Diamond Cut Diamond; The Last Man; A*

Good Night's Rest; The Freemason; The Savage and the Maiden; Shabby Gentility; High Life below Stairs; Charles II; The Yankee Duelist; Of Age Tomorrow; The Rake's Progress; Don Carlos; The Exile; Fazio; The Married Bachelor; The Wonder; Jane Shore; The Foundling of the Forest; Scotch Clans and Irish Chieftains; Naval Engagements; Hamlet; King Lear; St. Mary's Eve; The Wizard Skiff; Nathalie; The Escape; Suzanne; The Soldier's Dream; The New Colonel; The Wept of Wish-Ton-Wish; The Devil's Daughter; The Manager's Daughter; The Revenge; The Water Witch; Rory O'More; La sylphide; Luke, the Labourer; The Man about Town; The Gnome Fly; Jack Robinson and His Monkey; The Masquerade; Midshipman Easy; The Two Gregories; A Pleasant Neighbor; The Secret; The Wild Boy of Bohemia; Jack's the Lad; No!; The Loan of a Lover; The Smuggler; The Pirate of Hurlgate; Julius Caesar; Macbeth; Venice Preserved; The Flying Dutchman; Master Humphrey's Clock; The Poor Soldier; My Sister Kate; The Foulah Slave; The Little Tiger; The Spectre Pilot; Red Rover; Philip Quarl; The Mountain Savage; The Forty Thieves; The French Spy; The Muleteer of Palermo; The Daring Mariner; The Greek Fire; The Whistler.

1840–41: *The Greek Fire; Valentine and Orson; The Forty Thieves; The Innkeeper's Daughter; Timour, the Tartar; The Banditti of Corsica; Bluebeard; My Young Wife and My Old Umbrella; The Courier of the Ocean; The Yellow Kids; Robert Macaire; Is He Jealous?; Zelina; Out of Luck; The Mountain Minstrel; Joan of Arc; The Pirate of the Atlantic; Richard III; Seth Slope; The Yankee Pedlar; The Knight of the Golden Fleece; New Notions; A Wife for a Day; Jonathan in England; The Hypocrite; The Green Mountain Boy; The Forest Rose; The Hundred-Pound Note; Jumbo Jim; The Black Cupid; Uncle Pop; Wheugh! Here's a Go!; Black Hercules; The Cross of Death; The Mountain Nymph; Antoine the Savage; Peter Wilkins; The Hostler, the Innkeeper, and the Robber; Signs of the Times; The Serenade; A New Way to Pay Old Debts; King Lear; Hamlet; The Merchant of Venice; Julius Caesar; The Iron Chest; The Mountaineers; The Carpenter of Rouen; A Night in the Pyrenees; New York as It Is; The Devil's Ducat; The Alpine Hunters; Nantucket Will; Paul and Virginia; The Woodman's Hut; The Maniac; Thérèse; William Tell; The Mendicant, His Wife, and Family; Jonathan Bradford; Lo Zingaro; Janggaroo; The Gold Seekers of Anzasca; Damon and Pythias; The Stage-Struck Yankee; Columbus; The Avenger; The Brunswick Murder; Pizarro; The Witch of the Sea; Bone Squash Diavolo; The Mummy; A Dazzle by the Western; The Sea; The Condemned Student; The Peacock and the Crow; Jim Crow in London; Tom Cringle; The Saxon's Oath; She Would Be a Soldier; The Gambler's Fate; The Burning of the Caroline; Landsharks and Sea Gulls; Kaspar Hauser; Catch a Weazle Asleep; Cherry and Fair Star; The Hazard of the Die; The Watchword; My Uncle Oliver; Bob Buckeye in Florida; Oronaska; The Old Oak Chest; The Spectre Pilot; The Flying Dutchman; The Muleteer of Palermo; Androcles; Gil Blas; Rob Roy; The Foulah Slave; Robinson Crusoe; Montrose; A Soldier, A Sailor, a Tinker, and a Tailor; Abaellino; The Stranger; The Jewess; Is It a Wager?; Night and Morning; The Spy of Paris; Black Shakespeare; The Post Boy of Cornwall; Jack Sheppard; Peter Bell, the Waggoner; The Forest of Rosenwald; The Six Degrees of Crime; The Conquering Game; The Pirate's Doom; The Quadroone; The Rover's Bride; Old Jonathan and His Apprentices; Cassee Sing; Paul Clifford; Corse de Leon; Nymphs of the Red Sea; The Spitfire; Tom and Jerry; The Kinsman; The Battle of Stillwater; The Lady of the Lake; Walter Brand; Giovanni in New York; The Two Drovers;*

The Golden Farmer; The Bohemian Gipsy; Daughter of the Danube; The Bride of Abydos; John Stafford; Fifteen Years of a Drunkard's Life; Mark Laurence; The Knight and the Princess; The Wren Boys; The Huntsman and the Spy; Black Eyed Susan; The Truant Chief; The Fortune Teller; The Death Plank; A Cure for the Gout; The Wandering Boys; Love and Lucre; The Lady of Lyons; Macbeth; John de Procidi; The Brigand; The Wife; The Rent Day; The Children in the Wood; The Review; The Sledge Hammer; Jane Shore; Town and Country; The Miller's Maid; The Sarcophagus; Ugolino; The Seven Clerks; Deeds of Dreadful Note; The Dream at Sea; Out of Luck; The Maid of Croissey; The Gnome Fly; Aladdin; The Mother's Crime; Jocko, the Brazilian Ape; I'm Twenty-One To-morrow; A Good-Looking Fellow; The Loss of the Medusa; Charles II; The Haunted Inn; The Jester; Forty and Fifty; The Hunter of the Alps; The Surgeon of Paris; Man o' War; The Merchantman; The Siege of Beauvais; Napoleon; The Robber's Wife.

1841–42: *The Last Nail; Paul the Reprobate; The Siege of Beauvais; The Venetian; Valsha, the Slave Queen; Night and Morning; Isaac Ivy; The Lady of Lyons; Pizarro; William Tell; Gwynneth Vaughan; Seth Slope; Barnaby Rudge; The Sarcophagus; Calderoni, the Brigand; The Foreign Prince; The Shadow; Gaspardo, the Gondolier; The Convict's Child; My Wife's Dentist; Blanche; The Surgeon of Paris; The Carpenter of Rouen; Macbeth; King Lear; The Stranger; Othello; Hamlet; Koeuba; Brutus; Oberon; The Tower of Nesle; The French Spy; Hofer; The Black Ghost; The Wife; Richelieu; Tortesa, the Usurer; Brian Boroihme; Rienzi; Mabel's Curse; The Fatal Dowry; The King's Jester; The Maniac Lover; The Prophet of the Moor; Grace Huntley; New York Assurance; The Fisherman of Lisbon; Hermione; Alonzo, the Brave; Kehama; Aladdin; The Miller and His Men; Conancheota; Timour, the Tartar; Mazeppa; The Wraith of the Lake; The Robber of the Rhine; Julius Caesar; Sy Saco; A Wife for a Day; The Signet Ring; Guy Fawkes; The Vermonter; Josh Horseradish; Of Age Tonight; Catching a Weazle Asleep; Jonathan in England; The Tempter; Undine; The Mechanic and the Queen; My Charming Poll; Jacob Faithful; The Serenade; The Gamester of Milan; Charles, the Terrible; Sam Slick; Tom and Jerry; King John; The Provost of Bruges; El Hyder; Money; The Brigand; The Gunner and the Foundling; The Golden Farmer; Charles II; Sudden Thoughts; Guy Goodluck; The Two Friends; Mobb, the Outlaw; The Secret; Faustus; Catching an Heiress; The Spitfire; Abelard and Heloise; One Hour of a Soldier's Life; Natz Tieck; My Master's Rival; A Nabob for an Hour; The Incendiary; The Dead Shot; The Young Widow; The Night Hag; The Two Queens; A New Way to Pay Old Debts; The Shoemaker of Toulouse; Ten Miles from London; Clari; Deeds of Dreadful Note; The Muleteer of Palermo; Damon and Pythias; Zanoni; Orsini, the Banished; Rob Roy; The Avenger; Lo Studio; Philip Quarl; Beatrice Vivaldi; The Queen of Cyprus; Walter Brand; The Apostate; Coriolanus; Erasmus Bookworm; Open House; One Hour; The Courtier; Master and Man; London Assurance; Virginius; Landsharks and Sea Gulls; Metamora; Jack Cade; Zembuca; The Widow's Victim; Wilbert, the Reformed; The Railroad Station; Sam Patch in France; The Gamecock of the Wilderness; The Vermont Wool Dealer; The Secret; All the World's a Stage; Midshipman Easy; The Eye of Death; Ella Rosenberg; Jack Sheppard; Two London Locksmiths; The Free Trader; Fazio; Natty Nol; The Hunchback; Jane Shore; The Place Hunter; His Last Legs; The Water Witch; The Dead Shot; The Adopted Child; The Swiss Cottage; Henry IV; Edgar of Ravenswood; The Cataract of the Ganges; Love and Starvation; The Maid of Switzerland; The Rose of Aragon; Demetrius: The Renegade of Messina; A Good Night's Rest.*

1842–43: *The Lady of Lyons; Sweethearts and Wives; Othello; Richelieu; The Gladiator; Damon and Pythias; Jack Cade; Macbeth; Virginius; King Lear; Thérèse; The Broker of Bogota; Venice Preserved; The Turnpike Gate; Morley Ernstein; The Peacock and the Crow; Bone Squash Diavolo; The Foreign Prince; Jumbo Jim; Black Pompey; Wheugh! It's a Go!; The Sarcophagus; The Butchers of Ghent; The Spirit of '76; Life in New York; The King, the Innkeeper, and the Deserter; Antoine: The Mountain King; Sixteen String Jack; A New Way to Pay Old Debts; The Iron Chest; The Apostate; Richard III; The Mayor of Garratt; La Bayadère; Guy Mannering; John of Paris; The Escape; Don Juan; Fredolfo; His Last Legs; Aladdin; The Spectre Pilot; The Irishman in London; Cramond Brig; The Imposter; The Robber's Wife; The Renegade; The Irishman in China; Rehearsal for a Negro Ball; The Irish Lion; The Black Ghost; The Darkey in Livery; Croton Water; The Masquerade; Jack Sheppard; The Courier of the Ocean; The Loss of the Royal George; The Ogre of Brackenburg; The Clennaquoi Chief; Peter Wilkins; Timour, the Tartar; The Shipwrecked Orphan; Lo Studio; The Wreck Ashore; Black Eyed Susan; Jack's the Lad; The Gambler's Fate; Tom and Jerry; Eugene Aram; Darnley; Pizarro; The Man in the Iron Mask; The Shoemaker of Toulouse; The Surgeon of Paris; Arden, the Reckless; The Youthful Days of Richard III; The Field of the Forty Footsteps; H-ll on Earth; John Rock; Maurice, the Woodcutter; The Carpenter of Rouen; Six Degrees of Crime; The Last Days of Pompeii; Blue Jackets; The Prodigal Son; The Bottle Imp; Love, Faith, and Falsehood; Retribution; The Crown Prince; The Mariner's Dream; Normal Leslie; But, However; Adriani, the Brigand; A Match in the Dark; The Middle Temple; The King's Gardener; Deaf as a Post; Rinaldo Rinaldini; Venoni; The Terror of Normandy; Iron Jack; Fairly Hit and Fairly Missed; John di Procidi; The Dragon Knight; Charles O'Malley; La belle de la Brie; Bob Short; The Hunter of the Alps; The Executioners; The Ninth Statue; Does Your Mother Know You're Out?; The Water Party; The Maniac of Erin; The Young Widow; New Lights; The Coal-Black Rose; Wing and Wing; The King's Word; Mary: The Maid of the Inn; The Christening; The Wizard of the Glen; Helen Oakleigh; The Dumb Belle; A Pleasant Neighbor; The Floating Beacon; Melmoth; The Wife of Seven Husbands; The Sleep Walker; The Dragon Knight; Turning the Tables; Jacques Strop; Meet Me by Moonlight; The Village Doctor; A Nabob for an Hour; Married Life; Uncle John; Scan Mag; Mr. and Mrs. Pringle; Popping the Question; Bombastes Furioso; Charles XII; The Day after the Wedding; The Agreeable Surprise; The Anatomist; The Bohemian Mother; Blood for Blood; Claude Lorraine; La Coupée Gorge; The Golden Dream; Death's Bride; Crazy Jane; The Black Raven of the Tombs; The Blind Boy; The Brigand's Oath; The Bride of the Isles; The Four Mowbrays; Spoil'd Child; Cousin Lambkin; Romeo and Juliet; Rob Roy; The Siege of Mongatz; The Miller and His Men; The King and the Bandit; The Maid and the Magpie; The Spectre Pilot; El Hyder; The Smuggler's Dog; The Robbers of the Rhine; The Miser's Daughter; The Death of Christophe; The Hag of the Tombs; The Castle Spectre; The Dumb Man of Manchester; Knights of the Cross; The Siege of Corinth; Mutiny on the High Seas; The Ruffian Boy; The Foulah Slave; The Solitary of the Heath; Angelo, the Fratricide; Kill or Cure; Jonathan Bradford; Tom Tiller; Valentine and Orson; Love à la Mode; The Review; The Deserted; The Middy Ashore; The Flying Dutchman; The Merchant of New York;*

*Pills of Death; Raising the Wind; The Foundling of the Forest; Lost and Won;
Frankenstein; Rugantino; The First Fratricide; Jack Robinson; Joan of Arc; The
Devil to Pay; The Forged Will; The Omnibus; The Falls of Clyde; The Post Boy;
Ugolino; My Own Ghost; The Promissory Note; My Fellow Clerk; The Collegians;
Is He Jealous?; The Weathercock; The Devil's Ducat; A Woman's Life; The Outlaw
of Corsica; Rip Van Winkle; The Comet; Man o' War; Esmeralda; The Smuggler
of Bootle Bay; Black Angus; The Torrent of the Valley; Bertram; The Last of the
Mohicans; The Patrician Daughter; The Ladies' Club; The Love Chase; The Won-
der; His Last Legs; Honey Moon; Teddy, the Tiler; Rosina Meadows; Rory O'More;
My Poll; The Court of Queen Anne; The Wizard of the Moor; The Ancestress;
Marceline; The Nervous Man; Kaspar Hauser; The Maiden's Fame; Ahasuerus;
Peaceful Pelton; The Pride of the Ocean; The People's Lawyer; The Yankee in
Tripoli; Trial by Battle; The Fire Raiser; Belair, the Bandit; The Fall of Algiers;
False Colors; Yankee Land; The Beggar of Bethnal Green; The Vermont Wool
Dealer; Speculation; The Yankee at Niagara; Yankee Farmers; The Yankee in 1776;
The Yankee Preacher; The French Spy; The Soldier's Daughter; The Death Token;
The Bandit of Corsica; The New York Apprentice; The Honest Thieves; The Fatal
Dowry; The Maniac Lover; Hercules of Brittany; George Barnwell; She Would Be
a Soldier; Curiosities of Literature; Rule a Wife and Have a Wife; Julius Caesar.*

1843–44: *The Mummy; Paul Pry; The Wandering Minstrel; Der Nacht Wachter;
Wreck Ashore; The Rake's Progress; College Life; The Broken Heart; Love's Dis-
guises; A Woman's Life; The Poor Gentleman; Bumpology; The Lady of Lyons;
The Dumb Belle; New Notions; A Wife for a Day; The Pilot; The Rebel Chief; The
Hunchback; Romeo and Juliet; Thérèse; Jumbo Jim; Charles II; Perfection; Six
Degrees of Crime; The Cheesemonger and the Aristocrat; The Lawyer and His
Victim; John Jones; A Thumping Legacy; Boots at the Swan; The Rival Beauties;
The Wager; The Pickwick Club; Harlequin and the Ocean Imp; Larboard Fin; Mad
as a March Hare; The Dying Gift; The Dumb Man of Manchester; Freaks of Fortune;
Don Juan; Born to Good Luck; Bone Squash Diavolo; Fratricide; The Muleteer of
Palermo; The Spy in New York; The Stranger; The Dumb Savoyard; Valentine and
Orson; Cut and Come Again; Cramond Brig; Honest Roguery; Seth Slope; John
Bull; Accidental Honours; Signs of the Times; The Pretty Girls of Stillberg; The
Mysteries of Paris; The Wood Wolves; Hercules of Brittany; Family Jars; The Irish
Schoolmaster; Crime and Repentance; The Spy of St. Marc's; The Bohemians; Little
Red Riding Hood; The Star Queen; The Jewess; The Married Rake; A Lesson for
Ladies; The King's Gardener; The Virginia Mummy; William Tell; The King of the
Mist; Born to Good Luck; La tour de Nesle; A Match in the Dark; The Sergeant's
Wife; Richelieu; Money; The Sea Captain; Romeo and Juliet; The Heir-at-Law;
Marmaduke Wyvil; The Love Chase; Fazio; The Wife; Richard III; Lucille; Evadne;
The Somnambulist; The School for Scandal; She Stoops to Conquer; Macbeth;
Bumps; Sam Slick; Josh Doolittle; Handy Andy; The People's Lawyer; Seth Slope;
Richelieu in Love; A Blind Bargain; Pat Lyons: The Locksmith of Philadelphia;
The Carpenter of Rouen; The Butchers of Ghent; The Prince and the Watchman;
The Intemperate; Sweethearts and Wives; The Merchant and the Mechanic; Peter
the Great; The Fair One with the Golden Locks; Othello; Kinge Richarde ye Thirde;
The Golden Farmer; Jack Sheppard; Catching an Heiress; Dancing for the Million;
The Man about Town; Love and Revenge; The Siege of Mongatz; A Wife for a
Day; The Sarcophagus; The Dumb Belle; The Forest of Savoy; Homeward Bound;*

Grandfather Whitehead; The Mounting Sylph; A Tale of Pont Neuf; The Indian Girl; An Adonis of Sixty; The Irishman's Fortune; Hamlet; Stewart's Triumph; The Bridal; Quid pro Quo; Kehama; Putnam; Nell Gwynne; The Deep Deep Sea.

1844–45: *The Artful Dodger; The School for Scandal; The Gipsy King; 23 Chatham Street; The Eleventh Hour; The Rival Pages; Timour, the Tartar; El Hyder; Life in New York; Mandalzar, the Accursed; The Wandering Jew; Sketches in India; That Rascal Jack; The Drover Boy; The Seven Passions; A Christmas Carol; Windsor Castle; The Monks of Monks Hall; The Chimes; True Blue; The Devil in Paris; Hamlet; Jack Sheppard; Green Bushes; The Sealed Sentence; Monseigneur; The Doom of the Tory Guard; The Lady of Lyons; The Last Days of Pompeii; The French Spy; Beauty and the Beast; Masaniello; Time Works Wonders; The Bronze Horse; The Surgeon of Paris; Rookwood; The Female Horse Thief; La Fille du Régiment; Riches; Don Caesar de Bazan; Somebody Else.*

1845–46: *The Conscious Lovers; The Bohemian Girl; Masaniello; Hamlet; Lucrezia Borgia; Jonathan Bradford; The Bronze Horse; Virginius; Another Glass!; Jack Robinson and His Monkey; Montezuma; Macbeth; Thérèse; The Female Horse Thief; The Bull Fighter; Norman Leslie; Natural Curiosity; The Wizard of the Moor; The Brigand; The Shoemaker of Toulouse; The Surgeon of Paris; Wallace; The Rebel Chief; The Hunchback; Faust; The Smoked Miser; The King of the Beggars; The Old Oak Chest; Green Bushes; Thimblerig; Walter Brand; The Wife; The Lady of Lyons; Woman! Her Love! Her Faith! Her Trials!; Ion; The Welsh Girl; Spoil'd Child; Ups and Downs; The Irish Attorney; Modern Chivalry; The Bear Hunters; The Vermont Wool Dealer; Wat Tyler; Paul Jones; The Mountain Drover; The Wandering Minstrel; The Young Widow; Mother and Child Are Doing Well; Jack Sheppard; Lillian, the Show Girl; The Stranger; El Hyder; Red Rover; Rockwood; Cherry and Fair Star; Bluebeard; The School of Reform; The Wild Boy of Bohemia; Antoine, the Savage; Guy Mannering; The Wreck of the Rapid; Clarisse; Blackwell's Island; Love and Cash; Love, Law, and Physic; The Menageria; Susan Hopley; Honey Moon; Captain Kyd; The Emerald Isle; Born to Good Luck; The Irish Tutor; The Happy Man; Paddy's Trip to America; The Irish Lion; The Miser of Eltham; The Card Drawer; Kate Kearney; She Would Be a Soldier; The Child of the Regiment; The Cricket on the Hearth; The Ransom; Catching an Heiress; The Dead Shot; The Orange Girl of Venice; Minerali; Crime and Repentance; John of Paris; Oronaska; Rory O'More; Genevieve; The Golden Farmer; Othello; Jumbo Jum; The Earthquake; Richard III; A New Way to Pay Old Debts; The Apostate; King John; The Mayor of Garratt; Macbeth; King Lear; The Loan of a Lover; Trial by Battle; The Green Mountain Boy; A Wife for a Day; The Knight of the Golden Fleece; Cut and Come Again; The People's Lawyer; Jonathan Doubikins; Seth Slope; The Forest Rose; Kaspar Hauser; The Yankee Pedlar; Jonathan in England; New Notions; Honest Roguery; The Mummy; Catherine and Petruchio; The Minute Gun at Sea; The Flying Dutchman; The Hazard of the Heart; Rob Roy; Nick of the Woods; The Gnome Fly; The Shipwreck; Damon and Pythias; Tom Thumb; The Bastille; The Ruby Ring; The Review; Alive and Kicking; The Inchcape Bell; The Maiden's Fame; The Cabin Boy; New Lights; The Fairy Circle; The Dumb Belle; The Cherokee Chief; The Two Mechanics; Mobb, the Outlaw; Dancing Mad; Paul Clifford; The French Spy; The Dumb Savoyard; The Enchantress; The March of Freedom; The Western Heir; Cuffs and Kisses; Love's Sacrifice; Clari; The Day after the Wedding; Dominique, the Deserter; As You Like It; The Loan of a Lover;*

The King of the Commons; The Little Jockey; The White Boy of Ireland; Perfection; The Irish Tiger; The Irish Post Office; Charles XII; Woman; Landsharks and Sea Gulls; Money; The Floating Beacon; The Love Chase; Matrimony; The Love Hut; The Mutiny at the Nore; The Lioness of the North; The Scourge of the Ocean; The Shadow on the Wall; The Orphan's Legacy; The Adopted Child; The Married Rake; The Chain of Guilt; The Seven Escapes of Adelaide of Dresden.

1846–47: The Captain Is Not A-Miss; The King's Fool; The Fire Raiser; Matrimony; The Charcoal Burner; Claude Lorraine; Brutus; The Female Brigand; The Happy Man; The Robber's Wife; Teddy, the Tiler; Born to Good Luck; Ugolino; The Irish Lion; The Chain of Guilt; The Orphan's Legacy; Spoil'd Child; Jack Sheppard; Norah Creina; Jackets of Blue; Joe: The Orphan Found in a Haystack; Robert Macaire; That Rascal Jack; Cupid; I Can't Help It; Richard III; Richarde ye Thirde; The Alpine Maid; The Secret; The Man of the Mountain; The Governor's Wife; Blood Royal; Mary Melvyn; An American Manager in London; The Siege of Monterey; The Weaver of Lyons; The Murderer of Symon's Rock; Rob Roy; The Heart of Midlothian; The Rights of Women; Cramond Brig; The Merchant of Venice; Inheritance; Old Ironsides; Lestelle; The Way to Win Him; The Tower of Nesle; The Black Reefer; The Gipsy King; True Blue; Murderer's Leap; Did You Ever Send Your Wife to Hoboken?; Nix, the Cabman; Venice Preserved; The Poisoners of Paris in 1665; The Three Thieves; The Lapland Witch; The Iron Chest; The Stranger; Othello; Hamlet; Macbeth; The Wandering Minstrel; The Imp of Riches; Romeo and Juliet; Pizarro; The Wife; The First Night; The Lady of Lyons; The Gamester; The Apostate; A New Way to Pay Old Debts; Brutus; Wallace; Ali Pacha; The Marriage of Fool and Folly; The Queen of the Abruzzi; Lucrezia Borgia; Walter Brand; Honest Roguery; The Golden Farmer; The Floating Beacon; The Black Doctor; The Printer's Devil; The Irish Post; Teddy, the Tiler; The Omnibus; The Bashful Irishman; Sprigs of Ireland; Kate Kearney; The Robber's Wife; Johnny Atkins; The Irishman in London; Rory O'More; The Card Drawer; The Limerick Boy; The Snow Storm; The Witch; Ion; Susan Hopley; Hawk, the Highwayman; Infidelity; Border War; The Wandering Boys; Young Scamp; The Blind Boy; Perfection; The Highlander's Dream; The Youthful Brigand; The Hunter of the Alps; The Man about Town; March of Freedom; Black Beard: The Black Cruiser; The Roll of the Drum; Love in Humble Life; The Lady and the Devil; Of Age Tomorrow; Paul Jones; Frightened to Death; Raby Ratler; No Song, No Supper; The Purse; The Married Rake; Jenny Lind at Last; The Irishman in Difficulty.

1847–48: Grist to the Mill; His Last Legs; Life in the Clouds; The Trumpeter's Daughter; The Hamlet Travestie; The Married Rake; A Roland for an Oliver; Naval Engagements; Cher Ryan Dfairs Tar; My Grandfather's Will; The Cork Leg; Romeo and Giuletta; The Queen's Own; The Irish Pretender; The Return of the Volunteers; The Sailor's Return; The White Horse of the Peppers; The Widow's Victim; The Maid of Croissey; The Irish Dragoon; Our Tom Thumb; Luke, the Labourer; Young America; Used Up; Harlequin Punchinello; A Tompkins Blue; Damon and Pythias; The Imp of Riches; The Maniac Lover; London Assurance; The Follies of a Night; Charles XII; Victorine; Married and Settled; Antony and Cleopatra; Don Caesar de Bazan; The Young Scamp; The Stranger; Jumbo Jum; Ginger Blue; William Tell; Othello; The Castle of Limberg; The Lonely Man of the Ocean; Who's the Composer? The Savage and the Maiden; Used Up; Boots at the Swan; Asmodeus; The Bridge of Kehl; Don Juan; Richelieu; Pizarro; The Foreign Prince; The Wife;

The School for Scandal; Paul Jones; The Four Lovers; The Soldier's Daughter; Hofer; Jim Crow in London; The Mill of Ryland; The Dumb Belle; The Virginia Mummy; The Dumb Girl of Genoa; The Spirit of the Fountain; Aladdin; The Flying Dutchman; The Artful Dodger; The Idiot Witness; The Female Horse Thief; La Giselle; Teddy, the Tiler; The Bronze Horse; The Wept of Wish-Ton-Wish; Six Degrees of Crime; The King's Gardener; The Jacobite; The New Footman; My Poll; My Partner Joe; Othello; The Minute Gun at Sea; The Birthright of Freedom; Richard III; The Golden Key; Love and Madness; The Black Mantle; The Roll of the Drum; The Seaman's Log; The Wren Boys; The Yankee Duelist; The Momentous Question; The Yankee Lawyer; He Lies Like Truth; St. Clair of the Isles; Fazio; Agnes de Vere; The Bride of Abydos; Susan Ashfield; Tekeli; Who Do They Take Me For?; The Merchant of Venice; The Denouncer; Love's Sacrifice; The Texian Rangers; Metamora; Jonathan Bradford; The Turnpike Gate; Lillian: The Show Girl; The Hunter of the Alps; The New York Milliners; The Assassin of the Rocks; The Brigand's Son; Nix, the Cabman; The Heir-at-Law; The Whistler; Jack Robinson and His Monkey; The Golden Farmer; Thérèse; The Lion of the North; The Wandering Boys; The Man without a Head; A Pet of the Petticoats; Nicholas Nickleby; The Lost Son; The Iron Chest; A New Way to Pay Old Debts; Brutus; Faint Heart ne'er Won Fair Lady; Woman; Undine; The Man of the World; Forty and Fifty; Box, Cox, and Knox; New York as It Is; Paul and Virginia; Our National Defence; Sarah, the Jewess; The Sealed Sentence; The Fatal Snowstorm; The Loan of a Lover; The Morning of Life; The Brigand; The Rent Day; Crime and Repentance; Helen Oakleigh; A Glance at New York in 1848; Swiss Swains; Clari; The Idiot Witness; The Way to Get Married; Captain of the Watch; Ernestine; Honey Moon; My Aunt.

BIBLIOGRAPHY

Published Sources: T. Allston Brown, *A History of the New York Stage from the First Performance in 1732 to 1901* (New York: Dodd, 1903); Joseph N. Ireland, *Records of the New York Stage from 1750 to 1860*, 2 vols. (New York: T. H. Morrell, 1866–67); George C. D. Odell, *Annals of the New York Stage*, vol. 4 (New York: Columbia University Press, 1931).

George B. Bryan

CHESTNUT STREET THEATRE COMPANY. The Chestnut Street Theatre Company, also known as the Wignell and Reinagle Company, the Warren and Wood Company, and the Company of the New Theatre in Chestnut Street, operated in Philadelphia from 1794 until 1826. Besides running the parent theatre in Philadelphia, the managers operated summer theatres in Baltimore, Maryland; Washington, D.C.; and Alexandria, Virginia; and the company performed occasionally in New York City and in other towns along the Eastern Seaboard.

Theatrical activity in the American colonies concluded its infancy with the appearance of the Company of Players in Plumsted's Warehouse, Philadelphia, in 1749. This company, led by Walter Murray and Thomas Kean, was soon eclipsed by the arrival in 1754 of Lewis Hallam's Company of Comedians from London, and the theatre in America entered its adolescence. In 1766 the Hallam company returned to the colonies after a hiatus of seven years, under the management of Lewis Hallam's widow and David Douglass, her new husband. Renamed the American Company (1752–92)* (after the Revolution, [Old] American Company [1792–1806]*), the troupe played throughout the colonies and the states until, by 1792, it had all but lost its vitality.

But for visits from the Old American Company and occasional performances by troupes of itinerant actors, Philadelphia and its sister cities to the south were without entertainment following the Revolution. Religious opposition to the theatre had been largely quelled in Pennsylvania, and Philadelphia was rapidly becoming a center of trade and industry sufficiently large to support a first-rate theatrical company.

Internal squabbling signaled the Old American Company's eventual demise. In 1790, angered at his treatment by the managers, Thomas Wignell, an English comic actor of considerable talent, headed a defection that included several actors and Alexander Reinagle, conductor; personal friend of the younger Bach; well-known teacher of violin, harpsichord, and pianoforte; and a concert artist and composer of note.

In the summer of 1792, with Wignell in England recruiting actors and scenic artists for the new theatrical partnership of Wignell and Reinagle, work was begun on a magnificent new theatre building. Located on the northwest corner of Chestnut and Sixth streets in Philadelphia, the theatre was not, as has often been asserted erroneously, a "copy of the Royal Theatre at Bath" but was instead indebted to a large extent to London's Theatre Royal in Covent Garden and built from a model—and possibly from plans—supplied by John Inigo Richards, Wignell's brother-in-law and a scenic artist at Covent Garden.

From the opening of the Chestnut Street Theatre on February 17, 1794, with *The Castle of Andalusia* until the death of Thomas Wignell on February 21, 1803, the company was managed by Wignell and, to some extent, Alexander Reinagle. From 1803 until Reinagle's death in 1809, management was in the hands of Mrs. Ann Brunton Merry Wignell, Wignell's widow, and Reinagle, assisted regularly by William Warren, an English actor who had joined the troupe in 1796, and occasionally by William B. Wood, who had made his first stage appearance in Philadelphia in 1799. Following the deaths of the widow Wignell (by then Mrs. William Warren) and Alexander Reinagle, Warren and Wood became sole proprietors and managers of the company in 1810, a relationship that would continue for sixteen years.

Like their predecessors, Warren and Wood leased the Chestnut Street Theatre from the owners; the managers supplied all lighting fixtures, stage machinery, rigging, settings, and wardrobe and were responsible, moreover, for all maintenance to the building. Thanks to the efforts of Alexander Reinagle, the company owned the finest music library in the United States, a library that included the scores and libretti to the many operas produced by the company during its thirty-two-year history, as well as incidental, *entr'acte*, and ballet music and orchestrations for hundreds of popular airs performed as olio pieces between main production and afterpiece.

Although the music library was entirely consumed by the fire that destroyed the first theatre building, several of the company's prompt books survive. Most are for the standard repertory of the era, with pieces such as *The Carmelite, The Law of Lombardy, Rosina, Man of Ten Thousand, The Corsicans, The Disbanded Officer, The Distrest Mother, The Dramatist*, and a tantalizing fragment from the prompt book of *Tekeli*, which gives the particulars of a daring escape scene complete with puppet models of the actors.

The prompt books indicate clearly that production at the Chestnut Street Theatre followed closely British precedents, not surprisingly, perhaps, since many of the productions were copies almost in their entirety from productions at London's Covent Garden and Drury Lane theatres. The theatre boasted an excellent store of stock scenes, as well as special-effects machinery, set pieces, properties, and wardrobe. It productions were, in the eyes of many well qualified to make the comparison, the equal of anything to be seen on the London stage.

Music played an important role at the Chestnut Street establishment, its place in the philosophy of the managers having been well established by Alexander Reinagle. In later years, W. B. Wood would question the efficacy of musical productions, however, since the cost of these entertainments often exceeded the income they generated, their popularity notwithstanding. Between 1810 and 1824 the company produced an average of three operas, twelve comic operas, four "musical dramas," six "musical farces," and three ballets each year, with the season of 1818—biggest ever for music—boasting nineteen comic operas, four operas, five musical dramas, seven musical farces, and five ballets.

Shakespeare was extremely popular at the Chestnut Street. William Warren was noted for his Falstaff and Mrs. Merry for her Ophelia and Desdemona. The appearance of visiting stars such as George Frederick Cooke and Thomas Abthorpe Cooper in the years after 1810 heralded an annual surfeit of the Bard. In all, between 1794 and 1826 the company produced *As You Like It*; David Garrick's *Catherine and Petruchio* (but never *The Taming of the Shrew*); *Coriolanus; Cymbeline; Hamlet; Henry IV, Parts 1 and 2; Henry V; Henry VIII; Julius Caesar; King John; King Lear; Macbeth; The Merchant of Venice; The Merry Wives of Windsor; Much Ado about Nothing; Othello; Richard II; Richard III; Romeo and Juliet*; and John Dryden's version of *The Tempest*.

These works, with the balance of the repertory—farces, melodramas, tragedies, comedies, historical plays, and the like—were generally well received. Typically, the Chestnut Street Theatre company mounted seventy to one hundred pieces each winter in a season that might last from November until April, presenting successful works as often as five or six times throughout the season. Poorly received pieces rarely were given more than a single performance.

When critical disapprobation fell upon the company, it was most often directed at a specific performer. Actors who performed poorly were driven from the stage, often to a cacophony of hisses and a shower of fruit and lighted cigar butts. In the years immediately following the American Revolution and the War of 1812, patriotic sentiment ran high; several actors narrowly escaped serious injury at the hands of angry theatre patrons when they appeared to disparage the young nation through action or dialogue.

Until its declining years the Chestnut Street Theatre Company encountered little serious competition. The Old American Company retired from Philadelphia in December 1794 for New York City. The fall of 1795 saw the opening of the Art Pantheon, or Ricketts' Ampitheatre, which presented a combination of plays and circus and equestrian acts until December 1799, when the ampitheatre burned to the ground. April 1797 saw the grand opening of Lailson's Circus, an ill-fated enterprise whose ampitheatre collapsed only a year later. Neither John Bill Ricketts nor Mr. Lailson's enterprises seriously affected business at the Chestnut Street Theatre.

But for occasional impromptu performances at the old Southwark Theatre (built by David Douglass in 1766), the Chestnut Street establishment reigned unopposed until 1809, when the "Professors of the Art of Horsemanship and Agility," Messrs. Pepin and Breschard, opened their circus at Ninth and Walnut streets. Initially devoted solely to equestrian entertainment, in 1812 Pepin and Breschard's company undertook dramas at their renamed Olympic Theatre, in an attempt to survive in competition with Warren and Wood at the Chestnut Street Theatre. The Olympic would continue to offer limited competition to Warren and Wood until late in 1819, when it finally closed.

The years between 1794 and 1826 saw significant changes in the operation of the Chestnut Street Theatre company. Initially a resident company, relatively little turnover in personnel occurred in the years between 1794 and 1806; no other companies in the United States were of such excellence, and there was little incentive to leave. 1798 saw the opening of the Park Theatre in New York City, however, and under the management of William Dunlap (1798–1805), Thomas Abthorpe Cooper (1806–9), Cooper and Stephen Price (1809–15), and Stephen Price alone (after 1815), this splendid theatre in New York soon began to rival Philadelphia in the affections of American and visiting British actors. The years 1800–1810 saw increasing mobility among the actors and other artists of the Philadelphia and New York stages. Then in 1810, with the importation of George Frederick Cooke by Cooper and Price, there began a practice that in later years would become known as the "star system." The introduction of stars had an immediate effect upon the Warren and Wood company in Philadelphia. In an effort to combat the newly arrived Pepin and Breschard company at the Circus (Olympic Theatre), Warren arranged for an appearance of Cooke, thus beginning a practice that, in the fifteen years that followed, would see the Philadelphia appearances of Cooke, who played an average of twelve nights each season between 1810 and 1823, and luminaries from the English stage such as Thomas Abthorpe Cooper, who played regularly with the company between 1796 and 1798 and then made guest appearances in 1801, 1803, 1806, 1808, 1809, and 1819; and Mr. Hardinge, who did the same in 1804, 1805, 1810, 1811, 1813, 1814, and 1815.

Miss Agnes Holman played sixteen nights in 1812; Benjamin Charles Incledon, eight nights in 1817; and Henry James Finn, five nights in 1818. Thomas Philipps performed fifteen nights in 1818 and twenty-two in 1822, and James Wallack averaged seventeen nights each in 1819 and 1820. The years following the destruction of the first Chestnut Street Theatre saw guest appearances by Edmund Kean in 1821 (sixteen performances), Junius Brutus Booth (seven performances), and Charles Mathews (eighteen performances) in 1823.

Although the use of stars seemed at first an attractive prospect, and later became a necessity if the managers were to shut out competition, Warren and Wood profited little from star performances. Charges by the performers and by their managers as well bled off most of the profit. In the Baltimore season of 1821, for example, with star performances by Edmund Kean averaging $500 a night, the managers failed to make expenses.

With the introduction of stars came the demise of the resident company. Chestnut Street actors, displaced by star performers, sought star billings elsewhere, and many chose to appear, whether displaced or not, for part of each season at the numerous theatres that by 1820 had sprung up along the Eastern Seaboard.

On April 2, 1820, the Chestnut Street Theatre was destroyed by fire, and on April 19 a conflagration ravaged the company's theatre in Washington, D.C. Lost in the fires were the company's assets, including irreplacable sets painted by the English artists John Inigo Richards, William Hodges, and Michael Angelo Rooker. The disasters followed hard upon seasons that had been of little profit to Warren and Wood. The years 1816 and 1817 saw, respectively, the lighting by gas of the Chestnut Street and Baltimore theatres, the entire cost borne by the managers. Star appearances, and the introduction each year of numerous productions new to the repertory, had occasioned the purchase of an extensive and costly wardrobe and the construction of many new sets. Moreover, in 1818 the owners of the Chestnut Street Theatre building had raised the annual rent by nearly $2,000.

For the 1821–22 season, in dire straits, Warren and Wood leased the

Olympic Theatre, which they renamed the Walnut Street Theatre. There they remained until December 2, 1822, when the second Chestnut Street Theatre, leased from Joseph R. Ingersoll and Hartman Kuhn, agents for the stockholders, was opened.

The Walnut Street Theatre, under the management of Stephen Price and Edmund Simpson of the Park Theatre (New York City), appeared to be the Chestnut Street establishment's only competitor. But the forces that would bring an untimely end to the partnership of William Warren and W. B. Wood were to be found within the company itself, among the stockholders of the new enterprise. They forced business policies upon the partners—especially ticket pricing and complimentary ticket practices—that Wood found intolerable. Warren sided against Wood in dealing with the stockholders, and a wedge was driven between the managers. With regrets, Wood terminated his partnership with Warren at the conclusion of the 1825–26 season.

PERSONNEL

Management: Thomas Wignell, proprietor and manager (1792–1803); Alexander Reinagle, proprietor (1792–1809); Mrs. Ann Brunton Merry Wignell Warren, proprietor and manager (1803–8); William Warren, manager (1803–10), proprietor and manager (1810–26); William B. Wood, manager (1803–10), proprietor and manager (1810–26); Mr. Pullen, treasurer (c.1811–20); Henry Warren, production stage manager (c.1816–26).

Scenic Artists: Charles Ciceri (1793); M. C. Milborne (1793–96, 1799, 1802, 1803, 1805); John Pollard Moreton (1793–98); Luke Robbins (1794–96, 1806–9, 1811–1815, 1817); John Worrall (1794–1800, 1805); John Darley, Jr. (1794–98, 1801); John Joseph Holland (1796–1806); Jemmy (Jeremy) Stuart (1800, 1808); Hugh Reinagle (1803, 1806); Thomas Reinagle (c.1803, 1814–20); Smith (1806); Joseph Jefferson (1808 and occasionally until 1826); Henry Warren (c.1809–26); Tom Jefferson (1813, 1816, 1820).

Technical Staff: Mr. Evans; William Strickland; Mr. Flour (1794–96); Mr. McKenzie (occasionally, 1804–11); Mr. Cummins (Cummings?) (1815–18); Mr. Marks, "plaisterer" (1815); Mr. Bouvard (1816); Charles Ward (c.1816–18).

Costumes and Wardrobe: Mrs. Crosbye (c.1794?); Mr. McCubbins, master tailor (1801); J. Harbaugh (1816).

Prompters: Joseph Harris; Mr. Rowson (1794–96); Mr. L'Estrange (1796–1800); Charles Charnock (1810–11); Tom Scrivener (1817); Howard J. "Don" Lopez (1821 and probably through 1825).

Musical Directors: Alexander Reinagle (1792–1808); Mr. Gillingham (1804–10).

Actors and Actresses: Dates of activity for performers are given in three forms: From 1794–1800, a single date indicates that the performer was a member of the Chestnut Street Theatre Company throughout the year listed. Hypenated dates signify that the performer appeared as a member of the company throughout these inclusive dates. After 1800 it became customary for actors to move about from theatre to theatre. Unless dates between 1800 and 1820 are hypenated, dates given indicate that the performer merely appeared with the company for one or more performances during each year. When an actress married after joining the company, her married name is given in parentheses following the maiden name.

Miss Aaron (1804); Mr. Abercrombie (1814, 1817, 1818); Charlotte Abercrombie (1813); Sophia Abercrombie (1814, 1815); Mrs. Alsop (1821); Mr. Anderson (1818); Mrs. Anderson (1818); Miss Arnold (Mrs. Poe) (1799–1802, 1807); Mr. Ashton (1794); Mrs. Baker (1821); James Nelson Barker, playwright (1808, 1814); John Barnes (1821); Mrs. John Barnes (1821); Mrs. G. H. Barrett (1803, 1808, 1809, 1810, 1811); George Houton Barrett (1811, 1813, 1814, 1815, 1816, 1817, 1818, 1819); George Bartley (1809, 1819); Mrs. George Bartley (1809, 1819); Mr. Bartow (1816); Mr. Bason (1794); Master Bates (1795–96); *Mr. Bates* (1794–97); *Mrs. Bates* (1794–96); Mr. Beaumont (1810, 1811); Mrs. Beaumont (1810, 1811); Mr. Beete (1795–96); Bellona (1794); *John Bernard* (1797–1800, 1801, 1802, 1803, 1808); *Mrs. John Bernard* (1798–1800); Mr. Betterton (1818); Mr. Bibby (1815); *Francis Blissett* (1794–1800, 1802, 1803, 1804, 1805, 1806, 1808, 1811, 1813, 1814, 1815, 1819, 1820); Mrs. Bloxton (1817, 1820); Mr. Booth (1823); Mr. Bouchoni (1796–97); John Bray (1806, 1807, 1808, 1809, 1812, 1813, 1814); *Miss Broadhurst (1794–1800); Thomas Burke (1817, 1818, 1819, 1820); Mrs. Thomas Burke (1816, 1817, 1818, 1819, 1820, 1822, 1823); Master Byrne (1798); James Byrne (1796–99); Mrs. James Byrne (1796–98); Alexander Cain* (1799, 1801–8); Mr. Calbraith (1811, 1812); Mrs. Carter (1818, 1820); *James Chalmers* (1794–98); Mrs. Claude (1816, 1817); Thomas Cleveland (1794–95); Mrs. Thomas Cleveland (1794–95); *Spencer H. Cone* (1807, 1808, 1809, 1810, 1811, 1812); Mr. Con, Jr. (1808); Mr. Crampton (1820); Mr. Cross (1806, 1807, 1808); Master Cunningham (1807, 1808); Mrs. Cunningham (1806); *John Darley* (1794–1801, 1812, 1820); *John Darley, Jr.* (1794–98, 1801); Mrs. DeMarque (1794–96); Mr. Dennison (1811); *Sig. Joseph Doctor* (1795–1800); *Mrs. Joseph Doctor* (1796–1800); Mr. Downie (1799); Mrs. Downie (1804); Mr. Doyle (1813, 1814); Miss Drake (1821); Mr. Dubois (1798); John R. Duff (1812, 1813, 1814, 1815, 1816, 1817, 1819, 1823); Mrs. Mary Ann Duff (1812, 1813, 1814, 1815, 1816, 1817, 1823); Mr. DuMoulin(s), or De(s)Moulin(s) (1794); Master Durang (1805, 1806, 1807, 1808, 1809); Augustus Durang (1807); *Charles Durang* (1805, 1806, 1808, 1809); Miss Charlotte Durang (1816, 1821); *Ferdinand Durang* (1805, 1806, 1808, 1809, 1813, 1816); John Durang (1807, 1808); Mrs. John Durang (1804, 1808); Miss K. Durang (1816, 1821); Mr. Dwyer (1810, 1811); Mr. Entwisle or Entwistle (1815, 1816, 1817); Mrs. Entwisle or Entwistle, formerly Mrs. Mason (1816, 1817, 1819, 1820, 1822, 1823); Mr. Estinval (1798), *James Fennell* (1794–98, 1803, 1804, 1806, 1807, 1810, 1811, 1812, 1813, 1815); Mr. Fieron (1797–98); Mr. Finch (1794); Mrs. Finch (1794); Mr. Finn (1818); Edwin Forrest (1820, 1821); William Forrest (1822); *Gilbert Fox* (1796–98, 1803, 1804), *William Francis* (1794–1800, 1803, 1819, 1821); *Mrs. William Francis* (1800, 1802, 1807, 1811, 1812, 1814, 1817, 1818, 1819, 1821); Mme. Gardie (1794); Mr. Gibbon(s) (1795–96); Miss Gillespie, or Gilaspie (1795–96); *Mrs. Gillingham* (1796–1800); Mons. Giraud (1818); Mr. Glaize, or Gleise (1797–98); Miss Green (1809); Mr. Green (1794–96, 1802); Mrs. Green (*see* Miss Williams); Lewis Hallam (1807); Mirvan(?) Hallam (1803); Miss Hardinge (1797–98); Mr. Hardinge (1797–99, 1804, 1805, 1810, 1811, 1813, 1814, 1815); Mrs. Hardinge (1797–99); *Master Harris* (1799–1809); Mrs. Harris (1816, 1817, 1818, 1819); *John E. Harwood* (1794–98, 1800, 1806); Mrs. John E. Harwood (1797–98); John Herbert (1818, 1820, 1821); Mrs. Hervey or Harvey (1795–97); Miss F. Hodgkinson (1806); John Hodgkinson (1803);

Miss Agnes Holman (1812); Joseph George Holman (1812); Mr. Hughes (1818, 1819, 1820); *Miss Hunt* (Mrs. Bray) (1803–9, 1812); Mr. Hunter (1798–99); Mrs. Hunter (1798); Benjamin Charles Incledon (1817); Master Jefferson (1806, 1807); *Joseph Jefferson* (1804–23); Mrs. Joseph Jefferson (1804); T. Jefferson (1820, 1822); Mr. Jewitt (1817); Mr. Johnson (1797–98); Mr. Jones (1796–97, 1802, 1803); Mrs. Jones (1802, 1803); Edmund Kean (1821); Mr. Keene (1819); Mr. King (1820); Mr. Labasse (1822); Mr. Lafferty (1797–98); Mr. Lavancey, or Lavencey (1796–99); Mrs. Lavancey, or Lavencey (1799); Mr. Lee (1794); Mrs. Lefolle (1819); Mr. Lege (1795); Mrs. Lege (1795–96); *Master L'Estrange* (1797–1800); *Miss L'Estrange* (1796–1800); *Mr. L'Estrange (1796–1800); Mrs. L'Estrange* (1796–99); Mr. Lindsley (1813); Master Lynch (1802); *Mr. Marshall* (1794–1800); *Mrs. Marshall* (Mrs. Wilmot after 1807) (1794–1800, 1808, 1810, 1811); Mrs. Mason (1812, 1813, 1814, 1815); Mr. Matthew (1797–98); Matthews (1823); Robert Campble Maywood (1819); Mr. McDonald (1795–97, 1802); Mrs. McDonald (1799); Mr. McFarland (1816, 1817, 1818); Mr. McKenzie (1811); Mrs. McKenzie (1810); Mrs. Mechtler (1796–97); Mrs. Charlotte Melmoth (1806, 1807, 1808); *Mrs. Ann Brunton Merry* (Mrs. Wignell after 1803; Mrs. William Warren after 1806) (1796–1808); Mr. Mersier, or Mercer (1798–99); *Miss Milbourne* (1795–98); Mr. Mills (1807, 1808); Mrs. Mills (1807, 1808); Mr. Mitchell (1795–97, 1800); Mr. M'Lane (1798); *John Pollard Moreton* (1794–98); Mr. Morgan (1796–97); *Owen Morris* (1794–1800); *Mrs. Owen Morris* ("the second") (1794–1800, 1803); Miss Moses (1804); Miss Mullen (1807, 1808); Munto (1794); Mr. Nugent (1794–95); *Miss Oldfield* (1794–98); *Mrs. Oldmixon* (1794–1805); Master Parker (1794–95); John Howard Payne (1810, 1811); William Pelby (1821); Thomas Philipps (1818, 1822); Mr. Poe (1807); Mr. Poignand, or Poignard (1796–98); Mr. Price (1794–96); Mr. Quenet (Quesnay?) (1794); Miss Rachael (1804); Mr. Radcliff, or Ratcliff (1799–1800); Mrs. Riddle (1813); *Luke Robbins* (1795–96, 1803–5, 1807, 1808, 1811, 1813–16); Mr. Robertson (1817, 1818); Mr. Robertson (The Antipodean Whirligig) (1802); Mr. Robinson (1814); *Miss Rowson* (1794–96); *Mr. Rowson* (1794–96); *Mrs. Susannah Haswell Rowson* (1794–96); Mr. Rutherford (1806, 1808); Mr. St. Mare, or St. Marc (1796–97); Miss Scriven (1803, 1805, 1807); Mr. Serson (1808); Miss Seymour (1812, 1813, 1815, 1816, 1817); Mr. Seymour (1805); Mrs. Seymour (1806, 1807, 1808, 1810, 1812, 1813, 1814, 1815, 1816); *Mrs. Shaw* (1794–96, 1802, 1805); Mr. Simpson (1812); Master Smith; (1821); Mrs. Snowden (1804); *Miss Solomon(s)* (1794–96); *Mr. Solomon(s)* (1794–96); *Mrs. Solomon(s)* (1794–96); Miss C. Solomon(s) (1796); Mlle. Sophie (1796–97); Mrs. Stanley (1809); Mr. Steward (1816, 1817); Mrs. Stuart (1798–99); Mr. Tatin (1822); Mrs. Tetnall (1822, 1823); Mr. Taylor (1798–99, 1805, 1806, 1808); Mlle. Tesseire (1796–98); William Twaits (1804, 1805); Mrs. William Twaits (1810, 1811, 1812); Mr. Usher (1801, 1803); Mr. Viellard (1796–97); Henry Wallack (1819, 1820, 1822, 1823); Mrs. Henry Wallack (1819, 1820, 1822, 1823); James Wallack (1819, 1820, 1821, 1823); Mr. Waring (1814); *Master Harry Warrell* (1795–99); *John Warrell*, or Worrall (1794–1800, 1805); *Mrs. John Warrell*, or Worrell (1794–1800); *Master T. Warrell* (1794–1800, 1804); *William Warren* (1796–1820); Mr. Webster (1807, 1808); Miss Wells (1794–95); Francie Wemyss (1822); Mr. West (1810); *Miss Ellen Westray* (Mrs. John Darley) (1801–4, 1812, 1820, 1821); Miss Juliana Westray (1801); Master Whale (1810, 1811); Master W. Whale (1810); Frederick(?) Wheatley (1818); Mrs. S. Wheatley (1816, 1817); Miss White (1811, 1813, 1814, 1815, 1816); Mr. White (1818); *Mr. Whitlock* (1794–96); Elizabeth Kemble Whitlock (1794–96, 1802, 1812, 1814); *Thomas Wignell* (1794–1803); *Miss Williams*, or Willems (Mrs. Green after 1796) (1794–96, 1804, 1809, 1812, 1813, 1814, 1815); Mr. Williams (1808, 1820, 1821); Mrs. Williams (1816, 1820, 1821); Mr. Wilson (1823); Mrs. W. B. Wood (1812, 1813, 1814, 1816, 1820); *William B. Wood* (1799–1820); Mr. Woodham (1806, 1807); Mrs. Woodham (1806, 1807); Jacob Woodhull (1817).

REPERTORY

The following list is representative of plays, operas, and afterpieces performed each year by the Chestnut Street Theatre Company in Philadelphia between 1794 and 1823. For the most part, works introduced or repeated in the winter were also performed at the company's satellite theatres during the summer season. In the lists that follow, principal plays and operas given each season are listed first (1), followed by pantomimes, entertainments, and other afterpieces (2). The term afterpiece does not refer here to a type of dramatic work so much as it denotes that a piece followed the main presentation.

1794: (1) *As You Like It; The Battle of Hexham; The Carmelite; Robin Hood; Slaves in Algiers; The Surrender of Calais; The Woodman; The Castle of Andalusia; Cymbeline; Douglas; The Dramatist; The Fair Penitent; Hamlet; Macbeth; Othello; The Maid of the Mill; The Merchant of Venice; The Provok'd Husband; The Recruiting Officer; Richard III; Romeo and Juliet; The Tempest; Venice Preserved*; (2) *The Caledonian Frolic; The Embargo; La Forêt Noire; Peeping Tom of Coventry; Spoil'd Child; The Village Lawyer; The Critic; Harlequin Shipwrecked; Rosina; The Virgin Unmasked; Who's the Dupe?*

1794–95: (1) *The Female Patriot; The First Floor; Fontainville Forest; The Natural Son; The Triumphs of Love; As You Like It; Beaux Stratagem; The Beggar's Opera; The Castle of Andalusia; The Conscious Lovers; The Country Girl; Cymbeline; The Dramatist; George Barnwell; Hamlet; Inkle and Yarico; Macbeth; The Merry Wives of Windsor; Richard III; The Rivals; Romeo and Juliet; The School for Scandal; She Stoops to Conquer; Tamerlane; The Tempest; The West Indian*; (2) *The Devil in the Wine Cellar; The Elopment; or, Harlequin's Tour through the Continent of America; Harlequin Hurry Scurry; Les Armans d'Arcade; A New Way to Pay Old Debts; Set a Beggar on Horseback; The Birth of Harlequin; Comus; The Critic; The Devil to Pay; High Life below Stairs; Hob in the Well; The Lying Valet; The Miller of Mansfield; The Padlock; The Quaker; The Wrangling Lovers.*

1795–96: (1) *The Bank Note; Coriolanus* (John Philip Kemble's version); *The Disbanded Officer; Henry II; Rule a Wife and Have a Wife; The Suicide; The Wheel of Fortune; A Bold Stroke for a Wife; The Contrast; The Duenna; Every One Has His Fault; Hamlet; The Highland Reel; Inkle and Yarico; Jane Shore; Macbeth; The Maid of the Mill; The Merchant of Venice; The Merry Wives of Windsor; The Provok'd Husband; Richard III; The Rivals; Zara*; (2) *The American Tar; Both Sides of the Gutter; Un Divertissement Pastoral; The Doctor and the Apothecary; Gil Blas; Harlequin Doctor Faustus; The Maid of the Oaks; T'Other Side of the Gutter; Two Strings to Your Bow; All the World's a Stage; The Bird Catcher; The Critic; The First Floor; The Padlock; Robinson Crusoe; Tom Thumb, the Great; The Village Lawyer.*

1797–98: (1) *Cure for the Heart-Ache; Fatal Curiosity; The Italian Monk; The*

Shipwreck (George Colman, the younger); *The Spectre; Tancred and Sigismunda; Alexander the Great; The Belle's Stratagem; The Busy Body; Columbus; The Country Girl; The Fair Penitent; Hamlet; Henry IV, Part 1; He Would Be a Soldier; King Lear; Macbeth; The Orphan; Othello; Romeo and Juliet; Venice Preserved; The West Indian;* (2) *The Adventures of a Wit; The Advertisement; All in Good Humor; The Animated Statue; The Death of General Wolfe; Fortunatus; Marian; Richard Coeur de Lion; Tit for Tat; Animal Magnetism; The Castle of Andalusia; The Critic; The Death of Captain Cook; The Devil to Pay; La Forêt Noire; Inkle and Yarico; The Lying Valet; The Padlock; The Poor Soldier; Rosina; Robinson Crusoe; Two Strings to Your Bow.*

1799: (1) *Cheap Living; Duplicity; The Heir-at-Law; The Mysteries of the Castle; The Robbers; A Wedding in Wales; The Beggar's Opera; The Child of Nature; Columbus; The Conscious Lovers; The Disbanded Officer; The Dramatist; Jane Shore; The Natural Son; Romeo and Juliet;* (2) *American True Blue; The Battle of Trenton; The Catch Club; The History of John Gilpin; The Magic Fire; An Olio; William Tell; All the World's a Stage; The Castle of Andalusia; The Critic; The Death of General Wolfe, Harlequin Shipwrecked; Love à la Mode; The Mountaineers; The Padlock; The Poor Soldier; Rosina; Tom Thumb, the Great.*

1799–1800: (1) *Five Thousand a Year; The Secret; The Heir-at-Law; Lovers' Vows; The Roman Father; The Stranger; The School for Scandal; The Poor Soldier; King John; The Fair Penitent; Venice Preserved; Hamlet; Macbeth; Reconciliation; The Castle Spectre; Pizarro; The Double Disguise; Gustavus Vasa;* (2) *The Constellation; or, a Wreath for American Tars; The Naval Pillar; Bluebeard; The Critic; The Catch Club; Harlequin Freemason; The Horse and the Widow; The Jew and the Doctor; The Monody on Washington's Death; The Adopted Child; The Prize.*

1800–1801: (1) *Cato; Edwyn and Elgiva; The Law of Lombardy; The Siege of Belgrade; St. David's Day; The Votary of Wealth; Speed the Plough; Alexander the Great; Richard III; Othello; Macbeth; The Poor Soldier; Artaxerxes; The Corsicans; The Road to Ruin; The Will; The Castle Spectre;* (2) *The Critic; Bluebeard; The Siege of Exydrace; The Catch Club.*

1801–2: (1) *The Mountaineers; The Battle of Hexham; High Life below Stairs; Cure for the Heart-Ache; Hamlet; The London Hermit; Bunker Hill; The Election; The Poor Gentleman; Henry IV, Part I; Deaf and Dumb; The Purse; The Country Girl; Jane Shore; Speed the Plough; Il Bondacani; The Merchant of Venice; Cymbeline; The Merry Wives of Windsor; Macbeth; Pizarro;* (2) *Harlequin Recruit; A Trip to Fontainbleau; Bluebeard; St. David's Day; Obi; or, Three-Fingered Jack.*

1802–3: (1) *Bunker Hill; Lock and Key; The Rival Soldiers; The Way to Get Married; A Bold Stroke for a Husband; The Deaf Lover; The Poor Soldier; The Castle Spectre; The Sixty-third Letter; Henry IV, Part 2; Venice Preserved; Henry VIII; The Virgin of the Sun; The Tempest; Abaellino; The Belle's Stratagem; Speed the Plough; High Life below Stairs;* (2) *The Corsair; or, The Tripolitan Robbers; The Enterprise; or, A Wreath for American Tars; The Dramatist; Sancho Turned Governor; Harlequin Prisoner; Harlequin's Almanac.*

1803–4: (1) *The Heir-at-Law; The School for Scandal; She Wou'd and She Wou'd Not; The Marriage Promise; The Maid of Bristol; John Bull; A Tale of Mystery* (René Pixérécourt's *Coelina); Count Benyowsky; Raymond and Agnes* (M. G. Lewis' *Monk); Romeo and Juliet; Much Ado about Nothing; Richard III; Paul and*

Virginia; (2) *The Jew; Harlequin Restored; Blue Devils; The Scheming Milliners; Two Per Cent.*

1804–5: (1) *Cleone; Hamlet; Richard III; The Merchant of Venice; Macbeth; Romeo and Juliet; Henry IV, Part I; The Merry Wives of Windsor; Much Ado about Nothing; John Bull; A House to Be Sold; The Sailor's Daughter; The Point of Honour; Spoil'd Child; The Wife of Two Husbands; Speed the Plough; High Life below Stairs; The Mountaineers; A Tale of Mystery;* (2) *Liberty in Louisiana; A New Wreath for American Tars; Arthur and Emmeline; The Prospect of Columbia's Future Glory* (a masque); *American Tars in Tripoli; La Perouse; The Temple of Flora* (a masque); *Harlequin's Vagaries; The Catch Club.*

1805–6: (1) *The West Indian; Mary, Queen of Scots; The Road to Ruin; Douglas; The School for Scandal; Who Wants a Guinea?; The Purse; or, The Benevolent Tar; The Carmelite; Raising the Wind; Spoil'd Child; The Heir-at-Law; The Revenge; The Shipwreck; Othello; Paul and Virginia; The Brazen Mask; Romeo and Juliet; Honey Moon; Hamlet; Captain Smith and the Princess Pocahontas; The Fox Chase;* (2) *La Perouse; Cinderella; The Battle of Derne* (a scenic spectacle).

1806–7: (1) *He Would be a Soldier; Miss in Her Teens; Barbarossa; Love Makes a Man; Valentine and Orson; The Weathercock; Henry IV, Part I; The Merry Wives of Windsor; Lovers' Vows; The School of Reform; Peeping Tom of Coventry; Tears and Smiles; The Generous Farmers; Honey Moon; Speed the Plough; The Son-in-Law; Romeo and Juliet; The Clandestine Marriage; The Mayor of Garratt; The Distrest Mother; Love in a Village;* (2) *The Battle of Tripoli; The Carnival Masquerade of Venice; Cinderella; La Perouse; The Sons of Apollo.*

1807–8: (1) *The Indian Princess; Town and Country; Romeo and Juliet; Adrian and Orrila; The Embargo; To Marry or Not to Marry; The Fortress; The Country Girl; Rosina; The Rivals; George Barnwell; Venice Preserved; The Virgin Unmasked; The Poor Soldier; Speed the Plough; The Peasant of the Alps;* (2) *The Spirit of Independence; The Anniversary of Shelah; The Catch Club; Tom Thumb, the Great; Harlequin Dr. Faustus; Phantasmagori.*

1808–9: (1) *Pizzaro; The Provok'd Husband; Honey Moon; No Song, No Supper; The Soldier's Daughter; John Bull; The Heir-at-Law; Love à la Mode; Julius Caesar; The Forty Thieves; Adelgitha; The Lady of the Rock; The Wood Daemon; The School for Prodigals; The Wounded Huzzar; Bunker Hill; Who Pays the Piper; Hamlet; The Surrender of Calais; Speed the Plough; The School for Scandal;* (2) *The Critic; The Review; Glory of Columbia; The Spirit of Independence; The Independence of Columbia.*

1809–10: (1) *Lovers' Vows; Hamlet; Pizarro; The West Indian; The Foundling of the Forest; Miss in Her Teens; The Africans; Honey Moon; Town and Country; The Iron Chest; Spoil'd Child; The Lady of the Rock; Barbarossa; Romeo and Juliet; Henry IV, Part 1; The Robbers;* (2) *Mother Goose.*

1810–11: (1) *The Way to Get Married; Macbeth; The Foundling of the Forest; Isabella; Speed the Plough; The Belle's Stratagem; Ella Rosenberg; King Lear; Romeo and Juliet; Pizarro; Richard III; Othello; Henry IV, Part 1; The Castle Spectre; The Stranger; The School for Scandal; Hamlet; Venice Preserved; Douglas; The Distrest Mother; The Merchant of Venice; Coriolanus; A New Way to Pay Old Debts; Every Man in His Humor;* (2) *Modern Antiques; Raising the Wind; The Highland Reel; Who Wins; Hit or Miss; The Ghost; Catherine and Petruchio; Ways*

and Means; Love Laughs at Locksmiths; A Budget of Blunders; The Irishman in
London; Bluebeard; La Forêt Noire; The Spanish Barber; Don Juan.

1811–12: (1) Pizarro; Speed the Plough; Much Ado about Nothing; The Castle
Spectre; Hamlet; Richard III; Macbeth; Honey Moon; The Merry Wives of Windsor;
Adelgitha; The West Indian; Othello; The Merchant of Venice; Romeo and Juliet;
Venice Preserved; King John; King Lear; Henry IV, Part 1; Douglas; Speed the
Plough; The Lady of the Lake; The Robbers; The Country Girl; The Tempest;
Alexander the Great; (2) Of Age Tomorrow; Don Juan; Modern Antiques; Raising
the Wind; Bluebeard; The Invisible Girl; The Ghost; A Tale of Mystery; Catherine
and Petruchio; The Children in the Wood; Lyar; Matrimony; The Poor Soldier;
Tom Thumb, the Great; The Hunter of the Alps; Love à la Mode; The Forty Thieves;
Bluebeard; The Apprentice; Cinderella.

1812–13: (1) The Castle Spectre; Pizarro; Hamlet; Honey Moon; Douglas;
Alexander the Great; The Lady of the Lake; Macbeth; The Carmelite; The Foundling of the Forest; Henry IV, Part 1; She Stoops to Conquer; The Belle's Stratagem; The Sons of Erin; Hamlet; Venice Preserved; The Earl of Essex; Romeo and
Juliet; The Fair Penitent; Much Ado about Nothing; The Votary of Wealth; Town
and Country; The Dramatist; Barbarossa; William Tell; The Tempest; Marmion;
The Merry Wives of Windsor; Othello; Timour, the Tartar; The Rivals; The Merchant of Venice; Bunker Hill; Julius Caesar; Wild Oats; Coriolanus; (2) Monody
to Cooke; The Village Lawyer; Raising the Wind; The Constitution; A Budget of
Blunders; The Comet; The Forty Thieves; The Devil to Pay; Darkness Visible;
The Fortress; The Lady of the Lake; The Ghost; The Review; The Beehive; A Tale
of Mystery; The Return from a Cruise; Bluebeard; The Brazen Mask; Modern
Antiques; The Romp; The Critic; Cinderella; Little Red Riding Hood; The Quadrupeds of Quadlinburg.

1813–14: (1) Romeo and Juliet; Adelgitha; Macbeth; The Wonder; Much Ado
about Nothing; Marmion; The School for Scandal; The Robbers; Count Benyowski;
Wild Oats; The Foundling of the Forest; George Barnwell; The Ethiop; Hamlet;
Richard III; The Virgin of the Sun; Honey Moon; Henry IV, Part 1; Venice Preserved; The Wheel of Fortune; Othello; Education; The Birthday; The Exile; Remorse; The Sons of Erin; Town and Country; The Recruiting Officer; The Gamester;
(2) The Hero of the Lakes; The Sleepwalker; Cinderella; Little Red Riding Hood
(a ballet); The Critic; The Robber of Genoa; The Highland Reel; The Comet;
Darkness Visible; The Lady of the Lake; William Tell; The Children in the Wood;
Catherine and Petruchio; A Budget of Blunders; Tom Thumb, the Great; The
Spanish Barber; Catch Him Who Can; Who's the Dupe?; Transformation; Timour,
the Tartar; A Tale of Mystery; Tekeli.

1814–1815: (1) She Stoops to Conquer; Town and Country; The Heir-at-Law;
The Robbers; Count Benyowski; Wild Oats; The Recruiting Officer; The Ethiop;
The Exile; Pizarro; Peter the Great; Speed the Plough; Education; The Renegade;
George Barnwell; Romeo and Juliet; The West Indian; The Students of Salamanca;
Henry IV, Parts 1 and 2; Othello; Richard III; Hamlet; Honey Moon; Macbeth;
The Castle Spectre; Alexander the Great; The Man of Ten Thousand; John Bull;
The Poor Gentleman; The Stranger; Douglas; Tamerlane; Zorinski; King Lear; (2)
The Poor Soldier; The Beehive; The Turnpike Gate; The Highland Reel; The Tooth-
ache; 'Tis All a Farce; The Camp; The Comet; The Return from Camp; Darkness
Visible; Tom Thumb, the Great; The Widow's Vow; The Weathercock; The Ship-

wreck; Transformation; Catherine and Petruchio; The Fortress; The Miller and His Men; A Budget of Blunders; Timour, the Tartar; The Catch Club; Turn Out; Tekeli; The Lady of the Lake.

1815–16: (1) *The West Indian; The Mountaineers; Romeo and Juliet; The Foundling of the Forest; The Exile; The Robbers; The School for Scandal; Macbeth; The Stranger; Adelmorn; She Stoops to Conquer; Jane Shore; Speed the Plough; Zembuca; George Barnwell; The Forest of Bondy; Hamlet; Richrd III; Honey Moon; Macbeth; The Iron Chest; Othello; Much Ado about Nothing; The Belle's Stratagem; The Wonder; The Will; Henry IV, Part I; Columbus; Pizarro; Wild Oats; The Magpie and the Maid; Rosina; Romeo and Juliet; The Battle of Hexham; The Point of Honour; King Lear; Count Benyowski*; (2) *The Review; The Miller and His Men; The Devil to Pay; Sprigs of Laurel; The Fortune of War; The Lady of the Lake; The Hunter of the Alps; The Comet; The Beehive; Lock and Key; The Spanish Barber; Red Riding Hood; Three Weeks after Marriage; The Turnpike Gate; Catherine and Petruchio; Spoil'd Child; Raising the Wind; The Padlock; Love Laughs at Locksmiths; The Highland Reel.*

1816–17: (1) *The Foundling of the Forest; Pizarro; Zembuca; The Mountaineers; The Rivals; Romeo and Juliet; The Magpie and the Maid; Bertram; The Belle's Stratagem; Honey Moon; Rokeby; George Barnwell; The Fortune of War; Wild Oats; Aladdin; The Will; The Busy Body; Hamlet; Macbeth; Richard III; The School for Scandal; Coriolanus; Othello; Alexander the Great; The Robbers; Much Ado about Nothing; Henry IV, Part 1; Julius Caesar; The Castle Spectre; Gustavus Vasa; The Gamester; Guy Mannering; The Ethiop; The Man of Ten Thousand; The West Indian; The Tempest; King Lear; The Heir-at-Law; John Bull; Speed the Plough; The Dramatist;* (2) *Raising the Wind; No Song, No Supper; Paul and Virginia; The Miller and His Men; Turn Out; Timour, the Tartar; The Lady of the Lake; The Woodsman's Hut; Bombastes Furioso; The Prize; Catherine and Petruchio; The Hunter of the Alps; The Padlock; Transformation; Mr. H.; The Poor Soldier; The Irishman in London; Lyar; Bluebeard; The Ghost; The Comet; The Forty Thieves; A Tale of Mystery; The Armourer's Escape; Miss in Her Teens; The Surrender of Calais; The Catch Club.*

1817–18: (1) *Macbeth; The Magpie and the Maid; The Ethiop; Rosina; Love in a Village; The Fortune of War; The Maid of the Mill; The Poor Soldier; The Banditti of the Forest; As You Like It; Inkle and Yarico; Richard III; Henry IV, Part 1; The Broken Sword; The West Indian; Wild Oats; The Conquest of Taranto; Bertram; The Apostate; Lionel and Clarissa; The Duenna; Pygmalion; The Merry Wives of Windsor; Romeo and Juliet; The Surrender of Calais; The Robbers; The Stranger; Hamlet; She Stoops to Conquer; The Merchant of Venice; The Iron Chest; The Virgin of the Sun; The Snow Storm; Count Benyowski; The Slave;* (2) *The Beehive; The Forty Thieves; High Life below Stairs; The Turnpike Gate; How to Die for Love; Aladdin; My Landlady's Gown; The Hunter of the Alps; The Fortune of War; The Poor Soldier; Lovers' Quarrels; The Highland Reel; The Lady of the Lake; Of Age Tomorrow; Paul and Virginia; Raising the Wind; The Padlock; My Grandmother; Red Riding Hood.*

1818–19: (1) *The School for Scandal; The Conquest of Taranto; Honey Moon; The Merchant of Venice; The Snow Storm; John Bull; Pizarro; The Merry Wives of Windsor; The Apostate; The Robbers; Town and Country; The Exile; The Busy Body; Henry IV, Part 1; Bellamira; The Stranger; The Virgin of the Sun; The*

Foundling of the Forest; The Slave; Wild Oats; Macbeth; Hamlet; Richard III; Romeo and Juliet; Jane Shore; The Green Man; Alexander the Great; The Libertine; George Barnwell; Speed the Plough; Rob Roy MacGregor; Fazio; Bertram; Coriolanus; The Merchant of Venice; Richard II; Othello; King Lear; Venice Preserved; Bunker Hill; Accusation; The West Indian; Count Benyowski; Barbarossa; (2) *Lock and Key; A Budget of Blunders; The Kaleidoscope; Bluebeard; Love among the Roses; Turn Out; Little Red Riding Hood; The Magpie and the Maid; Darkness Visible; We Fly by Night; The Broken Sword; The Lady of the Lake; Wyandot Indians; Catherine and Petruchio; The Fortune of War; The Children in the Wood; My Aunt; The Review; My Uncle; High Life below Stairs; The Invisible Girl; Raising the Wind; The Miller and His Men; The Critic; The Blue Devils; Is He Alive?; The Scotch Ghost.*

1819–20: (1) *Much Ado about Nothing; Rob Roy MacGregor; The Exile; My Uncle; Brutus; Barmecide; The Stranger; The Robbers; The Heart of Midlothian; Henry IV, Part I; The Duenna; The Devil's Bridge; Jane Shore; The Foundling of the Forest; Town and Country; The School for Scandal; The Bride of Abydos; George Barnwell; Macbeth; Richard III; Marmion; Hamlet; Bertram; The Green Man; The Merry Wives of Windsor; Fazio; Douglas; Guy Mannering; She Would Be a Soldier; Speed the Plough; The Falls of Clyde; Altorf; Education; Pizarro; Coriolanus; The Carib Chief; Honey Moon; Fredolfo; The West Indian; She Stoops to Conquer; The Castle Spectre; A Short Reign and a Merry One; The Battle of Hexham; The Ethiop; Wild Oats; Adelgitha; The Rivals;* (2) *Of Age Tomorrow; Sigesmar, the Switzer; A Budget of Blunders; Paul and Virginia; The Romp; The Poor Gentleman; Zembuca; The Mayor of Garratt; Ella Rosenberg; Love Laughs at Locksmiths; Raising the Wind; The Ghost; The Review; Lyar; A Roland for an Oliver; Ode to the Passions; Love among the Roses; The Blue Devils; The Critic; Ways and Means; Turn Out; Where Shall I Dine?; The Lady of the Lake; The Deuce; The Children in the Wood; The Magpie and the Maid; Robinson Crusoe; Bluebeard; The Forest of Bondy; The Jew of Lubeck; The Ruffian Boy.*

1820–21: (1) *Wild Oats; The Poor Gentleman; As You Like It; The Road to Ruin; Henri Quatre; The Wonder; Douglas; The Busy Body; The Iron Chest; The Foundling of the Forest; The Heart of Midlothian; The Steward; She Stoops to Conquer; Virginius; Macbeth; Bertram; Hamlet; Richard III; The Fate of Calais; George Barnwell; Ivanhoe; The Robbers; The Mountaineers; Othello; The Merchant of Venice; Brutus; A New Way to Pay Old Debts; King Lear; Town and Country; The Child of the Mountains; The School for Scandal; The Belle's Stratagem; Romeo and Juliet; The Castle Spectre; Jane Shore; Honey Moon; Speed the Plough; The Merry Wives of Windsor; Riches; Venice Preserved;* (2) *Agreeable Surprise; Of Age Tomorrow; Rosina; A Budget of Blunders; Where Shall I Dine?; Little Red Riding Hood; High Life below Stairs; Turn Out; The Vampire; The Ruffian Boy; Belles without Beaux; Love among the Roses; The Magpie and the Maid; The Anatomist; Catherine and Petruchio; The Scotch Ghost; The Ghost; Raising the Wind; The Hunter of the Alps; The Dead Alive; The Actress of All Work; Matrimony; Sprigs of Laurel; The Broken Sword; The Falls of Clyde; Tom Thumb, the Great; The Turnpike Gate; A Mogul Tale; Inkle and Yarico; A Tale of Mystery.*

1821–22: (1) *The West Indian; The Point of Honour; The Devil's Bridge; Wallace; Rob Roy MacGregor; Henri Quatre; Wild Oats; Honey Moon; The Merry Wives of Windsor; Isabella; Macbeth; The Poor Gentleman; The Mountaineers; Hamlet;*

Pizarro; Bertram; Venice Preserved; Brutus; A Short Reign and a Merry One; The School for Scandal; Damon and Pythias; The Foundling of the Forest; The Warlock of the Glen; The Robbers; The Miller's Maid; Town and Country; Romeo and Juliet; George Barnwell; Undine; She Would Be a Soldier; De Montfort; The Green Man; Speed the Plough; The Iron Chest; Alexander the Great; Usef Caramalli; The Voice of Nature; Mahomet; The Cabinet; Brother and Sister; Guy Mannering; The Maid of the Mill; The Barber of Seville; Fontainebleau; Henry IV, Part 1; The Russian Imposter; The Spy; (2) *Helpless Animals; Too Late for Dinner; Spoil'd Child; Of Age Tomorrow; Valentine and Orson; The Vampire; The Ruffian Boy; Where Shall I Dine?; Miss in Her Teens; Belles without Beaux; My Grandmother; A Budget of Blunders; The Romp; The Highland Reel; Catherine and Petruchio; The Poor Soldier; The Deaf Lover; Love Laughs at Locksmiths; Turn Out; The Comet; The Children in the Wood; The Dead Alive; The Irishman in London; The Forty Thieves; The Magpie and the Maid; The Falls of Clyde; The Rendevous; High Life below Stairs; Modern Antiques; Ella Rosenberg; The Ghost; Little Red Riding Hood; Jealousy in a Seraglio.*

1822–23: (1) *The School for Scandal; Damon and Pythias; Venice Preserved; Honey Moon; The Dramatist; Pizarro; Much Ado about Nothing; Virginius; Wild Oats; The Apostate; Guy Mannering; The Belle's Stratagem; Rob Roy MacGregor; The Spy; Macbeth; Henry IV, Part 1; The Wood Daemon; The Robbers; The Law of Java; Adelgitha; Hamlet; Remorse; Bertram; Coriolanus; Fraternal Discord; The Gamester; Othello; Brutus; Bellamira; Venice Preserved; Douglas; Julius Caesar; King John; Richard III; The Iron Chest; A New Way to Pay Old Debts; William Tell; The Road to Ruin; Wild Oats; The Heir-at-Law; A Trip to Paris; Mail Coach Adventures; The Youthful Days of Mr. Mathews; Such Things Are; The Two Fascari; King Lear; Town and Country; The Mountaineers; The Distrest Mother; The Manager in Distress; The Falls of Clyde; Alexander the Great; Speed the Plough; Tom and Jerry; The North American;* (2) *Of Age Tomorrow; The Children in the Wood; The Comet; Modern Antiques; Miss in Her Teens; The Two Pages of Frederick the Great; Spoil'd Child; Who's the Dupe?; The Wandering Boys; The Mock Doctor; Three Weeks after Marriage; Lock and Key; The Blue Devils; The Phrenologist; A Tale of Mystery; The Prisoner at Large; My Aunt; Catherine and Petruchio; Fire and Water; A Christmas at Brighton; La Diligence; The Romp; Ella Rosenberg; Guy Fawkes; The Warlock of the Glen.*

No record survives for the 1823–24 season or for the seasons of 1824–25 and 1825–26.

BIBLIOGRAPHY

Dunlap, William. *History of the American Stage.* 2nd ed. New York: Burt Franklin, 1963.

James, Reese D. *Cradle of Culture: 1800–1810. The Philadelphia Stage.* Philadelphia: University of Pennsylvania Press, 1957.

———. *Old Drury of Philadelphia.* Philadelphia: University of Pennsylvania Press, 1932.

McKenzie, Ruth Harsha. "Organization, Production and Management at the Chestnut Street Theatre, Philadelphia from 1791 to 1820." Ph.D. diss., Stanford University, 1952.

Pollock, Thomas C. *The Philadelphia Theatre in the Eighteenth Century*. Philadelphia: University of Pennsylvania Press, 1933.

Pritner, Calvin Lee. "William Warren's Management of the Chestnut Street Theatre Company." Ph.D. diss., University of Illinois, 1964.

Stine, Richard D. "The Philadelphia Theatre, 1682–1829: Its Growth as a Cultural Institution." Ph.D. diss., University of Pennsylvania, 1951.

Wolcott, John R. "English Influences on American Staging Practice: A Case Study of the Chestnut Street Theatre, Philadelphia, 1794–1820." Ph.D. diss., The Ohio State University, 1967.

———. "Philadelphia's Chestnut Street Theatre: A Plan and Elevation." *Journal of the Society of Architectural Historians* 30, no. 3 (October 1971): 209–18.

———. "Apprentices in the Scene Room: Toward an American Tradition in Scene Painting." *Nineteenth Century Theatre Research* 4, no. 1 (1976): 23–39.

John R. Wolcott

[OLD] CHESTNUT STREET THEATRE STOCK COMPANY. (1826–55) At the end of the 1825–26 theatrical season, William Warren and William Burke Wood dissolved the partnership that had guided the Chestnut Street Theatre Stock Company since 1803. Warren assumed sole management of what had been Philadelphia's first permanent resident dramatic company. The Chestnut Street Theatre, sometimes referred to as the New Theatre, had recently been rebuilt on the site of the original theatre, which had been destroyed by fire in 1820. When the second Chestnut Street Theatre opened in 1822, it was the city's most convenient playhouse, located in the heart of Philadelphia at 605 Chestnut Street, less than one block from Independence Hall. It was also Philadelphia's most elegant theatre. Designed by renowned architect William Strickland, the building's ninety-two-foot frontage featured a restrained, Italianate, neoclassic design of marble columns and niches. Wooden statues of Tragedy and Comedy by famed sculptor William Rush occupied the largest niches. They became the theatre's emblems. (These statues are now in the Philadelphia Museum of Art.) The brick, iron, and wood construction contained a semicircular auditorium forty-six feet in diameter. It had three rows of boxes. The dress circle was covered by a canopy in the style of London's Covent Garden. According to the theatre's management, the unique form of the auditorium enabled the majority of audience members to be seated within thirty-five feet of the stage, closer than in the best European theatres (James, 40). The motto "To Raise the Genius and to Mend the Heart" was carved above the forty-six by twenty-five-foot proscenium arch opening. An ornamented dome ceiling and a magnificent chandelier completed the decor. The theatre seated about 1,500 persons. A scheme to admit patrons to the gallery from the alleylike Carpenter (Ranstead) Street, to the pit from Sixth Street, and to the boxes and the dress circle through the elegant Chestnut Street frontage aroused public outcry against a policy perceived as un-American. The builders abandoned their plan to segregate the classes before they entered the theatre. The new Chestnut ("Chesnut" until about 1850) Street Theatre, heated as it was with fireproof furnaces and fitted with comfortable lobbies, saloons, and coffee rooms, enabled the resident dramatic troupe to maintain its position as the city's foremost company and to appeal to fashionable audiences for several decades.

The tone of the theatre building, with its predominantly British and Continental style, paralleled and supported the company's personality during the 1820s and 1830s. Under the management of actor-manager William Warren (1767–1832), the company operated as a traditional stock organization. A resident company of approximately thirty-five actors and actresses, each adept at a particular stock role, formed a nucleus that was supplemented with infrequently hired "occasional actors" and by a large number of visiting stars. Many stars stayed for short engagements, but a few played such long periods, sometimes totaling several months in one season, that the only clear distinction between stars and regulars was the larger salary and greater number of leading roles granted to the stars. Generally, one full-length play and one or two shorter afterpieces were offered at each of six nightly performances each week. Novelty acts often were performed between dramas. The theatre was required by law to remain dark on Sunday. Most frequently, the plays presented were English in origin, or they were French or German dramas in English translation by London playwrights. The second Chestnut Street Theatre, nicknamed "Old Drury" after London's Drury Lane Theatre, was, like its predecessor, a conduit for aristocratic British and European theatrical traditions. To the stage were transplanted conventions such as Christmas Harlequin pantomimes and spectacle-laden processionals. The latest London plays were especially appealing to the theatre's fashionable clientele, always eager to absorb London tastes and fads. The Chestnut Street Theatre managers served their public by sending representatives to London in search of new plays and new talent. During the 1827–28 season alone, the company produced thirty-four new pieces. London stars of the first magnitude, including Junius Brutus Booth, William Charles Macready, Thomas Abthorpe Cooper, Lydia Kelly, and Mrs. Knight, appeared with the company. Many of the company's regulars had debuted on the London stage.

Warren's tenure, although artistically successful, was marred by disagreements with the theatre's stockholders over economic matters such as box-reservation procedures and artistic matters such as actor employment. Warren particularly resented the stockholders' refusal to allow his daughter Letty to appear with the company. The traditional company schedule of playing a main season in Philadelphia and short supplemental seasons in Baltimore and Washington had to be altered when Baltimore attendance fell to unacceptable levels. High salaries demanded by visiting stars threatened the traditionally low-margin profitability of resident stock theatre.

Then, too, the Chestnut Street Theatre experienced its first strong competition. For decades the company had been Philadelphia's only major troupe, but by 1828 the [Second] Walnut Street Theatre Company (1829– 34)* was making a permanent transition from equestrian to dramatic theatre, and the new Arch Street Theatre had commenced production. Perhaps most disturbing was Warren's demoralizing experience with English comedian and stage manager Joe Cowell. Cowell, a former employee of the rival Walnut Street Theatre, apparently used his trusted position with Warren to act secretly against the interests of the Chestnut Street Theatre Company. He was eventually found out, dismissed, and replaced by the highly capable Francis Courtney Wemyss, but the affair influenced the aging Warren's decision to retire from management. He took his farewell benefit on December 30, 1828, performing his most famed role, Falstaff, in *The Merry Wives of Windsor*. Warren sublet the theatre to Wemyss and his new partner and financial backer Lewis T. Pratt, but Warren stipulated that he be allowed to act with the company for $40 a week until the lease's termination. Warren stayed on only until November 1831, when his failing memory forced him to retire. He became the proprietor of a small Baltimore inn before his death in 1832.

Warren's decision to abandon management was fortuitous, for Philadelphia theatricals shortly entered a chaotic period of bankruptcies and experimentation. An expanding and changing population, particularly the rise of a large lower class, which accompanied industrial development, altered the audiences in the theatres. New nativist sentiments further altered audience expectations and stratified cultural tastes. The city in general and the Chestnut Street Theatre Stock Company in particular lost their status as the foremost in the nation. The growing dominance of New York and its Park Street Theatre during the 1820s prompted a certain atmosphere of pessimism in Philadelphia. The Chestnut Street Theatre troupe experienced a string of management failures from 1829 to 1831. First Wemyss and Pratt, then Pratt alone, and finally (most disastrous of all), Mr. Lamb, a singer-actor, and Mr. Coyle failed in leadership. The company's actors were forced to take one-half and later one-quarter salaries—"mere bread and cheese"—and some were compelled to live in the theatre for lack of funds. The undistinguished legacy of Lamb and Coyle was the appearance of three local Indian chiefs who exhibited their war dances and songs and carried out a mock ceremony of scalping.

Conservative Scottish emigrant Robert Campble Maywood, along with several financial backers, became manager and proprietor of the Chestnut Street Theatre Stock Company in 1831. Maywood set out to reestablish the troupe's old identity by bucking, whenever possible, the new trend toward Americanization of both plays and actors. Opera was to provide his means, and operating two Philadelphia theatres simultaneously was to be his method. Musical entertainment, long a component of the European stages, had always been highly popular at the Chestnut. So, too, had foreign companies, when they infrequently but profitably were booked into the house. The Chestnut offered Philadelphians their first bona fide Italian opera, *Il Trionfo della Musica*, on May 5, 1829. Although the management that presented it ultimately failed, the genre took hold. Maywood, who had extensive links with London and provincial British stages as well as a solid reputation as a Shakespearean tragedian in New York, leased both the Walnut and Chestnut Street theatres and created one company to fill both houses. Apparently assured that Philadelphians would not adequately support full-time companies at either house, Maywood employed one stable and reliable company to supply the two houses. Informally, this troupe was called the Chestnut Street Theatre Company when it performed at the Chestnut and the Walnut Street Theatre Company when it performed at the Walnut. However, Maywood maintained the Chestnut as the more elite theatre, charging full-price admission there (twenty-five cents to $1) while operating the Walnut as a half-price theatre. The Chestnut Street Theatre offered opera and operetta performances far more frequently than the Walnut.

Initially, Maywood attempted to operate his two houses with their one shared company on alternating nights. However, this plan proved unmanageable. He then devised a schedule whereby the troupe split a season between the Chestnut and the Walnut. The troupe played from September through January and May through early June at the Chestnut and from January through May and June through late July at the Walnut. During the winter, while the regular resident company played at the Walnut, a foreign opera company was booked into the Chestnut. During the years to come, the noted companies that appeared included the French Opera Company, German Opera Company, Italian Opera Company, and Italian Opera Company of Havana. However, Maywood did not adhere strictly to his schedule. Obviously preferring the Chestnut to the Walnut, he sporadically sublet the latter or left it vacant, as he did during the winter season of 1833–34. When the Arch Street Theatre's lease became available in 1834, Maywood opted to abandon the Walnut and to adopt the Arch as his adjunct theatre. He opened the Chestnut for longer periods than the Arch and favored it with better publicity and higher admission costs.

Although the Chestnut Street Theatre Stock Company continued to operate as a typical stock company, operas, spectacles, and pantomimes were its most outstanding and most profitable offerings. In 1835, for instance, the troupe had sixty operas or operettas in its repertory. In contrast, the rival American Theatre Company* at the Walnut Street Theatre performed only twenty musical pieces that year. W. Barrimore, the noted former stage director of Drury Lane, was hired to arrange the company's productions. English stars such as Charles and Fanny Kemble and Tyrone Power and noted London vocalists such as Mrs. Austin boosted attendance.

The Chestnut Street Theatre Company could not eschew totally the popular trend toward American dramatic themes and products, especially because its primary rivals—the Arch Street Company in the early 1830s and the American Theatre Company in the late 1830s—thrived on it. To compete, Maywood infrequently produced "Yankee" plays, booked "Yankee" stars, and had his orchestra produce programs of national melodies. On one occasion, he promoted a contest that offered a $300 prize for the best American comedy. However, when Maywood elected to redecorate the Chestnut Street Theatre in 1837, he chose not to match the American Theatre's elaborate Americanization; he chose rather an European theme and an European artist to maintain the theatre's elite, neoclassic atmosphere. When the company chose to give benefit performances for local causes, these causes included not only the usual orphan asylums, disaster victims, and volunteer fire companies but also interests of the upper class such as the American Institute of Letters and the American Library Institute.

During the 1830s and early 1840s, the talent in the Chestnut Street Theatre Stock Company received much critical praise. William Evans Burton (1804–60), a singer, comedian, and playwright, was known especially for writing and performing farces such as *Forty Winks, The Ladies' Man*, and *The Mummy*. Later Burton became a renowned manager of resident stock companies at Philadelphia's National Theatre, Arch Street Theatre, and Chestnut Street Theatre and in New York at the Chambers Street Theatre. James Edward Murdoch (1811–93), a resident of Philadelphia, began his career with the company and remained its most valued light comedian for seven seasons. Murdoch became a nationally known comedic talent, especially when he toured with Joseph Jefferson III. Celebrated Shakespearean interpreter E. L. Davenport, considered one of the finest actors of the day, was with the troupe for three seasons. From 1870 until 1874 he reestablished ties as the manager of the [New] Chestnut Street Theatre Stock Company (1863–80)*. Many other noted actors of the period were part of the troupe: D. P. Bowers, E. S. Conner, Susan Cushman, Mrs. Alexina Fisher Baker, E. N. Thayer, and Mrs. John Drew (then known as Mrs. Hunt).

Despite the company's apparent artistic excellence under Maywood, the increasing popularity of national feeling jeopardized the Chestnut's standing in the city. Although ostensibly driven from management and back to the London stage because of a personal lack of energy and financial resources, Maywood actually lost favor in the late 1830s due to his extreme prejudice against "native graces." The theatre's stockholders sought a new course for the theatre and regranted the theatre's lease to Lewis T. Pratt. Pratt, concerned primarily with financial matters, hired a string of competent comanagers, including William Dinsmore, Ethelbert A. Marshall, and William E. Burton, to help him operate the stock company during the next few years. However, no new policies of operation or philosophy materialized, and profits fell. In 1842–43 the stockholders invited Maywood to return from London to resume his management. Maywood rejected their offer but proposed that they engage his twenty-year-old daughter May Elizabeth Maywood. He would be her business consultant, and the respected stage manager Peter Richings would be her assistant. Their combined management lasted only a few months but was in effect long enough to provoke a nearly identical scheme for female management of the [Third] Walnut Street Theatre Stock Company* when young Charlotte Cushman was installed as manager.

Cushman's company, which included stage manager William Rufus Blake, apparently succeeded, for the Walnut's proprietor Ethelbert A. Marshall subsequently was given a lease of the Chestnut. With Blake as stage manager for both houses, Marshall operated the Chestnut and Walnut during 1843–44 in much the same manner as Maywood had operated the two in early 1830s: he shuffled one resident company of stock actors between the theatres, renting out the Chestnut to an opera company while the dramatic troupe played at the Walnut and subleting the Walnut to a Circus while the regular company performed at the Chestnut. The opera season proved especially disastrous, and Marshall retreated to sole management of the Walnut, where he remained for eighteen years.

A strategy for success continued to elude managers Pratt and Wemyss, who retook the reigns for the 1844–45 theatrical season, and Burton, who tried to halt the rapid decline of the Chestnut Street Theatre Stock Company in 1845 and 1846. Philadelphia's chaotic economic and social conditions during the period thwarted the Chestnut Street Theatre troupe's few, tentative attempts at change. A severe economic depression combined with the flight of the fashionable from the immediate Chestnut Street vicinity and an overall decline of aristocratic support forced the management to try to attract a broader-based audience. The troupe endeavored to make itself more available to the lower classes by lowering prices and by instituting a gallery for colored patrons. To shed its staid image, it occasionally scheduled fare designed to have popular, often sensational, appeal. However, the mid-1840s was a particularly unfortunate time to promote class, racial, and religious harmony. Gang violence and a succession of destructive riots betwen Negroes and Irish, between Irish and nativists, and between striking and nonstriking workers emphasized and intensified class stratification. The Chestnut Street Theatre Company's dilemma was heightened in the fall of 1844, when the management commissioned a stage adaptation, to be entitled *The Quaker City*, of George Lippard's serial exposé of Philadelphia's upper classes, *The Monks of Monk Hall*. The play sparked the attention the Chestnut Street Theatre sought and most probably would have endeared the troupe to the lower classes. However, the play was censored by the mayor and forbidden production. The company not only lost the time and financial support it had invested in the production, but its reputation with the city's elite was seriously marred. Meanwhile, its dream of appealing to the lower classes remained unrealized.

The Chestnut Street Theatre Company temporarily disbanded in January 1846. For the next three years, the theatre was used for temporary engagements only, primarily by opera companies but also by sundry traveling entertainers such as magicians, minstrels, German-language troupes, concert singers, and shuffle dancers. A brief revival of a resident dramatic company occurred during the summer of 1849, when W. E. Horn amassed an acting troupe to provide farces and vaudeville to supplement minstrel performances. However, the proprietor of the saloons in the theatre, James Quinlan, found his proceeds so reduced by the house's infrequent use that he financed a new resident dramatic company in the fall of 1850. With theatrical entrepreneur Joseph Foster as his partner, Quinlan's main goal was to fill the theatre to accumulate profits in his several bars located in the theatre's pit and on each of its tiers. To do so, he kept admission prices unnaturally low, charging only twenty-five and fifty cents. Quinlan's company endured through the 1849–50 season, but it was temporarily dissolved during the 1850–51 season. With new financial backing, it reassembled in 1851 and carried on for four seasons. Quinlan also operated a hotel and tavern at Ninth and Market streets, and he leased the saloons in the Walnut Street Theatre as well. After ending his association with Foster, Quinlan employed several stage managers and acting managers to attend to production details while he concentrated on business matters.

Quinlan's company featured actors new to the Chestnut Street Theatre, energetic young performers such as John E. McDonough, Lizzie Weston, and Conrad Clarke. Apparently, intent on breaking all links with the former Chestnut Street Theatre Stock Company, the company's repertory focused on American plays and on local theme pieces such as *Philadelphia as It Is, The Mysteries and Miseries of Philadelphia*, and *The Philadelphia Fireman*. Many plays concerned the low-life antics of the "b'hoys" Mose and Jakey. The preponderance of Irish plays and farces—twenty-five during 1849–50 alone—reflected this troupe's appeal to a lower-class audience, especially the large wave of Irish immigrants who had settled in Philadelphia during the 1840s. Stars such as Frank S. Chanfrau, H. Lindon, and Redmond Ryan, who were the idols of factory lads, appeared. Gossipy, topical pieces such as *Lola Montez in New York* and *Lola Montez in Bavaria* drew well. Plays featuring animals, such as *The Butcher's Dog of Kent, Mazeppa, Dog of the Ferry House*, and *The Dogs of Mount St. Bernard*, appealed to popular taste. The European pretentions of opera were spoofed in pieces such as *Lah-Buy-It-Dear* (Andre Deshaye's *La Bayadère*, 1831) and *La Som-Am-Bull-Ah* (Vincenzo Bellini's *La sonnambula*, 1831). One overt vestige of earlier regimes was the continuing popularity of Harlequin pantomimes.

Quinlan's company continued to operate in the typical stock-company mode of six performances each week with two plays a bill. The company operated year round from 1851 until 1854 and was a resounding financial success. Ironically, it was the deterioration of the Chestnut Street Theatre's immediate neighborhood that drove even Quinlan to give up his lease on the theatre in 1854 in favor of the more fashionably located National Theatre (located three blocks west of the Chestnut). S. E. Harris, originator of the role of the blackfaced Uncle Tom in *Uncle Tom's Cabin*, then assumed management, changing the theatre into a minstrel house and part-time dramatic facility, but he failed shortly after opening. The theatre's last managers, C. H. Griffith and J. Wayne Olwine, survived only four weeks. The farewell performance of the Chestnut Street Theatre Stock Company was held on May 1, 1855, and the theatre permanently closed. Spurred on by the erection of the lavish new opera facility on Broad Street, the Academy of Music, the stockholders had decided the city no longer needed its Old Drury and voted its demolition. A new theatre bearing the name Chestnut Street Theatre was erected in 1863. It was located nearly seven blocks west of the old theatre, at Twelfth and Chestnut streets, and was never again to bear the name "Old Drury." However, this new theatre did become the home of another long-lived resident company, the [New] Chestnut Street Theatre Stock Company.

PERSONNEL

Proprietors–Managers: William Warren (1826–28); Lewis T. Pratt, Francis Courtney Wemyss (1829); Lewis T. Pratt, H. H. Rowbotham (1829–30); Lewis T. Pratt (1829–30); Mr. Lamb, Mr. Coyle (1830–31); Robert Campble Maywood and Company, including Lewis T. Pratt, H. H. Rowbotham, Thayer Dinsmore (1831–39); Lewis T. Pratt (1839–40); Lewis T. Pratt, William R. Dinmore (1840–41); Lewis T. Pratt, William E. Burton, Ethelbert A. Marshall (1841–42); Mary Elizabeth Maywood (1842–43); Ethelbert A. Marshall (1843–44); Lewis T. Pratt, Francis Courtney Wemyss (1844–45); William E. Burton (1845–46); W. E. Horn (1849); James Quinlan, Joseph Foster (1849–50); James Quinlan (1851–54); S. E. Harris (1855); C. H. Griffith, J. Wayne Olwine (1855).

Scenic Artists: Henry Warren, Mr. Lewis, Charles Lehr, W. T. Russell Smith, Peter Grain, Jr., George Heilge, Mr. Hackurt, Cadwallader Griffiths.

Music Directors: J. T. Norton, C. Ben Cross, Jr., Signor La Manna, Mr. Mueller.

Directors: Joe Cowell, stage manager (1826–27); Francis Courtney Wemyss, stage manager (1827–29); William Burke Wood, stage manager (1830–31); W. Barrimore, stage director (1831–c.39); William E. Burton, acting manager (1835–38); William Burke Wood, acting manager, and G. F. Jervis, stage manager (1839–40); James E. Murdoch, acting manager (1840–41); Peter Richings, acting and stage manager (1841–42); Peter Richings, acting manager, and William Rufus Blake, stage manager (1842–43); John Sefton, Charles Durang, stage managers (1844–45); Charles Burke, Henry Wallack, stage managers; William Fredericks, C. Logan, acting managers; and Mr. Lingard, deputy stage director (1851–52); John G. Gilber, acting manager, and Mr. Addis, stage director (1853–54); William F. Johnson, acting and stage manager (1854–55).

Actors and Actresses: Mr. Adams; A. Addams; Mr. Aiken; Mr. Allen; Andrew Allen; Miss Anderson, later Mrs. Thomas; Mrs. Anderson; Miss Anderton; A. Andrews; Miss Appoline; Miss Archer; Mr. Archer; Miss Armstrong; Miss Ayres; Miss Baker; J. S. Baker; Mr. and Mrs. John S. Balls; *Mrs. N. H. Bannister* (1854–55); Mr. Barnes; Mr. and Mrs. Barrett; G. Barrett; Mr. Barton; Mr. Bateman; Mrs. Bell; Mr. and Mrs. Bellamy; Mr. Bernard; Mr. Bignall; Little Lavinia Bishop; William Rufus Blake; Miss Booth; *D. P. Bowers* (1842–43, 1854–55); Mr. Braun; Mr. Brazier; Mrs. Broad; Mr. Brough; *John Brougham* (1845–46, 1852–53); *Mrs. John Brougham* (1845–46, 1852–53, 1854–55); Miss Brown; Mr. Brown; Mr. Brunton; Miss Bryant; *Charles Burke* (1851–52); *Mrs. Charles Burke* (1849–50); Mr. Burroughs; *William E. Burton* (1834–39); Miss Cappell; Samuel Chapman; William Chapman; J. S. Charles; Mr. Chippendale; *Conrad Clarke* (1853–55); *N. B. Clarke* (1849–50); Mrs. N. B. Clarke; Josephine Clifton; T. S. Cline; Miss Collingbourne; Mrs. Conduit; *E. S. Conner* (1837–38, 1854–55); *Mrs. E. S. Conner* (1854–55); Mrs. Cornish; Mr. and Mrs. Joe Cowell; Mr. Coyle; Mr. Craddock; Mrs. H. Cramer; Mr. Crocker; Mr. Crowley; Mr. Cuddy; Mr. Curtis; *Susan Cushman* (1843–44); Julia Daly; Mr. and Mrs. John Darley; *A. H. Davenport,* also known as H. A. Davenport (1853–55); *E. L. Davenport* (1838–40, 1843–44); *Jean Margaret Davenport* (1851–52, 1853–54); Mrs. Davis; Mrs. Dawes; Miss Gertrude Dawes; Mr. Dawson; Blanche DeBar, later Mrs. Junius Brutus Booth; Mr. De Camp; Mr. Delarue; Mr. and Mrs. Thayer Dinsmore; Mr. Dixon; Mr. Donaldson; Miss Downes; *Mrs. Frank Nelson Drew* (1854–55); *Mr. and Mrs. John Drew* (1852–53); Mr. Drummond; Mr. Duff; *Mrs. Mary Ann Duff* (1830–31); *Jno. Dunn* (1845–46); Mr. and Mrs. Charles Durang; Mr. Dwyer; Mr. and Mrs. Dyott; Miss A. Eberle, later Mrs. Y. Leonard; David Eberle; Miss E. Eberle; Mr. Edwards; Clara Ellis; Miss Elphinstone; Mr. and Mrs. Elssler; J. Elssler; Miss Emery; Mrs. English; Mr. Eytinge; *Mrs. Henry Farren* (1854–55); Mr. and Mrs. Faulkner; A. W. Fenno; Mrs. Ferrai; J. M. Field; Henry J. Finn; Miss A. Fisher; *Mrs. Alexina Fisher*, later *Mrs. Lewis Baker* (1833–34, 1835–40, 1843–44); Clara Fisher; John Fisher; Mrs. Fitzwilliam; Mr. and Mrs. Flynn; Mr. and Mrs. Forrest; William Forrest; C. Foster; Miss Fox; Mrs. Francis; William Fredericks; Mr. Gale; Mr. Gallot; Mr. Gamble; Mr. Gann; Mr. Garner; Miss George; Mrs. Gibbs; *John Gilbert* (1851–54); Mrs. John Gilbert; Mr. Gile; Mrs. Gilfert; Mr. Glenroy; Mr. Godden; Miss Gonzales; Mr. and Mrs. Charles Green; *Mr. and Mrs. John Greene* (1826–27, 1845–46); Mr. Grierson; Mr. and Mrs. G. H. Griffiths; Miss Grove; Mrs. Hackett; Mr. and Mrs. Hackurt; *Mr. Hadaway* (1833–34, 1843–44); John Hallam; Mr. Haller; Mr. and Mrs. R. Hamilton; Mr. and Mrs. Harrington; S. E. Harris; Mr. Harrison; Miss Hathwell; Mr. Hathwell; Mr. Hatton; Mrs. Hautonville; Miss Hawthorn; H. Henkins; Mr. Henrie(y); L. Heyl; Miss Hildreth; Mr. Hildreth; Mr. Hines; Mr. Holland; Mr. and Mrs. C. E. Horn; Mr. Hosack; Mr. and Mrs. Houpt, formerly Emily Mestayer; Mrs. Howard; Charles Howard; Miss Hughes; Mr. Hughes; Mr. Hunt; Mr. Hunt, the singer; *Mrs. Hunt*, later Mrs. John Drew (1839–40); Mr. Hutchings; D. Ingersoll; W. Isherwood; Mr. Jack; Mrs. Jamar; Mr. James; George Jamieson; *Fanny Jarman*, later Mrs. Ternan (1835–36); Mr. Jarvis; Miss E. Jefferson; John Jefferson; *Joseph Jefferson I* (1826–28); *Joseph Jefferson II* (1853–54); *Mrs. Joseph Jefferson*, formerly Mrs. Charles Burke (1826–28); G. F. Jervis; W. F. Johnson; R. Johnston; Miss Jones; Mr. Jones; Mrs. George Jones; Mrs. Melinda Jones; Mr. and Mrs. W. G. Jones; Mr. and Mrs. H. C. Jordan; G. Kaimes; Mr. and Mrs.

Keeley; Mr. Kelley; Miss Kelly; Mr. Kelly; Miss Kerr; Mr. Kerr; Mrs. Kent; Mr. Klett; Master Kneass; Miss Kneass; *J. P. Knight* (1839–40); Mrs. A. Knight, formerly Miss Povey; Mr. Lamb; Mrs. Lambert; Mrs. Langdon; Mr. Latham; Miss Lee; Walter M. Leman; J. A. Leonard; H. Linden; Mr. Lindon; Mr. Lindsay; Mr. Logan; Miss C. Logan; Eliza Logan; Mr. Lomas; Miss Ludwig; Mr. Macarthy; Miss Mack; Mrs. Maddox; Mr. and Mrs. Martin; *Charles Mason* (1841–42, 1844–45, 1853–54); *Mrs. Charles Mason*, formerly Emma Wheatley (1845–46); T. Mathews; Miss H. Matthews; Augusta Maywood; Mary Elizabeth Maywood; *Robert Campble Maywood* (1831–39, 1842–43); *Mrs. Robert Campble (Martha) Maywood*, formerly Mrs. H. Williams (1835–38, 1842–43); Miss McBride; Mr. McCahen; *John E. McDonough* (1851–52); Mr. McDougall; J. McDowel; Mr. McFarland; Mrs. McLean; D. McMillan; Mr. and Mrs. Meer; Master Mercer; Mr. Mercer; Rose Merrifield; Mr. and Mrs. Charles Mestayer; Mrs. Meyers; Mr. Miller; Mr. Milnor; Mr. Milot; Miss Virginia Monier; C. Moorhouse; Mrs. Moreland; Miss Morgan; Mr. Morrow; Monsieur Mossie; Mr. and Mrs. Mossop; Miss F. Mowbray; Laura Mowbray; Mr. Mulholland; Mr. Mullikin; *James E. Murdoch* (1831–36, 1838–40, 1852–53); Mrs. Murray, formerly Miss Parker; Euphemia Murray; Mr. Murstack; Mrs. Frederick S. Myers; J. E. Nagle; Miss Nelson; Miss Norman; Mr. Norton; Mr. O'Brien; J. T. O'Brien; J. Wayne Olwine; *John E. Owens* (1845–46, 1851–52, 1854–55); Mr. and Mrs. Page; Miss Palmer; Mr. and Mrs. Palmer; Miss Parker; Mr. Parker; Mr. Pearman; Sidney Pearson; Miss Pelham; Mr. Perring; Mrs. Pindar; *T. Placide* (1833–34, 1835–37, 1838–43); Mr. Plantou; Mr. and Mrs. Plum(m)er; Mr. Polby; Mr. C. Porter; Mr. and Mrs. J. G. Porter; Mr. Potter; Mrs. Estelle Potter; Lewis T. Pratt; Miss C. Price; Mr. and Mrs. J. J. Prior; Mr. Radcliffe; Mr. Raffile; Mr. Rasimi; Mr. Rea; John Reeve; Mr. Reynolds; Mr. Reynoldson; *Thomas D. Rice* (1833–34); *Peter Richings* (1841–43, 1844–45); Miss Riddle; Mr. Riley; James Roberts; Miss Rock; Mrs. Rogers; B. Rogers; Miss Rosalie; *Mr. and Mrs. H. H. Rowbotham* (1832–37); Mr. Roys; G. C. Ryan; Redmond Ryan; Miss St. Clair; Mr. Scharf; Mr. Scott; *John R. Scott* (1833–34, 1852–53); Miss Seele; Mrs. Ann Sefton; Joseph O. Sefton; Mrs. Sharpe; Mrs. Shaw; E. Shaw; Mr. Shepard; Miss Shireff; Mr. Shrival; Mr. Singleton; *Mr. and Mrs. Sloman* (1827–28); Miss Smith; C. J. Smith; Mrs. W. H. Smith; Mr. Solomon; Mr. Southwell; Mr. Spear; Mr. Stafford; Mr. Stanl(e)y; Mr. Stearns; Mr. Stone; C. Stuart; Mr. Studley; Mr. Sullivan; Mr. Tayleure; J. H. Taylor; Mr. and Mrs. Ternan; *E. N. Thayer* (1835–40, 1845–46); *Mrs. E. N. Thayer* (1835–40, 1841–42, 1843–44); Mr. and Mrs. Thoman; Miss Thompson; E. Thompson; Mr. Thorne; Mr. and Mrs. Tyrell; Mr. Uhl; Miss Vincent; Miss Wagstaff; Mrs. Walker; Fanny Wallack; Mr. and Mrs. Walstein; Mr. Walton; Mr. Ward; Kate Warnick; *Mr. and Mrs. William Warren* (1826–28); Miss Watson, later Mrs. W. H. Bailey; Mr. and Mrs. C. Watson; Mr. and Mrs. John Weaver; Mr. Webb; *Francis Courtney Wemyss* (1827–29, 1831–32, 1844–45); *Lizzie Weston* (1853–55); Mr. Wheatleigh; Mr. Wheatley; Emma Wheatley, later Mrs. Charles Mason; Mr. White; Mr. and Mrs. G.B.S. Wilkes; Mr. Wilkinson; Mr. Willis; Mrs. Willis; Mrs. Wills; Miss Wilson; Elizabeth Wood; *Joseph Wood* (1833–39, 1840–43, 1844–45); Mrs. Joseph Wood; *W. Wood* (1850–52); W. F. Wood; *William Burke Wood* (1826–28, 1831–34); Mrs. William Burke Wood; Mr. Woodhull; Miss Workman; Mrs. Workman; Mr. Wright; Mrs. Young; Benjamin Young.

Guest Artists: Signora Albertazzi; Madame Alfred; Caradori Allan; Signor Angrisani; Diavolo Antonio; Mlle. Arreline; Mrs. Austin; Mrs. Alexina Fisher Baker;

Mr. and Mrs. J. S. Balls; Monsieur Barbere; Junius Brutus Booth; Mr. Brough; J. S. Browne; J. B. Buckstone; Master Burke; Mr. Butler; Mlle. Celeste; Frank S. Chanfrau; Mr. and Mrs. Checkini; Josephine Clifton; Herr Cline; Thomas Abthorpe Cooper; Charles W. Couldock; Mrs. H. Cramer; Charlotte Cushman; Susan Cushman; E. L. Davenport; Kate Denin; Susan Denin; Mr. Dowton; Mrs. F. A. Drake; Miss Mary Duff; Mrs. Mary Ann Duff; Fanny Elssler; Madame Fe(a)ron; Clara Fisher; Mr. Fleming; Mr. and Mrs. William J. Florence; Mrs. Flynn; Edwin Forrest; Oliver Francia; Mrs. Gilfert; S. W. Glenn; Mrs. Hackett; James H. Hackett; Thomas Sowerby Hamblin; Mr. Hess; Miss Hildreth; George H. Hill; Mr. Holland; C. E. Horn; Miss Horton; Mr. Howes; Miss Hughes; Mr. Hunt; Madame Hutin; Davis Jackson; Mr. and Mrs. George Jones; J. Jones; Charles Kean; Mr. and Mrs. Keeley; Lydia Kelly; Charles Kemble; Fanny Kemble; Mr. Kilner; Mrs. Knight; James Sheridan Knowles; Madame Labasse; Madame Le Compte; Jenny Lind; Mr. and Mrs. G. E. Locke; William Charles Macready; Charles Mason; Mr. and Mrs. Charles Mathews, formerly Mlle. Lucia Elizabetta Vestris; John E. McDonough; C. Moore; Anna Cora Mowatt; Mr. Mulligan; Brian O'Flagherty; Madame Otto; [Little] Louisa Parker; T. S. Parsloe; Mr. and Mrs. Pearman; Miss S. Phillips; H. Placide; Tyrone Power; Mr. Ranger; the Ravel family; John Reeve; Thomas D. Rice; J. B. Roberts; Agnes Robertson; Miss Rock; Mrs. Rogers; Madame Rosalie; Master Russell; Master St. Luke; Miss St. Luke; Signor Giovanni Sciarra; J. R. Scott; Mr. and Mrs. Sequin; Mrs. Shaw; Joshua S. Silsbee; John Sinclair; Mr. and Mrs. Sloan; Mr. and Mrs. Sloman; Fitzgerald Tasistro; Mr. Taylor; Mr. and Mrs. Ternan, formerly Fanny Jarman; Ellen Tree; Mr. Turpin; Miss Vandenhoff; George Vandenhoff; the Villalave family; Miss Vos; Mr. Walbourne; Mr. and Mrs. Henry Wallack; James Wallack, Jr.; James Wallack, Sr.; Master Wells; Miss Wells; Mr. and Mrs. Wells; Mr. Williams; Barney Williams; Master Wills; Mr. and Mrs. Joseph Wood.

SAMPLE REPERTORY

1827–28: *Romeo and Juliet; Is He Jealous?; The Poor Gentleman; Rosina; Venice Preserved; The Young Widow; Guy Mannering; Spoil'd Child; Hamlet; The Romp; The Mountaineers; How to Die for Love; Richard III; My Grandmother; Fazio; The Shipwreck; William Tell; The Wonder; A Roland for an Oliver; Bombastes Furioso; The Day after the Wedding; The Rencontre; The Maid and the Magpie; Evadne; Where Shall I Dine?; Love in a Village; Rob Roy; The Village Lawyer; The Cabinet; Fortune's Frolic; Love, Law, and Physic; Abon Hassan; The Jealous Wife; The Highland Reel; Town and Country; Cherry Bounce; The Sergeant's Wife; Sylvester Daggerwood; Virginius; My Spouse and I; Simpson and Co.; Douglas; The Haunted Tower; Bellamira; The Siege of Belgrade; Turn Out; Isabella; The Stranger; The Ghost; 102!; Jane Shore; No Song, No Supper; The Gamester; A Fish Out of Water; Henri Quatre; The Provok'd Husband; Family Jars; Charles the Second; George Barnwell; Don Giovanni; The Usurper; Artaxerxes; The Irishman in London; Deaf as a Post; Peter Wilkins; Stories; Monsieur Tonson; Paul Pry; Brutus; Damon and Pythias; Sprigs of Laurel; The Marriage of Figaro; The Lady and the Devil; Ella Rosenberg; The Iron Chest; The Padlock; 'Twas I; Pizarro; The Apostate; John Rock; Paul and Virginia; The Devil's Bridge; The Agreeable Surprise; Inkle and Yarico; The Hundred-Pound Note; Tom and Jerry; Much Ado* about Nothing; The Inconstant; The Belle's Stratagem; The Prize; The Cossack and the Volunteer; Wives as They Were and Maids as They Are; She Wou'd and She Wou'd Not; The Review; She Stoops to Conquer; The Actress of All Work; Of Age Tomorrow; Honeymoon; (also spelled Honey Moon); As You Like It; Thérèse; The School for Scandal; Ladies at Home; The Bridge of Abydos; The Sleep Walker; The Will; Old and Young; The Red Rover; The Rivals; The Merchant of Venice; Lovers' Vows; The Dead Shot; The Wandering Boys; The Rendezvous; The Country Girl; The Ten Mowbrays; Winning a Husband; Raising the Wind; The Soldier's Daughter; Know Your Own Mind; Dances; The Bride of Lammermoor; The Citizen; Clari; The Broken Sword; Deaf and Dumb; Gambler's Fate; 'Tis All a Farce; The Innkeeper's Daughter; The Prisoner at Large; The Serf; The Lie of the Day; Who's Who?; Barbarossa; Adelgitha; Mr. H.; A Budget of Blunders; Folly as It Flies; Three-Fingered Jack; Malvina; The Vampire; The Two Gregories; Turnpike Gate; The Road to Ruin; The School of Reform; The Adopted Child; High Life below Stairs; The Foundling of the Forest; Tom Thumb; Macbeth; Othello; Crazy Jane; Matrimony; Julius Caesar; Foscari; Der Freischutz; Lovers' Quarrels; The Lottery Ticket; The Barber of Seville; The Blue Devils; Song; Quite Correct; Intrigue; Animal Magnetism; Gnome King; Man and Wife; Warlock of the Glen; Must Be Buried.

1830–31: The Heir-at-Law; The Lottery Ticket; The Young Widow; The Devil's Bridge; The Lady and the Devil; Much Ado about Nothing; Rosina; Damon and Pythias; Winning a Husband; Wives as They Were and Maids as They Are; The Prize; Macbeth; The Poor Soldier; The Jealous Wife; Walk for a Wager; Rule a Wife and Have a Wife; Seven's the Main; The School for Scandal; The Revenge; The Highland Reel; She Stoops to Conquer; Popping the Question; Imitations; Virginius; The Actress of All Work; The Wonder; The Dead Shot; All in the Wrong; No Song, No Supper; Henri Quatre; Don Giovanni; Venice Preserved; Isabella; Inkle and Yarico; Youth; Love and Folly; Adrian and Orrila; The Wedding Day; Guy Mannering; Jane Shore; The Falls of Clyde; Aladdin; Of Age Tomorrow; The Gamester; The Magpie and the Maid; Gretna Green; The Bohemian Mother; The Cabinet; Raising the Wind; The East Indian; The Sleep Walker; Perfection; The Invincibles; 'Twas I; Home Sweet Home; Adelgitha; The Apostate; Turn Out; The Avenger of Sicily; The Hundred-Pound Note; Twelfth Night; Richard III; Family Jars; Hamlet; The Provok'd Husband; Down East; Monsieur Tonson; The Distrest Mother; The Rendezvous; The Merchant of Venice; Metamora; The Iron Chest; Clari; William Tell; A Roland for an Oliver; Sertorius; The Hunter of the Alps; Pizarro; Three and Deuce; Teddy, the Tiler; Othello; Love à la Mode; Bertram; Too Late for Dinner; The Yankee in England; The Romp; My Grandmother; King Lear; The Times; Touch and Take; The Water Witch; Paul Pry; The Comedy of Errors; Henry IV, Part 1; Cure for the Heart-Ache; Lovers' Quarrels; The Hypocrite; Rip Van Winkle; Tom and Jerry; Jacko: The Brazilian Ape; The Harper's Daughter; X.Y.Z.; Speed the Plough; Sweethearts and Wives; The Merry Wives of Windsor; How to Die for Love; Two Eyes Between Two; Deaf as a Post; The Suspicious Husband; Free and Easy; Town and Country; A New Way to Pay Old Debts; Richard II; Where Shall I Dine?; Brutus; Warlock of the Glen; The Clandestine Marriage; The Master's Rival; As You Like It; 102!; The Belle's Stratagem; The Will; The Wandering Boys; The Poor Gentleman; Know Your Own Mind; The Happiest Day of My Life; Montgomery; The Soldier's Daughter; The Way to Keep Him; Ladies at Home; Simpson and Company; Tom Thumb; Married and Single; The Day after the Wedding; High Life below Stairs; La Perouse; The Way to Get Married; The Midnight Hour; A Bold Stroke for a Husband; Honey Moon; She Would Be a Soldier; Man and Wife; The Broken Sword; The Prisoner at Large; Cherry and Fair Star; The Stranger; The Foundling of the Forest; The Two Thompsons; Animal Magnetism; The Slave; Cheap Living; Valentine and Orson; Barbarossa; The Exile; Two Friends; Fontainebleau; Charles the Second; Maid or Wife; Lock and Key; The Review; Turnpike Gate; Werner; The Children in the Wood; The Weathercock; Catherine and Petruchio; The Siamese Boys; Spoil'd Child; The Fair American; The Busy Body; Alp, the Renegade; The Roman Actor; The Wept of Wish-Ton-Wish; A Race for Dinner; Education; Brag's a Good Dog but Hold Fast's a Better; Nature and Philosophy; The Ethiop; Love Laughs at Locksmiths; A Tale of the Sea; Bluebeard; Miantonimoh; Evadne; The Honest Thieves; Black Eyed Susan; The Vampire; Roses and Thorns; The Two Pauls; Two Gregories; Zembuca; The Beggar on Horseback; The Lady of the Lake; The Bride of Abydos; The Spectre Bridegroom; Abaellino; The Heart of Midlothian; The Village Lawyer; Red Rover; The Blind Boy; Patriotic Banquet; Cetera; Columbus; The Flying Dutchman; The Irish Widow; Rumfustian; State Secrets; El Hyder; Fortune's Frolic; Douglas; Three Ears; The Philadelphia Market; The Miller and His Men; The Butchers; The Irish Tutor.

1833–34: The Promissory Note; The Nervous Man; Born to Good Luck; The Two Thompsons; The Irish Ambassador; The Irish Tutor; John Bull; Love à la Mode; Teddy, the Tiler; The Bold Dragoons; The Rendezvous; The Irishman in London; Fortune's Frolic; The West Indian; The Green Mountain Boy; John of Paris; Abon Hassan; East and West; The Man of the World; Music and Prejudice; The Tempest; No Song, No Supper; Napoleon; How to Die for Love; Love in a Village; Animal Magnetism; The Inquisitive Yankee; The Barber of Seville; The Dead Shot; Jonathan in England; Cinderella; Raising the Wind; The Prisoner at Large; The Marriage of Figaro; Guy Mannering; The Waterman; The Foundling of the Sea; The Slave; Rob Roy; The Purse; Masaniello; The Stranger; A Fish Out of Water; The Wonder; Fazio; The Hunchback; Gretna Green; The Wife; The Provok'd Husband; Turnpike Gate; The Merchant of Venice; The Midnight Hour; The Jealous Wife; Charles the Second; The Grecian Daughter; Of Age Tomorrow; Red Rover; Turn Out; The Point of Honour; Catherine and Petruchio; Hamlet; The Day after the Wedding; The Rent Day; Mr. and Mrs. Pringle; Mazeppa; Modern Antiques; Damon and Pythias; The Gambler's Fate; William Tell; Ambrose Gwinett; My Aunt; More Blunders Than One; Two Strings to Your Bow; Virginius; Pizarro; Town and Country; St. Patrick's Eve; Luke, the Labourer; The Review; Othello; Etiquette Run Mad; The Foundling of the Forest; A Mogul Tale; The Heir-at-Law; Whirligig Hall; The Poor Gentleman; Brutus; Speed the Plough; The Review; The Weathercock; Barney Brallaghan; The March of Intellect; Columbus; Honey Moon; The School for Scandal; 'Tis All a Farce; Romeo and Juliet; Deaf as a Post; Much Ado about Nothing; The Lottery Ticket; The Spectre Bridegroom; Monsieur Tonson; Paul Pry; Jane Shore; Three and the Deuce; King John; William Thompson; Adelgitha; Turning the Tables; Isabella; The Agreeable Surprise; The Bride of Lammermoor; The Bohemian Mother; Mahomet; The Omnibus; Family Jars; Lovers' Quarrels; The Harp; The Clutterbucks; The Robber's Wife; The Invincibles; The Rivals; The Field of Forty Footsteps; Der Freischutz; Fra Diavolo; The Duenna; The Robbers; My Aunt; The Devil's Bridge; The Quaker; High, Low Jack and the Game; The Maid of Judah; Clari; Rule a Wife and Have a Wife; Of Age Tomorrow;

Macbeth; Henry VIII; The Purse; The Gamester; The Inconstant; Cure for the Heart-Ache; No!; Rosina; Tam O'Shanter; The Mountaineers; George Barnwell; Rip Van Winkle; The Kentuckian; Monsieur Mallet; John Doubikins; Lady Carey; Inkle and Yarico; Plot and Counterplot; Married Lovers; The Recruiting Officer; The Secret; Comfortable Lodgings.

1836–37: *Married Life; Gnome King; The Rent Day; Rob Roy; Comfortable Lodgings; Point of Honour; Masaniello; Speed the Plough; Rosina; The Mountaineers; Othello, Travestie; The Soldier's Daughter; The Hunchback; The Stranger; Comfortable Service; The Jealous Wife; Cheap Boarding; The Wife; The Wonder; No Song, No Supper; The Merchant of Venice; The Mummy; Damon and Pythias; The Gladiator; Raising the Wind; John Jones; The Belle's Stratagem; Turn Out; Wept of Wish-Ton-Wish; The French Spy; Wizard Skiff; The Devil's Daughter; Moorish Page; Prince Lee Boo; Andreas Zell; The Dumb Sailor Boy; The Flying Dutchman; Orphan of Russia; Man about Town; Spirit Bride; Second Thoughts; Irish Ambassador; John Bull; The Nervous Man; The Irishman in London; The Rivals; Irish Tutor; Hamlet; How Do You Manage?; St. Patrick's Eve; The Omnibus; Born to Good Luck; Teddy, the Tiler; The Young Widow; Is He Jealous?; The West Indian; Paddy Carey; The Review; The Waterman; Etiquette; Lucille; Loan of a Lover; No!; The Maid and the Magpie; My Master's Rival; The Purse; She Stoops to Conquer; The Swiss Cottage; Love in a Village; Ransom; My Husband's Ghost; The Farmer's Story; 'Twas I; Hide and Seek; Spring and Autumn; Pizarro; My Aunt; The Gamester; The Dead Shot; The Wolf and the Lamb; The Poor Gentleman; Of Age Tomorrow; The Wandering Minstrel; Henry IV; The School for Scandal; The Road to Ruin; The Hypocrite; Scotch Cooper; Three Weeks after Marriage; Macbeth; Honey Moon; The Happiest Day of My Life; King O'Neil; Crossing the Line; More Blunders Than One; Maid of Cashmere; Sleeping Draught; Deaf as a Post; Kill or Cure; Make Your Wills; Turning the Tables; My Fellow Clerk; Cramond Brig; Day after the Fair; Stag Hall; The Three Gladiators; Vol-au-Vent; The Picnic; The Weathercock; The First Fratricide; Godenski; Tam O'Shanter; Whirligig Hall; Bedouin Arabs; The Green Man; La Fête Champêtre; Italian Brigands; Pongo; Riever's Ransom; All the World's a Stage; As You Like It; The Provok'd Husband; The Youthful Queen; Much Ado about Nothing; Animal Magnetism; Romeo and Juliet; High Life below Stairs; The Ladies' Man; Perfection; A Roland for an Oliver; The Scapegoat; A Bold Stroke for a Husband; Twelfth Night; The Daughter; Duddlestones; Cinderella; State Secrets; John of Paris; Brother and Sister; The Four Lovers; Clari, The Apostate; Fazio; Harlequin and the Magic Trumpet; Une Passion; Monsieur Mallet; The Kentuckian; Rip Van Winkle; Job Fox; Jonathan in England; Richard III; John Buzzby; Forty Winks; O'Flannigan and the Fairies; The Married Bachelor; Arabella; Fire and Water; The Pirate Boy; La sonnambula; The Rendezvous; Gretna Green; Spoil'd Child; Guy Mannering; The Grenadier; Der Freischutz; One O'Clock; Damon and Pythias; Black Eyed Susan; Pleasant Neighbors; Laugh When You Can; Three and the Deuce; Cure for the Heart-Ache; Wild Oats; 23 John Street; Fontainebleau; Ion; Barrack Room.*

1840–41: *The School for Scandal; Popping the Question; Weak Points; A Kiss in the Dark; Turning the Tables; Married Life; Chaos is Come Again; Our Mary Ann!; Perfection; The Single Life; Fire and Water; Rural Felicity; The Ladder of Love; The Duke's Bride; The Lottery Ticket; Fashionable Friends; Uncle John; The Duke's Progress; The Conquering Game; Simpson and Co.; Poor Jack; The Magpie; King*

John; Comfortable Service; Nicholas Nickleby; Scan. Mag.; The Innkeeper of Calais; Thérèse; Richelieu; Damon and Pythias; The Lady of Lyons; The Master's Rival; Metamora; Richard III; A Good Night's Rest; The Gladiator; The Broker of Bogata; Animal Magnetism; Turn Out; Wild Oats; The Jealous Wife; Love; The Storm; The Irish Ambassador; The Irish Tutor; The Dead Shot; The Nervous Man; The Irish Lion; How to Pay the Rent; Born to Good Luck; The Omnibus; His Last Legs; My Aunt; Is He Jealous?; John Bull; Teddy, the Tiler; Rory O'More; Paddy Carey; St. Patrick's Eve; The Irish Attorney; The Happy Man; The Irish Haymakers; Cinderella; Married Rake; La sonnambula; Fra Diavolo; Lucille; Guy Mannering; My Neighbor's Wife; The Christening; The Maid of Judah; The Poor Soldier; The Quaker; No Song, No Supper; The Waterman; Englishmen in India; The Roof Scrambler; La tarentule; La sylphide; Shocking Events; Nathalie; The Young Widow; Tom Noddy's Secret; Othello; Petticoat Government; Virginius; Mr. and Mrs. Pringle; She Would Be a Soldier; King Lear; The Happiest Day of My Life; Macbeth; Marco Bombo; The Flying Dutchman; My Fellow Clerk; Naval Engagements; A Day after the Wedding; Ice Witch and Sun Spirit; The Bride of Abydos; A Bold Stroke for a Husband; The Ladies' Club; The Irish Widow; The Banished Star; Fortune's Frolic; A Kiss in the Dark; Widow Wiggins; Town and Country; Nipped in the Bud; Thérèse; Castle Spectre; The Agreeable Surprise; Valentine and Orson; Hints for Husbands; Norma; Wheel of Fortune; King and the Mimic; The Soldier's Daughter; Honey Moon; How to Die for Love; The Heir-at-Law; Bride of Lammermoor; Catherine and Petruchio; Brian Boroihme; Laugh When You Can; The Last Man; The Poor Gentleman; Gustavus III; La Gazza Ladra; Delusion; H. B.; Don Giovanni; Maid of Cashmere; L'Elsire d'amore; My Sister Kate; Zampa; La Bayadère; Close Siege; Faint Heart ne'er Won Fair Lady; Midas; Wives as They Were; Charles the Second; Victorine; Money.

1844–45: Mountain Sylph; Robert Macaire; Blue Domino; The Young Widow; Christine of Sweden; The Country Girl; Nature and Philosophy; The Robber's Wife; Black Eyed Susan; The Loan of a Lover; Our Old House at Home; The Lady of Lyons; Bamboozling; He's not a-miss; Judith of Mont Blanc; Othello; Grandfather Whitehead; Bone Squash Diavolo; The Patrician's Daughter; Macbeth; The Virginia Mummy; The Stranger; Monsieur Jacques; Richard III; La chapeau du general; The President; Incog.; Pizarro; The Irish Tutor; Virginius; The Lottery Ticket; George Barnwell; The Golden Farmer; The School for Scandal; Simpson and Co.; Dumb Boy of the Pyrenees; Fazio; Hunting a Turtle; Romeo and Juliet; The Sleepwalker; The Hunchback; Thérèse; Aladdin; Hamlet; Catching an Heiress; Much Ado about Nothing; Sleeping Draught; Wags of Windsor; John Jones; Ion; Honey Moon; Sixteen String Jack; Laugh When You Can; G.T.T.; Catherine and Petruchio; Dumb Girl of Genoa; Jim Crow in London; The Bohemian Girl; Fra Diavolo; La sonnambula; The People's Lawyer; The Green Mountain Boy; A Wife for a Day; The Yankee Pedlar; Jonathan in England; Seth Slope; Jonathan Doubikins; New Notions; Old Heads and Young Hearts; Perfection; Shocking Events; Fortunio; The Busy Body; A Christmas Carol; Rob Roy; The Hunchback; Born to Good Luck; The Wonder; A Roland for an Oliver; Love's Sacrifice; The Youthful Queen; Kaspar Hauser; The Old Manor House; The American Farmer; Cut and Come Again; The Roué; The Hypocrite; The Fall of Kessiclak; Charles the Second; The Broken Sword; Postillion of Longjumeau; Lenora; Norma; The Dramatist; A Veteran; The Traitor.

1849–50: Black Eyed Susan; The Day after the Wedding; A Glance at Philadelphia;

Two Gregories; Agnes de Vere; The Lady of Lyons; Love in Humble Life; John Bull in France; The Stranger; Ambrose Gwinett; The Shipwrecked Mariner; The Old Guard; Jakey's Visit to his Aunts; Mr. and Mrs. White; Bobby Breakwindow; My Poll and my Partner Joe; Faint Heart ne'er Won Fair Lady; A Kiss in the Dark; Loan of a Lover; Turning the Tables; The Miser of Philadelphia; Love's Sacrifice; The Hunchback; Honey Moon; Hamlet; Poor Pillicoddy; Richard III; The Omnibus; Macbeth; Slasher and Crasher; Pizarro; Make Your Wills; Richelieu; The Golden Farmer; Sea King's Vow; The Infidelity; The Fighting Brothers of Rome; Philadelphia as It Is; The Faithful Slave; Crimson Crimes; Paul Pry; A New Way to Pay Old Debts; Water Witches; The Merchant of Venice; The Apostate; Chloroform; Romeo and Juliet; The Wife; The School for Scandal; Simpson and Co.; Ion; Uncle Sam; The Poor Gentleman; Married Life; Benjamin Franklin; Forty Thieves; Ups and Downs of a Student's Life; Hearts Are Trumps; Mose in China; Black Raven of the Tombs; Mose and Jakey's Visit to the Chestnut; Jack Sheppard; The Miner of Pottsville; Harlequin and Mother Goose; The Pride of the Ocean; Female Forty Thieves; The Brigadier's Horse; Naiad Queen; Mad Anthony Wayne; Lola Montez; His Last Legs; Spectre Bridegroom; Asmodeus; Rascal Jack; Swamp Steed; Joe, the Orphan; Sketches in India; The Jewess; A Ghost in Spite of Himself; Night Dancers; The Mountain Devil; Giselle; The Vampire; Harlequin and the Monster of St. Michael; Bird of Passage; Dancing Bears of Cashmere; Midshipman Easy; The Somnambulist; Tiger Horde; Marmion; Will Watch; Don Caesar de Bazan; The Philadelphia Fireman; Morgan: The Jersey Wagoner; Rake's Progress; The Three Guardsmen; Lucrezia Borgia; The French Spy; Wept of Wish-Ton-Wish; The Indian Girl; Esmeralda; Black Brig of Bermuda; Life in Alabama; Captain of the Watch; The Spectre Pilot; Tour de Nesle; The Whistler; Zelina; Ivanhoe; Rob Roy; The Serious Family; Siege of Comorn; Madeline; Sadak and Kalasrade; Whose Is It?; Leap Year; Born to Good Luck; The Limerick Boy; Rory O'More; Sprigs of Ireland; Paddy's Trip to America; Ireland as It Is; Teddy, the Tiler; The Happy Man; The Irish Post; The Irish Ambassador; The Irish Lion; The Robber's Wife; The Irish Tiger; Catching an Heiress; Emerald Isle; The Irish Farmer; In and Out of Place; Sudden Reformation; Grist to the Mill; Zindel; Seven Clerks; Valsha; Dumb Man of Manchester; Grub Mudge and Company; Launch of the Susquehanna; El Melechor; Alarming Sacrifice; Hernani; Who Speaks First?; Mazeppa; Trumpeter's Wedding; Winning a Husband; Changes; Married Rake; High Life In Philadelphia; The Reprobate; The Mechanic and the Queen; Knight of the Lion Heart; A Quiet Day; The Leprechaun; Gentleman Harry: The Terror of the Road; Willful Murder; The Hunter of the Pyrenees; An Awful Verdict; Things in the Next Century; The Last Nail; Sleeping Beauty; Henriette; Pet of the Petticoats; William Tell; Soldier's Progress; The Flying Highwayman; Queen of the Abruzzi; No. 333 Locust Street; Mysteries and Miseries of Philadelphia; Tom and Jerry; The Wrong Flue; The Duke's Wager; Delicate Ground; Post of Honor; Blanche Heriot; Zanthe; Romance and Burlesque; How to Die for Love; Married Bachelor; A Coroner's Verdict; The Devil's Ducat; Out on a Lark; Cure for the Heart-Ache; Rent Day; Maharajah Surovy Seing; The Irish Tutor; Thalaba; Irish Wager; Irish M.D.; Thirty Years of a Woman's Life; Ladies' Man; Pat Rooney; King O'Neil; Honor and Honesty; Isabelle; Who's the Father?; Philadelphia Boys and Girls in 1776; The World Reformed; Damon and Pythias; Nick of the Woods; The Iron Chest; Rose of Ettrick Vale; Red Rover; Tipperary Legacy; Wizard of the Moor; The Irish

Dragoon; The Bride of Lammermoor; The Eddystone Elf; Jakey in California; Evadne; The Robbers; Ole Bull; Forty Years of Life; Friend Waggles.

1852–53: She Wou'd and She Wou'd Not; Miseries of Human Life; Old Heads and Young Hearts; Eton Boy; Love's Sacrifice; The Wife; Nature and Philosophy; Romeo and Juliet; The Wandering Boys; Hamlet; An Irish Engagement; Othello; A New Way to Pay Old Debts; The Irish Tutor; The Merchant of Venice; Town and Country; The Corsican Brothers; Sketches in India; Child of the Regiment; Naval Engagements; Good for Nothing; Crown Diamonds; The Road to Ruin; Taking by Storm; Henry IV; Black Domino; The School for Scandal; The Lady of Lyons; The Enchantress; Valet de Sham; The Stranger; Don Caesar de Bazan; Money; An Alarming Sacrifice; Daughter of the Regiment; Catherine and Petruchio; Lola Montez in Bavaria; Delicate Ground; Charlotte Corday; Forty and Fifty; Uncle John; Maritana; Lola Montez in New York; Kill or Cure; Tender Precautions; Much Ado about Nothing; Wild Oats; Cure for the Heart-Ache; Irish Lion; The Belle's Stratagem; Perfection; The Wedding Day; Tom Noddy's Secret; Swiss Swains; Ask No Questions; As You Like It; Somebody Else; Slasher and Crasher; The Hunchback; The Banker's Wife; Honey Moon; The Actress of Padua; The School of Reform; Heir-at-Law; The Miller's Maid; Fortune's Frolic; Dombey and Son; A Row at the Chestnut; David Copperfield; Romance and Reality; Robert Macaire; The Irish Emigrant; The Maid of Croissey; Simpson and Company; The Last Man; Frightened to Death; The Knight of Arva; Mr. and Mrs. White; Ingomar; Carlo the Minstrel; The Irish Secretary; Satan in Paris; The Devil's in It; Giant of the Cave; Merry Wives of Windsor; Married Life; Wives as They Were; The Golden Farmer; He's not a-miss; Jemmy Twitcher in France; Two of the B'hoys; Women's Rights; St. Mary's Eve; Handy Andy; The Siamese Twins; The Review; Wept of the Wish-Ton-Wish; An Object of Interest; Doctor Dilworth; A Nabob for an Hour; The Dead Shot; The Young Scamp; The Little Devil; The Maid of Honor; The Forest Rose; Matheo Falcone; Douglas; Ion; Rob Roy; The Elder Brother; The Dramatist; My Aunt; The Gamester; The Robbers; The Inconstant; The Ladder of Love; De Soto; Pizarro; Hunting a Turtle; Laugh When You Can; The New Footman; Uncle Sam; The Spectre Bridegroom; The Veteran; Evadne; Our Mary Ann; Fazio; Walter Tyrrel; Love; Lady and the Devil; Lucrezia Borgia; Clandare; Richard III; The Bridal; Macbeth; Werner; Gisippus; King of the Commons; The Wind Mill; Betsy Baker; William Tell; The Love Chase; Grandfather Whitehead; George Barnwell; Jenny Lind; My Little Adopted; The Forest of Bondy; The Cattle Stealer; Three Thieves; The Butcher's Dog of Kent; My Poor Dog Tray; Don Juan; The Cross of Death; The Murdered Boatman; Myra Alwynn; Pauline; Dog of the Ferry House; Little Jockey; Napoleon; The Dogs of Mount St. Bernard; Born to Good Luck; The Irish Swan; Lord Barney; The Limerick Boy; Ireland as It Is; Our Gal; Irish Assurance and Yankee Modesty; Brian O'Lynn; In and Out of Place; The Happy Man; The Haunted Chamber; Uncle Pat's Cabin; Our Jemima; Sprigs of Ireland; Cavaliers and Roundheads; The Sea Captain; Raising the Wind; The Nervous Man; 'Tis All a Farce; Who Speaks First?; His Last Legs; St. Patrick's Eve; The Secret; Pride of the Market; All the World's a Stage; The Rivals; Rival Pages; The Philadelphia Fireman; Wine Works Wonders; Lucille; A Roland for an Oliver; Used Up; The Declaration of Independence; Bamboozling; A Wife for an Hour; The Fast Man; The Maid of Munster; Dumb Belle; Stage-Struck; Yankee Gal; Paddy, the Piper; Shandy Maguire; Mischievous Annie; Adrienne, the Actress; Loan of a Lover; Lola Montez.

BIBLIOGRAPHY

Published Sources: Reese D. James, *Old Drury of Philadelphia* (Philadelphia: University of Pennsylvania Press, 1932); Francis Courtney Wemyss, *Twenty-Six Years in the Life of an Actor and Manager* (New York: Burgess, Stringer, and Company, 1847); Arthur Herman Wilson, *A History of the Philadelphia Theatre, 1835–1855* (Philadelphia: University of Pennsylvania Press, 1935); William Burke Wood, *Personal Recollections of the Stage* (Philadelphia: Henry Carey Baird, 1855).

Unpublished Sources: Julia Curtis, "Philadelphia in an Uproar: 1844" (Paper presented at the American Theatre Association Convention, San Francisco, California, August 12–15, 1984).

Archival Sources: Chestnut Street Theatre File and Chestnut Street Theatre Programs File, Philadelphia Theatre Collection, Free Library of Philadelphia (Logan Square). The Philadelphia Theatre Collection also has files on many of the managers and performers connected with the Chestnut Street Theatre.

Mari Kathleen Fielder

[NEW] CHESTNUT STREET THEATRE STOCK COMPANY. (1863–80) Philadelphia, long known for its Chestnut Street Theatre and its accompanying resident stock company, had been without both since 1855. In that year, the Chestnut Street Theatre, located at 605 Chestnut Street and affectionately nicknamed "Old Drury," was demolished and the [Old] Chestnut Street Theatre Stock Company* (1826–55) disbanded. By the 1860s, however, several Philadelphia businessmen, headed by businessman William Cochrane and theatrical manager William Wheatley, deemed the city in need of a new theatre on Chestnut Street: only two "first-class" dramatic theatres remained, the Arch Street and the Walnut Street, and Philadelphia's theatrical reputation suffered. (The newest major addition, the Academy of Music, was considered far too large for ordinary dramatic performance, especially by its ex-manager Wheatley.) Local critics called it a rash move, when in 1862 a row of houses known as Boston Row, on the north side of Chestnut Street between Twelfth and Thirteenth streets and a full seven blocks to the west of the old theatre, was torn down to make way for the proposed Theatre; they assessed this locale as too removed from the city's theatrical hub to engender business. However, the locale proved to be the theatre's primary attribute. Although still considered a residential area in the early 1860s, the rapid westward expansion of center-city Philadelphia soon made the new Chestnut Street Theatre the city's most fashionably located theatrical facility.

The new Chestnut Street Theatre, 1211–15 Chestnut Street, was built in three months, despite the unsteady economic conditions caused by the darkest period of the Civil War. Smaller than average, the cast-iron and brick neoclassical-style exterior measured 56 feet wide, 150 feet deep, and 55-1/2 feet high. Inside, the house consisted of a parquet, parquet circle, dress circle, and family circle as well as the usual private and proscenium boxes. The stage—66 feet wide, 64 feet deep, with a 27-foot curtain opening—was decorated in a florid mixture of Victorian and neoclassic design elements: gold-leafed moldings ornamented with leaves, brackets, and scrolls; a white, gold, and red color scheme; a proscenium arch busily decorated with wreaths and classical figures; and a central medallion head of Shakespeare done in relief. The building was touted initially for its ultra-modern conveniences: steam heating, steam-engine-powered ventilating blowers, and a large steam fan.

William Wheatley (1816–76), himself well known as a handsome tragedian and graceful player of light comedy, was manager of the new theatre. Long associations with both the Philadelphia and New York stages—he had been a member of New York's Park Theatre Company as a child and young man; had managed Philadelphia's Arch Street Theatre, Academy of Music, and lesser Continental Theatre; and had been involved with Edward Davenport and James W. Wallack, the younger, in their Niblo's Garden venture—enabled Wheatley to amass a highly qualified resident stock company for the Chestnut Street Theatre as well as a sterling lineup of visiting stars. This practice of implementing a resident company of actors who assumed typed or stock roles with guest star performers was fairly common by the 1860s, although purists lamented the havoc this wreaked on the traditional stock company strengths: ability to choose appropriate plays for local audiences and to play in ensemble fashion. (Stars generally dictated the repertory, chosen from their own personal vehicles, and rarely rehearsed with the company before performance.)

The new Chestnut Street Theatre Stock Company opened on January 26, 1863, with a production of James Sheridan Knowles' heroic tragedy *Virginius*. For the opening weeks, Wheatley managed to secure both Philadelphia's native son and America's premier tragedian Edwin Forrest and the equally prominent comedian James H. Hackett. Forrest remained with the company throughout most of the season, and the stock company concentrated its repertory on Forrest's manly heroic tragedies such as *Metamora; Spartacus, the Gladiator;* and *Brutus; or, The Fall of Tarquin.* The Chestnut Street Theatre Stock Company followed the standard practice of the day and interspersed weeks of several plays in repertory each week with longer runs of one play. For instance, during the period from February 16–28, 1863, the company performed eight plays in repertory (*The Broker of Bogata, Hamlet, Damon and Pythias, Richelieu, Merry Wives of Windsor, Henry IV, East Lynne,* and *Brutus*) and rotated three stars (Forrest, Hackett, and Lucille Western). In contrast, during the period from April 13 to May 2, the company performed only one play, *Leah the Forsaken,* with one guest star, Kate Bateman.

Wheatley's management of the Chestnut Street Theatre Stock Company continued through the summer of 1863, interrupted only for a few weeks of variety performances in August. The 1863–64 theatrical season began early, on August 31, with yet another stellar performer, Edwin Booth. Stars, including Mlle. Felicita Vestvali, Forrest, and John Collins, continued to stud the roster until late January 1864, when Wheatley's management collapsed. The local press reported his losses at $12,000 and blamed his failure primarily on the theatre's high rent of $14,000 a year and on the high salaries and share of receipts demanded by his prominent stars, notably Forrest. Then, too, the physical theatre had proven a supreme disappointment to Philadelphia playgoers. Built in haste and under wartime conditions of scarce supplies and workmanship, its ugliness, isolated spaces, and poor sightlines earned it the nickname "The Morgue." Critics called its decoration crude and gaudy, more reminiscent of a restaurant than a theatre, and patrons complained of backaches due to uncomfortable seats and headaches and nausea caused by the poor ventilation and foul smells that emanated from cellar kitchens (apparently installed for the convenience of the actors). Poor insulation allowed street and house noises as well as sharp drafts to penetrate the auditorium. The upper tier was so steep, narrow, and dizzying that it eventually had to be closed permanently. Wheatley returned to Niblo's Garden, and his lucrative partnership in that theatre's 1866 production of the notorious *Black Crook* enabled him to retire.

Leonard Grover assumed management in January 1864 and immediately imposed substantial changes in operation and ideology on the company. These changes became all the more defined when Grover took on a partner, Colonel William E. Sinn, in the fall of that year. Grover, a playwright noted for his popular farce-comedies such as *Our Boarding House*, and Sinn, a manager (rather than actor-manager) long associated with the Brooklyn Theatre, set out to attract a broader-based audience by abandoning the emphasis on heroic or romantic acting and star performers. Instead, they concentrated on lighter, popular fare, and scenic effects and on creating a local following for the company's own actors. This demanded a new troupe, the only holdover being leading man Frank Mordaunt. Mordaunt, Walter Lennox, Mr. and Mrs. W. A. Chapman, and leading lady Josie Orton were to remain the company's stalwarts for several years. Breaking with the standard Philadelphia stock company practice of six evening performances weekly with occasionally scheduled special matinees, the Grover-Sinn management inaugurated a regular, bargain-priced Saturday matinee aimed directly at the workmen of Philadelphia. Calling this the "Grand Family Matinee," admission to seats in all parts of the house, regularly priced at twenty-five cents to $1.50, were offered for thirty cents for adults and twenty-five cents for children. When guest performers were sparingly used, it is significant that several were juvenile performers such as Jennie Parker and Little Katie Barker, and others often were actors associated more with the Philadelphia than New York or national stages such as native Philadelphian John E. McDonough.

Although Shakespeare's plays remained prominent in the company's repertory, popular melodramas abounded; the most-produced plays included *The French Spy, The Octoroon, Angel of Midnight,* and *Satan in Paris.* Local theme plays—*The Workmen of Philadelphia; or, The Curse of Drink; The Streets of Philadelphia; The Firemen of Philadelphia; Dead Sea Fruit; or, A Story of Philadelphia; Down at Cape May;* and *Did You Ever Take Your Wife to Germantown?* among them—were also apparent favorites. A staggering number of plays were produced by the stock company under Grover and Sinn: fifty-seven in 1864–65, seventy-three in 1865–66, sixty-five in 1866–67, all during seasons that were interrupted for approximately one month each summer when a touring minstrel show appeared or the theatre remained dark. The Chestnut Street Theatre Stock Company's staging was generally lauded by local critics during the Grover-Sinn years, and the company was credited, in 1867, with introducing the technical innovations of colored screens and colored footlights. However, critics generally found the offerings themselves uninspired and were sometimes aghast at the breaks with "first-class dramatic theatre" decorum the management undertook, as in 1866–67 when they raffled off prizes of cottage furniture, silverware, and china tea sets to boost attendance. It was indicative of the company's general personality that it was the first Philadelphia troupe to produce the naughty but extremely popular extravaganza *The Black Crook* in 1868.

After Grover retired in 1866 and Sinn assumed sole management, an increasing number of visiting stars were booked, notably during the 1866–67 season, when Felicita Vestvali, John E. Owens, Joseph Jefferson, Matilda Heron, Catherine Reignolds, and James E. Murdoch performed with the troupe, and Mr. and Mrs. Barney Williams virtually controlled the company's repertory for two months when they played the Williams' noted Irish-theme pieces exclusively. By the 1868–69 theatrical season, Sinn reported accumulated losses of $48,000 and disbanded the stock company, blaming the financial failure on the theatre's unpleasant physical environment and high rental fees. For the remainder of the season, the theatre was turned over to "lower" touring attractions such as the Hanlon Brothers' trapeze act and the Equestrian, Gymnastic, and Acrobatic Corps.

Yet the excellent location of the Chestnut Street Theatre, by now in the midst of new, fashionable shops and hotels and down the block from the prestigious Union League clubhouse, continued to lure managers intent on making it and its resident company a success. In 1869 famous actress-manager Laura Keene took control and aimed to elevate it to the ranks of a first-class, elite theatre geared to a delicate, polite, and feminine artistic sensibility. Keene, who had gained prominence as Edwin Booth's charming and graceful leading lady and had previously managed her own companies in Baltimore and Washington and at New York's Laura Keene's Varieties (1855–56) and Laura Keene's New Theatre (1856–63), was known as a particularly strong manager who anticipated the modern director in her blending of all theatrical elements into a personally envisioned artistic whole. Her first endeavor at the Chestnut Street Theatre was to remedy as many as possible of the building's defects by installing new, large velvet and satin-padded seats, repositioning both seats and boxes, and revamping the ventilation system. She replaced the theatre's vulgar appointments with baskets of natural flowers and plants, crystal chandeliers, and pastel drawings, advertising the refurbished theatre as a place of "beauty and refinement with homelike comfort." Keene offered as a special attraction frequent Saturday children's matinees; specific children's plays, often based on traditional folk or fairy tales, were produced exclusively for the matinees, and admission prices were lowered to the twenty-five- to seventy-five-cent range. Her company of actors blended previous Chestnut Street Theatre Stock Company members and other Philadelphia favorites, including Mordaunt, Charles McManus, William Wallis, and Mr. and Mrs. T. A. Creese, with actors new to the city. But it was Keene herself as the leading lady, renowned for her emotional, poetic acting, who was the primary attraction.

Despite Keene's financial investment and personal devotion to the Laura Keene's Chestnut Street Theatre Stock Company, losses forced her to relinquish management in March 1870 after less than a full season's operation. Her failure was speculated to stem from her overly refined and erudite taste in plays and from her own progressively deteriorating health. (Keene was the performer President Lincoln had come to see at Ford's Theatre on the evening of his assassination in 1865, and despite her blameless position, the incident deeply affected both her career and physical condition.) Keene never managed another company or theatre, although she continued acting until her death, caused by consumption, in 1873.

Apparently undaunted by the theatre's legacy, noted Shakespearean actor Edward Loomis Davenport (1815–77) assumed management in the fall of 1870, opening on December 12 with a repertory of Shakespeare's comedies. Davenport went to the Chestnut Street Theatre with an extensive reputation as a classical actor—the leading man of Anna Cora Mowatt in the 1840s, a key supporting player to Macready in the 1850s, and then a national star especially lauded by influential critic William Winter—and several only marginally successful previous experiences of stock-company management in Boston, Washington, and New York. Davenport wisely retained some of the most successful actors associated with the Chestnut Street Theatre such as Charles R. Thorne, Walter Lennox, and H. B. Phillips and added prominent actors from other Philadelphia resident companies. (At this time, it was not unusual for actors in Philadelphia and elsewhere to establish regional reputations and spend their careers moving amongst local resident companies. Actors with particularly large followings who had left one company for another were often brought back for sporadic appearances as guest stars.) Davenport also employed several members of his well-known theatrical family, including his wife, Fanny Vining Davenport, and his daughters Lily Vining, May, and the famous Fanny. For the 1872–73 season, young Augustin Daly, later to become one of the late nineteenth century's most renowned directors, was Davenport's "director of amusements": the creation of this new position (previously divided between stage manager and actor-manager or star performer) reveals Davenport's openness to the theatre's new demands for realistic, artistic staging.

Davenport was the company's leading actor, and the repertory immediately reflected his predilection for "the old, legitimate drama": Shakespeare; eighteenth- and nineteenth-century British romantic and heroic pieces; and light, witty comedies. Occasionally, however, Davenport interspersed popular melodramas or lower comedies, obviously understanding the financial necessity to do so. In this regard, Davenport apparently alienated some on both fronts: those who found his pandering to popular taste vulgar and those who found his typical fare too high brow and literary. By the 1870s Davenport, although still considered an extremely talented actor, had a difficult time drawing audiences in the face of the popular mass tastes that increasingly prevailed in urban markets.

Although select local critics and prominent citizens praised the Davenport company and offered publicly given tokens of appreciation, Davenport lost money in his Chestnut Street Theatre enterprise. Operating initially without benefit of visiting stars and with a large number of vehicles including most of his own past successes, Davenport tried both hiring stars and producing newer, more popular plays in his final full season of 1872–73. By December 1873, however, mounting losses exacerbated by a nationwide economic depression forced Davenport to retire from his management and disband the Chestnut Street Theatre Stock Company. He subsequently rented the theatre for short periods during the 1874–75 season, when the theatre was lent out for individual performances only. Those of the Chestnut Street Theatre's stock actors who had not found other employment were called in to work "as needed," but the proliferation of the full touring company minimized their opportunities. Meanwhile, Davenport experienced his one remaining highly acclaimed success before his death in 1877—the famed 1875 H. C. Jarrett and A. M. Palmer production of *Julius Caesar* in which Davenport played Brutus to Lawrence Barrett's Cassius.

The Chestnut Street Theatre Stock Company was revived in 1875 to the surprise of many Philadelphians. By this date, both the Arch Street and the Walnut Street theatres were giving up the resident stock mode and were relying instead on more and more full touring combination troupes. Many deemed stock an outworn institution. Obviously, William D. Gemmill, a fledgling actor who had inherited a small family fortune, did not agree. With two secondary partners, fellow young actors F. F. Mackay and J. Frederick Scott, Gemmill took control of the theatre in the late summer of 1875 and planned his "real old-fashioned stock company": a company in which all talent was supplied from the ranks and tasks were relatively interchangeable. Gemmill, known as "Billy" and considered somewhat of an urbane man-about-town, strongly injected his personality into the company from the start, with the repertory initially dominated by light, breezy comedies and glamorous romances but few of the old heavy-handed melodramas or low-life dramas. A sampling of the company's play titles reflects this shift in tone: *Lemons, Our Boys, Flirtation, Sweethearts, My Foolish Wife*. Occasionally, Gemmill adopted the New York stock companies' recent policy of producing a new play and then allowing it to run for as long as it engendered business. The long run of the Chestnut Street Theatre Stock Company's *Our Boys*—June 26 to November 18, 1876—testifies to the troupe's wide scope of appeal. However, because core, weekly-attending audiences usually were the staples of resident companies and an unchanging bill discouraged their support, many stock companies found this policy problematic. Under Gemmill, the stock company produced far fewer plays each season than under previous managements (approximately twenty-five or thirty); however, for the most part bills rarely remained stagnant for more than one or two weeks.

The company was comprised of several past regulars as well as several new younger, handsome performers such as Lillie Glover, Otis Skinner, George Holland, Jr., and Lydia Yeamans. That Gemmill had an astute eye for theatrical talent is attested to by the future careers of several of his actors: Skinner (1858–42) became one of the major comedic stars of the Broadway stage whose successful vehicles ranged from Booth Tarkington to Shakespeare; Annie Yeamans and daughter Lydia, having already appeared with Ned Harrigan, went on to become major figures in his entire Mulligan Guard series; George Holland, Jr., became one of Philadelphia's foremost managers and helped create the new stock company institution of the 1890s with his Girard Avenue Stock Company. Augustin Daly's brother, William H. Daly, was elevated from assistant stage manager to stage manager in 1877, although local press accounts intimate that he was primarily responsible for the company's effective staging throughout.

The usual large range of admission prices—from twenty-five cents to $1.50—was available, although in later years the top price was lowered to $1.00. For a time, the troupe's position as Philadelphia's only remaining first-class resident company and apparently effective management enabled the company to prosper. However, the city's lesser theatres soon offset the resident stock dearth by creating competitive companies. Furthermore, in 1878 severe internal difficulties began, and the Chestnut Street Theatre Stock Company's favorable position quickly eroded. Gemmill, in full power after the retirement of his partners, elevated himself to the position of leading actor despite his lack of experience and audience following. Many of the company's best actors resigned in protest, and this, coupled with a depressed nationwide economic situation, dramatically decreased the Chestnut Street Theatre's patronage. Ticket prices were lowered again (matinee prices were scaled down to fifty cents), but the theatre's rent continued to increase, its annual rental fee having escalated $4,000 since the theatre's opening. Thirteen theatres operated in Philadelphia by the late 1870s, many of which offered low-priced "lower" forms of entertainment such as burlesque, minstrelsy, and opera bouffe, and created hefty competition for theatres committed to the legitimate drama.

Despite these circumstances, Gemmill inaugurated a series of magnificently staged Shakespearean revivals, starring himself, which seriously injured the company's financial stability. Although the stock troupe continued for two more seasons, apparently operating on Gemmill's inheritance, it was immediately abandoned when Gemmill was forced to take on a partner, prominent and pragmatic Philadelphia saloon keeper Alexander Bunn. A week of farewells to the "Great Stock Company" occurred in late March 1880, when the company appropriately offered its most successful vehicle, *Our Boys*. Thereafter the Chestnut Street Theatre followed the city's other major theatres in becoming a combination house. Philadelphia was never again to have a Chestnut Street Theatre Stock Company, although the theatre did host the resident dramatic stock company the Orpheum Players during the 1907–13 period. The theatre was demolished in 1917 and an office building erected on its site.

PERSONNEL

Proprietor-Managers: William Wheatley (January 1863–January 1864); Leonard Grover (1864); Leonard Grover, William E. Sinn (1864–66); William E. Sinn (1866–69); Laura Keene (1869–70); Edward Loomis (E. L.) Davenport (1870–74); William D. Gemmill, J. Frederick Scott and Company, proprietors, and Gemmill, Scott, and F. F. Mackay, managers (1875–78); William D. Gemmill (1878–80).

Treasurers-Business Managers: Philip Warren, treasurer (1863–64); George R. Thompson, business manager, and M. Nunan, treasurer (1869–70); P. E. Abel, treasurer and business agent (1870–74); Henry M. Kieter, treasurer (1878–80).

Scenic Technicians: Russell Smith, H. Hillyard (1863–64); Russell Smith (1864–68); J. S. Schell, T. S. Plaisted, J. B. Price (1869–70); W. J. Fetters (1870–73); Harley Merry (1875–80).

Musical Directors: Mark Hassler (January 1863–January 1864), Charles Koppitz (1864–65), Adolph Birgfeld (1865–66), Benjamin E. Woolf (1866–68), C. W. Reinhart (1868–69), Mark Hassler (1869–70); T. E. Boettger (1870–71); Carl Sentz (1871–73); Simon Hassler (1875–80).

Stage Directors-Stage Managers: J. B. Wright, stage manager (January 1863–January 1864); S. C. DuBois, stage manager (1864); Lewis Baker, stage manager (1864–65); Joseph C. Foster, stage manager (1865–67); William H. Smith, stage manager (1867–69); [George] Vining Bowers, B. A. Baker, stage managers (1869–70); William S. Fredericks, stage manager (1870–72); Augustin Daly, director, and

J. H. Selwyn, stage manager (1872–73); F. F. Mackay, stage manager, and William H. Daly, assistant manager (1875–77); William H. Daly, stage manager (1877–80).

Actors and Actresses: Charlotte Adams; Viola Alexander; Mrs. J. H. Allen; Louisa Allen; Jennie H. Anderson; Mary Anderson; H. Archer; Leonie Arlington; Miss A. Atkins; W. H. Bailey; Emily Baker; Katie Baker; Mrs. S. A. Baker; Frank C. Bangs; Nellie Barbour; L. F. Barrett; Charles Barron; Ernest Bartram; Harry Bave; J. W. Blaisdell; Kitty Blanchard; William A. Booth; S. Bowen; [*George*] *Vining Bowers* (1873–74); Mrs. Boyce; J. B. Bradford; Charles H. Bradshaw; Mrs. F. Brelsford; T. F. Brennan; Virginia Buchanan; James G. Burnett; John Burns; Clara Cale; Violet Campbell; A. H. Canby; J. Canoll; Cordelia Cappelle; L. E. Carland; Mary Carr; Helen Cary; Edith Challis; Mr. and Mrs. William A. Chapman; Mrs. A. R. Chapon; George H. Clarke; Estelle Clayton; George H. Cohill; J. W. Collier; W. Connelly; Mrs. F. B. Conroy; J. F. Constans; Hart Conway; *Lillian Conway* (1876–77); L. Cooper; John Costello; Robert Craig; Mr. and Mrs. T. A. Creese; Bertha Cross; C. Cross; C. J. Dade; J. V. Dailey; *E. L. Davenport* (1870–74); *Mrs. E. L. Davenport*, formerly Fanny Elizabeth Vining (1870–74); Fanny Davenport; Lily Vining Davenport; May Davenport; William Davidge; C. P. DeGroat; Miss Delaney; Louis deLange; *Susan Denin* (1863–64); Annie DeVere; W. A. Donaldson; I. N. Drew; S. C. Dubois; Anabel Dudley; Dora Dufour; J. Durfie; Ada Dyas; T. F. Egberts; J. Ellis; George D. Erroll; Fanny Erwin; J. B. Evers; *Rose Eytinge* (1863–64); J. T. Fannin; Owen Fawcett; A. W. Fenno; W. J. Ferguson; Alex Fisher; P. A. Fitzgerald; *Edwin Forrest* (1863); *Frank Foster* (1866–67); Annie Fox; C. H. Frye; *William D. Gemmill* (1877–80); Effie Germon; J. Germon; Mrs. G. H. Gilbert; George Gilbert; Ada Gilman; Sophie Gimber, later Sophie Gimber Kuhn; Leonard Glover; *Lillie Glover* (1876–80); G. P. Goldie; Dora Goldwaithe; Annie Gossin; Lillian Graham; Mrs. H. P. Grattan; Ella Grayson; C. Gregory; *George H. Griffiths* (1875–80); J. Gurley; Alan Halford; J. S. Hall; Miss Hamilton; W. H. Hamilton; *James M. Hardie* (1879–80); Lizzie Harold; W. A. Haupt; Harry Hawk; Sam Hemple; Ettie Henderson; Mr. and Mrs. Charles Henri; Mrs. J. Henry; Imogene Herring; Phyllis Glover Hirschfield; George Hoey; J. S. Hoffman; *George Holland, Jr.* (1875–80); Joseph J. Holland; E. B. Holmes; Miss Hope; May Howard; Henrietta Irving; John Henry Jack; Billie Jackson; Minnie Jackson; Fannie Jacobs; Annie James; Louis James; Cornelia Jefferson; Ida Jeffreys; J. W. Jennings; J. Johnson; Mrs. George Jordan; Harry Josephs; Mrs. E. F. Keach; *Laura Keene* (1869–70); Thomas W. Keene; Frances Kemble; H. C. Kennedy; T. H. Knight; Addie Kunkel; George Kunkel; Miss Lancaster; J. W. Lanergan; *Harry Langdon* (1870–72); Josephine Laurens; W. B. Laurens; *W. H. Leak* (1867–68); *Henry W. Lee* (1878–80); Annie Leicester; Emily Leicester; *Walter Lennox* (1864–68, 1870–71); H. Lewis; Herman Linde; E. A. Locke; George E. Locke; *F. F. Mackay* (1875–78); E. Mackway; Mary Maddern; L. Mahon; Alice Mansfield; G. W. Marcellus; Emma Markley; J. Martin; B. F. Matlack; D. R. Matthews; J. P. Maylin; Miss Dean McConnell; J. McCullough; T. McKeon; Charles A. McManus; B. McNulty; T. E. McSorely; George Metkiff; May Montella; Clara Montello; *Frank Mordaunt* (1863–66, 1869–70, 1873–74); Mrs. Frank Mordaunt; Clara Morris; Louisa Morse; Mary Morse; C. H. Morton; H. W. Moyer; Frank Murdoch; H. S. Murdoch; W. Murillo; E. F. Nagle; J. Nagle; Kate Newbon; Isabella Nixon; Charles Norris; James W. Norris; *Josie Orton* (1865–68); W. H. Otis; Harry Pearson; Mrs. H. A. Perry; Clareen Petrea; W. H. Phelps; Mrs. E. J.

Phillips; *H. B. (Harry) Phillips* (1870–74); Alice Placide; *Mme. Elizabeth Ponisi* (1863–64); C. S. Porter; Julia Porter; Lizzie Price; Susan Price; Mrs. J. J. Prior; James F. Prior; Katie Putnam; *McKee Rankin* (1876–77); W. C. Raymond; Andrew J. Redifer; Clara Reed; Roland Reed; Ruth Rich; Florence Richmond; Emily Rigl; E. T. Ringgold; J. B. Roberts; Fred P. Robinson; *Katherine Rogers* (1879–80); F. W. Sanger; F. O. Savage; May Saville; Ida Savory; Laura B. Scanlan; Susie Schenck; *W. H. Sedley-Smith* (1865–66, 1867–68); Anna Schindel; James Seymour; Robert Sheridan; *William E. Sheridan* (1869–70, 1875–80); L. R. Shewell; E. T. Sinclair; Mrs. G. Skerrett; Otis Skinner; Mark Smith; *Charles Stanley* (1875–77, 1878–80); W. J. Stanton; Fanny Stockton; H. F. Stone; Clara Stoneall; A. H. Stuart; J. B. Studley; James Taylor; Charlotte Thompson; E. F. Thorne; *Charles R. Thorne, Jr.* (1870–72); E. L. Tilton; Hetty Tracey; Helen Tracy; Agnes Vache; A. R. Vanhorn; F. F. Varnum; Ada Vernon; Alex Vincent; E. Wallace; G. Wallis; William Wallis; *Annie Ward*, later Annie Ward Tiffany (1863–64); J. T. Ward; Ella Warren; L. Watson; Henrietta Wells; Mary Wells; Charles Wheatleigh; *William Wheatley* (1863–64); George White; C. M. Wilkins; E. P. Wilks; Bedford Williams; Emma Wilmot; Francis Wilson; Frank B. Wilson; J. S. Wilson; L. Wilson; Bertha Winans; Nellie Wisdom; *Annie Yeamans* (1875–76); *Lydia Yeamans* (1875–76); Benjamin Young.

Guest Artists: Edwin Adams; John Allen; (Little) Katie Baker; Daniel E. Bandmann; Kate Bateman; Edwin Booth; Junius Brutus Booth; Mrs. D. P. Bowers; Mlle. Johanna Claussen; Coleman Sisters; John Collins; C. W. Couldock; Lotta Crabtree; Charlotte Cushman; Julia Daly; Fanny Davenport; Susan Denin; Henry Dunbar; Charles Fechter; Mr. and Mrs. William J. Florence; Edwin Forrest; Ada Gray; James Henry Hackett; Ada Harland; Alice Harrison; James A. Herne; Matilda Heron; Jean Hosmer; Miss Leo Hudson; Fanny Janauschek; Joseph Jefferson; Avonia Jones; Paul Juignet; Sophie Gimber Kuhn; Herman Linde; Olive Logan; Frank Mayo; John McCullough; John E. McDonough; Robert McWade; Maggie Mitchell; James E. Murdoch; (Little) Nell; John E. Owens; Jennie Parker; Catherine Reignolds; J. B. Roberts; Mrs. Scott-Siddens; W. H. Sedley-Smith; Mlle. Felicita Vestvali; James W. Wallack; Warren Family; Webb Sisters; Helen Western; Lucille Western; Mr. and Mrs. Barney Williams; Mrs. John Wood; Mlle. Marie Zoe.

REPERTORY

1862–63 (Company first appeared in January 1863): *Virginius; Merry Wives of Windsor; Henry IV; Richelieu; The Broker of Bogata; Hamlet; Damon and Pythias; East Lynne; Brutus; or, The Fall of Tarquin; Macbeth; Richard III; King Lear; Jack Cade; The Merchant of Venice; Spartacus, the Gladiator; Narcisse; or, The Last of the Pompadours; Metamora; Leah the Forsaken; Fair One with the Golden Locks; Pocahontas; Pride of the Market; Lady Audley's Secret; The World of Fashion; Camille; The Lady of Lyons; Peep O' Day.*

1863–64: *The Iron Chest; Hamlet; Ruy Blas; The Fool's Revenge; Loan of a Lover; Don Caesar de Bazan; The Duke's Motto; Cynthia; or, The Lingara's Vow; Gemea: The Hebrew Mother; Lucrezia Borgia; Medea; Evadne; The Stranger; Catherine and Petruchio; Aurora Floyd; The Lady of Lyons; Macbeth; Honeymoon;* (originally spelled *Honey Moon*); *Richelieu; Damon and Pythias; Richard III; The*

Little Treasure; Othello; Virginius; Brutus; or, The Fall of Tarquin; The Broker of Bogata; Jack Cade; The Child of Nature; Spartacus, the Gladiator; King Lear; Metamora; Romeo and Juliet; Camille; Pizarro; William Tell; The Brigands; The Veteran; The Ticket-of-Leave Man; All That Glitters Is Not Gold; The Colleen Bawn; Pure Gold; The Accusing Spirit; The Octoroon; The Romance of a Poor Young Man; Leap Year; Naval Engagements; The Poor of Philadelphia; The Chimney Corner; The Seven Sisters; The Pirates of Savannah; Count Monte Leone; or, The Spy in Society.

1864–65: *Aladdin and the Wonderful Lamp; The Sea of Ice; Dunduckeity's Picnic; The Rivals; The School for Scandal; She Stoops to Conquer; Paul Pry; Nursery Chickweed; Babes in the Wood; London Assurance; Poor Pillicoddy; Look before You Leap; The Breach of Promise; The Hunchback; The Lottery Ticket; The Stranger; Romeo and Juliet; Youth Who Never Saw a Woman; Camille; The Monastery of St. Just; Jane Shore; Lady Audley's Secret; East Lynne; Pauvrette; Jessie Brown; The Octoroon; The Lady of Lyons; Sweethearts and Wives; The Serious Family; Richard III; Retribution; The Robbers; The Marble Heart; Katherine and Petruchio; Hamlet; The Three Guardsmen; The Flowers of the Forest; Satan in Paris; Don Caesar de Bazan; The Pet of the Petticoats; The French Spy; My Pleasant Neighbor; The Wept of the Wish-Ton-Wish; Asmodeus; The Workmen of Philadelphia; Uncle Tom's Cabin; The Colleen Bawn; Turn Him Out; Jenny Lind; Wild Oats; Oliver Twist; The Corsican Brothers; Pocahontas; Ivanhoe; The Seven Daughters of Satan; The Ticket-of-Leave Man; Arrah-na-Pogue.*

1865–66: *Naval Engagements; Peg Woffington; Antony and Cleopatra; As You Like It; Romeo and Juliet; Camille; The Sea of Ice; The French Spy; The Drunkard; Flowers of the Forest; Green Bushes; Don Caesar de Bazan; The Actress of Padua; The Angel of Midnight; Monte Cristo; Eleanor's Victory; Masks and Faces; Oliver Twist; East Lynne; Lucrezia Borgia; Gemea: The Hebrew Mother; Atonement; or, The Child Stealer; The Workingmen of Philadelphia; or, The Curse of Drink; The Octoroon; Satan in Paris; Mary Tudor, the Bloody Queen; The Spy of St. Marc; A Nation's Destiny; Still Waters Run Deep; The Sleeping Beauty; Red Rover; or, Murder on the Dolphin; Arrah-na-Pogue; Uncle Tom's Cabin; Blackmail; or, The Hour of Ten; Henry Dunbar; or, The Outcasts; Ice Witch, or, The Sea King's Bride; Ten Nights in a Barroom; The Three Guardsmen; Charles XII; or, The Siege of the Stralsund; The Firemen of Philadelphia; Cartouche; or, The Stolen Jewels; Betrayer and Betrayed; or, Crossing the Quicksands; Caught in the Toils; or, Only a Clod; The Rivals; The Heir-at-Law; Married Life; She Stoops to Conquer; Never too Late to Marry; Fanchon, the Cricket; The Pearl of Savoy; The Flying Dutchman; Little Barefoot; The Hut of the Red Mountain; The Heretic; Man of the Day; The Sculptor's Dream; The Robbers; The Dead Heart; Wild Oats; The Ticket-of-Leave Man; Hamlet; Richard III; The Lady of Lyons; Pocahontas; The Mother's Dying Child; Forty Thieves; Delicate Ground; Baccarat; or, The Knaves of the Pack; Our Mutual Friend.*

1866–67: *Fanchon, the Cricket; Romeo and Juliet; Bel Delmonio; The Marriage Certificate; Gemea: The Hebrew Mother; Fazio; or, The Italian Wife; Dot; Uncle Solon Shingle; The Victims; The Fast Family; Janet Pride; Did You Ever Send Your Wife to Germantown? Rip Van Winkle; Our American Cousin; Woodcock's Little Game; Victorine; The Long Strike; The Gunmaker of Moscow; Isabelle; Henrietta; Arrah-na-Pogue; Camille; Griffith Gaunt; The Fairy Circle; Born to Good Luck;*

Custom of the Country; All Hallow's Eve; Connie Soogah; Ireland as It Was; The Rough Diamond; Married Life; The Idiot Witness; The Three Red Men; Rory O'More; The Flowers of the Forest; Don Caesar de Bazan; The Corsican Brothers; Green Bushes; Satan in Paris; The Star-Spangled Banner; Thesbe; The French Spy; The Actress of Padua; Jenny Lind; The Windmill; Queen of the Silver Ivy; Armadale; The Streets of Philadelphia; Shamus O'Brien; Captain Kyd; Hamlet; Wild Oats; Money; Wine Works Wonders; The School for Scandal; Much Ado about Nothing; The Stranger; The Dramatist; The Gamester; The Elder Brother; After Many Days; or, An Inventor's Dream; The Colleen Bawn; Cendrillon; Cool as a Cucumber; Monte Cristo.

1867–68: Caste; Handy Andy; Wine Works Wonders; The School for Scandal; Hamlet; Mary Stuart; Lady Audley's Secret; Down at Cape May; Hunted Down; Dora; The French Spy; The Dumb Girl of Partiri; Medea; Adrienne Lecouvreur; Egmont; No Thoroughfare; The Public Press; Dot; The Victims; Everybody's Friend; Self; The Mikado; The Flying Scud; Dead Sea Fruit: A Story of Philadelphia; Dearer Than Life; The Black Crook; Humpty Dumpty.

1868–69: The White Fawn; Undine; or, The Nymphs of Lubleiberg; Foul Play; The Grand Duchess; La Belle Helene; The Good-for-Nothing; Barbe Bleue; The Lancashire Lass; Blow for Blow.

1869–70: The Marble Heart; Rachel, the Reaper; Our American Cousin; Home; Hunted Down; An Unequal Match; Bogus; School; Little Red Riding Hood; The Saucy Housemaid; Bold Jack: The Giant Killer; Patrice; or, The White Lady of Wicklow; Christmas Carol; Champagne; or, Step by Step; Blow for Blow; Two Can Play at That Game; Mercy Dodd; Is She Mad?; Fanchon, the Cricket; Streets of New York; The Three Guardsmen; Victorine; Everybody's Friend; The Demon of Paris; The Dangerous Game; Frou-Frou; Little Beauty and the Beast; or, The Kind Fairy of the Roses.

1870–71: As You Like It; "Favorite Character Sketches"; Romeo and Juliet; Much Ado about Nothing; The Merchant of Venice; Born to Good Luck; Thrice Married; The Ticket-of-Leave Man; The Colleen Bawn; Dombey and Son; Inshavogue; At Last; Handy Andy; The Wife; Hamlet; Richard III; Love's Sacrifice; Wild Oats; Katherine and Petruchio; The Marble Heart; The Hunchback; The Robbers; Black Eyed Susan; Michael Erle; The Jealous Wife; The Old Man of the Mountain; Honey Moon; A New Way to Pay Old Debts; Delicate Ground; Comedy and Tragedy; St. Marc; The Lady of Lyons; Turn Him Out; Town and Country; Don Caesar de Bazan; Robert Macaire; Damon and Pythias; London Assurance; Frou-Frou; The Marquis; School; The Serious Family; The Two Friends; Married Life; Othello; The Apostate; Dreams of Delusion; She Stoops to Conquer; Saratoga; All That Glitters Is Not Gold.

1871–72: Money; The Hunchback; The Rivals; The Lady of Lyons; Married Life; The Heir-at-Law; A Bull in a China Shop; The Marble Heart; Toodles; The Widow's Victim; As You Like It; The Road to Ruin; A New Way to Pay Old Debts; Damon and Pythias; Saratoga; The Castle Spectre; Hamlet; Alexander the Great; Comedy and Tragedy; Much Ado about Nothing; The Wife; Everybody's Friend; St. Marc; The Stranger; Othello; Raymond, the Patriot; Peril on the Beach at Long Branch; Fashion; Birds in a Cage; Brutus; School; The Coming Woman; The Three Guardsmen; Cinderella; A Dream of Life; The Iron Chest; The School for Scandal; The Colleen Bawn; Richelieu; Caste; The Robbers; The Serious Family; A Child of the

Regiment; A Great Bell; The Spirit of '76; The French Spy; The Merchant of Venice; The Ticket-of-Leave Man; Camille; Julius Caesar; King Henry VIII; Macbeth; Guy Mannering; The Waterman; How She Loves Him; Breakers; London Assurance; Dark Friday; or, The King and Queen of Erie; Jacquette; Uncle Tom's Cabin.

1872–73: *Horizon; Man and Wife; Article 47; Diamonds; Blunders; The Colleen Bawn; Money; A New Way to Pay Old Debts; The Ticket-of-Leave Man; Virginius; Merry Wives of Windsor; The Wonder; Thérèse; The Iron Chest; The Stranger; Arrah-na-Pogue; Othello; Damon and Pythias; Tom Cringle; Fidelia, the Waif; Under the Gaslight; Macbeth; Oliver Twist; Kind to a Fault; La sonnambula; The Artful Dodger; Saved by Chance; Robert Macaire; Laugh When You Can; The Golden Farmer; Bertha: The Sewing Machine Girl; The Boy Detective; Hamlet; Wild Oats; Don Caesar de Bazan; Ruy Blas; Driven from Home; The Rising Generation; The Doctor of Alcantara; Cataract of the Ganges; Richard III; The Flowers of the Forest; Ill-Treated Il Travatore; Pat Lyon: The Philadelphia Locksmith; "F"; or, Branded; Rip Van Winkle; The Irish Ambassador; His Last Legs; How to Pay the Rent; Rory O'More; The Happy Man; The Nervous Man; The Serious Family; The Angel of Midnight; The French Spy; Dick Turpin; The Broken Sword; The Flying Dutchman.*

1873–74: *Money; Wives as They Are and Maids as They Were; Love's Sacrifice; The Marble Heart; Toodles; Divorce; Fernande; Frou-Frou; Hamlet; The Merchant of Venice; The School for Scandal; Jack Cade; Julius Caesar; Fidelia, the Waif; The Hidden Hand; A New Way to Pay Old Debts; The Iron Chest; Macbeth; Katherine and Petruchio; The Twelve Temptations; Richelieu; The Wife; Damon and Pythias; Othello; Henry VIII; The Drunkard; Don Caesar de Bazan.*

1875–76: *Our Boys; Sweethearts; Tom Cobb; Weak Women; Tichborne; Married in Haste; Caste; Young Wives and Old Bachelors; Helen; or, One Hundred Years Ago; Daisy Farm; A Romance of a Poor young Man; Ours; She Stoops to Conquer; Saratoga; She Wou'd and She Wou'd Not; Old Heads and Young Hearts; Still Waters Run Deep; How She Loves Him; John Bull; or, An Englishman's Fireside.*

1876–77: *Our Boys; Money; Flirtation; Masks and Faces; Love's Sacrifice; Our Boarding House; The Two Orphans; Three Days; She Wou'd and She Wou'd Not; Quits; Sweethearts; Married in Haste; Everybody's Friend; A Regular Fix; Blow for Blow; Married Life; Caste; Jenny Lind.*

1877–78: *New Men and Old Acres; The Remarkable History of Lipset; My Foolish Wife; Her Second Husband; Much Ado about Nothing; The Rivals; The Four Sisters; The Lyons Mail; The Hunchback; Married in Haste; The Red Light; Cricket on the Hearth; As You Like It; Divorce; The Fast Family; The Craiga Dhoul; The Duke's Motto; School; Peep O' Day; The Corsican Brothers; Pauline; Louis XI; Serpent and Dove; The Marble Heart; Rip Van Winkle; The New Magdalen; Othello; Macbeth; The Three Guardsmen; Oliver Twist; Mathilde; Jack Cade; The Sea of Ice; East Lynne; The Child Stealer.*

1878–79: *London Assurance; She Stoops to Conquer; Wild Oats; The School for Scandal; The Willow Copse; The Inconstant; My Son; Our Boys; Our Club; Rob Roy; As You Like It; The Merchant of Venice; Within an Inch of His Life; Ours; Woman's Loyalty; Caste; The Tower of Babel; Camille; Henry IV; Money; Othello; Engaged; Robert Macaire; A Scrap of Paper; The Hunchback; Romeo and Juliet; The Lady of Lyons; Hamlet; Playing with Fire; Fatinitza.*

1879–80: *Horrors; Hiawatha; Babes in the Wood; Robinson Crusoe; Esquire;*

The Galley Slave; A Romance of a Poor Young Man; The Unequal Match; Cuba; The Wife: or, A Tale of Mantua; The Girls; Our Boys; Wives; Dr. Clyde; Hamlet; A Scrap of Paper; Pygmalion and Galatea; Hunted Down; Follies of a Night; A Rogue's Luck; The Wedding March; Louis XI; Camille; As You Like It; Richelieu; Shylock; School; Oliver Twist; My Neighbor's Wife; The School for Scandal; The Stranger; Wild Oats; The Inconstant; East Lynne; My Son-in-Law.

BIBLIOGRAPHY

Published Sources: Derek Naabe, "Philadelphia's Theatre Heritage: The Third Chestnut Street Theatre," *Germantowne Crier* 19 (March 1967): 16–21; *Philadelphia Inquirer*; Philadelphia *Public Ledger*.

Unpublished Sources: William Dickey Coder, "A History of the Philadelphia Theatre, 1856–1878" (Ph.D. diss., University of Pennsylvania, 1936); Thomas F. Marshall, "The History of the Philadelphia Theatre, 1878–1890" (Ph.D. diss., University of Pennsylvania, 1941).

Archival Sources: Chestnut Street Theatre File, Chestnut Street Theatre Programs File, and Philadelphia Theatre Index, Philadelphia Theatre Collection, Free Library of Philadelphia (Logan Square). The Philadelphia Theatre Collection also has files on many of the managers and performers connected with the Chestnut Street Theatre.

Mari Kathleen Fielder

CHICAGO THEATRE COMPANY. See ILLINOIS THEATRICAL COMPANY.

CITY THEATRE COMPANY. "Les comediens Francaise" originated as a group of French performers under the management of Alexander Placide (1750–1812), invited to Charleston in 1794 by Charleston entrepreneur John Sollee. Sollee was a French Huguenot, born into Norman aristocracy but forced by religious persecution to flee his country in 1791. Sollee took with him to the New World a significant fortune, which he used to buy a plantation near Charleston. His fortune was supplemented by the dowry of a well-to-do American girl, Harriet Neyle. Sollee may have witnessed performances by a French company while visiting Newport, Rhode Island, in the summer of 1793. Impressed with the group's talent and aware of the needs of the growing community of French refugees in Charleston, Sollee apparently invited Placide's troupe to South Carolina. Alexander-Placide Bussart, a dancer, acrobat, and pantomimist, had twenty year's experience performing in France and Great Britain. His first American engagement (with Mme. Placide) was in New York with the [Old] American Company (1792–1806)* in January 1792.

The history of Charleston's French, later City, Theatre Company is inextricably interwoven with the story of the company that opposed them, the West Company*. After an initial benefit played in the Charleston Theatre on February 8, 1794, through the generosity of Thomas Wade

West, Sollee and the French players erected their own theatre on Church Street, which they opened April 10, 1794. Intense competition ensued, not only for audience but also for the service of performers, dancers, musicians, and scenic artists.

The great success of the first season was a pantomime devised by Placide and other company members, *The Attack on Fort Moultrie*, based on a military incident in the American Revolution. The pantomime drew well, especially after the Charleston Theatre's season ended June 30, and Sollee prospered. But West soon struck back, stripping Sollee of the major performers in his company by offering better salaries. The Placides, the Couvilliers, the Vals, and Messrs. Francisqui and Spinacuta defected. Sollee was devastated. He acquired Mr. and Mrs. Hayden Edgar, Mr. and Mrs. Henderson, and part of the Sully family from the rival troupe, but his company lost much artistic appeal in the exchange.

Sollee's second season was delayed until December 20, 1794, by an intransigent Charleston city committee, which balked at licensing his theatre for performances in English. After two months of deliberation, a license was granted, and Sollee opened his theatre, then called the City Theatre. The English season lasted but nine weeks. Inflation undermined the value of currency, Sollee's actors were barely competent, and Sollee knew little of English dramatic literature or theatrical production techniques. His dependence on the judgment of the ambitious but intemperate Hayden Edgar was ill-advised, for Edgar selected plays that offended the political and cultural sensibilities of Charlestonians. The second season closed February 28, 1795. While Sollee again struggled with city hall to keep his license, the company disbanded.

Sollee went north to hire more actors for the winter season of 1795–96. A group led by Edward Jones of the Boston ["Federal Street"] Theatre Company* accepted Sollee's invitation, as did a group driven out of New York by a yellow-fever epidemic. The engagement of Mrs. Mary Ann Pownall and her daughters Charlotte and Mary Wrighten filled the ranks of this new and heterogeneous company, which opened what was to be a brilliant musical season at the City Theatre on November 10, 1795. Mrs. Pownall (formerly Mrs. Wrighten of London's Drury Lane Theatre), in the last year of her life, was a strong addition to the company, as were her daughters. In January 1796 Sollee introduced a second star, James Chalmers, most recently seen in Philadelphia with the Chestnut Street Theatre Company*. The company headed by Pownall and Chalmers yielded little to the group West introduced at the Charleston Theatre on February 16, 1796, despite the presence of attractive French performers in West's troupe. Sollee had regained the upper hand, and West was forced to abandon Charleston, his new theatre, and ten excellent performers, including the Placides. In the summer of 1796, while fires and disease ravaged Charleston, Sollee's actors joined with those at the Charleston for a brief season in

July. In August five of Sollee's actors died, including Mrs. Pownall and her daughter Mary. Other performers fled to the North.

Mrs. Pownall's place was taken by Elizabeth Kemble Whitlock of England's provincial theatre but most recently seen in starring engagements in Philadelphia and Boston. Assisted by her husband, Charles Whitlock (more drawn to dentistry than to acting), and supported by Alexander and a new Mrs. Placide (the former Charlotte Pownall) and Mr. and Mrs. James West, Mrs. Whitlock led an otherwise weak company into the winter season of 1796–97. Sollee reneged on salary agreements with the Whitlocks, used Charles Whitlock beyond the man's capacity to be effective, and generally mismanaged the resources of the group. Disenchanted elements in Charleston attacked Sollee and his manager, Edward Jones, in the press. Charles Whitlock, a seasoned manager of English provincial theatres, was touted to replace Jones, but Sollee resisted. In May 1797 the company dispersed, for Sollee could offer them no summer and autumn employment.

Sollee again went north, this time with a group of performers, which he promoted, at great expense but unsuccessfully, in New York and Boston, in an effort to keep his company intact. On November 7, 1797, the Whitlocks and Mr. and Mrs. John Brown Williamson led a troupe managed by Edward Jones in yet another fall season at the City Theatre, believing the only way to collect their back wages from Sollee was to continue to work for him. Sollee moved the group to the more luxurious Charleston Theatre on January 1, 1798, but this could not stem the rising tide of discontent in the company and in the city. Sollee further entangled himself in legal disputes with his employees. They finally petitioned for their unpaid salaries in publicly circulated handbills. The actors threatened to strike, and this split the company, especially offending Alexander Placide. Sollee paid off his performers and then sued them for damages done by the handbills. The situation was a shambles. Sollee was deeply in debt, beset on all sides by detractors, accused of squandering his wife's dowry, and under court order to sell his theatre to pay the mortgage. Whitlock, Jones, and Placide paid the mortgage arrears to keep the theatre from being confiscated and closed. Then in March 1798 Sollee struck an agreement to rent the theatre to Placide, Jones, and John Brown Williamson, late of the Boston Theatre, for four years. Sollee's retirement seemed to revitalize the company for the remainder of the season, which ended about March 31.

Williamson, Jones, and Placide reinforced the City Theatre Company in the next few months, opening January 9, 1799, with five new members and eventually building it up until about twenty performers were employed. French dancers returned to the ranks, and pantomimes and ballets were produced with greater frequency in the season ending April 19, 1799. The company was forced to move to the Charleston Theatre in February, when a portion of the City Theatre collapsed, injuring several patrons.

The managerial alliance returned to the City Theatre in October 1799, sporting the testimony of master builders about the structural safety of the building. Again recruits from the North were added to the company, including James Chalmers, former leading man in Sollee's company. Chalmers led off the season on October 28 in *Hamlet*. Shortly, the troupe and the city was shocked by the unexpected death of twenty-six-year-old Louisa Fontenelle Williamson, the company's popular soubrette and the wife of the senior manager. Charlotte Sully Chambers was engaged to replace her. The troupe was further grieved by the death November 21 of comanager and leading comedian Edward Jones. Placide was thrust into solo management, although Williamson rejoined the company in late December. The sad season ended December 31, 1799, the company having presented sixty-five productions, including six pieces new to Charleston.

On January 1, 1800, a period of mourning for the recently deceased George Washington closed theatres and depressed business everywhere in the United States. A memorial was celebrated at the City Theatre January 18. Shortly thereafter, a winter season got slowly underway, never rising to any considerable height. It closed May 8 with a benefit for the children of Edward Jones. Some of the company spent the summer at a resort on Sullivan's Island, where they performed for vacationers. Others worked for Placide at his Vaux-Hall Gardens resort in Charleston. Placide never renewed his lease on the City Theatre, electing instead to occupy the more splendid Charleston Theatre, where his company flourished when they were not engaged for brief seasons in the theatres of Savannah and Richmond.

The Charleston Theatre was built in 1792–93 by James Hoban and Thomas Wade West at the corner of Broad and Middleton (now New Street) streets, on Savage's Green. A sturdy but plain brick structure with an elegant interior, the Charleston was the city's only theatre until 1833, the City Theatre having been converted to a concert hall in 1800.

Placide's company presented no fall season in 1800. Not until January 23, 1801, were they ready to open the Charleston Theatre. Their intitial effort was a production of Susannah Centlivre's comedy *The Wonder, a Woman Keeps a Secret* (1714) and Samuel Birch's musical drama *Adopted Child* (1795).

Placide's company is exhaustively calendared in W. Stanley Hoole's *Ante-Bellum Charleston Theatre* (1946), but the history of the company is only lightly sketched. Placide seems to have been an innovative manager, insofar as he introduced a variety of stunts and novel attractions to keep the Charleston public interested in his theatre. Placide also produced seven plays by native Charlestonians, two by William Ioor (*Independence* and *The Battle of Eutaw Springs*), three by John Blake White (*Foscori, The Mysteries of the Castle*, and *Modern Honor*), one by Isaac Harby (*The Guardian Knot*), and one by James Workman (*Liberty in Louisiana*). He kept his company fully employed by using members of the troupe as entertainers at his Vaux-Hall Gardens, a fashionable summer resort in Charleston, and by organizing tours to Savannah, Richmond, and Petersburg. The repertoire of the Placide Company was no more or less distinguished than that of any American theatre of the time. For most of the period 1800–1813, Placide's troupe performed three of four nights each week, presenting a main piece (comedy or melodrama) and one or two afterpieces (short farces, burlettas, and pantomimes). As was usual for the time, he depended heavily on a varied bill of fare each evening, and a new bill each time the theatre opened. He also depended on a competent ensemble of players cast in strict lines of business, an inventive "scenist," and a small but tuneful orchestra. Performers in Placide's company might specialize in the dramatic roles he or she played (leading man or woman, soubrette, juvenile, comedian, and so on), but most offered the manager a variety of performance skills to be used in *entr'acte* presentations or wherever the manager designated. Actors and actresses were at least modestly skilled dancers (ballet and folk), singers (opera and popular), jugglers, tightrope and slackrope dancers, or swordsmen. Matthew Sully, one of Placide's most popular performers, acted a gymnastic Harlequin to Placide's clown in frequently produced pantomimes and filled other comedic roles.

The special achievement of the Placide company (really the personal achievement of Mr. and Mrs. Placide) was the introduction to theatre of five Placide children. Elizabeth (Eliza, later Mrs. Sheridan Mann, 1814–69) debuted in 1802 and continued to perform in Charleston until 1822. Jane (1804–35) left Charleston in 1813 and was, for ten years, the leading lady of the New Orleans stage. Henry Placide (1799–1870), destined to become one of the finest low comedians on the nineteenth-century American stage, debuted as a dancer and actor in 1809; Caroline (1798–1881) debuted in 1807 and, as Mrs. Leigh Waring and Mrs. William Rufus Blake, was a leading lady of stock companies on the Eastern Seaboard for the next forty years. Thomas (1808–77) was too young to perform when the company folded in 1813 but became a low comedian of national reknown.

Placide made little use of visiting stars, although Thomas Abthorpe Cooper (1776–1849) impressed and thrilled Charlestonians when he introduced the star system in Charleston in April 14, 1806. Cooper visited Charleston again in 1807, 1809, and 1810 during Placide's reign and regularly until about 1830.

Sometime between June and September 1812, shortly after the United States declared war on Great Britain, Alexander Placide died. His widow tried to carry on despite social and economic chaos brought by war and competition from two nondramatic theatres in Charleston. A company, reduced in size, struggled from December 7, 1812, to January 18, 1813, and then closed the theatre and disbanded.

PERSONNEL

Management: John Sollee, proprietor, 1794–98; Alexander Placide, manager, 1794; Hayden Edgar, manager, 1794–95; Edward Jones, manager, 1795–98; Mr. Mayberry, box-office keeper, 1797–1801; John Brown Williamson, Alexander Placide, Edward Jones, lessees and manager, 1798–1800; Alexander Placide, lessee and manager, 1800–1812; Charlotte Wrighten Placide, lessee and manager, 1812–13.

Acting Managers: John Hodgkinson, 1803–5; Mr. Villiers, 1802–3; William Bates, 1805–7; J. William Green, 1808–10; William Twaits, 1810–12.

Scene painters: M. Audin, 1795–98; Mr. Jones, 1800–1803; J. West, 1803–5, 1806–9, 1811–12; Mr. Holmes, 1806–7, 1808–9, 1811–12.

Orchestra leader: Mr. Graupner, 1795–96, Mr. Leumont, 1804–5, 1806–8, 1810–12; J. Eckhardt, 1805–6; Mr. Remoussin, 1808–10.

Actors and Actresses: James Anderson; Miss Arnold; Mr. and Mrs. Ashton; Mr. Bachelier; *C. G. Bailey*, boxkeeper and actor (1804–9); Master George Barrett; *Mrs. and Mrs. Giles L. Barrett* (1800–1802, 1804–5, 1807–8); Mr. Barrymore; Mr. Bartlett; Mr. Barton; John Beete; John Bernard; Mr. Berry; Mr. Boree, dancer; Mr. Branthwaite; Mr. and Mrs. J. Bray; Mrs. Brett; Miss Broadhurst; Mr. Burd; *Thomas Burke* (1802–3, 1811–13); *Mr. Caulfield* (1809–13); *James Chalmers* (1796, 1799–1801, 1802–3); Charlotte Sully Chambers; *Mr. Charnock* (1802–5); Miss Chaucer; Mr. Church; *Mr. Clarke* (1805–13); *Mrs. Clarke* (1806–13); Caroline Clarke; J. W. Clarke; *Mr. and Mrs. John Claude* (1805–7, 1808–9); *Mr. and Mrs. Cleveland* (1797–98); Mr. Clifford; Mr. Clough; Mr. and Mrs. Collins; Mlle. Cortes; Signor Cortez; Mr. Cromwell; Mr. and Mrs. John Darley, Jr.; Mr. and Mrs. John Darley, Sr.; M. Dainville; Mr. Davis; Mr. Dickinson; James Dickson; Mr. and Mrs. Douglas; M. and Mme. Douvillier; Miss Downie; Mr. and Mrs. Downie; Master Duport; J. Durang; Mlle. Duthe; *Mr. and Mrs. Dykes* (1802–6); *Mr. and Mrs. Hayden Edgar* (1794–95); Mr. Falkland; Mr. Fawcett; Mr. Field; Mr. Foster; M. Founiaud; Mr. Fournier; Mr. Fox; Mr. Frances; M. Francisqui; Mr. Garelli; Mr. Gray; Master Green; Miss Green; Mr. and Mrs. J. William Green; Miss Hamilton; Mr. Hamilton; Mr. Hanna; Mr. Hardinge; Mr. and Mrs. Harper; Mr. and Mrs. Hatton; Mr. Hayman; Mr. Heeley; Mr. and Mrs. Heelyer; Mr. Helmbold; Mr. and Mrs. Henderson; *Charles Hipworth* (1795–96); *Mrs. John Hodgkinson* (1803–5); *Mrs. John Hogg* (1803–5); Mr. Holland; Mr. Huntingdon; Mr. Jackson; Mr. Jacobs; *Edward Jones* (1795–99); *Mrs. Edward Jones* (1795–1801); Mr. and Mrs. J. Jones; *William Jones* (1805–6, 1807–8, 1809–11); Mr. and Mrs. King; Mr. Knox; J. K. Labotierre; M. Latte; Mr. Lavalette; Mrs. Lawrence; M. and Mme. Lege; Master C. Lege; Mr. Lewis; Mr. Lindsey; Mrs. Lipman; Mr. Lotti; Mr. MacDonald; Mr. and Mrs. Marriott; *George Marshall* (1800–1804); *Mrs. George Marshall* (1800–1805, 1806–7); Mr. McClough; Mr. McKenzie; Miss Miller; Mr. and Mrs. Miller; Mr. Morden; Mr. Mork; Mr. Morse; Movray; Mr. Nelson; Mr. Nugent; Mrs. Oldmixon; Mr. Patterson; Mr. and Mrs. Perkins; *Alexander Placide* (1794, 1796–1812); *Caroline Placide* (1807–10); *Charlotte Wrighten Placide* (1795–1813); *Eliza Placide* (1802–7, 1808–9, 1810–12); *Henry Placide* (1809–13); *Jane Placide* (1808–13); Mr. and Mrs. David Poe; *Mary Ann Pownall* (1795–96); Mr. and Mrs. Prigmore; Mr. and Mrs. Radcliffe; Mr. Rice; Mr. Ricketts; *Mr. Ringwood* (1806–10); Hopkins Robertson; Mrs. Robinson; Mr. and Mrs. Rowson; Mr. Rutherford; Mr. and Mrs. Rutley; Mr. Ryder; Mr. Santford; Mr. and Mrs. Seymour; Mr. Sierson; Mrs. Simpson; Miss Solomon; Mr. Solomon; Mr. and Mrs. Spear; M. and Mme. Spinacuta; Miss Stephens; Mr. Stephens; Mr. and Mrs. Story; Mrs. Stowell; Mrs. Stuart; Chester Sully; *Elizabeth Sully* (1799–1800, 1804–10); *Matthew Sully, Jr.* (1794, 1808–10); *Matthew Sully, Sr.* (1794, 1803–11); *Sara Sully* (1804–5, 1806–10); Thomas Sully; Mr. Swain; Mr. Taylor; *Miss Thomas*, later *Mrs. Thomas Burke* (1807–8, 1810–13); William H. Torrans; Mr. Tubbs; *Mrs. Tubbs* (1797–98); *John Turnbull* (1800–1807, 1812–13); *Mrs. John Turnbull* (1800–1808); *Mrs. and Mrs. Utt* (1807–13); M. and Mme. Val; M. Vandeville; Mr. Verguin; *Mr. Villiers* (1801–3); Mr. Watts; Mr. Webster; Mr. and Mrs. James West; H. Western; *Elizabeth Westray*, later *Mrs. Villiers* (1802–5); *Charles Whitlock* (1796–98, 1803–6); *Elizabeth Kemble Whitlock* (1796–98, 1803–6); *John Brown Williamson* (1797–1802); *Louisa Fontenelle Williamson* (1797–99); Mr. Wilmot; Mr. Wilson; Mrs. Winson; Mr. Woodham; Mrs. Woodville; Mary Wrighten; *Mr. and Mrs. Charles Young* (1806–9, 1810–12); Julia Sully Zolbins.

REPERTORY

Figures in parentheses indicate number of presentations this season.

1794 (April to August): *Pygmalion* (Rousseau) (2); *The Three Philosophers* (2); *One Does as One Can; The Bird Catchers* (2); *Harlequin Robbed* (3); *Robinson Crusoe* (3); *The Counsellor-at-Law; The Rose and the Bud* (3); *Amorous Disguises* (2); *Useless Resolution; Harlequin Doctor* (2); *Le père Duchèsne* (3); *Harlequin Supposed Nobleman* (2); *The Reasonable Fool* (2); *The Milliner* (4); *The Plebian Raised to Fortune; The Old Soldier* (4); *Le Baron Trenck* (2); *Les deux billets; La jeune indienne* (3); *The Two Wood Cutters* (2); *The Two Hunters and the Milk Maid* (4); *Parisian Gone into the Country; Harlequin Balloonist* (4); *The Waters of Oblivion; La belle Dorothée* (3); *Beverly; Aesop at the Faire; Boniface Pointu; Mizra and Lindor* (3); *The Way of the World; The Barber of Seville; The Deserter* (3); *The Two Game Keepers; The Speaking Picture* (2); *The Dog Magician* (2); *The Pessimist; The Grand Italian Shades* (2); *Orpheus and Euridice* (2); *Eugenia; The Besieged Castle; Jeanette; The Attack on Fort Moultrie* (4); *Annette and Lubin* (2); *The Seeker after Sense; The Fusilier; The Village Soothsayer; Nina* (2); *Blaise and Babet* (2); *Linco's Travels* (2); *Harlequin Statue; American Independence; Zémire and Azore; The Lamenting Statue; Genevieve of Brabant; The Dressing Room.*

1794–95 (December to February): *Tancred and Sigismunda* (3); *The Sultan; The Disbanded Officer* (3); *The Citizen; Douglas* (3); *The Earl of Essex* (2); *St. Patrick's Day* (3); *All in Good Humour* (3); *The Miller of Mansfield* (3); *The Farm House* (3); *The Sultana; Jane Shore; The Old Maid* (2); *Zara; Polly Honey Comb; Provok'd Husband; The Romp* (2); *The Deuce Is in Him* (3); *The Country Girl* (2); *All the World's a Stage* (2); *She Stoops to Conquer* (2); *The Virgin Unmasked; The Fair Penitent; Thomas and Sally; The Contrast; Louis XVI* (2); *George Barnwell; The Highland Reel, Harlequin Balloonist; Tristram Shandy; Oroonoka; Lyar.*

1795–96 (November to July): *Every One Has His Fault* (3); *Double Disguise* (2); *The Dramatist* (3); *The Poor Soldier* (4); *Such Things Are; The Romp* (3); *The Jealous Wife; Barnaby Brittle* (2); *Love in a Village* (2); *Miss in Her Teens* (2); *The Jew* (3); *She Stoops to Conquer* (2); *The Highland Reel; Bon Ton; The Citizen;*

Love in a Village; Modern Antiques (2); *Castle of Andalusia* (3); *The Lying Valet* (2); *The School for Scandal* (2); *The Farmer* (3); *Heighho for a Husband* (2); *The Midnight Hour; The Child of Nature; Catherine and Petruchio* (3); *The Belle's Stratagem; Robin Hood* (5); *All the World's a Stage; George Barnwell; The True-born Irishman* (3); *The West Indian* (4); *The Purse* (3); *The Suspicious Husband* (2); *The Quaker* (4); *Beaux Stratagem; Bold Stroke for a Wife; Irish Fine Lady; Miller of Mansfield; Village Lawyer; Lyar* (3); *Hamlet* (3); *No Song, No Supper* (3); *The Rage; Douglas; The Provok'd Husband; The Devil to Pay; The Gamester; Peeping Tom of Coventry* (2); *The Virgin Unmasked; The Busybody; The Merchant of Venice; Romeo and Juliet; Agreeable Surprise* (2); *Mountaineers* (4); *The Young Quaker; Rosina* (2); *Richard III* (3); *The Fair Penitent* (2); *Love à la Mode* (4); *Notoriety* (2); *The Irishman in London; The Orphan; The Deuce Is in Him; High Life below Stairs; Macbeth; Children in the Wood* (3); *Duenna* (2); *The Natural Son; The Grand Masque of Comus; The Road to Ruin; Laterna Magica* (2); *Two Strings to Your Bow; A Bold Stroke for a Husband; The Standard of Liberty; The Recruiting Officer; The Irish Taylor; The Critic* (2); *The Apprentice; Midas* (2); *Apotheosis of Franklin* (2); *The Son-in-Law; Chrononhotonthologos; Chapter of Accidents; Doctor and Apothecary* (2); *Fontaineville Forest; The Manager in Distress* (2); *My Grandmother; The Gentle Shepard; Scotch Pastoral; Inkle and Yarico.* In addition, Mary Julia Curtis reported a performance of *The Mayor of Garratt.*

1797 (January to July): See Eola Willis for a complete calendar. New plays added to the repertory: *The First Floor; The Carmelite; Don Juan; All in the Wrong; Alcesta; or, The Force of Love and Friendship; Lock and Key; Cleone; The Deserted Daughter; Belles Have at Ye All; The Sicilian Romance; Rule a Wife and Have a Wife; Fortune's Fool; Almeyda; Tom Thumb; or, the Downfall of Giants; The Princess of Galatea.*

1797–98 (October to May, plays new to Charleston): *New Hay at the Old Market; The Battle of Bunker Hill; The Will; The Town before You; The Spanish Barber; Next Door Neighbours; How to Grow Rich; Americania and Eleutheria; Speculation; The Prisoner; First Love; La bonne fille; The Welsh Heiress; The Sculptor; The Female Duellist; Better Late Than Never; Telemachus; L'Américain; ou, L'Homme raisonable.*

1799 (January to April, plays new to Charleston): *Cheap Living; Battle of Hexham; Secrets Worth Knowing; The Birthday of General G. Washington; The Pilgrim; The Stranger; He's Much to Blame.*

1799–1800 (October to May, plays new to Charleston): *Lovers' Vows; The Generous Cottager; King Henry IV; Harlequin Skeleton; The Jew and the Doctor; The Wonder; The Heir-at-Law; Pizarro; Laugh When You Can; Columbus; or, America Discovered; The Count of Narbonne; The Lypthora; Virgin of the Sun; School for Citizens; False Shame; Rinaldo and Armida; Preservation; Man and Wife; The Man of Fortitude.*

1801 (January to May, plays new to Charleston): *Speed the Plough; Bluebeard; Surrender of Calais; Know Your Own Mind.*

1801–2 (November in Charleston, December and January in Savannah, January 20 to May 17 in Charleston; plays new to Charleston): *Poor Gentleman; Happy Family; Honest Thieves; Sighs; Point of Honour; Life.*

1802–3 (November 5 to December 24 in Charleston, January in Savannah, January 31 to May 10 in Charleston; plays new to Charleston): *Carmelite, Adelmorn, Countess of Salisbury, Il Bondocane.*

1803–4 (November 9 to December 22 in Charleston, January in Savannah, January 31 to June 12 in Charleston; plays new to Charleston): *Gustavus Vasa; Robbers; Undescribable Something; Voice of Nature; Ladies' Race; Much Ado about Nothing; Marriage Promise; Rivers; Hampton Court Frolics; Touchstone of Truth; Liberty in Louisiana; Maid of Bristol; Charlotte and Werther; Charlotte Corday; Which Is the Man?; New Way to Win Hearts.*

1804–5 (November 12 to December 28 in Charleston, January in Savannah, February 7 to May 31 in Charleston; plays new to Charleston): *Alfonso of Castile; Review; Fraternal Discord; Wheel of Fortune; Guilty or Not Guilty; Sailor's Daughter; Independence; Glory of Columbia; Tale of Terror; Comet; Inconstant; Paul and Virginia; Hearts of Oak; Management; Family Picture.*

1805–6 (November 13 to May 27 in Charleston, plays new to Charleston): *Wife of Two Husbands; Who Wants a Guinea?; Blind Bargain; Sprigs of Laurel; Honey Moon; Gil Blas; Foscari; School of Reform; Secret; Flora; What Is She? Valentine and Orson; Castle of Sorrento; Barbarossa.*

1806–7 (November 10 to June 5, plays new to Charleston): *Weathercock; Finger Post; Mysteries of the Castle; Hunter of the Alps; Battle of Eutaw Springs and the Evacuation of Charleston; House to be Sold; Cinderella; Clemence and Waldemar; Sylvester Daggerwood; Iron Chest; Lodoiska; King Charles I; Coriolanus.*

1807–8 (November 11 to May 28, plays new to Charleston): *Adrian and Orrila; Town and Country; Too Many Cooks; Curfew; Tekeli; Brazen Mask; Prior Claim; Travellers; Arbitration; Fashionable Lover; Zorinski.*

1808–9 (November 11 to April 11, plays new to Charleston): *Time's a Tell-Tale; World; Fortress; Adelgitha; Ella Rosenberg; Wood Demon; Invisible Girl.*

1809–10 (No fall season; February 6 to May 16, plays new to Charleston): *Man and Wife; Begone Dull Care; Gordian Knot; Catch Him Who Can.*

1810–11 (No fall season; January 7 to May 20, plays new to Charleston): *Doubtful Son; Yes or No; The Winter's Tale; Hit or Miss; Poor Lodger.*

1811–12 (No fall season; January 31 to May 15; then the company moved to Augusta, Georgia; plays new to Charleston): *Lady of the Lake; Modern Honor; Ourselves; Blind Boy; Exile; Kiss.*

1812–13 (December 7 to January 18, plays new to Charleston): None.

BIBLIOGRAPHY

Mary Julia Curtis. "The Early Charleston Stage: 1703–1798." Ph.D. diss., Indiana University, 1968.

———. "John Sollee and the Charleston Theatre." *Educational Theatre Journal* 21 (October 1969): 285–98.

W. Stanley Hoole. *The Ante-Bellum Charleston Theatre.* University: University of Alabama Press, 1946.

Charles S. Watson. *Antebellum Charleston Dramatists.* University: University of Alabama Press, 1976.

Eola Willis. *The Charleston Stage in the XVIII Century*. Columbia, S.C.: The State
    Company, 1924.

Weldon B. Durham

CLEVELAND ACADEMY OF MUSIC. See ACADEMY OF MUSIC
COMPANY.

CLEVELAND THEATRE. See ACADEMY OF MUSIC COMPANY.

COATES OPERA HOUSE STOCK COMPANY. The Coates Opera House
Stock Company, Kansas City, Missouri's first resident organization, opened
at the new Coates Opera House in Edward Bulwer-Lytton's *Money* on
October 8, 1870. The company and the theatre were the property of Colonel
Kersey Coates, one of Kansas City's foremost citizens. The theatre and
the Coates House, Kansas City's newest and finest hotel, stood practically
alone on Coates Hill near what is presently the corner of Tenth Street and
Broadway. Sketches always included a few cows grazing near the dirt paths
and roads approaching the buildings. Coates built the theatre, which was
all brick and two stories high, at a cost of $105,000. The Opera House
occupied the second floor over Day's Grocery and Feed Store. Modeled
after the Detroit Opera House, the edifice featured a grand Mansard roof
with heavy iron cornices and niches for dramatic statuary. It faced east
with an imposing view of the bustling river town (population, 32,260 in
1870). The auditorium accommodated 2,000 in dress circle, parquet, balcony,
and family circle. The proscenium stage, thirty-six feet wide and seventy-
two feet deep, was equipped with gaslight and machinery for lowering drop
curtains and shifting scenery.

    The group's first manager was Charles Pope. He also played leading
roles. The acting company, numbering twenty-four, including Pope, featured
performers with experience in several of the best stock companies of the
day. The leading lady was Alice Grey, well known at the time in New
Orleans. Frank Murdoch of the Boston Museum Company* played second
leads. Patrons in large numbers paid $10 for private boxes and $2 for
admission to orchestra seats. Although local accounts indicate the first
season was an artistic success, the owner's daughter Laura Coates Reed
recalled that the venture was a financial failure, with Colonel Coates paying
the deficit.

    Charles Pope resigned in May 1871 to join Benjamin DeBar's company
in St. Louis. He was succeeded by John A. Stevens, who installed a much
smaller stock company for the 1871–72 season. Its chief members were
Florence Noble, Thomas E. Jackson, Charles Thornton, Annie Jamison,
and H. A. Hales. Steven's first company was much less active than had
been the first Coates Opera House group. His second company, installed
for the 1872–73 season, was the artistic equivalent of the first organization.

It featured Augustus Pitou and Florence Noble, but Mark Price, later leading man of the Boston Theatre Stock Company* and George Holland, a prominent comedian in the stock organizations of Philadelphia in the 1880s and 1890s, also added to the effectiveness of the company.

All three organizations shared the stage of the Coates Opera House with a parade of stars, some well known. In 1870–71 Kansas Citians saw Annie Ward Tiffany, Methua Scheller, Leona Cavender, Lawrence Barrett, Robert McWade, Lucille Western, Fanny Janauschek, Joseph K. Emmett, and Edwin Adams. In 1871–72 Annie Wait and W. H. Leake appeared, as did Stuart Robson, Janauschek, McWade, Joe Emmett, and Lucille Western (with James A. Herne) returned to the Kansas City stage, which also saw F. S. Chanfrau, Edwin Forrest, and Lotta Crabtree. Steven's new company depended heavily upon stars such as Joe Murphy, Edwin Adams, Lillie Eldridge, Johnny Allen, Maggie Mitchell, McWade, and Chanfrau.

Throughout the three years of stock operations at the Coates Opera House, Kansas City drifted toward financial disaster, a trend that dampened the hopes for financial success in the theatre venture. In 1873 the local economy, as well as the national, broke down, with the result that the city could no longer support a resident organization.

PERSONNEL

Builder and Proprietor: Colonel Kersey Coates.
Managers: Charles Pope (1870–71), John A. Stevens (1871–73).
Treasurer: Charles E. Locke (1870–73).
Business Manager: W. W. Austin (1870–73).
Actors and Actresses: 1870–71: H. C. Andrews; G. M. Ciprico; Miss F. Edstrom; Susie Edwin; W. H. Everett; George Gaston; Alice Grey; Mr. Lloyd; Annie Maston, or Moston; Ella Moyer; Frank Murdoch; Mrs. Agnes Naylor; W. Naylor; Mr. Pierce; Charles Pope; Lena Prentice; Emma Price; Mr. Robey; W. D. Shields; Mr. Slate; Mr. and Mrs. C. H. Thompson; Mr. Wallace; Jennie Workman. 1871–72: H. A. Hales; Thomas E. Jackson; Annie Jamison; Florence Noble; John A. Stevens; Charles Thornton. 1872–73: Marion Clifton; George R. Dixon; Minnie Oscar Gray; H. A. Hales; W. Harwood; George Holland; Annie Jamison; James Johnson; Florence Noble; Augustus Pitou; Mark Price; Gussie Raymond; Edward Smith; John A. Stevens; Annie Ward.

REPERTORY

Figures in parentheses indicate the number of performances this season.
1870–71: *Money* (2); *Lady of Lyons* (2); *East Lynne; Ingomar; The Hunchback; The Stranger; Richard III; London Assurance* (2); *Belphegor; The Mountebank; The Serious Family; Man and Wife; Faint Heart ne'er Won Fair Lady; Hidden Hand.* In support of Annie Ward Tiffany: *Little Treasure; Katty O'Sheil* (2); *Jessie Brown; Arrah-na-Pogue* (2); *Hidden Hand* (2); *Unequal Match* (2); *Sketches in India* (2); *Ireland as It Was; Rough Diamond.* Stock: *The Long Strike; A Kiss in the Dark.* In support of Annie Ward Tiffany: *Lucrezia Borgia; Toodles; Macbeth.* In support of Methua Scheller: *Romeo and Juliet; Pearl of Savoy; Morning Call;*

Child of the Regiment; The Colleen Bawn (2); *The Robbers; Under the Gaslight; Cinderella.* In support of Leona Cavender: *Minnie's Luck; Kate Kearney* (2); *Little Treasure; Cinderella* (3); *Nan: The Good-for-Nothing* (2); Stock with Charles Pope and Alice Grey in: *Under the Gaslight.* In support of Lawrence Barrett: *Hamlet; Richelieu; Othello; The Serious Family; Richard III; The Marble Heart; The Duke's Motto; Rosedale.* Stock: *London Assurance; Damon and Pythias; A Morning Call; Rough Diamond; The Love Chase; Madeline.* In support of Zavistowski Sisters: *Ixion* (2); *The Wandering Minstrel; The Morning Call; Pocahontas* (2); *Ticket-of-Leave Man; Little Rebel; Water Witches; Found on the Door-Step.* Stock: *Don Giovanni* (2); *Little Rebel; Rough Diamond; Naval Engagements; Camille; Don Caesar de Bazan; That Blessed Lady; Foul Play; Much Ado about Nothing.* In support of Annie Tiffany: *Fanchon, the Cricket* (2); *Camilla's Husband; Ireland as It Was; Married Life; The Irish Immigrant; Honey Moon; Jessie Brown.* In support of Robert McWade: *Rip Van Winkle* (3); *Handy Andy; Richard III in Dutch* (4); *Rory O'More* (2); *All that Glitters Is Not Gold.* Coates Company to Wyandotte, Kansas, January 19–20, 1871. Stock: *Ruy Blas; Maid of Munster.* In support of Robert McWade: *Flowers of the Forest; Dick Turpin; Toodles; Paddy Miles; The Lilac Blossom; Rip Van Winkle* (2); *Richard III in Dutch.* In support of Oliver D. Byron: *Across the Continent.* In support of Lucille Western and James A. Herne: *East Lynne* (2); *Leah the Forsaken* (2); *Oliver Twist; Much Ado about Nothing; Handy Andy; Rag Pickers of Paris.* Stock in *Foul Play; Green Bushes; Loan of a Lover; Streets of New York; Rob Roy.* In support of Fanny Janauschek: *Mary Stuart* (2); *Deborah; Fazio; The Winter's Tale; Macbeth.* In support of Madame Scheller: *Pauvrette; Life of an Actress; Child of the Regiment; Mazeppa* (3); *La sonnambula; Solon Shingle* (2); *Roll of Drums; Conjugal Lesson; His Last Legs.* In support of Lucy Rushton: *Red Hands* (2); *The School for Scandal; Sea of Ice* (2) *As You Like It.* In support of Mrs. F. W. Lander: *Elizabeth; Adrienne, the Actress; Mary Stuart; Macbeth.* Stock: *The Robbers.* In support of Joseph K. Emmett: *Fritz: Our German Cousin.* In support of Rose Evans: *Romeo and Juliet; Ingomar; Lady Audley's Secret* (2); *Hamlet; Female Spy; A Happy Pair; The Lady of Lyons.* In support of Edwin Adams: *Wild Oats; Enoch Arden* (2); *Hamlet; Dead Heat.* Company disbanded c. April 23, 1871.

1871–72 (Beginning September 23, 1871): *Uncle Tom's Cabin.* In support of Annie Waite: *Under the Willows; The Three Guardsmen* (2); *Branded.* In support of Stuart Robson: *Married Life;* scenes from *Jone's Baby; Benecia Boy; Camille; Skeleton Captain; Very Odd.* Stock displaced until November 18. In support of Birdie Van Dusen: *Uncle Tom's Cabin.* In support of Robert McWade: *Rip Van Winkle* (2); *Richard III in Dutch; Paddy Miles.* Stock displaced until December 13. In support of F. S. Chanfrau: *Sam* (3); *Ticket-of-Leave Man; Stage Struck Barber;* scenes from *Glances of New York; Toodles; Jumbo Jim.* Stock displaced until December 26. In support of Edwin Forrest: *Richelieu; Othello; King Lear; Jack Cade; Hamlet.* January 6, 1872, in support of Mrs. F. S. Chanfrau: *Dora.* From January 17, in support of Joe Murphy: *Help; Handy Andy; Colored Help.* Stock: *Octoroon.* Displaced until January 29; then in *Damon and Pythias.* In support of Joseph K. Emmett: *Fritz: Our German Cousin; Carl the Musician.* In support of Ettie Henderson: *Far West.* Displaced to February 26, when in support of Lucille Western: *Leah the Forsaken; The Mendicant* (2); *East Lynne; The Child Stealer; Oliver Twist.* In support of T. G. Riggs: *Shin Fane.* Displaced until March

18; then in support of Lotta Crabtree: *Little Detective* (2); *Old Curiosity Shop; Heartsease; Captain Charlotte; Family Jars.* In support of James W. Wallach; *The Man in the Iron Mask; Still Waters Run Deep; King of the Commons; Henry Dunbar.* Company disbanded after April 6, 1872.

1872–73 (Opening September 26, 1872): Steven's new company in support of Joe Murphy: *Help; Maum Cre* (2); *More Blunders Than One* (2); *Handy Andy* (2); *Murphy Changes.* In support of Edwin Adams: *Wild Oats; Enoch Arden; Hamlet.* Stock: *Marble Heart.* In support of Lillie Eldridge: *Mignon; Alma; Cricket on the Hearth; Elfie.* Displaced until November 4; then in support of Johnny Allen: *Schneider; Rip Van Winkle.* From November 18, stock: *The Long Strike; The School for Scandal; Enoch Arden* (2); *The Merchant of Venice; Richelieu; Damon and Pythias.* In support of Joe Murphy: *Colleen Bawn; Ireland and America; Barney, the Baron.* Displaced until December 16; then in support of Maggie Mitchell: *Fanchon, the Cricket; Jane Eyre* (2); *Little Barefoot; Pearl of Savoy.* In support of Robert McWade: *Rip Van Winkle; Richard III in Dutch.* Displaced until January 23, 1873; then in support of Little Nell: *Fidelia, the Waif* (2); *Hidden Hand.* In support of Dominic Murray: *Escaped from Sing Sing; Gambler's Crime.* In support of Miss Leo Hudson and her mare, Black Bess: *Mazeppa; Dick Turpin's Ride to New York.* In support of F. S. Chanfrau: *Kit: The Arkansas Traveller; Sam; Toodles; Spectre Bridegroom; Stage Struck Barber.* Off until March 19; then in support of Mrs. D. P. Bowers: *Lady Audley's Secret; Elizabeth: Queen of England; Mary Stuart; Macbeth.* Company disbanded after March 22, 1873.

BIBLIOGRAPHY

Unpublished Sources: Louis Jean Rietz, "History of the Theatre of Kansas City, Missouri from the Beginnings Until 1900," 3 vols. (Ph.D. diss., State University of Iowa, 1939).

Weldon B. Durham

THE COMPANY. See ILLINOIS THEATRICAL COMPANY.

COMPANY OF COMEDIANS FROM ENGLAND. See AMERICAN COMPANY (1752–92).

COMPANY OF COMEDIANS FROM LONDON. See AMERICAN COMPANY (1752–92).

COMPANY OF THE NEW THEATRE IN CHESTNUT STREET. See CHESTNUT STREET THEATRE COMPANY.

D

DALY STOCK COMPANY. Augustin Daly organized his stock company in 1869. Renting the Fifth Avenue Theatre (which was actually located on Twenty-fourth Street near Broadway) in New York City from James Fisk, Jr., for $25,000 a year, Augustin Daly opened August 16, 1869, with his version of T. W. Robertson's *Play*.

During the nineteenth century, Daly's work as a manager, director, and playwright contributed to the emergence of the *regisseur*, and as a result, he helped establish the director as a major component in the theatre. His abandonment of "lines of business" (a then-dominant method of casting) in favor of an ensemble company with no "stars"; his demand for natural acting (or as one critic phrased it, "acting with the act left out"); and his insistence on historically accurate sets, costumes, and properties marked the Daly Stock Company as the most progressive in America and one of the finest ensemble companies in the world.

Born on July 20, 1838, in Plymouth, North Carolina, Augustin Daly's first venture into the theatre began in 1856, when he hired the old Brooklyn Museum. Presenting the Melville Troupe of Juvenile Comedians in *Poor Pillicoddy, Toodles,* and the second act of *Macbeth*, Daly's yield for the one evening's performance was $11.25, whereas his expenses were $76.00. That same year Daly tried his hand at playwriting; in fact from 1856 to 1862, he wrote four plays that all proved unsuccessful. In 1862, however, the Batemans accepted his play, *Leah the Forsaken*, which provided him with his first dramatic success as well as his first managerial experience in that he managed the production's tour and its publicity.

With *Leah*'s success, Daly divided his time between playwriting and writing the drama reviews for five New York newspapers. At the end of 1867, he resigned from all of the newspapers except the *New York Times*. In addition to developing his writing and managerial skills, Daly gained more exposure by directing his plays *Griffith Gaunt* (1866) and *Under the Gaslight* (1867). Thus when the opportunity presented itself, Daly, believing that he had the necessary experience, opened his first theatre and with it formed the Daly Stock Company. With this opening Daly became one of the first nonactors to manage a successful stock company in America, and thus his management marks departure from the actor-management tradition in American stock companies.

Daly's first season lasted until July 9, 1870. During that period, the Daly Stock Company performed twenty-five plays: three were adaptations from the French, three were by Shakespeare, and five were Restoration comedies. Salaries ranged from $30 to $200 paid to E. L. Davenport. From the beginning, Daly established the guidelines that his company would follow until its demise in 1899: no lines of business, a frequent change of bill, touring, only those directly connected with the production allowed backstage, lengthy rehearsals, no stars (although he broke with this concept in 1870, when he starred Mr. and Mrs. Charles Mathews, and in 1894–95, when he starred Ada Rehan), absolute control over every item of production, every member to obey all rules under penalty of payment, emphasis on motivated stage movement, hiring and training of inexperienced actors, emphasis on comedy, and lavish care to realistic visual detail.

In 1872 Daly extended his managerial duties to include the Grand Opera House (New York), where he remained until 1874. A fire on January 1, 1873, burned his Fifth Avenue Theatre, forcing the company to temporary quarters at the New York Theatre, 728 Broadway, an address celebrated in the play *Seven-Twenty-Eight*. Refurbishing this theatre in three weeks, Daly renamed it Daly's Fifth Avenue Theatre and opened January 21 with his play *Alixe*. The season ended in June, whereupon the company toured to keep financially solvent.

That summer (1873) Daly's Fifth Avenue Theatre reopened as Daly's Broadway Theatre. Daly was now responsible for three theatres and three companies: the Grand Opera House, Daly's Broadway Theatre, and the New Fifth Avenue Theatre under construction in which the Daly Stock Company would be housed.

The New Fifth Avenue Theatre opened on December 3, 1873. Located on Twenty-eighth Street near Broadway, this new structure could seat 1,500 but could accommodate 2,000, which was an improvement over the first Fifth Avenue Theatre, which seated 900 but could hold 1,500. In an effort to place the new theatre on a sound financial basis, Daly based the company's repertory upon Restoration comedies, his modifications of Shakespeare, and his adaptations of novels and European dramas. Inasmuch as Daly could not read French, German, or Spanish, he would have a literal translation made and then adapt the parts to the company's members. In thirty-five years Daly's Stock Company performed sixty-five French plays— forty-four of which Daly adapted at least in part: thirty-five to forty German farces, and one Spanish play (*Yorick*). The company's play list also includes ten of Daly's adaptations of novels and sixteen Restoration comedies. Despite Daly's efforts to maintain his theatrical ship on a firm financial basis, the $30,000 rent plus other debts totaling $15,000 forced him to withdraw from the management of his theatre. Settling his $45,000 bill for $8,300, Daly closed his theatre on September 15, 1877.

Daly's Stock Company remained generally inactive between the years 1877 and 1879. They toured briefly during 1878, but in May Daly sailed for Europe—alone. He returned in the spring of 1879 to present *L'Assommoir* in April and May at the Olympic Theatre. This production marks Ada Rehan's first appearance in a Daly production. She remained with Daly until his death in 1899.

Daly spent large sums to improve and decorate his theatres. Therefore, upon buying the old Broadway Theatre on Broadway and Thirty-ninth Street, Daly made extensive alterations and on September 17, 1879, advertised not only the opening of Daly's Theatre but also that it was the only theatre in New York without doors. In the Daly Stock Company's history, the period that it occupied this theatre (1879–99) proved to be the most important. During this era, the company's reputation as having "no equal outside of Paris" and Daly's fame as a regisseur were established.

The company's policy to tour was not effectuated until 1884. At that time the Daly Stock Company went to Boston, Philadelphia, and Chicago and in July, instituted the first of its many trips to London. The productions were given first at Toole's Theatre and then at the Crystal Theatre, representing the first performances by an American stock company in London. With its success in London, the Daly Company began to tour Europe in the even years and the United States during the odd years. Thus in the summer of 1885 the company toured Philadelphia (two weeks), Boston (two weeks), Brooklyn (one week), Chicago (five weeks), and San Francisco (three weeks) and in the summer of 1886 returned to London to perform at the Strand Theatre. After the London engagement, Daly extended the tour to include Germany (Hamburg: Thalia Theatre; Berlin: Wallner Theatre), Ireland (Dublin: Gaiety Theatre), France (Paris: Théâtre des Vaudeville), Liverpool (Royal Alexandre Theatre), Scotland (Edinburgh: Princess or Lyceum), and Brighton (Theatre Royal). Between May 27 and September 15 the Daly Company gave 105 performances: London (68), Hamburg (5), Berlin (6), Dublin (7), Paris (3), Liverpool (7), Edinburgh (7), and Brighton (2).

In May 1888 the company made its third visit to London, where its *Taming of the Shrew* at the Gaiety Theatre marked the first time an American stock company had presented a Shakespearean comedy in London. Upon the company's return that fall, Daly initiated a new concept in American theatrical management—a series of subscription performances. According to Joseph Daly: "The subscription book was filled six weeks before the first performance" (Daly, 483).

The company's touring policy changed in 1891 with its visit to London and Paris and in the summer of 1892 with its tour to San Francisco. During this visit to London, Ada Rehan laid the cornerstone for Daly's London Theatre, which was built on Cranbourne Street off Leicester Square by George Edwardes for a reported 40,000 pounds. With the opening of Daly's Theatre (London), on June 27, 1893, the Daly Stock Company had two homes. It would make regular summer visits to London for the 1894–95, 1895–96, 1896–97 (made an English provincial tour as well), and 1897–98 seasons. With Augustin Daly's death on June 7, 1899, the company disbanded.

The composition of the Daly company included a business manager, treasurer, musical director, set designer, and at times a costumer. Membership in Daly's company was never set at a particular number—it changed from season to season—but it did possess a core of members whose tenure dated in some instances from the company's founding: Mrs. G. H. Gilbert (thirty years); George Clarke (seventeen years); John Drew (seventeen years); William Beekman (thirteen years); Charles Fisher, or Fischer (sixteen years); Sidney Herbert (eleven years); William J. Gilbert (ten years); James Lewis (twenty-six years); Charles Leclercq (sixteen years); George Parkes (fourteen years); and Ada Rehan (twenty-one years).

The Daly Stock Company was more than just another American stock company. Daly's work as a regisseur and the company's dedication to the ensemble concept made it a pioneer in American theatrical annals and enabled it, of all American companies, to achieve the ideal of ensemble playing established by the Meininger Company, the famous troupe residing at the court of George II, Duke of Saxe-Meiningen.

PERSONNEL

Manager: Augustin Daly (1869–99).

Stage Managers: D. H. Harkins (1869), George Clarke, Herbert Gresham, John Moore, George Devere, Edward Wilks.

Business Managers: Richard Dorney, George Bashford, William Terriss, John Farrington, Joseph H. Tooker.

Musical Directors: Henry Widmer, Harvey Dodworth, Frederick Ecke.

Set Designers: James Roberts, T. E. Ryan, Bruce Smith, Charles Duflocq, Walter Hann, Henry Hoyt, John Reed, Ernest Albert, E. Mollenhauer, Mr. Amalde, Mr. Bunnell, Walter Johnstone.

Treasurers: James W. Morrissey, Aaron Appleton.

Costume: W. Graham Robertson.

Actors and Actresses: Mrs. C. D. Abbott; Mrs. Louise Allen; Elizabeth "Amy" Ames (1869–70); Little Angelica (1881–82); Blanche Astley; Ida Aubrey; Alan Aynsworth; Mr. Ayres; Clement Bainbridge; Helen Bancroft; Maggie Barns; Lawrence Barrett; Olive Barry; *Maurice Barrymore* (1874–77); Miss Barton; E. Bartram; *Mr. Bascomb* (1870–71); Blanche Bates; Charles Bates; W. Bedell; *William Beekman* (1869–85); Digby Bell; E. Hamilton Bell; *Frank Bennett* (1876–80); Kate Best (1889–90); Sadie Bigelow; Fred Bird; Helen Blythe, originally Helen Blye, later Mrs. J. F. Brien; W. H. Bokee; *Frederick Bond* (1884–91); Edwin Booth, visiting star (1875); *Hobart Bosworth* (1889–98); *Lulu Bosworth* (1895–96); Arthur Bouchier; G. Vining Bowers; May Bowers; Sidney Bowkett; *John E. Brand* (1879–81); *Thomas Bridgeland* (1891–96); J. F. Brien; Quincy Briggs; Virginia Brooks; Lena Brophy; *John Brougham* (1875–77); William P. Brown; G. Browne; Ida Bruce; Helen Bryant, daughter of Dan Bryant; *Wilfred Buckland* (1891–93); Jane Burke; *J. H. Burnett* (1870–73); N. S. Burnham; Jean Burnside; Ellen Burg; May Cargill; Mr. Carleton; Blanche Carlisle; Catherine Carlisle; Sybil Carlisle (1894–95); Francis Carlyle; Mr. Carroll; Maud Carter; Mary Cary; William Castle; Ann Caverly; Florence Cecil; Lucie Celeste; Frank Celli; *Sara Chalmers* (1888–90); Mrs. F. S. Chanfrau; *F. Chapman* (1870–77); *Kitty Cheatham* (1888–92); Marion Chester; *Wilfred Clark* (1897–99); Creston Clarke; *George Clarke* (1869–74, 1887–99); Estelle Clayton; *Kate Claxton* (1870–72); Katherine Clinton; Charles Coghlan; E. K. Collier; William Collier; *Stella Congdon* (1873–75, 1879–80); *Florence Conron* (1890–92, 1895); Marie Conron; Lila Convere; Silva Converse; *Hart Conway* (1873–75, 1879–80); Minnie Conway (1873–74); Augustis Cook; Rosa Cook; Evelina Cooke; Anna Cowell; *Sydney Cowell* (1875–77); Alethe Craig; Charles Craig; *John Craig* (1891–97); Edith Crane; Alice Crawford; *Henry Crisp* (1871–73, 1876–77); T. J. Cronin; Henrietta Crosman (1877, 1889); Regina Dace; Caroline Dagmar; Belle d'Arcy; Lillian Darley; Lloyd Daubigny; *E. L. Davenport* (1869–71, 1875–77); *Fanny Davenport* (1869–77); Lily Davenport; *William Davidge* (1869–79); Mr. de la Manning; Emily Denin; L. J. Deveau; Eddie Devere; *G. F. Devere* (1869–75); Chester Devonne; *Linda Dietz* (1870–73); Helen Dingeon; Henry Dixey; John Dixon; Arthur Donaldson; Miss Donaldson; J. J. Douglass; Louise Draper; *Virginia Dreher* (1882–88); Georgie Drew; *John Drew* (1875–92); Rankin Duval; Ada Dyas; Virginia Earle; Walter Edmunds; Henry Edwards; Paula Edwards; Samuel Edwards; W. S. Edwards; Mr. Eldridge; W. G. Elliot; Maxine Elliott (1895–96); Florence Elmore; Clara Emory; *Agnes Ethel* (1869–72); Flossie Ethel; F. Evans; *Isabelle Evesson* (1879–82); Rose Eytinge; Lettice Fairfax; W. Farren; Amy Fawcett, or Fawsitt; *Owen Fawcett* (1871–75, 1893); Ada Featherstone; Nina Felton; *Bijou Fernandez* (1883, 1886, 1888); *May Fielding* (1879–85, 1895); Grace Filkins; Belle Finch; *Charles Fischer* (1872–89); Georgine Flagg (Mrs. Mark Price); Douglas Flint; F. Francis; Thomas M. Francis; Anna Franosch; Grace Freeman; Max Freeman; Nina Freeth; Pauline French; Elizabeth Garth; Julie Gaylord; Effie Geron; *Mrs. G. H. Gilbert* (1869–99); George Gilbert; *William J. Gilbert* (1882–88, 1892–93, 1898); Maybelle Gillman; Valda Glynn; Campbell Gollan; Violet Goodall; *Jean Gordon* (1884–89); Marie Gordon; Annie Graham; Alice Gray; William Greet; George Greppo; Joseph Greppo; *Herbert Gresham* (1885, 1892–99); Mlle. Gretchen; *George Griffiths* (1871–73); William Griffiths (1896–97); Henry Gunson; Kate Gurney; Francesca Guthrie; James Hackett; Thomas Hadaway; Lillian Hadley; Miss Hamilton; William Hamilton; Laura Hansen; Miss Hapgood; *F. Hardenberg* (1873–77); *D. H. Harkins* (1869–76); Maggie Harold (Mrs. William Dandridge, Jr.); Belle Harper; Hamilton Harris; Robb Harwood; *Percy Haswell* (1885, 1892–97); Alonzo Hatch; Miss Hathaway; Joseph Haworth; *William Hazeltine* (1896–98); George Heath; Thomas Hengler; Joseph Herbert; *Sydney Her-*

bert (1889–99); *Bijou Heron*, daughter of Matilda Heron (1874–75, 1882–85); Alfred Hickman; Laura Hill; Emma Hinckley (Mrs. James Clute); Maud Hoffman; Sophie Hoffman; George Holland; Joseph Holland; Kate Holland; Alice Hood; Albert Hope; Ethel Hornick; George Howard; May Howard; Nellie Howard; Percy Hunting; Edith Hutchins; Henry Hyde; F. Ireton; *Isabel Irving* (1888–92); *May Irwin* (1884–86); C. Jackson; *Louis James* (1871–75); Ida Jeffreys; Maud Jeffries; Mrs. Clara Jennings; Dewitt Jennings; John W. Jennings; Eugene Jepson; Lizzie Jeremy; *Sara Jewett* (1872–75); Mabel Jordan; Laura Joyce; Collin Kemper; Emily Kiehl; Albert King; *Edith Kingdon* (1884–86); Jerome Kinsbury; Miss Kirkland; Miss Kirwin; Richard Knowles; Dora Knowlton; Heinrich Koeke; Wilton Lackaye; Harry Lacy; J. M. Laflin; Margaret Lanner; Sara Lascelles; L. F. Lawrence; Laura Le Claire; Carlotta Leclercq; *Charles Leclercq* (1879–95); W. J. Lemoyne; Adelaide Lennox; Agnes Leonard; *George Lesoir* (1891–97); *Catherine Lewis* (1879–80, 1885, 1893–94, 1898); Emily Lewis; Harold Lewis; *James Lewis* (1869–96); Jeffrey Lewis; Helen Leyton; A. L. Lipman; Nellie Liscomb; Rupert Lister; Stevens Lockie; Grace Logan; Marie Longmore; Henry Loraine; Lena Loraine; Frank Losee; Lloyd Lowndes; Lotta Lynne; James MaCauley; Harry Macdonough; J. Macdonough; J. A. Mackey; Mariam Mansfield; Mary Marcy; Mr. Marker; Miss Marshall; Rose Marston; Arthur Mathison; Charles Mathews, visiting star (1871); Mrs. Mathews, formerly Lizzie Weston; Gerald Maxwell; Kitty Maxwell; Frank Mayo (1875); Paul McAllister; Neil McCay; Burr McIntosh; Nancy McIntosh; E. McLoughlin; Fannie McNeil; Roland McQuarie; J. Meridan; George Middleton; Henry Miller; Ida Molesworth; Henry J. Montague; Sig. Montegriffo; H. W. Montgomery; Elsie Moore; *John Moore* (1873–75, 1880, 1882, 1886–88); *Fanny Morant* (1870–73; 1880; 1883); *Clara Morris* (1870–75, 1885); Fanny Morris; William Morris; *Nellie Mortimer (Mrs. George Devere)* (1871–75); George Morton; J. D. Murphy; Emma G. Murray; Virginia Navarro; Adelaide Neilson; Lucille Neilson; Helena Nelson; Sydney Nelson; W. H. Newborough; Kate Newton; Ralph Nisbet; Gertrude Norwood; Roberta Norwood; May Nunez; Nora O'Brien; Elizabeth Oldcastle; *Eugene Ormande* (1888–90); *William F. Owen* (1895–99); *George Parkes* (1870–87); Miss Parkhurst; Kitty Paterson; J. Patten; *J. G. Peakes* (1872–75); *Agnes Perring* (1881–85); Irene Perry; E. Pierce; H. M. Pitt; Eben Plympton; J. B. Polk; Mme. Ponisi (courtesy of Wallack); Charles Poole; Mrs. Charles Poole; Miss Porter; Frederic Powell; *Tyrone Power* (1891–98); James Powers; Dean Pratt; *Adelaide Prince* (1889–93); Hazel Pughley; *Ada Rehan* (real name Crehan) (1879–99); Ella Remetze; Hamilton Revell; *Charles Richman; (1896–99); Emily Rigl* (1874–77, 1880); George Rignold; J. H. Ring; *B. T. Ringgold* (1872–75, 1881); H. Roberts; George S. Robinson; *Charles Rockwell* (1872–76, 1881); Mabel Roebuck; Frances Ross; Frank Rushworth; Fulton Russell; Hattie Russell; Phoebe Russell; Sol Smith Russell; Grace Rutter; J. H. Ryley; H. Ryner; Rosa St. Clair; *Marie St. John* (1896–98); *Lizzie St. Quinten* (1886–89); Mr. Saleon; *William Sampson* (1891–92, 1895–97); Marie Sanger; Cyril Scott; Eric Scott; Mrs. Scott-Siddons; Effie Shannon; J. W. Shannon; Mary Shaw; Robert Shepherd; Maud Sherman; Marie Shotwell; Miss Sinnott; Laurence Skinner; *Otis Skinner* (1884–89); E. P. Smith; Louise Smith; Lulu Smith; Percy Smith; J. L. Solomons; J. Stapleton; *Yorke Stephens* (1882–84); Adelaide Sterling; E. Sterling; Edwin Stevens; Mr. Stieger; Amy Stuart; Lillie Stuart; Marian Stuart; William Stuart; J. B. Studley; Mr. Sullivan; Carrie Swain; J. H. Swinburne; Nita Sykes; Louise Sylvester; *May Sylvie* (1880–81, 1887, 1890–

92, 1895); Jean Taylor; *Fay Templeton* (1875); Mabel Thompson; W. H. Thompson; Blanche Thorne; Laura Thorpe; Helen Tracy; Jennie Trevor; *Frederick Truesdell* (1896–98); Emma Turner; Ruby and Ester Tyrrell; George T. Ulmer; Eugenie Upham; Zelma Valdimer; George Vandenhoff; Violet Vanbrugh; Nina Varian; *Edwin Varrey* (1877, 1896–98); Rosa Vera; Carrie Vinton; Ellie Vinton; Lillie Vinton; Louise Volmer, or Vollmer; Jennie Vorhees; Anna Wakeman; James Wallis; J. W. Walsh; Frederick Warde; Eveline Warren; Kathleen Warren; Lillie Waters; J. F. Watson; Blanche Weaver; H. A. Weaver; E. Tom Webber; Mary Wells; George Wharnock; *Belle Wharton* (1875–77, 1889, 1891); Minnie Wharton; *Charles Wheatleigh (1888–95); Mrs. Thomas Whiffen; David Whiting* (1870–76); White Whittlesey; Marie Wilkins; *Edward Wilks* (1879–92); Marie Williams; Sallie Williams; Jefferson Winter (1896–98); Lizzie Winter; Gerda Wisner; Lelia Wolstan; Florence Wood; John Wood; Frank Worthing; Ann Yeamans; Jennie Yemans; Ida Yearance, or Yerance; Augustus Yorke; D. R. Young.

REPERTORY

1869–70: Play; Dreams; Old Heads and Young Hearts; London Assurance; Twelfth Night; As You Like It; King René's Daughter; The Love Chase; She Wou'd and She Wou'd Not; Much Ado about Nothing; Caste; A New Way to Pay Old Debts; Everybody's Friend; Daddy Gray; Checkmate; Wives as They Were and Maids as They Are; Irish Heiress; A Poor Goose; The Duke's Motto; The Busybody; Surf; Frou-Frou; Don Caesar de Bazan; The Hunchback; Man and Wife; Saratoga; The Heir-at-Law.

1870–71: Man and Wife; The Hunchback; The Heir-at-Law; Fernande; London Assurance; Twelfth Night; Saratoga; Jezebel; Married for Money; Patter versus Clatter; The Critic; A Thousand a Year; A Conjugal Lesson; Used Up; A Bachelor of Arts; Mr. Catherwood; Not Such a Fool as He Looks; The Golden Fleece; The Comical Countess; Cool as a Cucumber; No Name; Delmonico's; The Savage and the Maiden; An Angel.

1871–72: Divorce; Old Heads and Young Hearts (played both in Philadelphia and New York); *Fernande; Wives as They Were and Maids as They Are; The Provok'd Husband; London Assurance; Frou-Frou; Article 47; Diamonds; The Road to Ruin; The Belle's Stratagem; Everybody's Friend; The Inconstant; The Merry Wives of Windsor; The School for Scandal; The Baroness; Married Life; A Bold Stroke for a Husband; New Year's Eve.* Theatre destroyed by fire, January 1, 1873.

1873, January to June (Daly's Fifth Avenue Theatre): *Alixe; New Year's Eve; Old Heads and Young Hearts; Divorce; Madeline Morel.* September to November: Daly renamed his fifth Avenue Theatre Daly's Broadway Theatre; his company, however, did not appear.

1873–74, from December 3 (New Fifth Avenue Theatre): *Fortune; Old Heads and Young Hearts; New Year's Eve; Alixe; London Assurance; The Parricide; Man and Wife; Saratoga; Folline; Charity; Uncle's Will; Monsieur Alphonse; Divorce; Love's Labour Lost; Oliver Twist.*

1874–75: What Should She Do?; Fast Family; The School for Scandal; The Hanging of the Crane; The Critic; The Two Widows; Belles of the Kitchen; Moorcroft; The Belle's Stratagem; Masks and Faces; Everybody's Friend; The Heart of Mid-

lothian; Yorick; She Stoops to Conquer; A New Way to Pay Old Debts; Pygmalion and Galatea.

1875–76: *The Merchant of Venice; Charity Women of the Day; The Big Bonanza; A Bull in the China Shop; A Happy Pair; Uncle's Will; The School for Scandal; Pretty as a Picture; London Assurance; The Good for Nothing; Belles of the Kitchen; His Own Enemy; A Bunch of Berries; Living Too Fast; The Wrong Man in the Right Place; Saratoga; Our Boys; Hamlet* (with Edwin Booth; Booth also starred in *The Apostate; Richelieu; Othell; Richard II; The Lady of Lyons; The Merchant of Venice; King Lear; The Stranger;* and *The Taming of the Shrew); The New Leah; Pique; Money; The Serious Family; Pocahontas; As You Like It; Weak Woman; Frou-Frou; Jenny Lind at Last; Divorce; Siamese Twins.*

1876–77: *Life; The School for Scandal; The American; The Lady of Lyons; Lemons; Hamlet; Blue Glass; London Assurance; Princess Royal; Twelfth Night; Cymbeline; Romeo and Juliet; The Hunchback; Vesta; Money; As You Like It; Ah, Sin; The Dark City.* September 15, 1877, Daly withdrew as manager. Daly Stock Company on tour in May 1878, not to return to a New York Theatre until 1879.

1879–80, from September 17 (Daly's Theatre): *Love's Young Dream; Divorce; Wives; An Arabian Night; Newport; A Royal Middy; The Way We Live; Man and Wife; Fernande; Charity.*

1880–81: *New Port; Love's Young Dream; Divorce; Wives; Fernande; Man and Wife; Charity; Cross Purposes; The Brook; Tiote; Our First Families; Needles and Pins; Cinderella at School; Zamina; All the Rage.*

1881–82: *Quits; Americans Abroad; Royal Youth; The Passing Regiment; Cinderella at School; Odetta; Gironetto; Raven's Daughter; Frou-Frou.*

1882–83: *The Passing Regiment; Mankind; The Squire; Our English Friends; An Arabian Night; She Wou'd and She Wou'd Not; Serge Panine; Seven-Twenty-Eight.*

1883–84: *Dollars and Sense; Girls and Boys; The Country Girl; Red Letter Nights; Seven-Twenty-Eight.*

1884–85: *A Wooden Spoon; Lords and Commons; Love on Crutches; The Recruiting Officer; She Wou'd and She Wou'd Not; The Country Girl; A Woman's Wont; A Night Off; Denise.*

1885–86: *The Magistrate; A Night Off; She Wou'd and She Wou'd Not; A Wet Blanket; The Country Girl; A Sudden Shower; Nancy and Company; The Merry Wives of Windsor.*

1886–87: *After Business Hours; Love in Harness; The Taming of the Shrew; The Country Girl; A Woman's Wit.*

1887–88: *Dandy Dick; The Railroad of Love; A Midsummer Night's Dream.*

1888–89: *The Lottery of Love; The Wife of Socrates; Seven-Twenty-Eight; She Wou'd and She Wou'd Not; Needles and Pins; A Tragedy Rehearsed; The Inconstant; Dollars and Sense; Nancy and Company; The Country Girl; A Woman's Wit; An International Match; The Squire; The Taming of the Shrew; Samson and Delilah; A Night Off; Seven-Twenty-Eight.*

1889–90: *The Golden Widow; The Great Unknown; The Passing Regiment; As You Like It; The Railroad of Love; Seven-Twenty-Eight; A Woman's Wont; The Country Girl; A Priceless Paragon; The Prayer; A Midsummer Night's Dream; The Taming of the Shrew; Haroun Alraschid and His Mother-in-Law; Miss Hoyden's Husband.*

1890–91: *The Last Word; The School for Scandal; The Prodigal Son; A Night Off; Love's Labour's Lost; The Railroad of Love.*

1891–92: *The Taming of the Shrew; The Last Word; As You Like It; The School for Scandal; The Cabinet Minister; Nancy and Company; Love in Tandem; The Foresters; A Woman's Wont; Little Miss Million; Dollars and Sense; A Test Case; The Hunchback; The Good for Nothing; A Woman's Wont; New Lamps for Old.*

1892–93: *Little Miss Million; Dollars and Sense; A Test Case; The Hunchback; A Woman's Wont; The Good for Nothing; As You Like It; The Belle's Stratagem; The Knave; The School for Scandal; The Foresters; The Taming of the Shrew; Twelfth Night.*

1893–94: The company resumed production August 17, 1894.

1893–94: Daly's Stock Company spent its fifteenth season (1893–94) at its London Theatre. See European Repertory (London).

1894–95: *A Night Off, Seven-Twenty-Eight; Twelfth Night; Love on Crutches; The Taming of the Shrew; The Heart of Ruby; The Railroad of Love; The Orient Express; A Tragedy Rehearsed; Two Gentlemen of Verona; Nancy and Company; A Bundle of Lies; Honey Moon; A Midsummer Night's Dream.*

1895–96: *The School for Scandal; The Transit of Leo; Twelfth Night; The Two Escutcheons; The Countess Gucki.*

1896–97: *As You Like It; London Assurance; The Geisha; The School for Scandal; Much Ado about Nothing; The Magistrate; Guy Mannering; The Wonder; The Circus Girl; The Tempest.*

1897–98: *The Taming of the Shrew; Number Nine; The Subtleties of Jealousy; As You Like It; The Merry Wives of Windsor; Twelfth Night; The Country Girl; Coming Events; Jealousy; Lilli Tse; The School for Scandal; La poupee.*

1898–99: *A Runaway Girl; The Merchant of Venice; Madame Sans Gene; The School for Scandal; The Taming of the Shrew; The Great Ruby.*

EUROPEAN REPERTORY

1884: *Seven-Twenty-Eight; Dollars and Sense;* The "Jenny O'Jones" scene from *Red Letter Nights; She Wou'd and She Wou'd Not* (London).

1886: *A Night Off; Nancy and Company; Love on Crutches; A Woman's Wont; The Country Girl; She Wou'd and She Wou'd Not* (London, Liverpool, Edinburgh, Dublin, Hamburg, Berlin, Paris, and Brighton).

1888: *The Railroad of Love; The Taming of the Shrew; Nancy and Company* (London, Glasgow, Stratford, Paris).

1890: *Casting the Boomerang; Nancy and Company; Miss Hoyden's Husband; The Taming of the Shrew; As You Like It; A Woman's Wont; The Great Unknown* (London).

1891: *A Night Off; The Last Word; As You Like It; The School for Scandal; The Railroad of Love; The Lottery of Love* (Paris, London).

1893–94: *The Taming of the Shrew; The Hunchback; Love in Tandem; Dollars and Sense; The Foresters; The Last Word; The Orient Express; The School for Scandal; Twelfth Night; As You Like It; The Ring of Polycrates; The Country Girl; Loan of a Lover; A Woman's Wont* (London).

1895–96: *The Railroad of Love; Two Gentlemen of Verona; A Midsummer Night's Dream; Nancy and Company; Honey Moon* (London).

1897: *As You Like It; The Taming of the Shrew; Twelfth Night; The School for Scandal; The Last Word* (Stratford, Newcastle, Birmingham, Nottingham, Edinburgh, Glasgow, London, Liverpool, Manchester).

BIBLIOGRAPHY

Published Sources: Joseph Daly, *The Life of Augustin Daly* (New York: Macmillan, 1917); Edward Dithmar, *Memories of Daly's Theatre* (New York: Privately printed, 1897); Marvin Felheim, *The Theatre of Augustin Daly* (Cambridge: Harvard University Press, 1956); *New York Times*, 1898–99.

Unpublished Sources: Marion Victor Michalak, "The Management of Augustin Daly's Stock Company" (Ph.D. diss., Indiana University, 1961); Mrs. G. H. Gilbert's Scrapbooks (author's collection).

Loren K. Ruff

DEBAR'S GRAND OPERA HOUSE STOCK COMPANY. St. Louis, Benedict DeBar inaugurated his St. Louis management career on May 1, 1855, when he opened a summer season at Bates' Theatre (built 1851 on Pine Street), a proscenium-equipped house that could seat 2,500. The opening production was *The Nervous Man and the Man of Nerve* starring John Collins, supported by stock players. In June 1856 DeBar purchased the building and renamed it the St. Louis Theatre, and in 1865 he renamed it again, this time DeBar's Opera House. In 1873 DeBar leased this property to another and purchased the 1,600 seat, proscenium-equipped Varieties Theatre (built 1851 on Market Street). Located in a more fashionable part of town, he rechristened this theatre DeBar's Grand Opera House, enlarged it to accommodate 1,800, and opened it on September 1, 1873.

Despite the word *opera* in his house titles, DeBar was devoted to the legitimate drama, and from 1855 to 1878 a resident stock company was employed to provide support for visiting stars. The various names of his company have been collectively grouped by theatre historians as the Grand Opera House stock company, the best known of his theatres.

Benedict DeBar (1814–77), commonly called Ben, born in London but raised in Ireland, made his acting debut in 1831 in England and went to the United States in 1834 with his sister Clementine to join James H. Caldwell's St. Charles Theatre in New Orleans, where he was employed as an "eccentric comedian." He made his St. Louis debut in 1838 as a "second comedy man" with the legendary Noah Ludlow and Sol Smith stock company at their St. Louis Theatre (torn down 1853). Between 1838 and 1855 DeBar appeared periodically as an actor in all of the St. Louis theatres, experience that would stand him in good stead as a manager in the city. In 1853 he began his career as an actor-manager by leasing the St. Charles Theatre in New Orleans. To attract the best stock personnel, DeBar had to play a longer season than the hot summer weather of New Orleans would permit, so in 1855 he leased Bates' Theatre in St. Louis and, from 1855 to 1861, when the outbreak of the Civil War ended this arrangement, he usually spent April to October in St. Louis. On September 9, 1861, he began full-time playing in the city.

DeBar hired most of his stock company out of New York, but he did use local actors if they were good enough, and he changed the personnel about every three years. DeBar sometimes starred his company or individual members of it, but he frequently starred himself (and from box-office receipts and reviews, St. Louisans liked it when he did). A good all-around performer, he was a highly respected Falstaff in *Henry IV* and *Merry Wives of Windsor*, a role in which he successfully toured nationwide from 1872 to 1877.

Ben DeBar was a shrewd judge of talent. For example, he was directly responsible for the stardom of Joseph K. Emmet (1841–91), a native St. Louisan whose genius for German-dialect performing DeBar was one of the first to spot and to nurture. DeBar's niece Blanche (Booth) DeBar, daughter of Clementine and Junius Brutus Booth, Jr., was first starred by her uncle in 1865 and went on to a successful career in the hinterlands. DeBar also presented to St. Louis three future stars who came from his stock company: Mark Smith, Stuart Robson, and Sol Smith Russell. Finally, he brought two men to St. Louis who were destined to be among the last of the actor-managers in the city: Charles Pope and John W. Norton.

Throughout his career, DeBar's theatres enjoyed a justifiable reputation as being one of the two best St. Louis houses devoted to English-language legitimate drama (the other being the Olympic Theatre). In 1878, a year after his death, the stock company was disbanded, primarily because the rise in traveling combinations obviated the necessity for resident actors. In 1879 DeBar's remaining interest in the Grand Opera House was auctioned off, and his name was removed from the theatre.

DeBar's rule as a manager was to offer a little of something for everyone; consequently, he usually changed the star weekly and rotated the plays several times a week. DeBar had to appeal to a broad segment of the population, because there was a great deal of competition, especially circuses, dances, concert rooms, dramatic readings, and variety shows (where a ten-cent ticket included two glasses of beer at the Salvator Beer Hall). However, in the realm of legitimate drama, DeBar's competitors were much fewer. In 1860 there were seven theatres in St. Louis, two for German-language dramas, two for amateur productions, and one for vaudeville, leaving only DeBar's St. Louis Theatre and Wood's Theatre for English-language plays. In 1866 St. Louis theatregoers paid out $272,462 for tickets to five theatres, three of them variety oriented, but DeBar's Opera House was the leading operation, gathering $78,187, while his by then chief rival, the Olympic Theatre, accumulated only $40,651. But despite his generally good box-office receipts, DeBar was in constant monetary distress throughout the 1870s because of national financial panics, the rise of combinations, inflation in the cost of providing good production values including stock actors, stars who took as much as 50–70 percent of the gross receipts, overextension in his personal finances, and the inability to raise ticket prices appreciably because of his lower-cost competition (in 1866 DeBar's admission ranged from seventy-five cents to twenty-five cents; by 1876 it was $1 to twenty-five cents). After 1872 DeBar began to tire of active management, and he let more and more of the decisions be made by subordinates while he concentrated on acting.

Not counting minstrel shows, variety troupes, and the like, DeBar produced 1,449 plays, pantomimes, operas, and ballets. Plays were normally accompanied by a short forepiece or afterpiece that starred the entire stock company, and most of these playlets were farcical. Of the full-length shows, dramas predominated, although comedies and tragedies had strong representation. The three most popular titles in each category (with the number of performances in parentheses) were dramas: Auguste Waldauer's *Fanchon, the Cricket* (87), Dion Boucicault's *Colleen Bawn* (60), and Edward Bulwer-Lytton's *Lady of Lyons* (58); comedies: John Tobin's *Honey Moon* (50), Boucicault's *London Assurance* (38), *Merry Wives of Windsor* (32), and *The School for Scandal* (32); tragedies: *Hamlet* (83), *Camille* (80), and *Macbeth* (52). In twenty-four years 387 playwrights were produced, with Shakespeare the most often seen. DeBar's corps presented 522 productions of twenty-three Shakespearean plays. Second place went to Dion Boucicault's 417 performances of thirty-six titles. Although the chief attraction at DeBar's was always legitimate drama, an analysis of his offerings shows that he followed his axiom as a manager: something for everyone. DeBar also followed this rule in his choice of stars.

Between 1855 and 1879 there were 308 starring attractions in seasons that averaged thirty-eight to forty-three weeks, September to June. Literally, any prominent actor who toured performed for Ben DeBar. Not counting Ben himself, Maggie Mitchell was the most popular star with 223 performances, appearing often in *Fanchon, the Cricket*, written for her in 1861 by Auguste Waldauer. Following Mitchell in popularity were Mr. and Mrs. W. J. Florence with 190 performances. Lotta Crabtree chose DeBar's theatre for her premiere productions and played 160 times. John Collins, a professional Irishman, accumulated 139 performances by 1872. Matilda Heron, who had total of 106 performances, appeared thirty-five times as Camille. Edwin Booth played to "standing room only" houses for 50 percent of the gross receipts and gave 81 performances. Mark Smith, son of Sol Smith, had 79 performances, opening both the newly named DeBar's Opera House in 1865 and the newly dedicated DeBar's Grand Opera House in 1873. Joseph K. Emmet played 77 times including 21 consecutive performances of *Fritz: Our Cousin German* in 1871, the longest run of a single play attraction at a DeBar theatre. A few more important or unique stars who appeared were Edwin Forrest, Little Nell, Ada Isaacs Menken, F. S. Chanfrau as *Kit: The Arkansas Traveller*, Tommaso Salvini, Helena

Modjeska, Fanny Janauschek, John Wilkes Booth, Mary Anderson, Joe Jefferson, Dion Boucicault, Agnes Robertson, Fanny Davenport, and even W. F. "Buffalo Bill" Cody.

Among the talented members of DeBar's stock company, many of whom proved their worth later at the national level, some deserve special mention here. Auguste Waldauer and Charles A. Krone, both St. Louisans, were with DeBar from the early beginnings of his sojourn in St. Louis. Waldauer was the orchestra leader for DeBar and a well-known playwright who saw nine of his plays produced by DeBar for a total of 162 performances. Krone, with the exception of one season, was a permanent member of the stock company, hired in 1857 on the advice of Waldauer. Krone began as a "respectable utility man" for $10 a week but later specialized in villain roles.

Charles Pope, a stock leading man from 1855 to 1861, who could and did play either Othello or Iago, later became the performing stage manager for the Olympic Theatre, and in 1879 he opened his own Pope's Theatre in St. Louis, which lasted until 1895. John W. Norton (1843–95) was hired by DeBar in 1875 as a leading man and acting manager. Norton, a superb actor in tragic roles, was the discoverer of Mary Anderson, whom he first starred at the Grand Opera House in 1876. Norton remained manager of the Grand into the 1890s, and from 1882 to 1889 he was the manager of both the Olympic and the Grand theatres. Mark Smith (1829–74), a member of DeBar's 1855 company, went on to become a star comedian with his portrayal of roles such as Sir Anthony Absolute and Dr. Pangloss. Sol Smith Russell (1848–1902), calling himself Sol Smith, Jr. (he was no relation), was a low comedian for DeBar in 1861 and became a national star with *Edgewood Folks* in 1880. Stuart Robson (1836–1903) also showed his skill as a comedian in 1861, and St. Louisans thought he had great potential, which he proved in his 1877–89 partnership with William H. Crane.

George DeVere, a leading man, and his wife, Nellie Mortimer, were hired by DeBar in 1863 upon the recommendation of John Wilkes Booth. Both enjoyed good notices in St. Louis, and by 1869 they had become members of the Daly Stock Company*. George D. Chaplin, a DeBar protégé, began by playing juveniles in 1857, left and returned as a leading man and stage manager in 1868, and eventually went on to support Fanny Janauschek in 1874. Louise Sylvester, hired in 1869, was an accomplished leading lady who did all of her roles well. Catherine Reignolds (Mrs. Henry Farren), a member of the 1857 company, starred in the 1860s under both her married and maiden names. Charlotte Wyette, a leading lady in the Civil War period, demonstrated her classical English training and garnered good reviews with Lady Macbeth and Portia. Hattie Vallee, DeBar's second wife, was an accomplished dancer and pantomimist. DeBar's sister Clementine (Booth) DeBar, hired as a "first old woman" in 1856, was an excellent character actress. William Wiggins, a low comedian, and Willie

Slocum, a "responsible," were very popular St. Louis actors. O. H. Barr from the late 1860s, who received consistently favorable reviews, later toured in support of Lawrence Barrett. Finally, Archie Boyd, hired in 1872, became a star in the 1890s in Denman Thompson's play *The Old Homestead*.

From 1855 to 1877 Ben DeBar was the premiere actor-manager in St. Louis, but his death did not end the importance of his theatre. From 1879 to 1890 the Grand and the Olympic were "pooled" to eliminate interhouse rivalry and thus command lower prices and better bookings from road shows. In 1881 the Grand was torn down and reopened on the same site with a much larger capacity. Burned down in 1884 and rebuilt in 1885, it lasted as a legitimate theatre until 1896, when it went variety. Later the Grand became a vaudeville house attracting some of the top name acts. Finally, it became the Grand Burlesque Theatre and was still offering this form of entertainment when it was demolished in the early 1960s as a part of the overall development for the St. Louis Gateway Arch. A "grand" part of St. Louis theatre history had come to an end.

PERSONNEL

Management: Benedict DeBar, proprietor and manager (1855–77); Pierre Chouteau, proprietor (1877–79); John W. Norton, manager (1877–79); Henri Corri (1855–66), Joseph P. Price (1866–67), John W. Norton (1875–77), acting managers.

Treasurers: Charles G. Chesley (1855–58); Patrick Gleason (1859–67, 1868–69); George J. Jones (1867–68, 1869–70, 1871–78); Gleason and Jones, cotreasurers (1870–71); Arden R. Smith (1878–79).

Secretary: Patrick Gleason (1876–78).

Stage Managers: W. McIntosh (1867–68), George D. Chaplin (1868–70, 1873–74), J. Wesley Hill (1870–71), William Harris (1870–73), George Metkiff (1874–75), Charles C. Jordan (1875–76), George B. Berrell (1877–79).

Scenic Technicians: Leon Pomarede, John Hilliker (local artists used only when needed).

Propertyman: Walter Butler.

Musical Director: Auguste Waldauer.

Prompter: G. W. Riddell.

Stage Directors: Benedict DeBar (stage manager or promptor in his absence) or star of the engagement.

Actors and Actresses: *Maggie Arlington* (1874–78), Louise Arnot, *O. H. Barr* (1866–70), *George Berrell* (1875–78), O. W. Blake, Vining Bowers, Archie Boyd (1872–74), Milly Bridges, *George D. Chaplin* (1857, 1868–70, 1873–74), Florence Chase, *Thomas L. Connor* (1861–63), Virginia Cunningham, *Ben DeBar*, Clementine (Booth) DeBar, Fanny Denham, *George DeVere* (1864–68), Emma Duchateau, Kate Duff, Mrs. Frederick Edstrom, H. A. Ellis, *Henry Farren* (1858), Mr. and Mrs. R. C. Grierson, William Hamblin, William Harris, *J. Wesley Hill* (1870–71), Laura Honey, Grace Jones, Constance Jordan, *Charles A. Krone* (1857–78), George Lascelles, *Laura Linden* (1872–74), Emma Maddern, Lizzie Maddern, Minnie Maddern (mother of Minnie Maddern Fiske), *George Metkiff* (1874–75),

Kitty Mills (1869–75), G. W. Mitchell, Nellie Mortimer (Mrs. George DeVere), H. B. Norman, *John W. Norton* (1875–78), Sally Partington, A. B. Pearson, *Miss M. A. Pennoyer* (1868–71), Fanny Pierson, *Charles Pope* (1855–61), Mrs. Sylvester Post, *Joseph P. Price* (1866–67), *Catherine Reignolds* (Mrs. Henry Farren) (1857–58), *Stuart Robson* (1861–62), Charles S. Rogers, *Sol Smith Russell* (1861), J. H. Schuette, Mary Shaw, *William J. Slocum* (1872–73), *Mark Smith* (1855–56), *William P. Smith* (1860–66), Emma Stone, *Louise Sylvester* (1869–72), *Hattie Vallee* (1855–57, 1862–64, 1876–77), Mr. and Mrs. D. B. Vanderin, *William J. Wiggins* (1865–69, 1871–73), *Charlotte Wyette* (1861–64).

REPERTORY

In the three seasons selected, play titles are listed only once, in the order of their appearance, regardless of any subsequent performances. A complete listing of the day-by-day attractions can be found in the late Grant Herbstruth's dissertation on DeBar's Grand Opera House. Herbstruth indicated that until 1872 the chief attraction at DeBar's was legitimate drama with a heavy reliance on British drama, translations (French and German primarily), and adaptations from novels (Charles Dickens being very popular). After 1872 DeBar allowed more and more musical and variety entertainments into the regular season, although most of his repertory continued to be the drama.

1855 (First summer season): *The Nervous Man and the Man of Nerve; The Happy Man; Jenny Lind; His Last Legs; Teddy, the Tiler; To Oblige Benson; How to Pay the Rent; Robert Macaire; The Irish Ambassador; The Dumb Girl of Genoa; Paul Jones; The Stage Struck Tailor; The Irishman's Fortune; The Bronze Horse; The Wrong Passenger; The Irish Attorney; Toodles* (by Auguste Waldauer); *Wife Hunters; Beauty and the Beast; The Irish Post; The Captive; Vol-au-Vent; Trying It On; The Green Monster; Nicodemus; A Kiss in the Dark; Three-Faced Frenchman; The Magic Trumpet; Magic Pills; Elopement; La Maja Sevelle; The Hunchback; Slasher and Crasher; Ingomar; Norma; Evadne; The Lady of Lyons; Lucrezia Borgia; Romeo and Juliet; A Morning Call; Love; Hercules; The Italian Wife; Rough Diamond; Madelaine; Married Rake; Pizarro; Mary of Mantua* (by Julia Dean); *The Priestess; My Young Wife and My Old Umbrella; The Love Chase; Honey Moon; Jack Sheppard; Esmeralda; Faint Heart ne'er Won Fair Lady; The Drunkard; Fortunio; The Artful Dodger; Two B'hoys; Maid with the Milking Pail; La Bayadère; Woman: Her Faith, Her Love, Her Trials; Wallace; Satan in Paris; The Dutch Broom Girl; or, Buy It, Dear* (a burlesque of *La Bayadère*); *The Child of the Regiment; Kate Kearney; Time Tries All; Little Devil's Gift; The Forty Thieves; Follies of a Night; The Corsican Brothers; Pet of the Petticoats; The Unprotected Female; Maid's Tragedy of the Bridal; Don Caesar de Bazan; The French Spy; Wept of the Wish-Ton-Wish; Nick of the Woods; The Irish Widow; Mose.* There was break from July 5 to August 6. *Lover; The School for Scandal; Ion; Camille; The Wife; Richelieu; Macbeth; Hamlet; Othello; Miss Fanny; The Betrothal; The Willow Copse; Katherine and Petruchio; Louis XI; Your Life's in Danger; Island of Calypso; King Henry VIII; The Factory Girl; Kill or Cure; Armand; The Indian Girl; Jane Shore; Born to Good Luck; The Irish Genius; Fortune Hunters; Balloon Ascension; The Wrong Passenger; The Serious Family; The Flying Dutchman; Wanted: 1,000 Spirited Young Milliners; Isaura of Castile; Koeck and Guste; The Gamester;*

The Stranger; Rag Picker of Paris; London Assurance; The Duck Merchant; Woman's Rights; Grieselda (by Waldauer); *Dream of Life; Mary Tudor; Adelgitha; Sketches in India; Jack Cade; Damon and Pythias; Julius Caesar; Civilization; Still Waters Run Deep; Oraloosa; St. Mary's Eve; The Wrecker's Daughter; La tour de Nesle; The Ladies' Battle; Jonathan Bradford; The Carpenter of Rouen; The Poor Gentleman.*

1861–62: (First year of full-time playing at the St. Louis Theatre): *Paul Pry; A Race for a Widow; Nick of the Woods; Jack Sheppard; A Kiss in the Dark; Toodles; The Hunchback; Lucrezia Borgia; Robert Macaire; Evadne; Mr. and Mrs. Peter White; Thérèse; The Spectre Bridegroom; Camille; The Italian Wife; William Tell; Adrienne; A Day after the Wedding; The Wonderful Woman; The Maid with the Milking Pail; Katty O'Sheil; Wept of the Wish-Ton-Wish; The Four Sisters; The Wandering Minstrel; The Hidden Hand; Bonnie Fishwife; Fanchon* (by Waldauer); *Benecia Boy; Satan in Paris; A Regular Fix; The French Spy; The Wild Irish Girl; Antony and Cleopatra* (burlesque); *A Husband at Sight; A Thumping Legacy; Pet of the Petticoats; Margot; Hamlet; Macbeth; The Corsican Brothers; Don Caesar de Bazan; Black Eyed Susan; Metamora; Hit Him: He Has No Friends; Jack Cade; Richelieu; Buried Alive; Richard III; The Soldier's Daughter; Lola Montez; Joan of Arc; A Day in Paris; The Female Brigand; The Whistler; The Unprotected Female; The Three Fast Women; Jenny Divers; The Captain is Not A-Miss; King Henry IV; Merry Wives of Windsor; Betsy Baker; His Last Legs, Monsieur Mallet; The Kentuckian; Acquainted from Infancy; The Fire Eater; The Female Gambler; The Devil in Paris; Love's Disguises; The Factory Girl; Esmeralda; The Willow Copse; Still Waters Run Deep; Poor Pillicoddy; The Chimney Corner; The Hypocrite; The Advocate; King Louis XI; The Young Prince; John Dobbs; Truth in the Rough; The Little Treasure; The Ladies' Stratagem; Love's Telegraph; Guardians and School Boys; The Wandering Boys; Our Female American Cousin; Daughter of the Regiment; In and Out of Place; Our Gal; False and True; The Fool of the Family; The Bronze Horse; Ireland as It Was; Perfection; Othello; The Apostate; The Robbers; The Wife; The Marble Heart; To Paris and Back for Five Pounds; The Lady of Lyons; Too Much for Good Nature; Paul Jones; The Spy of St. Mark; The Little Jockey; The Angel of Midnight; The Phantom; My Wife's Mirror; A Woman on a Frolic; Oliver Twist; Damon and Pythias; Adventures of Mr. and Mrs. White; Virginius; Gio; Out-ah-Lan-chet; The Warrior Captive; The Rebel Chief; Wallace; Our American Cousin; The People's Lawyer and the Yankee Farmer; The Stage Struck Barber; The Ocean Child; A Glance at New York; The Limerick Boy; Tableaux of Washington; Mysteries and Miseries of New York; O'Flanigan and the Fairies; The Debutante; Mose in California; Novelty; The Dumb Girl of Genoa; The Phantom Ship; The Female Horse Thief; The Windmill; Dick Turpin; Sixteen String Jack; Great Expectations; Tom and Jerry; The Jew of Frankfort; Grimshaw, Bagshaw, and Bradshaw; Osceolo; The Conjugal Lesson; The Fool's Revenge; One Touch of Nature; London Assurance; Stratagem of an Actress; One Hundred Years Ago; Roll of the Drum; Mazeppa; or, The Untamed Rocking Horse; Madelaine; The Bottle Imp; The Invisible Prince; Pocahontas; The Merchant of Venice; Boots at the Swan; Romeo and Juliet; The Bold Dragoons and the Poor Peasant Girl; The Home Fairy; The Young Prince; The Foundling; Wanted; Masaniello* (feature was the La Senorita Isabel Cubas Spanish Ballet company); *John Smith; The Wizard Skiff; The Man of the World; The Huguenots; Brian Boroihme; The Miller and His*

Men; The Stage Struck Tailor; The Ice Witch; My Young Wife and My Old Umbrella; Aline; Woman's Whims; Green Bushes; The Young Actress; A Day too Late; Noemie; Parisian Life; Beauty and the Beast; Nicholas Nickleby; Actress of all Work; Robert Heller and Master Freddie (magician and pianist).

1873–74 (First season at DeBar's Grand Opera House): The Rivals; London Assurance; The Poor Gentleman; Heir-at-Law; Comedy of Errors; The Old English Gentleman; Honey Moon; Enoch Arden; Wild Oats; Richard III; Fidelia, the Waif Lady Thornhurst's Daughter (by George D. Chaplin); Across the Continent; Ben McCullough; Richelieu; Hamlet; The Duke's Motto; Julius Caesar; Rosedale; The Maniac Lover; A Kiss in the Dark; Three Fast Men; Merry Wives of Windsor; King Henry IV; Mrs. Norma; Ingomar; Belles of the Kitchen; Jones's Baby; Betsy Baker; Poor Pillicoddy; Help; Maum Cre; His Last Legs; All That Glitters Is Not Gold; Kit: The Arkansas Traveller; Sam; Arrah-na-Pogue; Colleen Bawn; The Knight of Arva; Irish Assurance and Yankee Modesty; Rory O'More; Handy Andy; Don Caesar de Bazan; Ireland as It Was; Tempted; The Child of the Savanna; Nan; Lighthouse Cliffs; The Willow Copse; Louis XI; The Chimney Corner; Divorce, Article 47; Alixe; Man and Wife; La Traviata; Il Trovatore; Les Huguenots; Mignon; Aida; Faust; Notre Dame; Darling; Oliver Twist; Hearts Are Trumps; Samson; Elizabeth; Othello; The Merchant of Venice; La morte civile; An Object of Interest; Fanchon; The Pearl of Savoy (by Waldauer); Jane Eyre; Little Barefoot; Lorle; A Woman's Wrong; Jealousy; Little Detective; Pet of the Petticoats; Little Nell and the Marchioness; Zip; Fritz: Our Cousin German; Max; Monte Cristo; Much Ado about Nothing; Brutus; The Lady of Lyons; Rip Van Winkle; Silver Star (which featured a double and triple tongueing cornet duet by the stars); Driven from Home; Jenny Foster; The Little Sentinel; Toodles; On Hand; Dixie; Face to Face; Olive; The New House; Romeo and Juliet; The Grand Duchess of Gerolstein; Les Bavards; The Flower Girl of Paris; The Child of the Regiment; Madame Angot's Child; Fortunio and His Gifted Servants; Belles of the Kitchen; Nabob for an Hour; Fun in a Fog; Two Buzzards; The Wrong Man in the Right Place; Love, Law, and Physic; Strakosch Italian Opera Company with excerpts from Faust, Martha, and Les Huguenots; Bullock's Royal Marionettes; Professor S. S. Baldwin and "A Night with the Spirits," exposing spiritual humbuggery."

BIBLIOGRAPHY

Published Source: John Callahan, "Fritz Emmet: St. Louis's Favorite German," Missouri Historical Society Bulletin 35, no. 2 (January 1979): 69–82.

Unpublished Sources: Grant M. Herbstruth, "Benedict DeBar and the Grand Opera House in St. Louis, Missouri, from 1855 to 1879," 2 vols. (Ph.D. diss., State University of Iowa, 1954); Theodore C. Johnson, "A History of the First Olympic Theatre of St. Louis, Missouri, from 1866 to 1879" (Ph.D. diss., State University of Iowa, 1958); John Callahan, "A History of the Second Olympic Theatre of St. Louis, Missouri, 1882–1916" (Ph.D. diss., Kent State University, 1974); James Alan Hammack, "Pope's Theatre and St. Louis Theatrical History: 1879–1895" (Ph.D. diss., State University of Iowa, 1954).

Archival Sources: Newspapers and programs are available in St. Louis at the Mercantile Library, Missouri Historical Society, and the St. Louis City Public Library. Financial data is available at the Missouri Historical Society and in the

Grand Opera House Estate Papers, Probate Court of St. Louis. The Missouri Historical Society also houses the following collections dealing with Ben DeBar and other St. Louis theatres: Gundlach Collection, Ludlow-Maury-Field Collection, Sol Smith Collection, Miscellaneous Theatre Collection, and Charles A. Krone's manuscript copy of "Recollections of an Old Actor."

John M. Callahan

DRAKE COMPANY. Organized by Samuel Drake in Albany early in 1815 for the express purpose of performing in rapidly growing Kentucky, the Drake Company gave its first performance in the state capital, Frankfurt, on Monday, December 4, 1815. The bill included *The Mountaineers*, with *The Midnight Hour* as the afterpiece. The company quickly established a circuit including Louisville and Lexington, with occasional seasons in Cincinnati as well as in smaller Kentucky towns.

The Drake Company was the first professional troupe of actors to play west of Pittsburgh. Its immediate success in Kentucky and the rapid emergence of a profitable circuit attests to the demand for entertainment on the frontier, and the cultural maturity that the existence of a theatre company was believed to signal. The production policies followed by the Drake Company offer, in microcosm, a view of the major transition in American theatre during the early nineteenth century.

At its inception, the Drake Company was a small, self-sufficient troupe with a strong base in the members of the Drake family, all of whom performed, augmented by a handful of other barnstormers. As the frontier grew and as transportation became relatively easier, especially along the great waterways of the Ohio and Mississippi rivers, the Drake Company gradually turned into a stock company whose central function was to support traveling stars—including the most famed member of the Drake family itself, Mrs. Alexander Drake.

The founder of both company and family, Samuel Drake (1768 or 1772–1854), was born in England. With his wife, Drake immigrated to the United States in 1810. Drake was acting comic and character roles with the Green Street Theatre Company in Albany after his wife's death (in 1814), when he learned of the possibilities in Kentucky. With his sons Samuel, Jr., James, and Alexander and his daughters Julia and Martha, Drake set out for Kentucky. Accompanying the Drakes was Noah M. Ludlow, a youth of barely twenty who was to become a pioneering actor-manager in his own right, and several additional actors. Ludlow's autobiography, *Dramatic Life as I Found It* (1880), contains a vivid account of the company's travels down the Ohio on a raft, performing wherever it was likely an audience might appear. Ludlow's description has been widely quoted for its evocation of the perils and profits of the barnstorming frontier actors.

In addition to the Drakes and Ludlow, the company included Frances Ann Denny (1797–1875) as leading lady. Denny left the company in 1819, returning in 1822 to marry Alexander Drake (1798–1830), who had become the company's leading comic actor. Alexander Drake eventually, in 1824, took over the management of the company from his father. Mrs. Drake, hailed as the "Siddons of the West," toured extensively as a star after her husband's death.

Although all of the Drake children acted, at least in the early years of the company, only Alexander and his sister Julia Drake Fosdick Dean (1800–1832) matured into talented and popular performers. Julia Drake Dean was survived by her daughter Julia, who became a major touring star at the end of the 1840s. Alexander's daughter, also named Julia, married the actor Harry Chapman, thus connecting the Drakes to the theatrical family noted for its role in the development of showboats in the middle of the nineteenth century.

Upon its arrival in Kentucky, the Drake Company absorbed several additional pioneer performers already in the area. John Vaughan and John Vos both were peripatetic theatrical workers who acted, painted scenery, sang, and danced—whatever was necessary or desired on the theatrical frontier. Both joined the Drakes, Vaughan in Frankfort and Vos in Louisville early in 1816, where he was not only to act but to renovate the theatre.

In the years following their 1815 premiere, the Drake Company prospered. Presenting regular seasons in Frankfort, Lexington, and Louisville, the company featured a repertory reminiscent of late eighteenth-century provincial English companies. Some of the actors who joined the company during the early period were, in fact, provincial English actors, notably Mr. and Mrs. Palmer Fisher, who joined the company in 1818, and whose daughter Clara—a touring star by 1831—made her debut with the company in 1819. Also joining the company in 1818, as leading lady, was Mrs. Belinda Groshon, an English actress who spent much of her career in the American, rather than the English provinces. American-born actors provided the majority of the Drake Company performers, however, including a young Edwin Forrest, with the company in 1822 and 1823, and T. D. Rice, inventor of the "Jump Jim Crow" specialty act, who was with the company between 1830 and 1832.

The Drake Company's early years were spent in short seasons in the three primary Kentucky cities—always including Frankfort when the state legislature was in session—with additional short tours to other towns. By 1819 Drake had purchased the theatres in both Frankfort and Louisville. Lexington was dropped from the circuit in 1820—changes in transportation and business patterns had turned a bustling city into a pretty village. The Drake Company did occasionally present short seasons in Lexington in the 1820s but not on a regular basis. Cincinnati was added to the regular circuit in 1825; the Drake Company occupied the Columbia Street Theatre, which had been constructed in 1825 for other barnstorming managers.

By the time the Drake Company expanded its operations to Cincinnati on a regular basis, the phenomenon of the touring star had appeared. Although there had been touring stars in the American theatre from the beginning of the century, their numbers had been few. After 1822, however, stars (often of lesser magnitude than the term would suggest) appeared in greater numbers and, by the middle of the decade, the Drake Company had been transformed from a self-sufficient acting troupe to a stock company supporting visiting celebrities. The Drake Company could still mount creditable productions between star engagements, but they were relatively rare, most often occuring when, for whatever reason of health or travel difficulty, the visitor failed to appear on schedule. In 1829 during the Louisville season, for example, touring stars included Edwin Forrest, the infant prodigy Louisa Lane (who, as Mrs. John Drew, would dominate the theatre in Philadelphia for most of the century), Mrs. Knight, and Mlle. Celeste.

The Drake Company faced occasional competition, particularly in Cincinnati and Louisville. Equestrian troupes in both cities periodically opened in the summer months, and efforts were made to establish rival companies by Noah Ludlow in Louisville in 1829 and in 1830. The Drakes closed the Louisville Theatre in the autumn of 1829 for remodeling, in part because of the competition from Ludlow. It reopened as the City Theatre on March 26, 1830, the interior having been gutted and entirely replaced.

Six weeks previously, Alexander Drake had died suddenly in Cincinnati. His death marked the ending of the company's period of vitality. The Drake Company continued to operate in Cincinnati until the end of 1831 but then performed only in Louisville. Samuel Drake continued the company in Louisville until 1833, when, after the winter season, he leased the City Theatre to a company sent north by James H. Caldwell, then the most powerful theatrical manager in New Orleans and the South, under the management of Charles B. Parsons (who had taken over the Drake Company's management upon Alexander Drake's sudden death) and Richard F. Russell, later manager of the American, or Camp Street, Theatre in New Orleans.

Samuel Drake effectively retired after the winter season of 1833, thus ending the history of the Drake Company as a producing organization. Both Alexander Drake and Julia Drake Dean, the most proficient performers among his children, had died at relatively young ages. Mrs. Alexander Drake continued her career as a star, periodically playing in Louisville but not always at the City Theatre. Mrs. Drake returned to Louisville to manage the City in 1839 but remained only a year before returning to the more lucrative business of the star. The City Theatre was leased by Samuel Drake to a succession of managers in 1840 through 1843 but with little apparent success. The theatre burned to the ground on March 20, 1843; Drake did not rebuild. His only connection with the theatre for the remainder of his life was through the careers of his daughter-in-law, his grandchildren, and his great-granddaughters, the Chapman sisters, who continued the family traditions.

PERSONNEL

The following list is incomplete, since newspaper files are not complete. The dates represent those years when individual performers were definitely with the Drake Company; it is possible that performers were with the Drakes longer than indicated.

Managers: Mr. Lewis (1815–17), Alexander Drake (1824–30), Charles B. Parsons (1830–33).

Scenic Artists: Joe Tracy (1815), Joe Cowell, Jr. (1833).

Actors and Actresses: Mr. Anderson, Mr. and Mrs. Francis Blisset (1815–17), Miss Clarke (1830–33), Mr. and Mrs. Joe Cowell, Sr. (1833); Miss Charlotte Julia Crampton (1829–32), *Mrs. Creeke* (1832), *Julia Drake Fosdick Dean* (1815–31), James Douglas (1815–20), *Alexander Drake* (1815–30), Frances Ann Denny Drake (1815–19, 1822–31), James Drake, Martha Drake, Sam Drake, Jr., *Samuel Drake, Sr.* (1815–33), Clara Fisher (1819– ?), *Mr. and Mrs. Palmer Fisher* (1818– ?), Edwin Forrest (1822–23), Mr. and Mrs. William Forrest (1832), Mr. Frankland, *Mrs. Belinda Groshon* (1818–19), Mr. Henderson, Thomas Jefferson (1815–16), William Jones (1818–19), James O. Lewis (1818–19), Noah M. Ludlow (1815–17), Mrs. Victor F. Mongin (1818–22), *Mr. and Mrs. Muzzy* (1829–33), *Charles B. Parsons* (1830–33), Miss Petrie, *T. D. Rice* (1830–32), Miss Robbins, Miss Rowe, Mrs. George T. Rowe (1830–33), Mr. Stith (1831–33), Henry Vaughan (1815), *John Vaughan* (1815–17), *John Vos* (1816–18), Mr. and Mrs. Watson, Mr. Wilson.

REPERTORY

Sample years are given, since records are incomplete.

1819, Lexington, autumn season: *Pizarro; Fortune's Frolic; The Foundling of the Forest; Tit for Tat; The Iron Chest; Catherine and Petruchio; The Magpie and the Maid; The Midnight Hour; The Hunter of the Alps; The Jew; St. Patrick's Day; Honey Moon; The Miller and His Men; The Forty Thieves; Reconciliation; The Gamester; The Turnpike Gate; Isabella; Alfonso of Castile; 'Tis All a Farce; Town or Country—Which is Best?; Children in the Wood; The Voice of Nature; Sylvester Daggerwood; The Sleepwalker; The School for Scandal; The Old Maid; Henry IV; She Stoops to Conquer; Lock and Key; The Poor Gentleman; Ella Rosenberg; Sprigs of Laurel.*

1828–29, Cincinnati, autumn–winter season: *The Prisoner at Large; 102; Three and the Deuce; Pizarro; The Jew and the Doctor; The Apostate; Married Yesterday; Guy Mannering; Simpson and Co., Evadne; Family Jars; William Tell; The Poor Soldier; The Miser; The Lives of Robin Hood and Little John; Virginius; The Iron Chest; The Agreeable Surprise; King Lear and His Three Daughters; Wedding Day; A New Way to Pay Old Debts; Love in a Village; Fontainebleau; Maid or Wife; He Would Be a Soldier; Curfew; Monieur Tonson; The Rifle; The Young Widow; William Tell.*

1833, Louisville, winter season: *Every One Has His Fault; The Belle's Stratagem; The Married Bachelor; Rienze; Gretna Green; A New Way to Pay Old Debts; Spoil'd*

Child; Deaf and Dumb; The Wedding Day; The Maid and the Magpie; The Two Merchants; The Foundling of the Forest; Nothing Superfluous; The Death Fetch; Demetri; The Hypocrite; Perfection; Deaf and Dumb; The Prisoner at Large; The Wonder!; The Mrs. Smiths; Gilderoy; Catherine and Petruchio; Two Eyes between Two; The Gamester; The Bath Road; The Tempest; The Review; The Turnpike Gate; The Legion of Honor; Who's the Dupe?; The Promissory Note; Richard III; The Hunchback; The Young Widow; The Soldier's Daughter; The Lady and Devil; The Merchant of Venice; Fortune's Frolic; Virginius; The Happiest Day of My Life; Macbeth; The Lancers; My Uncle; Marion; or, The Hero of Lake George; She Would Be a Soldier; The Lottery Ticket; Evadne; Fazio; Fish Out of Water; Adrian and Orrila; Popping the Question; Brian Boroihme; Columbus; The Stranger; The Wandering Boys; Much Ado about Nothing; Victorine; Matrimony; Pizarro; A Husband at Sight; Man and Wife; Facing the Wind; Jane Shore; The Hotel; Adelgitha; Agreeable Surprise; The Apostate; High-Ways and By-Ways; Isabella; Undine; Black Eyed Susan; Charles II; Fire and Water; The Earthquake; Alonzo and Imogine; Othello; The Jew and the Doctor; Thérèse: The Orphan of Geneva; The Four Mowbrays; The Blind Boy; William Tell; The Actress of All Work; The Romp; The Lady of the Lake; The Miller and His Men; Ella Rosenberg; Tom and Jerry; Shade; Deformed; The Conquest of Taranto; Luke, the Labourer; The Falls of Clyde; Marco Savone; The Budget of Blunders; The House of Aspen; The Bride of Abydos.

BIBLIOGRAPHY

There is no published history of the Drake Company. The Drake family is the subject of George D. Ford's *These Were Actors* (1955), a fictionalized account of the Drake and Chapman families written by a descendent. West T. Hill, Jr., *The Theatre in Early Kentucky, 1790–1820* (Lexington: University of Kentucky Press, 1971) competently covers the first four years of the Drake Company's history. John J. Weisert, "The Curtain Rose: A Checklist of Performances at Samuel Drake's City Theatre and other Theatres at Louisville from the Beginning to 1843" (Louisville, Ky., *mimeographed*, 1958) provides as complete a listing as the newspapers permit. Unfortunately, *The Curtain Rose* is a privately issued publication and is very difficult to locate. Weisert did publish three articles, in the *Filson Club History Quarterly* (1965, 1969) and the *Register of the Kentucky Historical Society* (1968), that detail the theatre in Louisville during the period of the Drake Company's activities.

Four unpublished graduate theses document the history of the theatre in Lexington during this early period, one of which also covers Cincinnati. Otherwise there are no histories of the early theatre in Cincinnati available and none of the Louisville theatre.

Despite its having been published sixty-five years after the events described, Noah Ludlow, *Dramatic Life as I Found It* (St. Louis: n.p., 1880; reprint, New York: Benjamin Blom, 1966), remains the fullest and most evocative account of the beginnings of the Drake Company.

Alan Woods

DUFFY AND FORREST STOCK COMPANY. The Duffy and Forrest company, Albany, New York, listed in newspapers of the time as the "Albany Theatre," was organized by William Duffy, an Albany native, and was managed by him and his second-in-command, William Forrest, brother of actor Edwin Forrest. They assumed management in 1829 of the South Pearl Street theatre (which had housed seven managements since its premiere season in 1825 under Charles Gilfert), opening their first season with productions of *The Poor Gentleman* by George Colman, the younger, and *My Grandmother* by Prince Hoare.

During the prior managements, nationally known performers were employed as visiting attractions to work with the stock company, and the theatre was generally well attended, but the rent for the building was so high, and the competition with the spectacles and equestrian displays offered at the New Circus Ampitheatre was so acute, that little profit was realized. Duffy, who at twenty-six was a respected actor, was determined to become a successful businessman of the theatre. Starting his management career in his hometown, he was soon heading the Arch Street Theatre in Philadelphia and was initiating control of a newly constructed theatre in Buffalo, which he envisioned as part of a chain of theatres under his management from western New York to Albany, Philadelphia, and Pittsburgh.

Of the two actor-managers, Duffy proved to have greater artistic and business acumen as well as far greater emotional stability. Born in Albany in 1803 of Irish parents, young Duffy went to school in Baltimore and Washington under the aegis of an army officer who had befriended him in Albany. On his return to his home, Duffy studied chairmaking and then law and also began acting in amateur theatre productions. When the need to make his own living became imminent, he began a professional acting career with Caldwell's New Orleans Company on tours in the South and West. In that company he met and became friends with Edwin Forrest and his brother William. Born in Philadelphia, William Forrest had come to acting from the trade of printing. Primarily because of his poor voice, he never gained prominence as an actor.

The Albany company's first season averaged box-office receipts of $66 a night. The theatre was renting for $40 a week, and prices for seats were seventy-five cents for boxes, thirty-seven and a half cents for the pit, and twenty-five cents for the gallery. In six weeks of the second season, forty-four plays were presented, some twice. The company struggled for six years, trying to provide quality entertainment to a reluctant public, using visiting stars of national and international repute along with the stock players. Seemingly always readily available to help was Edwin Forrest, who came to play numerous times in *Metamora, The Gladiator, The Broker of Bogota*, or some Shakespeare offering. The musical plays *Clari: The Maid of Milan, Der Freischutz, Guy Mannering, Cherry and Fair Star*, and, with great anxiety and expenditure attendant, *Cinderella*, were produced. In further efforts to capture popular support, child stars were hired to appear, as well as trained dogs and monkey impersonators, all performing in scripted plays. Duffy himself, an accomplished rider, appeared in the equestrian spectacle *Mazeppa*, "riding up clattering stairs to the top of the stage." A so-called theatre riot occurred when Tyrone Power, the celebrated Irish comedian, noted the small size of his audience on opening night and refused to play. Two nights later, when he deigned to appear, incensed theatre patrons made the performance impossible.

Duffy and Forrest both appeared as actors in their Philadelphia Arch Street theatre as well as in Albany. It was after one of Forrest's performances there, on March 3, 1834, that he died suddenly. Duffy continued to manage without him until February 10, 1836, when John Hamilton, an actor in the Albany company, wounded him with a knife, causing his death on March 12, 1836.

PERSONNEL

Not available.

REPERTORY

Not available.

BIBLIOGRAPHY

Published Sources: *Albany Argus, Albany Evening Journal*, H. P. Phelps, *Players of a Century* (New York, 1890).

Archival Sources: Morange Collection of the Letters of William Duffy, Albany Institute of History and Art.

James M. Leonard

F

FEDERAL STREET THEATRE COMPANY. See BOSTON ["FEDERAL STREET"] THEATRE COMPANY.

FRENCH PLAYERS, 1794–1800. See CITY THEATRE COMPANY and [THOMAS WADE] WEST COMPANY.

FRENCH THEATRE COMPANY. See CITY THEATRE COMPANY.

G

GAIETY THEATRE STOCK COMPANY. See VARIETIES THEATRE STOCK COMPANY.

GERMAN STOCK COMPANY. See KURZ STADT THEATER COMPANY.

GERMANIA THEATRE COMPANY. The Germania Theatre Stock Company, New York City, a German-speaking company, was organized in the summer of 1872 by musician-actor Adolf Neuendorff. He leased a small theatre on Fourteenth Street near Third Avenue (Tammany Hall) with a proscenium stage that was equipped with three sets of wings, which allowed entrances and exits on one side of the stage only. The Germania Theatre opened on October 10, 1872, with *Ein Diplomat der alten Schule* by Hugo Müller. The building was extensively renovated during the second season and the stage enlarged. The Germania Theatre Stock Company occupied the building until 1881. In the fall of 1881 Adolf Neuendorff leased the old Wallack Theatre (located on Broadway and Thirteenth Street), renamed it the Germania Theatre, and opened on September 15, 1881, with a production of Adolphe L'Arronge's *Der Compagnon*.

Adolf Neuendorff, an emigrant from Hamburg, had served as director of the chorus and later as musical director at Otto Hoym and Eduard Hamann's Neues Stadt Theater or new Stadt Theater* (45–47 Bowery). Hamann went bankrupt in 1872, and Neuendorff hired many of the Neues Stadt Theatre Stock Company members for his newly organized Germania Theatre. His objectives in the creation of the Germania Theatre Stock Company were to improve the ensemble quality of German-speaking theatre productions and to place more emphasis on a classic repertory. The Neues Stadt Theater was under new management and produced opera almost exclusively. During the first years of Neuendorff's management, his competition was minimal. The German beer halls and gardens, with their small stages constructed for musical, variety, and dramatic performances by various amateur groups and guest performers, appealed primarily to the spectators seeking lighter entertainment. Neuendorff wanted a company capable of supporting prominent guest stars from abroad. He was successful in introducing many important German-speaking actors to America in an attempt to raise the overall standards of his stock company. Among the most important were Magda Irschick (1879), Fanny Janauschek (1873), Karl Sontag (1881), Friedrich Haase (1881), Franziska Ellmenreich (1881, 1882), and Alexander Kauffman (1882). These guest actors received critical attention not only in the German-language newspapers but in the American press. Haase's guest engagement was not financially successful, but it aroused special interest in the press. Haase appeared as Narciss, Hamlet, and Shylock and in popular comic roles. Two very important additions to the Germania company were Heinrich Conried, later to become the organizer and manager of the Thalia Theatre in 1879, whose success would eventually be responsible for the Germania Theatre's demise, and Leon Wachsner, later to become the director of Milwaukee's German theatre.

The rivalry between the Thalia Theatre and the Germania Theatre reached its peak during the 1880–81 season as both theatres featured prominent guest stars from German theatres abroad: Karl Sontag at the Germania and Marie Geistinger at the Thalia. The Germania Theatre was plagued by Conried's success in luring away many of its best actors. Although the German population of New York City grew tremendously during the 1880s and German immigration reached a peak of more than 250,000 in 1882, the city could not support two first-class, German-speaking theatres. The competition was so keen that Neuendorff resorted to tactics such as opening the same play as announced by the Thalia Theatre one day in advance (*Sodom und Gomorrha*, 1879) at reduced prices.

The repertory was extensive and usually included more than 200 performances of fifty or more plays during a season. Contrary to Neuendorff's original intent, the majority of the plays were comedies (*Lustspiele, Schwänke*), farces, folk plays (*Possen*), a few classics by authors such as Gotthold Lessing, Friedrich Schiller, and William Shakespeare, as well as lighter musical fare and operettas. Of the classics, Schiller's *Die Räuber* and *Maria Stuart*, Goethe's *Faust*, Moliere's *Tartuffe*, and Shakespeare's *Hamlet, The Merchant of Venice*, and *Othello* seemed to be most popular. Neuendorff presented many new plays popular in German theatres abroad and billed them as American premier productions. However, these new German plays were not always welcomed by the ever more Americanized Germans. For example, although Henrik Ibsen was welcomed by German audiences in Berlin, this was not the case in New York.

Possibly Neuendorff's most serious mistake in his management of the

Germania was his decision to move into a larger theatre, the old Wallack Theatre, in anticipation of attracting larger audiences at lower prices to compete with the 2,000-seat capacity of the Thalia Theatre. His insistence on a repertory of farce, while the Thalia produced newer popular plays, and the failure of his guest stars to attract large audiences led to the closing of the theatre. On March 24, 1883, Neuendorff appeared before the audience and announced that financial failure had forced him to disband his company. He stated that he had never let the "dollar" take precedent over his high standards for the art form. The following year he attempted to organize a company in the Star Theatre, but the venture was short lived, and he returned his lease to Lester Wallack.

PERSONNEL

Management: Adolf Neuendorff, proprietor and manager (1872–83); Gustav Heinz, business manager.

Scenic Technicians: Carl Mauthner, N. Egli.

Music Directors: Franz Strebel, Julius Bernstein.

Stage Directors: Eugenie Schmitz, Otto Meyer, Adolf Neuendorff, various company members.

Actors and Actresses (From the years 1878–83): Herr Bagab, Frl. Becker, Frl. Behringher, *Hedwig Beringer* (1878), *Helene Bernsberg* (1879–82), *Reinhold Bojock* (1878–79), Herr Bowman, *Heinrich Conried* (1878), Frl. Delgmann, Herr Dieckmann, N. Egli, *Franziska Ellmenreich* (1881–82), *Carl Ernst* (1882), *Adolph Feuchter* (1879), W. Fliegner, *Herr Fortner* (1878–80), A. Fronosch, *Marie Geistinger* (1882), Herr Gross, *Ell Gröger* (1878), Herr Haath, Herr Hahn, Herr Hartzheim, Frl. Hecken, *Herr Heinemann* (1879–82), *Fanny Heller* (1878), Julie Heller, *Johanna Honnef* (1882), Herr Hopf, *Magda Irschick* (1879), Herr Janson, *Georgine von Januschowsky* (1880–82), Herr Jonas, Herr Jurgens, *Herr Kästner* (1879), Frl. Kaselowska, *Alexander Kauffmann* (1882), *Albert Kessler* (1878–82), Frau Kierschner, Frl. Klühn, Herr Kruger, Frl. Kuch, *Helene Kuhse* (1878), *Herr Kummer* (1878–82), Emma Kuster, *Herr Lichtental* (1879–80), Hermann Linde, Fr. Lorenz, Herr Lothar, Herr Lücke, Herr Mauthner, *Anna Martorel* (1878), *Hans Meery* (1879–82), *Claudius Merten* (1880–82), A. Meyer, *Bertha Necker* (1878–81), *Anton Otto* (1878), *Josephine Pagay* (1879), Herr Pauli, Herr Pinow, Herr Pönitz, *Franziska Raberg* (1879–82), *H. Raberg* (1879–82), *Bernhard Rank* (1878–82), *Franz Reinau* (1878–81), Frl. Rocke, Frl. Romanns, *Herr Sauer* (1879–81), *Carl Schimke-Hermann* (1882), Frl. Schlag, *Frl. Eugenie Schmitz* (1878–82), Herr Seifensieder, Herr Senger, *Herr Setti* (1879–80), *Karl Sontag* (1880–81), Frl. Stange, Herr Steinbuch, Frl. Stöbner, Herr Strüvy, *Frl. Umlauf* (1878–82), Frl. von Kaler, *Leon Wachsner* (1880–81), *Frl. Henrietta Wagner* (1878–81), *Oscar Will* (1878), Frl. Wolff, *Mortiz Wolkenstein* (1878, 1882).

REPERTORY

The following list is not complete; classics and representative plays only are listed.

1872–73: *Ein Diplomat der alten Schule; Onkel Moses; Die Helden; Inspector*

Bräsig; Ein Stiftungsfest; Der verlorene Sohn; Der Meineidbaur; Ein Glas Wasser; Das Milchmädchen; Die Gräfin von Somerive.

1873–74: Aus der Gesellschaft; Die schöne Galatheé; Das Stiftungsfest; Der Pfarrer von Kirchfeld; Marcel; Die Räuber; Maria Stuart; Der Elephant; Geld; Medea; Emilia Galotti; Robert und Bertram.

1874–75: Adelaide; Archenbrödel; Czaar und Zimmermann; Anti-Xantippe; Cato von Eisen; Ein Erfolg; Ultimo; Die bezähmte Widerspänstige; Die Journalisten; Die Fledermaus; Die lustigen Weiber von Windsor; Biegen oder brechen.

1875–76: Rabagas; Monsieur Alphonse; Ehrliche Arbeit; Citronen, Der Vetter; Die bezähmte Widerspänstige; Viel Lärm um Nichts; Grethchen's Polterabend; Zopf und Schwert; Uriel Acosta; Die Valentine; Kabale und Liebe; Maria Magdalene; Donna Diana; Mein Leopold; Das Mädel ohne Geld.

1876–77: Luftschlösser; Ein Fallissement; Emilia Galotti; Egmont; Othello; Die Reise durch New York in 80 Stunden; Tartüffe; Clavigo; Der zerbrochene Krug; Don Carlos; Die Zärtlichen; Verwandten; Uriel Acosta.

1877–78: Ultimo (Daly's Big Bonanza); Don Cäsar; Die Frömmler; Gebrüder Bock; Der Kaufmann von Venedig; Der Hypochondor; Dorf und Stadt; Hasemann's Töchter; Die Journalisten; Mutter und Sohn; Nathan der Weise.

1878–79: Graf Essex; Das erste Mittagessen; Dorf und Stadt; Bummelfritze; Jane Eyre; Gringoire; Die Räuber; Der Kuss; Hotel Klingenbusch; Nette Leute; Das Wasser; Ja, so sind wir! Maria Stuart; H.M.S. Pinafore; Minna von Barnhelm; Othello; Zopf und Schwert.

1879–80: Die Frau ohne Geist; Luftschlösser; Sodom und Gomorrha; Brunhild; Donna Diana; Maria Stuart; Viel Lärm um Nichts; Die Waise von Lowood; Deborah; Rosenkranz und Guldenstern; Lumpaci Vagabundus; Faust; Don Carlos; Ein Blitzmädel; Onkel Knusperich; Inspector Bräsig; Die Räuber; Die Grille.

1880–81: Auf der Brautfahrt; Hasemann's Töchter; Mas Mädel ohne Geld; Der Elephant; Das Glas Wasser; Die Journalisten; Tartüffe; Pechschulze; Minna von Barnhelm; Egmont; Dorf und Stadt; Hans Lonei; Das Stiftungsfest; Die bezähmte Widerspänstige.

1881–82: Der Compagnon; Don Carlos; Der Wildschütz; Sie ist Wahnsinnig; Lorbeerbaum und Bettelstab; Hamlet; Krieg und Frieden; Don Quixote; Die Räuber; Lumpaci Vagabundus; Jane Eyre; La Traviata; Faust; Ill Travatore; Adrienne Lecouvreur; Kätchen von Heilbronn; Hazel Kirke; Donna Diana; Freund Fritz; Mein Leopold.

1882–83: Uriel Acosta; Graf Waldemar; Boccaccio; Drei Paar Schuhe; Der Pawnbroker von Harlem; Die Räuber; Faust; Wilhelm Tell; Egmont; Wallenstein's Lager; Die Piccolomini; Don Carlos; Deborah; Hasemann's Töchter; Götz von Berlichingen; Jane Eyre; Emilia Galotte.

BIBLIOGRAPHY

Published Sources: (German-language press) New Yorker Figaro, New Yorker Staats-Zeitung. (English-language press) New York Dramatic Mirror, New York Herald, New York Times, New York Tribune, The Spirit of the Times. See Deutsche-Amerikanische Geschichtsblätter 15 (1915): 255–309; "Das Deutsche Theater in New York," Sonntagsblatt des New Yorker Staats-Zeitung, April 16, 1905; Montrose J. Moses, The Life of Heinrich Conried (New York: Thomas Y. Crowell, 1916); Ludwig Barnay, Irinnerungen (Berlin: E. Fleischel, 1903).

Archival Sources: New York Public Library and the Harvard Theatre Collection, Cambridge, Massachusetts, have numerous programs and newspaper clippings.

Ron Engle

GLOBE THEATRE COMPANY. On the fourth of July 1870, J. H. Selwyn left his position as a manager of a successful Boston theatre, and the building that had borne his name, Selwyn's Theatre, was rechristened the Globe. Arthur Cheney maintained his proprietorship of the theatre, thus insuring the continued fortunes and high production standards of Selwyn's Theatre Company*. During the three seasons of this first Globe theatre, the numbers of both melodramas and Irish plays increased, as did the practice of having guest stars appear with the resident company. Guest performers included Mr. and Mrs. W. J. Florence, Madame Janauschek, Edwin Forrest, Charlotte Cushman, and E. A. Sothern.

The Globe opened on September 12, 1870, with a dramatization of Alexander Dumas' *Monte Cristo*. Charles Fechter, the new sole manager of the theatre, adapted the novel to the stage of the Globe. Fechter was to manage and act for only a few months, since an apparent disagreement with Cheney resulted in the termination of his work in January 1871. He was replaced by W. R. Floyd, another member of the acting company.

Cheney's initial intentions were successfully carried over from Selwyn's to the Globe. In May 1872 the city's cultural leaders honored his five-year proprietorship of the theatre. They praised his taste and applauded his public-spirited efforts to raise and sustain the level of Boston's interest in the best classic and modern drama.

The Globe's 1870–71 season included the popular and versatile Mary Cary as Oliver in *Oliver Twist*, an appearance of Charles Mathews in *Thousand a Year*, and E. L. Davenport as Hamlet. The popular fare consisted of burlettas, romantic dramas, and plays by Tom Taylor, J. R. Planché, and W. S. Gilbert.

Cheney renovated the theatre before the 1871–72 season. The Globe's program, "an illustrated theatrical paper," unabashedly reaffirmed the theatre's purpose to produce "the most popular and successful plays" and "a constant variety of first-class dramatic entertainments" with regard to both "novelty, new plays" and the "favorite standard authors."

Highlights of the 1871–72 season included plays by Dion Boucicault and Taylor and the performances of stars such as Charlotte Cushman as Lady Macbeth and Meg Merrilles and Edwin Forrest as Lear, Virginius, and Richelieu. During the summer, the theatre was let to touring companies, such as William P. Emerson's California Minstrels and George L. Fox's *Humpty Dumpty*.

The Globe company itself would take up the practice of touring during the 1872–73 season. While Lydia Thompson's burlesque company appeared at the Globe in October 1872, the Globe company played in about a dozen cities and towns throughout Massachusetts and Connecticut, in *Speed the Plough, The Lady of Lyons*, and *The School for Scandal*.

An 1872 program stated that the theatre was "a place of respectable and rational amusement" and that at the Globe "Elegance, Comfort, Security and Purity are combined" with "the class of patrons most respectible and the PERFORMANCE CHASTE." Indeed, Charles Danforth, in his dramatic reviews in the Boston *Daily Herald*, noted that the Globe's audience consisted of "the very best class of people that the city can boast."

Mary Cary continued as the favorite actress of the theatre, in spite of the presence of some very strong character actresses, such as Mrs. F. S. Chanfrau, Mrs. Thomas Barry, and Carlotta Leclercq. John E. Owens was cited as the starring comedian of the 1870–71 season. The following year, Charles Danforth named J. T. Raymond as the "comedian of the establishment." Stuart Robson returned to the Globe for the 1872–73 season to resume his comic reign. He also contributed to the theatre's repertory, as did H. F. Daly, by writing and adapting comic works.

What was to be the last season of this Globe theatre featured E. A. Sothern in his famous Dundreary roles, the Boucicaults in several Irish plays, Frank Mayo as Davy Crockett, and Madame Janauschek as Medea, Mary Stuart, and Adrienne Lecouvreur. The theatre remained, according to one advertisement, "this elegant and popular establishment, the acknowledged 'model theatre of America.' "

Unfortunately, this theatre, which had opened as Selwyn's in 1867 with "the most complete and powerful dramatic company ever assembled in Boston," was destroyed by fire on May 30, 1873. The date was the holiday known then as Decoration Day, which Charles Danforth dubbed "desecration day" in his eulogy of the building. In the *Daily Herald* of May 31, he mourned the loss of the "temple of drama which was the most elegant of its kind in New England . . . the pride of the theatrical profession and of Boston."

However, Arthur Cheney would recover from his artistic and architectural losses, as he financed the rebuilding of the theatre. A new Globe opened in December 1874, and it remained in operation for the next twenty years.

PERSONNEL

Management: Arthur Cheney, proprietor (1870–73); William R. Floyd, manager (1870–71); Charles Fechter (1871–73), George B. Farnsworth (1870–71), and C. E. Tucker, treasurers (1871–73); H. A. McGlenen, business manager (1870–73).

Scenic Artists: George Heister (1870–71), E. V. Voegeltin (1871–73), Thomas B. Glessing (1871–73).

Musical Director: Charles Koppitz (1870–73).

Stage Managers: Arthur LeClercq (1870–73), H. F. Daly (1871–73).

Actors and Actresses: A. Aldrich, Leslie Allen, Amy Ames, Miss Athena, *Mrs. Thomas Barry* (1871–73), *G. F. Boniface* (1871–72), T. Brown, *Mary Cary* (1870–

73), *Mrs. F. S. Chanfrau* (1870–71), J. H. Connor, C. W. Couldock, C. E. Creswick, I. Curtis, *H. F. Daly* (1870–73), Charles Fechter, *W. R. Floyd* (1870–73), E. F. Foster, J. B. Fuller, Ada Gilman, F. Goldthwaite, Miss Grahame, Miss Griffiths, *G. H. Griffiths* (1870–71), Miss Hall, Mrs. H. Hall, D. S. Harkins, *Amilie Harris* (1871–73), F. Harriss, Sarah Henley, Emma Hicks, Adeline Hind, E. B. Holmes, J. H. Howland, Lizzie Hunt, *Mrs. T. M. Hunter* (1870–73), J. W. Jennings, Melinda Jones, Lucy Kenway, *Carlotta Leclercq* (1870–71), Charles Leclercq, W. J. Lemoyne, Gustavus Levick, F. F. Mackay, Mr. McLaughlin, C. A. McManus, H. Melmer, T. Morris, Louisa Morse, Josephine Orton, W. F. Owen, William H. Page, James G. Peakes, Lizzie Queen, *J. T. Raymond* (1871–72), H. A. Rendle, J. W. Reynolds, *Stuart Robson* (1872–73), Frank Roche, Ida Savory, F. Scallan, Mrs. L. E. Seymour, William Seymour, *W. E. Sheridan* (1871–73), Miss Spear, C. Stedman, F. E. Stedman, L. R. Stockwell, Colin Stuart, C. H. Vandenhoff, James W. Wallack, J. Wentwoth.

REPERTORY

1870–71: *Monte Cristo* (dramatization of the Dumas novel by Charles Fechter); *Henry Dunbar; King of the Commons; Hamlet; The Lady of Lyons; Brigand; Solon Shingle; Plot and Passion; Don Caesar de Bazan; Lottery Ticket; Black and White; Boots at the Swan; A Sheep in Wolf's Clothing; Guy Blas; King René's Daughter; Honey Moon; As You Like It; Dora; My Young Wife and My Old Umbrella; The Merchant of Venice; Debutante; Phantom Breakfast; Spitfire; The Irish Heiress; Still Waters Run Deep; Irish Emigrant; How She Loves Him; Saratoga; Oliver Twist; The Iron Mask; Hunchback; Margery; Arrah-na-Pogue; Rent Day; Born to Good Luck; Hamlet; Damon and Pythias; Molly Deer; Robert Macaire; Randall's Thumb; Americans in Paris; Pretty Piece of Business; Handy Andy; Thousand a Year; Patter vs. Clatter.*

1871–72: *Victims; Married Life; Forty Winks; Turning the Tables; Heir-at-Law; Everybody's Friend; Grimaldi; The Rivals; Solon Shingle; Happiest Day of My Life; Dot; Live Indian; Still Waters Run Deep; Captain of the Watch; Divorce; Henry VIII; Guy Mannering; Macbeth; Simpson and Co.; Dreams of Delusion; Under the Willows; Marble Heart; London Assurance; The School for Scandal; Eileen Oge* (4 weeks); *As You Like It; Love Chase; Hunchback; Plot and Passion; The Lady of Lyons; Masks and Faces; A Scrap of Paper; Sheep in Wolf's Clothing; Honey Moon; Little Emily; King Lear; Richelieu; Virginius; The Ticket-of-Leave Man; Dombey and Son; Return of the Volunteers; Irish Lion; Thrice Married; Yankee Housekeeper; Colleen Bawn; Forbidden Fruit; Saratoga; Long Strike; Lady Audley's Secret; All That Glitters; Toodles; Soldier's Daughter; Conjugal Lesson; How She Loves Him; Nervous Man.*

1872–73: *Speed the Plough; The Bells; Creatures of Impulse; Chimney Corner; Old Phil's Birthday; Our American Cousin; Brother Sam; Dundreary Married; David Garrick; Boorampooter; Louis XI; Spectre Bridegroom; Willow Copse; Arrah-na-Pogue; Colleen Bawn; Kerry; Milly; Masks and Faces; Jones's Baby; Hunchback; John Wopps; Stranger; Irish Emigrant; As You Like It; The School for Scandal; Plot and Passion; Married Life; Pygmalion and Galatea; Dora; Handy Andy; Sheep in Wolf's Clothing; The Merchant of Venice; Camille* (burlesque); *Who's Who?; Richard III; The Ticket-of-Leave Man; No Thoroughfare; Agnes;*

Only a Jew; Milky White; Betsy Baker; Chesney Wold; Macbeth; Eileen Oge; Adrienne Lecouvreur; Mary Stuart; Deborah; Medea; Davy Crockett; Serious Family; Paul Pry; New Magdalen; Still Waters Run Deep.

BIBLIOGRAPHY

Published Sources: William W. Clapp, Jr., "The Drama in Boston," in *The Memorial History of Boston, 1630–1880*, vol. 4, ed. Justin Winsor (Boston: James R. Osgood and Company, 1881), pp. 377–78; *Boston Daily Herald*, 1870–73.

Archival Sources: Programs, playbills, and newspaper clippings from the Harvard Theatre Collection, Cambridge, Massachusetts, and the Boston Public Library.

Noreen C. Barnes

GREEN STREET THEATRE COMPANY. The Green Street Theatre Company, Albany, New York, was organized by John Bernard (1756–1828) in 1812 to occupy the new Green Street Theatre, then under construction. The theatre was opened January 18, 1813, with a production of *The West Indian*, the company headed by Leigh Waring, Albany's first visiting star.

Before the organization of this stock company, the only theatrical entertainments available in Albany had been occasional tours and a relatively permanent troupe, known as the Hayman Company, that performed at the Thespian Hotel in Albany. After establishment of the Green Street Company, Albany became a regular stopping point for traveling stars, often operating as a link between New York and the Canadian Provinces.

John Bernard, who began as an actor at London's Covent Garden Theatre, originally went to America to perform with the Chestnut Street Theatre Company* in Philadelphia. After comanaging the Boston ["Federal Street"] Theatre Company*, he went to Albany in hopes of tapping the city's burgeoning interest in establishing its own theatre. His initial attempts failed, and he joined the Hayman Company as an actor, but in March 1812 a group of Albany businessmen formed the Albany Theatre Company to raise funds for the construction of a theatre with Bernard as the manager.

The company was well received and supported by the citizens of Albany. Bernard did his best to bring the top stars and plays from England and America to his theatre. Reviews were almost always favorable, despite the protests of a strong religious element, which went as far as to attempt to make theatre illegal on the grounds that it was a public nuisance. The resolution was rejected by the Albany Law Committee.

Bernard continued for four seasons, plus a summer season in 1814, changing programs every evening, unless the popularity of a particular production warranted a second performance. The theatre was open three nights a week, Monday, Wednesday, and Friday, and seats sold at $1 for the boxes, seventy-five cents for the pit, and fifty cents for the gallery. The houses were generally full, with declining attendance only during the final season.

Bernard presented a varied repertoire, interspersing serious drama with the more popular spectacles, including T. E. Hook's *Tekeli* (1806), Thomas Morton's *Columbus* (1792), and an original pantomime, *Harlequin in Albany*. In these pieces he relied heavily on his scene designers for colorful scenery and special effects. In 1815 two notable novelties were performed: the anonymous spectacle *The Festival of Peace*, complete with transparency and apotheosis, and George Colman, the younger's *Bluebeard* (1798), featuring a 6,000-pound elephant, which wintered in Albany. The classics were abundantly represented, particularly Shakespeare (twenty-two performances of twelve Shakespearean plays), as well as the standard repertoire of the English-speaking theatre of the time.

Bernard ran the theatre almost single handedly, employing a small number of stagehands, an orchestra leader, and a scenist. Monsieur Mallet remained the orchestra leader for the company throughout its four-season history, continuing in Albany even after the theatre closed. For the first two seasons, Mr. Aceport served as scenist, Hugh Reinagle assuming that post for the final two seasons. In 1813 Samuel Drake, Sr., joined the company as stage manager, bringing with him his theatrical family, consisting of Mrs. Drake and five children. The stock company remained virtually the same until the end of the 1814–15 season, when many players left Albany to work elsewhere.

Bernard relied heavily on visiting stars, particularly for Shakespearean productions and "heavier" dramatic pieces, engaging three to five stars a season, usually for ten-night engagements. Leigh Waring opened the theatre, followed, during the initial winter season of 1813, by John Dwyer, Mrs. De Jersey Beaumont, and Joseph Holman and his daughter Agnes. The second season, 1813–14, he engaged Mrs. Eliza (Elizabeth Kemble) Whitlock, Mr. and Mrs. Beaumont, and Hopkins Robertson. Mrs. Charlotte Placide and her son Henry (both of whom remained for the entire season), Mr. Garner (a singer), John Duff and his wife, Mary Ann, played Albany during the season of 1814–15, as did Hopkins Robertson and Holman and his daughter. In the final season, Bernard used less visiting talent: Agnes Holman Gilfert, Hopkins Robertson, and Mrs. Burke of the Park Theatre. The stock company was drawn primarily from recruits of the Hayman Company, the Canadian Circuit, and the Boston Theatre. Esther Young remained the leading lady through 1815, supported by Bernard and visiting players.

The theatre began having financial difficulties during the 1814–15 season as a result of forgeries committed against the theatre. The migration of actors at the end of this same season forced Bernard to establish an almost entirely new stock company for his 1815–16 season. April 5, 1816, Bernard resigned as manager, giving the theatre over to the company on a "sharing system," and they continued under this arrangement until April 14, 1816, at which time the company disbanded. The theatre was briefly engaged by a Mr. Mortimer, who attempted a stock company, hiring an aging Thomas Betterton as his leading man, but this enterprise was abandoned. In June 1818, after having been unoccupied for a year, the Green Street Theatre was sold to the Baptist Society, which converted it into a church.

PERSONNEL

Management: John Bernard (1813–16).
Scenists: Mr. Aceport (1813–14), Hugh Reinagle (1814–16).
Orchestra Leader: Monsier Mallet (1813–16).
Stage Manager: Samuel Drake, Sr. (1813–15).
Actors and Actresses: *Mrs. Aldis* (1815–16); *Mrs. and Mrs. Andrew Allen* (1813–16); Mr. and Mrs. Anderson; Mr. Armstrong; Mr. and Mrs. Bernard; Mr. Charnock; Miss Cordell; Mrs. Dorion; *Drake Family*—Samuel Drake, Sr., Mrs. Drake, Samuel, Jr., Alexander, James, Julia, and Martha (1813–15); Mr. Drummond; Miss Ellis; Mr. Garner; Mr. Graham; Mr. Heyl; Mr. Johnson; *Mr. Samuel Legg* (1813–14); *Mr. and Mrs. Lewis* (1813–15); Mr. Lindsley; Mr. Ludlow; Mr. Moore; Mrs. Morris; Mr. Morse; Mr. Pierson; Mr. Pierce; *Mrs. Caroline Placide* (1814–15); *Henry Placide* (1814–15); W. Robertson; *Mr. Southey* (1813–14); *Joseph Tyler* (1813–14); *Mrs. Wheatley* (1813–14); *Esther Young* (1813–15); *Thomas Young* (1813–15).

REPERTORY

1813 (January to June): *The West Indian; Fortune's Frolic; Laugh When You Can; Speed the Plough; The Irishman in London; Romeo and Juliet; Tekeli; Columbus; Hamlet; The Provok'd Husband; The Earl of Essex; Honey Moon; Othello; Alexander the Great; The Gamester; King Lear; The Fair Penitent; Harlequin in Albany; Much Ado about Nothing; The Soldier's Friend; Passion and Love; Robin Hood; Wild Oats; The Wheel of Fortune; Ella Rosenberg; The Wedding Ring; The Road to Ruin; The Son-in-Law; Venice Preserved; Douglas.*

1813–14: *The Fatal Marriage; The Merchant of Venice; Cymbeline; Macbeth; The Stranger; The Winter's Tale; The Wanderer; Tekeli; Wheel of Fortune; Harlequin in Albany; Venice Preserved; The Iron Chest; The Benevolent Jew; The Purse; The Curfew; The Poor Soldier; The Forty Thieves; Gazette Extraordinary; Matrimony; Laugh When You Can; Inkle and Yarico; The Recruiting Manager; Abaellino, the Bandit; Columbus; The Mountaineers; Don Juan; Embargo; King Lear; Othello; The Suffield Yankee; La Perouse; The Young Quaker; The Devil to Pay; The Judgment of Solomon; Honest Thieves.*

1814 (Summer): *Hamlet; The Mountaineers; Richard III; Macbeth; The Highland Reel; Three Deuces; Foundling of the Forest; Paul and Virginia.*

1814–15: *The Soldier's Daughter; The Irishman in London; Richard III; Macbeth; Forty Thieves; Battle of Orleans; Bluebird; Robin Hood; Timour, the Tartar; Adelgitha; Ella Rosenberg; More Ways Than One; Matrimony; Ways and Means; The Voice of Nature; Obi; The Heir-at-Law; The School for Scandal; The Castle Spectre; Oscar and Malvina; Pizarro; Embargo; The Miser; Festival of Peace; Americans in Algiers; The Surrender of Calais; Julius Caesar; Richard III; The Tempest.*

1815–16: *The School for Scandal; Venice Preserved; The Jew and the Doctor; Honey Moon; Spoil'd Child; As You Like It; Lovers' Vows; The Highland Reel; The Mountaineers; My Grandmother; Pizarro; Tooth Ache; Abaellino, the Bandit; Tekeli; The Mountaineers; Paul and Virginia; The National Fete; Bluebeard; Zambuca; The Magpie and the Maid; Ella Rosenberg; The Miller and His Men; Abaellino; 'Tis All a Farce.*

BIBLIOGRAPHY

Muriel Arline Kellerhouse, "The Green Street Theatre, Albany, New York, under the Management of John Bernard, 1813–1816" (Ph.D. diss., Indiana University, 1973), cited the *Albany Advertiser*, 1815–17; the *Albany Argus*, 1813–17; the *Albany Gazette*, 1813–17; and the *Albany Register*, 1813–17.

Jerri Cummins Crawford

H

HARRIGAN AND HART COMPANY. See HARRIGAN'S COMPANY.

HARRIGAN'S COMPANY. Harrigan's Company, also known as the Harrigan and Hart Company, coalesced from a group of variety performers around 1876. The company, which was managed by Edward Harrigan and Martin Hanley, occupied four theatres in New York City between 1876 and 1895, when it ceased to be a permanent resident company. Harrigan and his partner Tony Hart (born Anthony Cannon), rented the Theatre Comique at 514 Broadway from Josh Hart in 1876 and occupied that 1,400-seat proscenium theatre for five seasons. In August 1881 the company moved uptown to the New Theatre Comique at 728 Broadway, a 1,200-seat proscenium theatre that remained their home until it was destroyed by fire in December 1884. The team and its company briefly occupied the Park Theatre at Broadway and Thirty-fifth Street until the partnership was dissolved in May 1885. Then in the fall of 1885, Harrigan reorganized the company at the Park Theatre, where it resided until 1890. Finally, in December 1880 the actor-playwright-manager opened the 915-seat Harrigan's Theatre at Thirty-fifth Street and Sixth Avenue and continued to produce plays there until February 1895, when bad business and personal tragedy forced him to close. Some members of Harrigan's Company continued to tour with their familiar repertory until their leader's retirement in 1908.

Harrigan's Company evolved from a group of performers who had specialized in ethnic comedy and musical sketches in the variety houses of the Lower East Side of New York. The company's work appealed primarily to the people that its plays sought to portray—the Irish and German immigrants and the blacks of lower Manhattan. Its only competition lay in the variety houses of the 1870s and the vaudeville houses that proliferated under Tony Pastor's influence in the 1880s. The company had the distinction of presenting only those plays written by Harrigan himself and featuring the playwright and Hart in the leading roles. The plays were never produced by any other nineteenth-century theatrical company, and with one exception, none of the company's standard repertory has been performed since the playwright-manager's death in 1911.

The plays of Edward Harrigan were extended versions of the standard variety sketch that incorporated the familiar characters from nineteenth-century New York's Lower East Side immigrant neighborhoods with popular songs and slapstick action. He borrowed heavily from the traditions of the variety and minstrel stage, the burlesque, and the traditional melodrama to form his own unique musical comedy. Usually three acts long, the plays always included some of the 200 songs written by Harrigan and his conductor (and father-in-law) David Braham. Although the plays often lacked constructive unity and always featured a generous amount of superfluous action, they rarely failed to win the public's approval. Among the most popular and successful comedies were *Squatter Sovereignty, McSorley's Inflation, Cordelia's Aspirations, Old Lavender, Pete, Waddy Googan, Reilly and the Four Hundred*, and the plays of the Mulligan Guard Series. The incorporation of music into the fabric of these farcical stories about down-and-out immigrants provided a step in the development of American musical comedy.

In the 1870s Harrigan's Company's primary audiences were the immigrants who attended variety and minstrel shows in lower Manhattan. This popularity was reflected in the popular papers of the era like *The Spirit of the Times* that gave little consideration to other theatrical stories. By the beginning of the 1880s, people from all aspects of New York society flocked to their theatre including illustrious politicians, famous theatrical personalities, and respected dramatic critics like William Winter and Brander Matthews. The *New York Times* regularly reviewed their shows and frequently encouraged the playwright and his company to refine and upgrade the quality of their work. William Dean Howells, the Dean of American literary criticism in the nineteenth century, was particularly impressed with the company's work, heralding its realism and truth to nature and calling it the "spring of true American comedy" (Howells, *Harper's Monthly*, July 1886, pp. 315–16).

In addition to acting as stage director and artistic manager of the company, Harrigan was its principal star. He had begun acting in minstrel and variety theatres in San Francisco in the 1860s and joined Hart in 1871 to form the popular variety team of Harrigan and Hart. After he began producing full-length plays, Harrigan usually played Irish protagonist roles such as Dan Mulligan or Jeremiah McCarthy. Tony Hart, acclaimed for his female impersonations, appeared in the "wench" roles, such as the Mulligan's popular black maid, Rebecca Allup, or as Harrigan's zany sidekick. Hart left the company in 1885 to pursue a solo career, but bad luck and failing health prevented him from achieving success, and he died in 1891.

The company's leading lady was Annie Yeamans, who always played opposite Harrigan as his Irish wife or girlfriend. A veteran of the circus as well as the comic stage, she remained with the company throughout its existence. Another principal actress with the company, Annie Mack, had appeared as Ophelia opposite Edwin Booth's Hamlet. For Harrigan, she played comic Irish soubrette roles. Johnny Wild, fresh from the minstrel stage, created many of Harrigan's most popular blackface roles, and Billy Gray was usually cast alongside him as a complementary blackface character. Harry A. Fisher was assigned the roles of German immigrants who antagonized the Irish heroes and heroines.

Filling out the casts, which usually included between twenty and thirty characters, were John Queen, William West, Ed Mack, Michael Bradley, Gertie Granville (later Hart's wife), George L. Stout, John Sparks, Joseph Sparks (who understudied Harrigan), and countless others. Most of the principal players performed exclusively with Harrigan's company after it was firmly established. Dan Collyer replaced Tony Hart in 1885, and Mrs. Yeaman's daughters, Jennie, Lydia, and Emily, occasionally joined the company along with Ada Braham, David Braham, Jr., and Edward Harrigan, Jr. Emma Pollack and Ada Lewis also appeared with the company in the 1890s, creating Harrigan's popular "tough-girl" roles.

Because the company derived from the variety tradition and appealed to an already-existing audience, it was popular and financially successful from the beginning. Ticket prices ranged from fifteen cents for gallery seats in the 1870s to $1.50 for seats in the parquet in the 1890s. The company generally performed to packed houses every evening except Sundays and at matinees on Tuesdays and Fridays. While Martin Hanley managed the company's business affairs, Harrigan took control of artistic decisions, fulfilling the role of the modern artistic director. William Harrigan, the playwright's father, acted as company treasurer. The management employed Charles Witham (who had designed scenery for Edwin Booth) as its scenic designer and Michael Bradley as its choreographer, while various people functioned as master machinist, stage manager, costumer, property manager, advertising agent, and master of mechanical, gas, and later, electrical effects throughout the company's twenty-year history.

In 1895 Harrigan decided to dismantle the permanent resident company and leased Harrigan's Theatre to Richard Mansfield, who remodeled it and renamed it the Garrick. Harrigan took his company on tour throughout the remainder of the decade, presenting revivals of the company's biggest hits and sketch-length versions of some of them in vaudeville shows. In 1904 he appeared in New York for the last time with some members of his company at the Murray Hill Theatre in his final play to be produced, *Under Cover*. He continued to write plays until 1908, and he died on June 6, 1911.

PERSONNEL

Management: Edward Green Harrigan, proprietor and manager (1876–95); Tony Hart, proprietor and manager (1876–84); John E. Cannon, manager (1876–81); Martin Hanley, business manager; William Harrigan, Sr., treasurer (1876–90); Archie Stalker, advertising agent; William J. Hanley, treasurer (1891–95).

Scenic Artists: Charles Witham (1879–90), D. Frank Doyle (1891–95).

Scenic and Lighting Technicians: Robert J. Cutler, Richard Doyle, Louis Filber, Samuel Gorbitt, Joseph A. Logan, William McMurray, Robert Pullar, Edward Willoughby, John Whalen.

Costumers: Annie Howard, Mrs. Mary Jack.

Musicians: David Braham, Sr., composer and conductor.

Choreographers: Michael Bradley, Edward Murphy.

Actors and Actresses: Isabelle Archer, James Barlow, William Barlow, Fanny Batchelder, Mary Bird, Stella Boniface, *Michael Bradley* (1876–88), David Braham, Jr., James Brevarde, Dan Burke, James Burke, Ed Burt, J. Callahan, R. Callahan, May Carlisle, Jennie Christie, *Dan Collyer* (1885–1904), Harry Davenport, Joseph Davis, John Decker, M. F. Drew, Welsh Edwards, Ada Farwell, Lizzie Finn, *Harry Fisher* (1876–1904), James Fitzsimmons, Michael Foley, James Fox, Peter Goldrich, Marie Gorenflo, Edward Gorman, Edward Goss, *Gertie Granville* (1881–85), Billy Gray, Harry Guion, Annie Hall, *Edward Harrigan* (1876–1904), *Tony Hart* (1876–85), Emil Heusil, Edward Hume, Nellie Jones, Annie Langdon, Kate Langdon, Amy Lee, Marion Lester, Ada Lewis, Etta Lyons, Laura Lyons, Annie Mack, *Ed Mack* (1879–93), John McCullough, George Merritt, William Merritt, Hattie Moore, Arthur Moreland, Marcus Moriarty, Sadie Morris, Edward Murphy, Edwin Murphy, Annie O'Neill, Fred W. Peters, Emma Pollack, Fred Queen, John Queen, Richard Quilter, James B. Radcliffe, Thomas Ray, James Rennie, Mamie (Minnie) Richards, Marion Roberts, William Scanlon, Harry Sinclair, Robert Synder, John Sparks, *Joseph Sparks* (1881–1904), Adele Stillwell, George L. Stout, Charles Sturgis, James Tierney, Gertie Tutthil, Lulla Tutthil, Alfred Waite, John Walsh, Ida Ward, *William West* (1876–93), Nellie Wetherhill, Bertha Wild, *John Wild* (1876–95), Esther Williams, Joseph Williamson, George H. Wood, Harry Wright, *Annie Yeamans* (1877–1904), Emily Yeamans, *Jennie Yeamans* (1877–1904).

REPERTORY

1876–77: *Iascaire; Christmas Joys and Sorrows*.

1877–78: *Old Lavender; The Rising Star; The Pillsbury Muddle; Sullivan's Christmas; The Logaire; The Celebrated Hard Case*.

1878–79: *My Wife's Mother; Our Law Makers; Mulligan Guard Ball*.

1879–80: *Mulligan Guard Chowder; Mulligan Guard Christmas; Mulligan Guard Surprise*.

1880–81: *Mulligan Guard Picnic; Mulligan Guard Nominee; Mulligan Silver Wedding*.

1881–82: *The Major; Squatter Sovereignty*.

1882–83: *The Blackbird* (by G. L. Stout); *Mordecai Lyons; McSorley's Inflation; Muddy Day.*

1883–84: *Mulligan Guard Ball; Mulligan Guard Picnic; Cordelia's Aspirations; Dan's Tribulations.*

1884–85: *Investigation; McAllister's Legacy; The Major; Cordelia's Aspirations; Are You Insured?*

1885–86: *Old Lavender; The Grip; The Leather Patch.*

1886–87: *Investigation; The O'Reagans; McNooney's Visit.*

1887–88: *The Leather Patch; Cordelia's Aspirations; Pete.*

1888–89: *Waddy Googan; The Logaire; Pete; The O'Reagans; 4–11–44; The Grip.*

1890–91: *Reilly and the Four Hundred.*

1891–92: *Reilly and the Four Hundred; The Last of the Hogans; Reilly and the Four Hundred.*

1892–93: *Squatter Sovereignty; Mulligan Guard Ball; Cordelia's Aspirations; Reilly and the Four Hundred.*

1893–94: *Dan's Tribulations; The Woollen Stocking; Old Lavender; The Leather Patch; The Woollen Stocking.*

1894–95: *Notoriety; The Major.*

BIBLIOGRAPHY

Published Sources: E. J. Kahn, *The Merry Partners: The Age and Stage of Harrigan and Hart* (New York: Random House, 1955); Alicia Kae Koger, *A Critical Analysis of Edward Harrigan's Comedy* (Ann Arbor: UMI Research Press, 1984); Richard Moody, *Ned Harrigan: From Corlear's Hook to Herald Square* (Chicago: Nelson-Hall, 1980); *New York Times* (1879–95); George C. D. Odell, *Annals of the New York Stage*, vols. 10–15 (New York: Columbia University Press, 1938–49).

Unpublished Source: Warren Burns, "The Plays of Edward G. Harrigan: The Theatre of Intercultural Communication" (Ph.D. diss., Pennsylvania State University, 1969).

Archival Sources: Robinson Locke and Townsend Walsh Scrapbooks, Theatre Collection, New York Public Library, Lincoln Center; Harrigan Scrapbooks, Theatre Collection, New York Public Library, Lincoln Center; Harrigan Manuscripts, Rare Book Division, New York Public Library; Scrapbooks, photographs, and memorabilia, Theatre Collection, Museum of the City of New York; Scrapbooks, Player's Club Library, New York City; Manuscripts, Library of Congress, Washington, D.C.; Sheet Music, Lilly Rare Book Library, Indiana University, Bloomington, Indiana, and Music Collection, New York Public Library, Lincoln Center.

Alicia Kae Koger

THE HAYMARKET THEATRE COMPANY. Although Boston was too small to support two theatres at the time, rivalry between the pro-English Federalists and the pro-French Jacobins spread from politics to the arts, and during the spring of 1796, Charles Stuart Powell (d.1811), a previous and unsuccessful manager of the Boston ["Federal Street"] Theatre Company*, raised $12,000 to build a playhouse to rival his former company. Constructed during the summer and fall, the Haymarket opened to the public on December 26 with a double bill of *Belle's Stratagem* and *Mirza and Lindor*. The huge, wooden building stood near the corner of Tremont and Boylston streets, with most of the actors being newly imported from England.

In 1797 the new theatre with Powell's resident company ran steadily until June 14 and then housed a brief and financially unsuccessful season presented by John Hodgkinson and the [Old] American Company (1792–1806)* from New York. Having also lost money during his long season, Powell broke his lease on the house and disbanded the company.

In July 1798 Hodgkinson reopened the idle Haymarket with a performance of *Hamlet* starring Thomas Abthorpe Cooper (1776–1849), but the yellow-fever scare so decimated the audience that the run was cancelled at the second performance. Hodgkinson reopened the house in October, but a lack of business had darkened it again by the spring of 1799. Later the house was opened only sporadically to visiting companies. It was auctioned off in 1803 and razed by the new owner, who sold the lumber for firewood.

Since the Jacobins were the driving force behind the financing of the company, Powell produced a few plays to please them, including the premiere of John Burk's spunky *Battle of Bunker Hill* and William Brown's *West Point Preserved*. In the main, though, his taste ran to spectacular pantomimes and ballets to take advantage of the splendid scenery for which the theatre was noted.

PERSONNEL

Management: Charles Stuart Powell, manager (1796–97).

Scene Painters: Antony Audin, Antony Audin, Jr.

Actors and Actresses: Names that are followed by (P-B) indicate performers who were primarily seen in pantomimes and ballets. Mrs. Allen, Mr. Amean (P-B), Mrs. Barrett, *Mr. Giles S. Barrett*, Mr. Borier (P-B), Mr. Bowen (P-B), Miss Broadhurst, Mr. Clough, Mr. Cunnington, *Mr. James H. Dickenson*, Mr. Dubois (P-B), *Mr. Fawcett*, Mr. Francisquy (P-B), Miss Gowen, Miss Harrison, *Mr. Hughes*, *Mrs. Hughes*, Mr. Kenny, Madame Lege (P-B), Mr. Lege (P-B), *Mr. Marriott*, Mrs. Pick (P-B), Charles Powell, *Snelling Powell, Mrs. Snelling Powell*, Madame Sevens (P-B), Mr. Sevens (P-B), Master Shaffer (P-B), Mr. Simpson, Mrs. Simpson, Mr. Spinacuta (P-B), Mr. Spraque, Mr. Vale (P-B), Madame Val (P-B), Miss Westray, Eleanor Westray, Eliza Westray, *John Williamson*, Mr. Wilson.

REPERTORY

Numbers in parentheses indicate the number of times a play was presented.

Belle's Stratagem; Mirza and Lindor (2); *Suspicious Husband; Cooper; She Stoops to Conquer; Waterman* (2); *Beaux Stratagem; Padlock* (4); *Variety* (2); *Jew; Rosina; Upholsterer; New French Deserter* (4); *Alexander the Great* (3); *Way to Get Married* (2); *Deserter* (2); *Quaker* (2); *Battle of Hexham* (2); *Animal Magnetism* (2); *The Merchant of Venice* (2); *Mountaineers* (3); *Milliners* (3); *Miller of Mansfield; Richard III; Inkle and Yarico* (3); *Siege of Quebec* (2); *Two Hunters and the Milkmaid* (2);

Road to Ruin; Man of Ten Thousand; Wood Cutters (2); *Agreeable Surprise* (2); *Retaliation; Battle of Bunker Hill* (9); *Poor Jack* (3); *Prize* (3); *Deuce Is in Him* (2); *Bon Ton; Midnight Hour; Double Disguise* (3); *Robinson Crusoe* (2); *Child of Nature* (2); *Chrononhotonthologos; Adopted Child* (3); *George Barnwell; Every One Has His Fault; Ghost; Garden of Love* (3); *Columbus* (3); *Whims of Galatea; Love in a Village; West Point Preserved* (5); *Irish Widow; Harlequin Doctor; Lying Valet; He Would Be a Soldier; Irishman in London; Rule a Wife and Have a Wife* (2); *Quality Binding; Wrangling Lovers; Indian War Feast; Zorinski* (3); *Sportsman Outwitted; Romance of an Hour; Clemency of Charlemagne* (2); *Loves Makes a Man; Rage; Don Juan* (2); *Death of Louis XVI* (2); *Son-in-Law* (2); *Three and the Deuce; Destruction of the Bastille; Werter; Absent Man; The School for Scandal; Duplicity; Divorce; Medea and Jason; All in a Good Humour.*

BIBLIOGRAPHY

Published Sources: George O. Seilhamer, *History of the American Theatre*, vol. 3 (Philadelphia: Glove Printing House, 1891); Richard Stoddard, "The Haymarket Theatre, Boston," *Educational Theatre Journal* 27 (March 1975):63–69.

Larry D. Clark

HOWARD ATHENAEUM COMPANY. Located on the south side of Howard Street in Boston, the first "Old Howard" was a poorly constructed frame building erected in the early 1840s as a tabernacle by the followers of a doomsday sect headed by William Miller. The building was sold to restauranteur Thomas Ford and his partners, who converted it to a theatre, renamed it the Howard Athenaeum, and began its first season on October 13, 1845. The acting company was headed by William Ayling. The first season of eighty-nine pieces included ballet and English opera, a variety that typified the Howard and would eventually come to characterize it. It is notable that this theatre, unusual in the years before the Civil War, functioned from the first partially as a road house.

On February 23, 1846, the original Howard burned to the ground. Boston brewer Luke Beard bought the land and commissioned Isaiah Rogers to design a new theatre—with a bottling plant in the basement. The second Howard was a brick structure with a granite front pierced by three Gothic, church-style windows. The orchestra seating was raked and the seats spring cushioned; circular stairways carried patrons to the dress circle and to two additional tiers. Capacity varied between 1,800 and 2,000 persons. The original stage measured forty-three feet in depth, and the proscenium opening was thirty-six feet wide and thirty-two feet high. It is this building, opened on October 5, 1846, that was still standing at the midtwentieth-century mark, its exterior little changed, although the interior had been remodeled several times, notably in 1883 and 1895.

The 1846–47 season consisted of forty-one weeks: eight weeks of drama, one week of violin concerts, six weeks of Italian opera, six weeks of circus, four weeks of the Ravels in pantomime, and sixteen weeks of ballet. In his next season, beginning in August, Ford featured five weeks of drama, with starring visits by Junius Booth and Mrs. Mowatt, but gave over the rest of the season, lasting until June 1848, to opera, ballet, and variety. Barely into the 1848–49 season, Ford resigned and leased the theatre to John Brougham and William E. Burton. William Ayling continued intermittently as stage manager and then company manager, along with several others over the years, for the history of the Howard Athenaeum is marked neither by continuing management nor by a guiding philosophy. It functioned as a star-stock house, at times described as the best one in Boston, until the end of the 1867–68 season, after which it turned wholly to variety, and from 1918 by turns to vaudeville, movies, and burlesque. In its twenty-two seasons of star-stock existence, 1846–68, visiting dramatic stars and star companies included Junius Brutus Booth, Edwin Booth, Joseph Jefferson, Charlotte Cushman, William Charles Macready, Edwin Forrest, Fanny Davenport, William Warren, James H. Hackett, George Vandenhoff, Charles Kean, F. S. Chanfrau, Kate Fisher, James Murdock, Dan Marble, Mrs. Mossop (Louisa Lane Drew), Charles Dibden Pitt, Matilda Heron, and James W. Wallack.

PERSONNEL

Management: This list does not include managers of visiting companies, as far as they can be distinguished, nor management personnel of the variety bills featured after 1868. For these names, see the W. W. Clapp entry "The Drama in Boston," in *The Memorial History of Boston, Including Suffolk County, Mass.: 1630–1880.* As can be readily seen from the dates given, there was considerable overlapping of management personnel. Thomas Ford, W. F. Johnson, W. L. Ayling (1845–48); James H. Hackett, W. H. Chippendale, W. H. Crisp (1846–47); John Brougham, W. E. Burton, Wm. Ayling (1848–49); Charles R. Thorne, E. Eddy (1849–50); Messrs. Baker and English, Wm. Ayling (1850–51); Wyzeman Marshall (1851–52); Henry Willard (1852–55); W. Palmer, J. B. Strong, D. Swain (1854–55); J. M. Field, T. Placide, J. W. Buckland, Henry Farren, B. Duffy (1855–56); F. A. Munroe, J. Munroe, F. Harrington, E. B. Williams, H. Ashley, John Gilbert, E. L. Davenport, J. Barren (1856–57); H. Ashley, J. Barrow (1857–58); E. A. Sothern, T. E. Mills, E. L. Davenport (1858–59); E. L. Davenport (1859–62); W. M. Fleming, Wyzeman Marshall (1861–62); Wyzeman Marshall (1862–63); Henry Willard (1863–65); Isaac B. Rich (1865–68).

Scenery, Machinery, Costumes, Wardrobe, and Properties: R. Jones, G. Curtis, George Conover, G. W. Taylor, J. G. Gilbert (1845–46); G. Curtis, Adam Gailbraith, Mrs. Stafford (1846–47).

Prompter: T. Yeoman (1846–47).

Musical Direction: Mr. Meyrer (1845–47).

Actors and Actresses: 1845–46: Mr. Adams, W. L. Ayling, Mrs. W. L. Ayling, Mr. Binney, Miss Booth, Mr. Booth, Mrs. W. H. Chippendale, Mrs. H. Cramer, Mr. Davis, Miss Deluce, Miss Drake, Mr. Gilbert, Mr. G. Howard, Mrs. G. Howard, Mrs. C. W. Hunt, G. W. Jamieson, W. F. Johnson, Mr. Jones, Mrs. W. Jones, Mrs. Judah, Miss Mace, Mrs. Maeder, Mr. Munroe, J.A.J. Neafie, Mr.

Parker, A. J. Phillips, Mr. Resor, Mr. Russell, Mr. Sullivan, Mr. Taylor, C. H. Walcott, Mrs. C. H. Walcott, D. Whiting. 1846–47: W. L. Ayling, Mr. Bradshaw, Mrs. Crisp, H. H. Hall, Miss Hildreth, H. Hunt, Miss Maywood, Mrs. Maywood, Miss Phillips, C. H. Saunders, Mrs. Stone, Mary Taylor, William Warren. 1849–50: Mr. Bellamy, Mr. Eddy, Mr. G. Jordan, Mrs. Muzzy, Mr. Saunders, Mr. Skerrett, Mrs. Skerrett, Mr. and Mrs. Thorne, Miss Wagstaff, Mr. Ward, Mr. Watkins, Mr. C. Webb, Miss Fanny Wheeler. 1850–51: G. Arnold, John Brougham, Mrs. English, Mr. and Mrs. John Gilbert, S. Johnson, Mr. Raymond, Mrs. W. H. Smith, Mrs. H. M. Stephens, E. Warden. 1851–52: Mrs. Brand, Miss Cramer, Mrs. Cramer, Mrs. Groves, Mr. Hamblin, W. F. Johnson, Melinda Jones, Mr. Meeker, Mr. and Mrs. Sloane, W. H. Smith, Mrs. Whitman.

REPERTORY

1845–46: *The School for Scandal; Wives as They Were and Maids as They Are; Henry IV, Part I; The Kentuckian; Yankee in England; Man of the World; Merry Wives of Windsor; Rip Van Winkle; The Lady of Lyons; Honey Moon; Romeo and Juliet; Fashion; Bride of Lammermoor; The Stranger; Much Ado; Hamlet; As You Like It; The Gamester; Macbeth; Ion; Twelfth Night; The Hunchback; Othello; Money; The Barrack Room; La Bayadère; My Master's Rival; The Spectre Bridegroom; The Nervous Man; The Irish Ambassador; White Horse of the Peppers; Mysteries of Paris; Pizarro*, and others, including ballets and operas.

1846–47: *The Rivals; Hamlet; Honey Moon; Love's Sacrifice; Faint Heart ne'er Won Fair Lady; Used Up; Catherine and Petruchio; The Wonder; Romeo and Juliet; The Stranger; Fazio; Much Ado; The Hunchback; The Lady of Lyons; Love; La Bayadère; The Nervous Man; The Irish Post; The Irish Ambassador; The Wreck Ashore; Laugh When You Can; The Miller's Maid; Richard III; New Way to Pay Old Debts; Hamlet; The Iron Chest; The Merchant of Venice; King Lear; Venice Preserved; The Apostate; Guy Mannering; London Assurance; Henry IV; Merry Wives; Man of the World; The School for Scandal; The Vermont Yankee; The Kentuckian; Rip Van Winkle; The Devil in Paris; Clari; The Last Man; A Roland for an Oliver; Look before You Leap; A Kiss in the Dark*, and others, including numerous ballets, operas, and concerts.

1847–48: *The Rivals; Paul Pry; Henry IV; Don Caesar de Bazan; Wild Oats; The Wife; The Lady of Lyons; Hamlet; Richard III; The Apostate; A New Way to Pay Old Debts; Othello; King Lear; Macbeth; King of the Commons; The Hunchback; Much Ado; Romeo and Juliet; Armand; Vermont Wool Dealer; The Wolf and the Lamb; Spoil'd Child*, and others, plus operas, ballets, circus, and variety acts.

BIBLIOGRAPHY

The full history of the Howard Athenaeum stock-star period (1845–68) has never, to my knowledge, been thoroughly researched. As this entry makes clear, additional work is needed, especially to flesh out the acting companies and repertory at the Howard beyond its first years. Present available sources include John R. Woodruff's "Theatrical Venture in Boston as Exemplified by the First Seasons of the Howard Athenaeum" (Ph.D. diss., Cornell University, 1949), which concerns the Howard's first three seasons; Woodruff's "America's Oldest Living Theatre—The Howard Athenaeum," in *Theatre Annual*, 7 (1950):71–81; William W. Clapp's "Drama in

Boston," in *The Memorial History of Boston, Including Suffolk County, Mass.: 1630–1880*, vol. 4, ed. Justin Winsor (Boston: James R. Osgood and Co., 1881); and William W. Clapp's *Record of the Boston Stage* (Boston: James Monroe, 1853).

Rosemarie K. Bank

I

ILLINOIS THEATRICAL COMPANY. The Illinois Theatrical Company, Chicago, initially referred to as The Company or the Chicago Theatre Company, presented its first production in the fall of 1837. Organized by Harry Isherwood and Alexander McKenzie, the company was the first to present drama in the young city (the Indians were expelled in 1833). Their petition to the City Council for a theatrical license, one of the few official documents to survive the Great Fire of 1871, stated that their establishment was intended to "afford instruction as well as amusement" and that they proposed "to remain here during the winter, and that, consequently, they make no calculation to receive more money in the city than what they shall expend during their stay" (this last point was a plea for a low fee). The rate of the license was fixed at $125 for one year, a sum protested but paid. The exact date of the first production is not known, but the license is dated October 17, 1837, and it is generally believed that the first performance was given before the end of that month. The titles of the opening production have also been lost, but *The Idiot Witness, The Stranger,* and *The Carpenter of Rouen* were given early in the season.

Isherwood and McKenzie secured a lease for the recently vacated Sauganash Hotel, which stood on the southeast corner of Lake and Market streets. In his *History of Chicago*, A. T. Andreas described the "temple of dramatic art." "The room was not a model of theatric beauty. . . . Rough seats and chairs, upon the level floor where all men met in a spirit of equality; rude scenery, and smoking lamps—these were the most conspicuous characteristics of the furnishings" (1:474–75). According to Andreas, the room seated about 300 persons, the admission was seventy-five cents, and the curtain rose at 7:30 p.m. This first season lasted about six weeks, after which the company began a southern tour.

Isherwood and McKenzie evidently deemed their first Chicago season a success, for they returned in April 1838, petitioning the council to grant them a license for a new theater to be fitted in the "Rialto." The Rialto, originally an auction room measuring thirty by eighty feet, was located at Nos. 8 and 10 Dearborn Street (west side of street) between Lake and South Water streets. This was a prime location for a theatre. The only bridge over the Chicago River was at Dearborn Street; a principal hotel, the Tremont House, was in the same block; and the only public eating establishment, the City Refectory, was across the street. Critic Benjamin F. Taylor described the Rialto as "a den of a place, looking more like a dismantled grist-mill than a temple of *any*body. The gloomy entrance could have furnished the scenery for a nightmare, and the lights within were sepulchral enough to show up the coffin scene in *Lucrezia Borgia*" (Andreas, 1:476).

The petition to refurbish the Rialto as a theatre caused an uproar. A counterpetition, signed by thirty-five citizens, was submitted to the council on May 1, 1838. It requested that a license be denied on the grounds that the Rialto "is a wooden building, and surrounded by wooden and combustible buildings. Your petitioners would further represent that theaters are subject to take fire, and are believed to be dangerous on that account to property in their vicinity, and that insurance cannot be obtained on property in their vicinity except at greatly advanced premiums" (Andreas, 1:476). The council appointed a special committee to study and decide the matter. One of the committee members, Grant Goodrich, hopped on his moral highhorse and advocated denying a license on the grounds that theatres "were the nurseries of crime." (Although the original objections to the Rialto theatre were probably valid, Goodrich's accusations became the center of the short-lived debate. In defiance of Goodrich, the special committee recommended the granting of the license for a fee of $125; Goodrich received a further blow when the entire council voted to grant the license for $100.

Having been officially sanctioned, Isherwood and McKenzie turned the Rialto into an auditorium by adding boxes, gallery, and pit to seat approximately 400 persons. They renamed the building the Chicago Theatre. Again, records of the early productions have been lost. The season ran from late May to late October, after which the company left on a tour of other Illinois cities.

The company returned to Chicago in May 1839 without Isherwood (he eventually became the principal scenic artist at Wallack's in New York). Taking his place was Joseph Jefferson, Sr. It was at this time that McKenzie and his new partner renamed the company the "Illinois Theatrical Company." The first production of the 1839 season was given on August 31. It opened with *The Review; or, The Wags of Windsor*, a comedy with music, and closed with the farce *The Illustrious Stranger; or, Buried Alive!*

The Illinois Theatrical Company gave its final performance on November

2, 1839. Following this, the company (minus leading lady Mrs. Ingersoll, who remained to give dancing lessons) moved east, never to return. Although the company enjoyed successful short seasons in Chicago, the city (with a population of only 4,800 in 1839) could not support a permanent company. No major companies settled in Chicago until John B. Rice established a local company in 1847.

PERSONNEL

The following is probably a partial listing; complete records are not extant.

Management: Alexander McKenzie, proprietor and treasurer (1837–39); Harry Isherwood (1837–38); Joseph Jefferson II (1839).

Actors and Actresses: *A. A. Adams* (1838); Madame Analine (1837); Charles Burk (1837–38); William Childs (1838); C. G. Germon (1838–39); Charles L. Green (1839); Mrs. David Ingersoll (nee I. Jefferson), later Mrs. James Wright (1837, 1839); Mrs. Jefferson (1838–39); Joseph Jefferson II (1838–39); Joseph Jefferson III (1838–39); H. Leicester (1837–39); *Dan Marble* (1838); Mr. Mason (1839); *Mrs. McCluer*, star (1838), company member (1839); Alexander McKenzie (1837–39); Mrs. Hettie McKenzie (1837–39); Thomas Sankey (1837–39); A. Sullivan (1839); William Warren (1838–39); James S. Wright (1837–38).

REPERTORY

The following is a partial listing; complete records are not extant.

1837: *Thérèse; or, The Orphan of Geneva; The Hunchback; The Hypocrite; It Is the Devil; Everybody's Husband; Demon of the Desert; The Idiot Witness; The Stranger; The Carpenter of Rouen; The Polish Wife.*

1838: *The Lady of Lyons! or, Love and Pride; The Two Friends; The Stranger; Rob Roy; Damon and Pythias; Wives as They Were and Maids as They Are; Sam Patch; The Hypocrite; Honey Moon; Petticoat Government; Jane Shore; The Maid and the Magpie; The Idiot Witness.*

1839: *The Review; or, The Wags of Windsor; The Illustrious Stranger; or, Buried Alive!; The Warlock of the Glen; The Midnight Hour; Isabelle; or, Woman's Life; The Spectre Bridegroom; or, A Ghost in Spite of Himself; Simpson and Co.; Oliver Twist; The Golden Farmer; or, Vell, Vot of It?; The Sleeping Draught; The Magpie and the Maid; She Stoops to Conquer; Jane Shore; The Lady of Lyons; Cherry and Fair Star; or, The Children of Cyprus; Damon and Pythias; Is It a Lie?; Fazio; Taming of the Shrew; Romeo and Juliet; Macbeth; Hamlet; The Merchant of Venice; Tam O'Shanter; Pizarro; Uncle Sam; Poor Gentleman; Loan of a Lover; The Village Lawyer; The Irish Tutor; The Swiss Cottage; Sweethearts and Wives; Animal Magnetism; A Poor Soldier; My Heart's in the Highlands; The Idiot Witness; The Enraged Politician; A Wandering Boy; The Unfinished Gentleman; The Invincibles; It's All a Farce; Zembuca; Napoleon; The Wonder; Venice Preserved; Catherine and Petruchio; No Song, No Supper; The Wife; Aladdin and His Wonderful Lamp; Rendezvous; Vision of the Dead; Gilderoy; The Forest of Bondy; Black Eyed Susan; Bombastes Furioso; The Murderess; Don Juan; William Tell; Little Red Riding Hood; The Children of the Wood; Lafitte: Pirate of the Gulf; Joan of Arc; The Innkeeper's Daughter; The Rivals; The Devil's Ducat; Tom Cringle's Leg.*

BIBLIOGRAPHY

Andreas, A. T. *History of Chicago*. 3 vols. Chicago: A. T. Andreas Co., 1884–86.

McVicker, James H. *The Theatre: Its Early Days in Chicago*. Chicago: Knight and Leonard, 1884.

Sherman, Robert L. *Chicago Stage: Its Records and Achievements*. Chicago: Robert L. Sherman, 1947.

Linda Bandy-White

K

[LAURA] KEENE'S THEATRE. Laura Keene's Varieties opened December 17, 1855, and was the first of two theatres the manageress operated in New York. Located at Bond Street and Broadway, the Great Metropolitan (Tripler Hall) had been built for but never used by Jenny Lind. The initial production was *Old Heads and Young Hearts*. Keene lost this theatre in May 1856 and immediately began construction of her own theatre, known as Laura Keene's Theatre (622–24 Broadway), which opened November 18, 1856, with *As You Like It*.

Keene's management was typical of the New York stock company renaissance of the midnineteenth century. She avoided stars and relied on a core company of seasoned and well-known actors, presenting the play and her company as an ensemble attraction. She never billed herself above her employees. Competition during these years was fierce, and she and her rivals (William E. Burton, James W. Wallack, and E. A. Marshall) frequently ran productions of the same play against each other, sometimes opening on the same night. Keene in particular was not adverse to hiring actors away from her rivals, even in midseason. On the opening night of the Varieties, her scenery was slashed, causing a three-night postponement. Burton bought the Metropolitan Theatre and evicted her at the end of her first season. The financial panic of 1857 was disastrous, and although Keene was able to weather it, Burton's and the Broadway succumbed.

In eight seasons of management, Keene introduced two important innovations: the matinee and the long run. Instances of both can be traced to the 1820s, but it was Keene who introduced them as consistent operating policies. Any play that succeeded was run consecutively until its appeal was exhausted, and Wednesday and Saturday afternoon performances were added in 1857. Both innovations became standard in most American theatres shortly thereafter.

Laura Keene was born in England, probably in 1826, and is said to have been trained by her aunt for the stage. She made her debut as Juliet in Surrey in 1851. Her first London appearance was as Pauline in *The Lady of Lyons*, and she subsequently joined Mme. Vestris and Charles Mathews at their Lyceum, where she attracted the attention of James W. Wallack, who promptly hired her as his leading lady for his stock company opening in New York in September 1852. After a highly successful season, she left the company without notice and decamped to Baltimore, where she opened her own company at the Howard Athenaeum and Gallery of Art (Charles St. Theatre) on December 24, 1853. Keene's management there is a landmark in American theatre history, for she was (jointly with Catherine Norton Sinclair, the ex-Mrs. Edwin Forrest, who opened her Metropolitan Theatre in San Francisco on the same night) the first theatrical manageress of record in America. After a three-month season in Baltimore, she traveled to Australia (with Edwin Booth) and San Francisco, where she opened another company at the American Theatre in 1855. After a few months she returned to New York and, with this wealth of managerial experience behind her, began the Varieties.

The stock companies in New York at this time tended to specialize in one type of drama (Burton concentrated on low comedy, and Wallack's was known as the house for the old English comedies), but Keene was relentless in her appeal to all tastes. From Shakespeare she gave *Much Ado about Nothing, A Midsummer Night's Dream*, and *As You Like It*; from the popular melodrama, she presented *Camille, The Marble Heart, The Sea of Ice, The Corsican Brothers, Hunted Down*, and *Jane Eyre*; comedies included *The Rivals, The School for Scandal, Money*, and *London Assurance*. She had particular success with burlettas and spectaculars, and *The Elves, Seven Sisters* (long run record), and *Seven Sons* marked the commercial high tide and artistic low ebb of her management. New plays included *Blanche of Brandywine* (partially written by Joseph Jefferson), the world premiere of Dion Boucicault's *Colleen Bawn*, and, perhaps the most popular play of the period, Tom Taylor's *Our American Cousin*, which Keene personally disliked but was forced to present when a scheduled production was not ready. Taylor's play made stars of Joseph Jefferson and E. A. Sothern (both promptly left her organization and toured in separate companies of the play), and Keene's benefit in this play at Ford's Theatre in Washington on April 14, 1865, drew President Lincoln to the theatre, where he was assassinated.

Keene's production style was consistently lavish: "a wealth of fancy and an artistic finish that have never been equaled or even approached at any other New York theatre but her own" (*New York Times*, November 6, 1862). She spent more on advertising than had any previous manager, and her executive abilities touched every facet of her organization. She had an ability to hire first-rate talent, either established or nascent, and generally (despite an imperious attitude) to hold on to it. At various times her company included Dion Boucicault, Agnes Robertson, Mr. and Mrs. W. J. Florence, Mr. and Mrs. Charles M. Walcott, George Jordan, Mme. Ponisi, Charles Wheatleigh, C. W. Couldock, Frank Bangs, Catherine Reignolds, Ada Clifton, and Mrs. F. S. Chanfrau.

Keene's business affairs appear to have been managed by John Lutz, whom she married in 1860. The financial vicissitudes of the house were typical of the period: ticket prices for the boxes ranged from $1.50 to 75 cents, and the gallery hit a bottom of twelve and a half cents in lean times. Financial records do not exist, but in the best of times the theatre must have been extremely lucrative; Joseph Jefferson informs us in *Autobiography* that during the long run of *Our American Cousin* Keene herself began to blaze with diamonds. She regularly employed a company of about twenty actors, plus a full orchestra with leader and the largest scenic department in New York.

After the record-making runs of *Seven Sisters* and *Seven Sons*, the artistic prestige of the theatre was diminished. Keene temporarily suspended operations and toured Boston, Philadelphia, and Washington in early 1863, returning to New York for a series of farewell performances and benefits. The theatre was closed May 8, 1863, and taken over by Mrs. John Wood, who renamed it the Olympic.

PERSONNEL

Management: Laura Keene, proprietor and manager (1855–63); John Lutz, business manager (1855–63).

Scenic Technicians: Charles J. Hawthorne (1855–58), O. F. Almy (1855–57), Minard Lewis (1859–63).

Leader of the Orchestra: Thomas Baker (1855–60).

Ballet Master: Mons. Monplaisir.

Stage Manager: James G. Burnett.

Actors and Actresses: Mrs. J. H. Allen, J. D. Bilby, *Mr. and Mrs. William Rufus Blake* (1858–62), *James G. Burnett*, Mrs. F. S. Chanfrau, Ada Clifton, *C. W. and Eliza Couldock* (1858–61), H. F. Daly, Charles Fisher, Mr. and Mrs. W. J. Florence, Effie Germon, Mrs. H. P. Grattan, Frank Hardenberg, Cornelia Jefferson, T. B. Johnston, *George Jordan* (1856–62), D. Leeson, *Walter Lennox* (1858–63), Milnes Levick, George Lingard, Josephine Manners, Marion Macarty, Owen Marlowe, Polly Marshall, *Mme. Ponisi* (1859–61), John T. Raymond, *Catherine Reignolds* (1856–59), W. E. Richardson, Sol Smith Russell, Mark Smith, Sara Stephens, *J. H. Stoddart* (1856–58), Charlotte Thompson, F. A. Vincent, Mr. and Mrs. Charles Walcott, D. W. and Emma Waller, *F. C. Wemyss* (1856–58), Mary Wells, *Charles Wheatleigh* (1855–63).

REPERTORY

1855–56: *Old Heads and Young Hearts; Dreams of Delusion; Masks and Faces; King of the Courts; Perfection; The Love Chase; Still Waters Run Deep; The Lady of Lyons; Money; The Violet; Midas; School for Tigers; Belphegor, the Mountebank;*

or, The Pride of Birth; Serious Family; The Hunchback; Novelty; Look before You Leap; Two Loves and a Life; She Stoops to Conquer; Camille; The Bride of Lammermoor; The King's Rival; Faint Heart ne'er Won Fair Lady; St. Mary's Eve; The Unfinished Gentleman; The Marble Heart; Norma; Slightly Discovered; My Wife's Mirror; Diane; or, Hands, Not Hearts; The Daughter of the Regiment; Jane Eyre; The Rivals; It Takes Two to Make a Bargain; Married Rake; The Spitalfields Weaver; Clarissa Harlowe; The School for Scandal.

1856–57: As You Like It; Ladies Beware; Young New York; A Curious Case; School for Tigers; Second Love; Camille; Contentment vs. Riches; The Love Chase; The First Night; Marble Heart; Doing the Hansom; Young Bacchus; or, Spirits and Water; Rachel, the Reaper; Mary's Birthday; A Game of Speculation; Camomile; David Copperfield; The Wife's Mirror; Faust and Marguerite; Love in '76; The Black Book; The Aves; The Wielded Wife; or, The Reign of Terror; Living too Fast; The Love of a Prince; The Money Question; Like and Unlike; Nature and Art; Variety; or, The Picture Gallery; A Bird in the Hand is Worth Two in the Bush.

1857–58: The Heir-at-Law; The Spectre Bridegroom; A Conjugal Lesson; Angeline; Victims; Judith of Geneva, The Village Lawyer; An Affair of Honor; The Slain Light Guard; Nothing to Nurse; A Husband for an Hour; A Quiet Family; Splendid Misery; Birds of Prey; Lend Me Five Shillings; My Son Diana; The Sea of Ice; The Corsican Brothers; Take Care of Dowd; Harlequin Blue Bird; An Unequal Match; The Muleteer of Toledo; The Lighthouse; White Lies; The Lady of the Lions; The Courier of Lyons; All That Glitters Is Not Gold; Double-Faced People; Mind Your Own Business; An Unprotected Female; Captain Charlotte; Green Bushes; The Flowers of the Forest; Jonathan Bradford; To Parents and Guardians; She Stoops to Conquer; Poor Strollers; Blanche of Brandywine; An Unequal Match.

1858–59: The Willow Copse; The Advocate; or, The Lost Cause; Love and Lightning; or, The Telepath; Jenny Lind; London Assurance; Fra Diavolo; Our American Cousin; A Day in Paris; The Obstinate Family; Twenty Minutes with a Tiger; The Bonnie Fishwife; The Captain is Not A-Miss; The Loan of a Lover; The Married Rake; Aunt Charlotte's Maid; A Midsummer Night's Dream; The Pet of the Petticoats.

1859–60: House and Home; Our Clerks; Nine Points of the Law; World and Stage; The Election; Antony and Cleopatra; The Wife's Secret; Norma; Distant Relations; or, A Southerner in New York; The Heart of Midlothian; Vanity Fair; The Colleen Bawn.

1860–61: The Monkey Boy; Aileen Aroon; or, The Harp of Glanmire; Physic and Fancy; or, The Hypochondriac; The Beggar's Opera; An Unprotected Female; Toodles, a Father; The Seven Sisters; The Murderous Mother.

1861–62: The Seven Sons; Little Tom; or, A Christmas Carol; Robinson Crusoe; The Macarthy; or, The Peep of Day; Reason and Folly; or, Life in Paris; The Old Guard; The Post Boy.

1862–63: Old Heads and Young Hearts; Masks and Faces; Colleen Bawn; No Rest for the Wicked; A Conjugal Lesson; The Rough Diamond; Rachel, the Reaper; Blondette; Jessie McLove; Bantry Boy; Tib; or, The Cat in Crinoline.

BIBLIOGRAPHY

Published Sources: Seasonal accounts in Joseph Ireland, Records of the New York Stage, 1750–1860, 2 vols. (New York: T. H. Morrell, 1866–67); T. Allston Brown, A History of the New York Stage, 3 vols. (New York: Dodd, 1903); and

George C. D. Odell, *Annals of the New York Stage*, vol. 6 (New York: Columbia University Press, 1931).

Archival Sources: "The Letters of Laura Keene," Library of Congress, Washington, D.C. Both the New York Public Library and Harvard Theatre Collection, Cambridge, Massachusetts, have incomplete playbills. John Crehan, *The Life of Laura Keene* (Philadelphia: Rodgers, 1897), is the only published biography of the manageress. Dorothy Jean Taylor, "Laura Keene in America" (Ph.D. diss., Tulane University, 1966), is more comprehensive. Joseph Jefferson, *Autobiography* (New York: Century, 1897) is the only firsthand account of her theatre.

James Burge

KURZ STADT THEATER COMPANY. The Kurz Stadt Theater, Milwaukee, also known as the German Stock Company, was organized in the summer of 1868 by actor-manager Heinrich (Henry) Kurz. He built a proscenium-equipped theatre (217 Third Street) and opened it on October 11, 1868, with a production of Karl Görner's comedy *Tante Kobold und Onkel Satan, oder Der glückliche Familienvater.*

Kurz's stock company represents the first professional and most ambitious continuation of Milwaukee's German-language theatre tradition that had begun in 1850 and would extend into the 1930s. The phenomenon of German production in the United States was not unique to Milwaukee—witness similar theatres in New Orleans (1839), Baltimore (1840), St. Louis (1842), Cincinnati (1846), San Francisco (1853), New York (1854), Chicago (1856), and so on—but the support for Milwaukee's theatre was the most enduring. From its formation, the Stadt Theater operated in competition with other German-language companies, playing under a number of actor-managers at the North Side Turnhalle and at the South Side Turnhalle. The period of greatest competition was from 1880 to 1884, when the Thalia Theatre Company (North) and the Volkstheater (South) produced comparable repertoires with strong casts under competent directors, including Sigmund Selig and Louis Koch. Resorting to audience gifts and postperformance balls, these companies seriously affected the Stadt, but after 1884 the Kurz company dominated. For the 1878–79 season, the Kurz company was also performing in the Grand Opera House (144 East Wells), a larger proscenium theatre built in 1871 by Jacob Nunnemacher. To assist in the interchange of artists, the Stadt formed an alliance with the German theatres of Chicago and St. Louis in 1881, but it failed in 1883; thereafter a portion of the Milwaukee company performed regularly in Chicago on Sunday nights. The company also played in other cities of the upper Midwest; for example, ten performances were given at the Turner Opera House in Davenport, Iowa, 1888–89.

The Kurz family had been involved in German production in Milwaukee since they emigrated from Austria in 1847. Heinrich, his uncle Joseph, and his cousins formed a paraprofessional company that produced more than

480 works in three modified halls from 1853 to 1868. Those years of managerial experience and continued contact with the theatres of Europe reinforced Heinrich Kurz's successful career as a manager. He was also an able actor in musical comedies, such as *Der Postillion von Münchenberg* by Eduard Jacobson and Eduard Linderer. Under his direction the Stadt Theater provided entertainment and cultural continuity for Milwaukee's sizeable German population by producing the German classics and the latest success of Central European theatres.

The Kurz theatre, seating 1,300 following remodelings in 1879 and 1886, began with two performances a week on Wednesdays and Sundays at a top price of seventy-five cents. Friday performances were added after 1870, with the Wednesday offering devoted to serious or classical works for a large subscription audience. Generally, a new work or a revival would be staged for each performance. The first seasons were financially successful, but deficits soon became a regular and expected feature of the theatre. Like its European counterparts, the Stadt was never viewed as a financial enterprise; subsidy was expected from and willingly provided by Milwaukee's leading German families as part of their contribution to the city's German culture. For example, the 1878–79 season of eighty-one productions generated a deficit of $1,054.92, which would be covered by Milwaukee patrons.

Critical reaction in Milwaukee's German and English press varied according to the talents of directors and guests. During the directorship of Julius Collmer (1874–84), the repertoire, which depended upon minor comedies and farces, was repeatedly objected to but not the actual performances themselves. For example, a reviewer thought Eduard Jacobson and H. Wilden's *Goldene Berge*, a "Biographic Sketch with Song," was a poor choice for the Stadt, since it was "an unrelated 'mixtum compositum' of high nonsense, insipid jokes and music hall songs." Nonetheless it was "bearable and enjoyable through the quite adept playing of the principals" (*Freie Presse*, March 20, 1879, p. 4). Despite journalistic criticism of Collmer's artistic choices, he earned the support of his audiences: in an open letter, scores of German families called upon Collmer to award himself a benefit performance in recognition of his efforts "to provide the German population of Milwaukee with a good, German theatre." Collmer graciously accepted and subsequently donated his proceeds to offset that year's deficit (*Freie Presse*, March 27, 1879, p. 4; April 21, 1879, p. 4). During the directorship of Julius Richard, Ferdinand Welb, and Leon Wachsner (1884–90) there was a considerable improvement noted in the repertoire, casting, and direction. During the entire existence of the Stadt, individual actors were acclaimed as was the frequent practice of casting major players in supporting roles. Benefit performances for actors, directors, and production personnel would be given in the final months of the season or at the end of a guest's stay; such performances were well attended.

In twenty-two seasons, the Stadt offered nearly 1,800 productions, with minor repetition during a season. Farces and comedies maintained a strong hold on the repertoire, with operetta most popular during the Collmer directorship. The fantasy folk plays of Austria's Ferdinand Raimund (*Der Alpenkonig* and *Der Verschwender*) and Johann Nestroy (*Die verhängnisvolle Faschingsnacht* and *Lumpacivagabundis*) remained popular throughout as did the sentimental works of Charlotte Birch-Pfeiffer (*Die Waise aus Lowood* and *Der Pfarrherr*) and the salon comedies of Adolfe L'Arronge (*Mein Leopold* and *Hasemanns Töchter*). Alexander Dumas, Eugene Scribe, and Victorien Sardou were well represented and interest in the realists and naturalists brought performances of Friedrich Hebbel (*Genoveva* and *Maria Magdalena*), Björnstjerne Björnson (*Ein Fallissement*), and later Ludwig Fulda and Herman Sudermann. Eleven plays of Shakespeare, in the Friedrich von Schiller or August Wilhelm von Schlegel translations, were presented, sometimes repeatedly. Among the German classic playwrights, G. E. Lessing (*Nathan der Weise, Emilia Galotti, Minna von Barnhelm*) and Goethe (*Faust, Egmont, Götz von Berlichingen, Clavigo, Die Geschwister*) were overshadowed by Schiller: ten of his plays were produced for thirty-eight performances, the most frequent being *Die Räuber, Maria Stuart*, and *Don Carlos*. Normally Schiller would be produced in November in honor of the anniversary of his birth. The mainstay, however, of the Stadt and of its European counterparts was the prolific output of the popular farceurs Roderich Benedix, Oskar Blumenthal, Gustav Kadelburg, Wilhelm Mannstädt, Gustav von Moser, and Franz von Schönthan.

Kurz employed a business manager, musical director, small orchestra, scenic staff, and highly mobile cast of actors, employed for a season or for a limited series of productions. Actors tended to be engaged in standard lines of business, although such lines were not strictly adhered to, allowing leads to play minor roles and stronger vocalists to star in musical works. Actor-directors were generally engaged for their organizational and directorial abilities rather than their acting strengths. Supernumeraries were engaged irregularly as were guests for roles beyond the capacity of the existing company. Beginning with the second Stadt season, Kurz and his directors made concerted efforts to engage actors from German theatres in the United States and from European theatres. Summers would be spent in Germany and Austria contracting for the latest plays and hiring actors; frequently, the Stadt ensemble would include 30–50 percent German and Austrian nationals. Appearing with the Stadt company were notables such as Emil von der Osten from Dresden, a singer and lead actor; Franz Kirschner, a tragic actor from Vienna; Anna Martorel, who had leading roles in many German theatres; Ludwig Barnay, a member of the Meiningen troupe and of the original company at the Deutsches Theater in Berlin; Franziska Ellmenreich, also with the Meiningen troupe and then with the

Germania Theatre in New York; Friedrich Mitterwurzer, leading actor at
the Vienna Burgtheater and one of Germany's most noted interpreters of
Henrik Ibsen; the noted tragedienne Anna Haverland of Leipzig, Dresden,
and Berlin; and Ernst von Possart, an important figure in the history of
Munich theatre and, like Barnay, a member of the original company at
the Deutsches Theater. Most of these stars would move on to another
German company or would return to their European engagements; an
exception is the actress Hedwig Beringer, who joined the company in 1879,
premiering as Klärchen in Goethe's *Egmont*. She immigrated to the United
States after nineteen years on Germany's stages, including four years at
Berlin's Residenz Theater. With several minor interruptions, she stayed
on the Milwaukee stage for forty-seven years and serves as the major figure
linking the Kurz Theatre and the Pabst Stadt Theater, which succeeded
it. She earned her greatest praise and most frequent benefits for her
interpretations of comic aristocratic dowagers. Other leading ladies included
Hedwig Hesse, an eminent artist in tragic roles; Rosa Hagedorn, who won
critical acclaim in the title role of Victorien Sardou's *Cyprienne*; Elsie
Hagedorn, moving as Desdemona in the first Milwaukee production of
Othello in 1885; Freda Volgath (Velguth), a member of the original 1868
company, who starred in Michael Beer's historical tragedy *Struensee* for
her 1874 benefit; and Anna Wagner-Märtens, a member of the original
company, whose interpretation of the title role in Schiller's *Jungfrau von
Orleans* in 1871 was compared favorably to the acting of Marie Seebach,
guest from the Burgtheater and Munich.

Leading men at the Stadt included Eduard Härtung, an eminent artist,
who managed the company from 1868 to 1874; the comedians Ernst
Redwisch and Sigmund Selig; and Wilhelm Rieckhoff and Bernhard Moser,
who played Karl and Franz Moor in a gala performance of Schiller's *Die
Räuber*. Edward Brockmann, Louis Pelosi, and Theodor Pechtel were
other important principals. The Stadt performers were most adept at
maintaining a recognized ensemble responsible for a great variety of dramatic
genres, from the broadest farces to the romantic tragedies of Schiller.

The Kurz Stadt Theater came to an end when Heinrich Kurz sold the
theatre to brewer Captain Frederick Pabst, who was to provide the company
with an imposing new home. The last performance of the Stadt under
Kurz's lead was of *King Lear*, April 18, 1890, an offering that was repeated
at the McVicker's Theater in Chicago April 20.

PERSONNEL

Management: Heinrich Kurz, proprietor and manager (1868–90); business managers: Edward Härtung (1868–74), Julius Collmer (1874–84), Julius Richard, Ferdinand Welb, and Leon Wachsner (1884–90); Henry Bielfeld, treasurer.

Scenic Technicians: Louis Kurz, Ferdinand Kurz.

Music Director: Christian Bach (1868–90).

Stage Directors: Edward Härtung (1868–74), Ernst Redwisch (1871), Julius Collmer (1874–84), George Isenstein (1882), Alexander Wuster (1882), Joseph L'Hame (1882–83), Julius Richard, Ferdinand Welb, Leon Wachsner (1884–90).

Actors and Actresses: Parenthetical dates indicate year of first known activity with the group. Mary Ahlfeld, Margarethe Albrecht, Carl Artmann, Carl Bach, Paul Barthold, *Hedwig Beringer* (1879), Mila Bley, *Fritz Böckel* (1878), *A. Brockmann* (1873), Edward Brockmann, Adalbert Brüning, *Gustav Cohn* (1871), *Helene Collmer* (1878), *August Denzau (1884)*, *Heinrich Diekmann* (1879), *Heinrich Dietz* (1879), Ernst Ebert, Louis Eisenbach, Bertha Fiebach, Alwine Friehold, *Otillie Genee* (1880), Adolph George, Otto Gerlach, *A. Gschmiedler* (1885), Ernst Gschmiedler, Emmy Griebe, *Elsie Hagedorn* (1885), *Rosa Hagedorn* (1883), Gustav Hartzheim, *Fritz Hausen* (1884), Clara Hausmann, Sigmund Helfer, *Emmy Herwegh* (1886), *Hedwig Hesse* (1871), Franz Hillmann, *Frau Horowitz* (1868), Karl Huber, Gustav Kleman, *Lulu Klein* (1885), Marie König, *Georg Krüger* (1879), Mathilde Kühle-Catenhausen, *Lena Kuhn* (1871), Emil Lasswitz, *Aendery Lebius* (1888), Adolph Link, *Victoria Markham* (1880), Laura Mojean, *Bernhard Moser* (1879), Theresa Mundt-Mühlbach, Martha Neumann, *Theodor Pechtel, Johanna Pellesier* (1879), Louis Pelosi, Fred Rauch, Hans Ravene, *Ernst Redwisch* (1871), Wilhelm Rieckhoff, *Anna Richard* (1879), *Clara Schaumberg* (1878), Hermann Schmelzer, Auguste Schmidt, Julius Schmidt, Lina Schmitz, Norman Schmitz, Anna Schönherr, *Sigmund Selig* (1868), *Carl Sonntag* (1881), Robert Stengel, *Frieda Volgath* (1868), Henrietta Wagner, Lebius Wagner, *Anna Wagner-Märtens* (1868), *Adam Waldorf* (1879), *Lina Wassmann* (1878), Agathe Wilhelmy.

REPERTORY

Seasonal listings are available in the works of Lulu Bredlow and Norman J. Kaiser.

BIBLIOGRAPHY

Published Sources: J. C. Andressohn, "Die literarische Geschichte des Milwaukeer Deutschen Bühnenwesens, 1850–1911," *German American Annals*, n.s., 10 (1912):78–88, 150–70; Milwaukee newspapers: *Banner und Volksfreund* (1879–80), *Freie Presse* (1879–90), *Herold* (1869–90), *Sentinel*.

Unpublished Sources: Lulu Bredlow, "A History of the German Theater of Milwaukee, from 1850 to 1935" (M.A. thesis, Northwestern University, 1936); Norman J. Kaiser, "A History of the German Theatre of Milwaukee from 1850–1890" (M.S. thesis, University of Wisconsin—Madison, 1954).

Archival Sources: The Milwaukee County Historical Society has souvenir programs for 1885–86 and 1889–90, miscellaneous theatre programs, and incomplete manuscript histories of the Stadt.

Glen W. Gadberry

L

LAFAYETTE THEATRE COMPANY. The Lafayette Theatre Company (1825–29) was organized and operated by Major-General Charles W. Sandford as the resident troupe of the new Lafayette Theatre (first known as the Lafayette Circus and Lafayette Amphitheatre), which opened its doors on West Broadway in New York City in July 1825.

General Sandford was a soldier, lawyer, real-estate speculator and a colorful personality in New York who put up the Lafayette Theatre as the centerpiece of a large complex of shops and residences he was creating in the vicinity of Canal Street in what was then the northern limits of New York City. New York was rapidly expanding during the 1820s: its population doubled, and with the opening of the Erie Canal in 1825, its preeminence as the trading and financial center of the nation was firmly fixed. Most of the new residents were industrial workers who had the time and money to spend on entertainment that was vigorous, colorful, and uncluttered by literary subtleties. But in 1825 New York had only two winter houses, the Park and the Chatham, which usually offered the public revivals and imitations of plays from the eighteenth-century repertory. None of the theatres in New York could afford to ignore completely the popular new melodramatic forms of theatre, but their small stages and limited facilities could not accommodate the kind of spectacle General Sandford had in mind for the Lafayette.

The Lafayette Theatre opened on July 4, 1825, as a circus house with a large but undistinguished company whose efforts in minor drama on the stage were subordinate to the turns in the ring. The situation, however, soon changed. While his company was away in the spring of 1826 on a tour to Boston, Sandford began a series of renovations on the building that transformed the Lafayette into the largest theatre in the country with the most advanced stage facilities known to that time. The ring was replaced by a raked pit, increasing the capacity of the house to more than 3,000 persons. A water tank was installed at the rear of the huge stage (75 by 120 feet) for the production of nautical melodrama, and an all-overhead gas lamp system, the first of its kind anywhere, provided for stunning lighting effects and rapid changes of scenery. Twenty new players, most of them prominent in their lines, increased the size of the company to more than 70, augmented from time to time for the production of elaborate equestrian pieces, such as *El Hyder, The Bride of Abydos,* and *The Avenger,* when the stage swarmed with as many as 120 performers in addition to the stud of forty horses permanently attached to the company and several exotic animals, including at least one elephant, Tippoo Sultan, who had his own vehicles. A large staff of scenic artists, costumers, and technicians was hired by Sandford to insure that his theatre was the equal in scenic display to anything found in Europe. The most important addition, however, was Watkins Burroughs, who took over as theatrical manager of the company and its principal performer in melodrama and light comedy.

Burroughs was a touring English star whose handsome features, dashing appearance, and polished performances made him an effective leading man in a wide range of roles and, perhaps, "the most accomplished actor in the country" (*New York Globe and Emerald,* June 3, 1825). Having previously been associated with the Surrey, a melodramatic house in London, where he was T. J. Dibdin's successor as actor-manager, Burroughs was well qualified to make a success of the company in the most ambitious and wide-ranging program of theatre ever seen in New York.

The company that opened the Lafayette Theatre on July 4, 1826, for its third season in New York was unequaled in the city for talent, size, and range of repertory. Heading the list of players were Mary Ann Duff, Mrs. John Augustus Stone, and Mrs. Palmer Fisher as leading ladies; Westerfelt Walstein, Alexander Wilson, Robert Campble Maywood, and John Duff in tragedy; Arthur Keene, Mrs. Charles W. Sandford (the former Mrs. Joseph George Holman), and Mrs. Joseph Jefferson II in opera; Watkins Burroughs and William Dinneford as romantic leading men; Sarah Riddle, Miss Tilden, and Juliet Durang Godey as ingenues; and numerous high and low comedians, among them Paddy Doyne, James Roberts, W. R. Blake, Edward N. Thayer, and George Hyatt. The new, expanded repertory reflected the increased dimensions of the personnel. Burroughs brought out comedies, tragedies, operas, and several kinds of melodramas, in addition to the usual farces, ballets, pantomimes, and playlets that acted as curtain raisers for the main pieces. A series of fifteen tragedies and comedies from the standard repertory were produced in rapid succession, including *She Stoops to Conquer, Romeo and Juliet, The Rivals, Jane Shore, The Stranger, The Merchant of Venice,* and *Richard III.* Eight operas, among them *Guy Mannering, Rob Roy, The Young Hussar,* and the horse-opera *Lodoiska,* displayed the company's new vocal talent. One new play,

The Banker of Rouen, by John Augustus Stone, was commissioned, and twelve melodramas were added to the repertory in lavish mountings.

The new policy was a great success. The auditorium was often "crowded to suffocation" and the players greeted with "rapturous applause," especially Mrs. Duff, Mrs. Sandford, and Watkins Burroughs in their best roles. The critics, who largely ignored the company in its first season, were stunned by the sumptuous scenery, the realistic lighting effects, and the careful groupings of the performers, for Burroughs thoroughly prepared and rehearsed every major new production—often closing the theatre to do so—to obtain a polished effect from the first performance. This in contrast to the often slip-shod productions of the more fashionable Park Theatre, where dingy lamps and tattered scenery were the norm.

The company's success encouraged Sandford to expand his theatrical ventures. He built the Mount Pitt Circus on the East Side of Manhattan and opened it in November 1826, with a company of circus and variety performers. But after a year of such operation the Mount Pitt became an alternate home for the Lafayette company. All of the Lafayette's spectacles played at both theatres during the winter of 1827–28 as actors, costumes, scenery, horses, and all were transferred rapidly back and forth between the two houses. Sandford also took leases on a string of theatres in New England and sent both of his companies out on an extended tour (December 1826 to September 1827) to Albany, Boston, Providence, and other cities. Despite having excellent support from a string of engagements with famous stars, among them Edwin Forrest, J. B. Booth, and William C. Macready, the Lafayette company's tour was a total financial loss. Albany could not afford expensive daily theatre, and Boston was simply hostile to outsiders.

Back in New York for its fourth and longest season (September 1827 to September 1828), the Lafayette company had several excellent new players: Henry Wallack and James M. Scott as leading men; Peter Richings, Vincent DeCamp, and James Anderson as comedians; and Mary Wallack Hill and Matilda Twibill as leading ladies. Eighteen costly new spectacles were brought out, including *Joan of Arc, Ivanhoe, The Lady of the Lake, The Forty Thieves, The Battle of Waterloo, The Tiger Horde*, and the nautical melodramas *Red Rover* and *Paul Jones*, both of which featured battles at sea between ships floating on the theatre's water tank. The new season was well received and the audiences numerous, even during the usually slow summer period, but before the season came to an end in September the company suffered a blow from which it never recovered: General Sandford suddenly withdrew his support from both his companies.

Without the general's financial support the company quickly deteriorated. Watkins Burroughs announced his retirement, and nine of the troupe's most important players, including Mrs. Sandford, Mrs. Stone, and Henry Wallack, also left. The building was leased to James M. Scott, who took over the company as actor-manager for a fifth and last season beginning in December 1828. But the crippled company was able to perform only fitfully that winter and ceased altogether in March 1829. The unoccupied theatre burned to the ground on the morning of April 10, 1829. Its sister house, the Mount Pitt Circus, was destroyed by fire four months later.

PERSONNEL

Management: Charles W. Sandford, proprietor and general manager; Watkins Burroughs, theatrical manager; William Dinneford, stage manager.

Scene Designers: Thomas Reinagle; Mr. Grain; Mr. Jones; Mr. Huggins.

Costumers: Andrew Jackson Allen, Mr. Mead.

Machinery: Mr Buchannan.

Set Dressing: Mr. Blackmon.

Sword Play: George Jones.

Actors and actresses: Mr. Adams (1827), Mr. Allen (1828), Janey Anderson (1828–29), John Anderson (1827–28), *Mrs. John Barnes* (1827), *Mrs. George Barrett* (1827), Mr. Bernard (1826), Mr. Blaike (1827–28), *W. R. Blake* (1826–28), Mrs. W. R. Blake (1826–28), Mr. Blakeley (1828), Mr. Bogardus (1825), *J. Mills Brown* (1827), *Watkins Burroughs* (1825–28), Mr. Burton (1827), Mr. Byers (1827), Miss Campbell (1828–29), Mr. Carr (1827), Mr. Clark (1828–29), Mr. Collins (1826–29), Mrs. Collins (1827–28), Miss Conlon (1825–26), Mr. Conroy (1828–29), William Conway (1827–28), Mrs. Cooke (1825–26), Mrs. Costar (1828), Mr. Darley (1828), Mr. Davis (1828), *Vincent DeCamp* (1828), Miss Deblin (1828–29), Mr. Denman (1827–28), Mr. Dignall (1828–29), Mrs. W. Dinneford (1825–27), *William Dinneford* (1825–27), George W. Dixon (1828), *Paddy Doyne* (1826–27), *John Duff* (1826), *Mary Ann Duff* (1826), Mr. Duffy (1828–29), F. Durang (1828), *John H. Dwyer* (1827), David Eberle (1825–28), Elizabeth Eberle (1825–28), Henry Eberle (1825–28), Sophia Eberle (Mrs. La Forest) (1825–28), *Mrs. Edstrom* (1825–28), Mr. Eglee (1828–29), Mr. Emberton (1828), *Miss Emery* (1828–29), Mr. Faulkner (1827), Miss Favour (1829), Alexina Fisher (1825–28), Oceana Fisher (1825–28), Palmer Fisher (1825–28), *Mrs. Palmer Fisher* (1825–28), Mr. Forbes (1827–29), Mr. Ford (1827–28), Mr. Foster (1828–29), Mr. Garner (1828), Mr. Garson (1828–29), *Juliet Durang Godey* (1825–27), Mr. Gray (1828), *Mrs. Charles Greene* (1827–29), Mr. Harrington (1825), Mr. Harris (1827), Mr. Hart (1827), Mrs. A. Herbert (1826–27), August Herbert (1826–27), *Mary Wallack Hill* (1827–28), James Hunter (1825–26), *George Hyatt* (1826–28), A. W. Jackson (1828), Mr. James (1826–29), *Mrs. Joseph Jefferson* (1826), Mr. Johnson (1825–27), Mrs. Jones (1826–27), George Jones (1825–29), Mr. Keaton (1826–28), *Arthur Keene* (1826–27), John Kelly (1825), *Miss Kent* (1829), Mr. King (1828–29), Mr. Kinlock (1828), Mrs. Kinlock (1828), *Charles La Forest* (1825–28), Mr. Laidley (1828–29), Louisa Lane (1827–28), Mr. Lawson (1825–26), Mr. Lindsey (1826–29), Mr. MacQuire (1828), Mr. Madden (1825–26), Miss Marks (1829), *Robert C. Maywood* (1826), Mrs. McBride (1827), Mr. Mestayer (1825–28), Mrs. Mestayer (1825–28), Mrs. Mitchell (1828–29), *Mrs. Monier* (1825–26), Mr. Moore (1829), Mrs. Moreland (1828–29), Mrs. Morgan (1826–27), James Morrison (1826), Mr. Morton (1828–29), Mr. Neilson (1827–28), Mrs. Owens (1827), Mr. Page (1829), Ophelia Pelby (1825–26), *Rosalie Pelby* (1825–26), Mr. Petrie (1827), Mr. Phillips (1827–28), Miss Preston (1828–29), Mr. Quinn (1827), Mr. Reed (1827–29), *T. D. Rice* (1828), Mr. Richards

(1825–28), *Peter Richings* (1827–28), *Sarah Riddle* (1826), *James Roberts* (1826–28), *Miss Robertson* (1827–28), Mrs. Rogers (1828–29), *Mrs. Charles W. Sandford* (1826–28), Mr. Schinotti (1829), *James M. Scott* (1828–29), Miss Sibley (1829), Mr. Simmonds (1825), Mr. Simpson (1826–28), Mr. Sinclair (1829), *Mr. Somerville* (1826–27), Mrs. Spiller (1828), Mr. Stevenson (1828–29), Mrs. Stevenson (1828–29), Mr. Stickney (1825–28), *Mrs. John A. Stone* (1826–28), Mrs. Talbot (1828–29), Mrs. S. Tatnall (1825–26), *Samuel Tatnall* (1825–27), *Edward N. Thayer* (1826–28), *Miss Tilden* (1825–26), *William Thompson* (1825–28), Mr. Turnbull (1828–29), Mrs. Turner (1827), *Matilda Twibill* (1827–28), *Henry Wallack* (1827–28), *Mrs. Henry Wallack* (1827–28), Mrs. W. Walstein (1826–28), *Westerfelt Walstein* (1826–28), Mr. Whittaker (1825–26), *Alexander Wilson* (1826–27).

REPERTORY

First season (July–December 1825): *The Romp; Spoil'd Child; Miss in Her Teens; The Turnpike Gate; Raising the Wind; Sylvester Daggerwood; Catherine and Petruchio; The Rendezvous; The Adopted Child; The Irishman in London; The Midnight Hour; The Purse; Lovers' Quarrels; Modern Antiques; The Review; Ella Rosenberg; Honest Thieves; The Floating Beacon; Fortune's Frolic; How to Die for Love; The Sleep Walker; The Promissory Note; The Maid and the Magpie; Monsieur Tonson; Asleep and Awake; The Broken Sword; The Three Hunchbacks; Children in the Wood; Animal Magnetism; The Burning Forest; Descent of the Balloon; The Blind Boy; The Day after the Wedding; The Lady and the Devil; Beaux without Belles; The Forest of Bondy; My Benefit Night; Don Juan; Timour, the Tartar; Tom Thumb; The Review; The Mock Doctor; The Reprobate; The Miller's Frolic; No Song, No Supper; The Mountaineers; The Vampire; The Three Wives; Don Quixote; The Sultan; The Woodman's Hut; Bombastes Furioso; The Brave Soldier; Of Age Tomorrow; Millers and Coalmen; Abaellino.*

Second season (December–March 1825–26): *The Wedding Day; The Two Gregories; The Hunter of the Alps; The Miller's Frolic; The Sea Devil; Oscar and Malvina; The Three Hunchbacks; Raymond and Agnes; Timour, the Tartar; The Dumb Girl of Genoa; The Promissory Note; The Rendezvous; Children in the Wood; The Mayor of Garratt; El Hyder; The Strolling Manager; The Adopted Child; The Floating Beacon; Bluebeard; Intrigue; Richard III; The Broken Sword; The Turnpike Gate; Spoil'd Child; Tekeli; Rosina; The American Captive; The Shipwrecked Sailor; Five to One; The Review; The Reprobate; Tom and Jerry.*

First tour (April–July 1826): *Intrigue; The Review; Sponge Out of Town; No Song, No Supper; The Reprobate; The Hunter of the Alps; The Dumb Girl of Genoa; Children in the Wood; The Three Hunchbacks; The Adopted Child; The Sea Devil; The Two Gregories; El Hyder; The Miller's Frolic; Timour, the Tartar; The Shipwrecked Sailor; Rosina; The Purse; Tom Thumb; Cataract of the Ganges; Raymond and Agnes; The Three and Deuce; The Floating Beacon; The Turnpike Gate; The Sleepwalker; Bluebeard; Sylvester Daggerwood; Richard III; Modern Honor; Tekeli; Don Quixote; The Day after the Wedding; Tom and Jerry; George Barnwell; The Review; The Bride of Abydos; The Spectre Bridegroom.*

Third Season (July–December 1826): *The Dumb Girl of Genoa; The Three Hunchbacks; She Stoops to Conquer; The Hunter of the Alps; Catherine and Petruchio; The Floating Beacon; The Belle's Stratagem; The Budget of Blunders;*

George Barnwell; The Sea Devil; Matrimony; The Reprobate; The Rendezvous; Cure for the Heart-Ache; Raymond and Agnes; The Mountaineers; The Three and Deuce; Intrigue; Young and Old; The Castle Spectre; The Midnight Hour; The Dumb Girl of Genoa; Laugh When You Can; Family Jars; The Sultan; Romeo and Juliet; Two Strings to Your Bow; Sylvester Daggerwood; The Ruffian Boy; The Young Widow; Jane Shore; The Weathercock; The Apostate; The Spectre Bridegroom; The Rivals; Of Age Tomorrow; The Mogul Tale; The Irish Tutor; The Fair Penitent; The Stranger; The Promissory Note; Blue Devils; Is He Jealous?; Lyar; El Hyder; The Lying Valet; How to Die for Love; The Mock Doctor; The Busybody; The Day after the Wedding; Five to One; Nature and Philosophy; The Two Gregories; The Foundling of the Forest; The Lady and the Devil; Adrian and Orrila; The Sleepwalker; The Sleeping Draught; Irishman in London; Past Ten O'Clock; Too Late for Dinner; Agreeable Surprise; Douglas; The Avenger; High Life below Stairs; The Heart of Midlothian; The Turnpike Gate; The Idiot Witness; Honey Moon, Spoil'd Child; Turn Out; Tom and Jerry; The Maid and the Magpie; Ella Rosenberg; The Devil's Bridge; The Blind Boy; Love in a Village; My Grandmother; Alexander the Great; Guy Mannering; Brother and Sister; The Two Troubadours; Yard-arm and Yard-arm; Paul Pry; Richard III; The Young Widow; Rob Roy; The Merchant of Venice; The Falls of Clyde; A New Way to Pay Old Debts; The Innkeeper of Abbeville; Three Deep; Wandering Boys; Bertram; The Young Hussar; The Banker of Rouen; The Jew and the Doctor; The Iron Chest; Monsieur Tonson; Pizarro; Clari; The Old Oaken Chest; Children in the Wood; Michel et Christine; The Cataract of the Ganges; The Irish Tutor; The Miller's Maid, Lodoiska.

Second tour (December 1826–September 1827): *Pizarro; Lyar; The Devil's Bridge; The Promissory Note; The Inconstant; The Midnight Hour; Rob Roy; The Irish Tutor; The Rivals; Sponge Out of Town; Guy Mannering; The Jew and the Doctor; Virginius; The Young Widow; Matrimony; The Miller's Maid; The Two Troubadours; Clari; Modern Antiques; Cure for the Heart-Ache; Raymond and Agnes; A New Way to Pay Old Debts; Richard III; Brother and Sister; My Benefit Night; Of Age Tomorrow; The Merchant of Venice; Raising the Wind; The Idiot Witness; The Sea Devil; The Iron Chest; High Life below Stairs; Lodoiska; Othello; The Village Lawyer; Who's the Dupe?; Brutus; Tekeli; Venice Preserved; Intrigue; How to Die for Love; Honey Moon; The Falls of Clyde; Damon and Pythias; The Spectre Bridegroom; The Lady and the Devil; Tom and Jerry; William Tell; Honest Thieves; George Barnwell; Monsieur Tonson; Romeo and Juliet; Spoil'd Child; The Grecian Daughter; Laugh When You Can; The Three and Deuce; The Bride of Abydos; The Will; She Stoops to Conquer; No Song, No Supper; Three Weeks after Marriage; The Wedding Day; Blue Devils; The School for Scandal; Family Jars; The Belle's Stratagem; Is He Jealous?; The Soldier's Daughter; Agreeable Surprise; As You Like It; Sweethearts and Wives; The Turnpike Gate; The Maid and the Magpie; Deaf and Dumb; The Woodman's Hut; Sprigs of Laurel; The Hypocrite; Wives as They Were; The Devil to Pay; Evadne; Love, Law, and Physic; The Way to Keep Him; The Mogul Tale; Three Deep; The Provok'd Husband; The Actress of All Work; Old Bachelors; The Avenger; The Dumb Girl of Genoa; The Stranger; Ella Rosenberg; Five Miles Off; King Lear; The Mountaineers; Alexander the Great; The Unknown; The Virgin Unmasked; The Road to Ruin; The Way to Get Married; The Ninth Statue; 'Tis All a Farce; Fish Out of Water; The Sleeping Draught; The Merry Wives of Windsor; Paul Pry; The Poor Soldier; The Ruffian Boy; Love in a Village; The Two Gregories; Turn Out; The Young Hussar; Hamlet; Rule a Wife; Speed the Plough; The Fatal Dowry; Catherine and Petruchio; The Heir-at-Law; Brier Cliff; The Review; Children in the Wood; Lovers' Quarrels; Macbeth; The Weathercock; The Young Quaker; She Would Be a Soldier; A School for Grown Children; The West Indian; Animal Magnetism; Barbarossa; Douglas; The Bee Hive; The Innkeeper of Abbeville; The Poor Gentleman; Ways and Means; The Hunter of the Alps; El Hyder; Timour, the Tartar; The Romp; Rosina; The Miller and His Men; Prize Money; Smoked Miser; The Two Galley Slaves; Adeline; The Flying Dutchman; Ali Pasha; 'Twas I; The Burning Forest; Paul Pry at Dover; Dolly and the Rat; Fortune's Frolic; Bluebeard.*

Fourth season (September 1827–September 1828): *Honey Moon; The Wandering Boys; Rosina; The Bride of Abydos; Guy Mannering; The Young Widow; The Irish Tutor; Speed the Plough; The Warlock of the Glen; A Day after the Wedding; The Purse; Tom and Jerry; Town and Country; The Village Lawyer; The Promissory Note; The Heir-at-Law; The Poor Soldier; Intrigue; Charles II; Yard-arm and Yard-arm; The Floating Beacon; Blue Devils; Botheration; Fortune's Frolic; Robin Roughhead; Modern Antiques; Lodoiska; Is He Jealous?; The Spectre Bridegroom; X.Y.Z.; Returned Killed; She Stoops to Conquer; The Ruffian Boy; The Avenger; The Idiot Witness; Too Late for Dinner; Tekeli; The Spy; Saint Mark's Day; The Review; Kenilworth; The Pringles in Town; The Miller and His Men; How to Die for Love; The Battle of New Orleans; Rob Roy; The Rendezvous; Don Giovanni; The Ninth Statue; Douglas; Brier Cliff; Joan of Arc; El Hyder; The Cornish Miners; The Foundling of the Forest; A Day after the Fair; My Aunt; Matrimony; The Lady of the Lake; Prisoner-at-Large; High Life below Stairs; Family Jars; Love à la Mode; The Inconstant; Cherry Bounce; The Dumb Girl of Genoa; Gilderoy; The Barber of Seville; The Blood-Red Knight; The Tiger Horde; Of Age Tomorrow; Brian Boroihme; Richard III; Dolly and the Rat; The Reprobate; The Two Greg-ories; The Old Oaken Chest; The Murderer; Gil Blas; Who Owns the Hand?; False and True; The Forty Thieves; The Fisherman's Wife; Kouli Khan; The Cataract of the Ganges; The Boarding House; The Forest Rose; The Irish Valet; One Hundred-Pound Note; Lovers' Quarrels; Hide and Seek; The Father Outwitted; Rugantino; The Sons of Erin; Saint Patrick's Day; The Robbers; The Two Galley Slaves; The Two Wives; The Mountaineers; Honest Thieves; Raising the Wind; Paul Jones; The Weathercock; The Dramatist; Antoine, the Savage; The Broken Sword; The Lady and the Devil; The Battle of Waterloo; The Young Hussar; Children in the Wood; The Romp; The Wonder; The Turnpike Gate; Red Rover; Henry IV; Monsieur Tonson; Damon and Pythias; Miss in Her Teens; Actress of All Work; Meg Mur-dock; Laugh When You Can; The Three and Deuce; Clari; The Mayor of Garratt; Ivanhoe; No Dinner Yet; Tumble Up Stoop; Pizarro; My Spouse and I; Ireland Redeemed; The Comedy of Errors; The Hero of Lake George; Chimney Sweep; The Mogul Tale; Paul and Virginia; The Unknown; Military Manoeuvres; The Innkeeper's Daughter; Frightened to Death; The Lottery Ticket; William Tell; Ways and Means; The Forest of Bondy; The Sleep Walker; Barbarossa; Bluebeard.*

Fifth season (December 1828–April 1829): *Isabella; The Day after the Wedding; Paul Jones; The Review; Bertram; Adeline; The Lady and the Devil; Fazio; Intrigue; Town and Country; The Irishman in London; Douglas; Nature and Philosophy; Red Rover; Honest Thieves; The Floating Beacon; The Broken Sword; The In-quisition; Jane Shore; Crazy Jane; The Wandering Boys; The Battle of New Orleans;*

The Robbers; The Warlock of the Glen; Tekeli; William Tell; La Perouse; Blood for Blood; Raising the Wind; Damon and Pythias; Spoil'd Child; Rob Roy; Family Jars; Fortune's Frolic; Evadne; The Oudalun Arabs; El Hyder; The Spectre Bridegroom; The Rendezvous; The Slaves; Oscar and Malvina; The Fireman's Stratagem, The Elbow Shakers; Pizarro; Simpson and Co.; The Lady of the Lake; The Village Lawyer; The Glory of Columbia; Children in the Wood; Haunted Tower; The Heir-at-Law; The Round Tower; Tom and Jerry; Brian Boroihme; The Miller and His Men; She Would Be a Soldier; Ella Rosenberg; The Mountaineers; The Birthday; The Turnpike Gate; The Slave's Revenge; The Youthful Queen; The Cataract of the Ganges; The Vampire; The Lancers; The Stranger; The Weathercock.

BIBLIOGRAPHY

Published Sources: *Albany Argus, Boston Commercial Gazette, Essex, Massachusetts, Register, Gazette of Maine, New York American, New York Courier, New York Enquirer, New York Globe and Emerald, New York Post, New York Mirror and Ladies' Gazette*; promptbooks: John Farrell, *The Dumb Girl of Genoa* (New York: Elton's Dramatic Repository, 1829); Henry W. Wallack, *Paul Jones* (New York: Elton's Dramatic Repository, 1828).

Unpublished Sources: Robert B. Montilla, "The History of the Lafayette Theatre, 1825–29" (Ph.D. diss., Indiana University, 1974); Lafayette Theatre Account Books at Harvard College Library, Cambridge, Massachusetts.

Robert B. Montilla

LES COMEDIENS FRANCAISE. See CITY THEATRE COMPANY and [THOMAS WADE] WEST COMPANY.

LUDLOW AND SMITH COMPANY. The Ludlow and Smith Company was formed in 1835 by pioneer actor-managers Noah M. Ludlow (1795–1886) and Solomon F. Smith (1801–69). Ludlow and Smith presented two seasons annually in St. Louis, opening in the late spring and running into the autumn (with a break during the hottest weeks of late July) until 1851. In Mobile the pair presented winter seasons until 1840, returning in 1843 through 1848. Beginning in the late autumn of 1840, they also ran seasons during the cooler months in New Orleans, finally closing their company there and severing their business ties in April 1853.

Both Ludlow and Smith were among theatrical pioneers in what were then the western territories of the United States. Ludlow had traveled west with the Drake Company* in 1815, leaving Drake in 1817 to tour on his own. He both acted and managed theatres in Mobile, Natchez, Cincinnati, Louisville, and elsewhere before his association with Smith. Ludlow specialized in "high" comedy, particularly the "laughing comedy" of the late eighteenth century.

Smith, a popular "low" comedian affectionately known as "Old Sol" to audiences, began his career in 1823 at the Green Street Theatre Company* in Albany. Smith quickly joined the touring circuit and played with great success as both an actor and manager in theatres throughout the American West and Southeast. He was well received in his one engagement in the East, when he played both Philadelphia and New York in 1835.

Ludlow and Smith's theatres formed the major circuit of the 1840s in the American West. After a lengthy—and costly—battle with James H. Caldwell for dominance in both Mobile and New Orleans, Ludlow and Smith were the major theatrical force along the Mississippi River. Ironically, both Ludlow and Smith had worked as performers for Caldwell in the 1820s and early 1830s, and both men had managed theatres or companies for Caldwell. As partners, they supported a large stock company ranging between twenty-five and thirty-six performers during the eighteen years of the firm's existence. Their stock company most often provided support for the major touring stars of the period.

In St. Louis, the Ludlow and Smith company opened on July 3, 1835, in the "Salt Box" Theatre in Court Street, a former salt warehouse that had been converted into a theatre in 1825. The "Salt Box" burned to the ground on February 16, 1837, and was replaced by the New St. Louis Theatre that opened on July 3, 1837, and remained the firm's St. Louis home until 1851. Located on Third and Olive streets, the New St. Louis Theatre had the distinction of never having been completed: designed with an elaborate architectural facade to include monumental columns, money ran out before the facade could be erected.

The firm's theatres in both Mobile and New Orleans had more checkered careers. In Mobile, Ludlow and Smith opened on November 9, 1835, in the St. Emmanuel Street Theatre, which Ludlow had leased the previous year on his own. The St. Emmanuel Street Theatre burned to the ground on November 21, 1838, shortly after that year's season had begun. Ludlow, who maintained a home in Mobile, quickly leased an empty theatre on Government Street, which he opened on December 1, 1838. In the following year, on October 7, 1839, a major fire devastated much of Mobile, including the Government Street Theatre. It was replaced by the New Theatre, State Street, opening on December 31, 1839. Because the State Street Theatre was located on the outskirts of Mobile in a district untouched by the fire since it was underdeveloped and on marshy ground, Smith always referred to the building disparagingly as the "Swamp Theatre."

James H. Caldwell, then the dominant theatre manager in New Orleans and the Southwest, opened a new theatre (the Royal Street Theatre) in Mobile during the winter of 1840 in an attempt to drive Ludlow and Smith out of business. Caldwell was successful: unable to compete, Ludlow and Smith closed the "Swamp Theatre" in the spring of 1840 and temporarily left Mobile, although they did present occasional engagements of star performers there during the next two years.

In direct consequence of Caldwell's having invaded Mobile, Ludlow and Smith gained the lease of the New American Theatre on St. Francis Street in New Orleans, opening there on November 10, 1840, after their usual autumn season in St. Louis. Initially, the major attractions at the New American were equestrian dramas starring Master Hernandez, an eight-year-old rider.

Caldwell's New Orleans theatre, the St. Charles, burned down in the spring of 1842. On July 30, 1842, the New American also burned, amid reports that both fires were the work of antitheatre arsonists. Ludlow and Smith learned in the autumn of 1842 that Caldwell had obtained the lease to the rebuilt New American Theatre, which they had expected to be theirs. Smith promptly made arrangements with the owners of the building going up on the site of the St. Charles, and on January 18, 1843, Ludlow and Smith opened the New St. Charles Theatre. Caldwell, who had opened the New American Theatre six weeks earlier, was forced to close. Ludlow and Smith completed their victory over Caldwell when they won the lease of the Royal Street Theatre in Mobile and opened a new season there on November 18, 1843. Caldwell retired from the theatre. Ludlow and Smith so effectively dominated theatrical business in New Orleans for the rest of the decade that they managed the New American Theatre in 1845 and 1846, leasing the structure to equestrians while maintaining their own company at the New St. Charles.

Ludlow and Smith's professional partnership was, in the main, successful, despite a few losing seasons early in the decade of the 1840s, a period of general economic depression nationwide. Despite their professional success, personal relations between the two managers appear to have always been cool at best; indeed, as Joseph Jefferson noted, they "were in partnership for many years without exchanging a word except on business" (Jefferson, 89). Smith published his memoirs in 1868 (*Theatrical Management in the West and South for Thirty Years*), managing never to mention Ludlow by name. Ludlow retaliated by publishing *his* memoirs in 1880 (*Dramatic Life as I Found It*), in which he attempted to rebut every statement of Smith's that he found objectionable. The root of their mutual antipathy appears to have been financial, although there appears also to have been less-than-friendly rivalry between their wives, both of whom were actresses with the company. Smith maintained until his death that Ludlow had cheated him out of profits by taking the Mobile theatre for himself in 1834 and by transferring property to his wife and children to avoid having to repay money owed to Smith. Ludlow always insisted that Smith's accusations were unjust and unfounded. Later, biographers have extended the dispute by siding with one of the two.

The theatrical fare offered audiences in Ludlow and Smith's theatres was typical of the early nineteenth century. Their company contained core performers of widely varying experience (and capability) who served, most of the time, as support for traveling star performers. The visiting stars generally played a repertory of plays limited tightly to their own specializations. Thus Dan Marble, a popular interpreter of Yankee and sometimes Irish roles, who played in Ludlow and Smith's theatres every year from 1838 until 1849, performed a repertory in 1838 consisting of *The Forest Rose, Sam Patch, Black Eyed Susan, Jonathan in England, The Yankee in Time, The Vermonter*, and *The Bush Whacker*. Marble's final St. Louis season in 1849 included *Black Eyed Susan, Sam Patch in France*, and *An Hour in Ireland*, all plays similar in tone (if not identical) to his roles eleven years earlier.

Traveling stars such as Ellen Tree, William Macready, Edwin Forrest, Junius Brutus Booth, Julian Dean, Mrs. Alexander Drake, E. S. Conner, and Augustus A. Addams stressed the classical repertory: tragic plays, often in verse, ranging from the texts of Shakespeare to the quasi-Elizabethan works of J. S. Knowles and Edward Bulwer-Lytton. Infant phenomena such as Bertha Lewis, the Bateman sisters, the Heron family, Miss Meadows, and a young Joseph Jefferson performed in Shakespearean tragedy and in contemporary comedies such as *The Spoil'd Child, The Four Mowbrays*, and *Little Pickle*.

English performers of high comedy, including Mr. and Mrs. John Brougham, Fanny Fitzwilliam, and J. B. Buckstone, performed for the Ludlow and Smith theatres, as did their American counterparts, Anna Cora Mowatt, Henry Placide, Eliza Petrie, Mr. and Mrs. George H. Barrett, and Sarah Riddle Smith. Ludlow and Smith also regularly booked dancers, such as Mlle. Celeste, Hermine Blangy, Julia Turnbull, and even a rope dancer, Herr André Cline. Opera companies were rarely featured, although specialty troupes of variety entertainers frequently appeared, such as the Viennoise Children in 1847–48 and the Ravel family troupe, which filled Ludlow and Smith's theatres whenever they appeared. Indeed, the Ravels were the final attraction of Ludlow and Smith's management, playing the final thirty-six performances at the New St. Charles in New Orleans in March and April 1853.

The performers hired by Ludlow and Smith appear to have ranged from the barely competent to excellent. Notable among the resident performers were members of the Russell and Field families. Mary Ann Russell Farren was the company's leading lady from 1839 through 1847, when she became a touring star. Her husband, George P. Farren, acted leading and comedy roles during most of those seasons and frequently also served as the company's stage manager. Mrs. Farren's mother, Mrs. Richard F. Russell— widow of the manager of the American, or Camp Street, Theatre in New Orleans—joined the company in 1839, remaining until 1849 and specializing in character women roles. Dick Russell, her son, played juvenile leads and comedy roles from 1843 until his death in 1849. His wife first appeared with the company as Miss Sylvia, performing soubrette roles. After their marriage in 1846, the new Mrs. Russell occasionally played comic leads, such as Lady Teazle in *The School for Scandal*. She remained with Ludlow and Smith after her husband's death, acting until 1851.

Joseph M. Field and his wife, Eliza Riddle Field, performed both as members of the Ludlow and Smith company, first appearing in Mobile in 1836, and as visiting stars. Mrs. Field was a member of the Ludlow and Smith company in St. Louis as late as 1850. Field functioned as manager in St. Louis and Mobile after Ludlow and Smith retired. He was also a playwright; his comic plays were among the few original works produced by the Ludlow and Smith management, and were among the earliest examples of the American frontier drama.

Matthew C. Field, younger brother of Joseph, acted juvenile leads for four seasons, from 1837 to 1839, when he retired from the theatre to become a newspaper editor in New Orleans. Married to Ludlow's daughter, Matthew Field—who died in 1844—managed the St. Louis Theatre in 1838 during Ludlow and Smith's sole attempt to mount a winter season.

Ludlow and Smith had no consistent policy for the selection of plays during those periods between touring stars (or when touring stars failed to appear). Early in the partnership, such gaps in the schedule were frequently filled with plays that relied upon scenic spectacle to attract an audience, pieces such as *Der Freischutz* in 1837; *Cinderella* (the operatic version) in 1836, 1837, and 1838 in both St. Louis and Mobile; *The Flying Dutchman* in 1837; and *The Ice Witch; or, The Frozen Hand* in 1839. The company also used equestrian performers and troupes in both St. Louis and New Orleans, with standard horse dramas such as *Mazeppa; Timour, the Tartar; El Hyder*; and *The Cataract of the Ganges*.

Ludlow and Smith also relied heavily upon the comic repertory of the late eighteenth century, including plays such as John Tobin's *The Honey Moon* (which was often used to open seasons), *The Family Jars* (a frequent vehicle for Sol Smith), *She Stoops to Conquer* (Ludlow was particularly fond of performing Young Marlow, and did so until he retired), and *The Busy Body*. The company was quick to capitalize upon successful new plays: Dion Boucicault's *London Assurance* was mounted at the New American Theatre in New Orleans early in 1842, within three months of its first performance in New York. Ludlow and Smith did little experimentation, however. Tied as they were to the repertory of the touring stars, they most often offered familiar plays.

Ludlow and Smith represent the American theatre's transition from the strolling players of the frontier (which both Ludlow and Smith were at the beginnings of their careers) to well-established and stable theatre companies profitably based in the larger cities of the West. Ludlow and Smith's operations survived the vicissitudes of personal rancor, periodic ravages of cholera and yellow fever, and the rigors of performance under widely varying conditions.

PERSONNEL

The following is an incomplete list; Ludlow's biography includes lists of the company, although his information is frequently incorrect.

Management: Noah M. Ludlow, Solomon F. Smith, managers; A. B. Cook, treasurer (until at least 1844).

Scenic Artist: C. L. Smith (until at least 1842).

Orchestra Leaders: E. Woolf (1838–39), C. H. Mueller (1840–42).

Actors and Actesses: William Anderson; Mr. and Mrs. Bailey; Hezekiah L. Bateman (1839–40); Caroline and Therese Chapman (1843); Henry Chapman (1843, 1850–51); William Chapman (1843); W. H. Chippendale (1848–49); N. B. Clarke (1845–47); *Emily Coad* (1847–50); Joe Cowell, Sr. (1839–40); Miss Sidney Cowell (1839), as Mrs. Bateman (1840); Mr. Daugherty (1848–49); *Mr. and Mrs. Ben DeBar* (1840–46, 1849–53); Mr. and Mrs. Edward Eddy (1843–45); Mr. and Mrs. Foster (1838–44); Mr. and Mrs. Fuller (1848–49); Mr. and Mrs. Charles L. Green (1836–40); Mr. Hickmott (1847–51); Mr. and Mrs. Hubbard (1836–37); Mr. Huntley (1850–51); Mr. Jackson; Mr. and Mrs. and Miss Johnson (1836, 1840–41); *Mr. and Mrs. W. G. Jones* (1849–51); Mr. Kelly (1836–37); "Paddy" Larkin (1839–40); Mr. Lavette (1840–42); W. E. Leman (1849–50); Eliza Logan; Mr. Marsh (1838–40); Ellen Matthews; Mr. and Mrs. J. P. Maynard (1840–45); Mr. McConechy (1839–40); *J. H. McVicker* (1843–46); Mr. Morton (1848–49); *A. J. Neafie* (1843–46); Mr. and Mrs. Newton (1837–45); John E. Owens; Ada Parker (1849–51); *Eliza Petrie* (1836–42); Thomas Placide (1836–46); Miss E. Randolph (1844–45); Mr. Rose (1838–42); Mrs. Salzman (1837, 1844–45); Mr. Sankey (1840–42); Mr. Saunders (1840–45); Henry Schoolcraft (1848–50); Blanche Kemble Shea (1850–51); Mark (Marcus) Smith (1849–51); *Mary Vos Stuart* (1836–39, 1848–49); Mr. Sutherland (1840–41); *George Vandenhoff* (1848–50); Mrs. Warren (1840–45); Mr. Watson (1848–51); Charles H. Webb (1840–41, 1844–45); *J. M. Weston* (1845–51); Mr. and Mrs. James Wright (1840–50).

REPERTORY

Not available.

BIBLIOGRAPHY

Diaries, letters, account books, and other documents pertaining to the Ludlow and Smith company in St. Louis are located in the collections of the Missouri Historical Society, St. Louis. The New Orleans and Mobile operations of the company have been the subject of several unpublished graduate theses, as have Ludlow and Smith's sporadic attempts to establish permanent companies in Natchez, Cincinnati, and elsewhere. The major published works include pioneering works by William G. B. Carson, *The Theatre on the Frontier: The Early Years of the St. Louis Stage* (Chicago: University of Chicago Press, 1932; reprint New York: B. Blom, 1965); idem, *Managers in Distress: The St. Louis Stage, 1840–1844* (St. Louis: St. Louis Historical Documents Foundation, 1949). Joseph H. Dormon, Jr., in his *Theater in the Ante-Bellum South, 1815–1861* (Chapel Hill: University of North Carolina Press, 1967), provides a useful overview, particularly of Ludlow and Smith's barnstorming days. New Orleans theatres of the period are documented in published form in John S. Kendall's *Golden Age of the New Orleans Theatre*

(Baton Rouge: Louisiana State University Press, 1952); and in Nelle Smither's "History of the English Theatre in New Orleans, 1806–1842," *Louisiana Historical Quarterly* 28 (January–April 1945): 85–276, 361–572, and reprinted (New York: B. Blom, 1967) with a useful index. Noah Ludlow's autobiography *Dramatic Life as I Found It* (St. Louis: n.p., 1880) was reprinted (New York: B. Blom, 1966) with an excellent introduction by Francis Hodge. Solomon Smith's autobiography *Theatrical Management in the West and South for Thirty Years* (New York: 1868, reprinted New York: B. Blom, 1968) is a necessary complement to Ludlow. Smith is the subject of three unpublished graduate theses: Francis M. Bailey, "A History of the Stage in Mobile, Alabama from 1824 to 1850" (Master's thesis, University of Iowa, 1934); William S. Craig, "The Theatrical Management of Sol Smith: Organization, Operation, Methods, and Techniques" (Ph.D. diss., University of Illinois, 1964); and Larry E. Grisvard, "The Final Years: The Ludlow and Smith Theatrical Firms in St. Louis, 1845–51" (Ph.D. diss., Ohio State University, 1965). See also Joseph Jefferson, *Autobiography* (New York: Century, 1897).

Alan Woods

LYCEUM STOCK COMPANY. The resident company opened the first of its twelve seasons at the Lyceum Theatre in New York City on November 1, 1887. This was not the premier production at the little theatre on New York's Fourth Avenue. That first performance was of Steele MacKaye's *Dakolar* on April 6, 1885. MacKaye had been involved in the final stages of planning and constructing the theatre, and when it was sold in a foreclosure procedure in August 1885, the New York Theatre Company, which assumed ownership and control, appointed him its general manager. The theatre reopened for the season of 1885–86 as a combination house with Minnie Maddern in *In Spite of All*. MacKaye disagreed with the management about how to salvage the still-failing business, and he resigned as manager on November 9, 1885. Helen Dauvray assumed the management of the Lyceum and successfully produced *One of Our Girls* by Bronson Howard. With young E. H. Sothern in the leading role, it finished the season, ending exactly 200 performances on May 20, 1886. On May 28, 1886, Daniel Frohman was hired as general manager, and he continued to operate the Lyceum as a combination house through an unsuccessful season of 1886–87. The trustees of the New York Theatre Company agreed to organize a resident company in the winter of 1886–87, and they authorized Daniel Frohman to select and engage a company. With the help of David Belasco, the stage director, the company was selected, rehearsed, and readied to open in *The Wife*, a new play by Belasco and Henry C. DeMille.

Daniel Frohman, who was to guide the fortunes of the Lyceum Theatre and its stock company for the remainder of its existence, was the oldest of three theatrical Frohman brothers. All had begun their theatrical careers by selling programs on the sidewalks in front of New York theatres. Daniel was next an advance man for Callender's Original Georgia Minstrels, and, from that job, he moved to the Madison Square Theatre in 1879 as business manager for Steele MacKaye. After a year as manager of the Fifth Avenue Theatre, he returned in 1880–81 to the Madison Square as general manager, replacing Steele MacKaye. He remained there until A. M. Palmer acquired controlling interest in the theatre in 1884. Daniel then moved to the Lyceum Theatre as business manager and helped to prepare for the opening of the new theatre venture.

The idea for the establishment of the Lyceum was conceived in the mid–1860s by Phillip G. Hubert, a New York architect. In the early 1880s he contacted Franklin Sargent, "dramatic instructor" for the Madison Square road companies, and, together with Gustave Frohman, the third of the Frohman brothers, they formed a corporation with Gustave as the general manager. When MacKaye left the Madison Square, he too joined the Lyceum group. After MacKaye became associated with the Lyceum Theatre Corporation, the original concept of the Lyceum changed. What was at first intended as a school for amateur actors, with a small stage and auditorium to serve as a workshop, became a professionally oriented theatre. It was reported that the Lyceum was to produce a season of plays just as "regular places of amusement" did (*New York Times*, July 31, 1884). MacKaye now insisted that the little theatre Hubert had originally designed for his amateur students be altered to accommodate professional productions and larger audiences. MacKaye's original estimate of the expense of remodeling was $2,400. By the time the theatre opened in April 1885, MacKaye had spent $90,000 for changes and additions.

The theatre was in a three and a half story building of brick and gray stone. The first floor included offices and rooms for the Lyceum School for Actors (later the American Academy of Dramatic Arts) and dressing rooms for actors. The theatre itself occupied the upper level, and its 614 seats gave it the distinction of having the smallest seating capacity of any first-class theatre in New York City during the latter part of the nineteenth century. The stage was the first in this country to be lighted entirely by electricity, and part of the installation was supervised by Thomas A. Edison himself. Only minor changes were made in the theatre during its lifetime, and most of them were attempts to squeeze more seats into the auditorium. The little theatre was unique in American theatre history, but it was the excellence of the stock company that brought recognition and popularity to the Lyceum.

The Lyceum Theatre Stock Company, which appeared first on November 1, 1887, was strong and well balanced. The leading actors were relatively young but by no means inexperienced. For supporting actors, Frohman had selected a number of veteran performers who had already established their reputations.

Georgia Cayvan, the most popular actress who ever appeared with the Lyceum Company, was the leading actress from the beginning until illness forced her early retirement in November 1895. Before coming to the Lyceum her only other professional experience was as leading lady at the Madison Square. After Cayvan's retirement, her position was taken by Isabel Irving and later Mary Mannering. Playing opposite Cayvan in the original company was Herbert Kelcey, the leading man. He had played in provincial acting companies in his native England before being brought to the United States by Lester Wallack. He was appearing at the Madison Square under A. M. Palmer when Frohman hired him. He remained as the Lyceum's leading man until 1896, when he was replaced by James K. Hackett. In the fall of 1898, Hackett began a starring career and was replaced in the company by Edward J. Morgan.

Although the company's leading performers were talented and respected, its greatest strength and experience lay in the supporting actors. They included Mr. and Mrs. Charles Walcot, who had appeared at [Laura] Keene's Theatre* in New York and with Edwin Booth, not only in his 100-night run of *Hamlet* but also in the famous revival of *Julius Caesar* in which all three Booths appeared. The Walcots remained with the company for its entire existence. The only other performer to remain with the company for all twelve years was Mrs. Thomas Whiffen. She and her husband had originally come to this country as members of an opera company and later toured as members of various theatrical companies. She had appeared with James A. Herne and played Mercy Kirke in MacKaye's original production of *Hazel Kirke*.

William John Lemoyne was the oldest member of the company and had the most experience. His first important engagement was at the Troy Museum, where, with George C. Howard, he helped to make *Uncle Tom's Cabin* a success in 1852. He had also appeared with the Daly Stock Company*, the Boston Museum Company*, A. M. Palmer's Union Square Theatre Stock Company*, and the Madison Square Theatre Stock Company.

Among other members of the company were Henry Miller, the original "leading juvenile"; William Faversham; Effie Shannon; Louise Dillon; Grace Henderson; Katherine Florence; and Fritz Williams. In all, eleven performers who appeared with the Lyceum Company later toured as stars. Although the company had three leading men and three leading ladies during its twelve years of existence, some of the supporting actors changed more frequently. George C. D. Odell suggested, however, that the Lyceum Stock Company "was a more permanent organization than any other except Harrigan's in New York" (Odell, 15:292).

The Lyceum Company was seen in a relatively narrow repertory of plays. A variety of philosophical statements were issued from time to time suggesting policies of the management about play selection and scheduling. Nothing consistent emerges in these statements, but patterns of operation are apparent in retrospect. From the beginning the Lyceum was envisioned as a theatre for "fashionable" audiences. Daniel Frohman tended to select sentimental material, always with a strong love story focused on female characters. To each play he applied his rigid moral code. The second play that the Lyceum presented, *Sweet Lavender*, included, among the characters, a girl of illegitimate birth. Frohman thought he sensed an audience reaction, and after the play had run a week, he altered the story to legitimize her. Often plays were commissioned for his company and tailored to his requirements. With other plays he revised or deleted objectionable elements with the consent, but not always the blessing, of the playwright.

At one point Daniel Frohman indicated he would favor plays by American dramatists; yet only eight of thirty-two plays produced were by native authors. The larger portion of the plays were well-made, sentimental, society dramas of the popular French and English playwrights. Occasionally, one-act curtain raisers preceded featured plays. Almost without exception, Frohman produced new plays. He announced in 1890 that he intended to produce one "old comedy" a season. He staged *Old Heads and Young Hearts* by Dion Boucicault the next season and then abandoned the policy. All of the productions of American plays at the Lyceum were premier performances, and the English and French plays were usually presented at the Lyceum within a year of their production abroad.

The repertory at the Lyceum was not distinguished. It did, however, closely parallel the repertories of the other major stock companies active in New York during all or part of the Lyceum Stock Company's existence: the companies of Augustin Daly, A. M. Palmer, and Charles Frohman.

The New York Theatre Company, which managed the Lyceum and its stock company, showed a profit in each of its twelve years of operation. It became increasingly obvious, however, that more and more of the total profits were being reaped by summer tours of the basic company and by a number of other road companies that toured each year under the banner of the New York Lyceum Theatre.

The company was relatively strong and well balanced. The response from critics and audiences was generally warm and enthusiastic. Yet with all of this success, the company did not generate sufficient profits to warrant its continuation beyond the season of 1898–99.

PERSONNEL

Management: New York Theatre Company (1885–99); Pringle Mitchell, chairman, Board of Trustees; Daniel Frohman, general manager (1886–99); Frank D. Bunce, treasurer and business manager (1886–99).

Play Readers and Dramatic Advisers: Henry C. DeMille (1886–93), Abby Sage Richardson (1893–99).

Stage Directors: David Belasco (1886–90), Fred Williams (1890–99).

Scenic Technicians: W. H. Day, Frank King, E. G. Unitt, William Hawley.

Actors and Actresses: Louis Albion, George Alison, Harry Allen, Harriet Anbry, Helen Arnold, Vinton Ayre, Ralinda Bainbridge, H. Bayntun, *Walter Bellows* (1887–92), Josephine Bennett, Miss Berner, Albertina Bertram, George C. Boniface, Louise Brooks, W. Buckland, Clarence Bunce, Charles W. Burler, Rhoda

Cameron, Madge Carr, Evelyn Carter, R. Peyton Carter, E. Castano, *Georgia Cayvan* (1887–95), T. J. Clarke, Augustus Cook, Frazer Coulter, William Courtleigh, Edith Crane, Miss Creighton, Vida Croly, Henrietta Crosman, Ada Curry, Adrienne Dairolles, Merwyn Dallas, Charles S. Dickson, Louise Dillon, Millie Dowling, A. Dunton, W. Dupont, R. J. Dustan, Grace Elliston, David Elmer, William Eville, *William Faversham* (1887–88), John Findlay, Mr. Finney, *Katherine Florence* (1893–98), Josephine Forest, Grace Freeman, Alberta Gallatin, Seymour George, Arthur Giles, J. H. Gilmour, Vaughn Glaser, Charles A. Goettler, Ferdinand Gottschalk, Stephen Grattan, Grace Greeman, Adeline Grey, *James K. Hackett* (1896–98), Walter S. Hale, Mrs. H. Hall, John Hamersley, W. D. Hanbury, Charles Harbury, Maude Harrison, Earnest Hastings, Grace Henderson, Sophie Hoffman, J. Hollingsworth, Ethel Hornick, Miss Howell, *Isabel Irving* (1894–96), *Herbert Kelcey* (1887–95), Blanche Kelleher, Jennie Kenmark, C. W. King, Maude Knowlton, Norah Lamison, Bertha Lastall, Sadie Laver, *William J. Lemoyne* (1887–96), Dora Leslie, D. Lloyd, Helen Macbeth, Ada Terry Madison, Mathilde Madison, *Mary Mannering* (1896–99), Virginia Marlowe, Edwin Meyer, *Henry Miller* (1887–89), Frank Mills, Edward J. Morgan, Howard Morgan, Felix Morris, Nina Morris, Henry Muller, Francis Neilson, Helma Nelson, Don Von Neuvayer, Julie Opp, Eugene Ormonde, Elita Proctor Otis, Elliot Page, George Paxton, G. F. Platt, Edward J. Ratckiffe, Gertrude Rivers, Charles Robinson, Hyde Robson, *May Robson* (1890–93), Grace Root, W. R. Royston, Cyril Scott, *Effie Shannon* (1889–93), Winona Shannon, Frank Short, Marie Shotwell, Miss Sinnot, Alison Skipworth, Charles A. Smiley, Hilda Spong, Grant Stewart, H. S. Taber, Ernest Tarleton, J. Brandon Tynan, *Bessi Tyree* (1891–99), T. C. Valentine, Maude Venner, *Charles Walcot* (1887–99), *Mrs. Charles Walcot* (1887–99), Robert Week, Percita West, Percy West, *Nelson Wheatcroft* (1887–91), Joseph Wheelock, Jr., *Mrs. Thomas Whiffen* (1887–99), W. Whittlesey, Edward Wilke, E. H. Wilkerson, *Fritz Williams* (1889–96), Douglas J. Wood, Gertrude Wood, Henry Woodroff.

REPERTORY

1887–88: *The Wife.*
1888–89: *Sweet Lavender; The Marquise; The Wife* (revival).
1889–90: *The Charity Ball.*
1890–91: *The Idler; Nerves; The Open Gate* (one act); *Old Heads and Young Hearts.*
1891–92: *Lady Bountiful; Squire Kate; Merry Gotham; The Grey Mare; White Roses* (one act); *The Organist* (one act).
1892–93: *The Grey Mare* (revival); *White Roses* (revival); *Americans Abroad; The Guardsman.*
1893–94: *An American Duchess; Sweet Lavender* (revival); *Our Country Cousins; The Amazons; A Sheep in Wolf's Clothing* (one act).
1894–95: *A Woman's Silence; The Amazons* (revival); *The Case of Rebellious Susan; An Ideal Husband; Fortune.*
1895–96: *The Home Secretary; The Benefit of the Doubt; The Prisoner of Zenda.*
1896–97: *The Courtship of Leonie; The Late Mr. Castello; The Wife of Willoughby* (one act); *The White Flower* (one act); *The First Gentleman of Europe; When a Man's Married* (one act); *The Mayflower; The First Gentleman of Europe* (revival).
1897–98: *The Princess and the Butterfly; The Tree of Knowledge.*
1898–99: *Trelawny of the Wells; Americans at Home; John Ingerfield.*

BIBLIOGRAPHY

Published Sources: *New York Times* (1884–1900); Daniel Frohman, *Daniel Frohman Presents* (New York: Citadel, 1935); idem, *Encore* (New York: Citadel, 1937); idem, *Memories of a Manager* (New York: Doubleday, 1911); George C. D. Odell, *Annals of the New York Stage*, vol. 15 (New York: Columbia University Press, 1949).

Archival Sources: New York Public Library has minute books of the New York Theatre Company, 1885–94, and Daniel Frohman scrapbooks. An additional scrapbook is owned by nephew Charles Frohman in Sandusky, Ohio.

Unpublished Source: James L. Highlander, "Daniel Frohman and The Lyceum Theatre" (Ph.D. diss., University of Illinois, 1960).

James L. Highlander

M

MACAULEY STOCK COMPANY. On June 13, 1873, actor-manager Bernard "Barney" Macauley bought a plot of land in Louisville, Kentucky, measuring 110 feet wide and 160 feet deep, from William A. Merriwether for $40,000. Construction began on July 1, 1873, and Macauley's Theatre was completed in ninety days at a cost of $240,000. On October 14, 1873, he opened with sixteen of the twenty-five members of the Macauley Stock Company in J. Austin Sperry's play *Extremes*.

When Macauley began his operation, the prevailing method of theatre management was to engage a permanent resident company to perform a season in repertory. But Macauley must have seen the approaching end of the resident method, for he planned to operate differently. Instead of giving up lucrative theatrical interests in Cincinnati, Macauley planned to continue management of the Wood Theatre in Cincinnati and Macauley's in Louisville with the same company of actors. Because of tours by stars and the popularity of the combinations, he planned to use his stock company in Louisville while a combination played in his Cincinnati theatre.

At first, Macauley opened his theatre in September and ran through the last of May, but when this later proved to be unprofitable, he opened as late as October and closed as early as April. During the summer months, the theatre was occupied by occasional civic groups and amateur dramatic clubs, or it was closed. There was no real consistency in the scheduling of plays. Generally, one play ran the first three days of the week and a different play ran for the last three. Sometimes a third play was presented for the Saturday night performance. The two-play schedule was the norm, but neither the local company nor the visiting stars and combination companies strictly adhered to this schedule. Infrequently, a visiting star offered a different play every night. In this period, Macauley always presented Wednesday and Saturday afternoon matinees.

Macauley's method of operation for the stock company was basically the same as that of any other resident company. He employed a small orchestra, an orchestra leader, a treasurer, a business manager, a scenic artist, a machinist, a properties master, nine or ten actresses, and thirteen or fourteen actors, who played standard lines of business for a season. Rachel Macauley was always listed as leading lady, but frequently someone else in the company would play the starring role if Mrs. Macauley were playing in one of the other theatres managed by Macauley. Barney Macauley was a frequent leading man, depending upon the demands made upon his time and upon the star who happened to be appearing with the Macauley Stock Company. In addition to supporting their own company members in leading roles, the Macauley Stock Company regularly supported American stage luminaries such as Kate Fisher, Oliver Doud Byron, Edwin Booth, Frank Mayo, Lotta Crabtree, Lawrence Barrett, and Helena Modjeska. The most famous players in Macauley's company were Ada Rehan, William Griffith, and Mary Anderson, all of whom began their careers in the Macauley Stock Company. James O'Neill was listed on the stock roster for one season.

Barney Macauley, actor and theatre manager, had for some years been associated with theatrical interests in Louisville, Cincinnati, and Indianapolis. By the time he was twenty-one, he was one of the best leading men in the country. In 1857 he played in the old Buffalo Theatre; by 1859 he moved to the Memphis Theatre, where he played leading roles. Macauley began his theatre work in Kentucky in 1861 as a leading stock actor in the old Louisville Theatre playing the roles of Eccles in *Caste*, Fagin in *Oliver Twist*, Francis Levisson in *East Lynne*, and Bagshot in *A Bull in a China Shop*. He established himself as a stock player of some reputation and a local favorite. In 1863 he managed the Lexington Opera House before moving to Pike's Opera House in Cincinnati, where he was leading man. In that same year he made his New York debut in *Camille* with Matilda Heron at Niblo's Garden. In 1865 he married Rachel Johnson, a western actress of note. During the 1865–66 season Macauley acted in the New Orleans Varieties. During the latter part of the season he moved back to Louisville, along with Augusta Dargon, to head the stock company at the newly rebuilt Louisville Theatre. Almost constantly on the move, he managed theatres in Detroit and Toledo during 1867 and 1868. In November 1868 he was in Cincinnati, where he formed a partnership with R.E.J. Miles to manage the Wood and the National. In a two-year period of managing the two Cincinnati theatres, Macauley realized a profit of nearly $100,000. His success, and the desire of his Louisville-born wife to own a theatre in her native town, prompted Macauley to think he could repeat his success in Louisville.

Macauley espoused the "artistic" theatre and indicated a repugnance toward the "commercial," but he was also a part of the "commercial" theatre. Barney Macauley probably disliked the commercial theatre because he foresaw the approach of an era in which he would have to abdicate artistic control of the productions he presented. However, it was Macauley's goal to present productions of superior quality, and he felt that the stock system was the best method; certainly, the one most likely to succeed in his Louisville theatre. He was valiantly supported in his goals by the Louisville press. Reviewers enthusiastically responded to his espoused goals. Almost all of the reviews of the stock productions at Macauley's Theatre leaned toward lavish praise and encouragement.

Macauley's stock productions were smoothly presented because he did insist on organized rehearsal. His forceful personality seemed to be infectious. During his management, the stock companies were always strong, and the plays produced were finished and performed as professionally as the combinations. The stock companies performing at Macauley's Theatre seemed to be universally appreciated, and many members developed large local followings.

Nonetheless, the Macauley Stock Company was used infrequently in the five-year period of its existence, staging only forty-seven plays in 162 performances. The company acted varied bills of both short and full-length comedies, society and romantic dramas, melodramas, verse plays, and Shakespearean pieces. Popular writers of the period including Matilda Heron, James Sheridan Knowles, Dion Boucicault, John Brougham, and Thomas Robertson were represented, as well as popular older plays. Toward the end of the stock company era at Macauley's Theatre, the organization was seldom used as a unit but became simply a support company for visiting stars.

Although the first season at Macauley's Theatre was profitable, Barney Macauley had borrowed money to build and operate his theatre. He also had begun his managerial career in Louisville at possibly the worst time. The financial depression that choked the rest of the nation in 1873 finally hit Louisville in 1874 just at a time when Macauley needed full houses to retire many debts, including the mortgage on the theatre. During his five-year stint with the stock company in Louisville, Macauley managed to stay just ahead of his debtors. In 1877 he lost the Wood Theatre in Cincinnati when the lease ran out. He then leased Robinson's Opera House in Cincinnati, but that venture was financially disastrous.

Impending bankruptcy forced Macauley to give up his Louisville theatre. He had bought land and built a theatre with too little capital. Operating a stock company while spending large amounts to secure stars and combinations cost too much. Simultaneously, Macauley found it increasingly difficult to secure rights to new plays, and stricter enforcement of copyright laws hindered the pirating of new and potentially lucrative plays.

When the full Macauley Stock Company dispersed is unclear, but articles in the Louisville press indicate the presence of Macauley company members in newly formed combinations early in 1878. Although the company did support visiting stars almost to the end of the season, the last production by the full company was a play Macauley had bought for himself called *A Messenger from Jarvis Section*, a "down East" play in the manner of James A. Herne. Macauley's fifth season officially closed on May 1, 1878, after a three-day run by the Grand Opera House Company in support of George Rignold in *Henry V*, in Palgrove Simpson and Herman Merivale's *Alone*, and in D. W. Jerrold's melodrama *Black Eyed Susan*. The Macauley Stock Company was disbanded by May 1878, except for members of *The Messenger from Jarvis Section* company.

Barney Macauley continued his career as a prominent midwestern and southern actor for another six years. In March 1886 he died in Bellevue Hospital in New York City.

Macauley's Theatre remained open for another season under the management of William Warner, Barney Macauley's business manager, and then under the management of Col. John T. Macauley, brother of Barney, who later bought the theatre and continued operation, with the exception of a few years, until 1925, when the theatre was torn down to make way for a business establishment.

PERSONNEL

Management: Bernard Macauley, proprietor and manager (1873–78); William Warner, business manager (1873–78).

Treasurer: John Botto (1873–74).

Stage Manager: Harry Eytinge (1875–76).

Scenic Technicians: J. L. Malmsha, scenic artist (1873–74); Gasperd Maeder, scenic artist (1874–75); Mr. Blackburn, scenic artist (1877–78); A. Huffro, machinist (1873–74); P. Cummings, machinist (1874–75); P. Cummings, carpenter (1875–76); W. Davis, properties (1873–74); B. Whiton, properties (1875–76); F. T. Deneal, prompter (1875–76).

Musical Direction: Richard Maddern, orchestra leader (1873–74); J. M. Navore, musical director (1875–76).

Actors and Actesses: Mrs. V. Aldine (1877–78), May Arlington (1876–77), *Miss Arnold* (1874–76), G. Arnold (1874–75, 1876–77), Ella Bailey (1876–77), *Josie Bailey* (1874–77), Mrs. Bancroft (1876–77), H. Bancroft (1877–78), Mrs. Barrett (1874–75), *H. C. Barton* (1873–76), Laura Bascomb (1876–77), Marie Bates (1873–74), Miss Benjamin (1874–75), Frank Bosworth (1875–76), Nellie Boyd (1877–78), G. Brown (1873–74), T. S. Brown (1876–77), Mrs. Burroughs (1873–74), J. F. Charles (1874–75), A. Chipman (1873–75), Sally Cohen (1876–77), Miss Cooper (1874–75), Miss Courcelles (1875–76), Mrs. Charlotte Crampton (1875–76), *John Craven* (1873–77), Nellie Cummings (1875–76), Mary Davenport (1873–74), Lydia Denier (1877–78), Mr. DeVernon (1877–78), Ella Doyer (1875–76), E. Edwards (1875–76), R. Forsyth (1874–75), H. Foster (1873–74), Mr. Fox (1875–76), Fannie Francis (1877–78), Master Fred (1876–77), Hugh Fuller (1874–76), Mr. Garner (1877–78), F. Gavisk (1876–77), Master George (1876–77), *W. H. Gillette* (1876–78), *E. T. Goodrich* (1874–76), B. R. Graham (1876–77), J. Graham (1877–78),

William Griffith (1875–77), Mr. Gross (1875–76), W. B. Gross (1875–76), Miss Gunther (1876–77), J. Hamilton (1877–78), G. H. Henderson (1875–77), Ferd Hight (1873–75), Alfred Hudson (1873–74), Harry Hudson (1874–75), F. C. Huebner (1877–78), T. Humphries (1873–74), Nellie Jacobs (1874–75), C. V. James (1876–77), Mrs. C. Johnson (1876–77), Miss C. J. Johnson (1875–76), Flodie LeCompte (1874–75), H. V. Lingham (1874–75), Little Maud (1873–74), Frank Lloyd (1873–74, 1875–76); G. Lloyd (1876–77), Miss F. Lord (1875–76), *Rachel Macauley* (1873–78), J. A. MacKaye (1876–77), Emma Maddern (1873–74), Miss L. Maddern (1877–78), Mrs. R. Maddern (1873–74), Dolly Maeder (1875–76), Edwin Marble (1875–76), John Marble (1873–74, 1875–76), T. Martino (1874–75), Ella Mayer (1873–75, 1876–77), Jennie McClellan (1873–76), *Harry Mehan* (1874–78), Miss F. Mitchell (1877–78), H. W. Mitchell (1873–74), Mr. Morris (1877–78), Mr. Murphy (1877–78), C. T. Murphy (1877–78), *James O'Neill* (1874–75), W. F. Owen (1877–78), Emma Palmer (1876–77), Fred Percy (1874–75), Alferetta Perry (1873–74), Laura Phillips (1875–76), S. W. Pierce (1877–78), Sara Pierce (1877–78), Lizzie Pierson (1874–75), W.H. Powers (1873–75), Miss Price (1877–78), S. R. Reed (1877–78), *Ada Rehan* (1875–76), George Roberts (1873–74), Miss Ray Roberts (1876–77), Miss Rose (1874–75), Fulton Russell (1875–76), Mattie Russell (1875–76), T. Sardau (1877–78), Rufus Scott (1875–77), Mr. Sheldon (1875–76), Mrs. Sheldon (1875–76), Kitty Sheldon (1874–75), W. P. Sheldon (1874–75), Ames Shipley (1874–75), Minnie Shire (1875–76), F. O. Smith (1877–78), Randall Smith (1874–75), Wilda Smith (1873–74), Russell Soggs (1875–76), T. K. Spuckman (1875–76), Emma Stockman (1877–78), Amy Thorne (1876–77), Miss Tobitha Trump (1876–77), J. Waite (1873–74), I. F. Whitesides (1875–78), Robert T. Wilson (1876–78), W. N. Wilson (1877–78), Miss G. Wood (1876–77), Ella Wren (1877–78), W. Yearance (1877–78).

REPERTORY

1873–74: *Extremes; Caste; The Belle of the Season; East Lynne; Lucrezia Borgia; A Bull in a China Shop; Frou-Frou; The Hunchback; Lady Audley's Secret; Old Heads and Young Hearts; Surf; or, Life at Long Beach; The World of Fashion; Mr. and Mrs. Peter White; Oliver Twist; Hamlet; Rosedale; Marble Heart; Richelieu; Richard III; Julius Caesar; Garrick; Home; Colleen Bawn; Paul Clifford; Rory O'More; Wicked World; Robert Macaire; A Pretty Piece of Business; Jane Eyre; The Lady of Lyons; Delicate Ground; The Love Chase; The Stranger; The Rough Diamond; Chris and Lena; or, Life on the Upper Mississippi; Fritz: Our German Cousin; Kit: The Arkansas Traveller; Zip; The Little Detective; Mazeppa; The French Spy; Across the Continent; Ben McCullough; Much Ado about Nothing; The Merchant of Venice; Othello; Macbeth; On Hand; Dixie.*

1874–75: *Across the Continent; Ben McCullough; Donald McKay; The Irish Emigrant; Handy Andy; Colleen Bawn; Dombey and Son; The Ticket-of-Leave Man; Return of the Volunteers; Jane Eyre; East Lynne; Deborah; London Assurance; Oliver Twist; A Bull in a China Shop; Griffith Gaunt; The Belle of the Season; Romeo and Juliet; Hamlet; Wild Oats; Marble Heart; Enoch Arden; Othello; Macbeth; Chris and Lena; Led Astray; Pride; Model of a Wife; Off the Line; Ici on parle francais; The Dodger; Paul Pry; That Blessed Baby; Uncle Dick's Darling; Dearer Than Life; The School for Scandal; Lucrezia Borgia; As You Like It; The*

Hunchback; Nick of the Woods; Solon Shingle; Elizabeth, Queen of England; Marie Antoinette; Mary Stuart; Antony and Cleopatra; Ruy Blas; The Lady of Lyons; Hamlet; No Thoroughfares; Davy Crockett; Sampson; Belphegor, the Mountebank; Was She Right?; Van, the Virginian; Little Mother; Katty O'Sheil; Fanchon, the Cricket; The Pearl of Savoy; Kit: The Arkansas Traveller; Little Nell and the Marchioness; Musetta; Rip Van Winkle; Rory O'More; Richard III in Dutch; There's Millions in It; Minnie's Luck; Neck and Neck; Maum Cre; The Steeplechase; The Cricket on the Hearth; Sweethearts and Wives; Old Friends; Si Slocum; A New Way to Pay Old Debts; St. Marc: The Soldier of Fortune; Damon and Pythias; Macbeth; Clancarty; Whose Wife?; The Sea of Ice; Delicate Ground; Honey Moon.

1875–76: Ours; Tempted; Robin Gray's Wife; Under the Gaslight; Richelieu; Hamlet; Spartacus, the Gladiator; The Lady of Lyons; Romeo and Juliet; East Lynne; Nell Gwynne; Frou-Frou; Oliver Twist; Turn Him Out; The Geneva Cross; The New Magdalen; The Wandering Heir; There's Millions in It; Virginius; Othello; Jack Cade; Damon and Pythias; The Stranger; Richard III; Marble Heart; Harebell; The Merchant of Venice; David Garrick; The Hidden Hand; The Spy; Our Kate; Isa; Little Sunshine; Uncle Tom's Cabin; Across the Continent; Ben McCullough; Donald McKay; Davy Crockett; Wild Oats; Enoch Arden; The Robbers; Too Much Married; The Mighty Dollar; London Assurance; Camille; The Hunchback; Honey Moon; Ingomar; Beatrice (Much Ado about Nothing); Rosalind (As You Like It); Henry V; Fasio; Evadne; A Bull in a China Shop; Othello; King Lear; A New Way to Pay Old Debts; Richard II; Henry VIII; The Taming of the Shrew; Heinrich and Hettie; Zip; Musette; Maum Cre; Kerry Gow Dhuv.

1876–77: Saratoga; Caste; Evadne; Ingomar; Fazio; Romeo and Juliet; Guy Mannering; Arrah-na-Pogue; Escape from Sing-Sing; Our Boys; The Heir-at-Law; Happiest Days of My Life; Everybody's Friend; The Victims; Solon Shingle; A Crown of Thorns; Love and Duty; The Ticket-of-Leave Man; A Bull in a China Shop; The Mighty Dollar; Our American Cousin; Dundreary in a Hornet's Nest; David Garrick; Lady Audley's Secret; Mary Stuart; Macbeth; The School for Scandal; Parted; Jealousy; There's Millions in It; Seven Cakes; East Lynne; Oliver Twist; The Sea of Ice; School; Conscience; The Two Orphans; Mazeppa; The French Spy; Miss Multon; Jane Eyre; Tullamore; The Widow Concerned; Musette; Zip; Delicate Ground.

1877–78: Ingomar; Macbeth; The Lady of Lyons; Romeo and Juliet; Ion, a Foundling; Fazio; Our Boys; The Victims; Solon Shingle; Barnstable and Reform; Risks; There's Millions in It; Camille; As You Like It; Richelieu; Hamlet; Richard III; Henry VIII; The Taming of the Shrew; Brutus; The Merchant of Venice; Pink Dominoes; Our Bachelors; Across the Continent; Donald MacKay; The Mother's Secret; The Two Orphans; Conscience; Frou-Frou; A Messenger from Jarvis Section; Virginius; Othello; The Gladiator; A Heroine in Rags; The Sea of Ice; Adrienne; Davy Crockett; The Streets of New York.

BIBLIOGRAPHY

Published Sources: John J. Weisert, *Last Night at Macauley's: A Checklist, 1873–1925* (Louisville: University of Louisville Press, 1950); *Courier-Journal* (Louisville) (1873–1972); *Louisville Commercial* (1873–78); *Louisville Daily Courier* (1877); *Louisville Evening Post* (1873–1915).

Archival Sources: Louisville Public Library and the University of Louisville Library have scrapbooks, programs, and other memorabilia, and the University of Louisville Library has the Macauley family collection of photographs that once hung in the lobby of Macauley's Theatre. The Filson Club Library in Louisville also has scrapbooks of programs and other memorabilia.

Don Whitney Combs

MADISON SQUARE THEATRE STOCK COMPANY. A. M. Palmer had elicited interest in New York's Madison Square Theatre in the spring of 1883, while he was still managing the Union Square. When he entered a partnership with coproprietors (lessees) Marshall H. Mallory and the Reverend George S. Mallory on August 30 (effective September 1), 1884, he claimed, "I [do not] intend to step in and control the Madison-Square Theatre. . . . My interest will be financial, and . . . I certainly should not dream of throwing [Daniel and Gustave Frohman, the artistic directors] out" (*New York Times*, August 29, 1884). Yet from the outset, his interest was more than financial. After Daniel Frohman broke with the Mallorys, in late February 1885, Palmer assumed sole management of their theatre on March 13.

The Madison Square Theatre, on the south side of Twenty-fourth Street, between Broadway and Sixth Avenue, occupied ground where Amos R. Eno's Fifth Avenue Opera House (afterwards Fifth Avenue Theatre) had been erected in 1862. In January 1869 John Brougham leased the house and renamed it Brougham's Theatre; Augustin Daly took it over the following August, calling it Daly's Fifth Avenue; and the theatre was destroyed by fire on January 1, 1873. Proprietor Eno rebuilt the house in 1877; and in December of that year magician Robert Heller reopened it as the Fifth Avenue Hall. It was renamed Minnie Cummings' Drawing-Room Theatre in December 1878, and a new lessee and director, author-actor-inventor Steele MacKaye, rechristened it the Madison Square Theatre on April 23, 1879. The following spring, backed by the Mallory brothers, MacKaye spent seven weeks rebuilding and refurbishing the interior and installing his celebrated "double stage," a ventilating system, and patented folding chairs. Thus renovated, the theatre seated above 900 persons. MacKaye's drama *Hazel Kirke* was presented in this house February 4, 1880, and held the stage for 486 performances. Toward the end of this phenomenal run (May 31, 1881), trouble occurred between Steele MacKaye and the Mallorys. MacKaye withdrew from the Madison Square, and despite the playwright's efforts in the courts, *Hazel Kirke* remained the Mallorys' property.

After MacKaye's departure, the Mallory brothers kept the Madison Square filled with a succession of popular plays, mostly of American authorship, including William Gillette's *Professor*, Bronson Howard's *Young Mrs. Winthrop*, and David Belasco's *May Blossom*. When Palmer returned from Europe, on August 4, 1884, he brought with him a new play, C. H. Hawtrey's *The Private Secretary* (adapted from Gustav von Moser's *Der Bibliotheker*). This bright farce, with its comic clergyman, received its American premiere at the Madison Square Theatre September 29, 1884. It drew enthusiastic notices and large crowds and held the stage until mid-April 1885—by which time Palmer had undertaken management of the house. Julia Campbell Verplanck's melodrama of amatory and political intrigue, *Sealed Instructions*, followed from April 13 until June 6, after which the MacKaye-Mallorys resident company left the Madison Square stage for the first time since 1880.

Star comedian John T. Raymond and Company inaugurated the summer season with Arthur Wing Pinero's apprentice piece *In Chancery* on June 8; Raymond's mounting of David D. Lloyd's political satire *For Congress* lasted from July 6 through 25. Charles W. Couldock then brought *The Willow Copse* to this stage on August 3 for a month's run. Antonia Arco Janisch's production of *Anselma* (Leander Richardson's adaptation of Victorien Sardou's *Andrea*), introduced at the Madison Square on September 7 for only three weeks, was accounted a failure. When *Sealed Instructions* was restored to this stage for a month on October 5, the leading parts formerly played by Mathilde Madison, Jessie Millward, and Thomas Whiffen were now acted, respectively, by Agnes Booth, Maud Harrison, and James H. Stoddart, all from the ranks of Palmer's once great Union Square Theatre Stock Company*. Mme. E. J. Phillips would join them during the regular season. These players formed the nucleus of the superb company that was largely to remain at the Madison Square for several illustrious seasons.

The second Madison Square season under Palmer's management, and his first with a personally recruited acting company, opened November 7, 1885, with Henry Arthur Jones' drama of English country life, *Saints and Sinners*. The author directed rehearsals; former Union Square scenic artist Richard Marston (who had reenlisted under Palmer's banner for the production of *Sealed Instructions*) designed the settings. The cast was strong, for the regular company now included Mmes. Booth and Phillips, Misses Harrison, Marie Burroughs, Marie Greenwald, Annie Russell, J. H. Stoddart, Herbert Kelcey, W. J. Lemoyne, William Davidge, Walden Ramsey, Louis F. Massen, E. M. Holland, C. P. Flockton, Frank Drew, and Alfred Becks. The *New York Times* pronounced *Saints and Sinners* "noteworthy for smoothness and harmony" (November 8, 1885), and the production had a prosperous run through February 22, 1886.

W. S. Gilbert's experimental comedy *Engaged* followed on February 23 (it had been premiered three weeks earlier, on February 4, as the Madison Square's contribution to an extraordinary Actors' Fund matinee). Bronson Howard's curtain raiser *Old Love Letters* (an Agnes Booth vehicle since 1878) and Gilbert's poignant drama *Broken Hearts* ensued from March 30 through April 17. Clinton Stuart's *Our Society* (adapted from *Le monde où l'on s'ennuie*) sustained a profitable closing fortnight through May 1. Richard Mansfield's company was booked into the Madison Square with A. C. Gunter's comedy *Prince Karl* from May 3 until August 14, and William Gillette followed as principal actor in his own Civil War drama *Held by the Enemy*, a combination that played from August 16 through October 23.

Jim, the Penman, Sir Charles Young's powerful melodrama of London society (featuring Frederic Robinson and Agnes Booth), inaugurated the Madison Square's 1886–87 season on November 1 and ran steadily for six months. Palmer had rehearsed his company in this script during their summer in Chicago, and launched it there in late July for a successful month's run. The troupe presented Young's play before President Grover Cleveland and other government officials at the National Theatre, in Washington, D.C., April 18, 1887—an Actors' Fund benefit that reported proceeds of $3,000. After closing its New York run on April 30, *Jim, the Penman* was played for three months in Boston and one week each in St. Louis, Cincinnati, New Orleans, San Francisco, Baltimore, and Washington, D.C. *Our Society* returned to the Madison Square stage on May 2 and terminated the company's regular season on May 28. Richard Mansfield and Company then took over the house on May 30 for an eighteen-week engagement, through October 1.

The 1887–88 season opened on October 3, with a six-week revival of *Jim, the Penman*, followed on November 10 by A. R. Cazauran's *Martyr* (adapted from D'Ennery and E.J.L. Tarbé-des Sablons' *Martyre*), for which the indifferent business of a year before in Chicago was repeated in New York. But George Parsons Lathrop and Harry Edwards' *Elaine* (adapted from Lord Tennyson's *Idylls of the King*), which was launched December 6; Henry Arthur Jones' melodrama *Heart of Hearts*, which premiered January 16, 1888; and Robert Buchanan's *Partners* (adapted from Alphonse Daudet), which was introduced on May 2 and withdrawn for prior bookings at its peak of popularity, were all financial successes. Despite the auditorium's comparative smallness, this lackluster season reputedly cleared above $60,000, whereas Lester Wallack in his prime probably had not netted more than $50,000. It was "the remarkable Madison Square Company," according to Lewis C. Strang, "rather than the plays that were given, which brought such reputation to the house" (Strang, 208). But the Madison Square phase of Palmer's career effectually terminated with the 1887–88 season. In October 1888, Wallack having died in the preceding month, Palmer became proprietor of Wallack's Theatre and began to devote a major share of his attention to that new enterprise. He placed his brother Walter R. Palmer beside Wesley Rosenquist in charge of the Madison Square's business affairs during 1888–89, and he retained the management of this theatre until mid-September 1891.

The stock company's last three seasons at the theatre may be briefly summarized: three English plays and, belatedly, an American one. The 1888–89 regular season opened on November 14 with a three-week revival of *Partners* but was largely given over to the American premiere (December 4) of C. Haddon Chambers' *Captain Swift*, an English piece slightly altered and staged at the Madison Square by Dion Boucicault. The latter production, featuring Maurice Barrymore as Mr. Wilding, proved "one of the strongest attractions both in New York and on the road" (Stoddart, 216). Since *Captain Swift* called for a relatively small cast, Palmer dispatched a strong second company on a cross-country tour of *Partners* for most of 1888–89. The next season was launched on October 30 with another English import, Ralph R. Lumley's farce *Aunt Jack*, written expressly for Barrymore, preceded by American playwright (afterwards house-dramatist) Augustus Thomas' curtain raiser *A Man of the World*. That lively bill prospered through the season's close on April 26, 1890. The 1890–91 season opened October 30 with Sydney Grundy's *A Pair of Spectacles* (adapted from Eugene Labiche and Alfred-Charlemagne Delacour's *Les petites oiseaux*), paired successively with Bronson Howard's *Old Love Letters* and Thomas' *Afterthoughts* and *A New Year's Call*. Palmer had met the Madison Square Company in Chicago, en route east from California, and rehearsed them in Grundy's play in Philadelphia immediately before the new season's opening. *A Pair of Spectacles* held the stage through January 3, 1891, and was trailed by a string of English failures: Rosina Vokes and Company in Sydney Grundy's *Silver Shield* and the regular company in R. C. Carton's *Sunlight and Shadow* and J. A. Ritchie's *Dinner at Eight* coupled with Malcolm Watson and Mrs. Lancaster Wallis' *Social Fiction* and *The Pharisee*. That season's only real success was Thomas' compelling—yet long postponed—regional drama *Alabama*, which premiered on April 1.

But *Alabama*'s original cast departed the Madison Square stage after the April 18 performance; a second, less popular company filled out the month. Palmer then dispatched the regular troupe on an extensive tour and subleased the house for other, lesser attractions. Taking with him the Madison Square Company, the manager gave up his artistic interest in this theatre on September 15, 1891, and the house on that date passed into the hands of Charles Hoyt and Charles Thomas. Palmer retained a proprietary interest in the Madison Square—subleasing from the Mallorys—until January 11, 1894, when Hoyt and his new partner Frank McKee (Thomas had died the preceding year) took a nine-year lease on the property.

Albert Marshman Palmer (1861–1905) had earlier managed the Union Square Theatre, from June 1872, and guided the fortunes of its famous stock company through the season of 1882–83. These and the immediately ensuing years comprised an era of far-reaching change. As the foregoing summary partially attests, the Madison Square Theatre Stock Company's short heyday paralleled a sharp decline in American stock companies and the concurrent ascendancy of the combination house system. Palmer believed that his Union Square troupe's 1877 tour "was the precursor of all the noted expeditions . . . since then . . . to the Pacific Coast" (*Boston Sunday Herald*, May 9, 1880), and M. B. Leavitt also affirmed Palmer as "one of the first to institute the system of long summer tours for stock companies" (Leavitt, 100). Into the early 1880s, however, the Union Square company had remained nearly permanently established in New York. The case was different at the Madison Square. When Palmer approached the helm of this playhouse in fall of 1883, he and the Mallorys, in addition to managing their resident troupe, maintained no less than six formidable "Madison Square Theatre" traveling combinations: *The Private Secretary* (South), *The Private Secretary* (North), *Young Mrs. Winthrop, May Blossom, Called Back*, and *Hazel Kirke*. Palmer's own Madison Square company (afterwards "Mr. Palmer's Company") gradually expanded its activities in behalf of touring combinations, composed alternatively of first-string and pickup personnel. With the adoption of this system by an increasing number of metropolitan managers and by ranking stars, during the 1880s resident stock companies throughout the United States dwindled to a supernumerary status, many dying out.

By January 1882 the number of first-class American stock companies had diminished to three (of which the Union Square was one), giving employment to about 100 actors and actresses. "The remainder of the fraternity," wrote the *New York Times*, "must wander over the land for a livelihood, just as the strollers of old were wont to do" (January 1, 1882). There were upward of 3,500 theatres, opera houses, and places of amusement in the United States in 1887, giving employment to about 40,000 persons, and of this latter number, 10,000 adults were members of the then 500 traveling combinations (*New York Herald*, April 10, 1887).

"So it was that sooner or later the managers of stock-companies had to withdraw from a lost battle," as Brander Matthews recorded. "It was a swift and startling change . . . brought about by forces wholly beyond the control of those engaged in the business" (Matthews, 259–60). Richard Mansfield's *Prince Karl* combination had early capped the 1885–86 Madison Square season, and William Gillette's *Held by the Enemy* company then held its stage from mid-August until late October, pushing back the start of the next season to November 1. Rosina Vokes' three-week stint during 1890–91 ominously marks the first booking of a combination attraction during any regular Madison Square season. By 1888, when the stock company's eclipse was virtually complete, Palmer advanced "good and sufficient reasons" why that system should not be restored:

Theatre-going people . . . get . . . greater [variety and excellence] under the new system than they ever did under the old. The general length of an engagement, of a star or of a combination is one week, and the theatrical season extend[s] over about thirty-five weeks. Instead of . . . witnessing performances which, to say the least, come "tardy off," the patron of one of these theatres can now see new faces and listen to fresh voices every week, witnessing . . . a performance every participant in which is thoroughly drilled in his or her work. (*New York Journal*, September 30, 1888)

Palmer, who had seen *The Private Secretary* acted in London, presumably presided over rehearsals of C. H. Hawtrey's play, and also of *Sealed Instructions*, at the Madison Square. (After he had clashed with autocratic playwright-director David Belasco during the latter's rehearsals of *Called Back*, Belasco abruptly left the theatre's employ.) The manager rehearsed his actors out of town in both *Jim, the Penman* and *A Pair of Spectacles*; in Chicago, during July 1887, he also reportedly readied them for the coming season in Jones' *Welcome, Little Stranger*, but he did not bring this comedy into New York. Maud Harrison remembered Palmer as "a born stage director, [who] found things with a woman's intuition" (*New York Commercial*, September 5, 1905), and George Edgar Montgomery, writing in 1888, described his directorial *modus operandi*, as follows:

A play once accepted by Mr. Palmer, he assembles his entire company on the stage and reads it to them. The parts are then type-written and distributed; and the actors who are to appear in the play are afterwards repeatedly rehearsed by the acting stage manager. When they prove to be thoroughly familiar with the drift of the play and with the characters they are to assume, Mr. Palmer assembles them all again, and, from an orchestra chair, witnesses a rehearsal. From that time, until the production of the play, the conduct of the rehearsal is in his hands. His plan is to permit his actors to express, as far as possible, their own individualities. (*American Magazine*, November 1888)

Henry Arthur Jones personally directed his *Saints and Sinners* at the Madison Square in the fall of 1885. Gene W. Presbrey, first listed as "stage manager" for *Engaged*, later that season of 1885–86 continued in this crucial capacity (although never also a regular member of the acting company) for most other home and touring productions through 1890–91. Dion Boucicault, after revising and directing *Captain Swift* in the fall of 1888, stayed on to conduct Palmer's short-lived Madison Square School of Instruction for aspiring young actors. "The gentlemen were . . . awkward, stiff, ungainly, and slow; the ladies graceful, quick, and refined," Boucicault related. "Among the lady students we found twenty-two who aspired to be Juliets and Paulines and Parthenias, and one who consented to play old women. When faced with the result, Mr. Palmer could not refrain from Falstaff's bill of fare: 'Two gallons of sack to one half penny-worth of bread!' " (*North American Review*, October 1888, pp. 438–39). (Of the young women, only two hopefuls—Nannie Craddock and Nanette Comstock—achieved prominence in the Madison Square Company.)

Steele MacKaye's patented double stage was an essential, inescapable feature of Richard Marston's *mise-en-scène* at the Madison Square. By means of this contrivance, according to its inventor, the time formerly lost resetting scenes was saved, and the audience "spared the long and fatiguing waits . . . between the acts of eleborately mounted plays at modern theatres" (Patent No. 222,143, dated December 2, 1879; *Scientific American*, April 5, 1880). The vertically movable portion was thirty-one feet wide by twenty-nine feet deep, by twenty-five feet, two inches, high, affording two platform stages counterweighted above an excavation some thirty-four feet below street level (*New York Herald*, December 5, 1879). When its inner workings were demonstrated at a professional matinee, March 4, 1880, "the change between the heavy 'sets' was accomplished in forty seconds" (*Herald*, March 5, 1880). But by the time Marston arrived on the scene, four years later, the double stage's novelty had dissipated; indeed, Mac-Kaye's invention had acquired a reputation for often sluggish and refractory behavior.

Marston and Homer F. Emens' designs for *Sealed Instructions* were commended—"so deftly set that the small dimensions of the stage were not apparent" (*New York Times*, April 14, 1885)—as were Marston's initial solo assignments, the *For Congress* sets being described as "highly realistic" (*New York Tribune*, July 7, 1885), and his seven "handsome and appropriate" scenes for *Saints and Sinners* were pronounced "faultless . . . excepting, of course, those inevitable hitches in the stage machinery which cause long waits between the acts" (*Times*, November 8, 1885). James Stoddart, who played *Saints and Sinners'* somber minister Jacob Fletcher, also had reservations: "One evening, during the most pathetic scene of the play . . . , by some mistake of the carpenter, the stage . . . began to descend, and it continued to do so until only my head and shoulders were visible to the audience. . . . Of course the seriousness of the situation was done for, [and] I think I was the only one who did not see the joke" (Stoddart, 206–7). During his six Madison Square years, though, the scenic artist was less hampered by the double stage than by the relatively undemanding scenic aspect of most plays produced upon it. With the exceptions of scripts such as *Held by the Enemy* and *Alabama* (whose distinct regional qualities invited a strong pictorial element), only a few productions gave range to Marston's ability.

The Madison Square's repertory was preponderantly English (works by C. H. Hawtrey, Henry Arthur Jones, W. S. Gilbert, Charles Lawrence Young, Charles Haddon Chambers, Ralph R. Lumley, Sydney Grundy, and others) under Palmer's aegis. Jones wrote Stoddart an appreciative letter acknowledging that *Saints and Sinners'* American production (entailing script revisions) "surpassed that given in London" (Stoddart, 204). French imports were negligible, whereas, among a handful of American scripts, only Thomas' *Alabama* is notable. "Some of the papers carried editorials about the play," its author dourly recorded, "inquiring if New York managers had not made mistakes in leaning on the imported article when native subjects seemed so acceptable" (Thomas, 294–95). (Yet none of Palmer's thirteen vaunted authors' matinees, intermittent between the fall of 1886 and the spring of 1890, had yielded a dramatic gem.) Thomas, who succeeded Boucicault as the Madison Square patcher and adapter of plays (at $50 a week) in the spring of 1890, disclosed that *Alabama* was finished "under pressure" and twice put into rehearsal and then withdrawn; both he and Stoddart described how this piece eventually scored its instant success against the manager's better judgment, only to be summarily taken off while playing to capacity. Perhaps the retiring Palmer no longer cared, in that last season, about the destinies either of this house or of the plays produced there.

PERSONNEL

Management: Marshall H. Mallory and George S. Mallory, proprietors (1880–1903?); Steele MacKaye, manager (1879–81); Gustave and Daniel Frohman, managers (1881?–85); A. M. Palmer, manager (1884–91); Charles Hoyt and Charles Thomas, managers (1891–93), Charles Hoyt and Frank McKee, managers (1894–?); business manager (1885–87); Walter R. Palmer and Wesley Rosenquist, business managers (1887–91).

Musical Direction: Frank A. Howson, musical director (1884–?).

Dramaturgy: Dion Boucicault, house dramatist (1888–90); Augustus Thomas, house dramatist (1890–91).

Mise-en-scène: Charles Witham and Homer F. Emens, scenic artists (1884–85); Richard Marston and Homer F. Emens, scenic artists (1885–91).

Stage Direction: David Belasco, stage director (1884); A. M. Palmer, manager-director (1885–91); Henry Arthur Jones, author-director (1885); Gene W. Presbrey, stage manager (1885–91); Dion Boucicault, author-director (1888).

Actors and Actresses (incomplete list): Fanny Addison (1884–85), Harry Allen (1884–85), *Maurice Barrymore* (1885?–91), Alfred Becks (1885–?), *Agnes Booth* (1885–91), Ethel Brandon (1884–85), Olga Brandon (1884–85), Marie Burroughs (1884–?), F. Caffrey (1884–85), W. B. Cahill (1884–85), Bessi Cameron (1884–85), Frank Carlyle (1884–85), Agnes Carter (1884–85), Georgia Cayvan (1884–85), George Clarke (1884–85), Frank Colfax (1884–84), Nanette Comstock (c. 1888–?), Charles Coote (1884–85), Charles W. Couldock (1884–85), Sydney Cowell (1884–85), Nannie Craddock (c. 1888–?), W. H. Crompton (1884–85), Henrietta Crosman (1884–85), Frank Currier (1884–85), Mrs. E. L. Davenport (1884–85), *William Davidge* (1885–?), J. Delamater (1884–85), W. L. Denison (1884–85), Frank Drew (1885–?), Lizzie Duroy (1884–85), Ada Dwyer (1884–85), Ada Dyas (1884–85), W. J. Ferguson (1884–85), C. P. Flockton (1884–?), May Gallagher (1884–85), Marie Greenwald (1885–?), Leonard Grover (1884–?), Leonard Grover, Jr. (1884–85), George Gruening (1884–85), Maud Harrison (1885–?), Maud Haslam (1884–85), Mary Henderson (1884–85), William Henderson (1884–85), Caroline Hill (1884?–87), A. C. Hilsdorf (1884–85), Harry Hogan (1884–85), *E. M. Holland* (1884–91), Gertie Homan (1888?–?), Lin Hurst (1884–85), J. T. Jackson (1884–85), *Her-*

bert Kelcey (1884–87), Jenny Kennark (1884–85), M. A. Kennedy (1884–85), Lena Langdon (1884–85), *W. J. Lemoyne* (1884–87), Nestor Lennon (1884–85), Archie Lindsay (1884–85), A. L. Lipman (1884–85), Charles E. Lothian (1884–85), Mathilde Madison (1884–85), Benjamin Maginley (1884–85), Charles Malley (1884–85), Kitty Malony (1888?–?), Louis F. Massen (1884–?), Annie Mayer (188?–?), E. A. McDowell (1884–85), J. T. McKever (1884–85), Jessie Millward (1884–?), Kate Morris (1884–85), M. Morton (1884–85), Mrs. E. J. Phillips (1885–?), Dolly Pike (1884–85), *Walden Ramsey* (1884–91), May Roberts (1884–85), Forrest Robinson (1884–85), Frederick Robinson (1886–?), May Robson (1884–85), Katherine Roberts (1888?–?), Fred Ross (1884–85), Annie Russell (1884–?), *Alessandro Salvini* (1888?–91), J. G. Saville (1884–85), Alice Sherwood (1884–85), Charles Stacey (1884–85), *James H. Stoddart* (1885–91), Ed Tannehill (1884–85), Frank Thornton (1884–85), Odette Tyler (1884–85), Charles Walcot (1884–85), Joseph Wheelock (1884–85), Thomas Whiffin (1884–85), Mrs. Thomas Whiffen (1884–85), *Percy Winter* (1887–91).

REPERTORY

The following list includes outside combinations and summer bookings in parentheses.

1884–85: *The Private Secretary; Sealed Instructions; (In Chancery); (For Congress); (The Willow Copse); (Anselma).*

1885–86: *Saints and Sinners; Engaged; Old Love Letters; Broken Hearts; Our Society; (Prince Karl); (Held by the Enemy).*

1886–87: *Jim, the Penman; Our Society; (Prince Karl); (Monsieur); (Dr. Jekyll and Mr. Hyde).*

1877–88: *Jim, the Penman; The Martyr; Elaine; Heart of Hearts; Partners; (A Possible Case); (Dr. Jekyll and Mr. Hyde); (A Parisian Romance); (The Keepsake); (Judge Not); (A Legal Wreck); (Beauty Abroad).*

1888–89: *Partners; Captain Swift; Featherbrain; Bootle's Baby; Aunt Jack; A Man of the World; (The Blue Officer); (A Parisian Romance); (Beau Brummel).*

1889–90: *A Pair of Spectacles; Old Love Letters; Afterthoughts; A New Year's Call; (The Silver Shield); Sunlight and Shadow; Social Fiction; Dinner at Eight; The Pharisee; Alabama; (The Merchant); (Jane).*

BIBLIOGRAPHY

Published Sources: Dion Boucicault, "My Pupils," *North American Review* 148 (November 1888): 438–39; M. B. Leavitt, *Fifty Years in Theatrical Management* (New York: Broadway Publishing Co., 1912); Percy MacKaye, *Epoch*, 2 vols. (New York: Boni and Liveright, 1927); Brander Matthews, *Playwrights on Playmaking and Other Studies* (New York and London: Scribner, 1923); *New York Commercial; New York Herald*; George Edgar Montgomery, "An American Theatre," *American Magazine* 9 (November 1888): 22; *New York Times; New York Tribune*; George C. D. Odell, *Annals of the New York Stage*, vols. 13–14 (New York: Columbia University Press, 1942–45); *Scientific American*, April 5, 1902; A. M. Palmer, " 'Star' vs. 'Stock,' " *New York Journal*, September 30, 1888; James H. Stoddart, *Recollections of a Player* (New York: Century, 1902); Lewis C. Strang,

Plays and Players of the Last Quarter Century, 2 vols. (Boston: L. C. Page, 1903); Augustus Thomas, *The Print of My Remembrance* (New York: Scribner, 1922).

Archival Sources: Harvard Theatre Collection, Cambridge, Massachusetts (clippings, playbills, scrapbooks, and so on); Library for the Performing Arts, Lincoln Center, New York (scrapbooks, playbills, clippings, and so on).

Pat M. Ryan

MARYLAND COMPANY OF COMEDIANS. The Maryland Company of Comedians, Baltimore, was organized in 1781 by actor-manager Thomas Wall. This was the first attempt to establish a permanent acting troupe in America after the Revolution. Between 1781 and 1785 the Maryland Company of Comedians centered its activities in Baltimore but also appeared in Annapolis, Richmond, Charleston, New York, and Philadelphia.

Thomas Wall arrived in Charleston from London in 1765 and performed with David Douglas' American Company (Willis, 85). He appeared in Baltimore in 1772, in the one recorded performance in that city before the Revolution. With the company he waited out the Revolution in Jamaica. After the war he selected Baltimore as his first base of operations after the state Council of Maryland voted on June 8, 1781, that "Thomas Wall is hereby permitted to exhibit Theatrical performances" (Steiner, xlv, 446).

The only records of the Maryland Company's early performance are six extant playbills published between June 22 and October 3, 1781 (Theatre Collection, Maryland Historical Society). The first playbill, "The Lecture on Heads," by G. A. Stevens, featured only two performers, Wall and Miss Wall, a child of seven. But by October 3 Wall had enlarged his company to eight players, including himself, and performed *The Recruiting Officer* and *A Miss In Her Teens* in Adam Lindsay's coffeehouse on Fell's Point, a section of Baltimore near the wharves.

Wall and Lindsay began construction of Baltimore's first theatre building during the summer and on Christmas Day, 1781, announced in Baltimore's *Maryland Journal* the opening of "A Well-regulated THEATRE." By January 15, 1782, they initiated their first regular season of theatrical activities, which extended until July 9. The company performed at least twenty-one plays and twelve farces in forty-four evenings, usually playing only on Tuesday and Friday nights. The repertoire contained traditional eighteenth-century English plays.

Between September 17, 1782, and June 9, 1783, the Maryland Company of Comedians produced at least sixty-three evenings of entertainment in Baltimore. This season brought twenty new performers to the Baltimore stage. Dennis Ryan, an actor from Ireland, was the most prominent. He was one of the few in the company who had performed in any other city. Both Ryan and his wife played leading roles in comedy and tragedy.

On February 11, 1783, Dennis Ryan announced in the *Maryland Journal* that he had undertaken the sole management of the Maryland Company of Comedians. None of the three men most involved in this transaction recorded a reason for the change in management. The transfer of the company from the control of Wall and Lindsay, who remained with the company, to that of Ryan seems to have been smooth. The company did not miss a performance, and the actors did not lose roles. On the date of the announcement, both Wall and Ryan played leading roles.

In the unsigned article "Observations on the Baltimore Theatre," which appeared in the *Maryland Journal* (March 28, 1783), a writer complained that under the management of Wall and Lindsay the performers took liberties by spicing scripts "with their own wit to make them more palatable." He also questioned the necessity of the "obscene blunderers and abominable interpolators [adding] any loose balderdash or gross obscenities of their own."

The Maryland Company of Comedians left Baltimore between April 11 and May 13, 1783, and performed five times in Annapolis between April 19 and April 26 (Playbills, New York Historical Society). The company played in New York City between June 19 and August 16, 1783, and also between October 11 and 25, 1783.

On November 10, 1783, Ryan petitioned the Pennsylvania legislature to repeal an ordinance against the theatre. Despite the legislature's failure to repeal the ordinance, Ryan and his company performed on November 20, 21, 22, what was announced as a selection of readings by the Reverend Mr. Home. Home was the author of *Douglas*, which the company performed at least six times in Baltimore. Ryan and company may have performed *Douglas* in Philadelphia under the guise of a reading (for more details on the Maryland Company of Comedians in Philadelphia, see Garrett, 73–78).

The players returned to Baltimore for eighteen performances between December 2, 1783, and February 14, 1784. During 1784 and 1785 the company toured Annapolis, Richmond, Charleston, and perhaps other cities along the coast. Ryan and his company performed in Charleston in March and presumably toured until arriving in Baltimore for performances on September 7, 13, and 17, 1785. The Maryland Company of Comedians did not perform again in its home city.

Adam Lindsay, at whose coffeehouse the company first performed in 1781, announced in 1784 his intention to open a coffeehouse in Norfolk, Virginia. Thomas Wall apparently retired from the stage at this point in his life. One story indicates that he remained in Baltimore and attempted to open a school for fencing.

The company apparently disbanded because of Ryan's poor health. Some of the members joined other companies, and others retired from the stage. Ryan died less than a year later, in March 1786.

PERSONNEL

Management: Thomas Wall, manager (1781–83); Adam Lindsay, manager (1781–83); Dennis Ryan (1783–85).

Actors and Actresses: *Mr. Atherton* (1782–85), Mr. Bale, Mrs. Bartholomew, Mrs. Bradshaw, Mr. Brown, Mr. Courtenay, Mr. Church, Mrs. Davids, Miss Edwards, Mrs. Edwards, Mrs. Elm, Mr. Ford, Mrs. Foster, Mr. Gadon, Mr. Hamilton, Dr. Harrison, *Mr. Heard* (1782–85), *Mrs. Hyde* (1783–85), Mr. Imlay, Mr. Jeremy, Mr. Jones, Mrs. Kenny, Mr. Kidd, Mrs. Kidd, Mr. Killgour, *Mr. Lewis* (1782–85), *Adam Lindsay* (1781–82), Mr. Lord, Mrs. Lyne, Mr. Murray, Mrs. Parsons, *Mr. Patterson* (1782–85), Mrs. Pileur, Mrs. Potter, Mrs. Powell, Mrs. Powers, Major Price, Mrs. Remington, Mrs. Robinson, Mr. Ross, *Mons. Roussell* (1782–84), Master Ryan, *Dennis Ryan* (1782–85), *Mrs. Dennis Ryan* (1782–85), Mr. Scotman, *Mr. Shakespeare* (1781–85), Dr. Shood, *Mr. Smith* (1782–85), Mrs. Smith, Master Snyder, Mr. Solomon, Lieutenant Street, Mr. Street, *Mr. Tilyard* (1781–82), Reverend James Twyford, Mr. Villier, *Miss Wall* (1781–85), *Thomas Wall* (1781–83), *Mrs. Thomas Wall* (1781–82).

REPERTORY

The following is a list of plays performed by the Maryland Company of Comedians in Baltimore. The number following the title indicates the number of performances of that play in Baltimore.

All in the Wrong (3); *All the World's a Stage* (1); *The Apprentice* (4); *Beaux Stratagem* (2); *The Beggar's Opera* (5); *A Bold Stroke for a Wife* (2); *The Brothers* (2); *The Busybody* (4); *Cato* (2); *The Chaplet* (1); *The Cheats of Scapin* (2); *Chrononhotonthologos* (2); *The Citizen* (6); *The Clandestine Marriage* (1); *Columbus; or, The Discovery of America* (3); *The Commissary* (1); *The Constant Couple* (3); *The Contract* (3); *Contrivances* (3); *A Critical Dissertation on Noses* (3); *The Devil to Pay* (2); *The Devil upon Two Sticks* (3); *Douglas* (4); *The Drummer; or, The Haunted House* (1); *An Epilogue* (2); *An Epilogue on Jealousy* (1); *The Fair Penitent* (6); *The Fatal Curiosity* (1); *Fatal Discovery* (4); *Flora; or, Hob in the Well* (1); *The Foundling* (1); *The Gamester* (3); *The Ghost* (3); *The Grecian Daughter* (4); *Gustavus Vasa* (2); *Hamlet* (2); *Harlequin Dance* (1); *Harlequin in Hell* (1); *Harlequin Landlord* (1); *High Life below Stairs* (2); *Inconstant; or, The Way to Win Him* (1); *Irish Widow* (5); *Isabella* (2); *Jane Shore* (2); *The King and the Miller of Mansfield* (4); *King Henry IV* (1); *King Lear* (2); *Léthé; or, Aesop in the Shade* (8); *Life and Death of King John* (2); *The London Merchant; or, George Barnwell* (4); *Love and a Bottle* (1); *Love for Love* (1); *Love in a Village* (3); *Lying Valet* (6); *Macbeth* (1); *Mahomet* (2); *Mayor of Garratt* (5); *The Merchant of Venice* (1); *The Miser* (1); *A Miss in Her Teens* (5); *Mock Doctor* (5); *A New Lecture on Heads* (2); *Old Ground Young* (2); *Old Lecture on Heads* (1); *Old Maid* (1); *Oroonoko* (1); *Orphan* (5); *Othello* (1); *The Padlock* (6); *Perez and Estifania* (2); *Provok'd Husband* (1); *Recruiting Officer* (3); *Revenge* (4); *Richard III* (6); *Roman Father* (3); *Romance of an Hour* (2); *Romeo and Juliet* (3); *The School for Scandal* (2); *She Stoops to Conquer* (2); *Shoemakers* (2); *Stage-Coach; or, The Humors of an Inn* (1); *Tamerlane, the Great* (2); *The Taming of the Shrew* (2); *Theodosius* (2); *Thomas and Sally* (7); *The Times* (1); *Too Civil by Half* (1); *Trick upon Trick* (2); *Trip to Scotland* (1); *Two Misers* (2); *Upholsterer; or, What News?* (2); *Venice*

Preserved (5); *Vintner Trick'd* (1); *Virgin Unmasked* (2); *Walking Statue* (1); *Wapping Landlady; or, Jack in Distress* (4); *West Indian* (4); *The Witches* (7); *The Wonder, A Woman Keeps a Secret* (3); *The Wonder, An Honest Yorkshireman* (4); *Wrangling Lovers; or, Like Master, Like Man* (6); *Zara* (6).

BIBLIOGRAPHY

Published Sources: Eola Willis, *The Charleston Stage in the Eighteenth Century* (Columbia, S.C.: State Co., 1924), p. 85; Bernard Christian Steiner, ed., *Journal of Correspondence of the State Council of Maryland, 1780–1781* (Baltimore: Maryland Historical Society, 1927), pp. 446; Kurt L. Garrett, "Dennis Ryan's Temple of Apollo," *Theatre Survey* 21 (May 1980): 73–78; David Ritchey, "The Maryland Company of Comedians," *Educational Theatre Journal* 24 (1972): 355–61.

Archival Sources: Theatre collections in Enoch Pratt Library, Baltimore; Maryland Historical Society, Baltimore (nine playbills for 1781, six recording performances in Baltimore and three recording performances in Annapolis); and New-York Historical Society, New York City (playbills).

David Ritchey

McVICKER'S FIRST THEATRE COMPANY. The McVicker Theatre, Chicago, opened November 5, 1857, with the assembled company singing "The Star-Spangled Banner" (a Chicago theatrical tradition) and with the comedies *The Honey Moon* and *Rough Diamond*. Both plays featured the proprietor-manager James Hubert McVicker, who had made his Chicago debut at Rice's Theatre in 1848. McVicker was a member of Rice's stock company until 1851. After the death of comedian Dan Marble in that year, McVicker purchased the rights to Marble's plays and toured as a star in the United States and England. He managed the People's Theatre in St. Louis before returning to Chicago in 1857.

McVicker built what was, at its opening, the largest theatre in the West. Situated on Madison Street near the intersection of State Street, the sixty-by ninety-seven-foot auditorium seated 2,500. The stage measured sixty by eighty feet; the proscenium was thirty-three feet high. The Chicago *Tribune* of November 6, 1857, described the theatre: "The exterior of the structure is plain but exceedingly tasteful. . . . The front, when completed, will be occupied for stores and offices. The rear of the building is the Theater, which is approached from the street by a spacious and well-lighted hall. The Theater itself is neither remarkable for brilliancy of decoration or grandeur of design, but it is beyond question exceedingly graceful." Eight large windows provided ventilation, and both the sight lines and acoustics were reportedly good. It cost McVicker $85,000 to build the theatre.

The venture proved an immediate success, and McVicker continued that success by following the standard operational procedures of the day—two or three plays and several divertissements on a given evening. McVicker maintained a large stock company—at one point the company was so large that he double-cast the comedy *Extremes* and alternated the casts for the run of the performance. Despite such a large company, McVicker imported an impressive list of stars: James E. Murdoch, Charlotte Cushman, Edwin Booth, Adah Isaacs Menken, E. A. Sothern, Jane Coombs, Caroline Richings, Peter Richings, J. Wilkes Booth, L. M. Gottschalk (pianist), Carlotta Patti, William Warren, J. H. Hackett, Daniel E. Bandmann (German tragedian), Lotta Crabtree, Mlle. Augusta (dancer), Olive Logan, Mr. and Mrs. Charles Kean, Joseph Jefferson, Mme. Celeste, Charles Dillon (English tragedian), Frank Mayo, Fanny Janauschek, Charles Fechter, Carlotta Leclercq. To exemplify the drawing power of a star it is noted that Lotta Crabtree drew more than 12,000 during the first week of a three-week engagement in 1864. Occasionally, the production itself was the star. In July 1867 *The Black Crook* made its Chicago debut at the McVicker under the personal supervision of J.E. McDonough. It enjoyed an uncommonly long run of fifty-six performances.

The principal competitors of McVicker's Theatre were Wood's (intermittently Aiken's) Museum, which opened an auditorium with a capacity of 1,500 in 1863, and Crosby's Opera House, an incredible structure that opened in 1865, housing businesses, artists' studios, a fine arts gallery, and an auditorium with a capacity of 3,000. Wood's Museum produced mostly sophisticated drama without star support. As such, it enjoyed modest success, and while providing competition for McVicker, it posed no real threat. Crosby's Opera House was intended to be exactly what its name implied—a theater devoted to the production of grand opera. (Uranas H. Crosby, whose brainchild the Opera House was, made his fortune as a distiller. Knowing nothing of contemporary theater management, he intended to produce nothing but traveling companies, so a stock company was not employed. The venture was a complete financial failure, and Crosby conceived of a plan to dispose himself of the edifice by holding a lottery. Several thousands of tickets were sold; the grand prize was won by a country gentleman, who, after numerous rumors of scandal, sold the theatre back to Crosby. The Opera House suffered financial ups and downs until finally, in 1869, the management resorted to the stock system. It continued its up-and-down success.)

Despite the sometimes fierce competition from the Opera House, McVicker's Theatre thrived. In 1871 McVicker decided that the growing importance of Chicago as a center of commerce warranted the renovation of his theater. The $90,000 alteration was extensive; only the walls of the original theatre remained unchanged. The remodeled structure opened August 29, 1871; it fell to the Great Fire on October 9 of that year. (McVicker did rebuild; Sarah Bernhardt made her Chicago debut at McVicker's sometime after the fire.)

PERSONNEL

The following is a partial list; a date in parentheses indicates the first mention by A.T. Andreas.

Management: James H. McVicker, proprietor and manager (1857); Samuel Myers, stage manager and partial owner (1864); F. Harrington, assistant stage manager (1857).

Musical Director: Louis Chatel (1857).

Actors and Actresses: R.J. Allen (1857); Mrs. R.J. Allen (1857); Mr. Bradley (1859); F.S. Buxton (1857); Mr. Cline (1859); Mrs. Cowell (1869); Mrs. E. DeClancey (1857); Julia DeClancey (1857); Mr. Dillon (1859); W.C. Forrester (1857); Mrs. W.C. Forrester (1857); Nellie Gay (1857); W. Gay (1857); Mrs. W. Gay (1857); A.J. Grayer (1857); David Hanchett (1857); F. Harrington (1857); Mr. Havelock (1857); W.S. Higgins (1857); Lottie Hough (1857); Mrs. Hough (1859); H.R. Jones (1857); Mr. Leighton (1859); Emma Logan (1857); Alice Mann (1857); Eliza Mann (1857); Mrs. Marble (1859); Anna Martin (1857); J. Martin (1857); J.H. McVicker (1857); Mary McVicker (1859); F.A. Munroe (1857); Mr. Myers (1859); Fanny Rich (1857); Jenny Secore (1857); J. Taylor (1857); Mr. Tilton (1859); J.B. Uhl (1857); Ada Webb, dancer (1861); Emma Webb, dancer (1861); Joseph Wheelock (1869); Miss Woodbury (1859); Mary Wright (1857).

REPERTORY

1857: *Honey Moon; Rough Diamond; Money; Man and Tiger; The Hunchback; The School for Scandal; Matrimonial Squabble; The Stranger; Laugh When You Can; Much Ado about Nothing; The Italian Bride; All the World's a Stage; The Lady of Lyons; Guy Mannering; Naval Engagements; Ingomar; Adrienne, the Actress; Betsy Baker; Camille; Armand; Love; Turning the Tables; Hamlet; Richelieu; Jack Cade; Fashionable Society; The Corsican Brothers; Forty and Fifty; Don Caesar de Bazan; Macbeth; Harolde: the Merchant of Calais; Richard III; Faint Heart ne'er Won Fair Lady; Money Crisis of 1857; Sam Patch in France; Wild Oats; The Inconstant; The Dramatist; The Robbers; The Elder Brother; De Soto: Hero of the Mississippi.*

1858: *Taking the Chances; Macbeth; An Object of Interest; The Stranger; As You Like It; The School for Scandal; Henry VIII; Romeo and Juliet; Guy Mannering; Simpson and Co.; Honey Moon; The French Spy; Ladies, Beware; La Giselle; Sweethearts and Wives; La fille de Danube; The Cross of Gold; Gamecock of the Wilderness; Love and Loyalty; Your Life's in Danger; Lend Me Five Shillings; Handwriting on the Wall; Return from Moscow; Ardvoirlich: The Highland Seer; Midnight Watch; Captain Charles; Othello; Damon and Pythias; Richard III; Iron Chest; Richelieu; Rough Diamonds; Pizarro; Hamlet; In and Out of Place; The Robbers; Breach of Promise; A New Way to Pay Old Debts; A Home in the West; Fazio; Lillie White; The Hunchback; Times That Try Us; Man of The World; All That Glitters Is Not Gold; Toodles; The New Footman; The Nervous Man; The Man of Nerve; Bachelor of Arts; Love and Murder; The Serious Family; David Copperfield; A Gentleman from Ireland; Columbus El Filibustere; The Most Unwarrantable Intrusion; Amateur Actors; Virginius; O'Neil, the Avenger; William Tell; Gio: The Amourer of Tyre; Nick of the Woods; Adelphia; Outaichet: The Lion of the Forest; Uncle Sam; Alexander the Great; Michael; She Stoops to Conquer; The Sea of Ice; A Thirst for Gold; Irish Emigrant; Lesson for Husbands; The Yankee Girl; A Pretty Piece of Business; The School of Reform; Louis XI; Bamboozling; Still Waters Run Deep; The Willow Copse; Jessie Brown; or, The Relief of Lucknow; The Advocate; A Hard Struggle; The Governor's Wife; A Conjugal Lesson; Cousin Lambkin; Retribution; The Flying Dutchman; The Golden Farmer; The Countess and the Serf; Adrienne, the Actress; Camille; Charlotte Corday; Linda: The Cigar Girl; Vo Kurt Martial; Maid of Mariendorpt; London Assurance; Brutus; Katherine and Petruchio; Who Owns the Baby?; The Mystic Cave; or, The Clown's Misfortune; Mazulum; or, The Raven; Aladdin; Facts and Fancies; Maid, Wife, and Mother; Lucrezia Borgia; A Hopeless Passion; Fool of the Family; Sketches in India; The Brigand; Uncle Tom's Cabin; Cousin Cheery; The Gladiator of Ravenna; A Night of Mirth; Masaniello; The Black Crook; Satan in Paris; The Mysterious Stranger; Green Bushes; or, Six Degrees of Crime; Marriage à la militaire; Maid of Croissey; Mehitable Ann; The Flower of the Forest; Douglas; The Duchess of Malfi; The Fool of the Family; Phillip of France; La sonnambula; Daughter of the Regiment; Crown Diamonds; The Barber of Seville; The Bohemian Girl; Fra Diavolo; Cinderella; Der Freischutz; or, The Seven Magic Bullets; Evadne; Armand; Ingomar; Bride of Lammermoor; Sybil; The Maid with the Milking Pail; Romeo and Juliet; La Tisba; Coriolanus; Much Ado about Nothing; The Huron Chief; The Robbers; The King and the Commoner; The Windmill; Jenny Lind; The Wandering Boy; Katy, the Hot Corn Girl; The Little Devil; Three Fast Men; or, The Female Robinson Crusoes; A Female Minstrel; Young Monarch; Dreams of Delusion; The Artful Dodger; Time Tries All; The Four Sisters; Henry IV; Mons. Mallet; The Kentuckian; Merry Wives of Windsor; Smiles and Tears; or, A Mother's Prayer; Skeleton Hand; or, The Demon Statue; The Bride of the Evening; The Pioneer Patriot; The Maniac; His Favorable Companion; The Wild Man of the Woods (Valentine and Orson).*

1859: The Bride of Lammermoor; Up Salt River; The Brigand; Retribution; Speed the Plow; My Cousin Tom; Rob Roy; Lucrezia Borgia; Uncle Tom's Cabin; London Assurance; The Willow Copse; A Social Scourge; Blanche's Dream; Sketches of India; Camille; Mathilde; Medea; Joan of Arc; The Four Sisters; Thérèse; The Fool of the Family; Cure for the Heart-Ache; Dearest Elizabeth; Time Tries All; Ladies in Love; Polly: The Young Quaker; Town and Country; Old Heads and Young Hearts; Turning the Tables; The Momentous Question; The Rivals; The Bottle Imp; Our American Cousin; Pike's Peak; The King's Son and His Privileges; Margot: The Poultry Dealer; Maid with the Milking Pail; French Spy; Pet of the Petticoats; Nan: The Good-for-Nothing; Antony and Cleopatra; Satan in Paris; Katty O'Sheil; The Private Prince; Richard III; Henry IV; The Kentuckian; A Man of the World; Born to Good Luck; Mischievous Annie; A Happy Man; A Lump of Gold; Irish Lover; Wild Oats; The Robbers; Money; The Dramatist; The Elder Brother; Sam Patch in France; The School for Scandal; Hamlet; The Avenger; Five Married Men and Their Wives; A Model Farmer (Writing on the Wall); Mons. Alexander; Adrienne, the Actress; Romeo and Juliet; The Belle's Stratagem; Misalliance; Masks and Faces; Czarina; or, The Court of Russia; Extremes; The Queen's Necklace; The Four Sisters; Marble Heart; Matrimonial Squabbles; Court and Stage; The Duchess of Malfi; Guy Mannering; Byways and Highways; The Patrician's Daughter; Who Speaks First; Macbeth; Kim-Ka-Bianco; or, The Magic Sword; Pinchillo, the Corrupt; Nature's Nobleman; A Serious Family; Irish Lion; Pocahontas; David Cop-

perfield; Twenty Minutes with a Tiger; The Gamester; The Merchant of Venice; Gianette; The Stolen Child; Speculation; Our Eastern Cousin in Chicago; Much Ado about Nothing; Ingomar; The Hunchback; The Wrecker's Daughter; The Glorious Minority; Coriolanus; Damon and Pythias; The Robbers; Clouds and Sunshine; The Wonder; Royal Command; Captain Charlotte; Soldier's Daughter; Roll of Drums; Black Eyed Susan; Pauline; Is It a Boy?; Little Piccolomini; Ladies' Battle; Little Nell.

1860: *Hidden Hand* (according to Robert Sherman, this was the first play produced in Chicago without an afterpiece); *The Love Chase; The Belle's Stratagem; St. Mary's Eve; Lucrezia Borgia; Grist to the Mill; Widow's Stratagem; Highways and Byways; Everybody's Friend; Mary Tudor; The Octoroon; Hidden Hand; Captain Kyd; Samuel in Search of Himself; Luke, the Labourer; Ladies' Battle; The Hunchback; Ingomar; Love; The Lady of Lyons; Fazio; A Wife's Secret; Love's Sacrifice; Old Heads and Young Hearts; Jeanie Deans; Taking the Chances; Our Irish Cousin; The Queen's Own; Romance of a Poor Young Man; Satan In Paris; The Marble Heart; Two Can Play at That Game; Retribution; As You Like It; Obstinate Family; Nine Points of the Law; London Assurance; Betsy Baker; Much Ado about Nothing; The Rivals; She Stoops to Conquer; The Nervous Man; Pauline; Our American Cousin; Husband to Order; Aline; or, The Rose of Killarney; Nicholas Nickleby; Bride of Lammermoor; The Limerick Boy; Lucille; The Corsican Brothers; Retribution; Too Much for Good Nature; The Willow Copse; The Adopted Child; Tom and Jerry; A Day in Paris; Speed the Plough; The Wife; Married Life; Love's Telegraph; Katty O'Sheil; French Spy; Heir of D'Arville; Geraldine; Evangeline; Nora O'Neil; An Irish Emigrant; Romance of a Poor Young Woman; Katy, the Hot Corn Girl; Bombastes Furioso; Handsome Husbands; Fashion and Famine; Brigand's Son; Spoil'd Child; Evadne; The School for Scandal; Ada; Colleen Bawn; Lear in Private Life; A Race for a Widow; The Quadroon; David Copperfield; Jenny Lind; An Object of Interest; Politicians; or, The Contest in Chicago; Camille; Romeo and Juliet; Guy Mannering; Othello; Macbeth; The Rag Picker of Paris; Richard III; Faust and Marguerite; The Female Brigand.*

1861: *The Writing on the Wall; or, The Model Farmer; A Woman's Whims; Beauty and the Beast; The Four Sisters; Hue and Cry; Invisible Prince; Aline; or, The Rose of Killarney; The Hunchback; Comedy and Tragedy; Joseph and his Brethern; or, The Hebrew Son; Barney the Baron; Rose Elmore; The Irish Lion; The Hidden Hand; Woman in White; Douglas; Jack Sheppard; Handy Andy; Riding in a Railroad Keer; The Young Actress; Dombey and Son; Lalla Rookh; Our American Cousin; The Flower of the Forest; Twenty Minutes with a Tiger; Our American Cousin at Home; Romance of a Poor Young Man; Tragic Revival; Wild Oats; or, The Strolling Gentleman; Money; Hamlet; Much Ado about Nothing; The Robbers; The School for Scandal; Pizarro; DeSoto: The Hero of the Mississippi; The Stranger; Michael Earl; The Female Brigand; Sam Patch in France; Augustus and Theodore; Putnam; American Volunteers in 1776; Hit Him, He Has No Friends; Son of the Republic; Too Much for Good Nature; The Nervous Man; How to Pay the Rent; Irish Ambassador; His Last Legs; The Daughter of the Regiment; Washington at Valley Forge; Marian; or, The Daughter of the States; Extremes; The Enchantress; The Brigand; Bamboozling; The Fair One with the Golden Locks; Nicholas Nickleby; Union of Old Virginia; Ladies' Battle; Ireland as It Is; A Day too Late; The Willow Copse; Box and Cox; The Chimney Corner; Rough Diamonds; Richelieu;*

*Samuel in Search of Himself; One Touch of Nature; An Ugly Customer; Louis XI;
The School of Reform; The Gamecock of the Wilderness; Take That Girl Away;
Bold Dragoons; My Neighbor's Wife; Grandfather Whitehead; Lend Me Five Shill-
ings; Suspense; Lucrezia Borgia; Louise de Liegonrolles; Christmas Eve; or, A Duel
in the Snow; The Golden Farmer; Man of the World; Obstinate Family; Babes in
the Wood; The Artful Dodger; The Persecuted Dutchman; Jack Cade; Your Life's
in Danger; The Corsican Brothers; Metamora; Boots at the Swan; Don Caesar de
Bazan; Henry IV; Merry Wives of Windsor; Henry VIII; A Yankee in England;
Mons. Mallet; or, The Post Office Mistake; Rip Van Winkle; The Kentuckian;
Toodles; The Widow's Victim; The Barrack Room; Flanigan and the Fairies; Novelty; Paddy Miles; The Ocean Child; A Glance at New York; Bull Run; The Dumb
Girl of Genoa; The Willow Copse; Trying It On; Peace and Quiet; Great Expec-
tations; Jocrisse, the Juggler; King Lear; Geraldine; Self; The Colleen Bawn.*

1862: *Irish Ambassador; Born to Good Luck; Boys of the Irish Brigade; How
to Pay the Rent; Husband to Order; Who Stole the Pocket Book; I've Written to
Brown; Macbeth; Othello; Nick of the Woods; Ambition; O'Neil, the Rebel; Wallace:
The Hero of Scotland; Richard III; Lend Me Five Shillings; The Lady of Lyons;
Romeo and Juliet; Hamlet; The Robbers; The Apostate; The Belle of the Season;
or, Finding the Level; Camille; Gemea, the Hebrew Mother; Judith of Geneva; The
Jealous Wife; Rob Roy; Black Eyed Susan; The Lady in Camp; Pauline; The Ruined
Abbey; Love; As You Like It: Day after the Wedding; Marble Heart; Mary Stuart;
The Morning Call; Our Female American Cousin; Our Gal; The Irish Immigrant;
Mazeppa; Child of the Regiment; Honey Moon; In and Out of Place; Off to the
War; The Lady and the Lions; Married Life; Scotto, the Scout; or, The Union
Rangers; The Quadroon; The Model Farm; Idiot Witness; Sam Patch in France;
Corsican Brothers; Julius Caesar; Jack Cade; Streets of New York; Mysteries and
Miseries of Human Life; The Widow's Mite; Linda: The Cigar Girl; O'Flanigan
and the Fairies; Look at That Door; Louis XI; Richelieu; The Willow Copse; Lion
of St. John; Great Expectations; Love in '76; The Horsebreaker; The Unknown;
Naval Engagements; The Floating Beacon; Esmeralda; A Day in Paris; King Henry
VIII; Merry Wives of Windsor; Man of the World; Mons. Mallet; Your Life's in
Danger; Shylock, the Jew; Love and Hunger; Ingomar; Time Tries All; Loan of a
Lover; The Stranger; The Robber's Wife; A Regular Fix; Peep O'Day Boys; Home
in the West; Shocking Events; Time Works Wonders; The Seven Sisters; Virginius;
Speed the Plough; Wandering Minstrel; Brother Bill and Me; Payable on Demand;
One Touch of Nature; Harvest Home; A Terrible Secret; The Lion of St. Marc;
Mose in California; The Octoroon; Toodles; New York as It Is; The Married Rake;
Ambition; Warrior Captive; Pizarro; Fanchon, the Cricket; Lucrezia Borgia; The
Barrack Room; Cure for Heart-Ache; Nipped in the Bud; The Merchant of Venice;
Josephine: Child of the Regiment; The Maniac Lover; The Man in the Iron Mask.*

1863: *The Jewess; or, The Council of Constance; Dick Turpin; or, The Two
Highwaymen; Handy Andy; Mischievous Annie; The Irish Emigrant; Dombey and
Son; Shandy McGuire; The Return of the Volunteers; Thrice Married; The Yankee
Housekeeper; Ireland as It Was; The Colleen Bawn; Eily O'Conner; The Bride of
Garry Owen; Toodles; Macbeth; Ingomar; The Duchess of Malfi; The Pretty Hou-
sekeeper; Guy Mannering; The Married Rake; Lucrezia Borgia; Fazio; The Stranger;
Our Female American Cousin; Caroline Martin and Jerusha; Absent Minded; Our
Gal; The Bohemian Girl; Child of the Regiment; In and Out of Place; The Emigrant*

Girl; I've Written to Brown; The Jealous Wife; A Regular Fix; Naval Engagements; A Southerner Just Arrived; The French Spy; Narramattah (Wept of Wish-Ton-Wish); The Wizard Skiff; St. Patrick's Eve; The Corsican Brothers; The Hunchback; Love; The Lady of Lyons; Slasher and Crasher; Romeo and Juliet; Wife's Secret; The School for Scandal; Love Chase; A World to Fashion; Hamlet; St. Marc; Othello; Macbeth; Little Barefoot; Fanchon, the Cricket; Margot: The Poultry Dealer; All That Glitters Is Not Gold; The Marble Heart; The Robbers; The Apostate; The Merchant of Venice; Richard III; Our American Cousin at Home; Aurora Floyd; Husbands to Order; Lady Audley's Secret; Wept of Wish-Ton-Wish; The Heir-at-Law; The Serious Family; Seeing Warren; The Poor Gentleman; Paul Pry; The Silver Spoon; London Assurance; Sweethearts and Wives; The Seven Sisters; Dot; A Kiss in the Dark; The Jew of Frankfort; Henry IV; Rip Van Winkle; Nell Gwynne; The Female Gambler; Lucia D'Arville; or, The Wife's Trials; The Ghost; Jerry Clip; Yankee Teamster; Mistletoe Bough; The World of Fashion; Rob Roy; Love's Sacrifice; Narcisse; or, The Last of the Pompadours; Robert Emmett; Follies of a Night; Lavaugro.

1864: She Stoops to Conquer; Young Hearts and Old Heads; Rachel, the Reaper; Our American Cousin; Wives of Ireland; The School for Scandal; The Smiths and Browns; The Hunchback; The Wife; Madelaine; or, The Belle of Forbourg; The Lady of Lyons; Sarah's Young Man; Clouds with a Silver Lining; The Forty Thieves; Clyshea, the Deserter; Fanchon, the Cricket; Margot: The Poultry Girl; Little Barefoot; Pearl of Savoy; Pure Gold; I've Written to Brown; Forsaken Bride; Betsy Baker; A Kiss in the Dark; Speed the Plough; Macbeth; Guy Mannering; Naomi, the Deserter; The Duchess of Malfi; Othello; East Lynne; The Ticket-of-Leave Man; Everybody's Friend; Solon Shingle; Paul Pry; Poor Gentleman; Forty Winks; Victims; Hamlet; Wild Oats; Romeo and Juliet; Richard III; Mazeppa; The Sea of Ice; Dot; Camille; Follies of a Night; Ingomar; Delicate Grounds; Swiss Swains; Peace and Quiet; Pauline; or, The Assassin's Bride; The Heir-at-Law; Sweethearts and Wives; The Serious Family; A Breach of Promise; Grimshaw, Bagshaw, and Bradshaw; All That Glitters Is Not Gold; The Seven Sisters; The Cross of Gold; The Octoroon; Narcisse; Richelieu; Fashion; The Merchant of Venice; Dick Turpin and Tom King; The Carpenter of Rouen; Rosedale; or, The Rifle Ball; Nell Gwynne; Waiting for the Verdict; Bel Demonia; Gemea; The Dead Heart.

1865: The French Spy; The Wizard Skiff; The Felon's Daughter; The Hunchback; Ingomar; The Lady of Lyons; The Stranger; Handy Andy; Mischievous Annie; Colleen Bawn; The Ticket-of-Leave Man; Kathleen Mavourneen; Ireland as It Was; The Yankee Housekeeper; Dombey and Son; The Irish Lion; The Young Actress; Fanchon, the Cricket; Pearl of Savoy; Margot: The Poultry Dealer; Little Barefoot; Adrienne, the Actress; The Serf and the Countess; Charlotte Corday; Mazeppa; Dick Turpin; The Willow Copse; The Chimney Corner; Jessie McLane; Supper in Dixie; The Milky Way; Rosedale; The Marble Heart; Richard III; Richelieu; Hamlet; Under the Palm; Enoch Arden; The Workingmen of Paris; The Robbers; A Yankee in Cuba; A Yankee Duelist; Lost Heir; Wife for a Day; Henry VIII; The Merchant of Venice; Louis XI; Old Heads and Young Hearts; Speed the Plough; Founded on Facts; The School for Scandal; Our American Cousin; Eustache Baudin; London Assurance; Laugh When You Can; Time Tries All; As You Like It; Money; Arrah-na-Pogue; King John; The Woman in Red; Zembuca; Mysterious Stranger; The

French Spy; Green Bushes; or, The Huntress of the Mississippi; Lucrezia Borgia; Carpenter of Rouen; The Hypocrite; Madeline; Inshavogue; or, The Outlaw of '98.

1866: *Ambition; or, The Tomb, the Throne, and the Scaffold; Nick of the Woods; Macbeth; Jack Cade; Flies in a Web; Playing with Fire; David Copperfield; His Last Legs; Ireland as It Was; Dombey and Son; The Serious Family; Pocahontas; The Sea of Ice; The Workingmen of New York; Richard III; The Marble Heart; The Heretic; Black Eyed Susan; Hamlet; Dreams of Delusion; Don Caesar de Bazan; The Merchant of Venice; A Gentleman from Ireland; Fifties; Ingomar; Jeanie Deans; Charlotte Corday; The Child of Nature; Woodland Wildfire; The Union Prisoner; Old Phil's Birthday; The Willow Copse; Richelieu; The Chimney Corner; King Lear; Virginius; Hamlet; Belphegor, the Mountebank; A New Way to Pay Old Debts; A Hard Struggle; Eustache Boudin; Our American Cousin; London Assurance; The Octoroon; The French Spy; The Wonder; Camille; As You Like It; The Angel of Midnight; Sam; Toodles; A Glance at New York; The People's Lawyer; or, Solon Shingle; O'Flanigan and the Fairies; Child of Savannah; The Ice Witch; The Falls of Clyde; The Island King; The Two Buzzards; Nell Gwynne; Paddy Miles' Boy; Taking the Chances; Clairvoyance; or, The Man with the Wax Figure; Fast People; Peg; or, Mask and Faces; She Stoops to Conquer; A Regular Fix; Wild Oats; The Fairy Story; The Customs of the Countess; Born to Good Luck; In and Out of Place; Henry VIII; Merry Wives of Windsor; Griffith Gaunt; Rosedale; The Female Gambler; The Unequal Match.*

1867: *Lillian May; or, Actress and Artist; Othello; The Italian Wife; Love's Sacrifices; The Child Stealer; Macbeth; Richelieu; King Lear; Belphegor; Cynthia (The Flower of the Forest); The French Spy; Long Strike; Arrah-na-Pogue; Handy Andy; The Irish Emigrant; Born to Good Luck; More Blunders Than One; The Irish Lion; The Irish Baron; Shamus O'Brien; or, The Bold Soldier Boy of Glengall; Del Dominos; The Marble Heart; Rob Roy; Uncle Tom's Cabin; Chevalier; Nell Gwynne; Ambition; Jack Cade; The Jibbenainosay; or, Nick of the Woods; Henry IV; Merry Wives of Windsor; The Robbers; Clairvoyance; Black Eyed Susan; Sam; The Streets of New York; Our American Cousin at Home; Hamlet; The Merchant of Venice; Romeo and Juliet; Richard III; Much Ado about Nothing; The Black Crook; Ours; Caste; The Pet of the Petticoats; Family Jars; The Corsican Brothers; Captain Charlotte; Jenny Lind; Nan: The Good for Nothing; Little Nell and the Marchioness; Under the Gaslight; Rip Van Winkle; The Fairy Circle; The Shamrock; Connie Soogah; The Hunchback; The Woman in White.*

1868: *Leap Year; Nick of the Woods; A Regular Fix; Ten Nights in a Barroom; Spooks; Under the Gaslight; The Irish Emigrant; Handy Andy; Rory O'More, More Blunders Than One; Irish Lion; Love and Murder; Shamus O'Brien; Arrah-na-Pogue; The Merchant of Venice; Hamlet; The Lady of Lyons; Othello; Romeo and Juliet; Richelieu; Macbeth; Richard III; The Stranger; Katherine and Petruchio; The French Spy; Wept of Wish-Ton-Wish; The Wizard Skiff; Norwood; Fanchon, the Cricket; Little Barefoot; The Pearl of Savoy; Sam; The Streets of New York; The Octoroon; Joe; Our American Cousin at Home; Toodles; The Black Crook; The Lottery of Love; The School for Scandal; Two Old English Gentlemen; London Assurance; The Post Boy and Milky White; Rip Van Winkle; The Rivals; A Midsummer Night's Dream.*

1869: *Little Nell and the Marchioness; The Female Detective; Uncle Tom's Cabin; Narcisse; or, The Vagrant; The Marble Heart; The Robbers; Richard III; The He-*

retic; Black Eyed Susan; Romeo and Juliet; As You Like It; Much Ado about Nothing; King René's Daughter; The Jealous Wife; The Hunchback; The Field of the Cloth of Gold; The Snare; Lady Audley's Secret; The Flask of Lightning; Ingomar; Lucrezia Borgia; Katherine and Petruchio; Bound; The Child Stealer; Camille; Lioness of the North; The Wonder; East Lynne; Don Caesar de Bazan; Green Bushes; Leah the Forsaken; Oliver Twist; Sam; Kit: The Arkansas Traveller; Toodles; She Stoops to Conquer; London Assurance; The Rivals; Old English Gentlemen; Nine Points of the Law; The Marble Heart; Enoch Arden; Red Light; or, The Danger Signal; Formosa; Arrah-na-Pogue; Lady Audley's Secret; Rip Van Winkle; Onah's Engagement; Marian's Crime; Robert Macaire; The Golden Bubble; The French Spy; Fanchon, the Cricket; Pearl of Savoy; Little Barefoot.

1870: *Margot: The Poultry Dealer; Katty O'Sheil; Our Cousin German; Colleen Bawn; The Irish Lion; Thrice Married; The Return of the Volunteers; Inshavogue; Lucrezia Borgia, M.D.; The Outcast; Billiards; or, Business before Pleasure; The Coming Man; Hamlet; Richelieu; Ingomar; The Robbers; Macbeth; Othello; Richard III; Belphegor, the Mountebank; Damon and Pythias; Fritz; East Lynne; Oliver Twist; Leah the Forsaken; The Child Stealer; Frou-Frou; Kit: The Arkansas Traveller; The Streets of New York; The Rose of Killarney; The Brigand Queen; Uncle Tom's Cabin; The French Spy; Taking the Chances; Rory O'More; Irish Ambassador; The Irish Attorney; The Colleen Bawn; The Widow Hunt; Toodles; Fox and Geese; Among the Breakers; Brutus; Much Ado about Nothing; The Fool's Revenge; Won at a Raffle; The Fat Boy; The Hidden Hand; Red Ribbon; Rosedale; Mystery of Edwin Drood; The Victor of Rhu; Pearl of Savoy; Fanchon, the Cricket; Lorle; Jane Eyre; The Serious Family; Your Life's in Danger.*

1871: *Our Cousin German; Mary Stuart; Camille; Leah the Forsaken; The Maid and the Magpie; Deborah; Handy Andy; East Lynne; Oliver Twist; The Child Stealer; The Lady of Lyons; Ruy Blas; Hamlet; Don Caesar de Bazan; Ariadne; Help; Othello; Richard III; The Marble Heart; Macbeth; The Streets of New York; The Minstrel Boy; or, The Old Home and the New; Solon Shingle; Married Life; The Little Detective; Little Nell and the Marchioness; Uncle Tom's Cabin; Extremes; Saratoga; Elfie; or, Cherry Tree Inn.*

BIBLIOGRAPHY

Andreas, A. T. *History of Chicago.* 3 vols. Chicago: A. T. Andreas Co., 1884–86.

McVicker, James H. *The Theater: Its Early Days in Chicago.* Chicago: Knight and Leonard, 1884.

Sherman, Robert L. *Chicago Stage: Its Records and Achievements.* Chicago: Robert L. Sherman, 1947.

Linda Bandy-White

[THE NEW] MEMPHIS THEATRE STOCK COMPANY. This Memphis stock company came into being in 1859, when the Gaiety Theatre, operated for two seasons by William H. Crisp, came under the management of William C. Thompson. Crisp had been denied renewal of his lease when he aroused the ire of local patrons and the owners by opening a saloon in the newly built (1857) proscenium playhouse, the first permanent theatre building in the city.

When the search for a new lessee proved fruitless, the stockholders of the Memphis Dramatic Society, led by attorney James Wickersham, undertook to operate the theatre themselves. They employed a local resident, William C. Thompson, as stage and general manager and retained Crisp's business manager, E.C. LeMoyne, in the same capacity and as secretary.

Thompson renovated and renamed the playhouse the New Memphis Theatre and embarked on an ambitious program of star engagements with a resident acting company in support. After visiting New York to employ stock-company performers and to engage star attractions, Thompson opened the first season on September 16, 1859, with a performance of Richard Sheridan's *School for Scandal* starring James Murdoch and the talents of the New Memphis Theatre Stock Company, with J.M. Dawson as resident stage director.

Resident stock companies were the mainstay of nineteenth-century American theatre, particularly in cultural outposts such as Memphis, far from the populous cities of the Northeast. It was a mean by which growing commercial centers such as those along the Ohio and Mississippi rivers could enjoy resident professional theatre, graced frequently with the glitter of New York stars. Theatrical activity in St. Louis, Memphis, New Orleans, and accessible inland towns grew and flourished with marked similarity. It was characterized by gradual transformation from stock and star operations to "combination" bookings of star groups in particular plays to the earliest of road show circuits, vestiges of which still survive in limited engagements on an irregular schedule.

From its inception, in 1859, The New Memphis Stock Company had only sporadic competition. As the city's only real theatre building, constructed with the support of the Memphis Dramatic Society, The New Memphis Theatre had strong connections with the town's establishment and early exhibited the strength of those ties. Locally owned and locally managed, The New Memphis Theatre began a decade as the city's cultural mirror, sharing and reflecting the ups and downs of the population with remarkable fidelity.

This relationship was one that William C. Thompson shrewdly used to insure financial success during his first season as general manager. He had been active in New Orleans and Mobile, Alabama, theatrical circles and had for a time managed the older Memphis Theatre. His local ties and experience led to a general operations plan in vogue among many theatres at the time. A resident company of twenty-four performers held forth at The New Memphis Theatre under contract for a full season. Thompson then signed stars to specific engagements during the season. The star, who usually traveled alone or perhaps with a costar, would act the leading characters in his or her repertoire, and The New Memphis Stock Company filled the remaining roles.

Under this system, and due in part to its family entertainment and cultural reputation, Thompson's 1859–60 season was financially profitable and socially successful. Following James Murdoch's two weeks of appearances in standard offerings such as *Wild Oats; or, The Strolling Gentleman*; *The Stranger*; *Hamlet;* and *Macbeth*, a pattern of presentations asserted itself in which Memphians developed a number of favorite stars whose appearances could be counted on to offset sluggish attendance from time to time. Among those favorites, Maggie Mitchell performed her multirole specialties in *Satan in Paris; or, The Mysterious Stranger* (as six characters) and in *The Four Sisters* (as four more), and Jean Davenport exhibited her skills in *Adrienne, the Actress* and *Camille*.

The year 1860 witnessed a continuation of star runs of two weeks, interspersed with social events and special benefits such as the one given to provide a Home for the Homeless, or for the organ fund of St. Mary's Church. The varied fare of star attractions featured appearances by Mr. and Mrs. W. J. Florence in Irish comedies like *Paudeen O'Rafferty; or, Born to Good Luck* and *Shandy Maguire; or, The Bould Boy of the Mountain*. Shakespeare was also presented often, with a late January 1860 engagement of Barry Sullivan, whose heavy schedule included *Hamlet, Macbeth, Richard III,* and *King Lear*. Edwin Booth repeated the same roles during his visit two weeks later. The remainder of the first season was given over, with notable success, to comedy and music. Perhaps surfeited with heavy drama, The New Memphis audience welcomed the change to lighter fare. In a series of appearances performers such as Miss Caroline Richings and her father, the actor Peter Richings, set a record engagement of twenty-nine days. Maggie Mitchell's reappearance closed out the star portion of the first season, although the Campbell Minstrels played a one-night stand in late April 1860.

The pattern of the next three years (1859–62) saw an accelerating degree of change in activities of The New Memphis Theatre Stock Company, involving mostly changes in personnel and repertory, reflective of the effects of the Civil War.

The three-year (1862–65) occupation by federal forces was a hiatus for The New Memphis Stock Company, although the theatre itself was the scene of continued public performance, with little change in quantity or kind. There were new faces, however, with Captain George Rayfield, an enrolled federal militiaman, leasing the confiscated theatre and performers who, if not New York professionals, were ambitious and apparently competent. The new management did not engage star performers, but the plays presented were almost identical to those offered during the prewar years. Thompson had presented 154 plays for 312 performances during the 1861–62 season. Rayfield, in 1862–63, offered 145 plays, but with 358 performances in an extended season. The plays performed were predominantly those written in the first half of the ninteenth century and a strong representation of Shakespeare's works. One noticeable change in production saw a steady move toward a greater number (74 performances in 1863–64) of novelties and spectacles. These plays, which aimed at elaborate scenery and startling effects, usually placed in an exotic locale, evidently pleased the audience of occupied Memphis, for newspaper reports invariably spoke of the heavy applause that greeted these performances.

Soon after hostilities ended in April 1865, control of the theatre was returned to James Wickersham and "the most competent impressario in Memphis, William C. Thompson" (*Memphis Public Ledger*, October 25, 1865). Thompson sought to attract his prewar patrons with two strategies: an unbroken line of star attractions and reassurances that once again the New Memphis Theatre Stock Company would perform in the city's "favorite resort" (ibid.).

To the newly remodeled playhouse, sporting "orchestra chairs" with an exclusionary price of $1.50 each came stage luminaries such as Matilda Heron in her famous *Camille* and in her own play, *Belle of the Season;* Charlotte Thompson in *The Lady of Lyons* and as Parthenia in *Ingomar, the Barbarian;* and J.H. Hackett as Nimrod Wildfire in *Experiments with Mesmerism.* Indicative of their popularity with New Memphis patrons was the number of performances that featured star actresses. Only four male stars appeared there in 1865–66, but fourteen star engagements featured actresses in 159 of the 286 performances during the regular season (*Memphis Daily Commercial*, May 22, 1866).

Although The New Memphis Theatre continued operations, the 1866–67 season marked the start of a decline in its fortunes, a three-year process that culminated with the dissolution of The New Memphis Theatre Stock Company at the end of the 1868–69 season. James Wickersham, the theatre's owner, died in 1866, and his heirs, absentee landlords, lacked the local connection to assist Thompson in rebuilding patronage. Then an ambitious attempt at competition was mounted by Frank A. Tannehill, a former actor in The New Memphis Company, presenting a shortened season in Greenlaw's Opera House during the 1866–67 season. This forced Thompson to present more spectacular productions, including eye catchers such as a real horse and carriage onstage and a cast of sixty in *Arrah-na-Pogue,* presented October 22, 1866 (*Memphis Daily Argus,* October 24, 1966).

Added expense and declining profits caused Thompson to schedule special attractions in an attempt to salvage the season. The Ghioni and Susini Grand Opera Company performed in late April 1867 (with an astronomical top ticket price of $2.50), followed by a visit from the entire stock company of the Mobile, Alabama, Theatre in support of the famed old actor Edwin Forrest. Although Forrest was accepted as "all right," the visiting company was greeted with scorn, and one critic described them as "the worst we have seen among professionals for years" (*Memphis Daily Appeal,* May 13, 1867). This, with the continued special $2.50, $1.00, fifty cents, price scale, caused attendance to decline, just when Thompson had to meet the regular New Memphis Theatre Stock Company payroll, although they were not performing.

After a shaky start in the 1867–68 season, with a cancellation by Avonia Jones and irritable reviews for the stock company as substitute, The New Memphis Theatre became a victim of circumstance. The city was declared under yellow-fever epidemic in late September, just as the season began, and although attempting to remain open, The New Memphis Theatre was as much a casualty as the 2,500 who fell ill. Even an appearance by Edwin Booth failed to rouse the distracted patrons, and only a desperate production of *The Black Crook,* with a chorus of "fifty young ladies," special imported scenic effects, and a return to the $1 ticket salvaged a mediocre season.

William C. Thompson died August 10, 1868, and although his widow, Rose, and his friend and treasurer, Chris Steinkuhl, attempted to continue The New Memphis Theatre Stock Company in 1868–69, the enterprise sorely missed the talents of its founder. A reduced company of ten began the season in support of Charlotte Thompson, a great attraction in prior visits. Attendance was poor. Uneven successes, such as John Brougham's popular drama *Lottery of Life* would be followed by a similar spectacle like *The White Fawn,* popularly attended by the public but scorned as trash by the newspaper critic (*Memphis Daily Appeal,* December 17, 1868).

Desperately trying to capture the public's patronage, The New Memphis turned more and more to variety-spectacular fare, with an occasional cultural bow to the past such as the engagement of Frank Mayo in *Hamlet* on February 15, 1869. The steady decline continued. The Greenlaw Opera House competition resumed, this time under the management of Gilbert Spaulding and David Bidwell, who also had theatre interests in St. Louis and New Orleans. They presented road show extravaganzas such as *Undine,* featuring their "mammoth troupe from the Academy of Music," their New Orleans Theatre (*Memphis Daily Appeal,* January 3, 1869). When The New Memphis attempted to meet the threat with increased spectacle, a critic attacked the management for presenting "trash" that even a good stock company could not redeem (*Memphis Daily Appeal,* March 15, 1869). The season finally closed with the Whitman Opera Company, whose manager skipped town owing some $3,000, leaving Mrs. Thompson with an uncollected account to handle.

It was the final blow to The New Memphis Theatre Stock Company, which went out of existence with the end of the 1868–69 season. Mrs. Thompson returned to her millinery shop, and The New Memphis Theatre came under the management of Gilbert Spaulding and David Bidwell, forming the center link in their circuit of New Orleans, Memphis, and St. Louis. Memphis no longer had a resident stock company, and an important aspect of the social and cultural history of the city ended.

PERSONNEL

Management: James Wickersham, principal stockholder (1859–66); William C. Thompson, stage and general manager (1859–62, 1865–68); Rose Thompson, general manager (1868–69); E.C. LeMoyne, business manager (1859–62); Chris D. Steinkuhl, treasurer (1865–69).

Scenic Technicians: J.B. Roberts (William J. Burton) (1859–60); J.W. Alexander (1859–60); B.W. Peterson (1859–60); George Graive (1860–61); William Reidenburg (1860–61); J.A. Jones (1860–61); Sam K. Gulick (1865–68); John C. Denham (1865–66); J. White (1865–66); John Jamison (1865–67); C.E. Rowe (1866–67); Harry J. Drew (1866–67); William DeMilt (1867–68).

Musical Directors: Professor Hessing (1859–60); *Carlo Patti* (1860–61); William Withers (1865–67); Professor Jacobi (1867–68); George Handwerker (1868–69).

Stage Directors: J.M. Dawson (1859–61); Joseph Huntley (1865–66); W.H. Drayton (1866–67); Mr. Shirley France (1867–68); Robert McWade (1868–69).

Actors and Actresses: Edwin Adams, George L. Aiken (1865–66), Mrs. D. H. Allen, A. P. Anderson (1867–68), J. Anderson (1860–61), Miss Joey Arnold (1867–68), J.B. Ashton (1866–67), Edgar J. Ballard (1859–60), *Lawrence W. Barrett* (1866–67), *Kate Bateman* (1860–61), Walter Benn (1859–60), Hattie Bernard (1859–61), *Edwin Booth* (1859–60, 1867–68), J. Boyce (1866–67), Mrs. Browne, J. H. Browne, J. D. Bryant (1865–66), R. B. Buck (1867–68), J. C. Carden, Miss Carmelyte (1865–66), J. W. Carpenter (1866–67), *Latonia Chandler* (1859–60), Mrs. T. S. Cline (1868–69), E. B. Coleman, *J. Collins, Jane Coombs* (1850–60), Mr. and Mrs. Couldock, *Lotta Crabtree*, (1868–69), Miss J. M. Davenport (1859–60), J. M. Dawson (1859–61), Kate Denin (1859–60), Thos. R. Duncan (1859–61), Fannie Edrian, William Ellerton (1867–68), Miss Ellsworth (1859–69), E. Evans (1866–67), *Fanny Fitz Farren* (1859–60), W. J. Ferguson (1867–68), *Mr. and Mrs. W. J. Florence* (1859–60), *Edwin Forrest* (1866–67), *Mr. Shirley France* (1867–68), Margaret Freal (1859–61, 1865–66), *Marie Fredericci* (1868–69), Helen Freeman (1859–60), Jennie Gourley (1865–66), J. D. Grace (1859–60), Mrs. H. P. Grattan (1860–61), George H. Griffiths (1859–61), Mrs. George H. Griffiths (1860–61), Mrs. Gulick (1865–68), J. F. Hagan (1859–61), Mrs. Hamilton (1868–69), J. C. Hamilton (1865–66), Theodore Hamilton, H. A. Hancker (1859–60), Mrs. Harwood (1867–68), C. Caroll Hicks (1865–66), Mr. Higgins (1868–69), Jennie Hight (1865–66), J. W. Hill (1866–67), Jean Hosmer, J. W. Howarth (1865–66), Miss Leo Hudson (1868–69), Annette Ince (1860–61), Miss Jamison (1865–67), J. Jamison (1865–66), Mrs. Jones (1867–68), *Laura Keene* (1865–66), C. Kingsland (1860–61), Louisa Laidlaw (1865–66), Annie Lanagan (1865–67, 1868–69), M. Lanagan, Mrs. A. Llewellyn (1865–67); D. Macauley (1860–61), Miss Malmbury (1868–69), E. W. Marston, Marguerite Marston (1866–67), *Frank Mayo* (1868–69), Isabel McCulloch (1867–68), *Robert McWade* (1865–66, 1868–69), J. Meagher (1866–67), *Maggie Mitchell* (1859–60, 1868–69), Mary Mitchell (1865–66), W. W. Mitchell, Mrs. H. Moore (1867–68), Mrs. Morrison (1866–67), Charles Morrison (1865–67), Miss A. Mowbray, S. K. Murdoch (1859–60), Miss Norton (1865–66), Mr. O'Keefe

(1868–69), J. Parker, Jennie Parker (1860–61), J. W. Parsons (1866–67), C. Peters, Millie Peters (1860–61), Miss Fannie Pierson (1867–68), Adele Plunkett, Viola Plunkett (1860–61), *Mrs. Coleman Pope* (1859–60, 1865–66), John Power, William Powers (1859–61), *Fannie Price* (1868–69), *Joseph Proctor* (1865–66, 1868–69). *Caroline Richings,* Peter Richings (1859–60), J. B. Roberts (1860–61), *Frank Roche* (1867–68), J. Rogers (1866–67), M. J. A. Ross (1860–61), *S. Ryan* (1859–60), J. M. Sloan (1867–68), M. Snyder (1866–67), Abbie Stanley, *Jennie Stanley* (1859–60), Mrs. Henry Stone (1859–61), Henry A. Stone, *Barry Sullivan* (1859–60), J. J. Sullivan (1865–66), *Frank A. Tannehill, Mrs. Frank A. Tannehill* (1859–61), Miss Nellie Taylor (1868–69), *Charlotte Thompson* (1866–69), Irene Walker, *Mr. and Mrs. Wallack* (1860–61), *Helen Western* (1865–66), James Whalley (1859–60), Mr. Wheelock (1866–67), W. J. Wiggins (1865–66), Mr. and Mrs. Barney Williams (1860–61), Miss Woods (1865–66).

REPERTORY

1859–60: *Hamlet; The Stranger; Honey Moon; Fazio; Margaret Elmore; The Maid with the Milking Pail; Satan in Paris; The Four Sisters; The Rivals; The School for Scandal; Ingomar, the Barbarian; The Hidden Hand; Adrienne, the Actress; Camille; Paudeen O'Rafferty; or, Born to Good Luck; Shandy Maguire; or, The Bould Boy of the Mountain; Macbeth; Richard III; King Lear; A New Way to Pay Old Debts; The Apostate; Washington.*

1860–61: *Woman in White; A Race for a Widow; Forty and Fifty.*

1865–66: *Camille; Adrienne, the Actress; Gemea: The Jewish Mother; Belle of the Season; The Lady of Lyons; The Little Barefoot; Ingomar, the Barbarian; Fanchon, the Cricket.*

1866–67: *The Duke's Motto; The Sea of Ice; Arrah-na-Pogue.*

1867–68: *The Hunchback; Under the Gaslight; The Black Crook.*

1868–69: *Lottery of Life; The White Fawn; Martha* (opera)*; Mazeppa; Hamlet; Ireland as It Was; Loan of a Lover; The Colleen Bawn; Rip Van Winkle; Humpty Dumpty.*

BIBLIOGRAPHY

Unpublished Sources: Sedon Faulkner, "The New Memphis Theatre of Memphis, Tennessee, from 1859 to 1880" (Ph.D. diss., The University of Iowa, 1967).

Seldon Faulkner

MITCHELL'S OLYMPIC THEATRE. Mitchell's Olympic Theatre, New York City, was hastily opened by William Mitchell (1798–1856) late in 1839, when he and several other members of J. W. Wallack's company found themselves jobless as a result of the conflagration that destroyed Wallack's New National Theatre on September 28, 1839. Mitchell leased the Olympic, located at 444 Broadway, halfway between Howard and Grand streets, for $100 a month and opened his first season as sole proprietor and manager on December 9, 1839. The theatre, which held only 1,100 patrons and had been built in 1837, in conscious imitation of Madame Vestris' London Olympic, was small by the standards of the day. During the two years from its construction to Mitchell's assumption of its management, the Olympic failed miserably under six managers to the point that "its character was sunk to the lowest pitch of theatrical degradation; ...none but visitors of the most irregular habits and meanest condition would condescend to congregate there" (*The Albion*, May 21, 1842, 248).

Mitchell's plan was to offer his audiences three or four short comic pieces each evening and occasionally import traveling stars. This choice of repertory was the result of his prior experience: he had earned his reputation as an excellent low comedian in the British minor theatres. Born in Billquay, Durham, England, the son of a merchant ship's captain, Mitchell was apprenticed to a West Indies merchant at fifteen. In 1820 he obtained his first professional acting engagement—playing for shares with a minor troupe in Kent. In 1822 he joined the company of Vincent DeCamp in Sheffield. This troupe contained several young actors—Thomas S. Hamblin, George Holland, and Thomas Flynn—who were later to become well known in this country. Mitchell established an enviable reputation as a low and eccentric comedian in the provinces and moved to London in 1831. Although he did obtain a limited engagement at Covent Garden, all of his other London experience was at the minor theatres. In 1836 he migrated to the United States, where he was initially employed by Thomas Flynn and Henry E. Willard as principal low comedian at their National Theatre in New York. Throughout 1837 and 1838 he played limited engagements as a star at several theatres. The fall of 1838 found him back at the National, then under the management of James Wallack, as principal low comedian and stage manager. He remained there until the theatre burned, ending his job in the autumn of 1839.

Having opened the Olympic on December 9, 1839, Mitchell found that during his first week of business his stock company playing topical burlesque and short farces outdrew George Mossop, the second-line Irish star he had engaged. Moreover, he rapidly discovered that he could do better business by dropping his admission prices to fifty cents for the dress circle, twenty-five cents for the gallery, and twelve and a half cents for the pit. This made the Olympic the first of New York's "shilling" theatres and established a trend that other managers were to follow during the depressed decade of the 1840s.

From his first season Mitchell relied on the strengths of his stock company in light musical and topical burlesques to draw the heterogeneous audience that made the Olympic the most successful theatre in New York during most of the 1840s. During the heyday of the touring star he operated the most successful theatre in the city without stars and without observing the time-honored strictures of lines of business, which had been observed since the days of Elizabeth in England and from the earliest days of theatrical development in this country. For these reasons George Odell credited

Mitchell with developing "the first distinctive stock company of modern times in New York" (9: 8).

The Olympic operated at a profit for nine of Mitchell's eleven seasons as manager during what was the most economically depressed decade in the history of the American theatre. Extant records indicate that it cost the manager about $100 an evening to run the theatre and that he grossed between $150 and $200 an evening. Thus the only estimate of the theatre's profits at $10,000 annually seems reasonable.

Mitchell also marks a radical departure in managerial function in the pre-Civil War American theatre. Beginning with the opening of the Olympic's 1844–45 season, all playbills carried at their head the phrase "Produced under the Direction of Mr. Mitchell." The manager supervised scenery and costumes with care unusual in the 1840s and had an uncanny ability to detect and nurture talent in young performers who had little experience before working in the Olympic's stock company. Lawrence Hutton maintained, "It was quite a common sentiment in the days of Mitchell that Mitchell *made* the brilliant people who first became prominent at his theatre" (Hutton, 29).

Richard Bengough, Mitchell's scenic artist, joined the company at the outset and had previously been J. W. Wallack's scene painter. The small Olympic had no wing space; thus Bengough used drops and perhaps even free plantation scenery in achieving his much heralded scenic effects. The treasury was initially in the hands of William Corbyn and later B. F. Tyron. Musical arrangements were handled by George Loder, who supervised an orchestra consisting of four to six members.

Throughout the history of Mitchell's management the forte of the Olympic was topical burlesque. He lampooned every imaginable subject of interest or fancy to his fellow New Yorkers. Among his favorite theatrical subjects were William Charles Macready, Charles Kean, T. S. Hamblin, and Fanny Elssler; P. T. Barnum, Charles Dickens, James Gordon Bennett; the events surrounding the opening of the Astor Place Opera House; and the rival claims of the "hard" and "soft" money men during the specie panic of 1837 were all subject to the Aristophanic manager's stinging satire.

Because famous performers as well as important people from the realm of politics and literature were ridiculed on the boards of the Olympic, certain members of the company had to excel at burlesque mimicry. An extension of this burlesque mimicry resulted in the most famous play to be presented under Mitchell's management: Ben Baker's *Glance at New York* in 1848 with a litte-known stock actor named Frank S. Chanfrau as the "Bowery B'hoy" hero Mose. The play opened on February 15, 1848, and catapulted Chanfrau to instant stardom while running for seventy-four out of a possible seventy-six evenings, the longest run of any play in New York before Barnum's production of *The Drunkard* in 1850.

At the end of the 1847–48 season, Mitchell's fortunes declined. Chanfrau had leased the Chatham and opened it under his own management in the spring of 1848, taking a number of Mitchell's key personnel and many of his former manager's patrons with him. By the time Mitchell reopened his theatre in the autumn of 1848, he was hard pressed by another new management, that of William E. Burton at the Chambers Street Theatre. Burton lured away additional members of Mitchell's stock company and was to capitalize on the same type of entertainment the Olympic had been providing for a decade. As a result, Mitchell broke his long-standing policy of relying exclusively on the efforts of his stock company to fill the theatre's coffers. He hired the yankee actors George H. Hill and Dan Marble in rapid succession, but as Odell noted, "Mitchell's, dependent on outsiders, was hardly Mitchell's" (Odell, 5:474).

Although he struggled valiantly until March 1850, Mitchell's chronic ill health, the desertion of key members of his company, and stiff competition from both Chanfrau and Burton caused him to lose money during the final two years of his management. He quit the field on March 9, 1850, and died in poverty in New York City six years later.

Mitchell's Olympic probably would have declined in popularity even without stiff competition from Burton and Chanfrau, for the short farces, burlesques, and extravaganzas that had been the mainstay of the Olympic's repertory were waning from popularity during the late 1840s. Burton, who initially aped Mitchell's repertory, sensed this and began producing Shakespeare and other dramas during his third season at Chambers Street.

Mitchell's position in the history of the American theatre is singularly important. His was the first of the shilling theatres to attract a heterogeneous audience by specializing in light comic entertainments. He amply demonstrated that more money could be made without stars than with them if one had an excellent stock company and attended to the visual details of production. By abolishing lines of business, emerging as the artistic conscience of the company, and contributing toward the development of the long run, he established managerial policies that were to characterize the subsequent managements of Burton, the Wallacks, and the early days of Augustin Daly.

PERSONNEL

Management: William Mitchell, manager (1839–50).
Treasurers: William Corbyn (1839–46); B. F. Tryon (1846–50).
Scenic Artist: Richard Bengough (1839–50).
Musical Director: George Loder (1839–46).
Prompter: Ben Baker (1839–50).
Actors and Actresses: James Anderson (1839–40), George Arnold (1847–50), Charlotte Bailey (1839–40), Mrs. Baldock (1841–46), Mrs. Barnett (1841– ?), Mrs. J. B. Booth, Jr. (1843–47), James S. Browne (1839–40), *F. S. Chanfrau* (1847–48), Mr. Clarke (1841– ?), *Constantia Clarke* (1842–47), Louisa Cooper (1842–43), Peter

Cunningham (1840–41; 1847–48), James C. Dunn (1842–43), Mr. Everard (1839–40), *Mary Gannon* (1848–50), George Graham (1841–47), *George Holland* (1843–49), *Henry Horncastle* (1839–42), Mr. Horton (1841– ?), Mr. Johnson (1839–40), Mrs. Jones (1839–40), Thomas McKean (1842–43), Miss Montgomery (1841–43), *Mrs. Mossop* (1841–46), *John Nickinson* (1841–46; 1849–50), Sidney Pearson (1839–40), Mrs. Plumer (1839–40), Miss Randall (1841– ?), Evelyn Randolph (1839–40), *William H. Reynolds* (1848–50), Mr. Roberts (1841– ?), William Rosenthal (1842–43), Mr. Russell (1839–50), *Lydia Singleton* (1839–40), Mrs. Streebor (1841–44), *Mary Taylor* (1840, 1842–45, 1847–49), *Sarah Timm* (1840–44, 1846–47), Julia Turnbull (1841– ?), *Charles Wolcot* (1842–47, 1849–50), Mrs. Watts (1841– ?).

REPERTORY

During his eleven years as manager of the Olympic, Mitchell produced three to four pieces nightly most of the time, for a total of 515 theatrical pieces. A complete list of the repertory is impossible here but may be obtained in David L. Rinear's dissertation "William Mitchell's Management of the Olympic Theatre, 1839–1850" (pp. 268–471). Of his offerings, 230 were the American premieres of British farces and extravaganzas. These works, coupled with the premieres of topical burlesques and extravaganzas penned by several writers associated with the company during its history, indicate that Mitchell produced significantly more premieres on the boards of his theatre than any other manager in the country during the 1840s. He did not, however, produce the regular drama.

His first season may be taken as representative. Brief by virtue of the fact that the Olympic did not open until December 9, 1839, Mitchell presented sixty-three pieces that were given a total of 565 performances. Of these sixty-three pieces, eight were played twenty times or more, and of the eight that received upwards of twenty performances, only two, *The Savage and the Maiden* and *The Unfortunate Miss Baily*, were farces. The others were all burlesques or extravaganzas.

BIBLIOGRAPHY

T. Allston Brown, *History of the New York Stage*, 3 vols. (New York: Dodd, Mead and Co., 1903); Joseph Ireland, *Records of the New York Stage*, 2 vols. (New York: T. H. Morrell, 1866–67); and George C. D. Odell, *Annals of the New York Stage*, vols. 4–5 (New York: Columbia University Press, 1928, 1931) are standard reference works. Newspapers consulted include *The Albion: A Journal of News, Politics and Literature*, New York, n.s. 1–9 (1842–50); *The Daily Herald*, New York, 1839–50; *The Knickerbocker; or, New York Monthly Magazine*, New York, 9–20 (1839–50), *The New York Mirror: A Weekly Gazette of the Fine Arts*, New York, 17–20 (1839–42); and *The Spirit of the Times: A Chronical of the Turf, Agriculture, Field Sports, Literature, and the Stage*, New York, 9–20 (1839–50). Two unpublished dissertations are germane: Leland Croughan, "New York Burlesque, 1840–1870: A Study in Theatrical Self-Criticism" (Ph.D. diss., New York University, 1968); and David L. Rinear, "William Mitchell's Management of the Olympic Theatre, 1839–1850" (Ph.D. diss., Indiana University, 1971). See also David L. Rinear, "Burlesque Comes to New York: William Mitchell's First Season at the Olympic," *Nineteenth Century Theatre Research* 2 (Spring 1974): 23–34; and idem, "Mr. Mitchell, Mr. Macready, and the 'Uproar House in Disaster Place,' "

Theatre Southwest 6 (February 1980): 12–18; and Lawrence Hutton, *Plays and Players* (New York: Hurd and Houghton, 1875). The Harvard Theatre Collection Cambridge, Massachusetts, holds eleven volumes of bound playbills and the Olympic Contract Books, 1842–44. The New York Public Library at Lincoln Center has a clipping folder, as does the Museum of the City of New York.

David L. Rinear

MRS. CONWAY'S PARK THEATRE. See PARK THEATRE COMPANY (1863–98).

MURRAY AND KEAN COMPANY. A company of actors managed by Thomas Kean and Walter Murray appeared in Philadelphia in August 1749. Their first and only recorded performance there, Joseph Addison's *Cato*, took place in Plumstead's Warehouse on Water Street. What other performances occurred in Philadelphia we do not know, but on January 8, 1750, the Common Council of the city condemned the performance of plays on the grounds that they "would be Attended with very Mischievous Effects" and ordered the magistrates to bind the actors "to their good Behaviour."

Faced with such hostility, the company next moved to New York for an engagement from March 5, 1750, until July 19, 1751, followed with a second season from September 13, 1750, to July 19, 1751. The company performed in a building in Nassau Street, owned by the recently deceased Rip Van Dam. Probably to fend off religious opposition to their performances, the Murray-Kean company presented *The Orphan* on April 27, 1750, "For the Benefit of The Charity School in this City." As the weather grew warmer, however, receipts fell off, and advertisements announced *Love for Love* as "The Last Night of Playing for the Season" on July 19, 1750.

When cool weather returned, the company reappeared with *The Recruiting Officer* on September 13. A week later *Cato* played to the largest audience ever to attend a theatrical performance in New York to that time. The *Weekly Post-Boy* of September 24, 1750 noted: "It may serve to prove that the taste of this place is not so much vitiated or lost to a sense of liberty but that they can prefer a representation of virtue to one of loose character" (cited in Odell, 1:37). A notable addition to the company this season was Robert Upton, "lately from London," a dancer who performed for them a Harlequin dance, a Pierrot, and the popular "Drunken Peasant." Upton had come to North America to make advance arrangements for the Hallam troupe, which would arrive in 1752, but instead threw in his lot with Murray and Kean.

On April 22 Thomas Kean held his benefit, substituting *The Busy Body* for the originally scheduled *Richard III*, and apparently left the company. The troupe continued to produce until July 8, 1751. The opportunistic

Robert Upton convinced some of the players to remain in New York and continue performing under his management.

The Murray-Kean company reappeared in Williamsburg, Virginia, October 1751. There, on October 24, the *Virginia Gazette* carried the following advertisement:

The Company of COMEDIANS have been at a greater Expense than they at first expected in erecting a THEATRE in the city of *Williamsburg*, and having an immediate Occasion for the Money expended in that Particular, in Order to procure proper Scenes and Dresses, humbly hope that those Gentlemen who are Lovers of theatrical Performances, will be kind enough to assist them, by Way of Subscription, for the Payment of the House and Lots, each Subscriber to have a Property therein, in Proportion to the Sum subscribed. As the Money is immediately wanted, we hope the Gentlemen will be kind enough to pay it as they subscribe, into the Hands of Messrs. *Mitchelson* and *Hynderson*, who have obliged us so far as to receive the same, and to whom Deeds will be delivered, on the Subscription being compleated, for the Purpose above-mentioned, Which shall be gratefully acknowledged by

> Their most obliged humble Servants,
>
> Charles Somerset Woodham,
> Walter Murray,
> Thomas Kean.

Apparently, Murray had done some advance work; in the *Virginia Gazette* of August 29, 1751, Alexander Finnie announced his support of the company and the proposed construction of a new theatre. The theatre arose on the east side of Eastern (Waller) Street; the company first performed in it on September 26, presenting *Richard III*.

After a brief season, the company moved to Norfolk, opening November 17, 1751, in "Captain Newton's Great Room" with *The Recruiting Officer*. Probably they played the rest of the month there, with a brief side trip to Suffolk. They returned in December to Williamsburg but left no records, save their intention to play Petersburg the next month. Their next recorded performance is in the spring of 1752, a benefit for Mrs. Becceley, *A Constant Couple; or, A Trip to the Jubilee*. Murray and Kean both appeared in support of Mrs. Becceley.

Two weeks later (April 30) the company announced it would perform at the courthouse from May 10 to 24 in Hobb's-Hole (Tappahannock) in the courthouse. From there they traveled to Fredericksburg, where they were seen by a young George Washington, who mentioned "the play House" in his ledger.

On June 18 Murray and Kean opened in Annapolis at the "New Theatre" on the Duke of Gloucester Street with *The Beggar's Opera* and *The Lying Valet*. They remained for two months and then opened on August 20 with the same bill in Upper Marlborough, after which they returned to Annapolis and disappointingly small audiences. They next opened in Chester, Maryland, on October 26 but announced their return to Annapolis for December 11. Although they made public their intention to perform in Port Tobacco and Piscataway later, the Murray-Kean company at this point disappeared as mysteriously as it had appeared.

Details of the company and its personnel are few and tantalizing. Arthur Hornblow posited that Murray and Kean, and perhaps others of the company, had emigrated from England and acted regularly in Jamaica and Barbados, possibly in the band of players brought from London in 1749 by John Moody. Kean vowed to return to his profession of writing upon leaving the stage, but no details of his life have surfaced. Comparable obscurity clouds Murray's background and life.

Evidently, the company operated on the traditional sharing repertory system of the time, exemplified by the later Hallams. They gave frequent benefits, the bills for which supply the names of company members; few other details have survived. Still, the Murray and Kean Company represents the first professional, or perhaps semiprofessional, company recorded in what would become the United States of America.

Theatrical criticism had not yet appeared, but various responses to the company have survived. One John Smith entered for August 22, 1749, in his diary: "Joseph Morris and I happened to be in at the Peacock Bigger's and drank tea there and his daughter being one of the company who were going to hear the tragedy of 'Cato' acted, it occasioned some conversation in which I expressed my sorrow that anything of the kind was encouraged" (Cited in Hornblow, 53). America's first man of the theatre, William Dunlap, recalled: "It is on record that the magistracy of the city has been disturbed by some young men perpetrating the murder of sundry plays in the skirts of the town; but the culprits had been arrested and bound over to their good behavior after confessing their crime and promising to spare the poor poets of the future" (Dunlop, 17).

Since we lack a complete schedule of specific plays performed by this company, speculation about the strengths and weaknesses of their repertory proves futile. Of those scripts recorded as having several performances, however, some observations might be made. *Cato*, a verse tragedy, Whig in politics and Tory in effect, had held the English stage from its 1713 debut. John Gay's *Beggar's Opera*, first performed in 1728, satirized the political scene as well as Italian opera. Ambrose Philips' *The Distrest Mother*, based on Jean Racine's *Andromaque*, written in 1712, ranked second only to *Cato* as a pseudoclassical work reflecting the tastes of the London audience. In the absence of competition, perhaps any script would draw an audience in colonial America at this time, but one notes that the Hallam company similarly imported several recent London successes in 1752.

Nevertheless, drama, quasiprofessional and pseudoclassical, expatriate to be sure, had established its presence and precedents on the North American continent.

PERSONNEL

Bills for benefits supply the names of the chief performers of the Murray and Kean Company. In New York the two managers took benefits, as did most of the company, among them Charles Somerset Woodham, who accompanied the group to Williamsburg and after retiring from the stage became a printer in Jamaica. A Mr. Jago asked for particular kindness from the New York audiences, as he had just been released from prison. Other actors receiving benefits included Mr. Scott, Mr. Leigh, Mr. Marks, Mr. Smith, Mr. Moore, Mr. Tremain, and one manager's son, Master Dickey Murray. Actresses included Nancy George (one of the principals), Mrs. Taylor, Mrs. Davis (who hoped with her benefit to buy up her time as an indentured servant), Mrs. Leigh, Mrs. Osborne, and Miss Osborne, a "chief lady" in tragedy. During the spring engagement of 1752 in Williamsburg, Mrs. Becceley appeared as the female singer and soubrette. When the company last appeared in Annapolis, Mr. Wynell and Mr. Herbert had joined them as leading players, having deserted the Hallam troupe, in which they played relatively small roles.

REPERTORY

The first New York season included six scripts: *Richard III*; *The Spanish Friar*; *The Orphan*; *Beaux Stratagem*; *The History of George Barnwell*; and *Love for Love*. No afterpiece titles have survived.

During the second New York season the company added the following scripts: *The Recruiting Officer*; *Sir Harry Wildair*; *The Distrest Mother*; *A Bold Stroke for a Wife*; *Cato*; *Amphitryon*; *The Beggar's Opera*; *The Fair Penitent*; and *The Busybody*. Afterpieces for this season included *The Beau in the Suds*; *The Mock Doctor*; *The Devil to Pay; or, The Wives Metamorphosed*; *The Walking Statue*; *The Old Man Taught Wisdom*; *Damon and Phillida*; *Hob in the Well*; *Miss in Her Teens*; and *The Virgin Unmask'd*.

BIBLIOGRAPHY

Coad, Oral Sumner, and Mims, Edwin, Jr. *The American Stage*. The Pageant of America Series. Vol. 14. New Haven, Conn.: Yale University Press, 1929.

Dormon, Joseph H., Jr. *Theatre in the Ante-bellum South, 1815–1861*. Chapel Hill: University of North Carolina Press, 1967.

Dunlap, William. *History of the American Theatre and Anecdotes of the Principal Actors*. New York: J. and J. Harper, 1832.

Hornblow, Arthur. *The History of the Theatre in America from its Beginnings to the Present Time*. Philadelphia: J. B. Lippincott and Co., 1919.

Odell, George C. D. *Annals of the New York Stage*. Vol. 1. New York: Columbia University Press, 1927.

Rankin, Hugh. *The Theatre in Colonial America*. Chapel Hill: University of North Carolina Press, 1960, 1965.

Seilhamer, George O. *A History of the American Theatre*. Philadelphia: Globe Printing House, 1888–91. Reprint. New York: Benjamin Blom, 1968.

Wright, Richardson. *Revels in Jamaica: 1682–1838*. New York: Dodd, Mead and Co., 1937. Reprint. New York and London: Benjamin Blom, 1969.

Stephen M. Archer

N

[BURTON'S NEW] NATIONAL THEATRE COMPANY. The New National
Theatre Company opened Monday, August 31, 1840, in Philadelphia under
the management of William E. Burton (1804–60), in a facility situated on
the foundation of Cooke's Circus, Chesnut (later Chestnut) Street, east of
Ninth Street. The London-born Burton had acted in the English provinces
from 1825 until he immigrated to the United States in 1834. In that year
he made his first professional appearance at the Arch Street Theatre,
Philadelphia. Burton, a popular comedian, prolific playwright, and
innovative manager, made his home in Philadelphia until 1848, managing
first the New National Theatre and then [Burton's] Arch Street Theatre
Company (1844–50)* before amassing a small fortune, which enabled him,
in 1848, to lease the Chamber's Street Theatre in New York City. There,
and at the Metropolitan Theatre, he established a company bearing his
name that flourished until 1858. Burton gained his reputation at
Philadelphia's Arch Street Theatre and enhanced it in New York by breaking
away from the established managerial practice of attracting the public with
regular engagements of star performers. He did so by reestablishing the
old stock company system of relying mainly upon a small but hard working
corps of talented performers in a wide variety of plays. Burton's run of
managerial success from 1844 to 1858 was preceded by crushing failure in
his first management experiment in 1840.

Burton opened the New National, proclaiming it the "first in the Union."
Philadelphia newspaper reports supported Burton's claim. The New National
seemed to be the finest theatre that had yet come to Philadelphia, and the
company Burton assembled was strong in the leads but mediocre thereafter.
Charlotte and Susan Cushman of New York's Park Theatre Company
(1826–48)* were budding young stars. Thomas Placide and Peter Richings
gave Burton strength based on long experience in the low-comedian and

character-man lines of business. James Thorne was a good comedian with a fine baritone singing voice as well. E. J. Shaw, a handsome Irishman, played genteel character roles, and Andrew Jackson Neafie drew attention for being so conspicuously dashing in appearance. The company opened with Richard Sheridan's *Rivals*, in which Burton played Bob Acres, the rustic trying so unsuccessfully to transform himself into a city dandy. Thomas Morton's farce *A Roland for an Oliver* (1819) was the afterpiece. Farce afterpieces were the staple of the New National Theatre Company. They were produced every evening. Sometimes a bill was made up of two or three farces, as on September 2, 1840, when Thomas H. Bayly's *Tom Noddy's Secret* (1838) premiered in Philadelphia, followed by Charles Selby's *Married Rake* (1835) and Henry Mayhew's *Wandering Minstrel* (1834). *The Lady of Lyons*, by Edward Bulwer, Lord Lytton, the most popular English play of the decade, was revived five times. An adaptation of Charles Dickens' *Nicholas Nickleby* was brought out eight evenings. Although initially vowing to throw off the shackles of the starring system, Burton depended heavily on stars as time wore on. James Henry Hackett (1800–1871), a fourteen-year veteran of the American stage; George Graham (d.1847); and John Baldwin Buckstone (1802–79), an English actor new to America, were expensive failures, as was the two-week stand of the sixty-eight year old singer-actor John Braham (1774–1856). Josephine Clifton (d.1847) was competent but well past her prime. *The Naiad Queen*, an anonymous nautical spectacle revived December 19, 1840, ran a profitable sixteen performances. Special scenic effects engineered by Joseph Foster and new scenery painted by John Russell Smith were partly responsible for the success of *The Naiad Queen*, as was a bare-legged chorus of fifty "Female Warriors," led by Charlotte Cushman and Eliza Petrie. *The Naiad Queen* was a season saver, but Vincenzo Bellini's opera *Norma*, opening January 11, 1841, failed profoundly. Moreover, the production, hurried to opening in time to undermine the business of the [Old] Chestnut Street Theatre Stock Company (1826–55),* which was producing the same piece, gained Burton the unwelcome reputation of an envious, dogged, vicious, and unfair competitor, which led the public to repudiate both him and his company.

In April 1841 he took some members of the Philadelphia company to New York, where he leased the National Theatre for a summer season. When the New York National burned May 29, 1841, Burton and his company suffered a great financial loss. Burton was undercapitalized. He had built his own theatre in Philadelphia on leased grounds, which stretched his resources to the breaking point. Then he lost money in the 1841 failure of a bank in Philadelphia, and he was devastated by the theatre fire in New York. He reassembled the company (which included eighteen-year-old John E. Owens, destined to become one of America's best-known interpreters of Yankee characters) and opened at the New National on

August 21, 1841, at cut prices. Again Burton relied heavily on stars. Edwin Forrest appeared twenty-six nights in this five-month season. *The Ocean Child*, a melodrama of anonymous origin, and Dion Boucicault's *London Assurance* (1841) highlighted this abbreviated season. The theatre closed January 29, 1842, and the company was permanently disbanded. Burton dropped out of management to recoup his losses by playing starring engagements. By June 1844 he was ready to put together another company at Philadelphia's Arch Street Theatre.

PERSONNEL

Manager and Proprietor: William E. Burton.
Stage Manager: Peter Richings (1840–41).
Orchestra Leader: Professor Woolf.
Chorus Master: E. Duggan.
Stage Mechanic: Joseph Foster.
Scene Painter: John Russell Smith.
Actors and Actresses: Thomas à Becket; Mrs. Beckett; Liz Boulard, singer; John Valentine Bowers; Mr. Brooks; Mrs. Brooks; *William E. Burton*; Mrs. Cantor; Miss Collingbourne; *Edmund S. Conner* (1841–42); *Charlotte Cushman* (1840–41); *Susan Cushman* (1840–41); Miss Delsmere; Mr. Ferrers, prompter; *Alexina Fisher* (1841–42); Miss Flanagan; Mrs. Flanagan; George Graham; Helen Kent Herbert; John Herbert, Jr.; Mr. and Mrs. Charles Hill; Emma Ince; Fanny Ince; George Jamison; Miss Jones; Mrs. George Jones; Mr. and Mrs. William Jones; Miss Mary Anne Lee; Miss Melton; Andrew Jackson Neafie; Miss Nicholson; Mr. Oakley, dancer and ballet master; John E. Owens; Eliza Petrie; Thomas Placide; Mrs. Plumer; Charles S. Porter; Mrs. Charles S. Porter; Peter Quayle; Master Reed, dancer; *Peter Richings* (1840–41); Mr. Roberts; John R. Scott; J. Smith; C. Stafford; William Thompson; James Thorne; Joseph or Jackson Van Stavoren; James W. Wallack, Jr.; David Whitney; Miss Wilks; Miss Wilson.

REPERTORY

Plays are listed in the order performed each season, with the number of presentations each season, if more than one, indicated by a figure in parentheses.
1840–41: *The Rivals* (3); *A Roland for an Oliver* (5); *The Patrician and the Parvenu*; *Swiss Cottage* (7); *Tom Noddy's Secret* (5); *The Married Rake* (5); *Wandering Minstrel* (3); *The Lady of Lyons* (5); *Oliver Twist* (3); *The Dumb Belle* (3); *Much Ado about Nothing*; *The Lottery Ticket*; *The Wife* (3); *More Blunders Than One* (9); *Nicholas Nickleby* (7); *The Poor Soldier*; *King Henry IV* (2); *Monsieur Mallet* (2); *King Lear* (5); *The Kentuckian* (3); *Venice Preserved*; *Othello* (2); *The Critic*; *The Hunchback* (2); *Susanne* (6); *Merry Wives of Windsor* (3); *Jonathan in England*; *Julius Caesar*; *The Tee-Total Society*; *A Militia Training*; *Poor Jack* (3); *Englishmen in India*; *Victorine* (3); *A Kiss in the Dark*; *My Young Wife and My Old Umbrella*; *Married Life*; *The Heir-at-Law*; *Out of Luck*; *Christening Isabelle*; *Old Guard* (2); *A Dream at Sea* (2); *Virginius*; *Cameleon* (2); *Washington* (5); *Water Party* (3); *Paul Pry*; *Richard III*; *Poor Soldier* (2); *The Artist's Wife* (2); *John of Procida* (4); *Romantic Widow* (2); *My Sister Kate* (5); *Budget of Blunders* (2); *Le preux chevalier* (2); *Father and Daughter* (2); *Monsieur Tonson*; *The Lover*

Husband; Humbug (2); *Blue Devils; Jane Shore* (2); *The Place Hunter* (4); *The Stranger; State Secrets* (5); *Pizarro; Catherine and Petruchio; Swiss Swains* (2); *Master Humphrey's Clock* (2); *The Maid of Mariendorpt; Solomon Smink* (2); *My Husband's Ghost; Ups and Downs* (2); *Rob Roy* (5); *Pleasant Neighbors* (4); *Irish Ambassador* (2); *Irish Tutor; The Nervous Man* (3); *Irish Lion* (3); *O'Flannigan and the Fairies* (3); *The Wags of Windsor; Happy Man* (3); *White Horse of the Peppers* (3); *His Last Legs; The First Lion; Peter Bell* (2); *My Friend the Governor* (4); *The Irish Attorney; Omnibus; Guy Mannering* (2); *Devil's Bridge* (2); *Love in a Village; Waterman; Masaniéllo* (4); *Blue Devils; Siege of Belgrade; The Slave* (2); *Cabinet; The Dutch Burgomaster* (2); *The Merchant of Venice* (2); *Fire Raiser; Brutus; Sleigh Driver* (4); *The Naiad Queen* (16); *The Dancing Scotchman; The Deserter* (2); *Town and Country; Der Nacht Wachter; Mother Goose* (4); *The King's Word* (2); *Foundling of the Forest; The Magic Bee; Maurice, the Woodcutter; Norma* (10); *Monster's Fate* (2); *Ataxerxes; Loan of a Lover* (3); *The Yankee Valet* (4); *John Jones; Money* (6); *The Mummy; No Song, No Supper; Rent Day; Adopted Child; The Exile; Fairmount Ghost; Killing No Murder* (2); *Rochester* (2); *1841 and 1891; or, 50 Years Hence* (9); *The Yankee Valet* (5); *Fireman's Life; The School for Scandal; Maid or Wife; Young Napoleon and His Father* (5); *Little Red Riding Hood; Harlequin's Nuptials; Charles II; Floating Beacon, Uncle John; Secret Service; Village Doctor* (3); *A Nabob for an Hour; Agreeable Surprise; Speed the Plough; My Fellow Clerk; The Rival Soldier; The Theater in an Uproar; The Bandit Merchant* (2); *Sweethearts and Wives* (2); *The Mummy; The Happy Man; His Last Legs* (2); *Teddy, the Tiler; Born to Good Luck; Tekeli; Fazio; Love Chase; Joan of Arc; Wife; The Rake's Progress* (2); *Hamlet; But, However* (2); *Horse Shoe Robinson* (4); *Rip Van Winkle; Second Part of Henry IV; Forty Winks* (3); *Turning the Tables* (2); *The Genoese; Gil Blas* (2); *Man and Wife; Night and Morning* (5); *The New President* (3); *Second Thoughts; The Spitfire* (2); *Turnpike Gate* (2); *The Wrecker's Daughter; Delusion; Alpine Maid; Quadroon; Thérèse; Dead Shot; Tipoo Saib* (4); *Caswallon; Light Ship; The Enchanted Chinese* (2); *Invasion of Russia* (2); *Life of Napoleon Bonaparte.*

1841–42: *Is He Jealous?; Damon and Pythias; Faint Heart ne'er Won Fair Lady; The Lady of Lyons; Love's Victory; Othello* (3); *Married Rake; Metamora* (2); *Turnpike Gate* (2); *Virginius; Wandering Minstrel* (2); *Gladiator* (3); *Animal Magnetism* (6); *The Wife* (2); *Louise; Jonathan in England; Maniac Lover* (2); *King Henry IV; First Murder; or, Death of Abel* (2); *Rip Van Winkle; Militia Training; Perfection; The Home Squadron* (6); *My Fellow Clerk* (3); *Tactic; Raphael's Dream* (2); *A Speck of War* (2); *Three Chips of the Old Block; Rent Day* (2); *Black Eyed Susan* (2); *The Heir-at-Law* (2); *Harlequin's Olio; Valsha: The Saxon Serf* (6); *Winning a Husband; The Home Squadron; Nick of the Woods* (3); *The Ocean Child* (11); *Barnaby Rudge; Douglas* (2); *One Glass More* (2); *Paul Pry* (2); *Ship Scene; Cabinet Secrets* (3); *Teddy Roe* (2); *Billy Taylor* (2); *Cleopatra* (7); *Alexander the Great; Osceola; Money* (2); *Richelieu* (3); *Turning the Tables; Weathercock* (3); *Pizarro; Jack Cade* (5); *Catherine and Petruchio* (2); *Raising the Wind* (2); *King Lear; Hamlet; Out of Place* (3); *Snapping Turtles* (4); *Foreign Arts and Native Graces* (3); *My Old Woman* (3); *M'Leod; Johan; Charles XII of Sweden; Yankees in China; My Little Adopted* (3); *The Banished Star; Irish Widow; Widow Wiggins* (2); *The Maid of Croissey* (2); *Scotch Widow; London Assurance* (9); *Mr. and Mrs. Pringle* (4); *Tom Noddy's Secret; Forty Winks; Popping the Question* (3); *Jonathan*

Bradford (3); *Lottery Ticket* (2); *The Lady and the Devil; Mischief Making; Middy Ashore; Mummy* (2); *High Life below Stairs*; *La tour de Nesle* (2); *My Aunt; Othello Travestie; The Captive; Giovanni in London; The Dutch Governor; State Secrets* (2); *Joan of Arc; Romeo and Juliet; The School for Scandal; Mabel's Curse* (2); *Robert Macaire* (2); *My Young Wife and My Old Umbrella; Wanted; A Wife; Wreck Ashore; The Ladies Man* (2); *Evadne; Ruffian Boy; Two Late for Dinner; Jacques Strop; The Dream at Sea; Wallace: The Hero of Scotland; Jane Shore; Sweethearts and Wives* (2); *John Jones; Richard III; King Lear; Hamlet; Coriolanus* (2); *Macbeth; Venice Preserved; Wags of Windsor; Tom Cringle's Log; Brutus; Maurice, the Woodcutter; Town and Country; Whirligig Hall; William Penn* (3); *Magic Head* (3); *Peter Bell; The Rivals; The Spitfire* (4); *Old Waxend* (2); *Halt of the Caravan* (4); *The Robbers; Luke, the Labourer; The Clown and the Cat; The Stranger; Speed the Plough; The Sleep Walker; Wild Boy of Bohemia; Charles O'Malley* (3); *Blind Boy; The Exile; Prize; Wild Oats; Family Jars; Honey Moon; Fish Out of Water; Rise of the Rothschilds* (2); *Cure for the Heart-Ache; The Green-Eyed Monster; The Miller's Maid.*

BIBLIOGRAPHY

Johnson, Rue C. "The Theatrical Career of William E. Burton." Ph.D. diss., Indiana University, 1967.

Keese, William L. *William E. Burton: Actor, Author, and Manager.* New York: G. P. Putnam's Sons, 1885.

Wilson, Arthur H. *A History of the Philadelphia Theatre, 1835 to 1855.* Philadelphia: University of Pennsylvania Press, 1935.

Weldon B. Durham

NATIONAL THEATRE STOCK COMPANY. (1832–52) The company commenced performances July 3, 1832, under William Pelby, in the Warren Theatre. Pelby returned to Boston from a tour of the South in the spring of 1832, adamant to redress the wrong he believed done him by the proprietor of the Tremont Theatre Company. Pelby leased the newly built American Amphitheatre, which had opened February 27, 1832, for equestrian performances. He enlarged the stage, altered the auditorium to meet the demands of legitimate drama, assembled a company, and opened with J. B. Buckstone's *Victorine; or, The Orphan of Paris* (1831) and Isaac Bickerstaffe's farce *Spoil'd Child* (1791). His receipts were a mere $60.75. Pelby's company operated at the Warren Theatre until 1836, breaking the monopoly of the Tremont Theatre and establishing a reputation that appealed to Boston's lower classes. In 1836 Pelby more completely reconstructed the theatre, reopening it August 15, 1836, as the National Theatre. His management continued until his death, May 28, 1850, by which time the National's reputation had altered to attract middle- and upper-class Bostonians. The change was largely due to the influence of his stage manager from 1848, Thomas Barry. Barry became acting manager for Pelby's widow, Rosalie, who surrendered the lease to Barry on February

28, 1851. On March 3, 1851, the theatre reopened under the proprietorship and management of Barry and John B. Wright. The Barry-Wright season ended June 1, 1851. In 1851–52 Wright; Henry W. Fenno, long-time National Theatre treasurer; and George Bird were managers. The theatre burned April 22, 1852, but it was quickly rebuilt by Joseph Leonard and reopened November 1, 1852. Leonard managed for one year and then was succeeded in 1852 by W. M. Fleming. Under Fleming the company operated until December 8, 1855, when Fleming abandoned the lease, leaving a commonwealth of actors struggling to keep the company in business. It failed December 26, and the company permanently disbanded. The theatre had a checkered existence thereafter, housing circuses, equestrian troupes, and single-play companies until it burned, March 24, 1863.

According to William Clapp's *Record of the Boston Stage*, Pelby's companies were invariably good. The stars appearing with the National were not the brightest of the day, for the theatre's reputation rested on the excellence of its resident company's productions, an excellence imparted to the group by a series of talented stage managers.

A notable feature of plays written for the English and American stage in the first half of the nineteenth century is the gradual increase in the playwrights' explicit stage directions—few directions were given, typically, in plays written early in the century, more given each decade as time passed. In the period of the National Theatre Company, the stage manager was in charge of rehearsals. Scripts produced in midnineteenth-century theatres were first given to him. When tradition or managerial edict did not determine casting, the stage manager did. The playwright's hints for stage business, movement, groupings of the *dramatis personae* and offstage effects, as well as details of characterization, passed through the stage manager to the performer. The stage managers' main task was to see that the specifications of the author were carried out by performers and by technicians. As playwrights' directions became more numerous and explicit in newer plays, the stage managers' interpretation and teaching tasks took on greater importance in the production process. Furthermore, emerging "realism" in the stage action of newer plays (for that is the apparent aim of the steadily increasing playwrights' directions) altered the approach to producing older plays. Thus the stage managers' opportunities for creative control were rapidly increasing. The stage managers' duties began to resemble the duties of the director as they were carried out in the early twentieth century. F. S. Hill was stage manager from 1832 to 1838. Clapp asserted that Hill was "not only competent to the discharge of his duties, but his literary qualifications were very respectable. He [Hill] wrote *Six Degrees of Crime* and other pieces which drew money into Mr. Pelby's treasury" (*Record of the Boston Stage*, p. 404). W. H. Smith (1806–72) succeeded him. Smith (or Sedley-Smith), author of *The Drunkard*, a popular temperance play, was an often-employed stage manager until his death in San Francisco, where he was stage manager for the California Theatre Stock Company.*

J. S. Jones, formerly lessee and manager of the Tremont Theatre, rendered valuable service as stage manager and house playwright. A Mr. Cartlitch succeeded Jones. Then followed James E. Murdoch, William Rufus Blake, Robert Hamilton, and Thomas Barry. Barry, formerly stage manager of the Park Theatre in New York and Boston's Tremont Theatre from 1833 to 1839, was reputedly the nation's best stage manager at midcentury. John B. Wright (1814–93), who succeeded Barry, began his theatrical career as a callboy at the Tremont. He was the National's prompter, the prototype of today's assistant director, under W. H. Smith.

The National was, for more than ten years, the favorite theatre of residents of Boston's North End, who looked upon it as "their theatre." Clapp concluded his brief treatment of the National with this assessment: "The standard of the theatre has been that of the second class, but it has occasionally aspired above 'blue fire and mysterious music,' and at times has been *the* theatre of Boston" (*Record of the Boston Stage*, p. 406).

PERSONNEL and REPERTORY

To date, the history of The National Theatre, Boston, has been little more than rudely sketched. Lists of personnel and plays produced have yet to be made.

BIBLIOGRAPHY

Clapp, William W., Jr. *A Record of the Boston Stage*. Boston: James Monroe and Co., 1853. Reprint. New York, Greenwood Press, 1969.
———. "The Drama in Boston." In *The Memorial History of Boston*. Vol. 4, pp. 357–82. Boston: James R. Osgood and Company, 1881.
Leverton, Garrett H. *The Production of Later Nineteenth Century American Drama*. New York: Teachers College, Columbia University, 1936.

Weldon B. Durham

NATIONAL THEATRE STOCK COMPANY. (1836–39) When Thomas Flynn and Henry E. Willard leased the defunct Italian Opera House at Leonard and Church streets, New York City and rechristened it the National Theatre, they inaugurated a bold enterprise. A raging fire in December 1835 had destroyed many fashionable blocks, rendering fiscal recovery difficult. Yet four theatres were in operation in the metropolitan area; the National made a fifth. Boldly commencing on the same night, August 29, 1836, as their main rival, the Park Theatre, Flynn and Willard presented Junius Brutus Booth in *The Merchant of Venice* as well as the afterpieces *The Man with the Carpet Bag* and *The Wandering Minstrel*.

Neither Tom Flynn, said by George Odell to be "too unstable to prop any concern" (4:136), nor Henry Willard was able to steer the company toward great renown, but among their accomplishments was the importing of British comedians William Mitchell and Charles Howard and scenic artist Richard Bengough. The combination of European talent, luxurious surroundings, and exquisite stage settings made their production of the ballet opera *The Maid of Cashmere* a great success that earned nearly $8,000 in its first six continuous nights. Charlotte Cushman's subsequent appearance also proved lucrative but powerless to avert disaster since the Panic of 1837 crushed businesses everywhere. The National Theatre, under Flynn and Willard, was the first to succumb, but it would not be the last. James H. Hackett picked up the managerial reins, but his two-month regime failed ignominiously. As Odell said, "Hackett had no policy, and the public had been lukewarm" (4:148).

In June 1837 James W. Wallack, the elder, departed for Europe in pursuit of personnel for the National Theatre, the direction of which he planned to assume. When he opened his doors on September 4, there were nine other theatres in New York, but despite this competition Wallack built an organization that was familiarly known as "the Covent Garden of New York." The National Theatre under Wallack's aegis gave the Park "its first real struggle for fashionable and artistic supremacy" (Odell, 4:136).

An Englishman by birth, Wallack (1791–1864) was born into a theatrical family. Progressing from supporting player to a leading actor, Wallack carved out tragic and melodramatic roles as his own special province. Early in his life he immigrated to the United States, where he became a citizen and a favorite actor. Joseph Ireland noted that "he was first in his line, but . . . his line was not first" (1:342). Wallack was always known for meticulous attention to detail, both as an actor and as a stage manager, the very quality that distinguished his productions at the National. According to the *Knickerbocker Magazine* of December 1837, Wallack's National Theatre was "second to none in the United States."

Flynn and Willard opted to fly in the face of the manager of the Park Theatre by charging identical rates for tickets: $1, fifty cents, and thirty-seven and one-half cents. Wallack evidently continued that policy but rented private boxes, of which the entire second tier of seats was composed, for $10. The fact that his theatre was elegant almost beyond description did not obviate the necessity of Wallack's exertions to make it fashionable. Its location in a disreputable neighborhood some distance from a major street was unfortunate. Hackett had tried to combat this stigma by installing gas streetlights to protect his patrons, but Wallack favored stressing the exclusivity of the house.

Audiences and critics alike were vociferous in their praise of the National. Even the technical staff received periodic ovations. The *Knickerbocker Magazine* of October 1838 bestowed the ultimate accolade upon Wallack and his troupe, calling it "the best stock company in the United States." Such verdicts spelled the end of the Park's domination of the metropolitan theatre.

Wallack opened with *The Rivals*, *The Day after the Wedding*, and *The*

Unfinished Gentleman, which indicated the complexion of future offerings. The repertory always thereafter included so-called "genteel comedy" and farcical afterpieces. From his first season Wallack featured operas, such as *La sonnambula*, and his company roster highlighted European performers. By 1838–39 a virtual craze for opera existed, and Wallack wisely catered to this demand. His most prodigious success was William Michael Rooke's opera *Amilie; or, The Love Test*; an all-star production of *The Marriage of Figaro* also flooded his coffers. In addition to operas, plays by native dramatists, such as N. P. Willis' *Tortesa, the Usurer*, graced the boards of the National.

The staff of the National Theatre was extensive: a stage manager, a prompter, a costumer, a scenic artist, a machinist, a properties master, an orchestra conductor, and a chorus leader. The acting troupe, though, was Wallack's pride. Henry Wallack played supporting roles, and the manager's nephew J. W. Wallack (the younger) served as leading man. Comic roles were sustained mainly by J. S. Browne, W. H. Williams, and Benedict DeBar; Mrs. Russell was the "old woman" of the company. Even the minor players often were praised.

Such an excellent company provided a superior setting for the talents of visiting performers, the reputations of many of whom are enshrined in the history of the theatre. There was, of course, Junius Brutus Booth, already lost to drink but still possessed of extraordinary powers. T. D. Rice presented his Jim Crow repertory, and Yankee Hill amused with his regional drollery. Mlle. Celeste danced and presented her popular *French Spy*. Josephine Clifton, E. S. Conner, J. R. Scott, Emma Wheatley, and the impressive British tragedian John Vandenhoff performed their specialties. Wallack could also claim credit for introducing the long-admired William E. Burton in his American debut. The outstanding event of the season of 1838–39 was the appearance of Charles Kean, who was slated to present a predictable series of tragedies and melodramas, but illness forced him to cancel after he was seen in *Hamlet*. This was not the aesthetic loss that it would be in ten years' time; in 1838 he was still a moderately talented son of a superior father. His important contributions to theatrical production lay in the future. That season Wallack also booked mighty Edwin Forrest.

On September 23, 1839, when it must have seemed to Wallack that the National was destined to make theatre history, fate intervened. The handsome theatre on Church and Leonard streets burned to the ground. The resourceful manager rallied his forces and arranged for performances in Niblo's Gardens, now closed for the season, but his company was unable to compete against the chill of oncoming winter. The National Theatre Company, consequently, was disbanded on November 18, 1839.

PERSONNEL

Management: Thomas Flynn, Henry E. Willard (August 1836–March 1837); James H. Hackett (March–May 1837); James W. Wallack, the elder (September 1837–November 1839).

Stage Directors: Henry Wallack (1837, 1839), William Mitchell (1838).
Prompter: Mr. Addis (1837).
Costumers: Mr. and Mrs. Bassanio, Mr. Flannery.
Scenic Technicians: Mr. Bengough, scenery; Mr. Hatch, machinery.
Properties Masters: Mr. DeJonge, Mr. Williams, Mr. Foster, Mr. Morrell.
Musicians: Mr. Ambroise, orchestra; Mr. St. Luke, chorus; W. Penson, chorus.
Actors and Actresses: William Abbott, *J. J. Adams* (1837), John B. Addis, *Andrew J. Allen* (1838), Mr. Ames, J. H. Amherst, Andrew Andrews, George H. Andrews, Mlle. Arreline, Mlle. Augusta, Jane Ayres, Charlotte Bailey, Mr. Baldock, Mrs. Baldock, J. S. Balls, Amelia G. Bannister, Charlotte Barnes, *John Barnes* (1837–38), *George Barrett* (1836–38), Mrs. George Barrett, Miss Bell, J. Bernard, Mrs. J. Bernard, Miss Bernett, Ben Blaike, T. H. Blakely, W. Blanchard, *James S. Browne* (1837–39), Mr. Bunner, Charles S. T. Burke, Mr. Carnes, Mrs. Cantor, Mrs. Carter, the Chekinis, Emilia Coad, Miss Coffin, Mr. Collins, *Mrs. Mauvaise Conduit* (1836), Barkham Cony, H. Cooke, W. Cooke, Miss W. Cooke, Mr. Cooke, Jr., Jean M. Davenport, *Benedict DeBar* (1837), Giuseppi de Begnis, Mlle. Desjardins, Mr. Duggan; Mrs. Henry Eberle, William Edwin, Mr. Everard, Mrs. Everard, Thomas Faulkner, Mrs. Fletcher, Mrs. Thomas Flynn, W. C. Forbes, Miss Galt, James Gann, Mary Gannon, William F. Gates, Mr. Gilbert, Miss Grove, Mrs. J. H. Hackett, Mr. Halton, T. S. Hamblin, Mrs. T. S. Hamblin, Miss Hanker, Mrs. Hardwick, Miss Harrison, Mrs. Harrison, Mr. Hautonville, Mr. Hayden, J. Hazard, Helen Herbert, Miss S. Hildreth, Henry Horncastle, Charles D. S. Howard, Mrs. D. Ingersoll, David Ingersoll, George Jamieson, Mrs. Jefferson, W. F. Johnson, Henry Erskine Johnston, *George Jones* (1836–37), Emanuel Judah, Mr. Keiffer, Miss S. Kemble, Miss Kerr, J. Hudson Kirby, Miss Kneass, Mr. Lambert, Mrs. Lambert, W. H. Latham, Mme. Lecomte, Miss Lindley, the Martins, Helen Matthews, Mary Matthews, Thomas Matthews, Mrs. McGuire, Miss Melville, Louisa Missouri, *William Mitchell* (1836–39), *Virginia Monier* (1837–39), Mr. Morley, Mr. Mudie; J.A.J. Neafie; N. H. Needham; Annette Nelson; Miss Newell; John Nickinson; Mme. Otto; John H. Oxley; Mrs. W. Penson; Mr. Percival; Lydia Phillips; Andrew L. Pickering; Thomas Placide; Mr. Plumer; Mrs. Plumer; *Tyrone Power* (1836); the Ravels; Miss Reynolds; Mrs. Rivers; Mr. Rogers; Mrs. Rogers; Robert Rue; Mrs. Russell; Arthur B. Salmon; Mr. Salter; Ann Sefton; *William Sefton* (136–39); Edward Seguin; Mrs. Edward Seguin; Mrs. Sharpe; Jane Shireff, Miss Singleton; De Witt Clinton Smith; C. W. Spencer; Mr. Stanley; Josephine Stephan; Mrs. G. G. Stevenson; George G. Stevenson; *Mrs. Stickney* (1838); Charles Western Taylor; Mary Cecelia Taylor; Mrs. C. R. Thorne; Charles R. Thorne; Master Titus; Mme. Trust; Miss Turpin; J. Van Amburg; Miss Vandenhoff; *Henry Wallack* (1837–39); *James W. Wallack, the elder* (1836–39); *James W. Wallack, the younger* (1836–39); Mr. Walton; Ann Waring; Miss Watson; Mrs. Watson; Mrs. Watts; Mr. Wells; Miss Williams; *W. H. Williams* (1837–39); John Wilson; Clara Woodhull; John Woodhull; E. Woolford; Mrs. E. Woolford.

REPERTORY

1836–37: *The Merchant of Venice; The Man with the Carpet Bag; The Wandering Minstrel; Richard III; The Loan of a Lover; Venice Preserved; The Wife; Lubin Log; The Waterman; Pizarro; The French Spy; My Husband's Ghost; The Wept of*

Wish-Ton-Wish; The Moorish Page; Spoil'd Child; The Way to Get Married; Much Ado about Nothing; The Somnambulist; The Wonder; The Rent Day; Rob Roy; The School for Scandal; The Gamester; The Wolf and the Lamb; The Stranger; Honey Moon; The Dead Shot; Macbeth; The Hunchback; Catherine and Petruchio; The Maid of Cashmere; Mr. and Mrs. Pringle; The Ransom; Forty and Fifty; La tentation; Making Your Wills; The Spirit Bride; The Pet of the Petticoats; The Death Plank; Henry IV; The Irish Tutor; Three Weeks after Marriage; Rip Van Winkle; The Kentuckian; The Castle of Andalusia; The Cherokee Chief; Jonathan in England; Monsieur Mallet; Trial by Battle; Horse Shoe Robinson; Sardanapalus; Hamlet; Romeo and Juliet; The Maid of Genoa; Ion; Prince Lee Boo; The Flying Dutchman; Harlequin and the Black Woodsman; Virginius; The Provost of Bruges; Damon and Pythias; The Solitary of the Heath; The Sledge Driver; Guy Mannering; The Four Mowbrays; Une passion; The Pirate Boy; Peter White; Ugolino; The Star-Spangled Banner; The Middy Ashore; Lalla Rookh; Walder, the Avenger; Dr. Foster in New York; Is He Jealous?; Cinderella; The Rendezvous; Raphael's Dream; St. George and the Dragon; Bonaparte Crossing the Alps; Puss in Boots; La sonnambula travestie; Paul Pry; The Poor Soldier; The Devil's Bridge; Win Her and Wear Her; Joe Miller; Maid or Wife; The Marriage of Figaro; Jane Shore; Clari; The Young Widow; The Golden Farmer; The Day after the Wedding; Brutus; Chances and Changes; Perfection.

1837–38: The Rivals; The Day after the Wedding; The Unfinished Gentleman; La sonnambula; The Happiest Day of My Life; The Busy Body; The Sleeping Draught; Coriolanus; Raising the Wind; Damon and Pythias; Rob Roy; Macbeth; Venice Preserved; Cato; Turn Out; The Merchant of Venice; The Carmelites; Othello; A Pleasant Neighbor; The Comedy of Errors; The Kentuckian; Julius Caesar; My Young Wife and My Old Umbrella; The Three Dutch Governors; Hamlet; Lyar; King Lear; Robin Roughhead; Cure for the Heart Ache; Honey Moon; The Wife; My Aunt; Robert Macaire; Henry IV; The Scholar; The Virginia Mummy; Black and White; Jim Crow in London; The School for Scandal; The Critic; Virginius; The Bridal; The Poor Gentleman; Richard III; The Old English Gentleman; Love à La Mode; A Tale of Mystery; The Two Thompsons; Family Jars; Octavia Bragaldi; Gulliver in Lilliput; A New Way to Pay Old Debts; The Hunter of the Alps; The Two Figaros; The Yankee Pedlar; The Maid of Cashmere; Esmeralda; Ginger Blue; Tom Thumb; Holy Rood House; Bone Squash Diavolo; The Bee Hive; Much Ado about Nothing; The Brigand; The Rent Day; Abaellino; The Slave; The Love Chase; Telemachus; A Day at an Inn; The Loan of a Lover; Wild Oats; Sudden Thoughts; Impulse; The Parole of Honor; As You Like It; The Assignation, Zazezizozu; The Rival Queens; Brutus; The Miller and His Men; Henry VIII; Riches; Ernest Maltravers; Midas; The Young Widow; Rule a Wife and Have a Wife; The Good-Looking Fellow; The Hunchback; Leila; The Bengal Tiger; Luke, the Labourer; Wanted: A Brigand; Monsieur Mallet; Perfection; Spoil'd Child; The Manager's Daughter; The Brigand Boy; The Dumb Boy of Manchester; The Wonder; Charles XII; Fazio; Our Mary Anne; Amateurs and Actors; Humphrey Clinker; The Boarder; The Man of the World; Cramond Brig; The Children in the Wood; The Rifle Brigade; The Belle's Stratagem; The Dumb Belle; The Way to Get Married; Tom and Jerry; Bluebeard; The Married Rake; She Would Be a Soldier.

1838–39: Damon and Pythias; Raising the Wind; The Lady of Lyons; Charles II; Othello; The Married Rake; Macbeth; Three Weeks after Marriage; Virginius; Me-

tamora; King Lear; Hamlet; The Gladiator; William Tell; Brutus; The Barber of Seville; Il Fanatico per la Musica; Shocking Events; Weak Points; Pizarro; The Brigand; St. Mary's Eve; The Child of the Wreck; The Indian Girl; Suzanne; The French Spy; Amilie; Robert Macaire; Luke, the Labourer; Naval Engagements; The Waterman; The Maid of Croissey; The Boarder; La Délivrance des Grecs; The Miller and His Men; Thérèse; The Wizard Skiff; The Star of the Forest; The Mother; The Maid of Cashmere; Valet de Sham; Fra Diavolo; La sonnambula; Cramond Brig; No Song, No Supper; Annette; Love's Frailties; Short Cuts and Long Cuts; Abaellino; Sylvester Daggerwood; Don Juan; The Battle of Austerlitz; The Irish Tutor; More Blunders Than One; Whirligig Hall; The Irish Ambassador; Old Heads on Young Shoulders; The Last Days of Pompeii, The Mountaineers; The Spirit of the Air; Nicholas Nickleby; Norman Leslie; Sardanapalus; Sweethearts and Wives; John Jones; The Breach of Promise; The Mummy; Married Life; The Spitfire; The Englishman in India; Begone, Dull Care; Conrad and Medora; Rob Roy; Cinderella; Lafitte; Love in a Village; Guy Mannering; The Marriage of Figaro; The Poor Soldier; Clari; Nick of the Woods; Tortesa, the Usurer; Adam Gray; John Dibbs; Peter the Great; My Great Aunt; State Secrets; Stag Hall; X.Y.Z.; The Mountain Sylph; John of Paris; Gilderoy; What Have I Done?; The Original; The Spaniard's Revenge; La Gazza Ladra; Der Freischütz; Octavia Brigaldi; Family Jars; The Comedy of Errors; Fazio; The Grecian Daughter; Personation; Sprigs of Laurel.

1839–40: *Virginius; Too Late for Dinner; Macbeth; The Schoolfellow; Richard III; Othello; The Lady of Lyons; Metamora; Hamlet; The Gladiator; An Affair of Honor; The Middy Ashore; King Lear; Damon and Pythias; Richelieu; Petty Sins and Pretty Sinners; The Rear Admiral; A New Way to Pay Old Debts; The Merchant of Venice; Tortesa, the Usurer; Robert Macaire; Latin, Love, and War; Jacques Strop; A Wife for a Day; The Hunchback; New Notions; The Stranger; The Wife; Lyar; The Hunter of the Alps; Amilie; La sonnambula; Gustavus III; La tarentule; Seth Slope; The Yankee Pedlar; The King's Gardener; Nicholas Flam; But, However.*

BIBLIOGRAPHY

Published Sources: T. Allston Brown, *A History of the New York Stage from 1732 to 1901* (New York: Dodd, 1903); Joseph N. Ireland, *Records of the New York Stage from 1750 to 1860*, 2 vols. (New York, T. H. Morrell, 1866–67); George C. D. Odell, *Annals of the New York Stage*, vol. 4 (New York: Columbia University Press, 1931); Francis C. Wemyss, *Chronology of the American Stage from 1752–1852* (New York: W. Taylor, 1852).

George B. Bryan

[CHANFRAU'S NEW] NATIONAL THEATRE COMPANY. (1848–50) Frank S. Chanfrau (1824–84) stepped into the breach when J. Fletcher failed at the [New] Chatham Theatre Stock Company,* New York City. Fletcher gave up on February 26, 1848; two days later Chanfrau began as actor-manager, but it was not until August 14 that the enterprise, then called Chanfrau's New National Theatre, opened. The first program presented J. R. Scott and Emily Mestayer in *Richelieu* and Charles Burke in *The Lady of the Lions*, a burlesque of Edward Bulwer-Lytton's drama.

Chanfrau's industry in 1848 cannot be faulted, for he acted at the Olympic

Theatre simultaneously with operating a theatre in Newark and managing the National. While at the Olympic, Chanfrau appeared in a sketch called *A Glance at New York,* in which he played Mose, the Fireboy; his future and fortune were assured as Mose's celebrity grew dizzyingly. It is not surprising, then, that on March 17, 1848, he inaugurated his term at the Chatham with another Mose play, *New York as It Is.* The reports that thousands of disappointed spectators were turned away may not be seriously exaggerated. When Chanfrau mounted a third Mosaic play on September 14, *The Mysteries and Miseries of New York* ran uninterruptedly until October 21 and was repeated frequently afterwards. Later in the season he introduced *Mose in California* and *Three Years After,* a sequel to *The Mysteries and Miseries of New York.* The mine of Mosaic gold was not yet exhausted, for on June 27 *Mose in a Muss* was brought out. Clearly, Mose was the centerpiece of Chanfrau's organization and was responsible for the most successful season the house would know until 1853 when *Uncle Tom's Cabin* would be presented. Indeed, 1848–49 was "the Mose season."

Mose's great popularity has effectively camouflaged the realization that F.S. Chanfrau was a highly versatile actor. His subsequent popularity as Kit Carson notwithstanding, Chanfrau is remembered as a single-role comedian. In his own theatre and elsewhere, Chanfrau assayed a wide range of roles. Joseph Ireland maintained that "his versatility . . . is almost unequaled in merit" (2:419). Educated in England, Chanfrau entered the profession through amateur theatricals, graduated into the supernumerary class, steadily progressed toward leading roles, and became a star with the advent of Mose.

William Mitchell (1798–1856), manager of the Olympic Theatre, was Chanfrau's chief competitor, largely because he had a clear, yet novel principle of management. The Olympic was a half-price house that specialized in farces, burlesques, and burlettas played in an intimate atmosphere by highly skilled comedians and musicians. Chanfrau's Mose first saw the light in such an ambiance. Chathamites, though, seemed to lack the sophistication necessary to the enjoyment of a steady diet of Olympian fare; they demanded home-cooked melodrama with an occasional savory of old-fashioned tragedy. The manager of the National, in return for their enthusiastic acceptance of Mose, was forced to cater to their taste, which had been formed by the ilk of William S. Deverna and Charles R. Thorne.

Chanfrau's tenure at the National, which ended in April 1850, was characterized by extended runs of several productions in addition to the Mosaic plays. Tragedian William Charles Macready was attracting vast audiences to the Astor Place Opera House. His airs and eccentricities were the subject of a burlesque, *Mr. Macgreedy at the National,* which ran for two weeks. A new adaptation of *Rosina Meadows* was seen continuously for two months early in 1849. *The Enchantress; or, The Wizard of the Moon* played to good houses for two weeks. The production of *The Female Forty Thieves* occupied Mrs. Charles Mestayer for four weeks in 1849–50, and Chanfrau himself played *Mose in China* for a month. The Olympian influence on these offerings is clear. Little remains to be said of the repertory, of which much was stale, much was novel but poor. Luckily the long runs sustained the venture until Chanfrau relinquished the management.

The dramatic corps at the National was acceptable but not outstanding. Leading roles were taken by Emily Mestayer, comic males by Charles Burke. Burke must have been pleased when his young relative Joseph Jefferson III joined the company. His engagement involved playing Knickerbocker to Burke's Rip in an early version of *Rip Van Winkle*. Little could the young man have imagined that his career would be identified chiefly by his later impersonation of Rip.

J. R. Scott, C. R. Thorne, Corson W. Clarke, Barney Williams, and T. B. Johnston augmented the offerings of T. D. Rice and George H. Hill. Daddy Rice and Yankee Hill had played so often at the Chatham that they must have felt entirely at home. The visiting stars, however, for the first time in the history of this theatre, were less profitable than the manager and the resident stock company.

PERSONNEL

Management: Frank S. Chanfrau.
Stage Director: Charles Burke.
Stage Manager: R. J. Jones.
Actors and Actresses: James Anderson, Mr. Barnett, Miss Bishop, Mrs. J.B. Booth, Jr., T. G. Booth, Mrs. D.P. Bowers, Charles Burke, Mrs. Burroughs, Mr. Callandine, Mrs. Canfield, Mr. Cartlitch, Mrs. G. Chapman, W.B. Chapman, Mary Ann Charles, J. S. Charles, J. W. Crocker, Sarah Crocker, P. C. Cunningham, Mr. Davis, Mr. Dawes, Gertrude Dawes, Miss Deering, J.C. Dunn, Mr. Forrester, Mr. Goodseault, Fanny Gordon, Miss Gray, Mr. Hamilton, J. Herbert, Mrs. J. Herbert, Mr. Hield, Miss E. Hildreth, Mrs. H. Isherwood, Joseph Jefferson III, Mr. Kneass, Mr. Linden, Miss Lockyer, Mrs. Maddison, Mr. Marsh, Mr. Mc-Farland, Mrs. McLean, Emily Mestayer, Julia Miles, Mrs. Millar, Mrs. Muzzy, Mr. Palmer, H.O. Pardey, Mr. Richardson, Mr. Rosenthall, Miss Scott, James Seymour, Miss Sinclair, Miss Smith, Mrs. Smith, Mr. Stark, Mrs. J. Stickney, Mrs. Sutherland, C.W. Taylor, E. Thompson, Mr. Tilton, John Winans, Mrs. Woodward.

REPERTORY

1848–49: *Richelieu; The Lady of the Lions; Charles II; The Adopted Child; Don Caesar de Bazan; Macbeth; Rob Roy; Virginius; The Spectre Bridegroom; Ole Bull; The Swiss Swains; The Vermont Wool Dealer; The Little Nun; His Last Legs; Zarah; Victorine; Helen Oakleigh; The King and I; The Widow's Victim; The Mysteries and Miseries of New York; A Glance at New York; New York as It Is; A Mistaken Story; The Idiot Witness; This House to Be Sold; The Pretty Girls of Stillberg; Mr. Macgreedy; Crossing the Line; Luke, the Labourer; Ivanhoe; Jack Sheppard; Richard III; The Virginia Mummy; The Golden Farmer; Military Execution; Esmeralda;*

The Miser of Southwark Ferry; Jumbo Jum; Othello; Otello; Damon and Pythias; Bone Squash Diavolo; The Invisible Prince; Murrell: The Land Pirate; Grandfather Whitehead; Deaf as a Post; The Omnibus; A Wife for a Day; New Notions; Cut and Come Again; Return Strong; The Yankee Pedlar; Seth Slope; The Green Mountain Boy; The Illustrious Stranger; The Twin Brothers; Undine; Maritana; The Avenger; The Swiss Cottage; The Wandering Boys; Ella Rosenberg; The King and the Deserter; Ernest Maltravers; Monseigneur; The Wife; The Irish Tutor; Founded on Facts; A Kiss in the Dark; Caroline Ferrar; The Patriot; The Children in the Wood; The Married Rake; My Wife's Out; The Omnibus; Wacousta; The Deserted Mill; Woman; Rosina Meadows; Joan of Arc; Poor Pillicoddy; Mose in California; The Pride of the Market; Madeleine; Slasher and Crasher; Tom and Jerry; The Loan of a Wife; The Village Phantom; Your Life's in Danger; Jackets of Blue; The Weaver of Lyons; Advice to Husbands and Hints to Wives; I'll Be Your Second; The Brigadier; The Last Kiss; Cousin Joe; Which Is the King; The Happy Man; The French Spy; Who Speaks First?; The Old Guard; Cockneys in California; A Dream of Life; The Lady of Lyons; Rights of Age; The Lost Diamonds; The Enchantress; His First Peccadillo; Wild Oats; The Rake's Progress; The Rival Captains; Jim Crow in London; The Plains of Chippewa; The Limerick Boy; Sprigs of Ireland; The Irish Lion; Ireland as It Is; The Irish Ambassador; Boots at the Inn; Kate Kearney; Paul Pry; Three Years After; The Jacobite; The Chimes; Jonathan Bradford; Norwegian Wreckers; The White Horse of Peppers; A Roland for an Oliver; Mose in a Muss; Buy It, Dear; Josey, the Spartan; The Lady and the Devil; The Trumpeter's Wedding; Jack Robinson and his Monkey; The Soldier's Daughter; That Rascal Jack; The Dumb Girl of Genoa; Mammon and Gammon; The Young Scamp; Lola Montez; The Lottery Ticket; Joe in London; A Separate Maintenance; The Morning of Life; The Poor Gentleman; John Dobbs; The Irish Dragoon; Rory O'More; Valet de Sham; The Honest Thieves; A Wonderful Woman; Whistle for Your Pay; A Most Unwarrantable Intrusion; The Midnight Watch; A Tipperary Legacy.

1849–50: Jonathan Bradford; In and Out of Place; The Poor Soldier; The Midnight Hour; Somebody Else; The Irish Lion; The Dumb Man of Manchester; Perfection; The Dumb Belle; His Last Legs; The Happy Man; Philip Quarl; The Flying Dutchman; The Murdered Boatman and His Dog; The Invincibles; Slasher and Crasher; Ole Bull; The Bottle Imp; Revolution; The Spectre Pilot; Hearts Are Trumps; The Female Forty Thieves; Josey, the Spartan; A Budget of Blunders; A Dead Shot; My Wife's Out; The Fair One with the Golden Locks; The Phantom Breakfast; Jemmy Twitcher in America; A Roland for an Oliver; Mother and Child Are Doing Well; The Attic Story; Agnes de Vere; Isabelle; The Omnibus; The Irish Tutor; The Irish Dragoon; The Rent Day; The Robber's Wife; Joan of Arc; Lucille; The Lady of Lyons; Teddy Roe; Paul Pry; Lamora: The Indian Wife; The Soldier's Daughter; The Duchess of Vaubalière; Honey Moon; Murrell: The Land Pirate; The Happiest Day of My Life; Linda: The Pearl of Chamounix; The Handsome Husband; The Female Guard; The Laughing Hyena; The Dumb Savoyard; Valentine and Orson; The Floating Beacon; Rip Van Winkle; The People's Lawyer; Born to Good Luck; Jumbo Jum; Teddy, the Tiler; The Foreign Prince; The Virginia Mummy; The Honest Thieves; The Naiad Queen; Lola Montez; Esmeralda, Undine; Buy It, Dear; Jenny Lind; The Mysteries and Miseries of New York; The Intrigue; Somebody Else; Black Eyed Susan; Three Years After; Wild Ducks; New York as It Is; Rob

*Roy; The Charcoal Burner; 'Twas I; Mose in California; Don Caesar de Bazan;
The Widow's Victim; The Model of a Wife; Richard Three Times; The Governor's
Wife; The Jewess; Eaton Stone; Mischief Making; The Loan of a Lover; An Alarm-
ing Sacrifice; Richelieu; Hamlet; The Swiss Cottage; Damon and Pythias; An Un-
protected Female; The Wife; Macbeth; Virginius; Brutus; Sketches in India; The
Surgeon of Paris; The Carpenter of Rouen; The Maniac Lover; The Bohemian Girl;
Wallace; Brian Boroihme; The Pride of the Market.*

BIBLIOGRAPHY

Published Sources: Joseph N. Ireland, *Records of the New York Stage from 1750
to 1860,* 2 vols. (New York: T. H. Morrell, 1866–67); George C. D. Odell, *Annals
of the New York Stage,* vol. 4 (New York: Columbia University Press, 1931).

George B. Bryan

[PURDY'S] NATIONAL THEATRE COMPANY. (1850–60) When Frank
S. Chanfrau tired of operating the National Theatre, Chatham Street, New
York City, in 1850 A. H. Purdy assumed and sustained its direction for
ten years. The transition to Purdy's management was so smooth that no
formal inauguration of the new regime occurred. Wyzeman Marshall was
a guest star in April 1850. His appearance in *The Tower of Nesle* and
Joseph Jefferson's in *My Precious Betsey* marked the beginning of Purdy's
term.

In 1850 there was much theatrical competition. The National had to vie
for the public's attention with the Broadway, Bowery, and Olympic Theatres
as well as with those of William E. Burton and P. T. Barnum. The Astor
Place Opera House, Niblo's, and Castle Garden claimed their share of
patronage as well. Purdy was able to survive largely because of the immense
popularity of *Uncle Tom's Cabin* staged at the National for the first time
in 1852. Between July 1854 and August 1858, the National's doors had
been open for 1,284 consecutive nights (exclusive of Sundays). When he
finally retired on March 21, 1859, Purdy could congratulate himself for
having earned "a secure niche in theatre history—humble, but secure"
(Odell, 5:548). His treasurer T. C. Steers took the house when Purdy left,
but his three-month tenure was not notable, nor was that of actress Bell
Carr, which lasted but a summer. The establishment subsequently became
the Union Theatre, the National Concert Hall, and the National Music
Hall before being razed in 1862.

Three events distinguished Purdy's first half-season (1850) at the National:
Chanfrau's month-long engagement as Mose, the Fireboy; the production
of *The New York Fireman,* which lasted a month; and the appearance of
William E. Burton. When the theatre reopened in the autumn, there was
nothing remarkable in the program, but when Junius Brutus Booth came
in September, he brought with him his seventeen-year-old son Edwin. On
September 23 Edwin acted Hemeya to his father's Pescara in *The Apostate.*
Who could have predicted the lofty heights to which this youth's gifts would

carry him? A mere month later there was another important debut, that of George L. Fox, the future Humpty Dumpty. Perhaps Fate sent Fox to Purdy, because it was the actor who encouraged the manager to hire his relatives, the Howards, to present *Uncle Tom's Cabin* at the National. That initial season also marked the debut of G. E. Locke, who quickly established himself as a portrayer of Yankee roles. In 1858 it was Locke who played the leading role in a play only slightly less important than *Uncle Tom's Cabin*, the melodramatic *Ten Nights in a Bar Room*.

Little is known of A. H. Purdy aside from his operation of the National. A benefit performance was given in 1846 at the Chatham Theatre (the National's previous incarnation) for "Ex-Captain Purdy," but whether he acted or served the theatre in some other capacity is unclear. It is as a man of business that Purdy is remembered. One of his innovations was the introduction of holiday matinees, the first of which fell on November 25, 1852; audiences gathered at ten, two, and seven o'clock. Here is an example of a matinee's actually occurring in the morning. Purdy used the matinee performance at its fullest potential once *Uncle Tom's Cabin* was produced.

C. W. Taylor, a sometime playwright, was an actor at the National Theatre. When Harriet Beecher Stowe's narrative about slave life appeared and attracted attention, Taylor began to make a dramatic adaptation. Purdy produced Taylor's adaptation of *Uncle Tom's Cabin* at the National on August 23, 1852. Its two-week run was eminently successful, and Purdy was satisfied. When G. L. Fox persuaded Purdy to ask the Howard family to appear in George L. Aiken's version, no one could have guessed what success lay ahead. As George Odell observed, Purdy's decision was "shaken from the dice-box of the gods" (5:237). On July 18, 1853, the Howards opened in *Uncle Tom's Cabin* and entered the realm of theatrical legend. Manager Purdy presented the play nightly and on Wednesday and Saturday matinees far into the season; it was eventually seen in more than 300 continuous performances. A month after the opening, Purdy decided that black people should have the opportunity to witness the spectacle as well. A segregated parquet was reserved for a small number of respectable colored persons who could raise the twenty-five-cent admission fee. T. D. Rice's darkey drollery accompanied Taylor's *Uncle Tom's Cabin*, but no farce at all competed with Aiken's.

In December 1853 Purdy decided to present little Cordelia Howard in another drama, *Katy, the Hot Corn Girl,* which was seen at matinees on Monday, Tuesday, Thursday, and Friday. The other two matinee days were reserved for the main attraction, which was still playing nightly. Sensing that interest in Uncle Tom's woes was diminishing, Purdy brought out an entirely new version, a third production, of Stowe's novel. This spectacle lasted until May 13, when the regular repertory was resumed. Uncle Tom reappeared frequently throughout subsequent seasons, but the furor definitely was over, not to be rekindled by a production of Stowe's

Dred: A Tale of the Dismal Swamp in September 1856. This piece had a respectable five-week run.

The Broadway Theatre ceased operations in 1858–59; Burton surrendered the management of his theatre. A. H. Purdy gave up the National. The financial Panic of 1857 was largely responsible for the epochal decisions, decisions that must have had an apocalyptic ring. Religion was in the air; the National Theatre was used for Sunday evening worship services. When a fire seriously damaged the building on July 9, 1859, its days as a theatre were limited.

Purdy's troupe was admirable in many respects. His leading players included J. H. Allen, Charles Burke, Anna Cruise, Charlotte Crampton, George L. Fox, G. C. Germon, Fanny Herring, Annie Hathaway, Joseph Jefferson III, Wyzeman Marshall, Emily Mestayer, Harry A. Perry, Mrs. J. J. Prior, and others of similar rank. The old stars of Chatham days, Junius Brutus Booth, Barney Williams, and T. D. Rice, visited and passed profitable days. J. R. Scott paid annual visits until his untimely death. The Wallacks came back: Henry; James W., the younger; and Lester. Naturally, the repertory reflected the stars' interests. Otherwise the standard group of plays was given with monotonous frequency.

PERSONNEL

Management: A. H. Purdy, April 1850–March 1859; T. C. Steers, March–June 1859; Bell Carr, June 1859.

Stage Director: George L. Aiken, March–June 1859.

Treasurer: T. C. Steers.

Scenery: Mr. Culbert, Mr. Whytal, W. T. Porter, J. R. Smith.

Machinery: J. O. Squires, H. Seymour, W. Crane.

Properties: J. Timony.

Music: W.T. Peterson.

Actors and Actresses: Mr. Addis, Frank E. Aiken, George L. Aiken, J. H. Allen, Mlle. Angela, Miss Armstrong, G. J. Arnold, Miss Axtel, Mrs. Bannister, Miss Barber, Mr. Barnett, J. L. Barrett, Julia Barton, Maria Barton, S. Barry, T. Barry, G. A. Beane, Lavinia Bishop, Sallie Bishop, Mr. Blake, E. Blanchard, G. C. Boniface, Mrs. J. B. Booth, Jr., S. W. Bradshaw, Mrs. S. W. Bradshaw, J. M. Brandon, John Bridgman, W. H. Brown, Charles Burke, Mr. Canito, J. Canoll, Felix Carlo, I. N. Carr, D. Carroll, C. Chapman, H. W. Chapman, W. B. Chapman, G. C. Charles, Mary Ann Charles, E. Chippendale, Agnes Clare, N. B. Clarke, Mr. Cline, Rosa Cline, Fanny Colburn, T. Cony, J. M. Cooke, Charlotte Crampton, W. H. Crane, Miss Crocker, J. Crouta, Anna Cruise, Asa Cushman, H. F. Daly, Rachel Denvil, Mr. De Silveria, John Diamond, Mr. Dingey, Sir William Don, Frank Drew, Mrs. Frank Drew, J. C. Dunn, Mrs. J. C. Dunn, G. Edeson, Louisa Eldridge, John A. Ellsler, L. H. Everitt, Miss Farmer, Miss M. Ferguson, A. Fitzgerald, W. M. Foster, C. K. Fox, Mrs. C. K. Fox, Miss E. Fox, George L. Fox, G. C. Germon, Mrs. Giubelle, Mr. Gowan, Mr. Granger, Mrs. H. P. Grattan, Josephine Griffiths, Mr. Grubb, J. F. Hagan, Charles Hale, T. Hampton, D. H. Harkins, Annie Hathaway, Mrs. Hautonville, W. Henderson,

Mr. Herbert, Fanny Herring, Miss Heywood, H. P. Hickey, Clarence Holt, Mrs. Clarence Holt, Professor Honey, Miss Horton, Cordelia Howard, Mrs. G. C. Howard, H. Howard, T. Howard, J. B. Howe, W. C. Hurry, Cornelia Jefferson, Joseph Jefferson, Mrs. Joseph Jefferson, Robert Johnston, T. B. Johnston, Mrs. George Jones, W. G. Jones, Mrs. W. G. Jones, Mrs. Kirby, Henrietta Lacy, Mr. La Favor, Edward Lamb, Miss Landers, Yankee Lefler, Miss Le Folle, Miss C. Leroy, Anna Levering, Mrs. H. Lewis, J. Lewis, Mrs. Lingard, G. Lingard, J. W. Lingard, Launce Lynwood, A. J. Lyons, B. Macaulay, Mr. Mack, C. MacMillan, Mrs. Madison, Miss Malvina, R. Marsh, Wyzeman Marshall, C. Mathews, Mr. McDonnell, Miss McWilliams, R. S. Meldrum, W. Melville, Emily Mestayer, W. Mitchell, M. S. Mortimer, B. Morton, Mrs. Muzzy, Mrs. Myers, T. Myron, Miss Nathan, Mrs. H. F. Nichols, John Nunan, D. Oakley, Betty O'Neill, H. H. Owen, Miss Packer, Miss E. Parker, Charles T. Parsloe, Jr., Miss C. Partington, Miss S. Partington, Miss Pauline, Mrs. R. Penniston, H. A. Perry, M.B. Pike, Mr. Planque, Viola Plunkett, L. Porter, Adelaide Price, E. C. Prior, Mrs. J. J. Prior, Mrs. Radinski, J. Read, W. M. Reeve, Miss Roberts, Mr. Rogers, Mr. Rose, C. P. Salisbury, Miss Salome, Mr. Schmidt, H. Seymour, Mrs. H. Seymour, James Seymour, Mr. Siple, G. Smith, C. Spurgeon, C. Stafford, Master Alfred Steward, H. F. Stone, Mr. Stout, Mrs. C. Strahn, C. W. Taylor, E. F. Taylor, J. B. Terry, Mlle. Thérèse, J. F. Thomas, E. Thompson, G. W. Thompson, Miss S. Thompson, C. Toulmin, Miss J. Tree, J. Turner, Mr. Walton, J. M. Ward, C. Warwick, Harry Watkins, T. Watkins, H. Weaver, T. Welsh, F. C. Wemyss, Lizzie Weston, Mr. Whytal, S. B. Wilkins, Mrs. S. B. Wilkins, S. Williams, Mr. Wilson, Mrs. Wilson, Mrs. Wray, Miss Wright, Mr. Yates, Miss Yeomans, A. W. Young, Mlle. Zilla.

REPERTORY

1850: *The Tower of Nesle; My Precious Betsey; Ireland as It Is; The Limerick Boy; In and Out of Place; The Irish Lion; Born to Good Luck; Sprigs of Ireland; Paddy's Trip to America; Our Gal; The Irish Farmer; The Female Forty Thieves; The Robber's Wife; The Omnibus; Spoil'd Child; Rip Van Winkle; Ole Bull; The Widow's Victim; Mose in California; Revolution; Jemmy Twitcher in America; Second Thoughts; Going to the Races; The Yellow Dwarf; The Forest Rose; Poor Cousin Walter; The Female Guard; The Invincibles; The Three Cuckoos; The French Spy; Jack Sheppard; Esmeralda; The Old Guard; Oh, Hush!; Jumbo Jum; The Drunkard; The Flying Dutchman; The Wept of Wish-Ton-Wish; Life in Alabama; The Lottery Ticket; Mose in China; Rochester Knockings; Othello; Peeping at 6 A.M.; Wild Oats; The Heir-at-Law; My Aunt; The Man about Town; The Day after the Wedding; Rosina Meadows; Open Sesame; Not to Be Done; The New York Fireman; The Rough Diamond; Married Life; The White Farm; Boots at the Swan; The Devil in Paris; The Great Original; Six Degrees of Crime; Cousin Joe; Jenny Lind in America; She's Come! Jenny's Come!; Fortune's Whim.*

1850–51: *The Lady of Lyons; The Card Drawer; Isabelle; The Spectre Bridegroom; The New York Clerk; The Midnight Banquet; The Last Glass; Sixteen String Jack; The Flying Dutchman; Richard III; Mesmerism; Othello; A New Way to Pay Old Debts; King Lear; The Iron Chest; The Forest Rose; Hamlet; Town and Country; An Irish Engagement; The Apostate; The Mountaineers; The Merchant of Venice; The Water Witch; The New York Fireman; Nick of the Woods; The Irish Rebel;*

Rob Roy; The Carpenter of Rouen; Richelieu; Mose in California; Don Caesar de Bazan; The Model of a Wife; The Mysteries and Miseries of New York; Thérèse; The Widow's Victim; A Glance at New York; Three Years After; Jonathan Bradford; Mose in China; The Pride of the Market; New York as It Is; The Idiot Witness; The King and I; Rory O'More; Paddy Miles' Boy; Paddy the Piper; Our Gal; Jenny Lind; In and Out of Place; The Dumb Man of Manchester; The Cherokee Chief; Philip Quarl; The Murdered Boatman and His Dog; The First Fratricide; Bertram; Pizarro; The Corsair's Bride; The Cockney in China; The People's Lawyer; Black Eyed Susan; Sweethearts and Wives; Ole Bull, Breach of Promise: Revolution; The Poor Gentleman; The Lady of the Lions; The Vermont Wool Dealer; The Magic Well; Children of Love; Nature's Nobleman; The Freebooter; The Frisky Cobbler; Farmer Graball; The Curate's Daughter; The Man in the White Coat; The Night Hag; The Golden Axe; The Drunkard; Old King Cole; The Wife; The Frolic of the Fairies; The Printer of New York; Rights of Women; Jack Robinson and His Monkey; The Dry Goods Clerk; The French Spy; The Rose of Sharon; Damon and Pythias; Virginius; Macbeth; Honey Moon; Pizarrobus; A Day in Paris; Jonathan in England; Freedom Suit; The Hermit of the Rocks; Dr. Faustus the Devil; Rosina Meadows; The Stage-Struck Yankee; Aladdin; The Seamstress of New York; Churubusco; Servants by Legacy; Ginger Blue; The Rebel Chief; The Rival Chieftains of Mexico; The Road to Riches; The Cadi's Daughter; Allow Me to Apologize; Sam Patch in France; Harry Burnham; Hurley and Burley; The Fugitive Slave; It Beats Barnum; All That Glitters Is Not Gold; Travelling by Telegraph; The Prairie Wolf; Werner; Romeo and Juliet; The Gamester; Catherine and Petruchio; Thalaba, the Destroyer; A Morning Call; Victimising; The Lady of the Lake; Gilderoy; Love's Sacrifice; Ion; Brutus; The Adopted Child; Susan Hopley; The Heart of the World; Ugolino; Pettyloons; Actress of All Work; Macbeth Travestie; Morlaix, the Student; The Review; Cheap Excursion; Ladies' New Costume; The Robbers; The Female Daughters of the Croton Waters; St. Clara's Eve; Three Wives of Bagdad; It's Only a Clod; The Mysterious Chief; AZL; The Fast Coach; The People's Candidate; The Seven Escapes of Adelaide of Dresden; The Maiden's Vow; The Old Commodore; Love and Charity; Grimshaw, Bagshaw, and Bradshaw; The Daughter of the Regiment; The Young Scamp; The Fire Eater; The Virginia Mummy; Jumbo Jum; Jim Crow in London; Othello; The Invasion of Cuba.

1851–52: *Queen Joanna; The Widow's Victim; Love and Charity; Grimshaw, Bagshaw, and Bradshaw; The Adopted Child; The Cattle Stealers; The Newsboy of New York; Othello; Richard III; The Apostate; King Lear; The Iron Chest; The Merchant of Venice; The French Spy; The Slave's Revenge; The Dumb Man of Manchester; Richard of the Lion Heart; The Wept of Wish-Ton-Wish; A Day in Paris; Richelieu; London Assurance; The Gamester; The Last Days of Pompeii; Ernest Maltravers; The Forest of Bondy; Honey Moon; The Dogs of the Ship; Mose in Town; Macbeth; Mabel: The Child of the Battlefield; The Watch Dogs; The Fisherman and His Dogs; Blanch, the Outcast; Mose in France; Nick of the Woods; The Student of Morlaix; The Exile of Siberia; Too Many Cooks Spoil the Broth; My Poor Dog Tray; The Female Highwayman; The Deserter and His Dog; Manvers: The Child of Crime; Wigs and Widows; Zelina; Ben, the Devil; The Hungarians and Their Struggle for Liberty; The Trooper's Revenge; Ingomar; The Marble Maiden; The Little Red Man; Pilgrims of Love; Brian O'Lynn; The Rough Diamond; Ireland as It Is; Our Gal; Shandy Maguire; Alive and Kicking; Ireland and America; Erin;*

The Irish Diplomat; Kate Kearney; Jenny Lind; Swallowing a Policeman; Highway Robbery; Yankee Jack; The Idiot Witness; The Warlock of the Glen; Paulee Cliffordee; The Evil Eye; Ambrose Gwinett; Jonathan Bradford; The Golden Farmer; The Irish Jonah; The Old Continental; The New York Fireman; Harry Burnham; Catherine Hayes; The Match Woman of Boston; The Bath Bun; The Gambler's Fate; Brian Boroihme; The Siege of Tripoli; The People's Lawyer; Pizarrobus; The Anchor of Hope; A Lear of Private Life; Columbia's Sons; The Blacksmith of Antwerp; The Dumb Sailor Boy; Lawyers' Clerks; The Jolly Ones; Salander: The Dragon-Slayer; The Raggedy School; The Carpenter of Rouen; The Coarse-Haired Brothers; Virginius; Damon and Pythias; Pizarro; The Slave's Revenge; Oliver Twist; Faint Heart ne'er Won Fair Lady; Guy Mannering; Don Caesar de Bazan; Rob Roy; Helos, the Helot; The Limerick Boy; Rebels and Tories; The Negro Astrologer; Tom Casey; The Rent Day; Rather Excited; The Willow Copse; The Harvest Home; Kenneth; The Stage-Struck Yankee; The Yankee Pedlar; The Yankee Footman; The Mighty Deeds of Atlas; Adrian Gray; The Jacobite; Poor Pillicoddy; All That Glitters Is Not Gold.

1852–53: Uncle Tom's Cabin; Laid Up in Port; Servants by Legacy; Who Stole the Pocketbook? Kenneth; The Phantom Nigger; The Rose of Ettrick Vale; Binks, the Bagman; The Blacksmith of Antwerp; Rebels and Tories; Adrian Gray; Shandy Maguire; The Magic Trumpet; The Miller of Whetstone; M. Dechalumeau; Paddy, the Piper; The Old Continental; The Enchanted Poppy; Ireland as It Was; The Evil Eye; The Irish Tutor; The Writing on the Wall; The Forest Rose; New Notions; The Young Widow; Eva, the Irish Princess; The Conjurer, the Showman, and the Monkey; The Monkey of Frankfurt; The North Pole; The Saxon Chief; The Monkey of Pitcairn's Island; The Spy; Hawk, the Highwayman; Brian Boroihme; The Mystic Lily; The Sicilian Bride; Gale Breezely; The Eve of Waterloo; Richelieu; The Willow Copse; The Lost Child; The Children in the Wood; O'Neal, the Great; The Middy Ashore; The Young Scamp; The Loan of a Lover; Jack Sheppard; The Green Mountain Boy; Too Late for the Train; The Yankee Duelist; The Hermit of the Rocks; Yankee Land; The Captive's Ransom; The Doomed Drunkard; The Old Oak Chest; The Chieftains of Churubusco; The Rake's Progress; Woman's Wrongs; Crime and Repentance; The Black Avenger; The Armourer of Tyre; The Miseries of Human Life; The Drunkard; Laugh When You Can; Romeo and Juliet; Rob Roy; Catherine and Petruchio; The Man about Town; The New York Fireman; The Stage-Struck Yankee; Knights of the Cross; Chloroform; A Strange History; The Soldier's Progress; The Turkish Lovers; The Lady of Lyons; Hamlet; A Desperate Game; The Stranger; Robert Macaire; Luke, the Labourer; The Widow's Victim; Ugolino; The Broken Sword; The Wife; The Revenge; Othello; Money; George Barnwell; The Lady of the Lake; The Yankee Gal; The Patrol of the Mountain; Irish Assurance and Yankee Modesty; The Irish Lion; The Good-for-Nothing; Uncle Mike's Cabin; The Poor Soldier; Turn Out; No Song, No Supper; Brother and Sister; Richard III; Nick of the Woods; Julius Caesar; The Tower of Nesle; The Adopted Child; The Pilgrim of Love; A.S.S.; Harvest Home; Uncle Tom's Cabin.

1853–54: Uncle Tom's Cabin; Katy, the Hot Corn Girl; Lost and Won; Six Degrees of Crime; The Child of Prayer; The Blacksmith of Antwerp; Steps to Crime; The Forest of Bondy; The Ourang Outang; The Irish Harper and His Dog; The Fairy Light Guard; Amy Lawrence; Eva: The Irish Princess; Mazeppa, the Second; Podijah B. Peasley His (X) Mark; Rebels and Tories; Pizarro; The French Spy; Richelieu; Plot and Personation; A Day in Paris; Charles II; The Student's Revenge; The Iron King; A-Lad-in a Wonderful Lamp; King Lear; Othello; Damon and Pythias; The Apostate; Macbeth.

1854–55: Honey Moon; The Man o'War's Man; The Female Forty Thieves; Hamlet; Fashion and Famine; Eustache Baudin; Ben Bolt; The Ragpicker of Paris; The Wizard Skiff; Macbeth; Othello; Hamlet; The Idiot Witness; The Devil's Daughter; The Heart of Gold; The Aethiop; The Cradle of Liberty; Mazeppa, the Second; The French Spy; Jonathan in England; El Hyder; The Golden Axe; Cherry and Fair Star; Sketches in India; The Magic Rose; The Captain is Not A-Miss; The Limerick Boy; Fortunio; The Savage and the Maiden; Peter Wilkins; Asmodeus; Ireland as It Is; The Lady of Lyons; Jack Sheppard; Beauty and the Beast; Cinder-Nelly; Eveleen Wilson; Estelle Grant; The Black Cat of Coventry; The Fate of War; Satan in Paris; The Female Highwayman; Buy It, Dear; The Spectre Pilot; The Dice of Death; The Spirit of the Wreck; The Trials of Jemmy Green; The Invisible Prince; Lovers in Trouble; The Seven Castles of the Passions; The Romance of the Nose; The Bottle; The White Cat; Kate Aylesford; The Dumb Girl of the Harem; The Fountain of Beauty; Uncle Tom's Cabin; The National Baby Show; Harry Burnham; The Lamplighter; 1955; Katy, the Hot Corn Girl; The Roll of the Drum; City Streets; Mother Bailey; Don Caesar de Bazan; Hell on Earth; To Parents and Guardians; Wacousta; Norman Leslie; Mazulme; O'Neal, the Great; The Magic Barrel; Richard III; The Wizard of the Wave.

1855–56: The Armourer of Tyre; The Green Monster; Rob Roy; The Magic Barrel; The Swiss Cottage; The Rose of Pekin; The Golden Axe; Honey Moon; A Morning Call; The Hunchback; Romeo and Juliet; Eva: The Irish Princess; The Blacksmith of Antwerp; Mabel: The Child of the Battlefield; The Magic Pills; Ireland as It Is; The New York Fireman; O'Neal, the Great; Macbeth; Tom Cringle; Nick of the Woods; Aben Hamet; Satan in Paris; The Brigand; El Hyder; Kenneth; The Flying Dutchman; The Idiot Witness; Moll Pitcher; Gipsy Bess; Captain Kyd; The Limerick Boy; The Fountain of Beauty; Nature and Philosophy; Rebels and Tories; King Charming; Harry Burnham; Brian Boroihme; The Female Privateer; Mazulme; The Tailor of Tamworth; The Knight of Arva; Asphodel; The Youthful Brigand; The People's Lawyer; The Wizard Skiff; Follies of a Night; The French Spy; The Idiot of the Mill; The Wept of Wish-Ton-Wish; Wallace; The Muleteer of Toledo; The Invasion of Ireland; The Ice Witch; Herne, the Humbug; Silver Knife; The Frisky Cobbler; Arabian Nights; The Savage and the Maiden; The Gold Seekers; The Hunter of the Alps; The Spirit of the Wreck; The New York Newsboy; Norah Creina; Jack Sheppard; Madeleine; Four Lovers; Cinder-Nelly; The Fire Raiser; O'Flannigan and the Fairies; The Last Nail; Shinderhannes; The Fatal Goblet; The Orange Girl of Venice; The Red Gnome and the White Warrior; That Blessed Baby; Temptation; Pedlar's Acre; Raoul; Esmeralda; The Secret; State Secrets; My Neighbor's Wife; Pongo: The Intelligent Ape; An Object of Interest; The Little Treasure; The Boatman and His Dog; The Lord of the Isles; Nicaragua; Damon and Pythias.

1856–57: The Fairy Spell; The Red Gnome; The Frisky Cobbler; The Idiot of the Shannon; The Cattle Stealers; The Dogs of St. Bernard; Dred: A Tale of the Dismal Swamp; Uncle Tom's Cabin; The Lamplighter; The Old Homestead; The Schoolmaster; Old and Young; Wealth and Worth; Asphodel; The School in an Uproar; Raoul; The Lord of the Isles; Perfection; Planche; The Orange Girl of Venice; Ireland as It Is; Wissahickon; The Surgeon of Paris; Mary, Queen of Scots; Orion:

The Gold-Beater; Excelsior; Medea and My-Deary; The Secret Foe; Who Pin'd Fox's Coat Tail; Mary's Dream; Clam-eel; Life in Brooklyn; Karmel, the Scout; Dublin in 1530; The Mystic Bride; Cleopatra; Pongo: The Intelligent Ape; The Wild Knight; Salmagundi; Ups and Downs of New York Life; Bonaparte; The Widow of Toledo; The Irishman in Bagdad; Clari; The Charcoal Burner; Pizarrobus; The Manager's Dream; The Youthful King; Fast Young Men of New York and Brooklyn; Bertram; Rob Roy; My Poll; My Partner Joe; The Magic Hands.

1857–58: *William Tell; Pizarro; El Hyder; Nick of the Woods; The Lady of the Lake; The Robbers of the Rhin(e) oh!; Rob Roy; La tour de Nesle; The Queen of the Abruzzi; Masaniello; Jack Robinson and His Monkey; The Magic Hands; Wallace; Guy Mannering; The Sons of Toil; Pongo: The Intelligent Ape; In and Out of Place; The Yankee Heiress; Lola Montez; Black Hugh, the Outlaw; Peter Bell, the Waggoner; Bion, the Wanderer; The Wept of Wish-Ton-Wish; Oniska; The Warning Hand; Yankee Courting; The Persecuted Dutchman; Wetamo; The Siege of Wexford; The Wizard Priest; Dutch Richard III; The Savage and the Maiden; O'Neal, the Great; St. Mary's Eve; The Gunmaker of Moscow; The Carpenter of Rouen; The Surgeon of Paris; Orion: The Gold-Beater; Karmel, the Scout; The Invasion of Ireland; The Prophetess; The Revolt in India; Boreas; The Pioneer Patriot; The Results of Crime; Wapping Old Stairs; The Knight of the Silver Cross; Linda: The Segar Girl; The Widow's Victim; The Toodles; O'Flannigan and the Fairies; Mose in California; Novelty; Rip Van Winkle; The Mysteries and Miseries of New York; The Last Days of Pompeii; Don Caesar de Bazan; A Glance at New York; The Sea; The First Night; New York as It Is; Almoni: The Scourge of the Missouri; The Galley Slaves; Carmilhan; The Red Gnome; Sarah, the Jewess; Comfortable Service; New York Girls and Brooklyn Boys; Herne, the Humbug; Wealth and Worth; Jessie Brown; Ben Bolt; Gale Breezely; The Flowers of the Forest; The Negro of Wapping; Macbeth; Life of the Mormons at Salt Lake; The Inquisition; The Necromancer; The Cattle Stealers; Ingomar; The Idiot of the Shannon; Cut for Partners; Hamlet; The Slave; Jack Cade; Rosalind Hubert; Darby, the Blast; The Sons of Malta; The Emerald Ring; The Indian King; Ban Oussel Dhu; Dame Trot and Her Comical Cat; The Dog of the Ferry; The Old Stone Cross; Captain Kyd; The Roman Traitor; The Dumb Sailor Boy; Laugh When You Can; Fortunio; The Way to Get Married; The Invisible Prince; The Right of Search; Ticklish Times; The Debutante; Brian O'Lynn; The Happy Man; Paddy, the Piper; Shandy Maguire; The Floating Beacon; Family Jars; A Beggar on Horseback; Nature and Philosophy; The Good-for-Nothing; Outahlanchet; Wallace; The First Peep at a Woman; Clandare; The Dead Boxer; The Wandering Minstrel; Nipt in the Bud; The Roman Slave; Ambition; The Phantom Bride; The Stranger; The Battle of the Heart; Warriors of the Harem; The Two Buzzards; The Two Gregories; The Three Thieves of Marseilles; Make Your Wills; The May Festival; The French Spy; Ten Nights in a Bar Room; Podijah B. Peasley; The Battle of Saratoga; Cut and Come Again; The Yankee Duelist; Churubusco; True Love Never Runs Smooth.*

1858–59: *Azim al Barmechi; Nick Whiffles; Brian O'Lynn; Churubusco; The Rent Day; Daniel O'Connell; Judith of Geneva; Romeo and Juliet; The Harvest Queen; The Ice Witch; The Limerick Boy; Guy Mannering; The French Spy; Richard III; Hamlet; Macbeth; King Lear; La tour de Nesle; His Last Legs; The Poor of New York; The Bridal; Civilisation; Richelieu; The Lady and the Devil; The Iron Mask; The Avalanche; Henry IV; Charles XII; Pizarro; The O'Connors; The Prize*

Fighters; Cherry and Fair Star; The Fiend of the Mountains; The Lost Treasure; Honey Moon; Wallace; Knights of the Mist; The Bleak Hills of Erin; The Ship on Fire; The Magic Harp of Altenburg; The Mysteries and Crimes of New York and Brooklyn; The Ragpicker of New York; The Tree of Death; The Bonnie Fishwife; Richard Hoffman; The Will and the Way; The Rover's Bride; The Gipsy Father; The Woman of the World; The Pirate's Legacy; Pierre, the Partisan; Gentleman Jack; Alaric; The Bohemians of Paris; Conscience; The Magic Barrel; Lucrezia Borgia; Mazeppa; The Maniac Lover; The Wild Rider of the Santee; Luke, the Labourer; Kit Carson, the Guide; Ye Atlantic Telegraph; The Sea of Ice; Jack Robinson and His Monkey; Harold Hawk; Linda: The Segar Girl; Aunt Charlotte's Maid; The Widow's Victim; The Debutante; Pocahontas; The Toodles; Novelty; Mose in California; Our Yankee Cousin; Captain Kyd; The Felon of Marseilles; Wallace; Naval Engagements; Rosina Meadows; The Spectre Bridegroom; The Soldier's Daughter; A Day in Paris; Asmodeus; Satan in Paris; The Swiss Cottage; Rory O'More; The Irish Hussar; Handy Andy; Ireland as It Is; Larry, the Blunderer; The Knight of Arva; The Butcher of Lisbon; The Iron Chest; A New Way to Pay Old Debts; Louis XI; Our Irish Cousin; Black Eyed Susan; The Red Man of Agar; Harry Montford; The Wandering Jew; Claude Duval; A Life's Revenge; O'Nolan's Vow; Master Humphrey's Clock; The Crown Jewels; The Progress of a Scamp; Amalderac: The Black Rover; The Young Scamp; Scarlet Mantle; The Black Walloon; Linda: Pearl of Savoy; The Actress of Padua; The Haunted Hotel; Damon and Pythias; The New York Fireman; Ingomar; Charles II; Military Promotion; The Revolt of Messene; Rash Bold Connor; The Statue Lover; Peter Bell, the Waggoner; The Siege of Rochelle; The Ape of the Philippine Islands; The Wandering Boys; Thérèse; Jack Sheppard; The Drunkard; A Dream at Sea; The Dream Spectre; Little Nelly; Four Lovers; Timour, the Tartar; The Hunter's Bride; Married Blind.

BIBLIOGRAPHY

Published Sources: Joseph N. Ireland, *Records of the New York Stage from 1750 to 1860,* 2 vols. (New York: T.H. Morrell, 1866–67); George C. D. Odell, *Annals of the New York Stage,* vols. 4 and 5 (New York: Columbia University Press, 1928, 1931).

George B. Bryan

NEUES STADT THEATER. See STADT THEATRE COMPANY.

NEW AMERICAN THEATRE COMPANY. See [CALDWELL'S] AMERICAN COMPANY (1819–43)

NEW STADT THEATER. See STADT THEATRE COMPANY.

O

OLD AMERICAN COMPANY. See [OLD] AMERICAN COMPANY (reorganized; 1792–1806) and AMERICAN COMPANY (1752–92).

P

PARK THEATRE COMPANY. (1806–26) The opening of The Theatre, as it was then called, for it had no competition, in the fall of 1806 in New York City, marked the beginning of a new era in its history. The year 1806–7 was its first season under the management of Thomas Abthorpe Cooper (1776–1849), the leading actor in America. His assistant was William Dunlap (1766–1839), playwright, who had failed as manager early in 1805. John Joseph Holland (1776–1820), who had apprenticed in London, was the chief scenic artist. The actors included many who had performed under previous managements. Visiting stars included John Bernard (1756–1828), comedian; James Fennell (1769–1816), who rivaled Cooper in tragedy; and Mrs. Warren (1769–1808), of the Philadelphia Theatre, the leading actress in America. The repertory consisted largely of classics presented in three or four performances a week with a nightly change of bill. Business was bad and the season ended three months early. During the summer the theatre was remodeled and redecorated under Holland's supervision.

When the 1807–8 season opened, the theatre probably held 2,372: 1,272 in three tiers of boxes, 500 in the pit, and 600 in the gallery. At prices of $1, fifty cents, and twenty five cents, it could produce about $1,600. The season offered few stars but many plays new to the company's repertory, of which the most popular were the melodrama *Ella Rosenberg,* the gothic thriller *The Wood Daemon,* and the spectacular *Cinderella,* with new scenery, machinery, costumes, and decorations by Holland. In the summer of 1808, Stephen Price (1782–1840), a young lawyer, bought into the management.

Cooper acted only part of the 1808–9 season, which was notable for the successful debut of American-born John Howard Payne (1791–1852) as a child prodigy and for the premiere of an American play, *The Indian Princess,* by James Nelson Barker. Elizabeth and David Poe, parents of Edgar Allan

Poe, joined the company for the 1809–10 season as did Edmund Simpson (1784–1840), from Dublin and Edinburgh, who played juvenile leads. Again the company presented few stars and many new plays, the most successful being *The Africans*, which combined sensational action, broad comedy, music, and spectacular scenery. In June Cooper went to England seeking actors to strengthen the company.

The fruits of his talent hunt enriched the 1810–11 season: John Dwyer (? –1843), veteran star in elegant comedy; Thomas Hilson (1784–1834), just beginning his career in a wide range of comic and serious characters; and especially, George Frederick Cooke (1775–1812), the brilliant if undependable tragedian. Cooke drew capacity audiences in October and did only less well in February and again in the spring. He was immensely profitable to Cooper and Price, for between New York engagements they farmed him out to Philadelphia and Boston.

Although alcoholism and illness often detracted from his acting, Cooke was a feature of the 1811–12 season also. In January, Joseph Jefferson I (1774–1832) and William B. Wood (1779–1861) starred for two weeks in exchange for Cooper and Simpson. Business was adversely affected by events leading to the war with England, by the disastrous Richmond Theatre fire in December, and by competition from the Olympic Theatre on Anthony Street.

The war was reflected in the offerings of 1812–13: a transparency of the capture of the Macedonian, a scene depicting the victory of the Constitution over the Guerriere, and two plays, *Yankee Chronology; or, Huzza for the Constitution*, and *America, Commerce, and Freedom*. The only stars were William Warren (1767–1832), comedian from Philadelphia; Joseph George Holman (1764–1817), leading man from Covent Garden; and his daughter, later Mrs. Charles Gilfert (1793– ?), comedienne. Cooper acted the entire season. In May Simpson became business manager.

The war continued to color the 1813–14 season. The theatre was especially illuminated for Perry's victory on Lake Erie, and for visits by General Harrison and Commodore Bainbridge. The stars were Miss Holman, John Duff (1787–1831), leading man, and Mary Ann Duff (1794–1856), just beginning a career in tragedy. Business was adversely affected by economic conditions and by competition from a sharing company in the Anthony Street Theatre November 1–January 1 and April 18–July 4.

Competition from Anthony Street marked the first weeks of the 1814–15 season. Stars included John Dwyer, William Warren, and Mrs. Gilfert. Mrs. Williams (1790–1872), later Mrs. S. Wheatley, comedienne from London and Dublin, made her debut as a member of the stock company. In the summer of 1815, Cooper sold his share in the management to Price and became a full time traveling star.

Price went to England in the fall of 1815 seeking actors to strengthen the company and returned in the spring with John Barnes (1761–1841), comedian; Mrs. Barnes, leading lady; Joseph Baldwin (1787–1820), eccentric comedian; and Mrs. Baldwin (? –1856), character woman. Cooper played two starring engagements. Two plays by Americans were produced: John Howard Payne's *Accusation; or, The Family of D'Anglade,* and William Dunlap's *Battle of New Orleans.*

When the 1816–17 season opened, six performances a week were tried and abandoned. The stock company was strong and the visiting stars few but undistinguished, except for Cooper. Equestrian dramas, featuring James West and his horses, were presented in January and February. Simpson bought a quarter interest in the management.

Six performances a week were tried and abandoned again in 1817–18. The season abounded in musical drama, for the two principal stars were singing actors, both popular in England: Charles Incledon (1757–1826) and Thomas Philipps (? –1841). *The Beggar's Opera* was hissed as vulgar and licentious. R.L. Sheil's tragedy *The Apostate* was a success, thus beginning a long life on the American stage. In the spring of 1818, Simpson visited England seeking actors, particularly stars.

Beginning in 1818–19 there were six performances a week. It was a season largely of stars: J.W. Wallack (1791–1864) from Drury Lane, beginning a long career in America; Cooper in his usual repertory; George Bartley (1784–1858), comedian, and Mrs. Bartley (1783–1850) tragedienne, from Covent Garden. Catherine Leesugg, later Mrs. James H. Hackett (1798–1845), made her debut as a member of the stock company. The season was marked by the New York premiere of the popular tragedy *Fazio* and by premieres of two plays by Americans: John Howard Payne's long popular *Brutus* and Mordecai M. Noah's *She Would Be a Soldier.*

Disaster after disaster plagued the 1819–20 season. After opening August 30, the company was forced by an epidemic of yellow fever to close September 18 to October 6. Bank failures and bankruptcies in November discouraged attendance and the theatre was closed again January 5 to February 21. The company was strong in men but stars were few and familiar. The night of May 24, the theatre was destroyed by fire. Five days later the managers continued the season at the smaller Anthony Street playhouse. Three plays by Americans were included in the extensive repertory: *The Mountain Torrent* by Samuel B.H. Judah, *The Wandering Boys; or, The Castle of Olival* and *Yusef Caramalli; or, The Siege of Tripoli,* both by Noah.

Edmund Kean (1787–1833), the controversial star tragedian from Drury Lane, dominated the 1820–21 season, which was played in the Anthony Street house. He opened on November 29, concluded a highly successful first engagement on December 28, and played two more weeks in March. Notable premieres were Sheridan Knowles' *Virginius* and Payne's *Thérèse; or, The Orphan of Geneva.* In spite of competition in September and

October from James West's equestrian company in the circus on Grand Street, the season was profitable. A period of prosperity had begun.

Meanwhile, John Jacob Astor and John K. Beekman were building a new theatre on the site of the old. In the spring of 1821, Price and Simpson leased it for seven years at the annual rent of $13,000.

The company opened in the New Park Theatre September 1, 1821. It fronted 80 feet on City Hall Park and extended 135 feet deep. The auditorium was lyre shaped and seated 2,500 in three full circles of boxes, two side tiers, pit, and gallery. The stage was 52 feet, 6 inches, wide at the stage boxes; 38 feet wide at the proscenium; 70 feet deep from the front of the apron; and 40 feet from floor to ceiling. There was a proscenium door on either side of the aprons. The auditorium was lighted by patent oil lamps in three chandeliers. The building was assessed in 1823 at $80,000. The 1821–22 season was notable for the New York debut of Junius Brutus Booth (1796–1852), the great romantic tragedian, father of Edwin, and by the return of Thomas Phillips and J.W. Wallack. Joe Cowell (1792–1863), comedian, was a popular addition to the stock company. A feature of the winter was *Henry IV, Part 2,* with the coronation scene from *Henry V,* appended. Costumes from the Covent Garden production highlighted the show produced to celebrate the accession of George IV. The repertory included an unusually large number of plays by Americans: *Marion; or, The Hero of Lake George* and the *Grecian Captive* by M.M. Noah; *The Rose of Arragon* and *Battle of Lexington* by S. B. H. Judah; *Adeline; or, The Fruits of a Single Error* by John Howard Payne; and Charles Clinch's dramatization of *The Spy* by James Fenimore Cooper. In May Price sailed for England again.

During the summer, the auditorium was redecorated in gray and gold; the iron hoops were replaced by glass chandeliers; the proscenium was raised and arched; and the apron was reduced. Price returned early in September with Charles Mathews (1776–1835), the witty and eccentric comedian, but because of the severe yellow-fever epidemic, Mathews did not appear until November 7. Then for eight nights he drew nearly capacity houses. He played further profitable engagements in December, April, and May before returning to England. Special attractions included a mirror curtain 33 feet by 17 feet, 6 inches, and weighing nearly two tons, lowered at the end of the play on February 9 for the audience to admire itself in; the New York premiere of the burletta *Tom and Jerry; or, Life in London,* a hit; and a series of equestrian dramas intended to meet competition from James West's circus company. Price and Simpson bought out West in the summer of 1823 and Cowell left the Park to manage the circus. Competition came also from Mrs. Baldwin's company in the small City Theatre on Warren Street and from the African Company* in the Negro Theatre on Mercer Street.

During September 1823 the Park had competition from the outdoor theatre in Chatham Garden, and from May 17, 1824, until it closed July 5, from the new Chatham Garden Theatre, which thereafter competed during the regular season. Henry Placide (1799–1870) joined the stock company, beginning a long and honorable career at the Park, where he played more than 500 roles ranging from Yorkshire clowns to fashionable gentlemen. William Pearman (1792–1837), popular English singing actor, headed the list of visiting stars. During his engagement, the opera *Clari; or, The Maid of Milan,* remembered for the song "Home Sweet Home," held its New York premiere. Other stars included J. B. Booth and Mrs. Duff, now a mature tragedienne. *The Tempest* was revived with spectacular scenery and effects.

In 1824–25 the Chatham Garden company provided strong competition except for a little over two months, February 28 to May 9. Price had been in London again and had hired Lydia Kelly (1795– ?), vivacious comedienne and singing actress, who proved very popular. The season was notable for the American premiere of *Charles II,* a comedy by John Howard Payne and Washington Irving, and three very popular spectaculars: *Cataract of the Ganges,* an equestrian melodrama; *Cherry and Fair Star,* "a grand Asiatic Melodramatic Romance"; and Weber's opera *Der Freischutz.*

The 1825–26 season was the most brilliant in this twenty-year period. Edmond Kean, on his second American tour, appeared in November, February, and May and, in spite of opposition on his first night, played to good houses. Beginning November 29, the Manuel Garcia Opera Company, the first to perform in America, playing twice a week presented Mozart's *Don Giovanni,* five operas by G.A. Rossini, and two by Manuel Garcia (1782–1836). The star was the young and beautiful Maria Garcia, soon to be Maria Malibran and the toast of Europe. On March 1 native American James H. Hackett (1800–1871) began a long career in Yankee roles, and Edwin Forrest (1806–72), the first American-born star tragedian, made his New York debut June 23.

The managers had settled on the policy of presenting a succession of visiting stars, most of them from England, in a repertory largely drawn from the London stage, punctuated by an occasional new melodrama or spectacular, featuring special scenery and effects. The stock company functioned primarily in support of the stars. With the Park operating successfully, Price became lessee and manager of London's Theatre Royal Drury Lane in July 1826, leaving to Simpson the day-to-day supervision of the Park.

Barnard Hewitt

PERSONNEL

Management: Thomas Abthorpe Cooper (1806–8); Stephen Price, Thomas Abthorpe Cooper (1808–15); Stephen Price (1815–21); Stephen Price, Edmund Simpson (1821– ?).

Scenic Artists: J. J. Holland (1807–13, 1816–21), Hugh Reinagle (1807–26), Mr. Melbourne (c.1807), Mr. Strickland (c.1807), Mr. Robbins (1816–25), John Evers (1821–26), H. Isherwood (c.1821).

Costumer: Mr. Gibbons (c.1807).

Orchestra Leaders, Composers: Mr. Kelly (c.1807), Mr. Hewitt (1816–21), Mr. Gillingham (c.1821–24), Mr. De Luce (1824–26).

Actors, Actresses, Dancers, Pantomimists: Andrew J. Allen (1805–8, 1810–14), Miss Alphonse (1821–22), Mrs. Anderson (1816–18), *Mr. James Anderson* (1809–10, 1816–24), Miss Andrews (1807–8), Mr. Baldwin (1816–21), Mrs. Baldwin (1816–20), *Mr. Bancker* (1811–26), *John Barnes* (1816–22, 1824–26), *Mrs. John Barnes* (1816–22, 1824–26), Mrs. George Barrett (1821–22), *Mrs. Battersby* (1821–23, 1825–26), Mr. Betterton (1816–c.20), Master Blackley (1822–23), Mr. Blair (1818–19), Mr. Blythe (1824–25), Mr. Bray (1809–11), Mrs. Bray (1809–11), Mr. Broad (1822–23), *Miss Brundage* (1816–26), Thomas Burke (1811–12, 1814–16), Mrs. Thomas Burke (1814–16), Mr. Carpender (1811–20), Miss Chamberlain (1821–23), Mr. Chambers (1807–9), Mr. Charnock (1813–14), Mr. Clark (1814–15), Mrs. Clark (1814–15), John S. Clarke (1823–26), Mrs. John S. Clarke (1823–25), Isaac Star Clason (1823–24), Mr. Claude (1807–8, 1810– ?), *Mrs. Claude* (1807–8, 1810–15), Mr. Collingbourne (1825– ?), Mrs. Collins (1809–10), Mr. Comer, (1807–8, 1818–19), *Thomas A. Cooper* (1806–15), *Joseph Cowell* (1821–23), *Mr. Darley* (1806–9, 1811–18), *Mrs. Darley* (1806–9, 1811–18), Miss Deblin (1825– ?), Miss Delamater (1808– ?), *Miss Dellinger* (1804–21), Mrs. DeLuce (1824– ?), Miss Denny (1820–21), Mr. Doige (1810– ?), Mr. Doyle (1807–12), Miss Julia Drake (1821– ?), Mr. Drummond (1813– ?), Charlotte Durang (1821–24), Juliet Durang (1821–24), John Dwyer (1819–20), Mr. Dykes (1807–8, 1818–19), Miss Ellis (1812– ?), John Forrester Foot (1822–26), Mr. Foster (1809–10), Mr. Garner (1818– ?); *Mrs. Charles Gilfert*, nee Holman (1816–?); Mrs. Goldson, later Mrs. Groshon (1813–18); Mr. Goll (1818– ?); Miss Gordon (1811– ?); Mr. Graham (1811–19); Mr. Green (1807–8, 1814– ?); Miss Haines (1810– ?); *Mirvan Hallam* (1806–11); Mr. Harwood (1806–9); *Thomas Hilson* (1810–17, 1823–26); Miss Fanny Hodgkinson (1806–7); *Mrs. Ann Storer Hogg* (1808–16); *John Hogg* (1806–7, 1808–12); *Mrs. Joseph George Holman* (1818–19, 1821–24); Mr. Hopper (1818–19); Mr. Horton (1812– ?); Mr. Howard (1818–19); Mr. Huntington (1808–9); Mr. Jervis (1824–26); *Miss Ellen Johnson*, later *Mrs. Thomas Hilson* (1817–26); *Mr. John Johnson* (1817–20); Miss Jones, later Mrs. Bancker (1820–26); Julia Jones (1807–8, 1812–13); *William Jones* (1811–14, 1815–18); Arthur Keene (1824–26); Lydia Kelly (1824– ?); Master Kent (1822– ?); Mr. Kent (1821–25); Mrs. Kent (1824– ?); *Thomas Kilner* (1818–21); *Mrs. Thomas Kilner* (1818–20); Mr. Kirby (1825– ?); Mr. Knox (1811–12); M. Labasse (1821– ?); Mr. Lamb (1822– ?); Mr. Lee (1824–26); *Catherine Leesugg*, later Mrs. *J.H. Hackett* (1818–19); Mr. Lindsley (1806–12); Mrs. Lipman (1808–9); Miss Martin (1806–11); John Martin (1806–8); Mrs. Mason, later Mrs. Entwistle (1809–11, 1818–19); *Robert Campble Maywood* (1819–24); Mr. McFarland (1810–13); Mr. McEnery (1810–15); Harry George Moreland (1818–21); Mr. Morrell (1810–12); Mr. Morse (1806–8); *Gilbert Nexsen* (1818–26); *Mrs. Oldmixon* (1806–14); Mr. Oliff, or Olliff (1806–23?); Mr. Parker (1818– ?); Mrs. Parker (1818– ?); Aaron J. Phillips (1815–16, 1821–23); Caroline Placide (1807), later Mrs. Leigh Waring (1823–26); Eliza Placide (1823–26); *Henry Placide* (1823– ?); David Poe (1809–10); Elizabeth Poe (1809–10); James Pritchard (1810–19, 1821–23); D. Reed

(1820–25); *Peter Richings* (1821–26); James Roberts (1823– ?); *Hopkins Robertson* (1806–11, 1812–19); Mr. Rutherford (1806–7, 1808–9); Miss Ryckman (1810–11); Miss A. Ryckman (1810–11, 1812–13); Mr. Saubare (1806– ?); Mr. Schinotti (1823– ?); Mr. Shapter (1806–9); *Mrs. Sharpe*, nee Leesugg (1825– ?); Mr. Sidney (1812– ?) Mrs. J. Simpson (1806– ?); *Edmund Simpson* (1809–26); Mrs. Smith (1825– ?); Mr. Spear (1807–8); Mr. Spiller (1811–12, 1814–16); Mrs. Spiller (1814–16); Mr. Stanley (1810–12, 1824–26); Mrs. Stanley, later Mrs. Aldis (1810–14, 1816–17); Mrs. Stevenson (1823–24); Mrs. B. Stickney, formerly Mrs. Battersby (1825– ?); Mrs. Stone (1823–24); Mr. Stuart (1822– ?); M. Tatin (1821–23); Edward N. Thayer (1823– ?); Mr. Thornton (1810–11); Mrs. Turner (1807–8); *William Twaits* (1806– 10); *Mrs. William Twaits* (1807–10), formerly *Miss E. A. Westray* (to 1806) and then *Mrs. Villiers* (1806–7); *Joseph Tyler* (1806–10); James Watkinson (1822–25); Mr. Went (1820–23); *Frederick Wheatley* (1811–12, 1821–22); *Mrs. F. Wheatley*, formerly Miss Ross (1805–7, 1811–16, 1821–26); Mary White (1806–11); *Mrs. Williams*, later *Mrs. S. Wheatley* (1814–19); *Jacob Woodhull* (1818–26); Mr. Yates (1811–14); Mrs. Young (1812–13); Charles Young (1809–10); Mrs. Charles Young (1809–10).

REPERTORY

The following are plays new to the Park Theatre Company; dates in parentheses indicate the date of first performance:

1806–7: *Of Age Tomorrow* (11/5); *'Tis All a Farce* (12/24); *The Invisible Girl* (1/26/07); *We Fly by Night* (2/27); *Mr. H* (3/16).

1807–8: *Town and Country* (11/2); *Adrian and Orrila; or, A Mother's Vengeance* (12/11); *Tekeli; or, The Siege of Mongatz* (12/21); *The Secret* (2/26/08); *The Curfew* (3/4); *Cinderella* (4/1); *Time's a Tell-Tale* (4/18); *The Fortress* (4/22); *The Wood Daemon; or, The Clock Has Struck* (5/9); *Arbitration; or, Free and Easy* (5/25); *Ladoiska* (6/13); *Ella Rosenberg* (6/17).

1808–9: *The World* (10/19); *Begone, Dull Care* (11/9); *Adelgitha; or, The Fruits of a Single Error* (11/14); *Plot and Counterplot* (11/18); *The Blind Boy* (12/7); *Spanish Patriots* (1/4/09); *Harlequin Panattahah* (1/4); *The Forty Thieves* (3/20); *The School for Authors* (3/27); *Man and Wife; or, More Secrets Than One* (5/5); *The Indian Princess; or, La belle sauvage* (6/14); *The Duke of Buckingham* (6/21).

1809–10: *Is He a Prince?* (9/13); *Princess and No Princess* (9/29); *To Marry or Not to Marry* (10/6); *Grieving's a Folly* (10/18); *The Foundling of the Forest* (11/27); *Venoni* (12/6); *John Bull at Fontainebleau* (12/8); *The Africans* (1/1/10); *Where Is He?* (1/10); *Who Wins? or, The Widow's Choice* (3/12); *The Exile* (4/18); *The City Madam* (5/16); *Not at Home* (5/23); *The Free Knights; or, The Edict of Charlemagne* (6/13); *The Caravan; or, The Driver and His Dox* (6/29).

1810–11: *The Doubtful Son; or, Secrets of the Palace* (10/12); *High Life in the City* (10/19); *Hit or Miss* (12/5); *Le Perouse; or, The Desolate Island* (1/1/11); *Alberto Albertini; or, The Robber King* (1/25); *Tricks upon Travellers* (3/18); *The Young Hussar; or, Love and Mercy* (5/31); *The Knight of Snowdoun* (6/12).

1811–12: *The Bee Hive* (10/23); *Ourselves* (12/7); *The Gazette Extraordinary* (12/27); *Killing No Murder* (1/24/12); *Darkness Visible* (2/17); *Oh! This Love!* (2/26); *Marmion* (4/13); *The Child of Nature* (4/20); *Lost and Found* (4/29); *The Lady of the Lake* (5/8); *The Boarding House* (6/5); *M. P.; or, The Blue Stocking* (6/12); *The Peasant Boy* (6/26).

1812–13: *Yankee Chronology; or, Huzza for the Constitution* (9/7); *The Lake of Lausanne; or, Out of Place* (10/9); *Sons of Erin; or, Modern Sentiment* (11/11); *Try Again* (11/13); *Timour, the Tartar* (11/20); *Right and Wrong* (12/11); *How to Die for Love* (12/14); *The Sleep Walker* (1/13/13); *All in a Good Humour* (1/13); *The Renegade* (2/24); *The Brazen Mask* (3/8); *The Aethiop; or, The Child of the Desert* (4/5); *The Budget of Blunders; The Students of Salamanca* (7/12).

1813–14: *Heroes of the Lake; or, A Tribute to the Brave* (10/20); *The Plain Dealer* (11/5); *Remorse* (12/6); *Turn Out* (12/8); *Speculation; or, A Touch at the Times* (1/31/14); *Education* (2/21); *Music Mad* (5/20); *The Cabinet* (5/25); *The Widow's Vow* (6/6); *The Miller and His Men* (7/4).

1814–15: *Who's to Have Her?* (11/16); *Champlain; or, The Army and Navy* (11/18); *The Festival of Peace; or, Commerce Restored* (2/20/15); *Pantaloon in the Suds* (3/27); *For Freedom Ho!* (4/5); *The Harper's Daughter; or, Love and Ambition* (4/17); *The London Hermit* (5/10); *Personation* (5/26); *Youth, Love, and Folly* (5/29); *The Devil's Bridge* (7/4); *Fourth of July; or, American Commerce and Freedom* (7/4).

1815–16: *Past Ten O'Clock* (9/8); *Intrigue* (10/14); *Debtor and Creditor* (10/13); *First Impressions; or, Trade in the West* (10/23); *Alladin; or, The Wonderful Lamp* (11/25); *Zembuca; or, The Net-Maker and His Wife* (1/1/16); *Brother and Sister* (1/5); *The Forest of Bondy; or, The Dog of Montargis* (3/18); *The Magpie; or, The Maid* (4/1); *Accusation; or, The Family of D'Anglade* (5/10); *Living in London* (5/24); *Smiles and Tears; or, The Widow's Stratagem* (6/10); *The Battle of New Orleans* (7/4).

1816–17: *Guy Mannering* (9/18); *Love, Law, and Physic* (9/23); *Bertram* (9/25); *Bombastes Furioso* (10/15); *Where to Find a Friend* (10/18); *The Woodman's Hut* (10/28); *John of Paris* (11/25); *Love for Love* (11/26); *What Next?* (12/13); *Transformation; or, Love and Law* (12/30); *The Ninth Statue; or, The Palace of Fire and Water* (1/1/17); *The Mogul Tale; or, The Descent of a Balloon* (1/6); *The Tiger Horde* (2/24); *St. David's Day* (3/1); *My Wife! What Wife!* (3/12); *Frederick the Great* (3/21); *Who's Who; or, The Double Imposture* (3/24); *The Guardians; or, The Faro Table* (4/9); *The Broken Sword* (4/28); *Exit by Mistake* (5/9); *The Watch Word; or, Quito Gate* (5/14); *The Day after the Wedding* (5/23); *Manuel* (6/2); *Frightened to Death* (6/6); *The Slave* (7/4).

1817–18: *The Bold Buccaneers; or, The Discovery of Robinson Crusoe* (9/11); *The Apostate* (9/22); *The Innkeeper's Daughter* (9/29); *The Ravens; or, The Force of Conscience* (10/6); *The Libertine* (11/7); *The Touchstone; or, The World as It Goes* (11/19); *The Conquest of Taranto; or, St. Clara's Eve* (11/25); *Lowina of Tobolskoi; or, The Snow-Storm* (1/1/18); *The Lord of the Manor* (2/1); *The Woodman; or, Fairlop Forest* (2/6); *The Good-Natured Man* (2/16); *The Father and His Children* (2/23); *My Landlady's Gown* (3/2); *Lionel and Clarissa* (3/14); *The Falls of Clyde* (4/3); *The Will for the Deed* (5/4); *The Bride of Abydos* (5/25); *Rob Roy* (6/8); *Who's My Father* (7/4).

1818–19: *X.Y.Z.* (10/27); *Retribution; or, The Chieftan's Daughter* (11/13); *My Spouse and I* (11/14); *Fazio* (11/26); *The Sleeping Draught* (12/8); *Bellamira; or, The Fall of Tunis* (12/14); *The Secret Mine* (1/1/19); *Fire and Water* (1/15); *Zuma; or, The Tree of Health* (2/3); *Is He Jealous?* (2/8); *The Castle of Paluzzi; or, The Extorted Oath* (2/15); *Altorf* (2/19); *Richard II* (2/27); *The Barmecide; or, The Fatal Off-spring* (3/3); *Don Giovanni* (3/8); *A Tale of Mystery* (3/10); *Brutus; or, The*

Fall of Tarquin (3/15); *The Invisible Girl* (4/19); *The Rendezvous* (4/19); *The English Fleet of 1342* (4/26); *Where Shall I Dine?* (5/13); *The Heart of Midlothian* (5/19); *Evadne* (5/24); *Dr. Bolus* (5/26); *The Recluse of the Moor* (5/31); *Adelaide; or, The Emigrants* (6/2); *Bobbinet the Bandit; or, The Forest of Montescarpini* (6/18); *She Would Be a Soldier; or, The Plains of Chippewa* (6/21).

1819–20: *A Roland for an Oliver* (9/6); *The Jew of Lubeck; or, The Heart of a Father* (10/8); *The Gay Deceivers; or, More Laugh Than Love* (11/10); *Wanted: A Wife; or, a Cheque on My Banker* (11/15); *My Uncle* (11/18); *The Steward; or, Fashion and Feeling* (11/18); *The Carib Chief* (11/25); *Swedish Patriotism; or, The Signal Fire* (12/1); *A Walk for a Wager; or, A Bailiff's Bet* (12/8); *Sinbad, the Sailor; or, The Valley of Diamonds* (12/30); *The Irish Haymakers* (2/24/20); *The Mountain Torrent* (3/1); *Helpless Animals; or, Bachelor's Fare* (3/9); *The Wandering Boys; or, The Castle of Olival* (3/16); *Rochester; or, King Charles II's Merry Days* (3/23); *High Notions* (3/29); *Henry IV, Part 2* (4/5); *A Short Reign and a Merry One* (4/11); *The Gnome King* (4/14); *The Forest of Rosenwald; or, The Travellers Benighted* (4/26); *The Youthful Days of Frederick The Great* (5/1); *Guilt; or, The Gypsy's Prophecy* (5/8); *The Quadrille; or, A Quarrel, for What (?)*; *Yusef Caramalli; or, The Siege of Tripoli* (5/15); *Too Late for Dinner* (5/22); at Anthony Street Theatre, *Actress of All Work* (6/12); *Adelbert; or, The Polish Exile* (6/14); *Ivanhoe; or, The Jew and His Daughter* (6/19); *The Dandy Races; or, The Delights of the Jockey Club* (6/28).

1820–21: *Virginius* (9/25); *The Promissory Note* (9/29); *Henri Quatre; or, Paris in the Olden Times* (10/9); *Twenty Per Cent; or, The Usurer Foil'd* (10/18); *The Vampire; or, The Bride of the Isles* (10/23); *The Boat Race; or, The Waterman's Folly* (11/11); *Exchange No Robbery; or, The Diamond Ring* (11/15); *The Fortune of War* (11/18); *Orai and Otago; or, Indian Love* (11/27); *Modern Collegians; or, Insolvents in London* (12/28); *The Lady and the Devil* (3/5/21); *The Jew of Malta* (3/26); *Wallace; or, The Regent of Scotland* (4/9); *The Warlock of the Glen; or, The Triumph of Justice* (4/12); *Mirandola* (4/25); *Thérèse: The Orphan of Geneva* (4/30); *Mary of Scotland; or, The Heir of Avenel* (5/18); *Conscience; or, The Bridal Night* (5/28); *Twelve O'Clock Precisely; or, A Night at Dover* (6/4); *Ladies at Home; or, Gentlemen, We Can Do without You* (6/11); *Hamlet Travestie* (6/13); *Kenilworth* (6/18).

1821–22: *Damon and Pythias* (9/10); *Marino Faliero* (9/26); *The Grand Tour; or, Stop at Rochester* (10/4); *The Spectre Bridegroom* (10/11); *Wine Works Wonders; or, The Way to Win Him* (10/25); *Love's Dream* (11/15); *Marion; or, The Hero of Lake George* (11/25); *The Miller's Maid* (12/7); *Nature and Philosophy* (12/10); *A Chip of the Old Block* (12/10); *Half an Hour in France* (12/14); *Match Breaking; or, The Prince's Present* (12/19); *The Innkeeper's Daughter* (12/19); *New Year's Gambols; or, The Blazing Sun* (1/1/22); *Maid or Wife; or, The Deceiver Deceived* (2/11); *Don John; or, The Two Violettas (?)*; *The Green Mountain Boys; or, The Sons of Freedom* (2/22); *The Spy; or, Tale of the Neutral Ground* (3/1); *Oh! Yes; or, The New Constitution* (3/4); *La belle Peruvienne* (3/18); *The Siege of Tripoli; or, Valour Triumphant* (4/1); *The Rose of Arragon; or, St. Mark's Vigil* (4/18); *The Two Pages of Frederick the Great* (4/19); *The Russian Impostor; or, The Siege of Smolensko* (4/26); *Adeline* (5/1); *The Manager in Distress* (5/3); *Le chaperon rouge* (5/3); *Montrose* (5/13); *The Antiquary* (5/17); *The Expelled Collegian* (5/24); *The*

Two Wives (6/1); *Fredolfo* (6/14); *The Grecian Captive* (6/17); *The Battle of Lexington,* later *A Tale of Lexington* (7/4).

1822–23: *Monsieur Tonson* (11/7); *The Actor of All Work* (11/18); Charles Mathews "At Home" (11/27); *All in the Dark; or, The Banks of the Elbe* (12/5); *The Law of Java* (12/20); *Guy Fawkes; or, The Gunpowder Plot* (1/1/23); *John Buzzby; or, A Day's Pleasure* (1/6); *Tom and Jerry; or, Life in London* (3/3); *The Irish Tutor; or, New Lights* (3/11); *El Hyder* (3/31); *The Pioneers; or, The Sources of the Susquehanna* (4/21); *Ali Pacha; or, The Signet Ring* (5/8); *The Invisible Witness* (5/26); *Simpson and Co.* (6/12).

1823–24: *The Duel; or, My Two Nephews* (9/25); *The Renegade; or, France Restored* (9/26); *Durazzo* (10/17); *Cent. per Cent.* (10/20); *The Two Galley Slaves* (10/27); *Clari* (11/12); *I Will Have a Wife* (11/21); *The Hebrew* (12/15); *Greece and Liberty* (1/8/24); *Maid Marion; or, The Merry Days of Robin Hood* (1/9); *Pigeons and Crows* (2/5); *LaFayette; or, The Castle of Olmutz* (2/23); *The Avenger's Vow* (3/25); *Harlequin's Frolics* (4/16); *The Little Thief; or, The Night Walker* (4/30); *Pride Shall Have a Fall* (5/22); *Fish Out of Water* (6/4); *Washington; or, The Orphan of Pennsylvania* (7/5); *Alexander the Great and Thalestries the Amazon* (7/5).

1824–25: *The Cataract of the Ganges* (9/1); *The Siege of Yorktown* (9/8); *Cherry Bounce* (10/2); *Family Jars* (10/14); *Charles II* (10/25); *The Pilot* (10/29); *Sweethearts and Wives* (11/23); *The Floating Beacon* (11/25); *Kenilworth* (new version) (11/27); *The Devoted Son; or, The Nuptial Eve* (12/8); *Sponge Out of Town; or, No Dinner Yet* (12/18); *The Two Prisoners of Lyons; or, The Duplicate Key* (12/15); *Alasco* (12/16); *Frankenstein* (1/1/25); *Cherry and Fair Star; or, The Children of Cyprus* (1/10); *The Secret* (1/10); *A Woman Never Vext* (1/27); *The Innkeeper of Abbeville* (1/17); *Der Freischutz* (3/12); *The Young Widow* (3/18); *Self-Sacrifice; or, The Maid of the Cottage* (4/27); *The Hypocrite* (6/1); *Phellis, King of Tyre; or, The Downfall of Tyranny* (6/13).

1825–26: *Tribulation; or, The Unwelcome Visitors* (9/20); *William Tell* (9/26); *The Vision of the Sun; or, The Orphans of Peru* (10/3); *'Twould Puzzle a Conjurer* (10/13); *The Widow's Son; or, Which Is the Traitor* (11/25); *My Uncle Gabriel* (12/2); *Music Mad* (12/14); *The Rival Valets; or, Mistakes and Blunders* (12/21); *Jocko; or, The Ourang Outang of Brazil* (12/26); *Harlequin and Talking Bird; or, Singing Trees and Golden Waters (1/2/26); Paul Pry* (1/11); *The Invasion of Russia; or, The Conflagration of Moscow* (2/22); *Mrs. Smith* (3/6); *Deaf as a Post* (3/22); *'Twas I; or, The Truth a Lie* (5/19); *Wool Gathering; or, The Absent Man* (6/8); *Pontiac; or, The Siege of Detroit* (7/4).

BIBLIOGRAPHY

Published Sources: George C. D. Odell, *Annals of the New York Stage,* vols. 2 and 3 (New York: Columbia University Press, 1927, 1928).

Weldon B. Durham

PARK THEATRE COMPANY. (1826–48) Edmund Shaw Simpson (1784–48) was acting manager of the Park Theatre in New York City from July 1826, the date of Stephen Price's departure for London, until 1840, when Price died, leaving Simpson in complete control of the company. Simpson was sole lessee and manager until June 1848, when he sold his Park Theatre

Company interests to Thomas S. Hamblin, manager of New York's Bowery Theatre. Hamblin employed a double company, using many former Simpson employees, to serve both the Park and the Bowery Theatre until the Park was gutted by fire on December 16, 1848.

Simpson had first appeared at the Park in 1809, became its stage manager in 1810 and the acting manager in 1821. During the nearly forty years of his association with the company, Simpson imparted to the group many of his personal qualities. In his early career as a performer, Simpson was noted for his ease, grace, and naturalness as a comedian in juvenile leads. His modulant and sonorous voice and his lively physical manner pleased audiences. Simpson, a studious, painstaking performer himself, headed a well-drilled and efficient stock that, nevertheless, felt its popularity and its profitability waning through these, its last, twenty-two years. Simpson suffered a crippling stage accident in December 1827, and as he aged, his appeal as a performer diminished. By 1833 he was acting only rarely. The devastating financial depression of 1837 to 1841 drove him deeply into debt. George Vandenhoff, a visiting star in 1842, described Simpson as plain, reticent, slow, and well meaning but irresolute—a man "with no remarkable business capacity," worn out by the tasks of management and defeated by circumstances beyond his control (*Leaves from an Actor's Notebook,* cited in Odell, 4:606). The wooden, barn-like theatre he leased from John Jacob Astor and John Beekman decayed rapidly, and the owners supported nothing but occasional minor remodeling. In its last years, the wings and drop scenery were cheaply constructed, costumes were flimsy and tinseled, and props were cheap, worn, and few. The auditorium, especially the gallery, was commonly filled with gas leaking from the stage lighting system. Bachelors, critics, and wits filled the half-price seats in the pit and shirt-sleeved gentlemen lounged in the first and second tier of boxes (respectable women seldom attended). The third tier attracted the dissolute of both sexes; half of the gallery was filled with boys, servants, and sailors, half with seating for blacks. Bars and apple, pie, and peanut stands served the pit and the third tier. In its last days, the theatre harbored a multitude of rats and evil smells; the pit floor was full of holes, and the once-elegant boxes had become little more than screened pens for beasts, fitted with crude benches with board backs and attended by groveling, often drunk, parasites.

Simpson's first season found the fortunes of the company at the zenith. The introduction of Italian opera pumped new vitality into the business, although the regular Park players were relegated to the circus, on Broadway, on the nights of opera. Following the opera season in September, Stephen Price sent Simpson one of the finest tragedians of his time, William Charles Macready (1793–1873), the equal to the fiery Edmund Kean. Macready played five starring engagements in this season, including a spectacular tandem engagement with William Augustus Conway (1789–1828), an English actor known as "Handsome" Conway.

Extravaganzas were the most successful commodity after Macready. *Giovanni in London* first appeared March 1, 1827, and remained a favorite for several seasons, as did *The Flying Dutchman; or, The Phantom Ship,* which premiered April 9. Simpson relied heavily on new pieces, producing twenty-seven in this season, to offset the growing popularity of the rival company at the new Bowery Theatre. He was also forced to reinstate half-price seating to counter the appeal of the commodious Bowery.

The Macready season was succeeded by the Clara Fisher season of 1827–28. Fisher, later Clara Fisher Maeder (1811-98), appeared at the Park in her sixteenth year, after ten years of playing boys and soubrettes in burlesques and extravaganzas on the English stage. At the Park, she appeared in operettas, light opera, and vaudeville during three long starring engagements. Her protean performances, involving sharp character contrasts and rapid changes of costume, along with her winsome singing of ballads such as "Home Sweet Home" won her instant success. Her lisping, buoyant style influenced a generation of young ladies wherever she performed in America during the few years of the "Clara Fisher craze." Other musical fare drew well for the Park company, which seldom appeared in a full-length drama or comedy without a star in the lead. Moreover, the public taste for musical theatre extended the company's actors and actresses beyond their basic skills.

Despite the installation of gas lights and some refurbishing of the theatre's interior, the season of 1828–29 was an artistic and business failure. Clara Fisher's popularity continued, and starring engagements by James William Wallack (1795–1864), James H. Caldwell (1793–1863), Thomas S. Hamblin (1800–1853), and Elizabeth Feron (1793 or 97–1853) allowed the Park, despite poor business, to outlast its competitors at the Bowery, the Lafayette, and the Chatham. For the season of 1829–30, the Park stood alone in New York, its competitors broken by bad business. Curiously, the Park continued to struggle for patronage. Simpson introduced forty-seven new pieces and mounted six important revivals and more than fifty other works in a season that lasted eleven months. Never again, after 1829–30, was the Park, or any other theatre, to operate without competition in New York City, by then a city of more than 200,000.

Renewed competition from the Bowery and the Chatham notwithstanding, the Park Theatre Company had a good season in 1830-31. As interest in the youthful Clara Fisher lapsed, it was replaced by amazement at the feats of the child prodigy Master Joseph Burke, whose continued and frequent engagements netted large returns for Simpson. The weary manager also mounted one of his greatest hits. *Cinderella* premiered January 24; it was reproduced fifty times the first season, eighty times in 1831–32, and regularly for years thereafter.

The appearance of Frances Ann (Fanny) Kemble (1809–93) imparted an unusual lustre to the season of 1832-33. She appeared at the head of the Park Theatre Company for sixty nights this season. Her thirteen nights in October averaged $1,095 a night; her ten nights in May netted only $695 a night, but the stock alone played to houses as small as $100. In the following season, appearances by Charles and Fanny Kemble alternated with engagements of the beloved Irish comedian and singer Tyrone Power (1795–1841). Although the talents of the stars were extolled by the press, the supporting stock was subject to increasingly venomous ridicule. In the following season the Kembles were gone, but Tyrone Power remained. The Park regulars hardly uttered a word outside the presence of a star, since Simpson arranged thirty-three starring engagements in the twelve-month season. In 1835-36 he contracted for thirty-nine engagements.

Dramatic offerings eclipsed operatic and musical presentations in popularity and profitability in 1836–37, ending, temporarily, the decade-long dominance of music in the group's repertory. The popularity of drama was in large part due to several starring engagements by Ellen Tree (1806–80). Tree's popularity sustained the company as the intensity of competition increased. In 1837-38 nine theatres vied for New York's business, including the popular Franklin, Bowery, Broadway, Richmond Hill, and Wallach's New National Theatre. Heavy reliance on stars continued for several seasons, but in 1838–39, the engagement of Lucia Elizabetta Vestris (1797–1856) and her consort Charles James Mathews (1803–78) failed to attract. The public seemed to reject the pair because of their tentative marital status. The major attraction of the season was the stock company in an adaptation of Charles Dickens' *Oliver Twist*.

Expensive starring engagements of the dancing sensation Fanny Elssler in 1840, 1841, and 1842 virtually bankrupted Simpson. Yet in January and February 1841, the Park regulars, dismissed during a season of concerts, organized as a commonwealth and leased the Franklin Theatre. For five weeks they appeared nightly, without stars, in revivals of the revered old comedies. They prospered; costs were low and patronage respectable. For 1841–42 Simpson strengthened the company and attempted for six weeks to subsist on revivals of old favorites. The "new" repertory attracted adequate patronage. Furthermore, on October 11, 1841, Simpson introduced Dion Boucicault's *London Assurance* with Henry Placide, longtime regular as Sir Harcourt Courtly, and Charlotte Cushman as Lady Gay Spanker. The play ran for three weeks, without interruption, a remarkable departure from the traditional policy of the Park. Despite another big hit on January 5, Mark Lemon's *What Will the World Say?* (in which the stock performed without a star), Simpson closed the theatre from January 26 to February 21. In the spring season, revivals of *The School for Scandal* and *The Rivals*, "with the ancient costumes," drew well, as did Boucicault's *West End; or, The Irish Heiress*. An expensive opera season and the final engagement of

Fanny Elssler were less profitable. Three comedies featuring the regular players were the highlights of the season.

The magic of the regulars failed in the season of 1842–43, as did every other expedient, including sharp ticket-price reductions (to a top of fifty cents). Simpson was seldom able to pay full salaries to his large company. Business turned up slightly in 1843–44, due largely to the engagement of William Charles Macready and a successful production of J. R. Planché's *Fortunio and His Seven Gifted Servants*. The season's length had shrunk steadily from eleven and one-half months in the mid-1830s to barely seven and one-half months in the mid-1840s.

The period 1839–43 was the hardest of the company's life. The financial panic of 1837 paralyzed business for years following, and the depression altered social customs, much to the detriment of the Park. Moreover, Simpson was exhausted and unable or unwilling to alter business procedures to accommodate changing social and financial conditions. When the Bowery was surviving on long runs of popular melodramas, the Park continued to change bills nightly; when the public taste for musical theatre and ballet increased, the Park emphasized dramatic forms. Simpson's company gradually weakened as the best and most popular players moved on to more secure and lucrative employment. Mrs. Henry Hunt, formerly Louisa Lane and later Mrs. John Drew (1820–97), played attractive leads for Simpson from 1842 to 1844 but left for more profitable positions at the Bowery and at the Chatham. Gone also was Sarah Ross Wheatley (1790–1872). Wheatley was first a company regular (as Mrs. Williams) from 1814 to 1819 and then from 1821 to 1843. Jane Marchant Fisher Vernon (1796–1869) and Wheatley were the finest actresses on the New York stage of the nineteenth century in shrewish old women; inquisitive, gossipy old maids; and aristocratic dowagers. Vernon, who first appeared at the Park in 1830, riding the tide of success achieved by her sister Clara Fisher, stayed with Simpson's company until 1847. The season of 1841–42 was the last in the Park fold for Charlotte Cushman and her sister Susan. After a debut at Boston's Tremont Theatre, Charlotte, destined to become the most powerful American actress of her time, briefly pursued an unpromising operatic career in New Orleans and then moved to New York State to become a legitimate actress. Brief appearances in Albany, where Susan Cushman had her debut, promised success in the wider theatrical field of New York City. Her first performance at the Park on August 26, 1837, was a token of the use made of her talents for the next two years: she played Patrick in *The Poor Soldier,* a role in which John Henry had scored heavily in 1785. The same evening she appeared as the Countess of Novara in *The Scheming Matron,* J.R. Planché's version of the one-act farce by Eugene Scribe and J.F.A. Bayard. Roles in farce and musical comedy dominated her first season. She had little to do in Edwin Forrest's first starring engagement, but her performance of Volumnia in Shakespeare's

Coriolanus showed promise of the power latent in an emerging talent. Her performance as Nancy Sykes in an adaptation of Dickens' *Oliver Twist* in February 1839 established her reputation as an actress in dramatic roles. Cushman spent a formative five years with the Park Company, during which time she originated at least two of her most famous roles, Nancy Sykes and Lady Gay Spanker. But the lure of greater freedom in role selection and greater income drew her, in 1842, to Philadelphia, where she became manager and leading actress of the [Third] Walnut Street Theatre Company*.

Susan Cushman (1822–59), who played second leads and ingenues at the Park from 1838 to 1842, went to Philadelphia with her sister. Susan, never as dynamic or popular as Charlotte, was, nevertheless, one of the best ingenues on the American stage in her time. Her efforts to look, speak, and dress prettily and to display the charming innocence and delicious insipidness of the "walking lady" were liberally approved by the New York press and public. Her Grace Harkaway in *London Assurance* was one of her most becoming roles.

Also lost at the end of the 1842 season was William Wheatley (1816–76). Wheatley, son of Sarah Ross and Frederick Wheatley, Park regulars, had debuted at the Park at age ten during a Macready engagement. He then toured the United States in Macready's company. In 1834, at age eighteen, he became the Park's chief walking gentleman and then advanced rapidly to the status of chief juvenile. His performances in the title role of *Nicholas Nickleby* in 1839 and as Charles in *London Assurance* in 1841 were highlights of his young career. But he left the Park at the end of the 1841–42 season to join Charlotte Cushman's company in Philadelphia. Wheatley went on to great wealth and notoriety as an actor and producer, especially at New York's Niblo's Gardens, where, in 1866, he produced the epochal *Black Crook*.

Peter Richings (1797–1871) joined Simpson's company in 1821, after a brief career in English provincial theatres. He served a long apprenticeship with the group, maturing into an efficient performer of fops, military officers, and melodramatic villains. By 1838 he had become one of the country's best general stock actors. His departure to Philadelphia in 1840, where he became the stage manager of the National Theatre, was a heavy loss to Simpson.

Julia Turnbull (1822–87), a company regular as an actress and a between-the-acts dancer from age twelve in 1834, became, in her late teens, a ballerina of enormous skill, rivaling, even in a period of great popularity for ballet, the European stars who toured the United States. She toured as a soloist with Fanny Elssler and on her own, becoming one of the earliest American ballerinas to dance classic roles in *Giselle* and *Esmeralda*. She left the Park in 1844 to join the company at the rival Bowery Theatre, where, in 1847, she scored her greatest success in *The Naiad Queen*.

However great the loss of Mrs. Wheatley, Charlotte and Susan Cushman,

William Wheatley, Peter Richings and Julia Turnbull, no defection was so insufferable as that of Henry Placide (1799–1870), who left the troupe in October 1843 after twenty-one virtually uninterrupted years. In a company most frequently noted for its excellence in comedy, Placide was the main force. He had more than 500 roles in his repertoire, having originated almost 200 of them. Very versatile in comedy, he was strongest in broader roles such as Dogberry and Dromio, but he excelled in high comedy as well and contributed a strong buffo in opera. More conscientious than gifted, he was a great favorite for his high standard of workmanship in consistently better-than-average performances.

In its last seasons, the Park company was sustained by the strong stage management of Thomas Barry (1798–1876). From 1841 Barry disciplined and directed the hopefuls, the rising young performers, the few hardy regulars, and the mass of worn-out or inept performers Simpson could attract to his decaying theatre with its stodgy reputation.

In the declining years of the Park Theatre are two notable seasons of recovery and resurgence. In 1845–46 Simpson's devotion to the old classics, coupled with his employment of visiting stars James E. Murdoch (1811–93) and the duo of Charles John Kean (1811–68) and Ellen Tree Kean (1806–80), did much to restore the artistic reputation of the company. Revivals of *Richard III, Every Man in His Humour,* and *Antony and Cleopatra* were well received. The following season again featured Mr. and Mrs. Charles Kean, whose splendid revival of *King John* played to moderate houses for three weeks. The theatrical event of the season, however, was the appearance with the Park company of forty-eight Les Danseuses Viennoises. The little girl chorus took the city by storm.

The final season of the Park company ended December 18, 1847. Simpson assembled a company for two weeks in March 1848 and for another two weeks in late May and early June, before selling out to Thomas S. Hamblin for an annuity. Hamblin's recruits for the double company servicing both the Park and the Bowery in 1848 included many former Simpson employees. The Park operated fifty-one seasons, and its roots tapped into the John Street Theatre Company of the period 1767–98 and the Old American Company of the period 1752–67. For most of its life, the Park housed the best stock company in the United States. As long as it catered to a posh clientele, it thrived. When the building decayed and the management lapsed into an insensitive routine, the group failed.

PERSONNEL

Management: Edmund S. Simpson (1826–48); Thomas S. Hamblin (1848).
Treasurer: W. R. Blake (1831–48).
Scene Painters: Mr. Walker, also costumer (1827– ?); Mr. Evers (1830–c.42); Henry Hillyard (1842–48); J. R. Smith (1842–44); A. Wheatley (1843–44).

Costumers: Mr. Mead (1830–c.42); *Mr. Louis* (1842–43); *Mr. Dejonge, decorator* (1843–48).

Machinists: Mr. Dunn (1830–42); *Mr. Speyers* (1842–48).

Decorator: Mr. Dejonge (1842–43).

Property Masters: Mr. Chambers (1830– ?); *Mr. Johnson* (1838– ?).

Prompters: Mr. Durie (1827–37); *A. Lewis* (c.1843– ?).

Orchestra Leaders: Mr. DeLuce (1830–c.34); *Sidney Pearson, singer* (1834–37); *Mr. Hughes* (1837–39); *Mr. Eliason* (1839–c.42); *Mr. Chubb* (c.1842– ?).

Composer-Arranger: William Penson (1836– ?).

Actors and Actresses, Dancers, Singers: William Abbott (1841–43); *D. Anderson* (1844–48); *A. Andrews* (1840–48); *George H. Andrews* (1845–48); *Mr. Archer, singer* (1835–36, 1840–41); *Mrs. Archer, later Mrs. Timm* (1833–34); *Mme. Arraline, dancer* (1839–41); *Mrs. Austin* (1828–29); *Miss Ayres* (1843–44); *Mrs. Bailey* (1840, 1847–48); *W. Bancker* (1811–27, 1830–36); *John Barnes* (1816–22, 1824–29, 1831–32); *Mrs. John Barnes* (1816–22, 1824–33); George H. Barrett (1845–48); *Thomas Barry* (1826–33, 1841–48); *Mrs. Thomas Barry* (1827–c.33, 1840–48); W. Barrymore (1831–32); Mrs. W. Barrymore (1831–32); Charles Bass (1845–48); Miss Bedford (1837–42); Mr. Bedford (1837–41); Mr. Bellamy (1841–48); Mr. Bernard (1847–48); Mr. Bissett (1828, 1830–31); *Caroline Placide Waring Blake* (1807, 1823–26, 1830–34); W. R. Blake (1830–31); *T. H. Blakeley* (1829–36, 1838–41); Miss Bland (1827); Humphrey Bland (1845–46); Mrs. Humphrey Bland (1845–46); Mr. Boulard (1845–46); Mrs. Boulard (1844–45); Mr. Boyle (1826–28); Mr. Bridges (1843); Mrs. Broadley (1839–41); *Miss Brundage* (1816–28); *Miss Buloid*, later Mrs. William Abbott (1841–48); Mrs. Burrows (1842–47); Frank S. Chanfrau (1846–47); *Elizabeth Jefferson Chapman* (Mrs. Samuel) (1834–35); W. B. Chapman (1847–48); William Adams Chapman (1839–41); William Chapman, Sr. (1829–30); Mr. Charlton (1830–31); M. Checkini, dancer (1837–38); Mme. Checkini, dancer (1837–38); *William Chippindale* (1836–42, 1843–45); Mrs. William Chippindale (1837–41); *Corson W. Clarke*, formerly Mr. Walton (1833–36, 1837–38, 1840–43); Fanny Clarke, later Mrs. W. Isherwood (1835–36); *John H. Clarke* (1823–27, 1831–38); Rosetta Clarke (1835–36); Miss Cohen, dancer (1844–45); *Mr. Collett*, dancer (1828–34); Mrs. Conduit (1835–36); E. H. Conway, dancer (1826); Mrs. E. H. Conway, dancer (1826, 1833–37); Miss Cooke (1846–47); Miss Coombe (1846–47); William Creswick (1839–40); Mrs. William Creswick (1834–40); W. H. Crisp (1844–45); J. Crocker (1842–46); *Charlotte Cushman* (1837–42); *Susan Cushman* (1838–42); Miss Deblin, dancer (1825–27); Mlle. Dejardins, dancer (1841–42); Mr. Delavanti, singer (1845–46); Mrs. DeLuce (1824–27); Kate Denin (1847–48); Susan Denin (1846–48); Mr. Denman (1826–27); Mr. Dennison (1842–43); Mr. DeWalden (1844–46); Miss Dolly (1830); Mr. Dougherty (1847–48); *Mrs. Durie* (1830–41); *John Dyott* (1844–48); *Mrs. John Dyott* (1844–48); William Edwin, singer (1839–40); Clara Ellis (1844–45); Master Eustace (1846–47); J. M. Field (1830–31, 1842–43); Amelia Fisher (1840–41); *John Fisher* (1832–47); Mr. Fleming (1844–46); Miss Flynn (1843–48); Thomas Flynn (1832–33); J. F. Foot (1826–27, 1830–31); Mr. Forbes (1843–44); *W. S. Fredericks* (1836–38, 1841–42); Mr. Freeland (1842–46); Mr. Fuller (1845–46); *Mr. Gallott* (1835–48); Mrs. Gallott (1846–47); James Gann (1838–41, 1843–45); Mr. Garland (1837–38); *Juliet Durang Godey* (1827–31); Fanny Gordon (1845–47); Mr. Gourlay (1843–46); John Greene (1826–27); Mrs. Griffith (1844–45); Mrs. Grover (1841–42); Mrs. Gurner, singer (1834–36); *Mrs. J. H. Hackett*

(1826–c.32); Miss Hall (1846–47); Mr. Harrison (1833–36, 1844–45); Mrs. Harrison (1833–36); Mr. Harvey (1832–36); Miss Hayden (1846–47); *Mr. Hayden* (1828–37); Mr. Heath (1845–48); John Hield (1847–48); William Hield (1838–41); Miss S. Hildreth (1836–37, 1842–43); Charles Hill (1840–41); Mrs. Charles Hill (1840–41); *Ellen Augusta Johnson Hilson* (1817–31, 1835–37); *Thomas Hilson* (1810–17, 1823–30); *Kate Horn* (1842–48); Mr. Horton (1828–29); *William Hoskins* (1842–43); J. Howard (1818–19, 1826–27, 1844–45); Mrs. Hughes (1837–38); Henry Hunt (1843–44), *Louisa Lane Hunt*, later Mrs. John Drew (1842–44, 1846–47); George F. Hyatt (1832–33); *William Isherwood* (1836–39); George Jamison (1843-44); Mr. Jervis (1824–28); Miss Jessop (1830–31); Mr. Johnson (1832–38); Louisa Johnson, dancer (1835–36); Miss Jones (1846–47); Mr. Jones (1840–41); Mr. Jones (1846–47); Mrs. George Jones (1844–48); *John Jones*, singer (1830–39); *William Jones* (1811–14, 1815–18, 1826–28); Mr. Judah (1829–30); W.H. Keppell (1832–34); *Mr. King* (1830–48); Miss King (1844–45); Mr. Kingsley (1847–48); Miss E. Kinlock (1843–44); Georgina Kinlock (1842–44); Miss Kneass (1835–36, 1839–40); *Mrs. Edward Knight*, formerly Miss Povey, vocalist (1826–30, 1841–47); Henry Knight (1827–28), Mr. Langton (1829–30); W.H. Latham (1834–35; 1836–41); Miss Lawrence (1847–48); Mlle. Lecomte, dancer (1837–38); Mr. Lee (1824–27); Mr. Leffler (1840–41); Mr. Lovell (1842–45); Mr. Lyne (1843–44); Clara Fisher Maeder (1840–41); Mr. Matthews (1846–47); *John Kemble Mason* (1833–36, 1837–38); Mr. Maywood (1828–29); Mary Maywood, later Mrs. Duvenee (1843–45); *Cecilia McBride* (1838–45); Mr. McDouall (1845–47); Mrs. McLean (1842–43); Mr. Meger (1840–41); Mr. Mercer (1829–30); Master Charles Mestayer (1837–38); E. Metz (1826, 1832–33); Julia Miles (1846–48); Mr. Milot (1846–47); Mrs. P.K. Moran (1826–27); Miss Moss (1845–46); Mr. Mossop (1841–42); Mr. Nelson (1842–43); *Gilbert Nexsen* (1818–42); Mr. Nickinson (1838–41); Mme. Otto (1832–33); Mr. Parker, dancer (1827–29); Miss S. Parker (1829–30); *Sidney Pearson*, singer (1841–48); Miss Phillips (1843–44); Eliza Placide (1823–27); *Henry Placide* (1823–43); *Thomas Placide* (1828–35); Mr. Porter (1828–29); *John Povey* (1827–48); Mrs. C. Pritchard, later Mrs. Lovell (1837–45); Miss Rae (1832–34); Mr. Rae (1832–34); Mr. Rea (1847–48); Mr. Reed (1828); Mr. Rees (1827–29); Mr. Reynoldson (1833–34); Mrs. Richardson (1837–40); *Peter Richings* (1821–27, 1828–39, 1840–41); James Roberts (1829–30, 1845–46); Miss Rogers (1830–31); Richard Russell (1834–37); J. R. Scott (1832–33, 1841–42); Mrs. Sharpe (1825–34, 1837); E. Shaw (1839–43, 1845–46); Mr. Shrival, singer (1842–43); John Sinclair (1833–34); Emma Skerrett (1844–45); George Skerrett (1844–45); Mrs. Sloman (1843–45); Miss Smith (1832–33); *Miss Smith* (1847–48); Mrs. Smith (1827–28); Mrs. Spiller (1814–16, 1830–33); Mr. Sprague (1846–47); James (John) Stark (1846–48); Mr. Stanley (1831–32); Mrs. B. Stickney, later Mrs. Battersby (1821–23, 1825–27); Mr. Sutherland (1846–47); Mrs. Sutherland (1846–47); Mrs. Sutton, singer (1840–41); Mary Taylor (1840–42); James Thorne (1830–32); Mr. Thornton (1830–31); Mr. Toomer (1843–44); *Eliza Turnbull* (1830–37); *Julia Turnbull* (1830–44); W. A. Vache (1843–46); Hattie Vallée, dancer (1845–46); Miss S. Verity (1836–38); *Jane Marchant Fisher Vernon* (1830–47); *Mrs. Henry Wallack* (1828–34); Julia Wallack (1842–43); Annie Walters (1842–43); Mr. Walton (1833–36); Mr. Weiland (1831–32); Miss Wells (1836–39); Mr. Wells (1836–39); Master Henri Wells, dancer (1836–39); *Emma Wheatley* (1830–37); *Frederick Wheatley* (c.1804–29); James Wheatley (1828); Julia Wheatley, singer (1830–32);

Sarah Ross Wheatley (1806–7, 1811–16, 1821–43); *William Wheatley* (1834–42, 1843–44); Mr. Wilkinson (1832–33); Miss Williams (1828–29); H. A. Williams (1827–28); Mr. Wilmot (1843–44); *Jacob Woodhull* (1818–32); Mr. Wray (1827–28).

REPERTORY

Dates of first performances of new works are indicated in parentheses.

1826–27: *Quite Correct* (9/18); *Oberon; or, The Charmed Horn* (9/20); *Malvina* (10/5); *Peter Smink; or, Which Is the Miller?* (10/14); *Three Deep* (10/19); *A Midsummer Night's Dream* (11/9); *Teasing Made Easy* (11/18); *Paul Pry at Dover* (12/7); *The Scapegoat* (1/8); *Native Land; or, Return from Exile* (1/27); *Honey Moon* (2/3); *The Conquest of Taranto* (2/5); *White Lies; or, The Major and Minor* (2/14); *Luke, the Labourer* (2/17); *Giovanni in London* (3/1); *The Two Houses of Granada* (3/12); *Twixt the Cup and the Lip* (3/13); *A School for Grown Children* (3/20); *Foscari; or, The Doge of Venice* (3/23); *Quadrupeds; or, The Manager's Last Kick* (3/31); *The Flying Dutchman; or, The Phantom Ship* (4/9); *The Dead Shot* (4/23); *The Englishman in India* (5/4); *The Disagreeable Surprise* (5/9); *The Eleventh Hour; or, Sixteen Years Ago* (6/9); *More Blunders Than One* (6/11); *A Tale of the Crusade* (6/25).

1827–28: *The Hundred-Pound Note* (9/29); *Comfortable Lodgings* (10/8); *Faustus* (10/11); *Abon Hassan* (11/5); *Bears, Not Beasts* (11/12); *The Gambler's Fate* (11/15); *Peter Wilkins* (11/23); *Brier Cliff* (11/26); *The Vespers of Palermo* (11/30); *The Cornish Miners*, also titled *The Illustrious Stranger; or, You Must Be Buried* (12/3); *The Eighth of January* (1/28); *The Sleeping Beauty; or, The Knights of Old* (1/8); *Artaxerxes* (2/2); *Alfred the Great* (2/13); *The Goldsmith; or, The Secret Assassin* (2/27); *The Sargeant's Wife* (3/3); *The Courier of Naples* (3/6); *Forget and Forgive; or, Recontre in Paris* (3/17); *The Knights of the Cross; or, The Hermit's Prophecy* (3/25); *The Haunted Inn* (4/1); *The Red Rover* (5/1); *Paris and London; or, A Trip to Both Cities* (5/16); *The Somnambulist* (5/22); *The Poachers* (7/17).

1828–29: *Ups and Downs; or, The Ladder of Life* (9/16); *The Lear of Private Life* (10/17); *The Dumb Savoyard and His Monkey* (11/5); *The Serf* (11/7); *Giordano* (11/13); *The Bottle Imp* (11/25); *Jonathan in England* (12/3); *Werner* (12/6); *Rienzi* (12/31); *The Temple of Death* (1/1); *The Green-Eyed Monster* (2/14); *The Youthful Queen* (2/19); *The Slave's Revenge* (2/23); *Charlotte Temple* (2/24); *High Notions* (3/4); *Charles III of Sweden* (3/9); *The Forest Rose* (3/11); *The Scapegrace* (4/11); *Caswallon* (4/15); *Peter the Great* (4/24); *No! or, The Glorious Minority* (5/4); *Home Sweet Home; or, The Ranz des vaches* (5/25); *My Wife! What Wife?* (6/3); *The Nymph of the Grotto* (6/10); *Gretna Green* (6/15); *Brian Boroihme* (6/18); *The Manhattoes* (7/4); *Peter Bell, the Wagoner* (7/14); *Ambrose Gwinett* (7/16); *The Two Sternbergs* (7/18); *Almachilde; or, The Lombards* (8/11).

1829–30: *Thierna-na-Oge; or, The Prince of the Lake* (9/2); *Black Eyed Susan* (9/18); *My Old Woman; or, The Russian Stratagem* (10/5); *The Lancers* (10/9); *Maneuvering* (10/12); *The Caliph of Baghdad* (10/14); *My Master's Rival; or, A Day at Boulogne* (10/29); *The Sister of Charity; or, The Nun of Santa Chiara* (11/13); *The Devil's Elixir; or, The Shadowless Man* (11/25); *Touch and Take* (12/4); *The Times; or, Life in New York* (12/10); *Metamora; or, The Last of the Wampanoags* (12/15); *The Mountain Robbers; or, The Bandit Merchant* (12/14); *Brag Is a Good Dog, but Holdfast Is a Better* (12/18); *The Happiest Day of My Life* (12/

21); *Leonidos, the Spartan; or, The Straits of Thermopylae* (12/25); *The Assassin of the Rocks* (12/25); *Uncle Ben* (1/1/30); *The Robber's Wife* (1/8); *Epicharis; or, The Grecian Freedwoman* (1/11); *Naramattah; or, The Lost Found* (1/15); *Thirty-Three John Street* (1/21); *The First of May; or, The Royal Love Match* (1/22); *Music and Prejudice* (1/27); *Dead Man's Shoes* (2/4); *Snakes in the Grass* (2/26); *Shakespeare's Early Days* (3/3); *The Brigand; or, The Banditi of Guadagnola* (3/8); *William Thompson; or, Which Is He?* (3/11); *The Bold Dragoons* (3/25); *The First of May in New York; or, Double or Quit* (3/26); *Down East* (4/17); *The Bohemian Mother* (4/19); *Rip Van Winkle* (4/22); *Humours of a Country Fair* (4/24); *Popping the Question* (4/26); *Nods and Winks* (5/1); *Rokeby; or, A Tale of the Civil Wars* (5/17); *The Indian Wife; or, The Falls of Montgomery* (6/4); *The House of Aspen; or, The Invisible Tribunal* (6/7); *Robert, the Devil: Duke of Normandy* (6/10); *A Daughter to Marry* (6/14); *The Wigwam; or, Templeton Manor* (7/3); *Down South; or, A Militia Training* (7/5).

1830–31: *France and Liberty* (9/7); *Perfection; or, The Maid of Munster* (9/8); *Past and Present; or, Scenes of the Revolution* (9/17); *Pop; or, Sparrow Shooting* (9/24); *Valmondi; or, The Tomb of Terrors* (10/11); *A Husband at Sight* (10/18); *The Spanish Husband; or, First and Last Love* (11/1); *The First of April* (11/15); *The March of Intellect* (11/29); *Charles the Terrible* (11/25); *Three Days in Paris* (11/25); *Rhyme without Reason* (12/22); *Pocahontas* (12/28); *The Field of the Cloth of Gold* (1/8); *Turning the Tables* (1/13); *Barney Brallaghan* (1/14); *The Wreck Ashore* (1/18); *Cinderella* (1/24); *The Carnival at Naples* (2/1); *The Force of Nature* (2/8); *The Water Watch* (2/24); *Separation and Reparation* (3/3); *Short Stages; or, The Convenience of an Inconvenient Distance* (3/9); *Tancred: King of Sicily* (3/16); *The Jenkins* (3/24); *The Deuce Is in Her* (3/24); *The Moderns; or, A Trip to the Springs* (4/18); *The Smuggler's Son and the Robber's Daughter* (4/18); *Was I to Blame?* (4/26); *Caius Marius* (5/9); *Comrades and Friends* (5/13); *Tuckitomba; or, The Obi Sorceress* (5/16); *Home for the Holidays* (6/1); *Highways and Byways* (6/16).

1831–32: *Innocent Deception* (9/12); *The Gladiator* (9/26); *The Conscript* (10/12); *Waldimar; or, The Massacre* (11/1); *The Lion of the West,* (J. A. Stone revision) (11/14); *Masaniello* (11/28); *Saul Braintree* (12/10); *Napoleon Buonaparte* (12/15); *The Female Brigand* (12/23); *Martha Willis* (12/26); *It Is the Devil!* (1/2/32); *The False Key* (1/24); *Victorine; or, I'll Sleep on It!* (2/14); *The Maid of Judah* (2/27); *The Bride of Ludgate* (3/6); *Lords and Commons* (3/15); *The National Guard* (3/30); *Traits of Napoleon Buonaparte* (4/5); *Werdenberg; or, The Forest Play* (4/24); *The Greek Festival; or, The Evil Eye* (c.5/5); *La dame blanche* (5/21); *The Chaste Salute; or, Pay to My Order* (6/13); *The Hunchback* (6/18).

1832–33: *Jocko; or, The Ape of the Brazils* (9/1); *The Rent Day* (9/5); *Freaks and Follies* (9/15); *Rhyme and Reason* (9/29); *The Golden Calf* (10/17); *My Own Lover* (10/29); *The Compact; or, The Bandit and the Bishop* (11/5); *The Wolf and the Lamb* (11/5); *Oralloossa: Son of the Incas* (12/7); *The Vision of the Bard* (12/20; *The Hero of Scotland* (12/25); *Call Again To-Morrow* (1/1/33); *Raphael's Dream; or, The Artist's Study* (1/11); *Mr. and Mrs. Pringle* (1/30); *My Eleventh Day* (2/4); *Petticoat Government* (c.2/11); *Damp Beds* (2/12); *Francis I* (2/10); *The Green Mountain Boy* (3/19); *The Magic Flute,* adaptation by Horn (4/17); *The Clutterbucks* (4/25); *Nell Gwynne; or, The Prologue* (5/9); *The Foundling of the Sea* (5/16);

Captain Stevens (5/23); *The Chimney Piece* (6/11); *Fra Diavolo* (6/20); *Cupid* (6/26).

1833–34: *The Irish Ambassador* (8/28); *Born to Good Luck; or, The Irishman's Fortune* (9/2); *The Nervous Man and the Man of Nerve* (9/6); *Rip Van Winkle* (version of Bayle Bernard) (9/4); *The Kentuckian* (9/4); *A Nabob for an Hour* (9/16); *Jonathan Doubikins* (9/18); *The Wife* (10/4); *The Haunted Inn* (10/11); *Monsieur Mallet; or, My Daughter's Letter* (10/16); *More Blunders Than One; or, The Irish Valet* (10/24); *St. Patrick's Eve; or, The Order of the Day* (10/29); *Etiquette Run Mad* (11/4); *Paddy Carey; or, The Boy of Clogheen* (1/2/34); *The Husband's First Journey* (1/3); *My Neighbor's Wife* (1/4); *The Eighth of January* (?)(1/8); *High, Low, Jack, and the Game* (1/9); *My Uncle John* (1/18); *Presumptive Evidence* (2/7); *Virginia* (2/19); *The Soldier's Courtship* (3/10); *Scan Mag; or, The Village Gossip* (3/15); *Robert the Devil* (4/7); *P. P.: or, The Man and the Tiger* (4/3); *The Wag of Maine* (4/16); *The Wedding Gown* (4/17); *The Old Gentleman* (4/28); *In the Wrong Box* (4/29); *Major Jack Downing; or, The Retired Politician* (5/10); *Henriette; or, The Forsaken* (6/18); *Gustavas III* (adaptation of T. P. Cooke) (7/21).

1834–35: *The Knight of the Golden Fleece* (9/10); *Married Lovers* (9/12); *Ovid and Obid; or, The Yankee Valet* (10/1); *The Bee Hive* (10/3); *Pleasant Dreams* (10/18); *Before Breakfast* (10/15); *Love Laughs at Bailiffs* (10/22); *The Deep, Deep Sea* (11/15); *The Dumb Belle* (12/4); *The Beggar of Bethnal Green* (12/15); *The Secret Service* (12/20); *Esmeralda* (1/1/35); *Married Life* (2/2); *My Friend the Governor* (2/7); *The Regent* (3/7); *John Jones* (3/10); *The Unfinished Gentleman* (3/11); *Teresa Contarini* (3/19); *The Red Mask; or, The Council of Three* (3/26); *The Loan of a Lover* (4/7); *My Wife's Mother* (Uncle Foozle) (4/24); *The Mountain Sylph* (5/11); *The Pet of the Petticoats* (5/21); *The King's Word* (5/28); *The Lion of the East* (6/10).

1835–36: *The King's Fool; or, An Old Man's Curse* (10/5); *My Fellow Clerk* (10/17); *The Brothers; or, The Vision* (10/31); *Win Her and Wear Her,* an adaptation of *A Bold Stroke for a Wife* (11/4); *The Married Rake* (11/9); *La sonnambula* (11/13); *The Adventure* (11/18); *Kaspar Hauser* (11/27); *The Climbing Boy* (12/1); *1, 2, 3, 4, 5 by Advertisement* (12/1); *The Mummy* (12/3); *The Married Bachelor* (12/4); *The Middle Temple* (12/7); *The Golden Farmer* (12/12); *Rural Felicity* (1/30/36); *The Hazards of the Die* (2/4); *His First Campaign* (2/13); *The Court of Intrigue* (2/23); *The Widow's Victim* (3/10); *The Jewess* (3/11); *A Gentleman in Difficulties* (4/18); *Joe Miller* (4/20); *The Handsome Husband* (4/30); *Personation* (4/30); *The Water Party* (5/21).

1836–37: *The Man about Town* (9/19); *Lucille; or, The Story of a Heart* (9/22); *The Farmer's Story* (9/28); *Too Late for Dinner* (9/30); *Manfred* (10/20); *King O'Neil* (10/28); *House Room; or, The Dishonoured Bill* (11/12); *The Housekeeper; or, The White Rose* (12/1); *Twice Killed* (12/1); *La Bayadère* (12/3); *The Ransom* (12/12); *The Massacre* (12/26); *State Secrets; or, The Tailor of Tamworth* (1/14/37); *Ion: The Foundling of Argos* (2/2); *The Wrecker's Daughter* (2/6); *My Husband's Ghost* (3/23); *Quite at Home* (4/8); *The Barrack Room* (4/14); *The Soldier's Courtship* (4/19); *The Yeoman's Daughter* (4/20); *Love and Reason* (4/24); *Julie; or, The Forced Marriage* (5/1); *Old Times in Virginia; or, The Yankee Pedlar* (5/10); *The Duchess de la Valliere* (5/15); *A Down East Bargain* (5/15); *Barbers at Court* (6/12); *Truth! or, A Glass too Much* (6/12); *The Mysterious Family* (6/12).

1837–38: *Bianca Visconti* (8/25); *A Peculiar Position* (3/31); *Speculations; or,*

Major Wheeler in Europe (9/4); *The Sentinel* (10/12); *The Bridal* (10/18); *Peaceful Pelton; or, The Vermonter* (11/4); *The Two Queens* (11/7); *The Rival Pages* (11/9); *The Genoese; or, The Bride of Genoa* (11/18); *Promotion; or, A Morning at Versailles* (11/24); *The Kentucky Heiress* (11/29); *The Love Chase* (1/13/38); *Woman Is the Devil* (1/25); *Patrician and Parvenu; or, Confusion Worse Confounded* (2/1); *Pocahontas* (Robert Dale Owen version) (2/8); *Zazezizozu; or, Cards, Dominoes, and Dice* (2/15); *Advice Gratis* (2/19); *Sam Weller; or, The Pickwick Papers* (3/15); *The Siege of Rochelle* (4/9); *The Dew Drop; or, La sylphide* (4/19); *Our Mary Anne* (4/23); *The Bengal Tiger* (4/30); *The Lady of Lyons* (5/14); *Court Favours* (6/15); *Shocking Events* (8/10); *Woman's Wit* (8/23).

1838–39: *The Irish Lion* (8/30); *Confounded Foreigners* (9/4); *Rory O'More* (9/6); *Mackintosh and Co.* (9/14); *The Introduction: An Interlude from the Drama's Levee* (9/17); *One Hour; or, The Carnival Ball* (9/17); *He Would Be an Actor* (9/18); *The Welsh Girl* (9/20); *Patter vs. Clatter* (9/24); *Love in a Cottage* (9/29); *The White Horse of the Peppers* (10/22); *A Dream of the Future* (11/3); *Free and Easy* (11/5); *The Twin Brothers; or, The Wolf and the Lamb* (11/17); *An Affair of Honour* (11/24); *Tom Noddy's Secret* (12/14); *Velasco* (12/20); *The Maid of Mariendorpt* (12/28); *La Gazza Ladra* (1/14/39); *Sons and Systems* (1/21); *Father and Son* (1/25); *Nicholas Nickleby* (1/30); *Oliver Twist* (2/7); *Rafael, the Libertine* (2/27); *Chaos Is Come Again* (3/1); *The Old Clock* (3/18); *Mr. Greenfinch* (4/2); *Hercules: King of Clubs* (4/25); *Anna Boleyn* (5/14); *My Little Adopted* (5/27); *The Buckle of Brilliants; or, The Crown Prince* (6/15); *The Miser's Daughter* (7/19); *Captain Kyd; or, The Witch of Castle More* (7/23); *My Sister Kate* (8/6).

1839–40: *The Romantic Widow* (8/27); *The Artist's Wife* (9/5); *Fidelio* (9/9); *Nathalie; or, La laitière Suisse* (9/12); *Venus in Arms* (9/14); *The Spitfire* (10/1); *Borrowed Feathers* (10/10); *The Village Doctor* (10/12); *Single Life* (10/21); *Foreign Airs and Native Graces* (12/5); *The Dancing Barber* (12/6); *The Gentleman and the Upstart* (1/2/40); *Le preux Chevalier* (1/2); *Richelieu* (1/10); *Love; or, The Countess and the Serf* (1/17); *Maidens Beware!* (2/3); *The Queen's Horse* (3/12); *A Wife for a Day* (3/21); *Mary Stuart* (3/23); *The Postillion of Longjumeau* (3/30); *The Court of Old Fritz* (4/3); *A Good Night's Rest* (4/11); *Curiosity Cured; or, Powder for Peepers* (5/10); *The Ladies' Club* (5/11); *La cracovienne* (5/14); *La tarentule* (5/14); *La cachucha* (5/18); *L'Amour; or, La rose animée* (5/22); *The Sea Captain; or, The Birthright* (6/9).

1840–41: *Weak Points; or, Nothing Like Wheedling* (8/17); *A Kiss in the Dark* (8/18); *His Last Legs* (9/1); *Capers and Coronets* (9/2); *How to Pay the Rent* (9/4); *The Happy Man* (9/15); *The Irish Attorney; or, Galway Practice in 1770* (9/16); *Touch and Take; or, The Law of the Kiss* (11/10); *Faint Heart ne'er Won Fair Lady* (11/12); *Naval Engagements* (11/14); *The Beggar's Opera* (11/27); *The Banished Star* (12/2); *Out of Place* (12/7); *Dr. Dilworth* (12/23); *The Place Hunter* (12/26); *Fifteen Years of a New York Fireman's Life* (1/15/41); *Money* (2/1); *The Alpine Maid* (2/8); *Norma* (2/25); *Horse Shoe Robinson* (3/19); *Henry IV, Part 2* (3/23); *Zampa* (3/29); *The School-Fellows* (4/3); *The Two Greens* (4/9); *The Gypsy's Warning* (4/20); *The White Milliner* (4/27); *Aylmere; or, The Kentish Rebellion* (later *Jack Cade*) (5/24); *The Railroad Station* (6/23).

1841–42: *London Assurance* (10/11); *The Avenger* (11/9); *Old Maids* (11/15); *The Boarding School* (11/17); *Oliver Cromwell* (12/9); *What Will the World Say* (1/5/42); *My Wife's Dentist* (1/17); *Nina Sforza* (2/21); *The Village Coquette* (3/4); *The*

Fiscal Agent (2/28); *Charles O'Malley* (2/28); *The West End; or, The Irish Heiress* (4/6); *The Prisoner at War* (4/18); *The Woman Hater* (4/30); *The Bronze Horse* (5/9); *The Maid of Saxony* (5/23); *The Fairy and the Prince* (6/14).

1842–43: *Such as It Is* (9/4); *Der Nocht [sic] Wachter* (9/9); *The Rose of Arragon* (9/26); *Love's Sacrifice* (10/24); *The Israelites in Egypt* (10/31); *Acis and Galatea* (11/21); *Boots at the Swan* (12/1); *Alma Mater; or, Life in Oxford* (12/5); *Blanche Heriot; or, The Chertsey Curfew* (12/8); *The People's Lawyer* (12/17); *The Broken Heart; or, The Toodles* (12/26); *Mothers and Daughters* (3/13/43); *The Attic Story; or, Carney, Blarney, and Co.* (3/13); *The Pretty Girls of Stillberg* (3/20); *Cousin Lambkin* (3/28); *A Thumping Legacy* (3/31); *The New York Merchant and His Clerks* (4/12); *Grandfather Whitehead* (4/24); *Binks, the Bagman* (5/9); *Yankee Land; or, The Foundling of the Apple Orchard* (6/7).

1843–44: *Werner* (10/4); *The Double-Bedded Room* (10/11); *The Lost Letter* (12/4); *The Bridal* (12/6); *Marino Faliero* (12/15); *Old Parr* (12/22); *The Bohemians in Paris* (3/6/44); *The Spirit of the Fountain; or, The Eve of St. Marc* (3/6); *Bamboozling; or, A Husband for Half an Hour* (3/11); *Fortunio and His Seven Gifted Servants* (4/16); *Olympic Revels* (4/29); *The Wedding Breakfast* (4/30); *The Fair One with the Golden Locks* (5/22); *City Wives and City Husbands* (5/31); *The Devil's in It* (6/15).

1844–45: *Gisippus; or, The Heart's Sacrifice* (9/13); *Dominique the Deserter and the Gentleman in Black* (9/14); *The Enchanted Horse* (9/30); *A-Lad-In the Wonderful Lamp* (10/7); *G.T.T., Gone to Texas* (10/7); *Grist to the Mill* (10/17); *The Millionaire; or, The Scottish Gold Mine* (10/22); *Rights of Women; or, The Rose and the Thistle* (10/29); *Tam O'Shanter; or, Alloway Kirk* (11/4); *The Inheritance; or, The Heir of Rossville* (11/8); *The Patrician's Daughter* (11/15); *The Elder Brother* (11/22); *The Bohemian Girl* (11/25); *Borrowing a Husband* (12/9); *Don Caesar de Bazan* (12/16); *A Christmas Carol* (Edward Sterling version) (12/25); *Murder in the First Degree (Wilful Murder)* (12/30); *The Battle of Austerlitz; or, Love and Honour* (1/1/45); *Old Heads and Young Hearts* (1/6); *Used Up* (1/9); *The Gallopade* (1/13); *Green Bushes* (3/12); *Fashion* (3/24); *Somebody Else* (3/31); *Mother and Child Are Doing Well* (5/2); *The House Dog* (5/19); *Time Works Wonders* (6/3); *A Match in the Dark* (6/10).

1845–46: *The Follies of a Night* (10/17); *The Sheriff of the County* (11/3); *The Old Soldier* (12/11); *Done Brown* (12/25); *Amilie* (12/29); *Remorse; or, The Paternal Malediction* (1/1/46); *Giselle* (2/2); *The Miseries of Human Life* (2/5); *The Violet* (2/9); *The Cricket on the Hearth* (2/21); *The Angel in the Attic* (2/24); *Hue and Cry* (3/10); *The Backwoodsman; or, The Gamecock of the Wilderness* (3/12); *Oregon* (3/17); *Le brasseur de Preston* (3/23); *Fleur de champs* (4/6); *Antony and Cleopatra* (4/27); *Lend Me Five Shillings* (4/27); *Nicholas Flam* (5/20); *A Beggar on Horseback* (5/21); *The Man without a Head* (6/1); *Did You Ever Send Your Wife to Newark?* (6/8); *Family Ties* (6/19); *The Devil in Paris* (7/3).

1846–47: *The Irish Post* (8/22); *Two Gentlemen of Verona* (10/6); *The Wife's Secret* (12/12); *The King of the Commons* (10/19); *The Eton Boy* (10/22); *The Soldier of Fortune* (11/2); *Spring Gardens* (11/30); *Matteo Falcone* (1/8/47); *Is She a Woman?* (1/19); *The Wife Hunters* (1/29); *Look before You Leap* (2/3); *Ask No Questions* (3/15); *Ernestine; or, Wrong at Last* (4/7); *Wissmuth and Co.; or, The Merchant and the Noble* (4/13); *The Stage-Struck Yankee* (4/15); *The Invisible Prince; or, The*

Island of Tranquil Delights (4/26); *Eugene Aram* (5/25); *The Trumpeter's Daughter* (5/27).

1847–48: *The Governor's Wife* (8/19); *The Wrong Passenger; or, Secrets of the Cotton Market* (9/20); *Love in the Livery* (9/23); *Armand; or, The Child of the People* (9/27); *The Maid of Artois* (11/5); *The Cavalier; or, England in 1660* (11/10); *The Bottle* (11/15).

BIBLIOGRAPHY

Published Sources: George C. D. Odell, *Annals of the New York Stage*, vols. 3–5 (New York: Columbia University Press, 1928–31); *Dictionary of American Biography; Notable American Women; Appleton's Cyclopedia of American Biography; National Cyclopedia of American Biography;* Louisa (Lane) Drew, *Autobiographical Sketch of Mrs. Drew* (New York: Scribner, 1899).

Weldon B. Durham

PARK THEATRE COMPANY. (1863–98) Gabriel Harrison's Park Theatre Company gave its first performance on September 14, 1863, in the 900-seat theatre on Fulton Street, opposite City Hall, in Brooklyn, New York. The theatre was one flight up in a new building called Benton's Aquarial Gardens because of the salt-water bathing facilities located in the basement. J.B. Buckstone's comedy *Married Life* (1834) and J. R. Planché's musical farce afterpiece *The Loan of a Lover* (1834) made up the opening bill.

Brooklyn had only one other theatre at the time, the Brooklyn Academy of Music, built in 1861. The Academy was a general cultural center and had no stock company in residence. Theatre was only a small part of its seasonal programming. Brooklyn was America's third largest city at the time, but without a permanent theatre company; local residents had to take a ferry to Manhattan to see plays. Many voices were raised in the effort to convince someone to provide Brooklyn with its own professional theatre. Gabriel Harrison (1818–1902), a local citizen with some theatrical background, including a stint as a theatre manager in Troy, New York, decided to take the risk in offering Brooklyn its first regular stock company at the newly erected Park. Brooklyn was a conservative city with a strongly Puritanical streak, and Harrison had his hands full attracting enough patronage to make his venture work. Those Brooklynites who were avid theatregoers normally preferred to travel to Manhattan, since the local product was no match for the offerings across the river. Many managers after Harrison were to run into the same problem in attracting audiences.

Harrison's theatre charged $5 for private boxes, $1 for orchestra seats, seventy-five cents for the parquet, fifty cents for the balcony, and twenty-five cents for the family circle. Business was rarely good during his tenure, and the company was often criticized for its mediocrity.

The company offered standard light comedies and farces. Among the more popular productions were *Jenny Lind, Beauty and the Beast, Faint Heart ne'er Won Fair Lady, Naval Engagements, Pride of the Market,*

Sketches in India, John of Paris, Sweethearts and Wives, The Serious Family,
and *The Ticket-of-Leave Man.*

Harrison himself acted in *The Wife, The Lady of Lyons,* and *Thérèse;
or, The Orphan of Geneva.* He also presented *The Imposter; or, Blind but
Vigilant,* a sensational melodrama by a local journalist, John J. Ryan, and
one of the first plays by a Brooklyn citizen to be presented in the city.

When business failed to pick up by the end of 1863, Harrison took Ryan's
suggestion and engaged an English opera company to alternate with his
dramatic troupe. Each occupied the theatre for three nights a week. The
opera did better business, and by the end of January 1864, Harrison released
the acting company. Its last performance was January 30, 1864. In mid-
February, several weeks later, Harrison abandoned theatre management
altogether.

Harrison's career at the Park received praise for its liberality and
tastefulness, but the general weakness of the company remained a sore
point. Aside from several talented performers such as Mary Shaw, Walter
Lennox, and George Metkiff, the company was severely limited in its range.
Harrison's stock company lasted precisely twenty weeks.

The Park Theatre remained without a stock company for two months
following the demise of Gabriel Harrison's venture. On April 2, 1864, it
was taken over by a company headed by Mr. and Mrs. Frederick B. Conway.
The Conways were established players; his father was the English tragedian
William Augustus Conway. The bill included Mrs. G. W. Lovell's *Ingomar,
the Barbarian* (1851) and A. Bunn's farce *My Neighbor's Wife* (1833), with
the Conways in leading roles.

Brooklyn had no other stock company at the time, despite its great
population. The Conways planned to present only the finest dramas, usually
starring themselves. Mrs. Conway soon became the sole manager, for she
possessed a better head for business, and the theatre was renamed Mrs.
Conway's Park Theatre.

Although business was slow at first, it soon improved, and the management
broke even after its brief initial season. Their program was diverse and,
for Brooklyn, exceptional, with frequent changes of the bill. For years,
Mrs. Conway ran the Park successfully, moving to the New Brooklyn
Theatre in 1871 in hopes of even larger audiences. She continued throughout
to present herself and her husband in legitimate drama. In an average
season, forty-two weeks of drama were presented during a ten-month period.
In 1867–68 the company presented 255 performances, in addition to
occasional extra and matinee showings. Mrs. Conway appeared in at least
100 performances and Mr. Conway in about 90. The theatre season lasted
from September through May and the house was rented to outside groups
for the summer.

When business needed a boost, Mrs. Conway reluctantly staged
sensational plays. If the public responded she let them run for several

weeks at a time, a rarity for Brooklyn in those days. Her usual runs were half a week or less. Popular works ran as long as possible. The press criticized her for being too commercial, and they criticized her companies for being inadequately prepared to perform. The actors were especially prone to carelessness when the manageress was not present, as when a visiting female star acted with the company. Rather than take a supporting role, Mrs. Conway would not appear with a female star. Mr. Conway played opposite the female stars, and Mrs. Conway did likewise for male stars.

Among the stars visiting the Park from 1864–71 were Mrs. Conway's sister, Mrs. D. P. Bowers, Charlotte Thompson, Lawrence Barrett, E. L. Davenport, John Brougham, Lucille Western, Mr. and Mrs. Barney Williams, Mr. and Mrs. Frank S. Chanfrau, and Catherine Reignolds. Most of these popular players were of the second rank, though. Stars were fairly infrequent during the early years of the management, and some seasons saw few, but in 1867–68 the number of star engagements increased.

The acting company changed its composition annually, as new actors joined and others left. No great stars emerged from this theatre under the Conways, but a number of players were well known at the time. The Conway's children, Frederick B., Jr., Minnie, and Lillian, all went on the stage, Minnie making her debut at the Park on May 2, 1870. Minnie's sons Godfrey and Conway Tearle became famous English actors.

The Conway management of the Park Theatre Company provided seven years of legitimate theatre, made up mainly of contemporary dramas and comedies, with a fair proportion of classical and other revivals. When the Conways left the Park in May 1871, their farewell engagement was Laura Keene in Dion Boucicault's *Hunted Down* (1866). In the fall of 1871 the Conways opened the new Brooklyn Theatre.

For a few months following the May 1871 transfer of Mr. and Mrs. Conway's management from the Park to the Brooklyn Theatre, the former playhouse was used by itinerant companies. In September 1871 Edward Lamb and J. J. McCloskey, a Brooklyn playwright, leased the house for a season of stock. The new company's leading lady was McCloskey's wife, Jennie Carroll. *Help* was the opening bill, September 11, 1871.

A season of sensational melodramas similar to those associated with New York's Bowery Theatre occupied the Park in 1871–72. Many of the plays were from McCloskey's own pen. They included *On Hand, The Trail of the Serpent, The Far West, Poverty Flat, Daring Dick: The Brooklyn Detective,* and *The Fatal Glass; or, The Curse of Drink.*

The average program ran a week, a change from the kaleidoscopic repertoire that the Conways had provided. A few moderately well known, but decidedly lesser stars, such as Joseph Murphy and J. W. Albaugh, occasionally appeared with the company.

On September 9, 1873, A. R. Samuells, a local billiard entrepreneur, became sole lessee and manager of the Park Theatre. He opened his stock season with Boucicault's *London Assurance*. Before his management, the theatre had been the home of several other stock companies, most recently the company managed by John P. Smith (1872–73).

Brooklyn had several theatres operating by the early 1870s, so Samuells faced a competition new to local theatricals. He wanted to bring the Park back to the prestige it enjoyed in its days of glory under the Conway management in the 1860s. A $45,000 reconstruction project lowered the playhouse to street level so that people would not have to climb steps to see a play.

Unfortunately for Samuells, financial panic reigned in the country in 1873. Although he offered excellent attractions, the public failed to attend. It was not long before he had to file for bankruptcy.

Samuells' policy at the Park was to do legitimate dramas of the day with popular stars in the major roles. Lester Wallack, Adelaide Neilson, Mrs. Henrietta Chanfrau, E. H. Sothern, Maggie Mitchell, Lawrence Barrett ("wretched business") and Lotta Crabtree ("best business of the season") were among them. The critics praised the season, the performers, and the management, but Samuells' financial problems were insurmountable.

Samuells soon got into trouble with his actors when he was unable to pay them their full salaries. When he paid, he paid tardily. Some threatened to quit in midseason. At one point, Samuells was criticized for poor management, but several months later the press excused him on the grounds of inexperience. The season ended on June 6, 1874.

On February 1, 1875, Col. William E. Sinn took over the struggling Park Theatre and introduced it to its greatest period of prosperity and fame. Sinn had been unsuccessful in several earlier attempts to obtain the theatre's lease, but when Edward Lamb's attempt at management fizzled out early in 1875, Sinn took over. He began a career in Brooklyn that lasted twenty-four years, twenty of them at the Park. He was probably the most successful theatre manager in Brooklyn history.

From 1861 to 1875 Sinn had been actively engaged in management in Washington, D.C., Cincinnati, Philadelphia, Baltimore, Chicago, and other cities. His experience taught him he could prosper only if he offered lightweight but competent entertainment, supported by a heavy advertising campaign. His first Park season was principally a succession of variety programs; they proved immensely popular, especially at the fifteen-cents-minimum charge per seat.

For 1875–76 Sinn installed a stock company picked up when they were left stranded at another local theatre by the failure of their manager, and he used it to balance his variety programming. The leading lady was Annie Ward Tiffany. An actor-stage manager in the company was George E. Edeson, whose son Robert debuted at the Park in the 1880s and later became a star of stage and screen. The stock company would often appear on a bill including a play, sketches, songs, acrobats, dances, and minstrelsy. The plays were mainly farces and melodramas. Occasionally, a melodrama star would appear with the troupe.

Business remained excellent into the 1876–77 season, when the Brooklyn Theatre burned on December 5, 1876, with an enormous loss of lives. In the weeks following, as patrons shied away, local playhouses lost thousands of dollars. Sinn calculated his losses at $20,000.

With Brooklyn's prime legitimate playhouse in ashes, Sinn determined to improve the quality of his own shows. By season's end he had done so and had also made up his financial losses. The Park was becoming a first-class legitimate theatre, employing its stock company along with a procession of visiting stars, including Lucille Western (who died while engaged at the Park), Rose Eytinge, James O'Neill, H. J. Montague, John T. Raymond, Ned Harrigan, and Tony Hart.

During the 1877–78 season the stock company had to share the stage with combination companies and variety shows, although there were thirty-five weeks of drama and only five weeks of variety. A new venture occupied the stock company when Sinn sent them touring to New Jersey and New England during the engagement of combination companies at the Park.

George C. D. Odell's *Annals of the New York Stage* mistakenly claims that the 1877–78 stock company was the last to play in Brooklyn for many years. Actually, a stock company appeared at the Park in 1878–79. During the following years the Park's stage was home to top combination companies touring the country.

An attempt to operate Brooklyn's old Park Theatre as a stock company was begun on August 28, 1897, when Louis Hyde and Richard Behman took over the theatre management. They opened with *Rosedale*.

Hyde and Behman had been purveyors of local variety shows and controllers of several Brooklyn theatres since 1876. One of them bore their name. Low-cost stock companies were back in vogue in the 1890s, and Hyde and Behman thought the Park was a suitable place to establish one. They offered two performances a day with a vaudeville show added to each bill. Prices were low; ten, twenty, and thirty cents were charged for admission.

The stock company must have had a difficult task on its hands. It had to play twice a day while rehearsing each morning for the next week's production. By October 25, 1897, the vaudeville was dropped from the bill. Several new actors joined the company in mid-January 1898, but the remainder of the troupe had grown weary of the routine and soon gave up. The last week of the stock company was in *The Galley Slave*, February 14–19, 1898.

The local populace wanted to keep the company on with an easier work schedule, but the management was disappointed in their rate of profits with the stock policy. Hyde and Behman shifted to a combination company policy thereafter.

The stock company hired by Hyde and Behman included some excellent performers, most notably Henrietta Crosman, but their talent could do little to lure sizeable audiences. Brooklyn had experienced a large-scale boom in theatre building in the 1880s and 1890s, and competition was simply too fierce to allow the Park to prosper. The theatre's location, once suitable, had deteriorated as the area had grown, and theatregoers preferred the newer and more fashionable theatres, such as the Montauk, Columbia, Amphion, Academy, Star, Empire, and Bijou. Leonard Grover attempted to establish a new company at the Park in late August 1898, but the group survived only nine weeks.

PERSONNEL

1863–64
Management: Gabriel Harrison, lessee and manager.
Stage Manager: B. A. Baker.
Scenic Artist: George Tirell.
Musical Director: John M. Loretz, Jr.
Actors and Actresses: George Andrews, Miss E. Burnett, Miss E. C. Couran, Miss Curtis, T. C. Gourlay, Delmon Grace, Henrietta Irving, Walter Lennox, George Metkiff, Miss Norton, Madame Pozzoni, George Rae, Mary Shaw, Miss Singleton, Mrs. Tyrell.

1864–71
Management: Mrs. Frederick B. (Sarah) Conway.
Actors and Actresses: Joseph Barrett, Marie Bates, J. W. Carroll, F. Chippendale, Lillian Conway, William Davidge, James Duff, William Harris, J. Z. Little, Lewis Mestayer, Belville Ryan, J. W. Shannon, T. C. Weymss.

1871–72
Managers: Edward Lamb, J. J. McCloskey.
Business Manager: J. W. Carroll.

1873–74
Manager: A. R. Samuells.
Business Manager: Thomas E. Morris.
Actors and Actresses: J. C. Dunn, Moses W. Fiske, W. E. Sheridan, T. J. Hind, M. Lanagan, F. G. Maeder, Owen Marlowe, Mrs. Frank Murdock, Eben Plimpton, W. E. Sheridan, Geraldine Stuart, Helen Tracy, Mrs. Charles M. Walcott.

1875–79
Management: Col. William E. Sinn.
Actors and Actresses (1878–79): Charles Dobson, George E. Edeson, William M. Frazier, James N. Harrde, G. R. Holmes, J. Z. Little, R. F. McLannin, C. T. Murphy, Frank Nelson, Mrs. J. J. Prior, Rosa Rand, A. H. Steward, Connie Thompson.

1897–98
Proprietors and Lessees: Louis Hyde, Richard Behman.
Resident Manager: Nick Horton.

Stage Director: J. C. Huffman.

Actors and Actresses: Lillian Allison, Billy Barry, Robert Barry, Charles Canfield, Jessie Cawthorn, Herbert Chapman, Henrietta Crosman, William Davidge, Jr., Barton Drew, Edward Esmond, Samuel Forrest, Howard Hansel, J. P. Hill, George A. D. Johnson, Anna B. Layng, Daisey Lovering, John Murphy, Robert Ransom, Walter Stuart, Lester Wallace.

REPERTORY

1897–98: *Rosedale; The Ensign; The Lottery of Love; Friends; The Club Men; Trilby* (three weeks); *Niobe; A Celebrated Case; A Fatal Card* (one week at Brooklyn's Amphion Theatre); *A Night Off; Mr. Barnes of New York; Young Mrs. Winthrop; Seven-Twenty-Eight; Uncle Tom's Cabin; Little Lord Fauntleroy* matinees and *Incog* evenings, *The Lights o'London; The Lost Paradise; The Streets of New York; The Ticket-of-Leave Man; The New Unknown; The Galley Slave.*

BIBLIOGRAPHY

Unpublished Source: Samuel L. Leiter, "The Legitimate Theatre in Brooklyn, 1861–1898" (Ph.D. diss., New York University, 1968).

Samuel L. Leiter

PLACIDE'S COMPANY. See CITY THEATRE COMPANY.

PROVIDENCE MUSEUM COMPANY. The Providence Museum Company was organized in the fall of 1848 in Providence, Rhode Island, by William C. Forbes. Forbes was hired by the proprietors of the Providence Museum, built a year earlier on Westminster Street, fronting on Orange Street. The original intent of the owners was that the playhouse would be an appendage to a museum of curiosities. The museum was never opened, but the auditorium in the rear portion of the building, apparently on the second floor, housed Forbes' company for almost six seasons. The front gallery of the structure became a billiards room and most of the lower floor housed various merchants and an eating establishment. The company opened its initial season on December 25, 1848, with *Honey Moon,* a dance interlude, and the farce *The Turnpike Gate.*

From David Douglass' appearance in Providence in 1762, presenting "Dialogues" and "Dissertations" at his makeshift Histrionic Academy on Meeting Street, to the present operation of the Tony Award-winning Trinity Square Repertory Theatre on Washington Street, theatre activities in Providence have been varied and numerous. Just before Forbes' operation, a small company under the management of George C. Howard and G. and J. A. Fox offered dramatic fare first at Brown Hall in South Main Street and then at Cleveland Hall, in North Main Street. At the time of the Providence Museum's opening, however, there was no permanent company in Providence. From time to time Forbes did receive competition from musicians, panoramists, and other visiting performers at one of three halls, Westminster, Howard, or Franklin. The appearance of the circus, usually Spalding and Roger's, seemed to be a yearly event, and twice during Forbes' tenure Jenny Lind appeared in concert at the Howard Hall. As the repertory of the Providence Museum indicates, Forbes' operation was not a standard stock company but was more specifically a repertory company with frequent bill changes, indeed almost nightly. A permanent company presented a wide variety of plays, musical productions, pantomimes, and equestrian dramas; they also frequently supported guest stars, the number of which increased each season. Initially, the owners instructed that no tragedy should be presented, believing that a strong prejudice against such offerings existed within the community. By January 1849, however, this policy was cast aside and productions of serious plays became commonplace.

Forbes, born in New York State, was reared in Rhode Island. Before establishing this company he had a successful acting career first in Albany, then in New Orleans under James H. Caldwell, and finally as a principal performer at the Tremont Theatre in Boston. Throughout this period and thereafter he was a frequent visitor to Providence. For the ten-year period before taking permanent residency in Providence, Forbes had managed theatres in Savannah, Charleston, Columbia, and Augusta.

Little specific has been discovered regarding the financial operation and policy of Forbes' company or the nature of the playhouse. Initially, it contained a parquet and gallery and a fixed entrance fee of twenty-five cents. Just before the fourth season (1851–52) the theatre was altered and improved with a circle of boxes added and a separate entrance to the gallery, leading from Museum Avenue. The original drop curtain, painted by G. Curtis and featuring a circle surrounded by draperies with a Turkish landscape, was replaced by a new curtain painted by James Lamb, scenic artist at the Bowery Theatre. By this time prices were set at fifty cents for private boxes, thirty-seven and a half cents for boxes, twenty-five cents for orchestra seats, and thirteen cents for the gallery. Prices were frequently raised for visiting star engagements.

After a disagreement with the proprietors during the first season, the Museum closed temporarily on March 29, 1849. Forbes arranged for a five-year lease in his name with a yearly rent of $3,000, and the season resumed in May, completing a summer season on July 23. Subsequent seasons were as follows: the second opened September 1, 1849, and closed July 6, 1850; the third opened September 2, 1850, and closed July 8, 1851; the fourth opened September 6, 1851, and closed July 10, 1852; the fifth opened September 4, 1852, and closed June 3, 1853. The final season at the Providence Museum began on September 9, 1853, and ended abruptly after performances of *The Wandering Minstrel* and *Paris and London* on October 26. At 11:30 p.m. a fire broke out in a dry-goods store in an area known as the Howard Block. By early morning the fire had spread to the Museum, and the conflagration continued until October 28. Forbes lost all of the theatre's scenery and properties, although some of the wardrobe and most of the music was saved. He estimated his loss at $2,000 to $3,000 (without insurance). This fire, according to contemporary newspaper accounts, was the worst in Providence in more than fifty years.

Throughout its history, the Providence Museum followed no specific policy regarding choice of material. The repertoire was eclectic in extreme, frequently offering complex bills of as many as four plays and numerous entr'actes in one evening. On several occasions four separate performances were given between 10 a.m. and 10 p.m. Plays received brief runs, frequently no more than one night, with repeats during a season (or several seasons) commonplace. A number of productions were popular enough to run for several nights. During the first season, the longest run was four consecutive nights for *Aethiop; or, The Child in the Desert*; the most popular pieces during the second season were *The Naiad Queen, Satan in Paris,* and *Rockwood; or, The Highwayman,* although none of these plays were presented more than a few nights. *The Naiad Queen* was revived for the third season. During the fourth season popular pieces included *Captain Kyd* and *The Winter's Tale.* The fifth season marked the first successful long run in the Museum's history, thirty-three performances of H.J. Conway's *Uncle Tom's Cabin.*

Forbes hired a permanent company each season. Several actors became local favorites and appeared each season. Few prominent names were regular company members; the major exceptions were John Drew, the elder, and Joe Cowell. Mrs. Forbes was the company's major leading lady, although Mrs. George Mossop, who became Mrs. Drew and later the important manageress of the Arch Street Theatre in Philadelphia, appeared regularly for two seasons (1849–51) and as a guest artist in 1852 along with her new husband. The list of guest stars appearing at the Museum is impressive. Among the better-known performers were Junius Brutus Booth (his son Edwin appeared as Titus to his father's Brutus on December 21, 1850), Kate and Ellen Bateman, William Warren, Jr., Mr. and Mrs. Barney Williams, Fanny Wallack, George Vandenhoff, T.D. Rice, Anna Cora Mowatt, Lola Montez, Clara Maeder, Mr. and Mrs. John Gilbert, George L. Fox, Julia Dean, Fanny Davenport, Charlotte Cushman, F.S. Chanfrau, Gustavus V. Brooke, and Madame Celeste. Lesser known guest stars included Mrs. Warner, Julia Turnbull, Lysander Thompson, George Spear, Mrs. Sinclair, J. R. Scott, Joseph Proctor, C. Dibdin Pitt, Charlotte and John Nickinson, J. A. Neafie, J. E. Murdoch, Mrs. C. Mestayer, Robert Jones, Anne Hathaway, Mrs. Frost, Sir William Don, Susan and Kate Denin, Anna Cruise, McKean Buchanan, Jr., J. B. Booth, Jr., W. H. Bland, Julia Bennett, George H. Barrett and Miss Barrett, Mr. and Mrs. J. P. Adams, H. L. Bateman, Mrs. Farren, Emma Fitzpatrick, Wyzeman F. Marshall, J. H. McVicker, J. H. Oxley, and Julia Pelby. Guest dancers and singers included Mr. Collins, Mr. Szollosy, Madam de Margueritte,

Mr. Alleyn, M. Durand, Mlle. Ciocca, M. Carese, and Mlle. Blangy. Novelties were always popular and frequent, including the Seguin Opera Troup; the Rousset Ballet Troupe with John Sefton; Redmon Ryan and the London Pantomimists (Agnes Raymond and Messrs. Evian, Lake, Davis, Stone); the Penobscot Indians; the Martinetti Troupe (with M. Ellsler); Herr Kist and his son Valentine (gymnasts); Harris and his Arabian horse Kossuth; the Franconi Troupe with J. F. O'Connell, the tatooed man; Irish dancers; S. Lee and his cannonball feats; Mr. Miller, a pyramid and bottle balancer; and E. T. Backus, violinist; the Fakir of Brama, an oriental magician; W. R. Derr and his Mexican coursers Abdel Kader and El Hyder; Coney and his dogs Hector and Yankee (with E. F. Taylor and Master E. Coney); Herr Cline, a tightrope walker; and E. Blanchard and his dogs Hector and Bruin.

After the Providence Museum burned, George A. Howard built Forbes' Theatre on the same site and opened it September 6, 1854, under Forbes' management. The company continued much as it had previously until April 28, 1858. In 1855 Edwin Forrest made his first appearance in Providence in eleven years. Other notable stars in this period included E.L. Davenport, Fanny Vining, Charlotte Crampton, J. W. Wallack, Maggie Mitchell, Lola Montez, Charlotte Cushman, the Drews, and F. S. Chanfrau. The Panic of 1857 ultimately forced the closing of the theatre, no star could fill the house, and Forbes lost all of his savings. Forbes Theatre remained vacant for several months, and the edifice finally burned on the evening of November 15, 1858. A new building, called the Phoenix (157 Westminster Street) and containing a theatre known as the Academy of Music, was erected on the same site.

PERSONNEL

Management: William C. Forbes, lessee and manager (1848–53); H. B. Matteson, treasurer (1849–50); W.A. Arnold, treasurer (1850–53).

Scene Painters: G. Curtis (1848); James Lamb (1851); J.B. White (1851–52).

Orchestra Leaders: W. F. Marshall (1848–52); H. Edkhardt (1852–53); G. Yonkers (1853).

Actors and Actresses: Miss C. A. Adams; Miss M. Allen; James (?) Anderson; A. Andrews; Isabella Andrews; J. Arlin; G. A. Bancroft; J. B. Barry; Mons. Bouvay; Mr. Bowman; *E.W. Bradbury* (1850–53); Mr. Bradshaw; Mr. Braithwaite; Miss Carman; Miss Carpenter; Mr. Carter; *W.B. Chapman* (1850–51); Miss Clarke; Mr. Clarke; H. Cowell; *Joseph Cowell* (1848–49); Mr. Cunningham; *Gertrude Dawes* (1848–50, 1851–52); *John Drew*, the elder (1849–52); *John Dunn* (1853); Miss Eberie; Miss C. Emmons; Miss E. Emmons; *A.W. Fenno*; H. W. Finn; Mr. Fish; Mr. Fiske; *William Forbes* (1848–53); *Mrs. William Forbes* (1848–53); Miss George; *W. R. Goodall* (1852–53); *J. D. Grace* (1851–53); Mary Ann Graham; Miss Granice; Mr. Greene; Mr. Gregg; Mr. Gregory; Mr. Hamilton; *Charles (J. G.) Hanly* (1851–52); Frank Hardenbergh; J. H. Harly; Mrs. Hathaway; Mr. Howard; Mrs. Howard; C. W. Hunt (1848–50); *Mrs. C. W. Hunt* (1848–53); Miss Isabella;

S.D. Johnson; Mr. Jones; *Mrs. Melinda Jones* (1851–52); H.C. Jordan; Miss Julien; E. F. Keach; Mr. Keene; Miss F. Kendall; Miss R. Kendall; Miss Kimberly; *Mrs. Kinlock* (1848–50, 1852–53); *Georgiana Kinlock* (1848–50, 1852–53); Mr. Kneap; S. Lake; *Miss Lemair* (1851–53); *Miss Julia Leonard* (1849–50, 1853); H. Linden; Mr. Macdonald; O. L. Marshall; Mr. Martin; Mr. Matthews; Mr. McClellan; John McCormick; Mr. McGowan; Mr. McGregor; *Mr. Meeker* (1848–53); *Emily Mestayer* (1850–51); Julia Miles; Mr. Minot; Mr. Moore; Peter Morris; Miss Morse; Mr. Mortimer; *Mrs. George Mossop*, later *Mrs. John Drew* (1849–51, 1852); Mrs. Munroe; Mr. Munson; Mr. Myers; Mrs. Myers; Mrs. Ollier; D.S. Palmer (1848–51); Master Pardey; *H. O. Pardey* (1849–51, 1852–53); Sarah Pentland; A. R. Phelps; Mrs. A. R. Phelps; H. B. Phillips; S. Plum; W.H.A. Pratt; Mr. Rae; Mrs. Rae; Mrs. E. Raymond; Mr. Read; Mrs. Reid; Mr. Rose; L. P. Roys; J. H. Ryder; T. Salmon; Mrs. Stickney; H. F. Stone; Mr. Strahan; Mr. Stuart; Mr. Studley; *Emma Taylor* (1853); Mr. Torrey; Mr. Townsend; Julia Vallee; *Edwin Varrey* (1849–52); Mrs. E. Varrey; Cecelia Waldegrave; *Emily Waldegrave* (1849–50, 1852–53); Mr. Ward; Mrs. W. Ward; Mr. Warden; Mr. Warner; Mr. Weston; *Charles A. Wharton* (1851–52); Mrs. Willis; J.(?) Willis; Miss Wilmot; John Winans; Mrs. Yeoman.

REPERTORY

Numerous repeats occurred each season at the Museum. Only initial presentations are listed.

1848–49: *The Stranger; Poor Pillicoddy; The Barrack Room; Austerlitz; or, The Cross of Gold; Bamboozling; Dove's Sacrifice; Thérèse; Two Strings to Your Bow; Nature and Philosophy; The Love Chase; A Dead Shot; The Heir-at-Law; The Young Widow; The Hunchback; Boots at the Swan; The Rendezvous; Clari; or, The Maid of Milan; The Jacobite; The Lady of Lyons; Uncle John; My Aunt; William Tell; The Hero of Switzerland; The Turn Out; London Assurance; My Wife's Second Floor; Lola Montez; Jane Shore; Sweethearts and Wives; The Turnpike Gate; Othello; My Handsome Husband; Charles II; Victorine; Virginius; The Pride of the Market; The Lady of Palermo; Damon and Pythias; Our Mary Anne; Lend Me Five Shillings; Mrs. White; Don Caesar de Bazan; Family Jars; My Young Wife and My Old Umbrella; The Miller's Maid; Naval Engagements; Macbeth; Spoil'd Child; Paul Pry; Pizarro; The Rivals; The Secret; Popping the Question; Romeo and Juliet; Catherine and Petruchio; Make Your Wills; The Iron Chest; Alma Mater; No Song, No Supper; The Wife; or, A Tale of Mantua; The School for Scandal; All about Love and Murder* (written by a native of Providence); *The Forest of Rosenwald; The Midnight Hour; Richard III, Miami; or, The Irish Immigrant; The Poor Gentleman; Fashion; Richelieu; Raising the Wind; The Soldier's Daughter; The New Footman; Box and Cox; John Jones; Nick of the Woods; The Review; La tour de Nesle; The Mummy; O'Neil; The Rent Day; The Incendiary; The Birthday; or, The Reconciliation; Valet de Sham; Swiss Cottage; In Place and Out of Place; Bachelor's Buttons; A Nabob for an Hour; Rob Roy; The Eaton Boy; Asmodeus; or, The Mysterious Patron; The Aethiop; or, The Child in the Desert; Speed the Plough; Queen's Own; Asmodeus; or, The Little Devil's Share; Presumptive Evidence; Murder Will Out; A Day after the Wedding; A Roland for an Oliver; Black Eyed Susan; Old and Young; Robert Macaire; Widow's Victim; The*

Mountaineers; Pretty John and Co.; The Married Rake; Mazeppa; Somebody Else; The Mysteries and Miseries of New York; Putnam; The Lottery Ticket; The Pleasant Neighbor; Timour, the Tartar; Valentine and Orson; Brutus; 'Twas I; or, The Truth a Lie; The Carpenter of Rouen; Why Don't She Marry?

1849–50: *Love's Sacrifice; Irish Tutor; The Pride of the Market; Make Your Wills; Charles II; The Waterman; My Handsome Husband; The Stranger; William Tell; The Wife; The Irish Engagement; The Lady of Lyons; The Object of Interest; The Love Chase; The Secret; Aline; The Rose of Killarney; A Nabob for an Hour; Ballet of Action; L'Illusion d'un peintre* (ballet); *The Dead Shot; The Barrack Room; La vivandiere* (ballet); *Popping the Question; Lovers' Quarrels; The Lottery Ticket; Giselle* (Act 1, ballet); *State Secrets; Box and Cox; A New Way to Pay Old Debts; Young England; Richard III; The Merchant of Venice; Othello; Shocking Events; King Lear; My Fellow Clerk; The Iron Chest; The Young Widow; Hamlet, Richelieu; Henry IV; Gisippus; or, The Forgotten Friend; Catherine and Petruchio; Oronaska; or, The Chief of the Mohawks; The Belle's Stratagem; Perfection; London Assurance; Loan of a Lover; Honey Moon; The Dumb Belle; As You Like It; Four Sisters; Faint Heart ne'er Won Fair Lady; Black Eyed Susan; Mazeppa; The Youthful Queen; Mike Martin: The Boston Highwayman; Cataract of the Ganges; White Horse of the Peppers; Rookwood; or, The Highwayman; Object of Interest; Dombey and Sons; Naval Engagements; Born to Good Luck; Rob Roy; Mill Girls of Lowell; The Artful Dodger; Floating Beacon; Naiad Queen; How to Pay the Rent; Slasher and Crasher; Water Witches; or, The Boat Club of Field's Point* (local farce); *Dream at Sea; Beauty and the Beast; The Nervous Man; Satan in Paris; The Eaton Boy; Romeo and Juliet; Love and Charity; The Gamester; The Hunchback; Fortunio; Perfection; Ion; A Day at Boulogne; Grist to the Mill; No!; The Irish Lion; The Follies of a Night; The Swiss Cottage; The Rifle Brigade; Mrs. White; Jane Shore; Spoil'd Child; A Wife's First Lesson; Forty Thieves; The Castle Spectre; Thérèse; The Pilot; The Golden Farmer; Victorine; Sweethearts and Wives; Mons. Jacques; The Heir-at-Law; Tom Noddy's Secret; The Scarlet Monster* (pantomime); *Your Life's in Danger; Mons. Duchalumeau* (pantomime); *Deux Milliners* (pantomime); *John Jones; Simpson and Co.; The Magic Trumpet* (ballet-pantomime); *The Married Rake; The Three Gladiators; Boots at the Swan; The Little Miseries of Human Life* (comic ballet); *The Two Friends; The Flying Dutchman; The Witch; or, A Legend of the Catskill; Wild Oats; The Conquest of Taranto; The Irish Dragoon; The Serious Family; The Haunted Yankee; The Laughing Hyena; Temptation; Rory O'More; Sketches in India; Julius Caesar; Nature and Philosophy; Don Caesar de Bazan; Lyar; Money; Venice Preserved; Look before You Leap; Hunting a Turtle; The Young Scamp; Cradle of Liberty; or, Boston Boys of '76; The Irish Tiger; The Prying Yankee; That Rascal Jack; Nipped in the Bud; The Lady of Lyons; Lucrezia Borgia; Evadne; A Day in Paris; Macbeth; The Venetian; or, The Bravo's Oath; Filial Love; Child of the Regiment; The King's Gardener; The Ransom; The Idiot Witness; Turning the Tables; Jack Sheppard; The Happy Man; The Poor Gentleman; The Omnibus; Lavater; Napoleon's Old Guard; Sudden Thoughts; Charles XII; Who Speaks First?; How to Pay the Rent; Raising the Wind; Old Honesty; Midnight Watch; Veteran of 1776; The Old English Gentleman; Mons. Tonson; The Serious Family; The School for Scandal; Irish Widow; Capt. Charlotte; Robert Macaire; The Rights of the Age* (by company member Pardey); *The Robber's Wife; Brutus; The Village Lawyer; In Place and Out of Place; The Limerick Boy; The Widow's*

Victim; Somnambula (opera); *Barber of Seville* (opera); *The Postilion of Longju-meau* (opera); *The Elixir of Love,* (opera); *Fra Diavolo* (opera); *The Bohemian Girl* (opera); *Cinderella* (opera); *Norma* (opera); *Olympic Revels; Douglas; Cousin Cherry; Delicate Ground; The Sentinel; Youthful Days of Richelieu; A Devilish Good Joke; Cecile; or, The Child of Mystery; Captain of the Watch; A Roland for an Oliver; The Carpenter of Rouen; The Bride of Lammermoor; The Boston Fire-man; Used Up; Tipperary Legacy; The Painter's Studio* (pantomime); *The Old Maids; The Village Barber* (pantomime); *The Rustic Bride; The Irish Post; The Fairy of the Golden Wheatsheaf* (pantomime); *The Youthful Queen; Teddy, the Tiler; Virginia Mummy; Jumbo Jum; His Last Legs; Othello; Foreign Prince; The Irish Haymaker; Jim Crow in London; Advice to Husbands; Mysterious Knockings; The Peacock and the Crow; The King's Own; The Brigand; Ouscousta; The Prophet of the Moor; Lend Me Five Shillings; Advice for Husbands; Agnes De Vere; Where There's a Will There's a Way; A Man without a Head; Lucille; A Story of the Heart; Providence as It Is and California as It Ought to Be; Aladdin; or, The Magic Lamp; Shocking Events; The Passing Cloud; The Brigand Chief; Mr. Torrey; Comedian Settlers* (new play by H.O. Pardey); *Young America; Six Degrees of Crime; The Two Gregories; Willful Murder; The Broken Sword; The Rochester Knockings; Forest Rose; Army and Navy; Mad as a March Hare; Maid of Munster; Don Juan* (pantomime).

1850–51: *Sweethearts and Wives; The Child of the Regiment; Advice to Husbands; Paul Pry; Kiss in the Dark; The Heir-at-Law; Young America; Jack Sheppard; State Secrets; Matrimony; Love in Livery; Perfection; Beauty and the Beast; Turning the Tables; Rosina Meadows; Milliner's Holiday; Friend; Waggles; Buy It, Dear; Es-meralda; Pride of the Market; Village Phantom; Follies of a Night; Kit Carson; Rookwood; Not to Be Done; Simpson and Co.; Mazeppa; Siege of Corinth; Willful Murder; Poor Pillicoddy; Mike Martin; Timour, the Tartar; Valentine and Orson; Putnam; The Wizard Steed; Tom and Jerry; John Dobbs; Aladdin; Sudden Thoughts; Hamlet; Macbeth; Slasher and Crasher; Richard III; The Savage and the Maiden; Othello; Lady of Lyons; Richelieu; Hamlet; The Merchant of Venice; Catherine and Petruchio; Pizarro; P. P.; The Quadroon of New Orleans; Your Life's in Danger; London Assurance; Deaf as a Post; Joan of Arc; The Highlander's Dream; Cherry and Fair Star; The Double-Bedded Room; The Old Guard; An Object of Interest; The Inconstant; William Thompson; Town and Country; Raising the Wind; Laugh When You Can; Tom Cringle; Black Eyed Susan; Honey Moon; The Fireman's Daughter; Wallace; A Bold Stroke for a Husband; Used Up; Lucille, or, The Story of the Heart; Ion; The Windmill; Daughter of the Stars; Grist to the Mill; Money; The Ladies Club; Sketches in India; The Review; The Hunchback; Romeo and Juliet; Love; Mose; or, A Glance at New York; Hint to Husbands; Mons. Jacques; Geraldi; Lavater; The Omnibus; The Veteran of '76; Who Speaks First?; The Won-derful Woman; Mons. Tonson; The val d'Andorme; Castle of Linburg; The Magic Shirt; Capt. Charlotte; Domestic Poultry; Born to Good Luck; The Irish Tutor; Aline; Rory O'More; Irish Lion; The Golden Farmer; Irish Tiger; The Robber's Wife; The Two Friends; Teddy, the Tiler; King Lear; The King and I; A New Way to Pay Old Debts; Brutus; Naiad Queen; The Woodman Spell; The Dumb Singers; George Barnwell; Irish Emigrant; The Robbers; My Precious Betsey; Mill Girls of Lowell; The Violet; The Hero of Scotland; The Irish Ambassador; The Sentinel; Shocking Events; The French Spy; Thérèse; The Stranger; How to Pay the Rent;*

Love's Sacrifice; Adrienne; Box and Cox; The Three Cuckoos; Mariendorpt; Isabella; Mysterious Knockings; Damon and Pythias; Nick of the Woods; Irish Haymaker; William Tell; Esmeralda; Soldier's Daughter; Love Chase; Clari; Wizard of the Wave; Irish Engagement; The Post of Honour; The Rent Day; Ondine; The Wife; The Falls of Clyde; Anti-Bacchus (by H.O. Parkey); *The Denouncer; or, The Seven Clerks; Demetri; The Broken Sword; The Star of Mexico; The Trumpeter's Wedding; The Turn Out; The Dumb Girl of Genoa; Satan in Paris; Cousin Cherry; The Eton Boy; Invincibles; Agnes De Vere; Alarming Sacrifice; Husband of the Heart; Rough Diamond; Day in Paris; Our Gal; Limerick Boy; Jenny Lind in America; Paddy, the Piper; Sprigs of Ireland; Ireland as It Is; In Place and Out of Place; Rights of Women; The Bashful Irishman; Irish Tiger; Kate Kearney; Rip Van Winkle; Yankee Speculation; My Thumping Legacy; Much Ado about Nothing; King of the Commons; Husband of My Heart; Napoleon; Mose; The Cabin Boy; Delicate Ground; Sam Patch; Forest Rose; Happy Results; Travelling by Telegraph; Freedom Suit; Widow's Victim; Yankee Duelist; Rough and Ready; Bashful Lovers; The Atlantic Is Safe; People and the Tiger; Yankee Pedlar; Mohammed; Old Valet; Don Caesar de Bazan; Factory Girl; Betsy Baker; The Warlock of the Glen; Fortune's Whim; Shandy Maguire; Alive and Kicking; The Weathercock; Crown Prince; The Rendezvous; Fazio; The World's Fair; The Floating Beacon; Rascal Jack; The Somnambulist; The Omnibus; Shaker Lovers; No!; Laecinna; The Roman Consel* (by Isaac C. Pray of Boston); *Morning Call; The Spirit of the Fountain; Barney O'Rourke; Why Don't She Marry?; The Rivals; Forty and Fifty; The School for Scandal; Speed the Plough; Uncle John; The Organist; Poor Gentleman; Naval Engagements; Doctor Dilworth; Love in a Maze; Siege of Monterey; Scourge of the Ocean; Henry IV; Married Life; Wife's First Lesson; Kill or Cure; Hunting a Turtle; Werner; Momentous Question; That Odious Capt. Cutter; Matrimony; The Toodles; Dumb Belle; Model of a Wife; Mose in California; New York as It Is; Idiot Witness; Barber; Amateur; His Last Legs; Maid of Munster; Mysteries and Miseries of New York; The Lady and the Devil; Is He Jealous?; Raby Rattler; The Bloomer Rig; School of Reform; Village Tale; Woman's Tricks; All That Glitters Is Not Gold; Merry Monarch.*

1851–52: *Honey Moon; Mr. and Mrs. White; Love's Sacrifice; My Fellow Clerk; All That Glitters Is Not Gold; Boots at the Swan; Idiot Witness; Cherry and Fair Star; Pizarro; The Drunkard; Rendezvous; The Hunchback; Sergeant's Wedding; Lady of Lyons; The Wandering Minstrel; As You Like It; The Loan of a Lover; The Stranger; Don Caesar de Bazan; Guy Mannering; Family Ties; Sam Patch in France; Hue and Cry; Wool Dealer; Home of the West; Followed by Fortune; Yankee in Time; People's Candidate; Armand; Faint Heart ne'er Won Fair Lady; Thérèse; Captain Kyd; State Secrets; Madelaine; Dearest Elizabeth; Rough Diamond; Paddy, the Piper; Limerick Boy; Ireland as It Is; Irish Tiger; Bryan O'Lynn; Teddy, the Tiler; Jenny Lind; The Yacht Race; Irish Tutor; Shandy Maguire; The Haunted Chamber; Rory O'More; Irish Lion; The Pilgrim of Love; Fortune's Whims; The Happy Man; Born to Good Luck; Cousin Cherry; The Irish Post; Alive and Kicking; Swigs of Ireland; Woman's Rights; Ladies Battle; Hypochondriac; Grimshaw, Bagshaw, and Bradshaw; Midnight Watch; Forest Rose; Romeo and Juliet; Richard III; The Merchant of Venice; Othello; Apostate; Memoirs of the D***L; Ole Bull; Naval Engagements; Innkeeper's Daughter; Painter's Illusion* (ballet); *Diana and Endymion* (ballet); *Dumb Belle; Mysterious Lady; Valet de Sham; La gitana* (ballet);

The Sea; La Zinigarella (ballet); *Damon and Pythias; The Adopted Child; Macbeth; Black Eyed Susan; Richelieu; Shoemaker of Toulouse; The Married Rake; Mazeppa; Alp, the Renegade; Eagle Eye; The Young Widow; Turn Out; Putnam; Tom Cringle; The Blind Boy; Why Don't She Marry?; Cool as a Cucumber; Lola Montez; Iron Chest; Esmeralda; King's Own; Alpine Maid; Spirit of the Fountain; Buy It, Dear; Venice Preserved; How to Pay the Rent; The Winter's Tale; Henry VIII; Fire Eater; Orphan of Paris; Married Bachelor; Ion; Spectre Bridegroom; Fazio; Jane Shore; Robinson Crusoe; Agnes De Vere; Perfection; Hamlet; Nature and Philosophy; Clari; Catherine and Petruchio; The Dumb Girl of Genoa; Woman; The School for Scandal; His Last Legs; The Bronze Horse; The Cattle Stealer; Forty and Fifty; Christine of Sweden; Watch Dog; The Elopement; A Cheap Excursion; Poor Dog Trey; Circumstantial Evidence; The Dumb Man of Manchester; Fisherman and His Dogs; The Barrack Room; Charles II; Queen's Own; The Letter Carrier's Dog; The Last Shilling; The Forest of Bondy; I've Eaten My Friend; Napoleon's Order; Time Tries All; Return from Moscow; Irish Artist; Much Ado about Nothing; The Wife; More Blunders Than One; Bride of Lammermoor; Wedding Breakfast; Mohammed; Oralloossa; William Tell; Rough Diamond; Barney Rourke; Harolde; The Gipsies' Haunt; The Spanish Lover; London Assurance; A New Way to Pay Old Debts; Swallowing a Policeman; The Last Days of Pompeii; My Young Wife and My Old Umbrella; Un jour de carneval à Seville* (ballet); *Daughter; or, The Blind Father; Mother Bailey; Moll Pitcher; Valeria; Ninth Statue; Wept of the Wish-Ton-Wish; Taming a Tartar; Virginius; Lord Darnley; Irish Immigrant; Who Is She?; Paul Pry; The Eton Boy; My Friend in the Straps; Tender Precautions; The Two Bonnycastles; Handy Andy; Miseries of Human Life; The Good-for-Nothing; Green Bushes; St. Mary's Eve; The Mysterious Stranger; Gentleman of Lyons; Shocking Events; Rob Roy; Ingomar; Somebody Else; Is He Jealous?; The Irish Ambassador; Nervous Man; Irish Genius; The Wrong Passenger; Butcher's Dog of Ghent; The Ourang Outang; The Dumb Slave; Planter's Pest; or, The Brazilian Ape; The Foulah Slave; Lick Her Bill; Queen's Husband; Sixteen String Jack; The Pilgrim of Love; In and Out of Place; Irish Broom Maker; Ireland and America; It Is the Custom of the Country; Evil Eye; Box and Cox; Lady of the Lake; Nick of the Woods; Slasher and Crasher; Lucille; The Windmill; Pet of the Petticoat; The Wife's Revenge; Captain of the Watch; A Day after the Wedding; Robert Macaire; Luke, the Labourer; Masaniello; Rent Day; The Statue Lovers* (comic ballet); *The Demon Jester; Kossuth in Providence; A Roland for an Oliver; Castle Spectre.*

1852–53: *Faint Heart ne'er Won Fair Lady; Sketches in India; Loan of a Lover; All That Glitters Is Not Gold; Wild Duck; Rob Roy; The Hunchback; Your Life's in Danger; The Love Chase; Virginia Mummy; All the World's a Stage; The Lady of Lyons; A Dead Shot; The Wife; Evadne; Love; A Morning Call; The Wrecker's Daughter; Ingomar; As You Like It; Armand; The Stranger; The Secret; Ion; Marie de Meranne; Much Ado about Nothing; King René's Daughter; Fashion; Soldier's Daughter; Thérèse; Victorine; Fish vs. Fight; Peter Wilkins; Ladies' Battle; Who Speaks First?; Nature's Nobleman; Highway Robbery; London Assurance; State Secrets; Robert Macaire; Rough Diamond; Wool Dealer; As You Like It; Turning the Tables; Love's Sacrifice; Double-Bedded Room; Actress of Padua; Honey Moon; Romeo and Juliet; The Baker's Daughter; The Widow's Victim; A New Way to Pay Old Debts; Mountain Maid; The Merchant of Venice; Hamlet; Macbeth; 'Twas I; Othello; The Greek Slave; Spoil'd Child; Young Couple; Alpine Maid; Richard III;*

The Good-for-Nothing; Why Don't She Marry?; Her Royal Highness; Bombastes Furioso; Naval Engagements; The Willow Copse; The Lottery Ticket; Wanted: 1,000 Spirited Young Milliners; Pizarro; Adopted Child; The Carpenter of Rouen; Black Eyed Susan; Richelieu; Damon and Pythias; Charles II; Nick of the Woods; Catherine and Petruchio; Hamlet; Forty Thieves; My Fellow Clerk; Money; Married and Settled; The Drunkard; Perfection; Corsican Brothers; Caught in His Own Trap; The Broken Sword; The Wandering Boys; A Youth Who Never Saw a Woman; Young Scamps; Douglas; Little Devil's Share; Fazio; The Young Brigands; Gil Blas; Life's Morning; Noon and Night; The Idiot Witness; Nix; The Cabman; Jack Sheppard; Lillian: The Show Girl; The Winter's Tale; Anne Blake; Henry VIII; Jane Shore; Castle Spectre; Tom Noddy's Secret; Uncle Tom's Cabin (33 performances); *She Wou'd and She Wou'd Not; Satan in Paris; His Last Legs; The Heir-at-Law; Miseries of Human Life; Irish Tutor; The Irish Immigrant; Delicate Ground; Born to Good Luck; John, Jean, and Jonathan; Married Rake; Joan of Arc; Poor Soldiers; The People's Lawyer; P. P.; or, Man and Tiger; Belle's Stratagem; Isabella; The Child of the Regiment; The Forest of Bondy; Children in the Wood; Rascal Jack; The Wandering Minstrel; Napoleon's Old Guard; Mr. and Mrs. White; My Precious Betsey; The Jacobite; Two Bonnycastles; Charcoal Burner; Kabria; or, The Wooden Shoemaker; Box and Cox; Young Brigand; Richard Ye Third; Follies of a Night; Old Folks at Home; Nature and Philosophy; Toodles; Momentous Question; Willful Murder; Writing on the Wall; Wife's First Lesson; Old Heads and Young Hearts; Luke, the Labourer; Venice Preserved; Phenomenon; The Gamester; The Jewess; The School for Scandal; Lend Me Five Pounds; The Last Nail; The School of Reform; Fortune's Frolic; The Yorkshire Brother; A Roland for an Oliver; Love's Frailties; Town and Country; Speed the Plough; Yorkshire Bumpkins; Miller's Maid; New Footman; Baa! Baa! Baa!; Floating Beacon; The Spectre Bridegroom; The Golden Farmer; The Millers* (comic ballet); *The Old Guard; Two of the B'hoys; Sketches in India; Catarina* (ballet); *He's Not a-miss; Giselle* (ballet); *The Siamese Twins; Separate Maintenance; Beacon of Death; Ingomar; Julius Caesar; Virginia Mummy; Putnam; Mazeppa; Dick Turpin; Valentine and Orson; Paul Pry; The Talisman; Deaf as a Post.*

1853: *Widow's Victim; The Young King; My Precious Betsey; The Gamester; Phenomenon; Love's Sacrifice; Pizarro; The Talisman; Follies of a Night; Box and Cox; Idiot Witness; Thérèse; Married Rake; Wandering Minstrel; Go to Bed, Tom; Uncle Tom's Cabin; Wool Dealer; Toodles; Hamlet; Grandmother's Pet; The Young Couple; Macbeth; Her Royal Highness; Spoil'd Child; Paul Pry; Spectre Bridegroom; Richard III; Nature and Art; The Merchant of Venice; Day after the Fair; State Secrets; William Tell; Ingomar; Two Bonnycastles; Used Up; Rough Diamond; The Jacobite; All That Glitters Is Not Gold; The Serious Family; Virginia Mummy; Make Your Will; Sweet Hearts and Wives; Poor Pillicoddy; The Orphan Boys; La sylphide; Wild Oats; The Good-for-Nothing; Married Life; The Creole; Othello; Bertram; Peacock and the Crow; Separate Maintenance; Sketches in India; Jim Crow in London; Paris and London; To Paris and Back for One Pound; The Woman I Adore.*

BIBLIOGRAPHY

Published Sources: Charles Blake, *An Historical Account of the Providence Stage* (Providence, R.I., 1868); George O. Willard, *History of the Providence Stage* (Providence, R.I., 1891); *Providence Daily Journal* (1848–53).

Archival Sources: The Library of the Rhode Island Historical Society in Providence has several useful scrapbooks of clippings, histories of Providence in manuscript, and the texts for "The Streets of the City" by Florence Parker Simister (in particular volume 1, June 2, 1952–May 29, 1953, p. 191).

Don B. Wilmeth

R

RICE'S THEATRE COMPANY. Rice's Theatre Company, Chicago, was organized in 1847 by John B. Rice, an actor-manager from Buffalo, New York. Rice's Theatre was the first building in Chicago constructed specifically as a theatre. Built by one of the city's leading architects, Alderman Updike, the building was situated on the south side of Randolph Street, just east of Dearborn Street. A June 1847 issue of the *Chicago Democrat* described the theatre: "The internal arrangements of the new theatre, now nearly completed, are admirable. A full view of the stage can be obtained from every part of the house, and the plan of the old Coliseum has been followed. The boxes are elegantly furnished and fitted up with carpets and settees, rather resembling a boudoir, or private sitting room in a gentleman's house, than an apartment in a place of public resort. The building has been completed in six weeks" (quoted in Andreas, 1:484). The theatre opened on June 28, 1847, with *The Four Sisters,* a play featuring a quadruple role, starring Mrs. Hunt (later Mrs. George Mossop and then Mrs. John Drew) and guest artist Dan Marble.

The opening of Rice's Theatre marked the ending of a seven-year dearth of dramatic fare in Chicago. The city had had a somewhat permanent company, the Illinois Theatrical Company, from 1837 to 1839, and several traveling entertainments, but Rice was the first to sustain a dramatic company successfully for a lengthy period. Chicago in the 1840s was still a boom town—the failure of the Illinois Theatrical Company was due to too small a population (4,800 in 1839) to support a theatre. But by 1849 the population had swelled to 17,000, and a permanent dramatic company became not only possible but profitable. This is not to say that Rice met with immediate success. Many of Chicago's citizens still harbored prejudices against the theatrical profession, and critics had to assure the ladies of the city that in the new theatre, "few of these evils are attendant" (*The Journal*, July 10,

1847). Although the first season proved to be moderately successful in financial terms, Rice doubted the city's ability to support a theatre year round. At the close of the first season, and for several seasons thereafter, he took the company to Milwaukee for their winter season.

Much of Rice's success in Chicago was due to the engagement of national stars. The list of artists appearing at Rice's Theatre is long and includes prominent names such as Dan Marble, Julia Dean, T. D. Rice (no relation), James E. Murdoch, Edwin Forrest, Junius Brutus Booth, dancer Julia Turnbull, the Ravel Family, Lola Montez, John Brougham, E. L. Davenport, C. W. Couldock, J. Wallack, Cordelia Howard, and Maggie Mitchell. Success can also be attributed to a nightly change of bill—typically, two plays and several divertissements were offered each evening—and to Rice's willingness occasionally to forego more serious endeavors in favor of vaudeville, minstrelsy (Christy's made their Chicago debut at Rice's in 1847), ballet, or even opera. Rice introduced ballet to the city in May 1849 with the engagement of a European company, the Monplaisir Ballet Troupe (also known as the French Ballet Company). A less successful experiment was the introduction of opera to the city on July 29, 1850. A company featuring Eliza Brienti, Mr. Guibelei, Mr. Manvers, and a local chorus and orchestra was engaged for a production of *La sonnambula*. Ironically, low attendance on the second night proved a blessing, for halfway through the performance, a fire from a nearby stable spread to the theatre, completely destroying it. Rice immediately moved his company to Milwaukee, where they played with mild success until January 1851. Following this season, the company ceased their Milwaukee performances.

While the company was in Milwaukee, Rice built his second Chicago theatre on Dearborn, between Randolph and Washington streets. The new theatre, designed by architect J. M. Van Osdel, measured 80 by 100 feet and was constructed of brick with galvanized iron cornices at a cost of $11,000. Rice's second theatre opened on February 3, 1851, with the complete company singing the "Star Spangled Banner" and three plays: *Love in Humble Life, Captain of the Watch,* and *The Dumb Belle.* This second theatre enjoyed great success until Rice's retirement from the stage in 1856. The management of the company fell to J. G. Hanley, who met with fierce competition from McVicker's Theatre when it opened in 1857. Rice's theatre struggled until 1861, at which time Rice found it most profitable to convert the building to business property.

Rice is worthy of a brief biographical note, since he held varied and (for his time) unusual careers. Born in Easton, Maryland, in 1809, he made his theatrical debut when he was about twenty-one as the Uncle in *George Barnwell* at the Boston Theatre. He toured extensively as an actor, going as far as the West Indies, before organizing his first stock company in Bangor, Maine. In 1837 he married Mary Ann Warren, daughter of William Warren, and the couple played together as stars until 1839. In 1839 Rice became manager of the companies at the Buffalo and Albany museums and remained as such until he began his Chicago career. John B. Rice did not retire from public life when he retired from the theatre in 1856. As the Union party candidate, he was elected mayor of Chicago in 1865 and reelected to that office in 1867. Having served the city well, he was elected to the Congress of the United States in 1872, a position he held until his death in 1874.

PERSONNEL

Management: John B. Rice, manager (1847–56) and proprietor (1847–61); M. Conklin, treasurer (1848); Perry Marshall, treasurer (1849) and lessee (1857); U. P. Harris, treasurer (1857); J. G. Hanley, manager (1857); William McFarland, lessee and manager (1857).

Musical Direction: C. Brookton (1848); Mr. LeBrun (1851).

Scenic Design and Technicians: J. D. Beckwith (1848–49); Mr. Beaver (1849–51).

Stage Manager: N. B. Clarke (1848–49); J. H. McVicker (early part of season, 1851); William McFarland (1856).

Actors and Actresses: Mrs. Altemus (1857); Mr. Archer (1851); J. W. Burgess (1848); F. S. Buxton (1852); James Carroll (1847); N. B. Clarke (1849); Mr. Clifford (1848); Mrs. Clifford (1849); E. S. Conner (1847); Mrs. Farren (1852); Mrs. Frary (1852); Mr. Gilbert (1851); Mrs. Gilbert (1851); J. Greene (1848); Mrs. J. Greene (1848); Mr. Hanley (1852); Mrs. Hanley (1852); Mr. Hann (1851); Edwin Harris (1847); Miss Homer (1847); Mrs. Hunt, later Mrs. Mossop and Mrs. Drew (1847); Mrs. Linden (1857); Mrs. Marble (1852); Miss Mary Marble (1853); Helen Matthews (1849); Mr. McFarland (1856); Mrs. McFarland (1856); Mr. McMillan (1852); James H. McVicker (1848–51); William Meeker (1847); Jerry Merrifield (1847); Mrs. Jerry Merrifield (1847); George Mossop (1847); Samuel Myers (1852); Mrs. Pennoyer (1857); G. W. Phillimore (1847); Mrs. Coleman Pope (1849); Mrs. Price (1848); Mrs. Putnam (1852); Mrs. J. B. Rice (1847); John B. Rice (1847–56); George Ryer (1847); Mr. Ryner (1852); Mrs. Ryner (1852); D. Sanford (1848); H. T. Stone (1852); William Taylor (1848); Miss Willis (1848); C. H. Wilson (1848); Mr. Wright (1852); Miss Woodbury (1857).

REPERTORY

1847: *Four Sisters; The Backwoodsman; The Stranger; Sam Patch in France; Somebody Else; Grist to the Mill; Family Ties; The Forest Rose; Jonathan Ploughboy; Black Eyed Susan; The Mummy; The Day after the Wedding; Lucille; Jumbo Jum; Othello; Wife; Youthful Queen; The Love Chase; Clari: The Maid of Milan; The Lady of Lyons; Uncle Sam; Jane Shore; The Hunchback; Ion; The Rendezvous; Hamlet; An Object of Interest; Romeo and Juliet; My Neighbor's Wife; The Omnibus; Pizarro; Perfections; Richelieu; The Maid of Croissey; The Dead Shot; Asea: or, The Ocean Child; Thérèse; Austerlitz.*

1848: *Sam Patch in France; Hunting a Turtle; The Wool Dealer; Hue and Cry; My Neighbor's Wife; The People's Candidate; The Beacon of Death; Home in the West; The Forest Rose; Fortune's Frolic; Tom Cringle's Leg; The Backwoodsman; A Pleasant Neighbor; Time Tries All; Fortune's Roughhead; Jonathan in England;*

Black Eyed Susan; A Yankee in Time; The Hunchback; Evadne; Fazio; The Wife; Faint Heart ne'er Won Fair Lady; The Irish Tutor; The Married Rake; Lady of Lyons; The Wrecker's Daughter; Douglas; Thérèse; or, The Orphan of Geneva; The Stranger; The Soldier's Daughter; Grist to the Mill; The Young Scamp; The Four Sisters; Satan in Paris; Valentine and Orson; The Jewess; Othello; Hamlet; Eton Boy; Richelieu; Virginius; Raising the Wind; Jack Cade; Make Your Will; Metamora; The Gladiator; King Lear; Fortunio and His Seven Gifted Servants; The Happy Man; The Follies of a Night; Lucille; Paul Pry; A Wife for a Day; Mons. Tonson; The King's Gardener; Yankee Duelist; Yankee in Time; New Notions; A New Way to Pay Old Debts; Fox and Geese; The Cavalier of England in 1840; A Happy Pair; Genevieve; Kill or Cure; The Dramatist; The Mummy; A Night of Expectation; Macbeth; Honey Moon; The Marriage Spectre; Richard III; The Wag of Windsor; Macbeth; The Merchant of Venice; The Apostate; The Lady and the Devil; The Limerick Boy; Handsome Husband; Teddy, the Tiler; Glance at New York; Born to Good Luck; The Irish Lion; A Bashful Irishman; The Spectre Bridegroom; Lucrezia Borgia; A Kiss in the Dark; The Wife; An Object of Interest.

1849: *Day after the Fair; Diana's Revenge; My Wife's Second Floor; A Capital Match; My Wife's Out; Duel in the Dark; Who's Your Friend?; Romeo and Juliet; Evadne; The Hunchback; Pizarro; Catherine and Petruchio; The Eagle Eye; The Wild Steed of the Prairie; Mazeppa; A Soldier's Daughter; Born to Good Luck; The Limerick Boy; A Glance at New York; Paddy's Trip to Ireland; Springs of Ireland; Richelieu; The Lady of Lyons; Richard III; The Merchant of Venice; Hamlet; Honey Moon; Isabelle; or, A Woman's Life; Handsome Husbands; Gilderoy; The Carpenter of Rouen; Wreck Ashore; Duchess de la Vallière; A Roland for an Oliver; Castle Spectre; The Valet de Sham; Wallace; The Hero of Scotland; The Pride of Aloodos; Paul Pry; The Bride of Lammermoor; Man about Town; Paul Jones; Hofer; The Wrecker's Daughter; Mr. and Mrs. Peter White; Lucrezia Borgia; Simpson and Co.; Matrimony Money; One Hour at the Carnival; The Robbers; William Tell; Wine Works Wonders; Perfection; Macbeth; The Taming of the Shrew; Your Life's in Danger; Walter Raymond; or, Lovers of Accomac; The Dramatist; Guy Mannering; Charles XII; Two Georges.*

1850: *Lady of Lyons; Swiss Swains; Money; Nipped in the Red; Othello; Perfection; Charles II; Sandy Jones; My Wife's Come; Rob Roy; The Stranger; My Aunt; Hamlet; Cousin Lambkins; Slasher and Crasher; Richelieu; The Robbers; Your Life's in Danger; Wine Works Wonders; William Tell; The Critic; Wild Oats; Jannette and Janot; A Day after the Wedding; Don Caesar de Bazan; A Glance at New York; The Shoemaker of Toulouse; Sam Slick: The Clock Maker; Celestial Empire; Happy Results; The Wool Dealer; Green Mountain Boy; Jonathan in England; The Queen's Fate; Chloroform; or, Chicago in 1850; Isabelle; Victoria's Fete; Kaspar Hauser; Stage Struck Yankee; Militia Training; Richard III; A Trip to Scotland; A New Way to Pay Old Debts; Bertram; Sketches in India; Robert Tyke; Catherine and Petruchio; Macbeth; Hunting a Turtle; Mose in California; Zanthe; Black Eyed Susan; Three Thieves of Marseilles; Born to Good Luck; Irish Ambassador; Teddy, the Tiler; The Nervous Man; A Seaside Story; Wilful Murder; King and Deserter; The Golden Farmer; Maid of Croissey; My Poll and Partner Joe; Hofer; Michael: The Maniac Lover; The French Spy; Our Gal; Irish Lion; Romeo and Juliet; Simpson and Co.; Honey Moon; The Gamester; Uncle Sam; The School for Scandal; The Hunchback; La sonnambula.*

1851: *Love in Humble Life; The Water Witch; Dumb Belle; Victorine; or, Dream on It; Simpson and Co.; Sudden Thoughts; The Serious Family; Captain of the Watch; The Stranger; Lend Me Five Shillings; The Sleep Walker; The Brigand; The Lady of Lyons; The Ghost of My Uncle; The Widow's Victim; The Jewess; Charles VII; The People's Lawyer; or, Solon Shingle; The Wool Dealer; Sam Patch in France; Celestial Empire; A Yankee in Time; The People's Candidate; Family Ties; A Home in the West; Followed by Fortune; Cinderella; or, The Fairy and the Little Glass Slipper; Rob Roy; Othello; The Rendezvous; Pizarro; Cousin Lambkin; The Broken Sword; Beauty and the Beast; Thérèse; or, The Orphan of Geneva; Lady of the Lake; Black Eyed Susan; How to Die for Love; The Married Rake; Guy Mannering; Forty Thieves; The Broken Sword; Richard III; William Tell; The Drunkard; Family Ties; The Spectre Bridegroom; The Carpenter of Rouen; The Beacon of Death; Gilderoy; The Blue Devils; Duchess de la Vaubalier; Ladies Beware; The Iron Chest; Tom Cringle's Leg; The Maid and the Magpie; The Jacobite; The Love Chase; Born to Good Luck; Cousin Cherry; The Irish Immigrant; The Wife; The Irish Tutor; The Hunchback; The Alarming Sacrifice; Fazio; The Irish Ambassador; Agnes de Vere; A Delicate Question; Satan in Paris; Betsy Baker; Lucrezia Borgia; My Friend on the Strap; Rough Diamonds; Follies of the Night; The New Footman; Faint Heart ne'er Won Fair Lady; Money; A Wandering Minstrel; A Thumping Legacy; The Robber's Wife; Does Your Mother Know You're Out?; Hamlet; New Way to Pay Old Debts; The Merchant of Venice; Macbeth; The Aloine Maid; Teddy, the Tiler; His Last Legs; How to Pay the Rent; The Wrong Passenger; The Happy Man; Wife Hunters; The Nervous Man; Charles II; Lola Montez; Jenny Lind in Chicago; The Spirit of the Fountain; The Fairy Lake; Masaniello; Edward III; The Dead Shot; The Witch Girl; No Song, No Supper; Robert Macaire; Jacques Strop; The Eton Boy; Wept of Wish-Ton-Wish; Stage Struck Sailor; Nick of the Woods; Seven Escapes; or, The Bride's Journey; A Kiss in the Dark; The Island of Calypso; Illusion; Jack Sheppard; The Bride's Journey; The Two B'hoys; The French Spy; A Glance at New York; Evadne; The Sea; or, The Ocean Child; Mr. and Mrs. White; Romeo and Juliet; Animal Magnetism; Love; or, The Countess and the Serf; Uncle Sam; Love's Sacrifice; Family Jars; Honey Moon; My Aunt; Money; Calaynos; The Windmill; Helen Lovett; The Love Chase; The Bath Road; She Stoops to Conquer; The Ladies' Battle; All That Glitters Is Not Gold; or, The Factory Girl; A Roland for an Oliver; London Assurance; Dream of the Sea; Box and Cox; The Apostate; A Tipperary Legend; King Lear; The Iron Chest; Wreck Ashore; The Elder Brother; Don Juan; Bluebeard; The Elder Brother; The Lady of the Lake; The Wandering Boys; Joe in London; The Young Scamp; Matteo Falerno; Little Devil; Ambition; Pirate of the Isle; Rob Roy; Spirit of the Fountain; Jack Sheppard; Red Rover; The Bohemian Gypsy Girl; Slasher and Crasher; Fall of Algiers; Tom and Jerry; Much Ado about Nothing; The Rivals; Loan of a Lover; The Wonder; The Belle's Stratagem; Perfection; The Housekeeper; Time Tries All; Black Eyed Susan; The Mistletoe Bough; Trials of Poverty; Don Caesar de Bazan; The Husband of Her Heart; Rent Day; The Heir-at-Law.*

1852: *Pizarro; The Bronze Horse; The Foundling of the Forest; Hungarian Freedom; Don Caesar de Bazan; Michael Earle; or, The Manic Lover; The Elder Brother; Fox and Geese; The Idiot Witness; Fazio; The Love Chase; The Wife; Jane Shore; The Lady of Lyons; Mazeppa; Rob Roy; Timour, the Tartar; The Carpenter of Rouen; The Merchant of Venice; Damon and Pythias; The Stranger; William*

Tell; A Serious Family; Putnam, the Iron Man; Grimshaw, Bagshaw, and Bradshaw; Rookwood; Swiss Cottage; The Young Widow; Luke, the Labourer; Chicago Firemen; Lochinvar; Sweethearts and Wives; The Alpine Maid; The Flying Dutchman; The Castle Spectre; Raymond and Agnes; The Forty Thieves; Werner; The Heir-at-Law; Cherry and Fair Star; Brutus; or, The Fall of Tarquin; Friends and Straps; The Patrician's Daughter; Leap Year; Fashion; Robert Emmett; The Widow's Victim; The Cricket on the Hearth; Tortesa, the Usurer; Sam Patch in France; Family Ties; Home in the West; A Serious Family; Mose in California; Happy Results; Celestial Empire; Money; Forest Rose; Times That Tried Us; A Glance at New York; The Ocean Child; Surgeon of Paris; The Pilot; Love's Sacrifice; Romeo and Juliet; The Climbing Boy; Lillian; The Showgirl; Honey Moon; Gil Blas; Nature and Philosophy; Ion; Idiot Witness; The Hunchback; The Brigand's Son; Pirates of the Isle; The Felon's Dream; Jack Sheppard in France; Wilful Murder; Richelieu; Hamlet; Richard III; Captain Copp; Black Eyed Susan; The Iron Chest; Student of Morlaix; The Winter's Tale; The Wrecker's Daughter; The Dead Shot; Macbeth; The Valet de Sham; Henry VIII; Ingomar, the Barbarian; The Dumb Belle; Cramond Brig; A Night in the Bastille; The Windmill; Lucrezia Borgia; Evadne; The Cattle Stealers; Ourang Outang; The Butcher's Dog of Ghent; Three Thieves; or, The Monkey of Frankfort; Twin Brothers; Conjurer, Showman, and Monkey; The French Spy; Toodles; Jack Sheppard; Peter Wilkins; Disowned; Esmeralda; A Duel in the Dark; The School for Scandal; Twelfth Night; The Fair One with the Golden Locks; The Belle's Stratagem; The Four Sisters; Othello; My Neighbor's Wife; Ambrose Gwinett; The Flying Dutchman; Mind Your Own Business; The Maid and the Magpie; The People's Candidate; Highways and Byways; Family Ties; Your Life's in Danger; All the World's a Stage; The Last Man; Tom Cringle's Leg; Bride of Lammermoor; A Day after the Wedding; Naval Engagements; Dumb Girl of Genoa; The Loan of a Lover; Warlock of the Glen; The Corsican Brothers; Thérèse; Comedy of Errors; The Yankee Trader; Gilderoy; Nan: The Good-for-Nothing; The Jewess; Uncle Tom's Cabin (Ann Marble's version).

1853: *Married Life; The Jacobite; Paul Pry; Ingomar; Sweethearts and Wives; The Wife; Toodles; Much Ado about Nothing; The People's Candidate; Writing on the Wall; The Hunchback; Ireland as It Is; The Limerick Boy; The Smugglers of Northumberland; The Child of the Regiment; Home in the West; Hue and Cry; Macbeth; Willow Copse; Hamlet; Othello; Richelieu; The Betrothal; The King and the Freebooter.*

1854: *Uncle Tom's Cabin; The Stranger; Sam Patch in France; Honey Moon; Ireland as It Is; The Limerick Boy; The Willow Copse; Hamlet; Richelieu; Richard III; The Betrothal; Harvest Home; Macbeth; Antoine du Vernet; A New Way to Pay Old Debts; Green Bushes; The Queen of the Abruzzi; Lady of Lyons; Jack Sheppard; Man of the World; Henry IV; Virginius; King Lear; The Robbers; Pizarro; The Corsican Brothers; Wanted: A Loan of a Wife; Harold: The Merchant of Calais; Rob Roy; London Assurance; A Capital Match; Satan in Paris; Dearest Elizabeth; Merry Wives of Windsor; The Maid with the Milking Pail; The Pet of the Petticoats; Pauline; Fortunia; The Belle's Stratagem; Ingomar; The Banker's Wife; The Wonder; The Hunchback; Love; Adrienne, the Actress; Camille; Evadne; The Duke's Wager; The Young Actress; All the World's a Stage; Milly; The Guardian Angel; Andy Blake; Bob Nettles; The Devil's in It; As You Like It; George Barnwell; The Actress of Padua; Dombey and Son; David Copperfield; Romance and Reality;*

Game of Life; My Cousin German; Love and Murder; His Last Legs; Daughter of the Regiment; Washington at Valley Forge; The Old Guard; Old Heads and Young Hearts; Faint Heart ne'er Won Fair Lady; Maritana; Extremes; The Secret; Your Life's in Danger; The Course of Love Never Did Run Smooth; The Rendezvous; Love; The Wife; Romeo and Juliet; Maid of Mariondorpt; Masks and Faces; Tony Lumpkin; Othello; The Advocate; All That Glitters Is Not Gold; To Oblige Benson; The School for Scandal; Louis XI; The Iron Chest; Richard III; William Tell; Captain Kyd; Boots at the Swan; A Wife's Revenge; Home in the West; The Courier of Lyons.

1855: *The Hermit of the Rock; Wife for a Day; Cherubusco; Everybody's Mess; People's Lawyer; Stage Struck Yankee; Rebels and Tories; The Yankee Pedlar; Telulah; Faint Heart ne'er Won Fair Lady; Black Eyed Susan; The Pirate Boy; Lafitte; Pirate of the Gulf; Fashion and Famine; Uncle Tom's Cabin; Katy, the Hot Corn Girl; The Lamplighter; Ingomar; Satan in Paris; The Maid with the Milking Pail; Asmodeus; A Husband at Sight; Wandering Boys; An Object of Interest; Douglas; Queen of Abruzzi; The Yankee Housemaid; Middy Ashore; Child of the Regiment; The Willow Copse; Hamlet; The Advocate; Macbeth; School of Reform; Richard III; King Lear; The Merchant of Venice; Richelieu; The Betrothal; Venice Preserved; Old Heads and Young Hearts; Louise Muller; The Lady of the Lake; Fashion; Napoleon's Old Guard; The Millionaire.*

1856: *Walter Tyrrell; or, The Better Blood; Black Eyed Susan; Mountain Sylph; Ernest Maltravers; The Idiot Witness; Richelieu; Valet de Sham; The Merchant of Venice; Othello; Richard III; Hamlet; Macbeth; King John; The Bridal; Royal Picnic; Podijah B. Peazley, His (X) Mark; John Bigelow's Courtship; Hermit of the Rocks; Wife for a Day; Yankee Duelist; The Corsican Brothers; Don Caesar de Bazan; Jack Cade; The Willow Copse; The Advocate; The Stranger; Still Waters Run Deep; Romeo and Juliet; Love's Sacrifice; Pizarro* (under the name *Rollo*); *The Wife; The Idiot Witness; Rob Roy; Dead Shot; Nan: The Good-for-Nothing; Lucrezia Borgia; Honey Moon; Fazio; Ingomar; The Stranger; Thérèse; Gamecock of the Wilderness; Sam Patch in France; Captain Kyd; All the World's a Stage; Adrienne, the Actress; John Dobbs; Dombey and Son; Sketches from India; Derwent Manor; The Prima Donna; Sudden Thoughts; Katherine and Petruchio; St. Marc; Perfection; Pizarro; The Young Actress; Born to Good Luck; A Lesson for Husbands; Romeo and Juliet; Asmodeus; Jack Sheppard; The Somnambulist; Two Gregories; The Young Scamp; Queen of Abruzzi; Lucille; The Idiot Witness; Daughter of the Regiment; A Roland for an Oliver; Betsy Baker; Extremes; Wife's Secret; The Muleteer; Evadne; The Hunchback; The Lady of Lyons; Adelgitha; Italian Bride; Satan in Paris; Katty O'Sheil; Husband on Sight; Captain Charlotte; Madeline; Eton Boy; French Spy; Mischief Making; Limerick Boy; A Widow's Victim; Bob Nettles; New York as It Is; People's Lawyer; Linda; Ireland as It Is; Toodles; Mose in California; The Drunken Combat; The School for Scandal; The Gunmaker of Moscow; The Bride of Lammermoor; Bob Tails and Wagtails; Tom and Jerry; The Gypsy Farmer; Buried Alive; La tour de Nesle; Dred: or, The Dismal Swamp; The Momentous Question; Chicago in 1812.*

1857: *The People's Lawyer* (better known as *Solon Shingle*); *Cherubusco; Green Mountain Boy; Hamlet; The Willow Copse; Richelieu; The Advocate; The Merchant of Venice; Home in the West; Hue and Cry; Man of the World; Your Life's in Danger; All the World's a Stage; Taking Chances; Sam Patch; King of the Commons;*

The Bridal; Werner; The Iron Mask; The Merchant of Venice; Richard III; The Irish Emigrant; A Lesson for Husbands; Irish American; Yankee Modesty; Satan in Paris; The Maid with the Milking Pail; The French Spy; Pet of the Petticoats; Little Treasure; Margot; The Poultry Dealer; The Gamester; Faint Heart ne'er Won Fair Lady; Jane Shore; Camille; The Rights of Women; Mary Tudor; Second Love; Geralda; Taming a Tiger; Peg Woffington; St. Mary's Eve; A True Kentuckian; Mons. Mallet; Henry IV; Fire Eater; Rip Van Winkle; Slasher and Crasher; Merry Wives of Windsor; Cool as a Cucumber; Richard III; Lola Montez in Bavaria; Rosalie Bouquet; The Irish Tutor; Macbeth; Ingomar; Naval Engagements; Jenny Lind; The Elder Brother; Much Ado about Nothing; The Robbers; The King's Gardener; My Neighbor's Wife; Othello; Money; Barney Bourke; King Lear; The Lady of Lyons; Love; The Hunchback; Adrienne, the Actress; An Alarming Sacrifice; Romeo and Juliet; The Swiss Cottage; Medea; Masks and Faces; London Assurance; The School for Scandal; Camille; The Willow Copse; Still Waters Run Deep; School of Reform; Ion; Shylock; The Stranger; Asmodeus; Rough Diamond; Teddy, the Tiler; Queen of Abruzzi; Born to Good Luck; The Good-for-Nothing; Robber's Wife; The Momentous Question; Jack Sheppard; Madeline; The Rival Pages; Alice; The Young Scamp; Honest Thieves; Landlords and Tenants; The Wandering Boys; The Somnambulist; The Idiot Witness; Louise; Harvest Home; Magic Trumpet; Elopement; A Day in Cadiz; Secret Marriage; Three Gladiators; Janet and Janette; Parquito; Rose and Pattilou; Conscript; John Jones; Wanted: 1,000 Spirited Young Milliners; Deeds of Dreadful Note; Jack Sheppard; Camille; Bamboozling; Faustus; The Marble Heart; Still Waters Run Deep; Ben, the Boatswain; Lucrezia Borgia; London Assurance; As You Like It; Swiss Swains; Retribution; My Wife's Diary; Female Gambler; A Lonely Man of the Ocean; Poor Gentleman; The First Night; Ocean Child; The Limerick Boy; The Windmill; Model of a Wife; Widow's Victim; Toodles; Black Eyed Susan; A Glance at New York; Dumb Girl of Genoa; The Last Days of Pompeii; Mose; Shoemaker of Toulouse; Children of the Wood; Adelgitha; Perfection; Evadne; The Barrack Room; The Wrecker's Daughter; Child of the Regiment; Rights of Women; Husband at Sight; La Fiarnia; A Gentleman from Ireland; Dombey and Son; A Fellow Clerk; Pocahontas; Binks the Bagman; The Fast Man; A Serious Family; Life in New York; The Clock Maker's Dream; The Pirates of Mississippi; Metamora; Romance and Beauty; The Italian Wife; My Neighbor's Wife; London Assurance; Macbeth; Miseries of Human Life; Rob Roy; The Lady and the Devil; Guy Mannering; The Winter's Tale; The Fire Eater; The Corsican Brothers; A Wonderful Woman; Napoleon's Old Guard; Six Degrees of Crime; Siamese Twins; Don Caesar de Bazan; Lafitte: The Pirate of the Gulf; William Tell; The Gamecock of the Wilderness; The Pilot; Wife for a Day; Yankee Land; Nick of the Woods; Stage Struck Yankee; Ernest Maltravers; Love and Loyalty; Captain Kyd.

1858: *La tour de Nesle; Poor Pillicoddy; A Thumping Legacy; Six Degrees of Crime; An Alarming Sacrifice; The Poor of Chicago (The Streets of New York); Dombey and Son; The Grand Admiral; Neighbor Jackwood; Catherine and Petruchio; The Old Guard; His Last Leg.*

BIBLIOGRAPHY

Andreas, A. T. *History of Chicago.* 3 vols. Chicago: A. T. Andreas Co., 1884–86.

Chicago Daily Journal, Selected issues, 1849–71.

McVicker, James H. *The Theatre: Its Early Days in Chicago*. Chicago: Knight and Leonard, 1884.

Sherman, Robert L. *Chicago Stage: Its Records and Achievements*. Chicago: Robert L. Sherman, 1947.

Linda Bandy-White

S

ST. CHARLES THEATRE COMPANY. See CALDWELL'S AMERICAN COMPANY (1819–43) and ST. CHARLES THEATRE STOCK COMPANY

ST. CHARLES THEATRE STOCK COMPANY. On May 7, 1853, Benedict DeBar (1812–77) acquired the lease on the St. Charles Theatre, a proscenium house located on St. Charles Street between Poydras and Gravier streets in New Orleans. During the summer and fall of 1853 DeBar organized a stock company, and on November 12, 1853, he opened his first season with Richard Sheridan's *The School for Scandal* and the farce *The Swiss Swains*.

DeBar's management of the St. Charles followed that of Noah Ludlow and Sol Smith, who rebuilt the theatre in 1843 after the original structure (home to James Caldwell's fine companies, 1835 to 1842) burned to the ground in 1842. Ludlow and Smith maintained a stock-star company until 1853, when they relinquished their lease to the New Orleans Gas and Light Company, which had acquired the theatre from Caldwell. DeBar, an actor and stage manager under Caldwell and then under Ludlow and Smith, continued the policies that had proved most successful for his former employers: he maintained a high-quality stock company that performed contemporary and classical comedies and dramas with visiting star attractions; he dotted his seasons with light musical entertainments, opera, melodrama, spectacles, ballet, and variety fare in order to appeal to a wide spectrum of the New Orleans populace; and he cleaned and renovated the theatre each season. His early success was so great that in 1855 DeBar purchased the St. Louis Theatre in St. Louis; each year thereafter his company played a summer season following the regular season in New Orleans.

DeBar's major competition in New Orleans during his first eight years of management was the Varieties (Gaiety) Theatre, which offered variety fare and animal and novelty acts to a public hungry for escapist entertainment. In the 1870s the Academy of Music became a major competitor when its owner-manager David Bidwell offered bigger stars, a better stock company, and more popular shows than did DeBar. But the St. Charles under DeBar was the outstanding theatre in New Orleans, presenting legitimate drama until it closed in 1861 with the onset of the Civil War.

From 1861 to 1864 DeBar maintained his company in St. Louis. When he reopened the St. Charles in 1864, the social, economic, and political forces at work in the city (and throughout the nation) wreaked havoc on his New Orleans enterprise. Despite a dismal financial outlook, DeBar purchased the St. Charles in 1865 and continued his efforts to provide New Orleans with quality theatrical fare and major stars. Beginning with the 1872–73 season, however, each year was a greater financial disappointment than the last, and each of the stock companies became progressively weaker. Moreover, DeBar did not devote himself exclusively to the St. Charles, but split his time between New Orleans and St. Louis, sometimes absenting himself from New Orleans for entire seasons and leaving the St. Charles in the hands of acting managers (see Personnel). In 1877 the gas company foreclosed on DeBar, and Robert Strong (an employee in DeBar's business office) assumed management for two financially disastrous seasons.

David Bidwell (1820–89), owner-manager of the Academy of Music, purchased the St. Charles in 1880, planning to run the Academy and the St. Charles as one enterprise. Bidwell had developed a kind of theatrical circuit, and the purchase of the St. Charles offered him a second major house in New Orleans. From 1880 to 1885 he presented popular variety fare and the finest starring combinations. During these years New Orleans audiences began crying out for a permanent stock company, and Bidwell answered their plea in 1885. For two seasons he alternated stock-company performances with starring combinations. When not at the St. Charles, his stock company (The Star Dramatic Company) played in other theatres, such as the Grand Opera House; in this way Bidwell profited from both stock-company and visiting-star performances. But Bidwell found it difficult to maintain a high-quality stock company in New Orleans, and he returned the theatre to road-house status in 1887. For the last twelve years of its life, the St. Charles remained a road house under the managements of Mrs. Bidwell, Marc Klaw and Abraham Erlanger, and Col. J. D. Hopkins.

Clearly, the St. Charles underwent a number of significant changes in both personnel and theatrical fare between 1853 and 1899. Ben DeBar's tenure is the most significant, since it encompassed twenty-four years and coincided with the apex and demise of the old nineteenth-century stock tradition. The management of David Bidwell is of secondary but substantial importance: Bidwell did maintain control of the theatre for nearly a decade, and his was the last successful effort to maintain a stock company at the St. Charles. Trained as a dancer in England, DeBar was brought to America in 1835 by James Caldwell to serve as acrobat and comedian in Caldwell's St. Charles company. DeBar was a superb low comedian and played a variety of roles, but he was especially noted late in his career for his outstanding interpretation of Falstaff, which he studied for nine years before performing the role. Having worked with Caldwell and with Ludlow and Smith, DeBar naturally adopted those managers' policies: he maintained a stock-star company organization and was a regular member of his companies between 1853 and 1861. But DeBar purchased the St. Louis Theatre in 1855, the St. Charles in 1865, and the Grand Opera House in St. Louis in 1873, and his managerial responsibilities limited his performances during the late 1860s and 1870s. Moreover, DeBar sensed the ultimate demise of the stock-company tradition and began depending more and more on starring attractions and variety entertainment in the 1870s. David Bidwell was essentially a businessman who entered theatre management from a business perspective. He had run a ship chandlery business in New Orleans with his brother in 1846 and subsequently had bought the Phoenix House, a hotel adjoining a theatre. He naturally drifted into theatre business and soon after built the Academy of Music with George Lawrason. Bidwell had a shrewd appreciation of the amusement requirements of the New Orleans audience, and he was able to satisfy those requirements for eight years. He also developed a burning desire to return high-quality drama to New Orleans, and he succeeded in bringing to that city the finest starring combinations and in organizing a highly competent stock company.

The St. Charles Theatre built by Ludlow and Smith was not as large and magnificent as Caldwell's original, but it was well equipped, had a lovely interior, and seated 1,600. DeBar's company performed nightly, and performances generally commenced sometime between 7:00 and 7:45 P.M.; Saturday matinees and special "toy matinees" at Christmas and New Years (when toys were given away to children in the audience) began at noon. Between 1853 and 1861 admission ranged from twenty-five cents for gallery seats to seventy-five cents for parquet and dress circle, to $6.00 for private boxes. In the late 1860s and the 1870s, prices rose slightly to $1.00 for parquet and dress circle. For special attractions (such as Fanny Janauschek) prices rose as high as $1.50 for parquet and dress circle and $10.00 for private boxes. Matinees generally ran fifty cents for adults and twenty-five cents for children and servants. The bill changed nightly, with the exception of occasional short runs and starring engagements, and the seasons (October to May) concluded with benefits for actors, staff, and charities. DeBar kept an expense log that reveals that his receipts ran high between 1853 and 1872. In the 1869–70 season, for example, DeBar grossed about $21,000 during the three-week engagement of Lydia Thompson, and he netted about half that amount (Krestalaude, 62).

During the 1870s DeBar enlarged the auditorium to hold 2,500 spectators, and he began to depend more and more on traveling companies; consequently, the quality of his stock company diminished, and the Academy of Music with its stronger company, bigger stars, and more popular shows began outdrawing the St. Charles. DeBar also began catering to the escapist interests of his patrons, enlisting stars of lighter entertainment (Lotta Crabtree, Lydia Thompson) and presenting equestrian and minstrel shows (Fred Wilson's Minstrels) and specialty acts (Martinetti-Ravel Pantomime Troupe). This trend to lighter entertainment began the financial and social deterioration of DeBar's theatre; for the 1873–74 season he claimed to have lost $15,000.

When David Bidwell assumed control of the St. Charles in 1880, he spent $20,000 on renovations, constructed new dressing rooms, and installed folding opera chairs, confident that New Orleans had a prosperous theatre future. (In 1884 Bidwell converted the theatre's lighting system to electricity.) Bidwell hired touring companies for one- or two-week engagements, and these companies also played at his Academy of Music. Admission ranged from twenty-five cents for gallery seats, fifty cents for family circle, $1 for dress circle, to $10 for private boxes. Bidwell offered Saturday matinees and used gimmicks to get people to attend the theatre. For example, he continued DeBar's "toy matinees" but did not limit them to holidays; gifts were given out during matinees of popular engagements (*Hearts of Oak*) and variety performances. Bidwell's seasons ran from October to May and usually ended with benefit performances.

Critics were seldom discerning in their reviews of DeBar's productions, and they always thrilled to scenic marvels in plays such as *After Dark; or, London by Night* and praised the lovely wardrobes of starring actresses (such as Janauschek). Reviewers seldom wrote insightful reviews regarding starring actors' performances, but one critic did remark that Edwin Forrest's King Lear had become a finer piece of acting for the old star than his Hamlet. Audiences and critics alike were most positive when DeBar remained at the St. Charles as manager and actor. New Orleans audiences delighted in the manager's comic performances; moreover, DeBar was a stronger manager than any of the men he engaged as acting managers. Audiences and critics were most negative when DeBar began relying on star attractions to sustain the theatre, neglected his managerial duties in New Orleans, and failed to organize a quality stock company. During the 1873–74 season a reviewer complained that DeBar relied too heavily on minor stars and presented a stock company "wonderful for its incapacity" (Kendall, 541). Although this reviewer's complaint may have been valid, it was also voiced during a period of transition in the American theatre. It should be noted that DeBar was dealing with a public that preferred Buffalo Bill to Lawrence Barrett; DeBar's tendency to present lighter fare and specialty acts in the 1870s was a response to his audience's preference.

When David Bidwell assumed control of the St. Charles the situation had not changed. Critics seldom offered specific comments regarding Bidwell's presentations at the St. Charles, but they voiced their appreciation that Bidwell's variety fare gave all of the audience something to enjoy. Audiences and critics often responded to the horses, seldom to the actors.

During DeBar's first two decades at the St. Charles the manager emphasized dramatic productions. Shakespeare's *Othello, The Merry Wives of Windsor, Comedy of Errors, King Henry IV, Macbeth, Romeo and Juliet, King Lear,* and *Hamlet* were popular throughout this period. Plays by Dion Boucicault (*The Willow Copse, Colleen Bawn, Streets of New York*), contemporary dramas (*The Iron Mask, Richelieu, Camille, Our American Cousin*), and standard comedies (*The School for Scandal, Honey Moon, The Lady of Lyons*) were also popular. But DeBar strove to satisfy the entire audience by securing other types of entertainment. He engaged various opera companies (Mme. Rosa Devries and the Italian Opera Company, Niblo's Operatic Company) that performed the most popular pieces (*Norma, Fra Diavolo, Cinderella*). The Ravel and Martinetti troupes performed plays in pantomime, ballet, and tightrope and acrobatic acts, and the Keller troupe presented living tableaux. Nixon's Royal Circus was a popular attraction at the St. Charles, as were various minstrel shows, equestrian dramas (*Mazeppa*), spectacles, and Irish plays with songs. When the St. Charles entered its most severe financial depression under DeBar in 1872, the theatre's dramatic fare diminished. More variety fare appeared (G. L. Fox's Humpty Dumpty Pantomime Troupe, Berger's Swiss Family Bell Ringers), and touring companies presented minor figures such as Mrs. D. P. Bowers and Little Nell Gibson, an imitator of Lotta.

When Bidwell first acquired the St. Charles, he emphasized light musical and variety fare and presented a few contemporary hit plays performed by visiting stars (*Hazel Kirke, Hearts of Oak*); but from 1882–85 he moved toward an emphasis on dramatic production. By his fifth season, he was offering twenty-five plays, mostly by American authors (Belasco, Gillette) and mostly melodramatic in style. Bidwell also offered musicals (William Gilbert and Arthur Sullivan's *Mikado*), operas (*Il Trovatore, Faust, William Tell*), spectacles (Percy Brooke and Louise Dickson's adaptation of P. Merritt, H. Pettitt, and Sir A. Harris' *The World*), and melodramas (Boucicault's *Arrah-na-Pogue*). During its two seasons of existence, the Bidwell stock company performed twenty-five plays, mostly American, but including recent New York successes (*Taken from Life, Arrah-na-Pogue*) and contemporary melodramas dealing with social problems of the day (*Youth, Man and Wife*).

Ben DeBar employed a treasurer, a musical director, a full thirty-piece orchestra, a scenic artist, a costumer, a stage manager, a prompter, and twenty to thirty actors and actresses engaged in standard lines of business. He also employed singers and dancers, star performers, and special attractions. Major stars engaged by DeBar included American tragediennes Eliza Logan, who performed roles such as *The Hunchback, Ingomar,* and *Macbeth;* and Julia Dean, who presented *Jane Shore* and *Lucrezia Borgia* among other works. English tragedian James A. Anderson performed his classical repertory; J. A. Neafie presented *The Corsican Brothers*; J. H. Hackett performed Falstaff in *King Henry IV* and the title role in *Rip Van Winkle*; James Murdoch presented *Macbeth, Hamlet,* and *The Stranger*; and E. L. Davenport, C. W. Couldock, Edwin Forrest, Edwin Booth, and Johns Wilkes Booth performed their repertories. Husband and wife teams also abounded: Mr. and Mrs. Dion Boucicault presented *The Career of an Actress,* English comedians Mr. and Mrs. John Wood performed *Pet of the Petticoats*, and Mr. and Mrs. Charles Kean presented Shakespeare, *Louis XI* and *The Jealous Wife.* The emotional school of drama was represented by Lucille Western, who played *East Lynne* and *Camille*, and whose Nancy Sykes (*Oliver Twist*) was noted as one of the greatest performances of that character ever on the American stage. Lotta Crabtree performed in *Little Nell* and *The Little Detective*, Maggie Mitchell appeared as *Fanchon, the Cricket*, John Owens appeared in *Cricket on the Hearth*, John Collins sang in Irish plays, and W. E. Burton, low comedian and manager of Burton's Theatre in New York, performed Toodles, Tony Lumpkin, and Paul Pry. The versatile Charlotte Cushman appeared in *Honey Moon, Romeo and Juliet*, and *As You Like It*; Kate Bateman appeared in *Romeo and Juliet*; and Laura Keene, Minnie Maddern, Jane Coombs, and Ellen Tree appeared in their popular roles. During the 1868–69 season German actress Fanny Janauschek performed *Marie Stuart* in German. In 1874 British tragedian Charles Fechter revealed his new and controversial interpretation of Hamlet. Bidwell engaged star attractions (James Wallack in *The Bandit King*, Ada Gray in *East Lynne*, Charlotte Thompson in *Jane Eyre*, Fanny Davenport in *Fedora*), but he also presented burlesque companies (The Kiralfy Brothers' production of *The Black Crook*), musicals (the Ford Opera Company's *Mikado*), and variety fare (Tom Thumb and Company, Haverly's Minstrels, Buffalo Bill's Wild West Show, lecturer Henry Ward Beecher, wrestling and boxing).

Among the more significant members of DeBar's stock companies were the men who served as managers or acting managers during DeBar's frequent absences from New Orleans: H. Corri, S. B. Duffield, A. L. Griffin, T. W. Davey, Edward Eddy, H. W. Riley, Charles R. Pope, and John W. Albaugh. Tragedian Edward Eddy managed theatres in New York before his arrival in New Orleans and was a member of Ludlow and Smith's St. Charles companies in the 1840s and 1850s. Charles Pope performed tragic leads for DeBar in 1854 and then toured the country as a star performer until 1866, when he returned to the St. Charles as the company's leading man. John W. Albaugh performed in New York and was owner-manager of several theatres in Washington, D.C., and Baltimore before his tenure at the St. Charles.

Almost without exception, the truly exceptional players appeared at the St. Charles before 1870; after that year the quality of DeBar's stock companies diminished considerably. Appearing during DeBar's first tenure (1853–61) were DeBar's wife, the dancer Hattie Vallee (who remained with the company throughout her husband's tenure); DeBar's sister Clementine Booth; low comedian Vining Bowers, who performed for the Varieties stock companies as well; William Crisp's sister Mary Gladstone; J. B. Studley, one of the finest supporting actors in America and the actor who played Bill Sykes to Charlotte Cushman's Nancy in *Oliver Twist*; and Catherine Reignolds, star actress of the western and southern theatres, who played Virginia to Edwin Forrest's Virginius in New York and was later a member of Laura Keene's company. Two of the outstanding actors in the St. Charles company between 1861 and 1870 were A. H. Davenport, who also played in the First and Second Varieties Theatres and later was a member of the stock company at Bidwell's Academy of Music; and Miss Lizzie Maddern, wife of St. Charles manager T. W. Davey. Only three of Bidwell's stock members are of note: Joseph Wheelock, who was previously a member of the New Orleans Grand Opera House, supported Edwin Booth in New York, and played in the first production of *The Two Orphans* in 1875; Marie Wainright, former member of Palmer's Union Square Company in New York; and Barton Hill, a popular actor at the Varieties Theatre, who later managed the California Theatre in San Francisco, where he gave Helene Modjeska her start on the American stage.

When David Bidwell died in 1888, his wife assumed ownership of the St. Charles and for four years ran the theatre as a popular priced ("ten-twenty-thirty cents") road house. In 1893 Klaw and Erlanger leased the St. Charles, brought it into their chain, and began booking their own road show attractions. The theatre's new owner, Colonel J. D. Hopkins, refused to renew Klaw and Erlanger's lease in 1898 and instead organized a very weak stock company that lasted only one season, presenting a different play each week along with traveling vaudeville artists. The St. Charles was destroyed by fire on June 4, 1899; it was rebuilt as a vaudeville house and several decades later became a movie house.

PERSONNEL

Management: Benedict DeBar, lessee and manager (1853–61, 1864), proprietor and manager (1865–76); H. Corri, acting manager (1853–55, 1856–61); S. B. Duffield, acting manager (1855–56); A. L. Griffin, acting manager (1864); T. W. Davey, manager (1864–66); Edward Eddy, acting manager (1864–66), manager (1866–67); H. W. Riley, acting manager (1867–68); Charles R. Pope, acting manager (1868–70); John W. Albaugh, manager (1870–71); Robert Strong, manager (1877–79); David Bidwell, proprietor and manager (1880–88); Mrs. David Bidwell, proprietor and manager (1889–93); Marc Klaw and Abraham Erlanger, managers (1894–98); Col. J. D. Hopkins, proprietor and manager (1898–99); C. Chesley, treasurer (1853–59); Pat Gleason, treasurer (1860–61, 1864–76).

Scenic Technicians: T. C. Nixon (1853–56), Mr. Boulet (1857–59), Mr. Gaufrey (1868–70), Angelo Wiser (1871–72).

Costumers: J. McMahon (1853–56), P. H. Gallagher (1856–57), Job Jamison (1857–61).

Musical Directors: August Waldauer (1853–57, 1858–61), Robert Meyer (1857–58), Louis Mayer (1868–70).

Stage Managers: John W. Albaugh (1870–71), Alexander Fitzgerald (1871–74).

Actors and Actresses: *J. W. Albaugh* (1870–71), *Mrs. Mary Mitchell Albaugh* (1870–71), Miss Alexander, Mrs. Andrews, *Stephen W. Ashley* (1869–70), *Mrs. Harriet Bernard* (1853–56), Miss Marie Boniface, *Mrs. Clementine Booth* (1853–56), *Vining Bowers* (1853–59), *A. H. Campbell* (1854–59), *George D. Chaplin* (1855–56, 1864–65), J. B. Curtis, H. B. Corri, *A. H. Davenport* (1865–67), T. W. Davey, John Davis, Mr. and Mrs. William Davis, *Benedict DeBar* (1854–61, 1864–76), J. S. Delaney, Miss Fannie Denham, R. Dorsey, *Mr. and Mrs. John Duff* (1854–55), *Mr. and Mrs. S. B. Duffield* (1853–55), *Edward Eddy* (1864–67), *Alexander Fitzgerald* (1871–72), Mrs. Alexander Fitzgerald, *Mary Gladstone* (1855–56), *M. Golden* (1855–61), Miss Graham, *Alice Grey* (1869–72), A. L. Griffin, W. H. Hamblin, *C. B. Hawkins* (1874–76), *William Hield* (1854–55), Ferd Hight, J. W. Hill, Mrs. Adeline Hind, T. Hind, Laura Honey, Mr. and Mrs. George Howard, Miss Belle Howitt, *Nat Hyams* (1868–69), *Henrietta Irving* (1864–67), *George W. Jamison* (1853–54), J. D. Kinlin, Florence LaFond, Emma Maddern, *Miss Lizzie Maddern* (1864–67), J. B. Magill, H. W. Mitchell, C. J. Murphy, Mr. and Mrs. J. E. Nagle, J. W. Osborne, *Miss Henrietta Osborne* (1868–69), W. H. Partello, F. R. Pearce, Mrs. F. R. Pierce, Alice Placide, *Charles Pope* (1853–61, 1865–70), Mrs. Estelle Potter, J. S. Potter, Mark Quinlin, A. A. Read, *Catherine Reignolds* (1857–58), W. H. Riley, Mrs. Rosewood, Tom St. Clair, J. C. Savage, Mrs. Annie Senter, Mary Shaw, Mrs. Kate Shubert, *Mark Smith* (1853–56), W. P. Smith, Sol Smith, Jr., J. A. Stevens, *Mrs. Mary Stuart* (1854–55), *J. B. Studley* (1855–56), Mrs. Thorpe, Hattie Vallee, *Mrs. August Waldauer* (1854–58), *Mrs. Walters* (1864–67), W. M. Ward, *Amelia Waugh* (1873–74), *J. W. Whiting* (1865–67), E. B. Williams, Robert G. Wilson.

David Bidwell's Star Dramatic Company: George Bakers, Kate Barret, Olive Berkeley, W. F. Blande, Junius B. Booth, Jr., Andrew Bowers, Frank Bowers, H. C. Brinker, Percy Brooke, May Brooklyn, *Hart Conway* (1886–87), Minnie Conway, Louise Dickson, Alice Duffield, Pauline Duffield, Louis Filbert, Kate Freeman, J. W. Hague, Harry Hawk, Harry Hazletine, *Barton Hill* (1885–87), Emma Maddern, *Luke Martin* (1886–87), Kate Matthews, Lewis Mitchell, Minnie Monk, Louise Muldener, Helen Ogelvie, Samuel Rodgers, Jenny Scolly, A. Scroggs, Anne Scully, Edgar Selden, Annie Sommers, A. Spencer, *Osmond Tearle* (1886–87), Hugh Tenis, J. H. Twing, Bessie Vivian, *Marie Wainright* (1885–86), Isabelle Waldron, Charles B. Weeles, *Charles Wheatleigh* (1885–87), *Joseph Wheelock* (1885–86), W. A. Whitecar.

REPERTORY

1871–72: This season under the management of Ben DeBar represents the transition from an early concern for legitimate drama to an emphasis on popular attractions; accordingly, it is a compromise season that is representative of both tendencies.

October 15, Lingard Combination begins: *Elfie; or, The Cherry Inn; Delicate Ground; Naval Engagements; David Garrick; Marriage at Any Price; Frou-Frou; Una; A Day after the Wedding; Who's to Have Him; Knight of Arva; Pocahontas.* October 30, Chapman Sisters and E. A. Locke engagement begins: *Checkmate; Cinderella* (burlesque); *Aladdin* (burlesque); *Nan: The Good-for-Nothing; Amrie's New Year; Little Don Giovanni; Forty Thieves; A Quiet Family; True; Pluto; Jenny Lind* (farce); *Margot: The Poultry Dealer; Fra Diavolo.* DeBar company begins playing: *Mormons; or, Brigham Young at Home; Midnight Watch; All That Glitters Is Not Gold; Jack Sheppard.* November 11, Edwin Forrest engagement begins: *King Lear; Virginius; Richelieu; Jack Cade; Tom and Jerry; Mr. and Mrs. Peter White; Hamlet; Damon and Pythias; Othello.* DeBar company plays: *Huntress of the Mississippi; or, Ireland and America; Mystery of Edwin Drood.* November 3, Jane Coombs engagement begins: *London Assurance; The School for Scandal; Wife's Secret; Love's Sacrifice; The Hunchback; The Love Chase; The Lady of Lyons; World of Fashion; Romeo and Juliet.* December 12, Chapman Sisters return: *His Last Legs; Toodles; Boarding School; Little Jack Sheppard.* December 12, John Collins engagement begins: *Paul Clifford; The Magic Skirt, The Magic Flute; Irish Fortune; How to Pay the Rent; Colleen Bawn; The Omnibus; Rory O'More; Robert Macaire; The Good-for-Nothing.* December 25, Lucille Western and James A. Herne engagement begins: *East Lynne; Oliver Twist; The Child Stealer; Leah the Forsaken; Masks and Faces; Handy Andy; Satan in Paris; Mendicant; or, Stricken Blind; Spy of St. Marc; or, The Actress of Padua; Jonathan Bradford; or, Murder at the Roadside Inn.* January 15, Lotta Crabtree engagement begins: *The Little Detective; Fire Fly; Little Nell and the Marchioness; Heartsease; Rainbow; Pet of the Petticoats; The Ticket-of-Leave Man; Beauty and the Beast; Andy Blake; Norma; Family Jars; Captain Charlotte.* February 17, Coleman Children engagement begins: *Stolen by Gypsies; Little Sentinel; Rising Generation; Maid with the Milking Pail; Cross of Gold; Soldier's Return; or, The Fortunes of War.* February 27, J. W. Wallack engagement begins: *The Iron Mask; Still Waters Run Deep; The Stranger; Henry Dunbar; Oliver Twist; Werner; or, The Inheritance; King of the Commoners; Much Ado about Nothing; Swiss Swains.* March 11, J. K. Emmett engagement begins: *Fritz; Carl, the Musician.* March 24, Wyndam Comedy Company engagement begins: *Lancers; Progress; The Debutante; Caste; Saratoga; Ours; Home; Mephisto's Mission* (operetta); *Friends.* DeBar Company plays: *Bertha; or, The Sewing Machine Girl; Boarding School.* April 15, Fanny Janauschek engagement begins: *Marie Stuart; Leah the Forsaken; Chesney Wold; Fazio; or, The Italian Wife; Macbeth; The Winter's Tale.* April 28, Martinetti-Ravel Pantomime Troupe engagement begins: *Jocko: The Brazilian Ape; Pat a Cake, Pat a Cake, Baker's Man; Paul and Virginia; The Misfortunes of Baby; The Zamphylion; or, The Leap for Life; Hungarian Rendevous; Battle Leap; Robert Macaire; Green Monster; Mystic Gift; The Tyrolean Echo; Rose and Butterfly.* May 15–21, Varieties Theatre engagement: *The Octoroon; or, Life in Louisiana* (Dion Boucicault).

1885–86: This is one of the two seasons in which David Bidwell alternated his stock company performances with touring combinations.

Devil's Auction (Charles Yale Co.); *The Mikado* (Ford Co.); *Burr Oakes; Zo Zo: The Magic Queen; Forty-Nine; The Danites in the Sierras; The Bandit King* (J. H. Wallack Co.). Star Dramatic Company engagement begins: *Taken from Life; Divorce; Pique; Youth; Man and Wife; Two Orphans, The World; Pavements of Paris; Victor Durand; M'liss* (Annie Pixley Co.); *Fedora* (Fanny Davenport Co.); *Princess Andrea* (Mme. Janish Co.). Charlotte Crabtree engagement begins: *M'lle Nitouche; The Little Detective; Little Nell and the Marchioness; Musette.* Star Dramatic Company plays: *Called Back; The Romance of a Poor Young Man; Tickets-of-Leave; Michael Strogoff* (Charles L. Andrews Combination); *Ours.*

BIBLIOGRAPHY

Kendall, John S. *The Golden Age of the New Orleans Theater.* Baton Rouge: Louisiana State University Press, 1952.

Krestalaude, James A. "A Day Book and a History of the St. Charles Theatre, 1868–72." Master's thesis, Louisiana State University, 1972.

Lawler, Jo Ann. "The St. Charles Theatre of New Orleans, 1888–99." Master's thesis, Louisiana State University, 1966.

Nugent, Beatrice. "Benedict DeBar's Management of the St. Charles Theatre in New Orleans, Louisiana, 1853–1861." Master's thesis, Louisiana State University, 1967.

Roden, Sally Ann. "A History of the St. Charles Theatre in New Orleans under the Management of David Bidwell, 1880–1888." Master's thesis, North Texas State University, 1969.

C. Alex Pinkston, Jr.

SALEM THEATRE COMPANY. In the summer of 1827, Major J. W. Barton, an enterprising landowner and son of the proprietor of a hotel often used as a theatre by traveling shows, formed a joint stock company for the purpose of erecting a permanent theatre for Salem. Subscribers were so interested in the proposal that plans for a wooden building were replaced by plans for one of brick. The theatre built on Crombie Street opened February 4, 1828, with Thomas Holcroft's comedy *The Road to Ruin* (1792) and J. T. Allingham's farce *Fortune's Frolic* (1799).

The reputation of Salem's citizens for puritanism and persecution of witches would seem to auger poorly for any interest in secular amusements. Actually, the people of this wealthy maritime community were liberal and cosmopolitan, capable of appreciating a variety of musical and theatrical presentations. After the American Revolution, Salem was host to a number of performers who had appeared in London's Drury Lane, Covent Garden, and Haymarket theatres. Salem supported traveling theatre companies at a time when the laws of Boston forbade such exhibitions in that city. In 1792 a Salem town meeting on the subject of theatrical entertainments advised the Massachusetts legislature that the townspeople of Salem regarded the state's antitheatrical laws as "unconstitutional, inexpedient and abused."

The state law was repealed in 1793; meanwhile, in defiance of state law, Salem offered an appreciative and discerning audience for performers who would have been arrested in Boston. After 1793 solo performers and theatrical troupes found Salem well worth their time and effort, for audiences there were both gracious and critical. Salem became the first and most important stop for a theatrical troupe that wished to explore New England north of Boston.

The proprietors of the Salem Theatre requested an Act of Incorporation from the General Court of Massachusetts in January 1828. Their request was denied. Despite this refusal, a company was established under the management of Aaron J. Phillips, who leased the building for $75 a week. Phillips had acted with the Drake Company* some ten years earlier, when it toured the Ohio Valley and the South. In 1817 Phillips joined Henry Vaughn and Noah Ludlow in establishing a theatre in Nashville, Tennessee. Two years later, he brought a company to New Orleans, where he found competition more rigorous than anticipated. He then joined forces with another company under John Davis.

With few exceptions, performances were held in the Salem Theatre every Monday, Wednesday, and Friday evening. Ticket prices, at seventy-five cents for the first tier, fifty cents for the second tier, and thirty-seven and one-half cents for the pit, were appreciably less than those charged at Boston theatres. Although the actors and actresses were not generally of the first rank, they were considered highly capable. After the opening week performances, the community's major criticism concerned the poor quality of plays chosen. However, the plays Phillips selected were those older comedies, farces, and melodramas conventionally seen at the best theatres in New York, Boston, and Philadelphia. The first season of the Salem Theatre Company ended in May 1828 with Phillips $325 in debt. To balance his accounts, Phillips signed over to the proprietors such "goods, scenery, apparatus, and implements" as would make up the amount owed. The company then moved to Gloucester, Massachusetts, and Portland, Maine, for the summer.

Phillips had hoped to return to Salem in the fall, but the renovated and redecorated Salem Theatre was leased to the trustees of the Tremont Theatre, Boston. The rental fee was now $1,200 a year (from September 1 through August 31), to be paid in three equal installments. In addition to the rent, the lessee would pay the proprietors one-half of the receipts of each evening's use of the theatre. A further stipulation required that all plays be selected by the Committee of the Stockholders. Under these onerous conditions, Alexander M. Wilson, an assistant manager of the Tremont Theatre, became the new manager of the Salem Theatre. For the most part, Wilson's company was drawn from the ranks of companies in Boston, with the addition of guest artists from elsewhere.

The Salem Theatre reopened October 6, 1828. Performance nights and ticket prices were unchanged. Despite an interesting repertoire, guest artists such as Edwin Forrest, and generally favorable reviews, the company lost money and was disbanded in January 1829. J. W. Barton later noted that the first season the small, select company was a novelty, so it appealed to the public and functioned efficiently. The next season, in Barton's view, the theatre was run too extravagantly for the size of the town. But surely the heavy demands made by the proprietors contributed to the failure of the company. Additionally, the insolvency of the Tremont Theatre Company* may have contributed to the decision to disband the Salem Theatre Company.

Another company under the management of Mr. Archer of the Tremont Theatre took up residence in Salem in April and May 1829. Both the performers and the management were praised, but the audiences were not large enough to keep the company working for any length of time. Wilson opened the theatre once again on July 6,1829, but this effort was no more auspicious than his last, and the theatre closed on August 19.

Wilson was still the ostensible manager of the Tremont Theatre when he reopened the Salem Theatre on November 18, 1829. Ticket prices remained the same, but the company presented only one program about every seven days. Junius Brutus Booth and Mary Ann Duff appeared with the company in December. Edwin Forrest joined Duff on the Salem stage in March 1830, and the company played a brief engagement in May. While the Salem Theatre was failing once again, the Tremont Theatre was realizing a handsome profit. In July Tremont Theatre performers, who had in the past used the Salem Theatre, reopened the Federal Street Theatre in Boston for a summer season. The Salem Theatre was dark the summer of 1830. Wilson, no longer with the Tremont Theatre, leased the Salem Theatre in December 1830 for a final, brief engagement. The Salem Theatre closed its doors for good (with one brief exception) after a performance of J. S. Knowles' *Virginius* on December 24, 1830. Eventually, the theatre became the Crombie Street Church.

PERSONNEL

Management: Aaron J. Phillips, actor-manager (1828); Alexander M. Wilson, actor-manager (1828–30); Mr. Archer, actor-manager (1829); Mr. Tucker, treasurer and box-office keeper (1828).

Scenic Technicians: Mr. Coyle (1828); Mr. Reinagle (1828).

Musical Directors: Mr. Parnell (1828); Mr. Barnitt (1828); Mr. Ostinelli (1829); Mr. Width (1830).

Stage Managers: Mr. Foot (1828); H. C. Charnock (1828–29); W. H. Smith (1829); Mr. Taylor (1830).

Actors and Actresses: Mr. Adams, Andrew J. Allen, Mr. Andrews, Mr. Archer, Mr. Ball, Mr. Banker, Mrs. Barnes, *Mr. and Mrs. G. H. Barrett* (1829–30), Mr. and Mrs. Bernard, Mr. Blaike, *Mrs. J. B. Booth* (1828), Mr. and Mrs. Brewster, Mrs. Broad, *F. Brown* (1828), *James H. Caldwell* (1828), Mr. and Mrs. Campbell,

H. C. Charnock, Mr. Chipp, Mr. Clarke, Mr. Clements, *Joshua Collins* (1829–30), Mr. Comer, *Thomas Cooper* (1828), *Mr. and Mrs. Joe Cowell* (1828), Mr. Coyle, Mad'l Constance, Mr. Dickson, *William Dinneford* (1828), Mr. Doyne, *Miss Eberle* (1828–30), Mr and Mrs. H. Eberle, Mrs. Fairchild, Mr. Fenno, Mr. Field, *Harry J. Finn* (1828–30), Mrs. Fisher, Miss A. Fisher, *Clara Fisher* (1828), Mr. Foot, Miss George, *John Gilbert* (1829), *James Henry Hackett* (1830), John Hallam, Miss Hamilton, Mr. Hart, Mr. Hazard, Mr. and Mrs. Herbert, *George Holland* (1828), Mr. Hyatt, Mr. Isherwood, Mr. Jackson, Miss Jones, Mrs. Jones, *G. Jones*, (1828–30), J. Jones, Miss Kelly, Mr. Kelly, Mrs. Thomas Kilner, *Mrs. La Forrest* (1828–30), *Miss Louisa Lane* (1828), Miss Laws, Mr. Leman, *Mr. Logan* (1828), Miss McBride, Mrs. Meer, Master Mestayer, Miss Mestayer, Mr. J. Mestayer, Miss Pelby, Mrs. Pelby, *Mr. William Pelby* (1829), *A. J. Phillips* (1828), *Miss Caroline Placide* (1828), *Miss Riddle (Mrs. W. H. Smith)* (1828–29), Mr. and Mrs. Riddle, *Elizabeth Riddle* (1828–29), Miss S. Riddle, Mr. Scott, Mr. Shaw, Mr. Simpson, *W. H. Smith* (1828–30), Mr. Stanley, Major Stevens, J. A. Stone, Miss Thayer, *Mr. Thayer* (1828–30), Mr. Thompson, Mr. Tryon, Mrs. Turner, Miss E. Turner, Miss J. Turner, Mr. Walstein, Mr. Walton, Mr. Webb, Mr. and Miss Wells, Mr. Whiting, *Alexander M. Wilson* (1828–29), Mr. Woodly.

REPERTORY

1828: *The Road to Ruin; Fortune's Frolic; The Spectre Bridegroom; John Bull; High Life below Stairs; The Soldier's Daughter; Raising the Wind; Sweethearts and Wives; The Lady and the Devil; The Stranger; Family Jars; The Hypocrite; The Weathercock; Wives as They Were and Maids as They Are; The Irishman in London; She Would Be a Soldier; The Spectre Bridegroom; Beaux without Belles; The Secret; A Day after the Fair; The Wedding Day; The Whims of a Comedian; The Assembly Ball; A Day after the Fair; Venice Preserved; The Weathercock; The Gamester; No Song, No Supper; Rob Roy; The Young Widow; Virginius; Spoil'd Child; The Will; Frightened to Death; Douglas; The Rendezvous; The Two Pages of Frederick the Great; William Tell; The Three and the Deuce; The Belle's Stratagem; The Prize; The School for Scandal; A Day after the Wedding; Two Wives; No Song, No Supper; Turn Out; George Barnwell; The Sea Serpent; or, The Gloucester Hoax; Paul Pry; One and All; The Irish Tutor; The Castle Spectre; The Shipwrecked Sailor; The Poor Gentleman; Of Age Tomorrow; The Forty Thieves; Love à la Mode; The Foundling of the Forest; Magpie and the Maid; The Broken Sword; Don Juan* (pantomime); *The Red Rover; Married and Single; Guy Mannering; Tom Thumb, the Great; The Wandering Boys; The One Hundred-Pound Note; Spoil'd Child; Paul Pry of Salem; The Mogul Tale; Town and Country; Helpless Animals; Richard III; 'Twas I; Charlotte Temple; Blue Devils; The Poor Soldier; Nature and Philosophy; Tom and Jerry; Isabella; The Jew and the Doctor; The Heir-at-Law; Luke, the Labourer.*

1828–29: *The Will; Raising the Wind; Speed the Plough; Spoil'd Child; Virginius; The West Indian; Of Age Tomorrow; Laugh When You Can; The Weathercock; Honey Moon; The Three and the Deuce; Town and Country; Lyar; The Merchant of Venice; 12 Precisely; The Iron Chest; Old and Young; Cure for the Heart-Ache; No Song, No Supper; Richard III; The Poor Soldier; The Poor Gentleman; Catherine and Petruchio; The Belle's Stratagem; Spoil'd Child; Romeo and Juliet; The Ren-*

dezvous; Much Ado about Nothing; Old and Young; Pizarro in Peru; Fire and Water; Macbeth; Othello; How to Die for Love; The Turnpike Gate; Magpie and Maid; The Lady and the Devil; The Wonder; Venice Preserved; The Blind Boy; Alexander the Great; or, The Rival Queens; Thérèse; The Foundling of the Forest; The Soldier's Daughter; Spoil'd Child; Charles II; The Mountaineers; The Review; The Young Widow; The Romp; The Road to Ruin; The Broken Sword; Nature and Philosophy; Speed the Plough; Turn Out; Damon and Pythias; The Blind Boy; Paul Pry; The Children in the Wood; Marion; Intrigue; Fire and Water; The Tale of Mystery; Fortune's Frolic; The Romp; The Comedy of Errors; Rumfustian Inamarato; 'Tis All a Farce; Married and Single; The Veteran and His Progeny; Honey Moon; Is He Jealous?; The Barber of Seville; The Marriage of Figaro; The Bath Road; Hamlet (one performance by guest artist Mr. James Wallack).

1829 (under Mr. Archer): *John Bull; No Song, No Supper; Animal Magnetism; Ella Rosenberg; Tekeli; Charles II; The Spectre Bridegroom; The Castle Spectre; The Village Lawyer; The Lady of the Lake; Matrimony; The Idiot Witness; The Young Widow; Timour, the Tartar; The Battle of New Orleans; The Road to Ruin; Sylvester Daggerwood; Peter Finn; Is It a Lie?; Tom and Jerry; Pizarro in Peru; The Mogul Tale; A Day after the Wedding; Thérèse; Is He Jealous?*

1829 (under Mr. Wilson): *The Foundling of the Forest; The Promissory Note; Ambrose Gwinett; Wandering Boys; The Miller's Maid; Monsieur Tonson; The Bohemian Mother; The Invincibles; The Blue Devils; The Purse; The Rendezvous; The Children in the Wood; King Lear; Touch and Take; Spoil'd Child; The Apostate; Nature and Philosophy; The Warlock of the Glen; Luke, the Labourer; The Prize.*

1819–30: *Sweethearts and Wives; 'Twas I; Bertram; Sylvester Daggerwood; The Weathercock; Richard III; Three Weeks after Marriage; The Foundling of the Forest; The Blue Devils; Is He Jealous?; A Year in a Hour; One Hundred-Pound Note; The Master's Rival; The Prize; The Purse; High Life below Stairs; Evadne; Gretna Green; The School for Courtship; Wool Gathering; Plot and Counterplot; The Times; All at Coventry; The Two Friends; Brag Is a Good Dog, but Holdfast Is Better; Virginius; The Turnpike Gate; Metamora; The Lady and the Devil; Catherine and Petruchio; The Weathercock; The Romp; Two Friends; The Soldier's Daughter; The Two Gregories; The Busy Body; The Dumb Girl of Genoa; William Tell; The Master's Rival; The Dramatist; All at Brighton; Virginius; The Adopted Child.*

BIBLIOGRAPHY

Published Sources: *Essex Register* (Salem, Mass.); *Salem Gazette* (1827–30).

Archival Sources: The Essex Institute in Salem, Massachusetts, has letters and contracts dealing with the Salem Theatre.

Unpublished Source: Patricia H. Sankus, "Theatrical Entertainments and Other Amusements in Salem, Massachusetts, from the Colonial Period through the Year 1830" (Ph.D. diss., Tufts University, 1981).

Patricia H. Sankus

SALT LAKE THEATRE STOCK COMPANY. The Salt Lake Theatre Stock Company, Utah, was organized in late 1861 by Mormon Church President Brigham Young to perform in the newly constructed Salt Lake Theatre. Until about 1867 it was known as the Deseret Dramatic Association.

The theatre opened on March 8, 1862, with J. R. Planché's romantic comedy *The Pride of the Market*.

The close connection between the company, the theatre, and the Mormon leader made it unique among theatre companies of its time. The Mormon Church and its leader regarded theatre with great favor. They had presented productions while they were located in Nauvoo, Illinois; Young had even appeared as the high priest in *Pizarro*. The first theatrical performance in Utah was given in 1850, just three years after they arrived. In 1852 a multipurpose building, the Social Hall, was built, and the Deseret Dramatic Association was organized to perform there. Construction of the Salt Lake Theatre was begun in May 1861, financed by Mormon Church funds. The architect was William H. Folsom, designer of the famed Mormon Tabernacle. The theatre's plan was typical of the time, with a proscenium of thirty-one feet and a backstage depth of sixty-one feet. It originally seated 1,500 in a parquet and three horseshoe balconies.

Young appointed John T. Caine and H. B. Clawson, both members of the Deseret Dramatic Association, to be comanagers of the theatre and the company. Clawson managed the business affairs and Caine was stage manager. Both acted in some of the productions during the first two years.

Young repeatedly said that the theatre's main functions were to provide positive moral instruction and, more importantly, to entertain the isolated, hardworking Mormons. At the same time, he expected a profit would be made to repay construction costs, which were reported to be $100,000. Although specific figures have not survived, a profit was made, probably in excess of $10,000 a year. Since cash was scarce, produce, livestock, and homemade goods were accepted at the box office and, during the first few years, accounted for about two-thirds of the total income.

A major change occurred in February 1867, when Clawson and Caine leased the theatre. Although rent continued to be paid to Young, the company was, for the first time, operated for profit. Exact figures do not exist, but all indications are that it made a comfortable profit during the next six years. In July 1873 the theatre was purchased for $100,000 by the Salt Lake Theatre Corporation, a six-man group headed by Clawson and Caine, who continued as comanagers. The stage was remodeled, and a larger company, which included several nonlocal actors and a new stage manager, was engaged. The 1873–74 season was a financial disaster for the new owners. The increased expenses coupled with the financial panic of 1873 resulted in substantial losses. The managers limped through a curtailed season with a greatly reduced company in 1874–75.

In May 1875 the corporation sold the theatre back to Brigham Young for $126,000, the original purchase price plus the cost of remodeling. Clawson and Caine ended their association with the theatre at that time.

Although Young repeatedly said that moral instruction was an important part of the theatre's purpose, specifically religious plays were not presented.

The repertory leaned heavily to family comedies and sentimental melodramas. Young did not want to see tragedies, because the Mormons' lives were hard enough without seeing disaster on stage. This stricture was broken during Thomas A. Lyne's first guest appearance, which began with J. S. Knowles' heroic tragedy *Virginius*. Thereafter, some tragedies were done. Most of the company's new plays were introduced by guest stars. The increasing popularity of sensational melodramas was reflected. *Under the Gaslight* received an unequaled seven straight performances in 1868.

In its thirteen years of existence, the company gave 2,005 performances of 874 full-length plays and afterpieces. From the opening until mid-1865, two performances were given weekly. This increased to three until 1868, when four to six became common. During the 1873–74 season, there were seven weekly performances. The first two seasons ran from fall to late spring, but thereafter summer seasons were given. By 1870 there was virtually no interruption in performances.

The original acting company was made up of members of the Deseret Dramatic Association and the Mechanic's Dramatic Association, a small group organized in 1860. Both groups, totaling thirty men and ten women, were entirely amateur. Few had acted before arriving in Utah. Only one, Bernard Snow, had appeared briefly with Junius Brutus Booth in California in the early 1850s. The company was organized by lines of business in the manner of professional companies of the time. From the beginning, the leading lines were hard to fill. The two leading men from the Social Hall days were restricted by business demands to only a few performances. The leading male roles were spread among several actors, including Caine, with limited success. The problem was finally solved late in the 1863–64 season, when David McKenzie, a young actor who had been doing old men's roles, did well in several leading roles. He became the company's leading man, a line he held with few interruptions until the company disbanded.

Actresses were in short supply from the beginning in Utah. There were never enough wives and daughters who, after a hard day's work, wanted to spend the evening in rehearsal or performance. The two leading ladies of the Social Hall company had left Utah before the theatre opened. None of the company women were very satisfactory in the leading roles until Lydia Gibson, a newly converted second wife of a Mormon patriarch, arrived from England. Although she had not acted before, she possessed natural talent and became the leading lady in the fall of 1863. She was a great favorite with audiences until her unfortunate early death in 1866. Her line was not adequately filled until a young Salt Lake native, Nellie Colebrook, began to play leading roles in late 1867.

Performing in the company was both an honor and a fulfillment of community and religious duties. Promising young performers in local church theatricals were recommended to the managers. On at least one occasion Brigham Young wrote to the parents of a young actress, requesting that she be allowed to join the company. Several of Young's many daughters performed.

The company received no pay until the end of the 1863–64 season, when two benefits, one each for the men and the women, were held. The shares for each actor ranged from $20 to $75. As the frequency of performances and rehearsals increased, actors and orchestra members began to complain about the income lost through missed work. When they met on April 30, 1864, to protest, Young tried to placate them, reminding them of the great service they were performing. He was not successful, however, and the protests continued until payment was begun sometime in late 1865 or early 1866. Salaries ranged from $12 to $40 a week. By this time the company had developed from a large, inexperienced group to an experienced core of about eighteen men and ten women.

It was Young's original intention that only Mormons act in the company, but this policy was soon changed. Soon after the theatre opened, Clawson learned that an old acquaintance, Thomas A. Lyne, was in Denver, stranded when the Platte Valley Theatre closed. Lyne, a Philadelphia-born actor of some note and a Mormon briefly in 1843 and 1844, had gone to Illinois, where he had organized and starred in several productions. He then left the Mormons before they moved west in 1846. Clawson invited Lyne to Salt Lake, ostensibly to coach the acting company. He arrived in December 1862 in time to prepare them for the second season. Reviews noted an obvious improvement. Lyne was not content only to coach and soon secured a guest-star engagement, which began February 11, 1863. Lyne settled permanently in Salt Lake and appeared as a guest star periodically until 1874.

Lyne's appearance opened the door to other guest stars. Young and the managers realized that guest stars were necessary to relieve the pressure on the local leads and to sustain audience interest. Traveling actors easily secured engagements ranging from a few performances to several weeks. Beginning in 1866 some were engaged as stock stars for as long as three months at a time. Some came from Colorado, where they had appeared with Jack Langrish's companies in Denver and Central City, and continued on to the mining camps of Montana and Nevada. Others stopped on their way to and from San Francisco. Most were itinerate actors of no great reputation who had gone west to play in the mining camps. A few had national fame or were to earn it later. Julia Dean, who had been a very popular ingenue in New York in the late 1840s and early 1850s, went to Salt Lake in the summer of 1865 with a small touring company from San Francisco led by John S. Potter. The company played a short engagement in the theatre, and then Mrs. Dean left the Potter company to play an extended starring engagement with the local company from September 16, 1865, until June 30, 1866. She was very popular with the audiences and a great favorite of Young. It was even rumored for a time that he intended to make her wife number twenty-two. Other early guest stars of national fame were James A. Herne, Edward L. Davenport, and Charlotte Crampton.

When the transcontinental railroad was completed in November 1869, the Salt Lake Theatre became a regular stop on the cross-country tours of well-known actors. J. B., Jr., and Agnes Booth, Johnny Allen, Frank Mayo, Mrs. Frank Chanfrau, Dion Boucicault, and the British Blondes all appeared in the early 1870s. Combinations began to appear at this time. The first group to use the term was the Lingard Combination, three actors and two actresses, which appeared in June 1871. The number of combinations increased steadily until, by the 1874–75 season, they filled the majority of the performing dates.

An important change occurred in 1873, when the new owners began an ambitious season with a company that included many of the local company plus ten nonlocal actors, most of whom had appeared at the theatre as guest or stock stars. The company was given contracts guaranteeing thirty weeks' work, the first time playing time had been guaranteed. The season was a financial disaster, and the management had to return to a week-by-week engagement for the company in 1874. Many touring combinations were booked. Faced with the prospect of limited playing dates, six of the leading players departed to Virginia City, Nevada, to play at John Piper's theatre. The remainder of the company played support to the combinations and visiting stars. Between these engagements the company continued stock performances. The last performance of the season, Tom Taylor's *Ticket-of-Leave Man*, given May 8, 1875, ended Clawson and Caine's management and, for all practical purposes, the Salt Lake Theatre Stock Company. Although the name continued to be used as late as 1879, the actors had either left Salt Lake or returned to their other professions since acting no longer provided a living. Those who remained in Salt Lake continued intermittently to play support to combinations and touring stars. The theatre remained an important stop on cross-country tours until it was torn down in 1928.

Several of the company members continued acting careers at other western theatres, but none achieved prominence. The only performer to do so made only one appearance on the Salt Lake Theatre stage. The infant daughter of the company's comic ingenue, Annie Adams, was carried on in 1873 as a babe-in-arms in the farce *The Lost Child*. That infant, Maude Adams, went on to become a great star, although she can hardly be claimed as a product of the Salt Lake company.

PERSONNEL

Management: Hyrum G. Clawson, comanager and business manager (1862–75), coowner (1873–75); John T. Caine, comanager and stage manager (1862–75), coowner (1873–75); Thomas Williams, treasurer (? –1875).

Scenic Artists: George G. Ottinger, William V. Morris, J. Guido Methua (1868–69), Alfred Lambourne (1868–75), George Tirrell (1873–74).

Musical Directors: C. J. Thomas (1862–65), George Careless (1865–75).

Stock Company Actors and Actresses: *Annie Adams* (1865–75); Sarah Alexander; Henry E. Bowring; Marion Bowring; John T. Caine; J. W. Carter; Alice Clawson; Dellie Clawson; H. B. Clawson; John R. Clawson; Margaret Clawson; Totty Olive; William J. Cogswell (1873–74); *Nellie Colebrook* (1866–75); Sarah Cook; Arrah Crosbie (1873–75); W. O. Crosbie (1873–75); Belle Douglas (1868–75); William C. Dunbar; John W. Dunne; Richard E. Evans; *James Ferguson; Lydia Gibson* (1863–66); *James H. Hardy;* Harry Horsely; John B. Kelly; *John S. Linday* (1863–75); Henry Maiben; *Phil Margetts*; Richard Mathews; Johnny Matson; John McAllister; Henry McEwan; D. J. McIntosh; *David McKenzie* (1863–75); Bert Merrill; W. H. Miles; Sarah Napper; R. F. Neslin; R. H. Parker; Frank Rea (1873–75); C. R. Savage; Joseph Simmons; Sam Sirrine; Henry Snell; Bernard Snow; George Teasdale; Maggie Thomas; James Thompson; *Al Thorne* (1872–75); *James Vinson* (1873–75); Mark Wilton; Mrs. Woodmansee; E. G. Wooley.

Guest Stars and Stock Stars: Edwin Adams (1871); Laura Alberta (1873); Johnny Allen (1871); Charlie Backus (1871); Rose Bain (1874); Daniel E. Bandmann (1871); Shiel Barry (1873); James J. Bartlet (1872); Mr. and Mrs. F. M. Bates (1872); Florence Bell (1864); Agnes Booth (1874); J. B. Booth (1874); Dion Boucicault (1874); Oliver Doud Byron (1871); Carrie Carter (1871–73); J. M. Carter (1871–73); Fanny Cathcart (1873); Mrs. Frank Chanfrau (1872); George D. Chaplin (1869, 1872); Blanche Clifton (1873); William J. Cogswell (1873); the Coleman Sisters (1874); Fannie Colville (1874); C. W. Couldock (1867, 1870, 1871); Eliza Couldock (1867, 1870, 1871); R. H. Cox (1874); Lotta Crabtree (1869); Charlotte Crampton (1868); Arrah Crosbie (1873); W. O. Crosbie (1873); Augusta Dargon (1873, 1874); E. L. Davenport (1868); Julia Dean (1865, 1866); Blanche DeBar (1872); Kate Denin (1869, 1870, 1873, 1874); J. K. Emmett (1871); Rose Evans (1871, 1872); Harry Eyting (1873); W. J. Florence (1874); Annie Graham (1874); Ada Grey (1872); M. E. Gordon (1874); Willie Gill (1875); W. T. Harris (1872); Alice Harrison (1871); Geoge W. Harrison (1873); Ida Hernandez (1871); James A. Herne (1869, 1874, 1875); Sally Hinckley (1870); William Hoskins (1874); Frank Hussey (1873); Annette Ince (1868, 1873); Maria Irwin (1863, 1864); Seldon E. Irwin (1863, 1864); Florence Kent (1873); Mrs. Lander (1871); John S. Langrish (1867, 1870); Horace, Alice, and Dickie Lindgard (1871, 1874, 1875); Annie Lockhart (1868, 1869); Thomas A. Lyne (1863–74); Frank Mayo (1874); W. A. Mestayer (1874); John McCullough (1868, 1871, 1874); Robert McWade (1871); Maggie Moore (1874); Marion Mordant (1873); Joe Murphy (1869, 1871–74); Kate Newton (1871); Milton Nobles (1871); Mille Palmer (1871); George Pauncefort (1864, 1866); Alonzo Phelps (1866); Kitty Planchard (1871); W. H. Power (1871); Rosa Rand (1874); McKee Rankin (1871); Marie Ravel (1871); John T. Raymond (1874); Frank Rea (1873); Harry Rickards (1874); Katherine Rogers (1874, 1875); Sol Smith Russell (1872); J. Al Sawtell (1873, 1874); Mme. Maria Scheller (1868, 1869); James Stark (1868); E. T. Stetson (1872); Amy Stone (1867, 1869); H. F. Stone (1867, 1869); Charlotte Thompson (1870); George W. Thompson (1870); Al Thorne (1872); Helen Tracy (1871); the Volkes Family (1874); George B. Waldron (1865–67); Clara Jean Walters (1872–74); Annie Ward (1872); J. M. Ward (1871); Ger-

aldine Warden (1869); Neil Warren (1869); Lucille Western (1869); Charles Wheatleigh (1871, 1872); Joseph Wheelock (1874); Richard White (1874); Johnny Williamson (1874); John Wilson (1869, 1870].

REPERTORY

Play titles between periods designate one evening's bill.

1862: *The Pride of the Market; State Secrets. The Serious Family; State Secrets;
Sarah's Young Man. The Porter's Knot; Sarah's Young Man; An Object of Interest.
Used Up; An Object of Interest; Paddy Mile's Boy. The Charcoal Burner; To Oblige
Benson; Pleasant Neighbor; Love in Livery. Lavator, the Physiognomist; Love in
a Livery; Betsy Baker. Love's Sacrifice; The Widow's Victim.*

1862–63: *Honey Moon; Paddy Miles' Boy; The Two Polts. Old Phil's Birthday;
The Two Polts; Simpson and Co.; The Charcoal Burner; Don't Judge by Appear-
ances. Virginius; Don't Judge by Appearances; That Blessed Baby. Ingomar, the
Barbarian; That Blessed Baby; Bombastes Furioso. Retribution; Domestic Econ-
omy; All That Glitters Is Not Gold. The Secret Agent; Domestic Economy; The
Artful Dodger. Damon and Pythias; The Secret; Nan: The Good-for-Nothing; The
Artful Dodger. Pizarro; Nan: The Good-for-Nothing; The Artful Dodger; Valet de
Sham. Naval Engagements; Lear of Cripplegate. William Tell; Binks, the Bagman;
The Stranger; Marriage at any Price; Marriage at the Inn. Virginius; Marriage at
any Price. The Porter's Knot; The Artful Dodger; Bombastes Furioso. Damon and
Pythias; The Secret. Pizarro; Our Gal. The Merchant of Venice; The Widow's
Victim; Our Gal.*

1863–64: *Senior Valiente. Raffaelle, the Reprobate; Marriage at any Price; My
Wife's Mother. Eustache Baudin, the Forsaken; Love in Livery; The Irish Tiger;
Bombastes Furioso. The Charcoal Burner; Mr. and Mrs. Peter White. The Lady of
Lyons; The Irish Tiger; The Secret. Ingomar, the Barbarian; The Two Polts. Evadne;
Mr. and Mrs. Peter White; The Omnibus. Faint Heart ne'er Won Fair Lady; The
Omnibus; In and Out of Place. The Warlock of the Glen; A Morning Ball; The
Swiss Girl; A Day in Paris. Ireland as It Was; My Preserver; Perfection. Marble
Heart; The Artful Dodger. The Chimney Corner; Katherine and Petruchio. Honey
Moon; The Married Rake. Marble Heart; Bombastes Furioso. The Octoroon. The
Maid with the Milking Pail; Katherine and Petruchio; The Frisky Cobbler. The
Octoroon; The Frisky Cobbler. The Stranger; Paddy Miles' Boy. The Hunchback;
The Preserver; Two Buzzards. Greenbushes; Two Buzzards; The Trials of Tomp-
kins; The Frisky Cobbler. Damon and Pythias. Love's Sacrifice; The Trials of
Tompkins. Othello; Valet de Sham. The Corsican Brothers; Faint Heart ne'er Won
Fair Lady. Jessie Brown; Naval Engagements; In and Out of Place; The Spectre
Bridegroom. Still Waters Run Deep; Eton Boy. Idiot Witness; Trying It On; The
Spectre Bridegroom. Retribution; Eton Boy. Satan in Paris; My Fellow Clerk; Who
Speaks First?. The Angel of Midnight; Nature and Philosophy; Who Speaks First?.
Ireland as It Was; Slasher and Crasher. The Corsican Brothers; Loan of a Lover.
The Colleen Bawn; The Widow's Victim. Evadne; The Spectre Bridegroom. The
Lady of Lyons; The Frisky Cobbler. The Colleen Bawn; The Mountain Sylph.
Aurora Floyd. The Golden Farmer; The Omnibus. The Jacobite; The Irish Tutor.
Raffaelle, the Reprobate; The Siamese Twins. Eustache Baudin. The Crock of Gold;
Toodles. Damon and Pythias. Pizarro. The Octoroon. William Tell; The Indes-*

cribable. *The Romance of a Poor Young Man. The Merchant of Venice. Black Eyed Susan; Used Up; The Little Treasure. Hamlet. Ben, the Boatswain; The Little Treasure. The Corsican Brothers. The Duke's Motto. Don Caesar de Bazan; Beauty and the Beast.*

1864–65: *Jessie Brown; The Two Polts; Slasher and Crasher. The Jacobite; Toodles. A New Way to Pay Old Debts; The Hole in the Wall; The Spectre Bridegroom. Richelieu. The Warlock of the Glen; The Maid of Croissey. Darnand, the Denouncer; The Maid of Croissey; Richelieu. Richard III. Don Caesar de Bazan; Barney, the Baron. Black Eyed Susan; A Bachelor of Arts. Hamlet. The Duke's Motto. Belphegor, the Mountebank. Macbeth. White Lies; Barney, the Baron. The Colleen Bawn; Nature and Philosophy; The Queen's Subject. Rob Roy; The Queen's Subject; Nature and Philosophy. A Husband to Order; The Crock of Gold; The Idiot Witness. The Charcoal Burner; A Yankee in Cuba. The Iron Chest; Out to Nurse. The Octoroon; Out to Nurse. The Porter's Knot; Family Jars. Camilla's Husband; Family Jars; The Clockmaker's Hat. The Avenger; Magic Toys. Uncle Tom's Cabin. The Heart of Midlothian; The Frisky Cobbler; Magic Toys. Uncle Tom's Cabin. Camilla's Husband; Out to Nurse. The Avenger; Family Jars. Old Phil's Birthday; Ali Baba. Time Tries All; Lear of Cripplegate; Macbeth; Bombastes Furioso; Ali Baba; The Ticket-of-Leave Man. The Rag Picker of Paris; How's Your Uncle. Camilla's Husband; Magic Toys. Madelaine; The Bachelor's Bedroom. The Ticket-of-Leave Man. Uncle Tom's Cabin. The Rag Picker of Paris; Turn Him Out. Ernest Maltravers; How's Your Uncle. Madelaine; Turn Him Out. Family Jars; Idiot Witness; Turn Him Out. Intrigue; Stage Struck Barber; Actress of All Work. The Enraged Policeman; Hunting a Turtle; Nan: The Good-for-Nothing. Time Tries All; Naval Engagements. The People's Lawyer; Toodles.*

1865–66: *Macbeth. Madelaine; Husband of an Hour. Ernest Maltravers; The Serious Family. The School for Scandal. East Lynne. Medea; Husband for an Hour. The Wife; Love in All Corners. Ingomar, the Barbarian; My Son Diana. Our American Cousin; In and Out of Place. Pauline; Nobbs Will Turn Him Out. The Wife; Out to Nurse. The Lady of Lyons; The Lost Child. Masks and Faces; The Lost Child; Love in Livery. The Wife's Secret; The Queen's Subject. Evadne; The Mummy. The Fatal Mask; The Omnibus. The Marble Heart; The Secret. Cloud and Sunshine; Marriage at Any Price. The Colleen Bawn; Jubilee House. Lesbia; My Son Diana. Green Bushes; My Son Diana. Lesbia; Loan of a Lover. Rob Roy; Jubilee House. The Octoroon; Eton Boy. Green Bushes; The Lost Child. The Merchant of Venice; The Captain is Not A-Miss. The Hunchback; The Artful Dodger. Pizarro; The Captain is Not A-Miss. Gemea; Loan of a Lover; The Spectre Bridegroom. She Would and He Wouldn't; Forty Thieves. All That Glitters Is Not Gold; She Would and He Wouldn't. Flowers in the Forest; Box and Cox; Magic Toys. Nick of the Woods; The Spectre Bridegroom; The Young Widow. Metamora; The Young Widow. The Duke's Wager; The Two Polts. Aladdin; Valet de Sham; Faint Heart ne'er Won True Lady; Follies of a Night; The Jealous Wife; Honey Moon. Eleanor de Vere; The Rival Lovers; The Irish Tiger. Aladdin; The Rival Lovers. The Wrecker's Daughter; Raising the Wind. Fazio; Raising the Wind. Adrienne; Turn Him Out; Pocahontas. Much Ado about Nothing; Pocahontas. Leah the Forsaken; Pocahontas. East Lynne; Where's Your Wife. Much Ado about Nothing; The First Night. London Assurance; The First Night. The Wife; Apartments. London Assurance; Lend Me Five Shillings. The Foundling; The Irish Tutor. The Creole;*

Handy Andy; Magic Spell. Lesbia; Magic Spell. The Creole; Handy Andy. Aladdin; Handy Andy. Camille; The Fool of the Family. The Stanger; Pocahontas. Foundling of the Forest; The Two Polts. Guy Mannering; Magic Spell. Osceola; Jubilee House. The Gamester; My Husband's Ghost. The Wife's Secret; The Yankee Pedlar. The Hunchback; My Husband's Ghost. Gemea. The Black Sheep; Bowl'd Out. The Ticket-of-Leave Man. Thisbe; Bowl'd Out; The Pope of Rome. Cinderella; The Conscript. The Gunmaker of Moscow; As Alike as Two Peas. Ireland as It Was; Wanted a Young Lady. The Willow Copse. The Gunmaker of Moscow; Ici on parle francaise. A Woman's Love; Handy Andy. The Colleen Bawn; The Rough Diamond. The Courier of Lyons; The Irish Broommaker. The Black Sheep; Ici on parle francaise. The Love Knot; The New Footman. The Rag Picker of Paris; Deaf as a Post. Gilderoy; The Artful Dodger. Camilla's Husband; Brother Bill and Me. Robert Macaire; As Alike as Two Peas. Time Tries All; A Woman's Love. Extremes.

1866–67: The Love Knot. The Old Chateau; Brother Bill and Me. Damon and Pythias; Wanted: A Young Man. Charles XII; Jeremy Didler. Pizarro; My Husband's Ghost. Grandfather Whitehead; The Toodles. Black Eyed Susan; Naval Engagements. A Wonderful Woman; Grandfather Whitehead. Grist to the Mill; Andy Blake. Satan in Paris; Sketches in India. Grimaldi; The Fool of the Family. Our American Cousin; Lola Montez. Grist to the Mill; Antony and Cleopatra; Andy Blake. The Hidden Hand. Grimaldi; Perfection. The Angel of Midnight; Advertising for a Wife. The Marble Heart; Advertising for a Wife. Fanchon; Quash; or, Nigger Practice. The Wild Irish Girl; A Day in Paris. Asmodeus. Plot and Passion; Sketches in India. Kate Kearney; Spoil'd Child; Follies of a Night. Dominique, the Deserter; Advertising for a Wife. The Gunmaker of Moscow; Poulter's Wedding. The Deal Boatman; Poulter's Wedding. The Courier of Lyons; Area Belles. The Deal Boatman; The Illustrious Stranger. The Old Chateau; The Illustrious Stranger. Ten Nights in a Barroom; Area Belles; John Wopps; Out to Nurse. The Willow Copse; John Wopps. Gilderoy; From Village to Court. The Avenger; From Village to Court. Flowers of the Forest; The Lost Child; The Love Knot; Solon Shingle. The Wife; Found in a Four Wheeler. The Brigand; Bowl'd Out; The Illustrious Stranger. Dot; or, The Cricket on the Hearth; The Elves. Time Tries All; The Elves. Temptation; The Elves. Ten Nights in a Barroom; Harlequin's Triumph. Extremes; Harlequin's Triumph. Uncle Tom's Cabin; Found in a Four Wheeler. Venice Preserved; Take Care of Little Charlie; The Highwayman's Holiday. Extremes; The Highwayman's Holiday. Giralda; Take Care of Little Charlie. The Octoroon; The Lost Child. Jessie Brown; Bombastes Furioso. Victims; The Spectre Bridegroom. Green Bushes; Nobbs Will Turn Him Out. Damon and Pythias; An Object of Interest. Pizarro; Too Much for Good Nature. Virginius; The Happy Man. Richelieu. Thérèse: The Orphan of Geneva; The Frisky Cobbler. Richard III. The Apostate; Too Much for Good Nature. Richelieu. Othello; A Kiss in the Dark. Macbeth. The Apostate; Your Life's in Danger. The Charcoal Burner; Cramond Brig. Spirit Child; Your Life's in Danger; Handy Andy. Victorine; The Wilful Ward. The Somnambulist; Cramond Brig. Ten Nights in a Barroom; Harlequin's Triumph. Victims; The Illustrious Stranger. Natural Curiosity; My Wife's Maid. Victorine; The Happy Man. Don Caesar de Bazan; The Practical Man. Black Eyed Susan; A Bachelor of Arts. Hamlet. Lavater the Physiognomist; Seeing Margaret. The Duke's Motto. The Man with the Iron Mask; Pocahontas. Black Eyed Susan; Pocahontas. The Duke's Motto. Hamlet. Still Waters Run Deep; The Wilful Ward. The Bride of Lammermoor; The Little

Treasure. Belphegor, the Mountebank. The Romance of a Poor Young Man. The Three Guardsmen; The Irish Post. Macbeth. The Dead Heart. The Streets of New York. Arrah-na-Pogue. The Pope of Rome. The Carpenter of Rouen. Jessie Brown; My Turn Next. Giralda; Paddy Miles' Boy. The Road of Life; Seeing Margaret. The Carpenter of Rouen. The Chimney Corner; His Last Legs. The Willow Copse; The Laughing Hyena. Kate Hayes; The Post Boy. Louix XI; Poor Pillicoddy. Dot; or, The Cricket on the Hearth; The Omnibus. Arrah-na-Pogue. The Jew of Frankfort; The Wilful Ward. Richelieu. Jocrisse, the Juggler; Sarah's Young Man. The Willow Copse. Waiting for the Verdict. The Advocate's Last Cause; Milky White. Othello. Rosedale. Fanchon. The Pearl of Savoy.

1867–68: The Hidden Hand. The Female Gambler; The Maid with the Milking Pail. Our American Cousin; State Secrets. The Long Strike. The Pearl of Savoy. The Long Strike; Pleasant Neighbors. Little Barefoot. The Sea of Ice. The French Spy; The Rough Diamond. Uncle Tom's Cabin. The Sea of Ice. The French Spy; Stone in a Regular Fix. The Sea of Ice. The Long Strike; The Maid with the Milking Pail. The Hidden Hand. The Drunkard. Caste. Miralda; The Wandering Boys. Caste; Matteo Falcone. Our American Cousin; Matteo Falcone. The Workmen of New York; The Two Pigeons. The French Spy; Sketches in India. The Sea of Ice; The Spectre Bridegroom. The Workmen of New York; My Turn Next. Little Barefoot; Sketches in India. Griffith Gaunt. The Soldier's Daughter; The Wandering Boys. Meg's Diversion; Sketches in India. The Black Sheep. Nobody's Daughter. The Ticket-of-Leave Man; The Lost Child. The Stranger; The Lost Child. The Merchant of Venice; A Kiss in the Dark. The Hunchback; Bowl'd Out. Henry IV. Old Phil's Birthday; The Porter's Knot. Henry IV. Richard III; My Wife's Maid. Self; Valet de Sham; The Double Bedded Room. The Chimney Corner; Naval Engagements. Waiting for the Verdict; The Frisky Cobbler. Rosedale; The Frisky Cobbler. Lesbia; Valet de Sham. Lost in London; One Touch of Nature. The Willow Copse; The Rival Lovers. Lost in London; Milky White. Brutus; Valet de Sham. Richelieu; The Double Bedded Room. Money; How's Your Uncle?. The Merry Wives of Windsor. Money and Misery; Katherine and Petruchio. Jack Cade. The Huguenot Captain; Nature and Philosophy. Extremes; The Two Polts. Time Tries All; The Forty Thieves. The Writing on the Wall; The Widow's Victim. The Huguenot Captain; Too Much for Good Nature. Hamlet; Boots at the Swan. The Sea of Ice; Found in a Four Wheeler. Arrah-na-Pogue. The Colleen Bawn; A Kiss in the Dark. Somebody Else; Aladdin. A Woman's Love; Aladdin. Jessie Brown; The Dead Shot. The Writing on the Wall; Somebody Else. Leah the Forsaken; Don't Judge by Appearances. The Streets of New York; Dandelion's Dodger. Macbeth; The Spectre Bridegroom. Leap Year; The Illustrious Stranger. The Octoroon; The Dead Shot. Man of Many Friends. Evadne; Don't Judge by Appearances. Victorine; Love in Livery. Arrah-na-Pogue. The Huguenot Captain; Slasher and Crasher. Leah the Forsaken; The Frisky Cobbler. Damon and Pythias; Deaf as a Post. Paul-a-Dhail. The Deal Boatman; Off and On. Ernest Maltravers; The Mummy. Richelieu. Nick of the Woods; Slasher and Crasher. The Island King; Off and On. The Robbers; Dandelion Dodger. Nick of the Woods; English Fair Scene. The Island King; The Wilful Ward. Nobody's Child; Leap for Life. King Lear; The First Night. Retribution; Mother and Child Are Doing Well. The Corsican Brothers. The Marble Heart. The Pearl of Savoy. Mathilde; Love in Livery. The Lady of Lyons; The Swiss Cottage. Enoch Arden. The Phantom; Ernestine. Hamlet. The Merchant of

Venice; When Women Weep. Don Caesar de Bazan; Ernestine. Richard III. Under the Gaslight (seven performances). *Mathilde; The Two Puddifoots. Lucille; The Two Puddifoots. Enoch Arden; Too Much for Good Nature. Lucille; Too Much for Good Nature. Cinderella* (five performances). *The Idiot of the Mill. The Pearl of Savoy. The Dead Shot. The Lady of Lyons. Child of the Regiment; The Wilful Ward; Nature and Philosophy. The Hunchback. Evadne. Medea; A Morning Call. Mary Stuart. Ion, the Foundling. As You Like It. Elizabeth* (two performances). *Camille. Richelieu. The Wife. Black Eyed Susan; Faint Heart ne'er Won True Lady. Love's Sacrifice.*

1868–69: *Medea; Don't Judge by Appearances. Hamlet. East Lynne. Wild Oats; The Day after the Wedding. Elizabeth; Fazio; Off and On. Love and the Serf. Madeline; A Morning Call. Pizarro; Mr. and Mrs. White. Jeanne Deans; The Smiths and Burns; Mr. and Mrs. White. Wild Oats; Race for a Widow. The Golden Farmer; Milky White; Rent Day. Louis XI; His Last Legs. Jack Cade; The Lost Child. The Carpenter of Rouen; His Last Legs. Under the Gaslight. Extremes; The Smiths and the Browns. The Rag Picker of Paris. Jack in the Water; A Roland for an Oliver. The Pride of the Market; An Unprotected Female. Green Bushes; Bombastes Furioso. Sweethearts and Wives; Wandering Steenie. The Road of Life; A Roland for an Oliver. The Rose of Eltrick Vale; Naval Engagements. Thérèse, the Orphan of Geneva; Nobbs Will Turn Him Out. The Sea of Ice. The Gunmaker of Moscow. The Child of the Regiment; The Spectre Bridegroom. The Somnambulist; Toodles. The Colleen Bawn. The Life of an Actress. The Lady of Lyons; The Spectre Bridegroom. Mathilde; Nobbs Will Turn Him Out. The Love Knot; Too Much for Good Nature. Armand; The Obstinate Family. The Avenger; The Rough Diamond. The Old Chateau; The Artful Dodger. Ireland as It Was; Time Tries All. Damon and Pythias; Deaf as a Post. Richelieu. The Marble Heart. Othello. Hamlet. The Merchant of Venice; The First Night. The Robbers. Richard III. Macbeth. Playing with Fire. Brutus. The Apostate; The Obstinate Family; Wild Oats; Playing with Fire. Romeo and Juliet. The Lady of Lyons; The First Night. The Lancashire Lass* (three performances). *The Three Guardsmen. The Life of an Actress. Under the Gaslight. Rosedale; When Women Weep. La sonnambula. Mathilde. The Idiot of the Mill. The Child of the Regiment; The Rough Diamond. The Broken Sword; A Roland for an Oliver; The Swiss Cottage. Giralda; A Roland for an Oliver. Pauvrette. The Streets of New York. The Pearl of Savoy. Cinderella* (three performances). *Our American Cousin. The Lottery of Life* (four performances). *Under the Gaslight. The Naiad Queen* (four performances). *The Octoroon. The Child of the Regiment; Slasher and Crasher. Beauty and the Beast; When Women Weep; Ernestine. Jessie Brown; A Kiss in the Dark; A Roland for an Oliver. Ingomar, the Barbarian. Camille. Lady Audley's Secret; The Dead Shot; Nan: The Good-for-Nothing. Masks and Faces. Jane Pride; A Fearful Tragedy. Belle's Stratagem; To Oblige Benson. World and Stage; A Handsome Husband; To Oblige Benson. Wonders; The Two Polts. Masks and Faces; A Handsome Husband. Two Loves and Life* (three performances). *The Shingawn. Wallace; A Sheep in Wolf's Clothing. The Unequal Match; A Handsome Husband. Rip Van Winkle* (four performances). *The Day after the Wedding; Handy Andy; Rip Van Winkle. East Lynne. Green Bushes. The Heart of the Stage; Solon Shingle. Oliver Twist. Flowers of the Forest. Leah the Forsaken. Our American Cousin; Paddy Miles' Boy. Babes in the Wood; Paddy Miles' Boy. Dombey and Son; Rosina Meadows. One Hundred Thousand Pounds;*

Wept of the Wish-Ton-Wish. The Child Stealer (three performances). *The Loan of a Lover. Camilla's Husband. Foul Play. Lucrezia Borgia. Lady Audley's Secret; A Sheep in Wolf's Clothing. Actress by Daylight. The Wild Irish Girl. Kate Wynsley; Somebody Else. The Soldier's Daughter; The Bonnie Fish Wife. Arrah-na-Pogue. The Ladies' Battle; Bonnie Fish Wife. Susan Hopely; Katty O'Sheil. Moll Pitcher* (three performances). *Nell Gwynne. Moll Pitcher. The Colleen Bawn; Under the Gaslight. The Octoroon. Two Loves and a Life. The White Slave; The Lost Child; Too Much for Good Nature. Lost in London; To Oblige Benson; The Lone House on the Heath. Jane Pride. Ingomar, the Barbarian. The Lottery of Life. After Dark; The Model of a Wife* (four performances). *La grand duchesse* (three performances). *Tromb-al-ca-zar. Perfection; Il Trovatore. Pierette. Kate Kearney; The Eton Boy. I Couldn't Help It; Kenilworth. Rural Felicity. The Little Ambassador from Berlin; Mrs. Norma. Billy Horsebreaker; Der Freishutz; Ben and the Orange Tree. Illusion* (six performances). *Honey Moon; Maniac Love. Macbeth. The Lady of Lyons. Rosedale. Black Eyed Susan; Maniac Love. Nick of the Woods; Family Jars. The School for Scandal. All That Glitters Is Not Gold; Nan: The Good-for-Nothing. Arma Dale; Pocahontas. Little Nell and the Marchioness* (three performances). *Captain Charlotte; Nan: The Good-for-Nothing. Firefly. Uncle Tom's Cabin. Seven Sisters. Ten Nights in a Barroom. The Lady of Lyons. The Drunkard; Pocahontas. Entertainment; Family Jars; An Object of Interest. Time Tries All; The Dead Shot. Delicate Ground; Andy Blake. The Gentleman in Black; The Illustrious Stranger; Beauty and the Beast.*

1869–70: *The Captain of the Vulture. True to the Core; Blow for Blow; The Phemonom in a Smock Frock; Country Cousin. Richard III. Richelieu. Ingomar, the Barbarian; Delicate Ground. Othello. Don Caesar de Bazan; Used Up. A New Way to Pay Old Debts. Macbeth. The Hunchback; The Phemonom in a Smock Frock. The Lady of Lyons; The Swiss Cottage. Love's Sacrifice. Hamlet; A Morning Call. The Iron Chest. The Ticket-of-Leave Man. The Corsican Brothers. Ingomar, the Barbarian; The Swiss Cottage. Virginius. The Wife. Black Eyed Susan; The Gamester. The Love Chase; Family Jars. Richard III. Richelieu; Nan: The Good-for-Nothing. Macbeth. The Hunchback; Delicate Ground. Hamlet; The Smiths and Browns. A New Way to Pay Old Debts. The Gentleman in Black. The Maid and the Magpie; The Loan of a Lover. The Child of the Regiment; Slasher and Crasher. The Roll of the Drum; The Two Polts. Enoch Arden; Nobbs Will Turn Him Out. Under the Gaslight. The French Spy; Marchioness or Nothing. Kathleen Mavourneen; A Pleasant Neighbor. The French Spy; The Four Sisters. The Hidden Hand. The Long Strike; Andy Blake. Fanchon, the Cricket; Meg's Diversion; State Secrets. Baccarat; The Tailor of Tamworth. Griffith Gaunt. Waiting for the Verdict. Jessie Brown; A Rough Diamond. The Romance of a Poor Young Man; The Swiss Swains. The Poor of New York. The White Slave; The Swiss Swains. Claude Marcel; Family Jars. Belle of the Laubourg; Who Killed Cock Robin?; The Soldier's Daughter. Lucrezia Borgia; Too Much for Good Nature. Masks and Faces; Nobbs Will Turn Him Out. The Soldier's Daughter. Paul: The Pet of the Petticoats; Pocahontas. Black Eyed Susan. Camille. Formosa. The Angel of Midnight. Ireland as It Was; Gisippins; Jenny Lind at Last. Griffith Gaunt. The Female Detective; The Two Polts. East Lynne; Mr. and Mrs. Peter White. The Actress of Padua. The Hidden Hand. She Stoops to Conquer. Fazio; Dunducketly's Picnic. Jack Cade; Jenny Lind at Last. Hunted Down; An Object of Interest. The Golden Farmer; The Governor's*

Wife. Christmas Eve; The Frisky Cobbler. Robert Macaire; Ixion. Belle of the Fauberg. Presumptive Evidence; Brother Bill and Me. Rob Roy; Jenny Lind and Me. The Octoroon. The Marble Heart. Asmodeus. Hunted Down; Brother Bill and Me. The Hunchback; Brother Bill and Me. Romeo and Juliet. The Sea of Ice. Leah the Forsaken. Court and Sage. Peep O'Day. The Golden Farmer; Asmodeus. The Field of the Cloth of Gold; A Husband at Sight. Henry IV. The Duel in the Snow. Rosedale. The Duke's Motto. Victims; Horatio Thomas Sparkins. The Pride of the Market; Make Your Will; The Ladies' Club; Toodles. Rose of Amiens; The Wandering Boys. Men of the Day; Aunt Charlotte's Maid. White Horse of the Peppers; Ixion. The Avenger; Rose of Amiens. Mazeppa. Rookwood. Sistus V; Wanted: A Young Lady. Eustace Baudin; Slasher and Crasher. Forty Thieves. William Tell. Sinbad, the Sailor. La sonnambula. The Huguenot Captain; Love in Livery. William Tell; Bragg vs. Plotter. Damon and Pythias; Bowl'd Out. Sweethearts and Wives; The Wilful Ward.

1870–71: Richard Carvel; The Married Rake. The Muleteer of Toledo; The Wilful Ward. Sweethearts and Wives; The Married Rake; The Carpenter of Rouen; John Buttercup. The Avenger; My Husband's Ghost. The Sergeant's Wife; John Duck. A Bird in the Hand Is Worth Two in the Bush; A Married Rake; Did You Send Your Wife to Lakeside. A Wonderful Woman; The Young Widow. Luke, the Labourer; Naval Engagements. Victorine; The Ductchman's Ghost. The Colleen Bawn; Brother Bill and Me. The Will and the Way; The Dutchman's Ghost; Raising the Wind. Richard Carvel; Did You Take Your Wife to Lakeside. The Gunmaker of Moscow. Extremes; Did You Take Your Wife to Lakeside. The Road of Life; The Artful Dodger. Uncle Tom's Cabin. Ireland as It Was; Benicia Bay. The Streets of New York. Self; Budget of Blunders. Americans in Paris; Simpson and Co.; Lochinvar; The Fatal Initials. The Poor Gentleman; The Irish Lion. The Chimney Corner; The Irish Swain. Dora; I'll Call Mab. Uncle Dick's Darling; The Omnibus. Willow Copse; The Fatal Initials. Louis XI; Uncle Sam. Man and Wife; The Persecuted Dutchman. Birth; The Dutchman's Ghost. Rapparee; The Happy Man; The Rival Dutchman. The Octoroon. Frou-Frou. The Lancashire Lass. Wine Works Wonders; Fortune's Follies. Catherine Howard; The Smiths and the Browns. Under the Gaslight. The Lost Ship. Evadne; Brother Bill and Me. The Rag Picker of Paris; The Artful Dodger. Ten Nights in a Barroom. The Ice Witch; A Kiss in the Dark; Larkin's Love Letter; Sophie's Supper. A Husband to Order; Larkin's Love Letter; The Frisky Cobbler. The Jacobite; Jack Robinson and His Monkey. The Ticket-of-Leave Man. The Lonely Man of the Ocean; Sophie's Supper. A Bird in the Hand Is Worth Two in the Bush; Two Bonny Castles. Ireland as It Was; Dandelions Dodger. The Wind and the Whirlwind; Jubilee House. Fanchon, the Cricket. Little Mother; The First Night. Rosedale. Nannie. Rip Van Winkle. Little Barefoot. The Colleen Bawn. Nicholas Nickleby; Who Killed Cock Robin?; The Hidden Hand. Romeo and Juliet. Lady Audley's Secret; Sophie's Supper. Ingomar, the Barbarian; The Dutchman's Ghost. Twixt Axe and Crown. Hamlet. Belphegor, the Mountebank; Mother and Child Are Doing Well. Robbers of the Pyrenees; Brother Bill and Me. Robert Emmett; Six Degrees of Crime. The Merchant of Venice; The Corsican Brothers; A Happy Pain. Narcisse; My Turn Next. Richard III. Fritz: Our German Cousin (four performances). Blow for Blow. Under the Gaslight. Uncle Tom's Cabin. The Six Degrees of Crime; Faraxicum Twitters. The Red Mask; Gisippius. After Dark; A Sunday on Wager. The Willow Copse. The Chimney Corner; The First Time. Dora; Faraxicum Twitters. Old Phil's Birthday; Milky White. The Helping Hand;

*Faraxicum Twitters. The Jew of Frankfort; Irish Assurance and Yankee Modesty.
The Willow Copse; John Strong. The Advocate's Last Cause; Hew of Primrose Hall.
Waiting for the Verdict; A Sunday on Wager. Uncle Dick's Darling; The Double
Bedded Room. Richelieu; Christien and Christine. The French Dancing Master; A
Night of Adventures. The Miser of Marseilles; Cow-bell-o-gians. Who's to Have
Him; Naval Engagements. Delicate Ground; Little Toddlekins. The Day after the
Wedding; The Loan of a Lover. Dechatmeau; The Boston Police Jubilee; Perfection.
Humpty Dumpty; The Lost Man. The School for Scandal; One Touch of Nature.
Ben Bolt; Lafitte. Everybody's Friend. Which Is Which. Chiro Magique. The En-
chanted Canopy. The Professor's Ghost. Black Eyed Susan; Wild Oats. Men of the
Day. King of the Commons. Stop Him Who Can; La tour de Nesle. Macbeth.
Damon and Pythias; The Swiss Chalet. Othello; The Fairy Font. The Marble Heart.
Hamlet. London Assurance; The Fairy Font. Richard III; The Illuminated Fountain.
Fanchon, the Cricket. The Sea of Ice. The Idiot Witness. The Serious Family. The
Rag Picker of Paris; The Swiss Chalet. Arrah-na-Pogue.*

1871–72: *Nick of the Woods; The Illuminated Fountain. The Captain of the Watch;
Who Speaks First; Marriage at Any Price. Caste; Heathen Chinese. Frou-Frou; The
Mischievous Nigger. Help* (five performances). *Ambition; John Buttercup. The
Octoroon. Married Life; Boots at the Swan. Miriam's Crime; To Oblige Benson;
Romantic Tendencies. Never too Late to Mend. No Thoroughfare. Miriam's Crime;
A Dutchman's Difficulties. Elizabeth: Queen of England. Mary Queen of Scots.
Marie Antoinette. Time and Tide. Married Life; The Lost Child; The Illuminated
Fountain. Time Tries All; Did You Ever Send Your Wife to Ogden. The Lost Ship;
Larkin's Love Letter. Rip Van Winkle* (five performances). *From Village to Court;
Handy Andy. The Foundling of the Forest; Our Gal. Rocambole; A Case for Court.
Blanche Herriot; The Jealous Wife. The Phantom of the Village; The Irish Tutor.
Wandering Steenie; Two Buzzards* and a scene from *The School for Scandal. Kate
Wynsley; A Shower of Cats. The Old Chateau; Turn Him Out. Schneider* (four
performances). *Captain Kyd. Claude Marcel; Mr. and Mrs. Peter White. Never too
Late to Mend; A Pleasant Neighbor. Born to Good Luck; The Somnambulist. A
Hand of Cards. The Poor of New York; A Jealous Wife. Sixtus V. The Hidden
Hand. The Ladies' Club; Pitcher and Tosser. Through by Daylight* (six perform-
ances). *His Last Legs; Larkin's Love Letter; Paddy Miles' Boy. Across the Continent*
(six performances). *Ben McCullough. Uncle Tom's Cabin. Molly Pitcher. The Ladies' Club; Family Jars. Joan of Arc; The Smiths and the Browns. The Palace of
Truth; Pitcher and Tosser. Sight and Darkness; The Highwayman's Holiday; Love
in All Corners. Above and Below. Hamlet; A Happy Pair. Lady Audley's Secret;
Above and Below. Nell Gwynne. East Lynne. The Band of Society. The Daughter
of the Regiment; Mary Price. A Hand of Cards; As Alike as Two Peas; The House
Dog. Neck and Neck* (six performances). *The Drunkard; The Highwayman's Hol-
iday. Pizarro; The House Dog. Illusion. The Will and the Way; The Omnibus.
Jessie Brown. The Duel in the Snow; The House Dog. Randall's Thumb. Paul Pry.
Pure Gold. Under the Gaslight. Frou-Frou; The Dead Shot. Camilla's Husband;
The Trials of Tompkins. Not Guilty. Sybilla; The Trials of Tompkins; As Alike as
Two Peas. Rosedale. Not Guilty; The Omnibus. A Wonderful Woman; A Hand of
Cards. Hamlet; The House Dog. A Dream at Sea. The Corsican Brothers. Horatio
Thomas Sparkins; Married Life. Pigeon, The Turncoat. Elizabeth: Queen of Eng-
land. The Secret of a Life; The Conjugal Lesson. Caste; The Married Rake. Camille;*

The Trials of Tompkins. The Hunchback; Sophie's Supper. Eustache Baudin. Ingomar, the Barbarian; Toodles. Frou-Frou. The Duke's Motto. London Assurance. The Lady of Lyons. The Marble Heart. East Lynne. Not Guilty. Pure Gold. London Assurance. The Man with the Iron Mask. Richelieu. Romeo and Juliet. Lucrezia Borgia; Bamboozling. The Palace of Truth. All That Glitters Is Not Gold; Pitcher and Tosser. Panorama; Ixion. Cinderella; The Trials of Tompkins; Pygmalion; The Dead Shot. Help. Handy Andy. Black Eyed Susan; Grecian Statues. True to the Cross. The Stolen Pocket Book. A Victim of Circumstances; Forty Winks. Arrahna-Pogue. The Octoroon. John Garth. The Lottery of Life. Flying Scud. Early California.

1872–73: *Buffalo Bill. Monte Cristo. Joseph and His Brethren. Enoch Arden. Ireland as It Was; Pocahontas. Lady Thornhurst's Daughter. Macbeth. Neck and Neck. Daring Dick. Illusion. The Fatal Glass. The Seven Sisters. Article Forty-Seven. Jezebel; The Rough Diamond. Whose Wife; Sketches in India. Little Emily; Enoch Arden; Pocahontas. Strathmore; Norma. Nick of the Woods; Norma. Ingomar, the Barbarian; The Invisible Prince. Money and Misery; The Rough Diamond. Richelieu; An Object of Interest. Macbeth. The School for Scandal. The Writing on the Wall. The Muleteer of Toledo; Area Belles. The Octoroon; Bombastes Furioso. The Charcoal Burner; Family Jars. The Poor Nobleman; Solon Shingle; Ireland as It Was; The Illustrious Stranger. The Colleen Bawn. Sogarth Aroon. Honey Moon; That Blessed Baby. Aladdin; The Phenomenon in a Frock Smock. Caste; The Artful Dodger. The Streets of New York. Richard III. East and West (five performances). Nobody's Child. Don Caesar de Bazan; Lend Me Five Pounds. The Hunchback; My Turn Next. Griffith Gaunt. Havel, the Unknown; Hit Him, He Has No Friends; My Turn Next. Maud's Peril; A Capital Match. Magdalen; A Capital Match. David Garrick; As Cool as a Cucumber. Married for Money. The Man with the Iron Mask. Maude's Peril; Larkin's Love Letter. Fate. Leah the Forsaken. East Lynne. Fettered. Love's Sacrifice. Elizabeth: The Queen of England. Camille. Ingomar, the Barbarian. The Stranger. Frou-Frou. Lucrezia Borgia; At the Club. The Duke's Motto. Macbeth. The Bells. The Three Guardsmen; Box and Cox. Othello; The Spectre Bridegroom. Illusion; A Wife's Ordeal; Honey Moon; Box and Cox. Fate. Everybody's Friend. Dot. Only a Jew; Hit Him, He Has No Friends. Rip Van Winkle. Married Life; A Kiss in the Dark. Schneider (four performances). The Little Rebel; Belle of the Kitchen. Poisoned; That Blessed Baby. The French Spy; Cynthia; The Frisky Cobbler. Romeo and Juliet. The Ticket-of-Leave Man. Moll Pitcher. London Assurance; The Language Lesson. The Ice Witch. The Lost Ship. Nick of the Woods. Days of '76. Sam Patch in France; A Capital Match; Brass Band Practice. Nathan Tucker; Storming Fort Fisher. A Yankee in China. Not Such a Fool as He Looks; The Dead Shot. The Hermit of the Cave. Kathleen Mavourneen; Ici on parle francais. The Serf; I've Written to Brown; Brass Band Practice. Aline; Ici on parle francais; A Kiss in the Dark. Irish Assurance and Yankee Modesty; I've Written to Brown; The Dead Shot. The Rapids; Mose and Lize. Stage and Steam (three performances). Hazard (four performances). The Merton Sisters; The Four O'Clock Train. Darling (four performances). Hearts Are Trumps. Camille. Deborah; Lady Macbeth. Guy Mannering; I've Written to Brown. Unmasked. Lucrezia Borgia. Cherry and Fair Star; Classical Changes (five performances). Stage and Steam. The Mountain Sylph; The Widow's Victim. Three Fast Men; An Evening in China. The Victims; Brother Bill and Me. My Turn Next;*

Crispin and the Goose. Unmasked. Deborah. The Rising of the Moon. Outwitted; Betsy Baker. Elizabeth: The Queen of England. Mary Stuart. The Hunchback. The Lady of Lyons. Medea; The Four Sisters. The Stranger; Honey Moon. A Bird in the Hand Is Worth Two in the Bush; Betsy Baker. Ben Bolt; A First and Second Hand Hotel; The Fairy Fountain. The Lone Horse on the Bridge; The Fairy Fountain. The Cross of Gold; Pocahontas. The Lonely Man of the Ocean; A First and Second Class Hotel. The Miser of Marseilles; To Parents and Guardians. Quits; The Quiet Family. Dora; Napoleon's Old Guard; That Radical Pat. The Shingawn. The Life of an Actress; The Wandering Minstrel. Ernani; The Old Guard; The Irish Immigrant.

1873–74: The School for Scandal; Hunted Down; The Wandering Minstrel. East Lynne; The Wandering Minstrel. Leah the Forsaken; The Terrible Tinker. After Dark. Master Simpson and Son. Uncle Tom (three performances). Out at Sea; My Precious Betsy. Berta the Midget. Twice Saved. The Heiress of Mercy; Area Belles. Man and Wife. The Woman in Red; The Mysteries of the Stage. Masks and Faces; The Mexican Tigress. The Happy Pair; The Mexican Tigress; The Mysteries of the Stage. The Stanger; Black Eyed Susan. The New Magdalen. Solid Silver. The Wandering Heir. Guy Mannering; That Precious Baby; The Wandering Minstrel. London Assurance. Good as Gold. Romeo and Juliet. Camille. Richard III; Katherine and Petruchio. Dark Deeds. Jane Pride. Oliver Cromwell. Rory O'More; Devotion. Esker Dree; The Happy Man. Faugh A'Ballagh. Arrah-na-Pogue. Oliver Cromwell. The Illusionist; Katherine and Petruchio; The Pride of the Market; Hunted Down. Lucrezia Borgia. Under the Gaslight. Pygmalion and Galatea; Jenny Lind at Last. Simpson and Co.; Jenny Lind at Last. The French Spy; An Object of Interest. Ireland as It Was. The Nymph of Lureyberg; Time Tries All; An Object of Interest; The Loan of a Lover; The Rough Diamond; The Quiet Family; The Day after the Wedding; The Sailor of France. Rip Van Winkle (three performances). The Light House Cliffs. Kathleen Mavourneen; The Loan of a Lover; Solon Shingle. Carlotta: Queen of the Arena. Charles O'Malley; Solon Shingle. The Corsican Brothers; An Object of Interest. Dombey and Son; Handy Andy. Oliver Twist; The Quiet Family; Jack Cade. Romeo and Juliet. Hamlet. Money. Richelieu. Richard III; The Gladiator. Damon and Pythias. The Marble Heart. Virginius. Macbeth. A Night of Peril; Family Jars. The Green Bushes; The Spectre Bridegroom. The Flowers of the Forest; Family Jars. The French Spy; The Lost Child. Rosedale; The Jones' Baby. The Colleen Bawn; Used Up. Arrah-na-Pogue; Kerry. Daddy O'Down; Used Up. The Child of the Regiment; The Chinese Invasion. Uncle Tom's Cabin. Struck Oil; The Chinese Invasion. Eileen Oge. A California Girl. The Streets of New York; Turn Him Out. Our American Cousin. Only a Jew; A Regular Fix. Divorce (three performances). Uncle Dick's Darling; A Conjugal Lesson. The Wicked World; Toodles. Romeo and Juliet. Leah the Forsaken; Turn Him Out. The Hunchback. Mimi. Led Astray (three performances). Love's Sacrifice. Mary Queen of Scots; The Unequal Match. Pygmalion and Galetea. The Ticket-of-Leave Man; Paddy's Mischief. Margarite of Burgundy; Pocahontas. Diamonds. Caught in a Snare; Our Cousin Hamlet. Married Life; Fools of the Family. Four Diamonds. The Prussian Spy; Sketches in India. Lucrezia Borgia; The Fool of the Family. Quits; The Old Guard. Rob Roy; Bowl'd Out. Article Forty-Seven. Shadows. The Geneva Cross. The Willow Copse. Lady Thornhurst's Daughter. The Lady of Lyons. Time Tries All; Kathleen Mavourneen. Elzina: The Cuban Heiress. Bertha: The Sewing Machine Girl; The

Married Rake. Cigarette. Elfie; Sketches in India. The Pearl of Savoy. The Nymph of the Lureyberg; Andy Blake; The Limerick Boy. William Tell. Hamlet. The Jealous Wife; The Woodcock's Little Game. A Comical Countess; The Heir-at-Law. The King's Rival. Is He Jealous?; Four Months after the Marriage. Eleanor de Vere. Three Fast Men. Rachael Ben Israel. Out of the Slope at Frisco. The Odd Tricks; Neilson Fever. The Octoroon. Don Caesar de Bazan. The School for Scandal. Monte Cristo. Nick of the Woods; Naval Engagements. Othello. The Game of Speculation; Pocahontas. The Lancashire Lass. Rip Van Winkle. Macbeth. Help; Magic Changes. Maum Cre; The Heathen Chinese. His Last Legs. Charles XII; The Little Sentinel; The Day after the Fair. Jenny Foster; Our Country Cousins. The Deal Boatman; The Day after the Wedding. The Dead Shot; The Day after the Fair. Driven from Home; The Wandering Minstrel. Luke, the Labourer; The Quiet Family. Pizarro; The Lottery Ticket. Grimaldi. Blow for Blow. Charles XII. Old Fidelity. Belles of the Kitchen; The Old Guard. Wrong Man in the Right Place. Nabob for an Hour; Fun in a Fog. Ingomar, the Barbarian; Won at Last. The Lady of Lyons; The Eton Boy. Jack Sheppard. Grand Hibernica; Kitty O'Conner. The Trump Card; The Bonnie Fishwife. Faith and Fidelity.

1874–75: *The Hunchback; Danele's Song. The Trump Card; Black Eyed Susan. London Assurance. Time and the Hour; Ici on parle francais. The Cameron Pride; Jack Harkaway. Opera Mad; Christie Johnson. The Robber's Wife; Michael Erle. Davy Crockett* (four performances). *The Streets of New York. Neighbor Jackson. Much Ado about Nothing. King John. Elene; Engaged. The Detective. Bells That Ring; Nellie. Married Life. All That Glitters Is Not Gold. Time and the Hour. The Single Life. The French Spy; The Actor's Studio. Midnight; Ici on parle francais. Dombey and Son; A Kiss in the Dark. No Thoroughfare. The Colleen Bawn; A Kiss in the Dark. The Octoroon; Jack Sheppard; All That Glitters Is Not Gold. Under the Gaslight. Victims; The Persecuted Chinaman. The Hidden Hand; He Would Be an Actor. Romeo and Juliet. The Hunchback. Leah the Forsaken; The Rough Diamond. The Lady of Lyons; Galatea. The Unequal Match. Masks and Faces; Ici on parle francais. Love's Sacrifice. Romeo and Juliet. As You Like It. The Gilded Age. Built on Sand; Box and Cox. Madge of Evanlee; Toodles. Camille; The Spectre Bridegroom. Rachael Ben Israel. Still Waters Run Deep; Betsy Baker. Lost in London; His Last Legs. The Little Mother; The Weavers. Alphonse. The Admiral; The Day after the Wedding. David Garrick; Sketches in India. Life's Dream. Charity. Alice. A Wonderful Woman; The Spectre Bridegroom. Camille. Still Waters Run Deep; Toodles. The Hidden Hand; Betsy Baker. A Serious Family. Sweethearts and Wives; A Fish Out of Water. The Ticket-of-Leave Man.*

BIBLIOGRAPHY

Published Sources: John S. Lindsay, *The Mormons and the Theatre* (Salt Lake City: Century Publishing Co., 1905); George D. Pyper, *The Romance of an Old Playhouse* (Salt Lake City: The Seagull Press, 1928); Salt Lake City, *Daily Telegraph* (1864–68); *Salt Lake Daily Herald* (1870–75).

Unpublished Source: Therald F. Todd, "The Operation of the Salt Lake Theatre, 1862–75" (Ph.D. diss., University of Oregon, 1973).

Archival Sources: University of Utah Library, Provo: Western Americana Collection, Papers of George D. Pyper (last manager of the theatre), and

Scrapbook of David McKenzie; L.D.S. (Mormon) Church Historian's Library, Salt Lake City: Deseret Dramatic Association Papers and Salt Lake Theatre Papers and Accounts.

Therald Todd

SELWYN'S THEATRE COMPANY. Selwyn's Theatre, Boston, later known as the Globe Theatre (1870–94), was built by the architect B. F. Dwight. Arthur Cheney and Dexter H. Follett assumed proprietorship of the theatre, which was erected on the corner of Washington and Essex streets. Dwight modeled the theatre after Wallack's Theatre in New York and Cheney and Follett promised it would feature a first class stock company producing legitimate drama.

The theatre was named for its manager, J. H. Selwyn. Selwyn had been the scenic artist for the Boston Theatre Stock Company before his tenure with the new stock company. At the termination of his management at the end of the 1869–70 season, Selwyn's name disappeared from the playbills, and on July 4, 1870, the theatre was renamed the Globe. Arthur Cheney became sole proprietor of the theatre in 1869.

Selwyn's, one of four large stock companies in Boston, became the theatre "where so many went and so few remained." The interchange of actors among the Boston theatres is reflected in the large turnover of actors each season. Selwyn did manage to spirit members of the Boston Theatre Stock Company to his new theatre, including Charles Koppitz, the musical director, who brought both his talent and entire orchestra to Selwyn's.

The theatre itself, noted for its lavish but tasteful furnishings, seated about 2,200. The stage was eighty-four feet wide and fifty-five feet deep, and its height was seventy-five feet. Ticket prices ranged from $1 for the stalls and balcony to seventy-five cents for the parquet and dress circles to thirty to fifty cents for the family circle.

The advertised endeavor of Cheney in the establishment of this new stock company was to make it "the model theatre of America" and to produce the standard comedies, most of which were English, as well as occasional domestic dramas and tragedies. Cheney asserted that he would not favor lurid melodrama and that he regarded the theatre as a temple dedicated to the drama.

Selwyn's opened on Monday night, October 28, 1867. The theatre's premier offering, *Fast Family,* was an adaptation of a play by Victorien Sardou. The event was commemorated by satin playbills. Dramatic critics would note Selwyn's as the leading theatre in the city, but the repertory, which relied heavily upon the works of T. W. Robertson, Tom Taylor, and Dion Boucicault, was not without its share of productions that were called "sensational" and "trashy." The standard fare was comedy and farce, supplemented by the occasional burlesque, extravaganza, or domestic drama.

The most popular productions included *Dora, Black Eyed Susan* (each of which was performed more than sixty times in the theatre's first season and frequently revived in the following years), classics such as *The Rivals* and *She Stoops to Conquer*, and the historical burlesque extravaganza *The Field of the Cloth of Gold*. The first season featured the American premiere of Robertson's *School*, which had a successful run of more than six weeks.

Attempts at Shakespeare are scattered throughout the repertory of Selwyn's. Several tragedies were subject to burlesque treatment. The comedies often included women in the so-called "breeches" roles, such as the 1870 production of *Midsummer Night's Dream*, in which actresses appeared as Puck and Oberon.

The most popular of Selwyn's performers were Mary Cary and Stuart Robson. Cary was a Boston favorite who had begun her career at the Boston Theatre in 1860. At Selwyn's she appeared in the title roles of *Black Eyed Susan* and *Little Emily* and was also seen in many of the "breeches" roles. Robson was acknowledged as the premier comic and burlesque actor of his time. He became well known for his work with several major acting companies, including that of Mrs. John Drew's at the Arch Street Theatre in Philadelphia.

During the summer seasons, the theatre was let to touring companies. Such groups included Bateman's Opera Bouffe, The San Francisco Minstrels, The Hanlon Brothers, Lingard's Company, Dunning's Burlesque Troupe, and Wallack's Company.

Theatrical records are scattered and scarce in regard to the operation of Selwyn's Theatre, since a fire destroyed the theatre in May 1873, three years after Selwyn left for New York to manage for Lawrence Barrett and the name of the Selwyn Theatre had been changed to the Globe.

PERSONNEL

Management: Arthur Cheney, proprietor (1867–70); Dexter H. Follett, proprietor (1867–68); J. H. Selwyn, manager (1867–70); G. B. Farnsworth, treasurer (1867–70).

Scenic Artist: George Heister (1867–70).

Musical Director: Charles Koppitz (1867–70).

Stage Managers: C. M. Davis (1867–68); Thomas Barry (1868–70).

Actors and Actresses: Louise Anderson, Miss Athena, *Thomas Barry* (1868–70), *Mrs. Thomas Barry* (1868–70), H. L. Bascomb, *Kittie Blanchard* (1867–70), H. D. Billings, L. Bowers, J. D. Bradford, Eva Brent, Virginia Buchanan, T. A. Burns, L. Carland, Caroline Carson, *Mary Cary* (1867–70), *Mrs. F. S. Chanfrau* (1868–69), Ella Chapman, A. Cole, R. Cole, E. Coleman, J. Conner, *H. F. Daly* (1867–70), Miss Danforth, Mrs. E. L. Davenport, C. M. Davis, E. F. Dawson, O. A. Dinsmore, G. K. Fortescue, G. W. Garrison, F. Goldthwaite, T. Grahame, Mrs. T. Grahame, Miss Griffiths, *G. H. Griffiths* (1867–70), Mrs. G. H. Griffiths, W. Hague, *Amilie Harris* (1867–69), Miss Hunt, Mrs. T. M. Hunter, E. Johnson, Miss Jones, H. Josephs, Mrs. Kenway, G. F. Kenway, G. Ketchum, Miss La

Forrest, W. J. Lemoyne, E. Long, J. Lothian, Miss Manning, J. Mills, *Fanny Morant*, (1868–69), H. S. Murdock, Eliza Newton, S. Newton, E. Oliver, Mr. Packard, G. Parkhurst, Miss Pearson, Harry Pearson, T. Peek, Miss Roberts, *Stuart Robson* (1867–70), I. Savory, L. R. Shewell, F. Skerett, J. Somerby, C. Steadman, A. Steele, A. Taylor, G. Telbin, C. R. Thorne, G. T. Ulmer, C. H. Vandenhoff, Mary Welles, Mrs. M. Wilkins.

REPERTORY

1867–68: *Fast Family; Dreams of Delusion; 100,000 Pounds; John Wopps; The Rivals; Poor Gentleman; Caste; The Lady of Lyons; Hunted Down; Mazeppa; Two Puddifoots; Old Heads and Young Hearts; Money; Still Waters Run Deep; Peggy Green; Dot; Maud's Peril; Easy Shaving; Wild Oats; Dora; Black Eyed Susan; The School for Scandal; She Stoops to Conquer; Dearer Than Life; Katherine and Petruchio; The Wife's Secret; Bachelor of Arts; Cinderella; Married Life; Who Speaks First; Debutante; Honey Moon; A Wife Well Won; London Assurance; Ladies' Battle; Rural Felicity; Spirit of '76; Light at Last; The Jealous Wife; Used Up; Peggy Green; Ours; Everybody's Friend.*

1868–69: *Belle's Strategem; Money; Rivals; Man and Wife; Irish Heiress; Married Life; Antony and Cleopatra; Follies of a Night; Fowl Play; Leap Year; Debutante; Ladies' Battle; Simpson and Co.; The Last Trump Card; Everybody's Friend; Merry Wives of Windsor; Hunchback; Caste; The Field of the Cloth of Gold; Dreams of Delusion; Wonderful Women; King René's Daughter; Hard Struggle; Charles II; Lancashire Lass; Dot; An Hour with Forty Thieves; Tame Cats; Jones' Baby; She Stoops to Conquer; Speed the Plough; Who Speaks First; Needful; Bold Stroke for a Husband; Rent Day; Othello; The Heir-at-Law; School; My Lady Clara; Much Ado about Nothing; Fool's Revenge; Loan of a Lover; Spitfire; Camille* (burlesque); *King Lear, the Cuss* (tragi-comic burlesque); *Pride of the Market; Actress by Daylight; Asmodeus; Dora; Black Eyed Susan; Minnie; Breach of Promise; Hunted Down; Little Treasure; Delicate Ground; Andy Blake; Ours; Billiards; His Last Victory; Sunshine through the Clouds; Spirit of '76; Mazeppa; Two Cadis; To Parents and Guardians; Sam; London Assurance; The Widow's Victim.*

1869–70: *Serpent on the Hearth; Follies of a Night; Betsy Baker; School; The Heir-at-Law; Everybody's Friend; Andy Blake; Marble Heart; She Wou'd and She Wou'd Not; Lady Audley's Secret; Midsummer Night's Dream; Extremes; Bombastes Furioso; Little Emily; A Cheerful Reception; The Hypocrite; Hamlet* (burlesque); *The Spectre Bridegroom; Masks and Faces; People's Lawyer; Frou-Frou; Toodles; Dot; Who Killed Cock Robin?; Sir Simon Simple; Lost At Sea; Prima Donna; A Wild Rose; Ours; Silverstone's Wager; Nicholas Nickleby; The Spitfire; Married Life; Faint Heart ne'er Won Fair Lady; Loan of a Lover; The School for Scandal; My Lady Clara; The Field of the Cloth of Gold; Jones' Baby; Camille* (burlesque); *Wandering Minstrel; John Wopps; Dora; Black Eyed Susan; Little Treasure.*

BIBLIOGRAPHY

Published Sources: *Boston Advertiser; Boston Evening Gazette;* Eugene Tompkins and Quincy Kilby, *The History of the Boston Theatre, 1854–1901* (Boston: Houghton Mifflin, 1908); William W. Clapp, Jr., "The Drama in Boston," in *The*

Memorial History of Boston, 1630–1880, ed. Justin Winsor (Boston: James R. Osgood and Co., 1881), 4:377-78.

Archival Sources: Playbills, programs, scrapbook materials, and newspaper clippings from the Harvard Theatre Collection, Cambridge, Massachusetts, and the Boston Public Library.

Noreen C. Barnes

STADT THEATER COMPANY. The Stadt Theater Stock Company, New York City, was organized in the summer of 1854 by actor-manager-director Otto Hoym, with his wife, Elise, and August Siegrist. Hoym and Siegrist leased and rebuilt the old Amphitheatre at 37–39 Bowery Street (built in 1833) and opened it on September 4, 1854, to a full house. On September 11 Friedrich von Schiller's *Die Räuber* was performed.

The Stadt Theater was the earliest successful German-speaking professional stock company in New York City. Ten years later the same company would move to a larger theatre to accommodate an increasing demand for German-speaking theatre. Although earlier attempts at producing German theatre took place in the 1840s, none had achieved commercial success, with the exception of the St. Charles Theatre (17–19 Bowery) under the management of Eduard Hamann in 1853. With the opening of the Stadt Theater, the St. Charles lasted only four weeks into the first season of 1854 before it closed. Hamann joined Hoym as joint proprietor in 1855. The sole competition for the Stadt Theater came from the German beer halls and gardens with their small stages constructed for musical, variety, and dramatic performances by various amateur groups and guest performers. One of the better known and ever popular beer halls was G. Eustachi's New-Yorker Volks Theater on Fourth Street. Rohrschneider's Bier Garten advertised "*Eintritt 6 cents, wofür ein Glas Bier . . .*" (Entrance fee 6 cents, includes one free beer . . .). Other theatrical ventures were short lived, such as the Deutsches Volks-Theater at 45 Bowery Street, which opened on September 8, 1862, for three short months.

Hoym and Hamann intended to provide German-speaking New Yorkers with a variety of theatrical experiences including operettas, *Possen,* farces, comedies, and the classics. The Stadt Theater provided the latest popular fare from German theatres abroad in an attempt to satisfy the demand of the constant and ever-increasing flow of German immigrants. Occasionally, new plays that satirized the "old country" or life in America were written by newly arrived immigrants, for example, *Anton in New York, oder Faust's Soll and Haben* and *Die Macht des Goldes, oder Deutschland und Californien.* On special occasions, the classics were given special attention, for example, during the tercentenary of Shakespeare's birth (1863–64 season), the Stadt Theater produced eight of the bard's plays: *The Taming of the Shrew, The Winter's Tale, A Midsummer Night's Dream, The Tempest, The Merchant of Venice, Richard III, Hamlet,* and *Macbeth.*. The number of plays in the Stadt Theater repertory was extensive; often a season would feature fifty to sixty productions. During the 1866–67 season the group produced more than 200 individual plays, including one-act plays. The most frequently performed classics were Schiller's *Die Räuber, Don Carlos, Wilhelm Tell,* Goethe's *Faust,* and Shakespeare's *Hamlet, Othello, Macbeth,* and *Richard III.* In the comic vein, Gustav Freytag, Molière, August Kotzebue, and J. N. Nestroy were always popular with audiences.

The acting company was large and included many aspiring amateurs, who found it easier to break into the theatre in this country than in Europe. During the first ten years, 1854–64, the group included a music director, a small orchestra, a dance master, a scenic designer and painter, and several directors. The theatre also attracted the German intellectual and artistic elite and provided a haven for the future founders of the Thalia Theater and the Germania Theater. Tragedian Daniel E. Bandmann appeared with the Stadt Theater Company and became a favorite guest. In 1863 he ceased to perform in German for a number of years and became somewhat popular performing in English. Other popular guests of the Stadt Theater were Rudolph Fallenbach, Marie Scheller, Emil Niemeyer, Rudolph Backowitz, Jean and Anne Klein, and Jenny Kress. Guest stars from German theatres abroad were more frequent during the later history of the company.

In anticipation of larger audiences, the Stadt Theater moved into a larger theatre in 1864 and became the Neues Stadt Theater or New Stadt Theater. The Neues Stadt Theater Stock Company was essentially the same group as at the Stadt Theater, but it now occupied a new theatre at 45–47 Bowery Street (the five-story renovated Hastmann Hotel) with a seating capacity of 3,500. Hoym and Hamann opened the new theatre on September 6, 1864, with *Heinrich von Schwerin, oder Deutschland und Dänemark* by Eduard von Meyern.

Hoym and Hamann envisioned a greater demand for German-speaking theatre as the number of German immigrants continued to increase in New York. Their major competition remained the beer-hall stages and various short runs in rented theatres, such as the Atlantic Garten Vaudeville-Theater at 50 Bowery Street. Eduard Härting, a member of the Stadt Theater Company, organized a company of German-speaking actors and leased the Wood's Theatre on Broadway, renamed it the German Thalia Theater (not to be confused with the later Thalia Theater), and opened on September 3, 1866, with *Der beste Ton* by Karl Töpfer. The venture failed, and Härting later returned to the Stadt Theater.

Of major significance was the interest of Hoym and Hamann in engaging foreign German stars for large amounts of money. This prompted a wave of guest actors to cross the ocean and perform in New York and other German-language centers, such as Chicago, Milwaukee, and St. Louis. In the 1866–67 season, the prominent German actor Bogumil Dawison was reportedly offered approximately $50,000 for fifty performances. He appeared in many classic roles, such as *King Lear, Richard III, Hamlet, Faust, Wallenstein's Tod,* and so on and appeared with Hoym in *Othello.* Dawison attracted the critical attention of all of the major newspapers in New York, especially when he appeared as Othello to Edwin Booth's Iago at the Winter Garden Theatre on December 29 and January 2 and 4. The *Tribune* hailed Dawison as the German Macready.

Following the retirement of Hoym in 1867, there was a decline in the offering of the classics and more popular novelty engagements were offered. One such popular success, not only in New York but also in Germany, was the appearance of the three German dwarf actors, Jean Piccolo, Jean Petit, and Kis Jozsi, in 1867. In contrast to the lighter fare, however, the following season of 1868–69 featured the guest engagement of the noted actor Friedrich Haase from Berlin in classic and popular roles. Although the press reported that the 3,500-seat auditorium was frequently sold out, other sources indicate that Hamann suffered severe losses.

By the end of the 1870–71 season, the Neues Stadt Theater had shifted its repertory to include more and more opera. During the 1871–72 season there were many dark weeks, and the repertory was almost exclusively opera. Hamann, after suffering a stroke, was unable to manage the theatre and went bankrupt in 1872. The regular company disbanded and joined Adolf Neuendorff, Hamann's music director, in his newly established Germania Theater Company*. The *New Yorker Staats-Zeitung* (August 22, 1872) reported that the building was sold at auction for $122,000, although records do not confirm this transaction. The theatre struggled on with various managers, short runs, and opera seasons under the name of the Stadt Theater, but the curtain had been lowered on the stock company in 1872.

PERSONNEL

Management: Otto Hoym, proprietor and manager (1854–67); August Siegrist, proprietor and manager (1854); Eduard Hamann, proprietor and manager (1855–67); A. Rosenberg (1868–72).

Scenic Technician: Herr Stöckel.

Musical Directors: Herr Ungar (1854), Franz Herwig (1855–67), Adolf Neuendorff (1867–72).

Ballet Master: Herr Wood.

Stage Directors: Otto Hoym, August Siegrist, Eduard Hamann, Herr Dardenne, Carl Worret, Ludwig Knorr, Elise Hoym, Adolf Dombrowsky, Ferdinand Klotz, Carl Jendersky.

Actors and Actresses (selected): *Herr Adler* (1866), *Ferdinand Ahlfeld* (1866), *Pauline Ahlfeld* (1866), *Herr Alström* (1870), *Johann Armand* (1869), *Rudolph Backowitz* (1861), *Daniel E. Bandmann* (1857, 1862, 1864–66), *Frl. Bardenheuer* (1870), *Herr Barena* (1864), *Pauline Beckel* (1863), *Frl. Becker* (1855), *Herr Beckier* (1870), *Amalie Becker-Grahn* (1860–68), *Herr Benleb* (1856, 1858), *Herr Berger*

(1869), *Frl. Berndt* (1855), *Bruno Berndt* (1856), *Frl. Bissinger* (1870), *Herr Bölten* (1858), *Herr Böttner* (1854–57), *Frl. Brandt* (1859), *Herr Brethauer* (1867), *Herr Brinkmann* (1870), *Herr Bucherer* (1869), *Herr Brüggemann* (1866–67), *Herr Brugmann* (1868), M. Busch, Frl. Busch I, Fr. Caradori, *Frank Castelli* (1868), *Elsa Chorherr* (1869), Herr Christe, *Johanna Claussen* (1863–64), *Julius Colmer* (1867–69), Josy Coustini, Herr Cruse, *Herr Czmock* (1854–55), Fr. Dantzy-Heussmann, *Herr Dardenne* (1854), *Bogumil Dawison* (1866), *Herr Deetz* (1857), Herr Deimling, Frl. Denham, *Heinrich Döbelin* (1868), Adolf Dombrowsky (1867–70), *Herr Dorn* (1861), *Fr. Dornbach* (1862–63), Herr Dorschel, Frl. Marie Dupré, Sophie Dziuba, *Frl. Dorothea Ebert* (1865–66), Fr. Esden, Herr Ezollösy, *Rudolph Fallenbach* (1859), Johanna Ficher, *Frl. Adelheid Fischer* (1860–61), Herr Föllger, *Wilhelm Formes* (1866–70), Cöcelia Fortner, *Joseph Fortner* (1854–69), Frl. Fouche, *Cäsar Frank* (1865–68), Celestine Frank, Herr Franosch, Herr Frei, Herr Freiss, Herr Freund, *Marie Fridericie* (1869–70), *Carl Fritze* (1863–66, 1869), Frl. Fuchs (1856–59), *Auguste Fuchs* (1856–59), Herr Fürst, Herr Gantzberg, Herr Gebhard, Herr Geleben, *Ottilie Genée* (1865–69), Franz Graff, Frl. Grahn, Fr. Gregorovius, *Herr Grieben* (1861–67), W. Groschel, Frl. Grosse, *Herr Grossmann* (1856), Herr Gruben, Frl. Gubry, *Albert Gühlen* (1863–64), Fr. Guthery, *Robert Guthery* (1869), *Oscar Guttmann* (1866), *Herr Haake* (1854), *Friedrich Hasse* (1868), *Fr. Louise Haase* (1864–65), Herr Habelmann, *Frl. Laura Haffner* (1867–70), W. Hahn (1862), *Ann Hamann-Klein* (1868–69), *Eduard Härting* (1864–65, 1869), *Fanny Härting* (1866), Frl. Heerwegen, Herr Heinemann, *Carl Heinsdorf* (1867), *Hermann Hendrichs* (1868), *Joseph Hermans* (1867–69), *Friedrich Herrmann* (1867–69), Julius Herrmann (1867, 1869), Franz Herwig, *Hedwig Hesse* (1869), Franz Himmer, H. Hochheim, *Frl. Auguste Höfl* (1867–68), Gustav Hölzel, Herr Homann, *Heinrich Horar* (1867), *Elise Hoym* (1854–67), *Otto Hoym* (1854–67), Theodor Hoym, *Herr Hübner* (1864–70), *Eleonre Hübner* (1861–70), *Fritz Hübner* (1855–59, 1863), Frl. Hübsch (1870), *Gustav Hübsch* (1865–71), *Magda Irschick* (1866), Herr Jacobi, Herr Janitsky, *Carl Jendersky* (1868), *Herr Jünger* (1856–59), *Johanna Kaiser* (1863–64), Richard Kaps, *Fr. Albertine Kenkel* (1864), *Alfred Kessler* (1869–70), Maximilian Kessler, Frl. Kleemann, *Frl. Anna Klein* (1861, 1867), *Jean Klein* (1854–70), *Ferdinand Klotz* (1865–68), *Ludwig Knorr* (1858–68), Carl Koppe, Aloyse Krebs-Michalesi, *Jenny Kress* (1854–56), Angelika Kronfeld, *Heinrich Kronfeld* (1856–58), *Anne Krüger* (1870), *Wilhelm Kunst* (1859–61), *Fr. Lange* (1866–69), Heinrich Lange (1864–70), Frl. Laroche, *Hedwig L'Arronge* (1867), *Theodor L'Arronge* (1866–67), *Emil Lasswitz* (1867), Herr Lehman II, Isidor Lehmann (1857–61), Otto Lehmann, Hugo Lennert (1864, 1866), Herr Lewens, Herr Lorey, *Wilhelm Lotti* (1869), *Josephine Lube* (1869), *Max Lube* (1869), Frl. Mandelsloh, Frl. Ida Mantius (1862–66), *Frl. Marchand* (1865–66), Anna Märtens, *Fr. Matzke* (1858, 1866), *Hermann Matzke* (1855–62), *Adolph Meaubert* (1855–60), Henriette Meaubert (1855–56, 1859–60, 1866), Carl Merbitz, Fr. Methua-Scheller, *Wilhelmine Meyer* (1862–63), Frl. Müller, Herr Müller, Bertha Müller, Veronika Neuburg, Frl. Neumann, *Emil Niemeyer* (1859–62), Herr Otto (1855–56), Clara Perl, Frl. Peterson, *Alexander Pfeiffer* (1857), *Jean Piccolo* (1867), Ignatz Pollak, Bernhard Porth, *Heinrich Pototzky* (1859), Herr Quint, *Laura Raumann* (1866), *Otto Reiffrath* (1863–67), Rosine Reiss, *Ernest Rethwisch* (1867–68), *Herr Risch* (1865), *Herr Rittig* (1857), *Herr Robeck* (1870), Wilhelmine Rohde, Francesca Rohland, Franziska Roland, *Bertha Römer* (1870), Johanna Rotter, Marie Sand, Johanna Schaumbach,

Marie Scheller (1859–61), *Leonhard Scherer* (1856–58, 1864), *Elise Schermann* (1867–71), *Heinrich Schmidt* (1854–64), Fr. Heinrich Schmidt, *Eugenie Schmitz* (1866–71), Sophia Scholz (1867–71), Friedrich Schwan (1854–57, 1861, 1866–67), Herr Schwegerle, *Marie Seebach* (1870), Natalie Seelig, Fr. Siedenburg, *August Siegrist* (1854–55, 1858), Herr Sington, Elise Spengler (1854–61), *Fr. Steglich-Fuchs* (1864–69), *Auguste Steglich-Fuchs* (1860–63), Anna Stein, Georg Stemmlar, Frl. Storch, Frl. Thyssen, Gretchen Tiby, Frl. Umlauf, F. Urchs, *Mathilde Veneta* (1870), A. Vestvali, Fr. Vestvali-Lund (1863), Herr Vincke, Herr Volkland, *Frau von Bärndorf* (1868), *Auguste von Bärndorf* (1868), *Fr. von Berkel* (1858–61), *Minna von Berkel* (1865), Fr. von Gary-Lichtmoy, Fr. Minna von Hedemann, Olga von Plittersdorf, *Henriette Wagner* (1869), *Frl. Waldau* (1868, 1870), Fr. Friedericke Walthe, Herr Wedderin, Herr Weinlich, Herr Weissheit, Frl. Wellmer, *Herr Wenzlawsky* (1862–64), Herr Wernicke, *Emma Weise* (1869–70), Frl. Wild, Fr. Wolf, *Fr. Wollenberg-Rohde* (1867), *Carl Worret* (1854–58), *Fr. Carl Worret* (1854–58), Herr Wüstrow, *Fr. Zerboni* (1865–66), *Herr Zerboni* (1865–66), Fr. Zülch, Frl. Zullich.

REPERTORY

The following list is not complete and includes classics and representative plays only.

1854–55: *Die Räuber; Prinz Lieschen, oder der Carneval; Die Jungfrau von Orleans; Dorf und Stadt; Der Freischütz; Kabale und Liebe; Maria Stuart; Die Waise von Lowood; Barbier von Sevilla; Götz von Berlichingen; Endlich hat er gut gemacht; Das Versprechen hinter'm Heerde; Der Zauberschleier; Faust; Tell Eulenspiegel; Martha; Domi, der amerikanische Affe; Das Forsthaus; Czaar und Zimmermann; Der reisends Student; Johanna von Montfaucon; Lumpaci Vagabundus; Sieben Mädchen in Uniform; Die corsikaneschen Brüder; Die Hugenotten; Königin Margot; Richard III; Anna von Oesterreich, oder die drei Musketiere; Der Fliegende Holländer; Der Glöckner von Notre Dame; Eifersüchtige Frau.*

1855–56: *Die Räuber; Der Verscwender; Maria Stuart; Der Jungfrau von Orleans; Das Irrenhaus zu Dijon; Der Freischütz; Die falsche Braut; Moses; 100,000 Thaler; Der Glöckner von Notre Dame; Katharine Howard; Der Liebestrank; Daniel in der Löwengrube; Neun Mädchen in Uniforn; Muttersegen; Prinz Lieschen; Der Fliegende Holländer; Ein Deutscher in Amerika; Kean; Dr. Faust's Zauberkäppchen; Don Cäsar von Bazano; Der Freischütz; Die Waise von Lowood; Moses; Die ewige Jude; Hans Kohlhaus; Uriel Acosta; Don Juan; Mariette und Jeanneton; Rip Van Winkle; Von sieben die Hässlichste; Lord und Räuber; Die Macht des Goldes, oder Deutschland und Californien; Drei Tage der Weltgeschichte, oder die Reise in der Türkei; Die Jäger.*

1856–57: *Donna Diana; Kabale und Liebe; Wallenstein's Tod; Stadt und Land; Der Teufel von Paris; Unter der Erde; Ein moderner Faust; Preciosa; New York und Berlin; Der Zauberschleier; Robert und Bertram; Wenn Leute Geld haben; Die Dame mit der Camelien; Hamlet; Kean; Richard III; Rosenmüller und Finke; Joseph in Egypt; Lorbeerbaum und Bettelstab; Ruy Blas; Die Grille.*

1857–58: *Adrienne Lecouvreur; Die Grille; Der Glöckner von Notre Dame; Preciosa; Lucrezia Borgia; Die Dame mit der Camelien; Wilhelm Tell; Der fliegende Holländer; Narciss; Die Armen von Paris; Die Drillinge; Die Sachsen in Preussen; Faust; Die Räuber; Zopf und Schwert; Don Carlos; Maximilian Robespierre; Die*

Hochzeitsreise; Geld! Geld! Geld! Stadt und Land; Wilhelm Tell; Die Hugenotten; Deborah; Maria Stuart; Jungfrau von Orleans; Barfüssle; Die Gefangenen der Czaarin; Der alte Feldherr.

1858–59: *Adrienne Lecouvreur; Graf Essex; Kean; Don Carlos; Faust; Wilhelm Tell; Narciss; Jocko, der brasilianische Affe; Kätchen von Heilbronn; Der Freischütz; Der Glöckner von Notre Dame; Martha; Turandot; Maria Stuart; Romeo und Julia; Die Walpurgisnacht; Deborah; Alexander Stradellerle; Die Jungfrau von Orleans; Die Grille; Hamlet; Kabale und Liebe; Der Graf von Monte Christo; Lumpaci Vagabundus; Prinz Lieschen; Die Zauberflöte; Der Freischütz; Nathan der Weise; Minna von Barnhelm; Treue Liebe; Der Wildschütz; Tannhäuser; Die Töchter Lucifer's Zriny.*

1859–60: *Heinrich von Schwerin; Undine; Adrienne Lecouvreur; Don Carlos; Der Kaufmann von Venedig; Donna Diana; Nacht und Morgen; Romeo und Julia; Kätchen von Heilbronn; Narciss; Deborah; Hamlet; Der Wildschütz; Anna-Liese; Der Freischütz; Faust; Wilhelm Tell; Graf von Essex; Fiesco; Die Räuber; Die Zauberflöte; Emilia Galotti; Mutter und Sohn; Die Walpurgis Nacht; Die Grille; Kabale und Liebe; Richard III; Dämonische Liebe; Don Juan; Tante Kobold und Onkel Satan; Herz und Dollar; Tannhäuser; Oberon; Berta am Clavier; Ein weisser Othello; Junker Otto; Marie Anne, des Weib aus dem Volk, Aladin.*

1860–61: *Tristan und Isolde; Deborah; Kabale und Liebe; Naciss; Die Räuber; Die Befreiung von Neapel; Donna Diana; Uriel Acosta; Der Glöcker von Notre Dame; Hamlet; Wen Leute Geld haben; Don Caesar von Bazano; Wilhelm Tell; Isidor und Olga; Herz und Dollar; Die Jungfrau von Orleans; Schiller und Goethe; Die Braut von Messina; König Lear; Die Grille; Graf Essex; Wildröschen, oder Leben und Treiben in Süd Carolina.*

1861–62: *Ein Glas Wasser; Das Mädchen von Dorfe; Czaar und Zimmermann; Hamlet; Der Freischütz, Die Stumme; Postillion von Lonjumeau; George Washington; Mozart's Geige; Kabale und Liebe; Die Jungfrau von Orleans; Narciss; Adrienne Lecouvreur; Romeo und Julia; Die Waise von Lowood; Don Carlos; Uriel Acosta; Richard III; Wilhelm Tell; Maria Stuart; Das Urbild des Tartüffe; Die Räuber; Die Zauberflöte; Maria Stuart; Ueber den Ocean; Der deutsche Michel; Der Präsident; Der Goldbauer.*

1862–63: *Jane Eyre; Graf Essex; Narciss; Die Räuber; Das Mädchen von Lyon; Richard III; Mephistopheles; Der Kaufmann von Venedig; Das Volk, wie es weint und lacht; Friedrich Schiller; Der Geiziger; Berlin bei Nacht; Herz und Dollar; Die lustigen Weiber von Windsor; Faust und Gretchen; Weib aus dem Volke.*

1863–64: *Narciss; Maria Stuart; Lumpaci Vagabundus; Der Glöckner von Notre Dame; Medea; Die Grille; Therese Krones; Kabable und Liebe; Macbeth; Lady Bell; Die Räuber; Der Graf von Monte Christo; Wallenstein's Lager; Der Gold Onkel; Der fliegende Holländer; Ein Berliner in Wien; Uriel Acosta; Ein Wintermärchen; Orpheus in der Unterwelt; Wilhelm Tell; Ein Sommernachtstraum; Salamo's Urteil; Faust; Der Spion; Der Sturm; Lore-Ley; Die Nixe des Rheins; Kätchen von Heilbronn; Hamlet; Margot und die Hugenotten; Der Kaufmann von Venedig; Richard III; Die Grille; Der vicomte de Letoriéres; Barfüssle; Mathhilde, oder ein Weib wie es sein soll.*

1864–65: *Jane Eyre; Die Räuber; Therese Krones; Die Grille; Kabale und Liebe; Narciss; Ein Glas Wasser; Muttersegen; Wilhelm Tell; Herz und Dollar; Don Carlos; Deborah; Der ewige Jude; Hamlet; Lumpaci Vagabundus; Die Mozartgeige; Don*

*Carlos; Der Kaufmann von Venedige; Richard III; Titus Feuerfuchs; Maria Stuart;
Faust; Macbeth; Wallenstein's Tod; Nacht und Morgen; Was ihr Wollt; Viel Lärm
um Nichts.*

1865–66: *Die Bastille; Die Memoiren des Satans; Die Schwäbin; Nathan der Weise;
Graf Essex; Die Drillinge; Die Grille; Kabale und Liebe; Henry IV; Mazeppa; Die
Räuber; Coriolanus; Uriel Acosta; King Cotton; Wilhelm Tell; Lumpaci Vagabun-
dus; Der Glöckner von Notre Dame; Narciss; Don Carlos; Genoveva; Muttersegen;
Der Kaufmann von Venedige; Julius Cäsar; Mosses in Egypten; Hamlet; Faust; Die
Waise von Lowood; Das Kätchen von Heilbronn; Anna, Nanni, Nina, Nattchen,
oder die Unschuld auf dem Lande; Dr. Robin; Richard III; Adrienne Lecouvreur.*

1866–67: *Emilia Galotti; Herz und Dollar; Der Geizige; Der Jude; Lumpaci
Vagabundus; Narciss; Deborah; Uriel Acosta; Stadt und Land; Othello; Die Räuber;
Der Kaufmann von Venedig; Der Königslieutenant; Lorbeerbaum und Bettelstab;
Maria Stuart; Der Geizige; Faust; Richard III; Hans Jurge; Die Unglücklichen; Graf
Essex; Zwei Tage aus dem Leben eines Fürstes; Die Unglücklichen; Kabale und
Liebe; Pech-Schulze; Orpheus in der Unterwelt; Ein Wintermärchen; Lumpaci Va-
gabundus; Egmont; Romeo und Julia; Hamlet; Martha; Der Tower von London;
Kean; Don Carlos; Uriel Acosta; Die Zauberflöte; Wallenstein's Tod; Don Jaun;
Der Lumpensammler von Paris; Donna Diana; Die lustigen Weiber von Windsor;
König Lear; Viel Lärmen um Nichts; 5000,000 Teufel; Leonore, oder die Todten-
braut; Iffland, oder Hannover, Mannhein, Berlin.*

1867–68: *Adrienne Lecouvreur; Donna Diana: Maria Stuart; Zehn Mädchen und
kein Mann; Wem gehört die Frau?; Robert und Bertram; Er ist nicht eifersüchtig;
Narciss; Die Räuber; Graf Essex; Wallenstein's Lager; Hamlet; Wilhelm Tell; Dorf
und Stadt; Faust* (a burlesque); *Braut von Messina; Der Zigeuner; Die Grille;
Dawison; Macbeth; Der Freischütz; Romeo und Julia; Papa Buddendörfer; French
Louis: Der Runnerkönig New Yorks; Unter der Erde; Kätchen von Heilbronn; Hans
Sachs, Barfüssle; Der ewige Jude; Michael Kohlhaus; Lieserl; Der Hahn im Dorf;
Ich ess bei meiner Mutter.*

1868–69: *Herzog Albrecht, oder Vater und Sohn; Wilhelm Tell; Egmont; Don
Carlos; Kätchen von Heilbronn; Julius Caesar; Dorf und Stadt; Deborah; Fiesco;
Faust; Die Grille; Die Räuber; Die Jungfrau von Orleans; Macbeth; Adrienne Le-
couvreur; Maria Stuart; Hamlet; Kabale und Liebe; Uriel Acosta; Die Frieschütz;
Narciss; Doctor und Friseur; Minna von Barnhelm; Emilia Galotti; Don Carlos;
Romeo und Julia; Ludwigs des XI letzte Tage; Don Caesar de Bazano; Der Clöckner
von Notre Dame; Der Kaufmann von Venedige; Hamlet; Der alte Magister; Der
Jude; Der Zerbrochene Krug; Die Hochzeitsreise; Die Erzählungen der Königin
von Navarra.*

1869–70: *Die Memoiren des Satans; Die Zauberflöte; Die Räuber; Faust; Fidelio;
Kätchen von Heilbronn; Don Juan; Die Dame mit den Camelien; Othello; Der
kleine Richelieu; Die Jungfrau von Orleans; Blaubart; Fra Diavolo; Die weisse
Dame; Stradella; Abraham Lincoln; Der Geldonkel; Ein weibliche Othello; Der
Steckbrief.*

1870–71: *Die schöne Galtheé; Fidelio; Faust* (opera); *Norma; Tannhäuser; Rigoletto; Wilhelm Tell; Maria Stuart; Narciss; Kabale und Liebe; Faust; Romeo und
Julia; Die Räuber; Egmont; Emilia Galotti; Kätchen von Heilbronn; Hamlet; Die
Waise von Lowood; Isabelle Orsini; Lohengrin; Die schöne Helena; Die Afrikan-
erin; Robert der Teufel; Hermann und Dorothea.*

1871–72: *Der Postillon von Lonjumeau; Die weisse Dame; Martha; Fra Diavolo; Lucia di Lammermoor; Die Zauberflöte; Die eiserne Maske; Richard III; Don Juan; Der Goldonkel; Die Hochzeitsreise; Die schöne Müllerin.*

BIBLIOGRAPHY

Published Sources: (German language press) *Belletristisches Journal; New Yorker Criminal Zeitung; New Yorker Figaro; New Yorker Staats-Zeitung.* (English language press) *New York Dramatic Mirror; New York Herald; New York Times; New York Tribune; The Spirit of the Times.* See *Deutsch-Amerikanische Geschichtsblätter* 15 (1915): 255–309; *"Das Deutsche Theater in New York," Sonntagsblatt des New Yorker Staats-Zeitung* 16 (April 1905).

Archival Sources: The New York Public Library and the Harvard Theatre Collection, Cambridge, Massachusetts, have numerous programs and newspaper clippings.

Ron Engle

T

THALIA THEATER COMPANY. The Thalia Theater Stock Company, New York City, a German-speaking group, was organized in the spring of 1879 by actor-director Heinrich Conried, actor-director Mathilde Cottrelly, business manager Gustav Amberg, and Wilhelm Kramer, proprietor and owner of Kramer's Theatre (formerly the Bowery Theatre). The company opened in Kramer's Theatre, renamed the Thalia Theater, on September 11, 1879, with a production of Friedrich von Schiller's *Kabale und Liebe*.

The Thalia Theater was to become the most prominent and successful German-speaking theatre in the history of New York City. The idea for the formation of the stock company was initiated by Heinrich Conried, who had been employed by Adolf Neuendorff at the Germania Theater as an actor and director. In Europe, Conried had performed at the Burg Theater in Vienna, the National Theater in Berlin, and the Leipziger Stadttheater. He wanted to establish a German-speaking theatre in New York modeled after major German theatres in Europe. Disappointed with Neuendorff's neglect of more serious plays in the repertory of the Germania Theater Company*, Conried sought to provide audiences with both the classics and modern popular comedies. He advocated quality productions with sufficient rehearsal periods, the engagement of top-quality actors in the company, and the use of the finest guest stars available from German theatres abroad. Conried was later to become the artistic director of the Metropolitan Opera House, where he was responsible for importing leading operatic stars and promoting the operas of Richard Wagner.

During the first season of 1879–80, Conried and Gustav Amberg controlled the artistic direction of the Thalia. The company staged fifty productions during the first season, which included many classics, popular comedies, and a few very successful operettas. The most popular was Richard Genée's *Der Seecadet* (*Der Seekadet*), later to become the model for Augustin Daly's

Royal Middy. This was followed by a highly successful production of *Die Fledermaus*. These productions helped the Thalia toward financial success by frequently filling the 2,000-seat auditorium. However, Conried and Amberg, unlike their competition at the Germania, included a substantial number of classics in the repertory.

The Thalia established a reputation as the home of operetta and the classics. Among the more popular plays in the serious vein were Schiller's *Die Räuber, Kabale und Liebe, Maria Stuart, Wilhelm Tell*, and *Wallenstein's Tod*; Goethe's *Faust*; Shakespeare's *Romeo und Julia* and *Der Kaufmann von Venedig*. On the lighter side, Johann Nestroy's *Lumpaci Vagabundus*, Gustav Freytag's *Die Journalisten*, and Franz Lehar's *Czaar und Zimmermann* were always well attended.

Many of the core company actors were lured away from the Germania by Conried. Among the most successful guest actors engaged by the Thalia were Marie Geistinger, Magda Irschick, Jenny Stubel, Kaethi Schatt, Josephine Gallmeyer, Wilhelm Knack, Franz Tewele, Antonie Janisch, Friedrich Mitterwurzer, Emil Thomas, and Marguerite Fish. But by far the most sensational guest actors from abroad were provided by the tour engagements of Ludwig Barnay in 1883 and 1888, Adolf Sonnenthal in 1884, and Ernst Possart in 1887–88. These tours attracted the attention of all major New York newspapers.

Ludwig Barnay had appeared in lead roles with the Meiningen Company in cities throughout Europe. In London, where he was well received as Antony in *Julius Ceasar*, Barnay became acquainted with Henry Irving, who was in New York during Barnay's second tour in 1888. Barnay's prime reason for going to America was the large amount of money Conreid offered him. Barnay returned to Germany after each tour with a sizable sum of money to finance his theatre ventures in Berlin. In New York he was billed as the "German Booth," and Conried received much publicity from the press, since Edwin Booth was touring Germany at the same time Barnay was appearing in New York. He was well received by both the German and American press, and the critics covered all of his opening performances.

Neuendorff at the Germania was overwhelmed by the success of his competition and in the spring of 1883 closed the doors of the Germania. In the season of 1883–84, the Thalia had no major competition, but ironically, critics called it the most disappointing season ever witnessed in New York. The triumph of Barnay's engagement during the previous year was difficult to follow.

Amberg returned after one year's leave of absence in 1883 to become the sole manager of the Thalia. Conried left to become stage manager for Rudolph Aronson at the new Casino Theatre. Amberg attempted to cut down on the number of comedies in the repertory, but the German audiences demanded an increasing number of lighter musical comedies and operettas.

Catering to their requests, Amberg added additional musicians to the small orchestra.

The final season of the Thalia Theater, 1887–88, was perhaps one of the most important in terms of the repertory and guest actors. The season offered many classics and the appearance of the popular German actor Ernst Possart. While Possart was featured at the Thalia, Conried, always ready for a lucrative theatrical business undertaking, contracted Barnay in Berlin for an engagement at the Academy of Music. However, Conried was unable to pay Barnay after the first week, so Amberg engaged him to appear at the Thalia with Possart. This was a most significant event in German theatre history, since it was the first time two of the most esteemed German tragedians of the German-speaking world acted together. They appeared together in *Othello, Uriel Acosta, Hamlet, Kean, Die Journalisten, Faust, Die Räuber, Wilhelm Tell, Wallenstein's Tod, Der Kaufmann von Venedig*, and other dramas.

In May 1888 the Thalia Theater Company disbanded. Although Possart and Barnay attracted large crowds, the cost was obviously more than Amberg had anticipated. He did not renew his lease on the Thalia Theater but instead opened a new theatre company in Irving Hall, renamed the Amberg Theatre, in December 1888.

PERSONNEL

Management: Heinrich Conried, manager (1879–83); Wilhelm Kramer, proprietor (1879); Gustav Amberg, business manager (1879–83), proprietor and manager (1880–88); Karl Hermann, business manager (1882–88).

Musical Director: Heinrich Griener (1879–88).

Stage Managers: Joseph L'Hamé (1879– ?), Emil Hahn.

Stage Directors: Heinrich Conried, Gustav Amberg, Mathilde Cottrelly (retired in 1881), Max Lube.

Actors and Actresses: *Gustav Adolfi* (1879–85), Frl. Ahl, *Simon Alexander* (1882–84), Cäcille Alma, Fr. Arnold, *Daniel E. Bandmann* (1883), *Ludwig Barnay* (1883, 1888), Frl. Barre, Herr Bassermann, Emilie Becker, Frl. Beeskow, Frl. Bensberg, Ada Bergen, John Beroni, *Fr. Bersing-Hauptmann* (1881), Herr Bettini, Frl. Bischoff, *Reinhold Bojock* (1880, 1886), *Herr Bollmann* (1881, 1882), *Jenny Boner* (1887), *Heinrich Bötel* (1887), *Marianne Brandt* (1886), Frida Brede, Paula Büchner, Wilhelm Burghardt, Hedwig Buschmann, Cora Cabella, Frl. Camara, Herr Castelli, *Fr. Cathenhausen-Kuhle* (1883), Camilla Clairmont, Eily Coghlan, *Lucie Colmar* (1886), *Heinrich Conried* (1879–83), *Franz Costa* (1887), Mathilde Cottrelly (1879–81), Betty Damhofer, Helene Delia, Minnie Dilthey, Fr. Dombi, Ada Dore, Adolf Drombrowsky (1879–82), Herr Ducenzi, Adele Eichberg, Herr Eichberger, *Eduard Elsbach* (1884–87), *Frl. Carola Engländer* (1883, 1887), Edmund Fabliani, *Frl. Hermine Fanto* (1885), *Emma Fiebach* (1890–80), Eduard Fischer, *Marguerite Fish* (1886), Karl Formes, *Wilhelm Frank* (1879, 1881, 1885), *Carl. A. Friese* (1883, 1886–87), Dora Friese (1883), Herr Fritze, *Josephine Gallmeyer* (1882), Herr Galster, *Marie Geistinger* (1880–83), *Hermann Gerold* (1884–87), *Ernst Seschmeidler* (1882–84), *Gertrud Giers* (1887), Herr Gotthardt, Jacob Graff, Präciosa Grigolatis,

Frl. Grothusen, Julius Grunbaum, Frl. Grünewald, Herr Grünewald, Albertine Habrich, *Elisabeth Hagedorn* (1884–87), Pauline Hall, *Eduard Härting* (1880), Herr Hartmann, Marie Hartmann, *Hugo Hasskerl* (1885–86), F. Hause, *Herr Hausen* (1879–81), Herr Hecht, Cäcilie Hecht, Anna Heineck, *Fanny Heller* (1885–87), *Frl. Julie Heller* (1880), *Fr. Herbert-Förster* (1887), Emmy Herwegh, Herr Herz, Frl. Hesse, *Hedwig Hesse* (1880), *Frl. Asta Hiller* (1884), *Franz Hillmann* (1887), Eduard Hirsch, *Fritz Hitzegrath* (1884–85), *Marie Hock* (1887), Walter Hoffmann, Alse Hofmann, Frl. Holzapfel, Fr. Auguste Horn, Fr. Hoveman-Koerner, *Luzie Höven* (1883), *Magda Irschick* (1879, 1883–84), *Sophie Janauscheck* (1884), *Antonie Janisch* (1883), Herr Jolanda, Anna Jordan, Emma Juch, Hermine Jules, Herr Junck, *Conrad Junker* (1883–84, 1886–87), *August Junkermann* (1887), Herr Jürgens, Herr Kammer, Herr Keller, *Charlotte Kelly* (1879–82), *Otto Kemlitz* (1886), Herr Kern, Franz Kern, Bertha Kierscher, *Herr Kierschner* (1881–82), *Alexander Klein* (1881, 1883), Franz Kloczinski, Herr Klühn, Wilhelm Knaack, *Marie König* (1880), *Herman Korn* (1882–87), *Marie Kraft* (1879–80), Herr Kreutzberg, Therese Krones, *Selma Kronold* (1885–87), *Oskar Krüger* (1887), Eugen Kubach, *Fritz Kugelberg* (1884–85), *Mathilde Kühle* (1881), Herr Kühn, Pauline L'Allemand, *Emanuel Lederer* (1887), Herr Lehmann, Adam Lellman, Herr Lenoir, *Rosa Lesseur* (1887), Herr Liberati, *Herr Lindau* (1882), Louise Lindau, Hermann Linde, Frl. Lindemann, *Adolf Link* (1881, 1886), Helene Livingston, Herr Loë, *Hermine Lorenz* (1884–85), *Fr. Lube* (1879–82), *Max Lube* (1879–87), *Herr Lüpschütz* (1882), Mathilde Madison, Herr Markovitz, Henrietta Markstein, Herr Matz, *Emmy Meffert* (1884–86), Ada Melrose, Herr Mendal, Frl. Menget, Johanna Meta, Karl Meyer, *Otto Meyer* (1879–87), *Frl. Michaelis* (1883–85), *Friedrich Mitterwurzer* (1885), Victoria Morosini, Karl Mühe, Herr Mühlbauer, Ida Mülle, Herr Müller, Anna Mann, Sophie Neuberger, *Adolf Neuendorff* (1886), Hannah Norbert-Hagen, *Sophie Offeney* (1886), L. Ottomeier, *Adele Palma* (1887), *Max Pategg, Elise Patti-Rosa* (1886), Herr Pege, Herr Peiser, Frl. Petri, *Bertha Pierson* (1886), Poldi Pietsch, *Eduard Possansky* (1885), *Ernst Possart* (1887), Herr Prätorius, Louis Prätorius, Herr Puls, Herr Pusch, Herr Raberg (1883–85), *Franziska Raberg* (1880–85), Bertha Rabowska, Anna Ragan, Charlotte Randow, *Bernhard Rank* (1883–87), Margarethe Raspe, Otto Rathjens, Hermine Reichenbach, Herr Reif, Herr Reinau, Frl. Reinhold, *Herr René* (1882), Carola Rennen, *Adelaide Ristori* (1884, one night), Herr Rohbeck, Herr Rothenstein, Herr Rothschild, Alexander Rüdinger, Herr Ruthenberg, Herr Saldau, Herr Schäfer, *Julie Schamberg* (1884), Frl. Schamidatus, Frl. Schätz, *Johann Schatz* (1883–87), Fanny Schegar, *Herr Schimke-Herrmann* (1881), *Anna Schlag* (1879–82, 1885), *Mary Schlag* (1886), *Herr Schliemann* (1879), *Eduard Schmitz* (1879–81), *Eugenie Schmitz* (1883–85), Herr Schneider, Felix Schnelle, Fritz Schnelle, *Max Schnelle* (1879–81), *Carl Schönfeld* (1879–82), Caroline Schötter, Katharina Schratt, Herr Schüler, *Bertha Schulz* (1884–85), *Herr Schultze* (1881, 1883), *Ferdinand Schütz* (1883–87), *Emma Seebold* (1881, 1883–84), Herr Seidl, David Sichel, Herr Silbernagel, Rudolf Sinnhold, Fr. Skubra, Lori Slubel, *Adolf Sonnenthal* (1884), Herr Sparge, Frl. Spitzner, Frl. Stäbner, Herr Steckel, *Emil Steger* (1887), Julius Steger, Theodor Steinar, Eduard Steinberger, Carl Steinbuch, Herr Steindorf, Herr Steiner, Ludwig Steingade, Herr Steppes, Wilhelm Stöckel, Herr Stolte, Frl. Stork, Sigismund Störk, Ella Stort, Herr Strakosch, *Jenny Stubel* (1881), Herr Szwirschina, Fr. Telle, *Franz Tewele* (1882), Herr Thaller, *Emil Thomas* (1886), Herr Uberti, Ferdinand Urban, Marie

Vanoni, F. Varena, *Emilie von Aichsberg* (1887), *Helene von Doenhoff* (1886), *Frl. von Hahn* (1884), *Georgine von Januschowsky* (1884, 1886), Selina von Krottnauer, Franz von Metsch, Frau von Moser-Sperner, Ida von Trautmann (1879–80), *Paula von Varndal* (1886–87), Ferdenand Wachtel, *Franz Wackwitz* (1885), Herr Wagner, *August Walter* (1884–87), Lena Wassman, Theodor Wegern, Herr Weinacht, Joseph Weinlich, Frl. Weiss, Lucie Werner, Adolf Werther, Herr Wiechert, *Hubert Wilke* (1879, 1882–83), *Carl Witt* (1886), *Fanny Witt* (1879–80), Herr Wohlmuth, Herr Wolff, Ludwig Ziechmann, *Heinrich Zilzer* (1882–84), Arthur Zolki.

REPERTORY

The following list is not complete and includes classics and representative plays only.

1879–80: *Kabale und Liebe; Quecksilber; Dr. Klaus; Der Pfarrer von Kirchfeld; Sodom und Gomorrha; Die Fledermaus; Der Seecadet; Medea; Maria Stuart; Gringoire; Deborah; Der verkaufte Schlaf; Narciss; Robert und Bertram; Die Sontagsjäger; Käthchen von Heilbronn; Christ und Jude; Die Jungfrau von Orleans; Romeo und Julia; Aschenbrödel; Orpheus in der Unterwelt; Hasemann's Töchter; Stradella; Boccaccio; Die schöne Glatheé; Die schöne Helena.*

1880–81: *Wilhelm Tell; Die Hexe; Girofle-Girofla; 500,000 Teufel; Faust; Der Seecadet; Die Fledermaus; Lumpaci Vagabundus; Fatinitza; Robert und Bertram; Drei Paar Schuhe; Madame Flott; Therese Krones; Die Cameliendame; Graf Essex; Donna Diana; Ich speise bei meiner Mutter; Die schöne Galatheé; Die Näherin; La belle Helene.*

1881–82: *Demetrius; Die Glocken von Corneville; Donna Juanita; Boccaccio; Adrienne Lecouvreur; Dorf und Stadt; Die Näherin; Camille; Die Fledermaus; Maria Stuart; Dr. Klaus; Der Glücksengel; Max und Moritz; Die Räuber; Cyprienne; Die Grille; Die kleine Mama; Seit hat ihr Herz entdeckt; Der lustige Krieg; Minna von Barnhelm; Der Seecadet; Drei Paar Schuhe; Die Töchter der Hölle; Damenkrieg; Die schöne Galatheé.*

1882–83: *Sarah und Bernhard; Romeo auf dem Bureau; Don Quixote; Ein Engel; Der Sohn auf Reisen; Ich werde mir den Major einladen; Fromme Wünsche; Mascot; Coriolanes; Die Räuber; Jane Eyre; Wilhelm Tell; Hamlet; Uriel Acosta; Die Bluthochzeit; Narciss; König Lear; Wallenstein's Tod; Luftschlösser; Gräfin Dubarry; Kean; Julius Caesar; Der Goldonkel; Clavigo; Die Fledermaus; Boccaccio.*

1883–84: *Das Spitzenbuch der Königin; Der Zigeuner; Der Bettelstudent; Die Fledermaus; Lili; Lumpaci Vagabundus; Hass und Liebe, Afrikareise; Deborah; Brunhild; Maria Stuart; Medea; Kabale und Liebe; Kätchen von Heilbronn; Narciss; 1776; Fatinitz; Die Räuber; Adelaide; Capitan Nicol; Die Waise von Lowood; Hochzeit bei Laternenschein.*

1884–85: *Die Karlsschüler; Der Freischütz; Wilhelm Tell; Boccaccio; Hasemann's Töchter; Lorbeerbaum und Bettelstab; Robert und Bertram; Der Bettelstudent; Die Journalisten; Tannhäuser; Schneewittchen; Nanon; Martha; Kabale und Liebe; Uriel Acosta; Kean; Hamlet; Die schöne Ungarin; Die Grille; Die Fledermaus; Czaar und Zimmermann; Mein Leopold; Der Feldprediger; Maria Stuart.*

1885–86: *Czaar und Zimmermann; Maria und Magdalena; Nanon; Die Freischütz; Der Bettelstudent; Martha; Der Walzer König; Fatinitza; Kean; Die Räuber;*

Narciss; Lumpaci Vagabundus; Der Seecadet; Gasparone; Die lustige Weiber von Windsor; Mikado; Kätchen von Heilbronn; Faust; Figaro's Hochzeit; Richard III; Hamlet; Die Auswanderer; Wahn und Wahnsinn; Miller und Müller; Reif Reiflingen; Die Jungfrau von Belleville; Liederspiel am Hochzeitstag.

1886–87: *Ein Taugenichts; Heimliche Liebe; Humpty Dumpty; Lumpaci Vagabundus; Nanon; Czaar und Zimmermann; Feuer in der Mädchenschule; Cyprienne; Monsieur Hercules; Hasemann's Töchter; Dr. Peschke; Luftschlösser; Undine; Don Caesar; Die Fledermaus; Hundert Jungfrauen; Wenn Frauen sparen; Der Teufel im Schloss.*

1887–88: *Fra Diavolo; Hanna Nüte; Travatore; Die weisse Dame; Die Fledermaus; Der Freischütz; Der Kaufmann von Venedig; Narciss; Nathan der Weise; Richard III; Egmont; Die Räuber; König Lear; Othello; Maria Stuart; Deborah; Kabale und Liebe; Don Carlos; Faust; Byron; Wilhelm Tell; Die Jungfrau von Orleans; Uriel Acosta; Die Journalisten; Hamlet; Bluthochzeit; Kean; Die Memoiren des Teufels; Heinrich Heine; Nathan der Weise; Der Probepfeil; Ein moderner Barbar; Wallenstein's Tod; Doctor Klaus; Robert und Bertram; Unsere letzte Saison.*

BIBLIOGRAPHY

Published Sources: (German language press) *New Yorker Figaro; New Yorker Staats-Zeitung.* (English language press) *New York Dramatic Mirror; New York Herald; New York Times; New York Tribune; Spirit of the Times.* See *Deutsch-Americanische Gescichtsblätter* 15 (1915): 255–309; "*Das Deutsche Theater in New York,*" *Sonntagsblatt des New Yorker Staats-Zeitung,* April 16, 1905: Montrose J. Moses, *The Life of Heinrich Conried* (New York: Thomas Y. Crowell, 1916); Ludwig Barnay, *Irinnerungen* (Berlin: E. Fleischel, 1903).

Archival Sources: The New York Public Library and the Harvard Theatre Collection, Cambridge, Massachusetts, have numerous programs and newspaper clippings.

Ron Engle

TREMONT THEATRE COMPANY. Interest in building a theatre to break the monopoly held by the Boston ["Federal Street"] Theatre Company* grew steadily after the Kean riot of 1825. Three forces converged to convert this interest into a reality. Conflict between William Pelby (1793–1850) and the managers of the Boston Theatre over Pelby's allegedly exorbitant salary demands led to aroused public support for the Boston-born Pelby. His public believed he was a victim of pro-English bias in the operation of the old theatre. Pelby supporters aligned themselves with a group of Boston businessmen identified with the so-called Middling Interest in Boston politics and social affairs. Vociferous patriots and harsh Anglophobes, they wanted an "American" company under an "American" management. Finally, the Boston Theatre, long the resort of the fashionable class, seemed to be, to the younger generation of Boston playgoers, insensitive to changing public taste.

Pelby agitated for a new theatre at a meeting of these factions in February 1827. In March a building committee was formed to secure land and select a plan for the theatre. Lots on Tremont (then Common) Street were purchased, and Isaiah Rogers was commissioned to design the theatre. The cornerstone was laid on July 4, 1827, and the theatre, only partly built, opened for business under Pelby's management on September 24. Roger's design resulted in a building many Bostonians thought was the city's most beautiful.

Pelby scoured the American market for performers, musicians, and technicians, offering large salaries for native talent. True to form, the Boston Theatre management went to England for new talent in the coming war of theatres. Pelby's new company featured himself and Mrs. Pelby in romantic and serious leads and William Rufus Blake in comic leads. Mrs. Inchbald's comedy *Wives as They Were and Maids as They Are*, with William Dimond's farce *The Lady and the Devil*, neither an American product, made up the opening bill. Shortly, the first of many quarrels between the contentious Pelby and his players resulted in the withdrawal of Mr. and Mrs. Blake to the rival Boston Theatre. Pelby promptly recruited his rival's best performers, Mr. and Mrs. John Barnes. Pelby's expensive company launched into a season that was profitable for the first five months. An extravagant production of the ballet *Undine* was a failure, but productions of the tragic *Charlotte Temple* and Monk G. Lewis' perennially attractive spectacle *Timour, the Tartar* were well attended. At the end of the third quarter of the first year of his ten-year lease, Pelby was pressured by the disgruntled stockholders to sell his lease to an association of Boston gentlemen headed by Francis W. Dana. Pelby left the Tremont Theatre Company at season's end, in debt; at odds with the company, the Boston press, and the Tremont's owners; and determined to establish a company to rival the Tremont and the Boston Theatre.

Dana and his associates engaged Junius Brutus Booth (1796–1852), English-born American tragedian and progenitor of the famous theatre family. Booth really starred only in his two months at the helm. He was succeeded by Joe Cowell (1792–1863), a fine low comedian. The large, well-salaried company produced a season of beautiful musical and dramatic attractions with the help of a procession of stars including Thomas Hamblin; the infant prodigy Louisa Lane; Mary Ann Duff; J. W. Wallack; T. A. Cooper; John Gilbert; Edwin Forrest; Madame Celeste, dancer; and Madame Feron, opera singer. Opera highlighted the season's offering, with productions of *The Barber of Seville, Der Freischutz, Beggar's Opera*, and *Rienzi*, a ballet. *The Caliph of Baghdad* drew well, as did the scenic spectacle *The Enchanted Castle; or, Knights of Old*. Dana and Cowell discovered that the house was too small, especially offering too few seats in the prestigious dress circle, to clear a profit with such a high-toned repertory. The management lost $27,000.

The following year, 1829, the Tremont stockholders leased the Old Boston Theatre in order to close it and stifle competition. The expensive remedy worked for a while. Dana's manager, Mr. Wilson, and his stage manager, W. H. Smith (1806–72), cut costs by using fewer stars and by staging more old English comedies. They turned a profit of nearly $18,000. Richard Russell, of [Caldwell's] American Company*, managed in 1830–31 and tried to restore some of the earlier splendor to the season, but his attractions did not draw well. His effort to suppress vice in and about the theatre were effective, however. The child actor Master Joseph Burke had an immense reception. Russell closed the theatre for the month of May so that he and some of the players could support Master Burke's tour to Salem and Providence. The season ended early, on June 20, with Russell a poorer but wiser man.

"Gentleman" George H. Barrett (1794–1860) led the Tremont forces the next two years, during which the company was a modest financial success. Splendid scenery and fine singing were keys to the success in 1831–32 productions of *Cinderella* and *Aladdin*. Edwin Forrest drew well in the Boston premiere of Robert Montgomery Bird's muscular tragedy *The Gladiator*. The season of 1832–33, Barrett's second, was the last of the Dana lease but the first for gaslight in the theatre and the first for competition with William Pelby's Warren Theatre Company, 1832–36. The appearance of Charles and Fanny Kemble in a starring engagement was the season's highlight.

For the next six seasons, 1833–39, the Tremont Theatre Company flourished artistically under the management of Thomas Barry (1798–1876). The former stage manager of New York's Park Theatre was reputedly the nation's most capable in this line of work, which involved a rudimentary artistic direction of the group's productions. Barry aimed in his tenure to use the best stars of his day in plays and operas selected for their high moral standard. He received great public and journalistic approval, but he suffered financial reverses every year, losing a total of $26,000 in five years. The problem was the design of the theatre. Built to image the balance of classes in a democracy, it offered too few seats for the rich and fashionable clientele in the expensive dress circle. Pelby's National Theatre Stock Company* (1832–52), housed in the enlarged, renamed Warren Theatre, had become the popular venue, leaving the Tremont to cater to the upper class. Barry was in an economic trap, driven by a personal commitment to excellence, he was perforce committed to the best in regular performers, stars, and scenic investiture. Moreover, the stockholders demanded a high rent of $9,500 a year, which guaranteed their dividend. Finally, he was challenged by the high expectations of his patrons but was unable to capitalize fully on their approval because of the seating plan of his theatre. Perhaps the greatest success of Barry's years were the starring appearances of Mr. and Mrs. Wood in English opera. Average receipts for the Woods in *La sonnambula* in 1835 were $675 a night, but expenses were $700 a night. In the Park Theatre, New York, which accommodated 411 persons in the dress circle (the Tremont seated but 132), the Woods grossed an average of $1,467 a night at the same admission scale. Typical annual expenses for salaries for the regular company, salaries for stars, and rent totaled about $65,000. Barry's box office would have had to take in $260 a night just to pay these basic expenses, which it could not do at a $1 top admission to the first tier of boxes. An average starring engagement would gross nearly $500 each night. The Boston debut of Ellen Tree (Mrs. Charles Kean) was a great success, but her twenty-six-night engagement averaged only $700 a night. Even Edwin Forrest, appearing in October 1837 after a four-year absence, averaged just $570 a night for twenty nights.

In 1837 the nation's business was all but halted by a raging financial panic. A deep economic depression followed, casting a pall over the Tremont Theatre Company's business for the remainder of its life. The Lyceum movement of the 1830s cut into the Tremont's audiences and profits, as did competition from Pelby's National Theatre Stock Company. Finally, in the late 1830s, an evangelical revival swept Boston, and the condemnations of the preachers checked theatre business.

J. S. Jones, an actor with the Tremont Theatre Company from 1828 to 1831, leased the Tremont for the last four seasons of the life of the company. John Gilbert (1810–89), an excellent comic actor with the company since 1834, managed it for two seasons, 1839–41. In both seasons, business was dismal, except for brief upturns during visits by the dancers Mrs. Fitzwilliam in 1839 and Fanny Elssler in 1840. An Elssler mania swept Boston during her spectacular thirteen-night engagement. Elssler cuffs, made of velvet with bright buttons, adorned the debutantes; Elssler boot-jacks graced the fashionable dressing table, and Elssler bread piqued conversation at the dining table. Jones paid Fanny Elssler $500 a night, but a premium admission scale and public auction of tickets brought in almost $1,100 each night. In 1840–41 the theatre charged full prices a little over half the season. After February 15, with prices cut to half, an equestrian company supported the actors in noisy productions of *The Cataract of the Ganges, Napoleon, Amaleh, the Arab*, and *Mazeppa*, the most famous equestrian drama of the period.

George H. Andrews, longtime actor with the Tremont Company, and John Preston subleased the theatre in 1841–42. Again, Fanny Elssler was the only attraction to draw well. The theatre closed in early December and reopened December 20 at half prices with a production of Dion Boucicault's *London Assurance*, but Andrews and Preston abandoned their lease after the twenty-fifth week, $10,000 in debt. Boston Museum Company* performances at twenty-five cents were further undermining the economy of the Tremont. A commonwealth of actors tried to operate the theatre; they made money briefly, but dissension impeded their efforts. They closed in June.

Jones managed the theatre in the final year of operation. Despite sharp cuts in salary for the last quarter, expenses exceeded receipts by almost

$3,000 at the end of a forty-two-week season. Meantime, the stockholders had negotiated the sale of the theatre to the Reverend Mr. Colver's Baptist Society. The last performance on June 22, 1843, concluded with an emotional singing of "Auld Lang Syne" by the company and speeches by John Gilbert and William Rufus Blake defending theatre and drama from the attacks of the evangelists.

The operation of the Tremont Theatre has not been calendared, so the precise nature of its repertory is unclear. However, William Clapp's account indicates that comedy, opera, and ballet were the main ingredients in the Tremont entertainment mix. Despite the early intentions of the founders of the company, it catered to Boston's elite through most of its life with music, dance, fantasy, spectacle, and comedy. Certainly, the strengths of the best, most-used company members supports this view.

Henry James Finn (1785–1840), a company regular from 1829 until his death in the burning of the SS *Lexington* in Long Island Sound, was an inimitable comic in eccentric characters such as Sir Andrew Aguecheek and his own Yankee, Sergeant Welcome Sobersides. Boston-born John Gilbert (1810–89) debuted at the Tremont in 1828, stayed a year, and then developed his craft in theatres in the West and South. While with the company from 1834 to 1842, he excelled in irascible old men, such as Sir Anthony Absolute and Sir Peter Teazle. George Barrett (1794–1860) made his reputation playing the young men in comedies by Richard Sheridan and Oliver Goldsmith, blades such as Young Absolute in *The Rivals*, Charles Surface in *The School for Scandal*, Puff in *The Critic*, and Young Marlow in *She Stoops to Conquer*. His wife, formerly Mrs. Anne Jane Henry (1801–53), was a dancer-actress who excelled in refined comedy and the lighter roles in tragedy. William H. Smith (1806–72), like Barry a skilled stage manager, was also a versatile actor in a wide range of parts. Joe Cowell wrote that Smith was "one of those pink-looking men with yellow hair, that the ladies always admire, and in his day was considered the best fop and light comedian on the continent" (Cowell, 81). George H. Andrews (1798–1866) was popular as a low comedian as was Thomas Comer (1790–1862). Comer, best known as the director of choral music at the Tremont, was also effective in eccentric and low Irish characters.

Born of desire to provide an "American" alternative to Boston playgoers, the Tremont Theatre soon displaced the Boston Theatre and appropriated the old theatre's clients. For three years it operated competition-free but made little money for its managers. The beautiful but small theatre, the excellent acting company, and the classy bill of fare appealed to a too-narrow segment of Boston society. Moreover, according to Boston theatre historian Clapp, the theatre was "too small to enable even crowded houses to meet the extraordinary expenses incidental to great attractions" (4: 369).

PERSONNEL

Management: William Pelby (1827–28), Junius Brutus Booth (1828), Joe Leathley Cowell (1828–29), Mr. Wilson (1829–30), Richard Russell (1830–31), George H. Barrett (1831–33), Thomas Barry (1833–39), J. S. Jones (1839–43).

Stage Manager: W. H. Smith.

Actors and Actresses: Mr. Adams (1830–31, 1838–39); Mr. Addams (1836–37); *Mrs. Ophelia Anderson* (nee Pelby) (1828–29, 1839–40); *George H. Andrews* (1829–37, 1839–42); Thomas Archer (1828–29); *Mr. and Mrs. Ayling* (1839–43); J. F. Barker, singer (1828– ?); Mr. Barnes (1830–31, 1833–34); Mr. and Mrs. John Barnes (1827–28); *George H. Barrett* (1830–33, 1834–37); *Mrs. George H. Barrett* (nee Anne Jane Stockwell) (1832–33, 1834–37); *Thomas Barry* (1831–32, 1833–39); W. M. Bayne, scenic artist and actor (1828–29, 1836–37, 1839–40); George Birch, singer (1828– ?); Mr. Blake (1828–30); Mr. and Mrs. Willian Rufus Blake (1827, 1833–34); Junius Brutus Booth (1828); Miss Bouquet (1839–40); Mr. and Mrs. Brewster (1827–28); Mr. Brown (1827–28); J. Mills Brown (1827–28); Mrs. Chapman (1842–43); Mr. Clements (1828–30); Mr. Clive (1837–38); *Mr. Collingbourne* (1827–34); *Thomas Comer*, actor, musical director, and composer (1828–43); Miss Courtney (1832–33); *Joseph Cowell* (1828–29); Mrs. H. Cramer (1840–42); *Mr. and Mrs. Creswick* (1840–42); Mr. Cunningham (1837–38); W. H. Curtis (1836–41); Mr. Davenport (1837–38); Mary Ann Duff (1833–34); Miss Eberle (1828–32); A. W. Fenno (1839–42); J. M. Field (1827–29, 1841–42); Mrs. J. M. Field (1841–42); *Henry James Finn* (1829–40); *Alexina Fisher* (1833–42); Mr. Forbes (1827–28, 1833–34); Mrs. Forbes (1827–28); *John Gibbs Gilbert* (1834–43); *Mrs. John Gibbs Gilbert* (1834–43); Phineas Glover, singer (1828); Mr. and Mrs. Greene (1842–43); John Hall, singer (1828– ?); Lewis Hallman, Jr. (1828–29); Miss Hamilton (1828–29); Mr. Hart (1827–28); Mr. Herbert (1827–28); Joseph E. Herman (1836); Mr. and Mrs. Hield and Master Hield (1836–37); Mr. Hill (1840–41); Miss Holden (1830–31); Mr. Holden (1830–31); Mrs. Holden (1833–34); Mr. Houpt (1836–37); J. C. Howard (1830–31, 1842–43); Mrs. Hughes (1833–34); Mr. Hyatt (1827–30); W. Isherwood (1827–28); Mr. Jervis (1828–29); S. D. Johnson (1830–34, 1840–42); W. F. Johnson (1841–42); Mr. Jones (1829–30); *Fanny Jones*, dancer (1838–42); G. Jones (1829–30); *J. S. Jones* (1828–31, 1839–43); Mr. and Mrs. William Jones (1828–29); Mr. Keene, vocalist (1829–30); Mr. Kelly (1827–28); Thomas Kilner (1836–37); Mrs. Lascombe (1828–29); Mr. Laws (1828–29); Mr. Lerman (1827–37, 1842–43); Mr. Lopez, prompter (1828–29); Anselm Lothrop, singer (1828–29); Mr. Martin (1827–28); *Miss McBride* (1828–37); *James Murdoch* (1836–38); Mr. and Mrs. Muzzy (1836–41); William B. Oliver, singer (1828– ?); Mrs. Papanti (1828–30); Mr. Pearson (1830–31); *William Pelby* (1827–28); Mrs. William Pelby (1827–29); Mr. Preston (1841–42); Mr. Reed (1827–28); Mr. Rice (1831–32); Miss Riddle (1827–29); Mrs. Riddle (1827–28); J. H. Ring (1839–41); Mrs. Roper (1828–29); *Richard Russell* (1830–31); Master, Miss, and Mrs. Russell (1830–31); D. A. Sarzedas (1836–40); Mr. Scott (1828–31); Mr. Sheridan (1839–40); *W. H. Smith* (1827–34, 1839–40); *Mrs. W. H. Smith* (nee Riddle) (1827–34, 1838–43); Mr. Spear (1840–41); Mr. and Mrs. Stone (1830–31); Mr. Thayer (1828–30); Mr. Walton (1831–32); Mr. Webb (1827–29); David Whiting, actor-singer (1828–30, 1833–34, 1838–40); J. F. Williamson (1833–34, 1839–40); Mr. Woodhull (1832–33); Mrs. Young (1827–28).

REPERTORY

Not available.

BIBLIOGRAPHY

Clapp, William W., Jr. *A Record of the Boston Stage*. Boston: James Monroe and
    Company, 1853. Reprint. New York: Greenwood Press, 1969.
Clapp, William W., Jr. "The Drama in Boston." In *Memorial History of Boston*.
    Vol. 4, pp. 357–82. Edited by Justin Winsor. Boston: James R. Osgood and
    Company, 1881.
Cowell, Joseph. *Thirty Years Passed among the Players in England and America*.
    New York: Harper, 1844.
Stoddard, Richard. "Isaiah Rogers' Tremont Theatre, Boston." *The Magazine
    Antiques* 105 (June 1974): 1314–19.

Weldon B. Durham

U

UNION SQUARE THEATRE STOCK COMPANY. The Union Square Theatre acting company was organized by A. M. Palmer for the New York playhouse's second year of operation. The tasteful, elegant, and ample Union Square Theatre was designed and built by architect H. M. Simons for brewer-politician Sheridan Shook. It occupied the center of the Union Place Hotel, on Fourteenth Street, in the middle of the block between Broadway and Fourth Avenue and on the south side of Union Square, the Rialto of the day. Launched as a theatre for reputable burlesque and vaudeville on September 11, 1871, the Union Square Theatre was taken over by A.M. Palmer, who was managing attractions already booked on June 1, 1872. Palmer renovated the theatre and transformed it into a home of legitimate drama.

To rival in merit the players controlled by Lester Wallack and Augustin Daly, yet with "not a single play in the locker," Palmer coaxed veteran comedian Dan H. Harkins away from Daly's Fifth Avenue Theatre to be his stage manager. With Harkins' guidance, he assembled a company and negotiated a short-term engagement with popular actress Agnes Ethel. Henry Tissington, the orchestra leader, had previously conducted the house orchestra of Wallack's Theatre, the Winter Garden, and the Grand Opera House. Victorien Sardou's new script *Agnes [Andrea]*, which Ethel had just acquired, was announced as the first production of the Union Square's 1872–73 season. Adapted by H. S. Olcott and N. Hart Jackson and premiered September 17, 1872, the drama was a success, fulfilling the manager's agreement with his star for 100 consecutive nights.

After *Agnes*, according to Palmer, the first season's productions "were of a tentative kind, and not always made with anything like a firm adherence to my own opinions" (Palmer, MS, 6). The theatre had lost something like $75,000 during 1872–73 (*Freund's Music and Drama*, May 1885). When

Harkins, on whose faulty counsel he had too often relied, suggested that Palmer retire, in his behalf, the manager readjusted his cabinet. He engaged John Parselle as his stage director (*vice* stage manager), reduced the annual budget of plays performed from a dozen to only four, and opened the 1873–74 season with a stronger company entirely of his own choosing. He also instituted a policy of delegating production responsibilities to a team of proficient specialists. "It was an unusual thing for Mr. Palmer to interfere in any way with the work on the stage," actress Rose Eytinge recalled. "He had surrounded himself with a company in whose work both he and the public had the fullest confidence, and he let them alone" (Eytinge, 226). A reporter for *Music and Drama*, on the other hand, wrote that "Mr. Palmer . . . watches every detail of his rehearsals" (January 12, 1883), and actress Ida Vernon asserted that he also "put on the finishing touches" (*New York Sun*, September 12, 1915). When actor-manager Edwin Booth was in bankruptcy, when the resolutely British Lester Wallack was retired from active management, and when Palmer's most formidable rival, Augustin Daly (by undertaking too much management, too many houses, and too many players), was driven from the New York scene $45,000 in debt, the Union Square Company—in a repertory dominated by high-class melodrama ("plays of contemporary life")—was progressively thriving.

Albert Marshman Palmer (1838–1905), a Baptist clergyman's son, born in North Stonington, Connecticut, was classically educated in nearby schools. He earned an LL.B. from New York University and briefly clerked for a Manhattan law firm. From 1869 until July 1872, he was librarian of the New York Mercantile Library before taking on managerial duties at the Union Square. Although he occasionally invested a little money in theatrical enterprises, he knew almost nothing of theatres behind the footlights, yet "had sat a great deal in front of them, and rightly believed that from that side the best understanding was to be obtained of the public's requirements" (*Boston Sunday Herald*, May 16, 1880; *The Theatre*, April 16, 1886). Following box-office losses in 1872–73, Palmer's Union Square company turned profits for a decade. After 1877 the manager annually dispatched lucrative Union Square touring companies across the country. About 1878 he ascended to sole proprietorship.

Midway through the 1878–79 season, Palmer could boast that in the preceding five years no other major theatre in the world, except the Théâtre Français, had so little change in its leading artists (*New York Tribune*, January 2, 1879), and the Union Square Company sustained that continuity while he retained control. He sent out traveling companies, because he was obliged to maintain "the largest theatrical company of first-class artists ever kept by any theatre in an English-speaking country" (*New York Tribune*, January 2, 1879). "His employees were always secure with him," Arthur Hornblow remembered. "He discharged no one. Entirely simple in his manners, habits, and dress, he conducted his business with a like direct frankness. To scheme was no part of his nature. As a rule, the members of his company were retained, year after year, on verbal contracts" (*Theatre Magazine*, April 1905).

Palmer also paid his actors more liberally than other New York managers then did. Charles Thorne, Jr., received $200 a week year round almost from the time of his entry into the Union Square Company in 1873; Rose Eytinge, "for a short season without benefit," earned a like sum; and Clara Morris, whose drawing power exceeded either Thorne's or Eytinge's, was paid upwards of $300 a week for starring engagements. All company salaries were proportionately higher on the road. By contrast, Daly in 1879 engaged Ada Rehan and John Drew for leading parts at his theatre at starting salaries of only $35 a week; more than a decade afterward, his players "started as low as $7 a week and averaged about $35" (Felheim, 33).

Palmer "could estimate the capacities of his actors much more accurately than could Mr. Daly and rarely miscast them," *Evening Post* critic John Ranken Towse asserted (Towse, 363). One of his first fractures of conventional stock-company usage "was to break down, in a great degree, the traditional lines separating performers, . . . a reform adopted from the French, and now also accepted in the best German theatres," another contemporary reporter claimed (*Boston Sunday Herald*, May 9, 1880). "He will not engage any actress distinctly as 'leading lady' and his company today has no one actress who can make her choice of juvenile parts" (*Boston Sunday Herald*, May 16, 1880). Union Square players had no excuse for refusing a part because it was "not in their line." The invidious comparison of rival managers is both relevant and valid: even the plea that Palmer "broke down . . . traditional lines," which others have made for almost every manager since David Garrick, is allowable by virtue of the mitigating phrase "in a great degree." Rehearsals of a new script at the Union Square were routinely greater in number than at any other American theatre—some pieces being readied for six successive weeks, except Sundays. "While a new play was in constant preparation, the current offering was kept on the boards as long as the public demanded it," actress Ida Vernon attested. "Nothing was done in a haphazard way" (*New York Sun*, September 12, 1915).

Notwithstanding its eventual first- and second-company tours, the Union Square troupe remained under Palmer's management "a stock company pure and simple, which does not 'go on the road,' in the regular combination style" after a successful home-theatre run (*Boston Sunday Herald*, May 9, 1880). When provincial managers noticed which of the house's actors were temporarily out of a long-running play, they often applied for their services as featured players on outlying stages; Palmer sent them forth, in the belief they were better at work than lounging around New York, thereby making money for the other managers, for his artists, and for himself. This system is notable not so much for its sheer magnitude as because it was new.

Palmer's first aim was the perpetuation of the best New York stock company that was possible; his means toward that goal were no longer those of the old-school manager but of a modern producer. He departed the Union Square in late April 1883, while Charles Wyndham's visiting comedy troupe was playing *Brighton [Saratoga]* there, transferring his entire interest in the theatre on April 30 to his former partner Shook.

Had Palmer ventured into producing plays of contemporary life without acute regard to the mores of American audiences, his enterprise might have quickly foundered. Thus the crucial changes the manager ordered, and his literary attachés wrought, for Sardou's *Agnes* (booked without Palmer's having first read this script) and successively for other controversial imported plays—for example, *Led Astray, Camille, The Two Orphans, Rose Michel, Miss Multon, Pink Dominos, Daniel Rochat, A Parisian Romance*—largely account for their public acceptance on the Union Square stage. *Camille* and *The Two Orphans* were perhaps the two most popular plays on the nineteenth-century American stage: Clara Morris at first vehemently "hated! hated! hated!" *Camille*, through whose Union Square production she achieved one of her most enduring successes; whereas, after several other New York managers had rejected *The Two Orphans*, Hart Jackson's Union Square adaptation of it earned Palmer a fortune and advanced Kate Claxton, as the blind Louise, to stardom. Bronson Howard's provocative American social comedy *The Banker's Daughter* (as reshaped by Union Square house dramatist A. R. Cazauran) became the most successful play of the 1878–79 New York season; this script, according to Palmer, "did more to establish American dramatic authorship in honor than anything that had yet occurred in the history of our stage" (*New York Times*, September 17, 1880; Palmer, MS., 73).

Of the 1872–73 Union Square repertory, most plays, new and old, were of American authorship; English imports ranked second, followed by adaptations from the French. The four French pieces were surpassingly favored, however, monopolizing twenty-seven weeks of that nine-month regular season. Classic English comedy and tragedy were rarely performed at the Union Square during Palmer's tenure, and emasculated Shakespeare (apart from intermittent scenes acted for benefits) was never played there. Most of the company's 1873–74 season was divided between two current French dramas, *Led Astray* (twenty-three weeks) and *Camille* (four weeks), trailed by George Fawcett Rowe's American entry, *The Geneva Cross* (six and one-half weeks). *The Sphynx* and *The Two Orphans* dominated 1874–75, the latter piece running from December 21 until mid-June; three contemporary French adaptations, respectively, divided most of both the 1875–76 and 1876–77 seasons, and four fresh French imports filled the entire 1877–78 agenda. The 1878–79 season was notable for a single American script, *The Banker's Daughter* (November 30–April 15), whereas 1879–80 was led by *Daniel Rochat* and *Felicia* (both French); 1881–82 by

The Lights o' London and *The New Magdalen* (both English) and *Article '47* (French); with 1882–83 comprising only *The Rantzaus* and *A Parisian Romance* (both French). Palmer personally scouted the French theatre scene, obtained playwrights' models and sketches of *mise-en-scène* for adaptation (not replication) at the Union Square, and sometimes had copies (for example, for *The Rantzaus*) of the original Parisian costumes made abroad.

Outlays for scenery ranged between $300 for *Led Astray*—"done out of stock, . . . but the mounting was excellent" (Palmer, MS., 22)—and the lavish, meticulous staging of *The Two Orphans*, which the manager and his artistic corps "costumed and put on with as much particularity and richness as ever were bestowed on a classical play; and that was the rule of the house the whole time I managed it" (*New York Herald*, February 29, 1888). Richard Marston's settings for *The Two Orphans*, incidentally, were consistently "boxed," rather than executed in drop, wing, and border fashion, and the curtain was dropped for every scenic change at the Union Square. Marston had come to this theatre from Shakespearean productions at Sadler's Wells, London, and the *Black Crook*, at Niblo's Garden, New York. The *Sunday Dispatch* acclaimed his last-act scenery for *Rose Michel* as "one of the most perfect triumphs of scenic art [on] the New York stage" (November 24, 1875), and the *Times* described his massive scenes for *Ferreol* as "simply magnificent" (March 22, 1876). Marston's subsequent mounting of *The Lights o' London*, modeled closely after the famous London production, was "the most elaborate . . . since *The Two Orphans*" (Palmer, MS., 102). This melodrama's playbill stated that "over one-hundred supernumeraries" were regularly employed.

From the first, Palmer employed a large staff: a treasurer, assistant treasurer, advertising agent, bill distributor, scene painter, two assistant scene painters, stage carpenter and machinist, gas man, property man, assistant property man, door keeper, orchestra leader, house orchestra, stable of house dramatists (in literary attachés), and, for 1872–73, an acting company of sixteen men (of whom Harkins functioned as stage manager and James Thorpe as prompter) and a dozen actresses (including Agnes Ethel—to be joined later by several more female players, and by two visiting stars). James H. Stoddart, presently to augment the acting company, made his first appearance at the Union Square in mid-June 1873 (a benefit night). Supernumeraries were occasionally employed, as were outside stars (for example, Joseph Jefferson, Tommaso Salvini, John T. Raymond, Mme. Janauschek, Charles Wyndham, Genevieve Ward, and Mrs. E. L. Davenport). Other troupes annually occupied the stage during summer months.

George Fawcett Rowe ably directed his script *The Geneva Cross* and actor-playwright Dion Boucicault expertly conducted rehearsals of his *Led Astray* (adapted from Octave Feuillet's *La tentacion*), in 1873; then each left the premises after the last rehearsal and first performance of his respective play. A. R. Cazauran evidently assisted John Parselle in rehearsing not only *Miss Multon* but other Union Square scripts (Morris, 391–94; *Chicago Tribune*, October 22, 1882). Author-actor-inventor Steele MacKaye was the playhouse's first American-born director (MacKaye, 1:243; Eytinge, 237–41). Twenty-year-old William Seymour (also native born) helped MacKaye direct his *Rose Michel* in 1875, served as prompter during that drama's Union Square run, and independently directed *Two Men of Sandy Bar, The Danicheffs*, and some touring revivals. Playwright-director David Belasco directed several Union Square productions in 1878 in San Francisco, and Charles Cathcart, Wilson Barrett's stage manager, was especially imported to direct *The Lights o' London* in 1882.

Among players newly engaged for the year 1873–74—Clara Morris, Maud Harrison, Kate Claxton, Rose Eytinge, Marie Wilkins, Charles Thorne, Jr., John Parselle, McKee Rankin, and Stuart Robson—some were already established stars, and others would soon rise to prominence. Most of them would remain at the Union Square for more than a decade. The ensuing five years would see the advent here of Agnes Booth, Fanny Morant, Ida Vernon, Kitty Blanchard, Maud Harrison, Sara Jewett, Bijou Heron, Frederic Robinson, Lysander Thompson, James H. Stoddart, W. J. Lemoyne, Charles Coughlan, and James O'Neill. Richard Mansfield had joined their number by 1882–83. There were no raw recruits, only seasoned, star-caliber professionals—an unmatched, versatile combination of histrionic power.

Palmer asked his players to appear in a wide variety of plays and in roles large and small. Even the most famous accepted small roles, for Palmer convinced his company to set aside personal aggrandizement and to pursue the success of the play. Kitty Blanchard recalled her first Union Square season as the happiest she had known. "There were no jealousies or squabbles, and lots of pleasure," she stated. "It would not have been so if our manager had been less amiable" (unidentified clipping, Harvard Theatre Collection, Cambridge, Massachusetts). Clara Morris, who had bolted Daly's company to join the Union Square, would remember Palmer in her autobiography (1901) as "still my honored friend," and said that "our relations were always kindly" (Morris, 378).

Under the regime of James Collier, Palmer's successor as manager, the Union Square fell quickly from former eminence. "Collier, whose experience had been gained in a broader and coarser field of work, was in no way [Palmer's] equal in either judgment of plays or stage management," leading man J. H. Barnes glumly recalled, "and I had a most disastrous season as regards plays and parts" (Barnes, 149). In the wake of an indifferent 1883–84 season, Shook and Collier staged three successive failures and one dubious success (*Three Wives to One Husband*) during 1884–85; then, during the money-making run of Louis Nathal's *Prisoner for Life* (adapted from Auguste Anicet-Bourgeois's *Stella*), in February 1885, they lowered admission prices for all parts of the house.

Besides the regular troupe, which of original personnel included only Messrs. Stoddart, Parselle, and Quigley; Misses Jewett and Harrison; and Mrs. E. J. Phillips, the new management in 1884–85 maintained five Union Square theatre companies—two playing *The Lights o' London*, two playing *Storm Beaten*, and one playing *Ruth's Devotion*. After *A Prisoner for Life* closed on April 6, 1885, Shook and Palmer surrendered the theatre to J. M. Hill and after a brief spring tour, the depleted Union Square Theatre Stock Company disbanded for all time. While under Hill's management, the Union Square Theatre was destroyed by fire a few minutes after 1 P.M. February 28, 1888.

PERSONNEL

Management: Sheridan Shook, proprietor (1871–78, 1883– ?); A. M. Palmer, manager and coproprietor (1872–78); manager and coproprietor with W. Henry Johnson (*c.*1878–79); manager and sole proprietor (*c.*1879–83); E. H. Gouge, treasurer (1872– ?); Charles Sutton, assistant treasurer (1872– ?); James C. Schofield, advertising agent (1872– ?); Isaac H. Weinberg, chief usher (1872– ?); I. E. Hodes, bill distributor (1872– ?).

Musical Direction: Henry Tissington, orchestra leader (1872– ?).

Dramaturgy: N. Hart Jackson, A. R. Cazauran, George Fawcett Rowe, Dion Boucicault, Steele MacKaye, John Parselle, house dramatists.

Mise-en-scène: Richard Marston, scene painter (1872–83 +); Charles H. Ritter and R. J. Moye, assistant scene painters (1872– ?); Charles Murray, gas man (1872– ?); Augustus H. Benedict, property man (1872– ?); George Kingsland, assistant property man (1872– ?); E. C. Chamberlain, door keeper (1872– ?).

Stage Direction: Dan H. Harkins (1872–73), John Parselle (1873–83 +), George Fawcett Rowe and Dion Boucicault (1873), A. R. Cazauran (intermittent), Steele MacKaye (1875), William Seymour (1875–83 +), David Belasco (1878), Charles Cathcart (1882), James W. Thorpe (1872– ?).

Actors and Actresses: Thomas Atkins (1872–73), Kitty Blanchard (1874– ?), W. H. Bokee (1873– ?), Agnes Booth, J. P. Burnett (1872–73), Claude Burroughs (1872–73), Charlotte Cave (1872–73), Kate Claxton (1873– ?), Charles Coghlan, Welsh Edwards (1872–73), Agnes Ethel (1872–73), Rose Eytinge (1873– ?), Imogene Fowler (1872–73), William Gillette (1875–76), Kate Girard (1876– ?), Phillis Glover (1872–73), Maud Granger (1872–73), Mary Griswold (1872–73), Dan H. Harkins (1872–73 + ?), Maud Harrison (1873–85), Fanny Hayward (1872–73), Bijou Heron, Kate Holland (1872–73), Clara Jennings (1872–73), Sara Jewett (1876–85), Ed Lamb (1872–73), Frank Lamb (1872–73), Josephine Laurens (1872–73), Jennie Lee (1872–73), W. J. Lemoyne, F. F. Mackay (1872– ?), Richard Mansfield (1882–83), Emily Mestayer (1872–73), Henry Montgomery (1872– ?), Plessy Mordaunt (1872–73), Clara Morris (1873– ?), James O'Neill (1876– ?), George Parkes (1872–73), John Parselle (1873–85), Mrs. E. J. Phillips, W. S. Quigley (1872–75), McKee Rankin (1873– ?), Frederic Robinson, Stuart Robson (1873–?), Alessandro Salvini (1881–82), Mark Smith (1872–73), James H. Stoddart (1875–85), W. Stuart (1872–

73), Lysander Thompson, Charles Thorne, Jr. (1873– ?), Hattie Thorpe (1872–
?), James W. Thorpe (1872– ?), Ida Vernon, Eliza Weathersby (1873– ?), Marie
Wilkins (1873– ?), W. H. Wilder (1872– ?).

REPERTORY

Titles in parentheses are the sources of adaptations.

1872–73: *Agnes; London Assurance; The School for Scandal; Money; Orange
Blossoms; A Son of the Soil (Lion Amoreux); Atherley Court; One Hundred Years
Old (Le Centennaire); A Business Woman; Cousin Jack; Micawber; Frou-Frou;
Without a Heart; Fernande; Caste; The Toodles; Everybody's Friend; Secret Mar-
riage; Americans in Paris; Jane Eyre; Fun in a Fog; Old Phil's Birthday; Milky
White; Belles of the Kitchen.*

1873–74: *The Geneva Cross; The Wicked World; Conjugal Tactics; A Regular
Fix; Led Astray (La tentacion); Camille (La dame aux camelias); Peril; With the
Tide; Jane Eyre.*

1874–75: *The Sphynx; The Hunchback; Jane Eyre; Love's Sacrifice; The Two
Orphans (Les deux orphelines); Two Can Play at That Game; Patchwork; The
Gilded Age.*

1875–76: *Led Astray; Rose Michel; Ferreol; Conscience; Queen Mab; A Wolf in
Sheep's Clothing; Belles of the Kitchen; The Post Boy; Fun in a Fog; Nan: The
Good-for-Nothing; Two Men of Sandy Bar.*

1876–77: *The Two Orphans; Miss Multon; The Danicheffs (Les Danicheffs),
Smike (Nicholas Nickleby); Poor Joe (Bleak House); Pink Dominos (Les dominoes
roses); Struck Oil; The Chinese Question.*

1877–78: *Pink Dominos; The Mother's Secret (Seraphine); The Man of Success
(Montjoie); A Celebrated Case (Un cause célèbre); The School for Scandal; The
Chimes of Normandy; The Bohemian Girl; Martha; Fra Diavolo; The Lady of
Lyons; Macbeth* [scene]; *Cymbeline* [scene]; *Frou-Frou* [Acts 3 and 4]; *Home from
the War; Olivia (The Vicar of Wakefield).*

1878–79: *Mother and Son (Le bourgeois de Pont d'Arcy); The Banker's Daughter;
The Lost Children (Les orphelins du Pont Nôtre Dame); The Babes in the Wood;
or, Who Killed Cock Robin?; Horrors; or, The Maharajah of Zogobad; My Partner.*

1879–80: *French Flats (Les locataires de M. Blondeau); The False Friend; The
Two Orphans; My Partner; Boccaccio; The Love of His Life; Two Nights in Rome;
The Sultan of Mocha; Deacon Crankett.*

1880–81: *Daniel Rochat; The Banker's Daughter; Miss Multon; Camille; The
Creole (Diane); The Danicheffs; Felicia; or, Woman's Love (Le fils de Coralie);
Raymonde (Mons. Alphonse); Cousin Joe; The Wrong Man in the Right Place;
Coney Island; or, Little Ethel's Prayer; The Rivals; Forget-Me-Not; Bleak House;
Mary Stuart; The Doctor of Lima.*

1881–82: *Daniel Rochat; Camille; The Lights o' London; The New Magdalen;
Article 47; Far from the Madding Crowd; Solange; Camille; The Lady of Lyons;
The Living Age; The Black Flag; The Rivals; Fourteen Days; Brighton (Saratoga).*

BIBLIOGRAPHY

Published Sources: J. H. Barnes, *Forty Years on the Stage* (London: Chapman
and Hall, 1914); *Boston Sunday Herald; Chicago Tribune*; Rose Eytinge, *Memories
of Fifty Years* (New York: Frederick A. Stokes, 1905); Marvin Felheim, *The Theater*

of Augustin Daly (Cambridge, Mass.: Harvard University Press, 1956); *Freund's Music and Drama*, vols. 1–17 (November 10, 1883 – January 23, 1892); Arthur Hornblow, "Albert M. Palmer—A Personal Tribute," *Theatre Magazine* 5 (April 1905): 101–2; A. E. Lancaster, "A. M. Palmer and the Union Square Theatre," *Theatre Magazine* 3 (March 1903): 62–65; Percy MacKaye, *Epoch*, vol. 1 (New York: Boni & Liveright, 1927); Clara Morris, *My Life on the Stage* (New York: McClure, Phillips, and Co., 1901); *Music and Drama*, vols. 2–5 (April 29, 1882 – January 6, 1883); *New York Herald; New York Sun; New York Times; New York Tribune*; George C. D. Odell, *Annals of the New York Stage*, vols. 9–11 (New York: Columbia University Press, 1937–39); idem, "Some Theatrical Stock Companies of New York," *Theatre Annual*, 1951, pp. 7–26; A. M. Palmer, "Charles R. Thorne, Jr.," in *Famous American Actors of Today*, vol. 1, ed. Frederic Edward McKay and Charles E. L. Wingate (New York: Thomas Y. Crowell and Co., 1896); idem, "Why Theatrical Managers Reject Plays," *Forum*, July 1893, pp. 614–20; Pat M. Ryan, "Albert Marshman Palmer," *Enciclopedia dello Spettacolo* 6 (Rome, 1961); idem, "Our Half-Forgotten Founders," *The Players Bulletin*, Winter 1959, pp. 18–19; James H. Stoddart, *Recollections of a Player* (New York: The Century Company, 1902); *The Theatre; Theatre Magazine*; John Rankin Towse, *Sixty Years of the Theatre* (New York and London: Funk and Wagnalls, 1916); Union Square Theatre, *Souvenir of the One-Hundredth Performance of Rose Michel* [New York, 1876]; Phillip Walker, "Mark Twain, Playwright," *Educational Theatre Journal* 8 (1956): 185–93.

Unpublished Source: Pat M. Ryan, "A. M. Palmer, Producer: A Study of Management, Dramaturgy, and Stagecraft in the American Theatre, 1872–96" (Ph.D. diss., Yale University, 1959).

Archival Sources: Harvard Theatre Collection, Cambridge, Massachusetts, (A. M. Palmer, MS., "History of the Union Square Theatre"; clippings; scrapbooks); Library for the Performing Arts, Lincoln Center, New York (scrapbooks, playbills, clippings, photographs, and so on); Walter Hampden-Edwin Booth Theatre Collection and Library, The Players, New York (A. M. Palmer's inlaid, voluminous Record of the Union Square Theatre, including autobiographies, playbills, clippings, and so on); William Seymour Theatre Collection, Princeton University Library, Princeton, N.J. (Union Square Daybook [fragment] and Notebook).

Pat M. Ryan

V

VARIETIES THEATRE STOCK COMPANY. In January 1849 Thomas Placide (1808–77) suggested to members of the New Orleans Histrionic Association the idea of erecting a theatre for the production of burlesque, vaudeville, and farce. His suggestion split the association's membership and resulted in the formation of the Variété Association, which acted on Placide's suggestion. The new group built a proscenium theatre in the fall of 1849 on Gravier Street between Carondelet and Baronne streets and leased it to Placide. Placide organized the Varieties Theatre Stock Company and presented it on December 8, 1849, in a program consisting of five numbers: "Stars in Variety" (variety acts with songs and dances written by Charles Bass for the occasion), a fancy dance by M. Mongin and Mlle. Barron, *A Day after the Fair* (a burletta), *A Festival of Terpsichore* (a dance number), and *Jenny Lind* (a musical extravaganza).

To build a theatre specializing in variety fare and novelty acts was smart business in 1849. Noah Ludlow and Sol Smith controlled the theatrical life of the city between 1843 and 1853, when they managed (or controlled) the New St. Charles and New American theatres. While the managing duo dotted their season with variety presentations (equestrian shows, circus and novelty acts, pantomimes, ballet), they emphasized classical and contemporary dramas and comedies performed by a high-quality stock company with visiting star actors. Placide, responding to the New Orleans audience's love for circus and variety entertainment (a national phenomenon), decided to operate his theatre along the lines of Mitchell's popular Olympic Theatre in New York and to offer opera, comedy, vaudeville, farce, and ballet, thereby evading direct competition with Ludlow and Smith. During the 1850s Dan Rice's Amphitheatre (later David Bidwell's Academy of Music) offered variety and circus entertainment, creating some competition for Placide. In his last three seasons, Placide adjusted his fare to include stars in repertory, as well as opera, but he continued to emphasize comedy, music, and dance. On November 21, 1854, Placide's Varieties Theatre burned, and Thomas Placide left New Orleans to pursue theatrical ventures in the North. George Holland became the company's acting manager for several months and engaged the American Theatre, which he called the Olympic. Then John Calder assumed the position of acting manager, moved the company to the Pelican Theatre (Dan Rice's Amphitheatre), and completed the 1854–55 season. In 1855 the Variété Association built a second Varieties Theatre on the site of the First Varieties, christened it the "Gaiety," and leased it to Dion Boucicault (1820–90), who organized a stock company starring the actor-manager and his wife and presented a financially disappointing season consisting primarily of Boucicault's own works. William Crisp (1820–74) leased the Gaiety Theatre in 1856, renamed it "Crisp's Gaiety," and presented standard dramas and comedies performed by visiting stars and stock actors. But Crisp suffered Boucicault's financial fate, and he was dismissed by the Variété Association in 1858. The Gaiety under Boucicault and Crisp never attained the place of affection in the hearts of New Orleans theatregoers that it had under Placide. Accordingly, the Variété Association recalled Thomas Placide to manage the theatre (then renamed the Varieties). During the 1858–59 season Placide maintained a stock company but did not offer starring engagements, and he returned the theatre's fare to comedy, ballet, and melodrama. When Placide vacated the Varieties, the Variété Association decided to be its own manager and hired John Owens (1823–86) as acting manager for two seasons (1859–61). Owens responded with an excellent stock company playing a varied repertory. With the advent of the Civil War in 1861, Owens left New Orleans, and the heyday of the Varieties came to an end.

From 1849 to 1861 the four Varieties (Gaiety) Theatre managers, each with a diverse theatre background and a unique talent, took distinct approaches to theatrical management. Thomas Placide, son of Charleston theatre manager Alexander Placide, was a comic actor who had appeared as a principal in the American Theatre Company* and St. Charles Theatre Stock Company* in New Orleans during the 1840s. Critics ranked him among the best comic actors in America and England, and they rated his Sir Harcourt Courtley in Boucicault's *London Assurance* to be the best on the American and English stage. Placide sought to bring lighter fare to a populace hungry for variety entertainment. Dion Boucicault, the internationally famous actor and writer of melodramas, chose to emphasize his own works and his own acting. William H. Crisp, an intelligent comic actor of English origin, chose to maintain the star system he had established in Georgia as manager of the Savannah theatres and on the Georgia circuit (Augusta, Macon, Columbus, and Rome, Georgia; and Montgomery, Alabama). John Owens, considered one of the most earnest and conscientious character actors in America during his long career, relied on a quality stock company playing standard comedies and dramas and contemporary melodramas. After his years of management in New Orleans, Owens toured for two decades as a starring actor-manager, often playing engagements in New York City.

Placide's Varieties Theatre was built at a cost of $29,000 with the investment of forty-two subscribers. Although Placide's first season was a financial success, it was not a success great enough to return the interest and profits he had promised the investors. Accordingly, the investors dropped their expectations of dividends after 1850 and were satisfied that the theatre provide high-class amusement for the benefit of the public. Placide's company performed each night at 7:00 with a Tuesday or Wednesday matinee. The other managers preferred a 7:30 curtain. Admission under Placide ranged from twenty-five cents for gallery seats to seventy-five cents for parquet seats and semiprivate boxes to $5 for private boxes. In 1856 Crisp increased the theatre's seating capacity to 1,700, and he raised ticket prices to $1 for dress circle and parquet and $5 to $8 for private boxes. Occasionally, prices were raised slightly for special starring engagements (for example, Lola Montez, the Corradi Opera Troupe). The bill changed nightly, with the exception of occasional short runs and starring engagements, and the seasons (which usually ran from November to late May or June) concluded with several benefits for actors and theatre staff and for various charities (the Fireman's Charitable Association, for example). Occasionally, the theatre opened during the summer for short seasons under other managers. As noted, Placide's first four seasons at the Varieties were financially rewarding, but Boucicault's only season and Crisp's second season were financial disappointments. Apparently, Crisp, after his easy first-year success, did not exert himself in the 1857–58 season to provide a good stock company or a good list of stars; accordingly, the public refused to patronize the house. Thomas Placide's return to management and John Owens' tenure (1858–61) were, artistically, the most brilliant years in the history of the Varieties. During this period, the managers produced a series of plays in which the most eminent Americans then living performed. Although moderately successful financially, these years failed to bring the high returns afforded Placide's Varieties in the early 1850s.

Critical reaction to the Varieties' (or Gaiety's) productions revealed the New Orleans audience's love of variety entertainment, visiting stars, and scenic splendors. Critics consistently praised visiting stars and Owens' careful attention to scenic effect. In general, reviewers appreciated all four managers' attempts to maintain the beauty of the theatre's interior, to enlarge the auditorium and the backstage, and to provide excellent scenery and effects. But discerning critics were always quick to complain when a manager failed to provide an adequate supporting company for visiting stars. The reviewer who praised Edwin Booth's Richelieu also complained that Crisp supported the star with a "poor" company, lacking in pronunciation skills and insufficiently rehearsed; indeed, such complaints occurred often during Crisp's tenure. Naturally, the reviewers were pleased when Placide returned to management, and they were most positive in their response to Owens' seasons.

Of the twelve seasons presented at the Varieties (or Gaiety) between 1849 and 1861, the first five managed by Placide offered the most diverse variety fare. Placide emphasized light comic pieces with singing and dancing (the premiere program is an excellent example), but he also offered standard English comedies (Shakespeare's *Merry Wives of Windsor, Comedy of Errors*, and *As You Like It; The Rivals; London Assurance*) in which he took leading comic roles. Farces were numerous (almost always following a full-length work), as were ballets (performed by visiting troupes such as the Montplaisir Ballet Troupe, as well as by company dancers), musicals (*Beauty and the Beast; Esmeralda; Home, Sweet Home*), operas (*Barber of Seville*), panoramas, melodramas (mostly by Boucicault), and stars appearing in repertories that included Shakespearean tragedy and comedy, standard English comedies, and popular contemporary plays. As noted, Boucicault's season (1855–56) presented a long series of familiar Boucicault plays (*London Assurance, Violet; or, The Life of an Actress*) as well as standard comedies and farces. Crisp presented stars in traditional repertories that included works such as *Camille, The Lady of Lyons, The School for Scandal, Charlotte Corday, Hamlet, Richard III, Macbeth*, and *King Lear*. Crisp also presented spectacular melodramas (*Pizarro*), musicals, and operas (*Rob Roy, Der Freischutz*). Indeed, during his second season (1857–58) not only did he engage opera troupes but he enlarged his own company by five singers so that it might perform operas. During Placide's one-season return (1858–59), the manager presented the acting company in standard comedies, farces, and musical dramas, and he engaged a few starring attractions. John Owens continued Placide's tradition of variety fare by offering contemporary dramas and comedies (*Camille, Louis XI, Our American Cousin*), standard comedies (*The School for Scandal, The Rivals*), Shakespearean comedies, and works by Boucicault. Boucicault's *Dot*, an adaptation of Charles Dickens' *Cricket on the Hearth*, was the most successful show of the 1859–60 season with a five-week run. Its presentation afforded Owens the opportunity to play Caleb Plummer, a role subsequently identified with his reputation. Owens also featured an orchestra, one of the finest in the nation, that played operatic overtures and popular songs.

Each manager employed a treasurer, a musical director, a full thirty-piece orchestra, a scenic artist, a costumer, a stage manager, a prompter, and twenty to thirty actors and actresses engaged in standard lines of business. Each manager also employed singers and dancers (particularly Placide and Crisp), supernumeraries (for spectacles), star performers, and special attractions. Major stars engaged by Thomas Placide include the Ravel Family of pantomime artists, Placide's brother Henry, who appeared with the manager in *Comedy of Errors* and *The Rivals*; Kate and Ellen Bateman, child stars who performed Shakespearean works such as *Richard III* and *Hamlet*; Lola Montez, who performed exotic dances and acted in works such as *The School for Scandal* and *Charlotte Corday*; Catherine Sinclair, who appeared in *The Provok'd Husband* and *Henry VIII*; the Boucicaults; and then-amateur Frederick Thayer (later Dion Boucicault's secretary and leading man in New York opposite Matilda Heron in *Camille*). Among the dancers employed by Placide were M. Plaisir, first dancer of major European theatres; Henrietta Vallee, Mlle. Barron, S. Vegas, and M. Mongin. William Crisp emphasized starring attractions, presenting Eliza Logan; Matilda Heron in *Camille*; Jean M. Davenport in *Camille* and *Charlotte Corday*; the celebrated English tragedian James Anderson in *Ingomar, Hamlet, Richard III, King Lear*, and *The Merchant of Venice*; Edwin Booth in his wide range of roles; Mr. and Mrs. John Drew; and H. L. Bateman.

With Placide in his regular company were Charles Bass (also stage manager), W. H. Chippendale, Jr. (a popular player in America who later managed the Haymarket in London), Barton Hill (later manager of the California Theatre Stock Company* in San Francisco and the man who gave Helen Modjeska her start on the American stage), popular low comedian George Holland (formerly actor and secretary-treasurer at Caldwell's St. Charles Theatre), and Thomas' sister Eliza Placide Mann. Mr. and Mr. Boucicault were the only names of note in that manager's company during the 1855–56 season. But William Crisp's troupe included the manager and his wife, Ben DeBar, comic actor John Owens, and Mrs. Eliza Place, who had performed in Caldwell's companies at the St. Charles. Placide's 1858–59 company featured A. H. Davenport, a popular American actor who made his New Orleans debut this season; low comedian George Holland; John Owens; and Mr. and Mrs. Charles Plunkett, English actors who made their American debut at the Varieties this season. The companies of John Owens were probably the most talented. As leading man for the 1959–60 season Owens engaged E. A. Sothern, who had recently made a hit in New York as Lord Dundreary in Tom Taylor's *Our American Cousin* starring Laura Keene. The 1859–60 season was organized to feature Sothern, who performed in *Louis XI, Camille,* and *The Rivals*, among other hits. Other notable company members were H. J. Wallack, cousin of Lester who later achieved fame as Fagin in a production of *Oliver Twist* in New York, and Charlotte Thompson, who later made her fame in New York as Jane Eyre.

Owens' final season (1860–61) was disturbed by prospects of war between the states; the arrival of war in 1861 caused the Varieties and all other New Orleans theatres to close during the 1861–62 season. Various managers attempted to reestablish the stock tradition at the Varieties during the next decade with only moderate success. Lewis Baker managed a company that featured Lawrence Barrett in 1863–64; A. W. Fenno managed a mediocre company in 1864–65; W. P. Floyd increased the frequency and number of starring visitors, raised ticket prices, and emphasized long-run hits between 1865 and 1870. After the Second Varieties Theatre burned in 1870, a Third Varieties was built, but by that time the stock tradition was fast disappearing. Indeed, various managers of the Third Varieties (for example, Thomas Hall) presented nothing but road shows. In 1881 the name of the theatre was changed to the Grand Opera House and, except for a brief attempt to resurrect the stock system there by David Bidwell in the mid–1880s, the theatre became a home for traveling combinations.

PERSONNEL

Management: Thomas Placide, manager (1849–54, 1858–59), Dion Boucicault, manager (1855–56), William H. Crisp, manager (1856–58), John Owens, manager (1859–61), W. H. Chippendale, acting manager (1850–51), John H. Calder, treasurer (1849–54), H. Corri, treasurer (1856), T. B. Clarke, treasurer (1856–57), Philip Warren, treasurer (1858–59), W. B. Chippendale, treasurer (1859–61).

Scenic Technicians: Sig. Alexander Boulet (1855–57); C. L. Smith (1858–59); John R. Smith (1859–60); Oscar Almy, Joseph Almy (1860–61).

Musical Directors: Sig. L. Gabici (1849–51), Robert Stoepel (1855–57), Mr. Meyer (1856–57), Mons. Gillet (1857–58), Mr. Meyer (1858–59, Sig. Carlo Patti (1859–61), Eugene Fenellen (1860–61).

Stage Managers: Charles Bass (1849–54), H. J. Conway (1855–56), Grattan Dawson (1856–57), R. F. McClannin (1857–58), John Sefton (1858–59), H. G. Wallack (1859–60), Charles Bass (1860–61).

Actors and Actresses under Placide (1849–55, 1858–59): *J. H. Allen* (1853–54), *Charles Bass* (1849–54), W. Birch, Emma Blake, Fanny Blake, Ada Brown, *Mrs. Browne* (1853–54), *James S. Browne* (1853–55), Mrs. J. Campbell, Mrs. Chippendale, *W. H. Chippendale, Jr.* (1849–51), F. Church, Miss A. E. Cook, H. B. Copland, Pauline Cushman, *A. H. Davenport* (1858–59), S. D. DuBois, T. S. Emmett, J. B. Gourlay, *Annie Graham* (1858–59), C. C. Hamilton, Mr. and Mrs. G. W. Heath, *Mr. and Mrs. Barton Hill* (1854–55), *George Holland* (1849–54), *Mr. and Mrs. Charles Howard* (1849–54), *Mrs. W. R. Johnson* (1850–51), *George Jordan* (1858–59), T. D. Kemble, Virginia Kemble, T. B. Logan, *Henry Lynne* (1853–54), *Eliza Placide Mann* (1855), *John E. Owens* (1858–59), *Thomas Placide* (1849–55, 1858–59), *Mr. and Mrs. Charles Plunkett* (1858–59), *Mr. and Mrs. Reeves* (1850–53), Miss S. V. Ross, *G. T. Rowe* (1850–54, 1858–59), *Mrs. G. T. Rowe* (1850–54), *John Sefton* (1858–59), *Mark Smith* (1858–59), G. C. Spear, H. W. Stuart, *Mary Stuart* (1853–54), *Kate Warrick* (1853–54), A. Watson, *G. W. White* (1853–54), W. Wright.

Actors and Actresses under Boucicault (1855–56): Emma Blake, Fanny Blake, *Mr. and Mrs. Dion Boucicault, W. F. Johnson, John Owens, Mrs. Eliza Place, G. W. Stoddart*, Helen Yates.

Actors and Actresses under Crisp (1856–58): W. Allen, Humphrey Bland, *J. S.*

Browne (1856–57), Charles Carroll, Howard Carlton, *G. C. Charles* (1857–58), *W. B. Chippendale* (1856), *Conrad Clarke* (1857–58), Jessie Clarke, H. Corri, *Mr. and Mrs. William Crisp* (1857–58), *Emma Courtney* (1857–58), *W. Davidge* (1856–57), *John Davis* (1856–57), *Grattan Dawson* (1856–58), *Benedict DeBar* (1856), Julia Dickens, Kate Duckworth, Marie Duckworth, *Rosalie Durand* (1856–57), John English, W. R. Floyd, Mr. Frazer, J. C. Fredericks, *Ellen Gray* (1857–58), Charles Hale, J. Hickmott, Henry Howard, Jane Laws, Charles Loveday, Harry Macarthy, *R. F. McClannin* (1857–58), D. J. Miller, A. T. Morton, Caroline Myers, *John E. Owens* (1856), H. Carlton Peters, *Eliza Place* (1856), Louise Reeder, Charles Sandford, Sallie Steel, *Fred N. Thayer* (1856–57), L. J. Vincent, *J. J. Wallace* (1856–57), W. H. Whalley, Emma Wilton.

Actors and Actresses under Owens (1859–61): Addie Anderson, *Charles Bass* (1860–61), George Becks, Sallie Benner, J. Biddles, *Mr. and Mrs. H. Bland* (1859–60), W. H. Briggs, *Fanny Brown* (1860–61), *Mr. and Mrs. W. A. Chapman* (1859–61), *H. B. Copland* (1859–60), *C. W. Couldock* (1859–60), *Eliza Couldock* (1859–60), *A. H. Davenport* (1860–61), *Anna Graham* (1860–61), Harry Hawk, Lottie Heiness, *George Jordan* (1860–61), R. Lanse, *Joey LeClerc* (1859–60), *Miron W. Leffingwell* (1859–61), *Mrs. W. H. Leighton* (1860–61), *George Lingard* (1859–60), *Polly Marshall* (1859–60), T. B. McDonough, *T. E. Morris* (1859–60), *Charles Morton* (1860–61), *John E. Owens* (1859–60), Mary Preston, Frank Rea, Mr. and Mrs. James Seymour, *Mark Smith* (1860–61), *E. A. Sothern* (1859–60), *Sara Stevens* (1859–60), *Charlotte Thompson* (1859–61), C. R. Thorne, Jr., *George W. Wallack* (1859–61), *J. H. Wallack* (1859–60), Ella Wesner, James Taylor.

REPERTORY

Representative seasons under Placide, Crisp, and Owens follow. The play titles are listed in the order presented; although popular plays were presented more than once during a season, their titles are only listed once. Starring engagements are indicated, and important long-runs are followed by the length of the run in parentheses. The lists do not include titles of all dances and songs that were performed almost nightly.

1852–53: *Old Heads and Young Hearts; The Good-for-Nothing; Who Speaks First; Hearts Are Trumps; The Rivals; Done on Both Sides; Paul Pry; Perfection; Sweethearts and Wives; Old Honesty; Black Eyed Susan; Double Bedded Room; Speed the Plough; The Day after the Fair; Lola Montez; King Henry IV; Time Tries All; The Welsh Girl; The New Footman; The Two B'hoys; The Factory Girl; Alarming Sacrifice; St. Mary's Eve; Christmas Party; The Mad Wag of Baghdad; Kate Karroway; Cavaliers and Roundheads; The Merry Wives of Windsor; The Belle's Stratagem; Cockneys in California; The Serious Family; Scenes in the Life of an Unprotected Female; The Toodles; The Fair One with the Golden Locks.* January 3, Lola Montez engagement begins: *Lola Montez in Bavaria* (one week) with various farces; *Charlotte Corday* (one week) with various farces and Montez's "Spider Dance," "Sailor's Dance," and "El Ole" dance; *Used Up; The Irish Widow; A Lady and Gentleman in a Peculiarly Perplexing Predicament; The New Footman; Clarissa Harlow; Martiana; The School for Scandal; Done on Both Sides; The Two Bonnycastles.* January 31, Placide's company returns: *The Rough Diamond; The Village Phantom; The Isle of Tranquil Delight; The Post of Honor; The Bride of*

Lammermoor; Pet of the Petticoats; Love and Reason; Mardi Gras; or, La bal costume; Slasher and Crasher; Twelfth Night; The Irish Tutor. February 14, Bateman Children engagement begins: *The Young Couple; Spoil'd Child*; the trial scene from *Merchant of Venice*; the dance "The Minuet de la Cour"; Act V of *Richard III; Her Royal Highness; The Swiss Family; Bombastes Furioso; Four Mowbrays*; excerpts from *Macbeth* and *Paul Pry; Sweethearts and Wives*; trial scene from *Merchant of Venice; My Grandmother's Pet; Why Don't She Marry* (during the Bateman Children engagement, the regular company played pieces such as *Grimshaw, Bagshaw, and Bradshaw; Charles II; Michael Erle; My Precious Betsey; One Hour; Christmas Party; The Secret; The Devil in Paris; The Jenkenses; Where There's a Will, There's a Way; Nature and Art; The Loan of a Lover; Love in Humble Life; Capital Match; La Bayadère; Rob Roy; Dead Shot*; and *North and South*. March 13, Mrs. Catherine Sinclair engagement begins: *The School for Scandal; The Lady of Lyons; Love's Sacrifice; Much Ado about Nothing; A Roland for an Oliver; Provok'd Husband; Follies of a Night*. April 6, Regular company returns: *Ingomar; London Assurance; The Stranger; Katherine and Petruchio; Matrimony; North and South; Laugh When You Can; Sketches in India; The Willow Copse; Wives as They Were and Maids as They Are; Beauty and the Beast; Money; Hamlet; Charles XII; Jack Sheppard; Time Tries All; Phenomenon; The Lunatic and the Lover; The Alpine Maid; Gudeman of Ballangiech; Writing on the Wall*. April 28, Professor Jocko—magician and necromancer—engagement begins: "Feats of Natural Magic"; "Dissolving Views" (with farces such as *Generous Soldier* and *An Alarming Sacrifice*). April 30, Regular company returns: *King Lear; The School of Reform; The Wonder, a Woman Keeps a Secret; Jenny Lind; The Two Queens; Guy Mannering; Dead Shot*.

1856–57: *The Bohemian Girl; Antony and Cleopatra* (farce); *Spring and Autumn; Pocahontas* (burlesque); *Simpson and Co.; The Merchant of Venice; Grandfather Whitehead; Fra Diavolo; Poor Pillicoddy; Rob Roy; Old Heads and Young Hearts; Dominique, the Deserter; Midas* (burletta); *Katherine and Petruchio; Lola Montez; or, The pas de fascination; Lady of the Lake; Helping Hands; The Deserter; Der Freischutz; The Wreck Ashore; Black Eyed Susan; The Boarding School; Miller and His Men; Carnival Revolt; The Toodles; A Day after the Wedding*. December 2, Matilda Heron engagement begins: *Camille; Masks and Faces; Medea; Vice and Virtue; The School for Scandal; Clari; The Hunchback; Fazio; or, The Italian Wife's Revenge* (Heron's performances followed with various dances, songs, and farces— *Dominique, the Deserter; My Young Wife and My Old Umbrella; The Two Bonnycastles; The Barrack Room*). Regular company returns: *Mary Stuart, Queen of Scots; The Village Story; or, Rough Hands with Gentle Hearts; The Vampire; The Elder Brother; Rake's Progress; London Assurance; Evadne; or, The Statue*. December 29, Mrs. Walter Cherri engagement begins: *A Day in Paris; The Weathercock; A Roland for an Oliver; The Belle's Stratagem; Youth, Love, and Folly; Perfection* (Cherri's performances followed with songs, dances, and farces—*Bobtails and Wagtails; Monsieur Tonson*). January 15, Eliza Logan engagement begins: *Evadne; The Hunchback; Adrienne; Lucrezia Borgia; Romeo and Juliet; The Lady of Lyons; The School for Scandal; The Italian Bride; Pizarro; or The Death of Rolla* (Logan's performances followed by farces such as *The Boarding School* and *My Precious Betsey*). January 26, Jane Margaret Davenport engagement begins: *Love; Adrienne; The Hunchback; Masks and Faces; Mona Lisa; or, Da Vinci's*

Masterpiece; Camille; The Stranger; Honey Moon; Charlotte Corday (Davenport's performances followed by dances and farces such as *Petticoat Government; Shocking Events; Bobtail versus Wagtail*). February 8, Logan return engagement begins: *Adelgitha; The Wife; Love's Sacrifice; Ion; Fazio; The Stranger* (Logan's performances followed by dances and plays such as *Don Caesar de Bazan; The Spectre Bridegroom*). February 15, James Anderson engagement begins: *Ingomar; Hamlet; Richard III; Othello; King Lear; The Lady of Lyons; Katherine and Petruchio; Money; Matrimony; The Robbers; Macbeth; Cloud and Sunshine; Virginius; The King of the Commons; The Elder Booth* (Anderson's performances followed by farces such as *Slasher and Crasher; The Swiss Cottage; The Loan of a Lover*). March 14, the Keller Troupe—with the Gaiety Opera Organization—engagement begins: "Living Pictures" (depicting famous sculpture and poetry); *Oberon; The Naiad Queen; Lucifer's Daughters.* Regular company returns: *The Jolly Cobbler; The Bride* and *Lorenz and His Sister* (both performed by the German Opera and Dramatic Company); *Robespierre; or, Two Days of the Reign of Terror; Naval Engagements; The Grumbling Englishman; Lafitte; or, The Battle of New Orleans; Mr. and Mrs. Peter White; Lucille; or, The Story of a Heart; Luke, the Labourer; Robert Macaire; Opposite Neighbors; Boots at the Swan.* April 13, Corradi-Setti Italian Opera Troupe engagement begins: *Ernani; or, The Bandit; Il Trovatore; La traviata; Lucia Di Lammermoor; Lucrezia Borgia; Barber of Seville; Romeo and Juliet; Marie Di Rohan; La sonnambula; La semiramide; Norma; Rigoletto.*

1859–60: Dances, songs, and special orchestra performances are not detailed in the following list. *Old Heads and Young Hearts; The Eton Boy; Catching a Governor; The Country Squire; The Little Treasure; The School for Scandal; Used Up; To Paris and Back for Five Pounds; Still Waters Run Deep; The Yankee Teamster; or, The Peoples' Lawyer; The Serious Family; All That Glitters Is Not Gold; Morning Call; The Victims; The Willow Copse; A Morning Call; Book Third, Chapter First; The Rivals; Twenty Minutes with a Tiger; A Bachelor of Arts; Forty Winks; Payable on Demand; John Dobbs; Camille; Young England; The Jacobite; Louis XI; Box and Cox; The Conjugal Lesson; The Road to Ruin; Sweethearts and Wives; The School for Reform; Retribution; Second Love; The Poor Gentleman; The Irish Tutor; Still Waters Run Deep; Dot; or, The Cricket on the Hearth* (five weeks, with farces such as *The Limerick Boy; Blue Devils; Paddy Miles' Boy; Going to the Races; The Two Bonnycastles; The Omnibus; The Rendezvous; The Two Gregories; The Two Buzzards; Grimshaw, Bagshaw, and Bradshaw; Poor Pillicoddy*; and *Betsy Baker*); *Our American Cousin* (two weeks); *Everybody's Friend; An Unprotected Female; The Advocate's Last Cause; The Flowers of the Forrest; The Marble Heart; My Wife's Dentist; She Stoops to Conquer; Two Can Play at That Game; The Life of an Actress; The Argument of Tears; Time Tries All; One Touch of Nature; The Tragic Revival; Charles XII; Married Life; The Heir-at-Law; Faint Heart ne'er Won Fair Lady; Pauvrette; or, The Avalanche* (one week); *As You Like It; Pretty Piece of Business; Dot* (one-week return with farces such as *The Critic; or, A Tragedy Rehearsed* and *Nine Points of the Law*).

BIBLIOGRAPHY

Dormon, James. *The Theatre in the Ante-Bellum South, 1815–1861.* Chapel Hill: University of North Carolina Press, 1967.

Kendall, John S. *The Golden Age of the New Orleans Theatre.* Baton Rouge: Louisiana State University Press, 1952.

Melebeck, Claude. "A History of the First and Second Variety Theatres in New Orleans, Louisiana from 1849 to 1870." Ph.D. diss., Louisiana State University, 1973.
Roppolo, Joseph Patrick. "A History of the English Language Theatre in New Orleans, 1845–1861." Ph.D. diss., Tulane University, 1950.

C. Alex Pinkston, Jr.

VIRGINIA COMPANY. SEE [THOMAS WADE] WEST COMPANY.

W

WALLACK'S THEATRE COMPANY. The organization known as Wallack's Theatre in New York City consisted of repertory companies at three theatres under the management of a father, James William Wallack (1795–1864), and his son, John Johnston (known as Lester) Wallack (1820–88). The elder Wallack was a noted British actor who managed companies in England and the National Theatre in New York (1837–39). In 1852 Wallack assumed the lease of Brougham's Lyceum at Broadway near Broome Street from a Major Rogers, renamed the theatre, and operated it as Wallack's Lyceum from September 8, 1852, until April 29, 1861. This theatre, built for actor-manager-author John Brougham in 1850, has been described as elegant though small. Little else is thus far known about its physical proportions, but it has been suggested that Wallack used a box set in this theatre in 1852 for a production of *London Assurance* (Swinney, 135–36).

Ample information exists about the second house, Wallack's Theatre on Broadway at Thirteenth Street, opened September 25, 1861, and home to the Wallack Company until July 2, 1881. James Wallack leased the land upon which this theatre was built for ten years, with a ten-year renewal, at an annual rent of $6,000. The theatre itself had a stage seventy-two feet wide by sixty-five feet deep by forty-five feet high from the stage floor to the machine loft, with a proscenium opening thirty-six feet wide by thirty-eight feet high. The seating capacity was evidently about 1,600—600 in the parquet, 455 in the first tier, 512 in the second tier, and 42 box seats. The theatre was lit by gas, and its dressing and green rooms were located under the stage. There is no indication that the theatre was ever remodeled, although it lacked traps or much ability to fly scenery and retained at least the older tormenter grooves (Swinney, 67–68). This theatre was renamed the Star and remained under Lester Wallack's management after the company moved uptown.

The third Wallack's Theatre was built at Broadway and Thirtieth Street. It opened, behind schedule, on January 4, 1882. Like its predecessors, it was cosy rather than opulent, with the smaller amenities—chairs rather than benches, or extra leg room. The stage in this theatre was trapped and had modern foot and side lights. It measured forty feet deep with a proscenium opening thirty-four feet wide by thirty-six feet high. The dressing, music, and green rooms were again under the stage, whose floor according to one account was flat (Swinney, 72–73). Lester Wallack's management ended in 1887, although the stock company that bore his name was not disbanded until 1888, the thirty-sixth year for a Wallack's Theatre. His was evidently the longest continuously operating stock company in New York City history.

Despite its longevity and successfulness, the Wallack Company lacked a national character. Neither Wallack supported the work of American playwrights, relying instead primarily upon imports from England. (L. C. Strang maintained that Lester Wallack never did an American play until forced to and then deliberately mounted the worst one he could find.) Both James and Lester Wallack paid royalties to playwrights and had exclusive U.S. rights to the new plays of Tom Taylor, Tom Robertson, H. J. Byron, and Watts Phillips, with permission to lease them to other U.S. theatres, with royalties paid to the playwrights (Jones, 48). Although celebrated in memory for playing the comic "classics"—Oliver Goldsmith and Richard Sheridan—they were infrequently performed signature pieces at Wallack's. The repertory actually consisted overwhelmingly of about half recent and half new light romantic comedies and romantic melodramas, the kinds of plays in which both Wallacks specialized as handsome and popular leading men. In the 1870s and 1880s, spectacular melodramas were added, which many reviewers loathed and which are assumed by some to have driven away Wallack's fashionable, aristocratic, and previously loyal audience. Although many new plays were done—180 new to New York—only 22 made it to a second season, and half of them were by Wallack, Robertson, and John Brougham (Jones, 82).

Similar in repertory to, although less native than, the Arch Street Theatre in Philadelphia and the Boston Museum, Wallack's shared with them the universal decline in the number of plays produced in the course of the nineteenth century. Initially, Wallack's policy was to change bills nightly except for popular plays, which were given eleven consecutive performances and then a broken run, a policy violated only a handful of times from 1852 to 1872. After 1872, however, the theatre gave way—although later than others—to longer continuous runs. Although there were two major points of decrease—in 1858 after the William Stuart management of Wallack's Lyceum and in 1872 after E. A. Sothern's year as leading man at Wallack's at Thirteenth Street—the decline in the number of plays presented each season was steady: seventy-six plays in 1852, fifty-five in 1862, twenty in 1872, and eleven in 1882. Beginning in 1860, again later than at other theatres, afterpieces began to disappear from the bills, which further reduced the overall size of the repertory (the length of an evening's performance seems to have held constant at three and a half hours, with or without an afterpiece), although special nights of afterpieces were still presented in the 1870s. When Lester Wallack abolished benefits in 1867, one of two innovations with which the otherwise conservative Wallack management is credited, the number of "standards" and of performances of them further declined, while the runs of remaining plays lengthened somewhat due to fewer interruptions. Clearly, Wallack's could withstand some pressures to change longer than most repertory companies—it did not, for example, add a regular Saturday matinee until the 1870–71 season and never did have a regular Wednesday matinee—but even with its prestige, Wallack's could not hold off longer runs of fewer plays forever (Jones, 37–41).

From the days when James Wallack managed the Old National and broke the supremacy of the Park Theatre, Wallack productions were noted for the care given to the mise-en-scene. Indeed, Wallack's is the theatre most frequently cited to support the claim that American theatre architecture and scenography surpassed London's in the 1860s. Wallack's productions combined built and painted elements in the stock scenery used throughout the theatre's repertory life. The longer the run or the more spectacular the scenes or effects required by the play, the more elaborate its set, and the mise-en-scene at Wallack's in the 1870s and 1880s was repeatedly celebrated for its attention to detail. Male actors were required by the management to furnish period tights, wigs, swords, boots, and all of contemporary costumes, while other costume pieces and presumably all of the women's costumes were furnished by the house and appear to have been of first quality, according to reviews. The oft praised beauty of Wallack productions offset modest though steady increases in ticket prices:

	1852	1864	1881
Family circle	$0.25	$0.30	$0.50
Dress circle	0.50	0.75	1.00
Reserved dress circle	none	none	1.50
Orchestra	1.00	1.50	2.00
Boxes	6.00–7.00	10.00	15.00

These prices refer to the regular September–June season and not to the non-repertory summer attractions that played while the Wallack Company was on vacation (Jones, 97–105).

Some confusion has surrounded the terms *stage director, acting director,* and *acting manager,* which appear in Wallack bills, advertisements, and records interchangably with one another and with the term *stage manager*. John Gilbert was the only person listed as acting director, but eight men were listed as stage directors from 1866, when the position first appeared, to 1887: the aforementioned John Gilbert, who also acted in the company and rotated stage director and stage manager titles with J. H. Selwyn and fellow actor J. G. Hanley from 1866 to 1869; James Schonberg, who had stage-director credit from 1869–71; Tom Robertson, Jr., who later acted with the company and is listed as stage director from 1871 to 1872 or 1873; W. R. Floyd, who was with the company for fourteen and one-half years in several capacities and served as stage director from 1873 to 1880; and Arthur Wallack and actor Harry Edwards, who rotated stage-director and stage-manager titles from 1880 to 1887 (Jones, 28–29; Swinney, 99–103). It has been argued that John Gilbert's acting-director title existed to justify a higher salary, but it is just as likely that he earned it by assuming some of Wallack's routine duties. The acting-manager position combined some of the traditional stage manager and prompter duties of the time and appears to speak more to a large management staff than to any real innovation. Similarly, the duties of stage director varied with specific plays for which the position was listed; for example, J. H. Selwyn was engaged "to insure additional completeness of detail," according to a playbill, and Tom Robertson, Jr.'s position allowed him to provide staging details about his father's plays, while in turn learning management from Lester Wallack. Only with the ascendancy of W. R. Floyd, who is generally conceded to have had more responsibility during his term than did the others, does the position of stage director appear to have moved to a higher management level; yet his tenure was followed by a final rotation of stage-director and stage-manager duties between Arthur Wallack and Harry Edwards, which suggests only a difference in duties rather than the centralization of power that the term director signifies today.

The critical reception it received suggests that Wallack's was the leading company in New York City from 1855 to 1875 and equal to the Daly Company from 1875 to 1880. It is generally conceded by critics and historians that at the last theatre from 1881 to 1888, the actors were unable to sustain the earlier traditions and reputation of Wallack repertory companies. Some of the causes cited for this decline include the absence of Lester Wallack's active management (he was frequently away on star tours), an inability to fill traditional lines of acting, and a decline in audience interest in older plays in rotating repertory. Despite its eventual difficulties, it was the brilliance of the ensemble acting at Wallack's that first created and then for decades sustained its fame, and for this success two factors were chiefly responsible.

As with the Arch Street but especially the Boston Museum, a number of Wallack actors and actresses of all ranks stayed with the company for many years: John Gilbert (twenty-six), John Brougham (five), Madelaine Henriques (nine), W. S. Leonard (sixteen), Elizabeth Ponisi (seventeen),

E. A. Sothern (five), George F. Browne (fifteen), A. W. Young (eleven), Mrs. Hoey (eleven), Mary Gannon (thirteen), Effie Germon (eighteen), Mrs. Vernon (fourteen), Fanny Morant (eight), Emma Blaisdell (seventeen), and Rose Coughlan (eight). In the mid-1860s, sixteen actors had played together for at least five years, some as many as twelve years, whereas in 1882 only five actors had been together for five years, and noticeable differences in playing style had appeared (Jones, 55–76). Experience in playing together affected the quality of the Wallack ensemble, which in its prime retained actors to a degree unequaled by any other American stock company.

The second factor contributing to a successful ensemble appears to have been unique to Wallack's in its day and stands as the major innovation in an otherwise conventional management history: Wallack's operated without stars. While the Boston Museum and a few other companies at midcentury tried to keep star visits to a minimum, James and Lester Wallack went on stage themselves when business was low or introduced different plays to bolster attendance but otherwise relied upon the quality of the company itself to attract audiences. In the seasons of 1856–57 and 1857–58, when the company was managed by William Stuart for James Wallack, short engagements were played by Matilda Heron, Agnes Robertson and Dion Boucicault, James Anderson, Agnes Ellsworthy, and Mrs. James Wallack, Jr. An average of three stars a season hardly indicates a major change in management policy, but even this much deviation never appeared again at Wallack's.

Operating without stars saved the Wallacks money, but it also benefited the players, whose lines of acting and possession of parts were thereby confirmed, and certainly, secure and ample work would be an inducement to longevity. The lines and major holders of them at Wallack's were:

Leading Men: Frederick C. P. Robinson, Harry J. Montague, Osmond Tearle, Owen Marlowe, Charles F. Coughlan, Maurice Barrymore, Charles Wyndham, Charles Stevenson, Eben Plympton, E. L. Davenport, J. W. Wallack, Jr., Lester Wallack

Juveniles: John Dyott, William R. Floyd, Mark Smith, Charles Fisher, Gerald Eyre, Harry Pitt, Edward Arnott, Harry Edwards.

Old Men: William Rufus Blake, John Gilbert

Eccentric Comedians: John Brougham, J. H. Stoddart, Charles M. Walcott, Lysander Thompson

Low Comedians: George Holland, Harry Beckett, William Elton

Walking Gentlemen: H. B. Phillips, Felix Vincent, A. H. Davenport, E. A. Sothern, A. W. Young, W. H. Norton, John Sefton, Benjamin Ringgold, W. H. Reynolds, Joseph B. Polk, C. H. Rockwell, Edward Holland

Utility Men: George F. Browne, W. S. Leonard

Leading Women: Laura Keene, Mrs. John Hoey, Clara Jennings, Rose Eytinge, Ada Dyas, Rose Coughlan, Jeffreys Lewis, Stella Boniface, Georgina Hodson

Juveniles: Mary Gannon, Madelaine Henriques, Sara Stevens, Mrs. Charles Walcot, Ione Burke, Mrs. John Sefton

Old Women: Mrs. William R. Blake, Mrs. John Brougham, Mrs. George Vernon, Mme. Elizabeth Ponisi, Fanny Morant
Soubrettes: Kate Saxon, Mrs. Conover, Effie Germon
Utility Women: C. Carman, Emma Blaisdell (Jones, 55–57)

It has been argued that because the Wallacks favored employing English actors over American ones—a charge that seems valid in James Wallack's case but less so during Lester Wallack's management—it was very hard to advance in line at Wallack's. Actually, internal promotions were rare in any of the major companies of the day, except in an emergency, and Wallack's cannot fairly be singled out in this regard despite its document-able Anglophilia. The usual mode of advancement was to join another company, sometimes of lower status, at a higher rank.

As one would expect in a repertory company of Wallack's caliber, re-hearsals and performances were well regulated. The Wallacks were noted for their attention to detail and expected actors to rehearse as they intended to play. Rehearsals were usually held from 10 A.M. to 2 P.M. six or seven days a week. In the 1860s, new plays were rehearsed six to nine times, but in the 1870s ten to fourteen days would be allowed. Revivals in the 1860s were rehearsed two to four times, and in the 1870s five to eight rehearsals would be allowed for an old piece. Fewer plays and longer runs made a longer rehearsal period possible. Spectacular plays required as many as thirteen to twenty-one rehearsals, and according to existing Wallack rec-ords, properties, music, and sets were required to be present for rehearsals. Plays were cut after opening nights, which made additional rehearsals of them necessary, as did illnesses, scenes with supers that needed work (these rehearsals were usually held after performances), and playing or line mem-orizations that were not satisfactory (Jones, 42–47; Swinney, 106–13). Ac-cording to existing promptbooks, blocking in an arc was used for big scenes and triangular positions for tableaus at Wallack's, as elsewhere. Grouping tended to keep center stage clear, but existing sources are not otherwise explicit about stage movement.

The content of rehearsals and the amount of actor training provided by Wallack's has occasioned some controversy, but the evidence indicates that acting was consistently taught there, with some decline in later years. Actors who worked for Wallack's and have attested to its teaching include E. A. Sothern, Edward Holland, J. H. Stoddart, John Gilbert, Madelaine Henriques, Rose Coughlan, and Rose Eytinge (Jones, 76–78; Swinney, 54–60), and many critics also recognized Wallack's as a school for acting. The negative evaluations of Wallack's actor training by T. A. Brown, George C. D. Odell, and their disciples, who have either maintained that no one grew artistically at Wallack's or, curiously, that only experienced actors and never beginners were trained there, appear demonstrably unsubstan-tiated in light of existing testimony.

Actors at Wallack's learned their art by working together, and the benefits of long association and a varied repertory appear to have offset what might have been gained in the way of experience by working with stars. The major repertory companies of the period have an above-average permanence in common, not just among actors but among management staff as well, from whence training was also derived. The exact content of rehearsals is not preserved by promptbooks or the manager's timebook, but actors attest that rehearsals involved characterization as well as line retention, motivated movement as well as blocking, and attention to the dramatic as well as the scenic milieu. The preponderance of comedy and the lighter melodrama in the repertory created its own problems at Wallack's—ad libs, gags, restoring cut business, addressing the audience—against which the theatre regulations inveighed and for which, along with missed rehearsals and entrances, drunkenness, failure to be off book by the last rehearsal, copying plays, inviting visitors behind the scenes, and refusing parts, fines were imposed or dismissal could result. Onstage liberties appear to have occurred rarely at Wallack's, and considerable evidence attests to the discipline that prevailed throughout the company's history.

Wallack's salaries were higher than at comparable repertory companies during the period, and the generosity of father and son seems universally accepted. Two salary lists exist that attest to the financial benefits of working at Wallack's. Salaries are per week, benefits per season (Odell, 7:19). The first list covers 1857: Lester Wallack, actor and stage manager, $100 plus two benefits (one clear one-half and one one-third of the net); W. R. Blake, actor, $80 plus two benefits (one-third and one-third); Mrs. Hoey, actress, $55 plus two clear benefits (one-third and one-third); George Holland, actor, $40 plus two benefits (one-third and one-third); Mary Gannon, actress, $35 plus one clear benefit (one-third); H. B. Phillips, actor and prompter, $25 plus one benefit (one-third); Theodore Moss, treasurer, $20 plus one benefit (unspecified); actors and actresses D. Whiting, W. H. Norton, Mrs. Vernon, and conductor Robert Stoepel, $30; actors and actresses Joseph Grosvenor, A. H. Davenport, Mrs. J. H. Allen, and scene painter Harry Isherwood, $25; actors Mr. Levere, Mr. Russell, and property master Mr. Timoney, $18; carpenter Mr. Sanders and wardrobe assistant Mr. Flanigan, $15; wardrobe assistant Mr. Benschoten and scene painter Mr. Wallace, $12; actors and actresses Mr. Rea, Mrs. Reeves, Miss Carman, Mrs. Phillips, $10; actors Mr. Colby, Mr. Oliver, and Mr. Parsloe, $8; actors and actresses Mr. Jeffries and Miss Tree, $7; actresses Miss Pine and Miss Orton, $6.

The second salary list from 1862 indicates considerable raises for Lester Wallack ($125), Mr. Hoey ($100), and Theodore Moss ($50); modest increases for Mary Gannon ($40), Mr. Timoney ($23), and Harry Isherwood ($30); and decreases for W. R. Blake ($60) and George Holland ($25), which are difficult to explain, since a trade of salary even for increased benefits seems unlikely in a period of wartime inflation. The 1862 list also shows a larger number of actors in the $25 salary range (Jones, 28–37). When Lester Wallack abolished benefits after the 1866–67 season, he added to each salary the amount the actors told him each had made from benefits. Wallack said he undertook this innovation because benefits were "degrading . . . begging, appeals from actors and actresses who already received what they conceived an adequate return for their services, and who had no reason to call upon the public for something extra" (Wallack, 54–55), but Lester Wallack's expenses would certainly have been stabilized and, over time, reduced by discontinuing this "obnoxious system."

For thirty-six seasons the Wallack Theatre Company enjoyed critical and financial success. For most of those years Wallack's was the premier company in New York City and, some have said, in the United States, its hallmark a strong acting ensemble and a beautiful mise-en-scene. Wallack's was the only later nineteenth-century stock company to preserve rotating repertory throughout most of its history without the use of stars, and it is generally conceded to have exemplified the best of the old stock system, despite anachronisms such as Lester Wallack playing Young Marlowe in *She Stoops to Conquer* when he was in his fifties. First among many, Wallack's stands second only to the Boston Museum as the longest-lived theatre company in the last half of the nineteenth century, a period it did much to enhance artistically.

PERSONNEL

Management: James William Wallack, manager 1852–c.64; Lester Wallack, manager c.1864– c.87; company leased to William Stuart, 1856–58; Theodore Moss, treasurer 1856–88; James S. Wright, H. B. Phillips, prompters and stage managers 1852–mid-1860s; J. H. Selwyn, John Gilbert, J. G. Hanley, stage managers, 1866–69; W. R. Floyd, stage manager; Arthur Wallack, Harry Edwards, stage managers, 1880–87. See the text for a discussion of the positions "acting director," "stage director," and "acting manager" and the persons who held them.

Mise-en-scene: scenic artists-scene painters, Harry Isherwood (twenty-eight years), Philip Goatcher, Mr. Wallace; costumes and wardrobe, Mr. Flanagan, Mr. Benschoten; properties, Mr. Timoney; carpenter, Mr. Sanders.

Conductors: Robert Stoepel (1856–63), Mr. Mollenhauer, Thomas Baker.

Actors and Actresses: A partial list of actors at Wallack's according to their lines is presented in the text. For a season by season list of acting personnel, see Appendix D of Jones' dissertation (pp. 155–60).

REPERTORY

Like its personnel, the Wallack Company's repertory has been well documented. See Jones, pp. 84–85, for a list of the "standard" comedies in Wallack's repertory; see his Appendix E for a year-by-year list of the number of plays, afterpieces, and novelties done (and number by native authors); and see his Appendix F for a list of the plays produced at Wallack's in order of total seasons, with a list of total performances (the date of first appearance is also provided). Consult Appendix B of Swinney's dissertation for a list of twelve "typical" seasons at Wallack's—1852–53, 1853–54, 1858–59, 1861–62, 1862–63, 1866–67, 1871–72, 1876, 1877, 1880–81, 1881–82, 1882–83, 1885–86—which illustrates the contents of the repertory, its decline in size, and the increase in lengths of runs over the company's history.

BIBLIOGRAPHY

The Wallack Theatre Company has been well documented by two dissertations making extensive use of primary information, such as eighty-two promptbooks (Harvard Theatre Collection, Cambridge, Massachusetts; New York Public Library), programs and scrapbooks (New York Public Library; Matthews Museum of Columbia University, New York City), the Wallacks letters, catalogues of their possessions, and notices from them to the company (Harvard Theatre Collection; New-York Historical Society, New York City; Hampden Library at the Players Club, New York City; New York Public Library). The stage manager's timebooks from 1863 to 1886 are at the Matthews Museum of Columbia University, New York City; Wallack's personal account books are at the Billy Rose Theatre Collection, New York Public Library. The two pertinent Ph.D. dissertations are Cecil D. Jones, Jr., "The Policies and Practices of Wallack's Theatre, 1852–1888" (Illinois University, 1959); and Donald H. Swinney, "Production in the Wallack Theatres, 1852–1888" (Indiana University, 1961). Lester Wallack's account of his and his father's careers as actors and managers was recorded by Laurence Hutton, whose introduction to Lester Wallack, *Memories of Fifty Years* (New York: Scribner, 1889) helps fill in some gaps in this scattered although interesting memoir, interrupted by Wallack's death. Numerous other sources, including autobiographies of actors who worked at Wallack's, can be found in the bibliographies of the Jones and Swinney dissertations.

                                                                Rosemarie K. Bank

WALNUT STREET THEATRE COMPANY. See [FIRST] WALNUT STREET THEATRE COMPANY (1820–22); [SECOND] WALNUT STREET THEATRE COMPANY (1829–34); and [THIRD] WALNUT STREET THEATRE COMPANY (1840–79).

[FIRST] WALNUT STREET THEATRE COMPANY. (1820–22) The Chestnut (also spelled Chesnut) Street Theatre had been Philadelphia's only home of true resident dramatic theatre for nearly three decades, when it burned to the ground on April 2, 1820. The only theatre of feasible size and accommodation in the city was the Olympic Theatre, built in 1809 as a circus amphitheatre and centrally located at the northeast corner of Ninth and Walnut streets. Although several of its managers had tried to intersperse the Olympic's regular equestrian, ballet, pantomime, and circus fare with legitimate dramatic entertainment, most efforts had failed; no dramatic company had appeared for more than eight weeks each theatrical season since the theatre's first stage was installed in 1811. However, to retain Philadelphia as their primary residence, the Chestnut Street Theatre

Company* managers William Warren and William Burke Wood secured the theatre for the 1820–21 season, despite mandatory extensive remodeling. Luckily, the theatre, which was without a tenant, was offered on easy terms, for Warren and Wood continued to experience severe financial difficulties, having lost all of the company's uninsured scenery, props, wardrobe, and library; its music, piano, and organ; and the models of scenery and machinery. Philadelphia architect William Strickland provided a new entranceway, enlarged the stage, removed the dome and replaced it with a ceiling, erected a pit, and improved the lobbies, boxes, dressing rooms, and the green room. Various accounts indicate an approximate seating capacity of 1,500. The renovated Olympic Theatre was renamed the Walnut Street Theatre. The little-altered Chestnut Street Theatre Company, returning from an autumn engagement in Baltimore, was similarly renamed the Walnut Street Theatre Company (also called the Walnut Street Theatre Stock Company). It opened on November 10, 1820, with John O'Keeffe's comedy *Wild Oats* and O'Keeffe's comic opera *Agreeable Surprise*.

External circumstances hampered the company from the start: a particularly severe winter; a shortage of firewood; a drafty, uncomfortable theatre; and an unusual incidence of actor illness. Rumors that the new theatre was unsafe circulated around the city, and management was forced to make additional improvements, such as installing seventy-foot support beams. Even written testimonials by local fire companies about the building's security had only moderated Philadelphia's fear of the theatre. Edmund Kean's much-touted starring engagement with the company in January 1821 enticed audiences and alleviated prejudices to some degree; however, the company continued to lose money. In April the Walnut Street Theatre Company traveled to Baltimore's Holliday Street Theatre for its usual spring season, returning to the Walnut for a short summer season in July. Brief seasons in Washington, D.C., and Baltimore followed before the company opened its 1821–22 season at the Walnut in November. Problems were complicated by unexpected competition from the resident company at the small Prune Street Theatre, where manager Stanislaus Surin had secured several of the Walnut's valued players, including Mr. and Mrs. H. Williams, Charlotte and Katharine Durang, John Herbert, and Mr. Pelby. Because the company's seasons at the Walnut were, in manager Wood's terms, "ruinous," Warren and Wood pressed for rebuilding the Chestnut Street Theatre. With the newly constructed theatre promised for the fall of 1822, the managers relinquished the Walnut Street Theatre's lease. The company's last spring performance at the Walnut on April 24, 1822, ended its first forty-eight weeks in Philadelphia.

The company operated primarily in the resident mode established by the earliest permanent stock companies of the 1790s. Each actor specialized in a regular stock role such as low comedian, leading man, or juvenile.

"Occasional actors" supplemented a permanent company of approximately fifteen, when necessary. The company usually performed two plays each evening, six nights a week, with the theatre dark on Sundays. A main serious piece and a comic afterpiece were most usual, although this combination certainly was not the rule. Generally, bills changed nightly, although a play often was repeated several times during a brief period when first introduced and then added to the company's repertory for revival at later dates. Plays performed most often emanated from the London stage, but translations of French and German pieces were increasingly popular. New, American-authored plays were still infrequent, and the Walnut Street Theatre Company produced only one locally conceived work, H. McMurtie's *Author's Night*. Musical and ballet pieces also were favored: most company members could sing, dance, or play an instrument as well as act, and several of the company's visiting artists were ballet masters, such as Monsieurs Labasse and Tatin of the Royal Academy of Paris. Well-known vocalists, Mr. Philipps and Mr. Nichols, played with the regular company. An orchestra was engaged to play overtures and to accompany musical plays or *entr'acte* entertainments such as character songs or fencing displays.

Increasingly, traveling stars were engaged at the Walnut, some remaining for a single performance, others for a week or two, and others for several months (the ones remaining several months generally functioned as leading players with the regular company). Despite the Walnut Street Theatre's shortcomings, the company briefly engaged several of the most noteworthy stars of the period, including Edmund Kean and Thomas Abthorpe Cooper. The strictly stock nights at the Walnut produced less revenue overall than those supplemented by stars, although, ironically, the high salary required by a star often depleted the returns and made the star's engagement unprofitable. Manager Wood was known for his vehement criticism of the star system and for a pessimistic vision of the resident company's imminent demise; however, in comparison with conditions in years to come, the resident company was still a healthy institution. The Walnut Street Theatre Company's regular actors, such as eccentric comedian Joseph Jefferson I and versatile comedian Henry Wallack, were local favorites, as evidenced by their profitable benefits. In contrast, the outlandish behavior of visitors, such as Kean and the opiated Mrs. Alsop, prompted Philadelphia audiences to pelt the stage with apples, oranges, and other "light missiles." Regular company actors were often adorned by admirers with such an array of wreaths, bouquets, vases, goblets, cups, and rings that their dressing rooms were completely filled.

During the first Walnut Street Theatre Company's brief existence, it debuted one of the nineteenth century's most acclaimed actors and the one deemed America's first native star, Edwin Forrest. Billed as "Master Forrest," the fourteen-year-old performer, a native of Philadelphia, first appeared on November 27, 1820, as Young Norval in John Home's tragedy *Douglas*. Later, he also acted Frederic in *Lovers' Vows* and Octavian in *The Mountaineers*. He was critically praised for his noble figure and powerful, expressive style, both inordinately developed in such a young performer. However, his appearances, hampered by bad weather and scheduled between the engagements of Cooper and Kean, were financially unsuccessful. Forrest remained with the company until January 1822, when he opted to tour the western theatres as an apprentice actor, thereby abandoning his initial plan to emerge in the eastern theatres immediately as a "Young Roscius," as the popular juvenile stars of the day were called. Edwin's brother William Forrest debuted with the Walnut Street Theatre Company the following season.

The Walnut Street Theatre Company, in an attempt to woo Philadelphia audiences, on several occasions created spectacular new scenic effects for their productions, most carried out under the supervision of Joseph Jefferson II. The most elaborate was the first American production of the melodramatic romance *Undine* on January 1, 1822, which presented a huge flying fish and a bridge that changed into a "car drawn by horses" amid atmospheric displays of water and moonlight. On March 22 and 23, 1822, the management provided a live elephant for its production of *The Forty Thieves*, advertising it as the largest animal of its kind ever exhibited in America. In *The Snowstorm*, trained dogs in complete harness appeared with a driver. In December 1821 a deputation of six area Indian tribes (Grand Panis, Panis Republic, Panis Loups, O'Mahais, Kanzas, and Ottoes) was invited to attend the Walnut Street Theatre, and the visit created much local excitement. Despite these efforts, returns remained so low—averaging only $418.50 a night during 1820–21 and $309.75 in 1821–22 before stars and benefits—that the actors agreed to take partial salaries to prevent the company's bankruptcy. Instead, the actors opted to rely on their benefits to provide their necessary finances, and, as testimony of the popularity of company regulars, benefits were almost always well attended and profitable. The sporadic benefits accorded local causes, such as fire companies and disaster victims, also were well patronized. Observed William Wood of a benefit given by the Walnut Street Theatre Company for the recently razed Philadelphia Orphan Asylum, "in forty-seven years in the theatre . . . this is the only instance [in which] I have ever witnessed *a full house*" (Wood, 275). In contrast to the company's average nightly receipts, this benefit produced $1,760.00.

The Walnut Street Theatre reverted to its former name, the Olympic Theatre, in September 1822, when it once again became an equestrian theatre. Subsequently called the Walnut Street Circus and the Philadelphia Theatre, it hosted temporary resident companies during the next few years.

Gradually, the house was reestablished as a legitimate theatre and, by 1829, again hosted a permanent [Second] Walnut Street Theatre Company* (1829–34).

PERSONNEL

Management: William Warren, William Burke Wood, proprietors and managers.
Scenic Artists: Joseph Jefferson II, Henry Warren.

Actors and Actresses: Mr. Baker; *Mrs. Baker*; *Mr. and Mrs. John Barnes*; Mr. Bernard; Francis Blissett; Mr. and Mrs. Thomas Burke; John Darley; Mrs. John Darley, formerly Ellen Westray; Charlotte Durang; Katharine Durang; Edwin Forrest; William Forrest; Mr. and Mrs. William Francis; John Herbert; *Mr. and Mrs. Joseph Jefferson I*; Mr. Nichols; Mr. Pelby; *Mr. Philipps*; Miss Seymour; Miss Tilden; *Mr. and Mrs. Henry Wallack; William Warren*; William Wheatley; H. Williams; Mrs. H. Williams, later Mrs. Robert C. Maywood; *William B. Wood; Mrs. William B. Wood*, formerly Juliana Westray; Mrs. Young.

Guest Artists: Mrs. Alsop, Thomas Abthorpe Cooper, Mrs. Alexander Drake, Edmund Kean, Monsieur Labasse, Master George Frederick Smith, Monsieur Tatin.

REPERTORY

1820–21: *Wild Oats; Agreeable Surprise; The Poor Gentleman; Of Age Tomorrow; As You Like It; Rosina; The Road to Ruin; A Budget of Blunders; Henri Quatre; Where Shall I Dine?; Short Reign and a Merry One; Little Red Riding Hood; High Life below Stairs; Turn Out; The Wonder; The Vampire; Rob Roy; The Anatomist; Douglas; Three Weeks after Marriage; The Busy Body; The Iron Chest; Helpless Animals; The Ruffian Boy; The Foundling of the Forest; Belles without Beaux; The Heart of Midlothian; Love among the Roses; The Steward; She Stoops to Conquer; The Magpie and the Maid; Wanted: A Wife; Virginius; Macbeth; The Wedding Day; Bertram; The Review; Hamlet; Richard III; The Hunter of the Alps; Catherine and Petruchio; The Fate of Calais; Killing, No Murder; George Barnwell; The Scotch Ghost; Lovers' Vows; Ivanhoe; The Robbers; Raising the Wind; The Adopted Child; The Mountaineers; The Village Lawyer; Othello; The Merchant of Venice; Brutus; A New Way to Pay Old Debts; King Lear; Rule a Wife and Have a Wife; Town and Country; The Dead Alive; The Comet; The Actress of All Work; The Country Girl; The Devil to Pay; The Child of the Mountain; The School for Scandal; The Romp; Belle's Stratagem; The Day after the Wedding; The Rivals; Matrimony; The Midnight Hour; Fortune's Frolic; The Will; Romeo and Juliet; She Would Be a Soldier; Sprigs of Laurel; Isabella; The Castle Spectre; Ella Rosenberg; Jane Shore; The Broken Sword; Honey Moon; The Falls of Clyde; The Stranger; The Wandering Boys; The Author's Night; The Exile; Tom Thumb, the Great; Lovers' Quarrels; The Merry Wives of Windsor; The Turnpike Gate; Bold Stroke for a Husband; Collins' Ode; A Mogul Tale; Exchange No Robbery; Who's the Dupe?; The Heir-at-Law; Spoil'd Child; Inkle and Yarico; A Tale of Mystery; The Clandestine Marriage; The Highland Reel; Riches; Venice Preserved; The Deaf Lover.*

1821–22: *The West Indian; The Review; The Point of Honour; Helpless Animals;*

Too Late for Dinner; The Devil's Bridge; Spoil'd Child; Wallace; Of Age Tomorrow; Rob Roy; The Ghost; Henri Quatre; The Anatomist; Valentine and Orson; Wild Oats; The Vampire; Honey Moon; The Merry Wives of Windsor; The Ruffian Boy; Isabella; Paul and Virginia; Macbeth; Where Shall I Dine?; The Poor Gentleman; She Stoops to Conquer; Thérèse; The Mountaineers; Miss in Her Teens; Hamlet; Fortune's Frolic; Belles without Beaux; Pizarro; My Grandmother; Bertram; A Budget of Blunders; The Romp; The Clandestine Marriage; The Poor Soldier; Venice Preserved; The Highland Reel; Brutus; Catherine and Petruchio; The Weathercock; Damon and Pythias; A Short Reign and a Merry One; The Children in the Wood; The School for Scandal; The Comet; The Foundling of the Forest; The Deaf Lover; The Warlock of the Glen; The Devil to Pay; The Robbers; Love Laughs at Locksmiths; The Miller's Maid; Turn Out; The Libertine; Town and Country; George Barnwell; Romeo and Juliet; The Dead Alive; Undine; The Irishman in London; She Would Be a Soldier; The Thieves; The Village Lawyer; De Montfort; The Green Man; The Magpie and the Maid; The Follies of a Day; The Wedding Day; Speed the Plough; The Falls of Clyde; The Iron Chest; Alexander the Great; The Rendezvous; Usef Caramalli; The Voice of Nature; St. Patrick's Day; Mahomet; High Life below Stairs; Love in a Village; The Cabinet; Modern Antiques; Brother and Sister; Guy Mannering; The Maid of the Mill; The Prisoner at Large; Marion and Sigesmar the Switzer; Lionel and Clarissa; A Tale of Mystery; The Barber of Seville; Ella Rosenberg; Fontainebleau; The Wandering Boys; Henry IV (first part only); *The Forty Thieves; The Russian Imposter; The Adopted Child; All the World's a Stage; The Duenna; Alfonso; The Snow Storm; Little Red Riding Hood; Love Makes a Man; Robin Hood; The Peasant Boy; Rugatino; Love among the Roses; Jealousy in Seraglio; The Spy.*

BIBLIOGRAPHY

Published Sources: Reese D. James, *Old Drury of Philadelphia* (Philadelphia: University of Pennsylvania Press, 1932); William B. Wood, *Personal Recollections of the Stage* (Philadelphia: Henry Carey Baird, 1855).

Unpublished Source: Mary Helps, "The Walnut Street Theatre" (Paper presented as partial fulfillment of the M.L.S. degree, Drexel University, Philadelphia, 1966).

Archival Sources: Walnut Street Theatre File and Walnut Street Theatre Programs File, Philadelphia Theatre Collection, Free Library of Philadelphia (Logan Square). The Philadelphia Theatre Collection also has files on many of the managers and performers connected with the Walnut Street Theatre.

Mari Kathleen Fielder

[SECOND] WALNUT STREET THEATRE COMPANY. (1829–34) When Philadelphia's Walnut Street Theatre was abandoned by actor-managers William Warren and William Burke Wood, whose permanent [First] Walnut Street Theatre Company* had occupied the house for two unsuccessful theatrical seasons, 1820–22, the theatre reverted temporarily to its former name, the Olympic Theatre, and to its former occupation, circus and equestrian entertainment. The theatre came under the management of New York's Park Theatre operators, Stephen Price and Edmund Simpson, in the fall of 1822. The two tried varying modes and policies of operation during their seven years as managers, intent on making a profitable enterprise of the seemingly ill-fated theatre at Ninth and Walnut streets. Price, a New York-based lawyer and businessman, and Simpson, an actor-manager, managed their Philadelphia theatre *in absentia*, electing to hire English-born Joe Cowell, a former actor at the Park, to manage for them. Variously calling their theatre the Olympic, the Walnut Street Circus, and Simpson's Circus, the management concentrated on circus entertainment, as had previous managements from 1809 to 1820. However, Cowell increasingly produced equestrian dramas, such as Monk Lewis' *Timour, the Tartar* (1811) and William Moncrieff's *Cataract of the Ganges!* (1823), as well as standard afterpieces, such as Thomas Knight's comic opera *Turnpike Gate* (1799) and Moncrieff's burletta *Tom and Jerry* (1821). To act in both the equestrian dramas and afterpieces, Cowell employed a small troupe of resident actors and a larger band of occasional actors. However, because Cowell's operation was active only a total of about four months each year and because the bills each brief season were divided between circus and drama, the house could not be termed a home of permanent resident theatre.

By 1827 Cowell was a full partner of Simpson, Price having abandoned his interest and moved to London to manage the Drury Lane. (Price reportedly did so to acquire English starring actors more readily for the Park Theatre.) Cowell and Simpson, too, were sensitive to the rising popularity of stars who traveled from one resident stock to another, performing featured roles with the company and remaining for as little as a few days to as long as several months. Because Simpson and Cowell had well-developed links to the London theatre and because they thought Philadelphia had grown enough to accommodate a second regular dramatic house, they began gradually to convert their theatre. (The only permanent resident company in Philadelphia at the time was the long-lived Chestnut Street Theatre Company*.) Simpson and Cowell dispatched their circus on tour with increasing frequency, while they enlarged their dramatic troupe. They sent a representative, John Hallam, to London to secure regular actors, visiting stars, and new playscripts. In the fall of 1827, they remodeled the theatre, replacing the circus ring with a spacious pit, and officially renamed it the Philadelphia Theatre. This name, however, did not gain wide acceptance; the theatre was commonly called the Walnut Street Theatre.

The 1827–28 fall and winter season at the Walnut Street Theatre lasted only ten weeks, as had been the previous practice. Significantly different, however, was its devotion to legitimate drama, highlighted by the appearances of stars Thomas Abthorpe Cooper, Thomas Sowerby Hamblin, and Junius Brutus Booth as well as the debuts of many noted English actors in the regular company, including Mr. and Mrs. John Sefton and Mr. and

Mrs. W. H. Sedley-Smith. Most auspicious for the city was the American debut of seven-year-old Louisa Lane as the Duke of York to Booth's Richard III in September, 1827; later known as Mrs. John Drew, she was to become one of the nineteenth century's most prominent actress-managers, known primarily for her decades-long proprietorship of Philadelphia's Arch Street Theatre Company* (1861–76). The Walnut's low prices of twenty-five and fifty cents, its high production standards, and an extended summer season finally appeared to augur a permanent status for its company. In the spring of 1828 however, reliable local sources reported that the theatre was to be torn down, and Cowell and Simpson abruptly relinquished the lease.

In the fall of 1828 the decision to demolish the theatre was reversed, and it was refurbished for its new tenants, John A. Inslee and William Rufus Blake. When they took control in December 1828, the carefully plotted strategy to create a second permanent Walnut Street Theatre Company (also called the Walnut Street Theatre Stock Company) was realized. The company debuted on January 4, 1829, and was well received. However, local critics qualified their praise, attributing the company's power to its excellent actor personnel, which the management had been able to amass only because the city's other theatres temporarily were inactive. The Philadelphia theatrical scene was in great flux at this time. The Chestnut Street Theatre had recently undergone its first management changeover in twenty-five years; a rash of new managements, changing season schedules, and bankruptcies demoralized actors and audiences alike, and a new Arch Street Theatre exacerbated local competition. Despite their much-touted opening, the Walnut Street Theatre Company, which operated as a traditional resident stock company with supplemental visiting stars, novelty performers, dancers, and vocalists, lost money immediately in competition with the other companies. Its intitial failure in April 1829 was blamed on relatively inexperienced management, insufficient financial backing, and the continued inability of the managers to heat the theatre properly.

Actors Samuel Chapman and John Greene, former members of the Chestnut Street Theatre Company, assumed management in May. They retained essentially the same actors, policies, and operating schedule of six performances a week of two and occasionally three plays each. (Theatres in Pennsylvania traditionally and by law remained dark on Sundays.) Because the other theatres again were inactive, the company's ranks included favorite Philadelphia performers such as William Warren and William Wood. Chapman was considered a highly competent manager. He had the experience of a long career at London's Covent Garden before immigrating to America in 1827, and he had shown exceptional ability as the stage manager and director of amusements at the Arch during the 1827–28 theatrical season. However, under Chapman, the Walnut Street Theatre Company continued to succeed only when competition was nonexistent and to fail when it materialized. Apparently, Philadelphia simply could not support three permanent companies at this time. Chapman tried various new partners—first Mr. Edmonds and later his brother William Chapman—and he divested himself of his old partners, but the company floundered. It did, however, manage a nine-week 1829 summer season and a full September 1829 through August 1830 season, with only a brief four-week recess caused by winter weather conditions. In the unstable environment of the Philadelphia theatrical scene, this longevity indicated unusual company strength and management capability. However, Samuel Chapman's sudden death in May 1830 left the company under the sole management of William Chapman, who was forced to relinquish the theatre and temporarily to disband the company in December 1830. William Chapman's subsequent career as a showboat impresario along the Ohio and Mississippi rivers proved far more successful.

The Walnut Street Theatre Company spent its next five seasons under the management of Scottish emigrant Robert Campble Maywood and as an adjunct to the [Old] Chestnut Street Theatre Stock Company* (1826–55). Maywood, a former star tragedian of the Drury Lane and Park theatres and former actor-manager of Philadelphia's Arch Street Theatre, gained control of both the Chestnut and Walnut Street theatres during the 1831–32 theatrical season. Ostensibly, he was the leading partner in the firm of Maywood and Company, which included silent financial backers such as Lewis T. Pratt. Maywood created one basic stock company, which he dispatched between the two houses, informally calling the troupe the Chestnut Street Theatre (Stock) Company, when it performed at the Chestnut, and the Walnut Street Theatre (Stock) Company when it performed at the Walnut. Maywood seemed to see marked class differences in his two theatres' clientele, for he maintained the Chestnut as a full-priced house and operated the Walnut as a half-priced facility, admission costs there ranging from eighteen and three-quarters to fifty cents. Opera, considered to be in the domain of the upper classes, was produced far more frequently by the company at the Chestnut.

Maywood attempted to operate his two houses with one company, using it at the Walnut one night and at the Chestnut the next, but this proved far too cumbersome and caused a "severe and disastrous" financial situation, the nightly receipts averaging only $175, while the average nightly expenses were $300. Instead, he devised a schedule that slated the troupe at the Chestnut from September through January and again during May through early June and at the Walnut from January through May and again during late June through July. Each theatre, according to this plan, operated in the dramatic resident mode for approximately twenty-three weeks a season. However, Maywood did not adhere strictly to this schedule, for he occasionally sublet his theatres to other managers. He made it a standard policy to book a foreign opera company, such as the French Opera Company or Italian Opera Company of Havana, into the Chestnut during the resident company's winter months at the Walnut.

Guest artists continued to be featured and included dramatic actors such as Charles and Fanny Kemble, Tyrone Power, and Master Burke; vocalists such as John Sinclair; dancers and pantomimists such as the Ravel family; and specialty artists such as rope-performer Herr Cline. However, the company's regular performers were its mainstays and included many Philadelphia favorites as well as many new performers predominantly from London, New York, Boston, and Baltimore. The company's most popular performer was Thomas D. Rice, a star who appeared with the troupe almost as frequently as did company regulars. Rice was known especially for his specialty jump dances, which he performed in burnt-cork makeup as the Negro character Jim Crow, an act considered the precursor to the minstrel show.

Maywood was known for his conservative leanings toward British theatrical traditions and for his distaste of the emerging American genre and theme plays. The Walnut's repertory, predominantly from the London stage, reflected his predilections. However, Maywood was forced to retreat somewhat from this stance when the Arch Street Theatre began building a reputation and an accompanying financial success as the city's "American theatre," known for its cultivation of native plays and talent. To compete, Maywood employed several delineators of American characters, such as Rice, and Yankee-specialist George H. Hill, and he infrequently presented American plays such as *The Forest Rose; or, American Farmers* and *The Inquisitive Yankee*. Politically, however, the company extolled American ideals of nationalism and republicanism by holding benefit performances for the Polish revolutionaries who were, in 1831, fighting against monarchical Russian domination of their homeland.

Because the Walnut Street Theatre continued to be considered Philadelphia's least physically desirable theatre—it was still without gas lighting and adequate heating systems—Maywood opted to abandon it when the Arch Street Theatre's lease became available to him in August 1834. Maywood had already rearranged the Walnut's operating schedule in 1833–34 to bypass it during the winter months. He went on to operate both the Arch and Chestnut Street theatres for several seasons. The Walnut came under the management of Francis Courtney Wemyss, who changed the theatre's name and called its company the American Theatre Company*. In 1840 the Walnut Street Theatre nomenclature was restored, and the [Third] Walnut Street Theatre Stock Company* commenced production.

PERSONNEL

Management: John A. Inslee, William Rufus Blake, proprietors and managers (1829); Samuel Chapman, John Greene, proprietors and managers (1829); Samuel Chapman, John Greene, Mr. Edmonds, proprietors and managers (1829–30); Samuel Chapman, William Chapman, proprietors and managers (1830); William Chapman, proprietor and manager (1830); Robert Campble Maywood and Company, proprietor, Robert Campble Maywood, manager, and Thayer Dinsmore, treasurer (1831–34).

Stage Director: W. Barrimore.

Actors and Actresses: A. Allen; Mr. Barbiere; Mr. Barnes; Mr. and Mrs. Barrett; Mr. Barton; *William Rufus Blake* (1828–29); Miss Booth; J. S. Brown; William E. Burton; George Chapman; Samuel Chapman; William Chapman; *Miss Clifton* (1831–32); Mrs. Conduit; Samuel Cowell; Mr. Coyle; Mr. Cuddy; Mr. De Camp; Mr. and Mrs. Thayer Dinsmond; Mr. Dixon; Mr. Dwyer; Miss Elphinstone; Mr. Faulkner; *Alexina Fisher*, later known as Mrs. Alexina Fisher Baker (1832–33); Clara Fisher; *Mr. and Mrs. Flynn* (1832–33); Mrs. Frances; Mr. Gale; Mr. Gallot; Mr. Gamble; Mr. and Mrs. Charles Green; *Thomas Hadaway* (1833–34); Mr. Hamilton; Mr. Henkins; Mr. Horn; Mr. Howard; Mr. Hughes; Mr. Hunt; *D. Ingersoll* (1833–34); Mr. Jones; Miss Kelly; Miss Kent; Miss Kerr; Mrs. Knight; Charles Mason; Robert Campble Maywood; Mr. McDougall; Mr. Mercer; Mrs. Moreland; Mr. Mossie; *James E. Murdoch* (1831–34); Mr. and Mrs. Pearman; Mrs. Pindar; Mr. Porter; Mr. Pratt; *Mr. Proctor* (1832–33); *Mr. Reynoldson* (1832–33); *Thomas D. Rice* (1832–34); Mr. Riley; Mr. Roberts; Mr. Rosalie; *Mrs. and Mrs. Rowbotham* (1832–34); *J. R. Scott* (1833–34); Mr. and Mrs. John Sefton; Mr. and Mrs. William H. Sedley-Smith; Rachel Stannard; Sarah Stannard; Miss Vincent; Mr. Walstein; Mr. Walton; William Warren; Mr. Watson; Francis Courtney Wemyss; *William Burke Wood* (1832–34).

Guest Artists: Augustus A. Addams, Signor Angrisani, Mrs. Austin, Junius Brutus Booth, Mme. Brichita, Master Burke, Herr Cline, Mrs. F. A. Drake, Mme. Feron, H. J. Finn, Mrs. Fanny Fitzwilliam, T. Francisco, Thomas Sowerby Hamblin, George H. Hill, Miss Hughes, Charles Kemble, Fanny Kemble, Mr. Norton, Tyrone Power, Ravel family, Thomas D. Rice, Signor Sciarra, John Sinclair, Mr. Wilkinson.

SAMPLE REPERTORY

1831–32: *The Heart of Midlothian; Raising the Wind; Paul Pry; The Sleepwalker; Turn Out; The School of Reform; Charles XII; Wreck Ashore; Matrimony; The Colonel's Come; Fraternal Discord; The Devil to Pay; Rob Roy MacGregor; Lovers' Quarrels; The Marriage of Figaro; Sprigs of Laurel; Guy Mannering; A Day after the Wedding; Agreeable Surprise; John of Paris; The Hebrew; Fish Out of Water; The School for Scandal; The Slave; The Young Widow; Tancredi; The Spectre Bridegroom; The Fair Penitent; As You Like It; The Actress of All Work; The Foundling of the Forest; The Lottery Ticket; Romeo and Juliet; Spoil'd Child; A Bold Stroke for a Husband; Perfection; The Will; The Dead Shot; Richard III; Turnpike Gate; Much Ado about Nothing; Frederick the Great; Othello; 'Tis All a Farce; She Wou'd and She Wou'd Not; Husband at Sight; Hamlet; Is He Jealous?; A New Way to Pay Old Debts; The Prize; Macbeth; Fortune's Frolic; The Bride of Lammermoor; The Broken Sword; King Lear; The Two Gregories; The Wedding Day; The Castle Spectre; Douglas; The Rendezvous; Der Freischutz; The Comet; The Highland Reel; The Tempest; No Song, No Supper; The Hero of Scotland; The Robbers; Pizarro; Venice Preserved; The Evil Eye; Bertram; The Water Witch;*

George Barnwell; Alexander the Great; My Aunt; Down East; The Innkeeper's Daughter; Tom and Jerry; Jocko: the Brazilian Ape; Wives as They Were and Maids as They Are; Washington; Pitcairn's Island; Paul Jones; The Press Gang; The Recluse of the Hulk; Jack Robinson and His Monkey; The Midnight Hour; Everybody's Husband; Polichinelle Vampire, The Mountaineers; Harlequin and Mother Goose; The Old Soldier of the Revolution; Meg Murnoch; The Forty Thieves; High Ways and By Ways; Charles II; Thérèse; Industry and Idleness; The Navigator; The Blue Devils; The Jenkins; The Dream of Christopher Columbus; Julius Caesar; The Hypocrite; The Bold Dragoons; Napoleon; Family Jars; St. Patrick's Day; The Happiest Day of My Life; The Flying Dutchman; Dominique; It Is the Devil; No!; King John; William Thomson; The Iron Chest; Brutus; Masaniello; The Irishman in London; Town and Country; Catherine and Petruchio; How to Die for Love; Hernani; William Tell; Victorine; The Lion of the West; Of Age Tomorrow; The Hundred-Pound Note; The Master's Rival; The Africans; Winning a Husband; The Gamester; The Bohemian Mother; Jane Shore; The Peasant Boy; The Miller and His Men; Separation and Reparation; Cherry and Fair Star; Touch and Take; The Hunter of the Alps; The Plains of the Chippewa; Turning the Tables; The Good-Natured Man; Don Giovanni; The East Indian; Midas; Bluebeard; The Beggar's Opera; The Merchant of Venice; Education; The Dumb Girl of Genoa; The Fair American; Whirligig Hall.

BIBLIOGRAPHY

Published Sources: Mrs. John Drew, *Autobiographical Sketch* (New York: Charles Scribner's Sons, 1899); Reese D. James, *Old Drury of Philadelphia* (Philadelphia: University of Pennsylvania Press, 1932); William Burke Wood, *Personal Recollections of the Stage* (Philadelphia: Henry Carey Baird, 1855).

Unpublished Source: Mary Helps, "The Walnut Street Theatre" (Paper presented as partial fulfillment of the M.L.S. degree, Drexel University, Philadelphia, 1966).

Archival Sources: Walnut Street Theatre File, Philadelphia Theatre Collection, Free Library of Philadelphia (Logan Square). The Philadelphia Theatre Collection also has files on many of the managers and performers connected with the Walnut Street Theatre.

Mari Kathleen Fielder

[THIRD] WALNUT STREET THEATRE COMPANY. (1840–79) Philadelphia's Walnut Street Theatre, located at the northeast corner of Ninth and Walnut streets and built in 1808, had endured a checkered career as a dirt-floored equestrian amphitheatre, a circus ring, and a dramatic facility with several names before beginning an uninterrupted thirty-nine-year tenure as the home of the Walnut Street Theatre Stock Company in 1840. A short-lived first Walnut Street Theatre Company* (1820–22) had occupied the house from 1820 to 1822, while the Chestnut (then spelled Chesnut) Street Theatre, the city's regular home of dramatic stock, was rebuilt after a fire. A second continuous stock company, informally named the Walnut Street Theatre Company* (1829–34), appeared sporadically and under steadily changing managements from 1829 to 1834. Then in 1834 new management, a renovated facility, and a name change—to the American Theatre and an accompanying American Theatre Company*—finally earned the theatre a reputation as a feasible, permanent home for legitimate drama.

When the proprietor and manager of the American Theatre Company, Francis Courtney Wemyss, dropped the theatre's lease after a financial dispute with the theatre's stockholders, Ethelbert A. Marshall and William Dinneford became its new lessees and restored the location-based name and created a new Walnut Street Theatre Stock Company to occupy the theatre. Many of the players were new to Philadelphia, recruited from New York, Boston, Baltimore, and Washington; this epitomized a growing trend toward a less strictly local theatrical scene in the city and was due, in part, to the rapidly expanding theatrical activity there. The new troupe substantially lowered its prices, slashing in half the prevailing admission cost by charging only twelve and one-half cents for the pit and twenty-five cents for the second tier of boxes. Despite these core changes, the company did retain the patriotic symbol of an eagle with spread wings that had been adopted by the American Theatre's management, and this eagle was to remain the trademark of theatre and company throughout most of the nineteenth century.

The new Walnut Street Theatre Stock Company opened on October 14, 1840, in John Tobin's comedy *Honey Moon* and Thomas Morton's farce *A Roland for an Oliver*. Marshall's interest in the theatre apparently was primarily financial, since he was disinterested in either acting in or directing the plays. Rather, Marshall devoted his energies to securing other theatres to lease and manage. Divesting himself of his early partners, Marshall had enough capital by the 1843–44 season to lease both the Chestnut and Walnut Street theatres, two of the city's four main playhouses. He produced operas at the Chestnut and dramas at the Walnut, moving the dramatic company to the Chestnut when no operas were scheduled and closing the Walnut. The plan proved unsuccessful, and Marshall did not again attempt to manage two theatres simultaneously in the same city. He did, however, become the manager of New York's Broadway Theatre in 1847 and remained there until 1858, this period overlapping with Marshall's management of the Walnut Street Theatre.

Marshall experimented with various managerial assistance modes during his early years as proprietor of the Walnut Street Theatre Stock Company. During the 1842–43 season he appointed the company's new leading lady, Charlotte Cushman, as actress-manager of the troupe. Local critics speculated that Marshall did so to compete with the new female management at the Chestnut Street Theatre under twenty-year-old Mary Elizabeth Maywood. Controversy concerning who actually controlled both theatres was rampant: many claimed that Robert Campble Maywood, Mary's father, managed the Chestnut behind the scenes, and William Rufus Blake supervised the Walnut Street troupe. In fact, Cushman was given the lesser title of "acting manager" under Blake's "manager" the following season. At any rate, Cushman (1816–76) was still in the earliest phase of her career when she came to the Walnut, although she had already played with various stock companies in Boston, New Orleans, New York, Albany, and Philadelphia for seven years. The tall, dignified, powerful Cushman was highly praised for her acting with the Walnut Street Theatre Stock Company and especially for her portrayal of Romeo to the Juliet of her sister Susan in May 1843; in later years she was deemed by many the first great American actress.

After 1844 Marshall apparently did not appoint a specific manager each season but did entrust much of the company's management to Blake and his successor Peter Richings, both called simply "stage manager." William Rufus Blake was both a seasoned performer and manager, having performed at New York's Old Chatham Theatre as early as 1824 and stage managed the Tremont Theatre Company* of Boston as early as 1827. Blake also had stage managed briefly for the Walnut Street Theatre Stock Company in 1829 and toured extensively as a traveling star. His work as stage manager consistently was lauded by local critics, and the Walnut Street Theatre Stock Company became known for its lavish, detailed, polished staging. When the company produced *London Assurance*, audiences were amazed to discover the garden scene laid out with natural flowers, grass plots, and real orange and lemon trees (on loan from several of the city's noted horticulturalists). The company's *Water Queen* used 5,000 jets of real water and 6,000 jets of multicolored liquid fire to create a grand display of "fairy illusion." During this period the company excelled in the production of costly pantomimes such as *The Black Raven of the Tombs* and *Harlequin and the Silver Tower*, which depended in large part on spectacular scenic effects. Peter Richings, who succeeded Blake in 1848 when he left to stage manage Marshall's Broadway Theatre in New York, was also an extremely experienced performer and stage manager and maintained Blake's high standards as both a director of the stage and of the actors. Richings' role in the Walnut Street Theatre Stock Company was pivotal to its continued success at this point, for Marshall frequently was absent from his Philadelphia venture, preferring to oversee his new endeavors in New York.

The Walnut Street Theatre Stock Company operated in the standard vein of the day, with actors hired to perform stock "lines of business" in a basic repertory of plays called primarily from the contemporary London stage and from the annals of English dramatic literature. Melodramas, many set in Paris, became increasingly popular with the Walnut Street Theatre audiences during the period, as did dramas adapted from new novels and dramas in translation from the French and German stages. So-called national dramas with patriotic themes such as *1777, The Boston Tea Party, The Star-Spangled Banner*, and *The Battle of Germantown* played well as did pieces with local themes such as *The Philadelphia Fireman, Philadelphia as It Is*, and *The Young Quaker*. Irish-theme romantic dramas including *The Rose of Killarney, Kate Kearney*, and *Perfection; or, The Maid of Munster* and farces including *The Irish Attorney, Born to Good Luck*, and *The Irish Tutor* engendered much audience support as well. Tragedies lost favor. The Walnut Street Theatre did not present as many low-life dramas as the city's other theatres, undoubtedly indicating a slightly more elite audience.

Two plays generally were performed each night, one full-length and one afterpiece (although sometimes a play that was an afterpiece one night was a main offering on another evening). Occasionally, a portion of a full-length play was presented as the afterpiece. A serious piece and a comedic one usually comprised the bill, although this was not always the rule. The frequency with which a play was repeated also varied substantially. Sometimes a play would be presented for a full week with changing afterpieces each evening. During some weeks, the entire bill would change almost completely each night. For instance, during the week of November 30 to December 5, 1840, the company performed *Speed the Plough* (comedy) and *The Demon Dwarf* (melodrama) on Monday, *Archibald of the Wreck* and *The Demon Dwarf* on Tuesday, *Goblin Page* (melodrama) and *The Married Rake* (farce) on Wednesday, *Charles the Second* (comedy) and *Goblin Page* on Thursday, *Romeo and Juliet* and *Goblin Page* on Friday, and *Of Age Tomorrow* (musical farce) and *Spoil'd Child* (farce) on Saturday. In contrast, the troupe played the melodrama *The Carpenter of Rouen* every evening during the week of January 11 to January 16, 1841, with the comedic *Philadelphia as It Is* as the afterpiece on three evenings and three comedies, *Catching an Heiress, P.P.P.P.*, and *Laugh When You Can*, on the remaining nights. Additional entertainment sometimes was offered between the main piece and the afterpiece: most popular were character songs such as those of "Jim Crow" Rice, historical recitations, magic acts, dances, feats of contortion, and displays of strength.

Six evening performances a week was the standard, with the theatre always closed on Sunday. Occasionally, one of the regular nightly performances was set aside as a benefit for a company performer or staff member. As part of his or her contract, an actor negotiated a regular weekly salary plus a benefit performance from which he or she would retain from one-third to nine-tenths of the gross receipts, although the usual arrangement called for approximately one-half. For weeks before the benefit, the performer would circulate the news of the event and drum up support. Benefits generally were highly successful, and actors exerted their influence to keep the benefit system intact throughout most of the nineteenth century. The Walnut Street Theatre Stock Company also infrequently gave benefit performances for local causes such as the volunteer fire companies.

The Walnut Street Theatre Stock Company relied primarily on its resident actors and on occasionally engaged local actors to fill its bills during the Marshall years. Visiting stars, becoming more and more popular, did perform with the troupe and included notables such as Junius Brutus Booth, Sr., John Collins, James E. Murdoch, Dion Boucicault, John Brougham, and Ellen Tree. The Walnut's most frequent and favorite guest performer was Edwin Forrest, who maintained a residence in Philadelphia and played in the city for long periods during most seasons. Although the quantity of visiting stars and their influence on the resident company's repertory and general operation was negligible in comparison to later years, local critics already lamented the derogatory effects of the star system.

The Walnut Street Theatre infrequently was rented out for a week to another full company, most often opera or foreign-language troupes, and the resident company either toured or remained inactive. Sporadically, when ballet companies were engaged to provide the main offering, the resident company supplied one or two farcical afterpieces only. Theatrical seasons generally extended from late August or early September until late July or early August during the 1840s, although for three consecutive years, 1844 to 1846, the company performed all year. By the later part of the decade, a somewhat shorter theatrical year was established—from late August through late June or early July—and this was to remain the company's general policy for several decades. In keeping with the company's patriotic motifs, they often ended their season on July 4.

By 1844 the price of admission had been raised to the twenty-five- to seventy-five-cents range despite the lively and sometimes nasty competitiveness that existed among the city's theatres. Particularly sharp rivalry that endured for many years prevailed between the Walnut Street Theatre and Arch Street Theatre Company* (1861–76). In November 1848, for example, Forrest appeared at the Walnut and English star William Charles Macready at the Arch, and each pitted his respective version of *Macbeth, Othello, Richelieu, King Lear, Hamlet,* and *Virginius* against the other's on the same evenings. A Viennese dance troupe, highly publicized and scheduled to appear at the Arch Street Theatre, was lured to perform at the Walnut instead. Actors were constantly persuaded to abandon one company for the other, despite Marshall's ready access to actors from his New York theatre. In fact, Marshall often did hire members of his New York company to fill vacant Walnut Street Theatre Stock Company slots and frequently moved Walnut Street regulars to New York as well, but this did not daunt his rivalry for targeted Arch Street personnel.

The Walnut Street Theatre Stock Company was considered Philadelphia's finest at midcentury, the Arch having been abandoned by Burton and the Chestnut Street Theatre and company in a deteriorating state. The Walnut was substantially renovated in 1852 by celebrated architect R. Hoxie; the parquet was enlarged, orchestra compartments were installed, and the proscenium was widened considerably to provide better sightlines from the house. Considered novelties, heating units, a ventilating system, and a gas system were implemented. Mr. Barry's Patent Cool Air Machines eventually were added and were advertised to maintain the theatre at a comfortable seventy degrees even on Philadelphia's hottest and most humid nights. The management boasted that these alterations cost $10,000. Despite Marshall's overwhelming success as proprietor of the Walnut Street Theatre, he opted to move uptown to the Academy of Music, the city's new, lavish, 2,900-seat opera facility, for the 1857–58 season, leaving the Walnut Street Theatre available for new management for the first time in seventeen years. Marshall had accrued losses at New York's Broadway Theatre during his last few years of management in the mid–1870s, because rapid uptown movement there left his theatre in an unfashionable locale. Apparently, his move to the Academy was predicated, at least in part, on avoiding a repetition of this situation in Philadelphia.

Marshall took his farewell benefit at the Walnut on December 12, 1857, and by the following week, the theatre was open under its new manager, Mrs. David P. Bowers. Formerly known as Elizabeth Crocker and a native of Bridgeport, Connecticut, Mrs. Bowers had begun her career at New York's Park Theatre under E. Simpson, when she appeared as Amantis in *Child of Nature* (1846). However, after 1847 Mrs. Bowers made her career primarily in Philadelphia stock companies, appearing in nearly every local resident company including the Walnut, Chestnut, Arch, Philadelphia Museum, City Museum, Athenaeum National, and Barnum's Museum. She had appeared primarily as a partner with her late husband, David P. Bowers, a native Philadelphian who had spent most of his life appearing on the city's stages. His death in June 1857 apparently motivated her to expand into the managerial field.

Under Mrs. Bowers' management, play selection and operational policies remained essentially undistinguished from the former management, although acting personnel altered significantly. Mrs. Bowers retained many of the Walnut's core performers but also added several of her own family members, notably her sister and brother-in-law Mr. and Mrs. F. Bartlett Conway (formerly Sarah Crocker) and her niece Viola Crocker. She retaliated to the Arch Street Theatre management's "snatching" of Mme. Elizabeth Ponisi into their own ranks by persuading their exceedingly popular soubrette Anna Cruise to join her company in April 1858. Undoubtedly, her most astute move was to secure Mr. and Mrs. John Drew, always favorites with Philadelphia audiences, as company regulars. Mrs. Bowers' first year of management was considered extremely successful not only because it was lucrative but because she had chosen to buck the vogue and operate without guest stars.

However, the season of 1858–59 proved problematic from the start. The Drews were lured back to the Arch, and although Mrs. Bowers did secure the Arch's Mr. and Mrs. E. N. Thayer and John Drew's brother Frank N.

Drew (also a delineator of Irish characters), the loss remained uncompensated. Mrs. Bowers, apparently spurred on by her previous success, supervised extensive renovations on the Walnut Street Theatre during the summer of 1858, including the substitution of large, armed, cushioned seats spacious enough to accommodate the crinolines and hoops worn by ladies of the time. Repainting; repapering; adding new murals, portraits, and curtains; and much rearranging of boxes and circle partitions incurred high enough expenses to increase the theatre's annual rent by $1,000. The highly competent stage manager Peter Richings, whom Mrs. Bowers had cajoled back to the Walnut after his brief stint at the Academy of Music, left to join Burton's theatre. The additional rent plus the desertion of several of the company's most valued players—even the Conways left to tour England—resulted in diminished business and severe financial losses. Beginning in late November 1858 Mrs. Bowers added a star season in an attempt to reverse the situation, but this remedy proved ineffective, and her management collapsed in January 1859. She later managed Philadelphia's Academy of Music for several short-lived and financially unsuccessful seasons.

Mrs. M. Ann Garrettson took control of the Walnut Street Theatre Stock Company on January 24, 1859, basically retaining the resident acting personnel and immediately implementing a high-caliber star season, including James H. Hackett, Dion Boucicault, Emma Waller, James E. Murdoch, and Barry Sullivan. Of Mrs. Garrettson's few initial additions to the company, [George] Vining Bowers, a low comedian from New Orleans' St. Charles Theatre, and J. Sturton Wright, also from New Orleans, greatly pleased Philadelphia audiences. Later, her securing of Edwin Adams as leading man and occasional director for the 1860 to 1862 years helped boost the company's popularity further, and Mrs. Garrettson's management consistently was credited as a financial success. Adams (1834–77), known for his endearingly honest, clean-cut, and manly qualities, rose to the forefront of the American acting profession during the 1860s, touring as a star in roles such as Edward Middleton in *The Drunkard* and Robert Lantry in *The Dead Heart* and later as a Shakespearean actor with Edwin Booth. Another highly respected performer with the Walnut Street troupe was John McCullough (1832–85), who had resided in Philadelphia since his arrival from Ireland in 1847 and had gained his early exposure to acting in local amateur dramatic societies. His initial professional experience was as a member of the Arch Street Theatre Stock Company, where he debuted in 1857. It was yet another case of the enduring rivalry between the Arch and Walnut when Mrs. Garrettson persuaded McCullough to abandon the Arch and join her company for the 1860–62 theatrical seasons, although he left to join Edwin Forrest's tour before the end of the latter season. McCullough was to become inextricably linked with Forrest throughout the remainder of his career, duplicating Forrest's heroic, virile acting style and playing many of his mentor's roles.

Under Mrs. Garrettson, the Walnut Street Theatre Stock Company finally abandoned for the most part the practice of performing more than one play per performance. Because star's engagements followed each other in a basically uninterrupted sequence, the repertory reflected individual star's vehicles more than the management's predilections and was comprised of the usual mixture of higher-caste melodramas, Shakespearean pieces, comedies, and classics of the eighteenth- and ninteenth-century British stage. Irish-theme plays and their stars continued to draw large audiences: the vehicles associated with John Drew and Barney Williams inevitably appeared as part of the repertory during most seasons. By the 1860s overtly nationalistic dramas had lost favor, although plays with distinctly American themes began to prevail, including pieces such as *The Octoroon, Fashion*, and *Uncle Tom's Cabin*.

The Walnut Street Theatre Stock Company's reputation diminished after 1862, which local critics found both surprising and dismaying. First-rate stars such as Laura Keene, Mr. and Mrs. E. L. Davenport, and Mr. and Mrs. Barney Williams continued to appear, but the resident company lost several of its most valuable players and equal replacements were not secured. Critics found the company of "miserable character" and decried the "shabby manner" of production that had taken hold. Apparently, profits were seen as stemming from a star's popularity rather than from a sound company and proficient staging, for critics found cost cutting had occurred even in the theatre's lighting, now considered "meagre" and insufficient. Mrs. Garrettson countered the criticism somewhat by adding several new company regulars, notably James A. Herne, who proved especially popular. Herne (1839–1901) stayed with the Walnut Street Theatre Stock Company for two seasons before embarking on a career as a traveling star supporting female stars such as Susan Denin and the Western sisters in popular melodramas. Later Herne was known primarily as a pioneering playwright of realistic dramas such as *Margaret Fleming* (1890) and *Shore Acres* (1892).

In early 1865 the Walnut Street Theatre was bought by John Sleeper Clarke (1833–99) and Edwin Booth (1833–93). Clarke, considered one of Philadelphia's most prominent residents and, always a frequent performer on Philadelphia stages, was touted "Philadelphia's favorite actor." However, Clarke was not a native Philadelphian, having been raised in Harford County, Maryland, where he was Edwin Booth's closest boyhood friend and where the two began their theatrical careers by giving readings together at the local courthouse. Clarke began his professional career in 1851 at Boston's Howard Athenaeum. His success was rapid, especially in the realm of comedy, and only two years later, at the age of twenty, Clarke succeeded John Drew as the leading comedian in Philadelphia's [Old] Chestnut Street Theatre Stock Company* (1826–55). His most noted vehicles were to include the comedies *Everybody's Friend* and *Toodles*. He then moved to the Arch Street Theatre Stock Company, where, in 1858, he shared management duties with experienced actor-manager William Wheatley and for a short time managed the Academy of Music with him as well. In 1859 Clarke married Edwin Booth's sister Asia. Purportedly, Clarke persuaded Booth to join him in purchasing and managing the Walnut Street Theatre in order to bring him out of a period of deep melancholia. However, before their plan to assume immediate management could be realized, Booth's brother John Wilkes Booth assassinated President Lincoln. In the aftermath, both Clarke and Edwin Booth were arrested and detained by the government, and Clarke was held for questioning for an entire month. A perceived national hatred for the Booth family impelled Clarke to postpone accepting management duties at the Walnut until after the fall of 1865, and Booth remained a silent partner only. This was not the only Clarke-Booth management partnership, for the two, along with William Stuart, already managed the Winter Garden Theatre in New York and were soon to become partners in the Boston Theatre in 1866.

Fully committed to the star system, Clarke and Booth planned from the start to be visiting performers only at the Walnut, although the lengths of their engagements—sometimes three or four months—certainly equaled the employment lengths of many of the company regulars, and their status as "visitors" seemed only a matter of semantics during their first few seasons as proprietors. Clarke and Booth remodeled the theatre building yet again, reportedly making major alterations on both exterior and interior, so only the walls of the original building remained unchanged. Prices increased to a twenty-five-cents to $1 range. After 1868, however, Clarke became involved in various ventures in London, and Booth, occupied with his own Booth's Theatre in New York, eventually gave up his share in the Walnut in 1870. The Walnut Street Theatre then was left primarily in the hands of capable managers and stage managers. Clarke, upon assuming management, had revamped the entire company, keeping only James A. Herne. He secured many favored Philadelphia performers from other local stock companies, notably Effie Germon from the Chestnut and Annie Graham from the Arch. He also brought in performers new to the city such as low comedian Owen S. Fawcett, secured well-known performers such as Susan Denin and Charles Walcot, and hired John McCullough for another season as leading actor. However, despite the company's return to a stable and respectable reputation, it increasingly lost its position of importance, becoming instead a mere troupe of supporting players.

The Walnut Street Theatre was the first in Philadelphia to devote itself exclusively to star engagements on a permanent basis, and it was not surprising that the theatre's management succumbed rapidly to the combination system. By the 1871–72 theatrical season, the house was occupied from April until June by touring troupes, complete with sets and fully rehearsed vehicles, which did not need stock company support. During ensuing seasons a substantial number of the two- to three-week star-engagement slots were given over to such full touring companies. The Walnut Street Theatre Stock Company then either toured itself, often to the Pennsylvania coal regions near Scranton or the rural farm lands surrounding Lancaster, or remained inactive, its members forced to find other temporary employment. At the end of the 1878–79 theatrical year, the company was abandoned completely, and the theatre became a permanent combination house. The Walnut Street Theatre remained in Clarke's estate until the 1920s but was relegated to a movie, burlesque, and vaudeville house during the Depression. The Federal Theatre Project restored legitimate drama there in the late 1930s, and the Shubert organization purchased it in the 1940s. In subsequent years, the theatre was simultaneously a touring facility and home to the Philadelphia Drama Guild. Since 1983 its staff has been producing its own professional productions. The Walnut Street Theatre is considered the oldest continually operating theatre in the English-speaking world.

PERSONNEL

Proprietors-Managers: William Dinneford, Ethelbert A. Marshall (1840–41); Ethelbert A. Marshall, Lewis T. Pratt, proprietors, and Mr. Flynn, manager (1841–42); Ethelbert A. Marshall, proprietor, and Charlotte Cushman, manager (1842–43); Ethelbert A. Marshall, proprietor, William Rufus Blake, manager, and Charlotte Cushman, acting manager (1843–44); Ethelbert A. Marshall (1844–57); Mrs. D. P. Bowers (1857–59); Mrs. M. Ann Garrettson (1859–60); John Sleeper Clarke, Edwin Booth (1865–70); John Sleeper Clarke (1870–74); John Sleeper Clarke, proprietor, and Thomas A. Hall, manager (1874–75); John Sleeper Clarke, proprietor, and George K. Goodwin, manager (1875–79).

Treasurers-Business Managers: W. H. Stuart (c.1850s), James Hutchison (1857–58), William A. Arnold (1858–59), Joseph D. Murphy (1859–61), John T. Donnelly (1861–63), William H. Paul (1863–65), T. J. Hemphill (1865–72), Thomas A. Hall (1872–74), Charles K. Burns (1874–79).

Scenic Technicians: Peter Grain, Jr., J. Wiser, George Heister, Charles Witham, George Heilge, John Morton.

Musical Directors: William P. Cunnington, Simon Hassler, C. R. Dodworth.

Stage Directors: William Rufus Blake (1840–c.48), Peter Richings (1848–55, 1857–59), John O. Sefton (1855–56), E. F. Keach (1858–60), [George] Vining Bowers (1860–61), Edwin Adams (1860–61), William A. Chapman (1860–61, 1868–71), Benjamin Young (1861–62), J. P. Price (1862–63), E. L. Tilton (1863–64), W. S. Frederick (1864–66), J. B. Roberts (1866–68), Thomas A. Hall (1871–72), J. H. Browne (1873–74), B. W. Turner (1874–75), Charles Walcot (1875–79).

Actors and Actresses: Mr. Abbott; Mrs. William Abbott; *Thomas à Becket* (1841–42, 1845–47, 1849–55); Mrs. Thomas à Becket; A. J. Adams, *Edwin Adams* (1860–62); Miss Anderson; Mrs. J. Anderson; P. A. Anderson; Miss Andrews; Leonie Arlington; W. H. Bailey; Miss Baker; *Mrs. Alexina Fisher Baker*, formerly Miss A. Fisher (1842–43, 1844–48, 1849–50, 1856–57); John Baker; Mr. and Mrs. Lewis Baker; Nellie Barbour; Joseph Barrett; Mrs. Barry; Harry Bascomb; Mr.

Behin; Mr. and Mrs. Bellamy; Julia Bennett; Miss Bernard; William Rufus Blake; Mrs. William Rufus Blake, formerly Caroline Placide; Mr. and Mrs. George Boniface; *Edwin Booth* (1866–67); J. H. Boswell; D. P. Bowers (1852–53); *Mrs. D. P. Bowers* (1852–53, 1857–59); *[George] Vining Bowers* (1859–63); J. B. Bradford; Mrs. F. Brelsford; Mrs. J. P. Brelsford; Mrs. John Brougham; Miss Brown; Mr. Brunton; Mr. Brydges; Mr. Buchannan; Mrs. Charles Burke; Mr. Burnes; Mary Carr; W. B. Chapman; Mr. and Mrs. William A. Chapman, formerly Mrs. Martha Silsbee; Mr. and Mrs. J. S. Charles; Mr. and Mrs. S. K. Chester; Miss Chippendale; G. B. Clark; *John Sleeper Clarke* (1865–66, 1870–72, 1874–75); Mrs. Coad; E. Coleman; Miss Collingbourne; E. S. Conner; Mr. Conover; *F. Bartlett Conway*; *Mrs. F. Bartlett Conway*, formerly Sarah Crocker (1857–58); *Charles Walter Couldock* (1850–53); Mrs. Charles Walter Couldock; Lizzie Creese; Mr. and Mrs. T. A. Creese; Viola Crocker; Anna Cruise, later Anna Cowell; Mr. Curtis; *Charlotte Cushman* (1842–43); *Susan Cushman* (1842–43); Mr. Daly; Julia Daly; *A. H. Davenport*, also known as H. A. Davenport (1855–56); *E. L. Davenport* (1841–42, 1843–45, 1851–52, 1854–55); *Mrs. E. L. Davenport* (1875–76, 1878–79); *Mrs. Lizzie Weston Davenport* (1855–56); *May Davenport* (1875–76); Joseph F. Dean; Blanche De Bar; Julia De Lacy; Mr. Denby; *Susan Denin* (1866–68); Miss Dickens; Linda Dietz; Mr. Donaldson; Mrs. Drake; Mrs. Frank N. Drew; *Frank Nelson Drew* (1855–56, 1858–60); *John Drew* (1855–56, 1857–58); *Mrs. John Drew*, also known as Louisa Lane Drew (1855–56, 1857–58); S. C. DuBois; Mr. Duff; Mrs. Kate Wemyss Duffield; J. Dunn; J. P. Duval; David Eberle; Mr. Edward; Effie Ellsler; E. A. Emerson; Mr. Eytinge; H. Farren; Mr. Faulkner; Owen S. Fawcett; Mr. Ferrers; J. M. Field; A. Fisher; Mr. Fitzgerald; Emma Fitzpatrick; Mrs. Flynn; Mr. and Mrs. France; William S. Fredericks; Mary Gannon; Mrs. George; C. Germon; Effie Germon; Mrs. Greenbury; Mrs. Gibbons; Mrs. Mary Gladstone; Mr. and Mrs. William Gomersal; *Annie Graham* (1855–56, 1863–64, 1865–67, 1868–69); Lillie Graham; Alice Grey; G. H. Griffith; Mr. Hackurt; Mr. Hadaway; Mr. Haines; Charles B. Hale; Mrs. Hall; J. H. Hall; J. M. Hardie; Lizzie Harold; Mr. Harris; Lin Harris; Miss Harrison; Sam Hemple; Mr. Henkins; Louisa Henderson; Mr. and Mrs. Charles Henri; *James A. Herne* (1864–66); C. W. Hess; Mr. and Mrs. C. W. Hield; Barton Hill; Lillie Hinton; Mrs. John Hoey; Miss K. Horn; B. F. Hornig; Charles Howard; George W. Howard; Louisa Howard; Harry B. Hudson; Mr. and Mrs. Hutchings; Miss A. Ince; John Henry Jack; Lewis L. James; G. Jamison; Mrs. Cornelia Jefferson; George W. Johnson; W. F. Johnson; R. Johnston; S. Johnston; Mrs. G. Jones; W. H. Jones; G. Jordan; H. C. Jordan; E. F. Keach; Mrs. E. F. Keach, Mrs. Adah King; Mrs. Kinlock; Miss A. Kinlock; Mrs. La Forest; Mr. Lambert; J. F. Lane; Mr. and Mrs. Langdon; *Atkins Lawrence* (1878–79); Walter M. Leman; Miss Lemoyne; Mrs. Y. Leonard; Milnes Levick; Miss S. Lewis; M. V. Lingham; Cornelius A. Logan; Charles S. Long; Mrs. Maddox; Mrs. Clara Fisher Maeder, formerly Clara Fisher; E. Marbie; Mrs. Marsden; John B. Mason; Kate Mayhew; J. P. Maylin; Mr. McBride; *John McCullough* (1860–62, 1865–66), *John E. McDonough* (1853–54, 1856–57, 1858–60); Mr. McGowan; W. T. McKeon; D. McMillan; Harry Meredith; Miss Miles; Hattie Miller; Miss Mitchell; Frank Mordaunt; Lewis Morrison; Mrs. Mossop; Laura Mowbray; Mr. Murdock; Miss Murray; A. Murray; Mrs. Muzzy; F. S. Myers; J. E. Nagle; Mr. Oakey; Mr. O'Brien; John E. Owens; Willis H. Page; Murray Pearman; M. J. Pendleton; Mrs. Penson; Mrs. S. S. Perrin; Mr. and Mrs. H. A. Perry; Eliza

Petrie, later Mrs. Place; Emma Pierce; Augustus Pitou; Mrs. Plumer, *Mme. Elizabeth Ponisi* (1850–52, 1856–57); Julia Porter; N. Porter; Lena Prentice; Miss Price; Lizzie Price; Susan Price; Mrs. Proctor; J. Proctor; Mr. and Mrs. Radcliffe; Master Reed; Clara Reed; D. Reed; Miss E. Reed; John R. Reed; Julian Reed; Laura Reed; *Roland Reed* (1875–76); William Reed; D. E. Reilly; *Caroline Richings* (1855–59); *Peter Richings* (1845–53, 1855–59); C. S. Risley; J. B. Roberts; *Miss Rock* (1840–41); Benjamin G. Rogers; G. Rogers; C. Rush; T. B. Russell; J. Sandford; John Sefton; Mrs. John Sefton; Joseph O. Sefton; Mrs. W. Sefton; *W. E. Sheridan* (1873–74); Alice Sherwood; *L. R. Shewell* (1855–60, 1861–62); Mrs. L. R. Shewell; Otis Skinner; Mr. and Mrs. Sloman; Miss Smith; Mrs. W. H. Smith; Mr. Spear; Mrs. Stephens; H. E. Stevens; Mrs. Clara Stoneall; R. Struthers; Mr. Stull; Emma Taylor; Harry Taylor; James Taylor; Mr. Terry; Mr. and Mrs. E. N. Thayer; P. Thomas; E. L. Tilton; B. W. Turner; Josephine Tyson; Miss Tyte; Agnes Vache; W. A. Vache; Mr. Vanstavoreen; Ida Vernon; *Mr. and Mrs. Charles Melton Walcot* (1866–68, 1869–73, 1874–79); Fanny Wallack; *Mr. and Mrs. James Wallack, Jr.* (1846–49); Lester Wallack; William H. Wallis; Mr. Warden; Miss Watson; Mary Wells; Miss C. Wemyss; *Frances Courtney Wemyss* (1845–46); G. W. Wessell; Frank Weston; Mr. Wheatleigh; *William Wheatley* (1843–50); Mr. Whiting; Mrs. Wilford; Mr. and Mrs. G.B.S. Wilkes; Mrs. Wilks; Annie Wilks; Edward Wilks; Barney Williams; Mrs. C. W. Witham; Joseph Wood; *Rose Wood* (1869–74); Mrs. T. Worrell; J. Sturton Wright; Benjamin Young.

Guest Artists: Edwin Adams; A. A. Addams; Laura Addison; J. H. Anderson; Mary Anderson; Mrs. A. F. Baker; W. J. Barnes; Charles Barras; Lawrence Barrett; Charles Barron, Ellen Batemen; Kate Bateman; Julia Bennett; Mr. and Mrs. William Rufus Blake; Master Blanchard; Kitty Blanchard; Agnes Booth; Edwin Booth; Junius Brutus Booth, Jr., Junius Brutus Booth, Sr.; Mr. and Mrs. Dion Boucicault (Agnes Robertson); Mrs. D. P. Bowers; Mr. Brough; John Brougham; McKean Buchanan; Virginia Buchanan; J. B. Buckstone; Ella Burns; William E. Burton; Leona Cavender; Ada Cavendish; Mlle. Celeste; Mr. and Mrs. Frank S. Chanfrau; John Sleeper Clarke; Josephine Clifton; J. W. Collier; John Collins; Mr. and Mrs. F. B. Conway; Jane Coombs; Mr. and Mrs. C. W. Couldock; Lotta Crabtree; W. H. Crane; W. H. Crisp; Isabelle Cubas; Charlotte Cushman; Susan Cushman; Julia Daly; Mr. and Mrs. E. L. Davenport; Fanny Davenport; Jean Margaret Davenport; Grattan Dawson; Julia Dean; Noemie DeMarguerittes; Kate Denin; Susan Denin; Frank N. Drew; John Drew; Mrs. John Drew, formerly known as Mrs. Hunt; Edward Eddy; Julia Elliott; Joseph K. Emmett; Agnes Ethel; Rose Eytinge; Mrs. G. P. Farren; Charles Fechter; Fanny Fitzfarren; Mrs. Fitzwilliam; Mr. and Mrs. William J. Florence; Edwin Forrest; Joseph C. Foster; Isabelle Freeman; Mr. Freer; Mr. Gann; Nat Goodwin; Miss Joey Gougenheim; Maude Granger; Ada Gray; James H. Hackett; Ettie Henderson; Matilda Heron; Annette Ince; Emma Ince; Fanny Janauschek; Joseph Jefferson; J. S. Jones; Mr. and Mrs. Charles Kean (Ellen Tree); Laura Keene; Miss Kimberly; Mr. Klishing; Mrs. F. W. Lander; Josephine Laurens; Atkins Lawrence; Carlotta Leclerq; Milnes Levick; Olive Logan; Harry Lorraine; Mr. Lover; Rachel Macauley; Steele MacKaye; Alice Placide Mann; Dan Marble; Frank Mayo; J. C. McCollom (McCullum); John McCullough; John E. McDonough; Mary McVickers; Maggie Mitchell; Lola Montez; Clara Morris; Anna Cora Mowatt; James E. Murdoch; Dominick Murray; Miss Neilson; Adelaide Neilson; Julia Oatley; J. L. O'Toole; John E. Owens; Tony

Pastor; Mrs. Agnes Perry; James Pilgrim; Henry Placide; Thomas Placide; Louise Pomeroy; Mme. Elizabeth Ponisi; C. S. Porter; Joseph Proctor; Mary Provost; [Arthur] McKee Rankin; Ravel family; John T. Raymond; T. D. Rice; Caroline Richings; Peter Richings; J. B. Roberts; Stuart Robson; Katherine Rogers; Mrs. Rousby; G. F. Rowe; Sam Ryan; Sallie St. Clair; Tommaso Salvini; Dan Setchell; Annie Senter; E. A. Sothern; Emma Stanley; Beatrice Stafford; Barry Sullivan; Mr. Swinbourne; Charlotte Thompson; Minette Thompson; Charles R. Thorne; Miss Vandenhoff; George Vandenhoff; Felicita Vestvali; Mr. and Mrs. Herman Vezin; Lester Wallack; Mr. and Mrs. James Wallack, Jr., James Wallack, Sr.; Daniel W. Waller; Emma Waller; William H. Walley; Harry Watkins; Rose Watkins; Francis Courtney Wemyss; Lucille Western; Joseph Wheelock; Mr. and Mrs. Barney Williams; Miss E. Wood; Mrs. John Wood; William B. Wood.

SAMPLE REPERTORY

1840–41: *Honey Moon; A Roland for an Oliver; The School for Scandal; Winning a Husband; Faint Heart ne'er Won Fair Lady; The Rivals; Laugh When You Can; Othello; Family Jars; Married Rake; Wives as They Were; Paul Pry; Belle's Stratagem; Review; The Innkeeper's Daughter; Romeo and Juliet; Sprigs of Laurel; Foundling of the Forest; Comedy of Errors; Charles II; Perfection; Love and Madness; Sweethearts and Wives; Seven's the Main; The Last Man; Hunting a Turtle; Loan of a Lover; High Life below Stairs; George Barnwell; Deaf as a Post; Of Age Tomorrow; Mr. and Mrs. Peter White; Sailor's Revenge; The Prize; Black Eyed Susan; A Day after the Wedding; Is He Jealous?; The Lady and the Devil; Ship Wreck; Broken Sword; Archibald of the Wreck; Speed the Plough; Demon Dwarf; Rob Roy; Comfortable Service; Goblin Page; Spoil'd Child; Simpson and Co.; Three and Deuce; The Stranger; Agreeable Surprise; Agnes de Vere; Turn Out; The Heir-at-Law; Woman's the Devil; Nature and Philosophy; A Wife for a Day; Green Mountain Boy; Jonathan in England; Jumbo Jum; Cut and Come Again; Foreign Prince; Whew! Here's a Go!; Seth Slope; Uncle Pop; Virginny Mummy; Bone Squash Diavolo; Knight of the Golden Fleece; Richard III; New Notions; A New Way to Pay Old Debts; Hamlet; A Day in Paris; Norman Leslie; Forty Thieves; Stars and Stripes; Philadelphia as It Is; Carpenter of Rouen; Catching an Heiress; P.P.P.P.; Mazeppa; Like Father, Like Son; Douglas; The Golden Farmer; Kate Kearney; The Flying Dutchman; Rookwood; Cataract of the Ganges; The Widow's Victim; Rail Road Depot; The Fortune Teller; El Hyder; Timour, the Tartar; Black Castle of the Desert; Ransom; Gambler's Fate; Damon and Pythias; King and Deserter; Seven Voyages of Sinbad the Sailor; How to Pay the Rent; The Lady of Lyons; Wandering Boys; Oh! Hush!; Rum Old Commodore; Launch of the Mississippi; The Avenger; Pizarro; Virginius; Pet of the Petticoats; Unfinished Gentleman; The Star-Spangled Banner; Sudden Thoughts; Nicholas Nickleby; Soldier's Son; Turning the Tables; X.Y.Z.; Four Sisters; Irish Lion; Mrs. Normer; Dream at Sea; Mischief Making; Death Token; How to Die for Love; Glory of Columbia; Monsieur Tonson; Jack Robinson and His Monkey; Love, Law, and Physic; A Day Well Spent; The Waterman; Jocko; The Village Lawyer; Hofer; The Irish Tutor.*

1845–46: *The School for Scandal; The Young Widow; The Wife; Macbeth; Mummy; The Merchant of Venice; Romeo and Juliet; Black Eyed Susan; Cure for the Heart-Ache; Thimble Rig; Speed the Plough; The Robber's Wife; Point of Honour; William*

Tell; The Soldier's Daughter; Rob Roy; Old Heads and Young Hearts; The Poor Soldier; Bertram; High Life below Stairs; Hamlet; The Lady of Lyons; Agreeable Surprise; The Stranger; Deaf as a Post; Coriolanus; The West Indian; Fazio; The Wonder; The Heir-at-Law; Bridal; The Bohemian Girl; The Fatal Dowry; The Maid of Croissey; Young America; Much Ado about Nothing; P.P.P.P.; Othello; The Wandering Minstrel; A Roland for an Oliver; Mr. and Mrs. Pringle; Venice Preserved; My Aunt; Faint Heart ne'er Won Fair Lady; Wild Oats; Thérèse; Wedding Day; Mountain Drover; Uncle John; George Barnwell; Monseigneur; High, Low, Jack, and the Game; Naiad Queen; La Bayadère; Rent Day; The Spell of the Cloud King; The Bronze Horse; Prairie Bird; Dumb Belle; Fiend of the Golden Rock; Freedom's Martyrs; The Battle of Germantown, Pizarro; Abstraction; Money; Robert Macaire; The Deformed; Loan of a Lover; The Swiss Cottage; Laugh When You Can; Perfection; The Elder Brother; Henry IV; His Last Legs; Rendezvous; The Enchantress; Surgeon of Paris; Rogatino; Richard III; A New Way to Pay Old Debts; King John; Riches; Julius Caesar; Damon and Pythias; The Mountaineers; The Midnight Hour; The Last Man; Every One Has His Fault; Mr. Singleton; Paul Pry; Jacques Strop; Virginius; Werner; Lady of the Lake; King Lear; Brutus; London Assurance; The Mill of St. Aldervon; Gisippus; Glorious Minority; Giselle; La sonnambula; La Bayadère; Secret Service; The Elder Brother; Witchcraft; The New Footman; The Apostate; Did You Ever Send Your Wife to Germantown?; Rory O'More; Did You Ever Send Your Wife to Burlington?; The Jealous Wife; School for Soldiers; Monkey; Fashion; Campaign of the Rio Grande; Wyoming; Douglas; Yankee Wool Dealer; Spectre Bridegroom; Mother and Child Are Doing Well; Lessons for Lovers; Pocahontas; As You Like It; Joan of Arc; The Rivals; Smiles and Tears; The Devil's Bridge; Charles XII; Forty Thieves; Bears, Not Beasts; Putnam; Matrimony; Child of Nature; Honey Moon; Bold Stroke for a Husband; Satan in Paris; Young Scamp; Somebody Else; She Stoops to Conquer; The Eton Boy; The Hunchback; A Husband at Sight; Richelieu; Don Caesar de Bazan; Comedy of Errors; Rip Van Winkle; Yankee in England; Married Rake; Merry Wives of Windsor; Married Life; Yankee in Mississippi; The Chimes; A Poor Gentleman; Wizard of the Wave; Lend Me Five Shillings; Irish Lion; Town and Country.

1850–51: As You Like It; John Dobbs; Belle's Stratagem; P.P.P.P.; Leap Year; Katherine and Petruchio; A Wonderful Woman; Lend Me Five Shillings; Passing Cloud; The Hunchback; Lady Beware; Honey Moon; Retribution; Something Else; Our Mary Anne; Extremes; The Eton Boy; Hamlet; The Stranger; Wine Works Wonders; The Lady of Lyons; My Aunt; The Gamester; The Wonder; Money; The Dramatist; Adrienne, the Actress; Love; The Jacobite; The Apostate; The House Dog; Poor Pillicoddy; Romeo and Juliet; My Wife's Come; A Nabob for an Hour; Love's Sacrifice; Youthful Queen; Spectre Bridegroom; The Betrothal; Slasher and Crasher; An Alarming Sacrifice; Friend Waggles; The Wife; Daughter of the Stars; The Jealous Wife; Venice Preserved; The Irish Fortune Hunter; Teddy, the Tiler; His Last Legs; How to Pay the Rent; The Irish Post; The Serious Family; Clari; Don Caesar de Bazan; The School of Reform; Charles XII; The Mysterious Family; My Precious Betsey; Macbeth; London Assurance; Henry VIII; Guy Mannering; Much Ado about Nothing; Fazio; Platonic Attachment; Used Up; Rough Diamond; The Single Life; Box and Cox; Giralda; Riches; or, The City Madam; Wreck Ashore; Child of Air; Rascal Jack; The Mountaineers; Wild Oats; The Robbers; Cure for the Heart-Ache; Dead Shot; Calaynos; The School for Scandal; My Friend in the

Straps; Sent to the Tower; The Husband of My Heart; David Copperfield; The Nervous Man; The Irish Ambassador; Rory O'More; Wife Hunters; King O'Neil; Born to Good Luck; The Irish Attorney; The Wrong Passenger; The Soldier of Fortune; The Irish Guardian; The Happy Man; The Love Chase; Old Love and the New; My Uncle John; Betsy Baker; All That Glitters Is Not Gold; Loan of a Lover; The Housekeeper; A Roland for an Oliver; Belphegor; Allow Me to Apologize; An Object of Interest; The World a Mask; Twice Killed; The Teacher Taught; The Day of Reckoning; Robert Macaire; Town and Country; The Noble Heart; Patrician and Parvenu; Rob Roy; Richard III; A New Way to Pay Old Debts; Faustus; Faint Heart ne'er Won Fair Lady; The Adopted Child; Boots at the Swan; Without Incumbrances; Caecinna; Othello; A Morning Call; Paris and London.

1855–56: *Extremes; Lottery Ticket; The Sorceress; Blind Man's Daughter; Star of the North; Three Shaws; Magnolia; Love's Sacrifice; The Debutante; Barney, the Baron; Brian O'Lynn; Irish Assurance; Our Gal; Patience and Perseverance; Born to Good Luck; O'Flannigan and the Fairies; The Irish Tutor; Shandy Maguire; The Fairy Circle; Connecticut Courtship; The Irish Tiger; Much Ado about Nothing; The Young Widow; Ingomar; Mr. and Mrs. Peter White; The Hunchback; Camille; Hamlet; Richard III; Francesca da Rimini; William Tell; Beauty and the Beast; Rough Diamond; Loan of a Lover; Love and Murder; Two Gregories; Wandering Minstrel; Perfection; Faint Heart ne'er Won Fair Lady; Day after the Wedding; My Neighbor's Wife; The New Footman; Still Waters Run Deep; Married Rake; Mother and Child Are Doing Well; The Eton Boy; Masks and Faces; The Serious Family; Black Eyed Susan; Sweethearts and Wives; Rory O'More; Toodles; Knight of Arva; Good for Nothing; Naval Engagements; Pet of the Petticoats; The Blue Devils; Grist to the Mill; Time Tries All; Poor Pillicoddy; Angelo: The Tyrant of Padua; The Nervous Man; The Happy Man; How to Pay the Rent; Irish Genius; The Irish Ambassador; The Wrong Passenger; The Irish Fortune Hunter; Teddy, the Tiler; Paul Pry; Othello; Pizarro; Richelieu; Damon and Pythias; Don't Judge by Appearances; Jack Cade; Spectre Bridegroom; Nature and Philosophy; Family Jars; Metamora; Macbeth; The Gladiator; Virginius; Caught in a Trap; The Irish Emigrant; Fortunio; Delicate Ground; Il Trovatore; Norma; Follies of a Night; Lucrezia Borgia; Honey Moon; Comedy of Errors; The White Horse of the Peppers; Robert Macaire; Helping Hands; Irish Dragoon; Two Loves and a Life; The Omnibus; Leap Year; Satan in Paris; All That Glitters Is Not Gold; A New Way to Pay Old Debts; The Apostate; Fazio; Tender Precautions; Evadne; In and Out of Place; Ireland as It Was; Law for Ladies; Uncle Pat's Cabin; The Bashful Irishman; Yankee Courtship; Irish Thrush and Swedish Nightingale; Mephistopheles; Ireland and America; The Limerick Boy; Paddy, the Piper; Custom of the Country; Paddy's Blunders; Paddy Riley; Grimshaw, Bagshaw, and Bradshaw; That Blessed Baby; King Lear; King Charming; Cool as a Cucumber; Five Pounds Reward; Romeo and Juliet; Valet de Sham; The Love Chase; The Hypocrite; The Little Treasure; More Blunders Than One; Bob Nettles; The Road to Ruin; Goslings; Rob Roy; Prince for an Hour; The Game of Love.*

1858–59: *Romeo and Juliet; Evadne; Fashion; The Belle's Stratagem; Othello; Much Ado about Nothing; Pizarro; Smiles and Tears; Guy Mannering; The Foundling of the Forest; Louise de Lignerolles; Sweethearts and Wives; Asmodeus; Twelfth Night; The Single Life; Married Life; Camille; Our Wife; The Youth of Frederick the Great; The Inconstant; Naval Engagements; Jane Shore; The Cagot; Mathilde;*

The Marble Heart; The Son of the Night; Our Friend Peter; The Chaplain of the Regiment; Nothing Venture, Nothing Win; The Serious Family; Still Waters Run Deep; Court and City; Grist to the Mill; Retribution; The Lost Ship; Second Love; Love's Sacrifice; The Wife; The Stranger; All That Glitters Is Not Gold; Honey Moon; Macbeth; Pauline; or, The Abbey of Grandpre; Caius Marius; The Hunchback; Five Nights on the Delaware; Richard III; The Irish Ambassador; Handy Andy; The Knight of Arva; John Bull; Rory O'More; Comedy of Errors; Aline; or, The Rose of Killarney; The Irish Emigrant; The Irish Attorney; Terence O'Connor; Leap Year; St. Patrick's Eve; Love; Ingomar; Adrienne, the Actress; My Aunt; Medea; Misalliance; Nature vs. Art; The Czarina; The King's Rival; The Little Treasure; The Willow Copse; Daughter of the Regiment; King of the Commons; Helping Hands; The Love Chase; Cure for the Heart-Ache; Money; The Drunkard; The Beacon of Death; The Lady of Lyons; A Woman's Heart; The Robber's Wife; The Last Man; or, The Miser of Eltham Green; The Enchantress; Richelieu; Hamlet; The Merchant of Venice; Katherine and Petruchio; The Bold Dragoons; King Lear; Old Honesty; The Gamester; A New Way to Pay Old Debts; King Henry IV; The French Spy; The Merry Wives of Windsor; Extremes; Wild Oats; The Robbers; Andy Blake: The Irish Diamond; The Life of an Actress; The Phantom; Jessie Brown; Used Up; Charlotte Corday; Mona Lisa; or, Da Vinci's Masterpiece; Masks and Faces; Louis XI; Gamecock of the Wilderness; The Idiot of the Heath; The Widow's Stratagem; Fazio; Lucrezia Borgia; Adelgitha; Griselda: The Forest Child; Peg Woffington; Mary Tudor; Clari; or, The Maid of Milan; Simpson and Co.; The Young Heiress; The Dutchess of Malfi; The Patrician's Daughter; Don Caesar de Bazan; The Iron Chest; Laugh When You Can; Town and Country; The Heir-at-Law; Our Jersey Cousin in Philadelphia; Damon and Pythias; Jack Sheppard; The Wonder; Under Current to Still Waters; Wacousta; or, The Massacre of Fort Michilimackinac; Ladies' Battle.

1861–62: *Paul Pry; Babes in the Woods; Damon and Pythias; Too Much for Good Nature; The Chimney Corner; Robert Macaire; The Willow Copse; Richelieu; Jocrisse, the Juggler; The Widow's Victims; Horse Shoe Robinson; Married Life; The Men of the Day; Mr. and Mrs. Peter White; The Advocate; Great Expectations; A Quiet Family; Fashion; Presumptive Evidence; Second Love; The Surgeon of Paris; The Belle of the Season; Black Sheep; The Broken Sword; The Blind Man's Daughter; Black Eyed Susan; Virginius; Nick of the Woods; Alexander the Great; Toodles; Everybody's Friend; Our American Cousin; The Lonely Man of the Ocean; Bob Nettles; The Octoroon; My Neighbor's Wife; Faust and Marguerite; Green Bushes; Hamlet; The Lady of Lyons; The Four Phantoms; A Message from the Sea; The Hidden Hand; The Dead Heart; The Shoemaker of Toulouse; The Fairy Circle; All Hallow's Eve; Hour in Seville; Ireland as It Was; Law for Ladies; The Magic Joke; Irish Assurance and Yankee Modesty; The Lakes of Killarney; Uncle Pat's Cabin; Ireland and America; Shandy Maguire; Willie Reilly; The Laughing Hyena; Jumbo Jim; Money; The Rebel Privateer; King Henry IV; Merry Wives of Windsor; His Last Legs; The White Terror; The Latest from New York; A Yankee Courtship; The Irish Lion; Sketches in India; Retribution; All That Glitters Is Not Gold; Rough Diamond; Cricket on the Hearth; Camille; Romeo and Juliet; Madelaine; Edith and Zelida; Victorine; Eleanor of Cleves; The Stranger; Adelherd, the Disowned; Ion; Your Life's in Danger; The Hunchback; The Marquis of Belle Terre; Macbeth; The Governor's Wife; London Assurance; The Corsican Brothers;*

Lost and Found; Belphegor; Richard III; A New Way to Pay Old Debts; Angel of Midnight; A Night on the Stage; The Fool of the Family; King Cotton.

1864–65: *Lavaro: The Gypsy Brother; The French Spy; Masaniello; Lucrezia Borgia; The Wept of the Wish-Ton-Wish; Miami: The Huntress of the Mississippi; Masks and Faces; Loan of a Lover; East Lynne; Oliver Twist; The Heretic; The Drunkard; Wild Oats; Richard III; Lady of Lyons; The Dead Heart; The Gunmaker of Moscow; Camille; Honey Moon; The Stranger; The Carpenter of Rouen; Aspasia; Asia; Edith; The Robbers; The Last Days of Pompeii; Tom Cringle's Logs; The Rag Picker of Paris; His Last Legs; Pizarro; The Adopted Child; Nell Gwynne; Lucie D'Arville; The Female Gambler; Duelist; or, Heir de Clairville; As You Like It; The Widow's Stratagem; The School for Scandal; Our American Cousin; Everybody's Friend; Paul Pry; Babes in the Woods; Married Life; Luck; Giralda; or, The Invisible Husband; The Ticket-of-Leave Man; Don Caesar de Bazan; Satan in Paris; The Actress of Padua; Fanchon, the Cricket; The Guard; Kathleen Mavourneen; The Hidden Hand; The Flower Girl and the Convict Marquis; Wives of Ireland; Rachel, the Reaper; She Stoops to Conquer; London Assurance; The Sea of Ice; The Soldier's Daughter; Othello; Macbeth; Hamlet; The Adopted Child; Damon and Pythias; The Iron Mask; St. Marc; Still Waters Run Deep; Julius Caesar; Jane Shore; Handy Andy; Irish Emigrant; Ireland as It Was; Shandy Maguire; Leah the Forsaken; Uncle Tom's Cabin; The Surgeon of Paris; Naval Engagements; The Corsican Brothers; Cricket on the Hearth; The Chimney Corner; The Golden Farmer; Faust and Marguerite; The Iron Chest; The Moors of Spain.*

1869–70: *Duty; Trodden Down; The Pioneer Patriot; Reaping the Tempest; Snare; Hamlet; The Merchant of Venice; The Lady of Lyons; The Apostate; Much Ado about Nothing; Richelieu; Brutus; Othello; Richard III; Macbeth; The Fool's Revenge; The Stranger; Don Caesar de Bazan; The Taming of the Shrew; East Lynne; King Lear; Virginius; Uncle Tom's Cabin; The Gladiator; Jack Cade; Metamora; Enoch Arden; Mary Warner; Leah the Forsaken; Not Guilty; Narcisse, the Vagrant; Set in Gold; Ruy Blas; Henry VIII; Sam; Kit: The Arkansas Traveller; The Debutante; The Hidden Hand; The Widow's Victim; The Serious Family; The Heir-at-Law; Old Heads and Young Hearts; London Assurance; Speed the Plough; Pizarro; The Fairy Circle; Connie Soogah; The Emerald Ring; Ireland as It Was; Rip Van Winkle; The Lancers.*

1872–73: *Kind to a Fault; The Belles of the Kitchen; The Wrong Man in the Right Place; Notre Dame; Our American Cousin; Home; David Garrick; Pretty Piece of Business; Black Sheep; Brother Sam; An English Gentleman; The Squire's Last Shilling; Not if I Know It; Pygmalion and Galatea; Haunted Houses; Kerry; The Colleen Bawn; Arrah-na-Pogue; The Orange Girl; Not Guilty; Romeo and Juliet; As You Like It; The Lady of Lyons; Faust and Marguerite; The Elopement; Dora; Christie Johnstone; Agnes; The Marble Heart; Foul Play; Amos Clark; The Robbers of the Forest of Bohemia; Uncle Sam; Nemesis; Guy Mannering; King Henry VIII; Macbeth; Simpson and Co.; Chesney Wold; The Winter's Tale; Medea; Mary Stuart; Deborah: The Jewish Maiden; Tragedy and Comedy; The Debutante; Come Here; Davy Crockett; Law in New York; Barnaby Rudge; The Swamp Angels.*

1875–76: *The Two Orphans; Davy Crockett; Richelieu; Hamlet; The Stranger; Richard III; The Gamester; Macbeth; Lady of Lyons; Colonel Sellers; Henry V; Rouge et noir; The Apostate; Othello; A New Way to Pay Old Debts; Katherine and Petruchio; King Lear; Henry VIII; Richard II; Jane Eyre; The Hunchback; East Lynne; Camille; The Octoroon; Around the World in Eighty Days; Zip; The*

Pet of the Petticoats; Musette; Fire Fly; The Old Curiosity Shop; Uncle Tom's Cabin; The Little Detective; Monte Cristo; The Might Dollar; Faust and Marguerite; Julius Caesar; Marti; Lady Audley's Secret; Men of '76; The Golden Bubble; Romeo and Juliet; Victims; Everybody's Friend; Self; Dot; Oliver Twist; Thou Shall Not; The Child Stealer; Lonely Man of the Ocean; Our American Cousin; On the Beach at Cape May; David Garrick; The Household Fairy; The Happiest Day of My Life; Pygmalion and Galatea; Home!; Guy Mannering; Columbus Reconstructed; Stagestruck; Pocahontas; Captain Crosstree; Black Eyed Susan.

1878–79: *Billiards; Woman of the People; La cigale; Pink Dominoes; Charity; Mary Stuart; Chesney Wold; Macbeth; Medea; Brunhild; The Winter's Tale; Come Here; Catherine of Russia; Henry VIII; Jane Shore; Kit: The Arkansas Traveller; The Widow's Victim; Jerry Clip; Around the World in Eighty Days; The Hunchback; Evadne; Romeo and Juliet; The Lady of Lyons; Ingomar; M'Liss; Coriolanus; The Gladiator; Pizarro; The Laughing Hyena; Mother and Son; Cataract of the Ganges; The Exiles; Dan'l Druce; Cartouche; Our Candidate; A Ride for Life; An American Girl; Richelieu; Hamlet; Richard III; London Assurance; As You Like It; Divorce; Cymbeline; Struck Oil; The Chinese Question; The Emerald Ring; The Fool of the Family; The Marble Heart; Family Jars; Virginius; Shylock; St. Marc; Julius Caesar; There's Millions in It; Gilded Age; The Deluge; or, Paradise Lost; Post of Honour; Almost a Life; The Danites; Dreams of Delusion; The Serious Family; Leap Year; Custom of the Country; Connecticut Courtship; Under the Rose; Hobbies; The Soldier's Trust; Devotion; Rip Van Winkle; Hope and Ambition.*

BIBLIOGRAPHY

Published Sources: *Philadelphia Inquirer*; *Philadelphia Public Ledger*; Charles Durang, *The Philadelphia Stage, for the Years 1749–1855*. 7 vols. (Philadelphia: Philadelphia Sunday Dispatch, 1854, 1856, 1860), arranged and illustrated by Thomas Westcott, 1868; Manuel Kean, *The Walnut Street Theatre* (Philadelphia: Privately printed, 1971); Otis Skinner, "A Year in Stock at Philadelphia's Walnut Street Theatre," *Ladies Home Journal* 40 (November 1923): 46–52; Arthur Herman Wilson, *A History of the Philadelphia Theatre, 1835 to 1855* (Philadelphia: University of Pennsylvania, 1935).

Unpublished Sources: William Dickey Coder, "A History of the Philadelphia Theatre, 1856–1878" (Ph.D. diss., University of Pennsylvania, 1936); Mary Helps, "The Walnut Street Theatre" (Paper presented as partial fulfillment for the M.L.S. degree, Drexel University, Philadelphia, 1966); Thomas F. Marshall, "The History of the Philadelphia Theatre, 1878–1890" (Ph.D. diss., University of Pennsylvania, 1941).

Archival Sources: Walnut Street Theatre File, Walnut Street Theatre Programs File, and Philadelphia Theatre Index, Philadelphia Theatre Collection, Free Library of Philadelphia (Logan Square). The Philadelphia Theatre Collection also has files on many of the managers and performers connected with the Walnut Street Theatre.

Mari Kathleen Fielder

WARREN AND WOOD COMPANY. See CHESTNUT STREET THEATRE COMPANY.

WEST AND BIGNALL COMPANY. See [THOMAS WADE] WEST COMPANY.

[THOMAS WADE] WEST COMPANY. Thomas Wade West (1725–99) began his acting career in London in the 1770s and joined forces with John Bignall (d.1794), his brother-in-law, in Richmond, Virginia, in August 1790 to form a small company that toured Virginia in a repertory of plays including most of the standards of the day. The group moved to Charleston, South Carolina, in 1793 to occupy a theatre West was building on Broad Street. The Charleston Theatre opened February 11, 1793, with a production of *The Highland Reel*.

With the repeal, in 1792, of the Vagrancy Act of 1787, which had prohibited theatrical productions in Charleston, a vacuum was created that attracted two theatre companies: The Old American Company of Lewis Hallam and John Henry and West and Bignall's troupe. West and Bignall were first to secure a license. In Charleston they saw an opportunity to anchor themselves in the South's most vigorous city and to expand their southern circuit, which included Richmond, Fredericksburg, and Petersburg, Virginia.

Before the construction of the Charleston Theatre, dramatic production in Charleston had been sporadic at best. Plays had been performed in a room above Shepheard's Tavern as early as 1735. David Douglass had established his London Comedy of Comedians (later the [Old] American Company* [1792–1806]) in Charleston from 1763 to 1766. He returned in 1773 but soon fled to Jamaica to avoid the impending Revolutionary War. James Verling Godwin built a theatre known as Harmony Hall in Louisburg, a town just outside the Charleston city limits, in July 1786. Due to his difficulty in obtaining and keeping company members, Godwin abandoned the theatre in June 1787.

To raise funds for the construction of the Charleston Theatre, West sold shares to subscribers at 50 pounds a share, raising a total of around 2,500 pounds. The prices for seats in the theatre were initially six shillings for the boxes, five shillings for the pit, and three shillings, six pence for the gallery. The theatre was open Mondays, Wednesdays, and Fridays, except for Race Week (usually during February and the height of the social season), when it was open six consecutive nights. The first financial difficulties arose from defaults on subscription collections, but attendance was kept up through a variety of programs with different bills for every performance.

Serious problems in both management and profits arose with the opening of the French Theatre in 1794. On arrival in Charleston, the French Players (see City Theatre Company*), headed by M. Francesqui and John Sollee, had petitioned the Charleston Theatre to grant them a benefit for refugees from Santo Domingo. The benefit was granted, and the French Players presented a program on February 8, 1794, consisting of *Pygmalion*; two pastoral dances; a comedy, *The Plebian Becomes a Man of Consequence*; an English dance and a hornpipe; and *Two Hunters and the Milk Maid*. The company opened its own theatre in April 1794, thus presenting West and Bignall with serious competition. Soon after the opening of the French Theatre, the Charleston Company lost both orchestra and actors to the Frenchmen. By the end of the second season, the company was showing a loss of more than 10,000 pounds sterling and shares had dropped in value to 40 pounds.

In September 1794 West incorporated most of the French Players into his own company, but John Sollee remained as proprietor of the French, or City, Theatre, with Hayden Edgar as manager. In August 1794 John Bignall died, and his widow assumed the partnership. To compete with Edgar's company at the City Theatre, West lowered prices in December 1794, to five shillings for the boxes, four shillings for the pit, and two shillings for the gallery. There was the further financial hazard of the inflationary value of the dollar, necessitating both theatres to post notices that the dollar would be accepted only at the current prices of the day.

Thomas Wade West recognized a city that enjoyed and needed culture. He did everything possible to see to his patron's comforts and tastes. The theatre was opulently decorated, the scenery imaginative and well constructed. He managed to keep a sizeable company of varied talents and presented the finest in theatrical fare. But the city could not support two theatres, and the Frenchmen offered a strong attraction. Their pantomimes, spectacles, and rope dancing lowered the size of West's houses, when West needed full attendance to support his elaborate enterprise.

The opening bill for the Charleston Theatre included a prologue, a comic opera (*The Highland Reel*), and a farce (*Adventures of a Shawl*). This was the general format followed until competition from the City Theatre necessitated the addition of more spectacles and pantomimes. On February 25, 1793, the company presented the first American comedy performed by professional actors, *The Contrast*, by Royall Tyler, but the most popular playwrights were English: William Shakespeare, Richard Sheridan, and John O'Keeffe. They began a tradition of benefits for local charities (as a way to emphasize their contribution to the city) with a benefit performance of *George Barnwell* for the Orphan House. After the opening of the French (later City) Theater in 1794, the group began including more pantomimes and scenic spectacles in its repertory, notably *The Life and Death of Captain Cook* and *Don Juan; or, The Libertine Destroyed*. A further novelty, soon copied by the competition, was the use of uniformed townsmen in the military spectacles. After the French Players joined West's company, M. Francesqui created many new pantomimes, including a pantomime of the fall of the Bastille, *The 14th of July, 1789*. The company came to rely heavily on these original pantomimes and on Mme. Alexander Placide's solo dancing, presenting a French program every Saturday night. West also began, in 1794, the practice of a short midwinter season in Savannah, a practice that continued throughout Charleston's theatrical history and helped to support acting companies that Charleston could not have supported alone.

Thomas Wade West managed the company until 1799, with John Bignall as his partner until Bignall's death in 1794. There is no mention of acting managers or stage managers, so it is assumed that West himself performed all managerial duties. M. Audin, an accomplished painter, created scenery for the company from 1793 to 1794, when he became scene painter for the French Players. After that, Mr. Schultz began designing sets for the Charleston Company. With dancing and music a large part of the evening's entertainment, West employed a fairly large orchestra, usually thirteen to fifteen members.

West relied heavily on a strong and varied stock company, but each season had its high point. For the season of 1794, the high point was the Sully Family; indeed, almost the entire company was the Sully Family! Matthew Sully, Sr., with his wife Sarah and their nine children—all of them talented in theatre and the arts—arrived in Charleston while West, who had married Matthew's sister, was constructing his Charleston Theatre. All of the daughters married while in Charleston; notably, Charlotte Sully married A. A. Chambers, a distinguished British actor, in June 1793 and Julie Sully married M. Zolbins (later Belzon), a French miniaturist living in Charleston, in 1794. The only children to continue on the stage were Charlotte (as Mrs. Chambers), Matthew, Jr., and Elizabeth. A. A. Chambers arrived for the 1793–94 season from the Theatre Royal, Haymarket, and Drury Lane. He was primarily a singer, making his first American appearance at the Southwark Theatre, Philadelphia, October 10, 1793, in the comic opera *Rosina*. He specialized in romantic roles, such as Richard III, Doricourt in *The Belle's Stratagem*, and Belcour in *The West Indian*. In the 1794–95 season, the principal recruits were James West and Mr. and Mrs. F. Marriott. James West was a recruit from the Old American Company. He had made his American debut at the Southwark in September 1792, and he specialized in comic opera roles. Mr. and Mrs. Marriott were previously with the Simpson Company in London at the Red Lion Inn. They debuted in Charleston, Mr. Marriott as Belcour in *The West Indian* and Mrs. Marriott as Monimia in *The Orphan*.

After the close of the 1794–95 season in April, the theatre did not reopen until Race Week, February 15, 1796. West's troupe spent the summer in Norfolk and the autumn in Richmond. The year 1796, West's last in Charleston, brought increased competition from the City Theatre, three citywide fires, and a fever epidemic. West did not return for the 1796–97 season, moving rather to Richmond, Virginia, via Norfolk and Petersburg.

The West Company opened a season in Richmond in November 1796 lasting about ten weeks; then the company moved to Petersburg, opening a new theatre there on January 18, 1797. Again, they summered in Norfolk. In 1797 West had at least five theatres in operation or under construction in Richmond, Norfolk, Petersburg, Fredericksburg, and Alexandria. The poorest of them was the Richmond Theatre on Shockoe Hill, which burned after the season's close on January 30, 1798. By 1798 West's was mainly a strolling company, playing seasons of about eight weeks in length in each of about six sites in Virginia each year. In 1799 West died in a fall in his partly built theatre in Alexandria. His widow, Margaret Sully West, emerged temporarily as the group's leader, but she soon engaged J. W. Green to manage the organization of which she remained the proprietress.

Until 1806 the group continued its peripatetic ways, but when a new theatre was opened in Richmond, they made that city the hub of their Virginia circuit, playing seasons of three or four months in 1806 and 1807. The company left Richmond in July 1807 for other Virginia cities. Records of the subsequent two years are very scanty. Martin Shockley asserted that the company that returned to Richmond in 1809 was almost completely transformed. No record of its history after 1809 has been uncovered.

PERSONNEL

Management: Thomas Wade West, John Bignall, comanagers, 1790–94; Thomas Wade West, manager, 1794–99; Margaret Sully West, proprietor, and J. W. Green, manager, 1799 to c.1809.

Scenic Artists: M. Audin, 1793–94; Mr. Schultz, 1794–96.

Actors and Actresses: Mr. Andrews; Elizabeth Arnold; C. G. Bailey; Master George Barrett; Mr. and Mrs. Giles L. Barrett; Mr. Barrymore; Mr. Bartlett; M. Belzon (also Zolbins); *Charles Biddle* (1790–91); *Ann West Bignall* (1790–96); Issac Bignall; *John Bignall* (1790–94); Mr. and Mrs. John Bignall, Jr.; Mr. Briers; Alexander Cain; *A. A. Chambers* (1793–96); *Charlotte Sully Chambers* (1793–96); Mr. and Mrs. Clare; William Clarke; Mr. Cleaveland; Mr. Clifford; Mr. Comer; Mr. Collins; Mr. Copeland; Mlle. Cortes; M. and Mme. Cortez; Mr. Courtney; Richard Crosby; Master Davids; Mrs. Walter Davids; Miss Decker; Mr. and Mrs. Decker; Mr. and Mrs. Doctor; Mr. and Mrs. Downie; M. and Mme. Douvillier; M. Dubois; Mr. Dunham; Master Duport; Mlle. Duthe; Mr. and Mrs. Hayden Edgar; Mr. Falkland; Mr. Fayol; Mr. and Mrs. Fitzgerald; M. Founiaud; *M. Francesqui* (1794–96); Mr. Francis; Miss Gillespie; Mr. Gollier; Mrs. Graupner; Mr. Gray; *Mrs. Gray* (1793–95); *Mr. and Mrs. J. W. Green* (1796–1809); Nancy Green; Mr. Greenwood; *Mirvan Hallam* (1790–94); Mr. Hamilton; Mr. Heely; Mr. and Mrs. Henderson; Charles Hipworth; Charles Hopkins; Mr. Huntingdon; Mrs. Hyde; Mrs. John Johnson; Mrs. Jones; Mr. and Mrs. Kedey; Mr. and Mrs. J. Kenna; Mr. Lacot; M. Latte; Mrs. Lawrence; M. Lavalette; Mr. and Mrs. Lewis; Mrs. Lynch; *Mr. and Mrs. F. Marriott* (1793–94); John (?) Martin; Mr. McDonald; Mrs. Melford; Mr. and Mrs. Miller; Daniel M'Kenzie; Mrs. Moore; Mr. Morton; Mr. Munto; Mr. and Mrs. Murray; Mr. and Mrs. Samuel Nelson; Master Oliphant; Mrs. Oliphant; Mr. and Mrs. Pick; *M. and Mme. Alexander Placide* (1794–96); David Poe; W. H. Prigmore; Charles Lace Radcliffe; Mr. Riffetts (or Ricketts); Mrs. Robinson; Mr. Rutherford; Mr. Santford; Mr. Saubere; Mr. Sears; Mr. and Mrs. Sheldon; Miss Solomon; Mr. and Mrs. Solomon; *M. Spinacuta* (1794–96); Mr. and Mrs. Story; Elizabeth Sully; Lawrence Sully; Sarah Sully; Matthew Sully, Sr., Mr. Taylor; Mr. and Mrs. Gavin Trumbull; Mr. and Mrs. Tubbs; M. and Mme. Val; Miss Wade; Mr. Walpole; Mr. and Mrs. Watts; *James West* (1794–96); Harriet West; Mrs. James West; *Margaret Sully West* (1790–1809); *Thomas Wade West* (1790–99); Thomas Wade West, Jr.; Mr. Williams; Mr. and Mrs. Wilmot; Julia Sully Zolbins–Belzon (1793–96).

REPERTORY

1793 (February–May): *The Highland Reel; The Adventures of a Shawl; Douglas; The Contrast; Rosina; Venice Preserved; Beaux Stratagem; The West Indian; Richard III; The Romp; The Lying Valet; She Stoops to Conquer; The Poor Soldier; The Dramatists; Maid of the Mill; Barnaby Brittle; As You Like It; Agreeable Surprise; Inkle and Yarico; The School for Scandal; Hamlet; The Beggar's Opera; All the World's a Stage; The Flitch of Bacon; The Road to Ruin; The Tempest; Prisoner at Large; Surrender of Calais; The Critic; Wild Oats; No Song, No Supper; The Clandestine Marriage; Three Weeks after Marriage; The Fashionable Lover; The Devil to Pay; The Midnight Hour; George Barnwell; The Rivals; The Padlock; Romeo and Juliet; Shakespeare's Jubilee.*

1794 (January–June): *Earl of Essex; The Child of Nature; The Orphan; St. Patrick's Day; The Old Maid; The Merchant of Venice; Man of the World; King and the Miller; Jane Shore; Miss in Her Teens; The Way to Keep Him; Macbeth; School for Wives; Don Juan; High Life below Stairs; Chapter of Accidents; Barnaby Brittle; Spoil'd Child; The Mogul Tale; Death of Captain Cook; Robinson Crusoe; Alexander the Great; How to Grow Rich; Columbus; Barbarossa; The Duenna; Animal Magnetism; Countess of Salisbury; The Ghost; He Would Be a Soldier.*

1794–95 (September–April): *Pyramus and Thisbe; Jerome Pointu; The Tableau Parlant; The Whims of Galatea; L'Amant statue; The English Merchant; Nina; Harlequin Balloonist; Battle of Hexham; The Brothers; Cross Purposes; The Four Valiant Brothers* (pantomime); *The 14th of July, 1789* (pantomime); *A Bold Stroke for a Wife; The Irish Widow; La Forêt Noire; Zemire and Azor; The Inconstants; Le barbier de Seville; Lionel and Clarissa; The Miser* (Fielding); *Mayor of Garratt; Les deux arlequin; The Roman Father; La belle Dorothee; Mahomet* (Voltaire); *Devil on Two Sticks; Harlequin Skeleton* (pantomime); *Cymon and Sylvia; Love's Frailties; More Ways Than One; Modern Antiques; King Lear; Duplicity; Elopement; or, A Trip to the Charleston Races* (J. Kenna); *The Prize; or, 2, 5, 3, 8; Jupiter and Europa.*

1796 (February–June): *Richard III; Return of the Labourers* (pantomime); *Fontainebleau; Henry IV; The Wedding Day; Othello; All in a Good Humour; The Wheel of Fortune; The Natural Son; Comus; Maid of Orleans* (pantomime); *The Battle of Hexham; Richard I* (John Burgoyne); *Siege of Damascus; Oscar and Malvina; World in a Village; Echo and Narcissus; The Robbers; Death of Major André; Theodosius; Bank Notes; Rinaldo and Armida* (pantomime); *The Ladies' Frolic; Maid of the Oaks; A New Way to Pay Old Debts.*

BIBLIOGRAPHY

Curtis, Mary Julia. "The Early Charleston Stage: 1703–1798." Ph.D. diss., Indiana University, 1968.
Shockley, Martin S. *The Richmond Stage, 1784–1812.* Richmond: University Press of Virginia, 1977.

Willis, Eola. *The Charleston Stage in the Eighteenth Century*. Columbia, S.C.: The State Company, 1924.

Weldon B. Durham and Jerri Cummins Crawford

WIGNELL AND REINAGLE COMPANY. See CHESTNUT STREET THEATRE COMPANY.

WOOD'S MUSEUM STOCK COMPANY. Wood's Museum, Chicago, opened its doors on August 17, 1863. Originally housed in St. Louis, the Museum, located at 111–117 Randolph Street, featured historical curiosities (including the Zeugoldon, a ninety-six-foot prehistoric fossil), many works of art, and a panorama of London. The Museum began giving concerts in September 1863, the first concert featuring vocalist Madame Anna Bishop. Following Madame Bishop's engagement was the "Ghost," a mechanical trick that drew in the public but left the management unsatisfied. Wanting to take a more prominent place in Chicago's theatrical world, the Museum initiated a season of opera on November 26. *The Bohemian Girl* was presented by the Holman Troupe until November 30, when the Ravel Family began an engagement. *The Lady of Lyons*, featuring J. W. Lanergan and a stock company not associated with the Museum, was the first drama offered by the Museum. The play opened on December 14, 1863, and was followed by a financially unsuccessful season of standard works.

Colonel J. H. Wood became the proprietor of the Museum on January 25, 1864. He immediately arranged the services of a stock company and transformed two halls at the rear of the Museum into a proper theatre. The stage measured thirty by sixty feet: the seating capacity was about 1,500. The "Lecture Room" (as it was called) opened on March 22, 1864, under the management of A. D. Bradley. The first play given was *The Lady of Lyons*.

In 1868 the theatre was leased by Frank E. Aiken, a leading member of the Museum's stock company. Aiken remained at the helm until January 1869, producing mostly new English pieces and Irish drama. He was succeeded by John W. Blaisdell, who, after a short season of minstrelsy and burlesque, returned to the production of more serious drama. Aiken returned as proprietor in September 1869, and a month later he renamed the Museum after himself. Aiken retired in June 1871, the Museum reverting to the direction of Colonel Wood, who changed the name back to Wood's Museum.

In spite of all of the managerial changes, the Lecture Room maintained a high-quality product. The other major Chicago theatres of the period, McVicker's First Theatre Company* and Crosby's Opera House, featured star attractions and spectacle, respectively. Wood's relied on a strong stock company in quality plays. An indication of the success with which the small company operated is the fact that at one point Dion Boucicault's *Formosa* was enjoying simultaneous success at all three theatres.

Wood's Museum met the fate of all Chicago's theatres on October 9, 1871, when it was completely destroyed by the Great Fire. It was not rebuilt.

PERSONNEL

The following is a partial list.

Management: John O'Mellen, general manager of the Museum (1863–64); John W. Weston, manager of amusements (1863–64); B. L. McVickar, Museum treasurer (1863– ?); Colonel J. H. Wood, proprietor and manager (1864–68); A. D. Bradley, stock company manager (1864– ?); Frank E. Aiken, manager (1868–69); John W. Blaisdell, manager (January 1869–June 1871); Colonel J. H. Wood, proprietor and manager (June 1871–October 1871).

Technical Management: J. Z. Little (1869– ?).

Musical Director: Mr. Stevens (1864– ?).

Actors and Actresses: Frank E. Aiken (1864–January 1869, September 1869–June 1871), Miss Anderson (1864– ?), Miss Axtel (1864– ?), A. D. Bradley (1869– ?), Mr. and Mrs. John Dillon (1864– ?), Katy Fletcher (1869?), J. D. Germon (1869– ?), Alice Holland (1868– ?), Mary Howard (1869– ?), J. W. Jennings (1869– ?), M. V. Lingham (1869– ?), Anna Marble (1869– ?), Mrs. L. B. Perrin (nee Woodbury (1864– ?), McKee Rankin (1869– ?), Mr. Reed (1864– ?), Mr. Richards (1864– ?).

REPERTORY

The following is a partial list.

1863: *The Lady of Lyons, Still Waters Run Deep, Honey Moon.*
1864: *The Lady of Lyons.*
1868: *Foul Play.*
1869: *The School for Scandal, The Workingmen of Chicago, Formosa.*
1870: *Little Emily.*
1871: *Divorce.*

BIBLIOGRAPHY

Andreas, A. T. *History of Chicago*. 3 vols. Chicago: A. T. Andreas Co., 1884–86.

Linda Bandy-White

APPENDIX I

CHRONOLOGY OF THEATRE COMPANIES

1749   Murray and Kean Company

1752   American Company

1781   Maryland Company of Comedians

1790   [Thomas Wade] West Company

1792   [Old] American Company
Board Alley Theatre Company

1794   Boston ["Federal Street"] Theatre Company
Chestnut Street Theatre Company
City Theatre Company

1796   Haymarket Theatre Company

1806   Park Theatre Company

1813   Green Street Theatre Company

1815   Charleston Company of Comedians
Drake Company

1819   [Caldwell's] American Company
[First] Walnut Street Theatre Company

1821   African Theatre

1824   Chatham Garden Theatre Company

1825   Lafayette Theatre Company

1826   Bowery Theatre Company
[Old] Chestnut Street Theatre Stock Company
Park Theatre Company

1827   Tremont Theatre Company

1828   Salem Theatre Company

1829   American Opera House Company
        Duffy and Forrest Stock Company
        [Second] Walnut Street Theatre Company

1830   Blanchard's Amphitheatre Stock Company

1831   Chatham Theatre Company

1832   National Theatre Stock Company

1834   American Theatre Company

1835   Ludlow and Smith Company

1836   National Theatre Stock Company

1837   Illinois Theatrical Company

1839   [New] Chatham Theatre Stock Company
        Mitchell's Olympic Theatre

1840   [Burton's New] National Theatre Company
        [Third] Walnut Street Theatre Company

1842   [The "New"] Charleston Theatre Company

1843   Boston Museum Company

1844   [Burton's] Arch Street Theatre Company

1845   Howard Athenaeum Company

1847   Broadway Theatre Stock Company
        Rice's Theater Company

1848   Burton's Stock Company
        [Chanfrau's New] National Theatre Company
        Providence Museum Company

1849   American Museum Stock Company
        Varieties Theatre Stock Company

1850   Adelphi Theatre Company
        Brougham's Lyceum Theatre Stock Company
        [Purdy's] National Theatre Company

1852   Wallack's Theatre Company

1853   St. Charles Theatre Stock Company

1854   Boston Theatre Stock Company
        Stadt Theater Company

1855   Academy of Music Company
        DeBar's Grand Opera House Stock Company
        [Laura] Keene's Theatre

1857 McVicker's First Theatre Company

1859 [The New] Memphis Theatre Stock Company

1861 Arch Street Theatre Company

1862 Salt Lake Theatre Stock Company

1863 [New] Chestnut Street Theatre Stock Company
Park Theatre Company
Wood's Museum Stock Company

1867 Selwyn's Theatre Company

1868 Kurz Stadt Theater Company

1869 California Theatre Stock Company
Daly Stock Company

1870 Coate's Opera House Stock Company
Globe Theatre Company

1871 Brooklyn Theatre Company

1872 Germania Theater
Union Square Theatre Stock Company

1873 Macauley Stock Company

1875 Brooklyn Theatre Company

1876 Harrigan's Company

1879 Thalia Theater Company

1884 Madison Square Theatre Stock Company

1887 Lyceum Stock Company

THEATRE COMPANIES BY STATE

California	California Theatre Stock Company
Illinois	Illinois Theatrical Company
	McVicker's First Theatre Company
	Rice's Theatre Company
	Wood's Museum Stock Company
Kentucky	Drake Company
	Macauley Stock Company
Louisiana	[Caldwell's] American Company (1819–43)
	St. Charles Theatre Stock Company
	Varieties Theatre Stock Company
Maryland	Maryland Company of Comedians
Massachussetts	Board Alley Theatre Company
	Boston Museum Company
	Boston ["Federal Street"] Theatre Company
	Boston Theatre Stock Company
	Globe Theatre Company
	Haymarket Theatre Company
	Howard Athenaeum Company
	National Theatre Stock Company
	Salem Theatre Company
	Selwyn's Theatre Company
	Tremont Theatre Company
Missouri	Coate's Opera House Stock Company
	DeBar's Grand Opera House Stock Company
	Ludlow and Smith Company

New York	African Theatre
	[Old] American Company (1792–1806)
	American Museum Stock Company
	American Opera House Company
	Blanchard's Amphitheatre Stock Company
	Bowery Theatre Company
	Broadway Theatre Stock Company
	Brooklyn Theatre Company (1871–75)
	Brooklyn Theatre Company (1875–76)
	Brougham's Lyceum Theatre Stock Company
	Burton's Stock Company
	Chatham Garden Theatre Company
	Chatham Theatre Company
	[New] Chatham Theatre Stock Company
	Daly Stock Company
	Duffy and Forrest Stock Company
	Germania Theater
	Green Street Theatre Company
	Harrigan's Company
	[Laura] Keene's Theatre
	Lafayette Theatre Company
	Lyceum Stock Company
	Madison Square Theatre Stock Company
	Mitchell's Olympic Theatre
	National Theatre Stock Company
	[Chanfrau's New] National Theatre Company
	[Purdy's] National Theatre Company
	Park Theatre Company (1806–26)
	Park Theatre Company (1826–48)
	Park Theatre Company (1863–98)
	Stadt Theater Company
	Thalia Theater Company
	Union Square Theatre Stock Company
	Wallack's Theatre Company
Ohio	Academy of Music Company
Pennsylvania	American Company (1752–92)
	American Theatre Company
	[Burton's] Arch Street Theatre Company (1844–50)
	Arch Street Theatre Company (1861–76)
	Chestnut Street Theatre Company
	[Old] Chestnut Street Theatre Stock Company (1826–55)
	[New] Chestnut Street Theatre Stock Company (1863–80)
	Murray and Kean Company
	[Burton's New] National Theatre Company
	[First] Walnut Street Theatre Company (1820–22)
	[Second] Walnut Street Theatre Company (1829–34)
	[Third] Walnut Street Theatre Company (1840–79)

Rhode Island	Providence Museum Company
South Carolina	Charleston Company of Comedians (1815–24) [The "New"] Charleston Theatre Company City Theatre Company
Tennessee	Adelphi Theatre Company [The New] Memphis Theatre Stock Company
Utah	Salt Lake Theatre Stock Company
Virginia	[Thomas Wade] West Company
Wisconsin	Kurz Stadt Theater Company

Index of Personal Names and Play Titles

About the Contributors

STEPHEN M. ARCHER is a professor of theatre at the University of Missouri-Columbia, where he teaches theatre history and playwriting. He has published *American Actors and Actresses: A Guide to Information Sources* (Gale, 1983), *How Theatre Happens* (Macmillan, 1983), as well as numerous articles and reviews. He is presently preparing a comprehensive biography of J. B. Booth, Sr.

LINDA BANDY-WHITE is currently a freelance writer and researcher in New York City. She has taught dance and theatre theory and history in Chicago, Toronto, and Los Angeles. Articles and reviews by Ms. Bandy-White have appeared in various newspapers, newsletters, and *Women and Performance*.

ROSEMARIE K. BANK is associate professor in the School of Theatre at Kent State University, where she teaches American theatre history and drama; European theatre history and drama of the eighteenth, nineteenth, and twentieth centuries; dramatic theory; and criticism. Articles and reviews by Dr. Bank have appeared in *Theatre Journal, Nineteenth-Century Theatre Research, Women in American Theatre, Theatre Studies, Theatre History Studies, On-Stage Studies, Theatre Research International, Essays in Theatre, Ibsen News and Comment*, and *Exchange*. She is currently chair of the Theatre History Program of the American Theatre Association, a member of the ATA Commission on Theatre Research, and member of several committees of the American Society for Theatre Research.

NOREEN C. BARNES teaches at California State University, Northridge, where she is an instructor in both theatre history and women's studies. She has contributed to *Notable Women in the American Theatre*, the *Encyclo-*

pedia of World Biography, *The American Historical Review*, and *Theatre Journal*.

GEORGE B. BRYAN (associate professor) teaches courses in theatre history, criticism, and dramatic literature at the University of Vermont. In addition to articles that have appeared in *Theatre Survey*, *Shakespeare Quarterly*, *Vermont History*, and other journals and reference works, Bryan is the author of *Ethelwold and Medieval Music-Drama at Winchester* (1981), *An Ibsen Companion* (1984), and *Stage Lives* (1985). His forthcoming works include *A Galsworthy Companion* and *Stage Deaths*.

JAMES BURGE received his Ph.D. from the City University of New York in 1985. His dissertation, "Lines of Business: Casting Policies and Practices in American Theatre: 1752-1899," will be published in 1986 by Peter Lang, as will an entry in *Notable Women in the American Theatre*. An actor at the American Shakespeare Festival in Connecticut and on Broadway in *The Royal Family*, Dr. Burge also appeared in Woody Allen's film, *Annie Hall*, and in the television mini-series, "Kennedy." He taught at Queen's College and Hunter College, New York City.

JOHN M. CALLAHAN is professor of speech and theatre at Kutztown University, Kutztown, Pa., where he teaches a variety of theatre classes specializing in American and European theatre history, and stage combat. The author of *Barron's Simplified Approach to O'Neill: Mourning Becomes Electra*, he has authored articles in the Missouri Historical Society *Bulletin*, *Theatre Studies*, book reviews in *Theatre Journal*, and more than a dozen articles on stage combat in *The Fight Master* (the journal of the Society of American Fight Directors). He is a member of Actors' Equity Association and the SAFD.

LARRY D. CLARK is professor of theatre at the University of Missouri-Columbia where he teaches courses in American theatre history, acting, and directing. His articles have appeared in *Players*, *Theatre History Studies*, and other journals and he is co-author of the fifth edition of *Acting is Believing*.

DON WHITNEY COMBS is professor of communication and theatre at Western Kentucky University, Bowling Green. His doctoral dissertation (University of Illinois at Urbana-Champaign, 1977) covered the history of Macauley's Theatre, Louisville, Kentucky, from 1873 to 1925.

JERRI CUMMINS CRAWFORD is currently completing work on her Ph.D. at the University of Missouri-Columbia. Productions of her original scripts have been presented at Gentry Studio Theatre on the University of Missouri-Columbia campus, at Stephens College, and at Central Oklahoma State University. Ms. Crawford is chairperson of the university's lab theatre and has recently submitted articles on Ellen Burstyn and Kim Hunter for inclusion in *Notable Women in the American Theatre*.

WELDON B. DURHAM is associate professor of theatre at the University of Missouri-Columbia, where he teaches courses in American theatre history, in dramatic literature, and in dramatic theory and criticism. Articles by Dr. Durham have appeared in *Theatre Journal* and in *Theatre History Studies*.

RON ENGLE is professor of theatre history in the Theatre Arts Department at the University of North Dakota. Articles by Dr. Engle have appeared in journals such as *Theatre Journal, Literature in Performance, North Dakota Quarterly*, and *Slavic and East European Arts*. Dr. Engle is the founding editor of *Theatre History Studies*.

SELDON FAULKNER is professor of theatre arts at the University of Arkansas at Little Rock, where he teaches regularly and serves as Chairman of the Department of Theatre Arts and Dance. Articles by Dr. Faulkner have appeared in *Educational Theatre Journal, Dramatics*, and *The Quarterly Journal of Speech*.

MARI KATHLEEN FIELDER has published articles on American and Irish-American theatrical subjects in *Theatre Studies, Theatre History Studies, Eire-Ireland* and *Notable Women in the American Theatre*. Her reviews of books and productions appear regularly in *Theatre Journal*. She has taught courses on theatre history, dramatic literature, and psychological criticism at UCLA, California School of Professional Psychology, and Ohio State University.

GLEN W. GADBERRY is associate professor of theatre arts at the University of Minnesota-Twin Cities, where he teaches courses in theatre history, theatre research, and dramatic literature. Articles on the German drama and theatre have appeared in *Theatre Survey, Drama Review* and *Massenspiele* (problemata 58).

BARNARD HEWITT is professor of theatre, emeritus at the University of Illinois, Urbana-Champaign. He is the author of *A History of the Theatre from 1800 to the Present, Theatre U.S.A. 1665–1957*, and the essay on Stephen Price in *The Theatre Manager in England and America*.

JAMES L. HIGHLANDER is professor of theatre at Central Missouri State University in Warrensburg, Missouri. His major research and teaching interests include American theatre history, theatre architecture, and directing. Articles by Dr. Highlander have appeared in *Theatre Journal*.

DANIEL A. KELIN II is a student and practicing artist in theatre. He is working toward his MFA at the University of Hawaii and pursuing a professional career in Children's Theatre.

ALICIA KAE KOGER holds a Ph.D. in theatre history from the University of Michigan. She has presented scholarly papers at meetings of the American Theatre Association, the Southeastern Theatre Conference, and the Popular Culture Association and has published reviews in *Theatre Journal*.

SAMUEL L. LEITER is professor of theatre at Brooklyn College, CUNY. He studied in Japan under a Fulbright Research Fellowship in 1974–75, and has published articles in *Players*, *Educational Theatre Journal*, *Theatre Crafts*, *Literature East and West*, and elsewhere. His books include *The Art of Kabuki: Famous Plays in Performance*; *Kabuki Encyclopedia: an English Language Adaptation of Kabuki Jiten*; *The Encyclopedia of the New York Stage 1920–1930*; *Ten Seasons: New York Theatre in the Seventies*; and *Shakespeare Around the Globe: A Guide to Notable Postwar Revivals*.

JAMES M. LEONARD is professor of theatre at the State University of New York at Albany, where he teaches courses in acting, and in theatre theory and criticism. His graduate degrees are from the University of North Carolina and Cornell. His article on nineteenth-century Albany theatre appeared in *Theatre Survey*.

ROBERT B. MONTILLA has served on the faculty of Louisiana State University and the University of Portland. His doctoral dissertation (Indiana University, 1974) treated the history of the Lafayette Theatre, New York City, 1825–29.

C. ALEX PINKSTON, JR., has directed the acting program at Marquette University and is currently directing the theatre division at Florida School of the Arts. He has published articles in *Theatre History Studies* and *Nineteenth Century Theatre Research*, presented papers at meetings of the American Society for Theatre Research and at regional theatre conferences in the United States, and performed with professional companies in summer stock in Los Angeles, and at Florida's state-supported Hippodrome Theatre.

DAVID L. RINEAR is professor of drama at the University of Oklahoma where he directs plays and teaches in the areas of theatre history, dramatic literature, dramatic theory, and directing. Articles by Dr. Rinear have appeared in *Theatre Survey*, *Theatre Journal*, *Nineteenth Century Theatre Research*, and *Theatre Notebook*. His full-length study of Mitchell's Olympic Theatre will be in print in the spring of 1986.

DAVID RITCHEY is a free-lance writer living in Little Rock, Arkansas. He is author of *A Guide to the Baltimore Stage in the Eighteenth Century*. His articles on theatre history have appeared in the *Educational Theatre Journal*, the *Maryland Historical Magazine*, and the *Southern Speech Communication Journal*.

LOREN K. RUFF is associate professor of theatre at Western Kentucky University where he teaches courses in American theatre and drama, modern drama, theatre history, and theatre appreciation. The author of two books and numerous articles, Dr. Ruff is engaged presently in preparing two additional manuscripts for publication.

PAT M. RYAN is currently lecturer in American civilization at the University of Trondheim, Norway. His articles have appeared in the *Encyclopedia dello spettacolo*, *Dictionary of American Biography*, *Notable American Women*, and *Theatre Survey*.

PATRICIA H. SANKUS is associate professor and director of the theatre arts program at Stonehill College, North Easton, Mass., where she teaches acting, directing, and theatre history. Along with her work for Chamber Theatre Productions, a national touring company that specializes in adapting classic prose literature for the stage, Dr. Sankus is the director of the Magic Circle Children's Theatre at Tufts University, Medford, Mass.

CHARLES SCHULTZ is on the faculty of the Department of Theatre at Northwest Missouri State University, Maryville. Portions of his research on the history of theatre in Cleveland, Ohio, have been presented at the Theatre History Symposium of the Mid-America Theatre Conference.

THERALD TODD is on the performing arts faculty at Florida International University in Miami. His doctoral dissertation at the University of Oregon, 1973, traced the history of the Salt Lake Theatre of Salt Lake City, Utah.

DON B. WILMETH, professor of theatre arts and English and chairman of the Department of Theatre Arts at Brown University, has been the recipient of a Guggenheim Fellowship and has won the Barnard Hewitt Theatre History Award. He is a member of the College of Fellows of the American Theatre Association. He has written, edited, or co-edited seven books and is currently a contributing editor of *The Cambridge Guide to World Theatre*.

A former vice-president of the Theatre Library Association, he is currently on the Executive Committee of the American Society for Theatre Research.

JOHN R. WOLCOTT is professor of theatre at the School of Drama, University of Washington, Seattle. Essays by his hand have appeared in *Nineteenth Century Theatre Research*, the *Journal of the Society of Architectural Historians*, and *Theatre Research*.

ALAN WOODS is director of the Jerome Lawrence and Robert E. Lee Theatre Research Institute at the Ohio State University, where he also is an associate professor of theatre. His work has been published in *Theatre Survey* and *Theatre Journal*, and in numerous anthologies.